Visit classzone.com and get connected

Online resources for students and parents
ClassZone resources provide instruction, practice, and learning support.

eEdition Plus ONLINE
This interactive version of the text encourages students to explore science.

Content Review Online
Interactive review reinforces the big idea and key concepts of each chapter.

SciLinks
NSTA-selected links provide relevant Web resources correlated to the text.

Chapter-Based Support
Math tutorials, news, resources, test practice, and a misconceptions database help students succeed.

Now it all clicks!™

McDougal Littell

PHYSICAL SCIENCE

Standards and Benchmarks — xxiv
Introducing Physical Science — xxviii
Unifying Principles of Physical Science — xxx
The Nature of Science — xxxviii
The Nature of Technology — xlii
Using *McDougal Littell Science* — xliv

A Matter and Energy
Introduction to Matter
Properties of Matter
Energy
Temperature and Heat

B Chemical Interactions
Atomic Structure and the Periodic Table
Chemical Bonds and Compounds
Chemical Reactions
Solutions
Carbon in Life and Materials

C Motion and Forces
Motion
Forces
Gravity, Friction, and Pressure
Work and Energy
Machines

D Waves, Sound, and Light
Waves
Sound
Electromagnetic Waves
Light and Optics

E Electricity and Magnetism
Electricity
Circuits and Electronics
Magnetism

Scientific Thinking Handbook — R2
Lab Handbook — R10
Math Handbook — R36
Note-Taking Handbook — R45
Glossary — R52
Index — R71
Acknowledgments — R92

Acknowledgments: Excerpts and adaptations from *National Science Education Standards* by the National Academy of Sciences. Copyright © 1996 by the National Academy of Sciences. Reprinted with permission from the National Academies Press, Washington, D.C.

Excerpts and adaptations from *Benchmarks for Science Literacy: Project 2061.* Copyright © 1993 by the American Association for the Advancement of Science. Reprinted with permission.

Copyright © 2005 by McDougal Littell, a division of Houghton Mifflin Company.

No part of this work may be reproduced or transmitted in any form or by any means, electronic or mechanical, including photocopy and recording, or by any information storage or retrieval system without the prior written permission of McDougal Littell unless such copying is expressly permitted by federal copyright law. Address inquiries to Supervisor, Rights and Permissions, McDougal Littell, P.O. Box 1667, Evanston, IL 60204.

ISBN: 0-618-30369-3   2 3 4 5 6 7 8 VJM 08 07 06 05 04

Internet Web Site: http://www.mcdougallittell.com

Science Consultants

Chief Science Consultant

James Trefil, Ph.D. is the Clarence J. Robinson Professor of Physics at George Mason University. He is the author or co-author of more than 25 books, including *Science Matters* and *The Nature of Science*. Dr. Trefil is a member of the American Association for the Advancement of Science's Committee on the Public Understanding of Science and Technology. He is also a fellow of the World Economic Forum and a frequent contributor to *Smithsonian* magazine.

Rita Ann Calvo, Ph.D. is Senior Lecturer in Molecular Biology and Genetics at Cornell University, where for 12 years she also directed the Cornell Institute for Biology Teachers. Dr. Calvo is the 1999 recipient of the College and University Teaching Award from the National Association of Biology Teachers.

Kenneth Cutler, M.S. is the Education Coordinator for the Julius L. Chambers Biomedical Biotechnology Research Institute at North Carolina Central University. A former middle school and high school science teacher, he received a 1999 Presidential Award for Excellence in Science Teaching.

Instructional Design Consultants

Douglas Carnine, Ph.D. is Professor of Education and Director of the National Center for Improving the Tools of Educators at the University of Oregon. He is the author of seven books and over 100 other scholarly publications, primarily in the areas of instructional design and effective instructional strategies and tools for diverse learners. Dr. Carnine also serves as a member of the National Institute for Literacy Advisory Board.

Linda Carnine, Ph.D. consults with school districts on curriculum development and effective instruction for students struggling academically. A former teacher and school administrator, Dr. Carnine also co-authored a popular remedial reading program.

Donald Steely, Ph.D. serves as principal investigator at the Oregon Center for Applied Science (ORCAS) on federal grants for science and language arts programs. His background also includes teaching and authoring of print and multimedia programs in science, mathematics, history, and spelling.

Sam Miller, Ph.D. is a middle school science teacher and the Teacher Development Liaison for the Eugene, Oregon, Public Schools. He is the author of curricula for teaching science, mathematics, computer skills, and language arts.

Vicky Vachon, Ph.D. consults with school districts throughout the United States and Canada on improving overall academic achievement with a focus on literacy. She is also co-author of a widely used program for remedial readers.

Content Reviewers

John Beaver, Ph.D.
Ecology
Professor, Director of Science Education Center
College of Education and Human Services
Western Illinois University
Macomb, IL

Donald J. DeCoste, Ph.D.
Matter and Energy, Chemical Interactions
Chemistry Instructor
University of Illinois
Urbana-Champaign, IL

Dorothy Ann Fallows, Ph.D., MSc
Diversity of Living Things, Microbiology
Partners in Health
Boston, MA

Michael Foote, Ph.D.
The Changing Earth, Life Over Time
Associate Professor
Department of the Geophysical Sciences
The University of Chicago
Chicago, IL

Lucy Fortson, Ph.D.
Space Science
Director of Astronomy
Adler Planetarium and Astronomy Museum
Chicago, IL

Elizabeth Godrick, Ph.D.
Human Biology
Professor, CAS Biology
Boston University
Boston, MA

Isabelle Sacramento Grilo, M.S.
The Changing Earth
Lecturer, Department of the Geological Sciences
Montana State University
Bozeman, MT

David Harbster, MSc
Diversity of Living Things
Professor of Biology
Paradise Valley Community College
Phoenix, AZ

Richard D. Norris, Ph.D.
Earth's Waters
Professor of Paleobiology
Scripps Institution of Oceanography
University of California, San Diego
La Jolla, CA

Donald B. Peck, M.S.
Motion and Forces; Waves, Sound, and Light; Electricity and Magnetism
Director of the Center for Science Education (retired)
Fairleigh Dickinson University
Madison, NJ

Javier Penalosa, Ph.D.
Diversity of Living Things, Plants
Associate Professor, Biology Department
Buffalo State College
Buffalo, NY

Raymond T. Pierrehumbert, Ph.D.
Earth's Atmosphere
Professor in Geophysical Sciences (Atmospheric Science)
The University of Chicago
Chicago, IL

Brian J. Skinner, Ph.D.
Earth's Surface
Eugene Higgins Professor of Geology and Geophysics
Yale University
New Haven, CT

Nancy E. Spaulding, M.S.
Earth's Surface, The Changing Earth, Earth's Waters
Earth Science Teacher (retired)
Elmira Free Academy
Elmira, NY

Steven S. Zumdahl, Ph.D.
Matter and Energy, Chemical Interactions
Professor Emeritus of Chemistry
University of Illinois
Urbana-Champaign, IL

Susan L. Zumdahl, M.S.
Matter and Energy, Chemical Interactions
Chemistry Education Specialist
University of Illinois
Urbana-Champaign, IL

Safety Consultant

Juliana Texley, Ph.D.
Former K–12 Science Teacher and School Superintendent
Boca Raton, FL

English Language Advisor

Judy Lewis, M.A.
Director, State and Federal Programs for reading proficiency and high risk populations
Rancho Cordova, CA

Teacher Panel Members

Carol Arbour
Tallmadge Middle School,
Tallmadge, OH

Patty Belcher
Goodrich Middle School,
Akron, OH

Gwen Broestl
Luis Munoz Marin Middle School,
Cleveland, OH

Al Brofman
Tehipite Middle School,
Fresno, CA

John Cockrell
Clinton Middle School,
Columbus, OH

Jenifer Cox
Sylvan Middle School,
Citrus Heights, CA

Linda Culpepper
Martin Middle School,
Charlotte, NC

Kathleen Ann DeMatteo
Margate Middle School,
Margate, FL

Melvin Figueroa
New River Middle School,
Ft. Lauderdale, FL

Doretha Grier
Kannapolis Middle School,
Kannapolis, NC

Robert Hood
Alexander Hamilton Middle School,
Cleveland, OH

Scott Hudson
Coverdale Elementary School,
Cincinnati, OH

Loretta Langdon
Princeton Middle School,
Princeton, NC

Carlyn Little
Glades Middle School,
Miami, FL

Ann Marie Lynn
Amelia Earhart Middle School,
Riverside, CA

James Minogue
Lowe's Grove Middle School,
Durham, NC

Joann Myers
Buchanan Middle School,
Tampa, FL

Barbara Newell
Charles Evans Hughes Middle School,
Long Beach, CA

Anita Parker
Kannapolis Middle School,
Kannapolis, NC

Greg Pirolo
Golden Valley Middle School,
San Bernardino, CA

Laura Pottmyer
Apex Middle School,
Apex, NC

Lynn Prichard
Booker T. Washington Middle Magnet
School, Tampa, FL

Jacque Quick
Walter Williams High School,
Burlington, NC

Robert Glenn Reynolds
Hillman Middle School,
Youngstown, OH

Stacy Rinehart
Lufkin Road Middle School,
Apex, NC

Theresa Short
Abbott Middle School,
Fayetteville, NC

Rita Slivka
Alexander Hamilton Middle School,
Cleveland, OH

Marie Sofsak
B F Stanton Middle School,
Alliance, OH

Nancy Stubbs
Sweetwater Union Unified School District,
Chula Vista, CA

Sharon Stull
Quail Hollow Middle School,
Charlotte, NC

Donna Taylor
Okeeheelee Middle School,
West Palm Beach, FL

Sandi Thompson
Harding Middle School,
Lakewood, OH

Lori Walker
Audubon Middle School & Magnet Center,
Los Angeles, CA

Teacher Lab Evaluators

Andrew Boy
W.E.B. DuBois Academy,
Cincinnati, OH

Jill Brimm-Byrne
Albany Park Academy,
Chicago, IL

Gwen Broestl
Luis Munoz Marin Middle School,
Cleveland, OH

Al Brofman
Tehipite Middle School,
Fresno, CA

Michael A. Burstein
The Rashi School,
Newton, MA

Trudi Coutts
Madison Middle School,
Naperville, IL

Jenifer Cox
Sylvan Middle School,
Citrus Heights, CA

Larry Cwik
Madison Middle School,
Naperville, IL

Jennifer Donatelli
Kennedy Junior High School,
Lisle, IL

Melissa Dupree
Lakeside Middle School,
Evans, GA

Carl Fechko
Luis Munoz Marin Middle School,
Cleveland, OH

Paige Fullhart
Highland Middle School,
Libertyville, IL

Sue Hood
Glen Crest Middle School,
Glen Ellyn, IL

William Luzader
Plymouth Community Intermediate School,
Plymouth, MA

Ann Min
Beardsley Middle School,
Crystal Lake, IL

Aileen Mueller
Kennedy Junior High School,
Lisle, IL

Nancy Nega
Churchville Middle School,
Elmhurst, IL

Oscar Newman
Sumner Math and Science Academy,
Chicago, IL

Lynn Prichard
Booker T. Washington Middle Magnet
School, Tampa, FL

Jacque Quick
Walter Williams High School,
Burlington, NC

Stacy Rinehart
Lufkin Road Middle School,
Apex, NC

Seth Robey
Gwendolyn Brooks Middle School,
Oak Park, IL

Kevin Steele
Grissom Middle School,
Tinley Park, IL

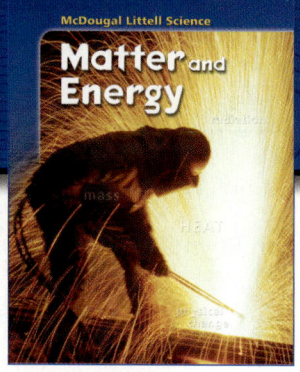

UNIT A
Matter and Energy

Unit Features

SCIENTIFIC AMERICAN FRONTIERS IN SCIENCE *Fuels of the Future* — A2

TIMELINES IN SCIENCE *About Temperature and Heat* — A96

1 Introduction to Matter — A6

the BIG idea
Everything that has mass and takes up space is matter.

- **1.1** Matter has mass and volume. — A9
  CHAPTER INVESTIGATION *Mass and Volume* — A14
- **1.2** Matter is made of atoms. — A16
  EXTREME SCIENCE *Particles Too Small to See* — A20
- **1.3** Matter combines to form different substances. — A21
  MATH IN SCIENCE *Making a Circle Graph* — A26
- **1.4** Matter exists in different physical states. — A27

2 Properties of Matter — A38

the BIG idea
Matter has properties that can be changed by physical and chemical processes.

- **2.1** Matter has observable properties. — A41
  MATH IN SCIENCE *Solving Proportions* — A49
- **2.2** Changes of state are physical changes. — A50
  CHAPTER INVESTIGATION *Freezing Point* — A56
- **2.3** Properties are used to identify substances. — A58
  CONNECTING SCIENCES *Separating Minerals* — A63

What properties could help you identify this sculpture as sugar? page A38

vi Physical Science

What different forms of energy are shown in this photograph? page A68

3 Energy A68

the BIG idea
Energy has different forms, but it is always conserved.

3.1 Energy exists in different forms. A71
　　THINK SCIENCE *Gasoline or Electric?* A77

3.2 Energy can change forms but is never lost. A78
　　CHAPTER INVESTIGATION *Energy Conversions* A84

3.3 Technology improves the ways people use energy. A86
　　MATH IN SCIENCE *Using Formulas* A91

4 Temperature and Heat A100

the BIG idea
Heat is a flow of energy due to temperature differences.

4.1 Temperature depends on particle movement. A103
　　MATH IN SCIENCE *Metric Conversions* A109

4.2 Energy flows from warmer to cooler objects. A110
　　SCIENCE ON THE JOB *Cooking with Heat* A115

4.3 The transfer of energy as heat can be controlled. A116
　　CHAPTER INVESTIGATION *Insulators* A122

Visual Highlights

States of Matter A29
Physical Changes A45
Converting Energy A81
Insulation A120

Table of Contents **vii**

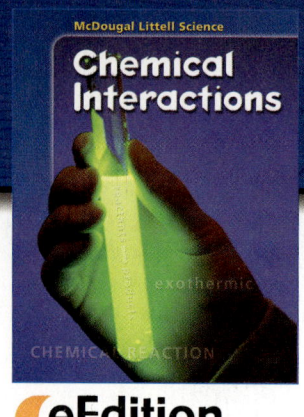

UNIT B
Chemical Interactions

Unit Features

FRONTIERS IN SCIENCE *Medicines from Nature* — B2

TIMELINES IN SCIENCE *The Story of Atomic Structure* — B104

1 Atomic Structure and the Periodic Table — B6

the BIG idea
A substance's atomic structure determines its physical and chemical properties.

- **1.1** Atoms are the smallest form of elements. — B9
  - CONNECTING SCIENCES *Elements of Life* — B16
- **1.2** Elements make up the periodic table. — B17
  - CHAPTER INVESTIGATION *Modeling Atomic Masses* — B24
- **1.3** The periodic table is a map of the elements. — B26
  - MATH IN SCIENCE *Using Scientific Notation* — B33

2 Chemical Bonds and Compounds — B38

the BIG idea
The properties of compounds depend on their atoms and chemical bonds.

- **2.1** Elements combine to form compounds. — B41
  - MATH IN SCIENCE *Calculating Ratios* — B46
- **2.2** Chemical bonds hold compounds together. — B47
  - THINK SCIENCE *Stick to It* — B55
- **2.3** Substances' properties depend on their bonds. — B56
  - CHAPTER INVESTIGATION *Chemical Bonds* — B60

How do these skydivers stay together? How is this similar to the way atoms stay together? page B38

viii Physical Science

3 Chemical Reactions — B66

the BIG idea
Chemical reactions form new substances by breaking and making chemical bonds.

3.1 Chemical reactions alter arrangements of atoms. — B69
  MATH IN SCIENCE *Analyzing Line Graphs* — B77

3.2 The masses of reactants and products are equal. — B78
  SCIENCE ON THE JOB *Chemistry in Firefighting* — B85

3.3 Chemical reactions involve energy changes. — B86
  CHAPTER INVESTIGATION *Exothermic or Endothermic?* — B92

3.4 Life and industry depend on chemical reactions. — B94

4 Solutions — B108

the BIG idea
When substances dissolve to form a solution, the properties of the mixture change.

4.1 A solution is a type of mixture. — B111

4.2 The amount of solute that dissolves can vary. — B117
  CONNECTING SCIENCES *Cool, Clear Water* — B124

4.3 Solutions can be acidic, basic, or neutral. — B125
  CHAPTER INVESTIGATION *Acids and Bases* — B132

4.4 Metal alloys are solid mixtures. — B134
  MATH IN SCIENCE *Calculating Percentages* — B139

5 Carbon in Life and Materials — B144

the BIG idea
Carbon is essential to living things and to modern materials.

5.1 Carbon-based molecules have many structures. — B147
  EXTREME SCIENCE *Stronger Than Steel* — B153

5.2 Carbon-based molecules are life's building blocks. — B154
  MATH IN SCIENCE *Making Bar Graphs* — B162

5.3 Carbon-based molecules are in many materials. — B163
  CHAPTER INVESTIGATION *Polymers* — B170

Visual Highlights

The Periodic Table of the Elements	B20
Comparing Bonds	B52
Balancing Equations with Coefficients	B83
Chemical Reactions in Catalytic Converters	B97
Common Acids and Bases	B130
Carbon Chains and Carbon Rings	B151
Nucleic Acid Structure and Function	B160
Using Petroleum	B165

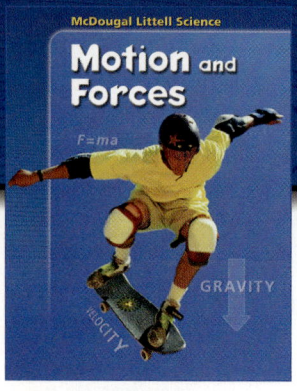

UNIT C
Motion and Forces

Unit Features

SCIENTIFIC AMERICAN   **FRONTIERS IN SCIENCE** *Robots on Mars*   C2

TIMELINES IN SCIENCE *Understanding Forces*   C108

1 Motion   C6

the BIG idea
The motion of an object can be described and predicted.

1.1 An object in motion changes position.   C9
     SCIENCE ON THE JOB *Physics for Rescuers*   C15
1.2 Speed measures how fast position changes.   C16
     MATH IN SCIENCE *Working with Units*   C24
1.3 Acceleration measures how fast velocity changes.   C25
     CHAPTER INVESTIGATION *Acceleration and Slope*   C32

2 Forces   C38

the BIG idea
Forces change the motion of objects in predictable ways.

2.1 Forces change motion.   C41
     THINK SCIENCE *Why Do These Rocks Slide?*   C48
2.2 Force and mass determine acceleration.   C49
     MATH IN SCIENCE *Using Significant Figures*   C56
2.3 Forces act in pairs.   C57
     CHAPTER INVESTIGATION *Newton's Laws of Motion*   C62
2.4 Forces transfer momentum.   C64

What must happen for a team to win this tug of war? page C38

What forces are acting on this snowboarder? on the snow? page C75

3 Gravity, Friction, and Pressure — C74

the BIG idea
Newton's laws apply to all forces.

3.1 Gravity is a force exerted by masses. — C77
EXTREME SCIENCE *Bending Light* — C84

3.2 Friction is a force that opposes motion. — C85
MATH IN SCIENCE *Creating a Line Graph* — C90

3.3 Pressure depends on force and area. — C91
CHAPTER INVESTIGATION *Pressure in Fluids* — C96

3.4 Fluids can exert a force on objects. — C98

4 Work and Energy — C112

the BIG idea
Energy is transferred when a force moves an object.

4.1 Work is the use of force to move an object. — C115
MATH IN SCIENCE *Working with Averages* — C120

4.2 Energy is transferred when work is done. — C121
THINK SCIENCE *How Do They Do It?* — C129

4.3 Power is the rate at which work is done. — C130
CHAPTER INVESTIGATION *Work and Power* — C136

5 Machines — C142

the BIG idea
Machines help people do work by changing the force applied to an object.

5.1 Machines help people do work. — C145
MATH IN SCIENCE *Changing Ratios to Percents* — C153

5.2 Six simple machines have many uses. — C154
CONNECTING SCIENCES *A Running Machine* — C163

5.3 Modern technology uses compound machines. — C164
CHAPTER INVESTIGATION *Design a Machine* — C170

Visual Highlights

Distance-Time Graph	C21
Velocity-Time Graphs	C30
Newton's Three Laws of Motion	C60
Orbits	C81
Conserving Mechanical Energy	C127
A Robot at Work	C168

Table of Contents xi

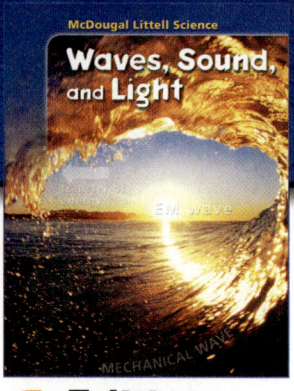

eEdition

UNIT D
Waves, Sound, and Light

Unit Features

SCIENTIFIC AMERICAN FRONTIERS IN SCIENCE *Sound Medicine* D2

TIMELINES IN SCIENCE *The Story of Light* D106

1 Waves D6

the BIG idea
Waves transfer energy and interact in predictable ways.

- **1.1 Waves transfer energy.** D9
  MATH IN SCIENCE *Mean, Median, and Mode* D15
- **1.2 Waves have measurable properties.** D16
  CHAPTER INVESTIGATION *Wavelength* D22
- **1.3 Waves behave in predictable ways.** D24
  CONNECTING SCIENCES *Tsunamis!* D29

2 Sound D34

the BIG idea
Sound waves transfer energy through vibrations.

- **2.1 Sound is a wave.** D37
  EXTREME SCIENCE *Sonic Booms* D44
- **2.2 Frequency determines pitch.** D45
- **2.3 Intensity determines loudness.** D52
  MATH IN SCIENCE *Interpreting Graphs* D57
- **2.4 Sound has many uses.** D58
  CHAPTER INVESTIGATION *Build a Stringed Instrument* D64

How is this guitar player producing sound? page D34

xii Physical Science

How does this phone stay connected? page D70

3 Electromagnetic Waves — D70

the BIG idea
Electromagnetic waves transfer energy through radiation.

- **3.1** Electromagnetic waves have unique traits. — D73
  - MATH IN SCIENCE *Using Exponents* — D78
- **3.2** Electromagnetic waves have many uses. — D79
  - THINK SCIENCE *Are Cell Phones Harmful?* — D87
- **3.3** The Sun is the source of most visible light. — D88
- **3.4** Light waves interact with materials. — D93
  - CHAPTER INVESTIGATION *Wavelength and Color* — D100

4 Light and Optics — D110

the BIG idea
Optical tools depend on the wave behavior of light.

- **4.1** Mirrors form images by reflecting light. — D113
  - MATH IN SCIENCE *Measuring Angles* — D118
- **4.2** Lenses form images by refracting light. — D119
  - CHAPTER INVESTIGATION *Looking at Lenses* — D124
- **4.3** The eye is a natural optical tool. — D126
- **4.4** Optical technology makes use of light waves. — D131
  - SCIENCE ON THE JOB *Optics in Photography* — D139

Visual Highlights

Graphing a Wave	D19
Sound Frequencies Heard by Animals	D47
How Musical Instruments Work	D61
The Electromagnetic Spectrum	D80
How a Convex Lens Forms an Image	D122
Microscopes and Telescopes	D133

Table of Contents xiii

UNIT E
Electricity and Magnetism

Unit Features

SCIENTIFIC AMERICAN   **FRONTIERS IN SCIENCE** *Electronics in Music*   E2

TIMELINES IN SCIENCE *The Story of Electronics*   E72

1 Electricity   E6

the BIG idea
Moving electric charges transfer energy.

1.1 Materials can become electrically charged.   E9
     CONNECTING SCIENCES *Electric Eels*   E17

1.2 Charges can move from one place to another.   E18
     CHAPTER INVESTIGATION *Lightning*   E26

1.3 Electric current is a flow of charge.   E28
     MATH IN SCIENCE *Using Variables*   E35

2 Circuits and Electronics   E40

the BIG idea
Circuits control the flow of electric charge.

2.1 Charge needs a continuous path to flow.   E43
     SCIENCE ON THE JOB *The Science of Electrical Work*   E50

2.2 Circuits make electric current useful.   E51
     MATH IN SCIENCE *Solving Percent Problems*   E56

2.3 Electronic technology is based on circuits.   E57
     CHAPTER INVESTIGATION *Design an Electronic Communication Device*   E66

How can circuits control the flow of charge? page E40

What force is acting on this compass needle? page E76

3 Magnetism — E76

the BIG idea
Current can produce magnetism, and magnetism can produce current.

3.1 Magnetism is a force that acts at a distance. — E79
  THINK SCIENCE *Can Magnets Heal People?* — E87
3.2 Current can produce magnetism. — E88
3.3 Magnetism can produce current. — E95
  CHAPTER INVESTIGATION *Build a Speaker* — E100
3.4 Generators supply electrical energy. — E102
  MATH IN SCIENCE *Using Significant Figures* — E107

Visual Highlights

How a Photocopier Works	E15
How Lightning Forms	E21
Batteries	E33
How a PC Works	E62
How Magnets Differ from Other Materials	E83
How a Motor Works	E93

Table of Contents xv

Features

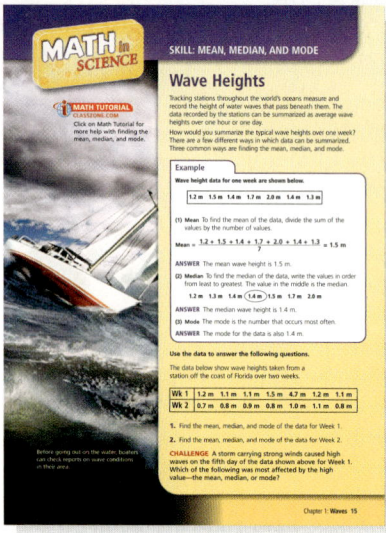

Math in Science

MATTER AND ENERGY
Making a Circle Graph	A26
Solving Proportions	A49
Using Formulas	A91
Metric Conversions	A109

CHEMICAL INTERACTIONS
Using Scientific Notation	B33
Calculating Ratios	B46
Analyzing Line Graphs	B77
Calculating Percentages	B139
Making Bar Graphs	B162

MOTION AND FORCES
Working with Units	C24
Using Significant Figures	C56
Creating a Line Graph	C90
Working with Averages	C120
Changing Ratios to Percents	C153

WAVES, SOUND, AND LIGHT
Mean, Median, and Mode	D15
Interpreting Graphs	D57
Using Exponents	D78
Measuring Angles	D118

ELECTRICITY AND MAGNETISM
Using Variables	E35
Solving Percent Problems	E56
Using Significant Figures	E107

Think Science

MATTER AND ENERGY
Finding Solutions	A77

CHEMICAL INTERACTIONS
Isolating Variables	B55

MOTION AND FORCES
Evaluating Hypotheses	C48
Isolating Variables	C129

WAVES, SOUND, AND LIGHT
Determining Relevance	D87

ELECTRICITY AND MAGNETISM
Evaluating Conclusions	E87

Connecting Sciences

MATTER AND ENERGY
Physical Science and Earth Science	A63

CHEMICAL INTERACTIONS
Physical Science and Life Science	B16
Physical Science and Earth Science	B124

MOTION AND FORCES
Physical Science and Life Science	C163

WAVES, SOUND, AND LIGHT
Physical Science and Earth Science	D29

ELECTRICITY AND MAGNETISM
Physical Science and Life Science	E17

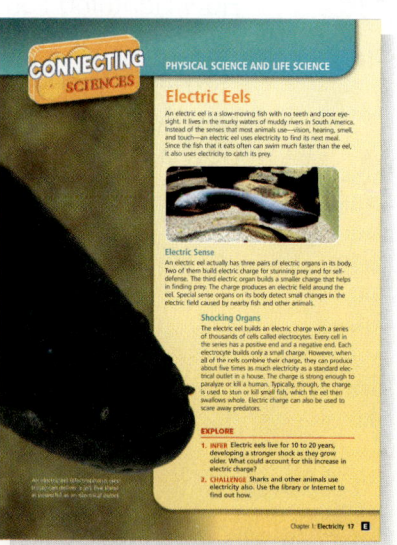

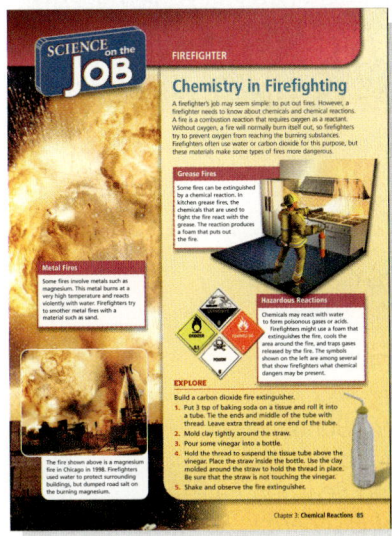

Frontiers in Science

MATTER AND ENERGY
Fuels of the Future — A2

CHEMICAL INTERACTIONS
Medicines from Nature — B2

MOTION AND FORCES
Robots on Mars — C2

WAVES, SOUND, AND LIGHT
Sound Medicine — D2

ELECTRICITY AND MAGNETISM
Electronics in Music — E2

Science on the Job

MATTER AND ENERGY
Cooking with Heat — A115

CHEMICAL INTERACTIONS
Chemistry in Firefighting — B85

MOTION AND FORCES
Physics for Rescuers — C15

WAVES, SOUND, AND LIGHT
Optics in Photography — D139

ELECTRICITY AND MAGNETISM
The Science of Electrical Work — E50

Timelines in Science

MATTER AND ENERGY
About Temperature and Heat — A96

CHEMICAL INTERACTIONS
The Story of Atomic Structure — B104

MOTION AND FORCES
Understanding Forces — C108

WAVES, SOUND, AND LIGHT
The Story of Light — D106

ELECTRICITY AND MAGNETISM
The Story of Electronics — E72

Extreme Science

MATTER AND ENERGY
Particles Too Small to See — A20

CHEMICAL INTERACTIONS
Stronger Than Steel — B153

MOTION AND FORCES
Bending Light — C84

WAVES, SOUND, AND LIGHT
Sonic Booms — D44

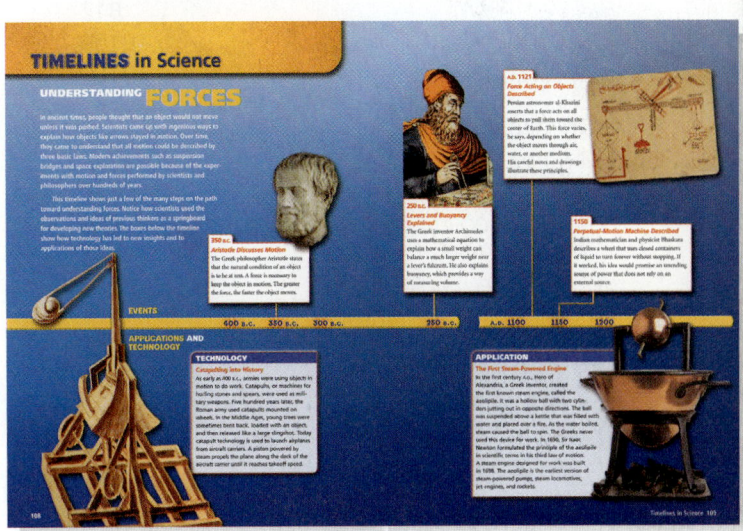

Table of Contents xvii

Internet Resources @ ClassZone.com

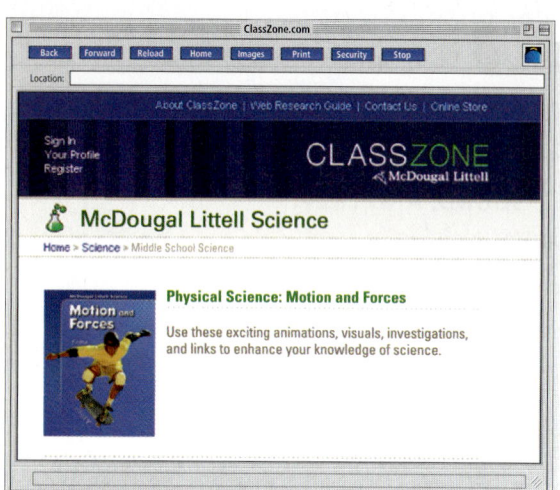

Simulations

MATTER AND ENERGY
Weight on Different Planets	A11
Gas Behavior	A33
Physical and Chemical Changes	A39
Potential Energy and Kinetic Energy	A69
Kinetic Energy and Temperature	A101
Conduction, Convection, or Radiation	A119

CHEMICAL INTERACTIONS
Build an Atom	B12
Mixing Alloys	B109
3-D Carbon Molecules	B150

MOTION AND FORCES
Changing Acceleration	C31
Applying Force	C39
Newton's Second Law	C50
Fluids and Pressure	C93
Work	C113
Mechanical Advantage	C161

WAVES, SOUND, AND LIGHT
Forces and Waves	D7
The Sun at Different Wavelengths	D71
Using Lenses to Form Images	D123

ELECTRICITY AND MAGNETISM
Static Electricity	E7
Ohm's Law	E29
Circuits	E41
Electromagnets	E77

Visualizations

MATTER AND ENERGY
Solar Cells	A88

CHEMICAL INTERACTIONS
Radioactive Decay	B32
Ionic and Covalent Bonds	B39
Polar Electron Cloud	B51
Concentration and Reaction Rate	B74
Endothermic and Exothermic Reactions	B90
Supersaturated Solutions and Precipitation	B118
Petroleum Distillation	B164

MOTION AND FORCES
Relative Motion	C7
Effect of Gravity in a Vacuum	C79
Transfer of Potential and Kinetic Energy	C126

WAVES, SOUND, AND LIGHT
Wave Graphing	D18
How Sound Travels	D35
Doppler Effect	D51
Electromagnetic Waves	D74
Reflection	D115

ELECTRICITY AND MAGNETISM
Hard Drive	E63
Motor	E92

Career Centers

Electrical Engineering	A5
Chemistry	B5
Physics and Engineering	C5
Audiology	D5
Music and Computer Science	E5

Resource Centers

MATTER AND ENERGY
Resources for the following topics may be found at ClassZone.com: *Scale Views of Matter; Volume; Scanning Tunneling Microscope Images; Mixtures; Chemical Properties of Matter; Melting Points and Boiling Points; Separating Materials from Mixtures; Kinetic Energy and Potential Energy; Electric Cars; Alternative Energy Sources; Temperature and Heat Research; Temperature and Temperature Scales; Thermal Energy.*

CHEMICAL INTERACTIONS
Resources for the following topics may be found at ClassZone.com: *Periodic Table; Atom; Elements Important to Life; Chemical Formulas; Properties of Ionic and Covalent Compounds; Balancing Chemical Equations; Catalysts in Living Things; Atomic Research; Aquifers and Purification; Acids and Bases; Alloys; Polymers; Nanotubes; Carbohydrates, Lipids, Proteins, and Nucleic Acids; Petroleum and Hydrocarbons.*

MOTION AND FORCES
Resources for the following topics may be found at ClassZone.com: *Finding Position; Acceleration; Inertia; Moving Rocks; Newton's Laws of Motion; Momentum; Gravity; Gravitational Lenses; Friction, Forces, and Surfaces; Force and Motion Research; Work; Power; Machines in Everyday Objects; Artificial Limbs; Nanomachines; Robots.*

WAVES, SOUND, AND LIGHT
Resources for the following topics may be found at ClassZone.com: *Waves; Wave Speed; Supersonic Aircraft; Sound Safety; Musical Instruments; The Electromagnetic Spectrum; Visible Light; Light Research; Optics; Microscopes and Telescopes; Lasers.*

ELECTRICITY AND MAGNETISM
Resources for the following topics may be found at ClassZone.com: *Lightning and Lightning Safety; Electrochemical Cells; Electrical Safety; Electronics; Electronic and Computer Research; Magnetism; Dams and Electricity; Energy Use and Conservation.*

Math Tutorials

MATTER AND ENERGY
Circle Graphs	A26
Solving Proportions	A49
Rates	A91
Temperature Conversions	A109

CHEMICAL INTERACTIONS
Scientific Notation	B33
Ratios	B46
Interpreting Line Graphs	B77
Understanding Percents	B139
Bar Graphs	B162

MOTION AND FORCES
Units and Rates	C24
Rounding Decimals	C56
Creating a Line Graph	C90
Finding the Mean	C120
Percents and Fractions	C153

WAVES, SOUND, AND LIGHT
Finding the Mean, Median, and Mode	D15
Interpreting Line Graphs	D57
Positive and Negative Exponents	D78
Measuring Angles	D118

ELECTRICITY AND MAGNETISM
Equations	E35
Percents and Proportions	E56
Rounding Decimals	E107

NSTA SciLinks

Codes for use with the NSTA SciLinks site may be found on every chapter opener.

Content Reviews

There is a content review for every chapter at ClassZone.com.

Test Practice

There is a standardized test practice for every chapter at ClassZone.com.

Explore the Big idea

Chapter Opening Inquiry

Each chapter opens with hands-on explorations that introduce the chapter's Big Idea.

Matter and Energy

What Has Changed? Where Does the Sugar Go?	A7
Float or Sink; Hot Chocolate	A39
A Penny for Your Energy; Hot Dog!	A69
Moving Colors, Does It Chill?	A101

Chemical Interactions

That's Far! Element Safari	B7
Mixing It Up; The Shape of Things	B39
Changing Steel Wool; A Different Rate	B67
Does It Dissolve? Acid Test	B109
Structure and Function; Sweet Crackers	B145

Motion and Forces

Off the Wall; Rolling Along	C7
Popping Ping-Pong Balls; Take Off!	C39
Let It Slide; Under Pressure	C75
Bouncing Ball; Power Climbing	C113
Changing Direction; Shut the Door!	C143

Waves, Sound, and Light

How Can Energy Be Passed Along? How Can You Change a Wave?	D7
What Gives a Sound Its Qualities? How Does Size Affect Sound?	D35
What Melts the Ice Cubes? What Is White Light Made Of?	D71
How Does a Spoon Reflect Your Face? Why Do Things Look Different Through Water?	D111

Electricity and Magnetism

How Do the Pieces of Tape Interact? Why Does the Water React Differently?	E7
Will the Flashlight Still Work? What's Inside a Calculator?	E41
Is It Magnetic? How Can You Make a Chain?	E77

xx Physical Science

Chapter Investigations

Full-Period Labs

The Chapter Investigations are in-depth labs that let you form and test a hypothesis, build a model, or sometimes design your own investigation.

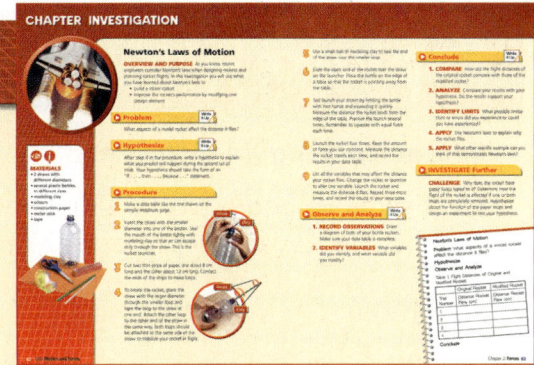

Matter and Energy

Mass and Volume	A14
Freezing Point	A56
Energy Conversions	A84
Insulators *Design Your Own*	A122

Chemical Interactions

Modeling Atomic Masses	B24
Chemical Bonds	B60
Exothermic or Endothermic?	B92
Acids and Bases	B132
Polymers	B170

Motion and Forces

Acceleration and Slope	C32
Newton's Laws of Motion	C62
Pressure in Fluids	C96
Work and Power	C136
Design a Machine *Design Your Own*	C170

Waves, Sound, and Light

Wavelength	D22
Build a Stringed Instrument *Design Your Own*	D64
Wavelength and Color	D100
Looking at Lenses	D124

Electricity and Magnetism

Lightning	E26
Design an Electronic Communication Device *Design Your Own*	E66
Build a Speaker	E100

Table of Contents **xxi**

Explore

Introductory Inquiry Activities

Most sections begin with a simple activity that lets you explore the Key Concept before you read the section.

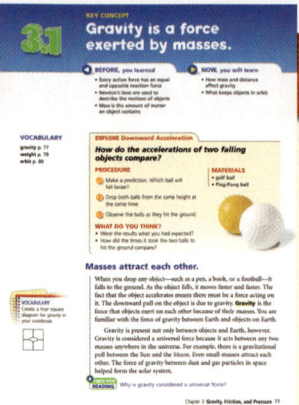

Matter and Energy

Similar Objects	A9
Mixed Substances	A21
Solids and Liquids	A27
Physical Properties	A41
Identifying Substances	A58
Energy	A71
Solar Cells	A86
Temperature	A103
Conduction	A116

Chemical Interactions

The Size of Atoms	B9
Similarities and Differences of Objects	B17
Compounds	B41
Bonds in Metals	B56
Chemical Changes	B69
Energy Changes	B86
Mixtures	B111
Solutions and Temperature	B117
Acids and Bases	B125
Carbon in Food	B154

Motion and Forces

Location	C9
Speed	C16
Changing Motion	C41
Acceleration	C49
Collisions	C64
Downward Acceleration	C77
Pressure	C91
Forces in Liquid	C98
Work	C115
Power	C130
Machines	C145
Changing Forces	C154

Waves, Sound, and Light

Waves	D9
Reflection	D24
Sound	D37
Pitch	D45
Echoes	D58
Electromagnetic Waves	D73
Radio Waves	D79
Light and Matter	D93
Reflection	D113
Refraction	D119
Focusing Vision	D126
Combining Lenses	D131

Electricity and Magnetism

Static Electricity	E9
Static Discharge	E18
Current	E28
Circuits	E43
Codes	E57
Magnetism	E79
Magnetism from Electric Current	E88
Energy Conversion	E95

Investigate

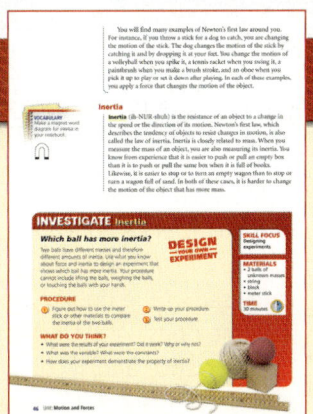

Skill Labs

Each Investigate activity gives you a chance to practice a specific science skill related to the content that you're studying.

Matter and Energy

Mass	Modeling	A17
Mixtures	Inferring	A24
Liquids	Measuring	A31
Chemical Changes	Measuring	A47
Separating Mixtures	Design Your Own	A61
Potential Energy	Design Your Own	A75
Solar Energy	Observing	A89
Temperature Measurements	Modeling	A107
Heat Transfer	Measuring	A112

Chemical Interactions

Masses of Atomic Particles	Modeling	B13
Radioactivity	Modeling	B31
Element Ratios	Modeling	B43
Crystals	Observing	B53
Chemical Reactions	Inferring	B74
Conservation of Mass	Measuring	B79
Sugar Combustion	Inferring	B95
Solutions	Observing	B113
Solubility	Design Your Own	B120
Alloys	Observing	B137
Carbon Bonding	Modeling	B149
Organic Molecules	Inferring	B158

Motion and Forces

Changing Positions	Observing	C12
Speed and Distance	Design Your Own	C19
Acceleration	Measuring	C27
Inertia	Design Your Own	C46
Motion and Force	Hypothesizing	C54
Newton's Third Law	Observing	C58
Momentum	Observing	C66
Gravity	Predicting	C82
Friction in Air	Design Your Own	C88
Bernoulli's Principle	Observing	C100
Work	Measuring	C118
Mechanical Energy	Analyzing Data	C125
Power	Measuring	C133
Efficiency	Analyzing Data	C151
Pulleys	Inferring	C157

Waves, Sound, and Light

Wave Types	Comparing	D13
Frequency	Collecting Data	D20
Diffraction	Predicting	D26
Sound Energy	Observing	D41
Sound Frequency	Inferring	D48
Loudness	Observing	D53
Wave Behavior	Design Your Own	D76
The Electromagnetic Spectrum	Drawing Conclusions	D84
Artificial Lighting	Design Your Own	D90
Mixing Colors	Observing	D98
The Law of Reflection	Analyzing	D115
Vision	Observing	D128
Optical Tools	Design Your Own	D134

Electricity and Magnetism

Making a Static Detector	Inferring	E14
Conductors and Insulators	Interpreting Data	E22
Electric Cells	Inferring	E31
Fuses	Making Models	E48
Circuits	Inferring	E54
Digital Information	Making Models	E59
Earth's Magnetic Field	Inferring	E85
Electromagnets	Observing	E90
Electric Current	Inferring	E98
Power	Making Models	E105

Table of Contents xxiii

Standards and Benchmarks

Each unit in **Physical Science** addresses some of the learning goals described in the *National Science Education Standards* (NSES) and the Project 2061 *Benchmarks for Science Literacy.* The following National Science Education Standards are also addressed in the book introduction, unit and chapter features, and lab investigations in all the units: A.9 Understandings About Scientific Inquiry, E.6 Understandings About Science and Technology, F.5 Science and Technology in Society, G.1 Science as a Human Endeavor, G.2 Nature of Science, G.3 History of Science.

National Science Education Standards

Content Standards

UNIT A Matter and Energy

B.1.a	A substance has characteristic properties, such as density, a boiling point, and solubility. A mixture of substances often can be separated into the original substances using these properties.	B.3.a	Energy is a property of substances and is often associated with heat, light, electricity, mechanical motion, and sound. Energy is transferred in many ways.
B.1.c	There are more than 100 known elements that combine to produce compounds.	B.3.b	Heat flows from warmer objects to cooler ones, until both reach the same temperature.

UNIT B Chemical Interactions

B.1.a	A substance has characteristic properties, such as density, a boiling point, and solubility, all of which do not depend on the amount of the sample.	B.1.c	Chemical elements do not break down during normal reactions involving heating, electric current, or acids. There are more than 100 known elements that combine in many ways to produce compounds. Compounds account for the living and non-living substances that we encounter.
B.1.b	Substances react chemically in characteristic ways with other substances to form new substances, or compounds. These compounds have different properties from the original substances. In chemical reactions, the total mass is conserved. Substances are placed in groups, such as metals, if they react in similar ways.	C.1.a	Living systems demonstrate the complementary nature of structure and function.
		D.1.h	The atmosphere is a mixture of nitrogen, oxygen, and small amounts of other gases such as water vapor.

xxiv Physical Science

UNIT C Motion and Forces

B.1.a	A substances has characteristic properties, such as density.	D.3.c	Gravity is the force that keeps planets in orbit around the Sun, governs motion within the solar system, holds us to Earth's surface, and produces tides.
B.2.a	An object's motion is described by its position, direction of motion, and speed. That motion can be measured and shown on a graph.	E.6.c	Science and technology often work together. Science helps drive technology. Technology is used to improve scientific investigations.
B.2.b	An object will move in a straight line at a constant speed unless a force acts on it.	E.6.d	Perfectly designed solutions do not exist. All technological solutions have trade-offs, such as cost, safety, and efficiency.
B.2.c	If more than one force acts on an object along a straight line, then the forces will reinforce or cancel each other.	E.6.e	All designs have limits, including those having to do with material properties, safety, and environmental protection.
B.3.a	Energy is often associated with heat, sound, and mechanical motion. Energy is transferred in many ways.		

UNIT D Waves, Sound, and Light

B.3.a	Energy is often associated with sound, light, and mechanical motion. Energy is transferred in many ways.	B.3.f	Energy from the Sun is transferred to Earth in the form of visible light, infrared light, and ultraviolet light.
B.3.c	Light interacts with matter by transmission, absorption, or scattering. To see an object, light from that object must enter the eye.		

UNIT E Electricity and Magnetism

B.3.a	Energy is the property of substances that is often associated with electricity. Energy is transferred in many ways.	B.3.e	In most chemical reactions, energy is transferred into or out of a system. Heat, light, motion, or electricity all might be involved in such transfers.
B.3.d	Circuits transfer electrical energy. Heat, light, sound, and chemical changes are produced.		

Process and Skill Standards

A.1	Identify questions that can be answered through investigation.	A.7	Communicate procedures, results, and conclusions.
A.2	Design and conduct a scientific investigation.	A.8	Use mathematics in scientific inquiry.
		E.1	Identify a problem to be solved.
A.3	Use appropriate tools and techniques to gather, analyze, and interpret data.	E.2	Design a solution or product.
		E.3	Implement the proposed solution.
A.4	Use evidence to describe, predict, explain, and model.	E.4	Evaluate the solution or design.
A.5	Use critical thinking to find relationships between results and interpretations.	E.5	Communicate the process of technological design.
A.6	Consider alternative explanations and predictions.	F.4.c	Use systematic thinking to estimate risks.

Project 2061 Benchmarks

Content Benchmarks

UNIT A Matter and Energy

4.D.1	All matter is made up of atoms.	4.E.4	Energy appears in different forms, including heat, mechanical, chemical, and gravitational.
4.D.2	Equal volumes of different substances usually have different weights.	8.B.1	The choice of materials for a job depends on their properties.
4.D.3	Atoms and molecules are always in motion.	8.C.1	Energy can change from one form to another. In the process, some energy is always converted to heat. Some systems transform energy with less loss of heat than others.
4.E.1	Energy cannot be created or destroyed, but it can be changed from one form to another.		
4.E.2	Most of what goes on in the universe involves energy transformations.		
4.E.3	Heat can be transferred through materials by the collisions of atoms or across space by radiation.		

UNIT B Chemical Interactions

4.D.1	All matter is made of atoms, which are far too small to see. The atoms of any element are alike but are different from atoms of other elements. Atoms may stick together in molecules or may be packed together in large arrays.	4.D.7	No matter how substances in a closed system interact with one another, the total weight of the system remains the same.
		10.F.3	The work of scientist Antoine Lavoisier led to the modern science of chemistry.
4.D.4	The temperature and acidity of a solution influence reaction rates.	10.F.4	Lavoisier tested the concept of conservation of matter by measuring the substances involved in burning.
4.D.6	There are groups of elements that have similar properties, including highly reactive metals, less-reactive metals, highly reactive nonmetals, and some almost completely nonreactive gases. Carbon and hydrogen are essential elements of living matter.	10.G.1	The discovery that minerals containing uranium darken photographic film led to the idea of radioactivity.
		10.G.2	Scientists Marie Curie and Pierre Curie isolated the elements radium and polonium.

UNIT C Motion and Forces

4.B.3	Everything on or near Earth is pulled toward Earth's center by the force of gravity.	4.G.2	The sun's gravitational pull holds the earth and other planets in their orbits. The planets' gravity keeps their moons in orbit around them.
4.E.1	Energy cannot be created or destroyed, but it can be changed from one form to another.	8.B.4	The use of robots has changed the nature of work in many fields, including manufacturing.
4.E.4	Energy appears in many different forms, including heat, chemical, mechanical, and gravitational.	10.A.1	An object's motion is relative to some other object or point in space.
4.F.3	An unbalanced force acting on an object changes its speed and/or direction of motion.	10.B.1	Newton's Laws describe motion everywhere in the universe.
4.G.1	Every object exerts the force of gravity on every other object.	11.C.2	A system may stay the same because no forces are acting on the system, or forces are acting on the system but they all cancel each other out.

UNIT D Waves, Sound, and Light

4.F.1	Light from the sun is made up of a mixture of many different colors of light, even though the light looks almost white.	4.F.4	Vibrations in materials set up wavelike disturbances that spread away from the source. Sound and earthquake waves are examples. These and other waves move at different speeds through different materials.
4.F.2	Something can be "seen" when light waves emitted or reflected by it enter the eye—just as something can be "heard" when sound waves from it enter the ear.	4.F.5	Human eyes respond to only a narrow range of wavelengths of electromagnetic radiation—visible light. Differences of wavelength within that range are perceived as differences in color.

UNIT E Electricity and Magnetism

1.C.6	Computers are important in science.	8.D.2	The ability to code information as electric currents in wires has made communication many times faster than is possible by mail or sound.
3.A.2	Technology is essential to science.		
3.A.3	Engineers and others who work in design and technology use scientific knowledge to solve practical problems.	8.E.1	Computers use digital codes containing only two symbols to perform all operations.
4.G.3	Electric currents and magnets can exert a force on each other.	9.A.6	Numbers can be represented by using only 1 and 0.
8.C.4	Electrical energy can be produced from a variety of energy sources and can be transformed into almost any other form of energy.		

Process and Skill Benchmarks

1.A.3	Some knowledge in science is very old and yet is still used today.	9.C.4	Graphs show patterns and can be used to make predictions.
1.C.1	Contributions to science and technology have been made by different kinds of people, in different cultures, at different times.	9.D.3	The mean, median, and mode tell different things about the middle of a data set.
2.B.1	Mathematics contributes to science and technology.	12.B.1	Find what percentage one number is of another.
3.B.1	Design requires taking constraints into account.	12.B.7	Determine the appropriate unit for an answer. Convert units.
3.B.2	Technologies have effects other than those intended.	12.B.8	Round a calculation to the correct number of significant figures.
3.C.4	Technology has influenced the course of history.	12.C.3	Use and read instruments that measure length, volume, weight, time, rate, and temperature.
8.B.1	The choice of materials for a job depends on their properties.		
9.A.3	How decimals should be written depends on how precise the measurements are.	12.D.1	Use tables and graphs to organize information and identify relationships.
9.B.3	Graphs can show the relationship between two variables.	12.E.3	Be skeptical of arguments based on very small samples for which there was no control group.

Introducing Physical Science

Scientists are curious. Since ancient times, they have been asking and answering questions about the world around them. Scientists are also very suspicious of the answers they get. They carefully collect evidence and test their answers many times before accepting an idea as correct.

In this book you will see how scientific knowledge keeps growing and changing as scientists ask new questions and rethink what was known before. The following sections will help get you started.

Unifying Principles of Physical Science   xxix

What do scientists know about matter and energy? These pages introduce four unifying principles that will give you a big picture of physical science.

The Nature of Science   xxxviii

How do scientists learn? This section provides an overview of scientific thinking and the processes that scientists use to ask questions and to find answers.

The Nature of Technology   xlii

How do we use what scientists learn? These pages introduce you to how people develop and use technologies to design solutions to real-world problems.

Using McDougal Littell Science   xliv

How can you learn more about science? This section provides helpful tips on how to learn and use science from the key parts of this program—the text, the visuals, the activities, and the Internet resources.

UNIFYING PRINCIPLES of Physical Science

What Is Physical Science?

In the simplest terms, physical science is the study of what things are made of and how they change. It combines the studies of both physics and chemistry. Physics is the science of matter, energy, and forces. It includes the study of topics such as motion, light, and electricity and magnetism. Chemistry is the study of the structure and properties of matter, and it especially focuses on how substances change into different substances.

The text and pictures in this book will help you learn key concepts and important facts about physical science. A variety of activities will help you investigate these concepts. As you learn, it helps to have a big picture of physical science as a framework for this new information. The four unifying principles listed below will give you this big picture. Read the next few pages to get an overview of each of these principles and a sense of why they are so important.

- **Matter is made of particles too small to see.**
- **Matter changes form and moves from place to place.**
- **Energy changes from one form to another, but it cannot be created or destroyed.**
- **Physical forces affect the movement of all matter on Earth and throughout the universe.**

the BIG idea

Each chapter begins with a big idea. Keep in mind that each big idea relates to one or more of the unifying principles.

Unifying Principles xxix

UNIFYING PRINCIPLE

Matter is made of particles too small to see.

This simple statement is the basis for explaining an amazing variety of things about the world. For example, it explains why substances can exist as solids, liquids, and gases, and why wood burns but iron does not. Like the tiles that make up this mosaic picture, the particles that make up all substances combine to make patterns and structures that can be seen. Unlike these tiles, the individual particles themselves are far too small to see.

What It Means

To understand this principle better, let's take a closer look at the two key words: *matter* and *particles*.

Matter

Objects you can see and touch are all around you. The materials that these objects are made of are called **matter.** All living things—even you—are also matter. Even though you can't see it, the air around you is matter too. Scientists often say that matter is anything that has mass and takes up space. **Mass** is a measure of the amount of matter in an object. We use the word **volume** to refer to the amount of space an object or a substance takes up.

Particles

The tiny particles that make up all matter are called **atoms.** Just how tiny are atoms? They are far too small to see, even through a powerful microscope. In fact, an atom is more than a million times smaller than the period at the end of this sentence.

There are more than 100 basic kinds of matter called **elements.** For example, iron, gold, and oxygen are three common elements. Each element has its own unique kind of atom. The atoms of any element are all alike but different from the atoms of any other element.

Many familiar materials are made of particles called molecules. In a **molecule,** two or more atoms stick together to form a larger particle. For example, a water molecule is made of two atoms of hydrogen and one atom of oxygen.

Why It's Important

Understanding atoms and molecules makes it possible to explain and predict the behavior of matter. Among other things, this knowledge allows scientists to

- explain why different materials have different characteristics
- predict how a material will change when heated or cooled
- figure out how to combine atoms and molecules to make new and useful materials

Unifying Principles xxxi

UNIFYING PRINCIPLE

Matter changes form and moves from place to place.

You see matter change form every day. You see the ice in your glass of juice disappear without a trace. You see a black metal gate slowly develop a flaky, orange coating. Matter is constantly changing and moving.

What It Means

Remember that matter is made of tiny particles called atoms. Atoms are constantly moving and combining with one another. All changes in matter are the result of atoms moving and combining in different ways.

Matter Changes and Moves

You can look at water to see how matter changes and moves. A block of ice is hard like a rock. Leave the ice out in sunlight, however, and it changes into a puddle of water. That puddle of water can eventually change into water vapor and disappear into the air. The water vapor in the air can become raindrops, which may fall on rocks, causing them to weather and wear away. The water that flows in rivers and streams picks up tiny bits of rock and carries them from one shore to another. Understanding how the world works requires an understanding of how matter changes and moves.

Matter Is Conserved

No matter was lost in any of the changes described above. The ice turned to water because its molecules began to move more quickly as they got warmer. The bits of rock carried away by the flowing river were not gone forever. They simply ended up farther down the river. The puddles of rainwater didn't really disappear; their molecules slowly mixed with molecules in the air.

Under ordinary conditions, when matter changes form, no matter is created or destroyed. The water created by melting ice has the same mass as the ice did. If you could measure the water vapor that mixes with the air, you would find it had the same mass as the water in the puddle did.

Why It's Important

Understanding how mass is conserved when matter changes form has helped scientists to

- describe changes they see in the world
- predict what will happen when two substances are mixed
- explain where matter goes when it seems to disappear

UNIFYING PRINCIPLE

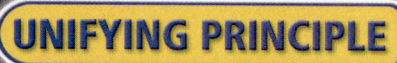

Energy changes from one form to another, but it cannot be created or destroyed.

When you use energy to warm your food or to turn on a flashlight, you may think that you "use up" the energy. Even though the campstove fuel is gone and the flashlight battery no longer functions, the energy they provided has not disappeared. It has been changed into a form you can no longer use. Understanding how energy changes forms is the basis for understanding how heat, light, and motion are produced.

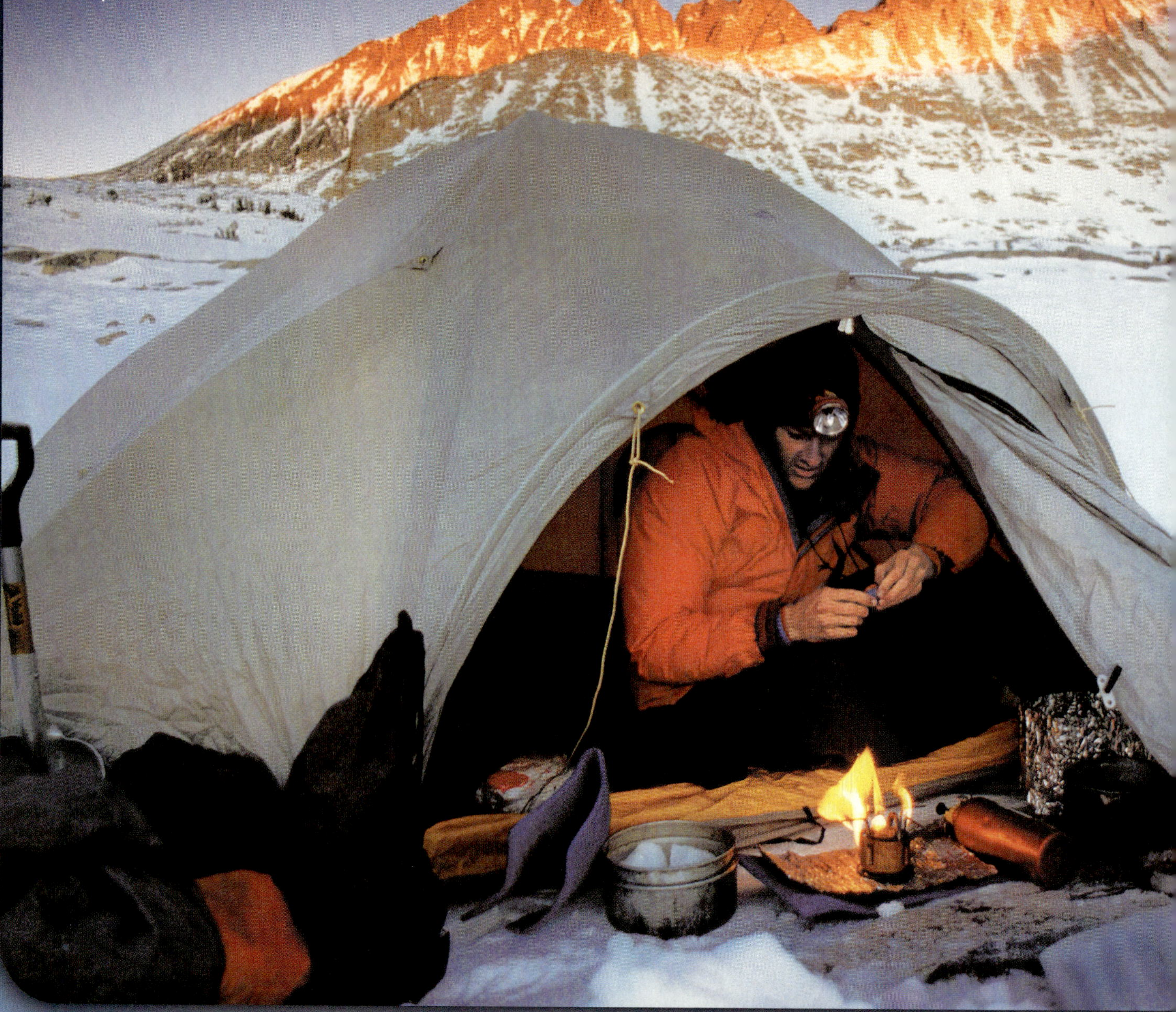

What It Means

Changes that you see around you depend on energy. **Energy,** in fact, means the ability to cause change. The electrical energy from an outlet changes into light and heat in a light bulb. Plants change the light energy from the Sun into chemical energy, which animals use to power their muscles.

Energy Changes Forms

Using energy means changing energy. You probably have seen electric energy changing into light, heat, sound, and mechanical energy in household appliances. Fuels like wood, coal, and oil contain chemical energy that produces heat when burned. Electric power plants make electrical energy from a variety of energy sources, including falling water, nuclear energy, and fossil fuels.

Energy Is Conserved

Energy can be converted into forms that can be used for specific purposes. During the conversion, some of the original energy is converted into unwanted forms. For instance, when a power plant converts the energy of falling water into electrical energy, some of the energy is lost to friction and sound.

Similarly, when electrical energy is used to run an appliance, some of the energy is converted into forms that are not useful. Only a small percentage of the energy used in a light bulb, for instance, produces light; most of the energy becomes heat. Nonetheless, the total amount of energy remains the same through all these conversions.

The fact that energy does not disappear is a law of physical science. The **law of conservation of energy** states that energy cannot be created or destroyed. It can only change form.

Why It's Important

Understanding that energy changes form but does not disappear has helped scientists to

- predict how energy will change form
- manage energy conversions in useful ways
- build and improve machines

UNIFYING PRINCIPLE

Physical forces affect the movement of all matter on Earth and throughout the universe.

What makes the world go around? The answer is simple: forces. Forces allow you to walk across the room, and forces keep the stars together in galaxies. Consider the forces acting on the rafts below. The rushing water is pushing the rafts forward. The force from the people paddling helps to steer the rafts.

What It Means

A **force** is a push or a pull. Every time you push or pull an object, you're applying a force to that object, whether or not the object moves. There are several forces—several pushes and pulls—acting on you right now. All these forces are necessary for you to do the things you do, even sitting and reading.

- You are already familiar with the force of gravity. **Gravity** is the force of attraction between two objects. Right now gravity is at work pulling you to Earth and Earth to you. The Moon stays in orbit around Earth because gravity holds it close.

- A contact force occurs when one object pushes or pulls another object by touching it. If you kick a soccer ball, for instance, you apply a contact force to the ball. You apply a contact force to a shopping cart that you push down a grocery aisle or a sled that you pull up a hill.

- **Friction** is the force that resists motion between two surfaces pressed together. If you've ever tried to walk on an icy sidewalk, you know how important friction can be. If you lightly rub your finger across a smooth page in a book and then across a piece of sandpaper, you can feel how the different surfaces produce different frictional forces. Which is easier to do?

- There are other forces at work in the world too. For example, a compass needle responds to the magnetic force exerted by Earth's magnetic field, and objects made of certain metals are attracted by magnets. In addition to magnetic forces, there are electrical forces operating between particles and between objects. For example, you can demonstrate electrical forces by rubbing an inflated balloon on your hair. The balloon will then stick to your head or to a wall without additional means of support.

Why It's Important

Although some of these forces are more obvious than others, physical forces at work in the world are necessary for you to do the things you do. Understanding forces allows scientists to

- predict how objects will move
- design machines that perform complex tasks
- predict where planets and stars will be in the sky from one night to the next

The Nature of Science

You may think of science as a body of knowledge or a collection of facts. More important, however, science is an active process that involves certain ways of looking at the world.

Scientific Habits of Mind

Scientists are curious. They are always asking questions. Scientists have asked questions such as, "What is the smallest form of matter?" and "How do the smallest particles behave?" These and other important questions are being investigated by scientists around the world.

Scientists are observant. They are always looking closely at the world around them. Scientists once thought the smallest parts of atoms were protons, neutrons, and electrons. Later, protons and neutrons were found to be made of even smaller particles called quarks.

Scientists are creative. They draw on what they know to form possible explanations for a pattern, an event, or an interesting phenomenon that they have observed. Then scientists create a plan for testing their ideas.

Scientists are skeptical. Scientists don't accept an explanation or answer unless it is based on evidence and logical reasoning. They continually question their own conclusions and the conclusions suggested by other scientists. Scientists trust only evidence that is confirmed by other people or methods.

Scientists cannot always make observations with their own eyes. They have developed technology, such as this particle detector, to help them gather information about the smallest particles of matter.

xxxviii Introducing Physical Science

Scientists ask questions about the physical world and seek answers through carefully controlled procedures. Here a researcher works with supercooled magnets.

Science Processes at Work

You can think of science as a continuous cycle of asking and seeking answers to questions about the world. Although there are many processes that scientists use, scientists typically do each of the following:

- Observe and ask a question
- Determine what is known
- Investigate
- Interpret results
- Share results

Observe and Ask a Question

It may surprise you that asking questions is an important skill. A scientific process may start when a scientist asks a question. Perhaps scientists observe an event or a process that they don't understand, or perhaps answering one question leads to another.

Determine What Is Known

When beginning an inquiry, scientists find out what is already known about a question. They study results from other scientific investigations, read journals, and talk with other scientists. A scientist working on subatomic particles is most likely a member of a large team using sophisticated equipment. Before beginning original research, the team analyzes results from previous studies.

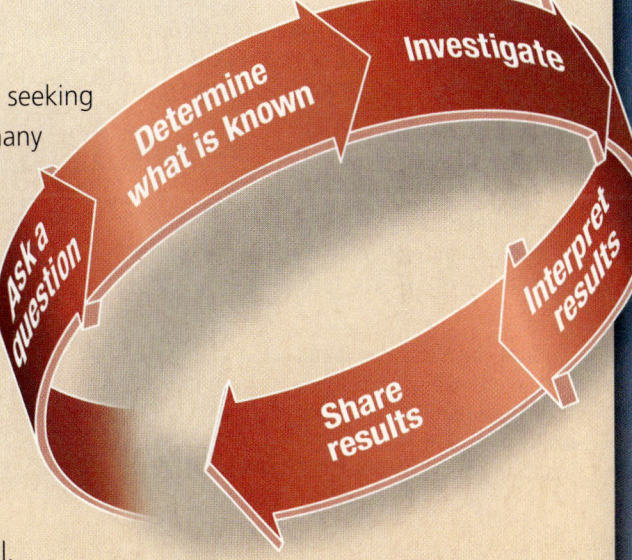

The Nature of Science xxxix

Investigate

Investigating is the process of collecting evidence. Two important ways of investigating are observing and experimenting.

Observing is the act of noting and recording an event, a characteristic, or anything else detected with an instrument or with the senses. A researcher may study the properties of a substance by handling it, finding its mass, warming or cooling it, stretching it, and so on. For information about the behavior of subatomic particles, however, a researcher may rely on technology such as scanning tunneling microscopes, which produce images of structures that cannot be seen with the eye.

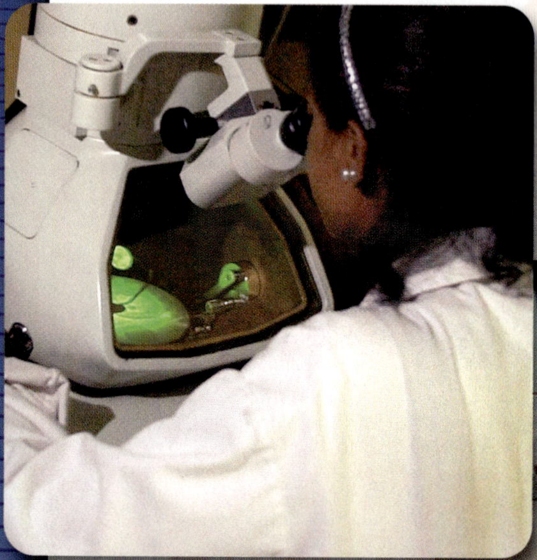

An **experiment** is an organized procedure to study something under controlled conditions. In order to study the effect of wing shape on the motion of a glider, for instance, a researcher would need to conduct controlled studies in which gliders made of the same materials and with the same masses differed only in the shape of their wings.

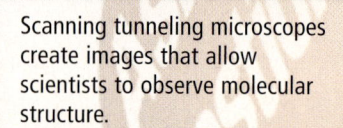

Scanning tunneling microscopes create images that allow scientists to observe molecular structure.

Physical chemists have found a way to observe chemical reactions at the atomic level. Using lasers, they can watch bonds breaking and new bonds forming.

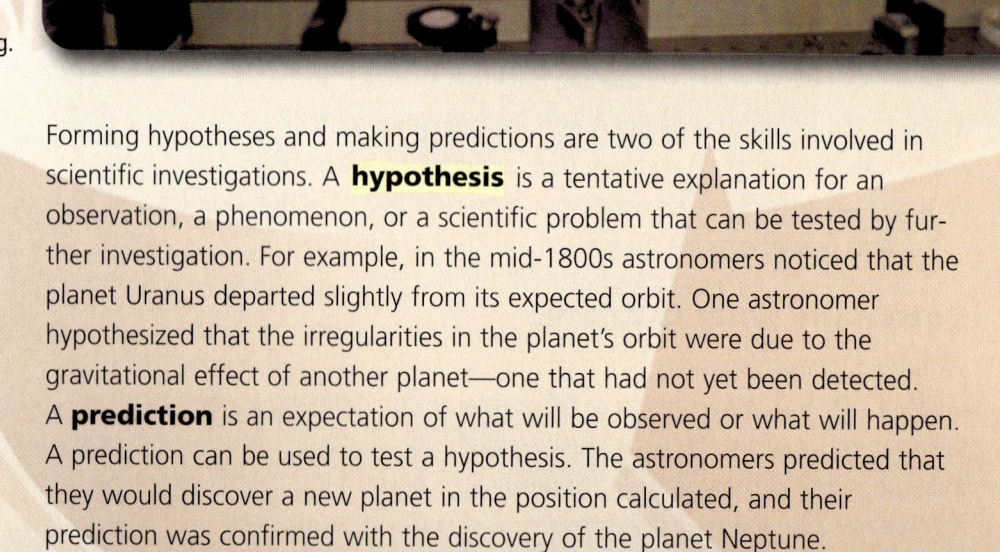

Forming hypotheses and making predictions are two of the skills involved in scientific investigations. A **hypothesis** is a tentative explanation for an observation, a phenomenon, or a scientific problem that can be tested by further investigation. For example, in the mid-1800s astronomers noticed that the planet Uranus departed slightly from its expected orbit. One astronomer hypothesized that the irregularities in the planet's orbit were due to the gravitational effect of another planet—one that had not yet been detected.
A **prediction** is an expectation of what will be observed or what will happen. A prediction can be used to test a hypothesis. The astronomers predicted that they would discover a new planet in the position calculated, and their prediction was confirmed with the discovery of the planet Neptune.

Interpret Results

As scientists investigate, they analyze their evidence, or data, and begin to draw conclusions. **Analyzing data** involves looking at the evidence gathered through observations or experiments and trying to identify any patterns that might exist in the data. Scientists often need to make additional observations or perform more experiments before they are sure of their conclusions. Many times scientists make new predictions or revise their hypotheses.

Often scientists use computers to help them analyze data. Computers reveal patterns that might otherwise be missed.

Scientists use computers to create models of objects or processes they are studying. This model shows carbon atoms forming a sphere.

Share Results

An important part of scientific investigation is sharing results of experiments. Scientists read and publish in journals and attend conferences to communicate with other scientists around the world. Sharing data and procedures gives them a way to test one another's results. They also share results with the public through newspapers, television, and other media.

The Nature of Science xli

The Nature of Technology

When you think of technology, you may think of cars, computers, and cell phones, as well as refrigerators, radios, and bicycles. Technology is not only the machines and devices that make modern lives easier, however. It is also a process in which new methods and devices are created. Technology makes use of scientific knowledge to design solutions to real-world problems.

Science and Technology

Science and technology go hand in hand. Each depends upon the other. Even designing a device as simple as a toaster requires knowledge of how heat flows and which materials are the best conductors of heat. Just as technology based on scientific knowledge makes our lives easier, some technology is used to advance scientific inquiry itself. For example, researchers use a number of specialized instruments to help them collect data. Microscopes, telescopes, spectrographs, and computers are just a few of the tools that help scientists learn more about the world. The more information these tools provide, the more devices can be developed to aid scientific research and to improve modern lives.

The Process of Technological Design

The process of technology involves many choices. For example, how does an automobile engineer design a better car? Is a better car faster? safer? cheaper? Before designing any new machine, the engineer must decide exactly what he or she wants the machine to do as well as what may be given up for the machine to do it. A faster car may get people to their destinations more quickly, but it may cost more and be less safe. As you study the technological process, think about all the choices that were made to build the technologies you use.

Identify a Need
Successful technology fills a need; it helps us perform a task we need or want to do. For example, as more cars appear on the road, noise and air pollution become serious threats to the environment and to people's health. Gas consumption also depletes precious petroleum resources. There is a need to find a fuel source for a car that will not pollute the air and that will never run out.

Design and Develop
Hydrogen fuel cells are a potential solution to this need. These cells combine hydrogen and oxygen into water, producing electricity in the process. Engineers have found a way to make fuel cells small enough to fit into a car, yet able to produce enough electricity to power an electric motor. Before arriving at this final design, engineers tried many others.

Test and Improve
Just because a technology works doesn't mean it cannot be improved. A fuel-cell-powered car has been driven from San Francisco to Washington, D.C., but it probably will be a while before it's in dealer showrooms. Engineers won't know how these cars will perform until they're driven in real-world conditions. Engineers also won't know if the average driver will be able to handle the necessary maintenance on the car until the car is made available to ordinary drivers. Improvements in the future may well bring cars powered by fuel cells into garages everywhere.

Using McDougal Littell Science

Reading Text and Visuals

This book is organized to help you learn. Use these boxed pointers as a path to help you learn and remember the **Big Ideas** and **Key Concepts**.

Read the Big Idea.
As you read **Key Concepts** for the chapter, relate them to **the Big Idea**.

Take notes.
Use the strategies on the **Getting Ready to Learn** page.

CHAPTER 1 — Atomic the Per...

the BIG idea
A substance's atomic structure determines its physical and chemical properties.

Key Concepts

SECTION 1.1 Atoms are the smallest form of elements.
Learn about the structure of atoms and how each element's atoms are different.

SECTION 1.2 Elements make up the periodic table.
Learn how the periodic table of the elements is organized.

SECTION 1.3 The periodic table is a map of the elements.
Learn more about the groups of elements in the periodic table.

Internet Preview
CLASSZONE.COM
Chapter 1 online resources: Content Review, Simulation, Visualization, three Resource Centers, Math Tutorial, Test Practice

B 6 Unit: Chemical Interactions

CHAPTER 1 Getting Ready to Learn

CONCEPT REVIEW
- Matter is made of particles called atoms that are too small to see with the eyes.
- Matter can be an element, a compound, or a mixture.
- Matter can undergo physical and chemical changes.

VOCABULARY REVIEW
See Glossary for definitions.
atom
compound
element

CONTENT REVIEW
CLASSZONE.COM
Review concepts and vocabulary.

TAKING NOTES

MAIN IDEA WEB
Write each new blue heading in a box. Then write notes in boxes around the center box that give important terms and details about that blue heading.

VOCABULARY STRATEGY
Write each new vocabulary term in the center of a **frame game** diagram. Decide what information to frame it with. Use examples, descriptions, parts, sentences that use the term in context, or pictures. You can change the frame to fit each term.

See the Note-Taking Handbook on pages R45–R51.

SCIENCE NOTEBOOK

- Atoms are made of protons, neutrons, and electrons.
- The atomic number is the number of protons in the nucleus.
- Each element is made of a different atom.
- Every element has a certain number of protons in its nucleus.

| Central part of atom |
| Contains most of an atom's mass | NUCLEUS | Electrons move about it |
| Is made of protons and neutrons |

B 8 Unit: Chemical Interactions

Read each heading.
See how it fits into the outline of the chapter.

1.1 KEY CONCEPT
Atoms are the smallest form of elements.

Remember what you know.
Think about concepts you learned earlier and preview what you'll learn now.

BEFORE, you learned
- All matter is made of atoms
- Elements are the simplest substances

NOW, you will learn
- Where atoms are found and how they are named
- About the structure of atoms
- How ions are formed from atoms

VOCABULARY
proton p. 11
neutron p. 11
nucleus p. 11
electron p. 11
atomic number p. 12
atomic mass number p. 12
isotope p. 12
ion p. 14

EXPLORE The Size of Atoms
How small can you cut paper?

PROCEDURE
1. Cut the strip of paper in half. Cut one of these halves in half.
2. Continue cutting one piece of paper in half as many times as you can.

MATERIALS
- strip of paper about 30 centimeters long
- scissors

WHAT DO YOU THINK?
- How many cuts were you able to make?
- Do you think you could keep cutting the paper forever? Why or why not?

Try the activities.
They will introduce you to science concepts.

All matter is made of atoms.

Think of all the substances you see and touch every day. Are all of these substances the same? Obviously, the substances that make up this book you're reading are quite different from the substances in the air around you. So how many different substances can there be? This is a question people have been asking for thousands of years.

About 2400 years ago, Greek philosophers proposed that everything on Earth was made of only four basic substances—air, water, fire, and earth. Everything else contained a mixture of these four substances. As time went on, chemists came to realize that there had to be more than four basic substances. Today chemists know that about 100 basic substances, or elements, account for everything we see and touch. Sometimes these elements appear by themselves. Most often, however, these elements appear in combination with other elements to make new substances. In this section, you'll learn about the atoms of the elements that make up the world and how these atoms differ from one another.

READING TIP
The word *element* is related to *elementary*, which means "basic."

Learn the vocabulary.
Take notes on each term.

Chapter 1: **Atomic Structure and the Periodic Table** 9 B

Chapter 1: **Atomic Structure and the Periodic Table** 7 B

Using McDougal Littell Science **xlv**

Reading Text and Visuals

Study the visuals.

- Read the title.
- Read all labels and captions.
- Figure out what the picture is showing. Notice colors, arrows, and lines.
- Answer the question. **Reading Visuals** questions will help you understand the picture.

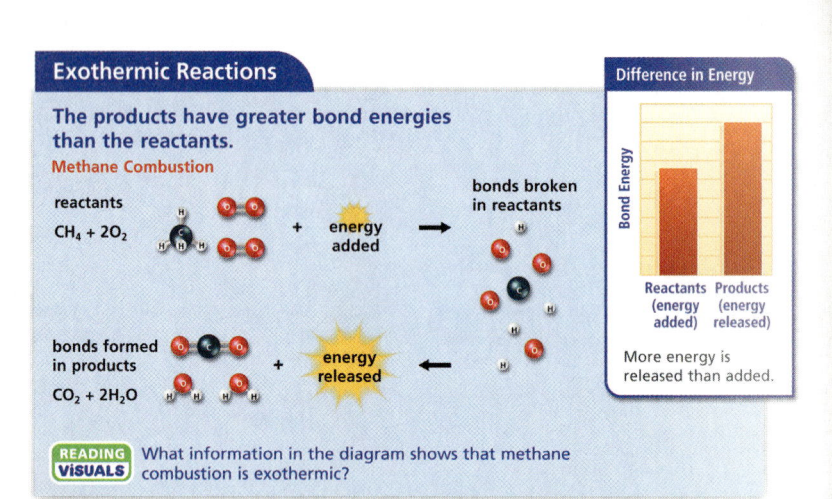

Exothermic Reactions

The products have greater bond energies than the reactants.

Methane Combustion

reactants
$CH_4 + 2O_2$ + energy added → bonds broken in reactants

bonds formed in products
$CO_2 + 2H_2O$ + energy released ←

Difference in Energy

Reactants (energy added) | Products (energy released)

More energy is released than added.

READING VISUALS What information in the diagram shows that methane combustion is exothermic?

Read one paragraph at a time.

Look for a topic sentence that explains the main idea of the paragraph. Figure out how the details relate to that idea. One paragraph might have several important ideas; you may have to reread to understand.

All common combustion reactions, such as the combustion of methane, are exothermic. To determine how energy changes in this reaction, the bond energies in the reactants—oxygen and methane—and in the products—carbon dioxide and water—can be added and compared. This process is illustrated by the diagram shown above. The difference in energy is released to the surrounding air as heat.

Some chemical reactions release excess energy as light instead of heat. For example, glow sticks work by a chemical reaction that releases energy as light. One of the reactants, a solution of hydrogen peroxide, is contained in a thin glass tube within the plastic stick. The rest of the stick is filled with a second chemical and a brightly colored dye. When you bend the stick, the glass tube inside it breaks and the two solutions mix. The result is a bright glow of light.

These jellyfish glow because of exothermic chemical reactions.

Exothermic chemical reactions also occur in living things. Some of these reactions release energy as heat, and others release energy as light. Fireflies light up due to a reaction that takes place between oxygen and a chemical called luciferin. This type of exothermic reaction is not unique to fireflies. In fact, similar reactions are found in several different species of fish, squid, jellyfish, and shrimp.

CHECK YOUR READING In which ways might an exothermic reaction release energy?

Answer the questions.

Check Your Reading questions will help you remember what you read.

B 88 Unit: Chemical Interactions

xlvi Introducing Physical Science

Doing Labs

To understand science, you have to see it in action. Doing labs helps you understand how things really work.

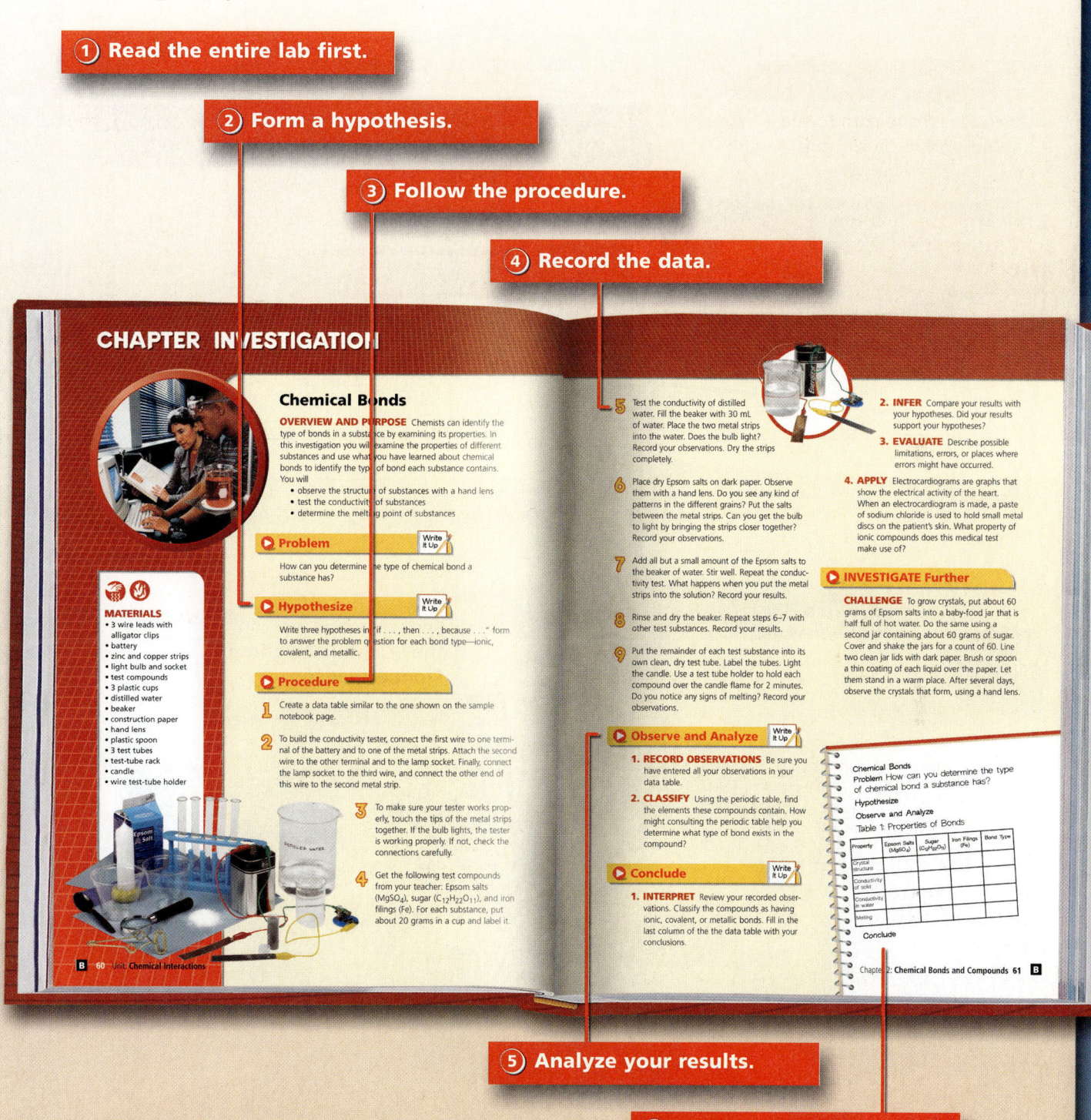

① **Read the entire lab first.**

② **Form a hypothesis.**

③ **Follow the procedure.**

④ **Record the data.**

⑤ **Analyze your results.**

⑥ **Write your lab report.**

Using McDougal Littell Science xlvii

Using Technology

The Internet is a great source of information about up-to-date science. The ClassZone Web site and SciLinks have exciting sites for you to explore. Video clips and simulations can make science come alive.

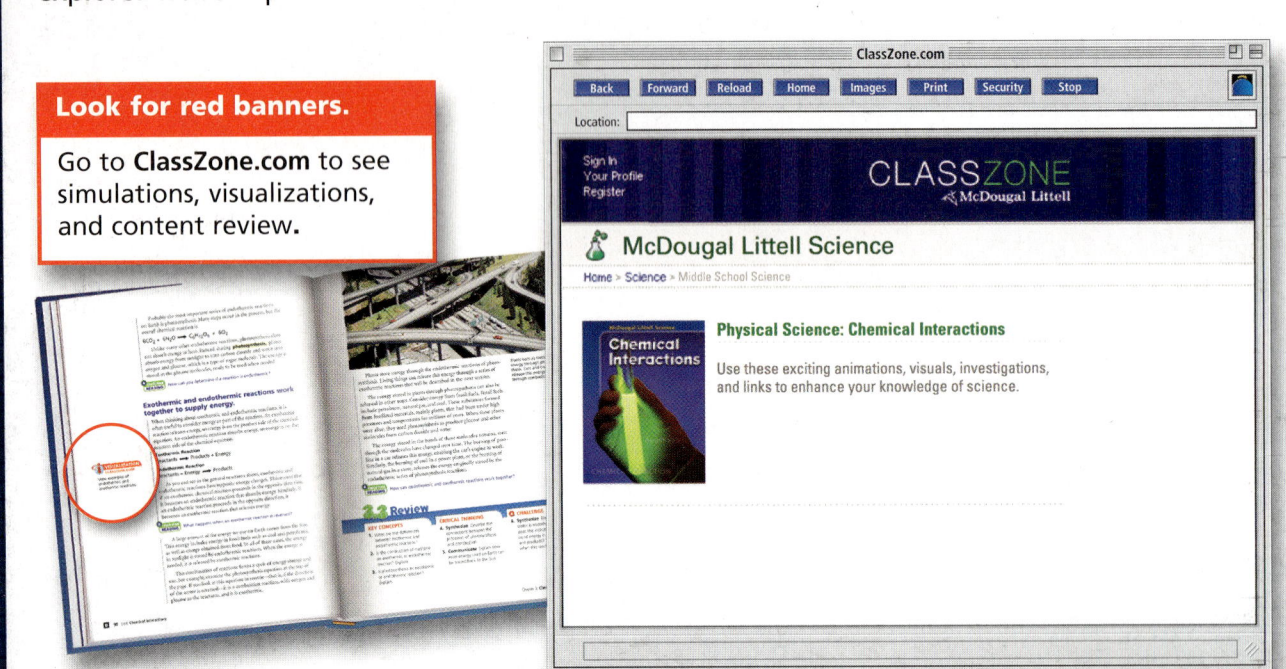

Look for red banners.

Go to **ClassZone.com** to see simulations, visualizations, and content review.

Watch the videos.

See science at work in the **Scientific American Frontiers** video.

Look up SciLinks.

Go to **scilinks.org** to explore the topic.

Forces **Code: MDL005**

xlviii Introducing Physical Science

UNIT A

Matter and Energy

radiation

mass

HEAT

physical change

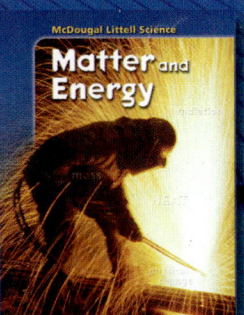

Matter and Energy
Contents Overview

Unit Features
FRONTIERS IN SCIENCE Fuels of the Future 2
TIMELINES IN SCIENCE About Temperature and Heat 96

1 Introduction to Matter　　6
the BIG idea
Everything that has mass and takes up space is matter.

2 Properties of Matter　　38
the BIG idea
Matter has properties that can be changed by physical and chemical processes.

3 Energy　　68
the BIG idea
Energy has different forms, but it is always conserved.

4 Temperature and Heat　　100
the BIG idea
Heat is a flow of energy due to temperature differences.

FRONTIERS in Science

FUELS of the FUTURE

Where does this spacecraft get its fuel?

SCIENTIFIC AMERICAN FRONTIERS

View the "Sunrayce" segment of your *Scientific American Frontiers* video to learn about a cross-country race in which cars use solar power instead of gasoline.

Deep Space 1 was an experimental design. Its successful mission prepared the way to the development of more ion-propelled spacecraft.

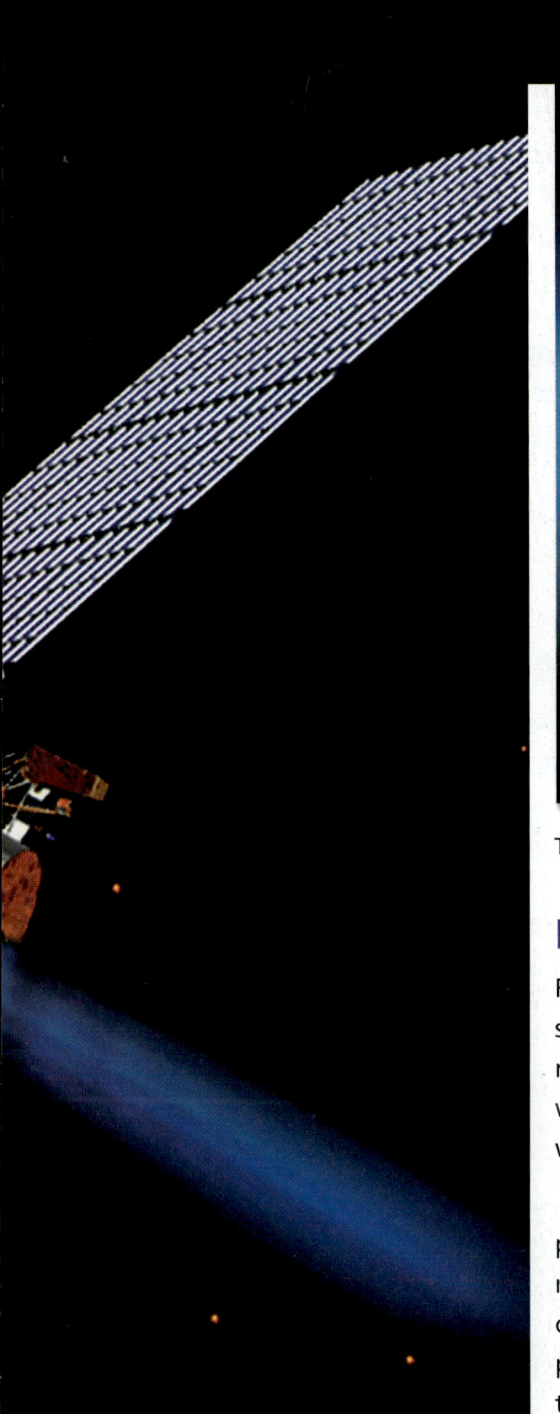

The stream of ions glows blue as it is shot out of an ion-propulsion engine.

Ion Engines for Long Voyages

Rocket engines must provide huge amounts of energy to move spacecraft away from Earth and keep them in orbit. The fuel required can weigh more than the spacecraft themselves. That is why scientists and engineers are always looking for more efficient ways to give spacecraft and other vehicles the energy to move.

One method of powering spacecraft uses electrically charged particles called ions. The atoms of a gas—usually xenon—are first made into ions. An electric field is then used to pull these ions out of the engine at a very high speed—faster than 100,000 kilometers per hour (62,000 mi/h). This stream of rapidly moving ions works like the gases coming out of a jet engine on a plane—propelling the spacecraft in the direction opposite to the ion stream.

An advantage of ion propulsion is that its fuel is much lighter than the chemical fuel used in rockets. Ion propulsion does not provide enough thrust to be used for a rocket launch, but it can be used to move a spacecraft through long distances in outer space. This method of propulsion provides a small force to the spacecraft; however, over time the spacecraft can reach great speeds.

The space probe *Deep Space 1* was the first to use an ion engine to travel between planets. The engine generated enough speed for the probe to follow and photograph comet Borrelly in 2001.

Solar sails will reflect sunlight to move a spacecraft through space.

Running on Sunlight

Solar energy is used for travel in outer space, where there is plenty of sunlight and very little friction to slow down a spacecraft. However, once a spacecraft travels far away from the Sun—as far as the outer planets Jupiter and Saturn—the amount of energy reaching it is far less than the energy it was getting near Earth. The sunlight can be helpful only if solar cells on the vehicle can collect enough of it. One solution is to reflect sunlight. Scientists are developing solar sails, which will act like enormous mirrors. The pressure of reflected sunlight on the sails can be used to move a large ship through space—even far from the Sun.

Beaming Energy from Earth

Another way to power a spacecraft is to send energy to it all the way from Earth. This idea is called beamed energy propulsion. A beam delivers energy to solar sails on the spacecraft. The energy can be in the form of microwaves—the same energy that heats food in a microwave oven or delivers calls on a cell phone. Or it can be in the form of laser light, a very concentrated beam of visible light. This method has already been used successfully to power very small vehicles, 10 centimeters (4 in.) long. Experiments are under way with larger spacecraft.

Combined Technologies

Some recent space flights have combined common and experimental technologies. For example, the *Cassini* space probe has two regular rocket engines for propulsion. Other energy comes from three generators powered by radioactive decay. This combination of engines allowed *Cassini* to be the largest and most complicated spacecraft ever launched. Its goal is to explore Saturn.

SCIENTIFIC AMERICAN FRONTIERS

View the "Sunrayce" segment of your *Scientific American Frontiers* video to see what is involved in solar-car racing.

IN THIS SCENE FROM THE VIDEO ▶
Students from California State University, Los Angeles, work on their solar car.

CATCHING THE SUN'S RAYS Since 1990 teams of college students have built and raced solar-powered cars. The races are held every two years to promote awareness of solar energy and to inspire young people to work in science and engineering.

Solar cells on the cars' bodies convert sunlight into electricity. The goal is to make lightweight cars that convert sunlight efficiently. Today's solar cars can reach speeds of up to 75 miles per hour, but the average racing speed is 25 miles per hour. On cloudy or rainy days, the teams conserve power by traveling more slowly—or risk running down their batteries.

In 2003 the American Solar Challenge took place on historic Route 66 from Chicago to Claremont, California. At 3700 kilometers (2300 mi), the ten-day event was the longest solar-car race in the world.

A 4 Unit: **Matter and Energy**

Alternative Fuels on Earth

Scientists and inventors have long been looking for practical alternative fuels to power vehicles on Earth as well as in outer space. Most vehicle engines on Earth use gasoline or other fossil fuels. These fuels are based on resources, such as petroleum, that are found in underground deposits. Those deposits will not be replaced for millions of years. Solar energy, by contrast, is endlessly renewable, so it seems to be a good alternative to nonrenewable fossil fuels.

Solar-powered cars rely on solar cells, which convert the energy of sunlight directly into electrical energy that can be stored in batteries. One outstanding solar car was built by Dutch students and entered in the 2001 World Solar Challenge.

The students' car, called the *Nuna*, used several technologies that had been developed for space travel. Its body was reinforced with Kevlar, a space-age material that is also used in satellites, space suits, and bulletproof vests. During the race, the *Nuna* covered 3010 kilometers of desert in Australia, breaking solar-car speed records, and won the race.

Does the development of solar cars like the *Nuna* mean that most people will be driving solar cars soon? Unfortunately, such cars run only when the Sun is shining unless they rely on batteries—and it takes hundreds of pounds of batteries to store the amount of energy in a gallon of gasoline. As with spacecraft, the goal is to design a vehicle in which the fuel doesn't outweigh the vehicle itself.

UNANSWERED Questions

Even as scientists and inventors solve problems in solar technology, new questions arise.

- Can solar technology be made affordable?
- Is solar technology practical for large-scale public transportation?
- Are there any hidden costs to the use of alternative fuels?

UNIT PROJECTS

As you study this unit, work alone or with a group on one of these projects.

Build a Solar Oven

Design and build a solar oven that can boil a quarter cup of water.

- Plan and sketch a design for a solar oven that can reach 100°C.
- Collect materials and assemble your oven. Then conduct trials and improve your design.

Multimedia Presentation

Create an informative program on solar race cars and the way they work.

- Collect information about solar race cars. Research how they are powered.
- Examine why solar cars have specific shapes. Learn how the solar panels and batteries work together.
- Give a multimedia presentation describing what you learned.

Design an Experiment

Design an experiment that compares how well two of the following alternative energy sources move an object: solar energy, wind power, biomass (fuel from plant material), waste-material fuel, hydrogen fuel cells, heat exchangers.

- Research the energy sources, and pick two types to compare.
- List materials for your experiment. Create a data table and write up your procedure.
- Describe your experiment for the class.

CAREER CENTER
CLASSZONE.COM

Learn more about careers in electrical engineering.

CHAPTER 1

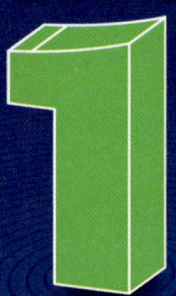

Introduction to Matter

the BIG idea

Everything that has mass and takes up space is matter.

What matter can you identify in this photograph?

Key Concepts

SECTION 1.1 Matter has mass and volume.
Learn what mass and volume are and how to measure them.

SECTION 1.2 Matter is made of atoms.
Learn about the movement of atoms and molecules.

SECTION 1.3 Matter combines to form different substances.
Learn how atoms form compounds and mixtures.

SECTION 1.4 Matter exists in different physical states.
Learn how different states of matter behave.

Internet Preview

CLASSZONE.COM

Chapter 1 online resources: Content Review, two Simulations, four Resource Centers, Math Tutorial, Test Practice

A 6 Unit: Matter and Energy

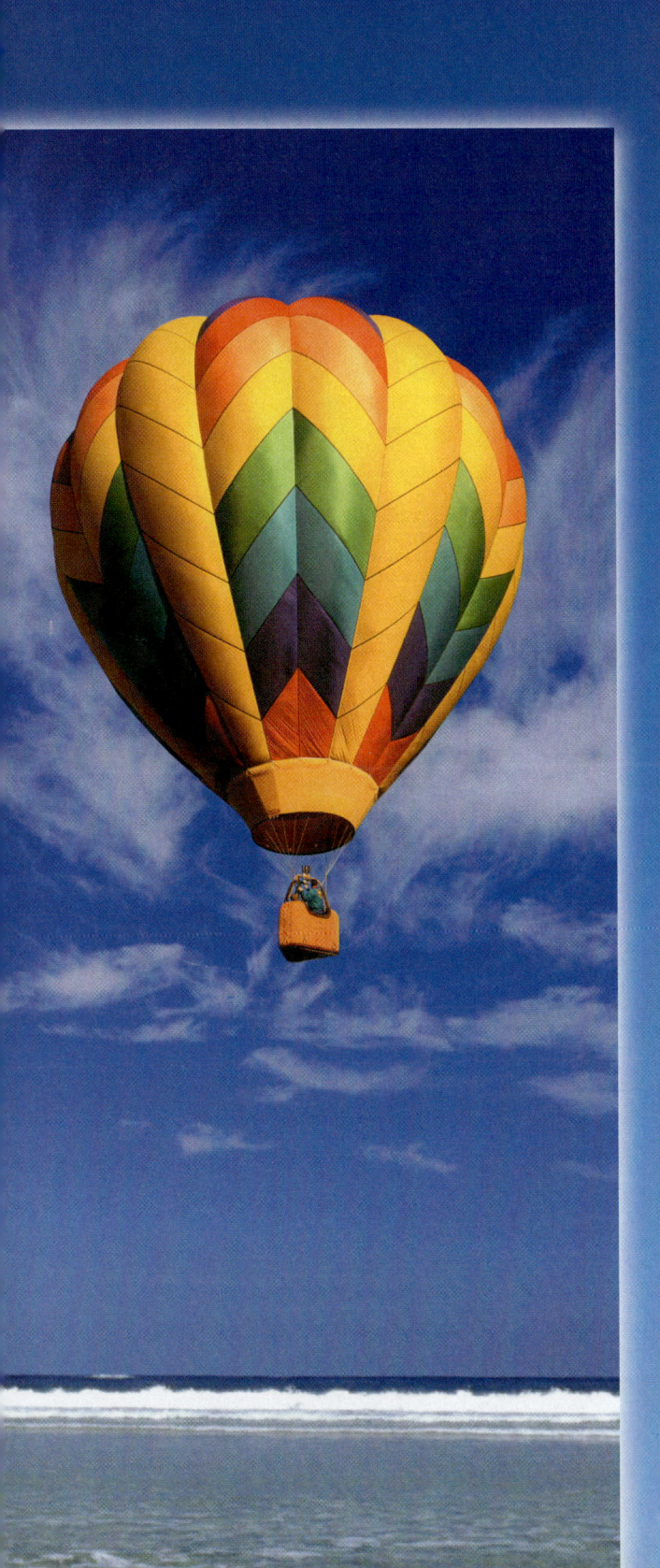

EXPLORE the BIG idea

What Has Changed?

Blow up a balloon. Observe it. Let the air out of the balloon slowly. Observe it again.

Observe and Think Did the amount of material that makes up the balloon change? Did the amount of air inside the balloon change? How did the amount of air inside the balloon affect the size of the balloon?

Where Does the Sugar Go?

Stir some sugar into a glass of water. Observe what happens.

Observe and Think What happened to the sugar as you stirred? Do you think you would be able to separate the sugar from the water? If so, how?

Internet Activity: Scale

Go to **ClassZone.com** to explore the smallest units of matter. Start with a faraway view of an object. Then try closer and closer views until you see that object at the atomic level.

Observe and Think Are all objects seen at faraway views made up of the same parts at an atomic level? Explain your answer.

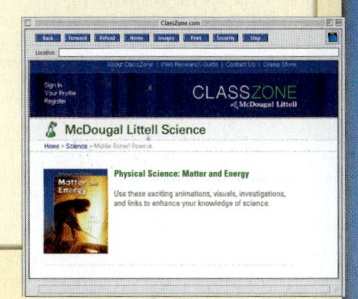

NSTA **SciLinks**
scilinks.org

Solids, Liquids, and Gases **Code: MDL061**

Chapter 1: **Introduction to Matter** 7

CHAPTER 1
Getting Ready to Learn

CONCEPT REVIEW

- Matter is made of particles too small to see.
- Energy and matter change from one form to another.
- Energy cannot be created or destroyed.

VOCABULARY REVIEW

See Glossary for definitions.

particle

substance

CONTENT REVIEW
CLASSZONE.COM
Review concepts and vocabulary.

TAKING NOTES

MAIN IDEA AND DETAIL NOTES

Make a two-column chart. Write the main ideas, such as those in the blue headings, in the column on the left. Write details about each of those main ideas in the column on the right.

VOCABULARY STRATEGY

Write each new vocabulary term in the center of a **four square** diagram. Write notes in the squares around each term. Include a definition, some characteristics, and some examples of the term. If possible, write some things that are not examples of the term.

See the Note-Taking Handbook on pages R45–R51.

SCIENCE NOTEBOOK

MAIN IDEAS	DETAIL NOTES
1. All objects are made of matter.	1. All objects and living organisms are matter.
	1. Light and sound are not matter.
2. Mass is a measure of the amount of matter.	2. A balance can be used to compare masses.
	2. Standard unit of mass is kilogram (kg).

Definition	Characteristics
the downward pull on an object due to gravity	• standard unit is newton (N)
	• is measured by using a scale

WEIGHT

Examples	Nonexamples
On Earth, a 1 kg object has a weight of 9.8 N.	not the same as mass, which is a measure of how much matter an object contains

A 8 Unit: Matter and Energy

1.1 KEY CONCEPT
Matter has mass and volume.

◄ **BEFORE, you learned**
- Scientists study the world by asking questions and collecting data
- Scientists use tools such as microscopes, thermometers, and computers

► **NOW, you will learn**
- What matter is
- How to measure the mass of matter
- How to measure the volume of matter

VOCABULARY
matter p. 9
mass p. 10
weight p. 11
volume p. 11

EXPLORE Similar Objects

How can two similar objects differ?

PROCEDURE

1. Look at the two balls but do not pick them up. Compare their sizes and shapes. Record your observations.

2. Pick up each ball. Compare the way the balls feel in your hands. Record your observations.

WHAT DO YOU THINK?
How would your observations be different if the larger ball were made of foam?

MATERIALS
2 balls of different sizes

All objects are made of matter.

Suppose your class takes a field trip to a museum. During the course of the day you see mammoth bones, sparkling crystals, hot-air balloons, and an astronaut's space suit. All of these things are matter.

Matter is what makes up all of the objects and living organisms in the universe. As you will see, **matter** is anything that has mass and takes up space. Your body is matter. The air that you breathe and the water that you drink are also matter. Matter makes up the materials around you. Matter is made of particles called atoms, which are too small to see. You will learn more about atoms in the next section.

Not everything is matter. Light and sound, for example, are not matter. Light does not take up space or have mass in the same way that a table does. Although air is made of atoms, a sound traveling through air is not.

VOCABULARY
Make four square diagrams for *matter* and for *mass* in your notebook to help you understand their relationship.

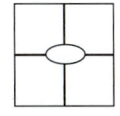

CHECK YOUR READING What is matter? How can you tell if something is matter?

Chapter 1: Introduction to Matter 9 **A**

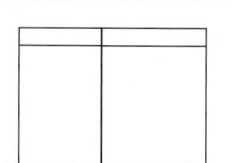

Mass is a measure of the amount of matter.

Different objects contain different amounts of matter. **Mass** is a measure of how much matter an object contains. A metal teaspoon, for example, contains more matter than a plastic teaspoon. Therefore, a metal teaspoon has a greater mass than a plastic teaspoon. An elephant has more mass than a mouse.

MAIN IDEA AND DETAILS As you read, write the blue headings on the left side of a two-column chart. Add details in the other column.

CHECK YOUR READING How are matter and mass related?

Measuring Mass

When you measure mass, you compare the mass of the object with a standard amount, or unit, of mass. The standard unit of mass is the kilogram (kg). A large grapefruit has a mass of about one-half kilogram. Smaller masses are often measured in grams (g). There are 1000 grams in a kilogram. A penny has a mass of between two and three grams.

How can you compare the masses of two objects? One way is to use a pan balance, as shown below. If two objects balance each other on a pan balance, then they contain the same amount of matter. If a basketball balances a metal block, for example, then the basketball and the block have the same mass. Beam balances work in a similar way, but instead of comparing the masses of two objects, you compare the mass of an object with a standard mass on the beam.

A bowling ball and a basketball are about the same size, but a bowling ball has more mass.

10 Unit: Matter and Energy

Measuring Weight

When you hold an object such as a backpack full of books, you feel it pulling down on your hands. This is because Earth's gravity pulls the backpack toward the ground. Gravity is the force that pulls two masses toward each other. In this example, the two masses are Earth and the backpack. **Weight** is the downward pull on an object due to gravity. If the pull of the backpack is strong, you would say that the backpack weighs a lot.

Weight is measured by using a scale, such as a spring scale like the one shown on the right, that tells how hard an object is pushing or pulling on it. The standard scientific unit for weight is the newton (N). A common unit for weight is the pound (lb).

Mass and weight are closely related, but they are not the same. Mass describes the amount of matter an object has, and weight describes how strongly gravity is pulling on that matter. On Earth, a one-kilogram object has a weight of 9.8 newtons (2.2 lb). When a person says that one kilogram is equal to 2.2 pounds, he or she is really saying that one kilogram has a weight of 2.2 pounds on Earth. On the Moon, however, gravity is one-sixth as strong as it is on Earth. On the Moon, the one-kilogram object would have a weight of 1.6 newtons (0.36 lb). The amount of matter in the object, or its mass, is the same on Earth as it is on the Moon, but the pull of gravity is different.

Gravity is pulling down on both the girl and the backpack. The heavier the backpack is, the stronger the pull of gravity is on it.

SIMULATION CLASSZONE.COM
Compare weights on different planets.

CHECK YOUR READING What is the difference between mass and weight?

Volume is a measure of the space matter occupies.

Matter takes up space. A bricklayer stacks bricks on top of each other to build a wall. No two bricks can occupy the same place because the matter in each brick takes up space.

The amount of space that matter in an object occupies is called the object's **volume.** The bowling ball and the basketball shown on page 10 take up approximately the same amount of space. Therefore, the two balls have about the same volume. Although the basketball is hollow, it is not empty. Air fills up the space inside the basketball. Air and other gases take up space and have volume.

Chapter 1: **Introduction to Matter** 11

Determining Volume by Formula

Find out more about volume.

There are different ways to find the volume of an object. For objects that have well-defined shapes, such as a brick or a ball, you can take a few measurements of the object and calculate the volume by substituting these values into a formula.

A rectangular box, for example, has a length, a width, and a height that can be measured. To find the volume of the box, multiply the three values.

$$\text{Volume} = \text{length} \cdot \text{width} \cdot \text{height}$$
$$V = lwh$$

If you measure the length, the width, and the height of the box in centimeters (cm), the volume has a unit of centimeters times centimeters times centimeters, or centimeters cubed (cm^3). If the measurements are meters, the unit of volume is meters cubed (m^3). All measurements must be in the same unit to calculate volume.

Other regular solids, such as spheres and cylinders, also have formulas for calculating volumes. All formulas for volume require multiplying three dimensions. Units for volume are often expressed in terms of a length unit cubed, that is, a length to the third power.

Calculating Volume

▶ **Sample Problem**

What is the volume of a pizza box that is 8 cm high, 38 cm wide, and 38 cm long?

What do you know?	length = 38 cm, width = 38 cm, height = 8 cm
What do you want to find out?	Volume
Write the formula:	$V = lwh$
Substitute into the formula:	V = 38 cm · 38 cm · 8 cm
Calculate and simplify:	11,552 cm · cm · cm = 11,552 cm^3
Check that your units agree:	Unit is cm^3. Unit of volume is cm^3. Units agree.
Answer:	11,552 cm^3

▶ **Practice the Math**

1. A bar of gold is 10 cm long, 5 cm wide, and 7 cm high. What is its volume?
2. What is the volume of a large block of wood that is 1 m long, 0.5 m high, and 50 cm wide?

Measuring Volume by Displacement

Although a box has a regular shape, a rock does not. There is no simple formula for calculating the volume of something with an irregular shape. Instead, you can make use of the fact that two objects cannot be in the same place at the same time. This method of measuring is called displacement.

① Add water to a graduated cylinder. Note the volume of the water by reading the water level on the cylinder.

② Submerge the irregular object in the water. Because the object and the water cannot share the same space, the water is displaced, or moved upward. Note the new volume of the water with the object in it.

③ Subtract the volume of the water before you added the object from the volume of the water and the object together. The result is the volume of the object. The object displaces a volume of water equal to the volume of the object.

You measure the volume of a liquid by measuring how much space it takes up in a container. The volume of a liquid usually is measured in liters (L) or milliliters (mL). One liter is equal to 1000 milliliters. Milliliters and cubic centimeters are equivalent. This can be written as 1 mL = 1 cm^3. If you had a box with a volume of one cubic centimeter and you filled it with water, you would have one milliliter of water.

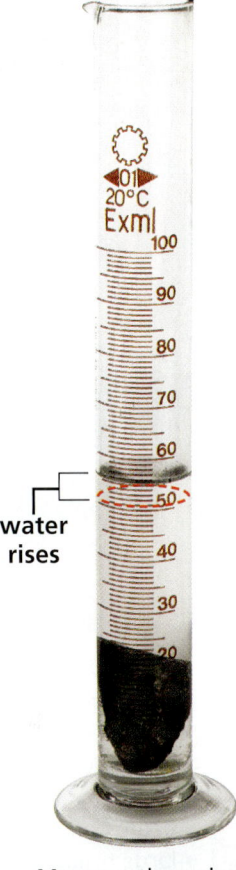

In the first photograph, the graduated cylinder contains 50 mL of water. Placing a rock in the cylinder causes the water level to rise from 50 mL to 55 mL. The difference is 5 mL; therefore, the volume of the rock is 5 cm^3.

Measure the volume of water without the rock.

Measure the volume of water with the rock in it.

1.1 Review

KEY CONCEPTS
1. Give three examples of matter.
2. What do weight and mass measure?
3. How can you measure the volume of an object that has an irregular shape?

CRITICAL THINKING
4. **Calculate** What is the volume of a box that is 12 cm long, 6 cm wide, and 4 cm high?
5. **Synthesize** What is the relationship between the units of measurement for the volume of a liquid and of a solid object?

CHALLENGE
6. **Infer** Why might a small increase in the dimensions of an object cause a large change in its volume?

Chapter 1: **Introduction to Matter** 13

CHAPTER INVESTIGATION

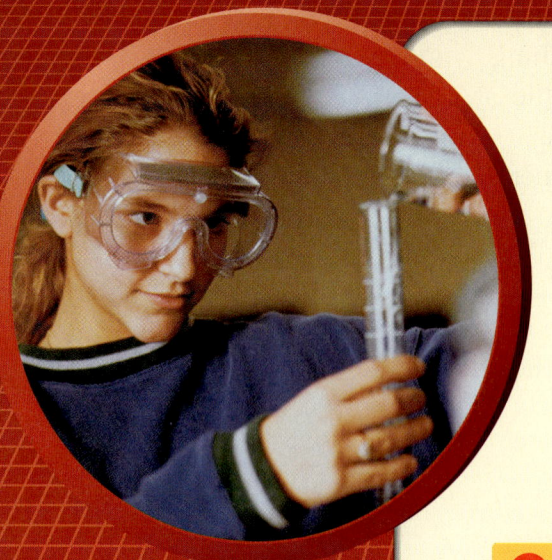

Mass and Volume

OVERVIEW AND PURPOSE In order for scientists around the world to communicate with one another about calculations in their research, they use a common system of measurement called the metric system. Scientists use the same tools and methods for the measurement of length, mass, and volume. In this investigation you will

- use a ruler, a graduated cylinder, and a balance to measure the mass and the volume of different objects
- determine which method is best for measuring the volume of the objects

▶ Procedure

1. Make a data table like the one shown on the sample notebook page.

2. Measure the mass of each object: rock, pennies, sponge, and tissue box. Record each mass.

3. For each object, conduct three trials for mass. Average the trials to find a final mass measurement.

4. Decide how you will find the volume of each object.

   For rectangular objects, you will use the following formula:

   Volume = length • width • height

   For irregular objects, you will use the displacement method and the following formula:

   Volume of object = volume of water with object − volume of water without object

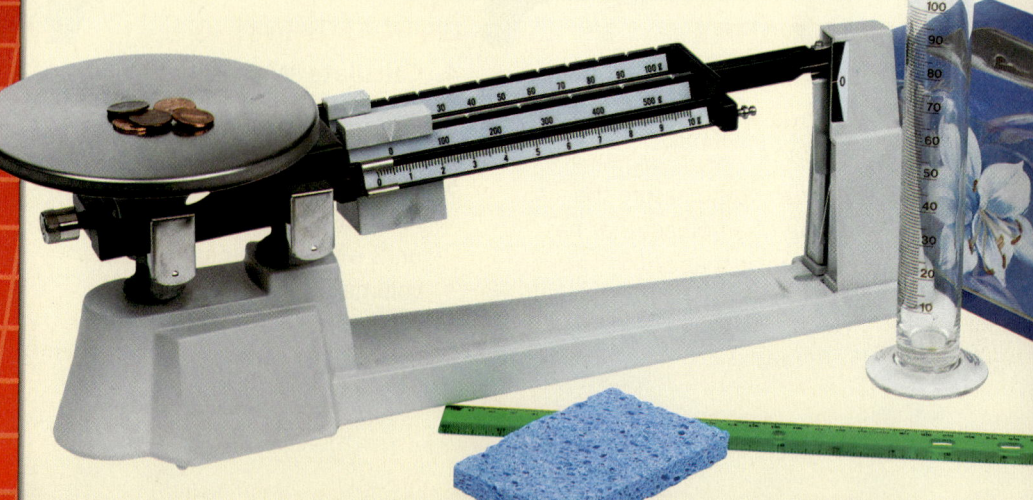

MATERIALS
- small rock
- 5 pennies
- rectangular sponge
- tissue box
- beam balance
- large graduated cylinder
- water
- ruler

Unit: **Matter and Energy**

5. For each object, you will conduct three trials for measuring volume. Average the trials to find a final volume measurement.

6. For rectangular objects, use metric units for measuring the length, width, and height. Record the measurements in your data table.

   step 6

7. For irregular objects, fill the graduated cylinder about half full with water. Record the exact volume of water in the cylinder. **Note:** The surface of the liquid will be curved in the graduated cylinder. Read the volume of the liquid at the bottom of the curve called the meniscus.

   step 7

8. Carefully place the object you are measuring into the cylinder. The object must be completely under the water. Record the exact volume of water in the cylinder containing the object by reading the meniscus.

Observe and Analyze   Write It Up

1. **RECORD OBSERVATIONS** Make sure you have filled out your data table completely.

2. **INTERPRET** For each object, explain why you chose a particular method for measuring the volume.

Conclude   Write It Up

1. **IDENTIFY LIMITS** Which sources of error might have affected your measurements?

2. **APPLY** Doctors need to know the mass of a patient before deciding how much of a medication to prescribe. Why is it important to measure each patient's mass before prescribing medicine?

3. **APPLY** Scientists in the United States work closely with scientists in other countries to develop new technology. What are the advantages of having a single system of measurement?

INVESTIGATE Further

CHALLENGE Measuring cups and spoons used in cooking often include both customary and metric units. Convert the measurements in a favorite recipe into metric units. Convert the amounts of solid ingredients to grams, and liquid ingredients to milliliters or liters. If possible, use the new measurements to follow the recipe and prepare the food. Were your conversions accurate?

Mass and Volume
Observe and Analyze
Table 1. Masses of Various Objects

Object	Mass (g)			Average
	Trial 1	Trial 2	Trial 3	
rock				
5 pennies				
sponge				
tissue box				

Table 2. Volumes of Various Objects

Object	Method Used	Volume (cm^3 or mL)			Average
		Trial 1	Trial 2	Trial 3	
rock					
5 pennies					
sponge					
tissue box					

Chapter 1: **Introduction to Matter** 15

1.2 Matter is made of atoms.

KEY CONCEPT

BEFORE, you learned
- Matter has mass
- Matter has volume

NOW, you will learn
- About the smallest particles of matter
- How atoms combine into molecules
- How atoms and molecules move

VOCABULARY

atom p. 16
molecule p. 18

THINK ABOUT

How small is an atom?

All matter is made up of very tiny particles called atoms. It is hard to imagine exactly how small these particles are. Suppose that each of the particles making up the pin shown in the photograph on the right were actually the size of the round head on the pin. How large would the pin be in that case? If you could stick such a pin in the ground, it would cover about 90 square miles—about one-seventh the area of London, England. It would also be about 80 miles high—almost 15 times the height of Mount Everest.

VOCABULARY
Make a four square diagram for *atom* that includes details that will help you remember the term.

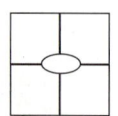

Atoms are extremely small.

How small can things get? If you break a stone wall into smaller and smaller pieces, you would have a pile of smaller stones. If you could break the smaller stones into the smallest pieces possible, you would have a pile of atoms. An **atom** is the smallest basic unit of matter.

The idea that all matter is made of extremely tiny particles dates back to the fifth century B.C., when Greek philosophers proposed the first atomic theory of matter. All matter, they said, was made of only a few different types of tiny particles called atoms. The different arrangements of atoms explained the differences among the substances that make up the world. Although the modern view of the atom is different from the ancient view, the idea of atoms as basic building blocks has been confirmed. Today scientists have identified more than 100 different types of atoms.

CHECK YOUR READING What are atoms? How are they like building blocks?

A 16 Unit: Matter and Energy

Atoms

It is hard to imagine that visible matter is composed of particles too tiny to see. Although you cannot see an individual atom, you are constantly seeing large collections of them. You are a collection of atoms. So are your textbook, a desk, and all the other matter around you. Matter is not something that contains atoms; matter is atoms. A desk, for example, is a collection of atoms and the empty space between those atoms. Without the atoms, there would be no desk—just empty space.

Atoms are so small that they cannot be seen even with very strong optical microscopes. Try to imagine the size of an atom by considering that a single teaspoonful of water contains approximately 500,000,000,000,000,000,000,000 atoms. Although atoms are extremely small, they do have a mass. The mass of a single teaspoonful of water is about 5 grams. This mass is equal to the mass of all the atoms that the water is made of added together.

READING TIP

The word *atom* comes from the Greek word *atomos,* meaning "indivisible," or "cannot be divided."

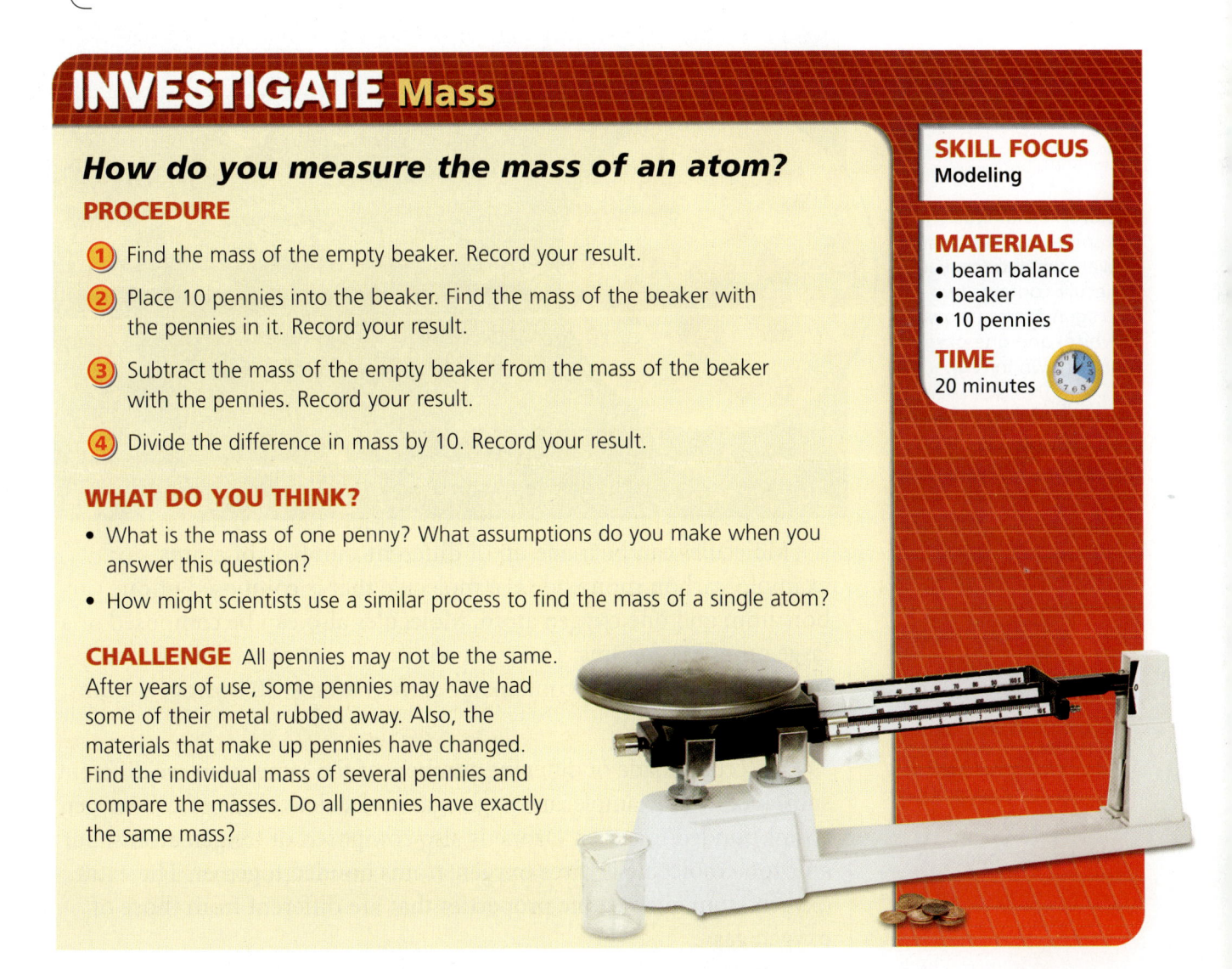

INVESTIGATE Mass

How do you measure the mass of an atom?
PROCEDURE

1. Find the mass of the empty beaker. Record your result.
2. Place 10 pennies into the beaker. Find the mass of the beaker with the pennies in it. Record your result.
3. Subtract the mass of the empty beaker from the mass of the beaker with the pennies. Record your result.
4. Divide the difference in mass by 10. Record your result.

WHAT DO YOU THINK?
- What is the mass of one penny? What assumptions do you make when you answer this question?
- How might scientists use a similar process to find the mass of a single atom?

CHALLENGE All pennies may not be the same. After years of use, some pennies may have had some of their metal rubbed away. Also, the materials that make up pennies have changed. Find the individual mass of several pennies and compare the masses. Do all pennies have exactly the same mass?

SKILL FOCUS
Modeling

MATERIALS
- beam balance
- beaker
- 10 pennies

TIME
20 minutes

Chapter 1: **Introduction to Matter** 17

Molecules

When two or more atoms bond together, or combine, they make a particle called a **molecule**. A molecule can be made of atoms that are different or atoms that are alike. A molecule of water, for example, is a combination of different atoms—two hydrogen atoms and one oxygen atom (also written as H_2O). Hydrogen gas molecules are made of the same atom—two hydrogen atoms bonded together.

A molecule is the smallest amount of a substance made of combined atoms that is considered to be that substance. Think about what would happen if you tried to divide water to find its smallest part. Ultimately you would reach a single molecule of water. What would you have if you divided this molecule into its individual atoms of hydrogen and oxygen? If you break up a water molecule, it is no longer water. Instead, you would have hydrogen and oxygen, two different substances.

READING TIP
Not all atoms and molecules have color. In this book atoms and molecules are given colors to make them easier to identify.

CHECK YOUR READING How is a molecule related to an atom?

The droplets of water in this spider web are made of water molecules. Each molecule contains two hydrogen atoms (shown in white) and one oxygen atom (shown in red).

hydrogen — oxygen
water

oxygen   **ozone**

Molecules can be made up of different numbers of atoms. For example, carbon monoxide is a molecule that is composed of one carbon atom and one oxygen atom. Molecules also can be composed of a large number of atoms. The most common type of vitamin E molecule, for example, contains 29 carbon atoms, 50 hydrogen atoms, and 2 oxygen atoms.

Molecules made of different numbers of the same atom are different substances. For example, an oxygen gas molecule is made of two oxygen atoms bonded together. Ozone is also composed of oxygen atoms, but an ozone molecule is three oxygen atoms bonded together. The extra oxygen atom gives ozone properties that are different from those of oxygen gas.

18 Unit: Matter and Energy

This photograph shows the interior of Grand Central Terminal in New York City. Light from the window reflects off dust particles that are being moved by the motion of the molecules in air.

Atoms and molecules are always in motion.

If you have ever looked at a bright beam of sunlight, you may have seen dust particles floating in the air. If you were to watch carefully, you might notice that the dust does not fall toward the floor but instead seems to dart about in all different directions. Molecules in air are constantly moving and hitting the dust particles. Because the molecules are moving in many directions, they collide with the dust particles from different directions. This action causes the darting motion of the dust that you observe.

Atoms and molecules are always in motion. Sometimes this motion is easy to observe, such as when you see evidence of molecules in air bouncing dust particles around. Water molecules move too. When you place a drop of food coloring into water, the motion of the water molecules eventually causes the food coloring to spread throughout the water.

The motion of individual atoms and molecules is hard to observe in solid objects, such as a table. The atoms and molecules in a table cannot move about freely like the ones in water and air. However, the atoms and molecules in a table are constantly moving—by shaking back and forth, or by twisting—even if they stay in the same place.

1.2 Review

KEY CONCEPTS

1. What are atoms?
2. What is the smallest particle of a substance that is still considered to be that substance?
3. Why do dust particles in the air appear to be moving in different directions?

CRITICAL THINKING

4. **Apply** How does tea flavor spread from a tea bag throughout a cup of hot water?
5. **Infer** If a water molecule (H_2O) has two hydrogen atoms and one oxygen atom, how would you describe the make-up of a carbon dioxide molecule (CO_2)?

CHALLENGE

6. **Synthesize** Assume that a water balloon has the same number of water molecules as a helium balloon has helium atoms. If the mass of the water is 4.5 times greater than the mass of the helium, how does the mass of a water molecule compare with the mass of a helium atom?

Chapter 1: **Introduction to Matter** 19

EXTREME SCIENCE

LOOKING AT ATOMS

Particles Too Small to See

Atoms are so small that you cannot see them through an ordinary microscope. In fact, millions of them could fit in the period at the end of this sentence. Scientists can make images of atoms, however, using an instrument called a scanning tunneling microscope (STM).

Bumps on a Surface

The needle of the scanning tunneling microscope has a very sharp tip that is only one atom wide. The tip is brought close to the surface of the material being observed, and an electric current is applied to the tip. The microscope measures the interaction between the electrically charged needle tip and the nearest atom on the surface of the material. An image of the surface is created by moving the needle just above the surface. The image appears as a series of bumps that shows where the atoms are located. The result is similar to a contour map.

Moving Atoms

Scientists also can use the tip of the STM needle to move atoms on a surface. The large image at left is an STM image of a structure made by pushing individual atoms into place on a very smooth metal surface. This structure was designed as a corral to trap individual atoms inside.

Scientists can manipulate individual atoms to build structures, such as this one made of iron atoms.

An STM maps the position of atoms using a needle with a tip that is one atom wide.

Tiny Pieces of Matter

- Images of atoms did not exist until 1970.
- Atoms are so small that a single raindrop contains more than 500 billion trillion atoms.
- If each atom were the size of a pea, your fingerprint would be larger than Alaska.
- In the space between stars, matter is so spread out that a volume of one liter contains only about 1000 atoms.

EXPLORE

1. **INFER** Why must the tip of a scanning tunneling microscope be only one atom wide to make an image of atoms on a surface?
2. **CHALLENGE** Find out more about images of atoms on the Internet. How are STM images used in research to design better materials?

RESOURCE CENTER
CLASSZONE.COM
Find more images from scanning tunneling microscopes.

KEY CONCEPT
1.3 Matter combines to form different substances.

BEFORE, you learned
- Matter is made of tiny particles called atoms
- Atoms combine to form molecules

NOW, you will learn
- How pure matter and mixed matter are different
- How atoms and elements are related
- How atoms form compounds

VOCABULARY
element p. 22
compound p. 23
mixture p. 23

EXPLORE Mixed Substances

What happens when substances are mixed?

PROCEDURE
1. Observe and describe a teaspoon of cornstarch and a teaspoon of water.
2. Mix the two substances together in the cup. Observe and describe the result.

MATERIALS
- cornstarch
- water
- small cup
- spoon

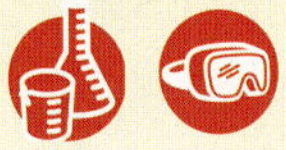

WHAT DO YOU THINK?
- After you mixed the substances, could you still see each substance?
- How was the new substance different from the original substances?

MAIN IDEA AND DETAILS
Continue to organize your notes in a two-column chart as you read.

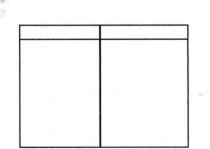

Matter can be pure or mixed.

Matter can be pure, or it can be two or more substances mixed together. Most of the substances you see around you are mixed, although you can't always tell that by looking at them. For example, the air you breathe is a combination of several substances. Wood, paper, steel, and lemonade are all mixed substances.

You might think that the water that you drink from a bottle or from the tap is a pure substance. However, drinking water has minerals dissolved in it and chemicals added to it that you cannot see. Often the difference between pure and mixed substances is apparent only on the atomic or molecular level.

A pure substance has only one type of component. For example, pure water contains only water molecules. Pure silver contains only silver atoms. Coins and jewelry that look like silver are often made of silver in combination with other metals.

Chapter 1: Introduction to Matter 21

> **REMINDER**
> A molecule consists of two or more atoms that are bonded together.

If you could look at the atoms in a bar of pure gold, you would find only gold atoms. If you looked at the atoms in a container of pure water, you would find water molecules, which are a combination of hydrogen and oxygen atoms. Does the presence of two types of atoms mean that water is not really a pure substance after all?

A substance is considered pure if it contains only a single type of atom, such as gold, or a single combination of atoms that are bonded together, such as a water molecule. Because the hydrogen and oxygen atoms are bonded together as molecules, water that has nothing else in it is considered a pure substance.

Elements

One type of pure substance is an element. An **element** is a substance that contains only a single type of atom. The number of atoms is not important as long as all the atoms are of the same type. You cannot separate an element into other substances.

You are probably familiar with many elements, such as silver, oxygen, hydrogen, helium, and aluminum. There are as many elements as there are types of atoms—more than 100. You can see the orderly arrangement of atoms in the element gold, on the left below.

> **CHECK YOUR READING**
> Why is an element considered to be a pure substance?

Element: Gold

The atoms in gold are all the same type of atom. Therefore, gold is an element.

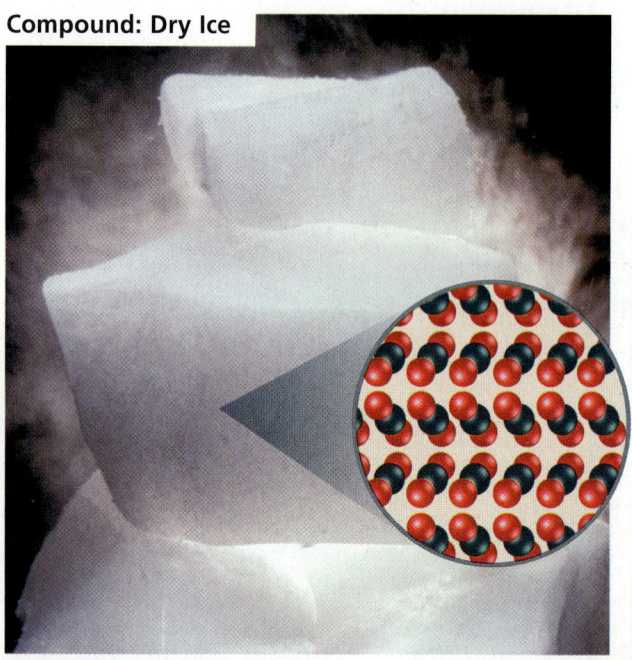

Compound: Dry Ice

Dry ice is frozen carbon dioxide, a compound. Each molecule is made of one carbon atom and two oxygen atoms.

22 Unit: Matter and Energy

Compounds

A **compound** is a substance that consists of two or more different types of atoms bonded together. A large variety of substances can be made by combining different types of atoms to make different compounds. Some types of compounds are made of molecules, such as water and carbon dioxide, shown on page 22. Other compounds are made of atoms that are bonded together in a different way. Table salt is an example.

A compound can have very different properties from the individual elements that make up that compound. Pure table salt is a common compound that is a combination of sodium and chlorine. Although table salt is safe to eat, the individual elements that go into making it—sodium and chlorine—are poisonous.

CHECK YOUR READING What is the relationship between atoms and a compound?

Mixtures

Most of the matter around you is a mixture of different substances. Seawater, for instance, contains water, salt, and other minerals mixed together. Your blood is a mixture of blood cells and plasma. Plasma is also a mixture, made up of water, sugar, fat, protein, salts, and minerals.

A **mixture** is a combination of different substances that remain the same individual substances and can be separated by physical means. For example, if you mix apples, oranges, and bananas to make a fruit salad, you do not change the different fruits into a new kind of fruit. Mixtures do not always contain the same amount of the various substances. For example, depending on how the salad is made, the amount of each type of fruit it contains will vary.

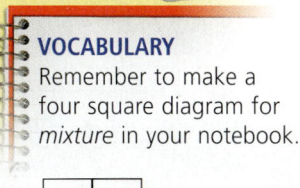

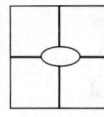

VOCABULARY
Remember to make a four square diagram for *mixture* in your notebook.

APPLY In what ways can a city population be considered a mixture?

Chapter 1: **Introduction to Matter** 23

INVESTIGATE Mixtures

How well do oil and water mix?

PROCEDURE

1. Add a few drops of food coloring to the water in the beaker. Swirl the water around in the beaker until the water is evenly colored throughout.
2. Pour the colored water from the beaker into the jar until the jar is about one-fourth full.
3. Add the same amount of vegetable oil to the jar. Screw the lid tightly on the jar.
4. Carefully shake the jar several times with your hand over the cover, and then set it on the table. Observe and record what happens to the liquids in the jar.
5. Turn the jar upside down and hold it that way. Observe what happens to the liquids and record your observations.

WHAT DO YOU THINK?

- Does water mix with food coloring? What evidence supports your answer?
- Do water and oil mix? What evidence supports your answer?
- What happened when you turned the jar upside down?
- Based on your observations, what can you infer about the ability of different liquids to mix?

CHALLENGE To clean greasy dishes, you add soap to the dishwater. Try adding soap to your mixture. What does the soap do?

SKILL FOCUS
Inferring

MATERIALS
- food coloring
- beaker of water
- jar with lid
- vegetable oil
for Challenge:
- dish soap

TIME
20 minutes

RESOURCE CENTER
CLASSZONE.COM
Find out more about mixtures.

Comparing Mixtures and Compounds

Although mixtures and compounds may seem similar, they are very different. Consider how mixtures and compounds compare with each other.

- The substances in mixtures remain the same substances. Compounds are new substances formed by atoms that bond together.
- Mixtures can be separated by physical means. Compounds can be separated only by breaking the bonds between atoms.
- The proportions of different substances in a mixture can vary throughout the mixture or from mixture to mixture. The proportions of different substances in a compound are fixed because the type and number of atoms that make up a basic unit of the compound are always the same.

CHECK YOUR READING How is a mixture different from a compound?

A 24 Unit: Matter and Energy

Parts of mixtures can be the same or different throughout.

It is obvious that something is a mixture when you can see the different substances in it. For example, if you scoop up a handful of soil, you might see that it contains dirt, small rocks, leaves, and even insects. You can separate the soil into its different parts.

Exactly what you see depends on what part of the soil you scoop up. One handful of soil might have more pebbles or insects in it than another handful would. There are many mixtures, such as soil, that have different properties in different areas of the mixture. Such a mixture is called a heterogeneous (HEHT-uhr-uh-JEE-nee-uhs) mixture.

In some types of mixtures, however, you cannot see the individual substances. For example, if you mix sugar into a cup of water and stir it well, the sugar seems to disappear. You can tell that the sugar is still there because the water tastes sweet, but you cannot see the sugar or easily separate it out again.

When substances are evenly spread throughout a mixture, you cannot tell one part of the mixture from another part. For instance, one drop of sugar water will be almost exactly like any other drop. Such a mixture is called a homogeneous (HOH-muh-JEE-nee-uhs) mixture. Homogenized milk is processed so that it becomes a homogeneous mixture of water and milk fat. Milk that has not been homogenized will separate—most of the milk fat will float to the top as cream while leaving the rest of the milk low in fat.

> **READING TIP**
> The prefix *hetero* means "different," and the prefix *homo* means "same." The Greek root *genos* means "kind."

1.3 Review

KEY CONCEPTS

1. What is the difference between pure and mixed matter?
2. How are atoms and elements related?
3. How are compounds different from mixtures?

CRITICAL THINKING

4. **Infer** What can you infer about the size of sugar particles that are dissolved in a mixture of sugar and water?
5. **Infer** Why is it easier to remove the ice cubes from cold lemonade than it is to remove the sugar?

CHALLENGE

6. **Apply** A unit of sulfuric acid is a molecule of 2 atoms of hydrogen, 1 atom of sulfur, and 4 atoms of oxygen. How many of each type of atom are there in 2 molecules of sulfuric acid?

Chapter 1: **Introduction to Matter** 25

MATH in SCIENCE

SKILL: MAKING A CIRCLE GRAPH

MATH TUTORIAL
CLASSZONE.COM
Click on Math Tutorial for more help with circle graphs.

A Mixture of Spices

Two different mixtures of spices may contain the exact same ingredients but have very different flavors. For example, a mixture of cumin, nutmeg, and ginger powder can be made using more cumin than ginger, or it can be made using more ginger than cumin.

One way to show how much of each substance a mixture contains is to use a circle graph. A circle graph is a visual way to show how a quantity is divided into different parts. A circle graph represents quantities as parts of a whole.

Example

Make a circle graph to represent a spice mixture that is 1/2 cumin, 1/3 nutmeg, and 1/6 ginger.

(1) To find the angle measure for each sector of the circle graph, multiply each fraction in your mixture by 360°.

Cumin: $\frac{1}{2} \cdot 360° = 180°$

Nutmeg: $\frac{1}{3} \cdot 360° = 120°$

Ginger: $\frac{1}{6} \cdot 360° = 60°$

(2) Use a compass to draw a circle. Use a protractor to draw the angle for each sector.

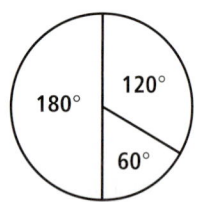

(3) Label each sector and give your graph a title.

ANSWER
Spice Mixture

Answer the following questions.

1. Draw a circle graph representing a spice mixture that is 1/2 ginger, 1/4 cumin, and 1/4 crushed red pepper.

2. A jeweler creates a ring that is 3/4 gold, 3/16 silver, and 1/16 copper. Draw a circle graph representing the mixture of metals in the ring.

3. Draw a circle graph representing a mixture that is 1/5 sand, 2/5 water, and 2/5 salt.

CHALLENGE Dry air is a mixture of about 78 percent nitrogen, 21 percent oxygen, and 1 percent other elements. Create a circle graph representing the elements found in air.

KEY CONCEPT
1.4 Matter exists in different physical states.

BEFORE, you learned
- Matter has mass
- Matter is made of atoms
- Atoms and molecules in matter are always moving

NOW, you will learn
- About the different states of matter
- How the different states of matter behave

VOCABULARY
states of matter p. 27
solid p. 28
liquid p. 28
gas p. 28

EXPLORE Solids and Liquids

How do solids and liquids compare?

PROCEDURE

1. Observe the water, ice, and marble. Pick them up and feel them. Can you change their shape? their volume?

2. Record your observations. Compare and contrast each object with the other two.

MATERIALS
- water in a cup
- ice cube
- marble
- pie tin

WHAT DO YOU THINK?
- How are the ice and the water in the cup similar? How are they different?
- How are the ice and the marble similar? How are they different?

Particle arrangement and motion determine the state of matter.

When you put water in a freezer, the water freezes into a solid (ice). When you place an ice cube on a warm plate, the ice melts into liquid water again. If you leave the plate in the sun, the water becomes water vapor. Ice, water, and water vapor are made of exactly the same type of molecule—a molecule of two hydrogen atoms and one oxygen atom. What, then, makes them different?

Ice, water, and water vapor are different states of water. **States of matter** are the different forms in which matter can exist. The three familiar states are solid, liquid, and gas. When a substance changes from one state to another, the molecules in the substance do not change. However, the arrangement of the molecules does change, giving each state of matter its own characteristics.

Chapter 1: Introduction to Matter 27

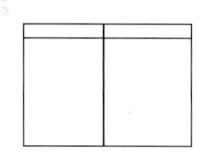

Solid, liquid, and gas are common states of matter.

MAIN IDEA AND DETAILS
Remember to organize your notes in a two-column chart as you read.

A substance can exist as a solid, a liquid, or a gas. The state of a substance depends on the space between its particles and on the way in which the particles move. The illustration on page 29 shows how particles are arranged in the three different states.

① A **solid** is a substance that has a fixed volume and a fixed shape. In a solid, the particles are close together and usually form a regular pattern. Particles in a solid can vibrate but are fixed in one place. Because each particle is attached to several others, individual particles cannot move from one location to another, and the solid is rigid.

② A **liquid** has a fixed volume but does not have a fixed shape. Liquids take on the shape of the container they are in. The particles in a liquid are attracted to one another and are close together. However, particles in a liquid are not fixed in place and can move from one place to another.

③ A **gas** has no fixed volume or shape. A gas can take on both the shape and the volume of a container. Gas particles are not close to one another and can move easily in any direction. There is much more space between gas particles than there is between particles in a liquid or a solid. The space between gas particles can increase or decrease with changes in temperature and pressure.

CHECK YOUR READING Describe two differences between a solid and a gas.

The particles in a solid are usually closer together than the particles in a liquid. For example, the particles in solid steel are closer together than the particles in molten—or melted—steel. However, water is an important exception. The molecules that make up ice actually have more space between them than the molecules in liquid water do.

The fact that the molecules in ice are farther apart than the molecules in liquid water has important consequences for life on Earth. Because there is more space between its molecules, ice floats on liquid water. By contrast, a piece of solid steel would not float in molten steel but would sink to the bottom.

Because ice floats, it remains on the surface of rivers and lakes when they freeze. The ice layer helps insulate the water and slow down the freezing process. Animals living in rivers and lakes can survive in the liquid water layer below the ice layer.

States of Matter

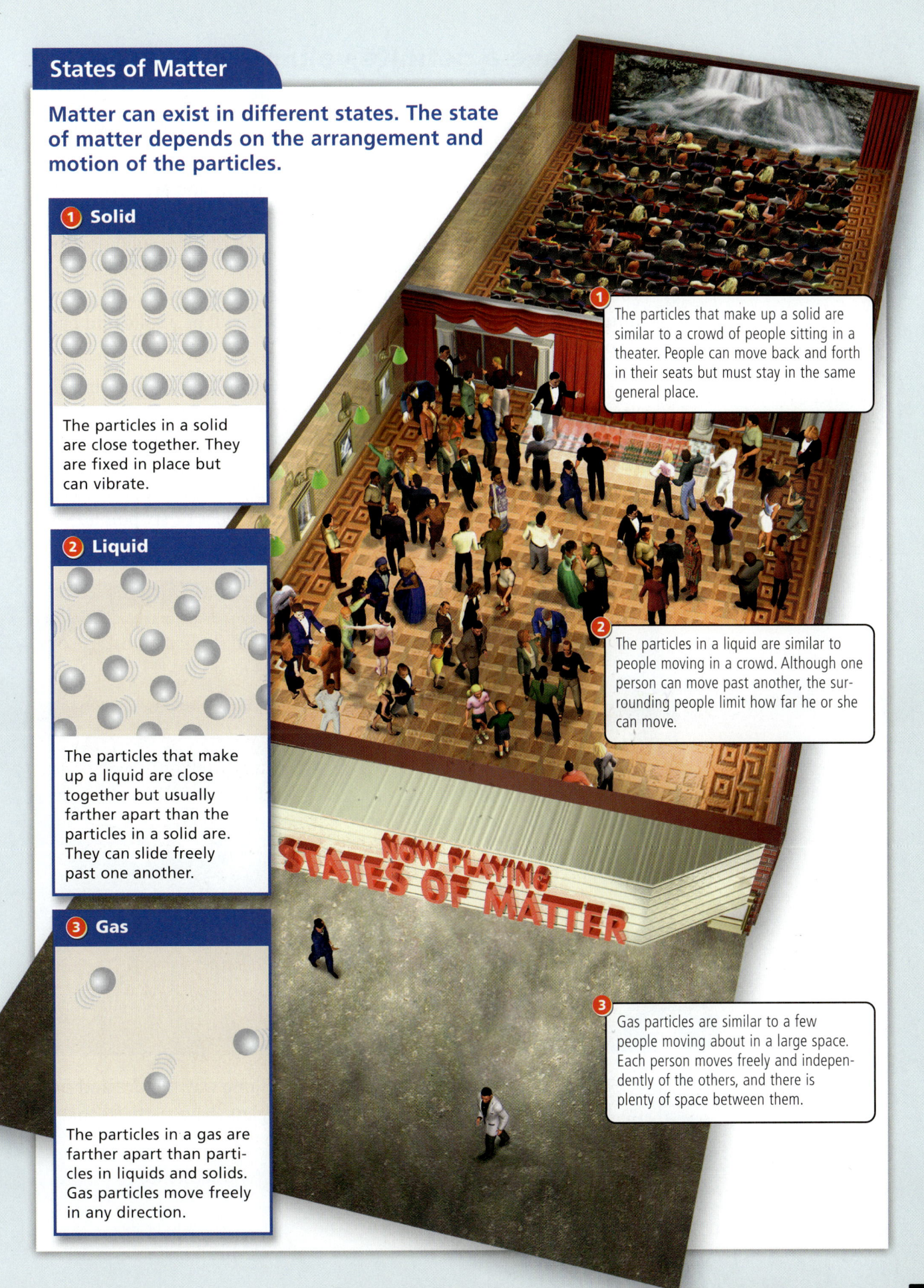

Matter can exist in different states. The state of matter depends on the arrangement and motion of the particles.

① Solid

The particles in a solid are close together. They are fixed in place but can vibrate.

① The particles that make up a solid are similar to a crowd of people sitting in a theater. People can move back and forth in their seats but must stay in the same general place.

② Liquid

The particles that make up a liquid are close together but usually farther apart than the particles in a solid are. They can slide freely past one another.

② The particles in a liquid are similar to people moving in a crowd. Although one person can move past another, the surrounding people limit how far he or she can move.

③ Gas

The particles in a gas are farther apart than particles in liquids and solids. Gas particles move freely in any direction.

③ Gas particles are similar to a few people moving about in a large space. Each person moves freely and independently of the others, and there is plenty of space between them.

Chapter 1: **Introduction to Matter** 29 **A**

> **REMINDER**
> Volume is the amount of space that an object occupies.

Solids have a definite volume and shape.

A piece of ice, a block of wood, and a ceramic cup are solids. They have shapes that do not change and volumes that can be measured. Any matter that is a solid has a definite shape and a definite volume.

The molecules in a solid are in fixed positions and are close together. Although the molecules can still vibrate, they cannot move from one part of the solid to another part. As a result, a solid does not easily change its shape or its volume. If you force the molecules apart, you can change the shape and the volume of a solid by breaking it into pieces. However, each of those pieces will still be a solid and have its own particular shape and volume.

The particles in some solids, such as ice or table salt, occur in a very regular pattern. The pattern of the water molecules in ice, for example, can be seen when you look at a snowflake like the one shown below. The water molecules in a snowflake are arranged in hexagonal shapes that are layered on top of one another. Because the molecular pattern has six sides, snowflakes form with six sides or six points. Salt also has a regular structure, although it takes a different shape.

The particles in many solids, such as the water molecules in this snowflake, have a regular pattern.

Not all solids have regular shapes in the same way that ice and salt do, however. Some solids, such as plastic or glass, have particles that are not arranged in a regular pattern.

> **CHECK YOUR READING**
> What two characteristics are needed for a substance to be a solid?

A 30 Unit: Matter and Energy

Liquids have a definite volume but no definite shape.

Water, milk, and oil are liquids. A liquid has a definite volume but does not have a definite shape. The volume of a certain amount of oil can be measured, but the shape that the oil takes depends on what container it is in. If the oil is in a tall, thin container, it has a tall, thin shape. If it is in a short, wide container, it has a short, wide shape. Liquids take the shape of their containers.

The molecules in a liquid are close together, but they are not tightly attached to one another as the molecules in a solid are. Instead, molecules in liquids can move independently. As a result, liquids can flow. Instead of having a rigid form, the molecules in a liquid move and fill the bottom of the container they are in.

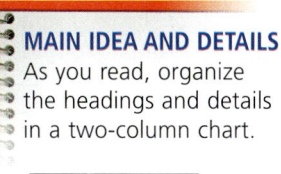

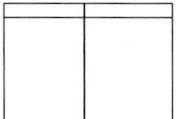

MAIN IDEA AND DETAILS
As you read, organize the headings and details in a two-column chart.

CHECK YOUR READING How is a liquid different from a solid?

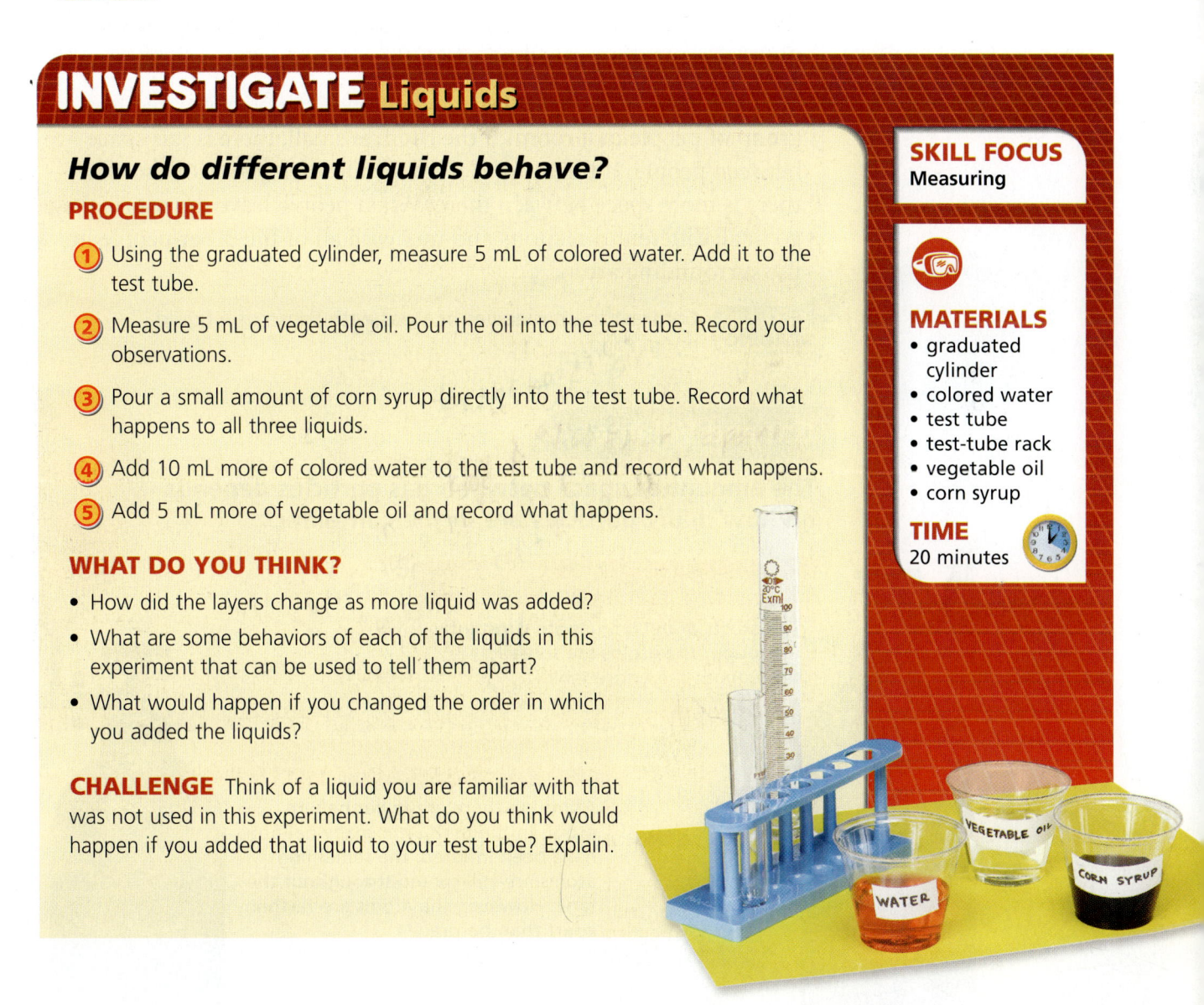

INVESTIGATE Liquids

How do different liquids behave?

PROCEDURE

1. Using the graduated cylinder, measure 5 mL of colored water. Add it to the test tube.
2. Measure 5 mL of vegetable oil. Pour the oil into the test tube. Record your observations.
3. Pour a small amount of corn syrup directly into the test tube. Record what happens to all three liquids.
4. Add 10 mL more of colored water to the test tube and record what happens.
5. Add 5 mL more of vegetable oil and record what happens.

WHAT DO YOU THINK?
- How did the layers change as more liquid was added?
- What are some behaviors of each of the liquids in this experiment that can be used to tell them apart?
- What would happen if you changed the order in which you added the liquids?

CHALLENGE Think of a liquid you are familiar with that was not used in this experiment. What do you think would happen if you added that liquid to your test tube? Explain.

SKILL FOCUS
Measuring

MATERIALS
- graduated cylinder
- colored water
- test tube
- test-tube rack
- vegetable oil
- corn syrup

TIME
20 minutes

Chapter 1: Introduction to Matter 31

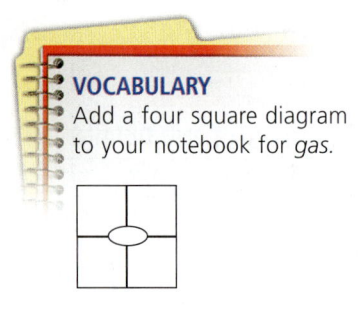

VOCABULARY
Add a four square diagram to your notebook for *gas*.

Gases have no definite volume or shape.

The air that you breathe, the helium in a balloon, and the neon inside the tube in a neon light are gases. A gas is a substance with no definite volume and no definite shape. Solids and liquids have volumes that do not change easily. If you have a container filled with one liter of a liquid that you pour into a two-liter container, the liquid will occupy only half of the new container. A gas, on the other hand, has a volume that changes to match the volume of its container.

Gas Composition

The molecules in a gas are very far apart compared with the molecules in a solid or a liquid. The amount of space between the molecules in a gas can change easily. If a rigid container—one that cannot change its shape—has a certain amount of air and more air is pumped in, the volume of the gas does not change. However, there is less space between the molecules than there was before. If the container is opened, the molecules spread out and mix with the air in the atmosphere.

As you saw, gas molecules in a container can be compared to a group of people in a room. If the room is small, there is less space between people. If the room is large, people can spread out so that there is more space between them. When people leave the room, they go in all different directions and mix with all of the other people in the surrounding area.

CHECK YOUR READING Contrast the molecules in a gas with those of a liquid and a solid.

Gas and Volume

The amount of space between gas particles depends on how many particles are in the container.

Before Use
The atoms of helium gas are constantly in motion. The atoms are spread throughout the entire tank.

After Use
Although there are fewer helium atoms in the tank after many balloons have been inflated, the remaining atoms are still spread throughout the tank. However, the atoms are farther apart than before.

A 32 Unit: **Matter and Energy**

Gas Behavior

Because gas molecules are always in motion, they are continually hitting one another and the sides of any container they may be in. As the molecules bounce off one another and the surfaces of the container, they apply a pressure against the container. You can feel the effects of gas pressure if you pump air into a bicycle tire. The more air you put into the tire, the harder it feels because more gas molecules are pressing the tire outward.

The speed at which gas molecules move depends on the temperature of the gas. Gas molecules move faster at higher temperatures than at lower temperatures. The volume, pressure, and temperature of a gas are related to one another, and changing one can change the others.

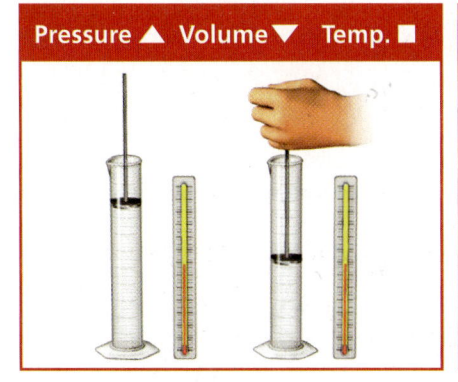

SIMULATION CLASSZONE.COM
Explore the behavior of a gas.

Pressure ▲ Volume ▼ Temp. ■	Pressure ▲ Volume ■ Temp. ▲	Pressure ■ Volume ▲ Temp. ▲
If the temperature of a gas stays the same, increasing the pressure of the gas decreases its volume.	If the volume of a gas stays the same, increasing the temperature of the gas also increases the pressure.	If the pressure of a gas stays the same, increasing the temperature of the gas also increases the volume.

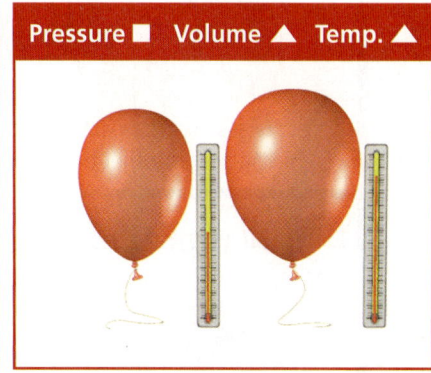

In nature, volume, pressure, and temperature may all be changing at the same time. By studying how gas behaves when one property is kept constant, scientists can predict how gas will behave when all three properties change.

1.4 Review

KEY CONCEPTS
1. What are the characteristics of the three familiar states of matter?
2. How can you change the shape and volume of a liquid?
3. How does gas behave inside a closed container?

CRITICAL THINKING
4. **Infer** What happens to a liquid that is not in a container?
5. **Synthesize** What is the relationship between the temperature and the volume of a gas?

CHALLENGE
6. **Synthesize** Can an oxygen canister ever be half empty? Explain.

Chapter 1: Introduction to Matter 33

Chapter Review

the BIG idea
Everything that has mass and takes up space is matter.

CONTENT REVIEW
CLASSZONE.COM

KEY CONCEPTS SUMMARY

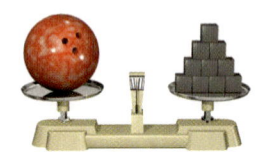

1.1 Matter has mass and volume.

Mass is a measure of how much matter an object contains.

Volume is the measure of the amount of space matter occupies.

VOCABULARY
matter p. 9
mass p. 10
weight p. 11
volume p. 11

1.2 Matter is made of atoms.

An atom is the smallest basic unit of matter. Two or more atoms bonded together form a molecule. Atoms and molecules are always in motion.

VOCABULARY
atom p. 16
molecule p. 18

1.3 Matter combines to form different substances.

Matter can be pure, such as an element (gold), or a compound (water).

Matter can be a mixture. Mixtures contain two or more pure substances.

VOCABULARY
element p. 22
compound p. 23
mixture p. 23

1.4 Matter exists in different physical states.

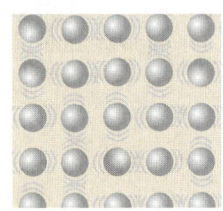

Solids have a fixed volume and a fixed shape.

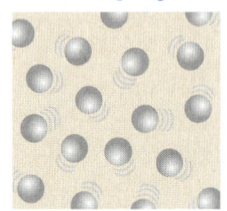

Liquids have a fixed volume but no fixed shape.

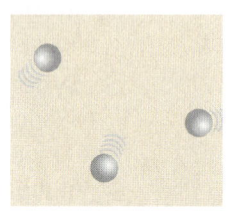

Gases have no fixed volume and no fixed shape.

VOCABULARY
states of matter p. 27
solid p. 28
liquid p. 28
gas p. 28

Reviewing Vocabulary

Copy and complete the chart below. If the right column is blank, give a brief description or definition. If the left column is blank, give the correct term.

Term	Description
1.	the downward pull of gravity on an object
2. liquid	
3.	the smallest basic unit of matter
4. solid	
5.	state of matter with no fixed volume and no fixed shape
6.	a combination of different substances that remain individual substances
7. matter	
8.	a measure of how much matter an object contains
9. element	
10.	a particle made of two or more atoms bonded together
11. compound	

Reviewing Key Concepts

Multiple Choice *Choose the letter of the best answer.*

12. The standard unit for measuring mass is the
    a. kilogram
    b. gram per cubic centimeter
    c. milliliter
    d. milliliter per cubic centimeter

13. A unit for measuring the volume of a liquid is the
    a. kilogram
    b. gram per cubic centimeter
    c. milliliter
    d. milliliter per cubic centimeter

14. The weight of an object is measured by using a scale that
    a. compares the mass of the object with a standard unit of mass
    b. shows the amount of space the object occupies
    c. indicates how much water is displaced by the object
    d. tells how hard the object is pushing or pulling on it

15. To find the volume of a rectangular box,
    a. divide the length by the height
    b. multiply the length, width, and height
    c. subtract the mass from the weight
    d. multiply one atom's mass by the total

16. Compounds can be separated only by
    a. breaking the atoms into smaller pieces
    b. breaking the bonds between the atoms
    c. using a magnet to attract certain atoms
    d. evaporating the liquid that contains the atoms

17. Whether a substance is a solid, a liquid, or a gas depends on how close its atoms are to one another and
    a. the volume of each atom
    b. how much matter the atoms have
    c. how free the atoms are to move
    d. the size of the container

18. A liquid has
    a. a fixed volume and a fixed shape
    b. no fixed volume and a fixed shape
    c. a fixed volume and no fixed shape
    d. no fixed volume and no fixed shape

Chapter 1: **Introduction to Matter** 35

Short Answer *Answer each of the following questions in a sentence or two.*

19. Describe the movement of particles in a solid, a liquid, and a gas.

20. In bright sunlight, dust particles in the air appear to dart about. What causes this effect?

21. Why is the volume of a rectangular object measured in cubic units?

22. Describe how the molecules in the air behave when you pump air into a bicycle tire.

Thinking Critically

23. **CLASSIFY** Write the headings *Matter* and *Not Matter* on your paper. Place each of these terms in the correct category: wood, water, metal, air, light, sound.

24. **INFER** If you could break up a carbon dioxide molecule, would you still have carbon dioxide? Explain your answer.

25. **MODEL** In what ways is sand in a bowl like a liquid? In what ways is it different?

26. **INFER** If you cut a hole in a basketball, what happens to the gas inside?

27. **COMPARE AND CONTRAST** Create a Venn diagram that shows how mixtures and compounds are alike and different.

28. **ANALYZE** If you place a solid rubber ball into a box, why doesn't the ball change its shape to fit the container?

29. **CALCULATE** What is the volume of an aquarium that is 120 cm long, 60 cm wide, and 100 cm high?

30. **CALCULATE** A truck whose bed is 2.5 m long, 1.5 m wide, and 1 m high is delivering sand for a sand-sculpture competition. How many trips must the truck make to deliver 7 cubic meters of sand?

Use the information in the photograph below to answer the next three questions.

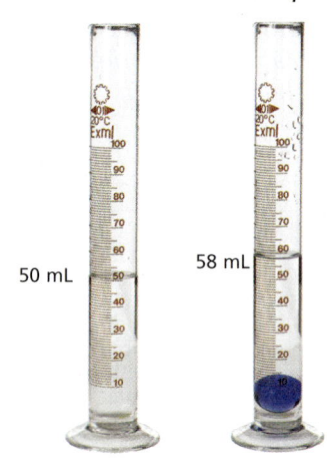

50 mL   58 mL

31. **INFER** One way to find the volume of a marble is by displacement. To determine a marble's volume, add 50 mL of water to a graduated cylinder and place the marble in the cylinder. Why does the water level change when you put the marble in the cylinder?

32. **CALCULATE** What is the volume of the marble?

33. **PREDICT** If you carefully removed the marble and let all of the water on it drain back into the cylinder, what would the volume of the water be? Explain.

the BIG idea

34. **SYNTHESIZE** Look back at the photograph on pages 6–7. Describe the picture in terms of states of matter.

35. **WRITE** Make a list of all the matter in a two-meter radius around you. Classify each as a solid, liquid, or gas.

UNIT PROJECTS

If you are doing a unit project, make a folder for your project. Include in your folder a list of the resources you will need, the date on which the project is due, and a schedule to track your progress. Begin gathering data.

Standardized Test Practice

For practice on your state test, go to...
TEST PRACTICE
CLASSZONE.COM

Interpreting Graphs

The graph below shows the changing volume of a gas as it was slowly heated, with the pressure held constant.

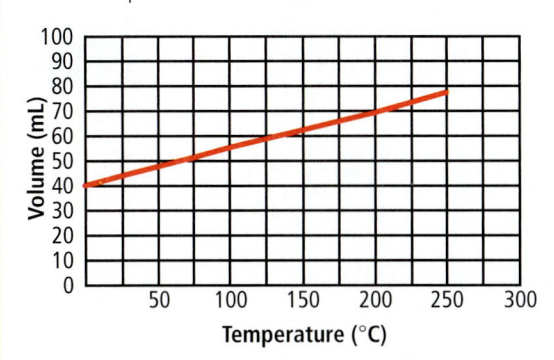

[Graph: Volume (mL) vs Temperature (°C), showing a line rising from about 40 mL at 0°C to about 80 mL at 250°C]

Use the graph to answer the questions.

1. As the temperature of the gas rises, what happens to its volume?
   a. It increases.
   b. It stays the same.
   c. It decreases.
   d. It changes without pattern.

2. What is the volume of the gas at 250°C as compared with the volume at 0°C?
   a. about three times greater
   b. about double
   c. about one-half
   d. about the same

3. What happens to a gas as it is cooled below 0°C?
   a. The volume would increase.
   b. The volume would continue to decrease.
   c. The volume would remain at 40 mL.
   d. A gas cannot be cooled below 0°C.

4. If you raised the temperature of this gas to 300°C, what would be its approximate volume?
   a. 70 mL   c. 80 mL
   b. 75 mL   d. 85 mL

5. If the volume of the gas at 0°C was 80 mL instead of 40 mL, what would you expect the volume to be at 200°C?
   a. 35 mL   c. 80 mL
   b. 70 mL   d. 140 mL

Extended Response

Answer the two questions below in detail. Include some of the terms from the word box. Underline each term you use in your answer.

| gravity | mass | molecule |
| states of matter | weight | |

6. An astronaut's helmet, measured on a balance, has the same number of kilograms on both Earth and the Moon. On a spring scale, though, it registers more newtons on Earth than on the Moon. Why?

7. Explain how water changes as it moves from a solid to a liquid and then to a gas.

Chapter 1: **Introduction to Matter** 37

CHAPTER 2
Properties of Matter

the BIG idea

Matter has properties that can be changed by physical and chemical processes.

What properties could help you identify this sculpture as sugar?

Key Concepts

SECTION 2.1 Matter has observable properties.
Learn how to recognize physical and chemical properties.

SECTION 2.2 Changes of state are physical changes.
Learn how energy is related to changes of state.

SECTION 2.3 Properties are used to identify substances.
Learn how the properties of substances can be used to identify them and to separate mixtures.

Internet Preview

CLASSZONE.COM
Chapter 2 online resources: Content Review, Simulation, three Resource Centers, Math Tutorial, Test Practice

A 38 Unit: Matter and Energy

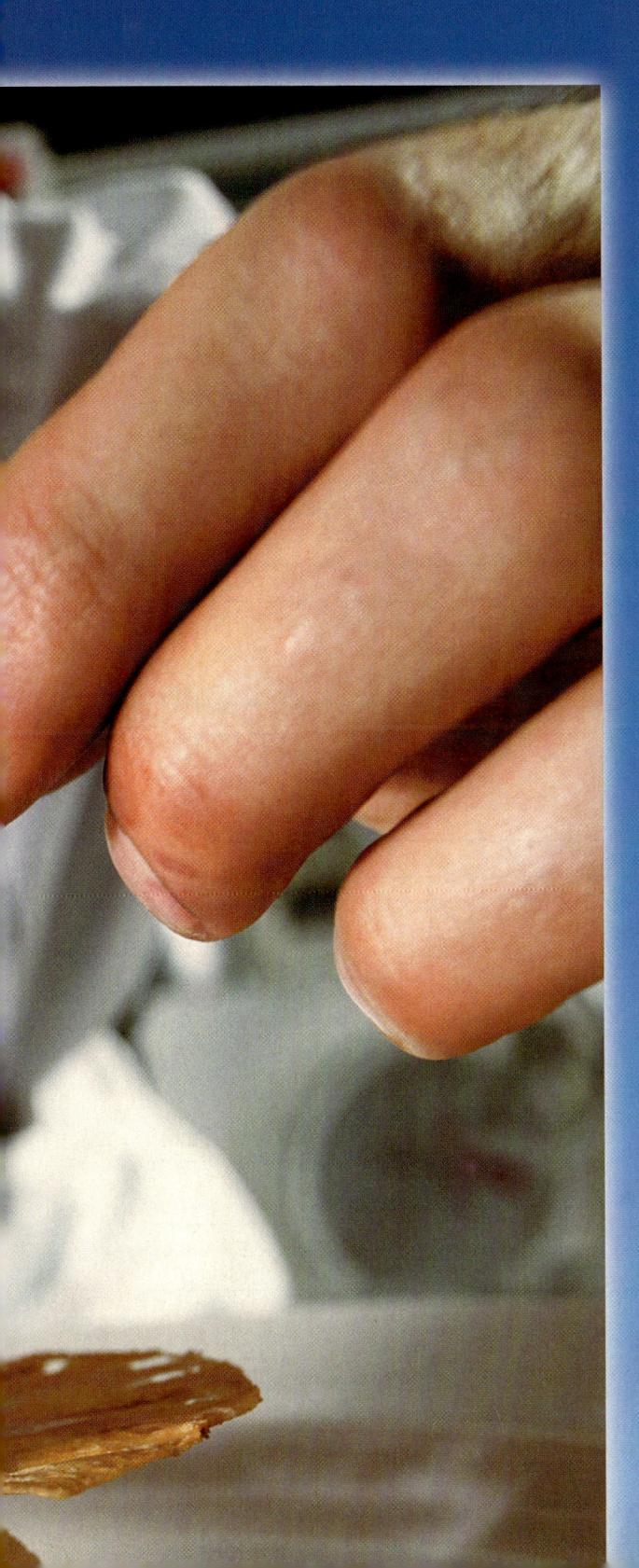

EXPLORE the BIG idea

Float or Sink

Form a piece of clay into a solid ball or cube. Place it in a bowl of water. Notice if it floats or sinks. Then mold the clay into a boatlike shape. Notice if this new object floats or sinks.

Observe and Think What did you change about the clay? What didn't you change? What would happen if you filled the boat with water?

Hot Chocolate

Place two candy-coated chocolates on a paper towel. Place two more in your hand and close your hand. Wait three minutes. Break open the candies and examine the chocolate.

Observe and Think What happened to the chocolate in your hand? on the towel? What do you think accounts for any differences you see?

Internet Activity: Physical and Chemical Changes

Go to **ClassZone.com** to see how materials can go through physical and chemical changes.

Observe and Think Think about each change. What can you infer about the difference between a physical change and a chemical change?

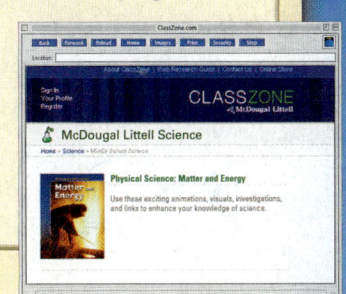

NSTA **scilinks.org** SCLINKS

Physical Properties of Matter **Code: MDL062**

Chapter 2: **Properties of Matter** 39 A

CHAPTER 2
Getting Ready to Learn

◁ CONCEPT REVIEW

- Everything is made of matter.
- Matter has mass and volume.
- Atoms combine to form molecules.

◁ VOCABULARY REVIEW

mass p. 10
volume p. 11
molecule p. 18
states of matter p. 27

CONTENT REVIEW
CLASSZONE.COM
Review concepts and vocabulary.

▷ TAKING NOTES

MAIN IDEA WEB

Write each new blue heading in a box. Then write notes in boxes around the center box that give important terms and details about that heading.

VOCABULARY STRATEGY

Think about a vocabulary term as a **magnet word** diagram. Write related terms and ideas in boxes around it.

See the Note-Taking Handbook on pages R45–R51.

SCIENCE NOTEBOOK

color, shape, size, texture, volume, mass

melting point, boiling point

Physical properties describe a substance.

density: a measure of the amount of matter in a given volume

burning — CHEMICAL CHANGE — change in temperature
rusting — change in color
tarnishing — formation of bubbles

A 40 Unit: Matter and Energy

KEY CONCEPT
2.1 Matter has observable properties.

BEFORE, you learned
- Matter has mass and volume
- Matter is made of atoms
- Matter exists in different states

NOW, you will learn
- About physical and chemical properties
- About physical changes
- About chemical changes

VOCABULARY

physical property p. 41
density p. 43
physical change p. 44
chemical property p. 46
chemical change p. 46

EXPLORE Physical Properties

How can a substance be changed?

PROCEDURE

1. Observe the clay. Note its physical characteristics, such as color, shape, texture, and size.
2. Change the shape of the clay. Note which characteristics changed and which ones stayed the same.

MATERIAL
rectangular piece of clay

WHAT DO YOU THINK?
- How did reshaping the clay change its physical characteristics?
- How were the mass and the volume of the clay affected?

Physical properties describe a substance.

What words would you use to describe a table? a chair? the sandwich you ate for lunch? You would probably say something about the shape, color, and size of each item. Next you might consider whether it is hard or soft, smooth or rough to the touch. Normally, when describing an object, you identify the characteristics of the object that you can observe without changing the identity of the object.

The characteristics of a substance that can be observed without changing the identity of the substance are called **physical properties.** In science, observation can include measuring and handling a substance. All of your senses can be used to detect physical properties. Color, shape, size, texture, volume, and mass are a few of the physical properties you probably have encountered.

VOCABULARY
Make a magnet word diagram in your notebook for *physical property*.

CHECK YOUR READING Describe some of the physical properties of your desk.

Chapter 2: Properties of Matter 41 A

Physical Properties

How do you know which characteristics are physical properties? Just ask yourself whether observing the property involves changing the substance to a different substance. For example, you can stretch a rubber band. Does stretching the rubber band change what it is made of? No. The rubber band is still a rubber band before and after it is stretched. It may look a little different, but it is still a rubber band.

Mass and volume are two physical properties. Measuring these properties does not change the identity of a substance. For example, a lump of clay might have a mass of 200 grams (g) and a volume of 100 cubic centimeters (cm^3). If you were to break the clay in half, you would have two 100 g pieces of clay, each with a volume of 50 cm^3. You can bend and shape the clay too. Even if you were to mold a realistic model of a car out of the clay, it still would be a piece of clay. Although you have changed some of the properties of the object, such as its shape and volume, you have not changed the fact that the substance you are observing is clay.

REMINDER
Because all formulas for volume involve the multiplication of three measurements, volume has a unit that is cubed (such as cm^3).

CHECK YOUR READING Which physical properties listed above are found by taking measurements? Which are not?

Physical Properties

Physical properties of clay—such as volume, mass, color, texture, and shape—can be observed without changing the fact that the substance is clay.

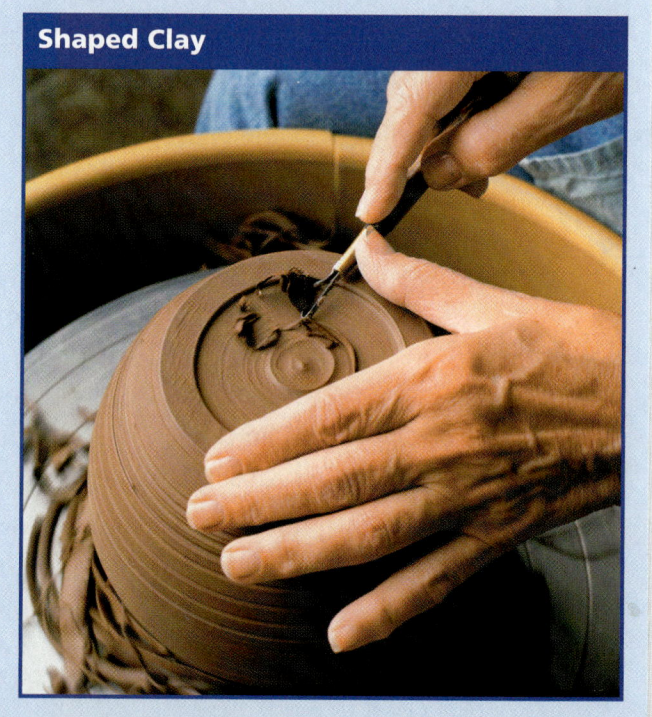

Block of Clay

Shaped Clay

READING VISUALS **COMPARE AND CONTRAST** Which physical properties do the two pieces of clay have in common? Which are different?

42 Unit: Matter and Energy

Density

The relationship between the mass and the volume of a substance is another important physical property. For any substance, the amount of mass in a unit of volume is constant. For different substances, the amount of mass in a unit of volume may differ. This relationship explains why you can easily lift a shoebox full of feathers but not one filled with pennies, even though both are the same size. A volume of pennies contains more mass than an equal volume of feathers. The relationship between mass and volume is called density.

Density is a measure of the amount of matter present in a given volume of a substance. Density is normally expressed in units of grams per cubic centimeter (g/cm^3). In other words, density is the mass in grams divided by the volume in cubic centimeters.

$$\text{Density} = \frac{\text{mass}}{\text{Volume}} \qquad D = \frac{m}{V}$$

How would you find the density of 200 g of clay with a volume of 100 cm^3? You calculate that the clay has a density of 200 g divided by 100 cm^3, or 2 g/cm^3. If you divide the clay in half and find the density of one piece of clay, it will be 100 g/50 cm^3, or 2 g/cm^3—the same as the original piece. Notice that density is a property of a substance that remains the same no matter how much of the substance you have.

READING TIP

The density of solids is usually measured in grams per cubic centimeter (g/cm^3). The density of liquids is usually measured in grams per milliliter (g/mL). Recall that 1 mL = 1 cm^3.

Calculating Density

▶ **Sample Problem**

A glass marble has a volume of 5 cm^3 and a mass of 13 g. What is the density of glass?

What do you know?	Volume = 5 cm^3, mass = 13 g
What do you want to find out?	Density
Write the formula:	$D = \frac{m}{V}$
Substitute into the formula:	$D = \frac{13 \text{ g}}{5 \text{ cm}^3}$
Calculate and simplify:	$D = 2.6$ g/cm^3
Check that your units agree:	Unit is g/cm^3. Unit of density is g/cm^3. Units agree.
Answer:	$D = 2.6$ g/cm^3

▶ **Practice the Math**

1. A lead sinker has a mass of 227 g and a volume of 20 cm^3. What is the density of lead?
2. A glass of milk has a volume of 100 mL. If the milk has a mass of 103 g, what is the density of milk?

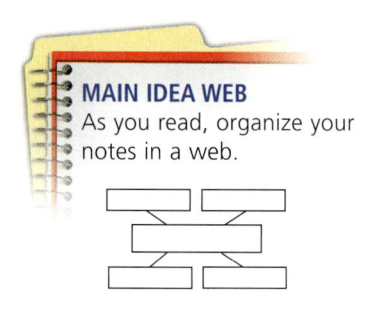

Physical Changes

MAIN IDEA WEB
As you read, organize your notes in a web.

You have read that a physical property is any property that can be observed without changing the identity of the substance. What then would be a physical change? A **physical change** is a change in any physical property of a substance, not in the substance itself. Breaking a piece of clay in half is a physical change because it changes only the size and shape of the clay. Stretching a rubber band is a physical change because the size of the rubber band changes. The color of the rubber band sometimes can change as well when it is stretched. However, the material that the rubber band is made of does not change. The rubber band is still rubber.

What happens when water changes from a liquid into water vapor or ice? Is this a physical change? Remember to ask yourself what has changed about the material. Ice is a solid and water is a liquid, but both are the same substance—both are composed of H_2O molecules. As you will read in more detail in the next section, a change in a substance's state of matter is a physical change.

CHECK YOUR READING How is a physical change related to a substance's physical properties?

A substance can go through many different physical changes and still remain the same substance. Consider, for example, the changes that happen to the wool that ultimately becomes a sweater.

① Wool is sheared from the sheep. The wool is then cleaned and placed into a machine that separates the wool fibers from one another. Shearing and separating the fibers are physical changes that change the shape, volume, and texture of the wool.

② The wool fibers are spun into yarn. Again, the shape and volume of the wool change. The fibers are twisted so that they are packed more closely together and are intertwined with one another.

③ The yarn is dyed. The dye changes the color of the wool, but it does not change the wool into another substance. This type of color change is a physical change.

④ Knitting the yarn into a sweater also does not change the wool into another substance. A wool sweater is still wool, even though it no longer resembles the wool on a sheep.

It can be difficult to determine if a specific change is a physical change or not. Some changes, such as a change in color, also can occur when new substances are formed during the change. When deciding whether a change is a physical change or not, ask yourself whether you have the same substance you started with. If the substance is the same, then the changes it underwent were all physical changes.

A 44 Unit: Matter and Energy

Physical Changes

The process of turning wool into a sweater requires that the wool undergo physical changes. Changes in shape, volume, texture, and color occur as raw wool is turned into a colorful sweater.

① Shearing

Preparing the wool produces physical changes. The wool is removed from the sheep and then cleaned before the wool fibers are separated.

② Spinning

Further physical changes occur as a machine twists the wool fibers into a long, thin rope of yarn.

③ Dyeing

Dyeing produces color changes but does not change the basic substance of the wool.

④ The final product, a wool sweater, is still wool.

READING VISUALS How does the yarn in the sweater differ from the wool on the sheep?

Chapter 2: Properties of Matter 45 A

Chemical properties describe how substances form new substances.

Resource Center CLASSZONE.COM
Learn about the chemical properties of matter.

If you wanted to keep a campfire burning, would you add a piece of wood or a piece of iron? You would add wood, of course, because you know that wood burns but iron does not. Is the ability to burn a physical property of the wood? The ability to burn seems to be quite different from physical properties such as color, density, and shape. More important, after the wood burns, all that is left is a pile of ashes and some new substances in the air. The wood has obviously changed into something else. The ability to burn, therefore, must describe another kind of property that substances have—not a physical property but a chemical property.

Chemical Properties and Changes

Chemical properties describe how substances can form new substances. Combustibility, for example, describes how well an object can burn. Wood burns well and turns into ashes and other substances. Can you think of a chemical property for the metal iron? Especially when left outdoors in wet weather, iron rusts. The ability to rust is a chemical property of iron. The metal silver does not rust, but eventually a darker substance called tarnish forms on its surface. You may have noticed a layer of tarnish on some silver spoons or jewelry.

INFER The bust of Abraham Lincoln is made of bronze. Why is the nose a different color from the rest of the head?

The chemical properties of copper cause it to become a blue-green color when it is exposed to air. A famous example of tarnished copper is the Statue of Liberty. The chemical properties of bronze are different. Some bronze objects tarnish to a dark brown color, like the bust of Abraham Lincoln in the photograph on the left.

Chemical properties can be identified by the changes they produce. The change of one substance into another substance is called a **chemical change.** A piece of wood burning, an iron fence rusting, and a silver spoon tarnishing are all examples of chemical changes. A chemical change affects the substances involved in the change. During a chemical change, combinations of atoms in the original substances are rearranged to make new substances. For example, when rust forms on iron, the iron atoms combine with oxygen atoms in the air to form a new substance that is made of both iron and oxygen.

A chemical change is also involved when an antacid tablet is dropped into a glass of water. As the tablet dissolves, bubbles of gas appear. The water and the substances in the tablet react to form new substances. One of these substances is carbon dioxide gas, which forms the bubbles that you see.

A   46   Unit: Matter and Energy

Not all chemical changes are as destructive as burning, rusting, or tarnishing. Chemical changes are also involved in cooking. When you boil an egg, for example, the substances in the raw egg change into new substances as energy is added to the egg. When you eat the egg, further chemical changes take place as your body digests the egg. The process forms new molecules that your body then can use to function.

CHECK YOUR READING Give three examples of chemical changes.

The only true indication of a chemical change is that a new substance has been formed. Sometimes, however, it is difficult to tell whether new substances have been formed or not. In many cases you have to judge which type of change has occurred only on the basis of your observations of the change and your previous experience. However, some common signs can suggest that a chemical change has occurred. You can use these signs to guide you as you try to classify a change that you are observing.

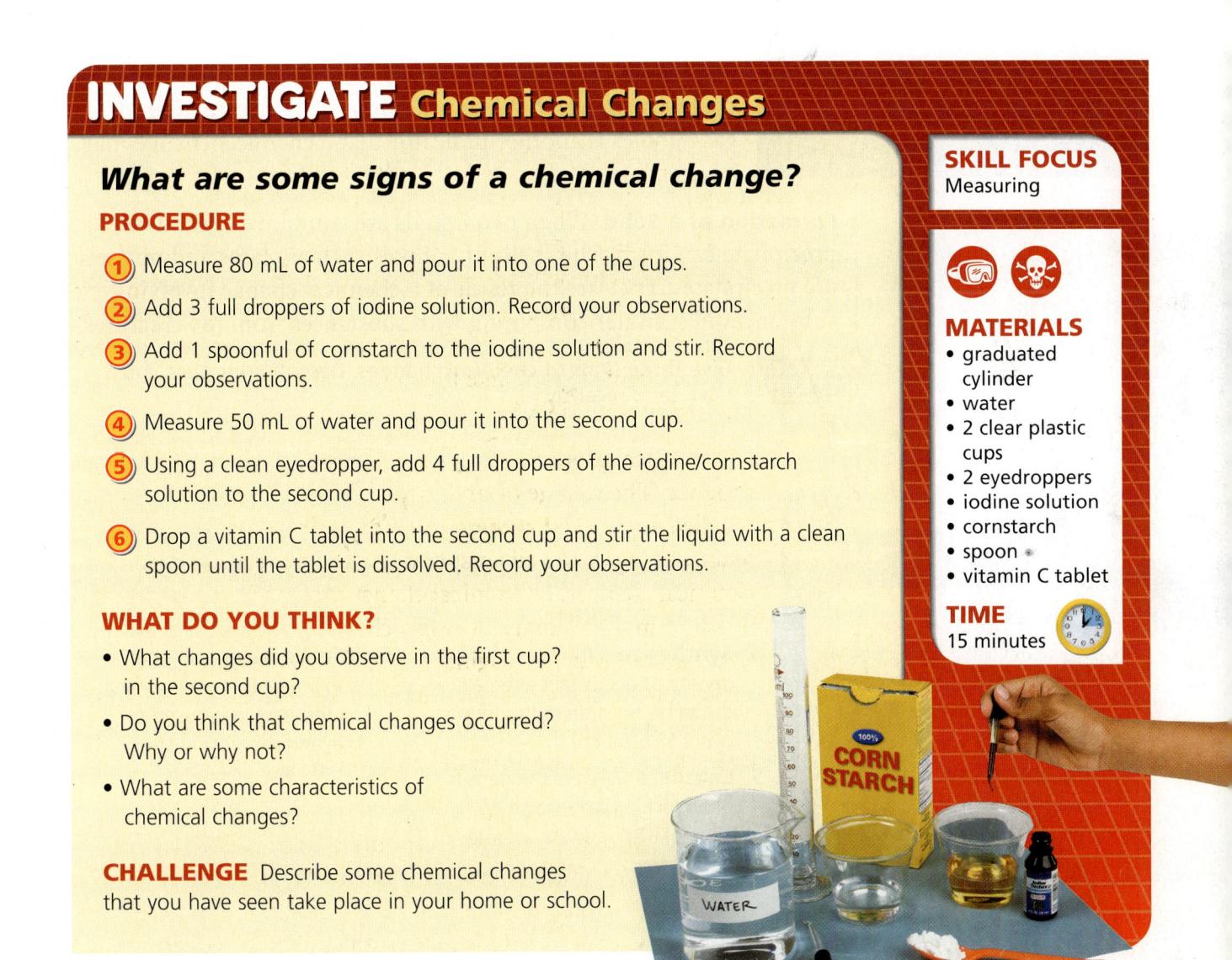

INVESTIGATE Chemical Changes

What are some signs of a chemical change?

PROCEDURE

1. Measure 80 mL of water and pour it into one of the cups.
2. Add 3 full droppers of iodine solution. Record your observations.
3. Add 1 spoonful of cornstarch to the iodine solution and stir. Record your observations.
4. Measure 50 mL of water and pour it into the second cup.
5. Using a clean eyedropper, add 4 full droppers of the iodine/cornstarch solution to the second cup.
6. Drop a vitamin C tablet into the second cup and stir the liquid with a clean spoon until the tablet is dissolved. Record your observations.

WHAT DO YOU THINK?
- What changes did you observe in the first cup? in the second cup?
- Do you think that chemical changes occurred? Why or why not?
- What are some characteristics of chemical changes?

CHALLENGE Describe some chemical changes that you have seen take place in your home or school.

SKILL FOCUS
Measuring

MATERIALS
- graduated cylinder
- water
- 2 clear plastic cups
- 2 eyedroppers
- iodine solution
- cornstarch
- spoon
- vitamin C tablet

TIME
15 minutes

Signs of a Chemical Change

Carbon dioxide bubbles form as substances in the tablet react with water.

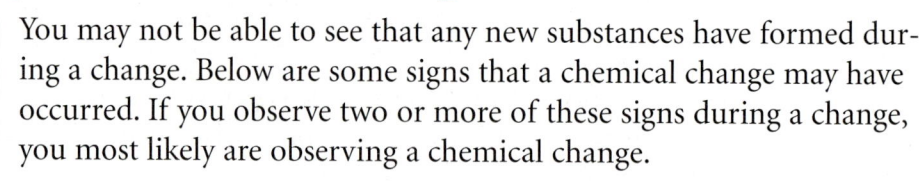

You may not be able to see that any new substances have formed during a change. Below are some signs that a chemical change may have occurred. If you observe two or more of these signs during a change, you most likely are observing a chemical change.

Production of an Odor Some chemical changes produce new smells. The chemical change that occurs when an egg is rotting produces the smell of sulfur. If you go outdoors after a thunderstorm, you may detect an unusual odor in the air. The odor is an indication that lightning has caused a chemical change in the air.

Change in Temperature Chemical changes often are accompanied by a change in temperature. You may have noticed that the temperature is higher near logs burning in a campfire.

Change in Color A change in color is often an indication of a chemical change. For example, fruit may change color when it ripens.

Formation of Bubbles When an antacid tablet makes contact with water, it begins to bubble. The formation of gas bubbles is another indicator that a chemical change may have occurred.

Formation of a Solid When two liquids are combined, a solid called a precipitate can form. The shells of animals such as clams and mussels are precipitates. They are the result of a chemical change involving substances in seawater combining with substances from the creatures.

> **CHECK YOUR READING** Give three signs of chemical changes. Describe one that you have seen recently.

2.1 Review

KEY CONCEPTS

1. What effect does observing a substance's physical properties have on the substance?
2. Describe how a physical property such as mass or texture can change without causing a change in the substance.
3. Explain why burning is a chemical change in wood.

CRITICAL THINKING

4. **Synthesize** Why does the density of a substance remain the same for different amounts of the substance?
5. **Calculate** What is the density of a block of wood with a mass of 120 g and a volume of 200 cm^3?

CHALLENGE

6. **Infer** Iron can rust when it is exposed to oxygen. What method could be used to prevent iron from rusting?

MATH in SCIENCE

SKILL: SOLVING PROPORTIONS

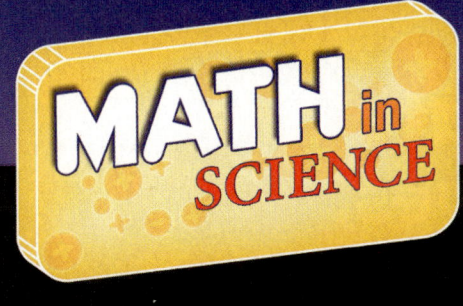

MATH TUTORIAL
CLASSZONE.COM

Click on Math Tutorial for more help with solving proportions.

Density of Materials

Two statues are made of the same type of marble. One is larger than the other. However, they both have the same density because they are made of the same material. Recall the formula for density.

$$\text{Density} = \frac{\text{mass}}{\text{Volume}}$$

Because the density is the same, you know that the mass of one statue divided by its volume is the same as the mass of the other statue divided by its volume. You can set this up and solve it as a proportion.

Example

A small marble statue has a mass of 2.5 kg and a volume of 1000 cm^3. A large marble statue with the same density has a mass of 10 kg. What is the volume of the large statue?

(1) Write the information as an equation showing the proportion.

$$\frac{\text{mass of small statue}}{\text{volume of small statue}} = \frac{\text{mass of large statue}}{\text{volume of large statue}}$$

(2) Insert the known values into your equation.

$$\frac{2.5 \text{ kg}}{1000 \text{ cm}^3} = \frac{10 \text{ kg}}{\text{volume of large statue}}$$

(3) Compare the numerators: 10 kg is 4 times greater than 2.5 kg.

(4) The denominators of the fractions are related in the same way. Therefore, the volume of the large statue is 4 times the volume of the small one.

volume of large statue = 4 · 1000 cm^3 = 4000 cm^3

ANSWER The volume of the large statue is 4000 cm^3.

Answer the following questions.

1. A lump of gold has a volume of 10 cm^3 and a mass of 193 g. Another lump of gold has a mass of 96.5 g. What is the volume of the second lump of gold?

2. A carpenter saws a wooden beam into two pieces. One piece has a mass of 600 g and a volume of 1000 cm^3. What is the mass of the second piece if its volume is 250 cm^3?

3. A 200 mL bottle is completely filled with cooking oil. The oil has a mass of 180 g. If 150 mL of the oil is poured into a pot, what is the mass of the poured oil?

CHALLENGE You have two spheres made of the same material. One has a diameter that is twice as large as the other. How do their masses compare?

If the marble statue and the marble bust both have the same density, their masses are proportional to their volumes.

Chapter 2: **Properties of Matter** 49

KEY CONCEPT
2.2 Changes of state are physical changes.

BEFORE, you learned
- Substances have physical and chemical properties
- Physical changes do not change a substance into a new substance
- Chemical changes result in new substances

NOW, you will learn
- How liquids can become solids, and solids can become liquids
- How liquids can become gases, and gases can become liquids
- How energy is related to changes of state

VOCABULARY
melting p. 51
melting point p. 51
freezing p. 52
freezing point p. 52
evaporation p. 53
sublimation p. 53
boiling p. 54
boiling point p. 54
condensation p. 55

THINK ABOUT

Where does dew come from?

On a cool morning, droplets of dew cover the grass. Where does this water come from? You might think it had rained recently. However, dew forms even if it has not rained. Air is made of a mixture of different gases, including water vapor. Some of the water vapor condenses—or becomes a liquid—on the cool grass and forms drops of liquid water.

MAIN IDEA WEB
Remember to place each blue heading in a box. Add details around it to form a web.

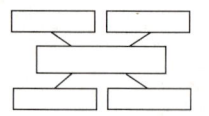

Matter can change from one state to another.

Matter is commonly found in three states: solid, liquid, and gas. A solid has a fixed volume and a fixed shape. A liquid also has a fixed volume but takes the shape of its container. A gas has neither a fixed volume nor a fixed shape. Matter always exists in one of these states, but it can change from one state to another.

When matter changes from one state to another, the substance itself does not change. Water, ice, and water vapor are all the same basic substance. As water turns into ice or water vapor, the water molecules themselves do not change. What changes are the arrangement of the molecules and the amount of space between them. Changes in state are physical changes because changes in state do not change the basic substance.

CHECK YOUR READING Why is a change in state a physical change rather than a chemical change?

A 50 Unit: Matter and Energy

Solids can become liquids, and liquids can become solids.

If you leave an ice cube on a kitchen counter, it changes to the liquid form of water. Water changes to the solid form of water, ice, when it is placed in a freezer. In a similar way, if a bar of iron is heated to a high enough temperature, it will become liquid iron. As the liquid iron cools, it becomes solid iron again.

Melting

Melting is the process by which a solid becomes a liquid. Different solids melt at different temperatures. The lowest temperature at which a substance begins to melt is called its **melting point**. Although the melting point of ice is 0°C (32°F), iron must be heated to a much higher temperature before it will melt.

VOCABULARY
Add magnet word diagrams for *melting* and *melting point* to your notebook.

Remember that particles are always in motion, even in a solid. Because the particles in a solid are bound together, they do not move from place to place—but they do vibrate. As a solid heats up, its particles gain energy and vibrate faster. If the vibrations are fast enough, the particles break loose and slide past one another. In other words, the solid melts and becomes a liquid.

Some substances have a well-defined melting point. If you are melting ice, for example, you can predict that when the temperature reaches 0°C, the ice will start to melt. Substances with an orderly structure start melting when they reach a specific temperature.

Melting a Solid

Steel melts at very high temperatures. Liquid steel can be poured into molds to form the beams that are used in bridges like the one shown on the left.

READING VISUALS What would happen to the steel in this bridge if it became as hot as the steel in the bucket?

Chapter 2: **Properties of Matter** 51

Other substances, such as plastic and chocolate, do not have a well-defined melting point. Chocolate becomes soft when the temperature is high enough, but it still maintains its shape. Eventually, the chocolate becomes a liquid, but there is no specific temperature at which you can say the change happened. Instead, the melting happens gradually over a range of temperatures.

CHECK YOUR READING Describe the movement of molecules in a substance that is at its melting point.

Icicles grow as water drips down them, freezes, and sticks to the ice that is already there. On a warm day, the frozen icicles melt again.

Freezing

READING TIP
On the Celsius temperature scale, under normal conditions, water freezes at 0°C and boils at 100°C. On the Fahrenheit scale, water freezes at 32°F and boils at 212°F.

Freezing is the process by which a liquid becomes a solid. Although you may think of cold temperatures when you hear the word *freezing*, many substances are solid, or frozen, at room temperature and above. Think about a soda can and a candle. The can and the candle are frozen at temperatures you would find in a classroom.

As the temperature of a liquid is lowered, its particles lose energy. As a result, the particles move more slowly. Eventually, the particles move slowly enough that the attractions among them cause the liquid to become a solid. The temperature at which a specific liquid becomes a solid is called the **freezing point** of the substance.

The freezing point of a substance is the same as that substance's melting point. At this particular temperature, the substance can exist as either a solid or a liquid. At temperatures below the freezing/melting point, the substance is a solid. At temperatures above the freezing/melting point, the substance is a liquid.

CHECK YOUR READING What is the relationship between a substance's melting point and freezing point?

A 52 Unit: Matter and Energy

Liquids can become gases, and gases can become liquids.

Suppose you spill water on a picnic table on a warm day. You might notice that the water eventually disappears from the table. What has happened to the water molecules? The liquid water has become water vapor, a gas. The water vapor mixes with the surrounding air. At the same picnic, you might also notice that a cold can of soda has beads of water forming on it. The water vapor in the air has become the liquid water found on the soda can.

Evaporation

Evaporation is a process by which a liquid becomes a gas. It usually occurs at the surface of a liquid. Although all particles in a liquid move, they do not all move at the same speed. Some particles move faster than others. The fastest moving particles at the surface of the liquid can break away from the liquid and escape to become gas particles.

As the temperature increases, the energy in the liquid increases. More particles can escape from the surface of the liquid. As a result, the liquid evaporates more quickly. This is why spilled water will evaporate faster in hot weather than in cold weather.

READING TIP
The root of the word *evaporation* is *vapor,* a Latin word meaning "steam."

CHECK YOUR READING Describe the movement of particles in a liquid as it evaporates.

It is interesting to note that under certain conditions, solids can lose particles through a process similar to evaporation. When a solid changes directly to a gas, the process is called **sublimation.** You may have seen dry ice being used in a cooler to keep foods cold. Dry ice is frozen carbon dioxide that sublimates in normal atmospheric conditions.

Evaporation

During evaporation, fast-moving particles escape from the surface of a liquid and become gas particles.

Chapter 2: **Properties of Matter** 53

Explore melting points and boiling points.

Boiling

Boiling is another process by which a liquid becomes a gas. Unlike evaporation, boiling produces bubbles. If you heat a pot of water on the stove, you will notice that after a while tiny bubbles begin to form. These bubbles contain dissolved air that is escaping from the liquid. As you continue to heat the water, large bubbles suddenly form and rise to the surface. These bubbles contain energetic water molecules that have escaped from the liquid water to form a gas. This process is boiling.

Boiling can occur only when the liquid reaches a certain temperature, called the **boiling point** of the liquid. Liquids evaporate over a wide range of temperatures. Boiling, however, occurs at a specific temperature for each liquid. Water, for example, has a boiling point of 100°C (212°F) at normal atmospheric pressure.

In the mountains, water boils at a temperature lower than 100°C. For example, in Leadville, Colorado, which has an elevation of 3094 m (10,152 ft) above sea level, water boils at 89°C (192°F). This happens because at high elevations the air pressure is much lower than at sea level. Because less pressure is pushing down on the surface of the water, bubbles can form inside the liquid at a lower temperature. Less energetic water molecules are needed to expand the bubbles under these conditions. The lower boiling point of water means that foods cooked in water, such as pasta, require a longer time to prepare.

Different substances boil at different temperatures. Helium, which is a gas at room temperature, boils at −270°C (−454°F). Aluminum, on the other hand, boils at 2519°C (4566°F). This fact explains why some substances usually are found as gases but others are not.

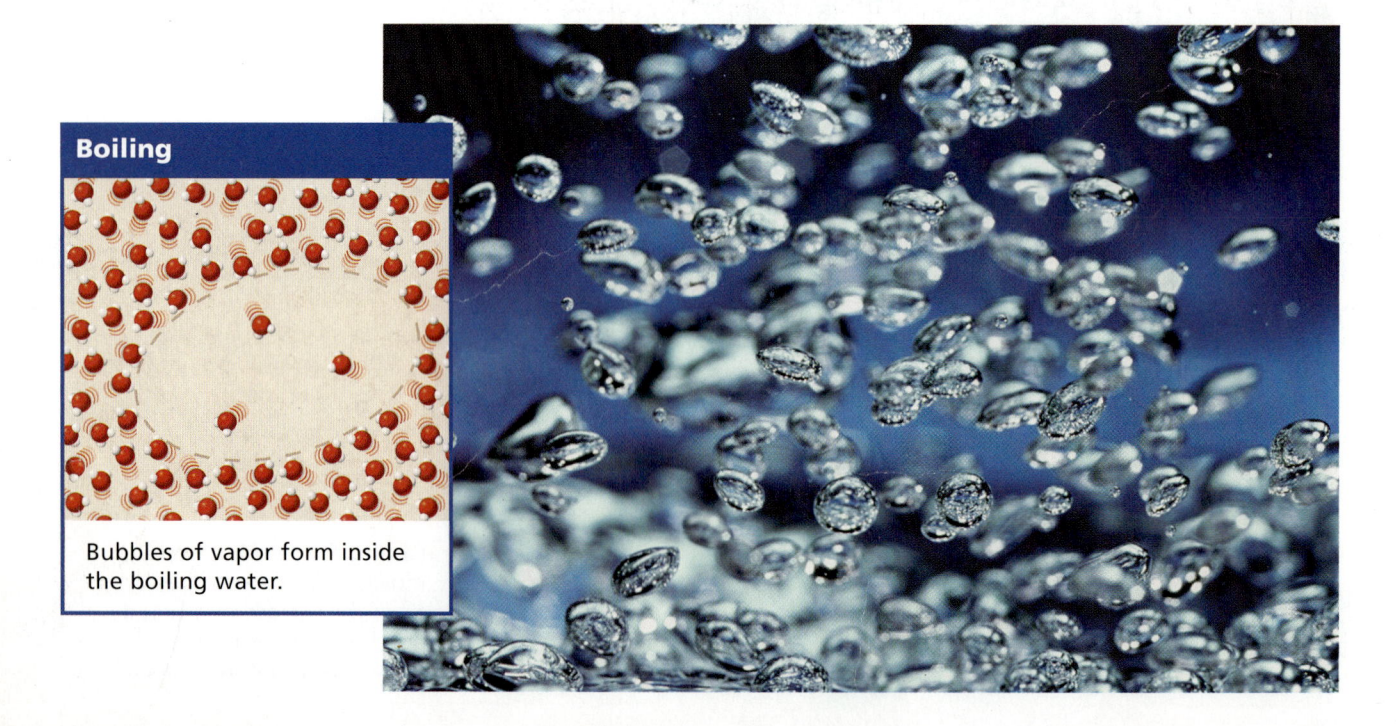

Boiling

Bubbles of vapor form inside the boiling water.

54 Unit: Matter and Energy

Tiny droplets of water form on a window as water vapor from the air condenses into liquid water.

Condensation

The process by which a gas changes its state to become a liquid is called **condensation.** You probably have seen an example of condensation when you enjoyed a cold drink on a warm day. The beads of water that formed on the glass or can were water vapor that condensed from the surrounding air.

READING TIP

The root of the word *condensation* is *condense*, which comes from a Latin word meaning "to thicken."

The cold can or glass cooled the air surrounding it. When you cool a gas, it loses energy. As the particles move more slowly, the attractions among them cause droplets of liquid to form. Condensed water often forms when warm air containing water vapor comes into contact with a cold surface, such as a glass of ice or ground that has cooled during the night.

As with evaporation, condensation can occur over a wide range of temperatures. Like the particles in liquids, the individual particles in a gas are moving at many different speeds. Slowly moving particles near the cool surface condense as they lose energy. The faster moving particles also slow down but continue to move too fast to stick to the other particles in the liquid that is forming. However, if you cool a gas to a temperature below its boiling point, almost all of the gas will condense.

2.2 Review

KEY CONCEPTS

1. Describe three ways in which matter can change from one state to another.
2. Compare and contrast the processes of evaporation and condensation.
3. How does adding energy to matter by heating it affect the energy of its particles?

CRITICAL THINKING

4. **Synthesize** Explain how water can exist as both a solid and a liquid at 0°C.
5. **Apply** Explain how a pat of butter at room temperature can be considered to be frozen.

CHALLENGE

6. **Infer** You know that water vapor condenses from air when the air temperature is lowered. Should it be possible to condense oxygen from air? What would have to happen?

Chapter 2: **Properties of Matter** 55

CHAPTER INVESTIGATION

Freezing Point

OVERVIEW AND PURPOSE Stearic acid is a substance used in making candles. In this experiment you will
- observe melted stearic acid as it changes from a liquid to a solid
- record the freezing point of stearic acid

▶ Problem

What is the freezing point of stearic acid?

▶ Procedure

1. Make a data table like the one shown on the sample notebook page.

2. Use the test-tube tongs to take the test tube of melted stearic acid and place it in the test-tube rack. Keep the test tube in the rack for the entire experiment.

3. Use the wire-loop stirrer and stir the liquid to make sure that it is the same temperature throughout.

4. Place the thermometer into the stearic acid to take a reading. Hold the thermometer so that it does not touch the sides or bottom of the test tube. Wait until the temperature stops rising. Then record the temperature on your data table. Also note whether the stearic acid is a liquid or a solid—or whether both states are present.

5. Take the temperature of the stearic acid every minute, stirring the stearic acid with the stirrer before each reading. To get an accurate reading, place the loop of the stirrer around the thermometer and use an up-and-down motion.

6. Continue taking temperature readings until two minutes after the acid has become totally solid or you are no longer able to stir it.

MATERIALS
- large test tube
- stearic acid
- test-tube tongs
- test-tube rack
- wire-loop stirrer
- thermometer

Unit: Matter and Energy

7. Make a note of the temperature on your data table when the first signs of a solid formation appear.

8. Make a note of the temperature on your data table when the stearic acid is completely solid.

9. Leave the thermometer and stirrer in the test tube and carry it carefully in the test-tube rack to your teacher.

Observe and Analyze — Write It Up

1. **RECORD OBSERVATIONS** Make a line graph showing the freezing curve of stearic acid. Label the vertical axis **Temperature** and the horizontal axis **Time**.

2. **RECORD OBSERVATIONS** Label your graph to show when the stearic acid was a liquid, when it was a solid, and when it was present in both states.

3. **ANALYZE** Explain how your graph tells you the freezing point of stearic acid.

Conclude — Write It Up

1. **INTERPRET** Answer the question in the problem.

2. **IDENTIFY** How does the freezing point of stearic acid compare with the freezing point of water?

3. **INFER** What happened to the energy of the molecules as the stearic acid changed from a liquid to a solid?

4. **INFER** From your observations, infer the melting point of stearic acid. How is the melting point of stearic acid related to its freezing point?

5. **APPLY** Why do you think stearic acid is used as an ingredient in bar soaps but not in liquid soaps?

INVESTIGATE Further

CHALLENGE What do you think would happen if you mixed in another substance with the stearic acid? How would that affect the freezing point? What experiment would you perform to find the answer?

Freezing Point
Problem What is the freezing point of stearic acid?
Observe and Analyze
Table 1. Freezing Point of Stearic Acid

Time (min)	Temperature (°C)	Liquid	Solid	Both
0.0				
1.0				
2.0				
3.0				
4.0				
5.0				
6.0				
7.0				

Chapter 2: **Properties of Matter** 57

KEY CONCEPT

2.3 Properties are used to identify substances.

◀ **BEFORE, you learned**
- Matter can change from one state to another
- Changes in state require energy changes

▶ **NOW, you will learn**
- How properties can help you identify substances
- How properties of substances can be used to separate substances

---

EXPLORE Identifying Substances

How can properties help you identify a substance?

PROCEDURE

1. Place some of substance A into one cup and some of substance B into the other cup. Label the cups.
2. Carefully add some water to each cup. Observe and record what happens.

WHAT DO YOU THINK?
- Which result was a physical change? a chemical change? Explain.
- The substances are baking soda and baking powder. Baking powder and water produce carbon dioxide gas. Which substance is baking powder?

MATERIALS
- substance A
- substance B
- 2 cups
- water

MAIN IDEA WEB
As you read, place each blue heading in a box. Add details around it to form a web.

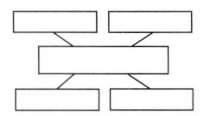

Substances have characteristic properties.

You often use the properties of a substance to identify it. For example, when you reach into your pocket, you can tell the difference between a ticket stub and a folded piece of tissue because one is stiff and smooth and the other is soft. You can identify nickels, dimes, and quarters without looking at them by feeling their shapes and comparing their sizes. To tell the difference between a nickel and a subway token, however, you might have to use another property, such as color. Texture, shape, and color are physical properties that you use all the time to identify and sort objects.

CHECK YOUR READING How can physical properties be used to identify a substance?

A 58 Unit: Matter and Energy

Identifying Unknown Substances

Suppose you have a glass of an unknown liquid that you want to identify. It looks like milk, but you cannot be sure. How could you determine what it is? Of course, you would not taste an unknown substance, but there are many properties other than taste that you could use to identify the substance safely.

To proceed scientifically, you could measure several properties of the unknown liquid and compare them with the properties of known substances. You might observe and measure such properties as color, odor, texture, density, boiling point, and freezing point. A few of these properties might be enough to tell you that your white liquid is glue rather than milk.

To determine the difference among several colorless liquids, scientists would use additional tests. Their tests, however, would rely on the same idea of measuring and comparing the properties of an unknown with something that is already known.

Properties Used for Identifying Substances

You are already familiar with the most common physical properties of matter. Some of these properties, such as mass and volume, depend upon the specific object in question. You cannot use mass to tell one substance from another because two very different objects can have the same mass—a kilogram of feathers has the same mass as a kilogram of peanut butter, for example.

Other properties, such as density, can be used to identify substances. They do not vary from one sample of the same substance to another. For example, you could see a difference between a kilogram of liquid soap and a kilogram of honey by measuring their densities.

The physical properties described below can be used to identify a substance.

Density The densities of wood, plastic, and steel are all different. Scientists already have determined the densities of many substances. As a result, you can conveniently compare the density of an unknown substance with the densities of known substances. Finding any matching densities will give you information about the possible identity of the unknown substance. However, it is possible for two different substances to have the same density. In that case, in order to identify the substance positively, you would need additional data.

Aerogel, an extremely lightweight material used in the space program, has such a low density that it can float on soap bubbles.

CHECK YOUR READING Why can't you identify a substance on the basis of density alone?

These fibers act as heat insulators to keep the inside of the sleeping bag warm.

Heating Properties Substances respond to heating in different ways. Some warm up very quickly, and others take a long while to increase in temperature. This property is important in selecting materials for different uses. Aluminum and iron are good materials for making pots and pans because they conduct heat well. Various materials used in household insulation are poor heat conductors. Therefore, these insulators are used to keep warm air inside a home on a cold day. You can measure the rate at which a substance conducts heat and compare that rate with the heat conduction rates of other substances.

Solubility Solubility is a measure of how much of a substance dissolves in a given volume of a liquid. Sugar and dirt, for instance, have very different solubilities in water. If you put a spoonful of sugar into a cup of water and stir, the sugar dissolves in the water very rapidly. If you put a spoonful of dirt into water and stir, most of the dirt settles to the bottom as soon as you stop stirring.

READING TIP
The root of the word *solubility* is the Latin word *solvere,* which means "to loosen."

Electric Properties Some substances conduct electricity better than others. This means that they allow electric charge to move through them easily. Copper wire is used to carry electricity because it is a good conductor. Materials that do not conduct easily, such as rubber and plastics, are used to block the flow of charge. With the proper equipment, scientists can test the electric conductivity of an unknown substance.

Iron filings are attracted by the magnet. The wood chips, however, are not.

Magnetic Properties Some substances are attracted to magnets, but others are not. You can use a magnet to pick up a paper clip but not a plastic button or a wooden match. The elements iron, cobalt, and nickel are magnetic—meaning they respond to magnets—but copper, aluminum, and zinc are not. Steel, which contains iron, is also magnetic.

Mixtures can be separated by using the properties of the substances in them.

Suppose you have a bag of cans that you want to recycle. The recycling center accepts only aluminum cans. You know that some of your cans contain steel. You would probably find it difficult to tell aluminum cans from steel ones just by looking at them. How could you separate the cans? Aluminum and steel may look similar, but they have different magnetic properties. You could use a magnet to test each can. If the magnet sticks to the can, the can contains steel. Recycling centers often use magnets to separate aluminum cans from steel cans.

Some mixtures contain solids mixed with liquids. A filter can be used to separate the solid from the liquid. One example of this is a tea bag. The paper filter allows the liquid water to mix with the tea, because water molecules are small enough to pass through the filter. The large pieces of tea, however, cannot pass through the filter and remain inside the tea bag.

INVESTIGATE Separating Mixtures

How can a mixture of sand, salt, and pepper be separated?

DESIGN YOUR OWN EXPERIMENT

Scientists often have to isolate a single substance from a mixture. Use your knowledge of the properties of sand, salt, and pepper to design a method for separating each of these substances from the mixture.

PROCEDURE

1. Examine the mixture and the materials provided. Design a procedure for separating the different substances in your mixture. Carefully consider the order in which you will try each step.

2. Write up your procedure. Explain why you chose the steps you did for each substance.

3. Carry out your procedure.

WHAT DO YOU THINK?

- Was your procedure successful? How would you modify your procedure if you were to perform the separation again?
- How does knowing the properties of matter help you separate the substances in mixtures?

SKILL FOCUS
Designing experiments

MATERIALS
- mixture of sand, salt, and pepper
- 2 index cards
- comb
- felt
- graduated cylinder
- spoon
- water
- coffee filter
- funnel
- small cup
- pie tin

TIME
30 minutes

Some mixtures are more difficult to separate than others. For example, if you stir sugar into water, the sugar dissolves and breaks up into individual molecules that are too tiny to filter out. In this case, you can take advantage of the fact that water is a liquid and will evaporate from an open dish. Sugar, however, does not evaporate. The mixture can be heated to speed the evaporation of the water, leaving the sugar behind.

There are many important reasons for separating substances. One reason is to make a substance safe to consume, such as drinking water. In order to produce drinking water, workers at a water-treatment plant must separate many of the substances that are mixed in with the water.

This water-treatment plant separates harmful substances from the water.

The process in water-treatment plants generally includes these steps:

- First, a chemical is added to the water that causes the larger particles to stick together. They settle to the bottom of the water, where they can be removed.
- Next, the water is run through a series of special molecular filters. Each filter removes smaller particles than the one before.
- Finally, another chemical, chlorine, is added to disinfect the water and make it safe to drink.

Water-treatment plants use the properties of the substances found in water to produce the clean water that flows from your tap.

CHECK YOUR READING What are two situations in which separating substances is useful?

2.3 Review

KEY CONCEPTS

1. How can properties help you distinguish one substance from another?
2. What are two physical properties that can help you identify a substance?
3. How can understanding properties help you separate substances from a mixture?

CRITICAL THINKING

4. **Apply** Why might an archaeologist digging in ancient ruins sift dirt through a screen?
5. **Synthesize** Suppose you had a mixture of iron pellets, pebbles, and small wood spheres, all of which were about the same size. How would you separate this mixture?

CHALLENGE

6. **Synthesize** You have two solid substances that look the same. What measurements would you take and which tests would you perform to determine whether they actually are the same?

Unit: Matter and Energy

Connecting Sciences

PHYSICAL SCIENCE AND EARTH SCIENCE

Separating Minerals

A few minerals, such as rock salt, occur in large deposits that can be mined in a form that is ready to use. Most minerals, however, are combined with other materials, so they need to be separated from the mixtures of which they are a part. Scientists and miners use the differences in physical properties to analyze samples and to separate the materials removed from a mine.

Appearance

Gemstones are prized because of their obvious physical properties, such as color, shininess, and hardness. Particularly valuable minerals, such as diamonds and emeralds, are often located by digging underground and noting the differences between the gemstone and the surrounding dirt and rock.

Density

When gold deposits wash into a streambed, tiny particles of gold mix with the sand. It is hard to separate them by appearance because the pieces are so small. In the 1800s, as prospectors swirled this sand around in a pan, the lighter particles of sand washed away with the water. The denser gold particles collected in the bottom of the pan. Some modern gold mines use the same principle in machines that handle tons of material, washing away the lighter dirt and rock to leave bits of gold.

Magnetism

Machines called magnetic separators divide a mixture into magnetic and nonmagnetic materials. In order to separate iron from other materials, rocks are crushed and carried past a strong magnet. Particles that contain iron are drawn toward the magnet and fall into one bin, while the nonmagnetic materials fall into another bin.

Melting Point

Thousands of years ago, people discovered that when some minerals are placed in a very hot fire, metals—such as copper, tin, and zinc—can be separated from the rock around them. When the ores reach a certain temperature, the metal melts and can be collected as a liquid.

Workers can identify garnets in a mine because their physical properties are different from the physical properties of their surroundings.

EXPLORE

1. **INFER** At a copper ore mine in Chile, one of the world's largest magnets is used to remove pieces of iron from the ore. What can you infer about the copper ore?

2. **CHALLENGE** Electrostatic precipitators are important tools for protecting the environment from pollution. Use the Internet to learn how they are used in power plants and other factories that burn fuels.

RESOURCE CENTER CLASSZONE.COM Find out more about separating materials from mixtures.

Chapter 2 Review

the BIG idea
Matter has properties that can be changed by physical and chemical processes.

CONTENT REVIEW
CLASSZONE.COM

KEY CONCEPTS SUMMARY

2.1 Matter has observable properties.

- Physical properties can be observed without changing the substance.
- Physical changes can change some physical properties but do not change the substance.
- Chemical properties describe how substances form new substances.
- Chemical changes create new substances.

VOCABULARY
physical property p. 41
density p. 43
physical change p. 44
chemical property p. 46
chemical change p. 46

2.2 Changes of states are physical changes.
Matter is commonly found in three states: solid, liquid, and gas.

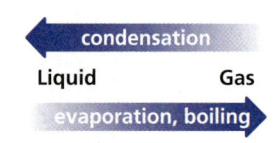

Solid ← freezing — Liquid
Solid — melting → Liquid

Liquid ← condensation — Gas
Liquid — evaporation, boiling → Gas

VOCABULARY
melting p. 51
melting point p. 51
freezing p. 52
freezing point p. 52
evaporation p. 53
sublimation p. 53
boiling p. 54
boiling point p. 54
condensation p. 55

2.3 Properties are used to identify substances.
Physical properties that can be used to identify substances include:
- density
- heating properties
- solubility
- electric properties
- magnetic properties

Mixtures can be separated by using the properties of the substances they contain.

A 64 Unit: Matter and Energy

Reviewing Vocabulary

Describe how the terms in the following sets of terms are related.

1. physical property, physical change
2. chemical property, chemical change
3. density, matter
4. melting, melting point, freezing point
5. boiling, boiling point, liquid
6. evaporation, condensation
7. sublimation, solid

Reviewing Key Concepts

Multiple Choice *Choose the letter of the best answer.*

8. Color, shape, size, and texture are
   a. physical properties
   b. chemical properties
   c. physical changes
   d. chemical changes

9. Density describes the relationship between a substance's
   a. matter and mass
   b. mass and volume
   c. volume and area
   d. temperature and mass

10. Dissolving sugar in water is an example of a
    a. physical change
    b. chemical change
    c. change in state
    d. pressure change

11. An electric current can be used to decompose, or break down, water into oxygen gas and hydrogen gas. This is an example of a
    a. physical change
    b. chemical change
    c. change in state
    d. pressure change

12. The formation of rust on iron is a chemical change because
    a. the color and shape have changed
    b. the mass and volume have changed
    c. the substance remains the same
    d. a new substance has been formed

13. The process by which a solid becomes a liquid is called
    a. boiling
    b. freezing
    c. melting
    d. evaporating

14. The process by which a liquid becomes a solid is called
    a. boiling
    b. freezing
    c. melting
    d. evaporating

15. Two processes by which a liquid can become a gas are
    a. evaporation and boiling
    b. melting and freezing
    c. sublimation and condensation
    d. evaporation and condensation

Short Answer *Answer each of the following questions in a sentence or two.*

16. When a sculptor shapes marble to make a statue, is this a physical or a chemical change? Explain your answer.

17. Describe and identify various physical changes that water can undergo.

18. Why does dew often form on grass on a cool morning, even if there has been no rain?

19. Describe the difference between evaporation and boiling in terms of the movement of the liquid's particles in each case.

20. What effect does altitude have on the boiling point of water?

Chapter 2: **Properties of Matter** 65

Thinking Critically

21. ANALYZE Whole milk is a mixture. When bacteria in the milk digest part of the mixture, changes occur. Lactic acid is produced, and the milk tastes sour. Explain why this process is a chemical change.

22. INFER Sharpening a pencil leaves behind pencil shavings. Why is sharpening a pencil a physical change instead of a chemical change?

23. ANALYZE Dumping cooked spaghetti and water into a colander separates the two substances because the liquid water can run through the holes in the colander but the solid spaghetti cannot. Explain how this is an example of separating a mixture based on the physical properties of its components.

24. INFER The density of water is 1.0 g/mL. Anything with a density less than 1.0 g/mL will float in water. The density of a fresh egg is about 1.2 g/mL. The density of a spoiled egg is about 0.9 g/mL. If you place an egg in water and it floats, what does that tell you about the egg?

Use the photograph below to answer the next three questions.

25. COMPARE Which physical properties of the puddle change as the water evaporates? Which physical properties remain the same?

26. ANALYZE Can water evaporate from this puddle on a cold day? Explain your answer.

27. PREDICT What would happen to any minerals and salts in the water if the water completely evaporated?

Use the chart below to answer the next two questions.

Densities Measured at 20°C

Material	Density (g/cm³)
gold	19.3
lead	11.3
silver	10.5
copper	9.0
iron	7.9

28. PREDICT Suppose you measure the mass and the volume of a shiny metal object and find that its density is 10.5 g/mL. Could you make a reasonable guess as to what material the object is made of? What factor or factors might affect your guess?

29. CALCULATE A solid nickel bar has a mass of 2.75 kg and a volume of 308.71 cm³. Between which two materials would nickel fall on the chart?

the BIG idea

30. PREDICT Look again at the photograph on pages 38–39. The chef has melted sugar to make a sculpture. Describe how the sugar has changed in terms of its physical and chemical properties. Predict what will happen to the sculpture over time.

31. RESEARCH Think of a question you have about the properties of matter that is still unanswered. For example, there may be a specific type of matter about which you are curious. What information do you need in order to answer your question? How might you find the information?

UNIT PROJECTS

Check your schedule for your unit project. How are you doing? Be sure that you have placed data or notes from your research in your project folder.

Standardized Test Practice

For practice on your state test, go to...
TEST PRACTICE
CLASSZONE.COM

Analyzing Experiments

Read the following description of an experiment together with the chart. Then answer the questions that follow.

Archimedes was a Greek mathematician and scientist who lived in the third century B.C. He figured out that any object placed in a liquid displaced a volume of that liquid equal to its own volume. He used this knowledge to solve a problem.

The king of Syracuse had been given a crown of gold. But he was not sure whether the crown was pure gold. Archimedes solved the king's problem by testing the crown's density.

He immersed the crown in water and measured the volume of water it displaced. Archimedes compared the amount of water displaced by the crown with the amount of water displaced by a bar of pure gold with the same mass. The comparison told him whether the crown was all gold or a mixture of gold and another element.

Element	Density (g/cm^3)
copper	8.96
gold	19.30
iron	7.86
lead	11.34
silver	10.50
tin	7.31

1. Which problem was Archimedes trying to solve?
   a. what the density of gold was
   b. what the crown was made of
   c. what the mass of the crown was
   d. how much water the crown displaced

2. Archimedes used the method that he did because a crown has an irregular shape and the volume of such an object cannot be measured in any other way. Which one of the following objects would also require this method?
   a. a square wooden box
   b. a cylindrical tin can
   c. a small bronze statue
   d. a rectangular piece of glass

3. Suppose Archimedes found that the crown had a mass of 772 grams and displaced 40 milliliters of water. Using the formula $D = m/V$, what would you determine the crown to be made of?
   a. pure gold
   b. half gold and half another element
   c. some other element with gold plating
   d. cannot be determined from the data

4. Using the formula, compare how much water a gold crown would displace if it had a mass of 579 grams.
   a. 10 mL
   b. 20 mL
   c. 30 mL
   d. 193 mL

5. If you had crowns made of each element in the chart that were the same mass, which would displace more water than a gold crown of that mass?
   a. all
   b. lead only
   c. tin only
   d. none

Extended Response

Answer the two questions below in detail.

6. What is the difference between a physical change and a chemical change? Include examples of each type in your explanation.

7. Why does someone cooking spaghetti at a high elevation need to boil it longer than someone cooking spaghetti at a lower elevation?

CHAPTER 3
Energy

the BIG idea

Energy has different forms, but it is always conserved.

What different forms of energy are shown in this photograph?

Key Concepts

SECTION 3.1 Energy exists in different forms.
Learn about several different forms of energy.

SECTION 3.2 Energy can change forms but is never lost.
Learn about the law of conservation of energy.

SECTION 3.3 Technology improves the ways people use energy.
Learn how technology can be used to make energy conversions more efficient.

Internet Preview

CLASSZONE.COM

Chapter 3 online resources: Content Review, Simulation, Visualization, three Resource Centers, Math Tutorial, Test Practice

EXPLORE the BIG idea

A Penny for Your Energy

Chill an empty glass bottle. Immediately complete the following steps: Rub a drop of cooking oil around the rim of the bottle. Place a coin on the rim so the oil forms a seal between the coin and the bottle. Wrap your hands around the bottle.

Observe and Think What happened to the coin? What do you think caused this to happen?

Hot Dog!

Cover a piece of cardboard with aluminum foil, and bend it into the shape of a U. Poke a wooden skewer through a hot dog, and through each side of the cardboard. Push corks over both ends of the skewer so the cardboard does not flatten out. Place your setup in direct sunlight for 30 minutes.

Observe and Think What happened to the hot dog? Were there any changes you had to make while the hot dog was in sunlight?

Internet Activity: Energy

Go to **ClassZone.com** to investigate the relationship between potential energy and kinetic energy.

Observe and Think How did you change potential energy? How do these changes affect kinetic energy?

NSTA scilinks.org
SciLINKS
Forms of Energy Code: MDL063

Chapter 3: Energy 69

CHAPTER 3
Getting Ready to Learn

CONCEPT REVIEW

- Matter has mass and is made of tiny particles.
- Matter can be changed physically or chemically.
- A change in the state of matter is a physical change.

VOCABULARY REVIEW

matter p. 9
mass p. 10
atom p. 16
physical change p. 44
chemical change p. 46

CONTENT REVIEW
CLASSZONE.COM
Review concepts and vocabulary.

TAKING NOTES

MIND MAP

Write each main idea, or blue heading, in an oval; then write details that relate to each other and to the main idea. Organize the details so that each spoke of the web has notes about one part of the main idea.

VOCABULARY STRATEGY

Write each new vocabulary term in the center of a **frame game** diagram. Decide what information to frame it with. Use examples, descriptions, parts, sentences that use the term in context, or pictures. You can change the frame to fit each term.

See the Note-Taking Handbook on pages R45–R51.

SCIENCE NOTEBOOK

DIFFERENT FORMS OF ENERGY HAVE DIFFERENT USES.
- ability to cause a change
- different changes from different forms
- sunlight — electromagnetic energy
- motion — mechanical energy
- food — chemical energy

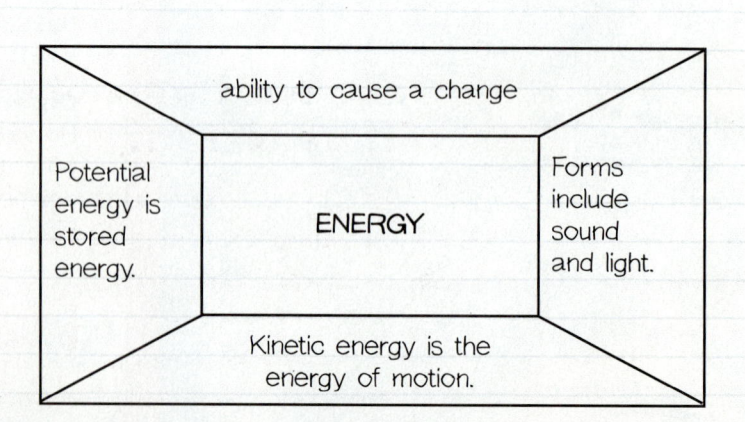

ENERGY
- ability to cause a change
- Potential energy is stored energy.
- Forms include sound and light.
- Kinetic energy is the energy of motion.

70 Unit: Matter and Energy

3.1 Energy exists in different forms.

KEY CONCEPT

◀ **BEFORE, you learned**
- All substances are made of matter
- Matter has both physical and chemical properties
- Matter can exist in different physical states

▶ **NOW, you will learn**
- How energy causes change
- About common forms of energy
- About kinetic energy and potential energy

VOCABULARY

energy p. 72
kinetic energy p. 74
potential energy p. 75

EXPLORE Energy

How can you demonstrate energy?

PROCEDURE

1. Fill the bowl halfway with sand. Place the bowl on the floor as shown. Make sure the sand is level.
2. Place a pebble and a rock near the edge of a table above the bowl of sand.
3. Gently push the pebble off the table into the sand. Record your observations.
4. Remove the pebble, and make sure the sand is level. Gently push the rock off the table into the sand. Record your observations.

MATERIALS
- large plastic bowl
- sand
- pebble
- rock

WHAT DO YOU THINK?
- What happened to the sand when you dropped the pebble? when you dropped the rock?
- How can you explain any differences you observed?

Different forms of energy have different uses.

Energy takes many different forms and has many different effects. Just about everything you see happening around you involves energy. Lamps and other appliances in your home operate on electrical energy. Plants use energy from the Sun to grow. You use energy provided by the food you eat to carry out all of your everyday activities—eating, exercising, reading, and even sitting and thinking. In this chapter, you will learn what these and other forms of energy have in common.

Chapter 3: Energy 71 **A**

Energy

All forms of energy have one important point in common—they cause changes to occur. The flow of electrical energy through a wire causes a cool, dark bulb to get hot and glow. The energy of the wind causes a flag to flutter.

You are a source of energy that makes changes in your environment. For example, when you pick up a tennis racquet or a paintbrush, you change the position of that object. When you hit a tennis ball or smooth paint on a canvas, you cause further changes. Energy is involved in every one of these actions. At its most basic level, **energy** is the ability to cause change.

VOCABULARY
Remember to use a frame game diagram for *energy* and other vocabulary terms.

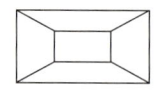

CHECK YOUR READING Provide your own example of energy and how it causes a change.

The photograph below shows a city street. All of the activities that take place on every street in any city require energy, so there are many changes taking place in the picture. Consider one of the cars. A person's energy is used to turn the key that starts the car. The key's movement starts the car's engine and gasoline begins burning. Gasoline provides the energy for the car to move. The person's hand, the turning key, and the burning gasoline all contain energy that causes change.

The motion of the cars and the glow of the streetlights are changes produced by energy.

Forms of Energy

Scientists classify energy into many forms, each of which causes change in a different way. Some of these forms are described below.

Mechanical Energy The energy that moves objects is mechanical energy. The energy that you use to put a book on a shelf is mechanical energy, as is energy that a person uses to turn a car key.

Sound Energy Sound results from the vibration of particles in a solid, liquid, or gas. People and other animals are able to detect these tiny vibrations with structures in their ears that vibrate due to the sound. So, when you hear a car drive past, you are detecting vibrations in the air produced by sound energy. Sound cannot travel through empty space. If there were no air or other substance between you and the car, you would not hear sounds from the car.

Chemical Energy Energy that is stored in the chemical composition of matter is chemical energy. The amount of chemical energy in a substance depends on the types and arrangement of atoms in the substance. When wood or gasoline burns, chemical energy produces heat. The energy used by the cells in your body comes from chemical energy stored in the foods you eat.

Thermal Energy The total amount of energy from the movement of particles in matter is thermal energy. Recall that matter is made of atoms, and atoms combined in molecules. The atoms and molecules in matter are always moving. The energy of this motion in an object is the object's thermal energy. You will learn more about thermal energy in the next chapter.

Electromagnetic Energy Electromagnetic (ih-LEHK-troh-mag-NEHT-ihk) energy is transmitted through space in the form of electromagnetic waves. Unlike sound, electromagnetic waves can travel through empty space. These waves include visible light, x-rays, and microwaves. X-rays are high energy waves used by doctors and dentists to look at your bones and teeth. Microwaves can be used to cook food or to transmit cellular telephone calls but contain far less energy than x-rays. The Sun releases a large amount of electromagnetic energy, some of which is absorbed by Earth.

Nuclear Energy The center of an atom—its nucleus—is the source of nuclear energy. A large amount of energy in the nucleus holds the nuclear particles together. When a heavy atom's nucleus breaks apart, or when the nuclei (NOO-klee-EYE) of two small atoms join together, energy is released. Nuclear energy released from the fusing of small nuclei to form larger nuclei keeps the Sun burning.

APPLY Where in this photograph can you find chemical, sound, and mechanical energy?

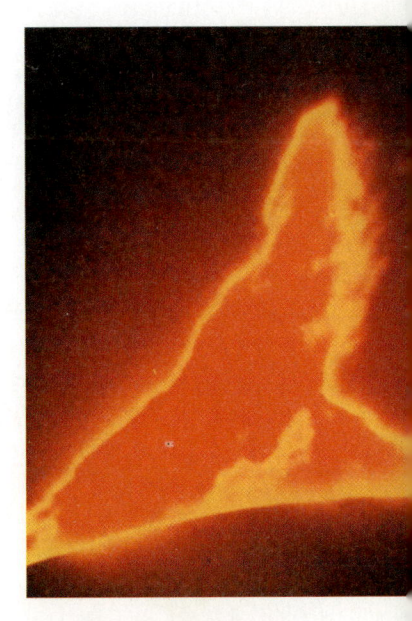

This solar flare releases electromagnetic energy and thermal energy produced by nuclear energy in the Sun.

CHECK YOUR READING How does chemical energy cause a change? What about electromagnetic energy?

Kinetic energy and potential energy are the two general types of energy.

RESOURCE CENTER
CLASSZONE.COM
Learn more about kinetic energy and potential energy.

All of the forms of energy can be described in terms of two general types of energy—kinetic energy and potential energy. Anything that is moving, such as a car that is being driven or an atom in the air, has kinetic energy. All matter also has potential energy, or energy that is stored and can be released at a later time.

Kinetic Energy

READING TIP
Kinetic means "related to motion."

The energy of motion is called **kinetic energy.** It depends on both an object's mass and the speed at which the object is moving.

All objects are made of matter, and matter has mass. The more matter an object contains, the greater its mass. If you held a bowling ball in one hand and a soccer ball in the other, you could feel that the bowling ball has more mass than the soccer ball.

- **Kinetic energy increases as mass increases.** If the bowling ball and the soccer ball were moving at the same speed, the bowling ball would have more kinetic energy because of its greater mass.

- **Kinetic energy increases as speed increases.** If two identical bowling balls were rolling along at different speeds, the faster one would have more kinetic energy because of its greater speed. The speed skater in the photographs below has more kinetic energy when he is racing than he does when he is moving slowly.

High Speed

This skater has a large amount of kinetic energy when moving at a high speed.

Low Speed

When the same skater is moving more slowly, he has less kinetic energy.

READING VISUALS APPLY How could a skater with less mass than another skater have more kinetic energy?

A 74 Unit: Matter and Energy

Potential Energy

Suppose you are holding a soccer ball in your hands. Even if the ball is not moving, it has energy because it has the potential to fall. **Potential energy** is the stored energy that an object has due to its position or chemical composition. The ball's position above the ground gives it potential energy.

The most obvious form of potential energy is potential energy that results from gravity. Gravity is the force that pulls objects toward Earth's surface. The giant boulder on the right has potential energy because of its position above the ground. The mass of the boulder and its height above the ground determine how much potential energy it has due to gravity.

It is easy to know whether an object has kinetic energy because the object is moving. It is not so easy to know how much and what form of potential energy an object has, because objects can have potential energy from several sources. For example, in addition to potential energy from gravity, substances contain potential energy due to their chemical composition—the atoms they contain.

Because the boulder could fall, it has potential energy from gravity.

CHECK YOUR READING How can you tell kinetic energy and potential energy apart?

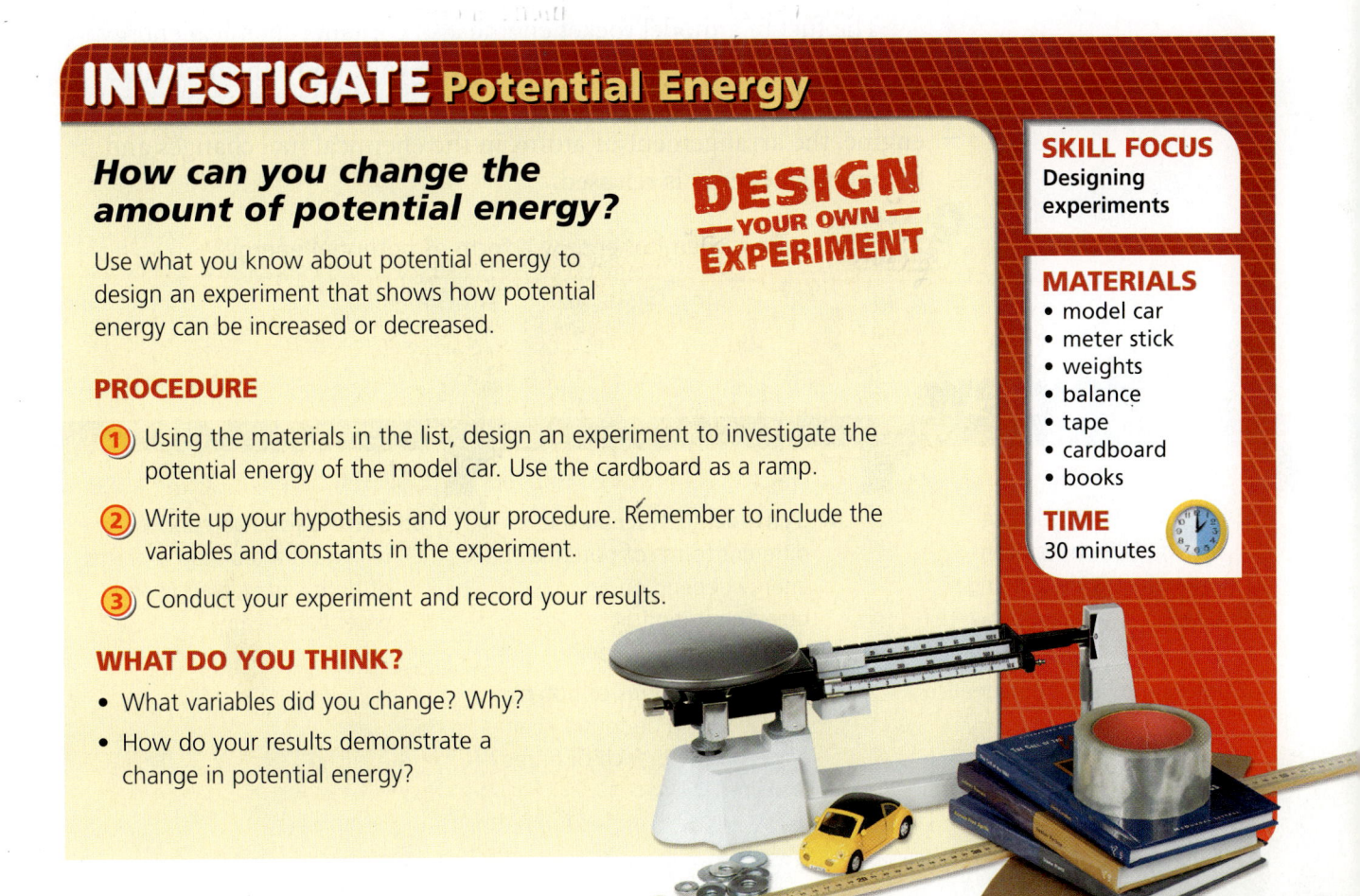

INVESTIGATE Potential Energy

How can you change the amount of potential energy?

Use what you know about potential energy to design an experiment that shows how potential energy can be increased or decreased.

DESIGN YOUR OWN EXPERIMENT

PROCEDURE

1) Using the materials in the list, design an experiment to investigate the potential energy of the model car. Use the cardboard as a ramp.

2) Write up your hypothesis and your procedure. Remember to include the variables and constants in the experiment.

3) Conduct your experiment and record your results.

WHAT DO YOU THINK?

- What variables did you change? Why?
- How do your results demonstrate a change in potential energy?

SKILL FOCUS
Designing experiments

MATERIALS
- model car
- meter stick
- weights
- balance
- tape
- cardboard
- books

TIME
30 minutes

Another form of potential energy related to an object's position comes from stretching or compressing an object. Think about the spring that is pushed down in a jack-in-the-box. The spring's potential energy increases when the spring is compressed and decreases when it is released. Look at the bow that is being bent in the photograph on the left. When the bowstring is pulled, the bow bends and stores energy. When the string is released, both the string and the bow return to their normal shape. Stored energy is released as the bow and the string straighten out and the arrow is pushed forward.

Pulling the string, which bends the bow, gives the bow potential energy.

When a rock falls or a bow straightens, potential energy is released. In fact, in these examples, the potential energy produced either by gravity or by bending is changed into kinetic energy.

Chemical energy, such as the energy stored in food, is less visible, but it is also a form of potential energy. This form of potential energy depends on chemical composition rather than position. It is the result of the atoms, and the bonds between atoms, that make up the molecules in food. When these molecules are broken apart, and their atoms rearranged through a series of chemical changes, energy is released.

Chemical energy in the fuel of a model rocket engine is potential energy.

The fuel in a model rocket engine also contains chemical energy. Like the molecules that provide energy in your body, the molecules in the fuel store potential energy. When the fuel ignites in the rocket engine, the arrangement of atoms in the chemical fuel changes and its potential energy is released.

CHECK YOUR READING Why is chemical energy a form of potential energy?

3.1 Review

KEY CONCEPTS

1. List three ways you use energy. How does each example involve a change?
2. What are some changes that can be caused by sound energy? by electromagnetic energy?
3. What two factors determine an object's kinetic energy?

CRITICAL THINKING

4. **Synthesize** How do the different forms of potential energy depend on an object's position or chemical composition?
5. **Infer** What forms of potential energy would be found in an apple on the branch of a tree? Explain.

CHALLENGE

6. **Synthesize** Describe a stone falling off a tabletop in terms of both kinetic energy and potential energy.

76 Unit: Matter and Energy

Think SCIENCE

SKILL: FINDING SOLUTIONS

Gasoline or Electric?

Cars use a significant amount of the world's energy. Most cars get their energy from the chemical energy of gasoline, a fossil fuel. Cars can also get their energy from sources other than gasoline. For many years, engineers have been working to design cars that run only on electricity. The goals of developing these new cars include reducing air pollution and decreasing the use of fossil fuels. So why have electric cars not replaced gasoline-powered cars?

▶ Advantages of Electric Cars

- Electric motors are more simple than gasoline engines.
- Electric cars use energy more efficiently than gasoline-powered cars, so they are cheaper to operate.
- Controlling pollution at power plants that produce electricity is easier than controlling pollution from cars.
- Electric motors are quieter than gasoline engines.
- Electric cars do not produce smog, which is a major health concern in large cities.

▶ Disadvantages of Electric Cars

- At this time, electric cars can travel only about 100 miles on a single battery charge.
- It takes several hours to recharge the batteries of an electric car using today's charging systems.
- The batteries of an electric car need to be replaced after being recharged about 600 times.
- An electric car's range is decreased by heating or cooling the inside of the car because, unlike batteries in gasoline-powered cars, its batteries are not recharged during driving.

▶ Finding Solutions

As a Group
What technology would need to be improved for electric cars to replace gasoline-powered cars? What facilities that do not exist today would be needed to serve electric cars?

As a Class
Compare your group's solutions to those of other groups. Use the Internet to research hybrid vehicles. How would these vehicles solve some of the problems that you identified?

RESOURCE CENTER
CLASSZONE.COM
Find out more about electric cars.

Chapter 3: **Energy** 77 **A**

3.2 Energy can change forms but is never lost.

KEY CONCEPT

BEFORE, you learned
- Energy causes change
- Energy has different forms
- Kinetic energy and potential energy are the two general types of energy

NOW, you will learn
- How energy can be converted from one form to another
- About the law of conservation of energy
- How energy conversions may be inefficient

VOCABULARY

law of conservation of energy p. 82
energy efficiency p. 83

THINK ABOUT

How does energy change form?

Potential energy is stored in the chemicals on the head of a match. The flame of a burning match releases that energy as light and heat. Where does the energy to strike the match come from in the first place?

MIND MAP
Use a mind map to take notes about how energy changes forms.

Energy changes forms.

A match may not appear to have any energy by itself, but it does contain potential energy that can be released. The chemical energy stored in a match can be changed into light and heat. Before the chemical energy in the match changes forms, however, other energy conversions must take place.

Plants convert energy from the Sun into chemical energy, which is stored in the form of sugars in their cells. When a person eats food that comes from plants—or from animals that have eaten plants—the person's cells can release this chemical energy. Some of this chemical energy is converted into the kinetic energy that a person uses to rub the match over a rough surface to strike it. The friction between the match and the striking surface produces heat. The heat provides the energy needed to start the chemical changes that produce the flame. From the Sun to the flame, at least five energy conversions have taken place.

CHECK YOUR READING How is a person's chemical energy changed into another form of energy in the lighting of a match?

78 Unit: Matter and Energy

Conversions Between Potential Energy and Kinetic Energy

The results of some energy conversions are obvious, such as when electrical energy in a light bulb is changed into light and heat. Other energy conversions are not so obvious. The examples below and on page 80 explore, step by step, some ways in which energy conversions occur in the world around you.

Potential energy can be changed into kinetic energy and back into potential energy. Look at the illustrations and photograph of the ski jumper shown below.

① At first, the ski jumper is at the top of the hill. This position gives him potential energy (PE) due to gravity.

② As the ski jumper starts moving downhill, some of his potential energy changes into kinetic energy (KE). Kinetic energy moves him down the slope to the ramp.

③ When the ski jumper takes off from the ramp, some of his kinetic energy is changed back into potential energy as he rises in the air.

When the ski jumper descends to the ground, his potential energy once again changes into kinetic energy. After the ski jumper lands and stops moving, how might he regain the potential energy that he had at the top of the hill? The kinetic energy of a ski lift can move the ski jumper back up the mountain and give him potential energy again.

Changing Potential Energy to Kinetic Energy

① Before starting down the slope, the ski jumper has potential energy (PE) but not kinetic energy (KE).

PE

② As the ski jumper moves down the slope, some potential energy is converted into kinetic energy.

PE   KE

③ When the ski jumper takes off from the ramp, some kinetic energy is changed back into potential energy.

PE   KE

READING VISUALS What would the colored bar look like just before the ski jumper lands on the ground?

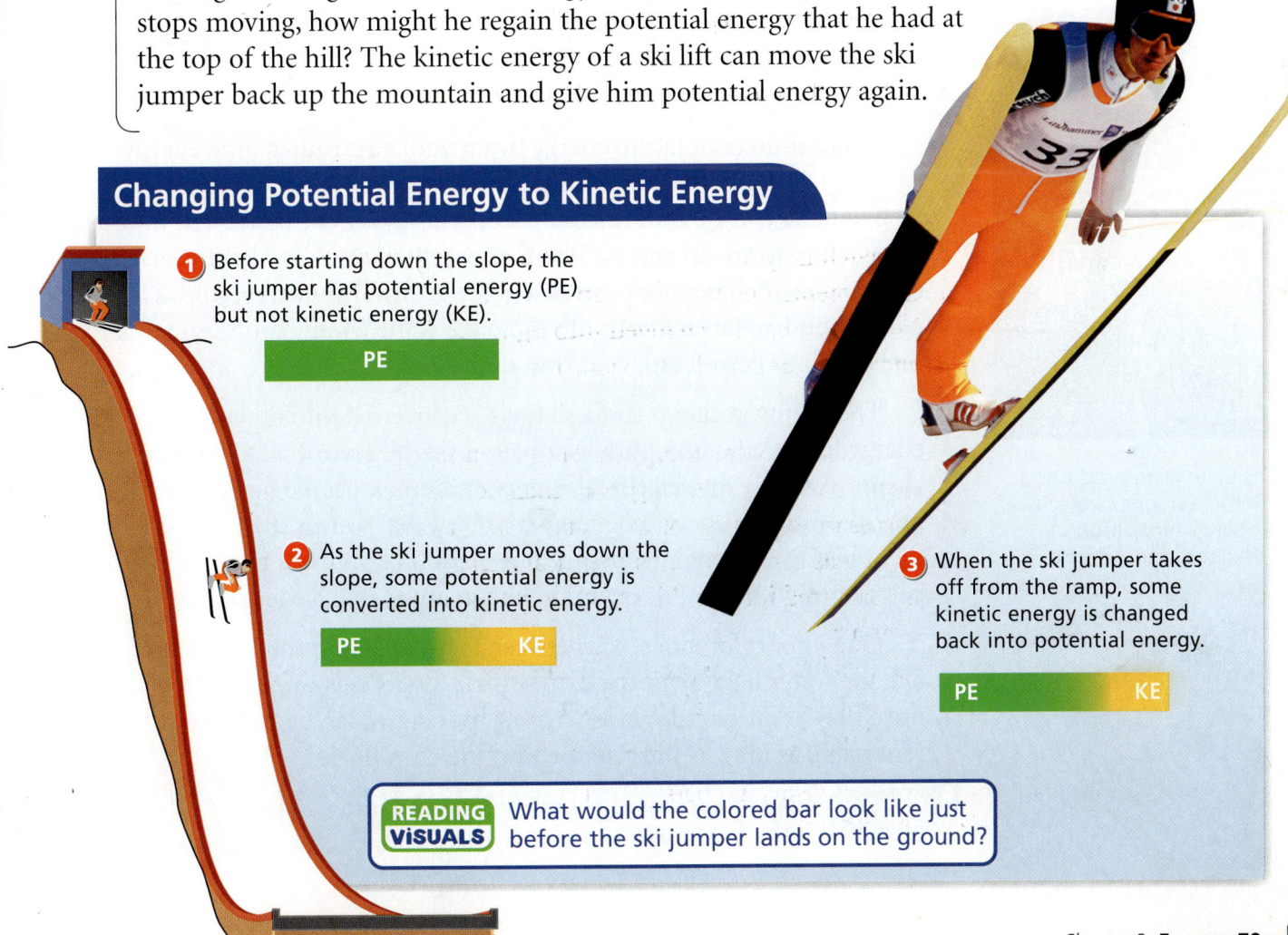

Chapter 3: **Energy** 79

Using Energy Conversions

People have developed ways to convert energy from one form to another for many purposes. Read about the energy conversion process below, and follow that process in the illustrations on page 81 to see how energy in water that is stored behind a dam is changed into electrical energy.

READING TIP

As you read about the process for producing electrical energy, follow the steps on page 81.

① The water held behind the dam has potential energy because of its position.

② Some of the water is allowed to flow through a tunnel within the dam. The potential energy in the stored water changes into kinetic energy when the water moves through the tunnel.

③ The kinetic energy of the moving water turns turbines within the dam. The water's kinetic energy becomes kinetic energy in the turbines. The kinetic energy of the turning turbines is converted into electrical energy by electrical generators.

④ Electrical energy is transported away from the dam through wires. The electrical energy is converted into many different forms of energy and is used in many different ways. For example, at a concert or a play, electrical energy is converted into light and heat by lighting systems and into sound energy by sound systems.

As you can see, several energy conversions occur in order to produce a usable form of energy—potential energy becomes kinetic energy, and kinetic energy becomes electrical energy.

Other sources of useful energy begin with electromagnetic energy from the Sun. In fact, almost all of the energy on Earth began as electromagnetic energy from the Sun. This energy can be converted into many other forms of energy. Plants convert the electromagnetic energy of sunlight into chemical energy as they grow. This energy, stored by plants hundreds of millions of years ago, is the energy found in fossil fuels, such as petroleum, coal, and natural gas.

The chemical energy in fossil fuels is converted into other forms of energy for specific uses. In power plants, people burn coal to convert its chemical energy into electrical energy. In homes, people burn natural gas to convert its chemical energy into heat that warms them and cooks their food. In car engines, people burn gasoline, which is made from petroleum, to convert its chemical energy into kinetic energy.

One important difference between fossil fuels and sources of energy like the water held behind a dam, is that fossil fuels cannot be replaced once they are used up. The energy of moving water, by contrast, is renewable as long as the river behind the dam flows.

Hoover Dam produces a large amount of electrical energy for California, Nevada, and Arizona.

CHECK YOUR READING How can potential energy be changed into a usable form of energy?

80 Unit: Matter and Energy

Converting Energy

Energy is often converted from one form to another in order to meet everyday needs.

1 Water held behind the dam has **potential energy.**

2 **Potential energy** is converted to **kinetic energy** when the water moves through the tunnel.

3 **Kinetic energy** is used to turn turbines. This **mechanical energy** is converted into **electrical energy** by generators.

4 **Electrical energy** is transmitted through wires, and then converted into many other forms of energy.

Potential Energy to Kinetic Energy

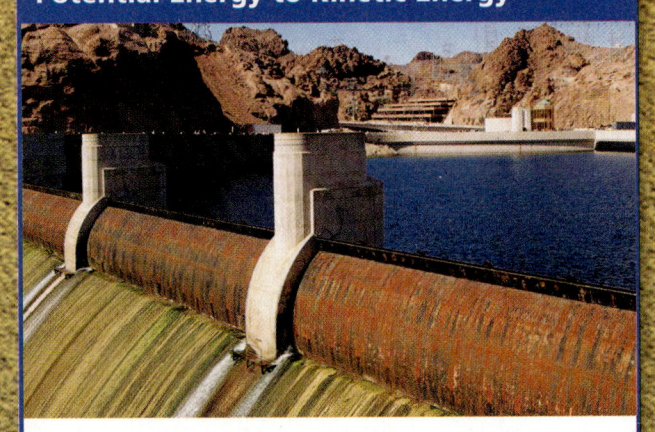

The potential energy of water behind the dam becomes the kinetic energy of moving water.

Kinetic Energy to Electrical Energy

The kinetic energy of turning turbines becomes electrical energy in these generators.

READING VISUALS How many different energy conversions are described in this diagram?

Chapter 3: Energy 81 A

Energy is always conserved.

When you observe energy conversions in your daily life, it may seem that energy constantly disappears. After all, if you give a soccer ball kinetic energy by kicking it along the ground, it will roll for a while but eventually stop. Consider what might have happened to the ball's kinetic energy.

As the ball rolls, it rubs against the ground. Some kinetic energy changes into heat as a result of friction. Some of the ball's energy also changes into sound energy that you can hear as the ball moves. Although the ball loses kinetic energy, the overall amount of energy in the universe does not decrease. The photograph below shows how the soccer ball's kinetic energy decreases.

The soccer ball's kinetic energy decreases as that energy is changed into sound energy and heat.

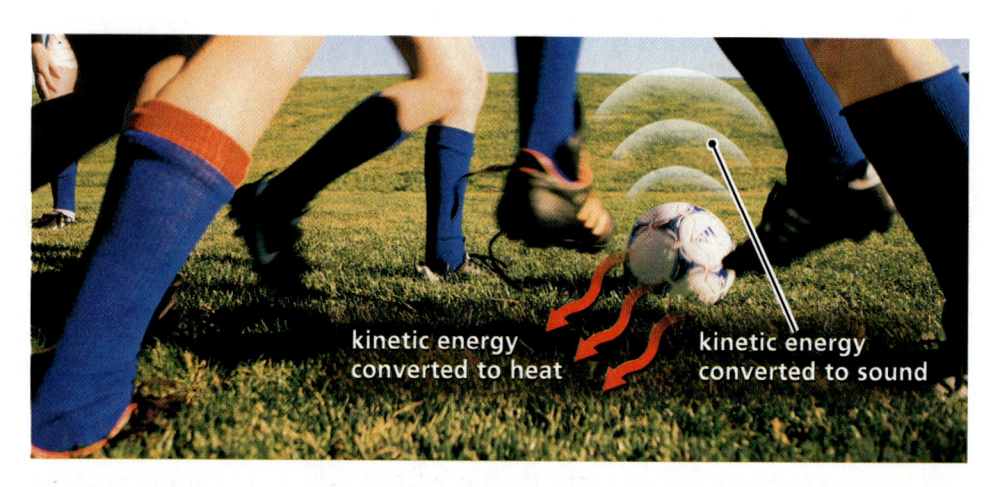

kinetic energy converted to heat

kinetic energy converted to sound

In the soccer ball example, the ball loses energy, but this energy is transferred to other parts of the universe. Energy is conserved. The **law of conservation of energy** states that energy can neither be created nor destroyed. Conservation of energy is called a law because this rule is true in all known cases. Although in many instances it may appear that energy is gained or lost, it is really only changed in form.

READING TIP
Conservation refers to a total that does not change.

CHECK YOUR READING Explain what is meant by the law of conservation of energy.

Conservation of energy is a balance of energy in the universe. When a soccer ball is kicked, a certain amount of energy is transferred by the kick. The ball gains an equal amount of energy, mostly in the form of kinetic energy. However, the ball's kinetic energy decreases as some of that energy is converted into sound energy and heat from the friction between the ball and the ground.

According to the law of conservation of energy, the amount of energy that a soccer player gives to the ball by kicking it is equal to the energy the ball gains. The energy the ball loses, in turn, is equal to the amount of energy that is transferred to the universe as sound energy and heat as the ball slows down.

82 Unit: Matter and Energy

Energy conversions may produce unwanted forms of energy.

When energy changes forms, the total amount of energy is conserved. However, the amount of useful energy is almost always less than the total amount of energy. For example, consider the energy used by an electric fan. The amount of electrical energy used is greater than the kinetic energy of the moving fan blades. Because energy is always conserved, some of the electrical energy flowing into the fan's motor is obviously changed into unusable or unwanted forms.

The fan converts a significant portion of the electrical energy into the kinetic energy of the fan blades. At the same time, some electrical energy changes into heat in the fan's motor. If the fan shakes, some of the electrical energy is being turned into unwanted kinetic energy. The more efficiently the fan uses electrical energy, though, the more energy will be transformed into kinetic energy that moves the air.

Energy efficiency is a measurement of usable energy after an energy conversion. You may be familiar with energy-efficient household appliances. These appliances convert a greater percentage of energy into the desired form than inefficient ones. The more energy-efficient a fan is, the more electrical energy it turns into kinetic energy in the moving blades. Less electrical energy is needed to operate appliances that are energy efficient.

Some electrical energy is converted into unwanted sound energy.

Some electrical energy is converted into kinetic energy of the fan blades.

Some electrical energy is converted into unwanted heat.

CHECK YOUR READING What does it mean when an energy conversion is efficient?

3.2 Review

KEY CONCEPTS
1. Describe an energy conversion you have observed in your own life.
2. Explain the law of conservation of energy in your own words.
3. Give an example of an energy conversion that produces unwanted forms of energy.

CRITICAL THINKING
4. **Synthesize** Suppose you are jumping on a trampoline. Describe the conversions that occur between kinetic energy and potential energy.
5. **Infer** Look at the ski jumper on page 79. Has all of his potential energy likely been changed into kinetic energy at the moment he lands? Explain.

CHALLENGE
6. **Communicate** Draw and label a diagram that shows at least three different energy conversions that might occur when a light bulb is turned on.

CHAPTER INVESTIGATION

Energy Conversions

OVERVIEW AND PURPOSE All foods contain stored chemical energy, but some foods contain more chemical energy than others. People need this chemical energy for all of their activities. The amount of chemical energy stored in foods like marshmallows can be measured by burning the foods. In this investigation, you will
- construct an apparatus to investigate the amount of energy in samples of food
- calculate the amount of energy released when the foods are burned

▶ Problem

How much energy is stored in different types of food?

▶ Hypothesize

Write a hypothesis to explain which type of food contains a greater amount of chemical energy. Your hypothesis should take the form of an "If . . . , then . . . , because . . ." statement.

▶ Procedure

1. Create a data table similar to the one shown on the sample notebook page.

2. Using the can opener, punch two holes directly opposite each other near the top of the can. Slide the dowel rod through the holes as shown in the photograph to the left.

3. Measure 50 mL of water with a graduated cylinder, and pour the water into the can. Record the mass of the water. (**Hint:** 1 mL of water = 1 gram)

4. Rest the ends of the dowel rod on the ring in the ring stand to hold the can in the air. Carefully place the thermometer in the can. Measure and record the initial temperature (T1) of the water in the can.

5. Make a collar of aluminum foil and tape it around the can as shown. Leave enough room to insert the burner platform and food sample.

MATERIALS
- can opener
- empty aluminum can
- dowel rod
- water
- graduated cylinder
- ring stand with ring
- thermometer
- aluminum pie plate
- aluminum foil
- tape
- large paper clip
- cork
- modeling clay
- crouton
- caramel rice cake
- balance
- wooden matches

84 Unit: **Matter and Energy**

6. Construct the burner platform as follows: Open up the paper clip. Push the straightened end into a cork, and push the bottom of the cork into the clay. Push the burner onto the pie plate so it will not move. Put the pie plate under the ring.

   step 6

7. Find and record the mass of the crouton. Place the crouton on the flattened end of the burner platform. Adjust the height of the ring so the bottom of the can is about 4 cm above the crouton.

8. Use a match to ignite the crouton. Allow the crouton to burn completely. Measure and record the final temperature (T2) of the water.

9. Empty the water from the can and repeat steps 3–8 with a caramel rice cake. The mass of the rice cake should equal the mass of the crouton.

Observe and Analyze   Write It Up

1. **RECORD OBSERVATIONS** Make sure to record all measurements in the data table.

2. **CALCULATE** Find the energy released from the food samples by following the next two steps.

   Calculate and record the change in temperature.
   change in temperature = T2 − T1

   Calculate and record the energy released in calories. One calorie is the energy needed to raise the temperature of 1 g of water by 1°C.
   energy released = (mass of water · change in temperature · 1 cal/g°C)

3. **GRAPH** Make a bar graph showing the number of calories in each food sample. Which type of food contains a greater amount of chemical energy?

Conclude   Write It Up

1. **INTERPRET** Answer the question posed in the problem.

2. **INFER** Did your results support your hypothesis? Explain.

3. **EVALUATE** What happens to any energy released by the burning food that is not captured by the water? How could you change the setup for a more accurate measurement?

4. **APPLY** Find out how much fat and carbohydrate the different foods contain. Explain the relationship between this information and the number of calories in the foods.

INVESTIGATE Further

CHALLENGE The Calories listed in foods are equal to 1000 calories (1 kilocalorie). Calculate the amount of energy in your food samples in terms of Calories per gram of food (Calories/g). Using a balance, find the mass of any ash that remains after burning the food. Subtract that mass from the original mass of the sample to calculate mass burned. Divide total calories by mass burned, then divide that value by 1000 to find Calories/g. Compare your results to those given on the product labels.

Energy Conversions

Problem How much energy is stored in different types of food?

Hypothesize

Observe and Analyze

Table 1. Energy in Food

	Sample 1	Sample 2
Mass of water (g)		
Initial water temp. (T1) (°C)		
Final water temp. (T2) (°C)		
Mass of food (g)		
Change in temp. (T2 − T1) (°C)		
Energy released (mass·change in temp.·cal/g°C)		

Conclude

KEY CONCEPT
3.3 Technology improves the ways people use energy.

BEFORE, you learned
- Energy can change forms
- When energy changes forms, the overall amount of energy remains the same
- Energy conversions usually produce unwanted forms of energy

NOW, you will learn
- How technology can improve energy conversions
- About advantages and disadvantages of different types of energy conversions
- How technology can improve the use of natural resources

VOCABULARY

solar cell p. 88

EXPLORE Solar Cells

Why does a solar calculator need a large solar cell?

PROCEDURE

1. Measure the area of the calculator's solar cell. (Hint: area = length • width)
2. Turn the calculator on. Make sure that there is enough light for the calculator to work.
3. Gradually cover the solar cell with the index card. Observe the calculator's display as you cover more of the cell.
4. Measure the uncovered area of the solar cell when the calculator no longer works.

MATERIALS
- solar calculator without backup battery
- ruler
- index card

WHAT DO YOU THINK?
- How much of the solar cell is needed to keep the calculator working?
- Why might a solar calculator have a solar cell that is larger than necessary?

MIND MAP Use a mind map to take notes about technology that improves energy conversions.

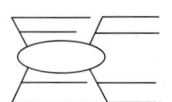

Technology improves energy conversions.

In many common energy conversions, most of the wasted energy is released as heat. One example is the common incandescent light bulb. Amazingly, only about 5 percent of the electrical energy that enters an incandescent light bulb is converted into light. That means that 95 percent of the electrical energy turns into unwanted forms of energy. Most is released as heat and ends up in the form of thermal energy in the surrounding air. To decrease this amount of wasted energy, scientists have investigated several more efficient types of lights.

A 86 Unit: Matter and Energy

Efficient Lights

Research to replace light bulbs with a more energy-efficient source of light has resulted in the light-emitting diode, or LED. LEDs have the advantage of converting almost all of the electrical energy they use into light.

The first LEDs were not nearly as bright as typical light bulbs, but over time scientists and engineers have been able to produce brighter LEDs. LEDs have many uses, including television remote controls, computer displays, outdoor signs, giant video boards in stadiums, and traffic signals. LEDs are also used to transmit information through fiber optic cables that connect home audio and visual systems.

CHECK YOUR READING How are LEDs more efficient than incandescent lights?

LEDs that produce infrared light are used in remote controls.

Efficient Cars

Another common but inefficient energy conversion is the burning of gasoline in cars. A large percentage of gasoline's chemical energy is not converted into the car's kinetic energy. Some of the kinetic energy is then wasted as heat from the car's engine, tires, and brakes. Here, too, efficiency can be improved through advances in technology.

Fuel injectors, common in cars since the 1980s, have improved the efficiency of engines. These devices carefully monitor and control the amount of gasoline that is fed into a car's engine. This precise control of fuel provides a significant increase in the distance a car can travel on a tank of gasoline. More recently, hybrid cars have been developed. These cars use both gasoline and electrical energy from batteries. These cars are very fuel efficient. Even better, some of the kinetic energy lost during braking in hybrid cars is used to generate electrical energy to recharge the car's batteries.

Hybrid cars may look very similar to typical gasoline-powered cars, but their engines are different.

Chapter 3: **Energy** 87

Technology improves the use of energy resources.

Much of the energy used on Earth comes from fossil fuels such as coal, petroleum, and natural gas. However, the supply of fossil fuels is limited. So, scientists and engineers are exploring the use of several alternative energy sources. Today, for example, both solar energy and wind energy are used on a small scale to generate electrical energy.

Solar energy and wind energy have several advantages compared to fossil fuels. Their supply is not limited, and they do not produce the same harmful waste products that fossil fuels do. However, there are also many obstacles that must be overcome before solar energy and wind energy, among other alternative energy sources, are as widely used as fossil fuels.

CHECK YOUR READING — What are the advantages of solar energy and wind energy as compared to fossil fuels?

Solar Energy

VISUALIZATION
CLASSZONE.COM
Observe how solar cells produce electricity.

Solar cells are important in today's solar energy technology. Modern **solar cells** are made of several layers of light-sensitive materials, which convert sunlight directly into electrical energy. Solar cells provide the electrical energy for such things as satellites in orbit around Earth, hand-held calculators, and, as shown below, experimental cars.

Solar Energy for Electricity

Solar cells can produce electricity to run a car.

A solar car requires 8 square meters of solar cells to provide sufficient electrical energy to power the car.

88 Unit: Matter and Energy

Solar cells produce electrical energy quietly and cleanly. However, they are not yet commonly used because the materials used to make them are very expensive. What's more, solar cells are not very efficient in producing electrical energy. Large numbers of solar cells produce only a relatively small amount of electrical energy. Typical solar cells convert only about 12 to 15 percent of the sunlight that reaches them into electrical energy. However, solar cells currently being developed could have efficiencies close to 40 percent.

In addition to converting the Sun's light directly into electrical energy, people have used the Sun's radiation for heating. In ancient Rome, glass was used to trap solar energy indoors so that plants could be grown in the winter. Today radiation from the Sun is still used to grow plants in greenhouses and to warm buildings. The photograph above shows a house that uses solar energy in both ways. The solar cells on the roof provide electrical energy, and the large windows help to trap the warmth. In fact, some solar power systems also use that warmth to produce additional electrical energy.

Solar energy can be used in homes to provide heat and electrical energy.

CHECK YOUR READING How can energy from the Sun be used by people?

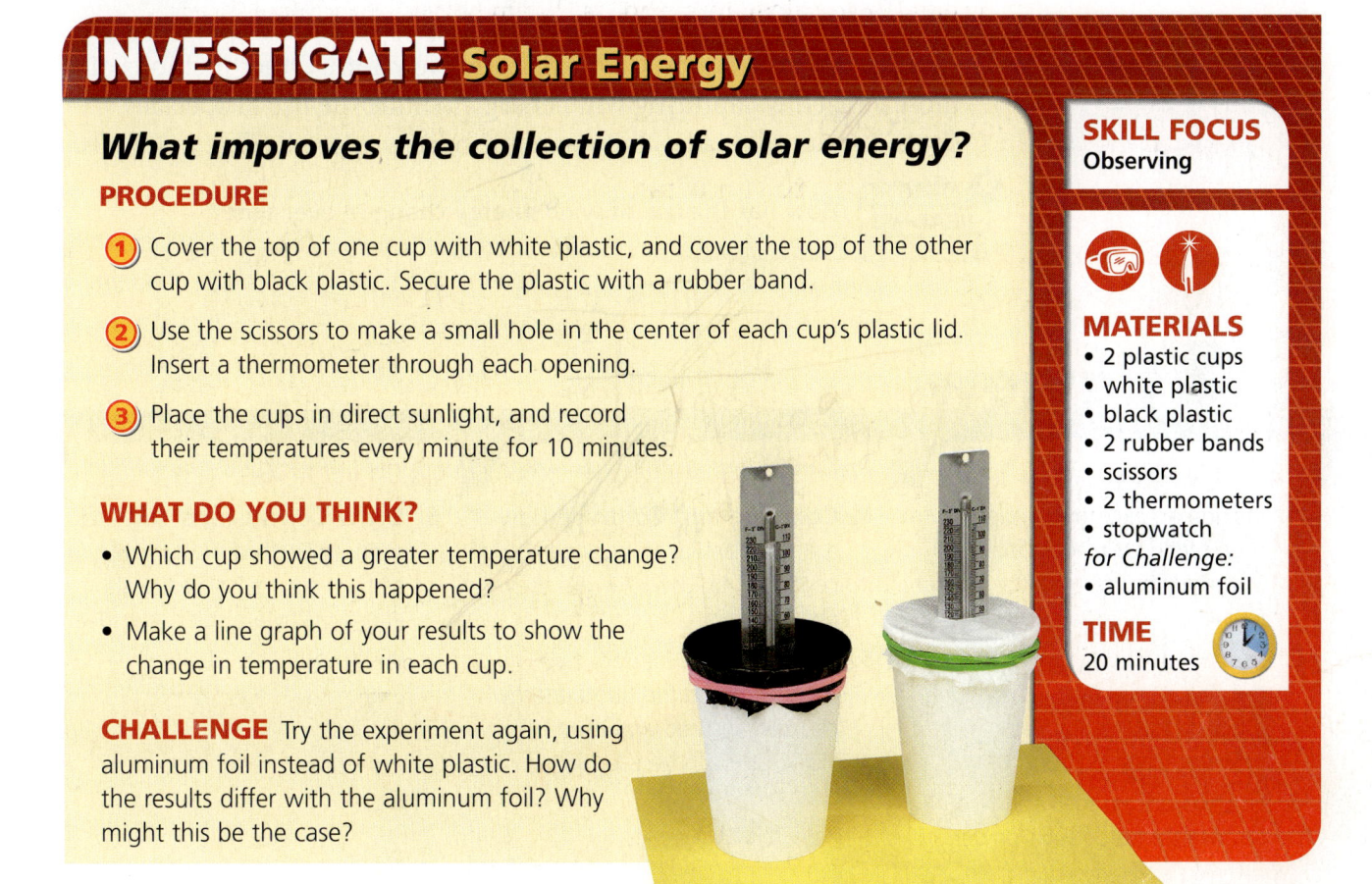

INVESTIGATE Solar Energy

What improves the collection of solar energy?

PROCEDURE

1. Cover the top of one cup with white plastic, and cover the top of the other cup with black plastic. Secure the plastic with a rubber band.

2. Use the scissors to make a small hole in the center of each cup's plastic lid. Insert a thermometer through each opening.

3. Place the cups in direct sunlight, and record their temperatures every minute for 10 minutes.

WHAT DO YOU THINK?

- Which cup showed a greater temperature change? Why do you think this happened?
- Make a line graph of your results to show the change in temperature in each cup.

CHALLENGE Try the experiment again, using aluminum foil instead of white plastic. How do the results differ with the aluminum foil? Why might this be the case?

SKILL FOCUS
Observing

MATERIALS
- 2 plastic cups
- white plastic
- black plastic
- 2 rubber bands
- scissors
- 2 thermometers
- stopwatch
for Challenge:
- aluminum foil

TIME
20 minutes

Chapter 3: Energy 89

INFER Why might so many windmills be needed at a windfarm?

RESOURCE CENTER
CLASSZONE.COM

Find out more about alternative energy sources.

Wind Energy

For many centuries, people have used the kinetic energy of wind to sail ships, and, by using windmills, to grind grain and pump water. More recently, windmills have been used to generate electrical energy. In the early 1900s, for example, windmills were already being used to produce electrical energy in rural areas of the United States.

Like the technological advances in the use of solar energy, advances in capturing and using wind energy have helped to improve its efficiency and usefulness. One way to better capture the wind's energy has been to build huge windmill farms in areas that receive a consistent amount of wind. Windmill farms are found in several states, including Kansas, California, and New York. Other methods of more efficiently capturing wind energy include the use of specially shaped windmill blades that are made of new, more flexible materials.

CHECK YOUR READING How has the use of wind energy changed over time?

3.3 Review

KEY CONCEPTS

1. Provide an example of a common technology that does not efficiently convert energy. Explain.

2. Describe two ways in which hybrid cars are more energy-efficient than gasoline-powered cars.

3. List two advantages and two disadvantages of solar power.

CRITICAL THINKING

4. **Compare and Contrast** How are LEDs similar to incandescent light bulbs? How are they different?

5. **Synthesize** What are two ways in which the Sun's energy can be captured and used? How can both be used in a home?

CHALLENGE

6. **Draw Conclusions** Satellites orbiting Earth use solar cells as their source of electrical energy. Why are solar cells ideal energy sources for satellites?

MATH in SCIENCE

MATH TUTORIAL
CLASSZONE.COM
Click on Math Tutorial for more help with rates.

SKILL: USING FORMULAS

Cool Efficiency

Energy efficiency is important because energy supplies are limited. The energy used by appliances such as air conditioners is measured in British thermal units, or BTUs. One BTU warms one pound of water by 1°F. The cooling ability of an air conditioner is measured by the number of BTUs it can move. Consider the number of BTUs that an air conditioning system must move in an ice rink.

An air conditioner typically has an energy efficiency ratio (EER) rating. The EER measures how efficiently a cooling system operates when the outdoor temperature is 95°F. The EER is the ratio of cooling per hour to the amount of electricity used, which is measured in watts. The higher the EER, the more energy efficient the air conditioner is.

$$EER = \frac{BTUs/hr}{watts\ used}$$

Example

Suppose an air conditioner uses 750 watts of electricity to cool 6000 BTUs per hour at 95°F. Calculate the air conditioner's EER.

(1) Use the formula above to calculate the EER.

$$EER = \frac{BTUs/hr}{watts\ used}$$

(2) Enter the known values into the formula.

$$EER = \frac{6000\ BTUs/hr}{750\ watts\ used}$$

(3) Solve the formula for the unknown value.

$$EER = \frac{6000\ BTUs/hr}{750\ watts\ used} = 8$$

ANSWER EER = 8 BTUs/hr per watt used

Answer the following questions.

1. What is the EER of a cooling system that uses 500 watts of electricity to move 6000 BTUs per hour at 95°F?

2. What is the EER of a cooling system that uses 1500 watts of electricity to move 12,000 BTUs per hour at 95°F?

3. Which air conditioner in the two questions above is more efficient?

CHALLENGE How many BTUs per hour would an air conditioner move at 95°F if it had an EER of 10 and used 1200 watts of electricity?

Indoor ice rinks require cooling systems that can keep ice frozen even when the outdoor temperature is 95°F.

3 Chapter Review

the BIG idea
Energy has different forms, but it is always conserved.

CONTENT REVIEW
CLASSZONE.COM

KEY CONCEPTS SUMMARY

3.1 Energy exists in different forms.
- Energy is the ability to cause a change.
- Different forms of energy produce changes in different ways.
- Kinetic energy depends on mass and speed.

Potential energy depends on position and chemical composition.

VOCABULARY
energy p. 72
kinetic energy p. 74
potential energy p. 75

3.2 Energy can change forms but is never lost.
- Energy often needs to be transformed in order to produce a useful form of energy.
- The law of conservation of energy states that energy is never created or destroyed.

Energy can be transformed in many different ways, including from potential energy (PE) to kinetic energy (KE) and back again.

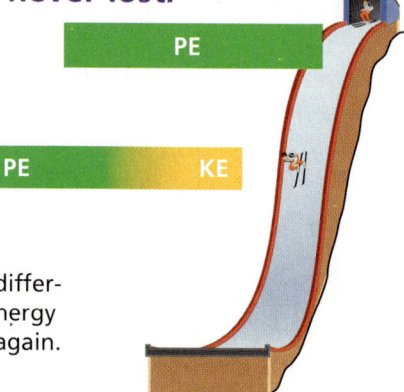

VOCABULARY
law of conservation of energy p. 82
energy efficiency p. 83

3.3 Technology improves the ways people use energy.
- Different forms of technology are being developed and used to improve the efficiency of energy conversions.
- Solar cells convert sunlight into electrical energy.

New solar cells convert light into electrical energy more efficiently than those in the past.

VOCABULARY
solar cell p. 88

A 92 Unit: Matter and Energy

Reviewing Vocabulary

Review vocabulary terms by making a four square diagram for each term as shown in the example below. Include a definition, characteristics, examples from real life, and, if possible, nonexamples of the term.

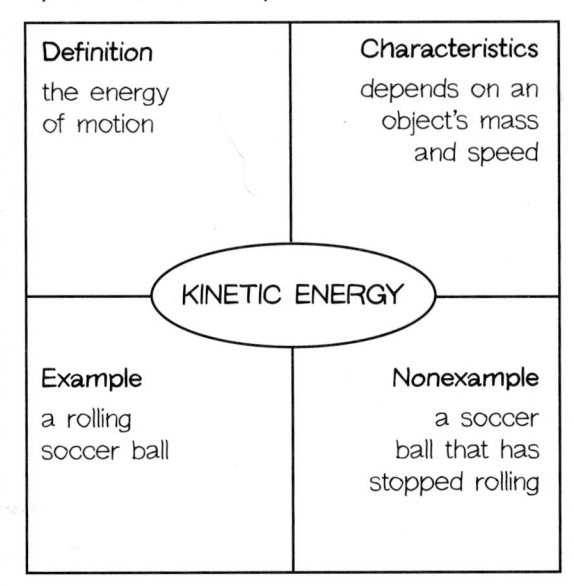

Definition	Characteristics
the energy of motion	depends on an object's mass and speed

KINETIC ENERGY

Example	Nonexample
a rolling soccer ball	a soccer ball that has stopped rolling

1. energy
2. potential energy
3. conservation of energy
4. energy efficiency

Reviewing Key Concepts

Multiple Choice *Choose the letter of the best answer.*

5. All forms of energy are a combination of
   a. mechanical energy and chemical energy
   b. chemical energy and kinetic energy
   c. potential energy and thermal energy
   d. potential energy and kinetic energy

6. Which type of energy is transmitted by vibrations of air?
   a. electromagnetic   c. nuclear
   b. sound   d. chemical

7. When energy is converted from one form to another, what is usually produced?
   a. chemical energy   c. heat
   b. gravity   d. nuclear energy

8. An object's kinetic energy is determined by its
   a. position and composition
   b. speed and position
   c. mass and speed
   d. height and width

9. Which of the following is a conversion from chemical energy to mechanical energy?
   a. a dark light bulb starting to glow
   b. food being heated in an oven
   c. a ball rolling down a hill
   d. a person lifting a weight

10. An energy-efficient electric fan converts a large portion of the electrical energy that enters it into
    a. an unwanted form of energy
    b. kinetic energy of the fan blades
    c. thermal energy in the fan's motor
    d. sound energy in the fan's motor

11. The energy in wind used to generate electricity is
    a. chemical energy
    b. sound energy
    c. potential energy
    d. kinetic energy

12. A skier on a hill has potential energy due to
    a. speed   c. compression
    b. energy efficiency d. position

Short Answer *Write a short answer to each question.*

13. Explain how the law of conservation of energy might apply to an energy conversion that you observe in your daily life.

14. Describe a situation in which chemical energy is converted into mechanical energy. Explain each step of the energy conversion process.

Chapter 3: **Energy** 93 **A**

Thinking Critically

The illustrations below show an in-line skater on a ramp. Use the illustrations to answer the next five questions.

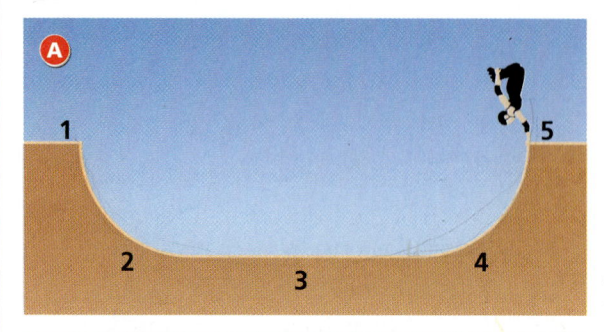

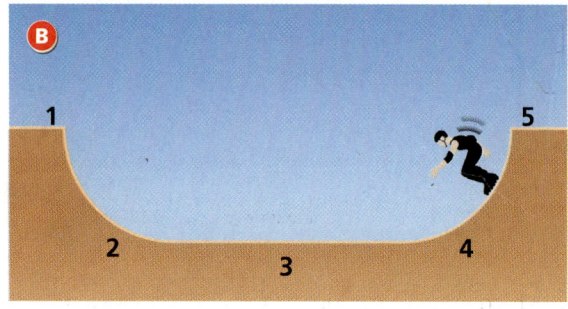

15. OBSERVE At what point in the illustrations would the skater have the most potential energy? the most kinetic energy? Explain.

16. SYNTHESIZE At what point in illustration B will the skater's kinetic energy begin to be changed back into potential energy? Explain.

17. INFER When the skater's kinetic energy is changed back into potential energy, will this amount of potential energy likely be equal to the skater's potential energy in illustration A? Why or why not?

18. PREDICT Describe how energy may appear to decrease in the example shown above. What energy conversions that produce unwanted forms of energy are occurring? Explain.

19. SYNTHESIZE Draw colored bars that might represent the potential energy and kinetic energy of the skater at each of the five labeled points on illustration A. Explain why you drew the bars the way you did. (**Hint:** See the illustration on p. 79.)

20. SYNTHESIZE How are plants and solar cells similar? How are the ways in which they capture sunlight and convert it into other forms of energy different? Explain.

21. COMPARE Explain how energy sources such as solar energy and wind energy have similar problems that must be overcome. How have scientists tried to address these problems?

22. INFER Suppose that one air conditioner becomes very hot when it is working but another air conditioner does not. Which air conditioner is more energy efficient? How can you tell?

23. DRAW CONCLUSIONS Suppose a vacuum cleaner uses 100 units of electrical energy. All of this energy is converted into thermal and sound energy (from the motor), and into the kinetic energy of air being pulled into the vacuum cleaner. If 60 units of electrical energy are converted into thermal energy and sound energy, how much electrical energy is converted into the desired form of energy? How do you know?

24. COMMUNICATE Describe a process in which energy changes forms at least twice. Draw and label a diagram that shows these energy conversions.

the BIG idea

25. APPLY Look again at the photograph on pages 68 and 69 and consider the opening question. How might your answer have changed after reading the chapter?

26. COMMUNICATE How have your ideas about energy and its different forms changed after reading the chapter? Provide an example from your life to describe how you would have thought of energy compared to how you might think about it now.

UNIT PROJECTS

If you need to do an experiment for your unit project, gather the materials. Be sure to allow enough time to observe results before the project is due.

Standardized Test Practice

For practice on your state test, go to...
TEST PRACTICE
CLASSZONE.COM

Interpreting Graphs

Study the graph below. Then answer the first five questions.

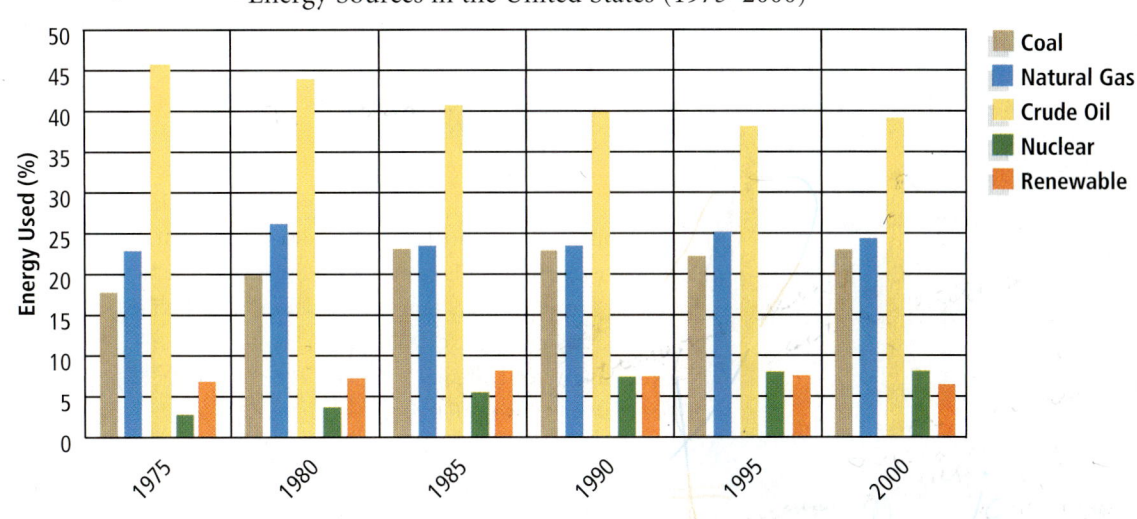

Energy Sources in the United States (1975–2000)

Legend: Coal, Natural Gas, Crude Oil, Nuclear, Renewable

Y-axis: Energy Used (%), 0 to 50
X-axis: Year (1975, 1980, 1985, 1990, 1995, 2000)

Source: U.S. Energy Information Administration, Monthly Energy Review (June 2003)

1. In which year did the greatest percentage of energy used in the United States come from crude oil?
   a. 1975
   b. 1980
   c. 1995
   d. 2000

2. What three sources of energy account for about 80 percent of all energy used in each year shown?
   a. coal, crude oil, nuclear
   b. natural gas, crude oil, renewable
   c. coal, natural gas, crude oil
   d. crude oil, nuclear, renewable

3. Which sources of energy show a greater percentage in 2000 as compared to 1980?
   a. crude oil, renewable
   b. natural gas, crude oil
   c. coal, nuclear
   d. coal, crude oil

4. The use of which energy source tended to decrease between 1975 and 2000?
   a. coal
   b. natural gas
   c. crude oil
   d. nuclear

5. The use of which source of energy steadily increased between 1975 and 1995?
   a. coal
   b. crude oil
   c. nuclear
   d. renewable

Extended Response

Answer the questions in detail. Include some of the terms from the word box on the right. Underline each term you use in your answers.

chemical energy	potential energy
electrical energy	sound energy
mechanical energy	thermal energy

6. When gasoline is burned in a moving car's engine, which forms of energy are being used? Which forms of energy are produced? Explain.

7. Name two appliances in your home that you believe are inefficient. What about them indicates that they may be inefficient?

Chapter 3: **Energy** 95

TIMELINES in Science

ABOUT TEMPERATURE AND HEAT

Most likely, the first fires early people saw were caused by lightning. Eventually, people realized that fire provided warmth and light, and they learned how to make it themselves. During the Stone Age 25,000 years ago, people used firewood to cook food as well as to warm and light their shelters. Wood was the first fuel.

This timeline shows a few of the many steps on the path toward understanding temperature and heat. Notice how the observations and ideas of previous thinkers sparked new theories by later scientists. The boxes below the timeline show how technology has led to new insights and to applications related to temperature and heat.

445 B.C.
Four Basic Substances Named
Greek philosopher Empedocles says that everything on Earth is made of some combination of four basic substances: earth, air, fire, and water. Different types of matter have different qualities depending on how they combine these substances.

350 B.C.
Aristotle Expands Theory of Matter
Greek philosopher Aristotle names four basic qualities of matter: dryness, wetness, hotness, and coldness. Each of the four basic substances has two of these qualities.

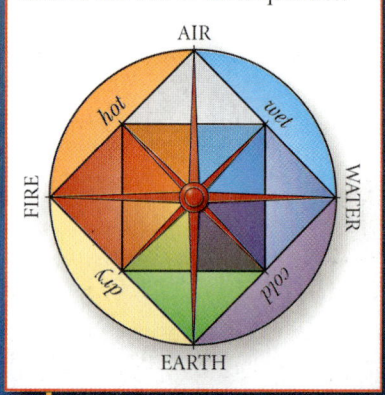

EVENTS
480 B.C.   440 B.C.   400 B.C.   360 B.C.   320 B.C.

APPLICATIONS AND TECHNOLOGY

People have been trying to understand and control heat since early times.

A 96 Unit: Matter and Energy

A.D. 1617
Heat Is Motion

English philosopher Francis Bacon uses observation and experimentation to demonstrate that heat is a form of motion. Most people remain unconvinced. They consider heat to be a fluid, which they call caloric.

1762
Calorimetry Founded

Scottish chemist Joseph Black founds the science of calorimetry, which describes the amount of energy as heat a substance can hold. His research in boiling and evaporation is valuable to his friend James Watt, who is making improvements to the steam engine.

1724
Mercury Used for Thermometer

Gabriel Fahrenheit, a German instrument maker, reports that mercury works well for measuring temperature. It expands evenly as temperature rises, and its silvery appearance makes it easy to see inside a glass tube. On Fahrenheit's scale, the boiling point of pure water is 212 degrees and the freezing point is 32 degrees.

1742
New Temperature Scale Used

Swedish astronomer Anders Celsius devises a scale for measuring temperature in which the freezing point of water is 0 degrees. The boiling point of pure water is 100 degrees. He calls this the Centigrade scale, from Latin words meaning "one hundred steps."

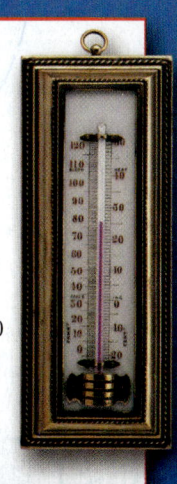

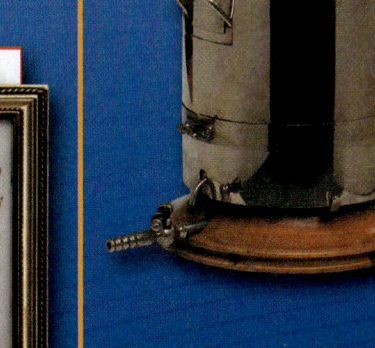

A.D. 1600   1640   1680   1720   1760

APPLICATION

Alchemy: The Quest to Create Gold

Alchemists, who hoped to turn less valuable metals into gold, took up the Greeks' theory of the four basic substances. They thought they could convert one substance into another by changing the balance of the four basic substances. Their ideas spread to the Byzantine Empire after A.D. 641, where these concepts were combined with advances in techniques for manipulating heat. Alchemy spread to Western Europe during the 1100s and 1200s.

Alchemists used chemical processes such as heating in furnaces, boiling in pots or cauldrons, distillation, pounding, and grinding. Because it was difficult to control the temperature, and thermometers had not yet been invented, alchemists usually had many different kinds of furnaces. Although alchemy is not considered a true science today, it did contribute methods and processes still used by chemists. It remained popular until around 1700.

Timelines in Science 97 A

1798
Heat and Friction Linked
While observing cannons at a weapons factory, American-born scientist Benjamin Thompson (Count Rumford) notices that friction between the cutting tools and the metal cannon barrels generates large amounts of heat. He concludes that friction is an unending source of heat. This observation helps put an end to the theory that heat is a fluid.

1906
Absolute Zero Identified
German physicist Walther Nernst suggests that absolute zero is the temperature at which the individual particles in an object would be practically motionless. Absolute zero, equivalent to –273°C, is the lowest temperature any object can reach. This limit was identified by British physicist Lord Kelvin in 1848. However, this temperature can never actually be reached by any real object.

1824
Heat Moves from Warmer to Cooler Objects
French physicist Nicolas Sadi Carnot shows that heat is a flow of energy from an object with a higher temperature to an object with a lower temperature. This explains why ice placed in a hot liquid melts and becomes a liquid rather than the liquid becoming ice.

1845
Various Energies Produce Heat
British physicist James Joule shows that mechanical energy can be converted to heat. Using a paddle-wheel device, he shows that the various forms of energy, such as mechanical and thermal, are basically the same and can change from one form to another. Joule also states that a given amount of energy of whatever form always yields that same amount of heat.

1800 1840 1880 1920

TECHNOLOGY
Keeping Heat In or Out
In 1892 Scottish physicist James Dewar invented the vacuum flask—a container in which warm fluids could be kept warm and cool fluids cool. A vacuum between the inner and outer walls of the container reduced conduction, which is the transfer of heat between two objects that are touching each other. Because a vacuum contains no matter, it does not conduct heat. Dewar's flask had silver walls to reflect radiated energy. As long as the flask was sealed, the vacuum was maintained and the temperature of a liquid inside the flask did not change much. A variation on Dewar's flask was produced in the early 1900s under the trade name Thermos. Today we call any vacuum container used for keeping beverages hot or cold a thermos.

This cutaway shows the inside of one of Dewar's experimental flasks.

2003
Wasps Stay Cool
Scientists in Israel have found evidence that some wasps have an internal air-conditioning system. Like a refrigerator, the wasp uses energy to stay cooler than the air around it. The energy may come from several sources, such as the energy generated by an electric current produced when the wasp's shell is exposed to sunlight. This ability to stay cool allows wasps to hunt for food even on very hot days.

RESOURCE CENTER
CLASSZONE.COM

Learn about current temperature and heat research.

1960   2000

APPLICATION
Using Thermal Energy from Ponds
Ponds can be used to store solar energy. The goal is to turn the solar energy into energy people can use. Salt must be added to the ponds, however, so that the water at the bottom is denser than the water at the top. This prevents thermal energy stored on the bottom from moving up to the surface, where it would be lost to the air through evaporation. A net on the surface helps prevent wind from mixing the water layers.

INTO THE FUTURE

As scientists are able to create colder and colder temperatures in the laboratory, they gain new insight into the scientific theories that explain temperature and heat. Advances in our knowledge of temperature and heat will lead to future applications.

- Scientists have developed a car that can run on hydrogen cooled into its liquid state. Before cars that run on this supercooled fuel become common, a system of refueling stations must be established.

- Understanding how some materials, such as silicon, conduct energy as heat may result in medical advances through better scanning and imaging technology.

- At temperatures approaching absolute zero (−273°C), a unique state of matter can be formed that is different from a solid, liquid, or gas. This rare state of matter could possibly be used to help produce extremely small circuits for use in miniature computers or other electronics.

ACTIVITIES

Design a Procedure
Many people claim that it is possible to determine the temperature by listening to the chirping of crickets. Crickets are sensitive to changes in air temperature and chirp more quickly when the temperature rises. To calculate the temperature in degrees Celsius, count the number of chirps in 7 seconds and add 5.

Write a procedure for an experiment that would test this claim. What factors would you consider testing? What range of temperatures would you test?

Writing About Science
Alchemy has fascinated people for centuries. Research its influence on both the technology and procedures of modern chemistry. Write a short report.

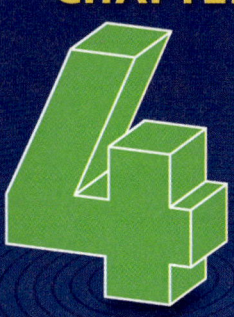

CHAPTER 4
Temperature and Heat

the BIG idea

Heat is a flow of energy due to temperature differences.

How does heat from the Sun increase this giraffe's temperature?

Key Concepts

SECTION 4.1 Temperature depends on particle movement.
Learn how kinetic energy is the basis of temperature.

SECTION 4.2 Energy flows from warmer to cooler objects.
Learn about differences between temperature and heat, and how temperature changes in different substances.

SECTION 4.3 The transfer of energy as heat can be controlled.
Learn how energy is transferred through heat, and how that transfer can be controlled.

Internet Preview

CLASSZONE.COM

Chapter 4 online resources: Content Review, two Simulations, two Resource Centers, Math Tutorial, Test Practice

EXPLORE the BIG idea

Moving Colors

Fill a clear plastic cup halfway with cold water. Fill another cup halfway with hot water. Using an eyedropper, place a drop of food coloring at the very bottom of each cup. Observe.

Observe and Think What happened to the drop of food coloring in cold water? in hot water? Why might this have happened?

Does It Chill?

Place an outdoor thermometer in an empty paper cup, and place the cup in the freezer. Check the thermometer every minute and record the time it takes for the temperature to reach 0°C (32°F). Remove the cup from the freezer. After it returns to room temperature, fill the cup with soil and repeat the experiment.

Observe and Think How long did it take for the temperature to reach 0°C each time? Why might there have been a difference?

Internet Activity: Kinetic Theory

Go to **ClassZone.com** to explore how temperature affects the speed of particles. Examine the effects of particle size as well.

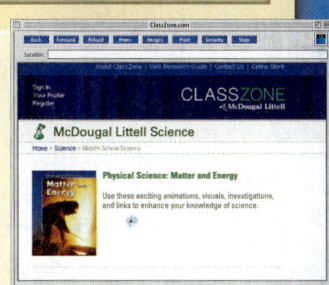

Observe and Think What is the relationship between temperature and kinetic energy? How does particle mass affect temperature?

NSTA scilinks.org
SCLINKS
Kinetic Theory **Code: MDL064**

Chapter 4: **Temperature and Heat** 101

CHAPTER 4
Getting Ready to Learn

CONCEPT REVIEW

- Matter is made of particles too small to see.
- Matter can be solid, liquid, or gas.
- Energy is the ability to cause a change.
- There are different forms of energy.

VOCABULARY REVIEW

matter p. 9
energy p. 72
kinetic energy p. 74

CONTENT REVIEW
CLASSZONE.COM
Review concepts and vocabulary.

TAKING NOTES

CHOOSE YOUR OWN STRATEGY

Take notes using one or more of the strategies from earlier chapters—**main idea and detail notes, main idea web,** or **mind map.** Feel free to mix and match the strategies, or use an entirely different note-taking strategy.

VOCABULARY STRATEGY

Place each vocabulary term at the center of a **description wheel** diagram. Write some words describing it on the spokes.

See the Note-Taking Handbook on pages R45–R51.

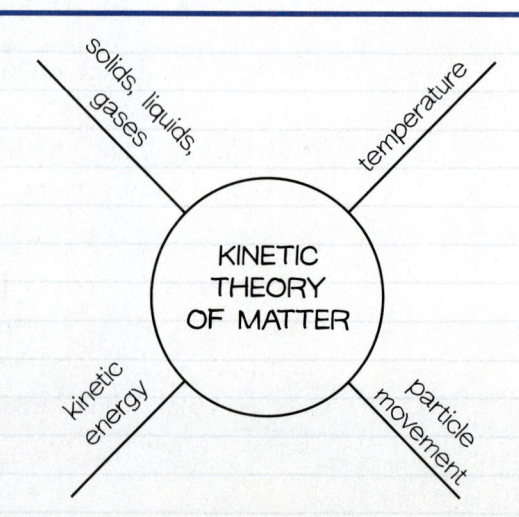

SCIENCE NOTEBOOK

Main Idea and Detail Notes

Mind Map

Main Idea Web

KINETIC THEORY OF MATTER
- solids, liquids, gases
- temperature
- particle movement
- kinetic energy

102 Unit: Matter and Energy

KEY CONCEPT
4.1 Temperature depends on particle movement.

BEFORE, you learned
- All matter is made of particles
- Kinetic energy is the energy of motion
- Energy can be transferred or changed but is never created or destroyed

NOW, you will learn
- How temperature depends on kinetic energy
- How temperature is measured
- How changes in temperature can affect matter

VOCABULARY
kinetic theory of matter p. 104
temperature p. 105
degree p. 106
thermometer p. 107

EXPLORE Temperature

What can cause a change in temperature?

PROCEDURE

1. Work with a partner. Hold the rubber band with both hands. Without stretching it, hold it to the underside of your partner's wrist.

2. Move the rubber band away, then quickly stretch it once and keep it stretched. Hold it to the underside of your partner's wrist.

3. Move the rubber band away and quickly let it return to its normal size. Hold it to the underside of your partner's wrist.

MATERIALS
large rubber band

WHAT DO YOU THINK?
- What effect did stretching the rubber band have on the temperature of the rubber band?
- What may have caused this change to occur?

NOTE-TAKING STRATEGY
You could take notes on the movement of particles in matter by using a main idea web.

All matter is made of moving particles.

You have read that any object in motion has kinetic energy. All the moving objects you see around you—from cars to planes to butterflies—have kinetic energy. Even objects so small that you cannot see them, such as atoms, are in motion and have kinetic energy.

You might think that a large unmoving object, such as a house or a wooden chair, does not have any kinetic energy. However, all matter is made of atoms, and atoms are always in motion, even if the objects themselves do not change their position. The motion of these tiny particles gives the object energy. The chair you are sitting on has some amount of energy. You also have energy, even when you are not moving.

Temperature can be measured.

RESOURCE CENTER
CLASSZONE.COM
Find out more about temperature and temperature scales.

You have read that a warmer temperature means a greater average kinetic energy. How is temperature measured and what does that measurement mean? Suppose you hear on the radio that the temperature outside is 30 degrees. Do you need to wear a warm coat to spend the day outside? The answer depends on the temperature scale being used. There are two common temperature scales, both of which measure the average kinetic energy of particles. However, 30 degrees on one scale is quite different from 30 degrees on the other scale.

Temperature Scales

To establish a temperature scale, two known values and the number of units between the values are needed. The freezing and boiling points of pure water are often used as the standard values. These points are always the same under the same conditions and they are easy to reproduce. In the two common scales, temperature is measured in units called **degrees** (°), which are equally spaced units between two points.

The scale used most commonly in the United States for measuring temperature—in uses ranging from cooking directions to weather reports—is the Fahrenheit (FAR-uhn-HYT) scale (°F). It was developed in the early 1700s by Gabriel Fahrenheit. On the Fahrenheit scale, pure water freezes at 32°F and boils at 212°F. Thus, there are 180 degrees—180 equal units—between the freezing point and the boiling point of water.

During a summer day in Death Valley, California, the temperature can reach 49°C (120°F).

The temperature scale most commonly used in the rest of the world, and also used more often in science, is the Celsius (SEHL-see-uhs) scale (°C). This scale was developed in the 1740s by Anders Celsius. On the Celsius scale, pure water freezes at 0°C and boils at 100°C, so there are 100 degrees—100 equal units—between these two temperatures.

Recall the question asked in the first paragraph of this page. If the outside temperature is 30 degrees, do you need to wear a warm coat? If the temperature is 30°F, the answer is yes, because that temperature is colder than the freezing point of water. If the temperature is 30°C, the answer is no—it is a nice warm day (86°F).

CHECK YOUR READING How are the Fahrenheit and Celsius temperature scales different? How are they similar?

A 106 Unit: Matter and Energy

Thermometers

Temperature is measured by using a device called a thermometer. A **thermometer** measures temperature through the regular variation of some physical property of the material inside the thermometer. A mercury or alcohol thermometer, for example, can measure temperature because the liquid inside the thermometer always expands or contracts by a certain amount in response to a change in temperature.

Liquid-filled thermometers measure how much the liquid expands in a narrow tube as the temperature increases. The distances along the tube are marked so that the temperature can be read. At one time, thermometers were filled with liquid mercury because it expands or contracts evenly at both high and low temperatures. This means that mercury expands or contracts by the same amount in response to a given change in temperature. However, mercury is dangerous to handle, so many thermometers today are filled with alcohol instead.

Some thermometers work in a different way—they use a material whose electrical properties change when the temperature changes. These thermometers can be read by computers. Some show the temperature on a display panel and are often used in cars and in homes.

CHECK YOUR READING How do liquid-filled thermometers work?

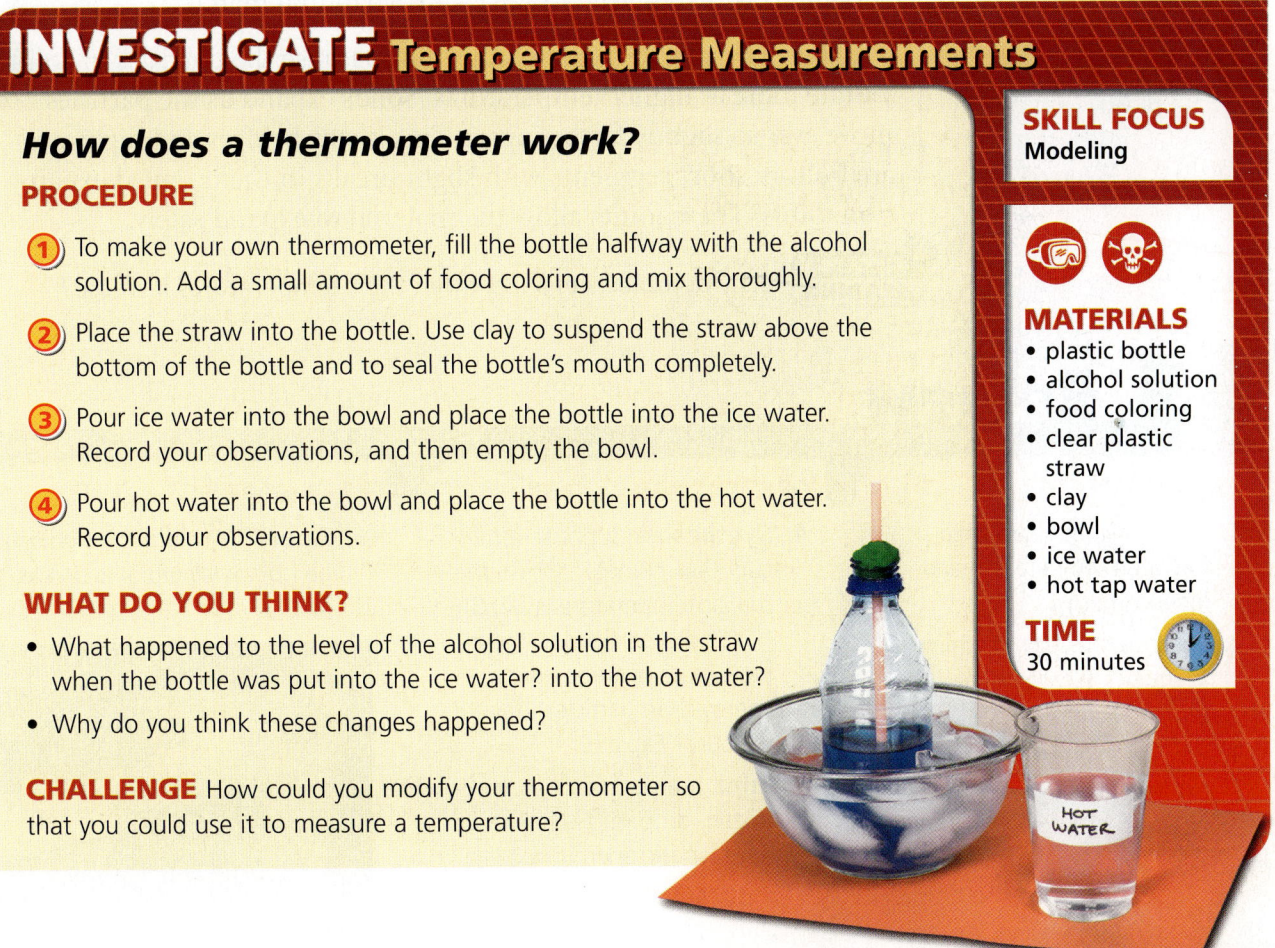

INVESTIGATE Temperature Measurements

How does a thermometer work?

PROCEDURE

1. To make your own thermometer, fill the bottle halfway with the alcohol solution. Add a small amount of food coloring and mix thoroughly.
2. Place the straw into the bottle. Use clay to suspend the straw above the bottom of the bottle and to seal the bottle's mouth completely.
3. Pour ice water into the bowl and place the bottle into the ice water. Record your observations, and then empty the bowl.
4. Pour hot water into the bowl and place the bottle into the hot water. Record your observations.

WHAT DO YOU THINK?
- What happened to the level of the alcohol solution in the straw when the bottle was put into the ice water? into the hot water?
- Why do you think these changes happened?

CHALLENGE How could you modify your thermometer so that you could use it to measure a temperature?

SKILL FOCUS
Modeling

MATERIALS
- plastic bottle
- alcohol solution
- food coloring
- clear plastic straw
- clay
- bowl
- ice water
- hot tap water

TIME
30 minutes

Thermal Expansion

The property that makes liquid-filled thermometers work is called thermal expansion. Thermal expansion affects many substances, not just alcohol and liquid mercury. All gases, many liquids, and most solids expand when their temperature increases.

Construction engineers often have to take thermal expansion into account because steel and concrete both expand with increasing temperature. An interesting example involves the construction of the Gateway Arch in St. Louis, which is built mostly of steel.

The final piece of the Arch to be put into place was the top segment joining the two legs. The Arch was scheduled to be completed in the middle of the day for its opening ceremony. However, engineers knew that the side of the Arch facing the Sun would get hot and expand due to thermal expansion.

This expansion would narrow the gap between the legs and prevent the last piece from fitting into place. In order to complete the Arch, workers sprayed water on the side facing the Sun. The water helped cool the Arch and decreased the amount of thermal expansion. Once the final segment was in place, engineers made the connection strong enough to withstand the force of the expanding material.

Thermal expansion occurs in solids because the particles of solids vibrate more at higher temperatures. Solids expand as the particles move ever so slightly farther apart. This is why bridges and highways are built in short segments with slight breaks in them, called expansion joints. These joints allow the material to expand safely.

During construction of the Gateway Arch in St. Louis, engineers had to account for thermal expansion.

CHECK YOUR READING Why do objects expand when their temperatures increase?

4.1 Review

KEY CONCEPTS
1. Describe the relationship between temperature and kinetic energy.
2. Describe the way in which thermometers measure temperature.
3. How can you explain thermal expansion in terms of kinetic energy?

CRITICAL THINKING
4. **Synthesize** Suppose a mercury thermometer shows that the air temperature is 22°C (72°F). Do particles in the air have more average kinetic energy than particles in the mercury? Explain.
5. **Infer** If a puddle of water is frozen, do particles in the ice have kinetic energy? Explain.

CHALLENGE
6. **Apply** Why might a sidewalk be built with periodic breaks in it?

MATH in SCIENCE

SKILL: METRIC CONVERSIONS

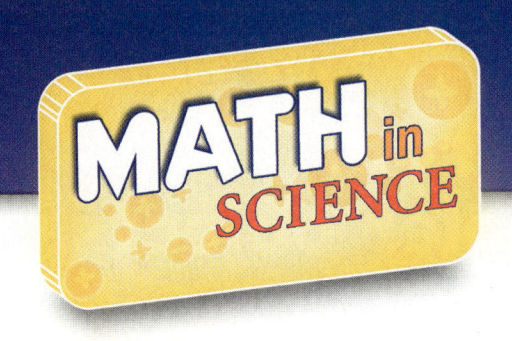

MATH TUTORIAL
CLASSZONE.COM
Click on Math Tutorial for more help with temperature conversions.

How Hot Is Hot?

Temperatures on Earth can vary greatly, from extremely hot in some deserts to frigid in polar regions. The meaning of a temperature measurement depends on which temperature scale is being used. A very high temperature on the Fahrenheit scale is equal to a much lower temperature on the Celsius scale. The table shows the formulas used to convert temperatures between the two scales.

Conversion	Formula
Fahrenheit to Celsius	$°C = \frac{5}{9}(°F - 32)$
Celsius to Fahrenheit	$°F = \frac{9}{5}°C + 32$

Example

The boiling point of pure water is 212°F. Convert that temperature to a measurement on the Celsius scale.

(1) Use the correct conversion formula.

$$°C = \frac{5}{9}(°F - 32)$$

(2) Substitute the temperature given for the correct variable in the formula.

$$°C = \frac{5}{9}(212 - 32) = \frac{5}{9} \cdot 180 = 100$$

ANSWER °C = 100

Use the information in the table below to answer the questions that follow.

Highest and Lowest Temperatures Recorded on Earth

Location	Highest Temp. (°F)	Location	Lowest Temp. (°F)
El Azizia, Libya	136	Vostok, Antarctica	−129
Death Valley, California	134	Oimekon, Russia	−90
Tirat Tsvi, Israel	129	Verkhoyansk, Russia	−90
Cloncurry, Australia	128	Northice, Greenland	−87
Seville, Spain	122	Snag, Yukon, Canada	−81

1. What is the highest temperature in °C?
2. What is the temperature difference in °C between the highest and second highest temperatures?
3. What is the difference between the highest and lowest temperatures in °F? in °C?

CHALLENGE The surface of the Sun is approximately 5500°C. What is this temperature in °F?

Temperatures on Earth, ranging from the extremes of frigid polar regions to the hottest deserts, can differ by more than 250°F.

Chapter 4: **Temperature and Heat** 109

KEY CONCEPT
4.2 Energy flows from warmer to cooler objects.

◀ **BEFORE, you learned**
- All matter is made of moving particles
- Temperature is the measurement of average kinetic energy of particles in an object
- Temperature can be measured

▶ **NOW, you will learn**
- How heat is different from temperature
- How heat is measured
- Why some substances change temperature more easily than others

VOCABULARY
heat p. 110
thermal energy p. 111
calorie p. 112
joule p. 112
specific heat p. 113

THINK ABOUT

Why does water warm up so slowly?

If you have ever seen food being fried in oil or butter, you know that the metal frying pan heats up very quickly, as does the oil or butter used to coat the pan's surface. However, if you put the same amount of water as you put oil in the same pan, the water warms up more slowly. Why does water behave so differently from the metal, oil, or butter?

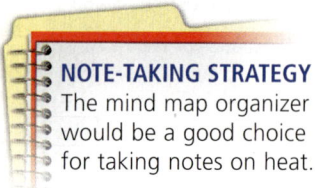

NOTE-TAKING STRATEGY
The mind map organizer would be a good choice for taking notes on heat.

Heat is different from temperature.

Heat and temperature are very closely related. As a result, people often confuse the concepts of heat and temperature. However, they are not the same. Temperature is a measurement of the average kinetic energy of particles in an object. **Heat** is a flow of energy from an object at a higher temperature to an object at a lower temperature.

If you add energy as heat to a pot of water, the water's temperature starts to increase. The added energy increases the average kinetic energy of the water molecules. Once the water starts to boil, however, adding energy no longer changes the temperature of the water. Instead, the heat goes into changing the physical state of the water from liquid to gas rather than increasing the kinetic energy of the water molecules. This fact is one demonstration that heat and temperature are not the same thing.

CHECK YOUR READING What is heat?

A 110 Unit: Matter and Energy

Heat and Thermal Energy

Suppose you place an ice cube in a bowl on a table. At first, the bowl and the ice cube have different temperatures. However, the ice cube melts, and the water that comes from the ice will eventually have the same temperature as the bowl. This temperature will be lower than the original temperature of the bowl but higher than the original temperature of the ice cube. The water and the bowl end up at the same temperature because the particles in the ice cube and the particles in the bowl continually bump into each other and energy is transferred from the bowl to the ice.

Heat is always the transfer of energy from an object at a higher temperature to an object at a lower temperature. So energy flows from the particles in the warmer bowl to the particles in the cold ice and, later, the cooler water. If energy flowed in the opposite direction—from cooler to warmer—the ice would get colder and the bowl would get hotter, and you know that never happens.

RESOURCE CENTER
CLASSZONE.COM
Learn more about thermal energy.

CHECK YOUR READING In which direction does heat always transfer energy?

When energy flows from a warmer object to a cooler object, the thermal energy of both of the objects changes. **Thermal energy** is the total random kinetic energy of particles in an object. Note that temperature and thermal energy are different from each other. Temperature is an average and thermal energy is a total. A glass of water can have the same temperature as Lake Superior, but the lake has far more thermal energy because the lake contains many more water molecules.

Another example of how energy is transferred through heat is shown on the right. Soon after you put ice cubes into a pitcher of lemonade, energy is transferred from the warmer lemonade to the colder ice. The lemonade's thermal energy decreases and the ice's thermal energy increases. Because the particles in the lemonade have transferred some of their energy to the particles in the ice, the average kinetic energy of the particles in the lemonade decreases. As a result, the temperature of the lemonade decreases.

Energy is transferred from the warmer lemonade to the cold ice through heat until their temperatures are equal.

CHECK YOUR READING How are heat and thermal energy related to each other?

Chapter 4: **Temperature and Heat** 111

Measuring Heat

VOCABULARY
Remember to make description wheel diagrams for *calorie, joule,* and other vocabulary terms.

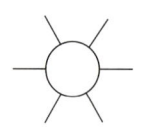

The most common units of heat measurement are the calorie and the joule (jool). One **calorie** is the amount of energy needed to raise the temperature of 1 gram of water by 1°C. The **joule** (J) is the standard scientific unit in which energy is measured. One calorie is equal to 4.18 joules.

You probably think of calories in terms of food. However, in nutrition, one Calorie—written with a capital C—is actually one kilocalorie, or 1000 calories. This means that one Calorie in food contains enough energy to raise the temperature of 1 kilogram of water by 1°C. So, each Calorie in food contains 1000 calories of energy.

How do we know how many Calories are in a food, such as a piece of chocolate cake? The cake is burned inside an instrument called a calorimeter. The amount of energy released from the cake through heat is the number of Calories transferred from the cake to the calorimeter. The energy transferred to the calorimeter is equal to the amount of energy originally in the cake. A thermometer inside the calorimeter measures the increase in temperature from the burning cake, which is used to calculate how much energy is released.

CHECK YOUR READING How is heat measured?

INVESTIGATE Heat Transfer

Which substances change temperature faster?
PROCEDURE

1. Using the graduated cylinder and the balance, separately measure 20 g of room-temperature water, 20 g of pennies, and 20 g of aluminum foil. Pour the water into a beaker until it is needed.

2. Using the graduated cylinder, pour 50 mL of hot water into each of the cups. Record the water temperature in each cup.

3. Pour the room-temperature water into one cup. Place the pennies in the second cup and the foil in the third. After 5 minutes, record the temperature of the water in each of the cups.

WHAT DO YOU THINK?
- How did the temperature changes in the three cups compare?
- What might account for the differences you observed?

CHALLENGE Why might items such as pots and pans be made of materials like copper, stainless steel, or iron?

SKILL FOCUS
Measuring

MATERIALS
- graduated cylinder
- balance
- room-temperature water
- pennies
- aluminum foil
- hot tap water
- 100 mL beaker
- 3 plastic cups
- thermometer
- stopwatch

TIME
30 minutes

112 Unit: Matter and Energy

Some substances change temperature more easily than others.

Have you ever seen an apple pie taken right out of the oven? If you put a piece of pie on a plate to cool, you can touch the pie crust in a few minutes and it will feel only slightly warm. But if you try to take a bite, the hot pie filling will burn your mouth. The pie crust cools much more quickly than the filling, which is mostly water.

Specific Heat

The amount of energy required to raise the temperature of 1 gram of a substance by 1°C is the **specific heat** of that substance. Every substance has its own specific heat value. So, each substance absorbs a different amount of energy in order to show the same increase in temperature.

If you look back at the definition of a calorie, you will see that it is defined in terms of water—one calorie raises the temperature of 1 gram of water by 1°C. So, water has a specific heat of exactly 1.00 calorie per gram per °C. Because one calorie is equal to 4.18 J, it takes 4.18 J to raise the temperature of one gram of water by 1°C. In joules, water's specific heat is 4.18 J per gram per °C. If you look at the specific heat graph shown below, you will see that 4.18 is an unusually large value. For example, one gram of iron has to absorb only 0.45 joules for its temperature to increase by 1°C.

A substance with a high specific heat value, like water, not only has to absorb a large quantity of energy for its temperature to increase, but it also must release a large quantity of energy for its temperature to decrease. This is why the apple pie filling can still be hot while the pie crust is cool. The liquid filling takes longer to cool. The high specific heat of water is also one reason it is used as a coolant in car radiators. The water can absorb a great deal of energy and protect the engine from getting too hot.

READING TIP

Joules per gram per °C is shown as $\frac{J}{g°C}$.

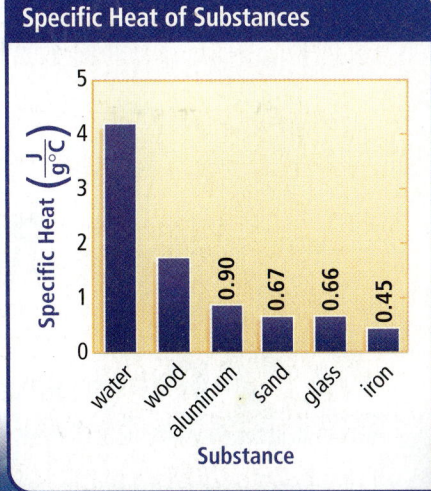

Specific Heat of Substances

- water: 4.18
- wood: ~1.7
- aluminum: 0.90
- sand: 0.67
- glass: 0.66
- iron: 0.45

CHECK YOUR READING How is specific heat related to a change in temperature?

APPLY More energy is needed to warm water than many other substances. What materials in this photograph might be warmer than the water?

Specific Heat and Mass

Recall that thermal energy is the total kinetic energy of all particles in an object. So, thermal energy depends on the object's mass. Suppose you have a cup of water at a temperature of 90°C (194°F) and a bathtub full of water at a temperature of 40°C (104°F). Which mass of water has more thermal energy? There are many more water molecules in the bathtub, so the water in the tub has more thermal energy.

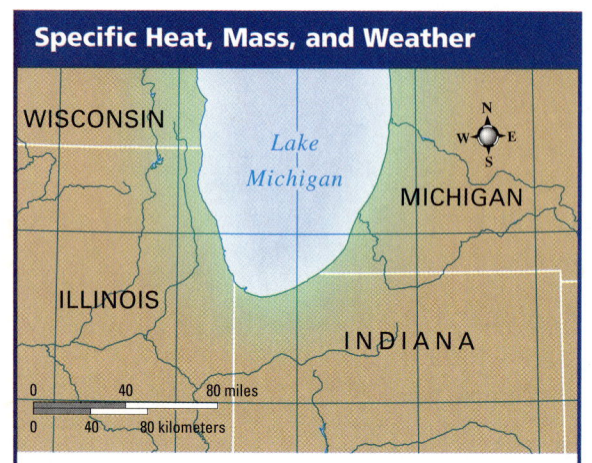

Specific Heat, Mass, and Weather

The temperature of a large body of water influences the temperature of nearby land. The green shading shows how far this effect extends.

The water in the cup has the same specific heat as the water in the tub. However, the cup of water will cool more quickly than the water in the bathtub. The tub of water has to release more thermal energy to its surroundings, through heat, to show a decrease in temperature because it has so much more mass.

This idea is particularly relevant to very large masses. For example, Lake Michigan holds 4.92 quadrillion liters (1.30 quadrillion gallons) of water. Because of the high specific heat of water and the mass of water in the lake, the temperature of Lake Michigan changes very slowly.

The temperature of the lake affects the temperatures on its shores. During spring and early summer, the lake warms slowly, which helps keep the nearby land cooler. During the winter, the lake cools slowly, which helps keep the nearby land warmer. Temperatures within about 15 miles of the lake can differ by as much as 6°C (about 10°F) from areas farther away from the lake.

As you will read in the next section, the way in which a large body of water can influence temperatures on land depends on how energy is transferred through heat.

CHECK YOUR READING How does an object's thermal energy depend on its mass?

4.2 Review

KEY CONCEPTS

1. How is temperature related to heat?
2. How do the units that are used to measure heat differ from the units that are used to measure temperature?
3. Describe specific heat in your own words.

CRITICAL THINKING

4. **Compare and Contrast** How are a calorie and a joule similar? How are they different?
5. **Synthesize** Describe the relationships among kinetic energy, temperature, heat, and thermal energy.

CHALLENGE

6. **Infer** Suppose you are spending a hot summer day by a pool. Why might the water in the pool cool the air near the pool?

SCIENCE on the JOB

CHEF

Cooking with Heat

A chef makes many decisions about cooking a meal based on heat and temperature. The appropriate temperature and cooking method must be used. A chef must calculate the cooking time of each part of the meal so that everything is finished at the same time. A chef also needs to understand how heat moves through food. For example, if an oven temperature is too hot, meat can be overcooked on the outside and undercooked on the inside.

Bread vs. Meat

Chefs have to understand how energy as heat is transferred to different foods. For example, the fluffy texture of bread comes from pockets of gas that separate its fibers. The gas is a poor conductor of energy. Therefore, more energy and a longer cooking time are needed to cook bread than to cook an equal amount of meat.

What Temperature?

Eggs cook very differently under different temperatures. For example, temperature is important when baking meringue, which is made of egg whites and sugar. A Key lime pie topped with meringue is baked at 400°F to make a meringue that is soft. However, meringue baked at 275°F makes light and crisp dessert shells.

Roasting and Heat

The shape of the food being roasted is just as important as what is being roasted. Heat moves more quickly through food with a thin shape than it will through food with a thicker shape.

EXPLORE

1. **COMPARE** Using a cookbook, find the oven temperatures for baking biscuits, potatoes, and beef. Could you successfully cook a roast and biscuits in the oven at the same time?

2. **CHALLENGE** Crack open three eggs. Lightly beat one egg in each of three separate bowls. Follow the steps below.
   1. Heat about two cups of water to 75°C in a small pan.
   2. Pour one of the eggs into the water in the pan.
   3. Observe the egg and record your observations.
   4. Repeat steps 1–3 twice, once with boiling water and then with room-temperature water.

   Describe the differences that you observed among the three eggs. What may account for these differences?

Chapter 4: **Temperature and Heat** 115

KEY CONCEPT

4.3 The transfer of energy as heat can be controlled.

BEFORE, you learned
- Temperature is the average amount of kinetic energy of particles in an object
- Heat is the flow of energy from warmer objects to cooler objects

NOW, you will learn
- How energy is transferred through heat
- How materials are used to control the transfer of energy through heat

VOCABULARY

conduction p. 117
conductor p. 117
insulator p. 117
convection p. 118
radiation p. 119

EXPLORE Conduction

How can you observe a flow of energy?

PROCEDURE

1. Fill the large beaker halfway with hot tap water. Fill the small beaker halfway with cold water. Place a thermometer in each beaker. Record the temperature of the water in each beaker.

2. Without removing the water in either beaker, place the small beaker inside the large beaker. Record the temperature in each beaker every 30 seconds for 2 minutes.

MATERIALS
- 500 mL beaker
- hot tap water
- 200 mL beaker
- cold water
- 2 thermometers
- stopwatch

WHAT DO YOU THINK?
- How did the water temperature in each beaker change?
- In which direction did energy flow? How do you know?

NOTE-TAKING STRATEGY
Main idea and detail notes would be a useful strategy for taking notes on how heat transfers energy.

Energy moves as heat in three ways.

Think about what you do to keep warm on a cold day. You may wear several layers of clothing, sit next to a heater, or avoid drafty windows. On a hot day, you may wear light clothing and sit in the shade of a tree. In all of these situations, you are trying to control the transfer of energy between yourself and your surroundings.

Recall that heat is always a transfer of energy from objects at a higher temperature to objects at a lower temperature. How does energy get transferred from a warmer object to a cooler one? There are three different ways in which this transfer of energy can occur—by conduction, convection, and radiation. So, in trying to control heat, it is necessary to control conduction, convection, and radiation.

A   116   Unit: Matter and Energy

Conduction

One way in which energy is transferred as heat is through direct contact between objects. **Conduction** is the process that moves energy from one object to another when they are touching physically. If you have ever picked up a bowl of hot soup, you have experienced conduction.

Conduction occurs any time that objects at different temperatures come into contact with each other. The average kinetic energy of particles in the warmer object is greater than that of the particles in the cooler object. When particles of the objects collide, some of the kinetic energy of the particles in the warmer object is transferred to the cooler object. As long as the objects are in contact, conduction continues until the temperatures of the objects are equal.

Conduction can also occur within a single object. In this case, energy is transferred from the warmer part of the object to the cooler part of the object by heat. Suppose you put a metal spoon into a cup of hot cocoa. Energy will be conducted from the warm end of the spoon to the cool end until the temperature of the entire spoon is the same.

Some materials transfer the kinetic energy of particles better than others. **Conductors** are materials that transfer energy easily. Often, conductors also have a low specific heat. For example, metals are typically good conductors. You know that when one end of a metal object gets hot, the other end quickly becomes hot as well. Consider pots or pans that have metal handles. A metal handle becomes too hot to touch soon after the pan is placed on a stove that has been turned on.

Other materials, called **insulators,** are poor conductors. Insulators often have high specific heats. Some examples of insulators are wood, paper, and plastic foam. In fact, plastic foam is a good insulator because it contains many small spaces that are filled with air. A plastic foam cup will not easily transfer energy by conduction. As a result, plastic foam is often used to keep cold drinks cold or hot drinks hot. Think about the pan handle mentioned above. Often, the handle is made of a material that is an insulator, such as wood or plastic. Although a wood or plastic handle will get hot when the pan is on a stove, it takes a much longer time for wood or plastic to get hot as compared to a metal handle.

> **VOCABULARY**
> Remember to make a description wheel diagram for *conduction* and other vocabulary terms.

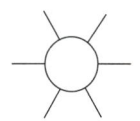

Conduction transfers energy from the cocoa to the mug to the person's hands.

CHECK YOUR READING How are conductors and insulators different?

Chapter 4: **Temperature and Heat** 117

Convection

Energy can also be transferred through the movement of gases or liquids. **Convection** is the process that transfers energy by the movement of large numbers of particles in the same direction within a liquid or gas. In most substances, as the kinetic energy of particles increases, the particles spread out over a larger area. An increased distance between particles causes a decrease in the density of the substance. Convection occurs when a cooler, denser mass of the gas or liquid replaces a warmer, less dense mass of the gas or liquid by pushing it upward.

Convection is a cycle in nature responsible for most winds and ocean currents. When the temperature of a region of air increases, the particles in the air spread out and the air becomes less dense.

① Cooler, denser air flows in underneath the warmer, less dense air, and pushes the warmer air upward.

② When this air cools, it becomes more dense than the warmer air beneath it.

③ The cooled air sinks and moves under the warmer air.

Convection in liquids is similar. Warm water is less dense than cold water, so the warm water is pushed upward as cooler, denser water moves underneath. When the warm water that has been pushed up cools, its density increases. The cycle continues when this more dense water sinks, pushing warmer water up again.

Recall that a large body of water, such as Lake Michigan, influences the temperature of the land nearby. This effect is due to convection. During the spring and early summer, the lake is cool and warms more slowly than the land. The air above the land gets warmer than the air over the water. The warmer air above the land is less dense than the cooler air above the water. The cooler, denser air moves onshore and pushes the warmer air up. The result is a cooling breeze from the lake.

REMINDER
Density = $\frac{mass}{Volume}$

READING TIP
As you read about the cycle that occurs during convection, follow the steps in the illustration below.

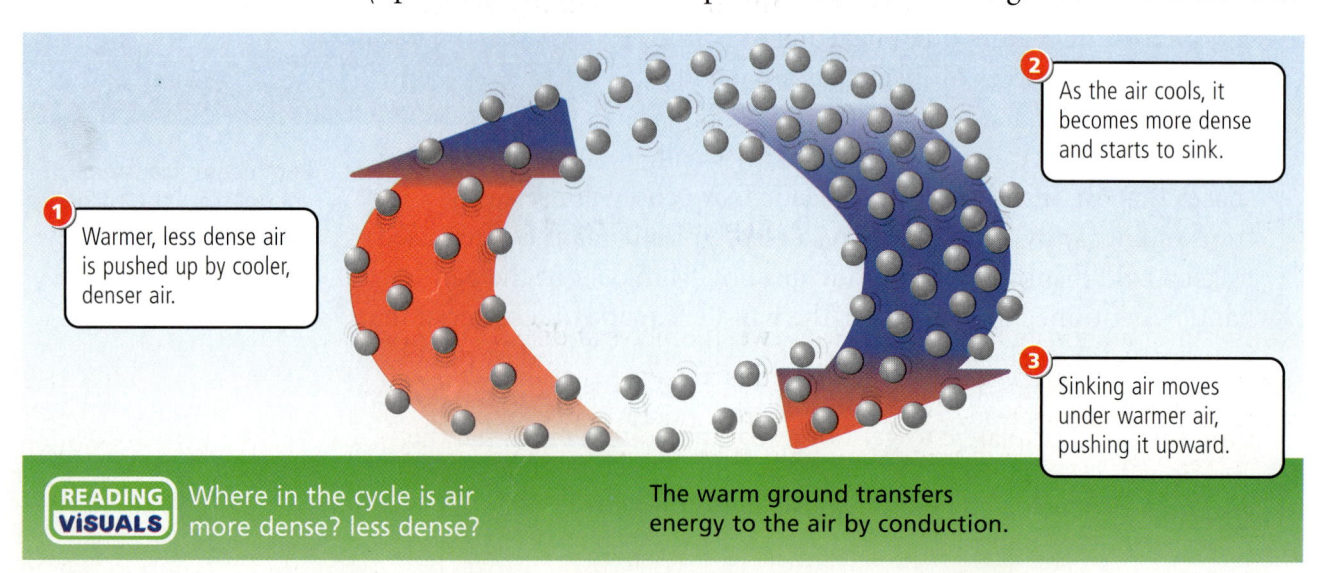

① Warmer, less dense air is pushed up by cooler, denser air.

② As the air cools, it becomes more dense and starts to sink.

③ Sinking air moves under warmer air, pushing it upward.

READING VISUALS Where in the cycle is air more dense? less dense?

The warm ground transfers energy to the air by conduction.

Radiation

Radiation is another way in which energy can be transferred from one place to another. **Radiation** is energy that travels as electromagnetic waves, which include visible light, microwaves, and infrared (IHN-fruh-REHD) light. The Sun is the most significant source of radiation that you experience on a daily basis. However, all objects—even you—emit radiation and release energy to their surroundings.

Consider radiation from the Sun. You can feel radiation as heat when radiation from the Sun warms your skin. The radiation emitted from the Sun strikes the particles in your body and transfers energy. This transfer of energy increases the movement of particles in your skin, which you detect as an increase in temperature. Of course, you are not the only object on Earth that absorbs the Sun's radiation. Everything—from air to concrete sidewalks—absorbs radiation that increases particle motion and produces an increase in temperature.

When radiation is emitted from one object and then is absorbed by another, the result is often a transfer of energy through heat. Like both conduction and convection, radiation can transfer energy from warmer to cooler objects. However, radiation differs from conduction and convection in a very significant way. Radiation can travel through empty space, as it does when it moves from the Sun to Earth. If this were not the case, radiation from the Sun would have no effect on Earth.

When radiation from the Sun is absorbed, energy is transferred through heat.

SIMULATION
CLASSZONE.COM
Identify examples of conduction, convection, or radiation.

CHECK YOUR READING How does radiation transfer energy?

Different materials are used to control the transfer of energy.

Energy is always being transferred between objects at different temperatures. It is often important to slow this movement of energy. For example, if energy were always transferred quickly and efficiently through heat, it would not be possible to keep a building warm during a cold day or to keep cocoa hot in a thermos.

Chapter 4: **Temperature and Heat** 119

Insulation

Insulators used by people are similar to insulators in nature. Polar bears are so well insulated that they tend to overheat.

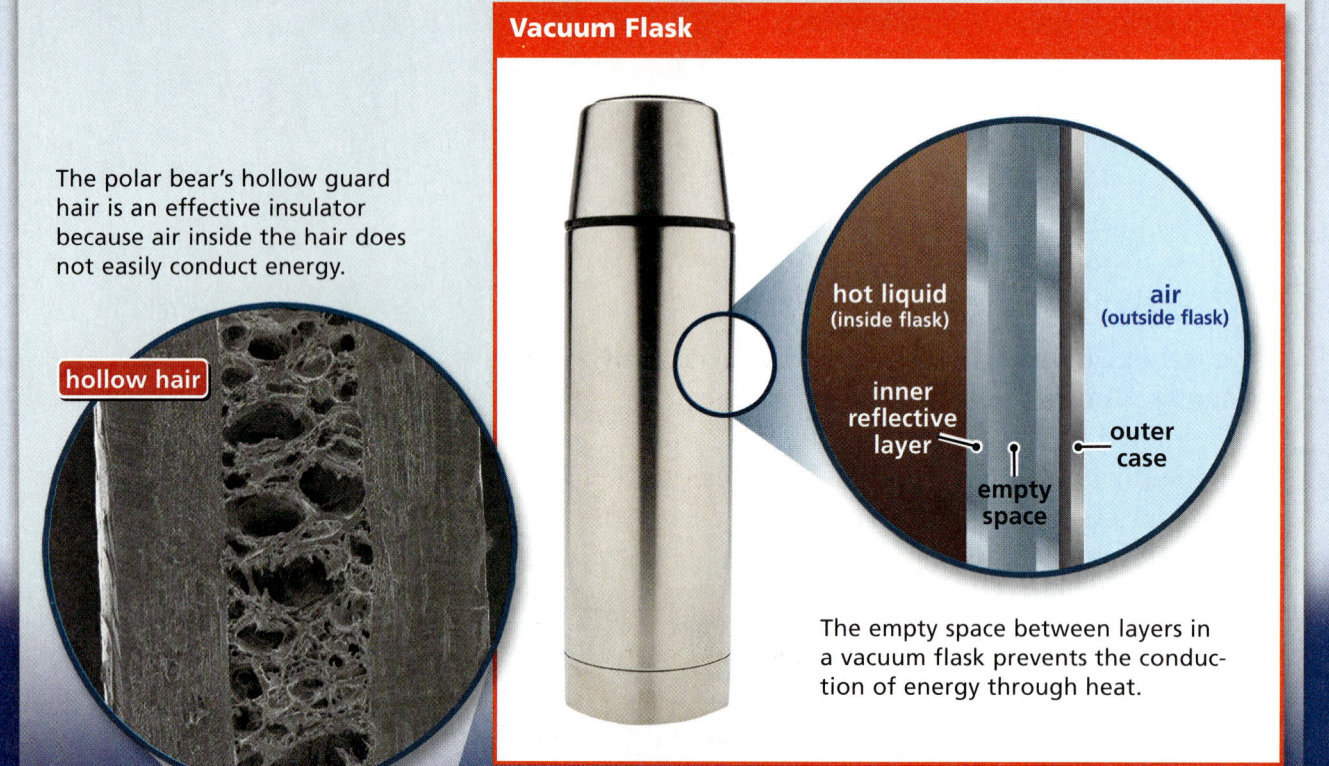

The polar bear's hollow guard hair is an effective insulator because air inside the hair does not easily conduct energy.

hollow hair

Vacuum Flask

hot liquid (inside flask)
air (outside flask)
inner reflective layer
outer case
empty space

The empty space between layers in a vacuum flask prevents the conduction of energy through heat.

Polar bears have several layers of insulation. They have a layer of fat up to 11 cm thick, a 2.5–5.0 cm thick layer of fur, and an outer layer of hollow guard hairs.

READING VISUALS How is the polar bear's hollow hair similar to the empty space in a vacuum flask? How is it different?

Insulators are used to control and slow the transfer of energy from warmer objects to cooler objects because they are poor conductors of energy. You can think of an insulator as a material that keeps cold things cold or hot things hot.

Sometimes people say that insulation "keeps out the cold." An insulator actually works by trapping energy. During the winter, you use insulators such as wool to slow the loss of your body heat to cold air. The wool traps air against your body, and because both air and wool are poor conductors, you lose body heat at a slower rate. Fiberglass insulation in the outer walls of a building works in the same way. The fiberglass slows the movement of energy from a building to the outside during cold weather, and it slows the movement of energy into the building during hot weather.

A vacuum flask, or thermos, works in a slightly different way to keep liquids either hot or cold. Between two layers of the flask is an empty space. This space prevents conduction between the inside and outside walls of the flask. Also, the inside of the flask is covered with a shiny material that reflects much of the radiation that strikes it. This prevents radiation from either entering or leaving the flask.

Insulators that people use are often very similar to insulators in nature. Look at the photograph of the polar bear on page 120. Because of the arctic environment in which the polar bear lives, it needs several different types of insulation. The polar bear's fur helps to trap a layer of air against its body to keep warmth inside. Polar bears also have guard hairs that extend beyond the fur. These guard hairs are hollow and contain air. Because air is a poor conductor, the bear's body heat is not easily released into the air.

CHECK YOUR READING How does insulation keep a building warm?

4.3 Review

KEY CONCEPTS

1. What are three ways in which energy can be transferred through heat? Provide an example of each.
2. Explain how convection is a cycle in nature.
3. Describe how an insulator can slow a transfer of energy.

CRITICAL THINKING

4. **Compare and Contrast** Describe the similarities and differences among conduction, convection, and radiation.
5. **Synthesize** Do you think solids can undergo convection? Why or why not? Explain.

CHALLENGE

6. **Infer** During the day, wind often blows from a body of water to the land. What do you think would happen at night? Explain.

CHAPTER INVESTIGATION

Insulators

DESIGN — YOUR OWN —

OVERVIEW AND PURPOSE
To keep warm in cold weather, a person needs insulation. A down-filled coat, such as the one worn by the girl in the photograph, is a very effective insulator because it contains a great deal of air. Energy is transferred rapidly through some substances and quite slowly through others. In this investigation, you will
- design and build an insulator for a bottle to maintain the temperature of the water inside
- test an unchanged bottle and your experimental bottle to see which maintains the water's temperature more effectively

▶ Problem   *Write It Up*

How can a bottle be insulated most effectively?

▶ Procedure

1. Create a data table similar to the one shown on the sample notebook page to record your measurements.

2. Set aside plastic bottles, thermometers, modeling clay, and a graduated cylinder. Decide whether you will test hot or cold water in your bottles.

3. From the other materials available to you, design a way to modify one of the bottles so that it will keep the temperature of the water constant for a longer period of time than the control bottle.

4. Build your modified bottle by using one or more of the insulating materials available.

MATERIALS
- 2 small plastic bottles
- 2 thermometers
- modeling clay
- graduated cylinder
- tap water (hot or cold)
- foam packing peanuts
- plastic wrap
- aluminum foil
- soil
- sand
- rubber bands
- coffee can
- beaker
- stopwatch

A 122 Unit: Matter and Energy

5. Fill each bottle with 200 mL of hot or cold water. Make sure that the water in each bottle is the same temperature.

6. Place a thermometer into each bottle. The thermometers should touch only the water, not the bottom or sides of the bottles. Use modeling clay to hold the thermometers in place in the bottles.

7. Record the starting temperature of the water in both bottles. Continue to observe and record the temperature of the water in both bottles every 2 minutes for 30 minutes. Record these temperatures in your data table.

step 6

Observe and Analyze
Write It Up

1. **COMMUNICATE** Draw the setup of your experimental bottle in your notebook. Be sure to label the materials that you used to insulate your experimental bottle.

2. **RECORD OBSERVATIONS** Make sure you record all of your measurements and observations in the data table.

3. **GRAPH** Make a double line graph of the temperature data. Graph temperature versus time. Plot the temperature on the vertical axis, or *y*-axis, and the time on the horizontal axis, or *x*-axis. Use different colors to show the data from the different bottles.

4. **IDENTIFY VARIABLES, CONTROLS, AND CONSTANTS** Which bottle was the control? What was the variable? What were the constants in both setups?

5. **ANALYZE** Obtain the experimental results from two other groups that used a different insulator. Compare your results with the results from the other groups. Which bottle changed temperature most quickly?

Conclude
Write It Up

1. **EVALUATE** Explain why the materials used by different groups might have been more or less effective as insulators. How might you change your design to improve its insulating properties?

2. **IDENTIFY LIMITS** Describe possible sources of error in the procedure or any points at which errors might have occurred. Why is it important to use the same amount of water in both bottles?

3. **APPLY** Energy can be transferred as heat by radiation, conduction, and convection. Which of these processes might be slowed by the insulation around your bottle? Explain.

INVESTIGATE Further

CHALLENGE We depend on our clothing to keep us from losing body heat when we go outside in cold weather. How might you determine the type of clothing that would provide the best insulation? Design an experiment that would test your hypothesis.

Insulators

Problem How can a bottle be insulated most effectively?

Observe and Analyze

Table 1. Water Temperature Measurements

Time (min)	Control Bottle Temperature (°C)	Experimental Bottle Temperature (°C)
0		
2		
4		
6		
8		
10		

Conclude

Chapter 4: **Temperature and Heat** 123

Chapter 4 Review

the BIG idea
Heat is a flow of energy due to temperature differences.

CONTENT REVIEW
CLASSZONE.COM

KEY CONCEPTS SUMMARY

4.1 Temperature depends on particle movement.
- All particles in matter have kinetic energy.
- Temperature is the measurement of the average kinetic energy of particles in an object.
- Temperature is commonly measured on the Fahrenheit or Celsius scales.

Particles in a warmer substance have a greater average kinetic energy than particles in a cooler substance.

VOCABULARY
kinetic theory of matter p. 104
temperature p. 105
degree p. 106
thermometer p. 107

4.2 Energy flows from warmer to cooler objects.
- Heat is a transfer of energy from an object at a higher temperature to an object at a lower temperature.
- Different materials require different amounts of energy to change temperature.

Energy is transferred from the warmer lemonade to the cold ice through heat.

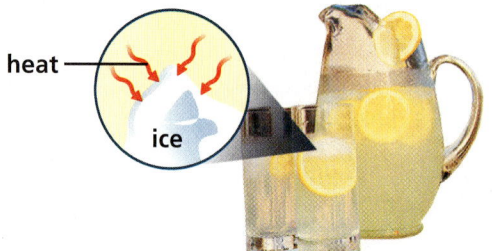

VOCABULARY
heat p. 110
thermal energy p. 111
calorie p. 112
joule p. 112
specific heat p. 113

4.3 The transfer of energy as heat can be controlled.
- Energy can be transferred by conduction, convection, and radiation.
- Different materials are used to control the transfer of energy.

VOCABULARY
conduction p. 117
conductor p. 117
insulator p. 117
convection p. 118
radiation p. 119

Types of Energy Transfer

Conduction	Convection	Radiation
• Energy transferred by direct contact • Energy flows directly from warmer object to cooler object • Can occur within one object • Continues until object temperatures are equal	• Occurs in gases and liquids • Movement of large number of particles in same direction • Occurs due to difference in density • Cycle occurs while temperature differences exist	• Energy transferred by electromagnetic waves such as light, microwaves, and infrared radiation • All objects radiate energy • Can transfer energy through empty space

A 124 Unit: Matter and Energy

Reviewing Vocabulary

Make a frame for each of the vocabulary terms listed below. Write the term in the center. Decide what information to frame it with. Use definitions, examples, descriptions, parts, or pictures.

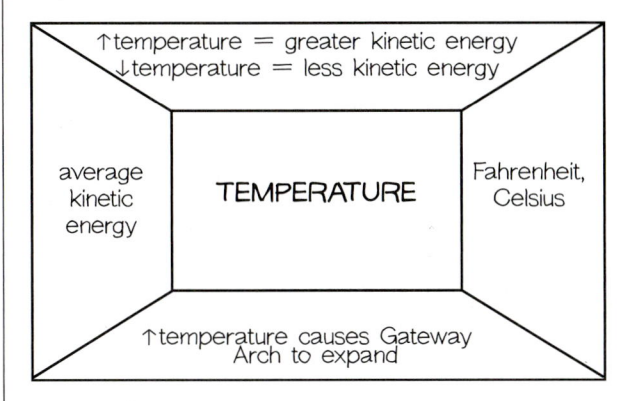

```
↑temperature = greater kinetic energy
↓temperature = less kinetic energy

average                          Fahrenheit,
kinetic       TEMPERATURE        Celsius
energy

↑temperature causes Gateway
        Arch to expand
```

1. kinetic theory of matter
2. heat
3. thermal energy
4. conduction
5. convection
6. radiation

In two or three sentences, describe how the terms in the following pairs are related to each other. Underline each term in your answers.

7. calorie, joule
8. conductor, insulator

Reviewing Key Concepts

Multiple Choice *Choose the letter of the best answer.*

9. What is the zero point in the Celsius scale?
   a. the freezing point of pure water
   b. the boiling point of pure water
   c. the freezing point of mercury
   d. the boiling point of alcohol

10. Energy is always transferred through heat from?
    a. an object with a lower specific heat to one with a higher specific heat
    b. a cooler object to a warmer object
    c. an object with a higher specific heat to one with a lower specific heat
    d. a warmer object to a cooler object

11. The average kinetic energy of particles in an object can be measured by its
    a. heat   c. calories
    b. thermal energy d. temperature

12. How is energy transferred by convection?
    a. by direct contact between objects
    b. by electromagnetic waves
    c. by movement of groups of particles in gases or liquids
    d. by movement of groups of particles in solid objects

13. The total kinetic energy of particles in an object is
    a. heat   c. calories
    b. thermal energy d. temperature

14. Water requires more energy than an equal mass of iron for its temperature to increase by a given amount because water has a greater
    a. thermal energy c. temperature
    b. specific heat   d. kinetic energy

15. Energy from the Sun travels to Earth through which process?
    a. temperature   c. radiation
    b. conduction   d. convection

16. An insulator keeps a home warm by
    a. slowing the transfer of cold particles from outside to inside
    b. increasing the specific heat of the air inside
    c. slowing the transfer of energy from inside to outside
    d. increasing the thermal energy of the walls

17. Conduction is the transfer of energy from a warmer object to a cooler object through
    a. a vacuum   c. direct contact
    b. a gas   d. empty space

Short Answer *Write a short answer to each question.*

18. How are kinetic energy and temperature related to each other?

19. What is the difference between heat and temperature?

Chapter 4: **Temperature and Heat** 125

Thinking Critically

The illustrations below show particle movement in a substance at two different temperatures. Use the illustrations to answer the next four questions.

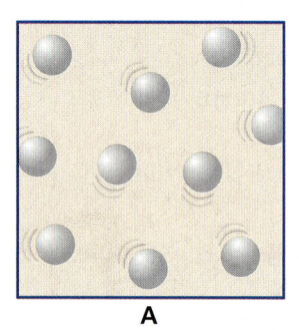

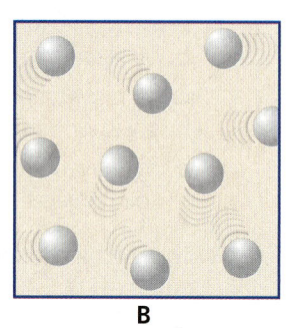

A   B

20. **OBSERVE** Which illustration represents the substance when it is at a higher temperature? Explain.

21. **PREDICT** What would happen to the particles in illustration A if the substance were chilled? What would happen if the particles in illustration B were warmed?

22. **PREDICT** If energy is transferred from one of the substances to the other through heat, in which direction would the energy flow (from A to B, or from B to A)? Why?

23. **COMMUNICATE** Suppose energy is transferred from one of the substances to the other through heat. Draw a sketch that shows what the particles of both substances would look like when the transfer of energy is complete. Explain.

24. **COMPARE AND CONTRAST** How are conduction and convection similar? How are they different?

25. **DRAW CONCLUSIONS** Suppose you are outdoors on a hot day and you move into the shade of a tree. Which form of energy transfer are you avoiding? Which type of energy transfer are you still feeling? Explain.

26. **COMMUNICATE** Draw a sketch that shows how convection occurs in a liquid. Label the sketch to indicate how the process occurs in a cycle.

Using Math Skills in Science

Use the illustrations of the two thermometers below to answer the next four questions.

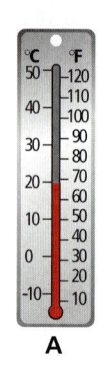

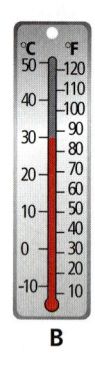

A   B

27. How much of a change in temperature occurred between A and B in the Fahrenheit scale?

28. Suppose the temperatures were measured in 10 g of water. How much energy, in calories, would have been added to cause that increase in temperature? (**Hint:** 1 calorie raises the temperature of 1 g of water by 1°C.)

29. Again, suppose the temperatures shown above were measured in 10 g of water. How much energy, in joules, would have been added? (**Hint:** 1 calorie = 4.18 joules.)

30. Suppose that the temperatures were measured for 10 g of iron. How much energy, in joules, would have been added to cause the increase in temperature? (**Hint:** see graph on p. 113.)

the BIG idea

31. **ANALYZE** Look back at the photograph and the question on pages 100 and 101. How has your understanding of temperature and heat changed after reading the chapter?

32. **COMMUNICATE** Explain the kinetic theory of matter in your own words. What, if anything, about the kinetic theory of matter surprised you?

UNIT PROJECTS

Evaluate all the data, results, and information from your project folder. Prepare to present your project.

Standardized Test Practice

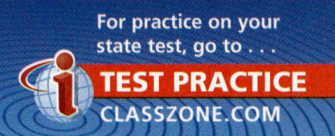

For practice on your state test, go to...
TEST PRACTICE
CLASSZONE.COM

Interpreting Diagrams

The diagrams below illustrate the process that occurs in sea and land breezes.

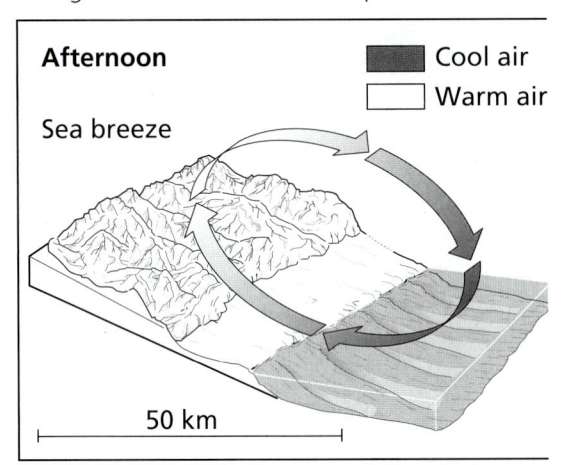

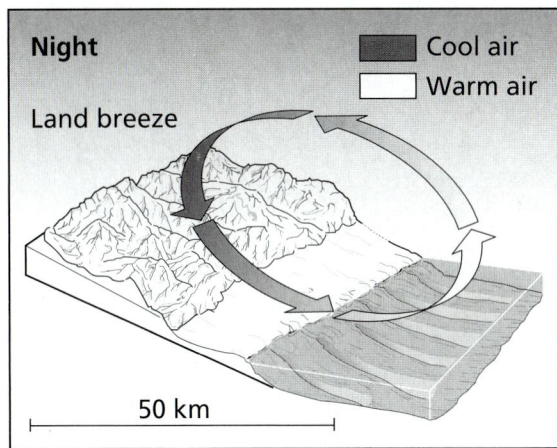

Afternoon — Sea breeze — Cool air / Warm air — 50 km

Night — Land breeze — Cool air / Warm air — 50 km

Use the diagrams above to answer the next five questions.

1. What happens during the day?
 a. Cool air from the land flows out to sea.
 b. Warm air from the land flows out to sea close to sea level.
 c. Cool air from the sea flows to the land.
 d. Warm air from the sea flows to the land.

2. What characteristic of large bodies of water explains why the seawater is cooler than the land in the hot afternoon sun?
 a. Water is liquid while the land is solid.
 b. Water has a higher specific heat than land.
 c. Land is a better insulator than water.
 d. Land has a higher specific heat than water.

3. What process causes the warm air to move upward over the land during the day?
 a. convection   c. evaporation
 b. condensation   d. radiation

4. Warm air is pushed upwards by cooler air during convection because the warm air
 a. is more dense   c. is less dense
 b. has more mass   d. has less mass

5. About how far over water does this land breeze extend?
 a. 1 kilometer   c. 25 kilometers
 b. 10 kilometers   d. 50 kilometers

Extended Response

Answer the two questions below in detail. Include some of the terms from the word box on the right. Underline each term that you use in your answer.

| boiling point | heat | specific heat |
| conduction | freezing point | zero point |

6. What are the differences between the Fahrenheit and Celsius temperature scales? Which one is used in science? Why might this be the case?

7. Suppose you place three spoons—one metal, one plastic, and one wood—into a cup filled with hot water. The bowl end of the spoon is inside the cup and the handle is sticking up into the air. On each handle, you place a bead, held to the spoon by a dab of margarine. From which spoon will the bead fall first, and why?

Chapter 4: **Temperature and Heat** 127

UNIT B
Chemical Interactions

reactants → products

exothermic

CHEMICAL REACTION

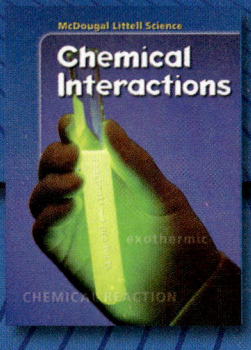

Chemical Interactions
Contents Overview

Unit Features
FRONTIERS IN SCIENCE Medicines from Nature   2
TIMELINES IN SCIENCE The Story of Atomic Structure   104

1 Atomic Structure and the Periodic Table   6
the BIG idea
A substance's atomic structure determines its physical and chemical properties.

2 Chemical Bonds and Compounds   38
the BIG idea
The properties of compounds depend on their atoms and chemical bonds.

3 Chemical Reactions   66
the BIG idea
Chemical reactions form new substances by breaking and making chemical bonds.

4 Solutions   108
the BIG idea
When substances dissolve to form a solution, the properties of the mixture change.

5 Carbon in Life and Materials   144
the BIG idea
Carbon is essential to living things and to modern materials.

FRONTIERS in Science

Medicines from Nature

Where have people found medicines?

SCIENTIFIC AMERICAN FRONTIERS

View the "Endangered Wonder Drug" segment of your Scientific American Frontiers video to see how chemicals found in nature can improve the health of people.

In Brazil, extracts from plants are used to treat everything from Parkinson's Disease to arthritis.

Finding Natural Remedies

In the 1960s, people were searching desperately for new cancer-fighting agents. Scientists tested over 35,000 compounds, some of which came from the bark of the Pacific yew tree, long known to have strong effects on the body. The tests indicated that something in the bark stopped the growth of cancerous tumors. Scientists eventually derived the drug Taxol from the compounds found in the yew tree.

Natural medicines are much more than simple folk cures, like the sapi karta leaves that the Kuna people of Panama believe increase creativity. Many powerful medicines are based on compounds found in nature. But even though these natural compounds may be very effective at treating diseases, they can be limited in supply and can have harmful side effects. Organic chemists must find ways to make these compounds safer and produce them in greater amounts.

Modeling the Molecule

To make a compound, a chemist must know what its molecule looks like, atom by atom. Many useful drugs have structures that contain many atoms arranged in complicated ways. The chemist must know exactly how many atoms of each kind are in the molecule and how they are arranged. One atom in the wrong place might mean that the drug won't work the way it should.

Frontiers in Science 3 B

To study the structures of molecules, chemists use a method called spectroscopy. Spectroscopy is a process that shows how the molecules of a compound respond to certain forms of radiation. Three important types of spectroscopy are

- NMR (nuclear magnetic resonance) spectroscopy, which allows chemists to identify small groups of atoms within larger molecules
- IR (infrared) spectroscopy, which shows the presence of certain types of bonds in molecules
- X-ray studies, which show details such as how much space there is between atoms and what the overall physical shapes of molecules are

Chemists put all this information together to determine the structure of a molecule. They might even build a model of the molecule.

Assembling the Puzzle

Once chemists know the structure of the molecule, they must figure out the starting reactants and the specific sequence of chemical reactions that will produce that molecule as a final product. It is a lot like doing a jigsaw puzzle when you know what the final picture looks like but still have to fit together all the pieces. Only in this case, the chemists may not even be sure what the little pieces look like.

Organic chemists often prefer to complete the process backward. They look at a model of the complete molecule and then figure out how they might build one just like it. How do chemists know what kinds of reactions might produce a certain molecule? Chemists have classified chemical reactions into different types. They determine how combinations of reactions will put the various kinds of atoms into their correct places in the molecule. Chemists may need to combine dozens of reactions to get the desired molecule.

Testing the Medicine

Once chemists have produced the desired drug molecule, the synthetic compound must be carefully tested to make sure it works like the natural substance does. The sequence of reactions must also be tested to make sure they produce the same compound when larger amounts of chemicals are used.

SCIENTIFIC AMERICAN FRONTIERS

View the "Endangered Wonder Drug" segment of your *Scientific American Frontiers* video to see how modern medicines can be developed from chemical compounds found in nature.

IN THIS SCENE FROM THE VIDEO
A researcher works with a substance found in bark.

SAVING LIVES THROUGH NATURE AND CHEMISTRY
Medicines from plants and other natural sources have been used by different cultures around the world for thousands of years. The ephedra plant contains the raw material for many decongestants, which help shrink swollen nasal passages. It was used by the Chinese more than 5000 years ago. Today, the bark of the Pacific yew tree is being used as the source of the anticancer drug Taxol. A large amount of bark from the tree, however, is needed to make just one dose of the drug, and very few Pacific yew trees are available. Chemists, therefore, are trying to make this medicine in the laboratory.

Once a potential new drug is found in nature, it may take several years, or even decades, to figure out how to produce the drug synthetically and test it for safety. Only a small percentage of drugs tested ever goes to market, because the drugs must undergo several stages of testing on both animals and humans. Today, chemists routinely search the seas and the forests for marine organisms and rare plants that might have the power to fight cancer, heart disease, or viruses.

Chemists often use computers to make models of drug molecules. Computers allow the chemists to see how the drug molecules will interact with other molecules.

UNANSWERED Questions

The search for new chemical compounds that can be used to treat human illnesses raises many questions. Scientists need to find ways to investigate, produce, and test new, more powerful drugs.

- How might scientists more quickly test the safety and effectiveness of new medicines?
- Can easily synthesized compounds be just as effective as natural medicines?
- Might the processes that produce these drugs in nature be duplicated in a lab?
- Can we discover other new sources of medicines in the natural world?

UNIT PROJECTS

As you study this unit, work alone or with a group on one of these projects.

Medicines Around You

Present a report about a plant in your region that has medicinal properties.

- Collect samples of a plant that has medicinal properties.
- Bring your plant samples into your classroom. Prepare and present a report about the plant and the way it is used in medicine.

Model Medicine

Build a scale model of a molecule that is used to treat a certain illness.

- Using the Internet or an encyclopedia, determine the structure of a compound that interests you.
- Using foam balls, toothpicks, water colors, string, and other materials, construct a model of the molecule. Describe your model to the class.

Remedies

Write a news report about a popular herbal remedy, such as Saint John's Wort.

- To learn more about the herbal remedy, try interviewing a personal fitness trainer or an employee of a health-food store.
- Deliver a news report to the class telling of the advantages of the remedy and warning of its potential dangers.

CAREER CENTER
CLASSZONE.COM

Learn more about careers in chemistry.

CHAPTER 1
Atomic Structure and the Periodic Table

the BIG idea

A substance's atomic structure determines its physical and chemical properties.

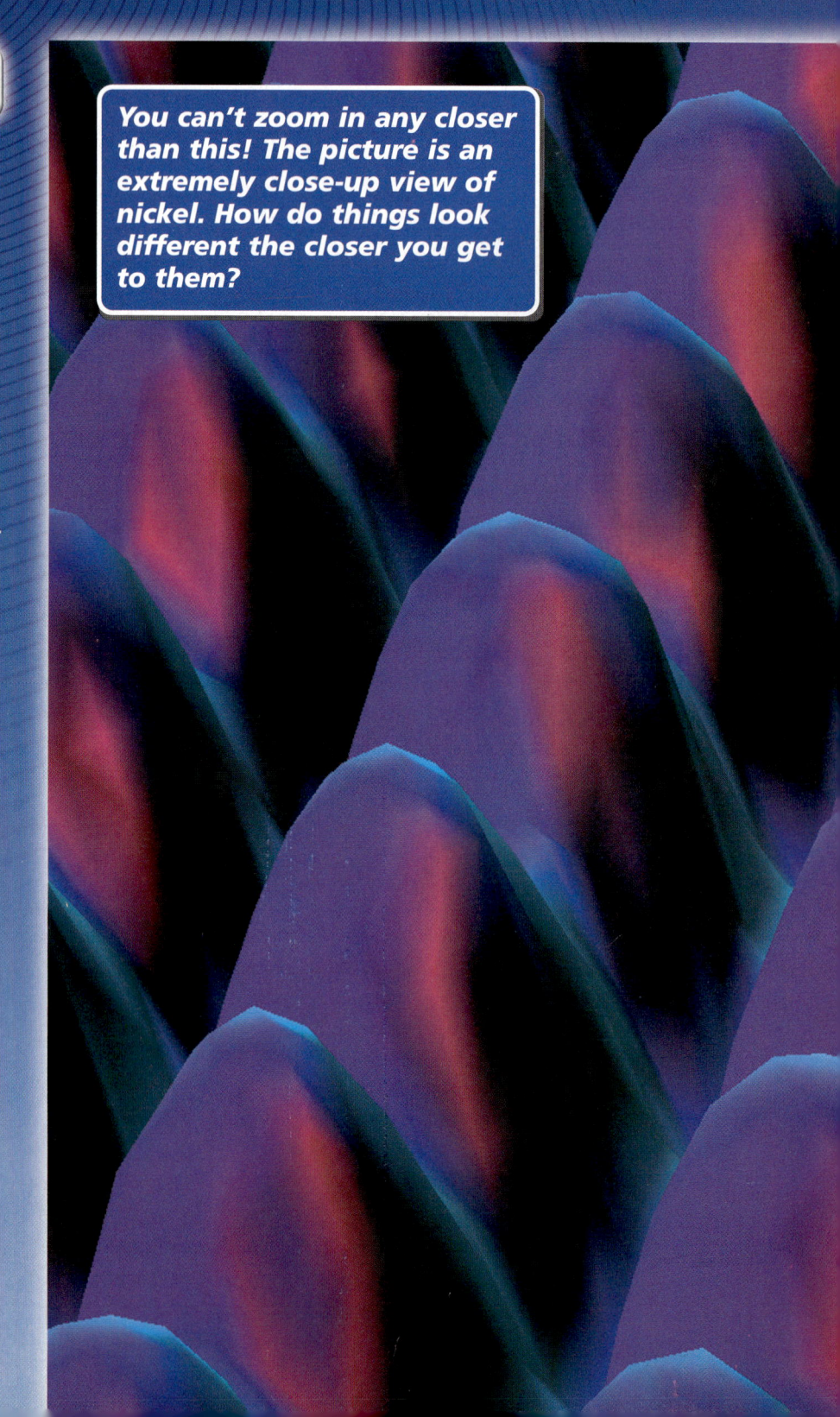

Key Concepts

SECTION 1.1 Atoms are the smallest form of elements.
Learn about the structure of atoms and how each element's atoms are different.

SECTION 1.2 Elements make up the periodic table.
Learn how the periodic table of the elements is organized.

SECTION 1.3 The periodic table is a map of the elements.
Learn more about the groups of elements in the periodic table.

You can't zoom in any closer than this! The picture is an extremely close-up view of nickel. How do things look different the closer you get to them?

Internet Preview

CLASSZONE.COM
Chapter 1 online resources: Content Review, Simulation, Visualization, three Resource Centers, Math Tutorial, Test Practice

EXPLORE the BIG idea

That's Far!
Place a baseball in the middle of a large field. Hold a dime and count off the number of steps from the baseball to the edge of the field. If the baseball were an atom's nucleus and the dime an electron, you would need to go about 6000 steps to walk the distance between the nucleus and the electrons.

Observe and Think How far were you able to go? How much farther would you need to go to model the proportion of an atom? What does this tell you about atomic structure?

Element Safari
Locate the following products in your home or in a grocery store: baking soda, vinegar, cereal flakes, and antacid tablets. You may examine other products if you wish. Look at the labels on the products. Can you recognize the names of any elements? Use your periodic table as a reference.

Observe and Think Which element names did you find?

Internet Activity: Periodic Table
Go to **ClassZone.com** to explore the periodic table. See different ways to set up the table and learn more about the listed elements.

Observe and Think How do atomic number and mass change as you move across the periodic table?

NSTA scilinks.org
SCLINKS
Atomic Theory **Code: MDL022**

Chapter 1: **Atomic Structure and the Periodic Table** 7 B

CHAPTER 1
Getting Ready to Learn

CONCEPT REVIEW

- Matter is made of particles called atoms that are too small to see with the eyes.
- Matter can be an element, a compound, or a mixture.
- Matter can undergo physical and chemical changes.

VOCABULARY REVIEW

See Glossary for definitions.

atom

compound

element

CONTENT REVIEW
CLASSZONE.COM
Review concepts and vocabulary.

TAKING NOTES

MAIN IDEA WEB

Write each new blue heading in a box. Then write notes in boxes around the center box that give important terms and details about that blue heading.

VOCABULARY STRATEGY

Write each new vocabulary term in the center of a **frame game** diagram. Decide what information to frame it with. Use examples, descriptions, parts, sentences that use the term in context, or pictures. You can change the frame to fit each term.

See the Note-Taking Handbook on pages R45–R51.

SCIENCE NOTEBOOK

- Atoms are made of protons, neutrons, and electrons.
- The atomic number is the number of protons in the nucleus.
- Each element is made of a different atom.
- Every element has a certain number of protons in its nucleus.

Frame game:
- Central part of atom
- Contains most of an atom's mass
- **NUCLEUS**
- Electrons move about it
- Is made of protons and neutrons

8 Unit: Chemical Interactions

KEY CONCEPT
1.1 Atoms are the smallest form of elements.

◀ **BEFORE, you learned**
- All matter is made of atoms
- Elements are the simplest substances

▶ **NOW, you will learn**
- Where atoms are found and how they are named
- About the structure of atoms
- How ions are formed from atoms

VOCABULARY

proton p. 11
neutron p. 11
nucleus p. 11
electron p. 11
atomic number p. 12
atomic mass number p. 12
isotope p. 12
ion p. 14

EXPLORE The Size of Atoms

How small can you cut paper?

PROCEDURE

① Cut the strip of paper in half. Cut one of these halves in half.

② Continue cutting one piece of paper in half as many times as you can.

WHAT DO YOU THINK?
- How many cuts were you able to make?
- Do you think you could keep cutting the paper forever? Why or why not?

MATERIALS
- strip of paper about 30 centimeters long
- scissors

All matter is made of atoms.

Think of all the substances you see and touch every day. Are all of these substances the same? Obviously, the substances that make up this book you're reading are quite different from the substances in the air around you. So how many different substances can there be? This is a question people have been asking for thousands of years.

About 2400 years ago, Greek philosophers proposed that everything on Earth was made of only four basic substances—air, water, fire, and earth. Everything else contained a mixture of these four substances. As time went on, chemists came to realize that there had to be more than four basic substances. Today chemists know that about 100 basic substances, or elements, account for everything we see and touch. Sometimes these elements appear by themselves. Most often, however, these elements appear in combination with other elements to make new substances. In this section, you'll learn about the atoms of the elements that make up the world and how these atoms differ from one another.

READING TIP

The word *element* is related to *elementary*, which means "basic."

Chapter 1: **Atomic Structure and the Periodic Table** 9

Atom Concentrations by Mass

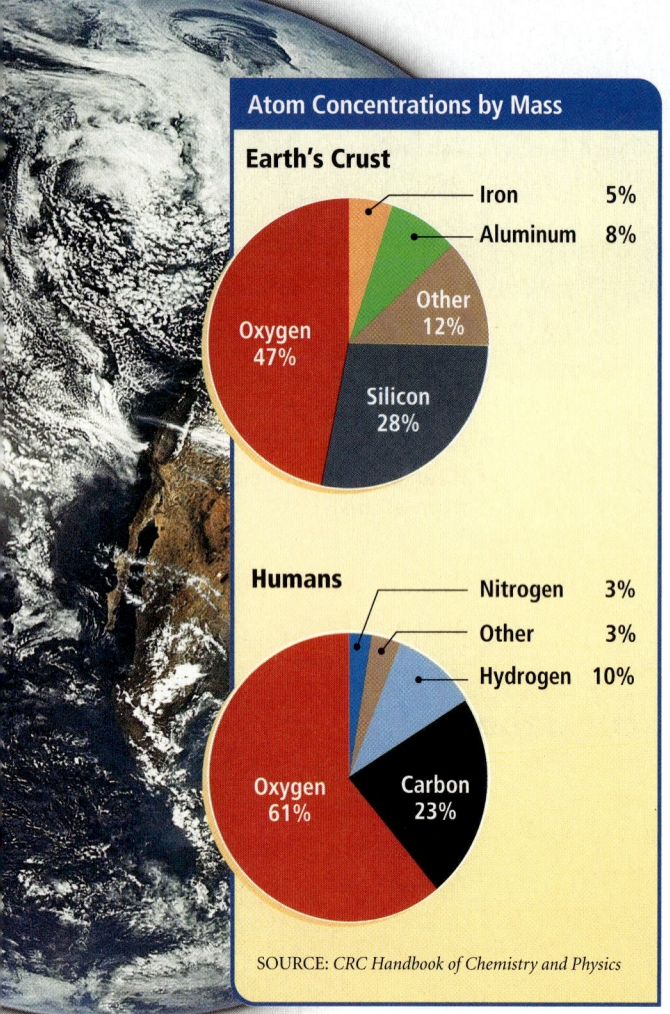

Earth's Crust
- Iron 5%
- Aluminum 8%
- Other 12%
- Silicon 28%
- Oxygen 47%

Humans
- Nitrogen 3%
- Other 3%
- Hydrogen 10%
- Carbon 23%
- Oxygen 61%

SOURCE: *CRC Handbook of Chemistry and Physics*

Types of Atoms in Earth's Crust and Living Things

Atoms of the element hydrogen account for about 90 percent of the total mass of the universe. Hydrogen atoms make up only about 1 percent of Earth's crust, however, and most of those hydrogen atoms are combined with oxygen atoms in the form of water. The graph on the left shows the types of atoms in approximately the top 100 kilometers of Earth's crust.

The distribution of the atoms of the elements in living things is very different from what it is in Earth's crust. Living things contain at least 25 types of atoms. Although the amounts of these atoms vary somewhat, all living things—animals, plants, and bacteria—are composed primarily of atoms of oxygen, carbon, hydrogen, and nitrogen. As you can see in the lower graph on the left, oxygen atoms account for more than half your body's mass.

CHECK YOUR READING What is the most common element in the universe?

Names and Symbols of Elements

Elements get their names in many different ways. Magnesium, for example, was named for the region in Greece known as Magnesia. Lithium comes from the Greek word *lithos,* which means "stone." Neptunium was named after the planet Neptune. The elements einsteinium and fermium were named after scientists Albert Einstein and Enrico Fermi.

Each element has its own unique symbol. For some elements, the symbol is simply the first letter of its name.

hydrogen (H)   sulfur (S)   carbon (C)

The symbols for other elements use the first letter plus one other letter of the element's name. Notice that the first letter is capitalized but the second letter is not.

aluminum (Al)   platinum (Pt)   cadmium (Cd)   zinc (Zn)

The origins of some symbols, however, are less obvious. The symbol for gold (Au), for example, doesn't seem to have anything to do with the element's name. The symbol refers instead to gold's name in Latin, *aurum.* Lead (Pb), iron (Fe), and copper (Cu) are a few other elements whose symbols come from Latin names.

Each element is made of a different atom.

In the early 1800s British scientist John Dalton proposed that each element is made of tiny particles called atoms. Dalton stated that all of the atoms of a particular element are identical but are different from atoms of all other elements. Every atom of silver, for example, is similar to every other atom of silver but different from an atom of iron.

Dalton's theory also assumed that atoms could not be divided into anything simpler. Scientists later discovered that this was not exactly true. They found that atoms are made of even smaller particles.

RESOURCE CENTER
CLASSZONE.COM
Learn more about the atom.

The Structure of an Atom

A key discovery leading to the current model of the atom was that atoms contain charged particles. The charge on a particle can be either positive or negative. Particles with the same type of charge repel each other—they are pushed apart. Particles with different charges attract each other—they are drawn toward each other.

Atoms are composed of three types of particles—electrons, protons, and neutrons. A **proton** is a positively charged particle, and a **neutron** is an uncharged particle. The neutron has approximately the same mass as a proton. The protons and neutrons of an atom are grouped together in the atom's center. This combination of protons and neutrons is called the **nucleus** of the atom. Because it contains protons, the nucleus has a positive charge. **Electrons** are negatively charged particles that move around outside the nucleus.

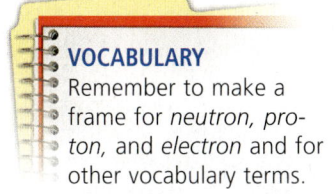

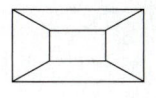

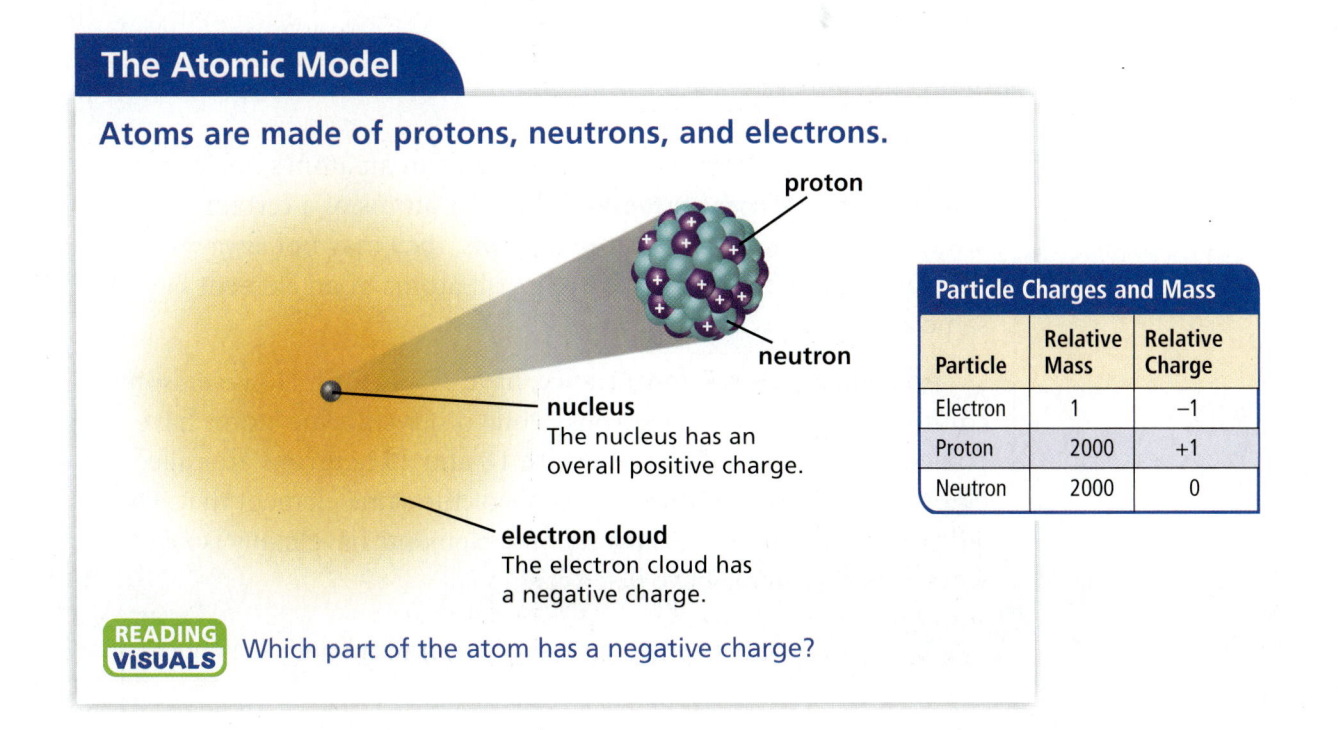

VOCABULARY
Remember to make a frame for *neutron*, *proton*, and *electron* and for other vocabulary terms.

The Atomic Model

Atoms are made of protons, neutrons, and electrons.

proton
neutron
nucleus
The nucleus has an overall positive charge.
electron cloud
The electron cloud has a negative charge.

Particle Charges and Mass		
Particle	Relative Mass	Relative Charge
Electron	1	−1
Proton	2000	+1
Neutron	2000	0

READING VISUALS Which part of the atom has a negative charge?

Chapter 1: **Atomic Structure and the Periodic Table** 11

SIMULATION
CLASSZONE.COM
Build a model of an atom.

Atoms are extremely small, about 10^{-10} meters in diameter. This means that you could fit millions of atoms in the period at the end of this sentence. The diagram on page 11, picturing the basic structure of the atom, is not drawn to scale. In an atom the electron cloud is about 10,000 times the diameter of the nucleus.

Electrons are much smaller than protons or neutrons—about 2000 times smaller. Electrons also move about the nucleus very quickly. Scientists have found that it is not possible to determine their exact positions with any certainty. This is why we picture the electrons as being in a cloud around the nucleus.

The negative electrons remain associated with the nucleus because they are attracted to the positively charged protons. Also, because electrical charges that are alike (such as two negative charges) repel each other, electrons remain spread out in the electron cloud. Neutral atoms have no overall electrical charge because they have an equal number of protons and electrons.

Atom Size

Millions of atoms could fit in a space the size of this dot. It would take you 500 years to count the number of atoms in a grain of salt.

Gold has 79 protons and 79 electrons.

Atomic Numbers

If all atoms are composed of the same particles, how can there be more than 100 different elements? The identity of an atom is determined by the number of protons in its nucleus, called the **atomic number.** Every hydrogen atom—atomic number 1—has exactly one proton in its nucleus. Every gold atom has 79 protons, which means the atomic number of gold is 79.

Atomic Mass Numbers

The total number of protons and neutrons in an atom's nucleus is called its **atomic mass number.** While the atoms of a certain element always have the same number of protons, they may not always have the same number of neutrons, so not all atoms of an element have the same atomic mass number.

All chlorine atoms, for instance, have 17 protons. However, some chlorine atoms have 18 neutrons, while other chlorine atoms have 20 neutrons. Atoms of chlorine with 18 and 20 neutrons are called chlorine isotopes. **Isotopes** are atoms of the same element that have a different number of neutrons. Some elements have many isotopes, while other elements have just a few.

READING TIP
The *iso-* in *isotope* is from the Greek language, and it means "equal."

CHECK YOUR READING How is atomic mass number different from atomic number?

Isotopes

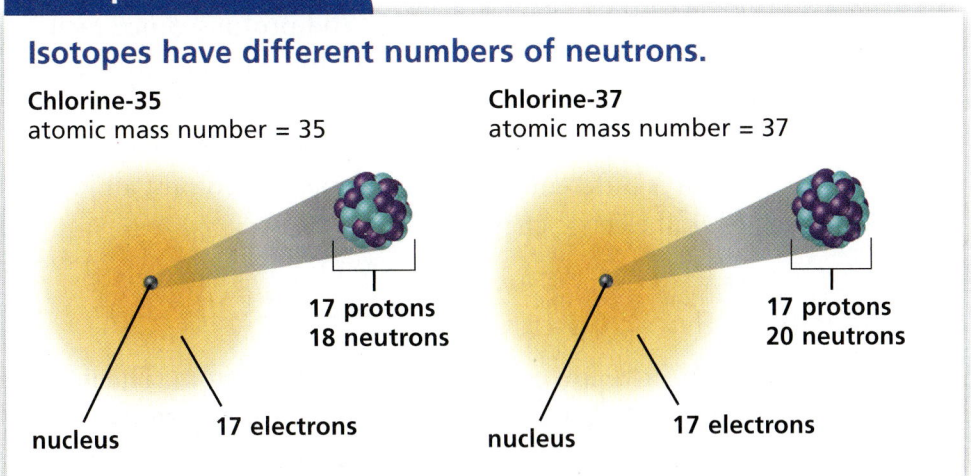

Isotopes have different numbers of neutrons.

Chlorine-35
atomic mass number = 35

17 protons
18 neutrons
nucleus
17 electrons

Chlorine-37
atomic mass number = 37

17 protons
20 neutrons
nucleus
17 electrons

A particular isotope is designated by the name of the element and the total number of its protons and neutrons. You can find the number of neutrons in a particular isotope by subtracting the atomic number from the atomic mass number. For example, chlorine-35 indicates the isotope of chlorine that has 18 neutrons. Chlorine-37 has 20 neutrons. Every atom of a given element always has the same atomic number because it has the same number of protons. However, the atomic mass number varies depending on the number of neutrons.

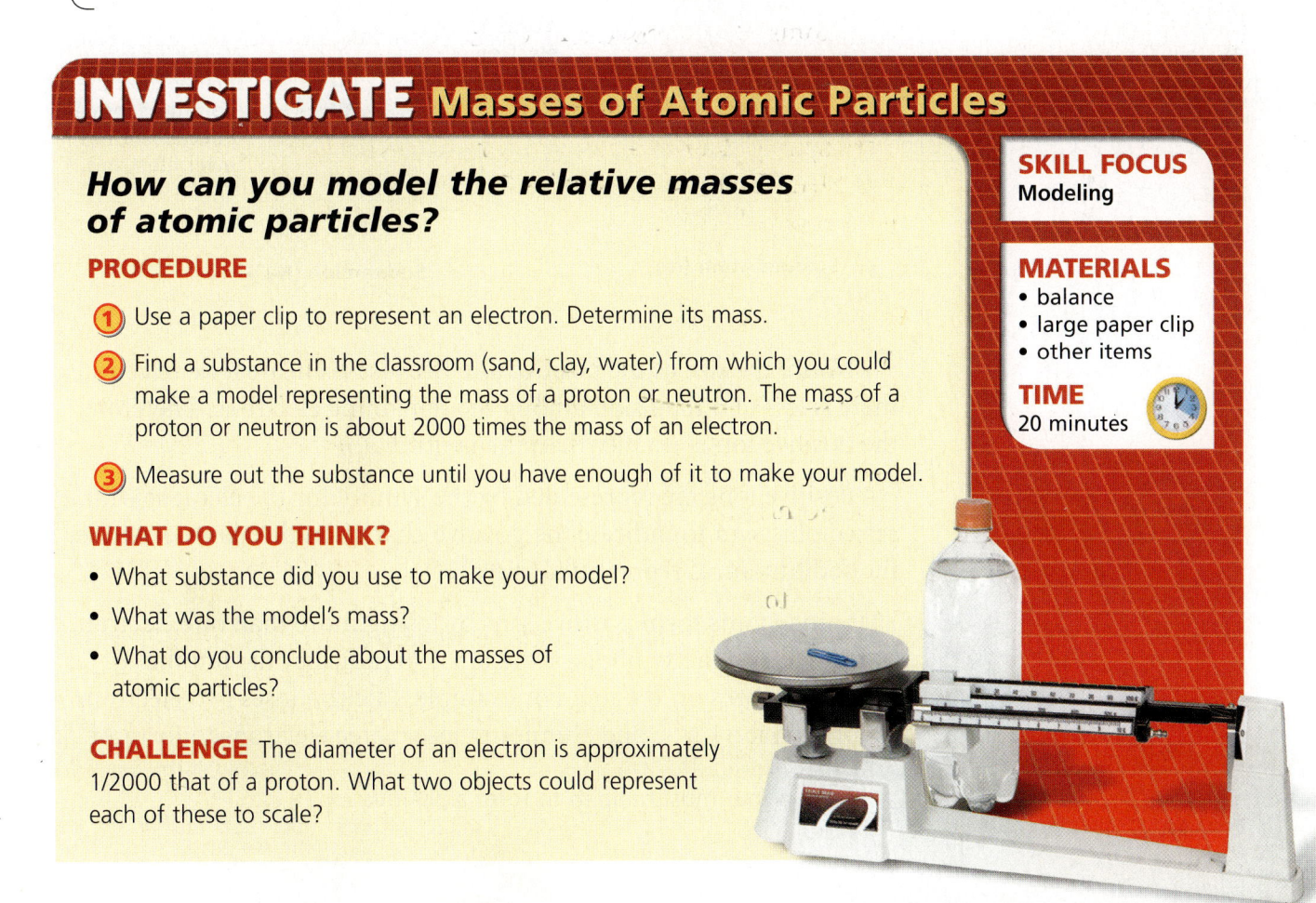

INVESTIGATE Masses of Atomic Particles

How can you model the relative masses of atomic particles?

PROCEDURE

1. Use a paper clip to represent an electron. Determine its mass.
2. Find a substance in the classroom (sand, clay, water) from which you could make a model representing the mass of a proton or neutron. The mass of a proton or neutron is about 2000 times the mass of an electron.
3. Measure out the substance until you have enough of it to make your model.

WHAT DO YOU THINK?
- What substance did you use to make your model?
- What was the model's mass?
- What do you conclude about the masses of atomic particles?

CHALLENGE The diameter of an electron is approximately 1/2000 that of a proton. What two objects could represent each of these to scale?

SKILL FOCUS
Modeling

MATERIALS
- balance
- large paper clip
- other items

TIME
20 minutes

Chapter 1: **Atomic Structure and the Periodic Table** 13 B

MAIN IDEA WEB
Make a main idea web to organize what you know about ions.

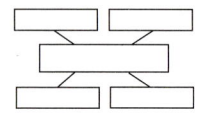

Atoms form ions.

An atom has an equal number of electrons and protons. Since each electron has one negative charge and each proton has one positive charge, atoms have no overall electrical charge. An **ion** is formed when an atom loses or gains one or more electrons. Because the number of electrons in an ion is different from the number of protons, an ion does have an overall electric charge.

Formation of Positive Ions

Consider how a positive ion can be formed from an atom. The left side of the illustration below represents a sodium (Na) atom. Its nucleus contains 11 protons and some neutrons. Because the electron cloud surrounding the nucleus consists of 11 electrons, there is no overall charge on the atom. If the atom loses one electron, however, the charges are no longer balanced. There is now one more proton than there are electrons. The ion formed, therefore, has a positive charge.

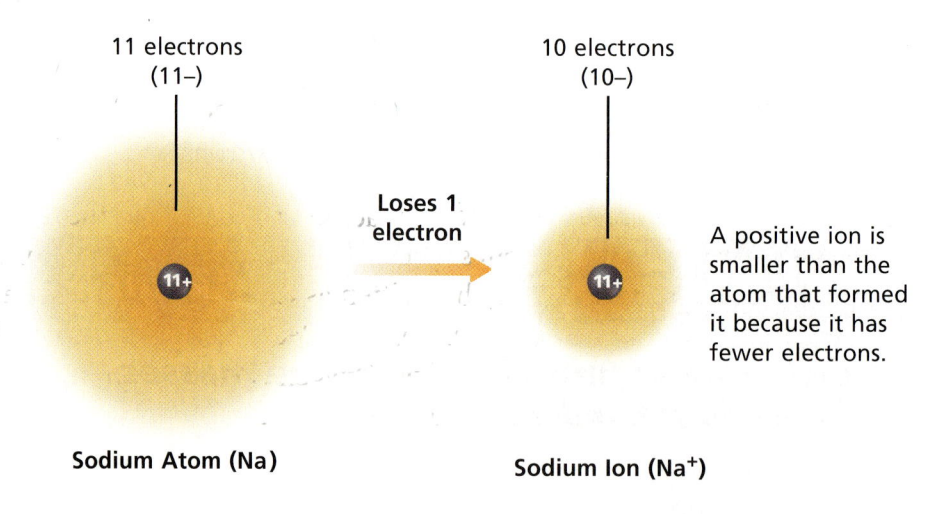

11 electrons (11–)   → Loses 1 electron →   10 electrons (10–)

11+   11+

Sodium Atom (Na)   **Sodium Ion (Na⁺)**

A positive ion is smaller than the atom that formed it because it has fewer electrons.

Notice the size of the positive ion. Because there are fewer electrons, there is less of a repulsion among the remaining electrons. Therefore, the positive ion is smaller than the neutral atom.

Positive ions are represented by the symbol for the element with a raised plus sign to indicate the positive charge. In the above example, the sodium ion is represented as Na^+.

Some atoms form positive ions by losing more than one electron. In those cases, the symbol for the ion also indicates the number of positive charges on the ion. For example, calcium loses two electrons to form an ion Ca^{2+}, and aluminum loses three electrons to form Al^{3+}.

CHECK YOUR READING What must happen to form a positive ion?

Formation of Negative Ions

The illustration below shows how a negative ion is formed. In this case the atom is chlorine (Cl). The nucleus of a chlorine atom contains 17 protons and some neutrons. The electron cloud has 17 electrons, so the atom has no overall charge. When an electron is added to the chlorine atom, a negatively charged ion is formed. Notice that a negative ion is larger than the neutral atom that formed it. The extra electron increases the repulsion within the cloud, causing it to expand.

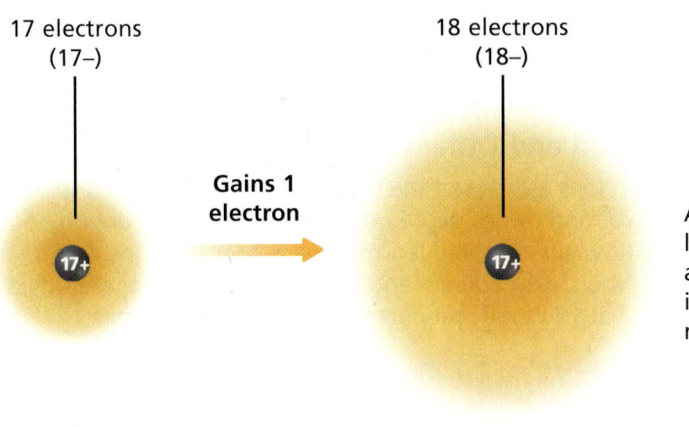

17 electrons (17−)

18 electrons (18−)

Gains 1 electron

A negative ion is larger than the atom that formed it because it has more electrons.

Chlorine Atom (Cl)

Chloride Ion (Cl⁻)

Negative ions are represented by placing a minus sign to the right and slightly above the element's symbol. The negative chloride ion in the example, therefore, would be written as Cl^-. If an ion has gained more than one electron, the number of added electrons is indicated by a number in front of the minus sign. Oxygen (O), for example, gains two electrons when it forms an ion. Its symbol is O^{2-}.

1.1 Review

KEY CONCEPTS

1. Which two atoms are most common in Earth's crust? in the human body?
2. What are the particles that make up an atom?
3. What happens when an atom forms an ion?

CRITICAL THINKING

4. **Infer** Magnesium and sodium atoms are about the same size. How does the size of a magnesium ion with a 2+ charge compare with that of a sodium ion with a single + charge?
5. **Compare** The atomic number of potassium is 19. How does potassium-39 differ from potassium-41?

CHALLENGE

6. **Analyze** When determining the mass of an atom, the electrons are not considered. Why can scientists disregard the electrons?

Chapter 1: **Atomic Structure and the Periodic Table** 15 **B**

CONNECTING SCIENCES

PHYSICAL SCIENCE AND LIFE SCIENCE

Elements of Life

There are more than 25 different types of atoms in the cells of your body. The table below shows the amount of atoms of some of the elements in a 50-kilogram human. Atoms of the element oxygen account for about 61 percent of a person's mass. Atoms of carbon account for about 23 percent of a person's mass. Although the atoms of some elements are present only in very small amounts, they play an important role in the chemical processes that occur in your cells.

Blood and Other Fluids

Iron ions are part of the hemoglobin that gives your blood its red color and carries oxygen to cells throughout your body. Sodium and potassium ions help regulate the amount and location of the water in your body. Sodium and potassium ions also make up part of the sweat your body produces to regulate temperature.

Mass of Elements in 50 kg Human

Element	Amount (kg)
Oxygen (O)	30.5
Carbon (C)	11.5
Hydrogen (H)	5.0
Nitrogen (N)	1.3
Calcium (Ca)	0.7
Phosphorus (P)	0.6
Potassium (K)	0.1
Sodium (Na)	> 0.1
Chlorine (Cl)	> 0.1

Other elements are in the body in very small amounts.
SOURCE: *CRC Handbook of Chemistry and Physics*

Bones and Teeth

The sturdier structures of your body get their strength from calcium, magnesium, and phosphorus. You have less than a kilogram of calcium in your body, almost all of which is in your bones and teeth. Fluoride ions make up part of the hard coating on your teeth. This is why you'll often find fluoride ions added to toothpaste.

Elements to Avoid

In some way, the atoms of every element in the periodic table play a role in human lives. Many of them, however, can be hazardous if handled improperly. For example, arsenic and mercury are poisonous.

EXPLORE

1. **CALCULATE** What percentage of your body is made up of oxygen, carbon, hydrogen, and nitrogen?
2. **CHALLENGE** Salt, made of sodium ions and chloride ions, is an essential part of your diet. However, too much salt can cause health problems. Use the Internet to find out about the problems caused by too much or too little salt in your diet.

RESOURCE CENTER CLASSZONE.COM Find out more about the elements important to life.

This photo shows a false color X-ray of the human skull. X-rays show the bones in the human body. Bones contain calcium.

KEY CONCEPT
1.2 Elements make up the periodic table.

BEFORE, you learned
- Atoms have a structure
- Every element is made from a different type of atom

NOW, you will learn
- How the periodic table is organized
- How properties of elements are shown by the periodic table

VOCABULARY
atomic mass p. 17
periodic table p. 18
group p. 22
period p. 22

EXPLORE Similarities and Differences of Objects

How can different objects be organized?

PROCEDURE

1. With several classmates, organize the buttons into three or more groups.
2. Compare your team's organization of the buttons with another team's organization.

MATERIALS
buttons

WHAT DO YOU THINK?
- What characteristics did you use to organize the buttons?
- In what other ways could you have organized the buttons?

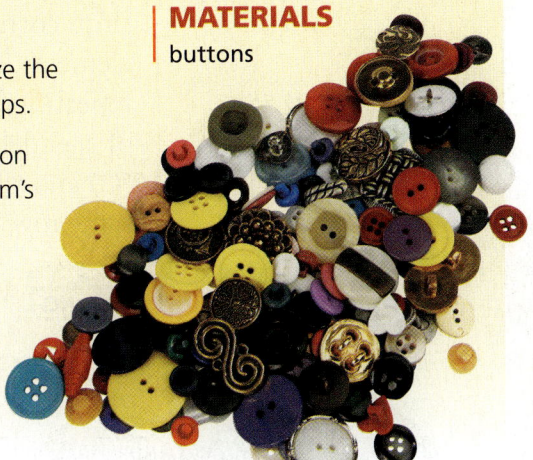

Elements can be organized by similarities.

One way of organizing elements is by the masses of their atoms. Finding the masses of atoms was a difficult task for the chemists of the past. They could not place an atom on a pan balance. All they could do was find the mass of a very large number of atoms of a certain element and then infer the mass of a single one of them.

Remember that not all the atoms of an element have the same atomic mass number. Elements have isotopes. When chemists attempt to measure the mass of an atom, therefore, they are actually finding the average mass of all its isotopes. The **atomic mass** of the atoms of an element is the average mass of all the element's isotopes. Even before chemists knew how the atoms of different elements could be different, they knew atoms had different atomic masses.

Chapter 1: **Atomic Structure and the Periodic Table** 17 B

Mendeleev's Periodic Table

In the early 1800s several scientists proposed systems to organize the elements based on their properties. None of these suggested methods worked very well until a Russian chemist named Dmitri Mendeleev (MENH-duh-LAY-uhf) decided to work on the problem.

In the 1860s, Mendeleev began thinking about how he could organize the elements based on their physical and chemical properties. He made a set of element cards. Each card contained the atomic mass of an atom of an element as well as any information about the element's properties. Mendeleev spent hours arranging the cards in various ways, looking for a relationship between properties and atomic mass.

The exercise led Mendeleev to think of listing the elements in a chart. In the rows of the chart, he placed those elements showing similar chemical properties. He arranged the rows so the atomic masses increased as one moved down each vertical column. It took Mendeleev quite a bit of thinking and rethinking to get all the relationships correct, but in 1869 he produced the first **periodic table** of the elements. We call it the periodic table because it shows a periodic, or repeating, pattern of properties of the elements. In the reproduction of Mendeleev's first table shown below, notice how he placed carbon (C) and silicon (Si), two elements known for their similarities, in the same row.

CHECK YOUR READING What organizing method did Mendeleev use?

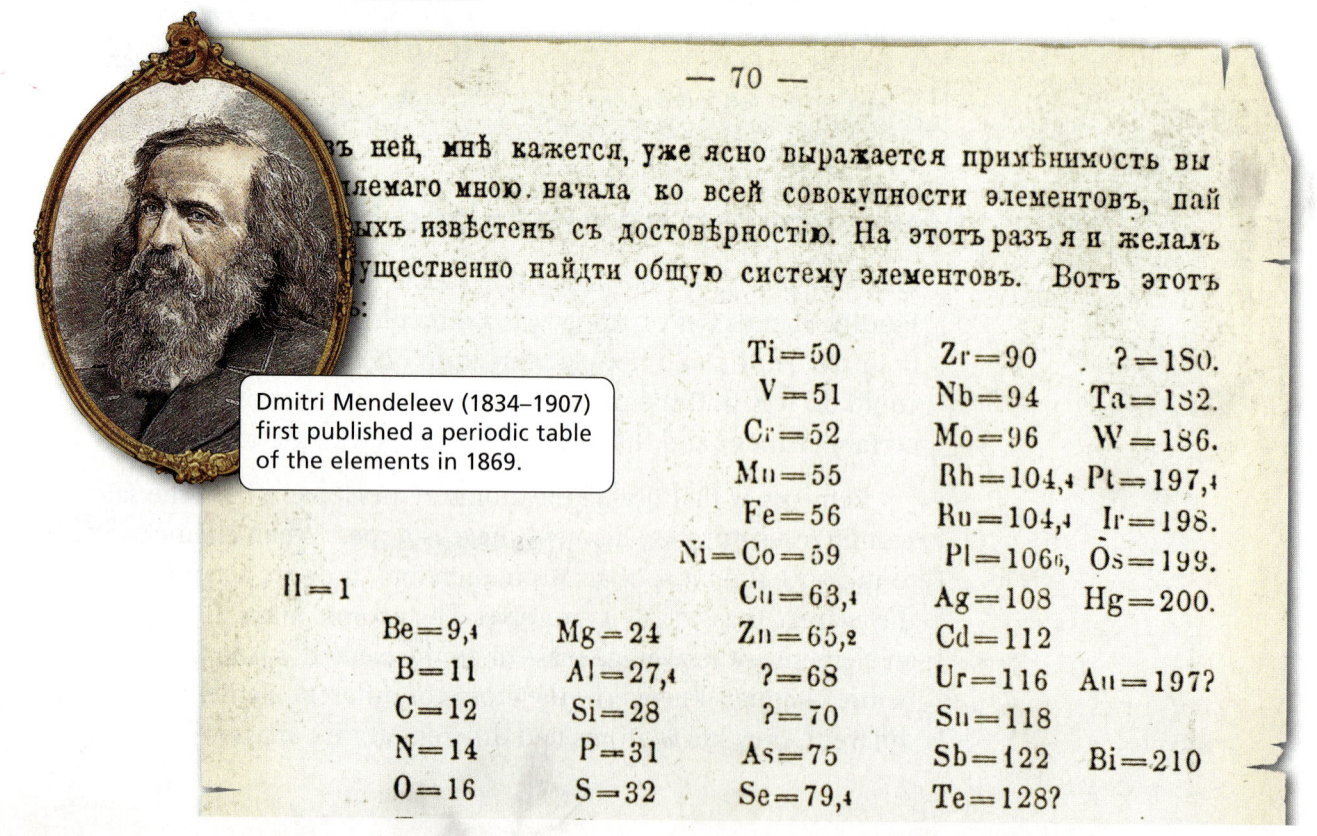

Dmitri Mendeleev (1834–1907) first published a periodic table of the elements in 1869.

— 70 —

ъ ней, мнѣ кажется, уже ясно выражается примѣнимость вы лемаго мною. начала ко всей совокупности элементовъ, пай ыхъ извѣстенъ съ достовѣрностію. На этотъ разъ я и желалъ ущественно найти общую систему элементовъ. Вотъ этотъ

				Ti=50	Zr=90	?=180.
				V=51	Nb=94	Ta=182.
				Cr=52	Mo=96	W=186.
				Mn=55	Rh=104,4	Pt=197,4
				Fe=56	Ru=104,4	Ir=198.
				Ni=Co=59	Pl=106,6	Os=199.
H=1				Cu=63,4	Ag=108	Hg=200.
	Be=9,4	Mg=24		Zn=65,2	Cd=112	
	B=11	Al=27,4		?=68	Ur=116	Au=197?
	C=12	Si=28		?=70	Sn=118	
	N=14	P=31		As=75	Sb=122	Bi=210
	O=16	S=32		Se=79,4	Te=128?	

18 Unit: Chemical Interactions

Predicting New Elements

When Mendeleev constructed his table, he left some empty spaces where no known elements fit the pattern. He predicted that new elements that would complete the chart would eventually be discovered. He even described some of the properties of these unknown elements.

At the start, many chemists found it hard to accept Mendeleev's predictions of unknown elements. Only six years after he published the table, however, the first of these elements—represented by the question mark after aluminum (Al) on his table—was discovered. This element was given the name gallium, after the country France (Gaul) where it was discovered. In the next 20 years, two other elements Mendeleev predicted would be discovered.

The periodic table organizes the atoms of the elements by properties and atomic number.

The modern periodic table on pages 20 and 21 differs from Mendeleev's table in several ways. For one thing, elements with similar properties are found in columns, not rows. More important, the elements are not arranged by atomic mass but by atomic number.

MAIN IDEA WEB
Make a main idea web to summarize the information you can learn from the periodic table.

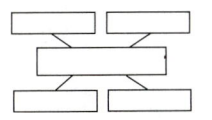

Reading the Periodic Table

Each square of the periodic table gives particular information about the atoms of an element.

1. The number at the top of the square is the atomic number, which is the number of protons in the nucleus of an atom of that element.

2. The chemical symbol is an abbreviation for the element's name. It contains one or two letters. Some elements that have not yet been named are designated by temporary three-letter symbols.

3. The name of the element is written below the symbol.

4. The number below the name indicates the average atomic mass of all the isotopes of the element.

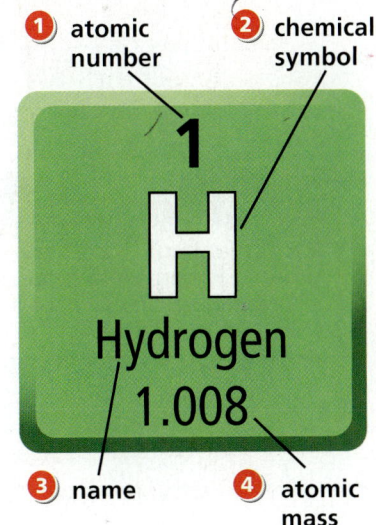

The color of the element's symbol indicates the physical state of the element at room temperature. White letters—such as the *H* for hydrogen in the box to the right—indicate a gas. Blue letters indicate a liquid, and black letters indicate a solid. The background colors of the squares indicate whether the element is a metal, nonmetal, or metalloid. These terms will be explained in the next section.

① atomic number
② chemical symbol
③ name
④ atomic mass

1
H
Hydrogen
1.008

Chapter 1: **Atomic Structure and the Periodic Table** 19

The Periodic Table of the Elements

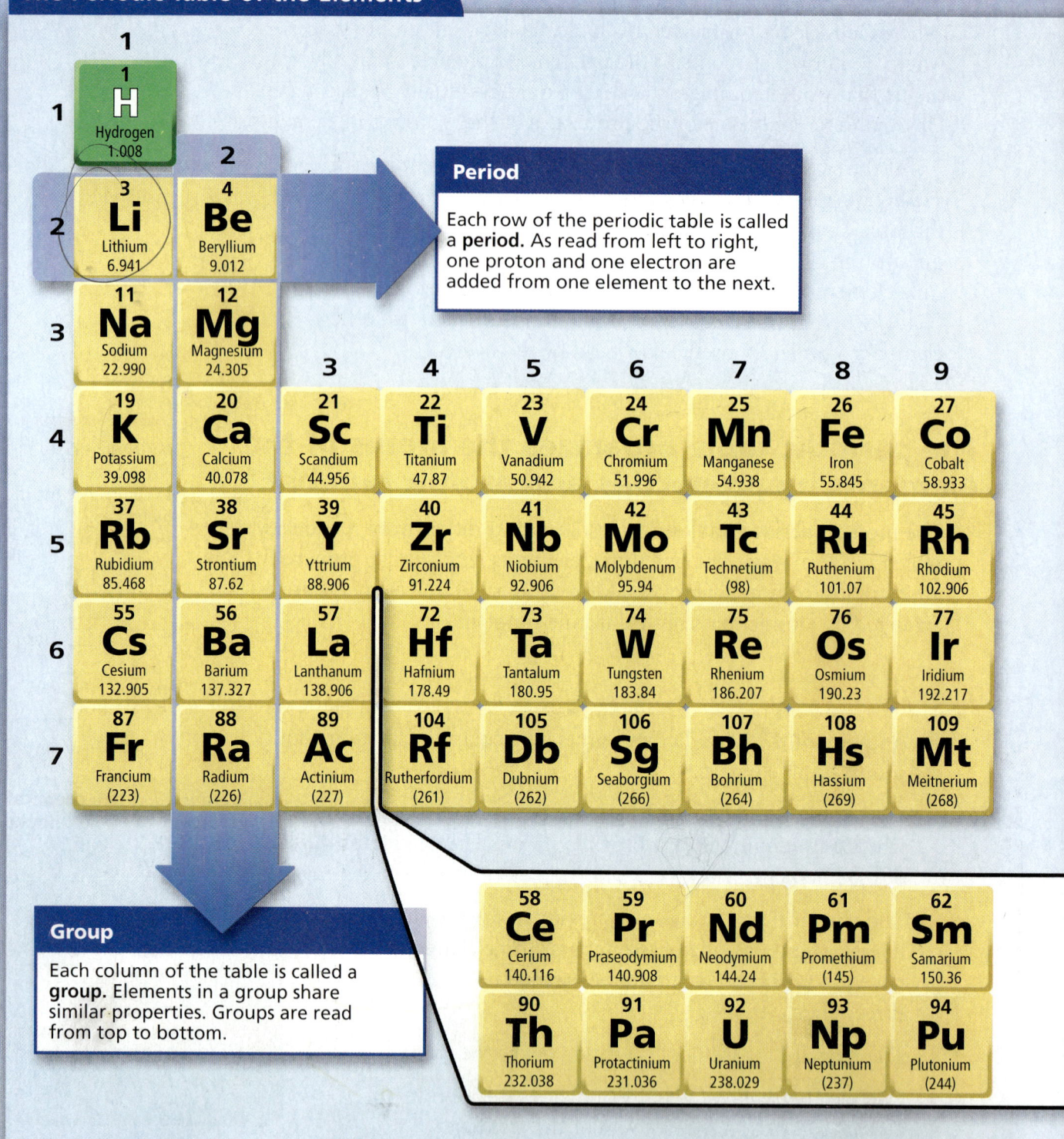

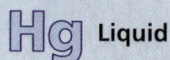

Period		
1	1 **H** Hydrogen 1.008	

Period

Each row of the periodic table is called a **period**. As read from left to right, one proton and one electron are added from one element to the next.

	1	2	3	4	5	6	7	8	9
1	1 **H** Hydrogen 1.008								
2	3 **Li** Lithium 6.941	4 **Be** Beryllium 9.012							
3	11 **Na** Sodium 22.990	12 **Mg** Magnesium 24.305							
4	19 **K** Potassium 39.098	20 **Ca** Calcium 40.078	21 **Sc** Scandium 44.956	22 **Ti** Titanium 47.87	23 **V** Vanadium 50.942	24 **Cr** Chromium 51.996	25 **Mn** Manganese 54.938	26 **Fe** Iron 55.845	27 **Co** Cobalt 58.933
5	37 **Rb** Rubidium 85.468	38 **Sr** Strontium 87.62	39 **Y** Yttrium 88.906	40 **Zr** Zirconium 91.224	41 **Nb** Niobium 92.906	42 **Mo** Molybdenum 95.94	43 **Tc** Technetium (98)	44 **Ru** Ruthenium 101.07	45 **Rh** Rhodium 102.906
6	55 **Cs** Cesium 132.905	56 **Ba** Barium 137.327	57 **La** Lanthanum 138.906	72 **Hf** Hafnium 178.49	73 **Ta** Tantalum 180.95	74 **W** Tungsten 183.84	75 **Re** Rhenium 186.207	76 **Os** Osmium 190.23	77 **Ir** Iridium 192.217
7	87 **Fr** Francium (223)	88 **Ra** Radium (226)	89 **Ac** Actinium (227)	104 **Rf** Rutherfordium (261)	105 **Db** Dubnium (262)	106 **Sg** Seaborgium (266)	107 **Bh** Bohrium (264)	108 **Hs** Hassium (269)	109 **Mt** Meitnerium (268)

Group

Each column of the table is called a **group**. Elements in a group share similar properties. Groups are read from top to bottom.

58 **Ce** Cerium 140.116	59 **Pr** Praseodymium 140.908	60 **Nd** Neodymium 144.24	61 **Pm** Promethium (145)	62 **Sm** Samarium 150.36
90 **Th** Thorium 232.038	91 **Pa** Protactinium 231.036	92 **U** Uranium 238.029	93 **Np** Neptunium (237)	94 **Pu** Plutonium (244)

Metal ■ Metalloid ■ Nonmetal ■ **Fe** Solid ■ Hg Liquid ■ O Gas

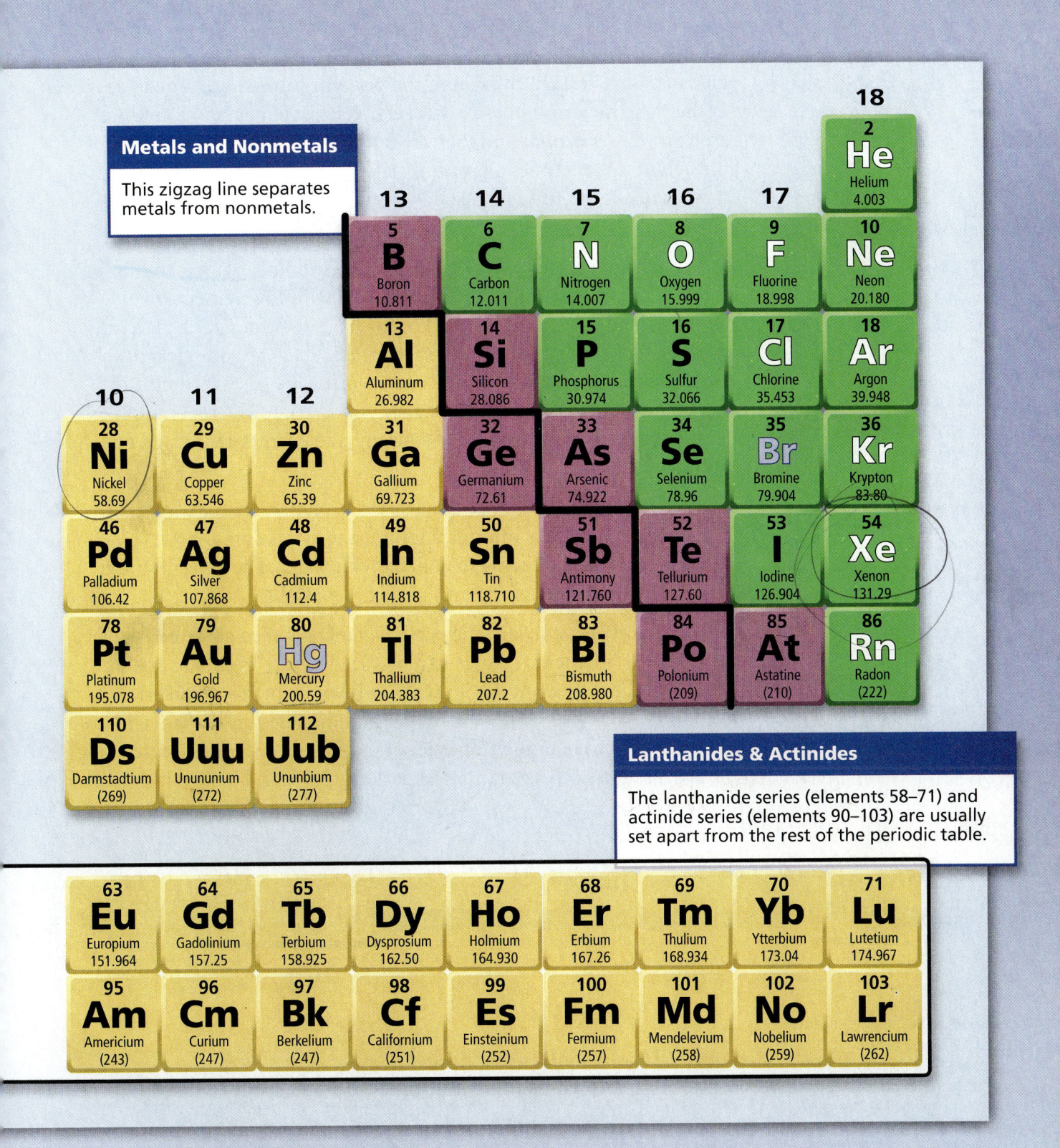

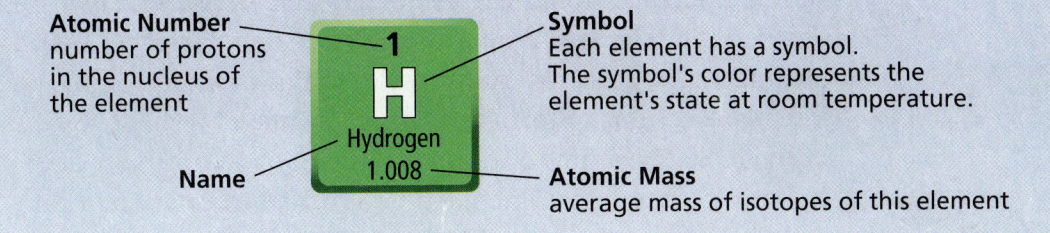

Metals and Nonmetals

This zigzag line separates metals from nonmetals.

18
2 **He** Helium 4.003

13	14	15	16	17
5 **B** Boron 10.811	6 **C** Carbon 12.011	7 **N** Nitrogen 14.007	8 **O** Oxygen 15.999	9 **F** Fluorine 18.998	10 **Ne** Neon 20.180
13 **Al** Aluminum 26.982	14 **Si** Silicon 28.086	15 **P** Phosphorus 30.974	16 **S** Sulfur 32.066	17 **Cl** Chlorine 35.453	18 **Ar** Argon 39.948

10	11	12
28 **Ni** Nickel 58.69	29 **Cu** Copper 63.546	30 **Zn** Zinc 65.39	31 **Ga** Gallium 69.723	32 **Ge** Germanium 72.61	33 **As** Arsenic 74.922	34 **Se** Selenium 78.96	35 **Br** Bromine 79.904	36 **Kr** Krypton 83.80
46 **Pd** Palladium 106.42	47 **Ag** Silver 107.868	48 **Cd** Cadmium 112.4	49 **In** Indium 114.818	50 **Sn** Tin 118.710	51 **Sb** Antimony 121.760	52 **Te** Tellurium 127.60	53 **I** Iodine 126.904	54 **Xe** Xenon 131.29
78 **Pt** Platinum 195.078	79 **Au** Gold 196.967	80 **Hg** Mercury 200.59	81 **Tl** Thallium 204.383	82 **Pb** Lead 207.2	83 **Bi** Bismuth 208.980	84 **Po** Polonium (209)	85 **At** Astatine (210)	86 **Rn** Radon (222)
110 **Ds** Darmstadtium (269)	111 **Uuu** Unununium (272)	112 **Uub** Ununbium (277)

Lanthanides & Actinides

The lanthanide series (elements 58–71) and actinide series (elements 90–103) are usually set apart from the rest of the periodic table.

| 63 **Eu** Europium 151.964 | 64 **Gd** Gadolinium 157.25 | 65 **Tb** Terbium 158.925 | 66 **Dy** Dysprosium 162.50 | 67 **Ho** Holmium 164.930 | 68 **Er** Erbium 167.26 | 69 **Tm** Thulium 168.934 | 70 **Yb** Ytterbium 173.04 | 71 **Lu** Lutetium 174.967 |
| 95 **Am** Americium (243) | 96 **Cm** Curium (247) | 97 **Bk** Berkelium (247) | 98 **Cf** Californium (251) | 99 **Es** Einsteinium (252) | 100 **Fm** Fermium (257) | 101 **Md** Mendelevium (258) | 102 **No** Nobelium (259) | 103 **Lr** Lawrencium (262) |

Atomic Number — number of protons in the nucleus of the element

Symbol — Each element has a symbol. The symbol's color represents the element's state at room temperature.

1 **H** Hydrogen 1.008

Name

Atomic Mass — average mass of isotopes of this element

Chapter 1: **Atomic Structure and the Periodic Table**

Groups and Periods

Elements in a vertical column of the periodic table show similarities in their chemical and physical properties. The elements in a column are known as a **group**, and they are labeled by a number at the top of the column. Sometimes a group is called a family of elements, because these elements seem to be related.

The illustration at the left shows Group 17, commonly referred to as the halogen group. Halogens tend to combine easily with many other elements and compounds, especially with the elements in Groups 1 and 2. Although the halogens have some similarities to one another, you can see from the periodic table that their physical properties are not the same. Fluorine and chlorine are gases, bromine is a liquid, and iodine and astatine are solids at room temperature. Remember that the members of a family of elements are related but not identical.

Metals like copper can be used to make containers for water. Some metals—such as lithium, sodium, and potassium—however, react violently if they come in contact with water. They are all in the same group, the vertical column labeled 1 on the table.

Each horizontal row in the periodic table is called a **period**. Properties of elements change in a predictable way from one end of a period to the other. In the illustration below, which shows Period 3, the elements on the far left are metals and the ones on the far right are nonmetals. The chemical properties of the elements show a progression; similar progressions appear in the periods above and below this one.

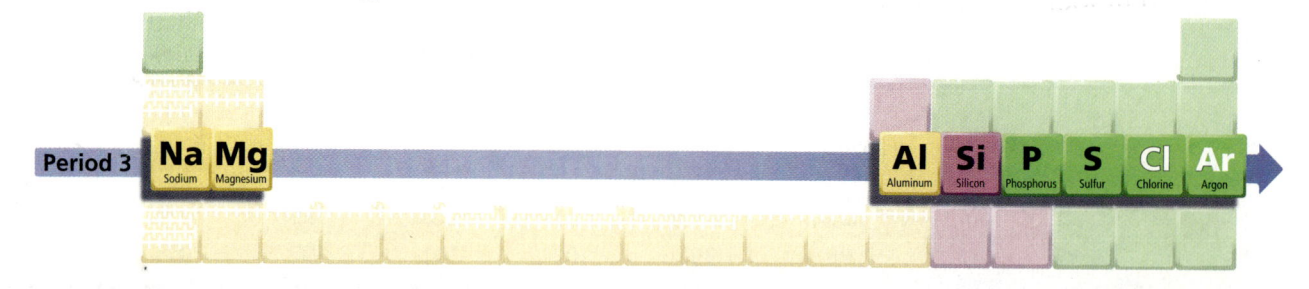

The elements in Group 17, the halogens, show many similarities.

Period 3 contains elements with a wide range of properties. Aluminum (Al) is used to make drink cans, while argon (Ar) is a gas used in light bulbs.

Trends in the Periodic Table

Because the periodic table organizes elements by properties, an element's position in the table can give information about the element. Remember that atoms form ions by gaining or losing electrons. Atoms of elements on the left side of the table form positive ions easily. For example, Group 1 atoms lose an electron to form ions with one positive charge (1+). Atoms of the elements in Group 2, likewise, can lose two electrons to form ions with a charge of 2+. At the other side of the table, the atoms of elements in Group 18 normally do not form ions at all. Atoms of elements in Group 17, however, often gain one electron to form a negative ion (1–). Similarly, the atoms of elements in Group 16 can gain two electrons to form a 2– ion. The atoms of the elements in Groups 3 to 12 all form positive ions, but the charge can vary.

Other information about atoms can be determined by their position in the table. The illustration to the right shows how the sizes of atoms vary across periods and within groups. An atom's size is important because it affects how the atom will react with another atom.

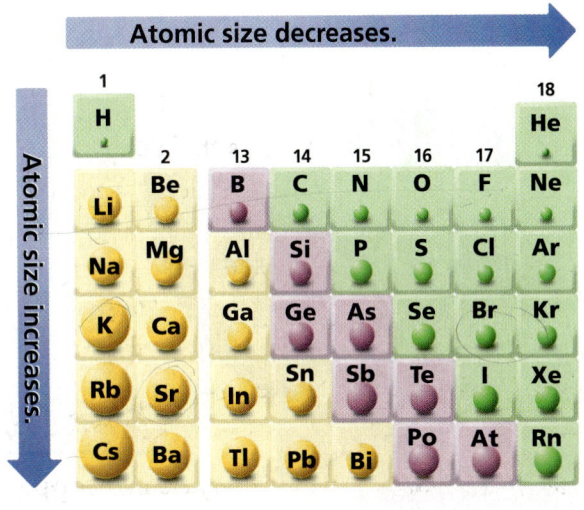

The densities of elements also follow a pattern. Density generally increases from the top of a group to the bottom. Within a period, however, the elements at the left and right sides of the table are the least dense, and the elements in the middle are the most dense. The element osmium (Os) has the highest known density, and it is located at the center of the table.

Chemists cannot predict the exact size or density of an atom of one element based on that of another. These trends, nonetheless, are a valuable tool in predicting the properties of different substances. The fact that the trends appeared after the periodic table was organized by atomic number was a victory for all of the scientists like Mendeleev who went looking for them all those years before.

Atomic size is one property that changes in a predictable way across, up, and down the periodic table.

CHECK YOUR READING What are some properties that can be related to position on the periodic table?

1.2 Review

KEY CONCEPTS

1. How is the modern periodic table organized?
2. What information about an atom's properties can you read from the periodic table?
3. How are the relationships of elements in a group different from the relationships of elements in a period?

CRITICAL THINKING

4. **Infer** Would you expect strontium (Sr) to be more like potassium (K) or bromine (Br)? Why?
5. **Predict** Barium (Ba) is in Group 2. Recall that atoms in Group 1 lose one electron to form ions with a 1+ charge. What type of ion does barium form?

CHALLENGE

6. **Analyze** Explain how chemists can state with certainty that no one will discover an element between sulfur (S) and chlorine (Cl).

Chapter 1: **Atomic Structure and the Periodic Table** 23 B

CHAPTER INVESTIGATION

Modeling Atomic Masses

OVERVIEW AND PURPOSE Atoms are extremely small. They are so small, in fact, that a single drop of water contains more atoms than you could count in a lifetime! Measuring the masses of atoms to discover the patterns in the periodic table was not an easy task for scientists in the past. This investigation will give you some sense of how scientists determined the mass of atoms. You will
- compare the masses of different film can "atoms"
- predict the number of washers in each film can "atom"

Procedure

1. Create a data table similar to the one shown on the sample notebook page.

2. Find the mass of one empty film can. Record this mass in the second row of the table.

3. Collect the four film cans labeled A, B, C, and D in advance by your teacher. Each can contains a different number of washers and represents a different atom. The washers represent the protons and neutrons in an atom's nucleus.

4. Measure the mass of each of the four film cans. Record the masses of the film can atoms in the first row of your data table.

5. Subtract the mass of an empty film can from the mass of each film can atom. Record the differences in the correct spaces in your data table. These masses represent the masses of the washers in your film can atoms. Think of these masses as the masses of the nuclei.

6. Divide the mass of the washers in can B by the mass of the washers in can A. Record the value under the mass of the washers in can B.

MATERIALS
- empty film can
- balance
- 4 filled film cans

24 Unit: Chemical Interactions

7. Repeat step 6 for film can atoms A, C, and D. Record the value under the masses of the washers in each can.

8. Round the values you obtained in steps 6 and 7 to the nearest whole number. Record the rounded figures in the next row of the table.

Observe and Analyze *Write It Up*

1. **RECORD OBSERVATIONS** Be sure your data table and calculations are complete. Double-check your arithmetic.

2. **ANALYZE DATA** Examine your data table. Do you notice any patterns in how the masses increase? Given that all the washers in the film can atoms have identical masses, what might the ratio of the mass of the washers to the smallest mass tell you?

3. **PREDICT** Assume there is only one washer in can A. Estimate the number of washers in the other cans and record your estimates in the last row of the table.

4. **GRAPH DATA** On a sheet of graph paper, plot the masses (in grams) of the washers in the film can atoms on the y-axis and the number of washers in each can on the x-axis. Connect the points on the graph.

5. **INTERPRET DATA** Compare the masses of your film can atoms with the masses of the first four atoms on the periodic table. Which represents which?

Conclude *Write It Up*

1. **IDENTIFY LIMITS** What can't this activity tell you about the identity of your film can atoms? (Hint: Protons and neutrons in real atoms have about the same mass.)

2. **INFER** Hydrogen has only a single proton in its nucleus. If your film can atoms represent the first four elements in the periodic table, what are the numbers of protons and neutrons in each atom?

3. **APPLY** Single atoms are far too small to place on a balance. How do you think scientists determine the masses of real atoms?

INVESTIGATE Further

CHALLENGE Use a periodic table to find the masses of the next two atoms (boron and carbon). How many washers would you need to make film can atom models for each?

Modeling Atomic Masses

Observe and Analyze

Table 1. Masses of Film Can Atoms

	A	B	C	D
Mass of film can atom (g)				
Mass of empty film can (g)				
Mass of washers (g)				
Mass of washers divided by can A				
Value rounded to nearest whole number				
Estimated number of washers in each can				

Atomic Structure and the Periodic Table 25 B

KEY CONCEPT
1.3 The periodic table is a map of the elements.

BEFORE, you learned
- The periodic table is organized into groups of elements with similar characteristics
- The periodic table organizes elements according to their properties

NOW, you will learn
- How elements are classified as metals, nonmetals, and metalloids
- About different groups of elements
- About radioactive elements

VOCABULARY
reactive p. 26
metal p. 27
nonmetal p. 29
metalloid p. 30
radioactivity p. 30
half-life p. 32

THINK ABOUT

How are elements different?

The photograph shows common uses of the elements copper, aluminum, and argon: copper in a penny, aluminum in a pie plate, and argon in a light bulb. Each element is located in a different part of the periodic table, and each has a very different use. Find these elements on the periodic table. What other elements are near these?

The periodic table has distinct regions.

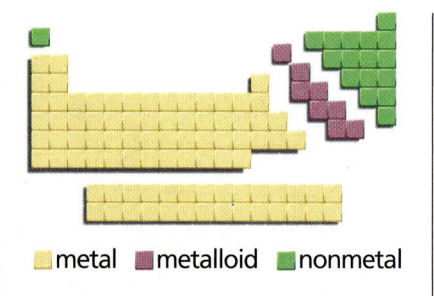

The periodic table is a kind of map of the elements. Just as a country's location on the globe gives you information about its climate, an atom's position on the periodic table indicates the properties of its element. The periodic table has three main regions—metals on the left, nonmetals (except hydrogen) on the right, and metalloids in between. The periodic table on pages 20 and 21 indicates these regions with different colors. A yellow box indicates a metal; green, a nonmetal; and purple, a metalloid.

metal metalloid nonmetal

An element's position in the table also indicates how reactive it is. The term **reactive** indicates how likely an element is to undergo a chemical change. Most elements are somewhat reactive and combine with other materials. The atoms of the elements in Groups 1 and 17 are the most reactive. The elements of Group 18 are the least reactive of all the elements.

CHECK YOUR READING How does the periodic table resemble a map?

26 Unit: Chemical Interactions

Most elements are metals.

When you look at the periodic table, it is obvious from the color that most of the elements are metals. In general, **metals** are elements that conduct electricity and heat well and have a shiny appearance. Metals can be shaped easily by pounding, bending, or being drawn into a long wire. Except for mercury, which is a liquid, metals are solids at room temperature.

Sodium is a metal that is so soft it can be cut with a knife at room temperature.

You probably can name many uses for the metal **copper**.

Aluminum is often used for devices that must be strong and light.

Reactive Metals

The metals in Group 1 of the periodic table, the alkali metals, are very reactive. Sodium and potassium are often stored in oil to keep them away from air. When exposed to air, these elements react rapidly with oxygen and water vapor. The ions of these metals, Na^+ and K^+, are important for life, and play an essential role in the functioning of living cells.

The metals in Group 2, the alkaline earth metals, are less reactive than the alkali metals. They are still more reactive than most other metals, however. Calcium ions are an essential part of your diet. Your bones and teeth contain calcium ions. Magnesium is a light, inexpensive metal that is often combined with other metals when a lightweight material is needed, such as for airplane frames.

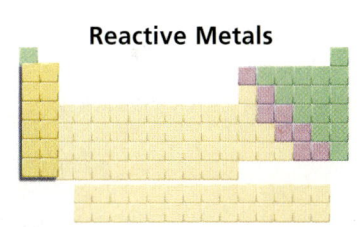

Transition Metals

The elements in Groups 3–12 are called the transition metals. Among these metals are some of the earliest known elements, such as copper, gold, silver, and iron. Transition metals are generally less reactive than most other metals. Because gold and silver are easily shaped and do not react easily, they have been used for thousands of years to make jewelry and coins. Ancient artifacts made from transition metals can be found in many museums and remain relatively unchanged since the time they were made. Today, dimes and quarters are made of copper and nickel, and pennies are made of zinc with a coating of copper. Transition metal ions even are found in the foods you eat.

Chapter 1: **Atomic Structure and the Periodic Table** 27

The properties of the transition metals make them particularly important to industry. Iron is the main part of steel, a material used for bridges and buildings. Most electric wires and many other electrical devices are made of copper. Copper is also used to make water pipes. Indeed, it would be hard to think of an industry that doesn't make use of transition metals.

Although other transition metals may be less familiar, many of them are important for modern technology. The tiny coil of wire inside incandescent light bulbs is made of tungsten. Platinum is in the catalytic converters that reduce pollution from automobile engines.

For many applications, two or more metals are combined to form an alloy. Alloys can be stronger, less likely to corrode, or easier to shape than pure metals. Steel, which is stronger than the pure iron it contains, often includes other transition metals, such as nickel, chromium, or manganese. Brass, an alloy of copper and zinc, is stronger than either metal alone. Jewelry is often made of an alloy of silver and copper, which is stronger than pure silver.

Rare Earth Elements

Rare Earth Elements

The rare earth elements are the elements in the top row of the two rows of metals that are usually shown outside the main body of the periodic table. Taking these elements out of the main body of the table makes the table more compact. The rare earth elements are often referred to as lanthanides because they follow the element lanthanum (La) on the table. They are called rare earth elements because scientists once thought that these elements were available only in tiny amounts in Earth's crust. As mining methods improved, scientists learned that the rare earths were actually not so rare at all—only hard to isolate in pure form.

More and more uses are being found for the rare earth elements. Europium (Eu), for example, is used as a coating for some television tubes. Praseodymium (Pr) provides a protective coating against harmful radiation in the welder's helmet in the photograph on the right.

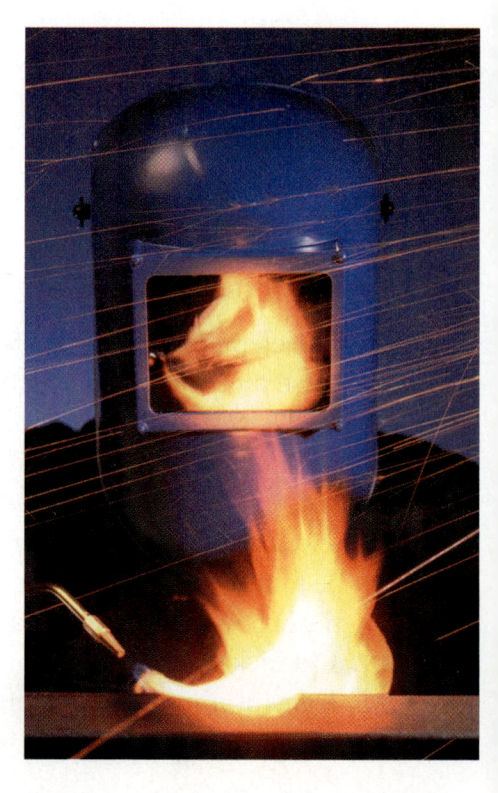

Nonmetals and metalloids have a wide range of properties.

The elements to the right side of the periodic table are called **nonmetals.** As the name implies, the properties of nonmetals tend to be the opposite of those of metals. The properties of nonmetals also tend to vary more from element to element than the properties of the metals do. Many of them are gases at room temperature, and one—bromine—is a liquid. The solid nonmetals often have dull surfaces and cannot be shaped by hammering or drawing into wires. Nonmetals are generally poor conductors of heat and electric current.

The main components of the air that you breathe are the nonmetal elements nitrogen and oxygen. Nitrogen is a fairly unreactive element, but oxygen reacts easily to form compounds with many other elements. Burning and rusting are two familiar types of reactions involving oxygen. Compounds containing carbon are essential to living things. Two forms of the element carbon are graphite, which is a soft, slippery black material, and diamond, a hard crystal. Sulfur is a bright yellow powder that can be mined from deposits of the pure element.

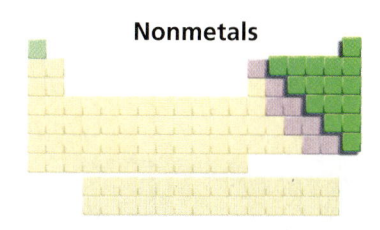

Halogens

The elements in Group 17 are commonly known as halogens, from Greek words meaning "forming salts." Halogens are very reactive nonmetals that easily form compounds called salts with many metals. Because they are so reactive, halogens are often used to kill harmful microorganisms. For example, the halogen chlorine is used to clean drinking water and to prevent the growth of algae in swimming pools. Solutions containing iodine are often used in hospitals and doctors' offices to kill germs on skin.

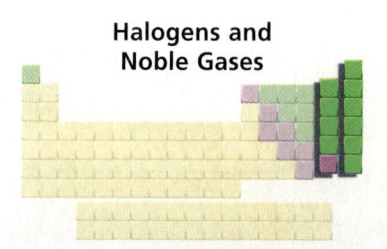

Noble Gases

Group 18 elements are called the noble, or inert, gases because they almost never react with other elements. Argon gas makes up about one percent of the atmosphere. The other noble gases are found in the atmosphere in smaller amounts. Colorful lights, such as those in the photograph on the right, are made by passing an electric current through tubes filled with neon, krypton, xenon, or argon gas. Argon gas also is placed in tungsten filament light bulbs, because it will not react with the hot filament.

CHECK YOUR READING Where on Earth can you find noble gases?

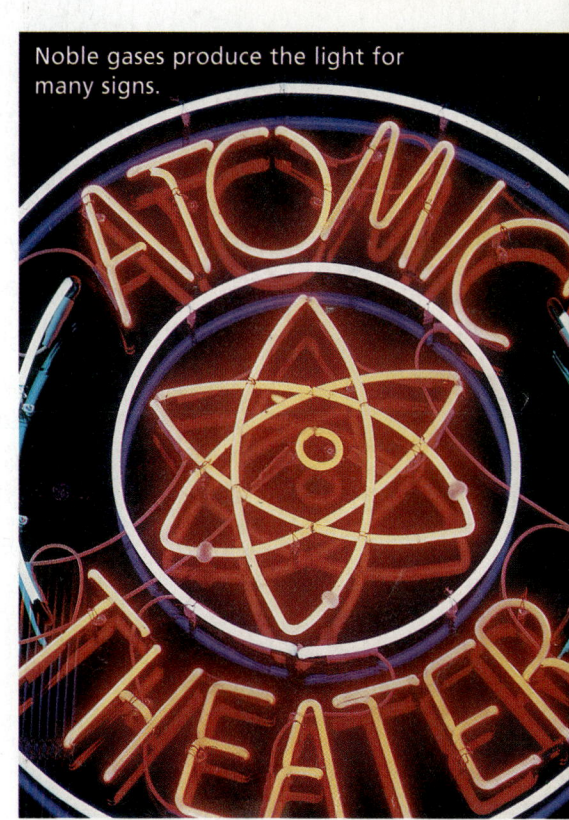

Noble gases produce the light for many signs.

Chapter 1: **Atomic Structure and the Periodic Table** 29

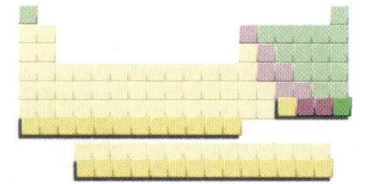

Metalloids

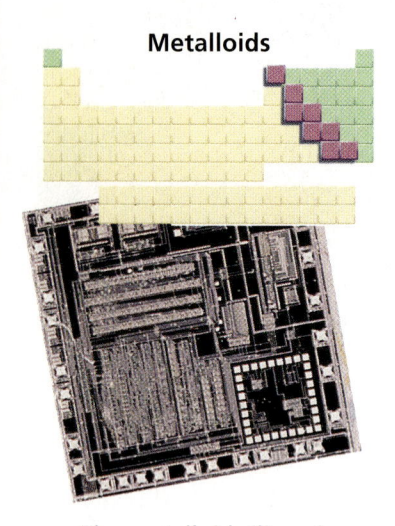

Metalloids are elements that have properties of both metals and nonmetals. In the periodic table, they lie on either side of a zigzag line separating metals from nonmetals. The most common metalloid is silicon. Silicon atoms are the second most common atoms in Earth's crust.

Metalloids often make up the semiconductors found in electronic devices. Semiconductors are special materials that conduct electricity under some conditions and not under others. Silicon, gallium, and germanium are three semiconductors used in computer chips.

The metalloid silicon is found in sand and in computer microchips.

Some atoms can change their identity.

The identity of an element is determined by the number of protons in its nucleus. Chemical changes do not affect the nucleus, so chemical changes don't change one type of atom into another. There are, however, conditions under which the number of protons in a nucleus can change and so change the identity of an atom.

Recall that the nucleus of an atom contains protons and neutrons. Attractive forces between protons and neutrons hold the nucleus together even though protons repel one another. We say an atomic nucleus is stable when these attractive forces keep it together.

Each element has isotopes with different numbers of neutrons. The stability of a nucleus depends on the right balance of protons and neutrons. If there are too few or too many neutrons, the nucleus may become unstable. When this happens, particles are produced from the nucleus of the atom to restore the balance. This change is accompanied by a release of energy.

If the production of particles changes the number of protons, the atom is transformed into an atom of a different element. In the early 1900s, physicist Marie Curie named the process by which atoms produce energy and particles **radioactivity**. Curie was the first person to isolate polonium and radium, two radioactive elements.

An isotope is radioactive if the nucleus has too many or too few neutrons. Most elements have radioactive isotopes, although these isotopes are rare for small atoms. For the heaviest of elements—those beyond bismuth (Bi)—all of the isotopes are radioactive.

Scientists study radioactivity with a device called a Geiger counter. The Geiger counter detects the particles from the breakup of the atomic nucleus with audible clicks. More clicks indicate that more particles are being produced.

CHECK YOUR READING How can an atom of one element change into an atom of a different element?

Uses of Radioactivity in Medicine

The radiation produced from unstable nuclei is used in hospitals to diagnose and treat patients. Some forms of radiation from nuclei are used to destroy harmful tumors inside a person's body without performing an operation. Another medical use of radiation is to monitor the activity of certain organs in the body. A patient is injected with a solution containing a radioactive isotope. Isotopes of a given atom move through the body in the same way whether or not they are radioactive. Doctors detect the particles produced by the radioactive isotopes to determine where and how the body is using the substance.

Although radiation has its benefits, in large doses it is harmful to living things and should be avoided. Radiation can damage or kill cells, and the energy from its particles can burn the skin. Prolonged exposure to radiation has been linked to cancer and other health problems.

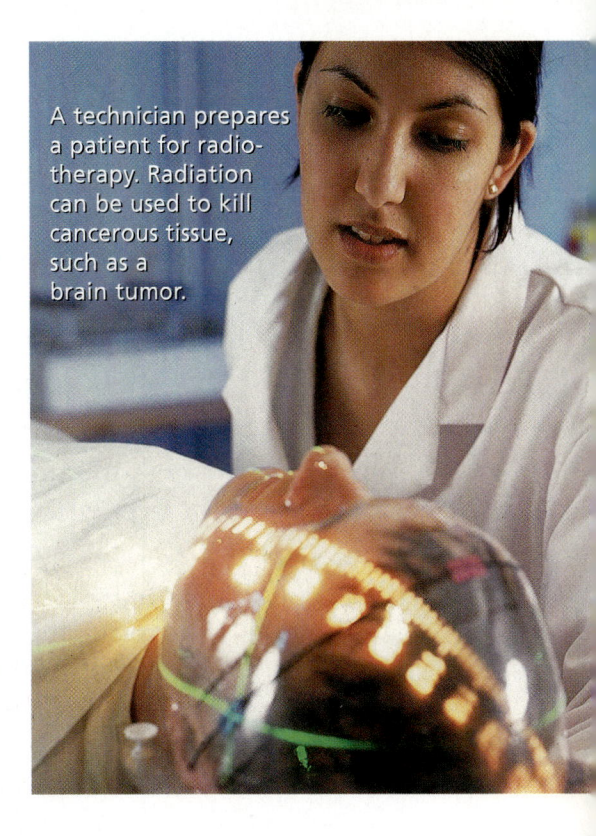

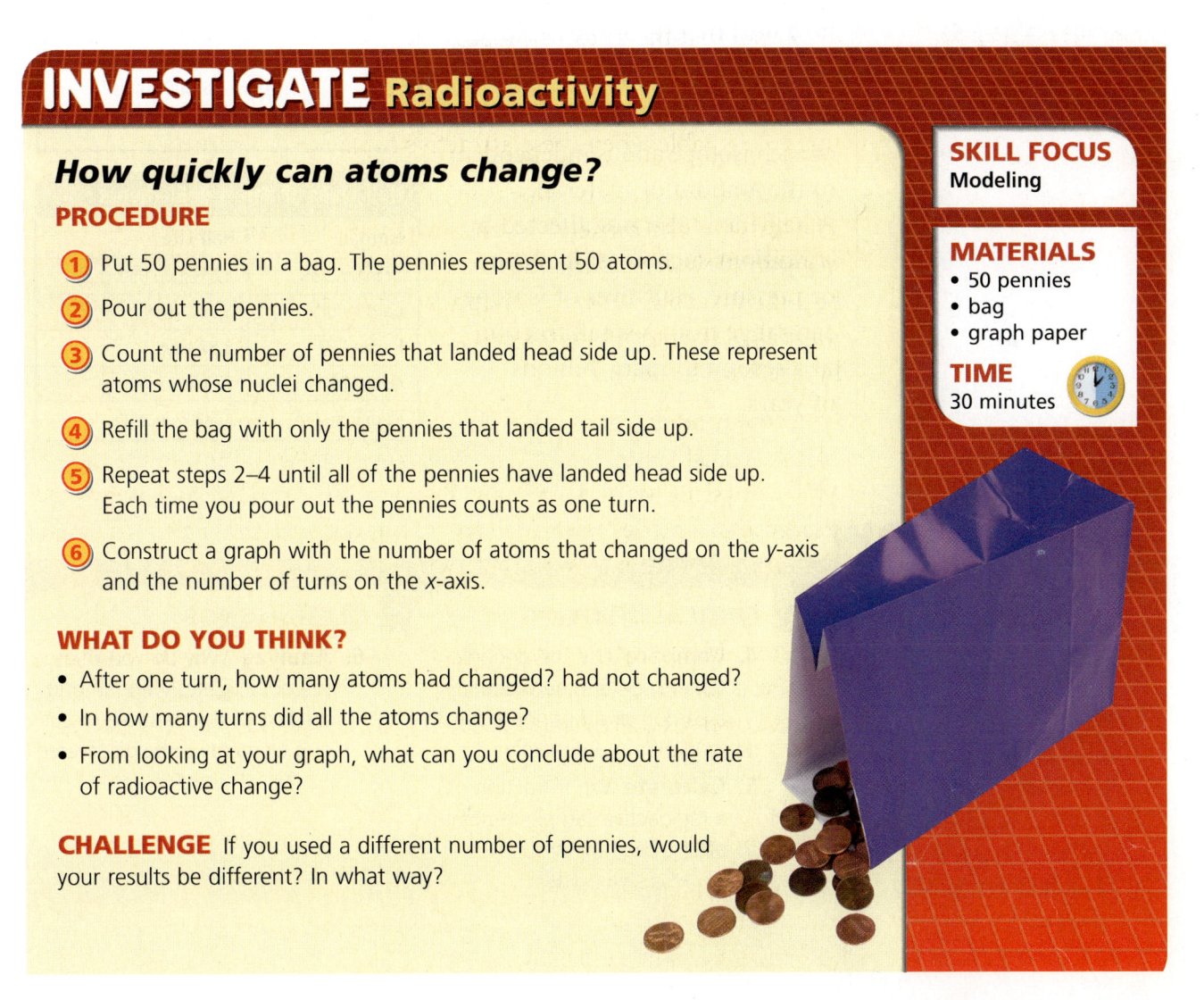

A technician prepares a patient for radiotherapy. Radiation can be used to kill cancerous tissue, such as a brain tumor.

INVESTIGATE Radioactivity

How quickly can atoms change?

PROCEDURE

1. Put 50 pennies in a bag. The pennies represent 50 atoms.
2. Pour out the pennies.
3. Count the number of pennies that landed head side up. These represent atoms whose nuclei changed.
4. Refill the bag with only the pennies that landed tail side up.
5. Repeat steps 2–4 until all of the pennies have landed head side up. Each time you pour out the pennies counts as one turn.
6. Construct a graph with the number of atoms that changed on the y-axis and the number of turns on the x-axis.

WHAT DO YOU THINK?

- After one turn, how many atoms had changed? had not changed?
- In how many turns did all the atoms change?
- From looking at your graph, what can you conclude about the rate of radioactive change?

CHALLENGE If you used a different number of pennies, would your results be different? In what way?

SKILL FOCUS
Modeling

MATERIALS
- 50 pennies
- bag
- graph paper

TIME
30 minutes

Chapter 1: **Atomic Structure and the Periodic Table** 31

Radioactive Decay

Watch how a radioactive element decays over time.

Radioactive atoms produce energy and particles from their nuclei. The identity of these atoms changes because the number of protons changes. This process is known as radioactive decay. Over time, all of the atoms of a radioactive isotope will change into atoms of another element.

Radioactive decay occurs at a steady rate that is characteristic of the particular isotope. The amount of time that it takes for one-half of the atoms in a particular sample to decay is called the **half-life** of the isotope. For example, if you had 1000 atoms of a radioactive isotope with a half-life of 1 year, 500 of the atoms would change into another element over the course of a year. In the next year, 250 more atoms would decay. The illustration to the right shows how the amount of the original isotope would decrease over time.

The half-life is a characteristic of each isotope and is independent of the amount of material. A half-life is also not affected by conditions such as temperature or pressure. Half-lives of isotopes can range from a small fraction of a second to many billions of years.

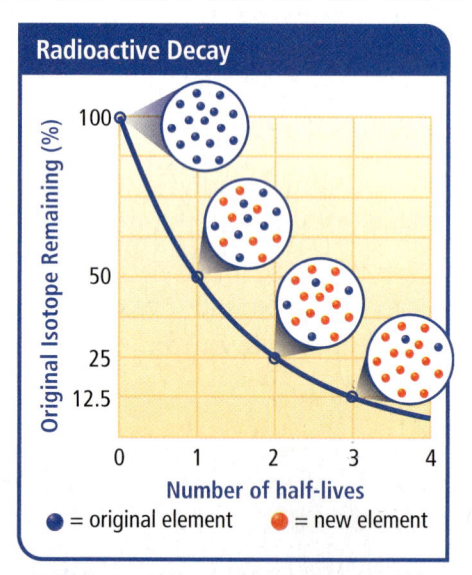

Radioactive Decay

● = original element   ● = new element

Half-Lives of Selected Elements

Isotope	Half-Life
Uranium-238	4,510,000,000 years
Carbon-14	5,730 years
Radon-222	3.82 days
Lead-214	27 minutes
Polonium-214	.00016 seconds

1.3 Review

KEY CONCEPTS

1. What are the three main classes of elements in the periodic table?
2. What are the major characteristics of metals?
3. How can an atom of one element change to an atom of another element?

CRITICAL THINKING

4. **Compare** Use the periodic table to determine whether a carbon or a fluorine atom would be more reactive.
5. **Calculate** What fraction of a radioactive sample remains after three half-lives?

CHALLENGE

6. **Analyze** Why do you think the noble gases were among the last of the naturally occurring elements to be discovered?

MATH in SCIENCE

SKILL: USING SCIENTIFIC NOTATION

MATH TUTORIAL
CLASSZONE.COM
Click on Math Tutorial for more help with scientific notation.

Numbers with Many Zeros

Semiconductor devices are at the heart of the modern personal computer. Today tiny chips can contain more than 42,000,000 connections and perform about 3,000,000,000 calculations per second. Computers have little problem working with such large numbers. Scientists, however, use a scientific notation as a shorthand way to write large numbers. Scientific notation expresses a very large or very small number as the product of a number between 1 and 10 and a power of 10.

Example

Large Number How would you express the number 6,400,000,000—the approximate population of the world—in scientific notation?

(1) Look at the number and count how many spaces you would need to move the decimal point to get a number between 1 and 10.

6, 4 0 0, 0 0 0, 0 0 0
  9 8 7 6 5 4 3 2 1

(2) Place the decimal point in the space and multiply the number by the appropriate power of 10. The power of 10 will be equivalent to the number of spaces you moved the decimal point.

ANSWER 6.4×10^9

Small Number How would you express 0.0000023 in scientific notation?

(1) Count the number of places you need to move the decimal point to get a number between 1 and 10. This time you move the decimal point to the right, not the left.

0. 0 0 0 0 0 2 3
  1 2 3 4 5 6

(2) The power of 10 you need to multiply this number by is still equal to the number of places you moved the decimal point. Place a negative sign in front of it to indicate that you moved the decimal point to the right.

ANSWER 2.3×10^{-6}

Answer the following questions.

1. Express the following numbers in scientific notation:
   (a) 75,000   (b) 54,000,000,000   (c) 0.0000064

2. Express these numbers in decimal form:
   (a) 6.0×10^{24} (b) 7.4×10^{22} (c) 5.7×10^{-10}

CHALLENGE What is 2.2×10^{22} subtracted from 4.6×10^{22}?

Chips like the one shown here can be smaller than a fingernail but contain millions of independent components.

Chapter 1: **Atomic Structure and the Periodic Table** 33 **B**

Chapter Review

the BIG idea
A substance's atomic structure determines its physical and chemical properties.

CONTENT REVIEW
CLASSZONE.COM

KEY CONCEPTS SUMMARY

1.1 Atoms are the smallest form of elements.
- All matter is made of the atoms of approximately 100 elements.
- Atoms are made of protons, neutrons, and electrons.
- Different elements are made of different atoms.
- Atoms form ions by gaining or losing electrons.

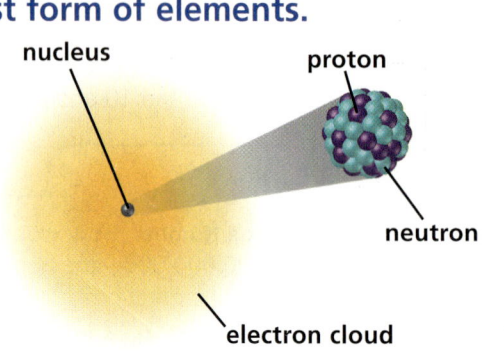

VOCABULARY
proton p. 11
neutron p. 11
nucleus p. 11
electron p. 11
atomic number p. 12
atomic mass number p. 12
isotope p. 12
ion p. 14

1.2 Elements make up the periodic table.
- Elements can be organized by similarities.
- The periodic table organizes the atoms of the elements by properties and atomic number.

Groups of elements have similar properties.
Elements in a period have varying properties.

VOCABULARY
atomic mass p. 17
periodic table p. 18
group p. 22
period p. 22

1.3 The periodic table is a map of the elements.
- The periodic table has distinct regions.
- Most elements are metals.
- Nonmetals and metalloids have a wide range of properties.
- Some atoms can change their identity through radioactive decay.

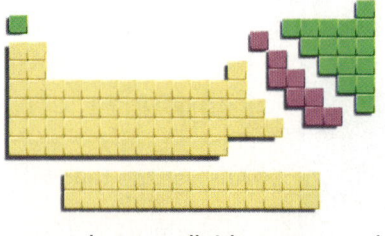

■ metal ■ metalloid ■ nonmetal

VOCABULARY
reactive p. 26
metal p. 27
nonmetal p. 29
metalloid p. 30
radioactivity p. 30
half-life p. 32

34 Unit: Chemical Interactions

Reviewing Vocabulary

Describe how the vocabulary terms in the following pairs are related to each other. Explain the relationship in a one- or two-sentence answer. Underline each vocabulary term in your answer.

1. isotope, nucleus
2. atomic mass, atomic number
3. electron, proton
4. atomic number, atomic mass number
5. group, period
6. metals, nonmetals
7. radioactivity, half-life

Reviewing Key Concepts

Multiple Choice Choose the letter of the best answer.

8. The central part of an atom is called the
   a. electron   c. proton
   b. nucleus   d. neutron

9. The electric charge on a proton is
   a. positive   c. neutral
   b. negative   d. changing

10. The number of protons in the nucleus is the
    a. atomic mass   c. atomic number
    b. isotope   d. half-life

11. Nitrogen has atomic number 7. An isotope of nitrogen containing seven neutrons would be
    a. nitrogen-13   c. nitrogen-15
    b. nitrogen-14   d. nitrogen-16

12. How does the size of a negative ion compare to the size of the atom that formed it?
    a. It's smaller.
    b. It's larger.
    c. It's the same size.
    d. It varies.

13. The modern periodic table is organized by
    a. size of atom
    b. atomic mass
    c. number of neutrons
    d. atomic number

14. Elements in a group have
    a. a wide range of chemical properties
    b. the same atomic radius
    c. similar chemical properties
    d. the same number of protons

15. Elements in a period have
    a. a wide range of chemical properties
    b. the same atomic radius
    c. similar chemical properties
    d. the same number of protons

16. From left to right in a period, the size of atoms
    a. increases   c. remains the same
    b. decreases   d. shows no pattern

17. The elements in Group 1 of the periodic table are commonly called the
    a. alkali metals   c. alkaline earth metals
    b. transition metals   d. rare earth metals

18. The isotope nitrogen-13 has a half-life of 10 minutes. If you start with 40 grams of this isotope, how many grams will you have left after 20 minutes?
    a. 10   c. 20
    b. 15   d. 30

Short Answer Write a short answer to each question. You may need to consult a periodic table.

19. Rubidium forms the positive ion Rb$^+$. Is this ion larger or smaller than the neutral atom? Explain.

20. How can you find the number of neutrons in the isotope nitrogen-16?

21. Explain how density varies across and up and down the periodic table.

22. Place these elements in order from least reactive to most reactive: nickel (Ni), xenon (Xe), lithium (Li). How did you determine the order?

Chapter 1: **Atomic Structure and the Periodic Table** 35

Thinking Critically

The table below lists some properties of six elements. Use the information and your knowledge of the properties of elements to answer the next three questions.

Element	Appearance	Density (g/cm³)	Conducts Electricity
A	dark purple crystals	4.93	no
B	shiny silvery solid	0.97	yes
C	shiny silvery solid	22.65	yes
D	yellow powder	2.07	no
E	shiny gray solid	5.32	semiconductor
F	shiny bluish solid	8.91	yes

23. **ANALYZE** Based on the listed properties, identify each of the elements as a metal, nonmetal, or metalloid.

24. **APPLY** Which would weigh more: a cube of element A or a same-sized cube of element D?

25. **HYPOTHESIZE** Which element(s) do you think you might find in electronic devices? Why?

26. **HYPOTHESIZE** The thyroid gland, located in your throat, secretes hormones. In 1924 iodine was added to table salt. As more and more Americans used iodized salt, the number of cases of thyroid diseases decreased. Write a hypothesis that explains the observed decrease in thyroid-related diseases.

27. **INFER** How does the size of a beryllium (Be) atom compare with the size of an oxygen (O) atom?

28. **PREDICT** Although noble gases do not naturally react with other elements, xenon and krypton have been made to react with halogens such as chlorine in laboratories. Why are the halogens most likely to react with the noble gases?

Below is an element square from the periodic table. Use it to answer the next two questions.

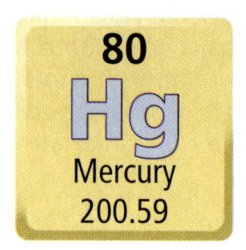

80
Hg
Mercury
200.59

29. **CALCULATE** One of the more common isotopes of mercury is mercury-200. How many protons and neutrons are in the nucleus of mercury-200?

30. **INFER** Cadmium occupies the square directly above mercury on the periodic table. Is a cadmium atom larger or smaller than a mercury atom?

31. **CALCULATE** An isotope has a half-life of 40 minutes. How much of a 100-gram sample would remain unchanged after two hours?

32. **APPLY** When a uranium atom with 92 protons and 146 neutrons undergoes radioactive decay, it produces a particle that consists of two protons and two neutrons from its nucleus. Into which element is the uranium atom transformed?

the BIG idea

33. **ANALYZE** Look again at the photograph on pages 6–7. Answer the question again, using what you have learned in the chapter.

34. **DRAW CONCLUSIONS** Suppose you've been given the ability to take apart and assemble atoms. How could you turn lead into gold?

35. **ANALYZE** Explain how the structure of an atom determines its place in the periodic table.

UNIT PROJECTS

If you are doing a unit project, make a folder for your project. Include in your folder a list of the resources you will need, the date on which the project is due, and a schedule to track your progress. Begin gathering data.

Standardized Test Practice

Interpreting Tables

The table below shows part of the periodic table of elements.

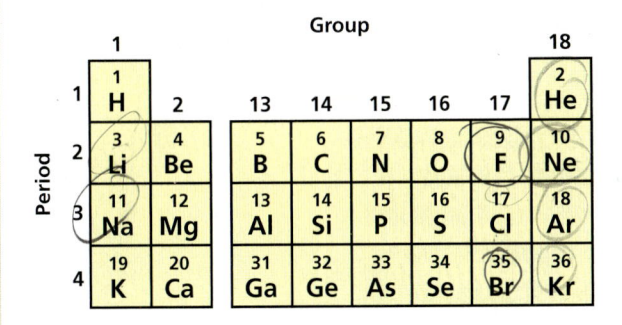

	Group 1	2	13	14	15	16	17	18
Period 1	1 H							2 He
Period 2	3 Li	4 Be	5 B	6 C	7 N	8 O	9 F	10 Ne
Period 3	11 Na	12 Mg	13 Al	14 Si	15 P	16 S	17 Cl	18 Ar
Period 4	19 K	20 Ca	31 Ga	32 Ge	33 As	34 Se	35 Br	36 Kr

Answer the questions based on the information given in the table.

1. What does the number above the symbol for each element represent?
   a. Its number of isotopes
   b. Its atomic number
   c. Its number of neutrons
   d. Its atomic mass

2. The atom of what element is in Period 4, Group 13?
   a. Na
   b. Ga
   c. Al
   d. K

3. What do the elements on the far right of the table (He, Ne, Ar, and Kr) have in common?
   a. They do not generally react with other elements.
   b. They are in liquids under normal conditions.
   c. They are metals that rust easily.
   d. They are very reactive gases.

4. How many electrons does a neutral chlorine (Cl) atom contain?
   a. 16
   b. 17
   c. 18
   d. 19

5. If a sodium (Na) atom loses one electron to form a positive ion, how many electrons would lithium (Li) lose to form a positive ion?
   a. 0
   b. 1
   c. 2
   d. 3

6. If a fluorine (F) atom gains one electron to form a negative ion, how many electrons would bromine (Br) gain to form a negative ion?
   a. 0
   b. 1
   c. 2
   d. 3

Extended Response

Answer the following two questions in detail. Include some of the terms shown in the word box at right. Underline each term you use in your answer.

| electron | nucleus | proton |
| isotope | neutron | radioactivity |

7. Democritus was an ancient Greek philosopher who claimed that all matter was made of tiny particles he called atoms. Democritus said that all atoms were made of the same material. The objects of the world differed because each was made of atoms of different sizes and shapes. How does the modern view of atoms differ from this ancient view? How is it similar?

8. Half-life is a measure of the time it takes half of the radioactive atoms in a substance to decay into other atoms. If you know how much radioactive material an object had to begin with, how could you use half-life to determine its age now?

CHAPTER 2
Chemical Bonds and Compounds

the BIG idea

The properties of compounds depend on their atoms and chemical bonds.

How do these skydivers stay together? How is this similar to the way atoms stay together?

Key Concepts

SECTION 2.1
Elements combine to form compounds.
Learn the difference between elements and compounds. Learn how to write and name chemical compounds.

SECTION 2.2
Chemical bonds hold compounds together.
Learn about the different types of chemical bonds.

SECTION 2.3
Substances' properties depend on their bonds.
Learn how bonds give compounds certain properties.

Internet Preview

CLASSZONE.COM

Chapter 2 online resources: Content Review, two Visualizations, two Resource Centers, Math Tutorial, Test Practice

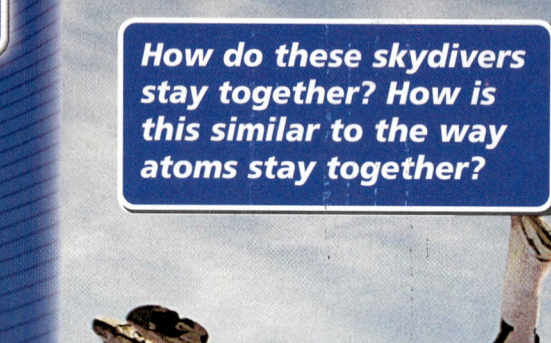

EXPLORE the BIG idea

Mixing It Up

Get some red and yellow modeling compound. Make three red and two yellow balls, each about the diameter of a nickel. Blend one red and one yellow ball together. Blend one yellow and two red balls together.

Observe and Think How different do your combinations look from the original? from each other?

The Shape of Things

Pour some salt onto dark paper. Look at the grains through a hand lens. Try to observe a single grain.

Observe and Think What do you notice about the salt grains? What do you think might affect the way the grains look?

Internet Activity: Bonding

Go to **ClassZone.com** and watch the animation showing ionic and covalent bonding. Observe the differences in the two types of bonding.

Observe and Think What's the difference between an ionic and a covalent bond? Explain how covalent bonding can have different characteristics.

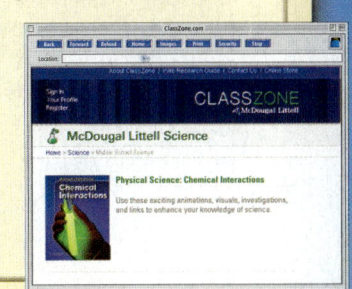

NSTA scilinks.org
SCILINKS
Compounds Code: MDL023

Chapter 2: **Chemical Bonds and Compounds** 39 **B**

CHAPTER 2
Getting Ready to Learn

CONCEPT REVIEW

- Electrons occupy a cloud around an atom's nucleus.
- Atoms form ions by losing or gaining electrons.

VOCABULARY REVIEW

electron p. 11

element *See Glossary.*

CONTENT REVIEW
CLASSZONE.COM
Review concepts and vocabulary.

TAKING NOTES

MAIN IDEA AND DETAIL NOTES

Make a two-column chart. Write the main ideas, such as those in the blue headings, in the column on the left. Write details about each of those main ideas in the column on the right.

VOCABULARY STRATEGY

Place each vocabulary term at the center of a **description wheel** diagram. Write some words describing it on the spokes.

See the Note-Taking Handbook on pages R45–R51.

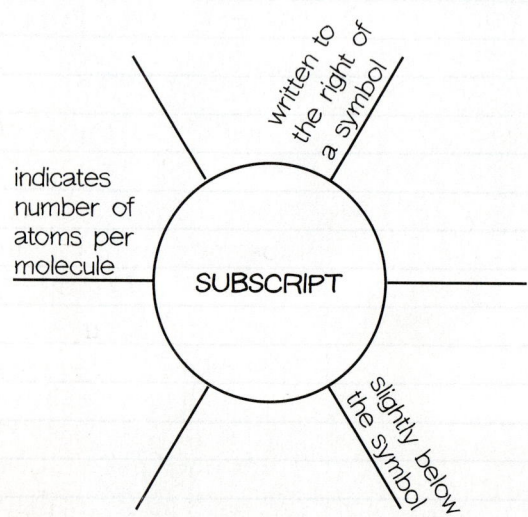

SCIENCE NOTEBOOK

MAIN IDEAS	DETAIL NOTES
Atoms combine in predictable numbers.	• Each compound has a specific ratio of atoms. • A ratio is a comparison between two quantities.
Writing chemical formulas	• Find symbols on the periodic table. • Note ratio of atoms with subscripts.

Description wheel for SUBSCRIPT:
- indicates number of atoms per molecule
- written to the right of a symbol
- slightly below the symbol

40 Unit: Chemical Interactions

2.1 Elements combine to form compounds.

KEY CONCEPT

◀ **BEFORE, you learned**
- Atoms make up everything on Earth
- Atoms react with different atoms to form compounds

▶ **NOW, you will learn**
- How compounds differ from the elements that make them
- How a chemical formula represents the ratio of atoms in a compound
- How the same atoms can form different compounds

VOCABULARY

chemical formula p. 43
subscript p. 43

EXPLORE Compounds

How are compounds different from elements?

PROCEDURE

1. Examine the lump of carbon, the beaker of water, and the sugar. Record your observations of each.

2. Light the candle. Pour some sugar into a test tube and heat it over the candle for several minutes. Record your observations.

MATERIALS
- carbon
- water
- sugar
- test tube
- test-tube holder
- candle
- matches

WHAT DO YOU THINK?
- The sugar is made up of atoms of the same elements that are in the carbon and water. How are sugar, carbon, and water different from one another?
- Does heating the sugar give you any clue that sugar contains more than one element?

MAIN IDEA AND DETAILS
Make a two-column chart to start organizing information on compounds.

Compounds have different properties from the elements that make them.

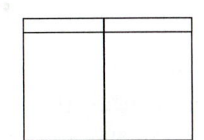

If you think about all of the different substances around you, it is clear that they cannot all be elements. In fact, while there are just over 100 elements, there are millions of different substances. Most substances are compounds. A compound is a substance made of atoms of two or more different elements. Just as the 26 letters in the alphabet can form thousands of words, the elements in the periodic table can form millions of compounds.

The atoms of different elements are held together in compounds by chemical bonds. Chemical bonds can hold atoms together in large networks or in small groups. Bonds help determine the properties of a compound.

Chapter 2: **Chemical Bonds and Compounds** 41 **B**

The properties of a compound depend not only on which atoms the compound contains, but also on how the atoms are arranged. Atoms of carbon and hydrogen, for example, can combine to form many thousands of different compounds. These compounds include natural gas, components of automobile gasoline, the hard waxes in candles, and many plastics. Each of these compounds has a certain number of carbon and hydrogen atoms arranged in a specific way.

The properties of compounds are often very different from the properties of the elements that make them. For example, water is made from two atoms of hydrogen bonded to one atom of oxygen. At room temperature, hydrogen and oxygen are both colorless, odorless gases, and they remain gases down to extremely low temperatures. Water, however, is a liquid at temperatures up to 100°C (212°F) and a solid below 0°C (32°F). Sugar is a compound composed of atoms of carbon, hydrogen, and oxygen. Its properties, however, are unlike those of carbon, hydrogen, or oxygen.

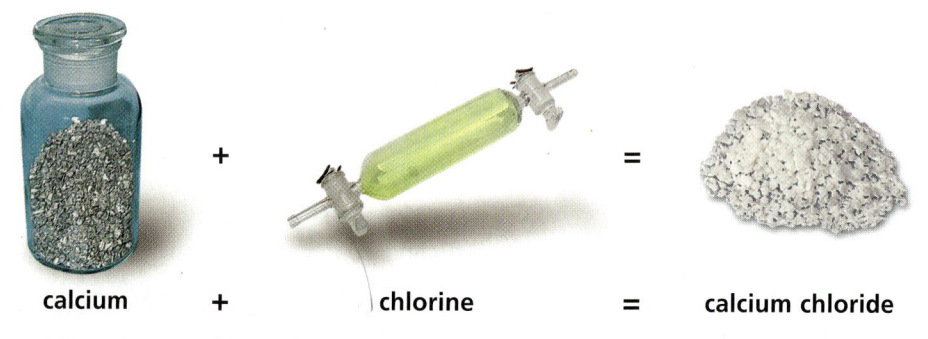

calcium + chlorine = calcium chloride

The picture above shows what happens when the elements calcium and chlorine combine to form the compound calcium chloride. Calcium is a soft, silvery metallic solid. Chlorine is a greenish-yellow gas that is extremely reactive and poisonous to humans. Calcium chloride, however, is a nonpoisonous white solid. People who live in cold climates often use calcium chloride to melt the ice that forms on streets in the wintertime.

CHECK YOUR READING How do the properties of a compound compare with the properties of the elements that make it?

Atoms combine in predictable numbers.

A given compound always contains atoms of elements in a specific ratio. For example, the compound ammonia always has three hydrogen atoms for every nitrogen atom—a 3 to 1 ratio of hydrogen to nitrogen. This same 3:1 ratio holds for every sample of ammonia, under all physical conditions. A substance with a different ratio of hydrogen to nitrogen atoms is not ammonia. For example, hydrazoic acid also contains atoms of hydrogen and nitrogen but in a ratio of one hydrogen atom to three nitrogen atoms, or 1:3.

READING TIP

A ratio is a numerical relationship between two values. If you had 3 apples for every 1 orange, you'd have a ratio of 3 to 1.

INVESTIGATE Element Ratios

How can you model a compound?
PROCEDURE

1. Collect a number of nuts and bolts. The nuts represent hydrogen atoms. The bolts represent carbon atoms.
2. Connect the nuts to the bolts to model the compound methane. Methane contains four hydrogen atoms attached to one carbon atom. Make as many of these models as you can.
3. Count the nuts and bolts left over.

WHAT DO YOU THINK?
- What ratio of nuts to bolts did you use to make a model of a methane atom?
- How many methane models did you make? Why couldn't you make more?

CHALLENGE The compound ammonia has one nitrogen atom and three hydrogen atoms. How would you use the nuts and bolts to model this compound?

SKILL FOCUS
Modeling

MATERIAL
- nuts and bolts
- Modeling Compounds Datasheet

TIME
20 minutes

Chemical Formulas

Remember that atoms of elements can be represented by their chemical symbols, as given in the periodic table. A **chemical formula** uses these chemical symbols to represent the atoms of the elements and their ratios in a chemical compound.

Carbon dioxide is a compound consisting of one atom of carbon attached by chemical bonds to two atoms of oxygen. Here is how you would write the chemical formula for carbon dioxide:

- Find the symbols for carbon (C) and oxygen (O) on the periodic table. Write these symbols side by side.
- To indicate that there are two oxygen atoms for every carbon atom, place the subscript 2 to the right of the oxygen atom's symbol. A **subscript** is a number written to the right of a chemical symbol and slightly below it.
- Because there is only one atom of carbon in carbon dioxide, you need no subscript for carbon. The subscript 1 is never used. The chemical formula for carbon dioxide is, therefore,

$$CO_2$$

The chemical formula shows one carbon atom bonded to two oxygen atoms.

VOCABULARY
Remember to create a description wheel for *chemical formula* and other vocabulary words.

READING TIP
The word *subscript* comes from the prefix *sub-*, which means "under," and the Latin word *scriptum*, which means "written." A subscript is something written under something else.

Chapter 2: **Chemical Bonds and Compounds** 43 B

Chemical Formulas

Chemical formulas show the ratios of atoms in a chemical compound.

Compound Name	Atoms	Atomic Ratio	Chemical Formula
Hydrogen chloride	H Cl	1:1	HCl
Water	H H O	2:1	H_2O
Ammonia	N H H H	1:3	NH_3
Methane	C H H H H	1:4	CH_4
Propane	C C C H H H H H H H H	3:8	C_3H_8

READING VISUALS How many more hydrogen atoms does propane have than methane?

Resource Center CLASSZONE.COM
Find out more about chemical formulas.

The chart above shows the names, atoms, ratios, and chemical formulas for several chemical compounds. The subscripts for each compound indicate the number of atoms that combine to make that compound. Notice how hydrogen combines with different atoms in different ratios. Notice in particular that methane and propane are made of atoms of the same elements, carbon and hydrogen, only in different ratios. This example shows why it's important to pay attention to ratios when writing chemical formulas.

CHECK YOUR READING Why is the ratio of atoms in a chemical formula so important?

Same Elements, Different Compounds

Even before chemists devised a way to write chemical formulas, they realized that different compounds could be composed of atoms of the same elements. Nitrogen and oxygen, for example, form several compounds. One compound consists of one atom of nitrogen attached to one atom of oxygen. This compound's formula is NO. A second compound has one atom of nitrogen attached to two atoms of oxygen, so its formula is NO_2. A third compound has two nitrogen atoms attached to one oxygen atom; its formula is N_2O. The properties of these compounds are different, even though they are made of atoms of the same elements.

water (H₂O)

hydrogen peroxide (H₂O₂)

There are many other examples of atoms of the same elements forming different compounds. The photographs above show two bottles filled with clear, colorless liquids. You might use the liquid in the first bottle to cool off after a soccer game. The bottle contains water, which is a compound made from two atoms of hydrogen and one atom of oxygen (H_2O). You could not survive for long without water.

You definitely would not want to drink the liquid in the second bottle, although this liquid resembles water. This bottle also contains a compound of hydrogen and oxygen, hydrogen peroxide, but hydrogen peroxide has two hydrogen and two oxygen atoms (H_2O_2). Hydrogen peroxide is commonly used to kill bacteria on skin. One way to tell these two compounds apart is to test them using a potato. A drop of hydrogen peroxide on a raw potato will bubble; a drop of water on the potato will not.

The difference between the two compounds is greater than the labels or their appearance would indicate. The hydrogen peroxide that you buy at a drugstore is a mixture of hydrogen peroxide and water. In its concentrated form, hydrogen peroxide is a thick, syrupy liquid that boils at 150°C (302°F). Hydrogen peroxide can even be used as a fuel.

CHECK YOUR READING What are the chemical formulas for water and hydrogen peroxide?

2.1 Review

KEY CONCEPTS

1. How do the properties of compounds often compare with the properties of the elements that make them?
2. How many atoms are in the compound represented by the formula $C_{12}H_{22}O_{11}$?
3. How can millions of compounds be made from the atoms of about 100 elements?

CRITICAL THINKING

4. **Apply** If a chemical formula has no subscripts, what can you conclude about the ratio of the atoms in it?
5. **Infer** How might you distinguish between hydrogen peroxide and water?

CHALLENGE

6. **Analyze** A chemist analyzes two compounds and finds that they both contain only carbon and oxygen. The two compounds, however, have different properties. How can two compounds made from the same elements be different?

Chapter 2: **Chemical Bonds and Compounds** 45

MATH in SCIENCE

SKILL: CALCULATING RATIOS

MATH TUTORIAL
CLASSZONE.COM
Click on Math Tutorial for more help with ratios.

Regarding Ratios

No pitcher gets a batter out every time. Sometimes even the worst pitchers have spectacular games. If you're a fan of professional baseball, you've probably seen the quality of certain players rated by using a ratio. A ratio is a comparison of two quantities. For a major league baseball pitcher, for example, one ratio you might hear reported is the number of strikeouts to the number of walks during a season. Chemical formulas are also ratios—ratios that compare the numbers of atoms in a compound.

Example

Consider the chemical formula for the compound glucose:

$$C_6H_{12}O_6$$

From this formula you can write several ratios. To find the ratio of carbon atoms to hydrogen atoms, for instance, do the following:

(1) Find the number of each kind of atom by noting the subscripts.

6 carbon, 12 hydrogen

(2) Write the first number on the left and the second on the right, and place a colon between them.

6:12

(3) Reduce the ratio by dividing each side by the largest number that goes into each evenly, in this case 6.

1:2

ANSWER The ratio of carbon to hydrogen in glucose is 1:2.

Use the table below to answer the following questions.

Compounds and Formulas	
Compound Name	**Chemical Formula**
Carbon dioxide	CO_2
Methane	CH_4
Sulfuric acid	H_2SO_4
Glucose	$C_6H_{12}O_6$
Formic acid	CH_2O_2

1. In carbon dioxide, what is the ratio of carbon to oxygen?

2. What is the ratio of carbon to hydrogen in methane?

3. In sulfuric acid, what is the ratio of hydrogen to sulfur? the ratio of sulfur to oxygen?

CHALLENGE What two chemical compounds in the table have the same ratio of carbon atoms to oxygen atoms?

A good strikeout-to-walk ratio for a baseball pitcher is 2:1. This means that for every two strikeouts achieved, the pitcher only allows one walk.

KEY CONCEPT
2.2 Chemical bonds hold compounds together.

BEFORE, you learned
- Elements combine to form compounds
- Electrons are located in a cloud around the nucleus
- Atoms can lose or gain electrons to form ions

NOW, you will learn
- How electrons are involved in chemical bonding
- About the different types of chemical bonds
- How chemical bonds affect structure

VOCABULARY
ionic bond p. 48
covalent bond p. 50
molecule p. 51
polar covalent bond p. 51

THINK ABOUT

How do you keep things together?

Think about the different ways the workers at this construction site connect materials. They may use nails, screws, or even glue, depending on the materials they wish to keep together. Why would they choose the method they do? What factors do you consider when you join two objects?

MAIN IDEA AND DETAILS
Make a two-column chart to organize information on chemical bonds.

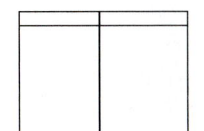

Chemical bonds between atoms involve electrons.

Water is a compound of hydrogen and oxygen. The air you breathe, however, contains oxygen gas, a small amount of hydrogen gas, as well as some water vapor. How can hydrogen and oxygen be water sometimes and at other times not? The answer is by forming chemical bonds.

Chemical bonds are the "glue" that holds the atoms of elements together in compounds. Chemical bonds are what make compounds more than just mixtures of atoms.

Remember that an atom has a positively charged nucleus surrounded by a cloud of electrons. Chemical bonds form when the electrons in the electron clouds around two atoms interact. How the electron clouds interact determines the kind of chemical bond that is formed. Chemical bonds have a great effect on the chemical and physical properties of compounds. Chemical bonds also influence how different substances interact. You'll learn more about how substances interact in a later chapter.

Chapter 2: **Chemical Bonds and Compounds** 47 B

Atoms can transfer electrons.

> **REMINDER**
> Remember that elements in columns show similar chemical properties.

Ions are formed when atoms gain or lose electrons. Gaining electrons changes an atom into a negative ion. Losing electrons changes an atom into a positive ion. Individual atoms do not form ions by themselves. Instead, ions typically form in pairs when one atom transfers one or more electrons to another atom.

An element's location on the periodic table can give a clue as to the type of ions the atoms of that element will form. The illustration to the left shows the characteristic ions formed by several groups. Notice that all metals lose electrons to form positive ions. Group 1 metals commonly lose only one electron to form ions with a single positive charge. Group 2 metals commonly lose two electrons to form ions with two positive charges. Other metals, like the transition metals, also always form positive ions, but the number of electrons they may lose varies.

Nonmetals form ions by gaining electrons. Group 17 nonmetals, for example, gain one electron to form ions with a 1– charge. The nonmetals in Group 16 gain two electrons to form ions with a 2– charge. The noble gases do not normally gain or lose electrons and so do not normally form ions.

CHECK YOUR READING What type of ions do metals form?

Ionic Bonds

What happens when an atom of an element from Group 1, like sodium, meets an atom of an element from Group 17, like chlorine? Sodium is likely to lose an electron to form a positive ion. Chlorine is likely to gain an electron to form a negative ion. An electron, therefore, moves from the sodium atom to the chlorine atom.

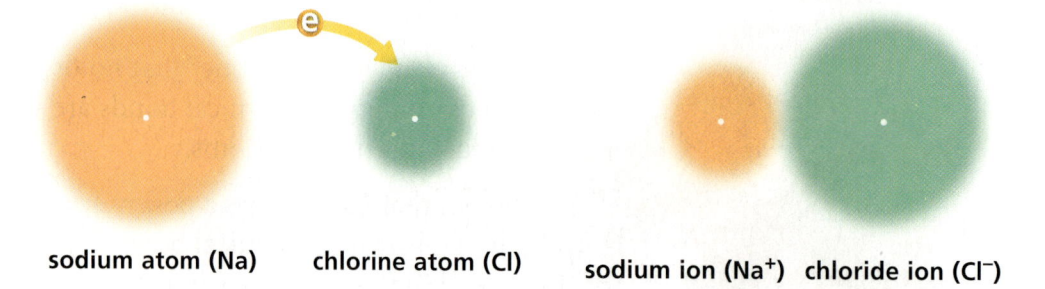

sodium atom (Na)   chlorine atom (Cl)   sodium ion (Na$^+$)   chloride ion (Cl$^-$)

Remember that particles with opposite electrical charges attract one another. When the ions are created, therefore, they are drawn toward one another by electrical attraction. This force of attraction between positive and negative ions is called an **ionic bond.**

Electrical forces act in all directions. Each ion, therefore, attracts all other nearby ions with the opposite charge. The next illustration shows how this all-around attraction produces a network of sodium and chloride ions known as a sodium chloride crystal.

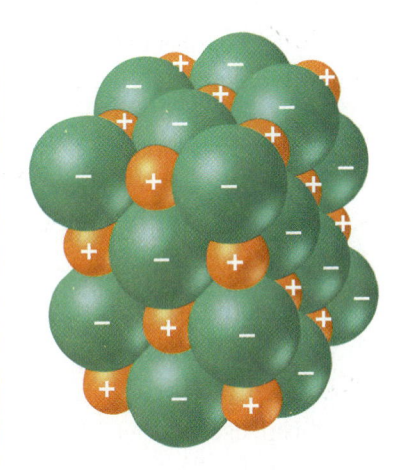

Notice how each positive ion is surrounded by six negative ions, and each negative ion is surrounded by six positive ions. This regular arrangement gives the sodium chloride crystal its characteristic cubic shape. You can see this distinctive crystal shape when you look at table salt crystals through a magnifying glass.

Ionic bonds form between all nearby ions of opposite charge. These interactions make ionic compounds very stable and their crystals very strong. Although sodium chloride crystals have a cubic shape, other ionic compounds form crystals with different regular patterns. The shape of the crystals of an ionic compound depends, in part, on the ratio of positive and negative ions and the sizes of the ions.

The cubic shape of sodium chloride crystals is a result of how the ions form crystals.

Names of Ionic Compounds

The name of an ionic compound is based on the names of the ions it is made of. The name for a positive ion is the same as the name of the atom from which it is formed. The name of a negative ion is formed by dropping the last part of the name of the atom and adding the suffix *-ide.* To name an ionic compound, the name of the positive ion is placed first, followed by the name of the negative ion. For example, the chemical name for table salt is sodium chloride. *Sodium* is the positive sodium ion and *chloride* is the negative ion formed from chlorine.

Therefore, to name the compound with the chemical formula BaI_2

- First, take the name of the positive metal element: barium.
- Second, take the name of the negative, nonmetal element, iodine, and give it the ending *-ide:* iodide.
- Third, combine the two names: barium iodide.

Similarly, the name for KBr is potassium bromide, and the name for MgF_2 is magnesium fluoride.

Chapter 2: **Chemical Bonds and Compounds**

Atoms can share electrons.

In general, an ionic bond forms between atoms that lose electrons easily to form positive ions, such as metals, and atoms that gain electrons easily to form negative ions, such as nonmetals. Another way in which atoms can bond together is by sharing electrons. Nonmetal atoms usually form bonds with each other by sharing electrons.

Covalent Bonds

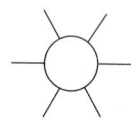

A pair of shared electrons between two atoms is called a **covalent bond**. In forming a covalent bond, neither atom gains or loses an electron, so no ions are formed. The shared electrons are attracted to both positively charged nuclei. The illustrations below show a covalent bond between two iodine atoms. In the first illustration, notice how the electron clouds overlap. A covalent bond is also often represented as a line between the two atoms, as in the second illustration.

Iodine (I_2)

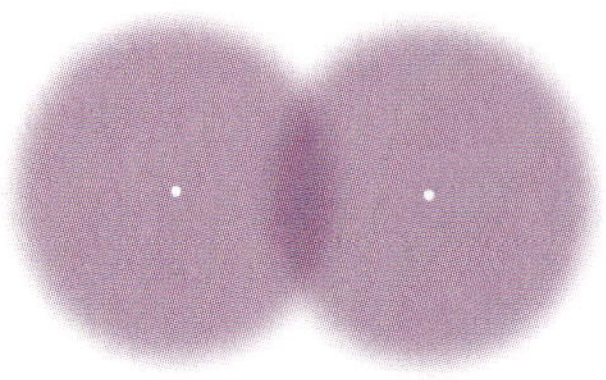

electron cloud model 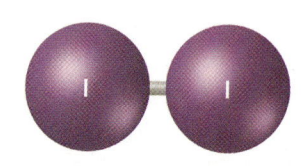   ball-and-stick model

VOCABULARY
Make a description wheel for *covalent bond* and other vocabulary words.

READING TIP
To help yourself remember that a covalent bond involves a sharing of electrons, remember that the prefix *co-* means "partner."

The number of covalent bonds that an atom can form depends on the number of electrons that it has available for sharing. For example, atoms of the halogen group and hydrogen can contribute only one electron to a covalent bond. These atoms, therefore, can form only one covalent bond. Atoms of Group 16 elements can form two covalent bonds. Atoms of the elements of Group 15 can form three bonds. Carbon and silicon in Group 14 can form four bonds. For example, in methane (CH_4), carbon forms four covalent bonds with four hydrogen atoms, as shown below.

Methane (CH_4)

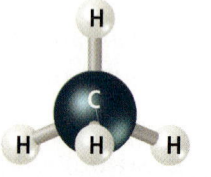

ball-and-stick model    space-filling model

We don't always show the lines representing the covalent bonds between the atoms. The space-filling model still shows the general shape of the bonded atoms, but occupies far less space on the page.

50 Unit: Chemical Interactions

Each carbon-hydrogen bond in methane is a single bond because one pair of electrons is shared between the atoms. Sometimes atoms may share more than one pair of electrons with another atom. For example, the carbon atom in carbon dioxide (CO_2) forms double bonds with each of the oxygen atoms. A double bond consists of four (two pairs of) shared electrons. Two nitrogen atoms form a triple bond, meaning that they share six (three pairs of) electrons.

Carbon Dioxide (CO_2)

Nitrogen (N_2)

READING TIP
Remember that each line in the model stands for a covalent bond—one shared pair of electrons.

A group of atoms held together by covalent bonds is called a **molecule.** A molecule can contain from two to many thousand atoms. Most molecules contain the atoms of two or more elements. For example, water (H_2O), ammonia (NH_3), and methane (CH_4) are all compounds made up of molecules. However, some molecules contain atoms of only one element. The following elements exist as two-atom molecules: H_2, N_2, O_2, F_2, Cl_2, Br_2, and I_2.

CHECK YOUR READING What is a molecule?

Polar Covalent Bonds

In an iodine molecule, both atoms are exactly the same. The shared electrons therefore are attracted equally to both nuclei. If the two atoms involved in a covalent bond are very different, however, the electrons have a stronger attraction to one nucleus than to the other and spend more time near that nucleus. A covalent bond in which the electrons are shared unequally is called a **polar covalent bond.** The word *polar* refers to anything that has two extremes, like a magnet with its two opposite poles.

READING TIP
To remind yourself that polar covalent bonds have opposite partial charges, remember that Earth has both a North Pole and a South Pole.

Water (H_2O)

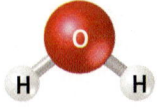

ball-and-stick model

space-filling model

In a water molecule (H_2O), the oxygen atom attracts electrons far more strongly than the hydrogen atoms do. The oxygen nucleus has eight protons, and the hydrogen nucleus has only one proton. The oxygen atom pulls the shared electrons more strongly toward it. In a water molecule, therefore, the oxygen side has a slightly negative charge, and the hydrogen side has a slightly positive charge.

VISUALIZATION
CLASSZONE.COM
Examine how electrons move in a polar covalent molecule.

Chapter 2: **Chemical Bonds and Compounds** 51 **B**

Comparing Bonds

In Salar de Uyuni, Bolivia, salt is mined in great quantities from salt water. The salt is harvested as the water evaporates into the air, leaving the salt behind. All types of chemical bonds are involved.

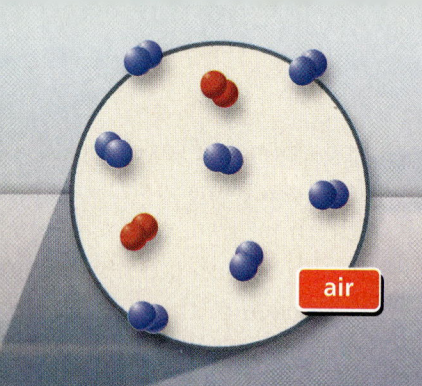

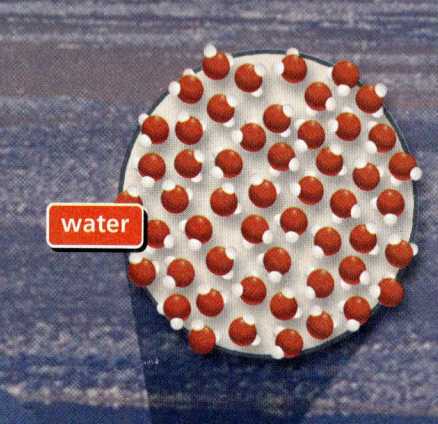

air

salt

water

Ionic Bonds (salt)

Sodium Chloride (NaCl)
A complete transfer of electrons produces the ionic bonds that hold sodium chloride (table salt) crystals together.

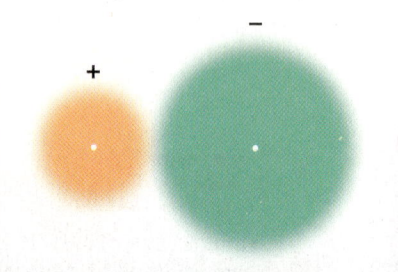

Covalent Bonds (air)

Nitrogen (N_2) and Oxygen (O_2)
Some molecules in air contain multiple covalent bonds. Nitrogen has triple bonds. Oxygen has double bonds.

Polar Covalent Bonds (water)

Water (H_2O)
The covalent bonds in water are very polar because oxygen attracts electrons far more strongly than hydrogen does.

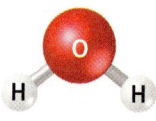

READING VISUALS Atoms of which element are shown both in the air and in the water?

Chemical bonds give all materials their structures.

The substances around you have many different properties. The structure of the crystals and molecules that make up these substances are responsible for many of these properties. For example, crystals bend rays of light, metals shine, and medications attack certain diseases in the body because their atoms are arranged in specific ways.

Ionic Compounds

Most ionic compounds have a regular crystal structure. Remember how the size, shape, and ratio of the sodium ions and chloride ions give the sodium chloride crystal its shape. Other ionic compounds, such as calcium chloride, have different but equally regular structures that depend upon the ratio and sizes of the ions. One consequence of such rigid structures is that, when enough force is applied to the crystal, it shatters rather than bends.

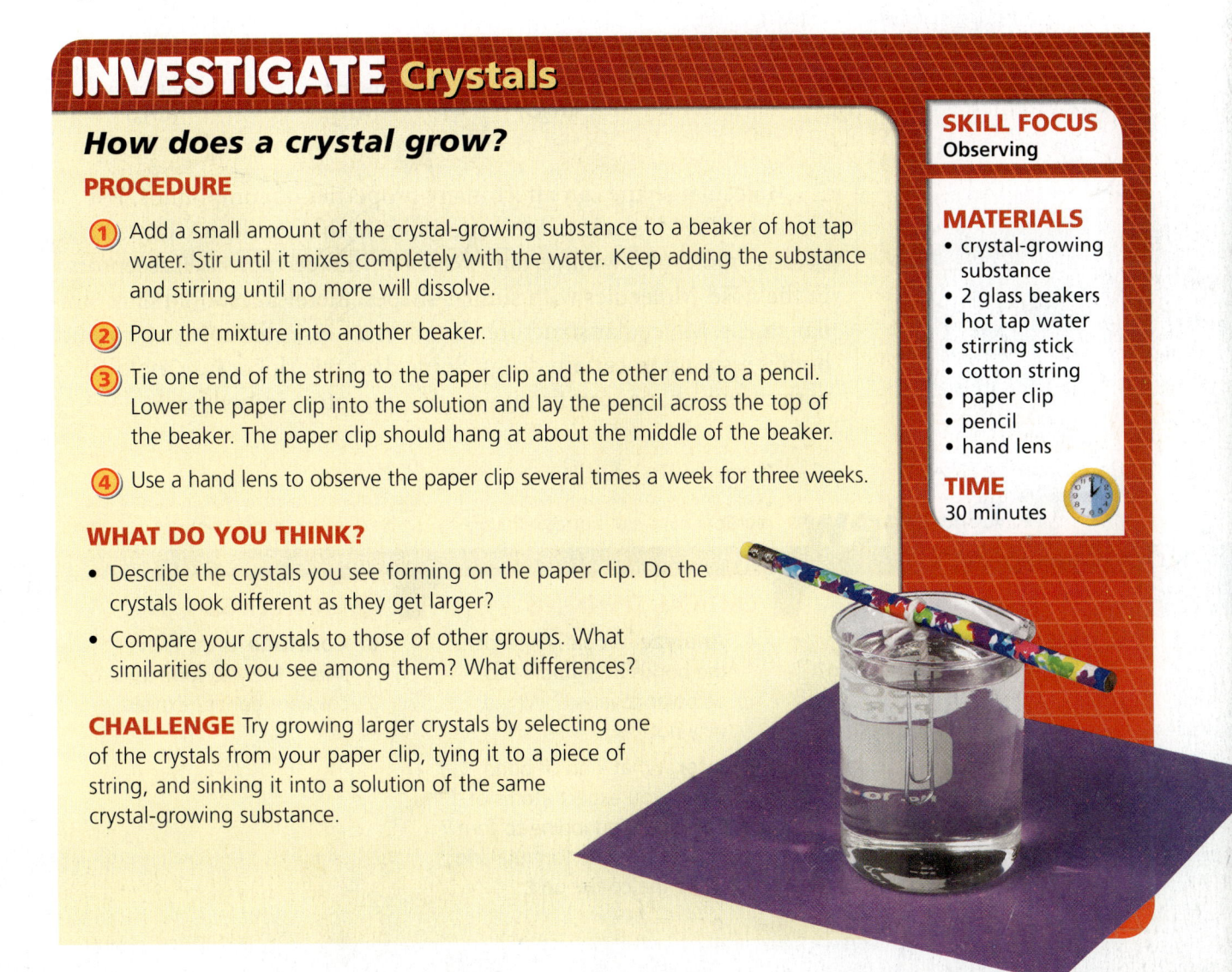

INVESTIGATE Crystals

How does a crystal grow?

PROCEDURE

1. Add a small amount of the crystal-growing substance to a beaker of hot tap water. Stir until it mixes completely with the water. Keep adding the substance and stirring until no more will dissolve.
2. Pour the mixture into another beaker.
3. Tie one end of the string to the paper clip and the other end to a pencil. Lower the paper clip into the solution and lay the pencil across the top of the beaker. The paper clip should hang at about the middle of the beaker.
4. Use a hand lens to observe the paper clip several times a week for three weeks.

WHAT DO YOU THINK?

- Describe the crystals you see forming on the paper clip. Do the crystals look different as they get larger?
- Compare your crystals to those of other groups. What similarities do you see among them? What differences?

CHALLENGE Try growing larger crystals by selecting one of the crystals from your paper clip, tying it to a piece of string, and sinking it into a solution of the same crystal-growing substance.

SKILL FOCUS
Observing

MATERIALS
- crystal-growing substance
- 2 glass beakers
- hot tap water
- stirring stick
- cotton string
- paper clip
- pencil
- hand lens

TIME
30 minutes

Chapter 2: **Chemical Bonds and Compounds** 53 B

Covalent Compounds

Unlike ionic compounds, covalent compounds exist as individual molecules. Chemical bonds give each molecule a specific, three-dimensional shape called its molecular structure. Molecular structure can influence everything from how a specific substance feels to the touch to how well it interacts with other substances.

A few basic molecular structures are shown below. Molecules can have a simple linear shape, like iodine (I_2), or they can be bent, like a water molecule (H_2O). The atoms in an ammonia molecule (NH_3) form a pyramid, and methane (CH_4) molecules even have a slightly more complex shape. The shape of a molecule depends on the atoms it contains and the bonds holding it together.

READING TIP
To help yourself appreciate the differences among these structures, try making three-dimensional models of them.

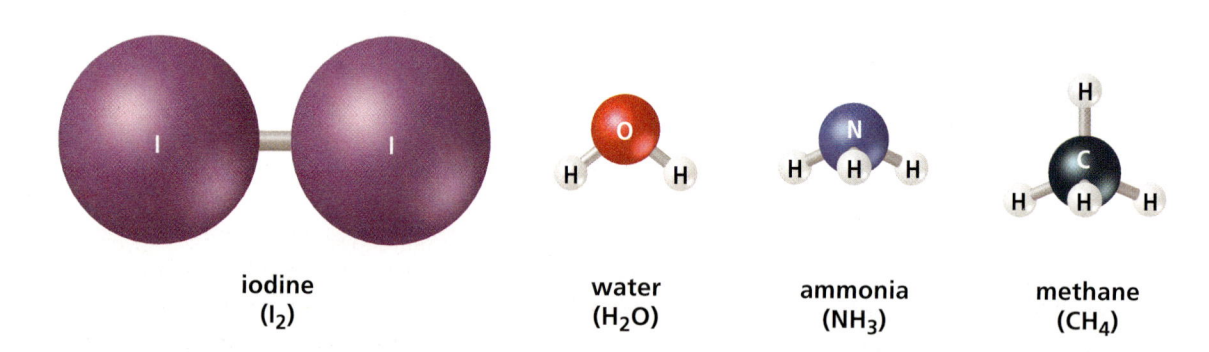

iodine (I_2)   water (H_2O)   ammonia (NH_3)   methane (CH_4)

Molecular shape can affect many properties of compounds. For example, there is some evidence to indicate that we detect scents because molecules with certain shapes fit into certain smell receptors in the nose. Molecules with similar shapes, therefore, should have similar smells. Molecular structure also plays an essential role in how our bodies respond to certain drugs. Some drugs work because molecules with certain shapes can fit into specific receptors in body cells.

2.2 Review

KEY CONCEPTS
1. What part of an atom is involved in chemical bonding?
2. How are ionic bonds and covalent bonds different?
3. Describe two ways that crystal and molecular structures affect the properties of ionic and covalent compounds.

CRITICAL THINKING
4. **Analyze** Would you expect the bonds in ammonia to be polar covalent? Why or why not?
5. **Infer** What kind of bond would you expect atoms of strontium and iodine to form? Why? Write the formula and name the compound.

CHALLENGE
6. **Conclude** Is the element silicon likely to form ionic or covalent bonds? Explain.

Think SCIENCE

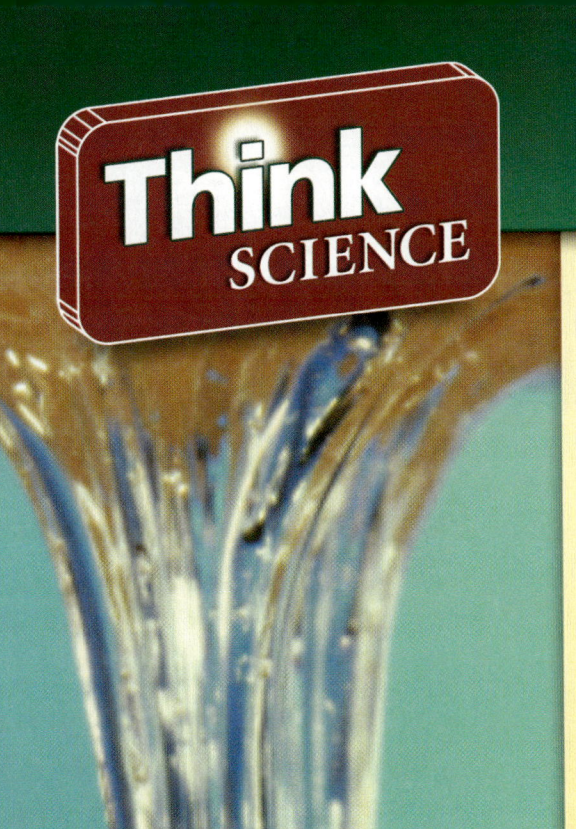

SKILL: ISOLATING VARIABLES

Stick to It

Glues join objects by forming something like chemical bonds between their surfaces. While glue manufacturers try to make glues as strong as possible, simply being strong does not mean that a glue will join all surfaces equally well. For example, a glue that will hold two pieces of wood together very well may not be able to form a lasting bond between two pieces of plastic piping or two metal sheets.

Variables

When testing a new glue, a scientist wants to know exactly how that glue will perform under all conditions. In any test, however, there are a number of variables that could affect the quality of the bonds formed by the glue. The scientist needs to discover exactly which of these variables most affects the glue's ability to form lasting bonds. Identifying these variables and the effects each has on the glue's strength and lifetime enables glue makers to recommend the best uses for the glue. Following are a few of the variables a glue maker may consider when testing a glue.

- What surfaces the glue is being used to join
- How much glue is used in a test
- How evenly the glue is applied to the surface
- How much force the glue can withstand
- Over how long a time the force is applied
- The environment the glue is used in (wet, dry, or dusty)

Variables to Test

On Your Own You are a scientist at a glue company. You have developed a new type of glue and need to know how specific conditions will affect its ability to hold surfaces together. First, select one variable you wish to test. Next, outline how you would ensure that only that variable will differ in each test. You might start out by listing all the variables you can think of and then put a check by each one and describe how you are controlling it.

As a Group Discuss the outlines of your tests with others. Are there any variables you haven't accounted for?

CHALLENGE Adhesive tapes come in many different types. Outline how you would test how well a certain tape holds in a wet environment and in a dry environment.

The glue on the back of a postage stamp must be activated somehow. This scanning electron microscope photo shows postage stamp glue before (green) and after (blue) it has been activated by moisture.

This highly magnified photograph shows the attachment formed by a colorless, waterproof wood glue.

Chapter 2: **Chemical Bonds and Compounds** 55

KEY CONCEPT
2.3 Substances' properties depend on their bonds.

BEFORE, you learned
- Chemical bonds hold the atoms of compounds together
- Chemical bonds involve the transfer or sharing of electrons
- Molecules have a structure

NOW, you will learn
- How metal atoms form chemical bonds with one another
- How ionic and covalent bonds influence substances' properties

VOCABULARY

metallic bond p. 56

EXPLORE Bonds in Metals
What objects conduct electricity?

PROCEDURE

1. Tape one end of a copper wire to one terminal of the battery. Attach the other end of the copper wire to the light bulb holder. Attach a second wire to the holder. Tape a third wire to the other terminal of the battery.

2. Touch the ends of both wires to objects around the classroom. Notice if the bulb lights or not.

WHAT DO YOU THINK?
- Which objects make the bulb light?
- How are these objects similar?

MATERIALS
- masking tape
- 3 pieces of copper wire (15 cm)
- D cell (battery)
- light bulb and holder
- objects to test

Metals have unique bonds.

REMINDER

Chemical bonds involve the sharing of or transfer of electrons.

Metal atoms bond together by sharing their electrons with one another. The atoms share the electrons equally in all directions. The equal sharing allows the electrons to move easily among the atoms of the metal. This special type of bond is called a **metallic bond.**

The properties of metals are determined by metallic bonds. One common property of metals is that they are good conductors of electric current. The electrons in a metal flow through the material, carrying the electric current. The free movement of electrons among metal atoms also means that metals are good conductors of heat. Metals also typically have high melting points. Except for mercury, all metals are solids at room temperature.

B 56 Unit: Chemical Interactions

Metallic Properties

Copper and other metals get their properties from metallic bonds.

The ability of electrons to move freely makes metals
- good conductors of electricity
- good conductors of heat
- easy to shape

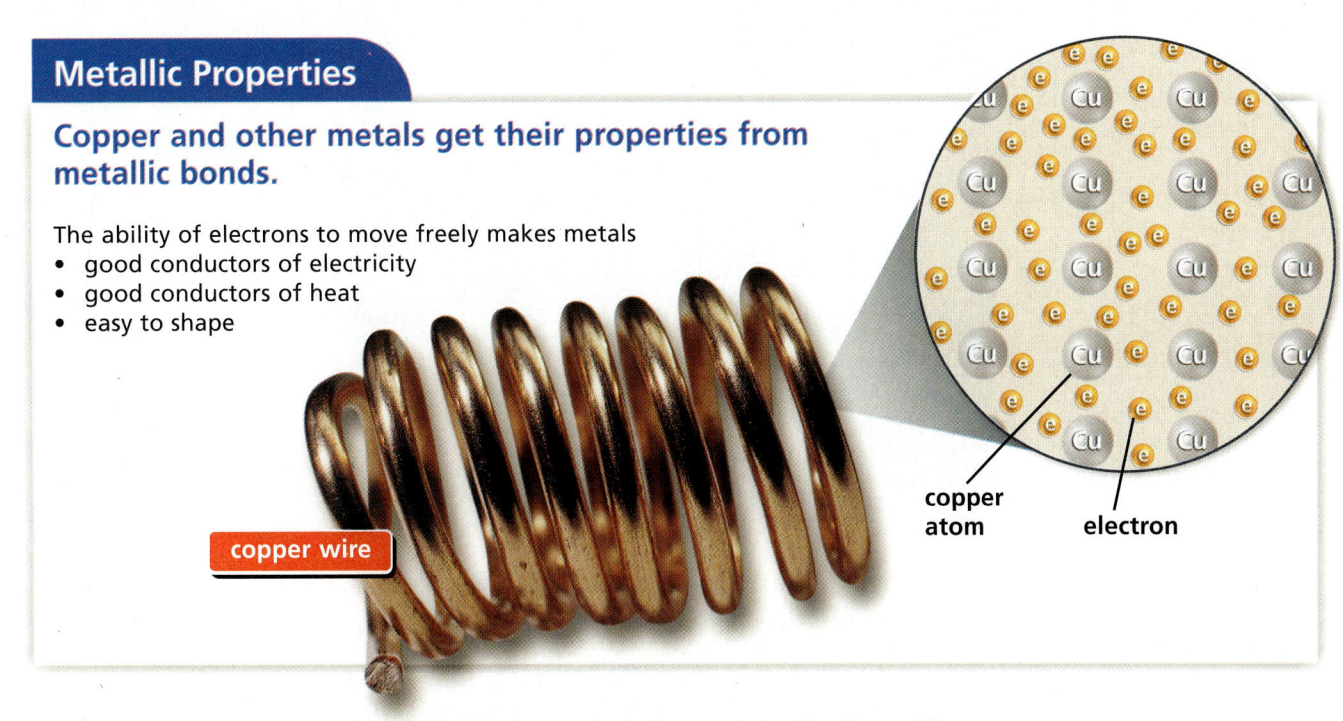

copper wire

copper atom   electron

Two other properties of metals are that they are easily shaped by pounding and can be drawn into a wire. These properties are also explained by the nature of the metallic bond. In metallic compounds, atoms can slide past one another. It is as if the atoms are swimming in a pool of surrounding electrons. Pounding the metal simply moves these atoms into other positions. This property makes metals ideal for making coins.

CHECK YOUR READING What three properties do metals have because of metallic bonds?

Ionic and covalent bonds give compounds certain properties.

The properties of a compound depend on the chemical bonds that hold its atoms together. For example, you can be pretty certain an ionic compound will be a solid at room temperature. Ionic compounds, in fact, usually have extremely high melting and boiling points because it takes a lot of energy to break all the bonds among all the ions in the crystal. The rigid crystal network also makes ionic compounds hard, brittle, and poor conductors of electricity. No moving electrical charges means no current will flow.

Ionic compounds, however, often dissolve easily in water, separating into positive ions and negative ions. The separated ions can move freely, making solutions of ionic compounds good conductors of electricity. Your body, in fact, uses ionic solutions to help transmit impulses between nerve and muscle cells. Exercise can rapidly deplete these ionic solutions in the body, so sports drinks contain ionic compounds.

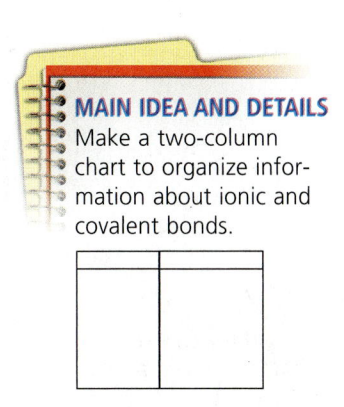

MAIN IDEA AND DETAILS Make a two-column chart to organize information about ionic and covalent bonds.

Chapter 2: **Chemical Bonds and Compounds** 57

A hot pool in Yellowstone Park's Upper Geyser Basin. These pools are often characterized by their striking colors.

RESOURCE CENTER
CLASSZONE.COM

Find out more about the properties of ionic and covalent compounds.

These compounds, such as potassium chloride, replace the ions lost during physical activity.

Mineral hot springs, like those found in Yellowstone National Park, are another example of ionic solutions. Many of the ionic compounds dissolved in these hot springs contain the element sulfur, which can have an unpleasant odor. Evidence of these ionic compounds can be seen in the white deposits around the pool's rim.

Covalent compounds have almost the exact opposite properties of ionic compounds. Since the atoms are organized as individual molecules, melting or boiling a covalent compound does not require breaking chemical bonds. Therefore, covalent compounds often melt and boil at lower temperatures than ionic compounds. Unlike ionic compounds, molecules stay together when dissolved in water, which means covalent compounds are poor conductors of electricity. Table sugar, for example, does not conduct an electric current when in solution.

Bonds can make the same element look different.

Covalent bonds do not always form small individual molecules. This explains how the element carbon can exist in three very different forms—diamond, graphite, and fullerene. The properties of each form depend on how the carbon atoms are bonded to each other.

Diamond is the hardest natural substance. This property makes diamond useful for cutting other substances. Diamonds are made entirely of carbon. Each carbon atom forms covalent bonds with four other carbon atoms. The pattern of linked atoms extends throughout the entire volume of a diamond crystal. This three-dimensional structure of carbon atoms gives diamonds their strength—diamond bonds do not break easily.

Another form of carbon is graphite. Graphite is the dark, slippery component of pencil "lead." Graphite has a different structure from diamond, although both are networks of interconnected atoms. Each carbon atom in graphite forms covalent bonds with three other atoms to form two-dimensional layers. These layers stack on top of one another like sheets of paper. The layers can slide past one another easily. Graphite feels slippery and is used as a lubricant to reduce friction between metal parts of machines.

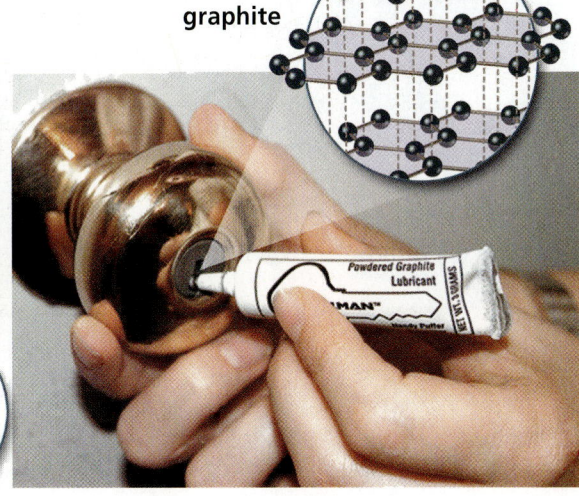

graphite

diamond

A third form of carbon, fullerene, contains large molecules. One type of fullerene, called buckminsterfullerene, has molecules shaped like a soccer ball. In 1985 chemists made a fullerene molecule consisting of 60 carbon atoms. Since then, many similar molecules have been made, ranging from 20 to more than 100 atoms per molecule.

buckminsterfullerene

2.3 Review

KEY CONCEPTS

1. How do metal atoms bond together?
2. Why do ionic compounds have high melting points?
3. What are three forms of the element carbon?

CRITICAL THINKING

4. **Apply** A compound known as cubic boron nitride has a structure similar to that of a diamond. What properties would you expect it to have?
5. **Infer** Sterling silver is a combination of silver and copper. How are the silver and copper atoms held together?

CHALLENGE

6. **Infer** Why might the water in mineral springs be a better conductor of electricity than drinking water?

Chapter 2: **Chemical Bonds and Compounds** 59

CHAPTER INVESTIGATION

Chemical Bonds

OVERVIEW AND PURPOSE Chemists can identify the type of bonds in a substance by examining its properties. In this investigation you will examine the properties of different substances and use what you have learned about chemical bonds to identify the type of bond each substance contains. You will
- observe the structure of substances with a hand lens
- test the conductivity of substances
- determine the melting point of substances

MATERIALS
- 3 wire leads with alligator clips
- battery
- zinc and copper strips
- light bulb and socket
- test compounds
- 3 plastic cups
- distilled water
- beaker
- construction paper
- hand lens
- plastic spoon
- 3 test tubes
- test-tube rack
- candle
- wire test-tube holder

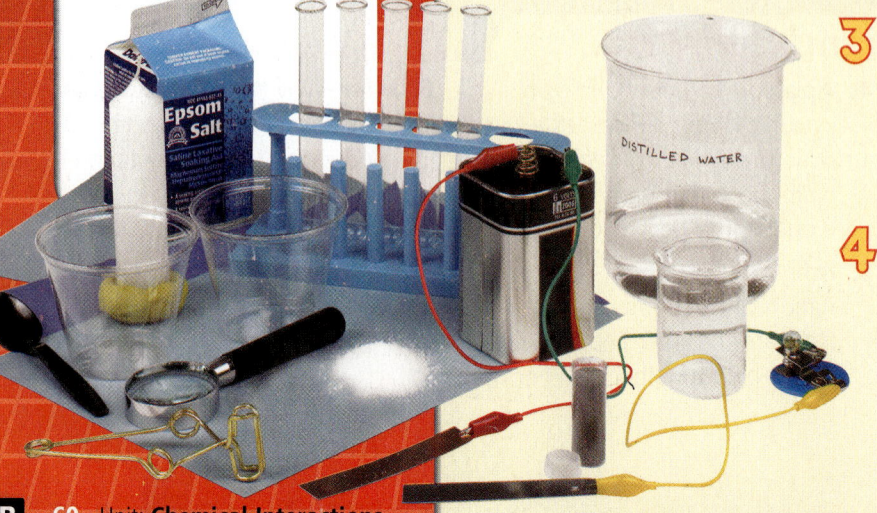

Problem
How can you determine the type of chemical bond a substance has?

Hypothesize
Write three hypotheses in "if . . . , then . . . , because . . ." form to answer the problem question for each bond type—ionic, covalent, and metallic.

Procedure

1. Create a data table similar to the one shown on the sample notebook page.

2. To build the conductivity tester, connect the first wire to one terminal of the battery and to one of the metal strips. Attach the second wire to the other terminal and to the lamp socket. Finally, connect the lamp socket to the third wire, and connect the other end of this wire to the second metal strip.

3. To make sure your tester works properly, touch the tips of the metal strips together. If the bulb lights, the tester is working properly. If not, check the connections carefully.

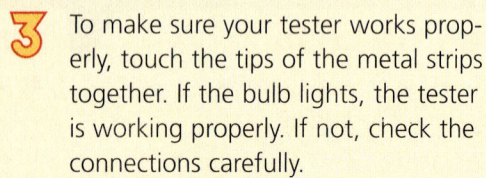

4. Get the following test compounds from your teacher: Epsom salts ($MgSO_4$), sugar ($C_{12}H_{22}O_{11}$), and iron filings (Fe). For each substance, put about 20 grams in a cup and label it.

Unit: Chemical Interactions

5. Test the conductivity of distilled water. Fill the beaker with 30 mL of water. Place the two metal strips into the water. Does the bulb light? Record your observations. Dry the strips completely.

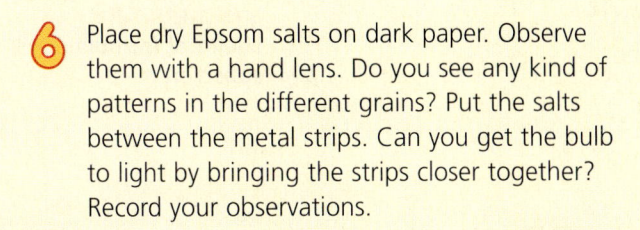

6. Place dry Epsom salts on dark paper. Observe them with a hand lens. Do you see any kind of patterns in the different grains? Put the salts between the metal strips. Can you get the bulb to light by bringing the strips closer together? Record your observations.

7. Add all but a small amount of the Epsom salts to the beaker of water. Stir well. Repeat the conductivity test. What happens when you put the metal strips into the solution? Record your results.

8. Rinse and dry the beaker. Repeat steps 6–7 with other test substances. Record your results.

9. Put the remainder of each test substance into its own clean, dry test tube. Label the tubes. Light the candle. Use a test tube holder to hold each compound over the candle flame for 2 minutes. Do you notice any signs of melting? Record your observations.

Observe and Analyze *Write It Up*

1. **RECORD OBSERVATIONS** Be sure you have entered all your observations in your data table.

2. **CLASSIFY** Using the periodic table, find the elements these compounds contain. How might consulting the periodic table help you determine what type of bond exists in the compound?

Conclude *Write It Up*

1. **INTERPRET** Review your recorded observations. Classify the compounds as having ionic, covalent, or metallic bonds. Fill in the last row of the data table with your conclusions.

2. **INFER** Compare your results with your hypotheses. Did your results support your hypotheses?

3. **EVALUATE** Describe possible limitations, errors, or places where errors might have occurred.

4. **APPLY** Electrocardiograms are graphs that show the electrical activity of the heart. When an electrocardiogram is made, a paste of sodium chloride is used to hold small metal discs on the patient's skin. What property of ionic compounds does this medical test make use of?

INVESTIGATE Further

CHALLENGE To grow crystals, put about 60 grams of Epsom salts into a baby-food jar that is half full of hot water. Do the same using a second jar containing about 60 grams of sugar. Cover and shake the jars for a count of 60. Line two clean jar lids with dark paper. Brush or spoon a thin coating of each liquid over the paper. Let them stand in a warm place. After several days, observe the crystals that form, using a hand lens.

Chemical Bonds

Problem How can you determine the type of chemical bond a substance has?

Hypothesize

Observe and Analyze

Table 1: Properties of Bonds

Property	Epsom Salts (MgSO4)	Sugar (C12H22O11)	Iron Filings (Fe)
Crystal structure			
Conductivity of solid			
Conductivity in water			
Melting			
Bond type			

Conclude

Chapter 2: **Chemical Bonds and Compounds** 61

Chapter 2 Review

the BIG idea
The properties of compounds depend on their atoms and chemical bonds.

CONTENT REVIEW
CLASSZONE.COM

KEY CONCEPTS SUMMARY

2.1 Elements combine to form compounds.
- Compounds have different properties from the elements that made them.
- Atoms combine in predictable numbers.

calcium (Ca)  + chlorine (Cl$_2$)  = calcium chloride (CaCl$_2$)

VOCABULARY
chemical formula p. 43
subscript p. 43

2.2 Chemical bonds hold compounds together.
- Chemical bonds between atoms involve electrons.
- Atoms can transfer electrons.
- Atoms can share electrons.
- Chemical bonds give all materials their structure.

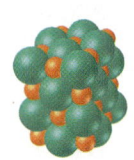

ionic bond 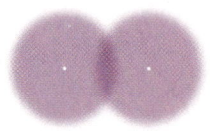   covalent bond

VOCABULARY
ionic bond p. 48
covalent bond p. 50
molecule p. 51
polar covalent bond p. 51

2.3 Substances' properties depend on their bonds.
- Metals have unique bonds.
- Ionic and covalent bonds give compounds certain properties.
- Bonds can make the same element look different.

copper    diamond fragment 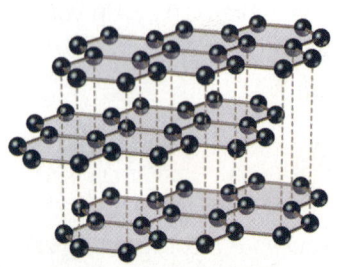   graphite fragment

VOCABULARY
metallic bond p. 56

Reviewing Vocabulary

Copy and complete the table below. Under each bond type, describe
- how electrons are distributed
- how the compound is structured
- one of the properties of the compound containing this type of bond

Some of the table has been filled out for you.

Ionic Bonds	Covalent Bonds	Metallic Bonds
1.	shared electron pair	2.
3.	4.	close-packed atoms in sea of electrons
have high melting points	5.	6.

Reviewing Key Concepts

Multiple Choice *Choose the letter of the best answer.*

7. Most substances are
   a. elements
   b. compounds
   c. metals
   d. nonmetals

8. All compounds are made of
   a. atoms of two or more elements
   b. two or more atoms of the same element
   c. atoms arranged in a crystal
   d. atoms joined by covalent bonds

9. The chemical formula for a compound having one barium (Ba) ion and two chloride (Cl) ions is
   a. BCl
   b. BaCl
   c. BaCl$_2$
   d. Ba$_2$Cl$_2$

10. The 4 in the chemical formula CH$_4$ means there are
    a. four carbon atoms to one hydrogen atom
    b. four carbon and four hydrogen atoms
    c. four hydrogen atoms to one carbon atom
    d. four total carbon CH combinations

11. The compound KBr has the name
    a. potassium bromide
    b. potassium bromine
    c. bromide potassium
    d. bromine potassium

12. An atom becomes a positive ion when it
    a. is attracted to all nearby atoms
    b. gains an electron from another atom
    c. loses an electron to another atom
    d. shares an electron with another atom

13. A polar covalent bond forms when two atoms
    a. share one electron equally
    b. share two electrons equally
    c. share one electron unequally
    d. share two electrons unequally

14. Metallic bonds make many metals
    a. poor conductors of heat
    b. liquid at room temperature
    c. difficult to shape
    d. good conductors of electricity

15. Three forms of carbon are
    a. diamond, graphite, and salt
    b. diamond, graphite, and fullerene
    c. graphite, salt, and carbonate
    d. diamond, salt, and fullerene

Short Answer *Write a short answer to each question.*

16. Why does a mixture of sodium chloride and water conduct electricity but a sodium chloride crystal does not?

17. Describe what makes diamond and graphite, two forms of the element carbon, so different.

Chapter 2: **Chemical Bonds and Compounds** 63

Thinking Critically

Use the illustration above to answer the next two questions.

18. IDENTIFY Write the chemical formula for the molecule pictured above.

19. ANALYZE The nitrogen atom has a far greater attraction for electrons than hydrogen atoms. Copy the molecule pictured above and indicate which parts of the molecule have a slightly positive charge and which parts have a slightly negative charge.

20. PREDICT The chemical formula for calcium chloride is $CaCl_2$. What would you predict the formula for magnesium chloride to be? [**Hint:** Find magnesium on the periodic table.]

21. INFER When scientists make artificial diamonds, they sometimes subject graphite to very high temperatures and pressures. What do you think happens to change the graphite into diamond?

22. SYNTHESIZE Why would seawater be a better conductor of electricity than river water?

23. ANALYZE How does the nature of the metallic bond explain the observation that most metals can be drawn into a wire?

24. EVALUATE Do you think the types of bonds you've studied occur on the planet Mars? Explain.

25. INFER Why don't we use the term *ionic molecule*?

Use the chemical formulas below and a periodic table to answer the next three questions.

Compound
I. K_2SO_4
II. CF_4
III. C_4H_{10}
IV. KCl

26. APPLY Name compound IV. Does this compound have ionic or covalent bonds?

27. ANALYZE Name the elements in each compound. Tell how many atoms are in each compound.

28. CALCULATE Express the ratio of atoms in compounds II, III, and IV. For compound I, express all three ratios.

29. APPLY By 1800 Alessandro Volta had made the first electric battery. He placed pieces of cardboard soaked in saltwater in between alternating zinc and silver discs. What properties of the metals and the saltwater made them good materials for a battery?

30. PREDICT What is the maximum number of covalent bonds that a hydrogen atom can form? Explain your answer.

the BIG idea

31. DRAW CONCLUSIONS Look at the photograph on pages 38–39 again. Can you now recognize any similarities between how the skydivers stay together and how atoms stay together?

32. APPLY Phosphorus can be a strange element. Pure phosphorus is sometimes white, black, or red. What can account for the differences in appearance?

UNIT PROJECTS

If you need to create graphs or other visuals for your project, be sure you have graph paper, poster board, markers, or other supplies.

Standardized Test Practice

Interpreting Tables

The table below lists some of the characteristics of substances that contain different types of bonds. Use the table to answer the questions.

Bond Type	Usually Forms Between	Electrons	Properties	Examples
Ionic	an atom of a metal and an atom of a nonmetal	transferred between atoms	• high melting points • conducts electricity when in water	BaS, $BaBr_2$, Ca_3N_2, $LiCl$, ZnO
Covalent	atoms of nonmetallic elements	shared between atoms but often not equally	• low melting points • does not conduct electricity	C_2H_6, C, Cl_2, H_2, $AsCl_3$
Metallic	atoms of metallic elements	freely moving about the atoms	• high melting points • conducts electricity at all times • easily shaped	Ca, Fe, Na, Cu, Zn

1. Which of these compounds would you expect to have the highest melting point?
   a. C_2H_6
   b. Cl_2
   c. $AsCl_3$
   d. $BaBr_2$

2. Which substance is likely to be easily shaped?
   a. $BaBr_2$
   b. $LiCl$
   c. Na
   d. C

3. In the compound $LiCl$, electrons are
   a. shared equally
   b. shared but not equally
   c. transferred between atoms to form ions
   d. freely moving among the atoms

4. Which of the following is an ionic compound?
   a. C_2H_6
   b. Cl_2
   c. $AsCl_3$
   d. ZnO

5. Which of the following compounds has a low melting point?
   a. Cl_2
   b. ZnO
   c. Cu
   d. $BaBr_2$

6. A solid mass of which substance would conduct electricity?
   a. Ca_3N_2
   b. $LiCl$
   c. Cu
   d. $AsCl_3$

Extended Response

Answer the next two questions in detail. Include some of the terms from the list in the box. Underline each term you use in your answer.

share electron	transfer electron
freely moving electrons	charge
compound	chemical formula

7. Compare how electrons are involved in making the three main types of bonds: ionic, covalent, and metallic.

8. Just about 100 elements occur naturally. There are, however, millions of different materials. How can so few basic substances make so many different materials?

CHAPTER 3
Chemical Reactions

the BIG idea

Chemical reactions form new substances by breaking and making chemical bonds.

What changes are happening in this chemical reaction?

Key Concepts

SECTION 3.1 Chemical reactions alter arrangements of atoms.
Learn how chemical reactions are identified and controlled.

SECTION 3.2 The masses of reactants and products are equal.
Learn how chemical equations show the conservation of mass.

SECTION 3.3 Chemical reactions involve energy changes.
Learn how energy is absorbed or released by chemical reactions.

SECTION 3.4 Life and industry depend on chemical reactions.
Learn about some chemical reactions in everyday life.

Internet Preview

CLASSZONE.COM

Chapter 3 online resources: Content Review, two Visualizations, two Resource Centers, Math Tutorial, Test Practice

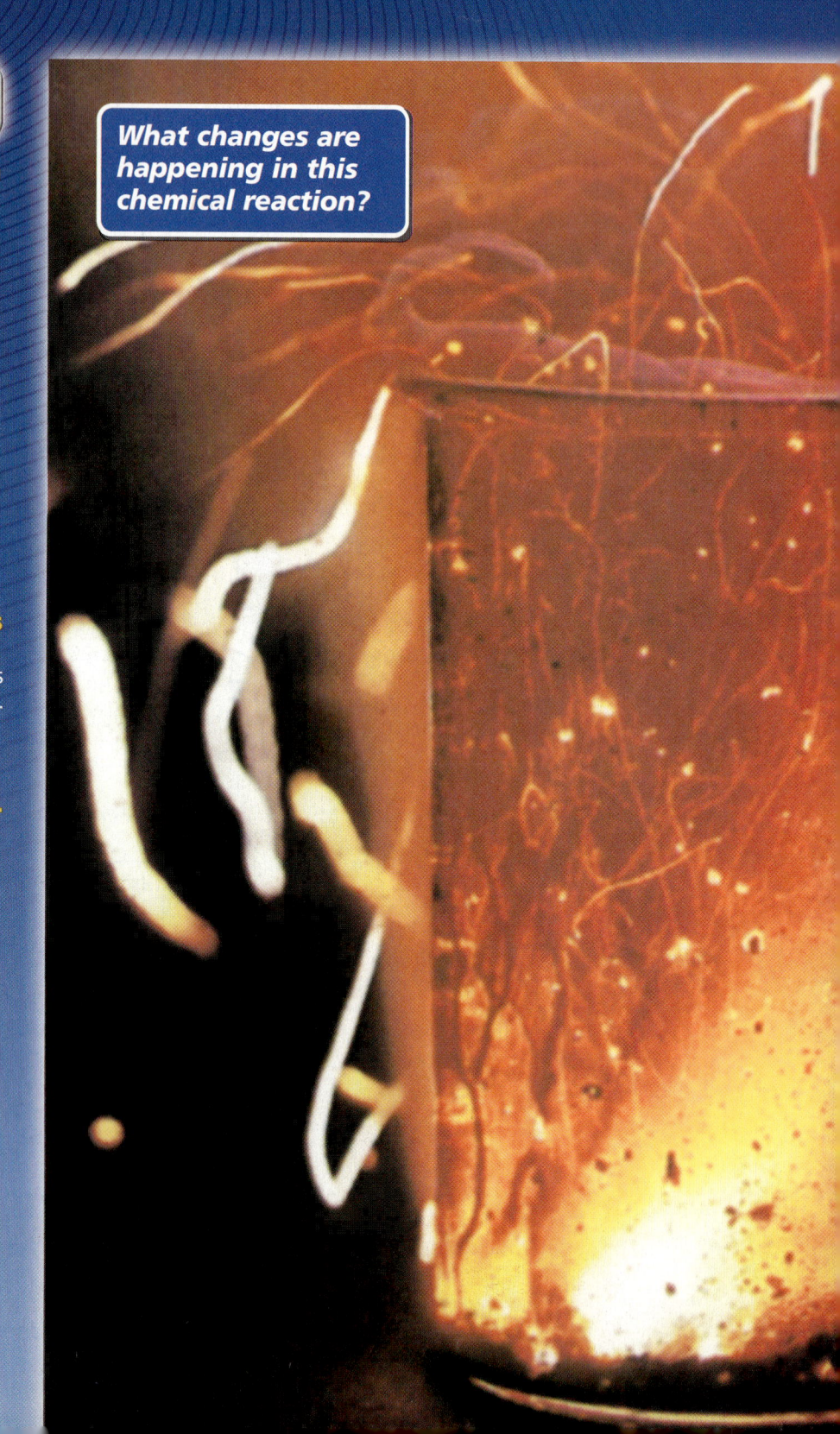

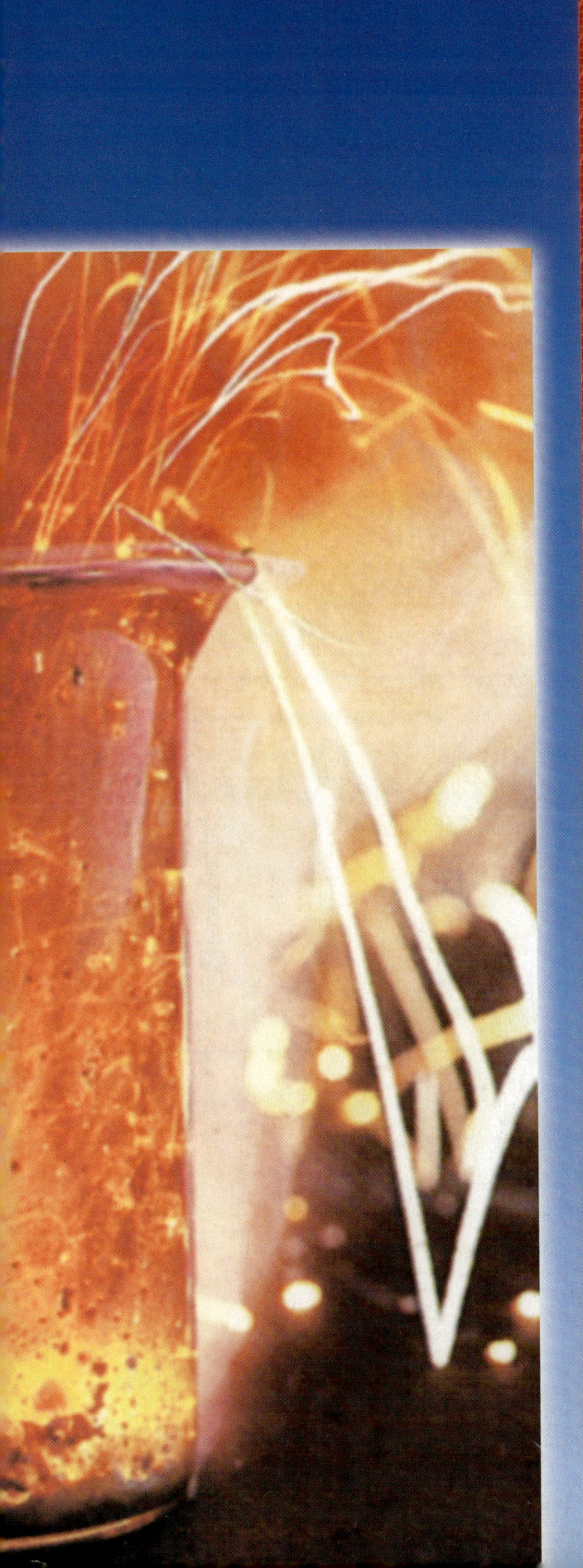

EXPLORE the BIG idea

Changing Steel Wool

Place a small lump of steel wool in a cup. Pour in enough vinegar to cover the steel wool. After five minutes, take the steel wool out of the vinegar. Shake the steel wool to remove any excess vinegar. Place the steel wool in a small plastic bottle, and cover the mouth of the bottle with a balloon. Observe the steel wool and balloon after one hour.

Observe and Think What happened to the steel wool and balloon? What might have caused this to occur?

A Different Rate

Half fill one cup with hot tap water and a second cup with cold tap water. Drop a seltzer tablet into each cup at the same time. Time how long it takes for each tablet to stop fizzing.

Observe and Think Which tablet fizzed for a longer period of time? How might you explain any differences?

Internet Activity: Reactions

Go to **ClassZone.com** to explore chemical reactions and chemical equations. Learn how a chemical equation can be balanced.

Observe and Think How do chemical equations show what happens during a chemical reaction?

NSTA scilinks.org
SCiLINKS
Chemical Reactions Code: MDL024

Chapter 3: Chemical Reactions 67 B

CHAPTER 3
Getting Ready to Learn

CONCEPT REVIEW

- Atoms combine to form compounds.
- Atoms gain or lose electrons when they form ionic bonds.
- Atoms share electrons in covalent bonds.

VOCABULARY REVIEW

electron p. 11
ionic bond p. 48
covalent bond p. 50

See Glossary for definitions.

atom, chemical change

CONTENT REVIEW
CLASSZONE.COM
Review concepts and vocabulary.

TAKING NOTES

COMBINATION NOTES

To take notes about a new concept, first make an informal outline of the information. Then make a sketch of the concept and label it so you can study it later.

VOCABULARY STRATEGY

Write each new vocabulary term in the center of a **four square** diagram. Write notes in the squares around each term. Include a definition, some characteristics, and some examples of the term. If possible, write some things that are not examples of the term.

SCIENCE NOTEBOOK

NOTES

Chemical reactions
- cause chemical changes
- make new substances
- change reactants into products

Evidence of Chemical Reactions

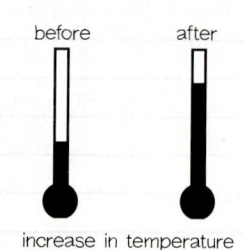

before / after

increase in temperature

Definition	Characteristics
substance present before a chemical reaction occurs	its bonds are broken during a reaction

REACTANT

Examples	Nonexample
oxygen in a combustion reaction	carbon dioxide in a combustion reaction

See the Note-Taking Handbook on pages R45–R51.

68 Unit: Chemical Interactions

3.1 KEY CONCEPT
Chemical reactions alter arrangements of atoms.

BEFORE, you learned
- Atoms of one element differ from atoms of all other elements
- Chemical bonds hold compounds together
- Chemical bonds may be ionic or covalent

NOW, you will learn
- About chemical changes and how they occur
- About three types of chemical reactions
- How the rate of a chemical reaction can be changed

VOCABULARY
chemical reaction p. 69
reactant p. 71
product p. 71
precipitate p. 72
catalyst p. 76

EXPLORE Chemical Changes
How can you identify a chemical change?

PROCEDURE

1. Pour about 3 cm (1 in.) of vinegar into the bowl. Add a spoonful of salt. Stir until the salt dissolves.
2. Put the pennies into the bowl. Wait two minutes, and then put the nail into the bowl.
3. Observe the nail after five minutes and record your observations.

WHAT DO YOU THINK?
- What did you see on the nail? Where do you think it came from?
- Did a new substance form? What evidence supports your conclusion?

MATERIALS
- vinegar
- clear bowl
- plastic spoon
- table salt
- 20 pennies
- large iron nail

COMBINATION NOTES
Use combination notes to organize information about how atoms interact during chemical reactions.

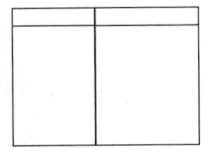

Atoms interact in chemical reactions.

You see substances change every day. Some changes are physical, such as when liquid water changes to water vapor during boiling. Other changes are chemical, such as when wood burns to form smoke and ash, or when rust forms on iron. During a chemical change, substances change into one or more different substances.

A **chemical reaction** produces new substances by changing the way in which atoms are arranged. In a chemical reaction, bonds between atoms are broken and new bonds form between different atoms. This breaking and forming of bonds takes place when particles of the original materials collide with one another. After a chemical reaction, the new arrangements of atoms form different substances.

Chapter 3: Chemical Reactions 69 B

Physical Changes

A change in the state of a substance is an example of a physical change. The substance may have some different properties after a physical change, but it is still the same substance. For example, you know that water can exist in three different physical states: the solid state (ice), the liquid state (water), and the gas state (water vapor). However, regardless of what state water is in, it still remains water, that is, H_2O molecules. As ice melts, the molecules of water move around more quickly, but the molecules do not change. As water vapor condenses, the molecules of water move more slowly, but they are still the same molecules.

Substances can undergo different kinds of physical changes. For example, sugar dissolves in water but still tastes sweet because the molecules that make up sugar do not change when it dissolves. The pressure of helium changes when it is pumped from a high-pressure tank into a balloon, but the gas still remains helium.

CHECK YOUR READING What happens to a substance when it undergoes a physical change?

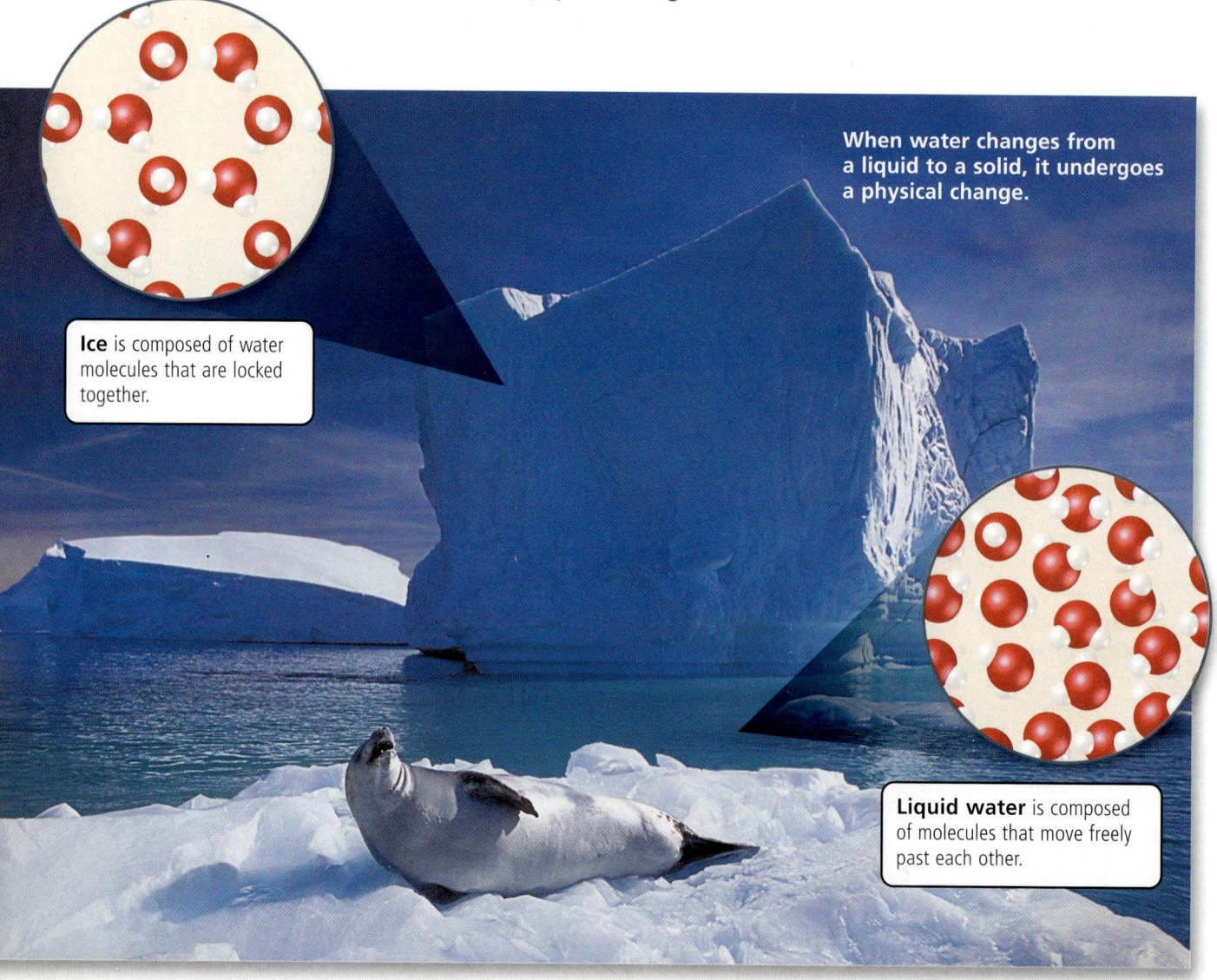

When water changes from a liquid to a solid, it undergoes a physical change.

Ice is composed of water molecules that are locked together.

Liquid water is composed of molecules that move freely past each other.

Chemical Changes

Water can also undergo a chemical change. Water molecules can be broken down into hydrogen and oxygen molecules by a chemical reaction called electrolysis. When an electric current is passed through liquid water (H_2O), it changes the water into two gases—hydrogen and oxygen. The molecules of water break apart into individual atoms, which then recombine into hydrogen molecules (H_2) and oxygen molecules (O_2). The original material (water) changes into different substances through a chemical reaction.

Hydrogen and oxygen are used as rocket fuel for the space shuttle. During liftoff, liquid hydrogen and liquid oxygen are combined in a reaction that is the opposite of electrolysis. This reaction produces water and a large amount of energy that helps push the shuttle into orbit.

CHECK YOUR READING How does a chemical change differ from a physical change?

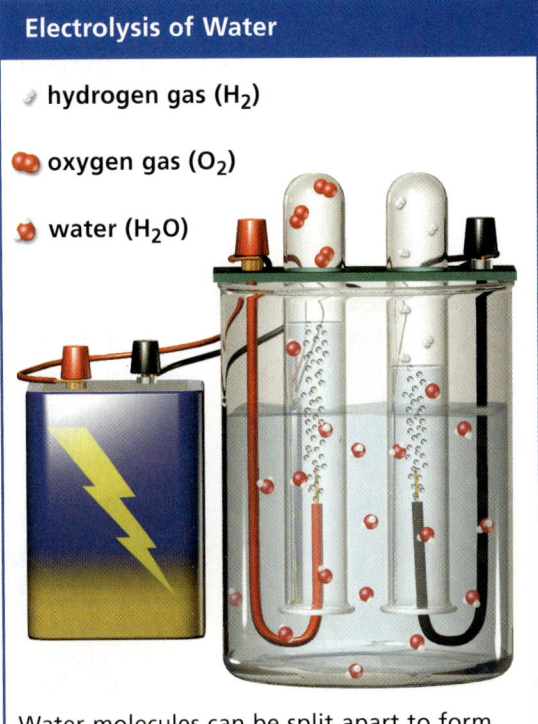

Electrolysis of Water

- hydrogen gas (H_2)
- oxygen gas (O_2)
- water (H_2O)

Water molecules can be split apart to form separate hydrogen and oxygen molecules.

Reactants and Products

Reactants are the substances present at the beginning of a chemical reaction. In the burning of natural gas, for example, methane (CH_4) and oxygen (O_2) are the reactants in the chemical reaction. **Products** are the substances formed by a chemical reaction. In the burning of natural gas, carbon dioxide (CO_2) and water (H_2O) are the products formed by the reaction. Reactants and products can be elements or compounds, depending on the reaction taking place.

During a chemical reaction, bonds between atoms in the reactants are broken and new bonds are formed in the products. When natural gas is burned, bonds between the carbon and hydrogen atoms in methane are broken, as are the bonds between the oxygen atoms in oxygen molecules. New bonds are formed between carbon and oxygen in carbon dioxide gas and between hydrogen and oxygen in water vapor.

Reactants—bonds broken	Products—new bonds formed
methane + oxygen (CH_4) (O_2)	carbon dioxide + water (CO_2) (H_2O)

CHECK YOUR READING What must happen for reactants to be changed into products?

Chapter 3: **Chemical Reactions** 71

VOCABULARY
Remember to use a four square diagram for *precipitate* and other vocabulary terms.

Evidence of Chemical Reactions

Some chemical changes are easy to observe—the products formed by the rearrangement of atoms look different than the reactants. Other changes are not easy to see but can be detected in other ways.

Color Change Substances often change color during a chemical reaction. For example, when gray iron rusts, the product that forms is brown, as shown in the photograph below.

Formation of a Precipitate Many chemical reactions form products that exist in a different physical state from the reactants. A solid product called a **precipitate** may form when chemicals in two liquids react, as shown in the photograph below. Seashells are often formed this way when a sea creature releases a liquid that reacts with seawater.

Color Change

Formation of a Precipitate

Formation of a Gas Chemical reactions may produce a gas, like that often formed when antacid pills are mixed with excess stomach acid. The photograph below shows an example in which carbon dioxide gas is produced by a chemical reaction.

Temperature Change Most chemical reactions involve a temperature change. Sometimes this change can be inferred from the observation of a flame, as in the burning of the metal magnesium in the photograph below. Other temperature changes are not immediately obvious. If you have touched concrete before it hardens, you may have noticed that it felt warm. This warmth is due to a chemical reaction.

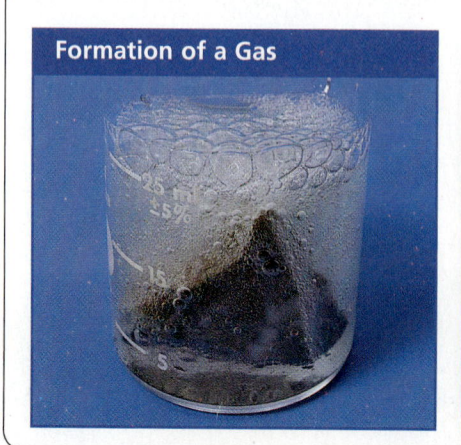

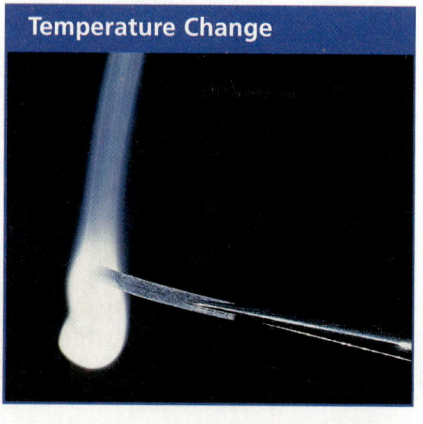

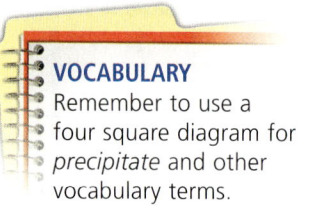

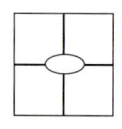

Formation of a Gas

Temperature Change

Chemical reactions can be classified.

Scientists classify chemical reactions in several ways to help make the different types of reactions easier to understand. All reactions form new products, but the ways in which products are made can differ.

Synthesis In a synthesis reaction, a new compound is formed by the combination of simpler reactants. For example, nitrogen dioxide (NO_2), a component of smog, forms when nitrogen and oxygen combine in the air.

READING TIP

Synthesis means "making a substance from simpler substances."

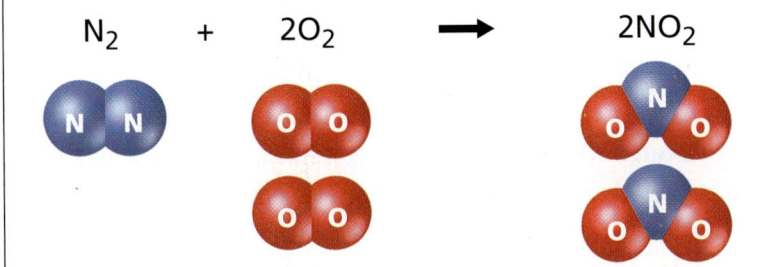

$$N_2 + 2O_2 \rightarrow 2NO_2$$

Decomposition In a decomposition reaction, a reactant breaks down into simpler products, which could be elements or other compounds. Decomposition reactions can be thought of as being the reverse of synthesis reactions. For example, water can be decomposed into its elements—hydrogen and oxygen.

READING TIP

Decomposition means "separation into parts."

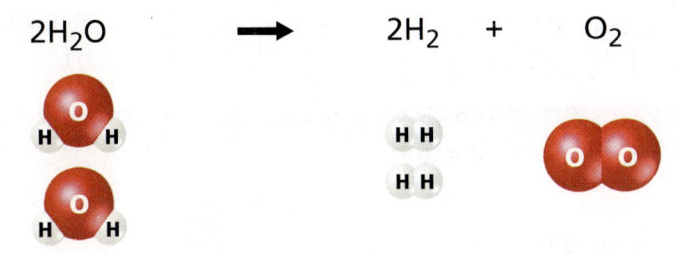

$$2H_2O \rightarrow 2H_2 + O_2$$

Combustion In a combustion reaction, one reactant is always oxygen and another reactant often contains carbon and hydrogen. The carbon and hydrogen atoms combine with oxygen, producing carbon dioxide and water. The burning of methane is a combustion reaction.

READING TIP

Combustion is the process of burning with oxygen.

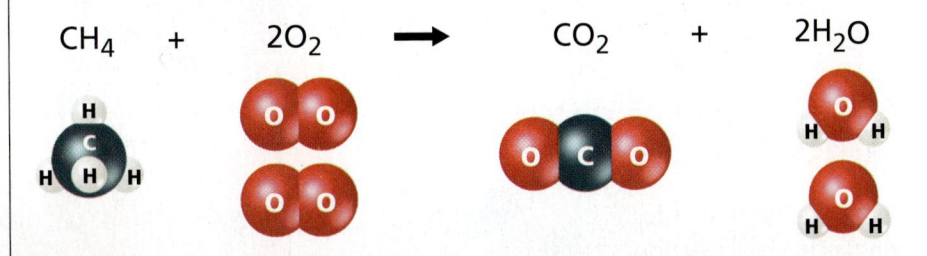

$$CH_4 + 2O_2 \rightarrow CO_2 + 2H_2O$$

CHECK YOUR READING How are synthesis reactions different from decomposition reactions?

Chapter 3: **Chemical Reactions** 73

The rates of chemical reactions can vary.

Most chemical reactions take place when particles of reactants collide with enough force to react. Chemical reactions can occur at different rates. Striking a match causes a very quick chemical reaction, while the rusting of an iron nail may take months. However, the rate of a reaction can be changed. For instance, a nail can be made to rust more quickly. Three physical factors—concentration, surface area, and temperature—and a chemical factor—a catalyst—can greatly affect the rate of a chemical reaction.

Concentration

VISUALIZATION
CLASSZONE.COM
Observe how changing the concentration of a reactant can change the rate of a reaction.

Concentration measures the number of particles present in a certain volume. A high concentration of reactants means that there is a large number of particles that can collide and react. Turning the valve on a gas stove to increase the flow of gas increases the concentration of methane molecules that can combine with oxygen in the air. The result is a bigger flame and a faster combustion reaction.

Surface Area

Suppose one of the reactants in a chemical reaction is present as a single large piece of material. Particles of the second reactant cannot get inside the large piece, so they can react only with particles on the surface. To make the reaction go faster, the large piece of material could be broken into smaller pieces before the reaction starts.

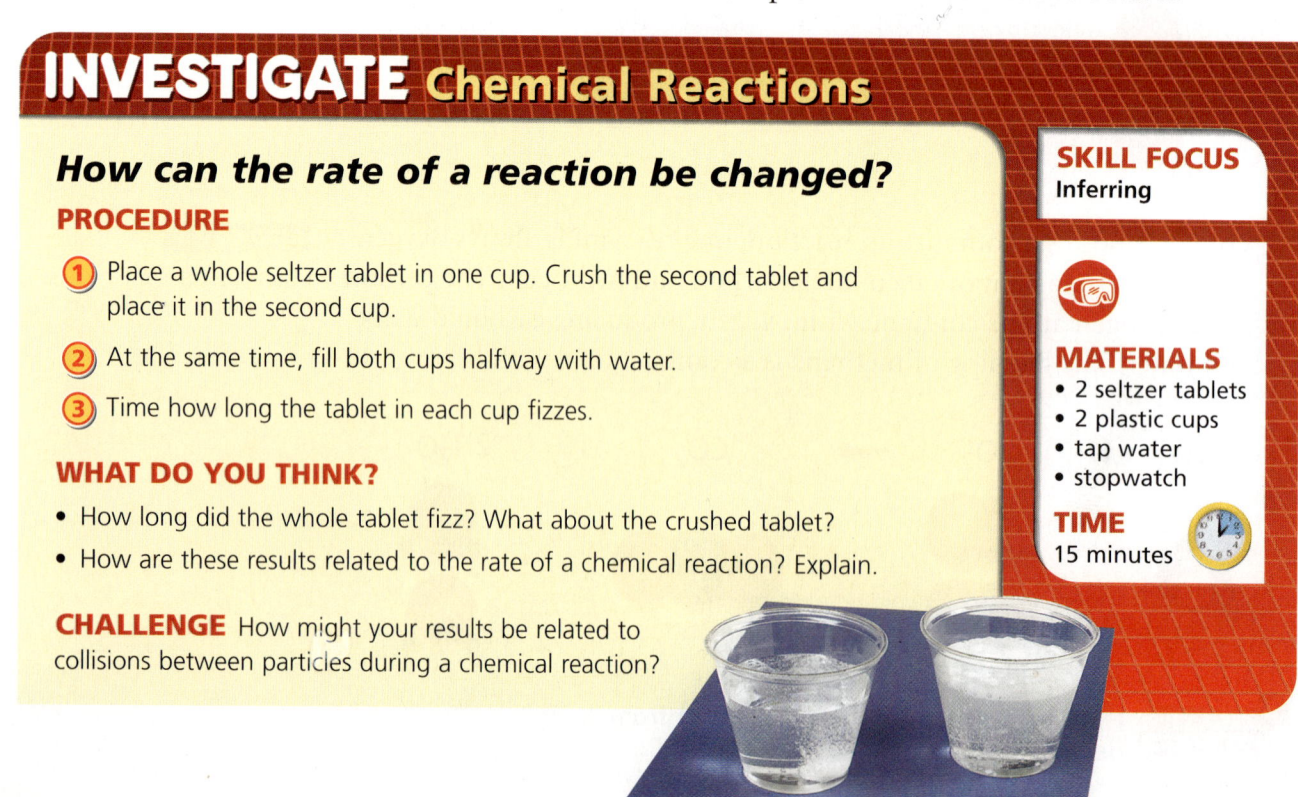

INVESTIGATE Chemical Reactions

How can the rate of a reaction be changed?
PROCEDURE

1. Place a whole seltzer tablet in one cup. Crush the second tablet and place it in the second cup.
2. At the same time, fill both cups halfway with water.
3. Time how long the tablet in each cup fizzes.

WHAT DO YOU THINK?
- How long did the whole tablet fizz? What about the crushed tablet?
- How are these results related to the rate of a chemical reaction? Explain.

CHALLENGE How might your results be related to collisions between particles during a chemical reaction?

SKILL FOCUS
Inferring

MATERIALS
- 2 seltzer tablets
- 2 plastic cups
- tap water
- stopwatch

TIME
15 minutes

B 74 Unit: Chemical Interactions

Breaking a large piece of material into smaller parts increases the surface area of the material. All of the inner material has no surface when it is inside a larger piece. Each time the large piece is broken, however, more surfaces are exposed. The amount of material does not change, but breaking it into smaller parts increases its surface area. Increasing the surface area increases the rate of the reaction.

CHECK YOUR READING Why does a reaction proceed faster when the reactants have greater surface areas?

Temperature

The rate of a reaction can be increased by making the particles move faster. The result is that more collisions take place per second and occur with greater force. The most common way to make the particles move faster is to add energy to the reactants, which will raise their temperature.

Many chemical reactions during cooking go very slowly, or do not take place at all, unless energy is added to the reactants. Too much heat can make a reaction go too fast, and food ends up burned. Chemical reactions can also be slowed or stopped by decreasing the temperature of the reactants. Again, think about cooking. The reactions that take place during cooking can be stopped by removing the food from the heat source.

REMINDER

Temperature is the average amount of kinetic energy of the particles in a substance.

Particles and Reaction Rates

Changes in Reactants	Normal Reaction Rate	Increased Reaction Rate
Concentration An increase in concentration of the reactants increases the number of particles that can interact.		
Surface area An increase in the surface area of the reactants increases the number of particles that can interact.		
Temperature Adding energy makes particles move faster and increases temperature. The increase in motion allows reactants to collide and react more frequently.		

Chapter 3: **Chemical Reactions** 75 B

Catalysts

Resource Center CLASSZONE.COM
Learn more about catalysts and how they work in living things.

The rate of a reaction can be changed chemically by adding a catalyst. A **catalyst** is a substance that increases the rate of a chemical reaction but is not itself consumed in the reaction. This means that after the reaction is complete, the catalyst remains unchanged. Catalysts are very important for many industrial and biological reactions. In fact, many chemical reactions would proceed slowly or not take place at all without catalysts.

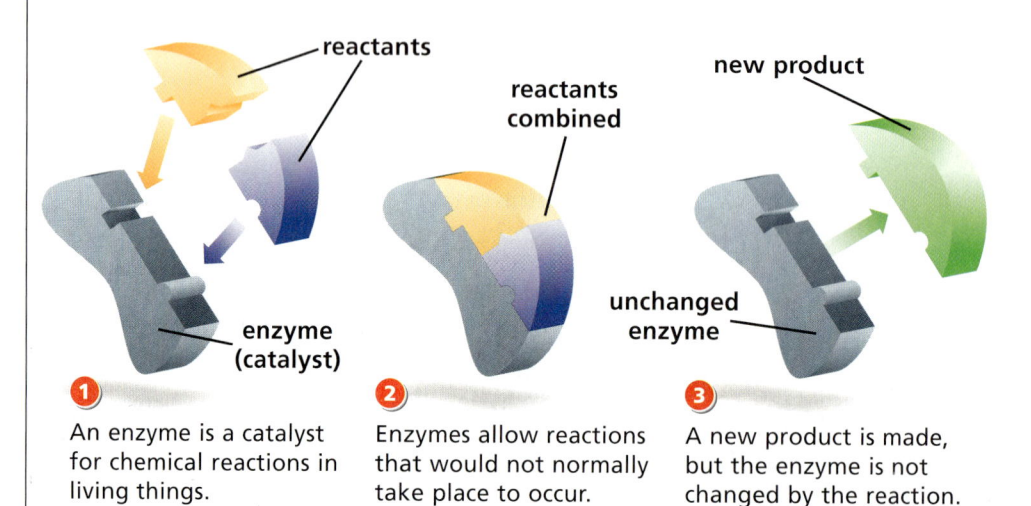

1 An enzyme is a catalyst for chemical reactions in living things.

2 Enzymes allow reactions that would not normally take place to occur.

3 A new product is made, but the enzyme is not changed by the reaction.

In living things, catalysts called enzymes are absolutely necessary for life. Without them, many important reactions could not take place under the conditions within your body. In fact, in 2003, scientists reported that they had discovered the slowest known chemical reaction in living things. This reaction would normally take one trillion years. Enzymes, though, allow the reaction to occur in 0.01 seconds.

CHECK YOUR READING Why are catalysts important in chemical reactions?

3.1 Review

KEY CONCEPTS
1. How do physical changes differ from chemical changes? Explain.
2. Describe four types of evidence of a chemical reaction.
3. Describe the ways in which the rate of a chemical reaction can be changed.

CRITICAL THINKING
4. **Synthesize** What evidence shows that the burning of methane is a chemical reaction?
5. **Compare** What about combustion reactions makes them different from either synthesis or decomposition reactions?

CHALLENGE
6. **Apply** How might the chewing of food be related to the rate of a chemical reaction—digestion—that occurs in your body? Explain.

MATH in SCIENCE

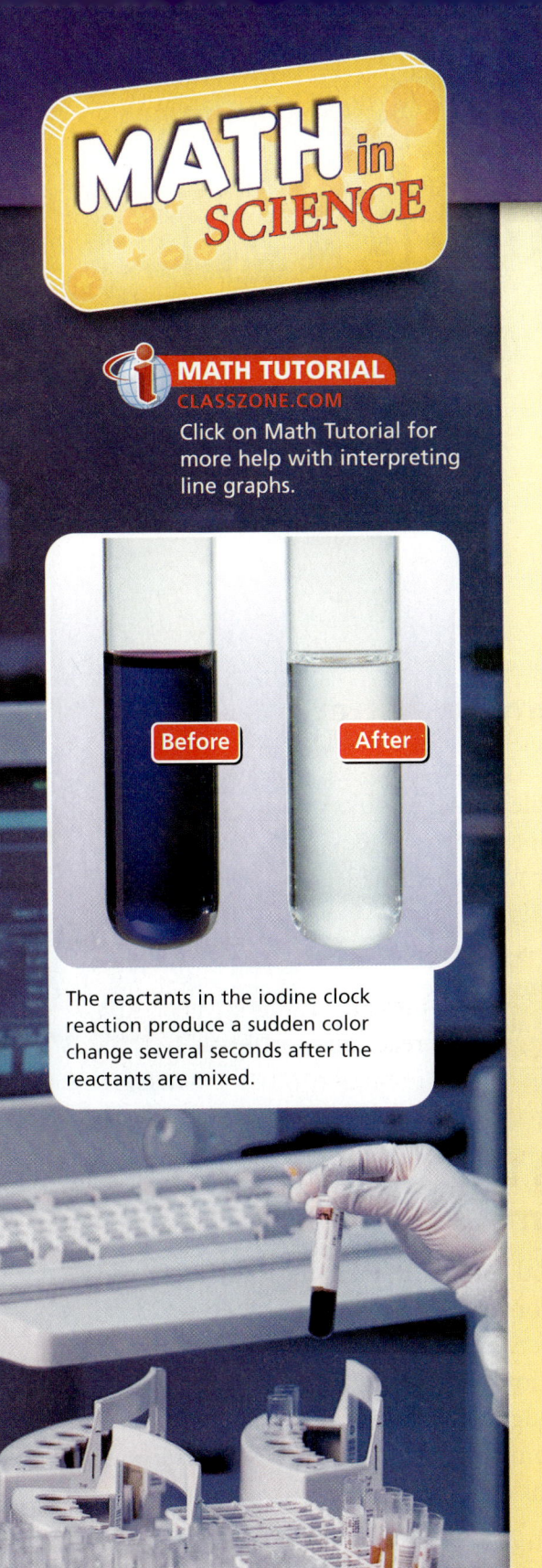

SKILL: ANALYZING LINE GRAPHS

MATH TUTORIAL
CLASSZONE.COM

Click on Math Tutorial for more help with interpreting line graphs.

Before / After

The reactants in the iodine clock reaction produce a sudden color change several seconds after the reactants are mixed.

The Iodine Clock

Can a chemical reaction be timed? In the iodine clock reaction, a sudden color change indicates that the reaction has occurred. The length of time that passes before the color changes depends on the concentration ratios of the reactants. As shown in the graph below, the greater the concentration of the reactants, the faster the reaction.

Example

Suppose you are given an unknown iodine concentration to test in the iodine clock reaction. What is the concentration ratio of the iodine if it takes 40 seconds for the color change to occur?

(1) Find 40 seconds on the *x*-axis of the graph below and follow the vertical line up to the plotted data.

(2) Draw a horizontal line from that point on the curve to the *y*-axis to find the iodine concentration ratio in your sample.

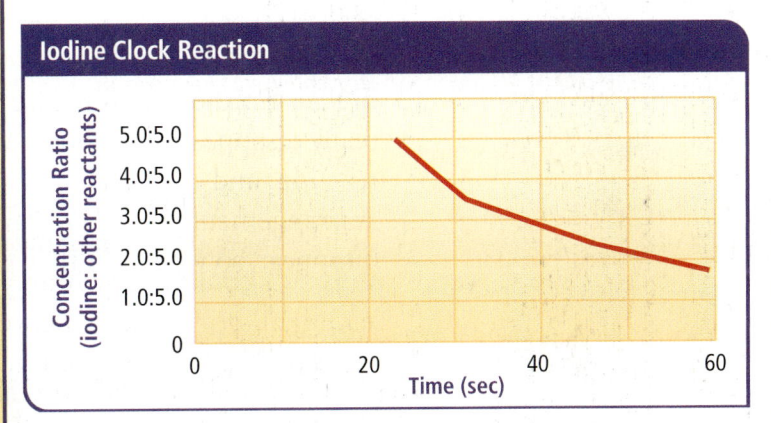

Iodine Clock Reaction

(graph: Concentration Ratio (iodine: other reactants) vs. Time (sec))

ANSWER The unknown concentration ratio is approximately 3.0:5.0.

Answer the following questions using the information in the graph above.

1. Approximately how long will it take for the reaction to occur if the concentration ratio is 4.0:5.0? 2.0:5.0?

2. Suppose you could extend the curve on the graph. If the reaction took 70 seconds to occur, what would be the approximate iodine concentration ratio?

CHALLENGE Using the following concentration ratios and times for another reactant, draw a reaction rate graph similar to the one shown above.

Concentration Ratios = 5.0:5.0, 4.0:5.0, 3.0:5.0, 2.0:5.0

Times = 24 sec, 25 sec, 43 sec, 68 sec

Chapter 3: **Chemical Reactions** 77

KEY CONCEPT
3.2 The masses of reactants and products are equal.

BEFORE, you learned
- Chemical reactions turn reactants into products by rearranging atoms
- Chemical reactions can be observed and identified
- The rate of chemical reactions can be changed

NOW, you will learn
- About the law of conservation of mass
- How a chemical equation represents a chemical reaction
- How to balance a simple chemical equation

VOCABULARY
law of conservation of mass p. 79
coefficient p. 82

THINK ABOUT

What happens to burning matter?

You have probably watched a fire burn in a fireplace, a campfire, or a candle flame. It looks as if the wood or candle disappears over time, leaving a small pile of ashes or wax when the fire has finished burning. But does matter really disappear? Combustion is a chemical reaction, and chemical reactions involve rearrangements of atoms. The atoms do not disappear, so where do they go?

COMBINATION NOTES
Take notes on the conservation of mass using combination notes.

Careful observations led to the discovery of the conservation of mass.

The ashes left over from a wood fire contain less mass than the wood. In many other chemical reactions, mass also appears to decrease. That is, the mass of the products appears to be less than the mass of the reactants. In other reactions, the products appear to gain mass. For example, plants grow through a complex series of reactions, but where does their extra mass come from? At one time, scientists thought that chemical reactions could create or destroy matter.

During the 1780s the French chemist Antoine Lavoisier (luh-VWAH-zee-ay) showed that matter can never be created or destroyed in a chemical reaction. Lavoisier emphasized the importance of making very careful measurements in his experiments. Because of his methods, he was able to show that reactions that seem to gain mass or lose mass actually involve reactions with gases in the air. These gases could not be seen, but their masses could be measured.

An example of Lavoisier's work is his study of the reaction of the metal mercury when heated in air. In this reaction, the reddish-orange product formed has more mass than the original metal. Lavoisier placed some mercury in a jar, sealed the jar, and recorded the total mass of the setup. After the mercury had been heated in the jar, the total mass of the jar and its contents had not changed.

Lavoisier showed that the air left in the jar would no longer support burning—a candle flame was snuffed out by this air. He concluded that a gas in the air, which he called oxygen, had combined with the mercury to form the new product.

Lavoisier conducted many experiments of this type and found in all cases that the mass of the reactants is equal to the mass of the products. This conclusion, called the **law of conservation of mass,** states that in a chemical reaction atoms are neither created nor destroyed. All atoms present in the reactants are also present in the products.

Lavoisier carefully measured both the reactants and the products of chemical reactions.

CHECK YOUR READING How did Lavoisier investigate the conservation of mass?

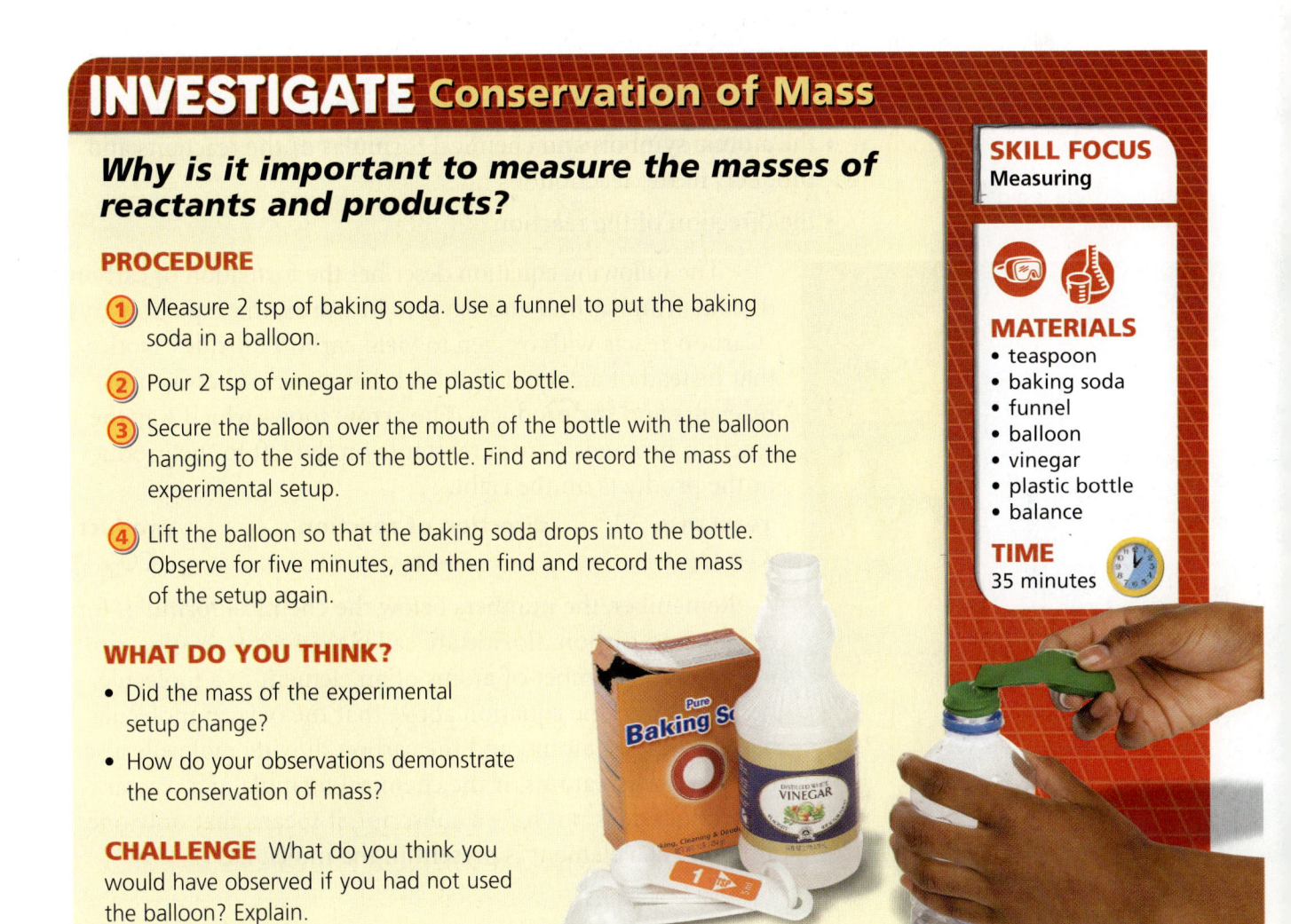

INVESTIGATE Conservation of Mass

Why is it important to measure the masses of reactants and products?

PROCEDURE

1. Measure 2 tsp of baking soda. Use a funnel to put the baking soda in a balloon.

2. Pour 2 tsp of vinegar into the plastic bottle.

3. Secure the balloon over the mouth of the bottle with the balloon hanging to the side of the bottle. Find and record the mass of the experimental setup.

4. Lift the balloon so that the baking soda drops into the bottle. Observe for five minutes, and then find and record the mass of the setup again.

WHAT DO YOU THINK?
- Did the mass of the experimental setup change?
- How do your observations demonstrate the conservation of mass?

CHALLENGE What do you think you would have observed if you had not used the balloon? Explain.

SKILL FOCUS
Measuring

MATERIALS
- teaspoon
- baking soda
- funnel
- balloon
- vinegar
- plastic bottle
- balance

TIME
35 minutes

Chapter 3: **Chemical Reactions** 79

Chemical reactions can be described by chemical equations.

The law of conservation of mass states that in a chemical reaction, the total mass of reactants is equal to the total mass of products. For example, the mass of sodium plus the mass of chlorine that reacts with the sodium equals the mass of the product sodium chloride. Because atoms are rearranged in a chemical reaction, there must be the same number of sodium atoms and chlorine atoms in both the reactants and products.

Chemical equations represent how atoms are rearranged in a chemical reaction. The atoms in the reactants are shown on the left side of the equation. The atoms in the products are shown on the right side of the equation. Because atoms are rearranged and not created or destroyed, the number of atoms of each different element must be the same on each side of the equation.

CHECK YOUR READING How does a chemical equation show the conservation of mass?

In order to write a chemical equation, the information that you need to know is

- the reactants and products in the reaction
- the atomic symbols and chemical formulas of the reactants and products in the reaction
- the direction of the reaction

Carbon dioxide is a gas that animals exhale.

The following equation describes the formation of carbon dioxide from carbon and oxygen. In words, this equation says "Carbon reacts with oxygen to yield carbon dioxide." Notice that instead of an equal sign, an arrow appears between the reactants and the products. The arrow shows which way the reaction proceeds—from reactants on the left to the product or the products on the right.

reactants	direction of reaction	product
$C + O_2$	$\longrightarrow$	CO_2

Remember, the numbers below the chemical formulas for oxygen and carbon dioxide are called subscripts. A subscript indicates the number of atoms of an element in a molecule. You can see in the equation above that the oxygen molecule has two oxygen atoms, and the carbon dioxide molecule also has two oxygen atoms. If the chemical formula of a reactant or product does not have a subscript, it means that only one atom of each element is present in the molecule.

Chemical equations must be balanced.

Remember, chemical reactions follow the law of conservation of mass. Chemical equations show this conservation, or equality, in terms of atoms. The same number of atoms of each element must appear on both sides of a chemical equation. However, simply writing down the chemical formulas of reactants and products does not always result in equal numbers of atoms. You have to balance the equation to make the number of atoms equal on each side of an equation.

Balancing Chemical Equations

To learn how to balance an equation, look at the example of the combustion of natural gas, which is mostly methane (CH_4). The reactants are methane and oxygen. The products are carbon dioxide and water. You can write this reaction as the following equation.

REMINDER
Oxygen is always a reactant in a combustion reaction.

Unbalanced Equation

$$CH_4 + O_2 \rightarrow CO_2 + H_2O$$

This equation is not balanced. There is one C on each side of the equation, so C is balanced. However, on the left side, H has a subscript of 4, which means there are four hydrogen atoms. On the right side, H has a subscript of 2, which means there are two hydrogen atoms. Also, there are two oxygen atoms on the left and three oxygen atoms on the right. Because of the conservation of mass, you know that hydrogen atoms do not disappear and oxygen atoms do not suddenly appear.

READING TIP
As you read how to balance the equation, look at the illustrations and count the atoms. The number of each type of atom is shown below the formula.

You can balance a chemical equation by changing the amounts of reactants or products represented.

- To balance H first, add another H_2O molecule on the right. Now, both C and H are balanced.
- There are now two oxygen atoms on the left side and four oxygen atoms on the right side. To balance O, add another O_2 molecule on the left.

Balanced Equation

$$CH_4 + O_2 + O_2 \rightarrow CO_2 + H_2O + H_2O$$

Chapter 3: **Chemical Reactions** 81

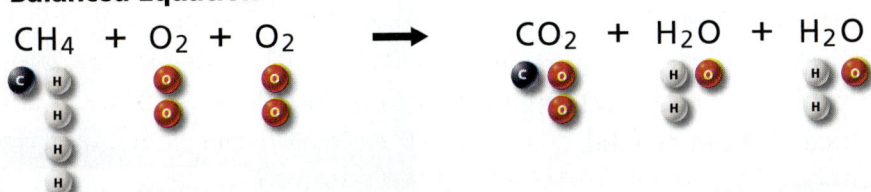

Using Coefficients to Balance Equations

The balanced equation for the combustion of methane shows that one molecule of methane reacts with two molecules of oxygen to produce one molecule of carbon dioxide and two molecules of water. The equation can be simplified by writing $2O_2$ instead of $O_2 + O_2$, and $2H_2O$ instead of $H_2O + H_2O$.

The numbers in front of the chemical formulas are called coefficients. **Coefficients** indicate how many molecules take part in the reaction. If there is no coefficient, then only one molecule of that type takes part in the reaction. The balanced equation, with coefficients, for the combustion of methane is shown below.

> **REMINDER**
> A subscript shows the number of atoms in a molecule. If a subscript is changed, the molecule represented by the formula is changed.

Balanced Equation with Coefficients

$$CH_4 + \underset{\text{coefficient}}{2}O_2 \longrightarrow CO\underset{\text{subscript}}{_2} + 2H_2O$$

Chemical formulas can have both coefficients and subscripts. In these cases, multiply the two numbers together to find the number of atoms involved in the reaction. For example, two water molecules ($2H_2O$) contain $2 \cdot 2 = 4$ hydrogen atoms and $2 \cdot 1 = 2$ oxygen atoms. Remember, coefficients in a chemical equation indicate how many molecules of each type take part in the reaction.

Only coefficients can be changed in order to balance a chemical equation. Subscripts are part of the chemical formula for reactants or products and cannot be changed to balance an equation. Changing a subscript changes the substance represented by the formula.

For example, the equation for the combustion of methane cannot be balanced by changing the formula CO_2 to CO. The formula CO_2 represents carbon dioxide gas, which animals exhale when they breathe. The formula CO represents carbon monoxide gas, which is a very different compound from CO_2. Carbon monoxide gas is poisonous, and breathing too much of it can be fatal.

CHECK YOUR READING Why are coefficients used to balance equations?

The combustion of methane (CH_4) is used to melt glass.

Balancing Equations with Coefficients

The steps below show how to balance the equation for the synthesis reaction between nitrogen (N_2) and hydrogen (H_2), which produces ammonia (NH_3).

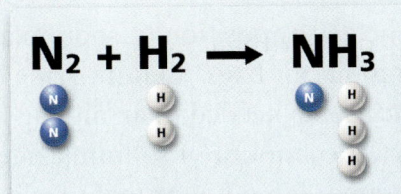

$$N_2 + H_2 \rightarrow NH_3$$

1 **Count the atoms.** Neither N nor H is balanced. The reactants contain two atoms each of N and H, but the product contains one N atom and three H atoms.

$N_2 + H_2 \rightarrow NH_3$

N = 2	N = 1
H = 2	H = 3

Tip: Listing the number of atoms of each element makes it easy to see which elements must be balanced.

2 **Use a coefficient to add atoms to one side of the equation.** A coefficient of 2 on NH_3 balances the number of N atoms.

$N_2 + H_2 \rightarrow 2\,NH_3$

N = 2	N = 2
H = 2	H = 6

Tip: When adding coefficients, start with the reactant or product that contains the greatest number of different elements.

3 **Add a coefficient to another reactant or product.** Adding a coefficient of 3 to H_2 on the left side of the equation balances the number of H atoms on both sides. Now the equation is balanced.

$N_2 + 3\,H_2 \rightarrow 2NH_3$

N = 2	N = 2
H = 6	H = 6

Tip: Make sure that the coefficients in your balanced equation are the smallest whole numbers possible—that is, they have no common factor other than 1.

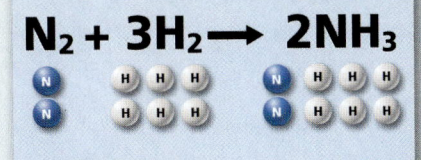

$$N_2 + 3H_2 \rightarrow 2NH_3$$

APPLY
Balance the following equations.
1. $Hg + O_2 \rightarrow HgO$
2. $Zn + HCl \rightarrow ZnCl_2 + H_2$

Using the Conservation of Mass

A balanced chemical equation shows that no matter how atoms are rearranged during a chemical reaction, the same number of atoms must be present before and after the reaction. The following example demonstrates the usefulness of chemical equations and the conservation of mass.

The decomposition of sodium azide (NaN_3) is used to inflate automobile air bags. Sodium azide is a solid, and the amount of sodium azide needed in an air bag fills only a small amount of space. In fact, the amount of sodium azide used in air bags is only about 130 grams—an amount that would fit in a large spoon. An inflated air bag, though, takes up much more space even though it contains the same number of atoms that entered the reaction. The reason is illustrated by the chemical equation for this reaction.

The decomposition of sodium azide is used to inflate air bags in automobiles.

Balanced Equation

$$2NaN_3 \longrightarrow 2Na + 3N_2$$

According to the balanced equation shown above, three molecules of nitrogen gas are formed for every two molecules of sodium azide that decompose. Because the nitrogen is a gas, it fills a much greater volume than the original sodium azide. In fact, 67 liters of nitrogen gas are produced by the 130 grams of sodium azide in the reaction. This amount of nitrogen is enough to quickly inflate the air bag during a collision—the decomposition of sodium azide to sodium and nitrogen takes 0.03 seconds.

CHECK YOUR READING Why must chemical equations be balanced?

3.2 Review

KEY CONCEPTS

1. State the law of conservation of mass.
2. Write the chemical equation that shows sodium (Na) and chlorine (Cl_2) combining to form table salt (NaCl).
3. Is the following equation balanced? Why or why not?

    $CO \longrightarrow C + O_2$

CRITICAL THINKING

4. **Communicate** Describe Lavoisier's experiment with mercury. How does this experiment show the law of conservation of mass?
5. **Synthesize** Suppose a log's mass is 5 kg. After burning, the mass of the ash is 1 kg. Explain what may have happened to the other 4 kg of mass.

CHALLENGE

6. **Synthesize** Suppose a container holds 1000 hydrogen molecules (H_2) and 1000 oxygen molecules (O_2) that react to form water. How many water molecules will be in the container? Will anything else be in the container? If so, what?

SCIENCE on the JOB

FIREFIGHTER

Chemistry in Firefighting

A firefighter's job may seem simple: to put out fires. However, a firefighter needs to know about chemicals and chemical reactions. A fire is a combustion reaction that requires oxygen as a reactant. Without oxygen, a fire will normally burn itself out, so firefighters try to prevent oxygen from reaching the burning substances. Firefighters often use water or carbon dioxide for this purpose, but these materials make some types of fires more dangerous.

Grease Fires

Some fires can be extinguished by a chemical reaction. In kitchen grease fires, the chemicals that are used to fight the fire react with the grease. The reaction produces a foam that puts out the fire.

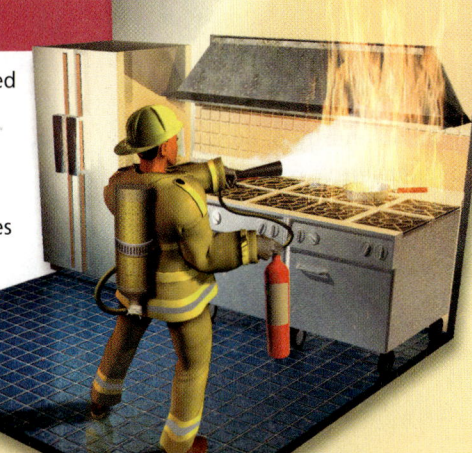

Metal Fires

Some fires involve metals such as magnesium. This metal burns at a very high temperature and reacts violently with water. Firefighters try to smother metal fires with a material such as sand.

Hazardous Reactions

Chemicals may react with water to form poisonous gases or acids. Firefighters might use a foam that extinguishes the fire, cools the area around the fire, and traps gases released by the fire. The symbols shown on the left are among several that show firefighters what chemical dangers may be present.

The fire shown above is a magnesium fire in Chicago in 1998. Firefighters used water to protect surrounding buildings, but dumped road salt on the burning magnesium.

EXPLORE

Build a carbon dioxide fire extinguisher.

1. Put 3 tsp of baking soda on a tissue and roll it into a tube. Tie the ends and middle of the tube with thread. Leave extra thread at one end of the tube.
2. Mold clay tightly around a straw.
3. Pour some vinegar into a bottle.
4. Hold the thread to suspend the tissue tube above the vinegar. Place the straw inside the bottle. Use the clay molded around the straw to hold the thread in place. Be sure that the straw is not touching the vinegar.
5. Shake and observe the fire extinguisher.

Chapter 3: **Chemical Reactions** 85 **B**

KEY CONCEPT
3.3 Chemical reactions involve energy changes.

◀ **BEFORE, you learned**
- Bonds are broken and made during chemical reactions
- Mass is conserved in all chemical reactions
- Chemical reactions are represented by balanced chemical equations

▶ **NOW, you will learn**
- About the energy in chemical bonds between atoms
- Why some chemical reactions release energy
- Why some chemical reactions absorb energy

VOCABULARY

bond energy p. 86
exothermic reaction p. 87
endothermic reaction p. 87
photosynthesis p. 90

EXPLORE Energy Changes

How can you identify a transfer of energy?

PROCEDURE

1. Pour 50 mL of hot tap water into the cup and place the thermometer in the cup.
2. Wait 30 seconds, then record the temperature of the water.
3. Measure 5 tsp of Epsom salts. Add the Epsom salts to the cup and immediately record the temperature while stirring the contents of the cup.
4. Continue to record the temperature every 30 seconds for 2 minutes.

MATERIALS
- graduated cylinder
- hot tap water
- plastic cup
- thermometer
- stopwatch
- plastic spoon
- Epsom salts

WHAT DO YOU THINK?
- What happened to the temperature after you added the Epsom salts?
- What do you think caused this change to occur?

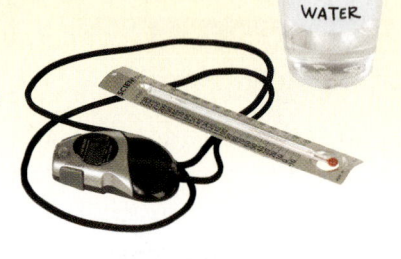

COMBINATION NOTES
Use combination notes to organize information on how chemical reactions absorb or release energy.

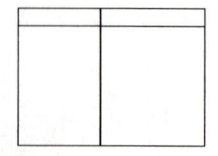

Chemical reactions release or absorb energy.

Chemical reactions involve breaking bonds in reactants and forming new bonds in products. Breaking bonds requires energy, and forming bonds releases energy. The energy associated with bonds is called **bond energy**. What happens to this energy during a chemical reaction?

Chemists have determined the bond energy for bonds between atoms. Breaking a bond between carbon and hydrogen requires a certain amount of energy. This amount of energy is different from the amount of energy needed to break a bond between carbon and oxygen, or between hydrogen and oxygen.

86 Unit: Chemical Interactions

Energy is needed to break bonds in reactant molecules. Energy is released when bonds are formed in product molecules. By adding up the bond energies in the reactants and products, you can determine whether energy will be released or absorbed.

If more energy is released when the products form than is needed to break the bonds in the reactants, then energy is released during the reaction. A reaction in which energy is released is called an **exothermic reaction.**

If more energy is required to break the bonds in the reactants than is released when the products form, then energy must be added to the reaction. That is, the reaction absorbs energy. A reaction in which energy is absorbed is called an **endothermic reaction.**

These types of energy changes can also be observed in different physical changes such as dissolving or changing state. The state change from a liquid to a solid, or freezing, releases energy—this is an exothermic process. The state change from a solid to a liquid, or melting, absorbs energy—this is an endothermic process.

CHECK YOUR READING How are exothermic and endothermic reactions different?

The white clouds of water vapor are formed by the exothermic reaction between hydrogen and oxygen.

$$2H_2 + O_2 \rightarrow 2H_2O$$

Exothermic reactions release energy.

Exothermic chemical reactions often produce an increase in temperature. In exothermic reactions, the bond energies of the reactants are less than the bond energies of the products. As a result, less energy is needed to break the bonds in the reactants than is released during the formation of the products. This energy difference between reactants and products is often released as heat. The release of heat causes a change in the temperature of the reaction mixture.

Even though energy is released by exothermic reactions, some energy must first be added to break bonds in the reactants. In exothermic reactions, the formation of bonds in the products releases more energy. Overall, more energy is released than is added.

Some reactions are highly exothermic. These reactions produce a great deal of heat and significantly raise the temperature of their surroundings. One example is the reaction of powdered aluminum metal with a type of iron oxide, a reaction known as the thermite reaction. The equation for this reaction is

$$2Al + Fe_2O_3 \rightarrow Al_2O_3 + 2Fe$$

This reaction releases enough heat to melt the iron that is produced. In fact, this reaction is used to weld iron rails together.

The thermite reaction releases enough heat to weld pieces of iron together.

CHECK YOUR READING What is evidence for an exothermic chemical reaction?

Chapter 3: **Chemical Reactions** 87

Exothermic Reactions

The products have greater bond energies than the reactants.

Methane Combustion

reactants
$CH_4 + 2O_2$

+ energy added →

bonds broken in reactants

bonds formed in products
$CO_2 + 2H_2O$

+ energy released ←

Difference in Energy

Bond Energy

Reactants (energy added) | Products (energy released)

More energy is released than added.

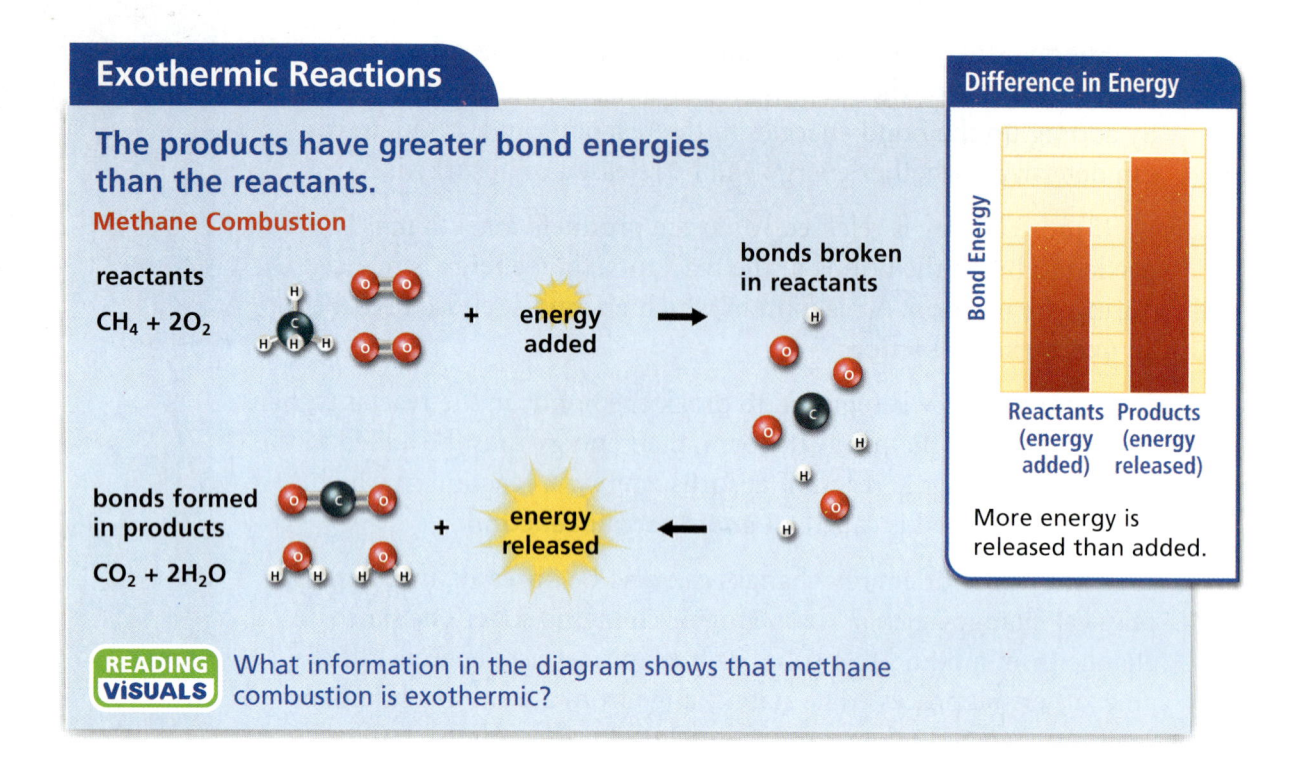

READING VISUALS What information in the diagram shows that methane combustion is exothermic?

All common combustion reactions, such as the combustion of methane, are exothermic. To determine how energy changes in this reaction, the bond energies in the reactants—oxygen and methane—and in the products—carbon dioxide and water—can be added and compared. This process is illustrated by the diagram shown above. The difference in energy is released to the surrounding air as heat.

Some chemical reactions release excess energy as light instead of heat. For example, glow sticks work by a chemical reaction that releases energy as light. One of the reactants, a solution of hydrogen peroxide, is contained in a thin glass tube within the plastic stick. The rest of the stick is filled with a second chemical and a brightly colored dye. When you bend the stick, the glass tube inside it breaks and the two solutions mix. The result is a bright glow of light.

These cup coral polyps glow because of exothermic chemical reactions.

Exothermic chemical reactions also occur in living things. Some of these reactions release energy as heat, and others release energy as light. Fireflies light up due to a reaction that takes place between oxygen and a chemical called luciferin. This type of exothermic reaction is not unique to fireflies. In fact, similar reactions are found in several different species of fish, squid, jellyfish, and shrimp.

CHECK YOUR READING In which ways might an exothermic reaction release energy?

The bombardier beetle, shown in the photograph on the right, uses natural exothermic reactions to defend itself. Although several chemical reactions are involved, the end result is the production of a hot, toxic spray. The most important reaction in the process is the decomposition of hydrogen peroxide into water and oxygen.

$$2H_2O_2 \rightarrow 2H_2O + O_2$$

When the hydrogen peroxide rapidly breaks down, the hot, toxic mixture made by the series of reactions is pressurized by the oxygen gas from the reaction in the equation above. After enough pressure builds up, the beetle can spray the mixture.

Endothermic reactions absorb energy.

Endothermic reactions often produce a decrease in temperature. In endothermic reactions, the bond energies of the reactants are greater than the bond energies of the products. As a result, more energy is needed to break the bonds in the reactants than is released during the formation of the products. The difference in energy is usually absorbed from the surroundings as heat. This often causes a decrease in the temperature of the reaction mixture.

All endothermic reactions absorb energy. However, they do not all absorb energy as heat. One example of an endothermic reaction of this type is the decomposition of water by electrolysis. In this case, the energy that is absorbed is in the form of electrical energy. When the electric current is turned off, the reaction stops. The change in energy that occurs in this reaction is shown below.

READING TIP
The prefix *endo-* means "inside."

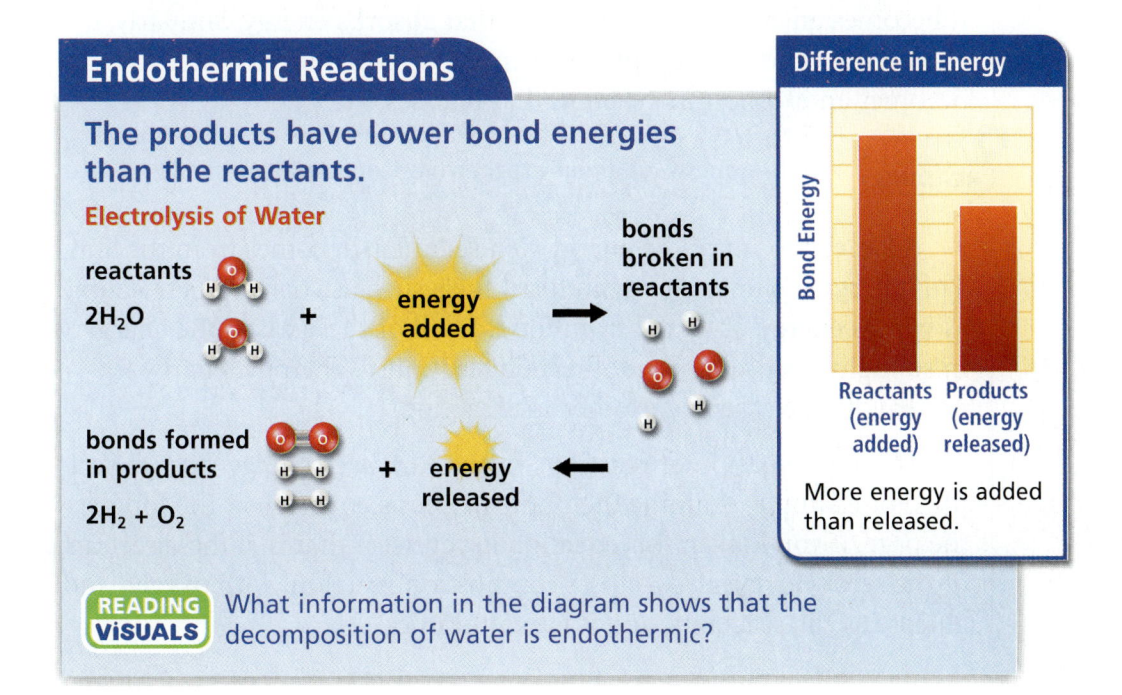

Endothermic Reactions

The products have lower bond energies than the reactants.

Electrolysis of Water

reactants
$2H_2O$
+ energy added → bonds broken in reactants

bonds formed in products
$2H_2 + O_2$
+ energy released ←

Difference in Energy

Reactants (energy added)   Products (energy released)

More energy is added than released.

READING VISUALS What information in the diagram shows that the decomposition of water is endothermic?

Chapter 3: **Chemical Reactions** 89

Probably the most important series of endothermic reactions on Earth is photosynthesis. Many steps occur in the process, but the overall chemical reaction is

$$6CO_2 + 6H_2O \longrightarrow C_6H_{12}O_6 + 6O_2$$

Unlike many other endothermic reactions, photosynthesis does not absorb energy as heat. Instead, during **photosynthesis,** plants absorb energy from sunlight to turn carbon dioxide and water into oxygen and glucose, which is a type of sugar molecule. The energy is stored in the glucose molecules, ready to be used when needed.

CHECK YOUR READING How can you determine if a reaction is endothermic?

Exothermic and endothermic reactions work together to supply energy.

When thinking about exothermic and endothermic reactions, it is often useful to consider energy as part of the reaction. An exothermic reaction releases energy, so energy is on the product side of the chemical equation. An endothermic reaction absorbs energy, so energy is on the reactant side of the chemical equation.

Exothermic Reaction
Reactants ⟶ Products + Energy

Endothermic Reaction
Reactants + Energy ⟶ Products

As you can see in the general reactions above, exothermic and endothermic reactions have opposite energy changes. This means that if an exothermic chemical reaction proceeds in the opposite direction, it becomes an endothermic reaction that absorbs energy. Similarly, if an endothermic reaction proceeds in the opposite direction, it becomes an exothermic reaction that releases energy.

CHECK YOUR READING What happens when an exothermic reaction is reversed?

A large amount of the energy we use on Earth comes from the Sun. This energy includes energy in fossil fuels such as coal and petroleum, as well as energy obtained from food. In all of these cases, the energy in sunlight is stored by endothermic reactions. When the energy is needed, it is released by exothermic reactions.

This combination of reactions forms a cycle of energy storage and use. For example, examine the photosynthesis equation at the top of the page. If you look at this equation in reverse—that is, if the direction of the arrow is reversed—it is a combustion reaction, with oxygen and glucose as the reactants, and it is exothermic.

VISUALIZATION
CLASSZONE.COM
View examples of endothermic and exothermic reactions.

Plants store energy through the endothermic reactions of photosynthesis. Living things can release this energy through a series of exothermic reactions that will be described in the next section.

The energy stored in plants through photosynthesis can also be released in other ways. Consider energy from fossil fuels. Fossil fuels include petroleum, natural gas, and coal. These substances formed from fossilized materials, mainly plants, that had been under high pressures and temperatures for millions of years. When these plants were alive, they used photosynthesis to produce glucose and other molecules from carbon dioxide and water.

The energy stored in the bonds of these molecules remains, even though the molecules have changed over time. The burning of gasoline in a car releases this energy, enabling the car's engine to work. Similarly, the burning of coal in a power plant, or the burning of natural gas in a stove, releases the energy originally stored by the endothermic series of photosynthesis reactions.

Plants such as trees store energy through photosynthesis. Cars and trucks release this energy through combustion.

CHECK YOUR READING How can endothermic and exothermic reactions work together?

3.3 Review

KEY CONCEPTS

1. What are the differences between exothermic and endothermic reactions?
2. Is the combustion of methane an exothermic or endothermic reaction? Explain.
3. Is photosynthesis an exothermic or endothermic reaction? Explain.

CRITICAL THINKING

4. **Synthesize** Describe the connections between the processes of photosynthesis and combustion.
5. **Communicate** Explain how most energy used on Earth can be traced back to the Sun.

CHALLENGE

6. **Synthesize** Electrolysis of water is endothermic. What does this indicate about the bond energy in the reactants and products? What happens when this reaction is reversed?

Chapter 3: **Chemical Reactions** 91 B

CHAPTER INVESTIGATION

Exothermic or Endothermic?

OVERVIEW AND PURPOSE A clue that a chemical reaction has taken place is a transfer of energy, often in the form of heat or light. The chemical reaction used to demolish an old building, as shown in the photograph to the left, is a dramatic example of energy release by a reaction. In this investigation, you will use what you have learned about chemical reactions to
- measure and record temperature changes in two processes
- compare temperature changes during the processes in order to classify them as exothermic or endothermic

Procedure

1. Make a data table like the one shown on the sample notebook page.

2. Work with a partner. One should keep track of time. The other should observe the thermometer and report the temperature.

PART 1

3. Pour 30 mL of hydrogen peroxide into a beaker. Put a thermometer into the beaker. Wait 2 minutes to allow the thermometer to reach the temperature of the hydrogen peroxide. During the time you are waiting, measure 1 g of yeast with the balance.

4. Record the starting temperature. Add the yeast to the beaker and immediately record the temperature while gently stirring the contents of the beaker. Continue to record the temperature every 30 seconds as you observe the process for 5 minutes.

MATERIALS
- graduated cylinder
- hydrogen peroxide
- 2 beakers
- 2 thermometers
- stopwatch
- measuring spoons
- yeast
- balance
- plastic spoon
- large plastic cup
- hot tap water
- vinegar
- baking soda

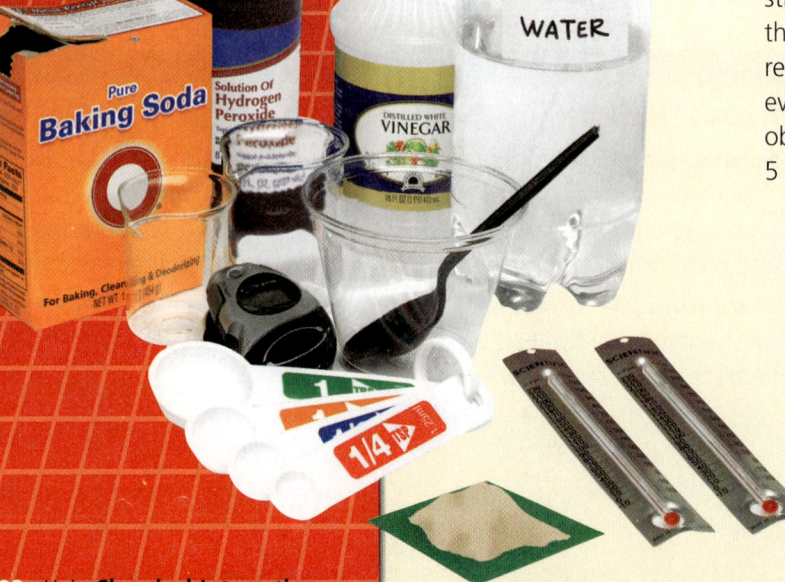

B 92 Unit: Chemical Interactions

PART 2

5. Make a hot water bath by filling a large plastic cup halfway with hot tap water.

6. Measure and pour 30 mL of vinegar into a small beaker. Set this beaker in the hot water bath and place a thermometer in the vinegar. Wait until the temperature of the vinegar rises to between 32 and 38°C (90 to 100°F). While waiting for the vinegar's temperature to increase, measure 1 g of baking soda.

7. Remove the beaker from the hot water bath. Record the starting temperature.

8. Add the baking soda to the vinegar and immediately record the temperature as you swirl the contents of the beaker. Continue to record the temperature every 30 seconds as you observe the reaction for 5 minutes.

Observe and Analyze

1. **RECORD OBSERVATIONS** Remember to complete your data table.

2. **GRAPH** Use the information from your data table to graph your results. Make a double-line graph, plotting your data in a different color for each part of the investigation. Plot temperature in degrees Celsius on the vertical, or y-axis. Plot the time in minutes on the horizontal, or x-axis.

3. **ANALYZE DATA** Examine the graph. When did the temperature change the most in each part of the investigation? When did it change the least? Compare the temperature at the start of each process with the temperature after 5 minutes. How do the temperature changes compare?

Conclude

1. **CLASSIFY** Is the mixture of hydrogen peroxide and yeast endothermic or exothermic? Is the reaction between vinegar and baking soda endothermic or exothermic? Provide evidence for your answers.

2. **EVALUATE** Did you have any difficulties obtaining accurate measurements? Describe possible limitations or sources of error.

3. **APPLY** What does the reaction between baking soda and vinegar tell you about their bond energies?

INVESTIGATE Further

CHALLENGE Repeat Part 2, but instead of using the hot water bath, add the hot water directly to the vinegar before pouring in the baking soda. Does this change in procedure change the results of the experiment? Why might your observations have changed? Explain your answers.

Exothermic or Endothermic?

Observe and Analyze

Table 1. Temperature Measurements

Time (min)	Hydrogen Peroxide and Yeast Temperature (°C)	Vinegar and Baking Soda Temperature (°C)
0		
0.5		
1.0		
....		
5.0		

Conclude

Chapter 3: **Chemical Reactions** 93

3.4 Life and industry depend on chemical reactions.

KEY CONCEPT

BEFORE, you learned
- Chemical reactions turn reactants into products by rearranging atoms
- Mass is conserved during chemical reactions
- Chemical reactions involve energy changes

NOW, you will learn
- About the importance of chemical reactions in living things
- How chemistry has helped the development of new technology

VOCABULARY

respiration p. 94

THINK ABOUT

How is a glow stick like a firefly?

When a firefly glows in the dark, a chemical reaction that emits light is taking place. Similarly, when you activate a glow stick, a chemical reaction that causes the glow stick to emit light occurs. Many reactions in modern life and technology adapt chemical reactions found in nature. Can you think of other examples?

Living things require chemical reactions.

In section 3, you saw that photosynthesis stores energy from the Sun in forms that can be used later. These forms of stored energy include fossil fuels and the sugar glucose. The glucose molecules produced by photosynthesis make up the basic food used for energy by almost all living things. For example, animals obtain glucose molecules by eating plants or eating other animals that have eaten plants.

Living cells obtain energy from glucose molecules through the process of **respiration**, which is the "combustion" of glucose to obtain energy. This series of chemical reactions is, in general, the reverse of photosynthesis. It produces carbon dioxide and water from oxygen and glucose. The overall reactions for both photosynthesis and respiration are shown on the top of page 95. From a chemical point of view, respiration is the same as any other combustion reaction.

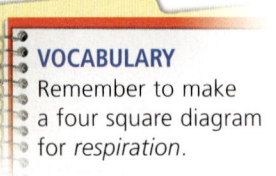

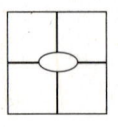

VOCABULARY
Remember to make a four square diagram for *respiration*.

B 94 Unit: Chemical Interactions

Photosynthesis
$6CO_2 + 6H_2O + \text{energy} \longrightarrow C_6H_{12}O_6 + 6O_2$

Respiration
$C_6H_{12}O_6 + 6O_2 \longrightarrow 6CO_2 + 6H_2O + \text{energy}$

The energy released by respiration can be used for growth of new cells, movement, or any other life function. Suppose that you are late for school and have to run to get to class on time. Your body needs to activate nerves and muscles right away, without waiting for you to first eat some food as a source of energy. The glucose molecules in food are stored in your body until you need energy. Then, respiration consumes them in a process that includes several steps.

To make these steps go quickly, the body uses catalysts—enzymes—for each step. Some enzymes break the glucose molecules into smaller pieces, while other enzymes break bonds within each piece. Still other enzymes help form the reaction products—carbon dioxide and water. With the help of enzymes, these reactions take place quickly and automatically. You do not have to think about breaking down glucose when you run—you just start to run and the energy is there.

CHECK YOUR READING How are photosynthesis and respiration opposites?

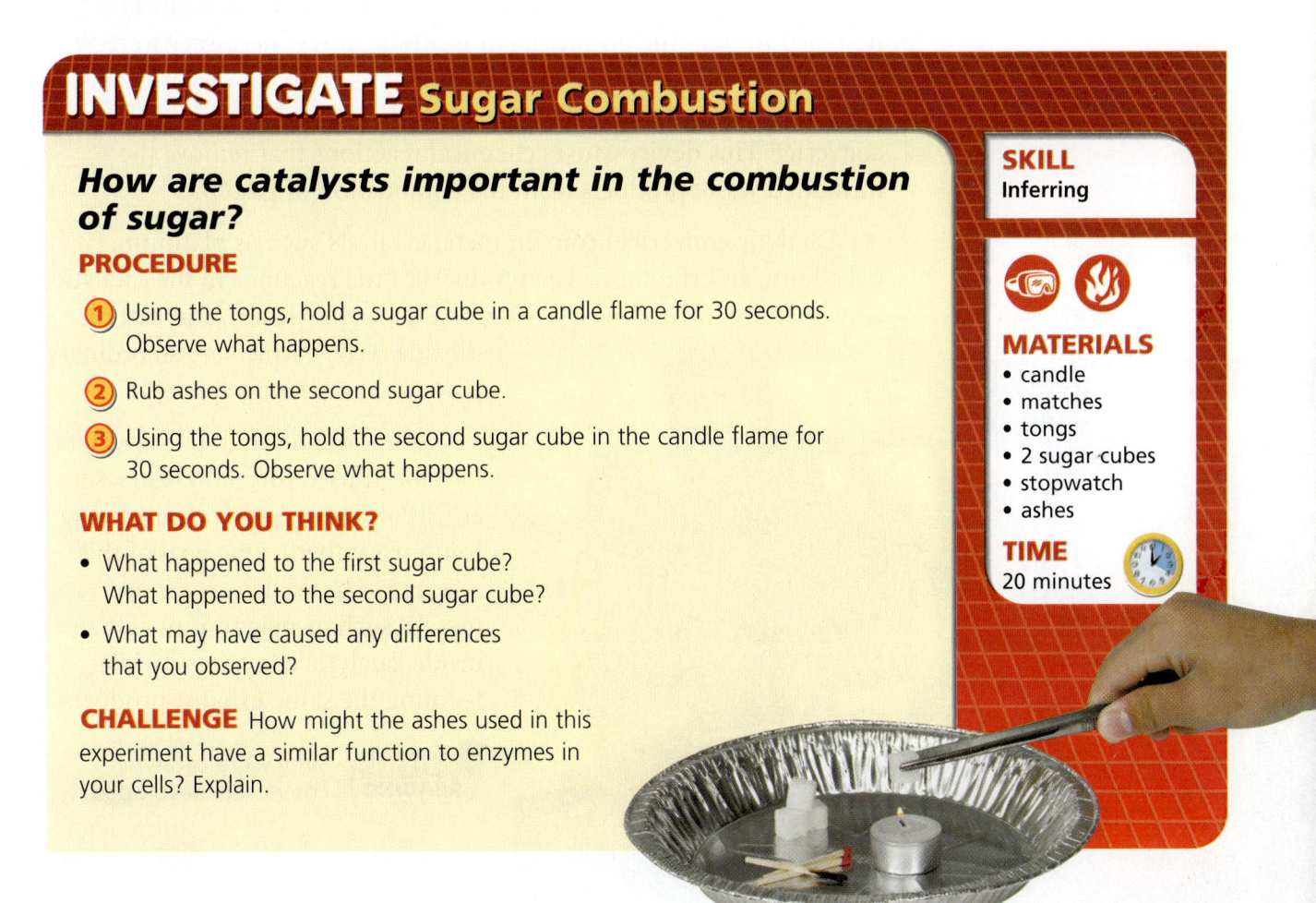

INVESTIGATE Sugar Combustion

How are catalysts important in the combustion of sugar?

PROCEDURE

1. Using the tongs, hold a sugar cube in a candle flame for 30 seconds. Observe what happens.
2. Rub ashes on the second sugar cube.
3. Using the tongs, hold the second sugar cube in the candle flame for 30 seconds. Observe what happens.

WHAT DO YOU THINK?
- What happened to the first sugar cube? What happened to the second sugar cube?
- What may have caused any differences that you observed?

CHALLENGE How might the ashes used in this experiment have a similar function to enzymes in your cells? Explain.

SKILL Inferring

MATERIALS
- candle
- matches
- tongs
- 2 sugar cubes
- stopwatch
- ashes

TIME 20 minutes

Chapter 3: **Chemical Reactions** 95 **B**

Chemical reactions are used in technology.

Every time your cells need energy, they essentially complete respiration—the "combustion" of glucose. The series of chemical reactions in respiration involves enzymes, which are catalysts. Every time someone drives a car, another combustion reaction occurs—the combustion of gasoline. While the combustion of gasoline does not require a catalyst, the chemical reactions that change a car's exhaust gases do use a catalyst.

No chemical reaction is ever completely efficient. It does not matter what the reaction is or how the reaction conditions are set up. There are always some reactants that do not change completely into products. Sometimes a chemical reaction makes unwanted waste products.

In the case of gasoline combustion, some of the original carbon compounds, called hydrocarbons, do not burn completely, and carbon monoxide gas (CO) is produced. Also, nitrogen in the air reacts with oxygen in a car's engine to produce compounds of nitrogen and oxygen, including nitric oxide (NO). The production of these gases lowers the overall efficiency of combustion. More importantly, these gases can react with water vapor in the air to form smog and acid rain.

Sometimes, as you can see with gasoline combustion, chemical technology causes a problem. Then, new chemical technology is designed to treat the problem. For example, it was necessary to reduce carbon monoxide and nitric oxide emissions from car exhaust. As a result, engineers in the 1970s developed a device called a catalytic converter. This device causes chemical reactions that remove the unwanted waste products from the combustion of gasoline.

Catalytic converters contain metal catalysts such as platinum, palladium, and rhodium. The products of the reactions in the catalytic converter are nitrogen (N_2), oxygen (O_2), water (H_2O), and carbon dioxide (CO_2), which are all ordinary parts of Earth's atmosphere.

Even though catalytic converters have been used for many years, scientists and engineers are still trying to improve them. One goal of this research is to use less expensive metals, such as magnesium and zinc, inside catalytic converters, while forming the same exhaust products.

Many states inspect vehicles to test the pollutants in their exhaust gases.

CHECK YOUR READING Why were catalytic converters developed?

Chemical Reactions in Catalytic Converters

The combustion of gasoline makes harmful waste products. Chemical reactions in catalytic converters make these waste products less harmful.

1 Into the Catalytic Converter When gasoline is mixed with air and burned in a car's engine, the reaction produces some unwanted waste products, such as
- carbon monoxide (CO)
- nitric oxide (NO)
- unburned hydrocarbons

2 Inside the Catalytic Converter Catalysts in a car's catalytic converter help change these unwanted products into other gases. The catalysts are metals that are bonded to a ceramic structure.

3 Out from the Catalytic Converter The final products are ordinary parts of Earth's atmosphere.
- nitrogen (N_2)
- oxygen (O_2)
- water (H_2O)
- carbon dioxide (CO_2)

engine
catalytic converter
muffler and tailpipe

The honeycomb shape of the metal-coated ceramic increases the surface area of the catalyst.

READING VISUALS What are CO and NO changed into by a catalytic converter?

Industry uses chemical reactions to make useful products.

No area of science and technology has changed today's society as much as the electronics industry has. Just think about all the common electronic products that did not even exist as recently as 30 years ago—from personal computers to CD players to cellular phones. All of these devices are based on the electrical properties of materials called semiconductors. A semiconductor is a material that can precisely control the conduction of electrical signals.

READING TIP
The prefix *semi-* means "partial," so a semiconductor partially conducts electricity.

The most common semiconductor material is the element silicon (Si). Silicon is the second most common element in Earth's crust after oxygen, and it is found in most rocks and sand. Pure silicon is obtained from quartz (SiO_2). The quartz is heated with carbon in an electric furnace at 3000°C. The chemical reaction that takes place is

$$SiO_2 + 2C \longrightarrow Si + 2CO$$

This reaction produces silicon that is about 98 percent pure. However, this silicon is still not pure enough to be used in electronics. Several other refining steps must be used to make silicon that is more than 99.999999999 percent pure.

CHECK YOUR READING What property makes silicon useful in electronic devices?

Quartz (SiO_2) is the source of silicon for chips.

Early electronic devices had to be large enough to fit various types of glass tubes and connecting wires inside. In the 1950s, however, engineers figured out how to replace all of these different tubes and wires with thin layers of material placed on a piece of silicon. The resulting circuits are often called microchips, or simply chips.

In order to make these chips, another reaction is used. This reaction involves a material called photoresist (FOH-toh-rih-ZIST), whose properties change when it is exposed to ultraviolet light. Silicon wafers are first coated with photoresist. A stencil is placed over the surface, which allows some areas of the wafer to be exposed to ultraviolet light while other areas are protected. A chemical reaction takes place between the ultraviolet light and the coating of photoresist. The exposed areas of photoresist remain on the silicon surface after the rest of the material is washed away.

The entire process is carried out in special clean rooms to prevent contamination by dust. A typical chip has electrical pathways so small that a single particle of smoke or dust can block the path, stopping the chip from working properly. The process is automated, and no human hand ever touches a chip.

From Quartz to Microchips

A chemical reaction makes the tiny circuits that are used to run electronic devices such as cellular phones.

1 After silicon is sliced into very thin wafers, it is coated with photoresist. The silicon is covered with a stencil and exposed to ultraviolet light, which reacts with the photoresist.

2 The entire process takes place in clean rooms, where workers wear special clothing to prevent dust from reaching the chips.

3 The areas of the chip that were exposed to ultraviolet light form tiny circuits used in electronic devices.

The reaction of photoresist with ultraviolet light is an important chemical reaction. The same type of material is used in the printing of books and newspapers. A similar reaction occurs in photocopiers and laser printers. This is an example of how one type of chemical reaction has helped change industry and society in important ways.

One of the many uses of silicon chips is in cellular phones.

CHECK YOUR READING Describe how chemical reactions are important in industry.

3.4 Review

KEY CONCEPTS

1. Explain how respiration and photosynthesis are chemically opposite from each other.
2. Provide an example of how catalysts are used in technology.
3. Describe two chemical reactions used in making silicon chips.

CRITICAL THINKING

4. **Compare and Contrast** How are respiration and the combustion of gasoline similar? How are they different?
5. **Analyze** In microchip manufacture, what would happen if the clean rooms had outside windows? Explain.

CHALLENGE

6. **Infer** The gases released from a catalytic converter include N_2, O_2, H_2O, and CO_2. The original reactants must contain atoms of which elements?

Chapter 3: **Chemical Reactions** 99 **B**

Chapter 3 Review

the BIG idea
Chemical reactions form new substances by breaking and making chemical bonds.

CONTENT REVIEW
CLASSZONE.COM

KEY CONCEPTS SUMMARY

3.1 Chemical reactions alter arrangements of atoms.
- Chemical changes occur through chemical reactions.
- Evidence of a chemical reaction includes a color change, the formation of a precipitate, the formation of a gas, and a change in temperature.
- Chemical reactions change reactants into products.

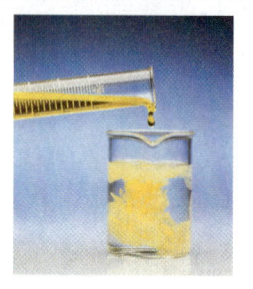

VOCABULARY
chemical reaction p. 69
reactant p. 71
product p. 71
precipitate p. 72
catalyst p. 76

3.2 The masses of reactants and products are equal.
- Mass is conserved in chemical reactions.
- Chemical equations summarize chemical reactions.
- Balanced chemical equations show the conservation of mass.

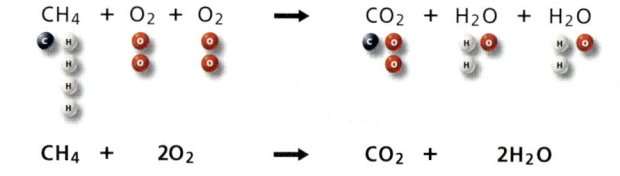

$$CH_4 + O_2 + O_2 \longrightarrow CO_2 + H_2O + H_2O$$

$$CH_4 + 2O_2 \longrightarrow CO_2 + 2H_2O$$

VOCABULARY
law of conservation of mass p. 79
coefficient p. 82

3.3 Chemical reactions involve energy changes.
- Different bonds contain different amounts of energy.
- In an exothermic reaction, more energy is released than added.
- In an endothermic reaction, more energy is added than released.

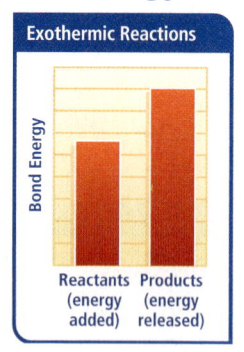

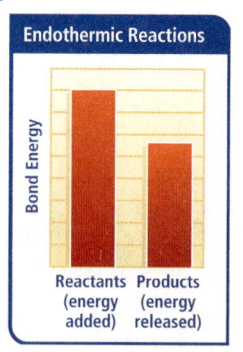

VOCABULARY
bond energy p. 86
exothermic reaction p. 87
endothermic reaction p. 87
photosynthesis p. 90

3.4 Life and industry depend on chemical reactions.
- Living things rely on chemical reactions that release energy from molecules.
- Different parts of modern society rely on chemical reactions.

VOCABULARY
respiration p. 94

Reviewing Vocabulary

Describe how the vocabulary terms in the following pairs are related to each other. Explain the relationship in a one- or two-sentence answer.

1. reactant, product
2. law of conservation of mass, chemical reaction
3. endothermic, exothermic
4. respiration, photosynthesis

Reviewing Key Concepts

Multiple Choice *Choose the letter of the best answer.*

5. During a chemical reaction, reactants always
    a. become more complex
    b. require catalysts
    c. lose mass
    d. form products

6. The splitting of water molecules into hydrogen and oxygen molecules is an example of a
    a. combination reaction
    b. chemical change
    c. synthesis reaction
    d. physical change

7. Combustion reactions
    a. destroy atoms   c. form precipitates
    b. require glucose   d. require oxygen

8. Which of the following will increase the rate of a reaction?
    a. breaking solid reactants into smaller pieces
    b. removing a catalyst
    c. decreasing the temperature
    d. decreasing the concentration

9. What does a catalyst do in a chemical reaction?
    a. It slows the reaction down.
    b. It speeds the reaction up.
    c. It becomes a product.
    d. It is a reactant.

10. During a chemical reaction, the total amount of mass present
    a. increases
    b. decreases
    c. may increase or decrease
    d. does not change

11. Chemical equations show summaries of
    a. physical changes
    b. changes of state
    c. chemical reactions
    d. changes in temperature

12. A chemical equation must
    a. show energy   c. use subscripts
    b. be balanced   d. use coefficients

13. What type of reaction occurs if the reactants have a greater total bond energy than the products?
    a. an endothermic reaction
    b. a synthesis reaction
    c. an exothermic reaction
    d. a decomposition reaction

14. Endothermic reactions always
    a. absorb energy
    b. make more complex products
    c. release energy
    d. make less complex products

Short Answer *Write a short answer to each question.*

15. Describe the differences between physical and chemical changes. How can each be identified?

16. Compare and contrast the overall chemical reactions of photosynthesis and respiration. How can these reactions be described in terms of bond energy in the reactants and products?

17. Describe an example of an advance in technology that makes use of a chemical reaction.

18. When you balance a chemical equation, why can you change coefficients of reactants or products, but not subscripts?

Thinking Critically

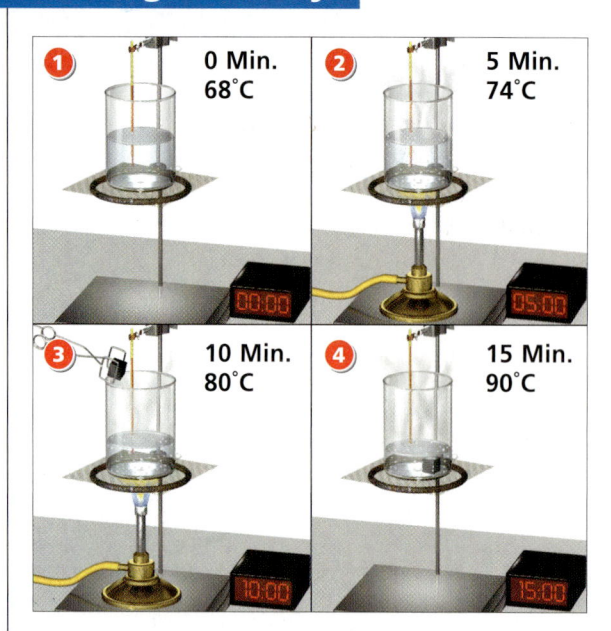

1 0 Min. 68°C
2 5 Min. 74°C
3 10 Min. 80°C
4 15 Min. 90°C

The series of illustrations above shows a chemical reaction at five-minute intervals. Use the information in the illustrations to answer the following six questions.

19. OBSERVE What happened to the temperature of the substance in the beaker from the beginning to the end of each five-minute interval?

20. ANALYZE Does the reaction appear to continue in step 4? What evidence tells you?

21. CLASSIFY Is this an endothermic or exothermic reaction? Explain.

22. INFER Suppose the metal cube placed in the beaker in step 3 is a catalyst. What effect did the metal have on the reaction? Why?

23. PREDICT If the metal cube is a catalyst, how much of the metal cube will be left in the beaker when the reaction is completed? Explain.

24. SYNTHESIZE Assume that the reaction shown is a decomposition reaction. Describe what happens to the reactants.

Using Math Skills in Science

Answer the following ten questions based on the equations below.

Equation 1 — $HgO \rightarrow Hg + O_2$

Equation 2 — $Al + O_2 \rightarrow Al_2O_3$

Equation 3 — $S_8 + O_2 \rightarrow SO_3$

25. Copy and balance equation 1.

26. What coefficients, if any, did you add to equation 1 to balance it?

27. How many Hg atoms take part in the reaction represented by equation 1 when it is balanced?

28. Copy and balance equation 2.

29. What coefficients, if any, did you add to equation 2 to balance it?

30. How many O atoms take part in the reaction represented by equation 2 when it is balanced?

31. Copy and balance equation 3.

32. What coefficients, if any, did you add to equation 3 to balance it?

33. How many S atoms take part in the reaction represented by equation 3 when it is balanced?

34. How many O atoms take part in the reaction represented by equation 3 when it is balanced?

the BIG idea

35. DRAW CONCLUSIONS Describe three ways in which chemical reactions are important in your life.

36. ANALYZE Look back at the photograph and question on pages 66 and 67. Answer the question in terms of the chapter's Big Idea.

UNIT PROJECTS

Check your schedule for your unit project. How are you doing? Be sure that you have placed data or notes from your research in your project folder.

Standardized Test Practice

For practice on your state test, go to...
TEST PRACTICE
CLASSZONE.COM

Analyzing Theories

Answer the questions based on the information in the following passage.

During the 1700s, scientists thought that matter contained a substance called phlogiston. According to this theory, wood was made of phlogiston and ash. When wood burned, the phlogiston was released and the ash was left behind.

The ash that remained had less mass than the original wood. This decrease in mass was explained by the release of phlogiston. However, when substances such as phosphorus and mercury burned, the material that remained had more mass than the original substances. This increase in mass did not make sense to some scientists.

The scientists who supported the phlogiston theory said that the phlogiston in some substances had negative mass. So, when the substances burned, they released phlogiston and gained mass. Other scientists disagreed, and their research led to the discovery of a scientific law. Antoine Lavoisier carried out several experiments by burning metals in sealed containers. He showed that mass is never lost or gained in a chemical reaction.

1. What did the phlogiston theory successfully explain?
   a. the presence of ash in unburned wood
   b. the apparent gain of mass in some reactions
   c. the chemical makeup of the air
   d. the apparent decrease in mass in some situations

2. Why did some scientists disagree with the phlogiston theory?
   a. Burning a substance always produced an increase in mass.
   b. Burning a substance always produced a decrease in mass.
   c. Burning could produce either an increase or decrease in mass.
   d. Burning wood produced ash and phlogiston.

3. What law did Lavoisier's work establish?
   a. conservation of energy
   b. conservation of mass
   c. conservation of momentum
   d. conservation of resources

4. To carry out his experiments, what kind of equipment did Lavoisier need?
   a. devices to separate the different elements in the air
   b. machines that could separate wood from ash
   c. microscopes that could be used to study rust and ash
   d. balances that could measure mass very accurately

Extended Response

Answer the following questions in detail. Include some of the terms from the list on the right. Underline each term you use in your answers.

catalyst	coefficient	concentration
temperature	reaction	subscript
surface area		

5. Suppose you wanted to change the rate of a chemical reaction. What might you change in the reaction? Explain each factor.

6. Is the chemical equation shown below balanced? Why or why not? How are balanced chemical equations related to conservation of mass?

$$6CO_2 + 6H_2O \rightarrow C_6H_{12}O_6 + O_2$$

Chapter 3: **Chemical Reactions** 103 B

TIMELINES in Science

THE STORY OF ATOMIC STRUCTURE

About 2500 years ago, certain Greek thinkers proposed that all matter consisted of extremely tiny particles called atoms. The sizes and shapes of different atoms, they reasoned, was what determined the properties of a substance. This early atomic theory, however, was not widely accepted. Many at the time found these tiny, invisible particles difficult to accept.

What everyone could observe was that all substances were liquid, solid, or gas, light or heavy, hot or cold. Everything, they thought, must then be made of only a few basic substances or elements. They reasoned these elements must be water, air, fire, and earth. Different substances contained different amounts of each of these four substances.

The timeline shows a few of the major events that led scientists to accept the idea that matter is made of atoms and agree on the basic structure of atoms. With the revised atomic theory, scientists were able to explain how elements could be basic but different.

1661
Boyle Challenges Concept of the Four Elements

British chemist Robert Boyle proposes that more than four basic substances exist. Boyle also concludes that all matter is made of very tiny particles he calls corpuscles.

EVENTS

1600   1620   1640   1660

APPLICATIONS AND TECHNOLOGY

TECHNOLOGY
Collecting and Studying Gases

Throughout the 1600s, scientists tried to study gases but had difficulty collecting them. English biologist Stephen Hales designed an apparatus to collect gases. The "pneumatic trough" was a breakthrough in chemistry because it allowed scientists to collect and study gases for the first time. The pneumatic trough was later used by such chemists as Joseph Black, Henry Cavendish, and Joseph Priestley to study the gases that make up the air we breathe. The work of these scientists showed that air was made of more than a single gas.

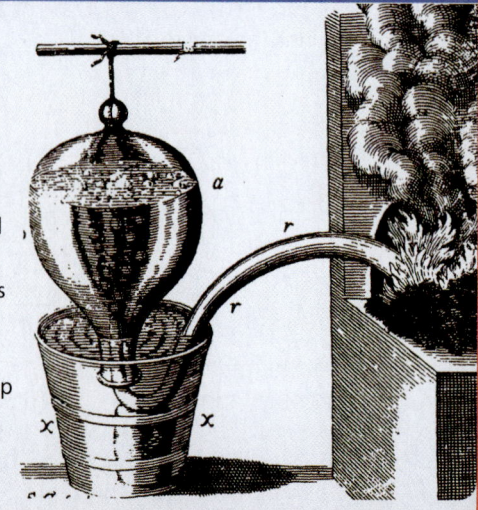

1808
John Dalton Says: "Bring Back the Atom"

English chemist John Dalton revives the ancient Greek idea that all matter is made of atoms. Dalton claims that each element has its own type of atom and that the atoms combine in fixed and predictable ratios with one another in different substances.

1897
It's Smaller Than the Atom!

English physicist Joseph John Thomson discovers the electron—the first subatomic particle to be identified. Thomson concludes that these tiny particles have a negative charge. Thomson will later propose that atoms are made of a great many of these negative particles floating in a sea of positive charge. Thomson suggests that each atom resembles a dish of pudding with raisins in it. The electrons are the raisins and the pudding the positive charge in which they float.

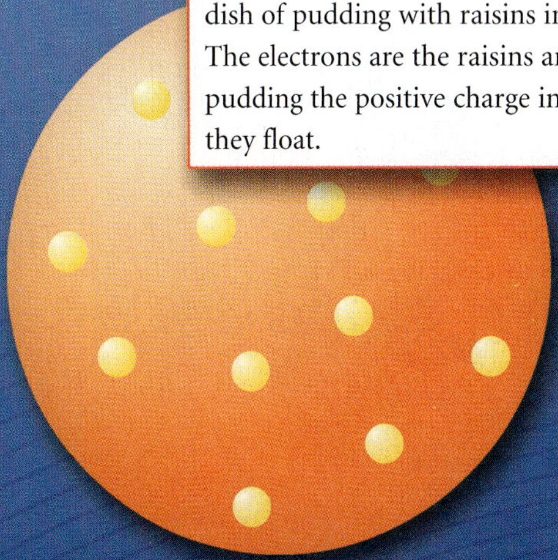

1808
Humphrey Davy Shocks Chemistry

English chemist Humphrey Davy applies an electric current to different materials. He discovers that many materials once thought to be elements break apart into even simpler materials. Davy succeeds in isolating the elements sodium, calcium, strontium, and barium.

1800   1820   1840   1860   1880

TECHNOLOGY

Chemistry and Electric Charge

In 1800 Italian physicist Alessandro Volta announced that he had produced an electric current from a pile, or battery, of alternating zinc and silver discs. Volta's invention was important for the study of atoms and elements in two ways. First, the fact that the contact of two different metals could produce an electric current suggested that electric charge must be part of matter. Second, the powerful electric current produced by the batteries enabled chemists to break apart many other substances, showing that there were more elements than previously thought.

Timelines in Science 105 B

1903
Atoms Release Energy
Polish-born French physicist Marie Curie and her husband, Pierre, have won the Nobel Prize for their isolation of the elements polonium and radium. These elements are unique because they release energy. Marie Curie names this trait "radioactivity." They share the award with Henri Becquerel, who previously observed this trait with the element uranium.

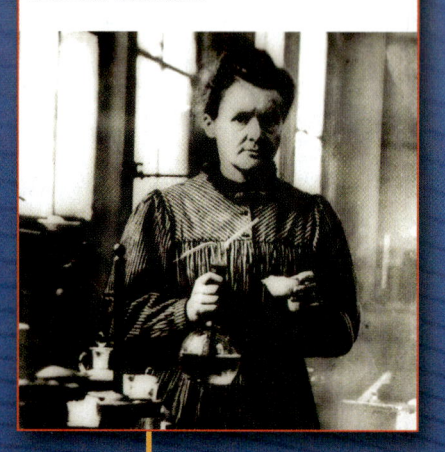

1911
Atoms Have a Center
By aiming a stream of particles at a piece of gold foil, New Zealand-born physicist Ernest Rutherford finds that atoms are not like a dish of pudding filled with raisins, as J. J. Thomson had suggested. Atoms must have a positive center because many of the particles bounce back. He calls the atom's center its nucleus.

1913
Bohr Puts Electrons into Orbit
Building on the work of Rutherford, Danish physicist Niels Bohr claims that electrons move about the nucleus only in certain, well-defined orbits. Bohr also says that electrons can jump to different orbits and emit or absorb energy when doing so.

1919
Atoms Share a Common Bond
U.S. chemists G.N. Lewis and Irving Langmuir suggest that atoms of many elements form bonds by sharing pairs of electrons. The idea that atoms could share electrons leads to a greater understanding of how molecules are structured.

1900 1905 1910 1915 1920 1940

APPLICATION
The Chemistry of Communication
The discovery of the electron resulted in more than a greater understanding of the atom. It also opened new ways of communicating. In 1906, U.S. inventor Lee De Forest invented a device for detecting and amplifying radio signals that he called the audion. The audion worked by producing a beam of electrons inside a vacuum tube. The beam was then made to respond to radio signals that it received from an antenna. The audion helped pave the way for later devices such as the transistor.

1960s
Smaller Particles Discovered

By smashing atoms into one another, scientists discover that protons and neutrons are themselves composed of even smaller particles. In a bit of scientific humor, these smaller particles are named "quarks," a nonsense word taken from a novel. Scientists detect these particles by observing the tracks they make in special detectors.

1980s
Tunneling to the Atomic Level

Scanning tunneling microscopes (STMs) allow scientists to interact with matter at the atomic level. Electrons on the tiny tip of an STM "tunnel" through the gap between the tip and target surface. By recording changes in the tunneling current, researchers get an accurate picture.

RESOURCE CENTER
CLASSZONE.COM
Explore advances in atomic research.

1960   1980   2000

TECHNOLOGY
Particle Accelerators

Particle accelerators speed up charged particles by passing them through an electric field. By smashing subatomic particles into one another, scientists are able to learn what these particles are made of as well as the forces holding them together. The H1 particle detector in Hamburg, Germany, can accelerate protons to 800 billion volts and is used to study the quarks that make up protons.

INTO THE FUTURE

Humans have gone from hypothesizing atoms exist to being able to see and move them. People once considered only four substances to be true elements; today we understand how there are more than a hundred simple substances. Not only have scientists learned atoms contain electric charges, they have also learned how to use these charges.

As scientists learn more and more about the atom, it is difficult to say what they will find next. Is there something smaller than a quark? Is there one type of particle from which all other particles are made? Will we one day be able to move and connect atoms in any way we want? Are there other kinds of atoms to discover? Maybe one day we will find answers to these questions.

ACTIVITIES

Explore a Model Atom

The discovery of the nucleus was one of the most important discoveries in human history. Rutherford's experiment, however, was a simple one that you can model. Take an aluminum pie plate and place a table tennis ball-sized piece of clay at its center. The clay represents a nucleus. Place the end of a grooved ruler at the edge of the plate. Hold the other end up to form a ramp. Roll a marble down the groove toward the clay. Move the ruler to different angles with each roll. Roll the marble 20 times. How many rolls out of 20 hit the clay ball? How do you think the results would be different if the atoms looked like pudding with raisins in it, as Thomson suggested?

Writing About Science

Suppose you are an atom. Choose one of the events on the timeline and describe it from the atom's point of view.

CHAPTER 4
Solutions

the BIG idea

When substances dissolve to form a solution, the properties of the mixture change.

Why might some substances dissolve in the seawater in this photograph, but others do not?

Key Concepts

SECTION 4.1
A solution is a type of mixture.
Learn how solutions differ from other types of mixtures.

SECTION 4.2
The amount of solute that dissolves can vary.
Learn how solutions can contain different amounts of dissolved substances.

SECTION 4.3
Solutions can be acidic, basic, or neutral.
Learn about acids and bases and where they are found.

SECTION 4.4
Metal alloys are solid mixtures.
Learn about alloys and how they are used.

Internet Preview

CLASSZONE.COM
Chapter 4 online resources: Content Review, Simulation, Visualization, three Resource Centers, Math Tutorial, Test Practice

108 Unit: Chemical Interactions

EXPLORE the BIG idea

Does It Dissolve?

Pour water into four small clear cups. Add a teaspoon of each of the following: in cup 1, powdered drink mix; in cup 2, vinegar; in cup 3, milk; in cup 4, sand. Stir briefly. Observe the contents of all four cups for five minutes.

Observe and Think Do all of the substances dissolve in water? How can you tell?

Acid Test

Rub a radish on three blank index cards until the marks on the cards become dark pink. Use cotton swabs to wipe lemon juice onto the mark on the first card, tap water onto the mark on the second card, and soda water onto the mark on the third card. Observe the color of the radish mark on each index card.

Observe and Think What happened to the color on each index card? How might the three liquids that you tested differ?

Internet Activity: Alloys

Go to **ClassZone.com** to investigate alloys. Explore the production of different varieties of an alloy by changing the percentages of the metals used to make them. Find out how different alloys have different properties.

Observe and Think How does changing the composition of an alloy change its properties? Why?

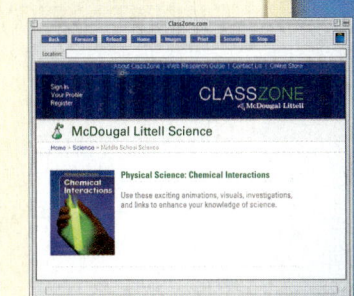

NSTA scilinks.org SCLINKS

Solutions Code: MDL025

Chapter 4: **Solutions** 109 B

CHAPTER 4
Getting Ready to Learn

CONCEPT REVIEW

- Matter can change from one physical state to another.
- A mixture is a blend of substances that do not react chemically.
- Particles can have electrical charges.

VOCABULARY REVIEW

proton p. 11
ion p. 14
molecule p. 51
chemical reaction p. 69
mixture See Glossary.

CONTENT REVIEW
CLASSZONE.COM
Review concepts and vocabulary.

TAKING NOTES

MIND MAP

Write each main idea, or blue heading, in an oval; then write details that relate to each other and to the main idea. Organize the details so that each line of the map has a note about one part of the main idea.

CHOOSE YOUR OWN STRATEGY

For each new vocabulary term, take notes by choosing one of the strategies from earlier chapters—**frame game**, **description wheel**, or **four square** diagram. You can also use other vocabulary strategies that you might already know.

See the Note-Taking Handbook on pages R45–R51.

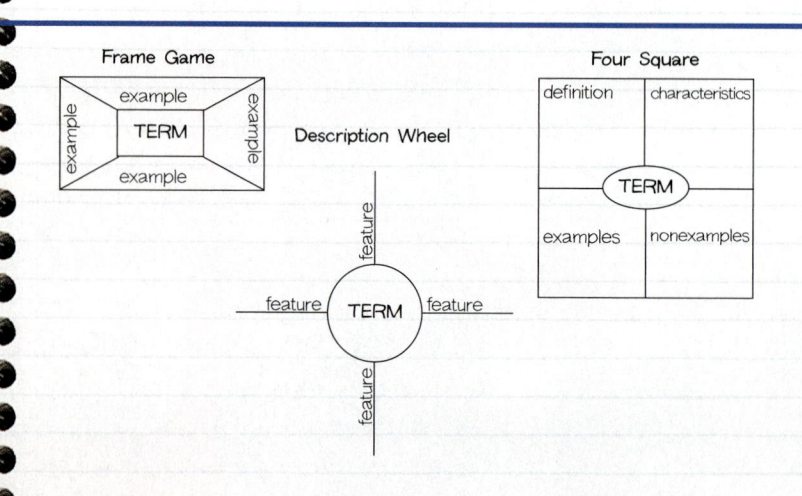

SCIENCE NOTEBOOK

parts not easily separated or differentiated
substances dissolved in a solvent

(A solution is a type of mixture.)

can be solid, liquid, or gas
physical properties differ from solvent

Frame Game: example / TERM / example / example

Description Wheel: feature / TERM / feature / feature

Four Square: definition / characteristics / TERM / examples / nonexamples

110 Unit: Chemical Interactions

KEY CONCEPT
4.1 A solution is a type of mixture.

BEFORE, you learned
- Ionic or covalent bonds hold a compound together
- Chemical reactions produce chemical changes
- Chemical reactions alter the arrangements of atoms

NOW, you will learn
- How a solution differs from other types of mixtures
- About the parts of a solution
- How properties of solutions differ from properties of their separate components

VOCABULARY

solution p. 111
solute p. 112
solvent p. 112
suspension p. 113

EXPLORE Mixtures

Which substances dissolve in water?

PROCEDURE

1. Pour equal amounts of water into each cup.
2. Pour one spoonful of table salt into one of the cups. Stir.
3. Pour one spoonful of flour into the other cup. Stir.
4. Record your observations.

MATERIALS
- tap water
- 2 clear plastic cups
- plastic spoon
- table salt
- flour

WHAT DO YOU THINK?
- Did the salt dissolve? Did the flour dissolve?
- How can you tell?

VOCABULARY
Remember to use the strategy of your choice. You might use a four square diagram for *solution*.

The parts of a solution are mixed evenly.

A mixture is a combination of substances, such as a fruit salad. The ingredients of any mixture can be physically separated from each other because they are not chemically changed—they are still the same substances. Sometimes, however, a mixture is so completely blended that its ingredients cannot be identified as different substances. A **solution** is a type of mixture, called a homogeneous mixture, that is the same throughout. A solution can be physically separated, but all portions of a solution have the same properties.

If you stir sand into a glass of water, you can identify the sand as a separate substance that falls to the bottom of the glass. Sand in water is a mixture that is not a solution. If you stir sugar into a glass of water, you cannot identify the sugar as a separate substance. Sugar in water is a common solution, as are examples such as seawater, gasoline, and the liquid part of your blood.

Chapter 4: **Solutions** 111

Solutes and Solvents

READING TIP
The words *solute* and *solvent* are both related to the Latin word *solvere*, which means "to loosen."

Like other mixtures, a solution has definite components. A **solute** (SAHL-yoot) is a substance that is dissolved to make a solution. When a solute dissolves, it separates into individual particles. A **solvent** is a substance that dissolves a solute. Because a solute dissolves into individual particles in a solvent, it is not possible to identify the solute and solvent as different substances when they form a solution.

In a solution of table salt and water, the salt is the solute and the water is the solvent. In the cells of your body, substances such as calcium ions and sugar are solutes, and water is the solvent. Water is the most common and important solvent, but other substances can also be solvents. For example, if you have ever used an oil-based paint you know that water will not clean the paintbrushes. Instead, a solvent like turpentine must be used.

CHECK YOUR READING What is the difference between a solute and a solvent?

Types of Solutions

Many solutions are made of solids dissolved in liquids. However, solutes, solvents, and solutions can be gases, liquids, or solids. For example, oxygen, a gas, is dissolved in seawater. The bubbles in carbonated drinks come from the release of carbon dioxide gas that was dissolved in the drink.

Gas Solution
Air is oxygen and other gases dissolved in nitrogen.

Solid Solution
Bronze consists of tin dissolved in copper.

Liquid Solution
Water often contains many dissolved substances.

In some solutions, both the solute and the solvent are in the same physical state. Vinegar, for example, is a solution of acetic acid in water. In a solution of different liquids, it may be difficult to say which substance is the solute and which is the solvent. In general, the substance present in the greater amount is the solvent. Since there is more water than acetic acid in vinegar, water is the solvent and acetic acid is the solute.

Although you may usually think of a solution as a liquid, solid solutions also exist. For example, bronze is a solid solution in which tin is the solute and copper is the solvent. Solid solutions are not formed as solids. Instead, the solvent metal is heated until it melts and becomes a liquid. Then the solute is added, and the substances are thoroughly mixed together. When the mixture cools, it is a solid solution.

Solutions made of combinations of gases are also common. The air you breathe is a solution. Because nitrogen makes up the largest portion of air, it is the solvent. Other gases present, such as oxygen and carbon dioxide, are solutes.

CHECK YOUR READING When substances in a solution are in the same physical state, which is the solvent?

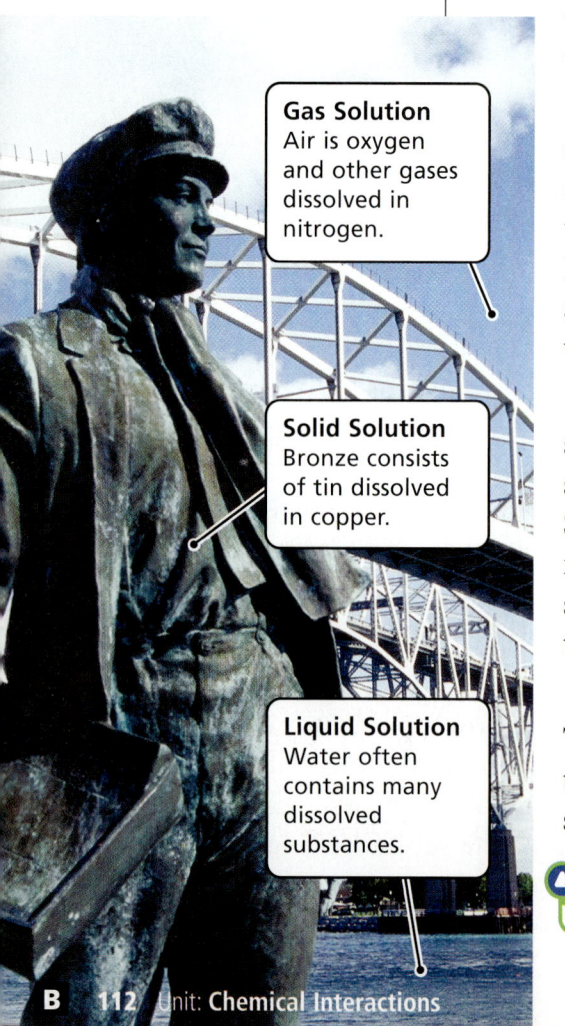

INVESTIGATE Solutions

How can you separate the parts of a solution?

PROCEDURE

1. Draw a solid black circular region 6 cm in diameter around the point of the filter.
2. Place the filter, point up, over the top of the bottle.
3. Squeeze several drops of water onto the point of the filter.
4. Observe the filter once every minute for 10 minutes. Record your observations.

WHAT DO YOU THINK?
- What happened to the ink on the filter?
- Identify, in general, the solutes and the solution in this investigation.

CHALLENGE Relate your observations of the ink and water on the coffee filter to the properties of solutions.

SKILL FOCUS
Observing

MATERIALS
- black marker
- coffee filter
- plastic bottle
- eyedropper
- tap water
- stopwatch

TIME
15 minutes

Suspensions

When you add flour to water, the mixture turns cloudy, and you cannot see through it. This mixture is not a solution but a suspension. In a **suspension**, the particles are larger than those found in a solution. Instead of dissolving, these larger particles turn the liquid cloudy. Sometimes you can separate the components of a suspension by filtering the mixture.

Solution Dissolved particles cannot be identified as a substance different from the solvent.

Suspension Particles that do not dissolve make a suspension look cloudy.

Chapter 4: **Solutions** 113 B

Solvent and solute particles interact.

The parts of a solution—that is, the solute and the solvent—can be physically separated because they are not changed into new substances. However, individual particles of solute and solvent do interact. When a solid dissolves in a liquid, the particles of the solute are surrounded by particles of the liquid. The solute particles become evenly distributed throughout the solvent.

The way in which a solid compound dissolves in a liquid depends on the type of bonds in the compound. Ionic compounds, such as table salt (NaCl), split apart into individual ions. When table salt dissolves in water, the sodium and chloride ions separate, and each ion is surrounded by water molecules. When a covalent compound, such as table sugar ($C_{12}H_{22}O_{11}$), dissolves, each molecule stays together and is surrounded by solvent molecules. The general processes that take place when ionic compounds dissolve and when covalent compounds dissolve are shown below.

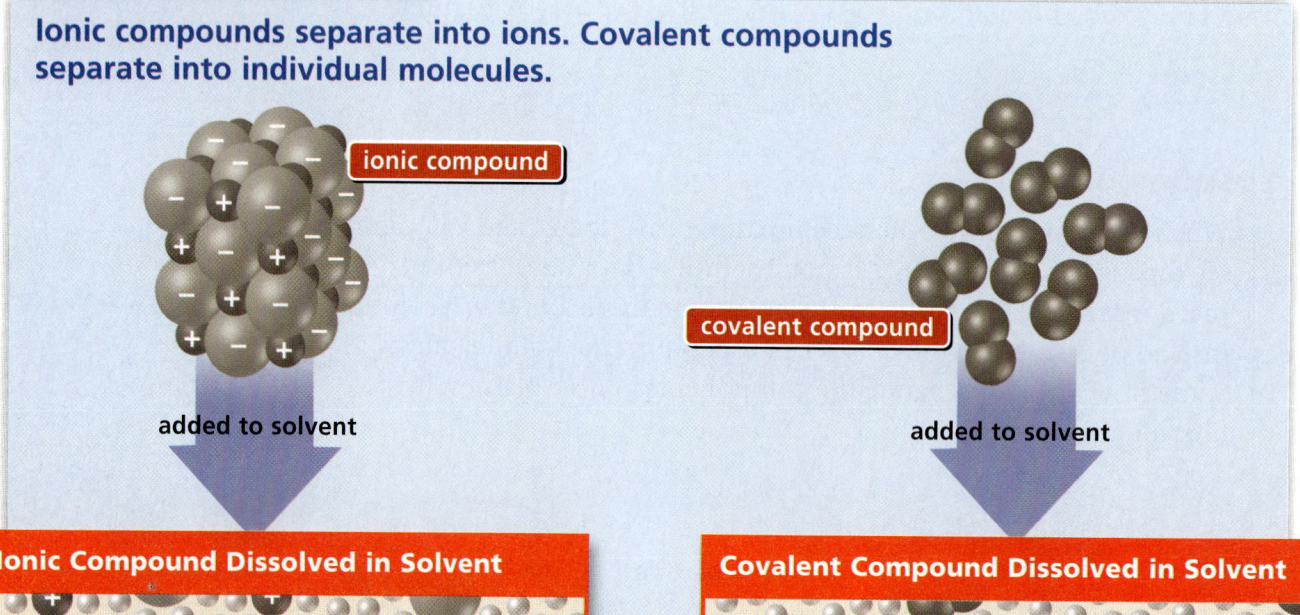

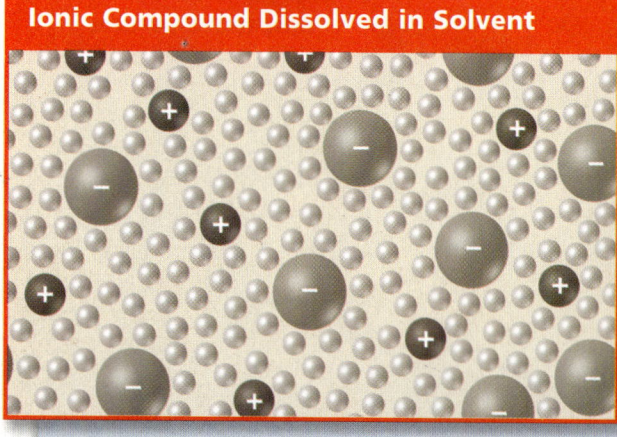

How Solutes Dissolve

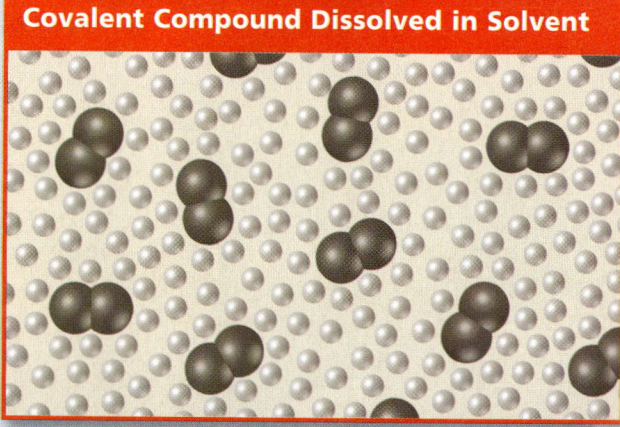

Ionic compounds separate into ions. Covalent compounds separate into individual molecules.

ionic compound

covalent compound

added to solvent

added to solvent

Ionic Compound Dissolved in Solvent

Covalent Compound Dissolved in Solvent

READING VISUALS What difference between the two illustrations tells you whether a compound is ionic or covalent?

Properties of solvents change in solutions.

In every solution—solid, liquid, and gas—solutes change the physical properties of a solvent. Therefore, a solution's physical properties differ from the physical properties of the pure solvent. The amount of solute in the solution determines how much the physical properties of the solvent are changed.

Lowering the Freezing Point

Recall that the freezing point is the temperature at which a liquid becomes a solid. The freezing point of a liquid solvent decreases—becomes lower—when a solute is dissolved in it. For example, pure water freezes at 0°C (32°F) under normal conditions. When a solute is dissolved in water, the resulting solution has a freezing point below 0°C.

Lowering the freezing point of water can be very useful in winter. Road crews spread salt on streets and highways during snowstorms because salt lowers the freezing point of water. When snow mixes with salt on the roads, a saltwater solution that does not freeze at 0°C is formed. The more salt that is used, the lower the freezing point of the solution.

Since salt dissolves in the small amount of water usually present on the surface of ice, it helps to melt any ice already present on the roads. However, there is a limit to salt's effectiveness because there is a limit to how much will dissolve. No matter how much salt is used, once the temperature goes below –21°C (–6°F), the melted ice will freeze again.

REMINDER
In temperature measurements, C stands for "Celsius" and F stands for "Fahrenheit."

CHECK YOUR READING How does the freezing point of a solvent change when a solute is dissolved in it?

Making ice cream also depends on lowering the freezing point of a solvent. Most hand-cranked ice cream makers hold the liquid ice cream ingredients in a canister surrounded by a mixture of salt and ice. The salt added to the ice lowers the freezing point of this mixture. This causes the ice to melt—absorbing heat from its surroundings, including the ice cream ingredients. The ice cream mix is chilled while its ingredients are constantly stirred. As a result, tiny ice crystals form all at once in the ice cream mixture instead of a few crystals forming and growing larger as the mix freezes. This whole process helps to make ice cream that is smooth and creamy.

Adding salt to lower the freezing point of ice helps to make ice cream.

Raising the Boiling Point

The boiling point of a liquid is the temperature at which the liquid forms bubbles in its interior and becomes a gas. Under normal conditions, a substance cannot exist as a liquid at a temperature greater than its boiling point. However, the boiling point of a solution is higher than the boiling point of the pure solvent. Therefore, a solution can remain a liquid at a higher temperature than its pure solvent.

For example, the boiling point of pure water is 100°C (212°F) under normal conditions. Saltwater, however, can be a liquid at temperatures above 100°C because salt raises the boiling point of water. The amount of salt in the water determines how much the boiling point is increased. The more solute that is dissolved in a solution, the greater the increase in boiling point.

APPLY Why might the addition of antifreeze to the water in this car's radiator have prevented the car from overheating?

CHECK YOUR READING How does the boiling point of a solution depend on the amount of solute in it?

A solute lowers the freezing point and raises the boiling point of the solvent in the solution. The result is that the solute extends the temperature range in which the solvent remains a liquid. One way in which both a decrease in freezing point and an increase in boiling point can be useful in the same solution involves a car's radiator. Antifreeze, which is mostly a chemical called ethylene glycol, is often added to the water in the radiator. This solution prevents the water from freezing in the winter and also keeps it from boiling in the summer.

4.1 Review

KEY CONCEPTS
1. How is a solution different from other mixtures?
2. Describe the two parts of a solution. How can you tell them apart?
3. How does the boiling point of a solvent change when a solute is dissolved in it? How does the freezing point change?

CRITICAL THINKING
4. **Contrast** Contrast the way in which an ionic compound, such as table salt, dissolves with the way in which a covalent compound, such as sugar, dissolves.
5. **Infer** Pure water freezes at 0°C and boils at 100°C. Would tap water likely freeze and boil at those exact temperatures? Why or why not?

CHALLENGE
6. **Synthesize** People often sprinkle salt on icy driveways and sidewalks. Would a substance like flour have a similar effect on the ice? Explain.

KEY CONCEPT
4.2 The amount of solute that dissolves can vary.

BEFORE, you learned
- Solutions are a type of mixture
- A solution is made when a solute is dissolved in a solvent
- Solutes change the properties of solvents

NOW, you will learn
- About the concentration of a solution
- How a solute's solubility can be changed
- How solubility depends on molecular structure

VOCABULARY
concentration p. 117
dilute p. 118
saturated p. 118
solubility p. 119

EXPLORE Solutions and Temperature

How does temperature affect a solution?

PROCEDURE
1. Pour cold soda water into one cup and warm soda water into another cup. Record your observations.
2. After 5 minutes, observe both cups of soda water. Record your observations.

WHAT DO YOU THINK?
- Which solution bubbled more at first?
- Which solution bubbled for a longer period of time?

MATERIALS
- soda water
- 2 clear plastic cups

MIND MAP
Remember to use a mind map to take notes on the concentration of a solution.

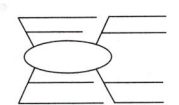

A solution with a high concentration contains a large amount of solute.

Think of water from the ocean and drinking water from a well. Water from the ocean tastes salty, but water from a well does not. The well water does contain salt, but in a concentration so low that you cannot taste it. A solution's **concentration** depends on the amount of solute dissolved in a solvent at a particular temperature. A solution with only a small amount of dissolved solute, such as the salt dissolved in well water, is said to have a low concentration. As more solute is dissolved, the concentration gets higher.

If you have ever used a powdered mix to make lemonade, you probably know that you can change the concentration of the drink by varying the amount of mix you put into a certain amount of water. Two scoops of mix in a pitcher of water makes the lemonade stronger than just one scoop. The lemonade with two scoops of mix has a higher concentration of the mix than the lemonade made with one scoop.

Chapter 4: **Solutions** 117

READING TIP

The word *dilute* can be used as either an adjective or a verb. A dilute solution has a low concentration of solute. To dilute a solution is to add more solvent to it, thus lowering the concentration of the solution.

Degrees of Concentration

A solution that has a low concentration of solute is called a **dilute** solution. Salt dissolved in the drinking water from a well is a dilute solution. The concentration of a solution can be even further reduced, or diluted, by adding more solvent. On the other hand, as more solute is added to a solution, the solution becomes more concentrated. A concentrated solution has a large amount of solute.

Dilute
solvent
solute
Less solute is dissolved in a dilute solution.

Concentrated
More solute is dissolved in a concentrated solution.

Have you ever wondered how much sugar can be dissolved in a glass of iced tea? If you keep adding sugar to the tea, eventually no more sugar will dissolve. The tea will contain as much dissolved sugar as it can hold at that temperature. Such a solution is called a **saturated** solution because it contains the maximum amount of solute that can be dissolved in the solvent at a given temperature. If a solution contains less solute than this maximum amount, it is an unsaturated solution.

CHECK YOUR READING How are the terms *dilute* and *saturated* related to the concept of concentration?

Supersaturated Solutions

VISUALIZATION
CLASSZONE.COM
Explore supersaturated solutions and precipitation.

Sometimes, a solution contains more dissolved solute than is normally possible. This type of solution is said to be supersaturated. A saturated solution can become supersaturated if more solute is added while the temperature is raised. Then if this solution is slowly cooled, the solute can remain dissolved. This type of solution is very unstable, though. If the solution is disturbed, or more solute is added in the form of a crystal, the excess solute will quickly solidify and form a precipitate. This process is shown in the photographs on the top of page 119.

1 A supersaturated solution contains more dissolved solute than is normally possible.

2 After a crystal of solute is added, or the solution is disturbed, a precipitate forms.

REMINDER
A precipitate is a solid substance that comes out of a solution.

One example of a supersaturated solution is a chemical heat pack that contains sodium acetate and water. The pack contains more sodium acetate than can normally dissolve at room temperature, but when the pack is heated in a microwave oven, all of the sodium acetate dissolves. The solution inside the pack is supersaturated. The heat pack is activated by bending it. This disturbs the solution, solidifying the sodium acetate and releasing a large amount of heat over a long period of time.

Solubility

The **solubility** (SAHL-yuh-BIHL-ih-tee) of a substance is the amount of that substance that will dissolve in a certain amount of solvent at a given temperature. For example, consider household ammonia used for cleaning. This ammonia is not pure ammonia—it is a solution of ammonia in water.

Because a large amount of ammonia can dissolve in water, ammonia is said to have a high solubility in water. However, other substances do not dissolve in such large amounts in water. Only a small amount of carbon dioxide will dissolve in water, so carbon dioxide has a low solubility in water. Oils do not dissolve at all in water, so oils are said to be insoluble in water.

READING TIP
The word *solubility* is related to the words *solute* and *solvent*, and means "ability to be dissolved." A substance that is insoluble will not dissolve.

The amount of solute needed to make a saturated solution depends on the solubility of a solute in a particular solvent.

- If the solute is highly soluble, a saturated solution will be very concentrated.
- If the solute has a low solubility, the saturated solution will be dilute.

In other words, a saturated solution can be either dilute or concentrated, depending on the solubility of a solute in a particular solvent.

CHECK YOUR READING How does solubility affect a solution?

Chapter 4: **Solutions** 119

The solubility of a solute can be changed.

The solubility of a solute can be changed in two ways. Raising the temperature is one way to change the solubility of the solute, because most solids are more soluble at higher temperatures. Another way to change solubility when the solute is a gas is to change the pressure. The solubility of gases in a liquid solvent increases at high pressure.

Temperature and Solubility

> **REMINDER**
> An increase in temperature means an increase in particle movement.

An increase in temperature has two effects on most solid solutes—they dissolve more quickly, and a greater amount of the solid dissolves in a given amount of solvent. In general, solids are more soluble at higher temperatures, and they dissolve faster.

The opposite is true of all gases—an increase in temperature makes a gas less soluble in water. You can see this by warming tap water in a pan. As the water approaches its boiling point, any air that is dissolved in the water comes out of solution. The air forms tiny bubbles that rise to the surface.

CHECK YOUR READING What effect does temperature have on most solid solutes? on gaseous solutes?

INVESTIGATE Solubility

How can you change solubility?
Use what you know about solubility to design an experiment that shows how a change in temperature can change the amount of table salt that will dissolve in water.

DESIGN YOUR OWN EXPERIMENT

PROCEDURE
1. Use the materials in the list to identify the relationship between temperature and solubility.
2. Write your procedure, identifying the constants and variables.
3. Perform your experiment and record your results.

WHAT DO YOU THINK?
- Which variable did you change? What were your constants? Why?
- How do your results demonstrate the effect of temperature on solubility?

SKILL FOCUS
Designing experiments

MATERIALS
- clear plastic cups
- thermometer
- tap water
- table salt
- balance
- plastic spoon
- hot-water bath
- cold-water bath

TIME
20 minutes

B 120 Unit: Chemical Interactions

Think back to the earlier discussion of supersaturated solutions. One way in which a solution can become supersaturated is through a change in temperature. For example, suppose that a solution is saturated at 50°C (122°F), and is then allowed to cool slowly. The solid is less soluble in the cooler solution, but the excess solute may not form a precipitate. As a result, the solution contains more of the dissolved solute than would be possible under normal conditions because of the change in temperature.

Temperature and Solubility		
Solute	Increased Temperature	Decreased Temperature
Solid	increase in solubility	decrease in solubility
Gas	decrease in solubility	increase in solubility

A change in temperature can produce changes in solutions in the environment. For example, a factory located on the shore of a lake may use the lake water as a coolant and then return heated water to the lake. This increase in temperature decreases the solubility of oxygen in the lake water. As a result, less oxygen will remain dissolved in the water. A decrease in the oxygen concentration can harm plant and animal life in the lake.

Changing Temperature Changes Solubility

More sugar dissolves in hot water than in cold water.

Solubility of Table Sugar (in 100 g H$_2$O)

The solubility of most solids increases with a rise in temperature.

READING VISUALS About how much sugar will dissolve in 100 g of water at 70°C?

Chapter 4: **Solutions** 121

Pressure and Solubility

A change in pressure does not usually change the solubility of solid or liquid solutes. However, the solubility of any gas increases at higher pressures and decreases at lower pressures.

When manufacturers make carbonated beverages, such as soda, they add carbon dioxide gas at a pressure slightly greater than normal air pressure. When you open the can or bottle, the pressure decreases and the carbon dioxide bubbles out of solution with a fizz.

Another example is shown in the photograph on the left. When a diver's tank contains regular air, about 79 percent of the air is nitrogen. People breathe air like this all the time without any problem, but the pressure underwater is much greater than on Earth's surface. The higher pressure increases the solubility of nitrogen in the diver's blood.

When a diver heads up to the surface too fast, the pressure decreases, and so does the solubility of the nitrogen. The nitrogen comes out of solution, forming bubbles in the diver's blood vessels. These bubbles can cause a painful and sometimes fatal condition called the bends.

Divers can avoid the bends in two ways. They can rise to the surface very slowly, so that nitrogen bubbles stay small and pass through the bloodstream more easily. They can also breathe a different mixture of gases. Some professional divers breathe a mixture of oxygen and nitrogen that contains only about 66 percent nitrogen. For very deep dives, the mixture can also include helium because helium is less soluble in blood than nitrogen.

INFER If these divers are breathing regular air, why might they be looking at their depth gauges?

Pressure and Solubility

Solute	Increased Pressure	Decreased Pressure
Solid	no effect on solubility	no effect on solubility
Gas	increase in solubility	decrease in solubility

CHECK YOUR READING How does pressure affect the solubility of solids? of gases?

Solubility depends on molecular structure.

Everyone knows that oil and water do not mix. When a tanker spills oil near shore, the oil floats on the water and pollutes the beaches. Why do oil and water not mix? The answer involves their different molecular structures.

When a substance dissolves, its molecules or ions separate from one another and become evenly mixed with molecules of the solvent. Recall that water contains polar covalent bonds. As a result, water molecules have a negative region and a positive region. Water molecules are said to be polar. The molecules of an oil are nonpolar— the molecules do not have positive and negative regions. This difference makes oil insoluble in water.

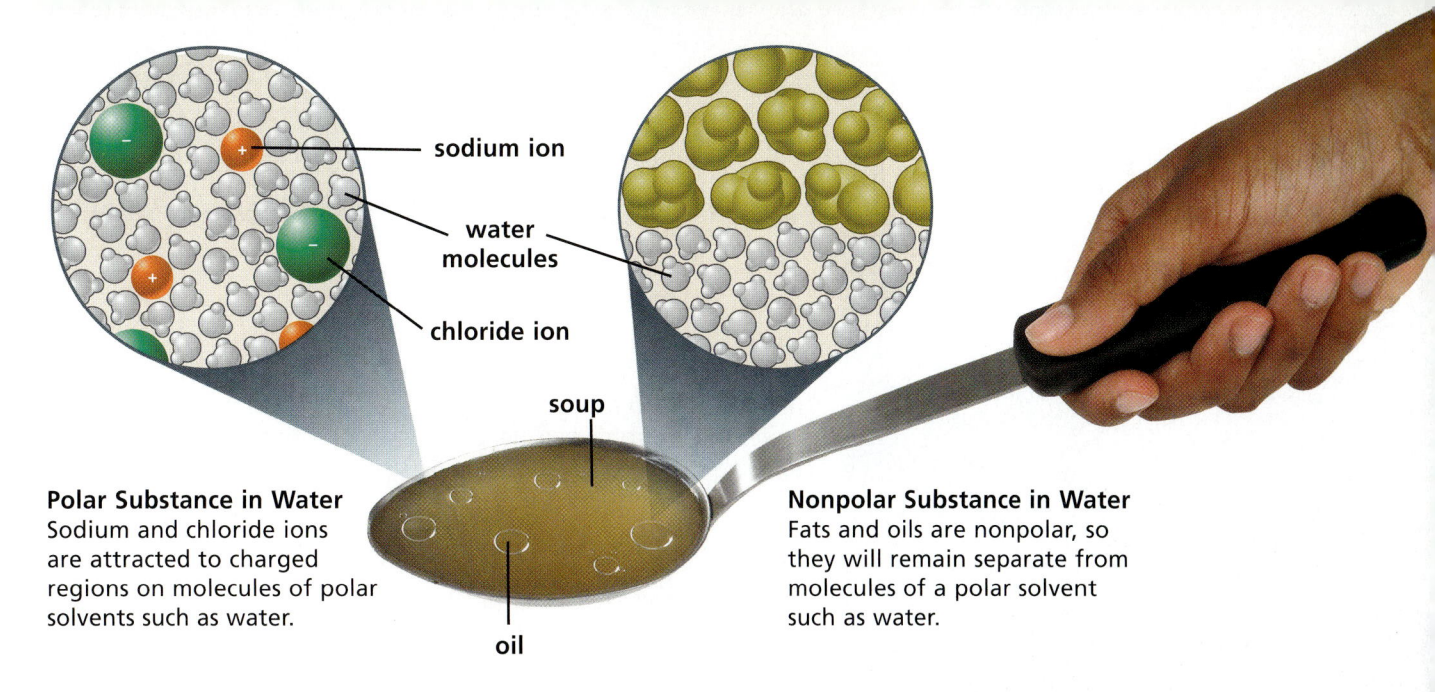

Polar Substance in Water
Sodium and chloride ions are attracted to charged regions on molecules of polar solvents such as water.

Nonpolar Substance in Water
Fats and oils are nonpolar, so they will remain separate from molecules of a polar solvent such as water.

Because water is polar and oil is nonpolar, their molecules are not attracted to each other. The molecules of a polar solvent like water are attracted to other polar molecules, such as those of sugar. This explains why sugar has such a high solubility in water. Ionic compounds, such as sodium chloride, are also highly soluble in water. Because water molecules are polar, they interact with the sodium and chloride ions. In general, polar solvents dissolve polar solutes, and nonpolar solvents dissolve nonpolar solutes. This concept is often expressed as "Like dissolves like."

So many substances dissolve in water that it is sometimes called the universal solvent. Water is considered to be essential for life because it can carry so many different ions and molecules—just about anything the body needs or needs to get rid of—through the body.

CHECK YOUR READING Why will a nonpolar substance not dissolve in a polar substance?

4.2 Review

KEY CONCEPTS

1. How can a solution be made more concentrated? less concentrated?
2. What two factors can change the solubility of a gas?
3. Are nonpolar compounds highly soluble in water? Why or why not?

CRITICAL THINKING

4. **Predict** Suppose you stir sugar into ice water. Some sugar remains on the bottom of the glass. After the glass sits out for an hour, you stir it again. What will happen? Why?
5. **Infer** A powder dissolves easily in water but not in oil. Are the molecules in the powder probably polar or nonpolar? Explain.

CHALLENGE

6. **Synthesize** If mixing a substance with water forms a suspension, does the substance have a high or a low solubility in water? Explain.

Chapter 4: **Solutions** 123

CONNECTING SCIENCES

PHYSICAL SCIENCE AND EARTH SCIENCE

Cool, Clear Water

Water that looks clear, clean, and pure may not be. The water you drink every day contains many dissolved substances.

The drinking water that comes out of a tap is a solution. Many minerals, chemicals, and even gases are dissolved in it. Some drinking water comes from rivers, lakes, or reservoirs, but about half of the drinking water in the United States is pumped from wells. Well water comes from underground aquifers. The water in aquifers flows through gaps in broken or porous rocks.

Filtering Impurities

The water in a puddle is not pure water. It contains suspended dirt and dissolved chemicals. This water can be cleaned underground. As the solution flows through soil and rocks, the soil and rocks filter and trap particles. Some chemicals in the water are removed from the solution by clay particles in the soil. Other chemicals, such as acids from acid rain, are neutralized by limestone and other rocks.

Adding Minerals

The rocks surrounding aquifers do not just remove chemicals from water. As water flows underground, minerals dissolve in the water. The solutes include compounds of calcium, magnesium, and iron. These compounds do not harm the quality of drinking water because they are necessary parts of your diet. Water with a high concentration of dissolved minerals is called hard water.

Copying Earth

Water that has been used by people must be cleaned before it is returned to the environment. Waste treatment plants copy some of the natural cleansing processes of Earth. Wastewater solutions may contain many dissolved impurities and harmful chemicals, but the water can be filtered through beds of sand and gravel. Water must be treated after it is used because so many substances dissolve in it.

Aquifer Layer

EXPLORE

1. **INFER** A white solid often forms around a tiny leak in a water pipe. Where does the white solid come from?
2. **CHALLENGE** Use the Internet or call your local water company to find out the source of your drinking water. Find out whether you have hard or soft water and what dissolved chemicals are in your drinking water.

RESOURCE CENTER
CLASSZONE.COM
Learn more about aquifers and water purification.

KEY CONCEPT
4.3 Solutions can be acidic, basic, or neutral.

BEFORE, you learned
- Substances dissolved in solutions can break apart into ions
- Concentration is the amount of a substance dissolved in a solution
- Water is a common solvent

NOW, you will learn
- What acids and bases are
- How to determine if a solution is acidic or basic
- How acids and bases react with each other

VOCABULARY
acid p. 126
base p. 126
pH p. 129
neutral p. 129

EXPLORE Acids and Bases

What happens when an antacid mixes with an acid?

PROCEDURE

1. Fill the cup halfway with vinegar.
2. Observe the vinegar in the cup. Record your observations.
3. Crush two antacid tablets and place them in the vinegar.
4. Observe the contents of the cup for 5 minutes. Record your observations.

WHAT DO YOU THINK?
- What did you observe before adding the antacid tablets?
- What happened after you added the tablets?

MATERIALS
- clear plastic cup
- vinegar
- 2 antacid tablets

Acids and bases have distinct properties.

Many solutions have certain properties that make us call them acids or bases. Acids are found in many foods, such as orange juice, tomatoes, and vinegar. They taste slightly sour when dissolved in water and produce a burning or itchy feeling on the skin. Strong acids should never be tasted or touched—these solutions are used in manufacturing and are dangerous chemicals.

Bases are the chemical opposite of acids. They tend to taste bitter rather than sour and often feel slippery to the touch. Bases are also found in common products around the home, including soap, ammonia, and antacids. Strong bases, like the lye used for unclogging drains, are also dangerous chemicals.

READING TIP
The prefix *ant-* means "against," so an antacid is a substance that works against an acid.

Chapter 4: **Solutions** 125

Acids, Bases, and Ions

RESOURCE CENTER
CLASSZONE.COM
Find out more about acids and bases.

Generally, a compound that is an acid or a base acts as an acid or a base only when it is dissolved in water. In a water-based solution, these compounds produce ions. Recall that an ion is a charged particle. For example, if a hydrogen atom, which consists of one proton and one electron, loses its electron, it becomes a hydrogen ion. The hydrogen ion is simply a proton and has a positive charge.

An **acid** can be defined as a substance that can donate a hydrogen ion—that is, a proton—to another substance. The diagram below shows what happens when the compound hydrogen chloride (HCl) is dissolved in water. The compound separates into hydrogen ions (H^+) and chloride ions (Cl^-). Hydrogen ions are free to react with other substances, so the solution is an acid. When hydrogen chloride is dissolved in water, the solution is called hydrochloric acid.

Acid

READING TIP
The H_2O above the arrow means the substance on the left is added to water and the substances on the right are dissolved in the water.

$$HCl \xrightarrow{H_2O} H^+ + Cl^-$$

In water, acids release a proton (H^+) into the solution.

A **base** can be defined as a substance that can accept a hydrogen ion from another substance. The diagram below shows what happens when the compound sodium hydroxide (NaOH) is dissolved in water. The compound separates into sodium ions (Na^+) and hydroxide ions (OH^-). The hydroxide ions are free to accept protons from other substances, so the solution is a base. The solution that results when NaOH is dissolved in water is called sodium hydroxide.

Base

$$NaOH \xrightarrow{H_2O} Na^+ + OH^-$$

In water, many bases release a hydroxide ion (OH^-), which can accept a proton.

On the atomic level, the difference between acids and bases is that acids donate protons and bases accept protons. When a proton—a hydrogen ion—from an acid is accepted by a hydroxide ion from a base, the two ions join together and form a molecule of water. This simple transfer of protons between substances is involved in a great many useful and important chemical reactions.

CHECK YOUR READING How are protons related to acids and bases?

Characteristics of Acids

As you read earlier, acids in foods taste sour and produce a burning or prickling feeling on the skin. However, since tasting or touching an unknown chemical is extremely dangerous, other methods are needed to tell whether a solution is an acid.

One safe way to test for an acid is to place a few drops of a solution on a compound that contains a carbonate (CO_3). For example, limestone is a rock that contains calcium carbonate ($CaCO_3$). When an acid touches a piece of limestone, a reaction occurs that produces carbon dioxide gas.

Acids also react with most metals. The reaction produces hydrogen gas, which you can see as bubbles in the photograph on the right. Such a reaction is characteristic of acids.

The feature of acids most often used to identify them is their ability to change the colors of certain compounds known as acid-base indicators. One common indicator is litmus, which is often prepared on slips of paper. When a drop of an acid is placed on litmus paper, the paper turns red.

Acids react with some metals, such as zinc, and release hydrogen gas.
$2HCl + Zn \rightarrow H_2 + ZnCl_2$

CHECK YOUR READING What are three safe methods to test for an acid?

Characteristics of Bases

Bases also have certain common characteristics. Mild bases in foods taste bitter and feel slippery, but as with acids, tasting and touching are not safe ways of testing whether a solution is a base. In fact, some strong bases can burn the skin as badly as strong acids.

Bases feel soapy or slippery because they react with acidic molecules in your skin called fatty acids. In fact, this is exactly how soap is made. Mixing a base—usually sodium hydroxide—with fatty acids produces soap. So, when a base touches your skin, the combination of the base with your own fatty acids actually makes a small amount of soap.

Like acids, bases change the colors of acid-base indicators, but the colors they produce are different. Bases turn litmus paper blue. A base will counteract the effect that an acid has on an acid-base indicator. You might put a few drops of acid on litmus paper to make it turn red. If you put a few drops of a base on the red litmus paper, the litmus paper will change colors again.

CHECK YOUR READING How do the characteristics of bases differ from those of acids?

Bases are found in many cleaning agents, including soap.

The strengths of acids and bases can be measured.

MIND MAP
Remember to use a mind map to take notes about acid and base strength.

Battery fluid and many juices contain acids. Many people drink some type of juice every morning, but you would not want to drink, or even touch, the liquid in a car battery. Similarly, you probably wash your hands with soap several times a day, but you would not want to touch the liquid used to unclog drains. Both soap and drain cleaners are bases. Clearly, some acids and bases are stronger than others.

Acid and Base Strength

Strong acids break apart completely into ions. For example, when hydrogen chloride (HCl) dissolves in water to form hydrochloric acid, it breaks down into hydrogen ions and chloride ions. No hydrogen chloride remains in the solution. Because all of the hydrogen chloride forms separate ions, hydrochloric acid is a strong acid.

A weak acid does not form many ions in solution. When acetic acid ($HC_2H_3O_2$), which is the acid in vinegar, dissolves in water, only about 1 percent of the acetic acid breaks up into hydrogen ions and acetate ions. The other 99 percent of the acetic acid remains unchanged. Therefore, acetic acid is a weak acid.

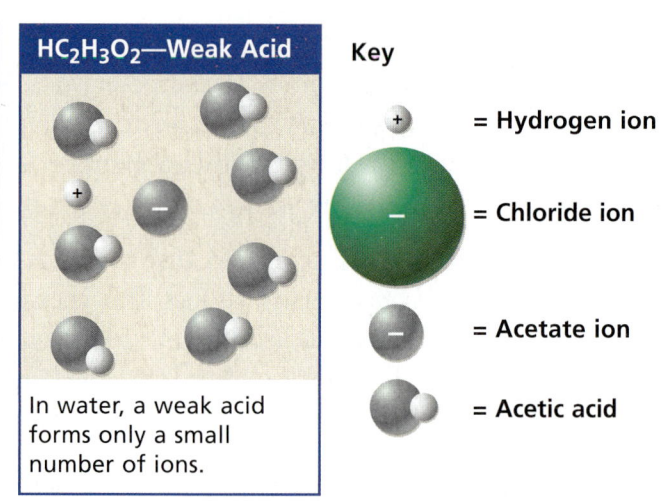

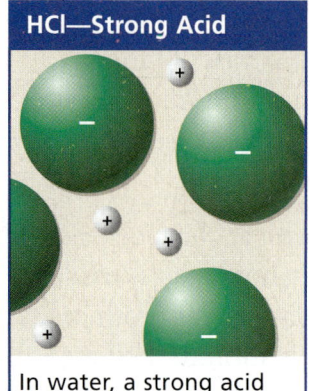

HCl—Strong Acid

In water, a strong acid dissolves completely into ions.

$HC_2H_3O_2$—Weak Acid

In water, a weak acid forms only a small number of ions.

Key
+ = Hydrogen ion
− = Chloride ion
− = Acetate ion
= Acetic acid

Bases also can be strong or weak. When sodium hydroxide (NaOH) dissolves in water, it forms sodium ions (Na^+) and hydroxide ions (OH^-). None of the original NaOH remains in the solution, so sodium hydroxide is a strong base. However, when ammonia (NH_3) dissolves in water, only about 1 percent of the ammonia reacts with water to form OH^- ions.

$$NH_3 + H_2O \rightarrow NH_4^+ + OH^-$$

The other 99 percent of the ammonia remains unchanged, so ammonia is a weak base. The ions formed when NaOH or NH_3 is dissolved in water are shown on the top of page 129.

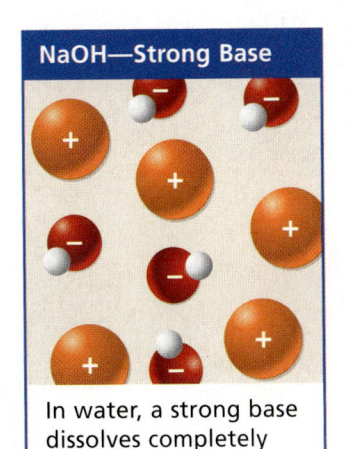

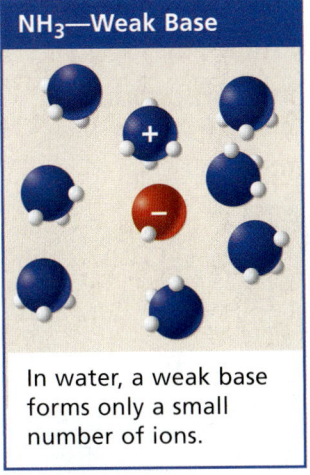

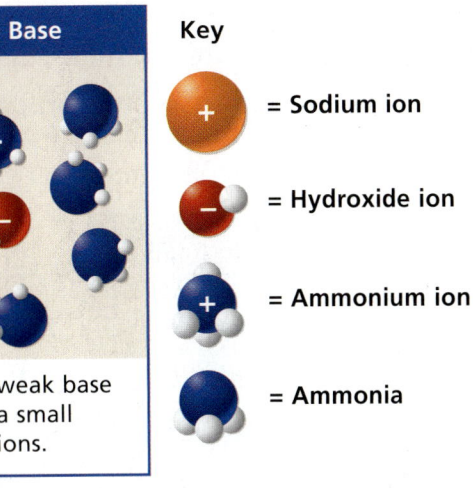

NaOH—Strong Base

In water, a strong base dissolves completely into ions.

NH₃—Weak Base

In water, a weak base forms only a small number of ions.

Key

+ = Sodium ion
− = Hydroxide ion
+ = Ammonium ion
= Ammonia

> **READING TIP**
> Look at the reaction on the bottom of page 128 for help with the illustration of NH₃ in water.

Note that the strength of an acid or base is not the same as its concentration. Dilute hydrochloric acid is still strong and can burn holes in your clothing, whereas acetic acid cannot. The strengths of acids and bases depend on the percentage of the substance that forms ions.

CHECK YOUR READING What determines acid and base strength?

Measuring Acidity

The acidity of a solution depends on the concentration of H^+ ions in the solution. This concentration is often measured on the **pH** scale. In this scale, a high H^+ concentration is indicated by a low number, and a low H^+ concentration is indicated by a high number. The numbers of the pH scale usually range from 0 to 14, but numbers outside this range are possible. The middle number, 7, represents a neutral solution. A **neutral** substance is neither an acid nor a base. Pure water has a pH of 7.

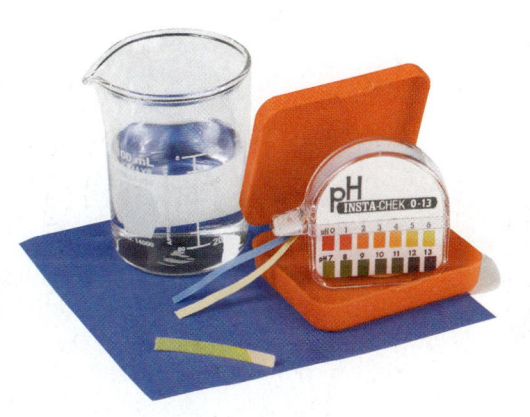

Numbers below 7 indicate acidic solutions. A concentrated strong acid has a low pH value—the pH of concentrated hydrochloric acid, for example, is less than 0. Numbers above 7 indicate a basic solution. A concentrated strong base has a high pH value—the pH of concentrated sodium hydroxide, for example, is greater than 14. The illustration on page 130 shows the pH values of some common acids and bases.

Today, electronic pH meters are commonly used to measure pH. A probe is placed in a solution, and the pH value is indicated by the meter. An older method of measuring pH is to use an acid-base indicator. You read earlier that acids turn litmus paper red and bases turn litmus paper blue. Other acid-base indicators, such as a universal pH indicator, show a variety of colors at different pH values.

The strip of universal indicator paper in the bottom front of the photograph shows a nearly neutral pH.

CHECK YOUR READING Is the pH of a base higher or lower than the pH of an acid?

Common Acids and Bases

Dilute acids and bases are found in many common products.

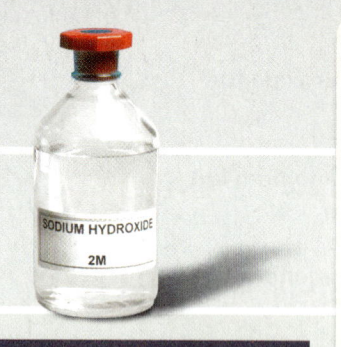

low H⁺ concentration

pH 14
13
12
11
10
9
8
7
6
5
4
3
2
1
pH 0

high H⁺ concentration

sodium hydroxide (NaOH)—pH > 14
Concentrated NaOH has a pH greater than 14 because it has a very low H⁺ concentration. Drain openers usually contain concentrated NaOH.

milk—pH 6.5
Milk contains molecules called fatty acids, which make milk slightly acidic.

lemon—pH 2
Lemons and other types of citrus fruit contain citric acid.

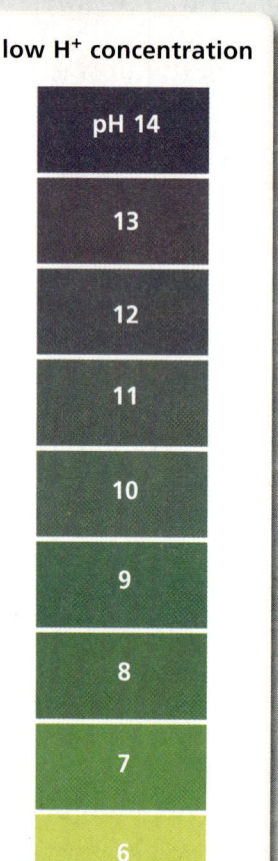

soap—pH 10
Soap is commonly made by mixing fats with NaOH. There is a relatively low concentration of NaOH in soap.

pure water (H₂O)—pH 7
In pure water, the H⁺ concentration is equal to the OH⁻ concentration. Pure water has a pH of 7 and is neutral.

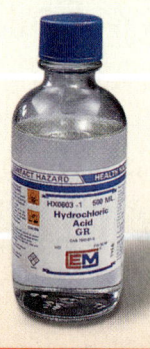

hydrochloric acid (HCl)—pH < 0
Concentrated HCl has a pH lower than 0 because it has a very high H⁺ concentration. HCl is used in many processes, including refining sugar from sugar cane.

READING VISUALS
Where are the strong acids on the chart? Where are the strong bases? How does the concentration of hydrogen ions change?

130 Unit: Chemical Interactions

Acids and bases neutralize each other.

Acids donate hydrogen ions, and bases accept hydrogen ions. Therefore, it is not surprising that acids and bases react when they come into contact with each other. Recall that when a hydrogen ion (H^+) from an acid collides with a hydroxide ion (OH^-) from a base, the two ions join to form a molecule of water (H_2O).

The negative ion of an acid (Cl^-) joins with the positive ion of a base (Na^+) to form a substance called a salt. Since both the salt and water are neutral, an acid-base reaction is called a neutralization (NOO-truh-lih-ZAY-shuhn) reaction. The reactants are an acid and a base, and the products are a salt and water.

A common example of a neutralization reaction occurs when you swallow an antacid tablet to relieve an upset stomach. The acid in your stomach has a pH of about 1.5, due mostly to hydrochloric acid produced by the stomach lining. If your stomach produces more acid than is needed, you may feel a burning sensation. An antacid tablet contains a base, such as sodium bicarbonate, magnesium hydroxide, or calcium carbonate. The base reacts with the stomach acid and produces a salt and water. This reaction lowers the acidity—and raises the pH—to its normal value.

Acid rain forms when certain gases in the atmosphere dissolve in water vapor, forming acidic solutions. During rainstorms these acids fall to Earth. They can harm forests by making soil acidic and harm aquatic life by making lakes acidic. Acid rain can also dissolve marble and limestone in buildings and statues, because both marble and limestone contain calcium carbonate, which is a base.

> **READING TIP**
> The salt produced by a neutralization reaction is not necessarily table salt.

CHECK YOUR READING How is neutralization an example of a chemical reaction?

4.3 Review

KEY CONCEPTS

1. Use the concept of ions to explain the difference between an acid and a base.
2. How do the properties of an acid differ from the properties of a base?
3. What happens when an acid and a base react with each other?

CRITICAL THINKING

4. **Infer** When an acid reacts with a metal, such as zinc, what is released? Where does that product come from?
5. **Infer** Suppose that you have 1 L of an acid solution with a pH of 2. You add 1 L of pure water. What happens to the pH of the solution? Explain.

CHALLENGE

6. **Synthesize** Suppose that equal amounts of solutions of HCl and NaOH with the same concentration are mixed together. What will the pH of the new solution be? What are the products of this reaction?

CHAPTER INVESTIGATION

Acids and Bases

OVERVIEW AND PURPOSE Acids and bases are very common. For example, the limestone formations in the cave shown on the left are made of a substance that is a base when it is dissolved in water. In this activity you will use what you have learned about solutions, acids, and bases to
- test various household substances and place them in categories according to their pH values
- investigate the properties of common acids and bases

▶ Procedure

1. Make a data table like the one shown on the sample notebook page.

2. Set out 7 cups in your work area. Collect the substances that you will be testing: baking soda, fruit juice, shampoo, soda water, table salt, laundry detergent, and vinegar.

3. Label each cup. Be sure to wear goggles when pouring the substances that you will be testing. Pour 30 mL of each liquid substance into a separate cup. Dissolve 1 tsp of each solid substance in 30 mL of distilled water in a separate cup. To avoid contaminating the test solutions, wash and dry your measuring tools and hands between measurements.

MATERIALS
- plastic cups
- baking soda
- fruit juice
- shampoo
- soda water
- table salt
- detergent powder
- vinegar
- masking tape
- marking pen
- measuring spoons
- graduated cylinder
- distilled water
- paper towels
- pH indicator paper

132 Unit: Chemical Interactions

4 Dip a piece of indicator paper into each solution. Compare the color of the test strip with the colors in the chart included in the package. Record the indicator color and the approximate pH number for each solution.

Step 4

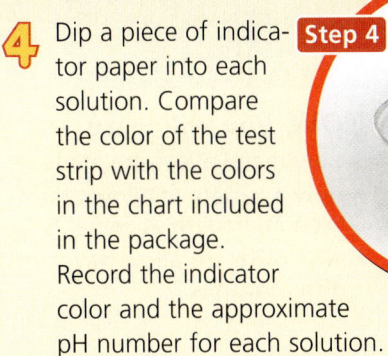

5 After you have tested all of the solutions, arrange the cups in order of their pH values.

Observe and Analyze   *Write It Up*

1. **RECORD DATA** Check to be sure that your data table is complete.

2. **ANALYZE DATA** What color range did the substances show when tested with the indicator paper? What do your results tell you about the pH of each substance you tested?

3. **CLASSIFY** Look for patterns in the pH values. Use your test results to place each household substance in one of three groups—acids, bases, or neutral.

4. **MODEL** Draw a diagram of the pH scale from 0 to 14. Use arrows and labels to show where the substances you tested fall on this scale.

Conclude   *Write It Up*

1. **GENERALIZE** What general conclusions can you draw about the hydrogen ion concentration in many acids and bases found in the home? Are the hydrogen ion concentrations very high or very low? How do you know?

2. **EVALUATE** What limitations or difficulties did you experience in interpreting the results of your tests or other observations?

3. **APPLY** Antacid tablets react with stomach acid containing hydrochloric acid. What is this type of reaction called? What are the products of this type of reaction?

INVESTIGATE Further

CHALLENGE Repeat the experiment, changing one variable. You might change the concentrations of the solutions you are testing or see what happens when you mix an acidic solution with a basic solution. Get your teacher's approval of your plan before proceeding. How does changing one particular variable affect the pH of the solutions?

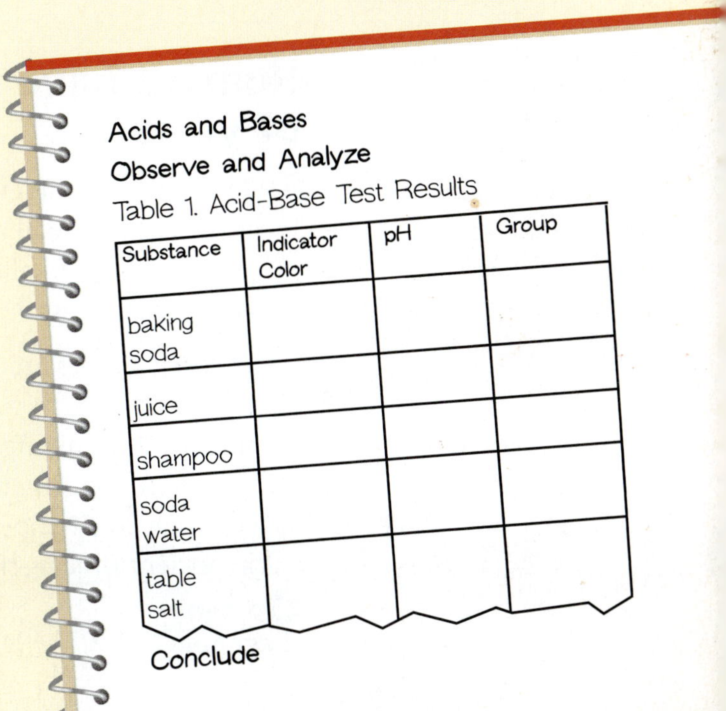

Acids and Bases
Observe and Analyze
Table 1. Acid-Base Test Results

Substance	Indicator Color	pH	Group
baking soda			
juice			
shampoo			
soda water			
table salt			

Conclude

Chapter 4: **Solutions** 133

KEY CONCEPT
4.4 Metal alloys are solid mixtures.

BEFORE, you learned
- A solution can be a solid
- Solutes change the properties of solvents
- The concentration of a solution can vary

NOW, you will learn
- How metal alloys are made
- How a variety of alloys are used in modern society
- Why different alloys have different uses

VOCABULARY

alloy p. 134

THINK ABOUT

If gold jewelry is not pure gold, what is it?

People have prized gold since ancient times—archaeologists have found gold jewelry that was made thousands of years ago. Gold is a very soft metal, and jewelry made of pure gold bends very easily. Today, most gold jewelry is about 75 percent gold and 25 percent other metals. Why might these metals be mixed in?

VOCABULARY
Remember to use the strategy of your choice. You might use a description wheel diagram for *alloy*.

Humans have made alloys for thousands of years.

The gold used in jewelry is an example of an alloy. An **alloy** is a mixture of a metal and one or more other elements, usually metals as well. The gold alloys used in jewelry contain silver and copper in various amounts.

Many alloys are made by melting the metals and mixing them in the liquid state to form a solution. For example, bronze is made by melting and mixing copper and tin and then letting the solution cool. Bronze is not difficult to make, because both copper and tin melt at relatively low temperatures. Bronze was probably the first alloy made in ancient times—historians say it was discovered about 3800 B.C.

CHECK YOUR READING How is an alloy usually made?

B 134 Unit: Chemical Interactions

Recall that the addition of a solute changes the properties of a solvent. The alloy bronze is harder than either copper or tin alone. This hardness made bronze a better material than stones or animal bones for making tools. The transition from the Stone Age to the Bronze Age, when humans first began to use metals, was an important period in human history.

Even though alloys have been made for thousands of years, new alloys with new properties are still being developed. One alloy with a very interesting property is nitinol, which is made of nickel and titanium. Nitinol is called a memory alloy because it can be given a particular shape and then reshaped. What makes nitinol unusual is that it will return to its original shape after being heated. Because of this property, nitinol is used in several common products, including eyeglass frames.

A short list of useful alloys is given in the table below. The percentages shown in the table are those for only one type of each alloy.

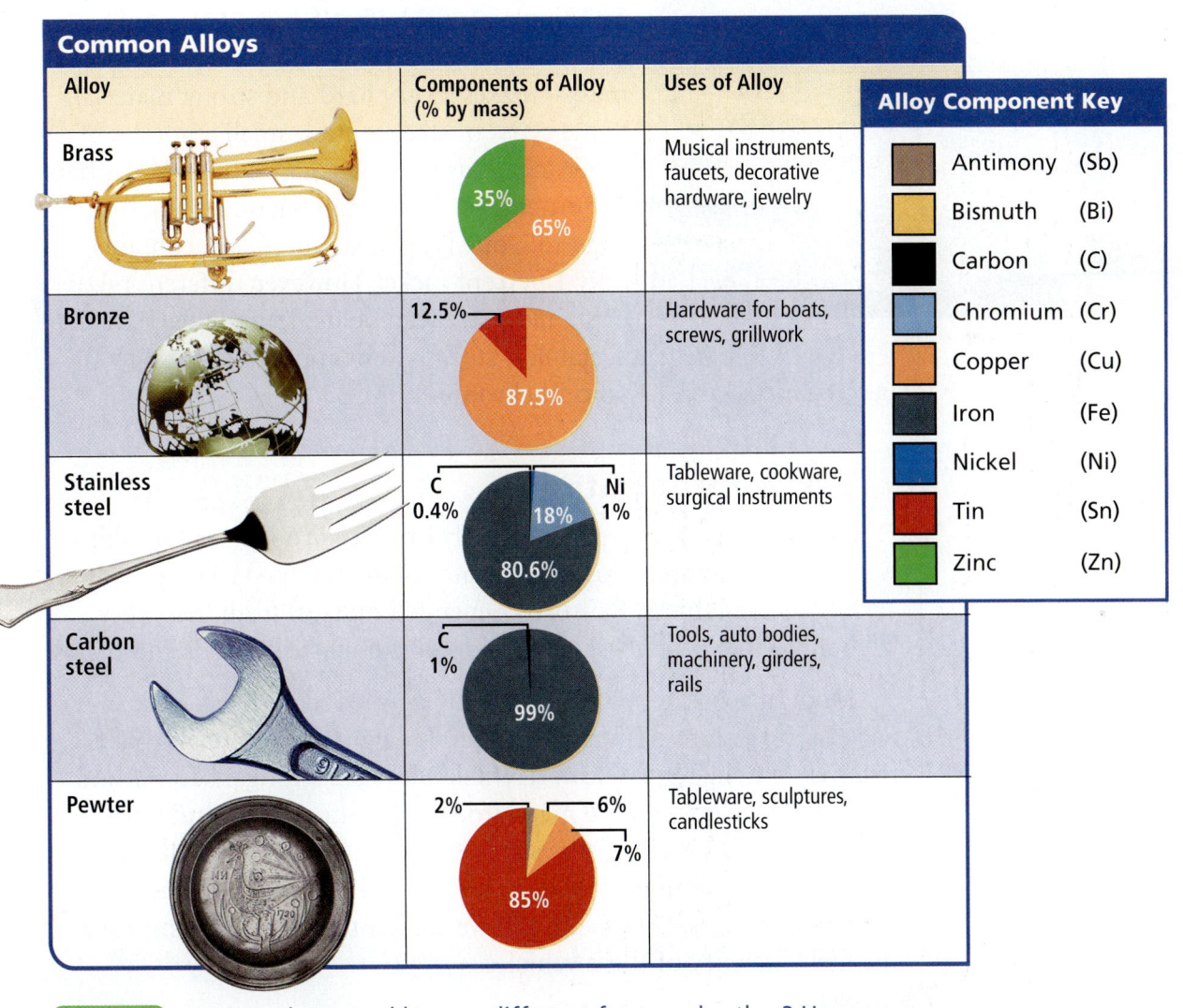

Common Alloys

Alloy	Components of Alloy (% by mass)	Uses of Alloy
Brass	35% Zn, 65% Cu	Musical instruments, faucets, decorative hardware, jewelry
Bronze	12.5% Sn, 87.5% Cu	Hardware for boats, screws, grillwork
Stainless steel	C 0.4%, 18% Cr, Ni 1%, 80.6% Fe	Tableware, cookware, surgical instruments
Carbon steel	C 1%, 99% Fe	Tools, auto bodies, machinery, girders, rails
Pewter	2% Cu, 6% Bi, 7% Sb, 85% Sn	Tableware, sculptures, candlesticks

Alloy Component Key
- Antimony (Sb)
- Bismuth (Bi)
- Carbon (C)
- Chromium (Cr)
- Copper (Cu)
- Iron (Fe)
- Nickel (Ni)
- Tin (Sn)
- Zinc (Zn)

READING VISUALS How are brass and bronze different from each other? How are stainless steel and carbon steel different from each other?

Explore alloys and their uses.

Alloys have many uses in modern life.

The advances in materials science that began with bronze almost 6000 years ago continue today. Modern industry uses many different alloys. Some alloys, based on lightweight metals such as aluminum and titanium, are relatively recent developments. However, the most important alloy used today—steel—has been around for many years.

A major advance in technology occurred in the 1850s with the development of the Bessemer process. This process made it possible to manufacture large amounts of steel in a short time. Until then, steel could be made only in batches of less than 100 pounds. The Bessemer process made it possible to produce up to 30 tons of steel in about 20 minutes. Since it began to be mass-produced, steel has been used in everything from bridges to cars to spoons.

Most steel used in construction is an alloy of iron and carbon. Iron is too soft to be a good building material by itself, but adding only a small amount of carbon—about 1 percent by mass—makes a very hard and strong material. Some types of steel contain small amounts of other metals as well, which give the alloys different properties. As you can see on the chart on page 135, one type of stainless steel contains only 1 percent nickel. However, different types of stainless steel can be made, and they have different uses. For instance, stainless steel used in appliances has 8 to 10 percent nickel and 18 percent chromium in it.

Steel is the main material used in the structure of this sphere at Epcot Center in Florida.

Alloys in Transportation

Different forms of transportation rely on steel. Wooden sailing ships were replaced by steel ships in the late 1800s. Today, steel cargo ships carry steel containers. Railroads depended on steel from their very beginning. Today's high-speed trains still run on steel wheels and tracks.

Modern vehicles use more recently developed alloys as well. For example, aluminum and titanium are lightweight metals that are relatively soft, like iron. However, their alloys are strong, like steel, and light. Airplane engines are made from aluminum alloys, and both aluminum and titanium alloys are used in aircraft bodies. Aluminum alloys are also commonly used in high-speed passenger ferries and in the bodies of cars. Because the alloys are light, they help to improve the fuel efficiency of these vehicles.

CHECK YOUR READING How are alloys used in transportation?

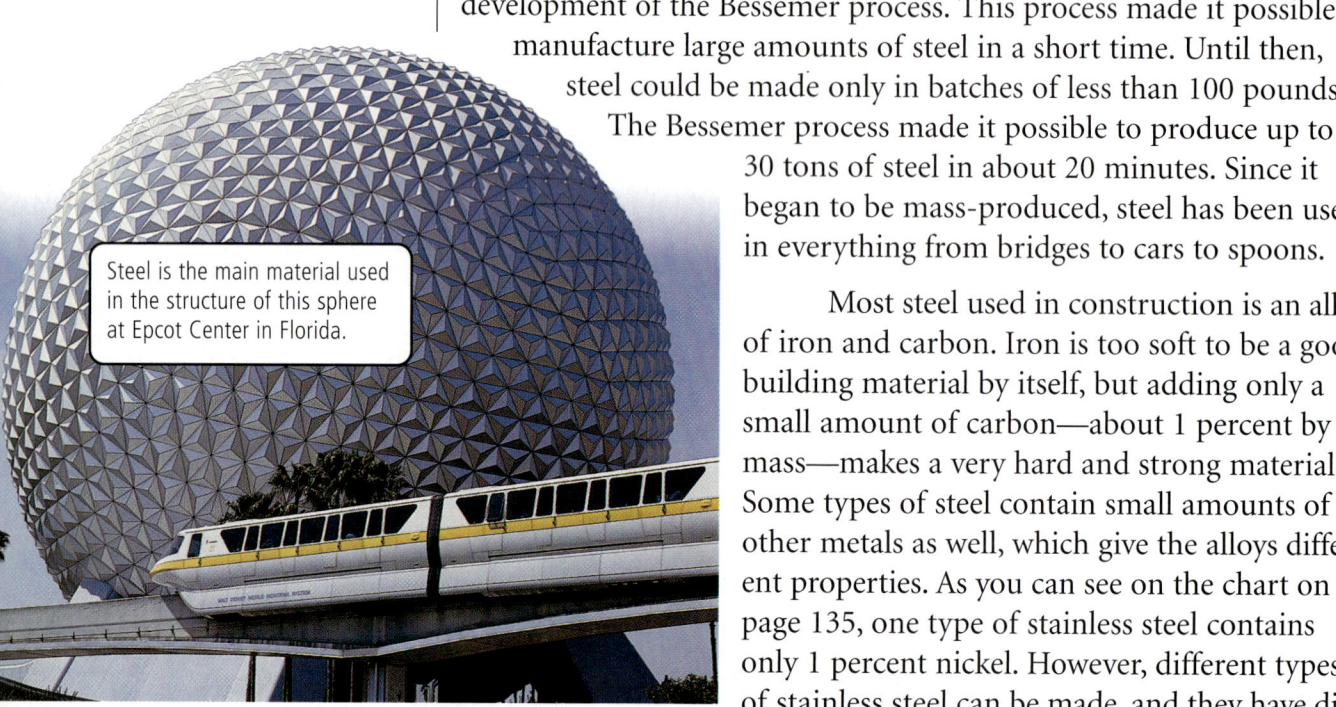

Alloys in Medicine

You may have noticed that most medical equipment is shiny and silver-colored. This equipment is made of stainless steel, which contains nickel and chromium in addition to iron and carbon. Surgical instruments are often made of stainless steel because it can be honed to a very sharp edge and is also rust resistant.

Cobalt and titanium alloys are also widely used in medicine because they do not easily react with substances in the body, such as blood and digestive juices. These alloys can be surgically placed inside the body with a minimum of harm to either the body or the metal. The photographs on the right show one use of alloys—making artificial joints.

Memory alloys similar to the nitinol alloy described earlier also have a wide range of medical uses. These alloys are used in braces for teeth, and as implants that hold open blocked arteries or correct a curve in the spine. Medical devices made of memory alloys can be made in a particular shape and then reshaped for implantation. After the device is in place, the person's body heat causes it to return to its original shape.

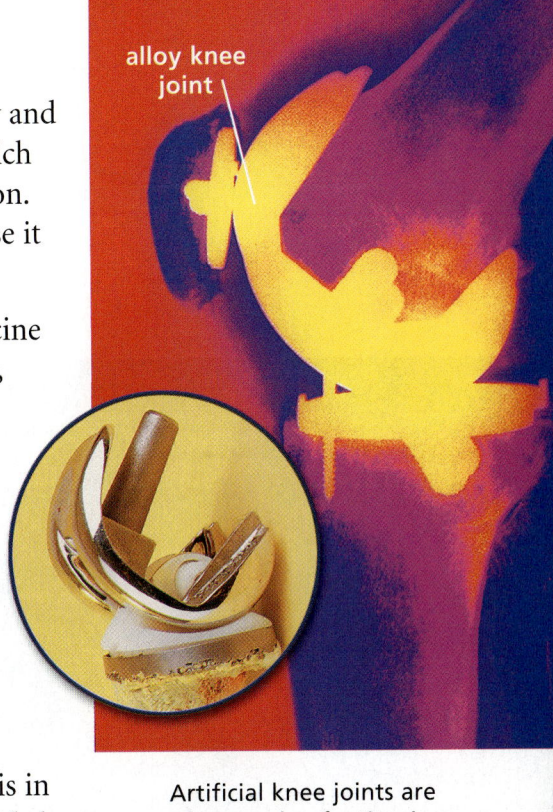

alloy knee joint

Artificial knee joints are often made of a titanium alloy. The x-ray image shows the device in place.

CHECK YOUR READING What properties make alloys useful in medicine?

INVESTIGATE Alloys

How is a pure metal different from its alloy?

PROCEDURE

1. Examine the iron nails and the alloy (steel or stainless steel) nails. Record your observations.

2. Find and record the mass of the three iron nails. Repeat with the three alloy nails.

3. Find the volume of the nails by displacement, as follows: Into the empty graduated cylinder, pour water to a height that is higher than the nails are long. Note the water level. Add the iron nails and record the change in water level. Repeat this step with the alloy nails.

4. Calculate the density of each type of nail. **Density** = $\dfrac{\text{mass}}{\text{Volume}}$

WHAT DO YOU THINK?

- Compare your observations of the metals contained in the nails.
- Which metal has the greater density? How might a metal's density be important in how it is used?

CHALLENGE How can you identify different alloys of a metal?

SKILL FOCUS
Observing

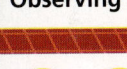

MATERIALS
- 3 iron nails
- 3 steel nails or 3 stainless steel nails
- balance
- graduated cylinder
- water

TIME
30 minutes

Chapter 4: **Solutions** 137 B

Alloys in Space Flight

The aerospace industry develops and uses some of the newest and most advanced alloys. The same qualities that make titanium and aluminum alloys useful in airplanes—lightness, strength, and heat resistance—also make them useful in spacecraft. Titanium alloys were used in the Gemini space program of the 1960s. Large portions of the wings of today's space shuttle are made of aluminum alloys.

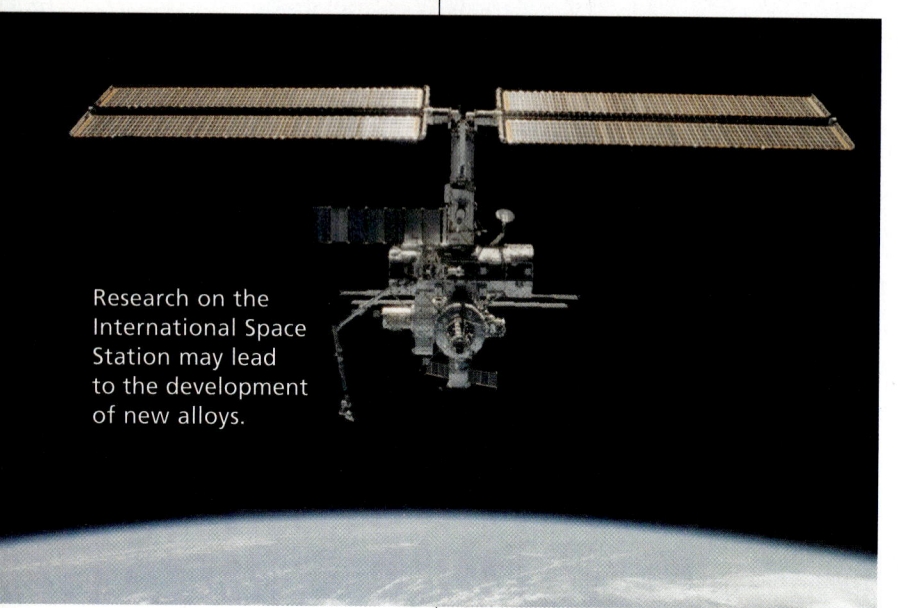

Research on the International Space Station may lead to the development of new alloys.

For more than 20 years, the heat shield on the shuttle's belly has been made from ceramic tiles. However, engineers have experimented with a titanium heat shield as well.

Construction of the International Space Station, which is shown in the photograph on the left, began in 1998. Alloys are a major part of the space station's structure. More important, research on the space station may lead to the development of new alloys.

One of the goals of research on the space station is to make alloys in a microgravity environment, which cannot be done on Earth. For example, astronauts have experimented with thick liquids, made with iron, that harden or change shape when a magnet is placed nearby, and then return to their previous shapes when the magnet is removed. These liquid alloys may be useful in robots or in artificial organs for humans.

CHECK YOUR READING Why is research into new alloys on the International Space Station important?

4.4 Review

KEY CONCEPTS

1. How can one metal be made to dissolve in another metal?
2. Name three metal alloys and a use for each one.
3. Why are alloys of cobalt or titanium, instead of pure iron, used for medical devices that are implanted inside people?

CRITICAL THINKING

4. **Infer** In industry, all titanium alloys are simply called titanium. What might this tell you about the use of pure titanium?
5. **Compare and Contrast** How are modern alloys similar to alloys made hundreds or thousands of years ago? How are they different?

CHALLENGE

6. **Synthesize** The melting point of copper is 1083°C. Tin is dissolved in copper to make bronze. Will bronze have a melting point of 1083°C? Why or why not?

138 Unit: Chemical Interactions

Math in Science

SKILL: CALCULATING PERCENTAGES

MATH TUTORIAL
CLASSZONE.COM
Click on Math Tutorial for more help understanding percents.

The Mixtures in Alloys

An alloy is a mixture of a metal with other substances. Because even a small change in the percentages of materials in an alloy can change its properties, alloys are made according to strict specifications. For example, steel is an alloy of iron and carbon. Steel that contains 0.6 percent carbon by mass is used in steel beams, whereas steel that contains 1.0 percent carbon by mass, which makes the steel harder, is used to make tools and springs. How can the percentages of materials in an alloy be calculated?

Example

Calculate the percentage of nickel in an alloy if a small portion of the alloy has 10 atoms, 3 of which are nickel.

(1) Convert the number of atoms into a fraction.

3 of 10 atoms in the alloy are nickel = $\frac{3}{10}$

(2) To calculate a percentage, first find an equivalent fraction that has a denominator of 100. Use x as the numerator.

$\frac{3}{10} = \frac{x}{100}$

(3) Convert the fraction into a percentage by using cross products

$3 \cdot 100 = 10 \cdot x$

$300 = 10x$

$30 = x$

ANSWER The percentage of nickel atoms in the alloy is 30%.

Answer the following questions.

1. A sample of an alloy contains 4 iron atoms, 3 zinc atoms, 2 aluminum atoms, and 1 copper atom.

   a. What percentage of the alloy is aluminum by number of atoms?

   b. What percentage is zinc by number of atoms?

2. A sample of an alloy contains 12 titanium atoms, 4 niobium atoms, and 4 aluminum atoms.

   a. What percentage of the alloy is titanium by number of atoms?

   b. What percentage is niobium by number of atoms?

CHALLENGE Suppose there is an alloy in which 2 of every 3 atoms are silver atoms, 1 of every 4 atoms is a copper atom, and 1 of every 12 atoms is a tin atom. What are the percentages of each metal in the alloy by number of atoms?

The steel in girders like these contains iron and 0.6 percent carbon by mass.

Chapter 4 Review

the BIG idea
When substances dissolve to form a solution, the properties of the mixture change.

CONTENT REVIEW
CLASSZONE.COM

KEY CONCEPTS SUMMARY

4.1 A solution is a type of mixture.
- A solution is a mixture in which one or more solutes are dissolved in a solvent.
- A solution is a homogeneous mixture.

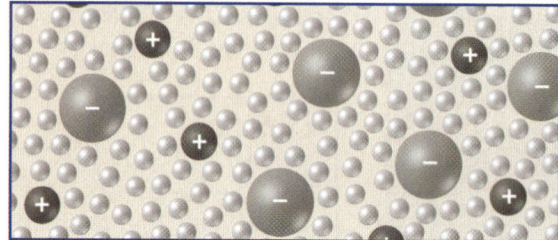

Ionic compound dissolved in solvent

VOCABULARY
solution p. 111
solute p. 112
solvent p. 112
suspension p. 113

4.2 The amount of solute that dissolves can vary.
- The amount of dissolved solute determines a solution's concentration.
- The more soluble a substance is, the more of it will dissolve in a solution.

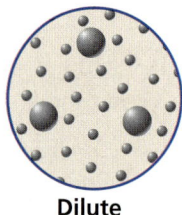

Dilute   Concentrated

VOCABULARY
concentration p. 117
dilute p. 118
saturated p. 118
solubility p. 119

4.3 Solutions can be acidic, basic, or neutral.
- Acids donate protons (H+) in solutions, and bases accept protons in solutions.
- Acidity is measured by the H+ concentration on the pH scale.

Acid   HCl $\xrightarrow{H_2O}$ H+ + Cl−

Base   NaOH $\xrightarrow{H_2O}$ Na+ + OH−

VOCABULARY
acid p. 126
base p. 126
pH p. 129
neutral p. 129

4.4 Metal alloys are solid mixtures.
- Many of the metals used in modern transportation and medicine are alloys.
- The properties of a metal can be changed by adding one or more substances to produce a more useful material.

VOCABULARY
alloy p. 134

B 140 Unit: Chemical Interactions

Reviewing Vocabulary

Draw a diagram similar to the example shown below to connect and organize the concepts of related vocabulary terms. After you have completed your diagram, explain in two or three sentences why you organized the terms in that way. Underline each of the terms in your explanation.

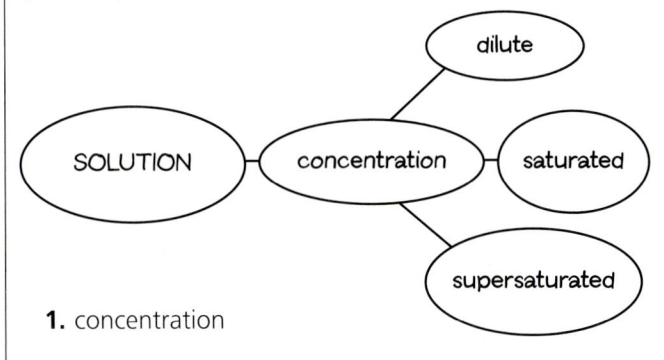

1. concentration
2. acid
3. base
4. neutral
5. pH

Latin Roots Several of the vocabulary terms in this chapter come from the Latin word *solvere*, which means "to loosen." Describe how each of the following terms is related to the Latin word.

6. solution
7. solute
8. solvent
9. solubility

Reviewing Key Concepts

Multiple Choice *Choose the letter of the best answer.*

10. What makes a solution different from other types of mixtures?
    a. Its parts can be separated.
    b. It is the same throughout.
    c. Its parts can be seen.
    d. It is a liquid.

11. When a solute is dissolved in a solvent, the solvent's
    a. boiling point decreases
    b. boiling point decreases and its freezing point increases
    c. freezing point increases
    d. freezing point decreases and its boiling point increases

12. When a compound held together by ionic bonds dissolves, the compound
    a. releases molecules into the solution
    b. forms a suspension
    c. releases ions into the solution
    d. becomes nonpolar

13. Water is called the universal solvent because it
    a. dissolves many substances
    b. dissolves very dense substances
    c. has no charged regions
    d. is nonpolar

14. How does an increase in temperature affect the solubility of solids and gases?
    a. It increases solubility of most solids and decreases the solubility of gases.
    b. It decreases solubility of most solids and gases.
    c. It increases solubility of gases and decreases the solubility of most solids.
    d. It increases solubility of both solids and gases.

15. A solution with a very high H^+ concentration has a
    a. very high pH   c. pH close to 5
    b. very low pH   d. pH close to 7

16. Why are oils insoluble in water?
    a. They are acids.   c. They are bases.
    b. They are polar.   d. They are nonpolar.

Short Answer *Write a short answer to each question.*

17. Describe the reaction that occurs when a strong acid reacts with a strong base.

18. How might an alloy be changed for different uses? Explain.

Chapter 4: **Solutions** 141

Thinking Critically

The illustration below shows the results of pH tests of four different solutions. Assume the solutions are made with strong acids or strong bases. Use the diagram to answer the next four questions.

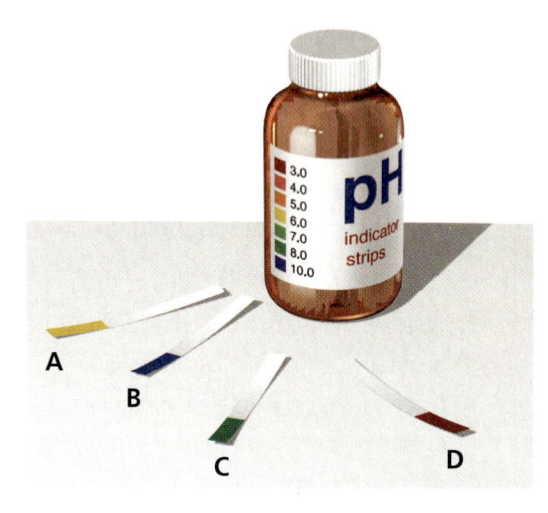

19. OBSERVE Which of the indicator strips show an acidic solution? Which show a basic solution?

20. INFER Which strip of indicator paper detected the highest concentration of H^+ ions? How do you know?

21. PREDICT What would happen if you mixed together equal amounts of the solutions that produced the results of strip B and strip D?

22. INFER Suppose you mix together equal amounts of the solutions that produced the results of strip C and strip D, then test the pH of this new solution. What color will the indicator paper be? Explain.

23. CAUSE AND EFFECT Suppose that you place a beaker containing a solution in a refrigerator. An hour later there is a white solid on the bottom of the beaker. What happened? Why?

24. INFER Do you think iron by itself would be a good material to use in the frame of a bridge? Why or why not?

25. SYNTHESIZE How might the concentration of a solute in an alloy be related to the properties of the alloy? Explain.

Using Math Skills in Science

Use the graph below to answer the next three questions.

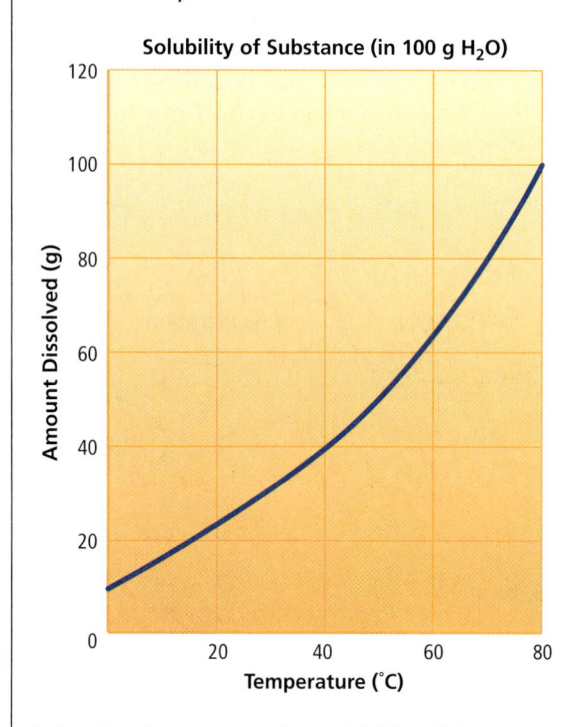

26. What happens to the solubility of the substance as the temperature increases? decreases?

27. Approximately how many grams of the substance dissolve at 20°C? 60°C?

28. Is the substance a solid or a gas? Explain.

the BIG idea

29. APPLY Look back at pages 108–109. Think about the answer you gave to the question about the photograph. How has your understanding of solutions and their properties changed?

30. COMPARE Describe the similarities and differences between solutions of table salt (NaCl) in water and sugar in water. Do both solutes have similar effects on the properties of the solvent? Explain.

UNIT PROJECTS

Check your schedule for your unit project. How are you doing? Be sure that you have placed data or notes from your research in your project folder.

Standardized Test Practice

For practice on your state test, go to...
TEST PRACTICE
CLASSZONE.COM

Interpreting Graphs

Use the information in the paragraph and the graph to answer the questions.

Acid rain is an environmental concern in the United States and in other countries. Acid rain is produced when the burning of fuels releases certain chemicals into the air. These chemicals can react with water vapor in Earth's atmosphere to form acids. The acids then fall back to the ground in either rain or snow. The acids can damage plants, animals, and buildings. Normally, rain has a pH of about 5.6, which is slightly acidic. But rain in some areas of the United States has a pH that is lower than 4.0. The graph shows the pH of water in several lakes.

Lake Water pH Values

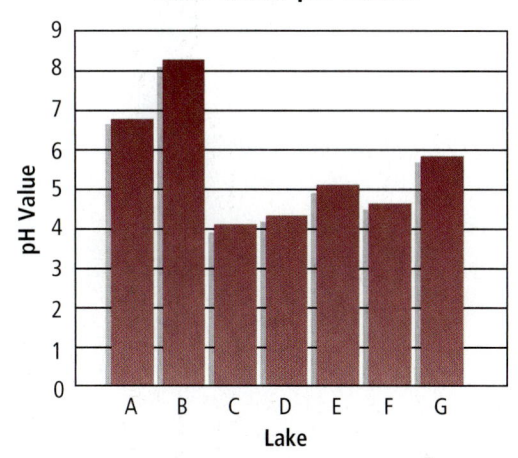

1. Which lake is the most acidic?
   a. Lake A
   b. Lake B
   c. Lake C
   d. Lake D

2. Which lake is the least acidic?
   a. Lake A
   b. Lake B
   c. Lake C
   d. Lake D

3. Which lake has water the closest to neutral?
   a. Lake A
   b. Lake B
   c. Lake E
   d. Lake G

4. Lakes that form on a bed of limestone are less likely to suffer from high acidity. The limestone reacts with acids to neutralize them. Which of the following lakes is most likely to have a limestone bed?
   a. Lake C
   b. Lake D
   c. Lake F
   d. Lake G

5. Lake trout are fish that live in many freshwater lakes. When the pH of the water in a lake drops below 5.5, this species of fish can no longer reproduce, because its eggs cannot hatch. Which of the following statements is most likely true?
   a. Lake trout have probably stopped reproducing in all the lakes.
   b. In terms of reproducing, lake trout are not in danger in any of the lakes.
   c. Lake trout will probably be able to reproduce in lakes A, B, and G but not in the others.
   d. Lake trout have probably stopped reproducing only in lakes C, D, and F.

Extended Response

Answer the following two questions in detail. Include some of the terms from the list in the box. Underline each term you use in your answers.

| concentration | solute | solubility |
| polar | solution | solvent |

6. Suppose you are trying to make two solutions. One contains water and salt. The other contains water and oil. What do you think will happen in both cases? How might charges on particles affect your results?

7. Explain why some substances dissolve more easily than others. How can this characteristic of a solute be changed by changing the temperature or pressure of a solution?

Chapter 4: **Solutions** 143 **B**

CHAPTER 5
Carbon in Life and Materials

the BIG idea
Carbon is essential to living things and to modern materials.

Where in this photograph might you find carbon-based molecules?

Key Concepts

SECTION 5.1 Carbon-based molecules have many structures.
Learn why carbon forms many different compounds.

SECTION 5.2 Carbon-based molecules are life's building blocks.
Learn about the four main types of carbon-based molecules in living things.

SECTION 5.3 Carbon-based molecules are in many materials.
Learn how common materials are made from carbon-based molecules.

Internet Preview
CLASSZONE.COM
Chapter 5 online resources: Content Review, Simulation, Visualization, four Resource Centers, Math Tutorial, Test Practice

Unit: Chemical Interactions

EXPLORE the BIG idea

Structure and Function

Drop a hollow rubber ball on the ground and observe what happens. Then cut the ball in half and glue the two pieces together back-to-back. Predict what will happen when you drop the glued ball. Will it bounce? If so, how high? Test your prediction.

Observe and Think What happened when you dropped the glued ball? How does the ball's behavior depend on its structure?

Sweet Crackers

Eat an unsalted cracker, but chew it for a long time. Keep the cracker in your mouth for a few minutes before you swallow it.

Observe and Think What happened to the taste of the cracker during the time it was in your mouth? What does the change in taste tell you about the molecules in the cracker?

Internet Activity: Polymers

Visit **ClassZone.com** to explore the Polymer Resource Center. Discover some of the common polymers that you use every day. Investigate how a change in a polymer's structure can make a very different material.

Observe and Think What things around you might be polymers? How might the variety of polymers be related to the way in which carbon atoms bond to each other?

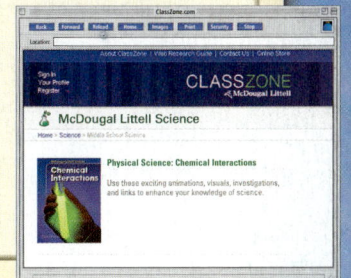

NSTA scilinks.org **SCLINKS**
Organic Compounds Code: MDL026

Chapter 5: **Carbon in Life and Materials** 145 **B**

CHAPTER 5
Getting Ready to Learn

CONCEPT REVIEW

- Atoms share electrons when they form covalent bonds.
- Some atoms can form multiple bonds with another atom.
- Chemical reactions alter the arrangement of atoms.

VOCABULARY REVIEW

electron p. 11
covalent bond p. 50
chemical reaction p. 69
catalyst p. 76

CONTENT REVIEW
CLASSZONE.COM
Review concepts and vocabulary.

TAKING NOTES

SUPPORTING MAIN IDEAS

Make a chart to show main ideas and the information that supports them. Copy each blue heading. Below each heading, add supporting information, such as reasons, explanations, and examples.

VOCABULARY STRATEGY

Think about a vocabulary term as a **magnet word** diagram. Write the other terms or ideas related to that term around it.

See the Note-Taking Handbook on pages R45–R51.

SCIENCE NOTEBOOK

Living and nonliving things contain carbon.
- All life on Earth is based on carbon.
- All organic compounds contain carbon.
- Compounds that do not contain carbon are inorganic.

compounds that contain the same atoms in different places — ISOMER — carbon-based molecules — butane and isobutane

146 Unit: Chemical Interactions

KEY CONCEPT
5.1 Carbon-based molecules have many structures.

BEFORE, you learned
- Atoms of one element differ from atoms of other elements
- The structure and properties of compounds depend on bonds
- Atoms of different elements can form different numbers of bonds

NOW, you will learn
- About the importance of carbon in living things
- Why carbon can form many different compounds
- About different structures of carbon-based molecules

VOCABULARY
organic compound p. 147
inorganic compound p. 148
isomer p. 152

THINK ABOUT
Where can you find carbon?

The wood of a pencil consists of carbon-based molecules. These molecules are considered to be organic. The graphite in the center of the pencil is also made of carbon. In fact, graphite is pure carbon, but it is not considered to be organic. What makes the carbon in wood different from the carbon in graphite?

VOCABULARY
Remember to make a magnet word diagram for *organic compound* and for other vocabulary terms.

Living and nonliving things contain carbon.

Just about every substance that makes up living things contains carbon atoms. In fact, carbon is the most important element for life. Molecules containing carbon atoms were originally called organic because a large number of carbon-based molecules were found in living organisms. Sugars are organic. They are formed by plants, which are living organisms, and they contain carbon. Notice that the term *organic* is closely related to the term *organism*.

Organic compounds are based on carbon. Besides carbon, organic compounds often contain atoms of the elements hydrogen and oxygen, but they can also contain atoms of nitrogen, sulfur, and phosphorus. Scientists once thought that organic compounds could be made only in living organisms by an organism's life processes. Then an organic compound was made in a laboratory. This discovery showed that organic substances were not unique to living things. Instead, organic compounds could be made in a laboratory just like all other chemical compounds.

CHECK YOUR READING Why were carbon compounds called organic compounds?

Chapter 5: Carbon in Life and Materials 147 **B**

Organic Compound

Sugar, shown here as cubes, is organic and contains carbon atoms. It is made by plants from inorganic substances.

Inorganic Compound

Carbon dioxide, shown here as dry ice, is inorganic even though it contains carbon atoms. It is used by plants to make sugars.

There are several exceptions to the rule that carbon-based molecules are organic. These include diamond and graphite, which are made entirely of carbon but are not considered to be organic. The same is true of other compounds, such as cyanides (which contain a CN^- group), carbonates (which contain a CO_3^{2-} group), and carbon dioxide (CO_2). These carbon-containing compounds, among others, and all compounds without carbon are called **inorganic compounds.**

READING TIP
The prefix *in-* means "not," so *inorganic* means "not organic."

Carbon forms many different compounds.

Millions of different carbon-based molecules exist. Consider the number of molecules that make up living things and all of the processes that occur in living things. Carbon-based molecules are vital for all of them.

The large variety of carbon-based molecules results from the number of bonds that each carbon atom forms in a molecule and from a carbon atom's ability to form bonds with atoms of many different elements. In compounds, carbon atoms always share four pairs of electrons in four covalent bonds. This means that one carbon atom can form single bonds with up to four other atoms. Carbon atoms can also form multiple bonds—the atoms can share more than one pair of electrons—with other atoms including, most importantly, other carbon atoms. Different ways of showing the same carbon-based molecules are illustrated below and on page 149.

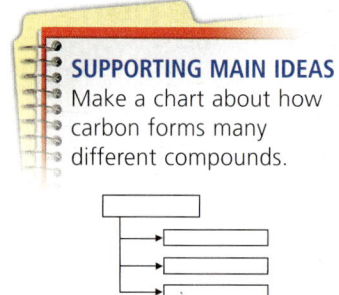

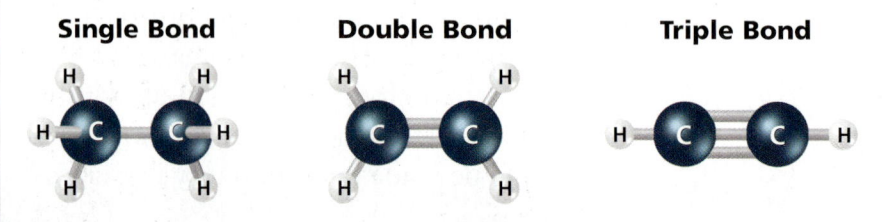

SUPPORTING MAIN IDEAS
Make a chart about how carbon forms many different compounds.

Single Bond   **Double Bond**   **Triple Bond**

CHECK YOUR READING How many bonds can one carbon atom form with another?

B 148 Unit: Chemical Interactions

As you can see in the compounds shown, two carbon atoms can form single, double, or even triple bonds with one another. The compounds have different numbers of hydrogen atoms and different numbers of bonds between their carbon atoms. Count the bonds for each carbon atom. Each carbon atom makes a total of four bonds and always makes just one bond with each hydrogen atom.

Organic molecules are often shown in a simplified way. Instead of models that include all of a molecule's atoms and bonds, structural formulas—such as those shown below—can be used.

> **REMINDER**
> One pair of electrons is shared in a single covalent bond.

Full Structural Formulas

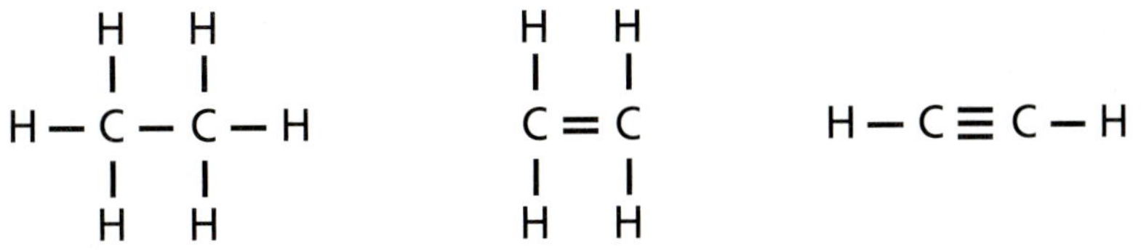

$$H-\underset{\underset{H}{|}}{\overset{\overset{H}{|}}{C}}-\underset{\underset{H}{|}}{\overset{\overset{H}{|}}{C}}-H \qquad \underset{\underset{H}{|}}{\overset{\overset{H}{|}}{C}}=\underset{\underset{H}{|}}{\overset{\overset{H}{|}}{C}} \qquad H-C\equiv C-H$$

Simplified Structural Formulas

$$CH_3-CH_3 \qquad CH_2=CH_2 \qquad CH\equiv CH$$

Carbon-based molecules can have many different structures. Some of the most important structures are molecules shaped like chains and molecules shaped like rings.

INVESTIGATE Carbon Bonding

How do carbon-based molecules depend on the number of bonds between carbon atoms?

PROCEDURE

1. Label the large foam balls "C" for carbon, and label the small foam balls "H" for hydrogen.
2. Using a toothpick to represent a bond, construct a model of a molecule with two carbons, six hydrogens, and seven toothpicks. Carbon has four bonds and hydrogen has one.
3. Make a new model, using two carbons, two hydrogens, and five toothpicks.

WHAT DO YOU THINK?

- How many bonds are there between carbon atoms in the first model? in the second model?
- Which molecule might be more tightly held together? Why?

CHALLENGE In the model on the right, would it be possible for an additional hydrogen atom to bond to each carbon atom? Why or why not?

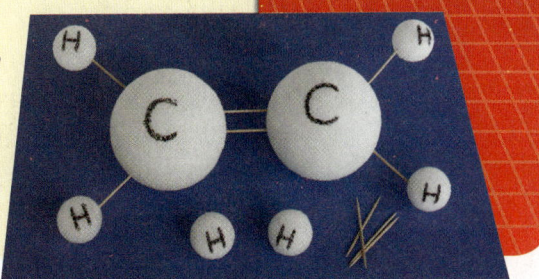

SKILL FOCUS
Modeling

MATERIALS
- marking pen
- 2 large foam balls
- 6 small foam balls
- toothpicks

TIME
10 minutes

Chapter 5: **Carbon in Life and Materials** 149 B

Carbon Chains

Unlike atoms of other elements, carbon atoms have the unusual property of being able to bond to each other to form very long chains. One carbon chain might have hundreds of carbon atoms bonded together. A carbon chain can be straight or branched.

Straight Chain

$CH_3 — CH_2 — CH_2 — CH_2 — CH_2 — CH_3$

Branched Chain

$$\begin{array}{c} CH_3 \\ | \\ CH_2 \\ | \\ CH_3 — CH — CH_2 — CH_3 \end{array}$$

In a branched carbon chain, additional carbon atoms, or even other carbon chains, can bond to carbon atoms in the main carbon chain. Straight chains and branched chains are both results of carbon's ability to form four bonds.

CHECK YOUR READING How is it possible for carbon atoms to form both straight and branched chains?

Carbon Rings

Carbon-based molecules also can be shaped like rings. Carbon rings containing either 5 or 6 carbon atoms are the most common ones, and carbon rings containing more than 20 carbon atoms do not occur naturally.

Just as there are different types of carbon chains, there are different types of carbon ring molecules. One of the most important carbon-based ring molecules is a molecule called benzene (BEHN–ZEEN). Benzene contains six carbon atoms and six hydrogen atoms. Benzene differs from other carbon-based rings because it contains alternating single and double bonds between carbon atoms, as shown below. The benzene molecule is often shown as a circle inside a hexagon.

Benzene Ring

Simplified Benzene Ring

Many compounds are based on benzene's ring structure. These carbon-based molecules often have very strong smells, or aromas, and so are called aromatic compounds. One aromatic compound that contains a benzene ring is a molecule called vanillin. Vanillin is the molecule that gives vanilla its distinctive smell.

SIMULATION CLASSZONE.COM
Observe and rotate three-dimensional models of carbon-based molecules.

Carbon Chains and Carbon Rings

Carbon-based molecules shaped like chains or rings are found in the world around you.

Carbon Chains

One of the carbon chains in the diesel fuel for this locomotive has the formula $C_{15}H_{32}$. It contains 13 CH_2 groups between the CH_3 groups that are on both ends of the molecule. This molecule can be written as $CH_3(CH_2)_{13}CH_3$.

$CH_3 - CH_2 - CH_2 - CH_2 - CH_2 - CH_2 - CH_2 - CH_2 - CH_2 - CH_2 - CH_2 - CH_2 - CH_2 - CH_2 - CH_3$

Carbon Rings

Vanilla ice cream gets its flavor from vanilla, which is also used to enhance other flavors. The molecule that gives vanilla its strong smell is based on the benzene carbon ring.

Carbon Chains and Rings

The molecules in polystyrene, which make up this foam container, contain carbon rings attached to a long carbon chain. The dashed lines at both ends of the structural formula tell you that the molecule continues in both directions.

$---CH_2 - CH - CH_2 - CH - CH_2 - CH---$

Chapter 5: **Carbon in Life and Materials** 151 B

Isomers

Another reason there is such a large number of carbon-based molecules is that carbon can form different molecules with the same atoms. The atoms in these molecules are in different places, and the molecules have different structures. Because the atoms are arranged differently, they are actually two different substances. Compounds that contain the same atoms, but in different places, are called **isomers.**

> **READING TIP**
> The prefix *iso-* means "equal," and the root *mer-* means "part."

The formulas below show a pair of compounds—butane and isobutane—that are isomers. Both molecules contain four carbon atoms and ten hydrogen atoms. However, butane molecules are straight chains of carbon atoms. Isobutane molecules are branched chains of carbon atoms. Even though both butane and isobutane contain the same atoms, the structures of the molecules are different, so they are isomers.

Butane

$$CH_3 - CH_2 - CH_2 - CH_3$$

Butane contains four carbon atoms and ten hydrogen atoms. It has a straight chain structure.

Isobutane

$$\begin{array}{c} CH_3 \\ | \\ CH_3 - CH - CH_3 \end{array}$$

Isobutane also contains four carbon atoms and ten hydrogen atoms. It has a branched chain structure.

Some carbon-based molecules can shift from one isomer to another, and then back to the original structure. For example, isomers of a molecule called retinal are necessary for your eyesight. When light strikes retinal, its structure changes from one isomer to another. The new isomer of retinal starts a process that sends a signal from the eye to the brain. After the retinal isomer starts the signaling process, the molecule shifts back to its original structure.

CHECK YOUR READING If two substances are isomers of each other, how are they the same? different?

5.1 Review

KEY CONCEPTS

1. Why were carbon-based compounds first called organic? How has the understanding of organic compounds changed?
2. How is the way in which carbon atoms bond to each other important for the number of carbon-based compounds?
3. Describe three structures of carbon-based molecules.

CRITICAL THINKING

4. **Infer** Could the last carbon atom in a carbon chain make bonds with four hydrogen atoms? Why or why not?
5. **Synthesize** Do you think molecules based on carbon rings can have isomers? Why or why not?

CHALLENGE

6. **Communicate** A molecule called naphthalene consists of ten carbon atoms and eight hydrogen atoms in two linked benzene rings. Draw a diagram of a molecule that could be naphthalene. Be sure to include the atoms and the bonds between the atoms.

Extreme Science

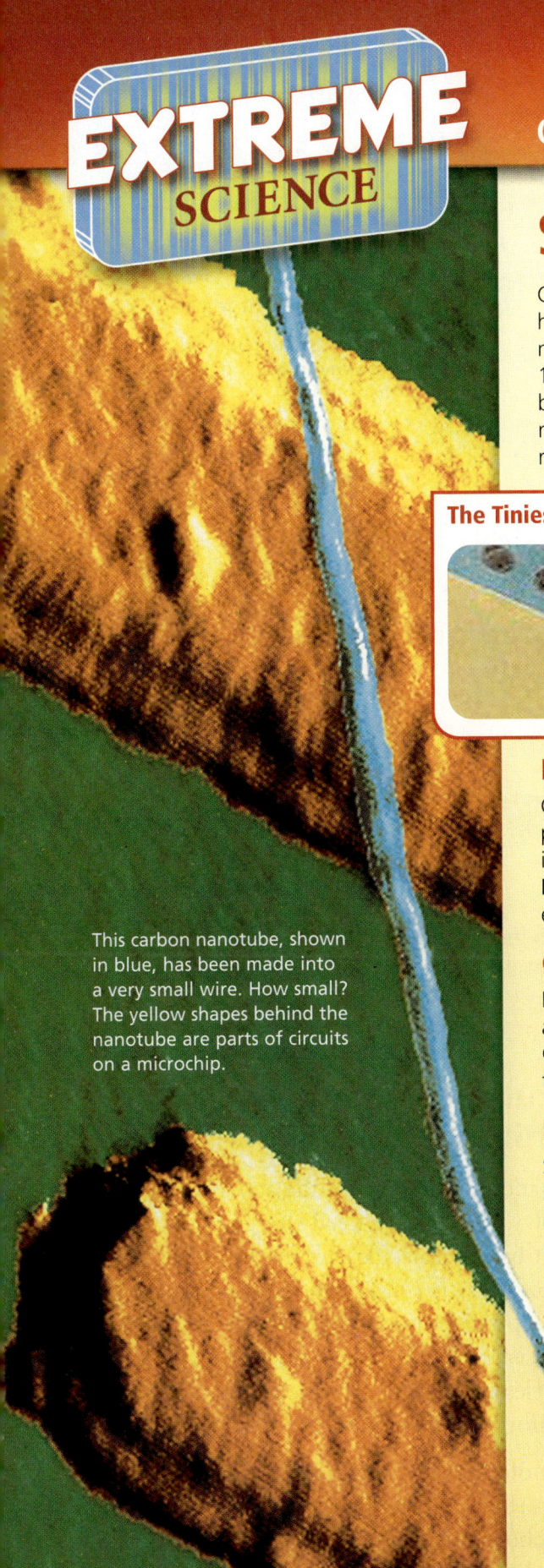

CARBON NANOTUBES

Stronger Than Steel

Can you imagine something that is much smaller than a human hair yet much stronger than steel? Welcome to the world of carbon nanotubes. Carbon nanotubes are made of pure carbon. They are 10 to 100 times as strong as the same weight of steel, but they can be 10,000 times smaller than a hair from your head. Carbon nanotubes were discovered in 1991 as a byproduct of a chemical reaction, but they may have many uses in the near future.

The Tiniest Test Tube

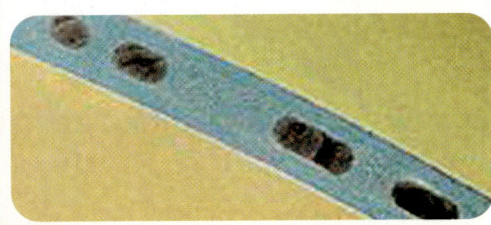

Because a carbon nanotube is hollow, atoms and small molecules can fit inside the tube. Chemists have even used them as tiny test tubes. This photograph shows beads of silver inside a carbon nanotube.

Really Tiny Axles

Carbon nanotubes are not all the same size. Smaller tubes can be placed inside larger tubes. The atoms of the two tubes do not interact much, so the inner nanotube can turn inside the outer one. Nested carbon nanotubes might one day be used as axles for extremely tiny machines.

Conductor or Insulator

Depending on their structure, some carbon nanotubes can conduct an electric current just as well as metal, whereas others will not. Computer scientists have built simple nanotube electrical circuits that could someday become the brains of new supercomputers.

Flash and It's Gone

Some carbon nanotubes are sensitive to bright flashes of light. In fact, when scientists tried to take flash photographs of fluffy masses of tubes, the material caught fire. This property might make them useful as a precise way to control explosives.

This carbon nanotube, shown in blue, has been made into a very small wire. How small? The yellow shapes behind the nanotube are parts of circuits on a microchip.

EXPLORE

1. **CLASSIFY** Is a carbon nanotube an element, a compound, or a mixture? Explain.
2. **CHALLENGE** Use the Internet to find information about carbon nanotube research. What are some of the uses, in addition to those listed above, that scientists have proposed for carbon nanotubes? Which of these possibilities is most interesting to you? Why?

RESOURCE CENTER
CLASSZONE.COM
Learn more about carbon nanotubes.

Chapter 5: **Carbon in Life and Materials** 153

KEY CONCEPT
5.2 Carbon-based molecules are life's building blocks.

BEFORE, you learned
- Carbon is the basis of life on Earth
- Carbon atoms can form multiple bonds
- Carbon can form molecules shaped like chains or rings

NOW, you will learn
- About the functions of carbohydrates and lipids in living things
- About structures and functions of proteins
- How nucleic acids carry instructions for building proteins

VOCABULARY
carbohydrate p. 155
lipid p. 156
protein p. 158
enzyme p. 159
nucleic acid p. 161

EXPLORE Carbon in Food
How can you see the carbon in food?

PROCEDURE

1. Place the candle in the pie plate and light the candle.
2. Use the tongs to hold each food sample in the candle flame for 20 seconds. Record your observations.

MATERIALS
- aluminum pie plate
- candle
- wooden matches
- tongs
- small marshmallow
- piece of carrot

WHAT DO YOU THINK?
- What changes did you observe in the samples?
- What type of chemical reaction might have caused these changes?

Carbon-based molecules have many functions in living things.

You depend on carbon-based molecules for all of the activities in your life. For example, when you play softball, you need energy to swing the bat and run the bases. Carbon-based molecules are the source of the chemical energy needed by your muscle cells. Carbon-based molecules make up your muscle cells and provide those cells with the ability to contract and relax. Carbon-based molecules carry oxygen to your muscle cells so that your muscles can function properly. Carbon-based molecules even provide the information for building new molecules.

The many carbon-based molecules in all living things have certain similarities. They all contain carbon and elements such as hydrogen, oxygen, nitrogen, sulfur, and phosphorus. Many of the molecules are also very large molecules called macromolecules. However, these molecules have different structures and different functions.

READING TIP
The prefix *macro-* means "large," so a macromolecule is a large molecule.

154 Unit: Chemical Interactions

Living things contain four major types of carbon-based molecules.

The organic molecules found in living things are classified into four major groups—carbohydrates, lipids, proteins, and nucleic acids. You may already be familiar with these types of molecules and their functions in living things.

Carbohydrates include sugars and starches found in foods such as bread and pasta. Many lipids are fats or oils. Proteins are necessary for many functions in the body, including the formation of muscle tissue. Nucleic acids are the molecules that carry the genetic code for all living things. As you read about each of these types of molecules, look for ways in which the molecule's function depends on its structure.

Carbohydrates

Carbohydrates (KAHR-boh-HY-DRAYTZ) include sugars, starches, and cellulose, and contain atoms of three elements—carbon, hydrogen, and oxygen. They serve two main functions. Carbohydrates are a source of chemical energy for cells in many living things. They are also part of the structural materials of plants.

One important carbohydrate is the sugar glucose, which has the chemical formula $C_6H_{12}O_6$. Cells in both plants and animals break down glucose for energy. In plants glucose molecules also can be joined together to form more complex carbohydrates, such as starch and cellulose. Starch is a macromolecule that consists of many glucose molecules, or units, bonded together. Many foods, such as pasta, contain starch. When starch is broken back down into individual glucose molecules, those glucose molecules can be used as an energy source by cells.

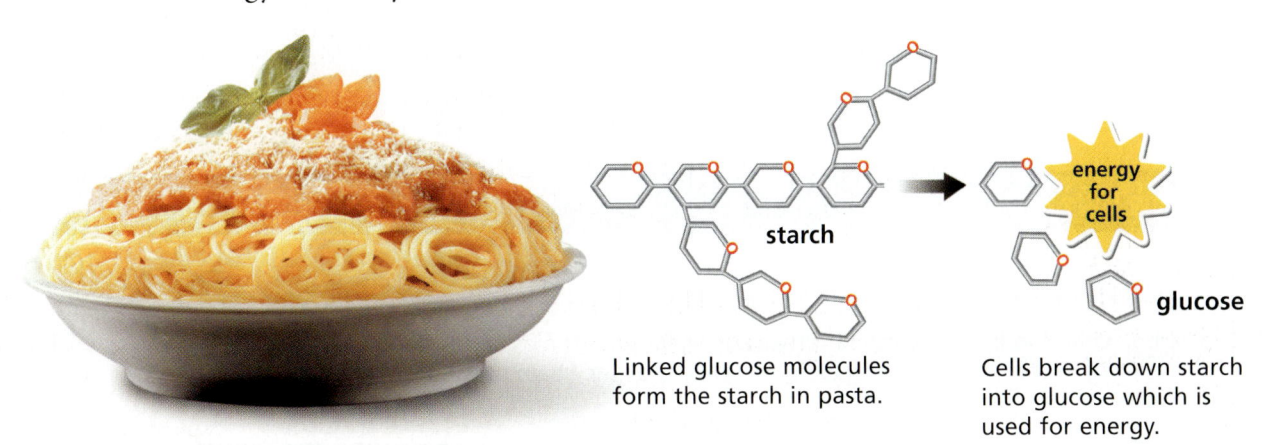

Modeling Glucose

The glucose molecule can be represented by a hexagon. The red O shows that an oxygen atom is in the ring.

Linked glucose molecules form the starch in pasta.

Cells break down starch into glucose which is used for energy.

Chapter 5: **Carbon in Life and Materials** 155

Moss Leaf Cells

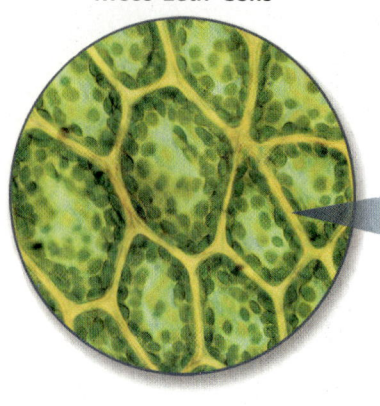

Plants make their own glucose through a process called photosynthesis, which you read about in Chapter 3. Some of the glucose made during photosynthesis is used to make the complex carbohydrate molecules that form a plant's structure.

Cellulose

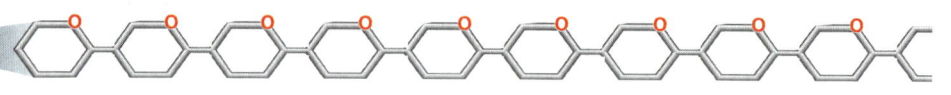

Cellulose is a long chain-like molecule that forms part of a plant's structure.

Unlike animal cells, plant cells have a tough, protective layer outside the cell membrane called the cell wall. Cellulose (SEHL-yuh-LOHS) is a macromolecule found in plant cell walls, and it is a large part of vegetables such as lettuce and celery. The illustration shows moss leaf cells with their cell walls, and a diagram of part of a cellulose molecule.

Cellulose and starch are both carbohydrates composed of glucose molecules, but the glucose molecules that make up these larger macromolecules are linked in different ways. Because of their different structures, starch and cellulose have different functions. In fact, this structural difference also prevents your body from breaking down and using cellulose as it would starch.

CHECK YOUR READING What are some functions of carbohydrates in animals? in plants?

Lipids

VOCABULARY
Make a magnet word diagram for *lipid* and for other vocabulary terms.

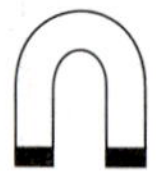

Lipids include fats and oils and are used mainly for energy and as structural materials in living things. Like carbohydrates, most lipids are made of carbon, hydrogen, and oxygen. Even though lipids and carbohydrates have many similarities, they have different structures and properties.

Animals store chemical energy in fat. Plants store chemical energy in oils, such as olive oil and peanut oil. Fats and oils store energy very efficiently—one gram of fat contains about twice as much energy as one gram of carbohydrate or protein. Fats and oils contain three carbon chains called fatty acids. The illustration below shows the general structure of a fatty acid.

Modeling Fatty Acids

$$CH_3-CH_2-CH_2\}\{CH_2-CH_2-CH_2-COOH$$

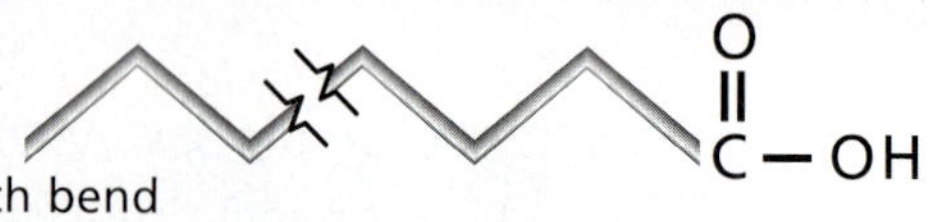

The carbon chains in lipids are called fatty acids. A carbon atom is at each bend of the zig-zag model above. The break in the middle of the chain shows that some carbon atoms have been left out.

B 156 Unit: Chemical Interactions

You may have heard the terms *saturated* and *unsaturated* in relation to fats. If all of the bonds between carbon atoms in the fatty acids are single bonds, the lipid is a saturated fat. If one or more of these bonds is a double bond, the lipid is an unsaturated fat. Most animal fats are saturated, and most oils from plants are unsaturated. Diets high in saturated fats have been linked to heart disease. Lipids in the butter in the photograph on the right are saturated fats.

Fat Structure

Fats in butter contain three fatty acids and are used for energy. Butter contains saturated fats.

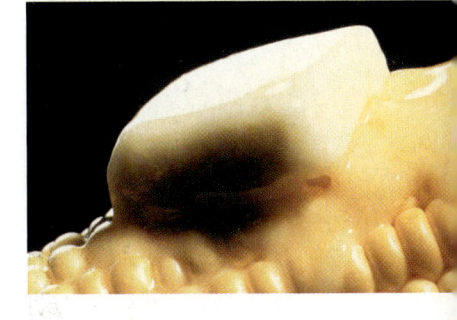

CHECK YOUR READING What is the difference between a saturated fat and an unsaturated fat?

Some lipids are important parts of cell structure. Structural lipids often contain the element phosphorus and are called phospholipids. Phospholipids are a significant part of cell membranes such as the one shown in the photograph of the nerve cell on the right.

Phospholipid Structure

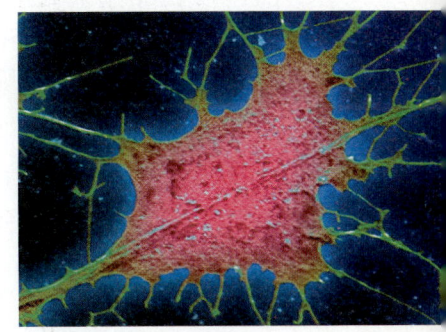

Some lipids in this nerve cell's membrane have two fatty acids and one phosphate group. These lipids are called phospholipids.

Another lipid involved in cell structure is cholesterol, which is a part of cell membranes. Cholesterol has other functions as well. It is necessary to make substances called hormones. Hormones, such as adrenaline, are chemical messengers in your body.

Your body makes some of the cholesterol that it needs, but it also uses cholesterol from foods you eat. Cholesterol is found in many foods that come from animals, such as meat and eggs. Even some plant products, such as coconut oil, can increase the amount of cholesterol in your body. Although you need cholesterol, eating too much of it—just like eating too much saturated fat—can lead to heart disease.

Chapter 5: **Carbon in Life and Materials** 157 B

INVESTIGATE Organic Molecules

Where can you find organic molecules?

PROCEDURE

1. Place a dropper of cornstarch solution into one jar lid and a dropper of liquid gelatin into a second jar lid.
2. Add a drop of iodine solution to the cornstarch sample and to the gelatin sample.
3. Examine the jar lids after 1 minute. Record your observations.
4. Using the remaining two jar lids, repeat steps 2 and 3 with the bread and the tofu instead of the cornstarch and gelatin.

WHAT DO YOU THINK?

- What changes occurred after the addition of iodine to the cornstarch and to the gelatin?
- Iodine can be used to detect the presence of starches. What carbon-based molecules might be in the bread and tofu? How do you know?

CHALLENGE
Suppose you tested a piece of pepperoni pizza with iodine. Which ingredients (crust, sauce, cheese, pepperoni) would likely contain starch?

SKILL FOCUS
Inferring

MATERIALS
- 4 small jar lids
- 3 eyedroppers
- cornstarch solution
- liquid gelatin
- iodine solution
- bread
- tofu
- stopwatch

TIME
20 minutes

Proteins

Proteins are macromolecules that are made of smaller molecules called amino acids. Proteins, like carbohydrates and lipids, contain carbon, hydrogen, and oxygen. However, proteins differ from carbohydrates and lipids in that they also contain nitrogen, sulfur, and other elements. Unlike carbohydrates and lipids, which are used primarily for energy and structure, proteins have many different functions.

Think of a protein as being like a word, with amino acids as the letters in that word. The meaning of a word depends on the order of letters in the word. For example, rearranging the letters in the word "eat" makes different words with different meanings. Similarly, proteins depend on the order of their amino acids.

Linked Amino Acids

tyrosine   lysine   cysteine   serine   leucine

B   158   Unit: Chemical Interactions

Just as 26 letters of the alphabet make up all words in the English language, 20 amino acids make up all of the proteins in your body. The structure of a protein is determined by the order of its amino acids. If two amino acids change places, the entire protein changes.

The function of a protein depends on its structure. There are at least 100,000 proteins in your body, each with a different structure that gives it a specific function. Some proteins are structural materials, some control chemical reactions, and others transport substances within cells and through the body. Still others are a part of the immune system, which protects you from infections.

CHECK YOUR READING How does the function of a protein depend on its structure?

Proteins that are part of the structure of living things are often shaped like coils. One coil-shaped protein, keratin, is part of human hair as shown on the left below. Proteins called actin and myosin are coil-shaped proteins that help your muscles contract.

Other types of proteins have coiled regions but curl up into shapes like balls. One example is hemoglobin, shown on the right below. Hemoglobin is a transport protein that carries oxygen in the blood.

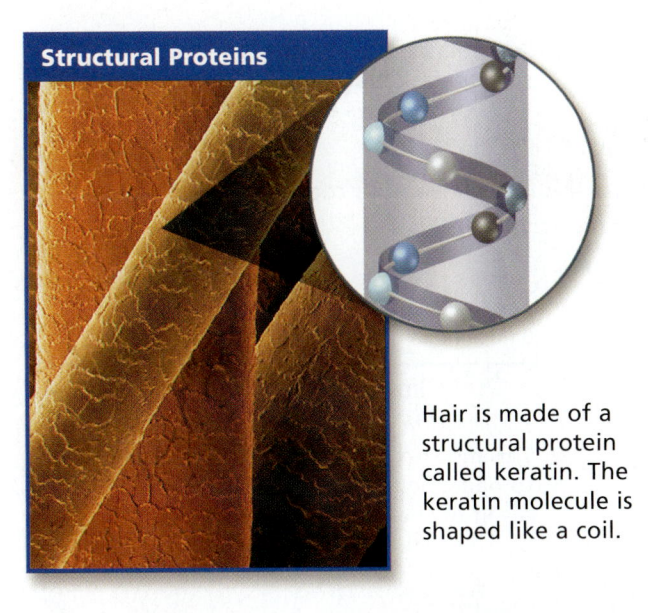

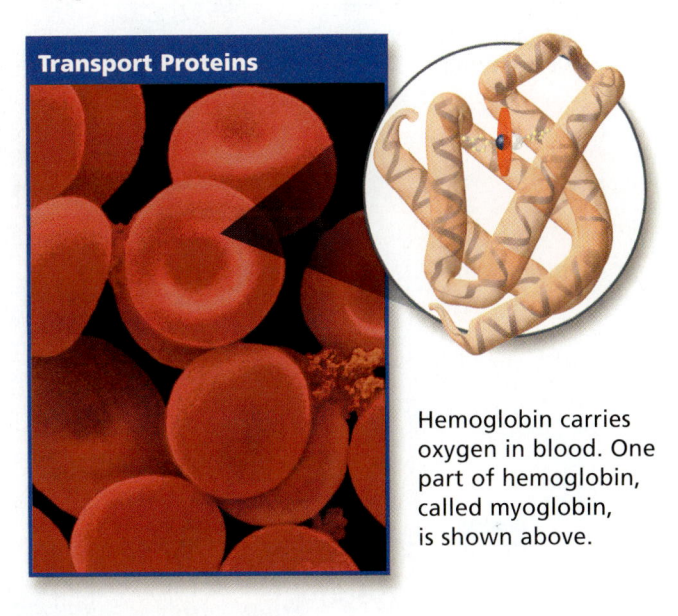

Structural Proteins

Hair is made of a structural protein called keratin. The keratin molecule is shaped like a coil.

Transport Proteins

Hemoglobin carries oxygen in blood. One part of hemoglobin, called myoglobin, is shown above.

Some proteins that curl up into a shape like a ball are enzymes. An **enzyme** (EHN-zym) is a catalyst for a chemical reaction in living things. Catalysts increase the rate of chemical reactions. Enzymes are necessary for many chemical reactions in your body. Without enzymes, these reactions would occur too slowly to keep you alive.

It is important to have proteins in your diet so that your body can make its own proteins. Proteins in foods such as meats, soybeans, and nuts are broken down into amino acids by your body. These amino acids are then used by your cells to make new proteins.

Chapter 5: **Carbon in Life and Materials** 159

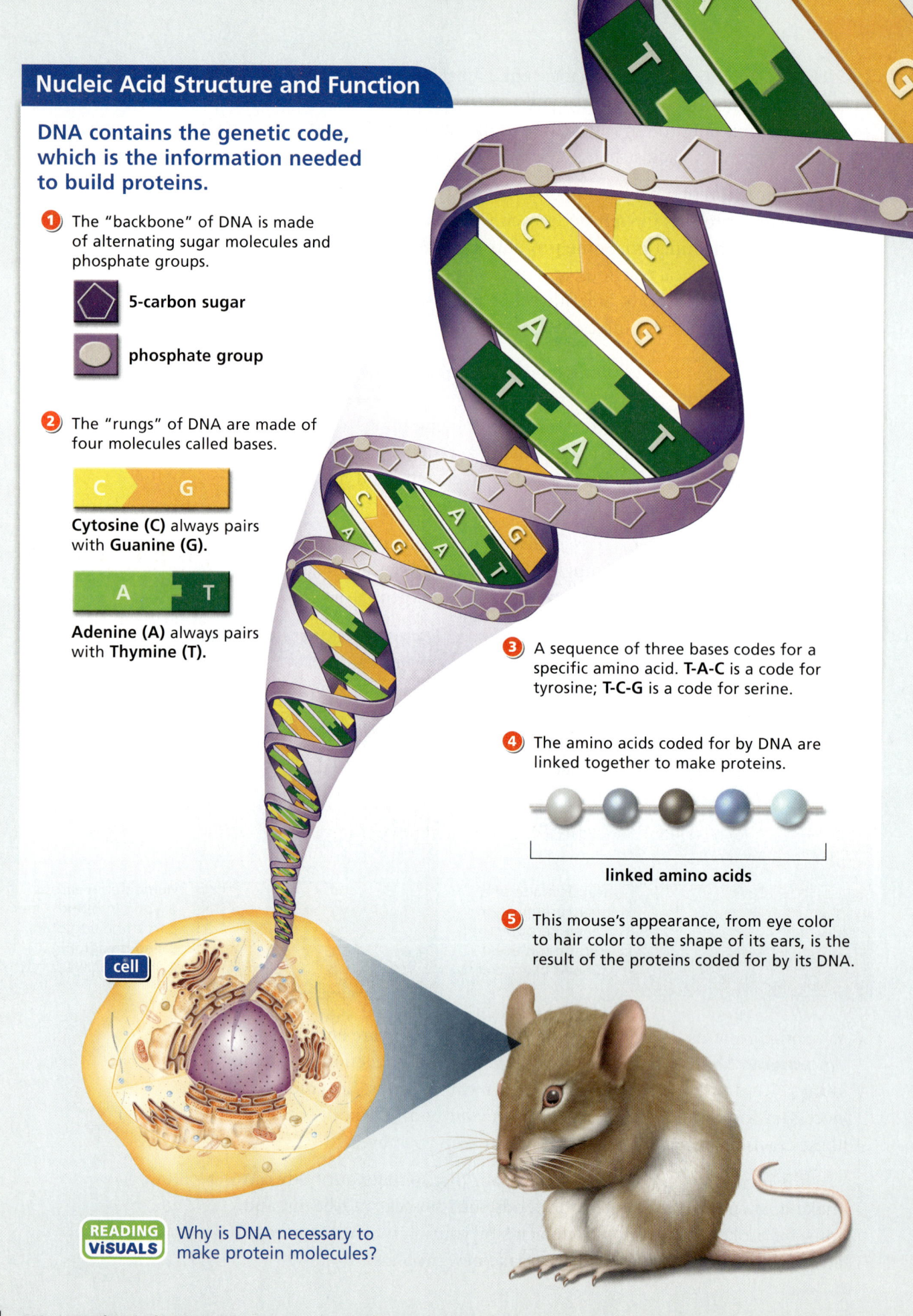

Nucleic Acid Structure and Function

DNA contains the genetic code, which is the information needed to build proteins.

① The "backbone" of DNA is made of alternating sugar molecules and phosphate groups.

- 5-carbon sugar
- phosphate group

② The "rungs" of DNA are made of four molecules called bases.

Cytosine (C) always pairs with **Guanine (G)**.

Adenine (A) always pairs with **Thymine (T)**.

③ A sequence of three bases codes for a specific amino acid. **T-A-C** is a code for tyrosine; **T-C-G** is a code for serine.

④ The amino acids coded for by DNA are linked together to make proteins.

linked amino acids

⑤ This mouse's appearance, from eye color to hair color to the shape of its ears, is the result of the proteins coded for by its DNA.

cell

READING VISUALS Why is DNA necessary to make protein molecules?

B 160 Unit: Chemical Interactions

Nucleic Acids

Nucleic acids (noo-KLEE-ihk AS-ihdz) are huge, complex carbon-based molecules that contain the information that cells use to make proteins. These macromolecules are made of carbon, hydrogen, and oxygen, as well as nitrogen and phosphorus. Each of the cells in your body contains a complete set of nucleic acids. This means that each cell has all of the instructions necessary for making any protein in your body.

The illustration on page 160 shows part of a nucleic acid molecule called DNA, which looks like a twisted ladder. The sides of the ladder are made of sugar molecules and phosphate groups. Each rung of the ladder is composed of two nitrogen-containing molecules called bases. DNA has four types of bases, represented by the letters A, C, T, and G. The order of the bases in a DNA molecule is the way in which DNA stores the instructions for making proteins. How do just four molecules—A, C, T, and G—carry all of this important information?

Recall that a protein is composed of amino acids that have to be linked in a certain order. Each of the 20 amino acids is represented by a particular series of three DNA bases. For example, the sequence T–A–C corresponds to—or is a code for—the amino acid tyrosine. There are 64 different three-base sequences in DNA, all of which have a specific meaning. This genetic code works in the same way in every living thing on Earth. It provides a complete set of instructions for linking amino acids in the right order to make each specific protein molecule. The DNA code is only one part of making proteins, though. Other types of nucleic acids, called RNA, are responsible for reading the code and assembling a protein with the correct amino acids.

READING TIP
The *NA* in DNA stands for nucleic acid. The *D* stands for deoxyribose, which is the type of sugar in the molecule.

RESOURCE CENTER
CLASSZONE.COM
Find out more about carbohydrates, lipids, proteins, and nucleic acids.

CHECK YOUR READING How many different types of bases make up the genetic code in DNA?

5.2 Review

KEY CONCEPTS
1. How does the function of a lipid depend on its structure?
2. What determines the structure of a protein?
3. What role does DNA perform in the making of proteins?

CRITICAL THINKING
4. **Synthesize** Give two examples of carbon-based molecules in living things that are based on a chain structure. Explain.
5. **Compare and Contrast** How are carbohydrates and lipids similar? How are they different?

CHALLENGE
6. **Infer** Suppose the order of bases in a DNA molecule is changed. What do you think will happen to the structure of the protein that is coded for by that region of DNA? Why?

Chapter 5: Carbon in Life and Materials 161 B

MATH in SCIENCE

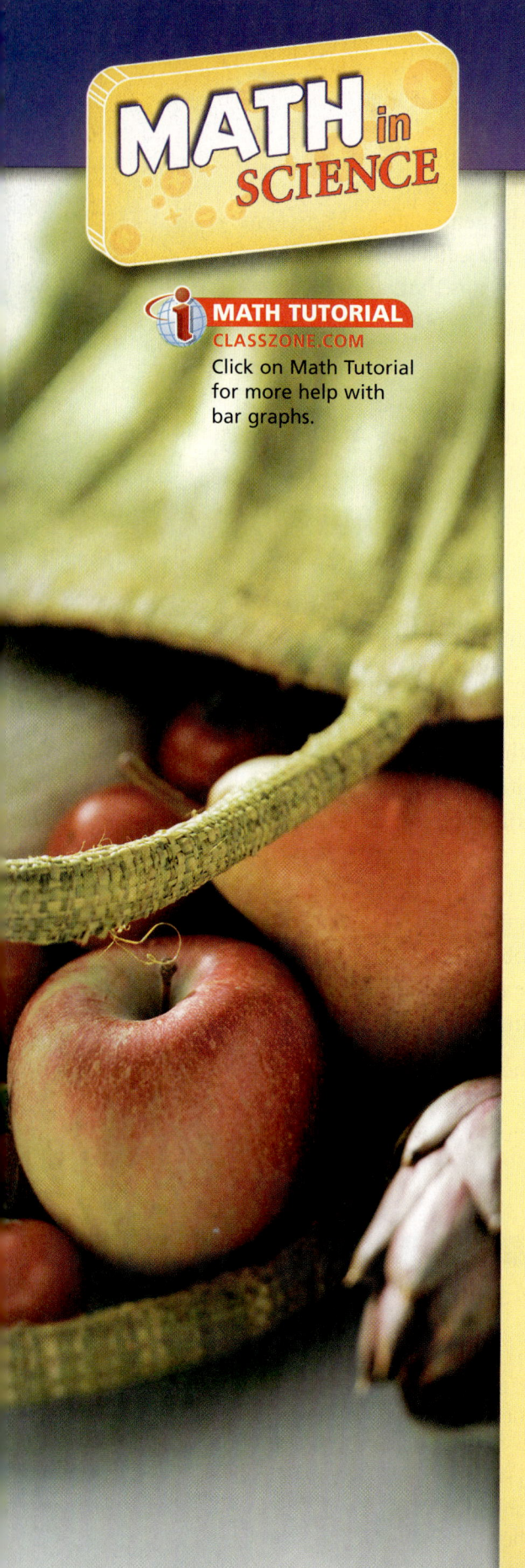

SKILL: MAKING BAR GRAPHS

MATH TUTORIAL
CLASSZONE.COM

Click on Math Tutorial for more help with bar graphs.

Graphing Good Food

People need to eat carbohydrates, proteins, and lipids to have a healthy diet. Different amounts of each type of organic molecule are recommended for different groups of people. In general, grains, vegetables, and fruits contain carbohydrates. Dairy products, meats, and beans contain proteins and lipids. The table on the right shows dietary recommendations. The information could also be shown in a bar graph.

Recommended Servings

Food group	Young children	Teen girls	Teen boys
Grains	6	9	11
Vegetables	3	4	5
Fruits	2	3	4
Dairy	3	3	3
Meats, beans	2	2	3

SOURCE: U.S. Department of Agriculture, Home and Garden Bulletin Number 252, 1996

Example

Create a bar graph that shows the dietary recommendation of grains for each group.

(1) Use the height of the bar to indicate the numerical value of a piece of data.

(2) Show the number of servings on the vertical axis. Label each group of bars on the horizontal axis.

(3) Use a different color for each group.

ANSWER

Daily Servings of Each Food Group

- Young Children
- Teen Girls
- Teen Boys

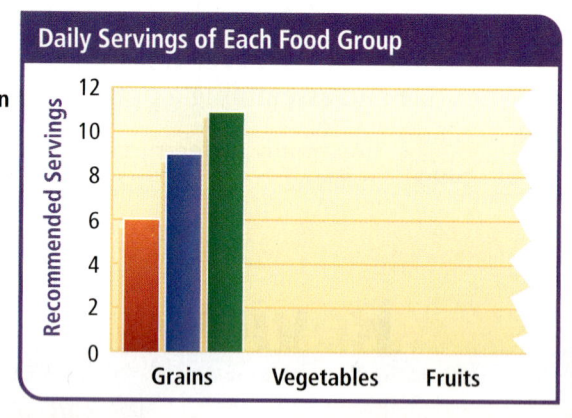

Use the Recommended Servings table above to answer the following questions.

1. Copy and complete the bar graph to show the dietary recommendations for the other four food groups.

2. Which group has the tallest bars on the graph? the shortest?

CHALLENGE Choose one group of people and make a pie graph showing recommendations for them. (**Hint:** First convert the numbers of servings into fractions of the whole diet.)

Unit: Chemical Interactions

KEY CONCEPT
5.3 Carbon-based molecules are in many materials.

BEFORE, you learned
- Organic compounds are based on carbon
- Carbon can form molecules shaped like chains or rings
- Four types of carbon-based compounds are common in living things

NOW, you will learn
- How carbon-based molecules are obtained from petroleum
- How carbon-based molecules are designed for specific uses
- How a material's properties depend on its molecular structure

VOCABULARY

hydrocarbon p. 163
polymer p. 166
monomer p. 166
plastic p. 167

THINK ABOUT

What do windbreakers and motor oil have in common?

Motor oil and windbreakers are both made of carbon-based molecules. The motor oil is composed mostly of carbon and hydrogen. The nylon windbreaker is also composed mostly of carbon and hydrogen. How can two materials that are so different be made of similar molecules?

RESOURCE CENTER
CLASSZONE.COM
Find out more about petroleum and hydrocarbons.

Carbon-based compounds from ancient organisms are used to make new materials.

Many of the things you see around you every day contain carbon-based molecules. Some, such as people, plants, and animals, are easy to spot. Others are not so easy to identify. These objects include clothing, furniture, packing materials, sports equipment, and more. You have read that a large number of substances that make up living things are based on carbon. Where do we get carbon-based molecules that we use to make modern materials?

The carbon-based compounds that are the basis of many materials are called hydrocarbons. A **hydrocarbon** is simply a compound made of only carbon and hydrogen. Many different hydrocarbons are found in large deposits underground and under the sea. The story of how they got there began a long time ago and is related to the way carbon moves through the environment in a cycle.

Chapter 5: Carbon in Life and Materials 163 B

SUPPORTING MAIN IDEAS
Make a chart about the carbon-based molecules in modern materials.

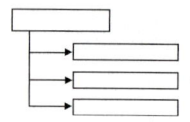

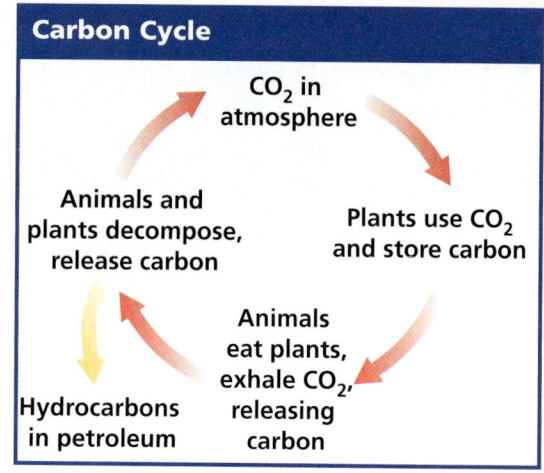

READING TIP
As you read the numbered steps, follow the process shown on page 165.

VISUALIZATION
CLASSZONE.COM
Observe the process involved in the separation of the hydrocarbons in petroleum.

In the carbon cycle, plants use carbon dioxide from the air to make carbohydrates. Animals eat plants and absorb carbon, and then release carbon dioxide into the air when they exhale. When animals and plants die, they decompose and carbon returns to the environment. Most carbon returns to the atmosphere as part of the

Carbon Cycle

- CO_2 in atmosphere
- Plants use CO_2 and store carbon
- Animals eat plants, exhale CO_2, releasing carbon
- Animals and plants decompose, release carbon
- Hydrocarbons in petroleum

carbon cycle, but some does not. This carbon is the source of the carbon-based compounds that are so important for modern life.

① **Obtaining Petroleum** Some living things that died hundreds of millions of years ago fell into mud or sediment. Instead of returning to the atmosphere, the carbon-based molecules from these organisms became trapped in the ground. Over time, and through a process of chemical changes, some of this organic material became petroleum, which is a mixture of hundreds of different hydrocarbons. People pump petroleum from underground and undersea deposits. Liquid petroleum is called crude oil.

② **Refining Petroleum** In its raw form, petroleum is not a useful substance. However, when it is processed at a refinery, it is separated into many useful parts.

③ **Using Products Made from Petroleum** Many products, including gasoline, plastics, and fibers such as nylon are made from the separated parts of petroleum.

The refining of petroleum is an example of the separation of a mixture based on physical properties. Each type of hydrocarbon in petroleum has a different boiling point. In general, each boiling point depends on the number and arrangement of carbon atoms in the molecule. For example, lubricating oil contains long carbon chains and boils at temperatures above 350°C. The hydrocarbons that make up gasoline are smaller molecules, and they boil between 35°C and 220°C.

At a refinery, petroleum is heated until all but the largest of the hydrocarbons are in gaseous form. This gaseous petroleum is released into a distillation tower. As the gases rise in the tower, they gradually cool. When each specific hydrocarbon cools to its boiling point, it condenses back into a liquid. Thus, lubricating oil cools to its boiling point quickly and is collected from a low level in the tower. Hydrocarbons in gasoline take longer to become liquids and are collected higher in the tower.

CHECK YOUR READING How are hydrocarbons in petroleum separated from each other?

B 164 Unit: Chemical Interactions

Using Petroleum

Carbon-based compounds in petroleum are used to make a wide range of products.

❶ Obtaining Petroleum

Petroleum is trapped underground between rock layers that it cannot move through. People have pumped petroleum out of the ground since the 1850s.

rock layer containing petroleum

❷ Refining Petroleum

Petroleum is separated into different parts, or fractions, at an oil refinery. Different fractions are used for different purposes.

Petroleum Products

Petroleum Fraction	Number of Carbon Atoms per Molecule	Uses
Gases	1 to 4	Cooking, heating, manufacturing
Gasoline	5 to 12	Automobile fuel
Kerosene	12 to 16	Airplane fuel
Fuel oil	15 to 18	Diesel fuel, heating oil
Greases	16 to 20	Lubrication

SOURCE: Mortimer, *Chemistry*, 6th edition

❸ Using Products Made from Petroleum

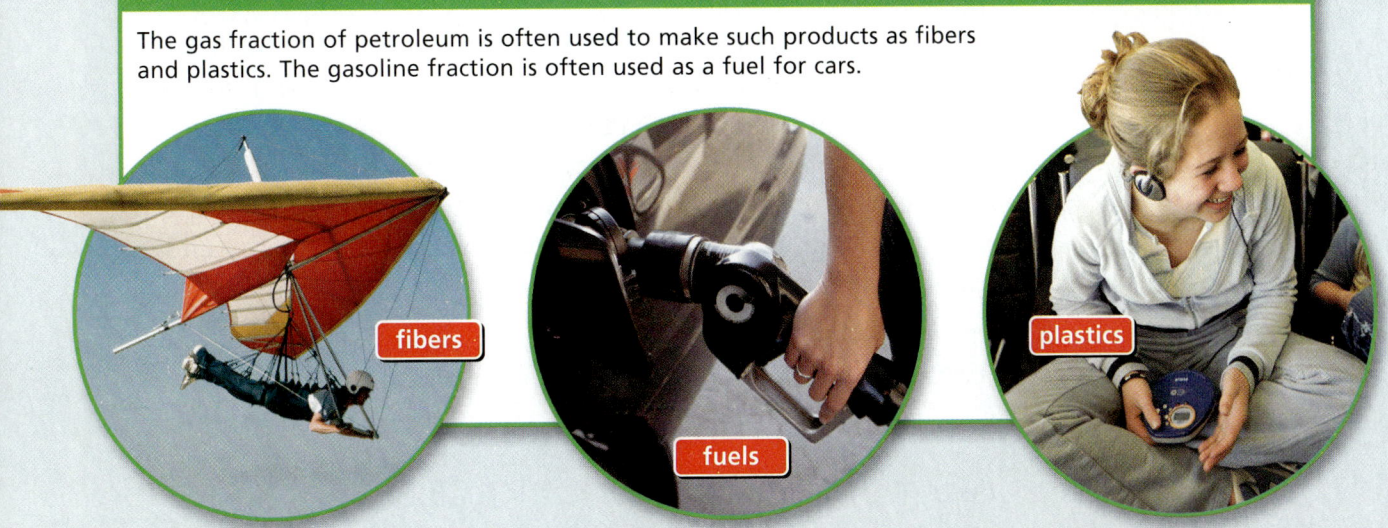

The gas fraction of petroleum is often used to make such products as fibers and plastics. The gasoline fraction is often used as a fuel for cars.

fibers

fuels

plastics

Chapter 5: **Carbon in Life and Materials** 165 B

Polymers contain repeating carbon-based units.

READING TIP
The prefix *mono-* means "one," and the prefix *poly-* means "many."

Many everyday materials made of carbon-based molecules contain macromolecules called polymers. **Polymers** are very large carbon-based molecules made of smaller, repeating units. These small, repeating units, called **monomers,** are linked together one after another. By themselves, monomers are also carbon-based molecules.

Some of the carbon-based molecules that you read about in the previous section are polymers. For example, both cellulose and starch are polymers. They are chains of linked glucose units. The glucose units are the monomers. Many common materials that are manufactured for specific purposes are polymers. Plastics and fibers are two examples of these kinds of polymers.

CHECK YOUR READING What do starch and plastic have in common?

Formation of Polymers

The properties of a polymer depend on the size and structure of the polymer molecule. The size and structure of a polymer depend both on its particular monomers and how many monomers are added together to make the final product.

The process of making a polymer involves chemical reactions that bond monomers together. Think back to the different types of reactions described in Chapter 3. The process of making a polymer is a synthesis reaction that yields a more complex product from simpler reactants.

The diagram on the top of page 167 shows one way in which a polymer can be made. The monomer that is the building block of the polymer in the illustration is called propylene (PROH-puh-LEEN). The propylene molecule consists of three carbon atoms and six hydrogen atoms. By itself, propylene is a gas. Notice that propylene has a double bond between two of its carbon atoms.

During the reaction that links the monomers, one of the bonds that makes up the double bond is broken. When that bond is broken, a new bond can form between two of the monomer units. A large number of the propylene monomers bonded together form a polymer called polypropylene. Polypropylene is a strong, solid plastic used to make such items as plastic crates, toys, bicycle helmets, and even indoor-outdoor carpeting.

CHECK YOUR READING How do the properties of polypropylene differ from those of propylene?

B 166 Unit: Chemical Interactions

Building Polymers

Polymers such as polypropylene are made by linking many monomers together.

① Propylene (C_3H_6) can be used as a monomer.

Monomer
$CH_2 = CH — CH_3$

② Propylene monomers are linked together.

Monomers Are Linked Together
$CH_2 = CH — CH_3 \quad CH_2 = CH — CH_3 \quad CH_2 = CH — CH_3$

③ Linked propylene monomers make polypropylene.

Polymer

$$CH_2 — CH — CH_2 — CH — CH_2 — CH \text{ ---}$$
$$\quad\quad\;\;|\quad\quad\quad\quad\;\;|\quad\quad\quad\quad\;\;|$$
$$\quad\quad CH_3\quad\quad\;\; CH_3\quad\quad\;\; CH_3$$

— = double bond changed to single bond
— = new bond formed between monomers

This bicycle helmet is made of polypropylene.

Polymers may be composed of more than one type of monomer. Polyester fabric is an example of a polymer that contains two different monomers. Protein is another example. In fact, as you read earlier, proteins in living things contain several different monomers. The monomers in proteins are amino acids.

Plastics

Polypropylene is one of many polymers that are called plastics. As an adjective, *plastic* means "capable of being molded or shaped." A **plastic** is a polymer that can be molded or shaped. If you look around, you can see how common plastics are in everyday life.

The first plastic made by chemists was celluloid, which was patented in 1870. It was based on cellulose molecules from cotton plants and was used to make such things as billiard balls and movie film. Celluloid is different from many of the plastics that are made today. It was made by chemically changing an existing, naturally occurring polymer—cellulose.

Many of today's plastics are made artificially, by building polymers from monomers. The first completely artificial polymer made by scientists was a plastic called Bakelite, which was invented in 1907. Chemists made Bakelite by linking individual monomers together. Because Bakelite is moldable and nonflammable, it was used for many household items such as pot handles, jewelry, lamps, buttons, and radio cases.

CHECK YOUR READING How does the term plastic describe a polymer's properties?

Chapter 5: **Carbon in Life and Materials** 167

Recycling Plastics				
Code	Chemical Name	Monomers	Properties	Uses
1	Polyethylene terephthalate (PET or PETE)	$C_2H_6O_2$ and $C_8H_6O_4$	Transparent, high strength, does not stretch	Clothing, soft-drink bottles, audiotapes, videotapes
2	High Density Polyethylene (HDPE)	C_2H_4	Similar to LDPE (code 4) but denser, tougher, more rigid	Milk and water jugs, gasoline tanks, cups
3	Polyvinyl chloride (PVC)	C_2H_3Cl	Rigid, transparent, high strength	Shampoo bottles, garden hoses, plumbing pipes
4	Low Density Polyethylene (LDPE)	C_2H_4	White, soft, subject to cracking	Plastic bags, toys, electrical insulation
5	Polypropylene (PP)	C_3H_6	High strength and rigidity, impermeable to liquids and gases	Battery cases, indoor-outdoor carpeting, bottle caps, auto trim
6	Polystyrene (PS)	C_8H_8	Glassy, rigid, brittle	Insulation, drinking cups, packing materials

SOURCE: *American Chemical Society*

The chart above lists some common plastics and their uses. You may have noticed the symbols shown in the first column of the chart on plastic bottles and containers that you have around your home. The numbers stand for different types of plastic, with different uses. After a plastic has been used in a certain way, such as in soft drink bottles, it can recycled and used again. When a plastic is recycled it can be made into a new product that has a different use. For example, recycled soft drink bottles can be made into fibers for carpeting.

Designing Materials

Chemists have been designing and making polymers for many years. However, new polymers are always being developed. One way in which scientists make new polymers is by chemically changing an original monomer. When scientists change a monomer and then link the monomers together, a new material is produced.

Teflon is very strong and light in weight. It was used to make the roof of this stadium in Minneapolis.

Teflon is a common polymer that is made by chemically changing a hydrocarbon monomer. Chemists replace the hydrogen atoms in the monomer with fluorine atoms and link the monomers together. You have probably seen Teflon as a nonstick coating on pots and pans. Teflon is also very strong, and it was used as a part of the structure of the stadium's dome in the photograph on the left.

$$--- CF_2 - CF_2 - CF_2 - CF_2 ---$$

Nomex is used to make fireproof clothing worn by firefighters.

Kevlar is used in bulletproof vests worn by police officers and police dogs.

Chemists have developed several other materials by changing the monomers in nylon, a polymer that is often used in clothing. By adding a carbon-based ring to the nylon monomer, chemists made Nomex, which is used in fireproof clothing. Then scientists changed the placement of this ring on the monomer. This change resulted in the polymer called Kevlar, which is used in bulletproof vests.

Nomex and Kevlar are isomers. The monomers that are the basis of each contain the same atoms but have different structures. As a result, the polymers have different properties and uses. The structure of the polymer in Nomex gives the fibers flexibility along with fire resistance. As a result, Nomex can be made into relatively comfortable fireproof clothing for firefighters and race car drivers. Kevlar, however, is very rigid because of its structure and is the strongest known fiber. In fact, Kevlar is five times stronger than an equal amount of steel, which helps explain why Kevlar is used in bulletproof vests.

CHECK YOUR READING Why are Nomex and Kevlar isomers?

5.3 Review

KEY CONCEPTS

1. What physical property allows the hydrocarbons in petroleum to be separated? Explain.
2. What are monomers? How are monomers related to polymers?
3. How are polymers such as Kevlar and Nomex similar to each other? How are they different?

CRITICAL THINKING

4. **Synthesize** What general type of chemical reaction makes polymers from monomers? Explain.
5. **Compare and Contrast** How are plastics such as polypropylene similar to celluloid, the first plastic? How are they different?

CHALLENGE

6. **Synthesize** A petroleum deposit is full of carbon compounds. How did that carbon get out of the atmosphere and into the petroleum?

Chapter 5: **Carbon in Life and Materials** 169 **B**

CHAPTER INVESTIGATION

Polymers

OVERVIEW AND PURPOSE Polymers are used in many common items. For example, the substance that is being pulled out of the beaker in the photograph on the left is raw nylon, which is a polymer. The properties of polymers are influenced by the way in which the chains are linked together. In this activity, you will use what you have learned about carbon-based molecules to
- make a polymer
- study the properties of a polymer

Procedure

1. Create a data table like the one shown on the sample notebook page.

2. Follow the instructions to mix the polymer called Glurch. After you have made the polymer, store it in a zip-top bag.

GLURCH
40 mL (8 tsp) water
40 mL (8 tsp) white glue
6 drops of food coloring
2 tsp powdered borax
30 mL (6 tsp) water

- Make a glue mixture by mixing 40 mL of water with 40 mL of white glue in a plastic container.
- Add food coloring and mix the color evenly.
- Make a borax solution by adding 2 tsp of borax to 30 mL of water. Shake the mixture in a covered jar for 30 seconds.
- Combine the borax solution with the glue mixture. Stir.
- Knead until the mixture is smooth, with a rubberlike consistency.

3. Remove some of the polymer from the bag. Try each test below in order. Observe each test and record your results.

4. **SQUEEZE TEST** Put some of the polymer in your hand. Squeeze the polymer to test its shape and its feel. Is it a solid, a liquid, or a little like both? Record your observations.

5. **PULL TEST** Hold the polymer between your hands and pull it apart slowly. Try again, and pull it apart very quickly. What happens to the polymer? Record the results of this test.

MATERIALS
- measuring spoons
- 2 plastic containers
- tap water
- white glue
- food coloring
- borax
- jar with lid
- plastic spoon
- zip-top plastic bags
- scissors
- 2 L plastic bottle
- ring stand with ring
- stopwatch
- straws

170 Unit: Chemical Interactions

6 BOUNCE TEST Roll some of the polymer into a ball between your palms. Test whether the polymer ball will bounce. Record your observations about the polymer's behavior.

7 CREEP TEST

Setup Cut the top off a 2 L bottle. Keep the bottle cap on. Set up a ring stand. To use the bottle top as a funnel, place it upside down in the ring. Put a plastic container under the funnel.

Trials Place approximately 100 mL of the polymer in the funnel. Remove the bottle cap and time how long it takes for the polymer to flow completely through the funnel. Record the time. If time allows, conduct one or two more trials.

8 BUBBLE TEST Take a small amount of the polymer and roll it into a ball around the end of a straw. Pinch the polymer closed around the straw. Hold the ball in one hand as you gently blow into the other end of the straw. Try to make a bubble by filling the polymer with air. Record your observations.

Observe and Analyze

1. **RECORD OBSERVATIONS** Be sure that your data table is complete. Describe how the polymer feels, as well as its state, shape, and behavior.

2. **COMMUNICATE** Include drawings of any observations for which a picture is helpful in understanding your results.

3. **INTERPRET DATA** Make a list of the polymer's physical properties. Which test was most helpful in identifying these properties? Which test was the least helpful?

Conclude

1. **INFER** The more complex a polymer is, the more rigid it is. Do you think that the polymer you made contains molecules with extremely long or complex carbon chains? Why or why not? What properties of your polymer provide evidence for your answer?

2. **EVALUATE** What limitations or difficulties did you experience in interpreting the results of your tests or other observations?

3. **APPLY** Based upon your results, what uses could you suggest for the polymer? What further tests would you need to do to make sure it would stand up to the demands of that use?

INVESTIGATE Further

CHALLENGE Investigate the properties of your polymer by varying the proportions of the ingredients. Change only one ingredient. Be sure to record the change you made in the polymer. Make a new data table. Record the results of the experimental tests. How do changes in the polymer recipe change the physical properties of the polymer?

Polymers
Observe and Analyze

Table 1. Polymer Properties

Test	Observations
Squeeze test	
Pull test	
Bounce test	
Creep test	Trial 1 (time) Trial 2 (time) Trial 3 (time)
Bubble test	

Conclude

Chapter 5: **Carbon in Life and Materials** 171

5 Chapter Review

the BIG idea

Carbon is essential to living things and to modern materials.

CONTENT REVIEW
CLASSZONE.COM

◀ KEY CONCEPTS SUMMARY

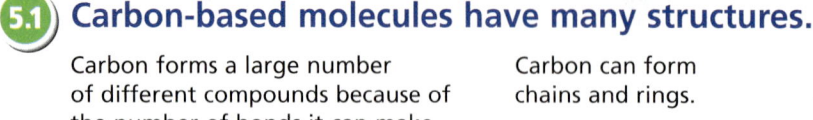

5.1 Carbon-based molecules have many structures.

Carbon forms a large number of different compounds because of the number of bonds it can make with other atoms.

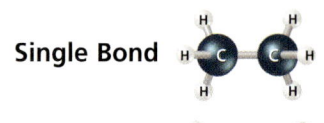

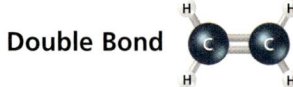

Single Bond

Double Bond

Triple Bond

Carbon can form chains and rings.

Hexane

$CH_3 - CH_2 - CH_2 - CH_2 - CH_2 - CH_3$

Vanillin

VOCABULARY
organic compound p. 147
inorganic compound p. 148
isomer p. 152

5.2 Carbon-based molecules are life's building blocks.

There are four main types of carbon-based molecules in living things.

Carbon-Based Molecules			
Carbohydrates	**Lipids**	**Proteins**	**Nucleic Acids**
• include sugars and starches • energy for cells • plant cell walls	• include fats and oils • energy for cells • cell membranes	• function depends on order of amino acids • structure, transport, immune system, enzymes	• DNA • carries genetic code • sequence of three DNA bases is the code for an amino acid

VOCABULARY
carbohydrate p. 155
lipid p. 156
protein p. 158
enzyme p. 159
nucleic acid p. 161

5.3 Carbon-based molecules are in many materials.

Carbon from ancient organisms is used to make many common items, such as clothing and plastics. These items are based on polymers.

Monomer $CH_2 = CH - CH_3$

Polymer $CH_2 - CH - CH_2 - CH - CH_2 - CH - - -$
                          | | |
                         CH_3 CH_3 CH_3

VOCABULARY
hydrocarbon p. 163
polymer p. 166
monomer p. 166
plastic p. 167

B 172 Unit: Chemical Interactions

Reviewing Vocabulary

Copy and complete the chart below. Fill in the blanks with the missing term, example, or function. See the example in the chart.

Term	Example	Function
inorganic compound	carbon dioxide	used by plants to make glucose
1. organic compound	glucose	
2. carbohydrate	sugar	
3.	fat	stores chemical energy
4.	keratin	found in hair and feathers
5. nucleic acid		instructions for proteins
6. plastic	polypropylene	

Greek Roots Describe how each of the following terms is related to one or more of the following Greek roots.

iso- means "equal" *mono-* means "one"
-mer means "part" *poly-* means "many"

7. isomer
8. polymer
9. monomer
10. polyunsaturated

Reviewing Key Concepts

Multiple Choice *Choose the letter of the best answer.*

11. All life on Earth is based on atoms of which element?
    a. oxygen
    b. nitrogen
    c. carbon
    d. hydrogen

12. One reason that carbon atoms can form large numbers of compounds is that a carbon atom forms
    a. two bonds with a hydrogen atom
    b. four bonds in its compounds
    c. ionic bonds in its compounds
    d. bonds with up to five hydrogen atoms

13. Which of the following is not found in living things?
    a. proteins   c. lipids
    b. petroleum   d. carbohydrates

14. What functions do carbohydrates and lipids perform in living things?
    a. They provide energy and instructions.
    b. They provide water and oxygen.
    c. They provide water and immunity.
    d. They provide energy and structure.

15. The molecules that carry instructions to make other molecules are called
    a. nucleic acids   c. carbohydrates
    b. proteins   d. lipids

16. Which kinds of molecules are best for storing chemical energy in living things?
    a. enzymes   c. lipids
    b. proteins   d. nucleic acids

17. The properties of artificial polymers are determined by
    a. the structure of the molecule
    b. the reaction used to make the polymer
    c. the time it took to make the polymer
    d. a series of DNA bases

Short Answer *Write a short answer to each question.*

18. Explain how carbon's ability to form isomers is related to the large number of carbon-based molecules that exist.

19. Describe the movement of carbon through the environment in a cycle. How does a break in the cycle provide carbon for modern materials?

Chapter 5: **Carbon in Life and Materials** 173 **B**

Thinking Critically

The illustration below models linked amino acids. Use the illustration to answer the next four questions.

20. SYNTHESIZE Why can the model shown by the illustration be considered to be a polymer?

21. CONCLUDE What would cause the amino acids in the illustration to be placed in that particular order? Explain.

22. APPLY If the order of amino acids shown in the illustration changes, would the protein formed likely still have the same function? Why or why not?

23. PREDICT Suppose the protein formed by the amino acids has a coiled shape. What might be the general function of that protein? What if the protein is coiled but also curls up into a ball?

24. COMPARE AND CONTRAST Copy and complete the chart below. Provide two similarities and two differences for each pair of items.

Items	Similarities	Differences
starch/cellulose	both carbohydrates; both polymers	starch used for energy, cellulose for structure; starch molecule branched, cellulose molecule straight
carbon chains/carbon rings		
proteins/lipids		
glucose/amino acids		

Using Math Skills in Science

The nutrition label below shows the Calories and the amount of fat, carbohydrates, and protein in a type of cracker. Use the information on the label to answer the following three questions.

Nutrition Facts

Servings Per Container   about 15

Amount Per Serving

Calories   150

Total Fat   6g

Total Carbohydrates   20g

Protein   2g

25. Fats contain about twice as many Calories per gram as carbohydrates and proteins. Assume that all of the Calories on the label come from the carbohydrates, fats, and proteins. About how many Calories come from each substance?

26. Make a pie chart that compares the number of Calories from carbohydrates, fats, and proteins contained in this food.

27. Adult athletes are recommended to eat a diet that provides 15% of its Calories from protein, 30% from fats, and 55% from carbohydrates. Does this food have the recommended balance of nutrients? Why or why not?

the BIG idea

28. DRAW CONCLUSIONS Look at the photographs on pages 144–145. Describe three ways in which carbon is important in the activities taking place.

29. SYNTHESIZE Write one or more paragraphs describing how plants, animals, and plastics are related to each other.

UNIT PROJECTS

Evaluate all the data, results, and information from your project folder. Prepare to present your project.

Standardized Test Practice

For practice on your state test, go to...
TEST PRACTICE
CLASSZONE.COM

Interpreting Tables

The following table contains information about some of the different products that can be separated from petroleum. Use the information in the table to answer questions 1–5.

Characteristics of Petroleum Products

Product	Number of Carbon Atoms per Molecule	Boiling Point (°C)
Natural gas	1 to 4	lower than 20
Gasoline	5 to 12	35 to 220
Kerosene	12 to 16	200 to 315
Jet fuel	12 to 16	200 to 315
Diesel fuel	15 to 18	250 to 375
Heating oil	15 to 18	250 to 375
Lubricating oil	16 to 20	350 and higher
Asphalt	More than 25	600 and higher

SOURCE: *Mortimer, Chemistry,* 6th edition

1. Which petroleum product has the lowest boiling point?
   a. diesel fuel
   b. gasoline
   c. kerosene
   d. natural gas

2. Which petroleum product has the highest boiling point?
   a. asphalt
   b. heating oil
   c. jet fuel
   d. kerosene

3. Petroleum is heated and turned into gas. The gas rises in a distillation tower. The lightest gases—those with the smallest molecules—rise highest. The heaviest gases—those with the largest molecules—stay lowest. Which of the following products would be found lowest in the tower?
   a. diesel fuel
   b. kerosene
   c. lubricating oil
   d. natural gas

4. Petroleum is split into fractions. Each fraction includes all the products that have the same boiling point. Which of the following pairs of products are in the same fraction?
   a. gasoline and natural gas
   b. jet fuel and kerosene
   c. lubricating oil and diesel fuel
   d. natural gas and asphalt

5. What might be the boiling point of a petroleum product that contains 22 carbon atoms?
   a. 100°C
   b. 300°C
   c. 500°C
   d. 700°C

Extended Response

Answer the following two questions in detail. Include some of the terms from the list in the box at right. Underline each term that you use in your answers.

atoms	carbon chains	carbon rings
molecules	properties	structure
function	monomer	

6. How are polymers made? Give examples of a natural polymer and an artificial polymer.

7. Carbohydrates, lipids, and proteins are all carbon-based molecules. How are they similar? How are they different?

Chapter 5: **Carbon in Life and Materials** 175 B

UNIT C

Motion and Forces

$F=ma$

GRAVITY

VELOCITY

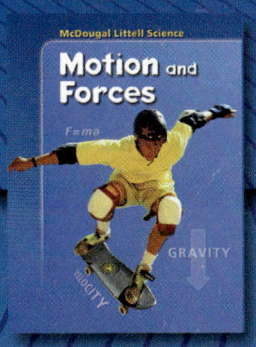

Motion and Forces
Contents Overview

Unit Features
FRONTIERS IN SCIENCE Robots on Mars — 2
TIMELINES IN SCIENCE Understanding Forces — 108

1 Motion — 6
the BIG idea
The motion of an object can be described and predicted.

2 Forces — 38
the BIG idea
Forces change the motion of objects in predictable ways.

3 Gravity, Friction, and Pressure — 74
the BIG idea
Newton's laws apply to all forces.

4 Work and Energy — 112
the BIG idea
Energy is transferred when a force moves an object.

5 Machines — 142
the BIG idea
Machines help people do work by changing the force applied to an object.

FRONTIERS in Science

ROBOTS on Mars

If you could design a robot to explore Mars, what would you want it to be able to do?

SCIENTIFIC AMERICAN FRONTIERS

Watch the video segment "Teetering to Victory" to learn about a competition that challenges students to use their knowledge of motion and forces to design a machine.

The surface of Mars looks rocky and barren today, but scientists have long wondered if life might have existed on Mars long ago. That would have been possible only if Mars once had water, which is necessary for all forms of life.

NASA's Mars Exploration Rover (MER) shown in a computer-simulated Martian landscape

The Design Challenge

It's still not possible to send scientists to Mars to search for signs of water, but in 1999 a team of scientists and engineers began to design two robots for NASA's 2004 mission to Mars. As the team worked, they relied on their scientific understanding of motion, forces, and machines to create and test a successful design.

To identify their goals, the team started by thinking about what scientists would want to do if they could go to Mars. First they would want to look around the landscape to find good areas to study. Then they would need to travel to those areas and analyze rock samples. Finally they would use a variety of tools to analyze the rocks, interpret their data, and communicate their findings back to Earth. Those goals set the basic plan for the Mars Exploration Rovers (MERs).

As you can see in the photograph, the MER team designed a rover with cameras for viewing the surface, wheels for moving around the landscape, and an extendable arm in front equipped with tools for drilling into, observing, and identifying rocks. The rover also has a computer to process information, an antenna for radio communication with Earth, and batteries and solar panels to provide energy for everything.

As in any technology project, the MER team had to work within specific constraints, or limits. The most basic constraints were time and money. They had to design rovers that could be built within NASA's budget and that would be ready in time for launch in 2003. But the team also faced some more challenging

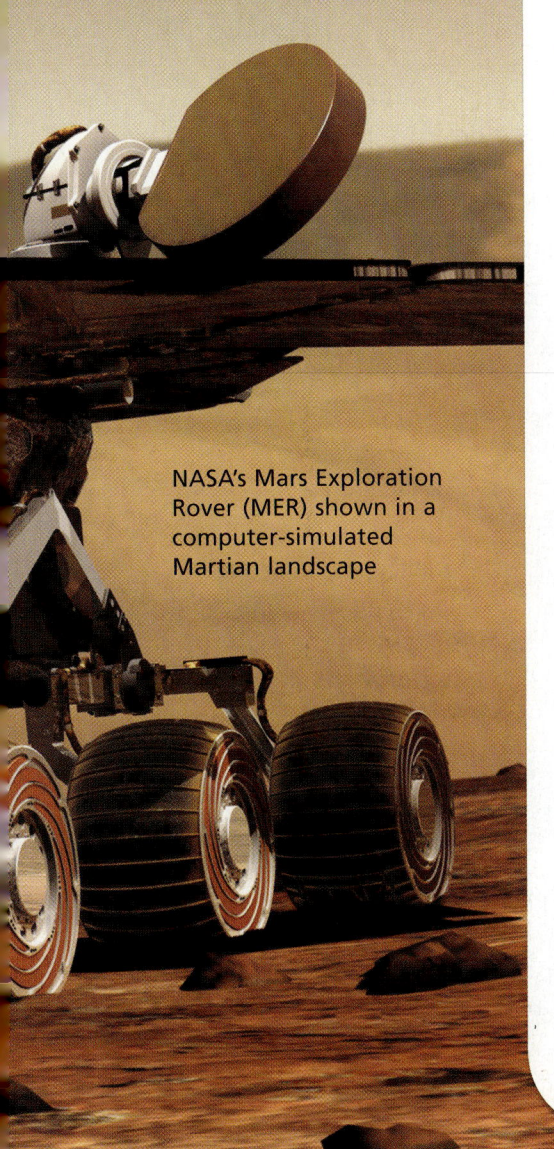

Frontiers in Science 3

Members of the project team stand with a MER and a replica of the much smaller *Sojourner*.

constraints. The rover must survive a rocket launch from Earth as well as a landing on the surface of Mars. This means it must be both lightweight and compact. Engineers designed the MER to fold up into a pyramid-shaped protective compartment, which drops down onto Mars by parachute. Air bags surrounding the compartment absorb the impact, and then the compartment opens and the MER moves down the compartment panels to the planet's surface.

Scientists built on some valuable lessons learned from an earlier robot, *Sojourner*, which explored the surface of Mars for 12 weeks in 1997. At the left you see one of the MERs next to a replica of *Sojourner*, which was only about 28 centimeters (about 11 in) tall. MER's mast rises up to 1.4 meters (almost 5 ft), giving the cameras, which can be angled up or down, a view similar to what a person would see when standing on the surface of Mars.

Testing the Model

Every part of the MER had to be tested to be sure it would work properly in the harsh conditions on Mars. For example, consider the Rock Abrasion Tool (RAT) at the end of the rover's extendable arm. The RAT is designed to grind off the weathered surface of rock, exposing a fresh surface for examination. Tests with the RAT showed that it worked fine on hard rocks, but its diamond-tipped grinding wheel became clogged with pieces of soft rock. The solution: Add brushes to clean the RAT automatically after each use.

Scientists were also concerned that the RAT's diamond grinding wheel might wear out if it had to grind a lot of hard rocks. An entry from the design team's status report explains why that turned out not to be a problem:

SCIENTIFIC AMERICAN FRONTIERS

View the "Teetering to Victory" segment of your Scientific American Frontiers video to learn how some students solved a much simpler design challenge.

IN THIS SCENE FROM THE VIDEO
MIT students prepare to test their machines.

BATTLE OF MACHINES Each year more than 100 engineering students at the Massachusetts Institute of Technology (MIT) compete in a contest to see who can design and build the best machine. The challenge this time is to build a machine that starts out sitting on a teeter-totter beam and within 45 seconds manages to tilt its end down against an opponent trying to do the same thing.

Just as the Mars rover designers had to consider the constraints of space travel and Mars' harsh environment, the students had constraints on their designs. They all started with the same kit of materials, and their finished machines had to weigh less than 10 pounds as well as fit inside the box the materials came in. Within these constraints, the student designers came up with an amazing variety of solutions.

The big question, of course, was how things would work under the very cold, dry, low-pressure atmospheric conditions on Mars. We put a RAT into a test chamber recently, took it to real Martian conditions for the first time, and got a very pleasant surprise. The rate at which our diamond studded teeth wear away slowed way down! We're still figuring out why, but it turns out that when you put this Martian RAT into its natural environment, its teeth don't wear down nearly as fast.

Engineers also needed to test the system by which scientists on Earth would communicate with and control the rovers on Mars. For this purpose, they built a smaller version of the real robot, nicknamed FIDO. In tests FIDO successfully traveled to several locations, dug trenches, and observed and measured rock samples.

Goals of the Mission

Technology like the Mars Exploration Rovers extends the power of scientists to gather data and answer questions about our solar system. One main goal of the MER missions is to study different kinds of rock and soils that might indicate whether water was ever present on Mars. From the data gathered by the MERs, scientists hope to find out what factors shaped the Martian landscape. They also hope to check out areas that have been studied only from far away so that the scientists can confirm their hypotheses about Mars.

UNANSWERED Questions

As scientists learn more and more about Mars, new questions always arise.

- What role, if any, did water, wind, or volcanoes play in shaping the landscape of Mars?
- Were the conditions necessary to support life ever present on Mars?
- Could there be bacteria-like life forms surviving below the surface of Mars today?

UNIT PROJECTS

As you study this unit, work alone or with a group on one of these projects.

Build a Mechanical Arm

Design and build a mechanical arm to perform a simple task.

- Plan and sketch an arm that could lift a pencil from the floor at a distance of one meter.
- Collect materials and assemble your arm.
- Conduct trials and improve your design.

Multimedia Presentation

Create an informative program on the forces involved in remote exploration.

- Collect information about the Galileo mission to Jupiter or a similar expedition.
- Learn how engineers use air resistance, gravity, and rocket thrusters to maneuver the orbiter close to the planet and its moons.
- Give a presentation describing what you learned using mixed media, such as a computer slide show and a model.

Design an Experiment

Design an experiment to determine the pressure needed to crush a small object.

- Select a small object, such as a vitamin C tablet, to use in your experiment.
- Collect other materials of your choosing.
- Plan and conduct a procedure to test the pressure required to crush the object. Vary the procedure until you can crush the object using the least amount of force.

CAREER CENTER
CLASSZONE.COM

Learn more about careers in physics and engineering.

CHAPTER 1: Motion

the BIG idea

The motion of an object can be described and predicted.

Where will these people be in a few seconds? How do you know?

Key Concepts

SECTION 1.1 An object in motion changes position.
Learn about measuring position from reference points, and about relative motion.

SECTION 1.2 Speed measures how fast position changes.
Learn to calculate speed and how velocity depends on speed and direction.

SECTION 1.3 Acceleration measures how fast velocity changes.
Learn about acceleration and how to calculate it.

Internet Preview

CLASSZONE.COM

Chapter 1 online resources: Content Review, Visualization, Simulation, two Resource Centers, Math Tutorial, Test Practice

6 Unit: Motion and Forces

EXPLORE the BIG idea

Off the Wall
Roll a rubber ball toward a wall. Record the time from the starting point to the wall. Change the distance between the wall and the starting point. Adjust the speed at which you roll the ball until it takes the same amount of time to hit the wall as before.

Observe and Think How did the speed of the ball over the longer distance compare with the speed over the shorter distance?

Rolling Along
Make a ramp by leaning the edge of one book on two other books. Roll a marble up the ramp. Repeat several times and notice what happens each time.

Observe and Think How does the speed of the marble change? At what point does its direction of motion change?

Internet Activity: Relative Motion
Go to **ClassZone.com** to examine motion from different points of view. Learn how your motion makes a difference in what you observe.

Observe and Think How does the way you see motion depend on your point of view?

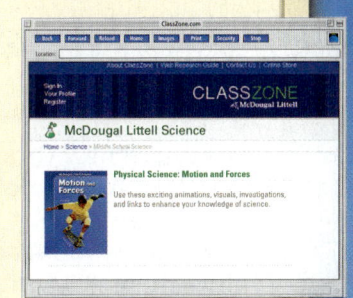

NSTA scilinks.org SciLINKS

Velocity Code: MDL004

Chapter 1: **Motion** 7

CHAPTER 1
Getting Ready to Learn

CONCEPT REVIEW

- Objects can move at different speeds and in different directions.
- Pushing or pulling on an object will change how it moves.

VOCABULARY REVIEW

See Glossary for definitions.

horizontal
meter
second
vertical

CONTENT REVIEW
CLASSZONE.COM
Review concepts and vocabulary.

TAKING NOTES

OUTLINE

As you read, copy the headings onto your paper in the form of an outline. Then add notes in your own words that summarize what you read.

VOCABULARY STRATEGY

Place each new vocabulary term at the center of a **description wheel** diagram. As you read about the term, write some words on the spokes describing the term.

See the Note-Taking Handbook on pages R45–R51.

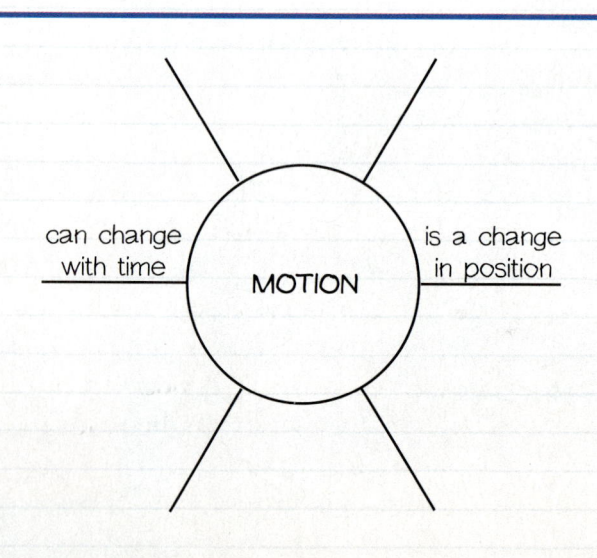

SCIENCE NOTEBOOK

OUTLINE

I. Position describes the location of an object.
   A. Describing a position
      1. A position is compared to a reference point.
      2. Position can be described using distance and direction.

MOTION
- can change with time
- is a change in position

8 Unit: Motion and Forces

KEY CONCEPT
1.1 An object in motion changes position.

◀ **BEFORE, you learned**
- Objects can move in different ways
- An object's position can change

▶ **NOW, you will learn**
- How to describe an object's position
- How to describe an object's motion

VOCABULARY
position p. 9
reference point p. 10
motion p. 11

EXPLORE Location

How do you describe the location of an object?

PROCEDURE

1. Choose an object in the classroom that is easy to see.
2. Without pointing to, describing, or naming the object, give directions to a classmate for finding it.
3. Ask your classmate to identify the object using your directions. If your classmate does not correctly identify the object, try giving directions in a different way. Continue until your classmate has located the object.

WHAT DO YOU THINK?
What kinds of information must you give another person when you are trying to describe a location?

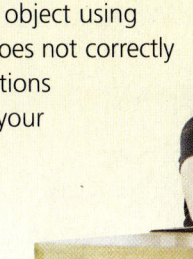

VOCABULARY
Make a description wheel in your notebook for *position*.

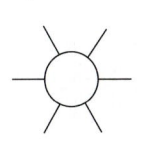

Position describes the location of an object.

Have you ever gotten lost while looking for a specific place? If so, you probably know that accurately describing where a place is can be very important. The **position** of a place or an object is the location of that place or object. Often you describe where something is by comparing its position with where you currently are. You might say, for example, that a classmate sitting next to you is about a meter to your right, or that a mailbox is two blocks south of where you live. Each time you identify the position of an object, you are comparing the location of the object with the location of another object or place.

CHECK YOUR READING Why do you need to discuss two locations to describe the position of an object?

Chapter 1: **Motion** 9

RESOURCE CENTER
CLASSZONE.COM

Learn more about how people find and describe position.

Describing a Position

You might describe the position of a city based on the location of another city. A location to which you compare other locations is called a **reference point.** You can describe where Santiago, Chile, is from the reference point of the city Brasília, Brazil, by saying that Santiago is about 3000 kilometers (1860 mi) southwest of Brasília.

You can also describe a position using a method that is similar to describing where a point on a graph is located. For example, in the longitude and latitude system, locations are given by two numbers—longitude and latitude. Longitude describes how many degrees east or west a location is from the prime meridian, an imaginary line running north-south through Greenwich, England. Latitude describes how many degrees north or south a location is from the equator, the imaginary circle that divides the northern and southern hemispheres. Having a standard way of describing location, such as longitude and latitude, makes it easier for people to compare locations.

Describing Position

There are several different ways to describe a position. The way you choose may depend on your reference point.

1 Reference Point: Brasília

2 Reference Point: 0° longitude, 0° latitude

To describe where Santiago is, using Brasília as a reference point, you would need to know how far Santiago is from Brasília and in what direction it is.

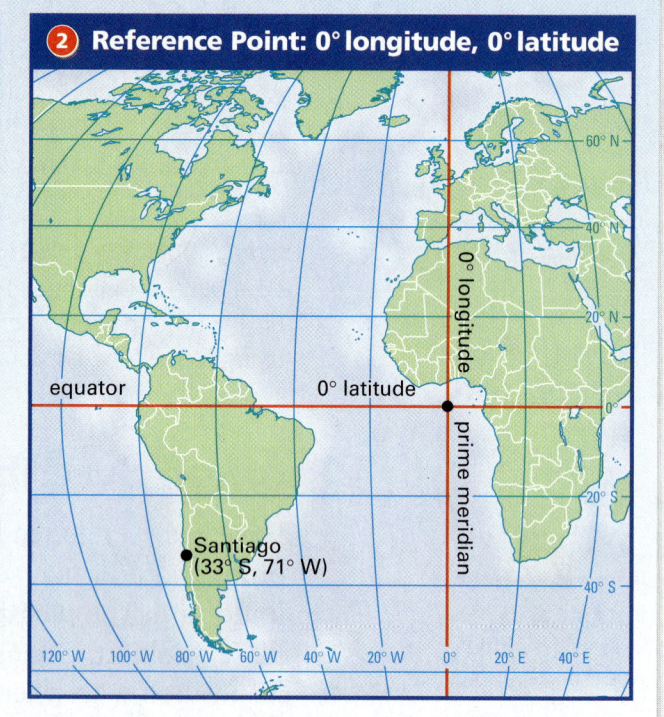

In the longitude and latitude system, a location is described by how many degrees north or south it is from the equator and how many degrees east or west it is from the prime meridian.

READING VISUALS Compare and contrast the two ways of describing the location of Santiago as shown here.

10 Unit: Motion and Forces

Measuring Distance

If you were to travel from Brasília to Santiago, you would end up about 3000 kilometers from where you started. The actual distance you traveled, however, would depend on the exact path you took. If you took a route that had many curves, the distance you traveled would be greater than 3000 kilometers.

The way you measure distance depends on the information you want. Sometimes you want to know the straight-line distance between two positions. Sometimes, however, you might need to know the total length of a certain path between those positions. During a hike, you are probably more interested in how far you have walked than in how far you are from your starting point.

When measuring either the straight-line distance between two points or the length of a path between those points, scientists use a standard unit of measurement. The standard unit of length is the meter (m), which is 3.3 feet. Longer distances can be measured in kilometers (km), and shorter distances in centimeters (cm).

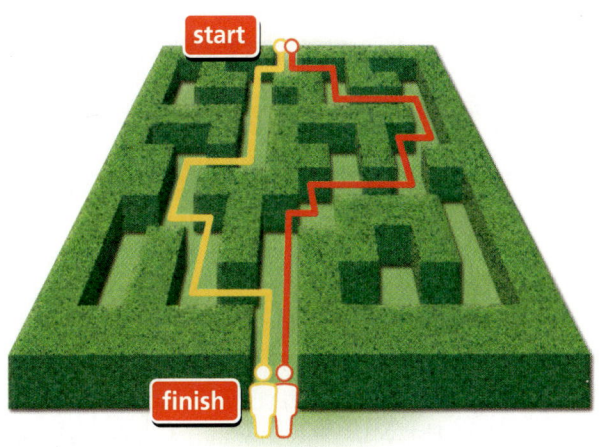

COMPARE How does the distance each person has walked compare with the distance each is from the start of the maze?

Motion is a change in position.

The illustration below shows an athlete at several positions during a long jump. If you were to watch her jump, you would see that she is in motion. **Motion** is the change of position over time. As she jumps, both her horizontal and vertical positions change. If you missed the motion of the jump, you would still know that motion occurred because of the distance between her starting and ending positions. A change in position is evidence that motion happened.

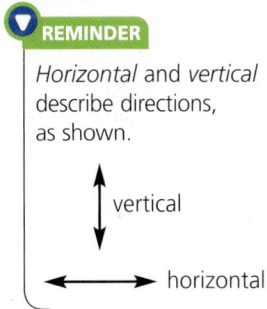

REMINDER

Horizontal and *vertical* describe directions, as shown.

↕ vertical

↔ horizontal

starting position

ending position

Chapter 1: **Motion** 11

INVESTIGATE Changing Position

How are changes in position observed?

PROCEDURE

1. Begin walking while tossing a ball straight up and catching it as it falls back down toward your hand. Observe the changes in the position of the ball as you toss it while walking a distance of about 4 m.

2. Make a sketch showing how the position of the ball changed as you walked. Use your own position as a reference point for the ball's position.

3. Watch while a classmate walks and tosses the ball. Observe the changes in the position of the ball using your own position as a reference point. Make a sketch showing how the ball moved based on your new point of view.

WHAT DO YOU THINK?

- Compare your two sketches. How was the change in position of the ball you tossed different from the change in position of the ball that your partner tossed?
- How did your change in viewpoint affect what you observed? Explain.

CHALLENGE How would the change in position of the ball appear to a person standing 4 m directly in front of you?

SKILL FOCUS
Observing

MATERIALS
- small ball
- paper
- pencil

TIME
20 minutes

Describing Motion

A change in an object's position tells you that motion took place, but it does not tell you how quickly the object changed position. The speed of a moving object is a measure of how quickly or slowly the object changes position. A faster object moves farther than a slower moving object would in the same amount of time.

The way in which an object moves can change. As a raft moves along a river, its speed changes as the speed of the river changes. When the raft reaches a calm area of the river, it slows down. When the raft reaches rapids, it speeds up. The rafters can also change the motion of the raft by using paddles. You will learn more about speed and changing speed in the following sections.

APPLY Describe the different directions in which the raft is moving.

Relative Motion

If you sit still in a chair, you are not moving. Or are you? The answer depends on the position and motion of the person observing you. You do not notice your position changing compared with the room and the objects in it. But if an observer could leave Earth and look at you from outer space, he could see that you are moving along with Earth as it travels around the Sun. How an observer sees your motion depends on how it compares with his own motion. Just as position is described by using a reference point, motion is described by using a frame of reference. You can think of a frame of reference as the location of an observer, who may be in motion.

Consider a student sitting behind the driver of a moving bus. The bus passes another student waiting at a street sign to cross the street.

① To the observer on the bus, the driver is not changing his position compared with the inside of the bus. The street sign, however, moves past the observer's window. From this observer's point of view, the driver is not moving, but the street sign is.

② To the observer on the sidewalk, the driver is changing position along with the bus. The street sign, on the other hand, is not changing position. From this observer's point of view, the street sign is not moving, but the driver is.

OUTLINE
Add relative motion to your outline, along with supporting details.

I. Main idea
   A. Supporting idea
      1. Detail
      2. Detail
   B. Supporting idea

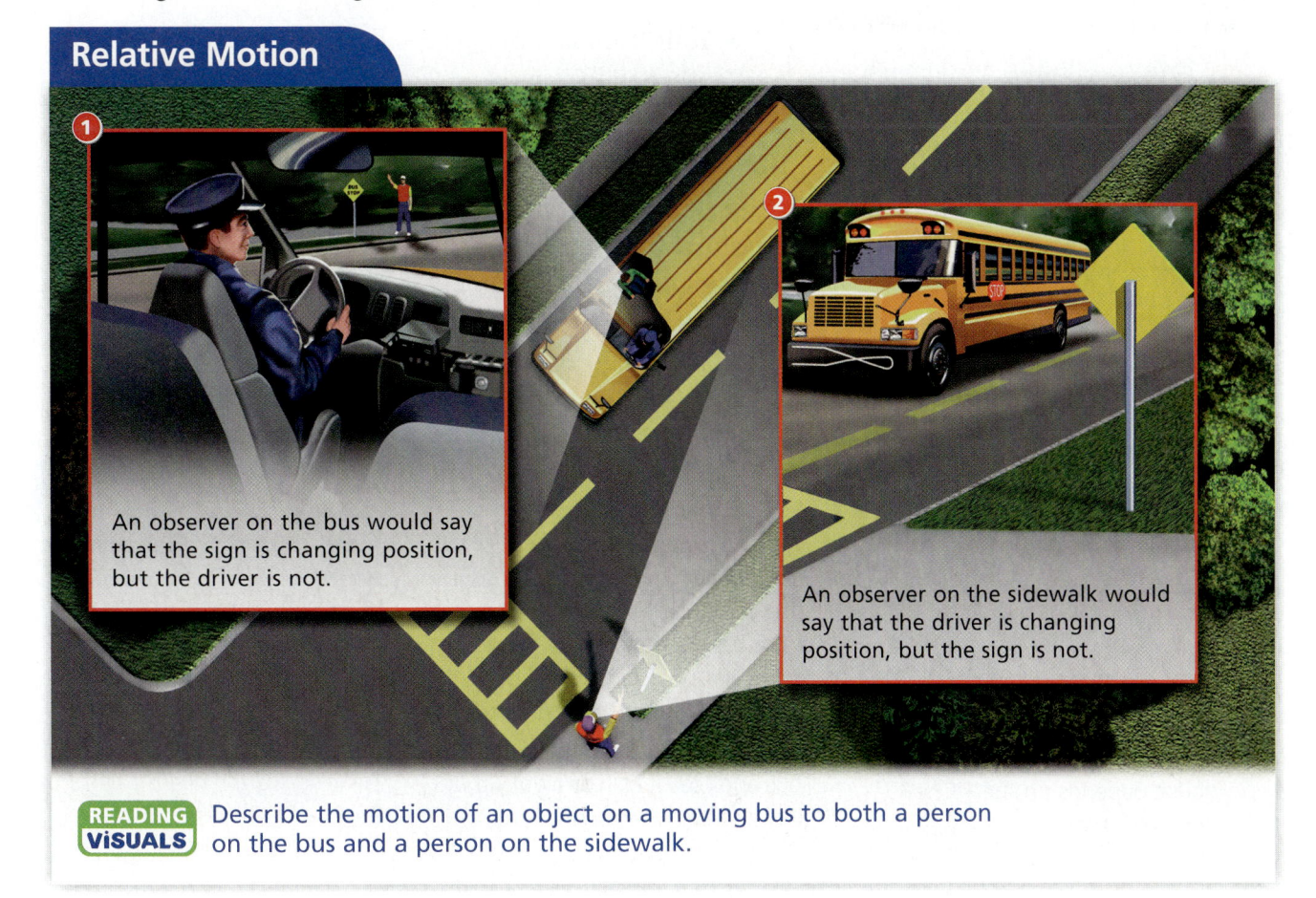

Relative Motion

An observer on the bus would say that the sign is changing position, but the driver is not.

An observer on the sidewalk would say that the driver is changing position, but the sign is not.

READING VISUALS Describe the motion of an object on a moving bus to both a person on the bus and a person on the sidewalk.

Chapter 1: **Motion** 13

When you ride in a train, a bus, or an airplane, you think of yourself as moving and the ground as standing still. That is, you usually consider the ground as the frame of reference for your motion. If you traveled between two cities, you would say that you had moved, not that the ground had moved under you in the opposite direction.

If you cannot see the ground or objects on it, it is sometimes difficult to tell if a train you are riding in is moving. If the ride is very smooth and you do not look out the window at the scenery, you might never realize you are moving at all.

Suppose you are in a train, and you cannot tell if you are stopped or moving. Outside the window, another train is slowly moving forward. Could you tell which of the following situations is happening?

- Your train is stopped, and the other train is moving slowly forward.
- The other train is stopped, and your train is moving slowly backward.
- Both trains are moving forward, with the other train moving a little faster.
- Your train is moving very slowly backward, and the other train is moving very slowly forward.

Actually, all four of these possibilities would look exactly the same to you. Unless you compared the motion to the motion of something outside the train, such as the ground, you could not tell the difference between these situations.

APPLY In the top picture, the train is moving compared with the camera and the ground. Describe the relative motion of the train, camera, and ground in the bottom picture.

CHECK YOUR READING How does your observation of motion depend on your own motion?

1.1 Review

KEY CONCEPTS

1. What information do you need to describe an object's location?
2. Describe how your position changes as you jump over an object.
3. Give an example of how the apparent motion of an object depends on the observer's motion.

CRITICAL THINKING

4. **Infer** Kyle walks 3 blocks south from his home to school, and Jana walks 2 blocks north from her home to Kyle's home. How far and in what direction is the school from Jana's home?
5. **Predict** If you sit on a moving bus and toss a coin straight up into the air, where will it land?

CHALLENGE

6. **Infer** Jamal is in a car going north. He looks out his window and thinks that the northbound traffic is moving very slowly. Ellen is in a car going south. She thinks the northbound traffic is moving quickly. Explain why Jamal and Ellen have different ideas about the motion of the traffic.

SCIENCE on the JOB

COAST GUARD RESCUE

Physics for Rescuers

Performing a rescue operation is often difficult and risky because the person in trouble is in a dangerous situation. Coast Guard Search and Rescue Teams have an especially difficult problem to deal with. As a rescue ship or helicopter approaches a stranded boat, the team must get close enough to help but avoid making the problem worse by colliding with the boat. At the same time, wind, waves, and currents cause changes in the motion of both crafts.

Finding the Problem

A stranded boater fires a flare to indicate his location. The observer on the Coast Guard ship tracks the motion of the flare to its source.

Avoiding Collision

As the boats move closer together, the captain assesses their motion relative to each other. The speeds of the boats must match, and the boats must be close enough that a rope can be thrown across the gap. If the sea is rough, both boats will move up and down, making the proper positioning even more difficult.

Rescue from Above

The helicopter pilot determines where to hover so that the rescue basket lands on target. A mistake could be disastrous for the rescuers as well as the people being rescued.

EXPLORE

1. **PREDICT** Tie a washer to a 30 cm piece of string. Using your hand as a helicopter, lower the rescue washer to a mark on the floor. Turn on a fan to create wind. Predict where you will need to hold the string to land the washer on the mark. Place the fan at a different location and try again. How accurate was your prediction? Does your accuracy improve with practice?

2. **CHALLENGE** Have a partner throw a baseball into the air from behind the corner of a wall. Using the motion of the ball, try to determine the position from which it was thrown. When is it easier—when the ball is thrown in a high arc or lower one?

Chapter 1: **Motion** 15

1.2 Speed measures how fast position changes.

KEY CONCEPT

◀ **BEFORE, you learned**
- An object's position is measured from a reference point
- To describe the position of an object, you can use distance and direction
- An object in motion changes position with time

▶ **NOW, you will learn**
- How to calculate an object's speed
- How to describe an object's velocity

VOCABULARY

speed p. 16
velocity p. 22
vector p. 22

EXPLORE Speed

How can you measure speed?

PROCEDURE

1. Place a piece of tape on the floor. Measure a distance on the floor 2 m away from the tape. Mark this distance with a second piece of tape.

2. Roll a tennis ball from one piece of tape to the other, timing how long it takes to travel the 2 m.

3. Roll the ball again so that it travels the same distance in less time. Then roll the ball so that it takes more time to travel that distance than it did the first time.

MATERIALS
- tape
- meter stick
- tennis ball
- stopwatch

WHAT DO YOU THINK?
- How did you change the time it took the ball to travel 2 m?
- How did changing the time affect the motion of the ball?

Position can change at different rates.

VOCABULARY
Make a description wheel in your notebook for *speed*.

When someone asks you how far it is to the library, you can answer in terms of distance or time. You can say it is several blocks, or you can say it is a five-minute walk. When you give a time instead of a distance, you are basing your time estimate on the distance to the library and the person's speed. **Speed** is a measure of how fast something moves or the distance it moves, in a given amount of time. The greater the speed an object has, the faster it changes position.

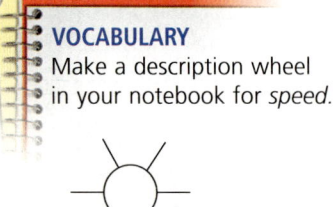

CHECK YOUR READING How are speed and position related?

16 Unit: Motion and Forces

The way in which one quantity changes compared to another quantity is called a rate. Speed is the rate at which the distance an object moves changes compared to time. If you are riding a bike to a movie, and you think you might be late, you increase the rate at which your distance changes by pedaling harder. In other words, you increase your speed.

Calculating Speed

To calculate speed, you need to know both distance and time measurements. Consider the two bike riders below.

① The two bikes pass the same point at the same time.

② After one second, the first bike has traveled four meters, while the second has traveled only two meters. Because the first bike has traveled four meters in one second, it has a speed of four meters per second. The second bike has a speed of two meters per second.

③ If each bike continues moving at the same speed as before, then after two seconds the first rider will have traveled eight meters, while the second one will have traveled only four meters.

Comparing Speed

Objects that travel at different speeds move different distances in the same amount of time.

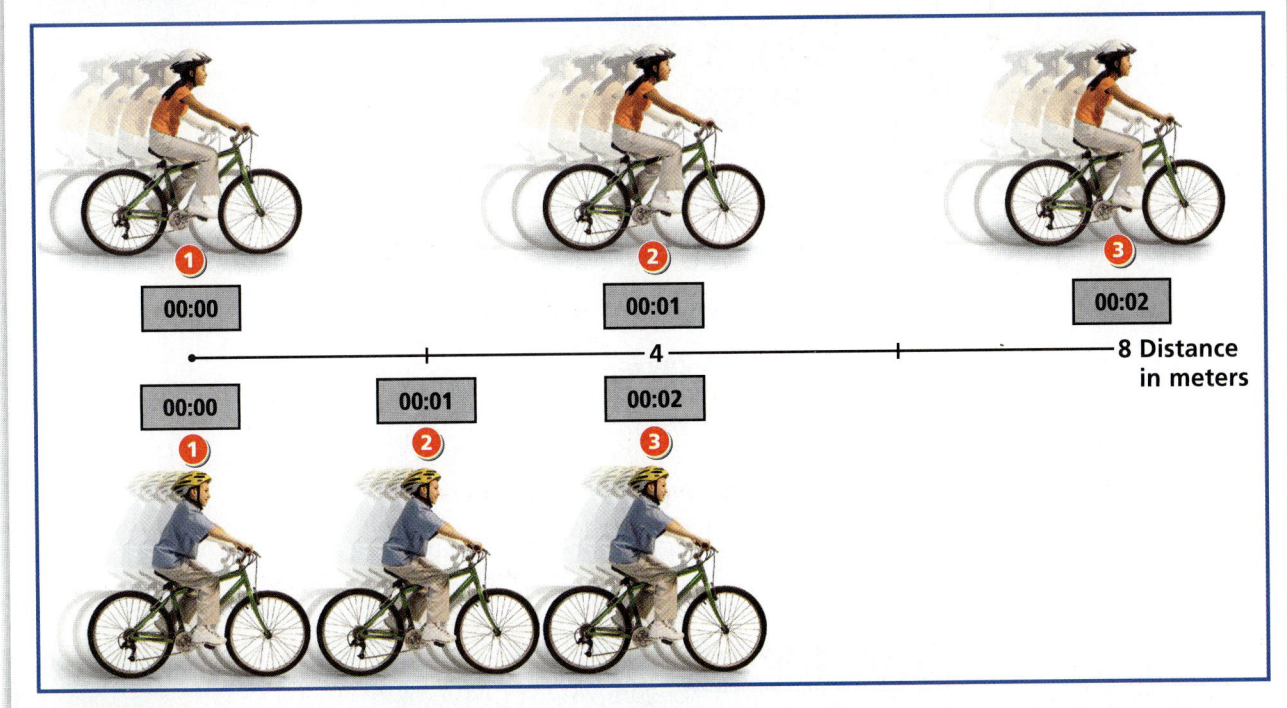

READING VISUALS How far will each rider travel in five seconds?

Chapter 1: **Motion** 17

Speed can be calculated by dividing the distance an object travels by the time it takes to cover the distance. The formula for finding speed is

$$\text{Speed} = \frac{\text{distance}}{\text{time}} \qquad S = \frac{d}{t}$$

Speed is shown in the formula as the letter S, distance as the letter d, and time as the letter t. The formula shows how distance, time, and speed are related. If two objects travel the same distance, the object that took a shorter amount of time will have the greater speed. Similarly, an object with a greater speed will travel a longer distance in the same amount of time than an object with a lower speed will.

The standard unit for speed is meters per second (m/s). Speed is also given in kilometers per hour (km/h). In the United States, where the English system of measurement is still used, speeds are often given in miles per hour (mi/h or mph). One mile per hour is equal to 0.45 m/s.

The man participating in the wheelchair race, at left, will win if his speed is greater than the speed of the other racers. You can use the formula to calculate his speed.

Racing wheelchairs are specially designed to reach higher speeds than regular wheelchairs.

CHECK YOUR READING If two runners cover the same distance in different amounts of time, how do their speeds compare?

Calculating Speed

Sample Problem

A wheelchair racer completes a 100-meter course in 20 seconds. What is his speed?

What do you know?	distance = 100 m, time = 20 s
What do you want to find out?	speed
Write the formula:	$S = \frac{d}{t}$
Substitute into the formula:	$S = \frac{100 \text{ m}}{20 \text{ s}}$
Calculate and simplify:	S = 5 m/s
Check that your units agree:	Unit is m/s. Unit of speed is m/s. Units agree.
Answer:	S = 5 m/s

Practice the Math

1. A man runs 200 m in 25 s. What is his speed?
2. If you travel 100 m in 50 s, what is your speed?

Average Speed

Speed is not constant. When you run, you might slow down to pace yourself, or speed up to win a race. At each point as you are running, you have a specific speed. This moment-to-moment speed is called your instantaneous speed. Your instantaneous speed can be difficult to measure; however, it is easier to calculate your average speed over a distance.

In a long race, runners often want to know their times for each lap so that they can pace themselves. For example, an excellent middle school runner might have the following times for the four laps of a 1600-meter race: 83 seconds, 81 seconds, 79 seconds, 77 seconds. The lap times show the runner is gradually increasing her speed throughout the race.

The total time for the four laps can be used to calculate the runner's average speed for the entire race. The total time is 320 seconds (5 min 20 s) for the entire distance of 1600 meters. The runner's average speed is 1600 meters divided by 320 seconds, or 5.0 meters per second.

READING TiP
The root of *instantaneous* is *instant*, meaning "moment."

INVESTIGATE Speed and Distance

How does design affect speed?

Cars are built in different shapes. How does the shape of the car affect the way it moves? Design your own car, and see how fast it can go.

DESIGN YOUR OWN EXPERIMENT

PROCEDURE

1. Use the clay, film container lids, and toothpicks to design a car that rolls when it is pushed. The car should have a total mass of 150 g or less.

2. Using any or all of the other materials, design an experiment to measure and compare the speed of your car with the speed of someone else's car. Your experiment should be designed so that the design of the car is the only variable being tested. Write up your procedure.

3. Perform the experiment using your car and another student's car. Record the data you need to calculate the speed of both cars.

4. Calculate the speed of each car, and record which car went faster.

WHAT DO YOU THINK?

- What were the constants in your experiment?
- How would you improve your design if you were to repeat the experiment?

SKILL FOCUS
Designing experiments

MATERIALS
- clay
- film container lids
- toothpicks
- beam balance
- board
- books
- string
- straw
- scissors
- stopwatch

TIME
20 minutes

Distance-Time Graphs

A convenient way to show the motion of an object is by using a graph that plots the distance the object has traveled against time. This type of graph, called a distance-time graph, shows how speed relates to distance and time. You can use a distance-time graph to see how both distance and speed change with time.

The distance-time graph on page 21 tracks the changing motion of a zebra. At first the zebra looks for a spot to graze. Its meal is interrupted by a lion, and the zebra starts running to escape.

In a distance-time graph, time is on the horizontal axis, or *x*-axis, and distance is on the vertical axis, or *y*-axis.

❶ As an object moves, the distance it travels increases with time. This can be seen as a climbing, or rising, line on the graph.

❷ A flat, or horizontal, line shows an interval of time where the speed is zero meters per second.

❸ Steeper lines show intervals where the speed is greater than intervals with less steep lines.

You can use a distance-time graph to determine the speed of an object. The steepness, or slope, of the line is calculated by dividing the change in distance by the change in time for that time interval.

> **REMINDER**
> The *x*-axis and *y*-axis are arranged as shown:

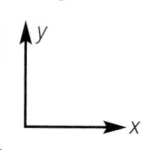

Calculating Speed from a Graph

▶ **Sample Problem**

How fast is the zebra walking during the first 20 seconds?

What do you know?	Reading from the graph: At time = 0 s, distance = 0 m. At time = 20 s, distance = 40 m.
What do you want to find out?	speed
Write the formula:	$S = \dfrac{d}{t}$
Substitute into the formula:	$S = \dfrac{40 \text{ m} - 0 \text{ m}}{20 \text{ s} - 0 \text{ s}}$
Calculate and simplify:	$S = \dfrac{40 \text{ m}}{20 \text{ s}} = 2 \text{ m/s}$
Check that your units agree:	Unit is m/s. Unit of speed is m/s. Units agree.
Answer:	$S = 2$ m/s

▶ **Practice the Math**

1. What is the speed of the zebra during the 20 s to 40 s time interval?
2. What is the speed of the zebra during the 40 s to 60 s interval?

Distance-Time Graph

A zebra's speed will change throughout the day, especially if a hungry lion is nearby. You can use a distance-time graph to compare the zebra's speed over different time intervals.

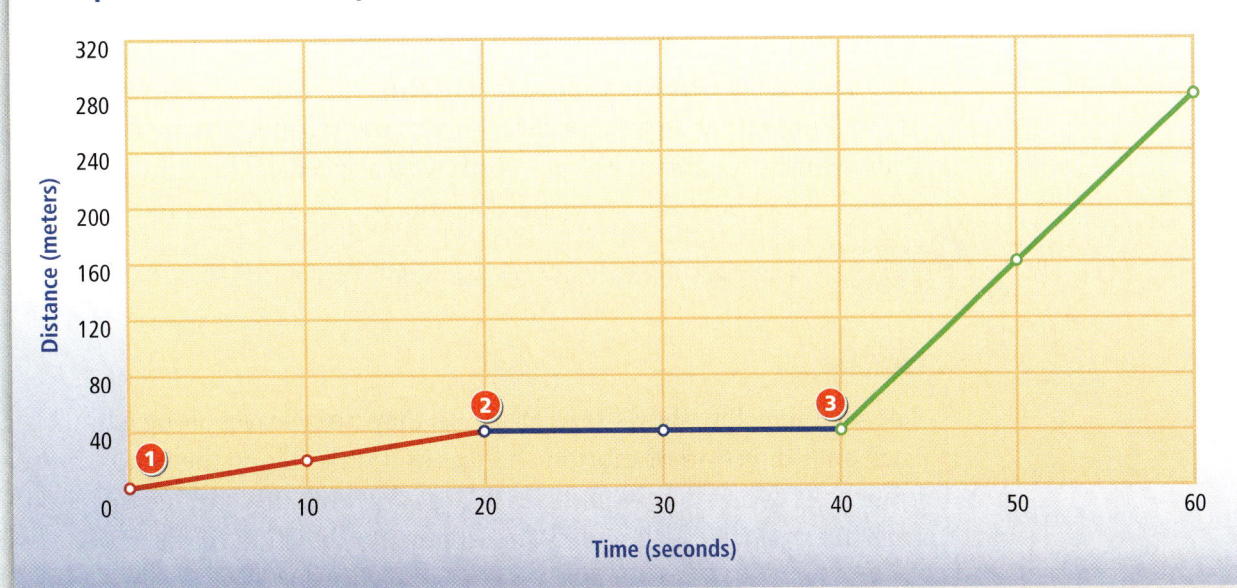

(1) When the zebra is walking, its distance from its starting point increases. You can see this motion on the graph as a climbing line.

(2) When the zebra stops to graze, it no longer changes its distance from the starting point. Time, however, continues to pass. Therefore, the graph shows a flat, or horizontal, line.

(3) As soon as the zebra notices the lion, it stops grazing and starts to run for its life. The zebra is covering a greater distance in each time interval than it was before the chase started, so the line is steeper.

READING VISUALS How do the distances change over each 10-second time interval?

Chapter 1: Motion 21 C

Velocity includes speed and direction.

Sometimes the direction of motion is as important as its speed. In large crowds, for example, you probably always try to walk in the same direction the crowd is moving and at the same speed. If you walk in even a slightly different direction, you can bump into other people. In a crowd, in other words, you try to walk with the same velocity as the people around you. **Velocity** is a speed in a specific direction. If you say you are walking east at a speed of three meters per second, you are describing your velocity. A person walking north with a speed of three meters per second would have the same speed as you do, but not the same velocity.

CHECK YOUR READING   What is velocity? Give an example of a velocity.

Velocity

The picture below shows several ants as they carry leaves along a branch. Each ant's direction of motion changes as it walks along the bends of the branch. As the arrows indicate, each ant is moving in a specific direction. Each ant's velocity is shown by the length and direction of the arrow. A longer arrow means a greater speed in the direction the arrow is pointing. In this picture, for example, the ant moving up the branch is traveling more slowly than the ant moving down the branch.

To determine the velocity of an ant as it carries a leaf, you need to know both its speed and its direction. A change in either speed or direction results in a change in velocity. For example, the velocity of an ant changes if it slows down but continues moving in the same direction. Velocity also changes if the ant continues moving at the same speed but changes direction.

Velocity is an example of a vector. A **vector** is a quantity that has both size and direction. Speed is not a vector because speed is a measure of how fast or slow an object moves, not which direction it moves in. Velocity, however, has a size—the speed—and a direction, so it is a vector quantity.

READING TIP

Green arrows show velocity.

A longer arrow indicates a faster speed than a shorter arrow. The direction of the arrow indicates the direction of motion.

ant moving slowly upward

ant moving quickly downward

INFER How does this ant's velocity compare with those of the other ants?

C 22 Unit: Motion and Forces

Velocity Versus Speed

Because velocity includes direction, it is possible for two objects to have the same speed but different velocities. If you traveled by train to visit a friend, you might go 30 kilometers per hour (km/h) north on the way there and 30 km/h south on the way back. Your speed is the same both going and coming back, but your velocity is different because your direction of motion has changed.

Another difference between speed and velocity is the way the average is calculated. Your average speed depends on the total distance you have traveled. The average velocity depends on the total distance you are from where you started. Going north, your average speed would be 30 km/h, and your average velocity would be 30 km/h north. After the round-trip ride, your average traveling speed would still be 30 km/h. Your average velocity, however, would be 0 km/h because you ended up exactly where you started.

INFER How do the speeds and velocities of these trains compare?

CHECK YOUR READING Use a Venn diagram to compare and contrast speed and velocity.

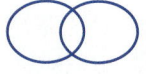

1.2 Review

KEY CONCEPTS

1. How is speed related to distance and time?
2. How would decreasing the time it takes you to run a certain distance affect your speed?
3. What two things do you need to know to describe the velocity of an object?

CRITICAL THINKING

4. **Compare** Amy and Ellie left school at the same time. Amy lives farther away than Ellie, but she and Ellie arrived at their homes at the same time. Compare the girls' speeds.
5. **Calculate** Carlos lives 100 m away from his friend's home. What is his average speed if he reaches his friend's home in 50 s?

CHALLENGE

6. **Synthesize** If you watch a train go by at 20 m/s, at what speed will the people sitting on the train be moving relative to you? Would someone walking toward the back of the train have a greater or lesser speed relative to you? Explain.

Chapter 1: **Motion** 23

MATH in SCIENCE

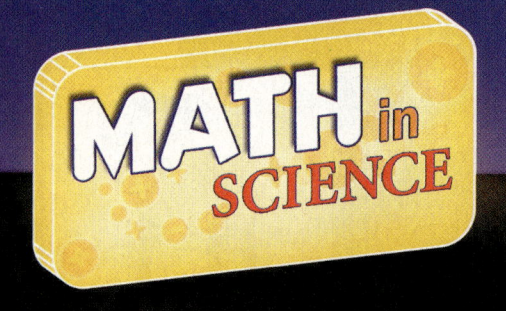

SKILL: WORKING WITH UNITS

MATH TUTORIAL
CLASSZONE.COM
Click on Math Tutorial for more help with units and rates.

Time, Distance, and Speed

If someone tells you the store is "five" from the school, you would probably ask, "Five what? Five meters? Five blocks?" You typically describe a distance using standard units of measurement, such as meters, miles, or kilometers. By using units, you help other people understand exactly what your measurement means.

When you work with a formula, the numbers that you substitute into the formula have units. When you calculate with a number, you also calculate with the unit associated with that number.

Example

A cheetah runs at a speed of 30 meters per second. How long does the cheetah take to run 90 meters?

The formula for time in terms of speed and distance is

$$\text{time} = \frac{\text{distance}}{\text{Speed}} \qquad t = \frac{d}{s}$$

(1) Start by substituting the numbers into the formula. Include the units with the numbers.

$$t = \frac{90 \text{ m}}{30 \text{ m/s}}$$

(2) When the units or calculations include fractions, write out the units as fractions as well:

$$t = \frac{90 \text{ m}}{\frac{30 \text{ m}}{\text{s}}}$$

(3) Do the calculation and simplify the units by cancellation:

$$t = 90 \text{ m} \cdot \frac{\text{s}}{30 \text{ m}} = \frac{90}{30} \cdot \frac{\text{m} \cdot \text{s}}{\text{m}} = 3 \cdot \frac{\cancel{\text{m}} \cdot \text{s}}{\cancel{\text{m}}} = 3 \text{ s}$$

ANSWER 3 seconds

Note that the answer has a unit of time. Use the units to check that your answer is reasonable. An answer that is supposed to have a unit of time, for example, should not have a unit of distance.

Answer the following questions.

1. How long would it take an object traveling 12 m/s to go 60 m? What unit of time is your answer in?

2. If a car travels 60 km/h, how long would it take the car to travel 300 km? What unit of time is your answer in?

3. If a man walks 3 miles in 1 hour, what is his speed? What unit of speed is your answer in? (Use the formula on page 18.)

CHALLENGE Show that the formula *distance = speed • time* has a unit for distance on both sides of the equal sign.

A cheetah can reach a speed of 30 meters per second, but only in short bursts.

24 Unit: Motion and Forces

1.3 Acceleration measures how fast velocity changes.

KEY CONCEPT

◀ **BEFORE, you learned**
- Speed describes how far an object travels in a given time
- Velocity is a measure of the speed and direction of motion

▶ **NOW, you will learn**
- How acceleration is related to velocity
- How to calculate acceleration

VOCABULARY

acceleration p. 25

THINK ABOUT

How does velocity change?

The photograph at right shows the path that a bouncing ball takes. The time between each image of the ball is the same during the entire bounce. Is the ball moving the same distance in each time interval? Is the ball moving the same direction in each time interval?

OUTLINE

Remember to use the blue and red headings in this chapter to help you make notes on acceleration.

I. Main idea
   A. Supporting idea
      1. Detail
      2. Detail
   B. Supporting idea

Speed and direction can change with time.

When you throw a ball into the air, it leaves your hand at a certain speed. As the ball rises, it slows down. Then, as the ball falls back toward the ground, it speeds up again. When the ball hits the ground, its direction of motion changes and it bounces back up into the air. The speed and direction of the ball do not stay the same as the ball moves. The ball's velocity keeps changing.

You can find out how much an object's position changes during a certain amount of time if you know its velocity. In a similar way, you can measure how an object's velocity changes with time. The rate at which velocity changes with time is called **acceleration**. Acceleration is a measure of how quickly the velocity is changing. If velocity does not change, there is no acceleration.

CHECK YOUR READING   What is the relationship between velocity and acceleration?

Chapter 1: Motion 25

The word *acceleration* is commonly used to mean "speeding up." In physics, however, acceleration refers to any change in velocity. A driver slowing down to stop at a light is accelerating. A runner turning a corner at a constant speed is also accelerating because the direction of her velocity is changing as she turns.

Like velocity, acceleration is a vector, which means it has both size and direction. The direction of the acceleration determines whether an object will slow down, speed up, or turn.

READING TIP

Orange arrows are used to show acceleration.

Remember that green arrows show velocity.

A longer arrow means greater acceleration or velocity.

① **Acceleration in the Same Direction as Motion** When the acceleration is in the same direction as the object is moving, the speed of the object increases. The car speeds up.

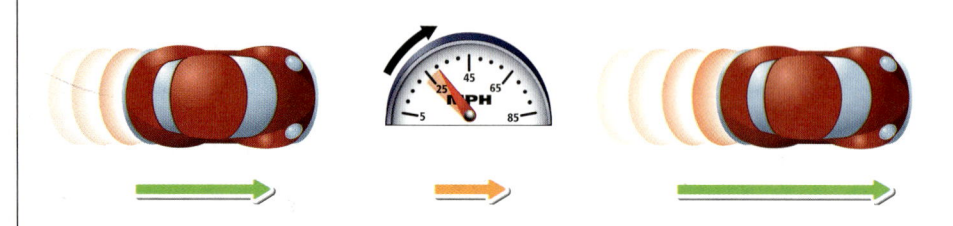

② **Acceleration in the Opposite Direction of Motion** When the acceleration is opposite to the motion, the speed of the object decreases. The car slows down. Slowing down is also called negative acceleration.

③ **Acceleration at a Right Angle to Motion** When the acceleration is at a right angle to the motion, the direction of motion changes. The car changes the direction in which it is moving by some angle, but its speed does not change.

CHECK YOUR READING How does acceleration affect velocity? Give examples.

C 26 Unit: Motion and Forces

INVESTIGATE Acceleration

When does an object accelerate?

PROCEDURE

1. Use the template and materials to construct an acceleration measuring tool.
2. Hold the tool in your right hand so that the string falls over the 0 m/s² mark. Move the tool in the direction of the arrow. Try to produce both positive and negative acceleration without changing the direction of motion.
3. With the arrow pointing ahead of you, start to walk. Observe the motion of the string while you increase your speed.
4. Repeat step 3, but this time observe the string while slowing down.
5. Repeat step 3 again, but observe the string while walking at a steady speed.

WHAT DO YOU THINK?
- When could you measure an acceleration?
- What was the largest acceleration (positive or negative) that you measured?

CHALLENGE If you moved the acceleration measuring tool backward, how would the measuring scale change?

SKILL FOCUS
Measuring

MATERIALS
- template for tool
- cardboard
- scissors
- glue
- piece of string
- weight

TIME
30 minutes

Acceleration can be calculated from velocity and time.

Suppose you are racing a classmate. In one second, you go from standing still to running at six meters per second. In the same time, your classmate goes from standing still to running at three meters per second. How does your acceleration compare with your classmate's acceleration? To measure acceleration, you need to know how velocity changes with time.

- The change in velocity can be found by comparing the initial velocity and the final velocity of the moving object.
- The time interval over which the velocity changed can be measured.

In one second, you increase your velocity by six meters per second, and your friend increases her velocity by three meters per second. Because your velocity changes more, you have a greater acceleration during that second of time than your friend does. Remember that acceleration measures the change in velocity, not velocity itself. As long as your classmate increases her current velocity by three meters per second, her acceleration will be the same whether she is going from zero to three meters per second or from three to six meters per second.

Chapter 1: **Motion** 27

Calculating Acceleration

If you know the starting velocity of an object, the final velocity, and the time interval during which the object changed velocity, you can calculate the acceleration of the object. The formula for acceleration is shown below.

$$\text{acceleration} = \frac{\text{final velocity} - \text{initial velocity}}{\text{time}}$$

$$a = \frac{v_{final} - v_{initial}}{t}$$

Remember that velocity is expressed in units of meters per second. The standard units for acceleration, therefore, are meters per second over time, or meters per second per second. This is simplified to meters per second squared, which is written as m/s^2.

As the girl in the photograph at left sleds down the sandy hill, what happens to her velocity? At the bottom of the hill, her velocity will be greater than it was at the top. You can calculate her average acceleration down the hill if you know her starting and ending velocities and how long it took her to get to the bottom. This calculation is shown in the sample problem below.

REMINDER

Remember that velocity is the speed of the object in a particular direction.

Calculating Acceleration

Sample Problem

Ama starts sliding with a velocity of 1 m/s. After 3 s, her velocity is 7 m/s. What is Ama's acceleration?

What do you know? initial velocity = 1 m/s, final velocity = 7 m/s, time = 3 s

What do you want to find out? acceleration

Write the formula: $a = \frac{v_{final} - v_{initial}}{t}$

Substitute into the formula: $a = \frac{7 \text{ m/s} - 1 \text{ m/s}}{3 \text{ s}}$

Calculate and simplify: $a = \frac{6 \text{ m/s}}{3 \text{ s}} = 2 \frac{\text{m/s}}{\text{s}} = 2 \text{ m/s}^2$

Check that your units agree: $\frac{\text{m/s}}{\text{s}} = \frac{\text{m}}{\text{s}} \cdot \frac{1}{\text{s}} = \frac{\text{m}}{\text{s}^2}$

Unit of acceleration is m/s^2. Units agree.

Answer: $a = 2 \text{ m/s}^2$

Practice the Math

1. A man walking at 0.5 m/s accelerates to a velocity of 0.6 m/s in 1 s. What is his acceleration?

2. A train traveling at 10 m/s slows down to a complete stop in 20 s. What is the acceleration of the train?

The sledder's final velocity was greater than her initial velocity. If an object is slowing down, on the other hand, the final velocity is less than the initial velocity. Suppose a car going 10 meters per second takes 2 seconds to stop for a red light. In this case, the initial velocity is 10 m/s and the final velocity is 0 m/s. The formula for acceleration gives a negative answer, –5 m/s². The negative sign indicates a negative acceleration—that is, an acceleration that decreases the velocity.

RESOURCE CENTER
CLASSZONE.COM
Learn more about acceleration.

CHECK YOUR READING What would be true of the values for initial velocity and final velocity if the acceleration were zero?

Acceleration over Time

Even a very small positive acceleration can lead to great speeds if an object accelerates for a long enough period. In 1998, NASA launched the *Deep Space 1* spacecraft. This spacecraft tested a new type of engine—one that gave the spacecraft an extremely small acceleration. The new engine required less fuel than previous spacecraft engines. However, the spacecraft needed a great deal of time to reach its target velocity.

The acceleration of the *Deep Space 1* spacecraft is less than 2/10,000 of a meter per second per second (0.0002 m/s²). That may not seem like much, but over 20 months, the spacecraft could increase its speed by 4500 meters per second (10,000 mi/h).

By carefully adjusting both the amount and the direction of the acceleration of *Deep Space 1*, scientists were able to control its flight path. In 2001, the spacecraft successfully flew by a comet, sending back images from about 230 million kilometers (140 million mi) away.

APPLY What makes the new engine technology used by *Deep Space 1* more useful for long-term missions than for short-term ones?

Chapter 1: **Motion** 29

Velocity-Time Graphs

Velocity-time graphs and distance-time graphs are related. This is because the distance an object travels depends on its velocity. Compare the velocity-time graph on the right with the distance-time graph below it.

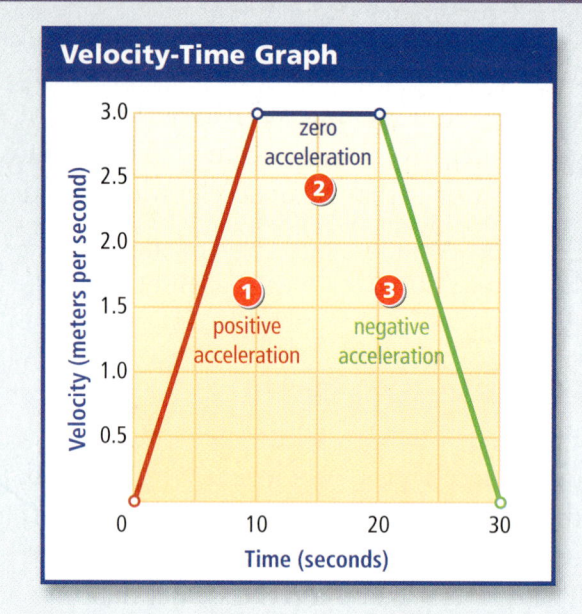

Velocity-Time Graph

Velocity (meters per second) vs. Time (seconds)

- ② zero acceleration
- ① positive acceleration
- ③ negative acceleration

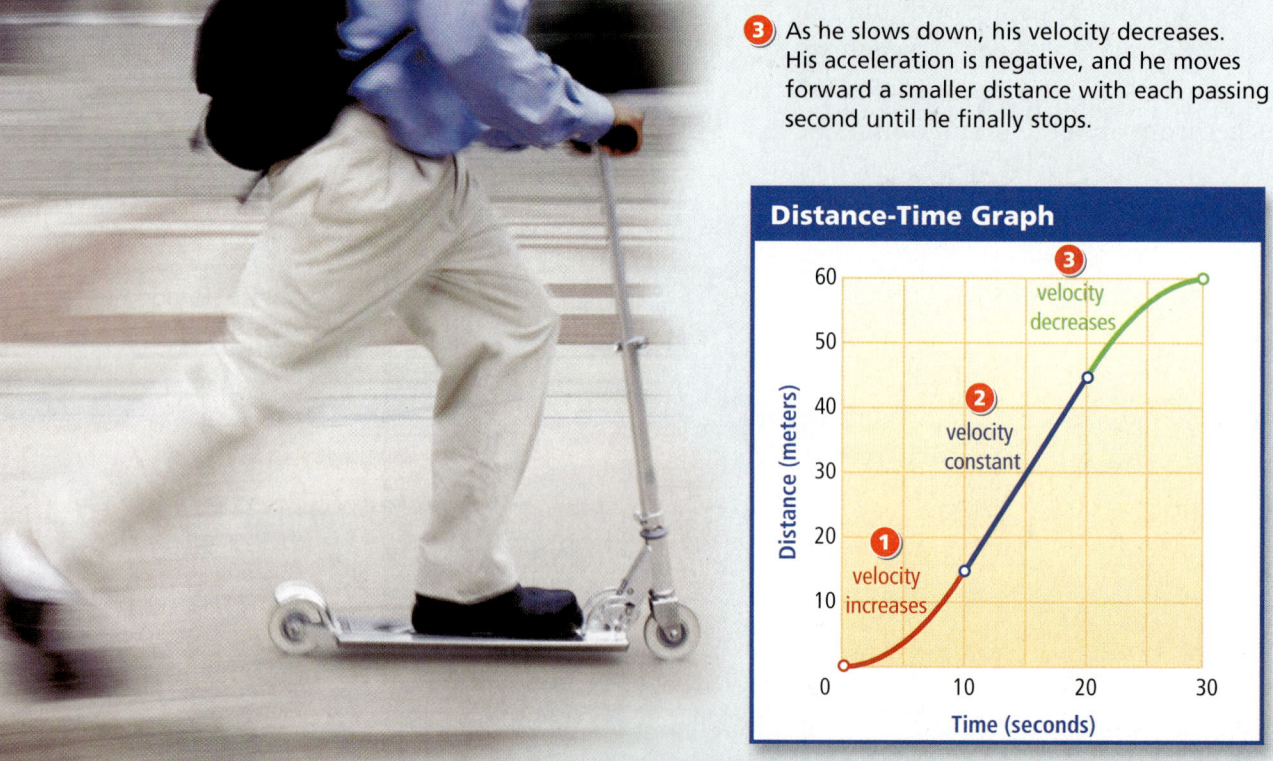

① As the student starts to push the scooter, his velocity increases. His acceleration is positive, so he moves forward a greater distance with each second that passes.

② He coasts at a constant velocity. Because his velocity does not change, he has no acceleration, and he continues to move forward the same distance each second.

③ As he slows down, his velocity decreases. His acceleration is negative, and he moves forward a smaller distance with each passing second until he finally stops.

Distance-Time Graph

Distance (meters) vs. Time (seconds)

- ③ velocity decreases
- ② velocity constant
- ① velocity increases

READING VISUALS What velocity does the student have after five seconds? About how far has he moved in that time?

30 Unit: Motion and Forces

Velocity-Time Graphs

Acceleration, like position and velocity, can change with time. Just as you can use a distance-time graph to understand velocity, you can use a velocity-time graph to understand acceleration. Both graphs tell you how something is changing over time. In a velocity-time graph, time is on the horizontal axis, or x-axis, and velocity is on the vertical axis, or y-axis.

The two graphs on page 30 show a velocity-time graph and a distance-time graph of a student riding on a scooter. He first starts moving and speeds up. He coasts, and then he slows down to a stop.

① The rising line on the velocity-time graph shows where the acceleration is positive. The steeper the line, the greater the acceleration. The distance-time graph for the same interval is curving upward more and more steeply as the velocity increases.

② The flat line on the velocity-time graph shows an interval of no acceleration. The distance-time graph has a straight line during this time, since the velocity is not changing.

③ The falling line on the velocity-time graph shows where the acceleration is negative. The same interval on the distance-time graph shows a curve that becomes less and less steep as the velocity decreases. Notice that the overall distance still increases.

Velocity-time graphs and distance-time graphs can provide useful information. For example, scientists who study earthquakes create these graphs in order to study the up-and-down and side-to-side movement of the ground during an earthquake. They produce the graphs from instruments that measure the acceleration of the ground.

SIMULATION CLASSZONE.COM

Explore how changing the acceleration of an object changes its motion.

CHECK YOUR READING What does a flat line on a velocity-time graph represent?

1.3 Review

KEY CONCEPTS

1. What measurements or observations tell you that a car is accelerating?
2. If an object accelerates in the same direction in which it is moving, how is its speed affected?
3. What measurements do you need in order to calculate acceleration?

CRITICAL THINKING

4. **Calculate** A car goes from 20 m/s to 30 m/s in 10 seconds. What is its acceleration?
5. **Infer** Two runners start a race. After 2 seconds, they both have the same velocity. If they both started at the same time, how do their average accelerations compare?

CHALLENGE

6. **Analyze** Is it possible for an object that has a constant negative acceleration to change the direction in which it is moving? Explain why or why not.

Chapter 1: Motion 31

CHAPTER INVESTIGATION

Acceleration and Slope

OVERVIEW AND PURPOSE When a downhill skier glides down a mountain without using her ski poles, her velocity increases and she experiences acceleration. How would gliding down a hill with a greater slope affect her acceleration? In this investigation you will
- calculate the acceleration of an object rolling down two ramps of different slopes
- determine how the slope of the ramp affects the acceleration of the object

Problem *Write It Up*

How does the slope of a ramp affect the acceleration of an object rolling down the ramp?

Hypothesize *Write It Up*

Write a hypothesis to explain how changing the slope of the ramp will affect acceleration. Your hypothesis should take the form of an "If . . . , then . . . , because . . ." statement.

Procedure

1. Make a data table like the one shown on the sample notebook page.

2. Make a ramp by laying two meter sticks side by side. Leave a small gap between the meter sticks.

3. Use masking tape as shown in the photograph to join the meter sticks. The marble should be able to roll freely along the groove.

4. Set up your ramp on a smooth, even surface, such as a tabletop. Raise one end of the ramp on top of one of the books. The other end of the ramp should remain on the table.

5. Make a finish line by putting a piece of tape on the tabletop 30 cm from the bottom of the ramp. Place a ruler just beyond the finish line to keep your marble from rolling beyond your work area.

MATERIALS
- 2 meter sticks
- masking tape
- marble
- 2 paperback books
- ruler
- stopwatch
- calculator

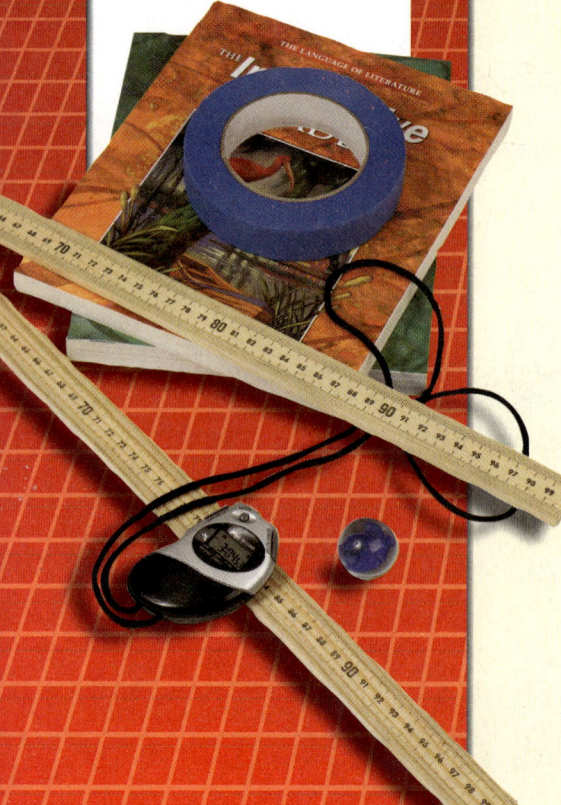

6. Test your ramp by releasing the marble from the top of the ramp. Make sure that the marble rolls freely. Do not push on the marble.

7. Release the marble and measure the time it takes for it to roll from the release point to the end of the ramp. Record this time under Column A for trial 1.

8. Release the marble again from the same point, and record the time it takes the marble to roll from the end of the ramp to the finish line. Record this time in Column B for trial 1. Repeat and record three more trials.

9. Raise the height of the ramp by propping it up with both paperback books. Repeat steps 7 and 8.

Observe and Analyze

1. **RECORD OBSERVATIONS** Draw the setup of your procedures. Be sure your data table is complete.

2. **IDENTIFY VARIABLES AND CONSTANTS** Identify the variables and constants in the experiment. List them in your notebook.

3. **CALCULATE**

    Average Time For ramps 1 and 2, calculate and record the average time it took for the marble to travel from the end of the ramp to the finish line.

    Final Velocity For ramps 1 and 2, calculate and record V_{final} using the formula below.

    $$v_{final} = \frac{\text{distance from end of ramp to finish line}}{\text{average time from end of ramp to finish line}}$$

    Acceleration For ramps 1 and 2, calculate and record acceleration using the formula below. (Hint: Speed at the release of the marble is 0 m/s.)

    $$a = \frac{v_{final} - v_{initial} \text{ (speed at release)}}{\text{average time from release to bottom of ramp}}$$

Conclude

1. **COMPARE** How did the acceleration of the marble on ramp 1 compare with the acceleration of the marble on ramp 2?

2. **INTERPRET** Answer the question posed in the problem.

3. **ANALYZE** Compare your results with your hypothesis. Do your data support your hypothesis?

4. **EVALUATE** Why was it necessary to measure how fast the marble traveled from the end of the ramp to the finish line?

5. **IDENTIFY LIMITS** What possible limitations or sources of error could have affected your results? Why was it important to perform four trials for each measurement of speed?

INVESTIGATE Further

CHALLENGE Design your own experiment to determine how the marble's mass affects its acceleration down a ramp.

Acceleration and Slope

Problem How does the slope of a ramp affect the acceleration of an object rolling down the ramp?

Hypothesize

Observe and Analyze

Table 1. Times for Marble to Travel down Ramp

Height of Ramp (cm)	Trial Number	Column A Time from release to end of ramp	Column B Time from end of ramp to finish line
Ramp 1	1		
	2		
	3		
	4		
	Totals		
		Average	Average

Chapter 1: **Motion** 33

Chapter Review

the BIG idea

The motion of an object can be described and predicted.

CONTENT REVIEW
CLASSZONE.COM

KEY CONCEPTS SUMMARY

1.1 An object in motion changes position.

Position is measured from a reference point.

Motion is measured relative to an observer.

start — finish

VOCABULARY
position p. 9
reference point p. 10
motion p. 11

1.2 Speed measures how fast position changes.

- Speed is how fast positions change with time.
- Velocity is speed in a specific direction.

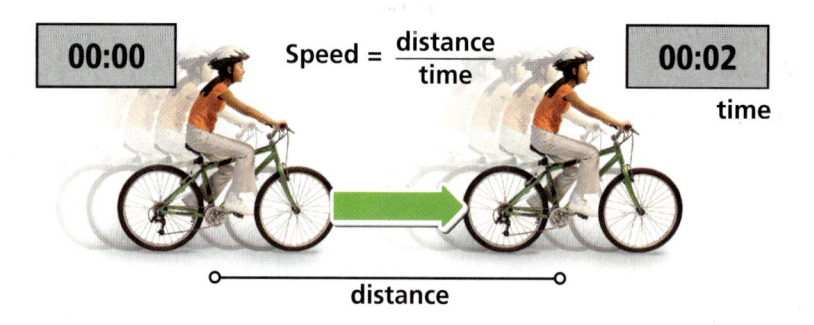

$$\text{Speed} = \frac{\text{distance}}{\text{time}}$$

00:00   00:02 time
distance

VOCABULARY
speed p. 16
velocity p. 22
vector p. 22

1.3 Acceleration measures how fast velocity changes.

$$\text{acceleration} = \frac{\text{final velocity} - \text{initial velocity}}{\text{time}}$$

initial velocity   acceleration   final velocity

VOCABULARY
acceleration p. 25

Unit: Motion and Forces

Reviewing Vocabulary

Copy and complete the chart below. If the left column is blank, give the correct term. If the right column is blank, give a brief description.

Term	Description
1.	speed in a specific direction
2.	a change of position over time
3. speed	
4.	an object's location
5. reference point	
6.	the rate at which velocity changes over time
7.	a quantity that has both size and direction

Reviewing Key Concepts

Multiple Choice *Choose the letter of the best answer.*

8. A position describes an object's location compared to
   a. its motion
   b. a reference point
   c. its speed
   d. a vector

9. Maria walked 2 km in half an hour. What was her average speed during her walk?
   a. 1 km/h
   b. 2 km/h
   c. 4 km/h
   d. 6 km/h

10. A vector is a quantity that has
    a. speed
    b. acceleration
    c. size and direction
    d. position and distance

11. Mary and Keisha run with the same constant speed but in opposite directions. The girls have
    a. the same position
    b. different accelerations
    c. different speeds
    d. different velocities

12. A swimmer increases her speed as she approaches the end of the pool. Her acceleration is
    a. in the same direction as her motion
    b. in the opposite direction of her motion
    c. at right angles to her motion
    d. zero

13. A cheetah can go from 0 m/s to 20 m/s in 2 s. What is the cheetah's acceleration?
    a. 5 m/s^2
    b. 10 m/s^2
    c. 20 m/s^2
    d. 40 m/s^2

14. Jon walks for a few minutes, then runs for a few minutes. During this time, his average speed is
    a. the same as his final speed
    b. greater than his final speed
    c. less than his final speed
    d. zero

15. A car traveling at 40 m/s slows down to 20 m/s. During this time, the car has
    a. no acceleration
    b. positive acceleration
    c. negative acceleration
    d. constant velocity

Short Answer *Write a short answer to each question.*

16. Suppose you are biking with a friend. How would your friend describe your relative motion as he passes you?

17. Describe a situation where an object has a changing velocity but constant speed.

18. Give two examples of an accelerating object.

Chapter 1: **Motion** 35

Thinking Critically

Use the following graph to answer the next three questions.

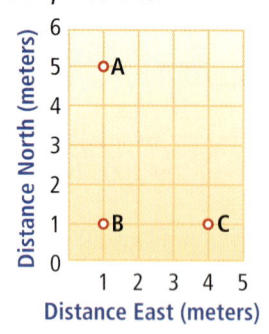

19. **OBSERVE** Describe the location of point A. Explain what you used as a reference point for your location.

20. **COMPARE** Copy the graph into your notebook. Draw two different paths an object could take when moving from point B to point C. How do the lengths of these two paths compare?

21. **ANALYZE** An object moves from point A to point C in the same amount of time that another object moves from point B to point C. If both objects traveled in a straight line, which one had the greater speed?

Read the following paragraph and use the information to answer the next three questions.

In Aesop's fable of the tortoise and the hare, a slow-moving tortoise races a fast-moving hare. The hare, certain it can win, stops to take a long nap. Meanwhile, the tortoise continues to move toward the finish line at a slow but steady speed. When the hare wakes up, it runs as fast as it can. Just as the hare is about to catch up to the tortoise, however, the tortoise wins the race.

22. **ANALYZE** How does the race between the tortoise and the hare show the difference between average speed and instantaneous speed?

23. **MODEL** Assume the racetrack was 100 meters long and the race took 40 minutes. Create a possible distance-time graph for both the tortoise and the hare.

24. **COMPARE** If the racetrack were circular, how would the tortoise's speed be different from its velocity?

25. **APPLY** How might a person use a floating stick to measure the speed at which a river flows?

26. **CONNECT** Describe a frame of reference other than the ground that you might use to measure motion. When would you use it?

Using Math Skills in Science

27. José skated 50 m in 10 s. What was his speed?

28. Use the information in the photograph below to calculate the speed of the ant as it moves down the branch.

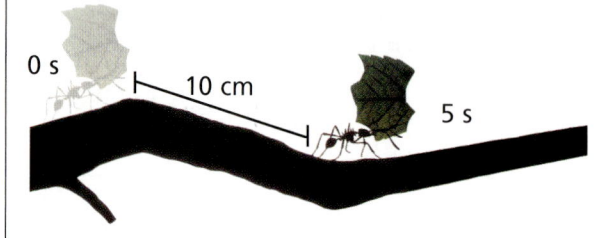

29. While riding her bicycle, Jamie accelerated from 7 m/s to 2 m/s in 5 s. What was her acceleration?

the BIG idea

30. **PREDICT** Look back at the picture at the beginning of the chapter on pages 6–7. Predict how the velocity of the roller coaster will change in the next moment.

31. **WRITE** A car is traveling east at 40 km/h. Use this information to predict where the car will be in one hour. Discuss the assumptions you made to reach your conclusion and the factors that might affect it.

UNIT PROJECTS

If you are doing a unit project, make a folder for your project. Include in your folder a list of the resources you will need, the date on which the project is due, and a schedule to keep track of your progress. Begin gathering data.

Standardized Test Practice

Interpreting Graphs

The graph below is a distance-time graph showing a 50-meter race.

Distance-Time Graph of Foot Race

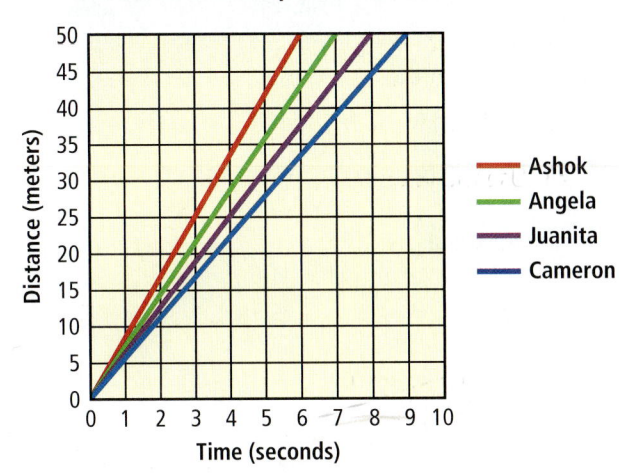

(Lines shown: Ashok, Angela, Juanita, Cameron)

Study the graph and then answer the questions that follow.

1. Which runner reached the finish line first?
   a. Ashok
   b. Angela
   c. Juanita
   d. Cameron

2. How far did Juanita run in the first 4 seconds of the race?
   a. 5 m
   b. 15 m
   c. 25 m
   d. 35 m

3. How much time passed between the time Angela finished the race and Cameron finished the race?
   a. 1 s
   b. 2 s
   c. 3 s
   d. 4 s

4. Which of the following setups would you use to calculate Angela's average speed during the race?
   a. $\dfrac{7 \text{ m}}{50 \text{ s}}$
   b. $\dfrac{7 \text{ s}}{50 \text{ m}}$
   c. $\dfrac{50 \text{ m}}{6 \text{ s}}$
   d. $\dfrac{50 \text{ m}}{7 \text{ s}}$

5. What can you say about the speed of all of the runners?
   a. They ran at the same speed.
   b. They ran at a steady pace but at different speeds.
   c. They sped up as they reached the finish line.
   d. They slowed down as they reached the finish line.

Extended Response

Answer the two questions below in detail.

6. Suppose you are biking. What is the difference between your speed at any given moment during your bike ride and your average speed for the entire ride? Which is easier to measure? Why?

7. Suppose you are riding your bike along a path that is also used by in-line skaters. You pass a skater, and another biker passes you, both going in the same direction you're going. You pass a family having a picnic on the grass. Describe your motion from the points of view of the skater, the other biker, and the family.

Chapter 1: **Motion** 37

CHAPTER 2 Forces

the BIG idea

Forces change the motion of objects in predictable ways.

What must happen for a team to win this tug of war?

Key Concepts

SECTION 2.1
Forces change motion.
Learn about inertia and Newton's first law of motion.

SECTION 2.2
Force and mass determine acceleration.
Learn to calculate force through Newton's second law of motion.

SECTION 2.3
Forces act in pairs.
Learn about action forces and reaction forces through Newton's third law of motion.

SECTION 2.4
Forces transfer momentum.
Learn about momentum and how it is affected in collisions.

Internet Preview

CLASSZONE.COM

Chapter 2 online resources: Content Review, two Simulations, four Resource Centers, Math Tutorial, Test Practice

38 Unit: Motion and Forces

EXPLORE the BIG idea

Popping Ping-Pong Balls

Place a Ping-Pong ball in front of a flexible ruler. Carefully bend the ruler back and then release it. Repeat with a golf ball or another heavier ball. Be sure to bend the ruler back to the same spot each time. Predict which ball will go farther.

Observe and Think
Which ball went farther? Why?

Take Off!

Blow up a balloon and hold the end closed. Tape the balloon to the top of a small model car. (Put the tape around the car and the balloon.) Predict what will happen to the car when you set it down and let go of the balloon. Will the car move? If so, in what direction? How far?

Observe and Think
What happened to the car? If you try it again, will you get the same results? What do you think explains the motion of the car?

Internet Activity: Forces

Go to **ClassZone.com** to change the sizes and directions of forces on an object. Predict how the object will move, and then run the simulation to see if you were right.

Observe and Think What happens if two forces are applied to the object in the same direction? in opposite directions? Why?

NSTA scilinks.org SCLINKS
Forces Code: MDL005

Chapter 2: Forces 39

CHAPTER 2
Getting Ready to Learn

CONCEPT REVIEW

- All motion is relative to the position and motion of an observer.
- An object's motion is described by position, direction, speed, and acceleration.
- Velocity and acceleration can be measured.

VOCABULARY REVIEW

velocity p. 22
vector p. 22
acceleration p. 25
mass *See Glossary.*

CONTENT REVIEW
CLASSZONE.COM
Review concepts and vocabulary.

TAKING NOTES

COMBINATION NOTES

When you read about a concept for the first time, take notes in two ways. First, make an outline of the information. Then make a sketch to help you understand and remember the concept. Use arrows to show the direction of forces.

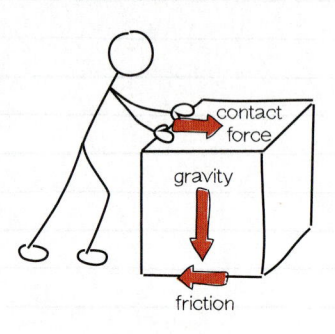

VOCABULARY STRATEGY

Think about a vocabulary term as a **magnet word** diagram. Write the other terms or ideas related to that term around it.

See the Note-Taking Handbook on pages R45–R51.

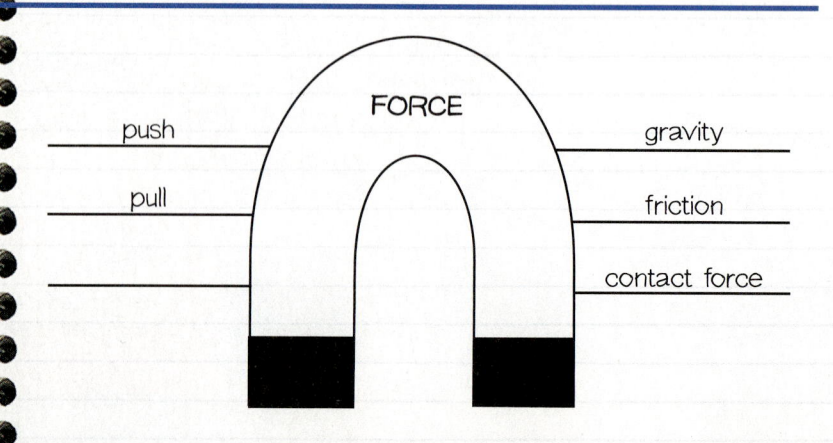

SCIENCE NOTEBOOK

NOTES

Types of forces
- contact force
- gravity
- friction

forces on a box being pushed
- contact force
- gravity
- friction

FORCE
- push
- pull
- gravity
- friction
- contact force

40 Unit: Motion and Forces

KEY CONCEPT
2.1 Forces change motion.

BEFORE, you learned
- The velocity of an object is its change in position over time
- The acceleration of an object is its change in velocity over time

NOW, you will learn
- What a force is
- How unbalanced forces change an object's motion
- How Newton's first law allows you to predict motion

VOCABULARY

force p. 41
net force p. 43
Newton's first law p. 45
inertia p. 46

EXPLORE Changing Motion

How can you change an object's motion?

PROCEDURE

1. Choose an object from the materials list and change its motion in several ways, from
   - not moving to moving
   - moving to not moving
   - moving to moving faster
   - moving to moving in a different direction

2. Describe the actions used to change the motion.

3. Experiment again with another object. First, decide what you will do; then predict how the motion of the object will change.

MATERIALS
- quarter
- book
- tennis ball
- cup
- feather

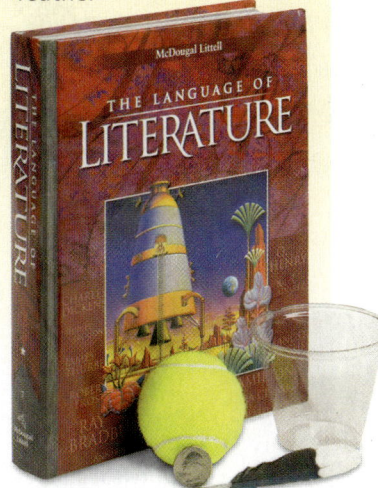

WHAT DO YOU THINK?
In step 3, how were you able to predict the motion of the object?

A force is a push or a pull.

Think about what happens during an exciting moment at the ballpark. The pitcher throws the ball across the plate, and the batter hits it high up into the stands. A fan in the stands catches the home-run ball. In this example, the pitcher sets the ball in motion, the batter changes the direction of the ball's motion, and the fan stops the ball's motion. To do so, each must use a **force**, or a push or a pull.

You use forces all day long to change the motion of objects in your world. You use a force to pick up your backpack, to open or close a car door, and even to move a pencil across your desktop. Any time you change the motion of an object, you use a force.

> **REMINDER**
> Motion is a change in position over time.

Types of Forces

A variety of forces are always affecting the motion of objects around you. For example, take a look at how three kinds of forces affect the skater in the photograph on the left.

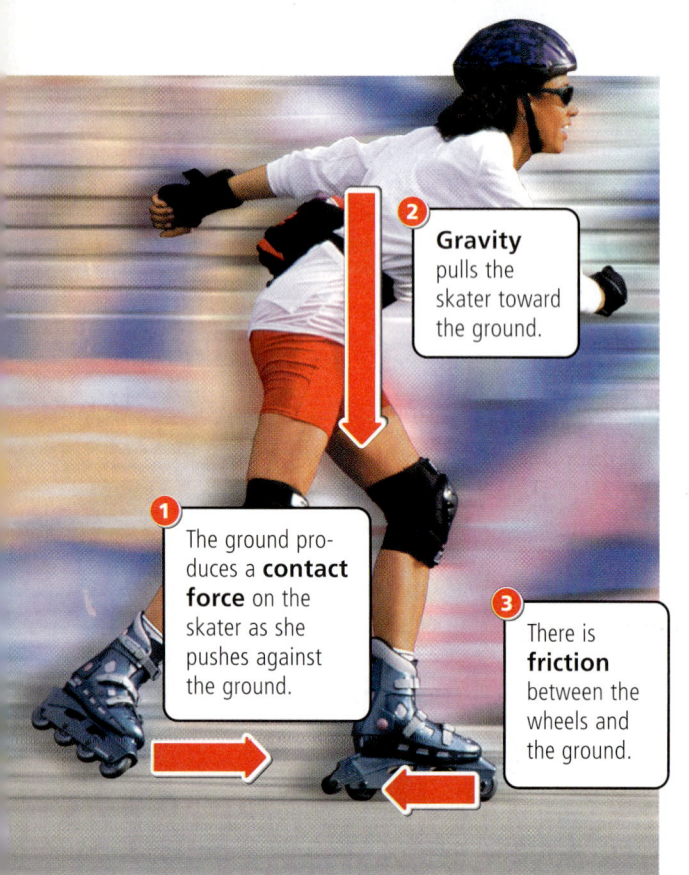

❶ Contact Force When one object pushes or pulls another object by touching it, the first object is applying a contact force to the second. The skater applies a contact force as she pushes against the ground. The ground applies a contact force that pushes the skater forward.

❷ Gravity Gravity is the force of attraction between two masses. Earth's gravity is pulling on the skater, holding her to the ground. The strength of the gravitational force between two objects depends on their masses. For example, the pull between you and Earth is much greater than the pull between you and a book.

❸ Friction Friction is a force that resists motion between two surfaces that are pressed together. Friction between the surface of the ground and the wheels of the skates exerts a force that resists the skater's forward motion.

You will learn more about gravity and friction in Chapter 3. In this chapter, most of the examples involve contact forces. You use contact forces constantly. Turning a page, pulling a chair, using a pencil to write, pushing your hair away from your eyes—all involve contact forces.

❶ The ground produces a **contact force** on the skater as she pushes against the ground.

❷ **Gravity** pulls the skater toward the ground.

❸ There is **friction** between the wheels and the ground.

CHECK YOUR READING — What is a contact force? Give an example of a contact force.

Size and Direction of Forces

Like velocity, force is a vector. That means that force has both size and direction. For example, think about what happens when you try to make a shot in basketball. To get the ball through the hoop, you must apply the right amount of force to the ball and aim the force in the right direction. If you use too little force, the ball will not reach the basket. If you use too much force, the ball may bounce off the backboard and into your opponent's hands.

In the illustrations in this book, red arrows represent forces. The direction of an arrow shows the direction of the force, and the length of the arrow indicates the amount, or size, of the force. A blue box represents mass.

READING TIP

Red arrows are used to show force.

Blue boxes show mass.

42 Unit: Motion and Forces

Balanced and Unbalanced Forces

Considering the size and the direction of all the forces acting on an object allows you to predict changes in the object's motion. The overall force acting on an object when all the forces are combined is called the **net force.**

If the net force on an object is zero, the forces acting on the object are balanced. Balanced forces have the same effect as no force at all. That is, the motion of the object does not change. For example, think about the forces on the basketball when one player attempts a shot and another blocks it. In the photograph below on the left, the players are pushing on the ball with equal force but from opposite directions. The forces on the ball are balanced, and so the ball does not move.

Only an unbalanced force can change the motion of an object. If one of the basketball players pushes with greater force than the other player, the ball will move in the direction that player is pushing. The motion of the ball changes because the forces on the ball become unbalanced.

It does not matter whether the ball started at rest or was already moving. Only an unbalanced force will change the ball's motion.

COMBINATION NOTES
Make an outline and draw a diagram about balanced and unbalanced forces.

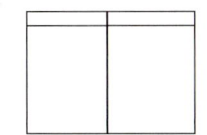

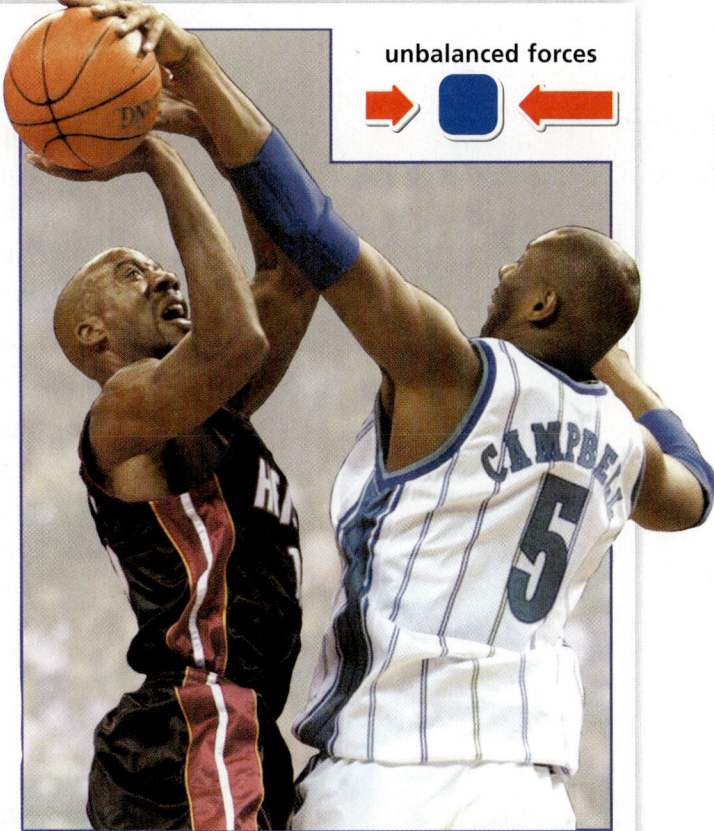

balanced forces

unbalanced forces

READING VISUALS **COMPARE** Compare the net force on the balls in these two photographs. Which photograph shows a net force of zero?

Chapter 2: **Forces** 43

Forces on Moving Objects

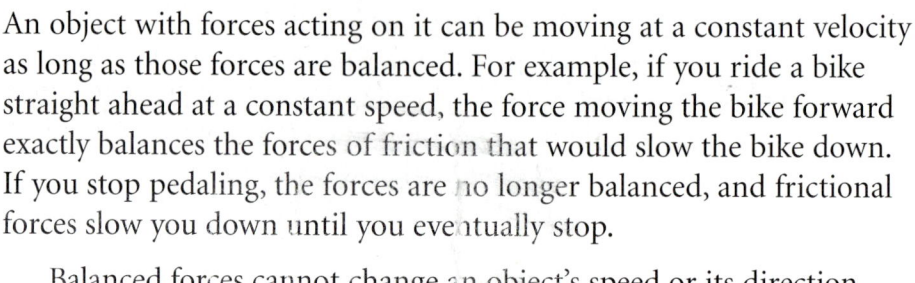

An object with forces acting on it can be moving at a constant velocity as long as those forces are balanced. For example, if you ride a bike straight ahead at a constant speed, the force moving the bike forward exactly balances the forces of friction that would slow the bike down. If you stop pedaling, the forces are no longer balanced, and frictional forces slow you down until you eventually stop.

Balanced forces cannot change an object's speed or its direction. An unbalanced force is needed to change an object's motion.

- To increase the speed of your bike, you may exert more forward force by pedaling harder or changing gears. The net force moves the bike ahead faster.
- To turn your bike, you apply an unbalanced force by leaning to one side and turning the handlebars.
- To stop the bike, you use the extra force of friction that your bike brakes provide.

CHECK YOUR READING What happens to a moving object if all the forces on it are balanced? Which sentence above tells you?

Newton's first law relates force and motion.

In the mid-1600s, the English scientist Sir Isaac Newton studied the effects of forces on objects. He formulated three laws of motion that are still helping people describe and predict the motions of objects today. Newton's ideas were built on those of other scientists, in particular the Italian scientist Galileo Galilei (gal-uh-LEE-oh gal-uh-LAY). Both Galileo and Newton overturned thinking that had been accepted since the times of the ancient Greek philosophers.

The ancient Greeks had concluded that it was necessary to apply a continuous force to keep an object in motion. For example, if you set a book on a table and give the book a quick push, the book slides a short way and then stops. To keep the book moving, you need to keep pushing it. The Greeks reasoned that the book stops moving because you stop pushing it.

Galileo's Thought Experiment

In the early 1600s, Galileo suggested a different way of interpreting such observations. He imagined a world without friction and conducted a thought experiment in this ideal world. He concluded that, in the absence of friction, a moving object will continue moving even if there is no force acting on it. In other words, it does not take a force to keep an object moving; it takes a force—friction—to stop an object that is already moving.

READING TIP
Contrast the last sentence of this paragraph with the last sentence of the previous paragraph.

Objects at rest and objects in motion both resist changes in motion. That is, objects at rest tend to stay at rest, and objects that are moving tend to continue moving unless a force acts on them. Galileo reasoned there was no real difference between an object that is moving at a constant velocity and an object that is standing still. An object at rest is simply an object with zero velocity.

CHECK YOUR READING How were Galileo's ideas about objects in motion different from the ideas of the ancient Greeks?

Newton's First Law

Newton restated Galileo's conclusions as his first law of motion. **Newton's first law** states that objects at rest remain at rest, and objects in motion remain in motion with the same velocity, unless acted upon by an unbalanced force. You can easily observe the effects of unbalanced forces, both on the ball at rest and the ball in motion, in the pictures below.

Newton's First Law

Objects at rest remain at rest, and objects in motion remain in motion with the same velocity, unless acted upon by an unbalanced force.

An Object at Rest

An object at rest **(the ball)** remains at rest unless acted upon by an unbalanced force **(from the foot)**.

unbalanced force
object at rest

unbalanced force (from the foot) → object at rest (ball)

An Object in Motion

An object in motion **(the ball)** remains in motion with the same velocity, unless acted upon by an unbalanced force **(from the hand)**.

object in motion
unbalanced force

object in motion (ball) ← unbalanced force (from the hand)

READING VISUALS What will happen to the ball's motion in each picture? Why?

Chapter 2: **Forces** 45

You will find many examples of Newton's first law around you. For instance, if you throw a stick for a dog to catch, you are changing the motion of the stick. The dog changes the motion of the stick by catching it and by dropping it at your feet. You change the motion of a volleyball when you spike it, a tennis racket when you swing it, a paintbrush when you make a brush stroke, and an oboe when you pick it up to play or set it down after playing. In each of these examples, you apply a force that changes the motion of the object.

VOCABULARY
Make a magnet word diagram for *inertia* in your notebook.

Inertia

Inertia (ih-NUR-shuh) is the resistance of an object to a change in the speed or the direction of its motion. Newton's first law, which describes the tendency of objects to resist changes in motion, is also called the law of inertia. Inertia is closely related to mass. When you measure the mass of an object, you are also measuring its inertia. You know from experience that it is easier to push or pull an empty box than it is to push or pull the same box when it is full of books. Likewise, it is easier to stop or to turn an empty wagon than to stop or turn a wagon full of sand. In both of these cases, it is harder to change the motion of the object that has more mass.

INVESTIGATE Inertia

Which ball has more inertia?
Two balls have different masses and therefore different amounts of inertia. Use what you know about force and inertia to design an experiment that shows which ball has more inertia. Your procedure cannot include lifting the balls, weighing the balls, or touching the balls with your hands.

DESIGN YOUR OWN EXPERIMENT

SKILL FOCUS
Designing experiments

MATERIALS
- 2 balls of unknown masses
- string
- block
- meter stick

TIME
30 minutes

PROCEDURE

1. Figure out how to use the meter stick or other materials to compare the inertia of the two balls.
2. Write up your procedure.
3. Test your procedure.

WHAT DO YOU THINK?
- What were the results of your experiment? Did it work? Why or why not?
- What was the variable? What were the constants?
- How does your experiment demonstrate the property of inertia?

Unit: Motion and Forces

Inertia is the reason that people in cars need to wear seat belts. A moving car has inertia, and so do the riders inside it. When the driver applies the brakes, an unbalanced force is applied to the car. Normally, the bottom of the seat applies an unbalanced force—friction—which slows the riders down as the car slows. If the driver stops the car suddenly, however, this force is not exerted over enough time to stop the motion of the riders. Instead, the riders continue moving forward with most of their original speed because of their inertia.

RESOURCE CENTER
CLASSZONE.COM
Find out more about inertia.

1 As a car moves forward, the driver—shown here as a crash-test dummy—moves forward with the same velocity as the car.

2 When the driver hits the brakes, the car stops. If the stop is sudden and the driver is not wearing a seat belt, the driver keeps moving forward.

3 Finally, the windshield applies an unbalanced force that stops the driver's forward motion.

If the driver is wearing a seat belt, the seat belt rather than the windshield applies the unbalanced force that stops the driver's forward motion. The force from the seat belt is applied over a longer time, so the force causes less damage. In a collision, seat belts alone are sometimes not enough to stop the motion of drivers or passengers. Air bags further cushion people from the effects of inertia in an accident.

CHECK YOUR READING If a car makes a sudden stop, what happens to a passenger riding in the back seat who is not wearing a seat belt?

2.1 Review

KEY CONCEPTS

1. Explain the difference between balanced and unbalanced forces.
2. What is the relationship between force and motion described by Newton's first law?
3. What is inertia? How is the inertia of an object related to its mass?

CRITICAL THINKING

4. **Infer** Once a baseball has been hit into the air, what forces are acting upon it? How can you tell that any forces are acting upon the ball?
5. **Predict** A ball is at rest on the floor of a car moving at a constant velocity. What will happen to the ball if the car swerves suddenly to the left?

CHALLENGE

6. **Synthesize** What can the changes in an object's position tell you about the forces acting on that object? Describe an example from everyday life that shows how forces affect the position of an object.

Chapter 2: Forces 47

Think SCIENCE

SKILL: EVALUATING HYPOTHESES

Why Do These Rocks Slide?

In Death Valley, California, there is a dry lakebed known as Racetrack Playa. Rocks are mysteriously moving across the ground there, leaving tracks in the clay. These rocks can have masses as great as 320 kilograms (corresponding to 700 lb). No one has ever observed the rocks sliding, even though scientists have studied their tracks for more than 50 years. What force moves these rocks? Scientists do not yet know.

A playa was once a shallow lake. The water in it evaporated, leaving a dry lakebed.

▶ Observations

Scientists made these observations.

a. Some rocks left trails that are almost parallel.
b. Some rocks left trails that took abrupt turns.
c. Sometimes a small rock moved while a larger rock did not.
d. Most of the trails are on level surfaces. Some trails run slightly uphill.
e. The temperature in that area sometimes drops below freezing.

This rock made a U-turn.

▶ Hypotheses

Scientists formed these hypotheses about how the rocks move.

- When the lakebed gets wet, it becomes so slippery that gravity causes the rocks to slide.
- When the lakebed gets wet, it becomes so slippery that strong winds can move the rocks.
- When the lakebed gets wet and cold, a sheet of ice forms and traps the rocks. Strong winds move both the ice sheet and the trapped rocks.

▶ Evaluate Each Hypothesis

On Your Own Think about whether all the observations support each hypothesis. Some facts may rule out some hypotheses. Some facts may neither support nor contradict a particular hypothesis.

As a Group Decide which hypotheses are reasonable. Discuss your thinking and conclusions in a small group, and list the reasonable hypotheses.

CHALLENGE What further observations would you make to test any of these hypotheses? What information would each observation add?

RESOURCE CENTER
CLASSZONE.COM
Learn more about the moving rocks.

48 Unit: Motion and Forces

KEY CONCEPT
2.2 Force and mass determine acceleration.

BEFORE, you learned
- Mass is a measure of inertia
- The motion of an object will not change unless the object is acted upon by an unbalanced force

NOW, you will learn
- How Newton's second law relates force, mass, and acceleration
- How force works in circular motion

VOCABULARY
Newton's second law p. 50
centripetal force p. 54

EXPLORE Acceleration
How are force and acceleration related?

PROCEDURE

1. Tie a paper clip to each end of a long string. Hook two more paper clips to one end.
2. Hold the single paper clip in the middle of a smooth table; hang the other end of the string over the edge. Let go and observe.
3. Add one more paper clip to the hanging end and repeat the experiment. Observe what happens. Repeat.

MATERIALS
- paper clips
- string

WHAT DO YOU THINK?
- What happened each time that you let go of the single paper clip?
- Explain the relationship between the number of hanging paper clips and the motion of the paper clip on the table.

Newton's second law relates force, mass, and acceleration.

Suppose you are eating lunch with a friend and she asks you to pass the milk container. You decide to slide it across the table to her. How much force would you use to get the container moving? You would probably use a different force if the container were full than if the container were empty.

If you want to give two objects with different masses the same acceleration, you have to apply different forces to them. You must push a full milk container harder than an empty one to slide it over to your friend in the same amount of time.

REMINDER
Acceleration is a change in velocity over time.

CHECK YOUR READING What three concepts are involved in Newton's second law?

Chapter 2: Forces 49

Newton's Second Law

SIMULATION
CLASSZONE.COM

Explore Newton's second law.

Newton studied how objects move, and he noticed some patterns. He observed that the acceleration of an object depends on the mass of the object and the size of the force applied to it. **Newton's second law** states that the acceleration of an object increases with increased force and decreases with increased mass. The law also states that the direction in which an object accelerates is the same as the direction of the force.

The photographs below show Newton's second law at work in a supermarket. The acceleration of each shopping cart depends upon two things:

- the size of the force applied to the shopping cart
- the mass of the shopping cart

In the left-hand photograph, the force on the cart changes, while the mass of the cart stays the same. In the right-hand photograph, the force on the cart stays the same, while the mass of the cart varies. Notice how mass and force affect acceleration.

Newton's Second Law

The acceleration of an object increases with increased force, decreases with increased mass, and is in the same direction as the force.

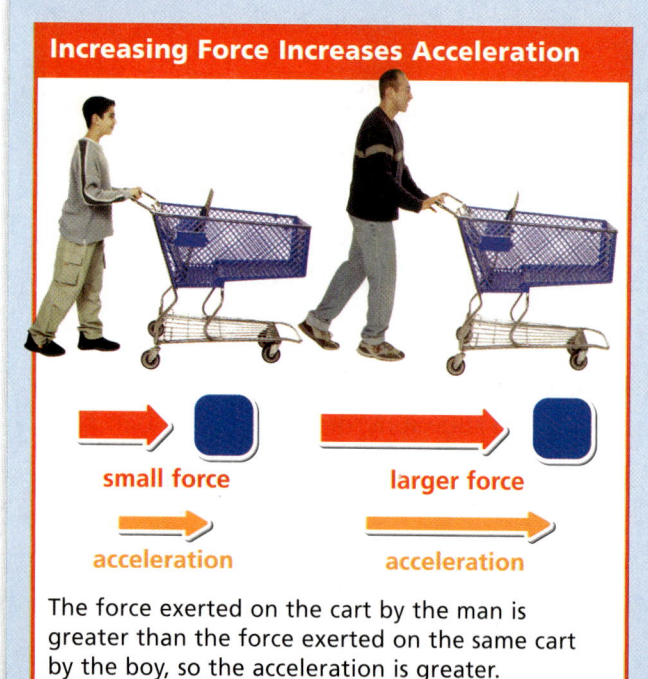

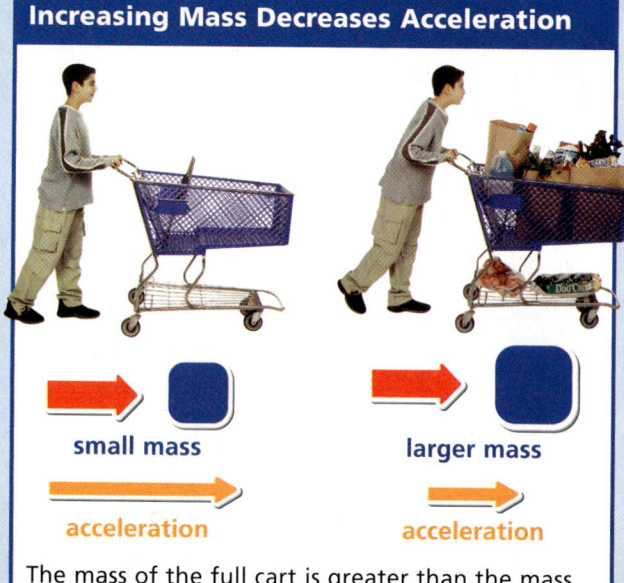

Increasing Force Increases Acceleration

small force → acceleration

larger force → acceleration

The force exerted on the cart by the man is greater than the force exerted on the same cart by the boy, so the acceleration is greater.

Increasing Mass Decreases Acceleration

small mass → acceleration

larger mass → acceleration

The mass of the full cart is greater than the mass of the empty cart, and the boy is pushing with the same force, so the acceleration is less.

READING VISUALS What do the arrows in these diagrams show?

50 Unit: Motion and Forces

Force Equals Mass Times Acceleration

Newton was able to describe the relationship of force, mass, and acceleration mathematically. You can calculate the force, the mass, or the acceleration if you know two of the three factors. The mathematical form of Newton's second law, stated as a formula, is

Force = mass · acceleration
F = ma

To use this formula, you need to understand the unit used to measure force. In honor of Newton's contribution to our understanding of force and motion, the standard unit of force is called the newton (N). Because force equals mass times acceleration, force is measured in units of mass (kilograms) times units of acceleration (meters per second per second). A newton is defined as the amount of force that it takes to accelerate one kilogram (1 kg) of mass one meter per second per second (1 m/s^2). So 1 N is the same as 1 kg · m/s^2.

> **REMINDER**
> *Meters per second per second* is the same as m/s^2, which can be read "meters per second squared."

CHECK YOUR READING If the same force is applied to two objects of different mass, which object will have the greater acceleration?

The mathematical relationship of force, mass, and acceleration allow you to solve problems about how objects move. If you know the mass of an object and the acceleration you want to achieve, you can use the formula to find the force you need to exert to produce that acceleration. Use Newton's second law to find the force that is needed to accelerate the shopping cart in the sample problem.

Calculating Force

▶ **Sample Problem**

What force is needed to accelerate a 10 kg shopping cart 3 m/s^2?

What do you know?   mass = 10 kg, acceleration = 3 m/s^2
What do you want to find out?   Force
Write the formula: F = ma
Substitute into the formula: F = 10 kg · 3 m/s^2
Calculate and simplify: F = 10 kg · $\frac{3m}{s^2}$ = 30 kg · m/s^2
Check that your units agree: Unit is kg · m/s^2.
   Unit of force is newton, which is also kg · m/s^2. Units agree.
Answer: F = 30 N

▶ **Practice the Math**

1. If a 5 kg ball is accelerating 1.2 m/s^2, what is the force on it?
2. A person on a scooter is accelerating 2 m/s^2. If the person has a mass of 50 kg, how much force is acting on that person?

This team of 20 people pulled a 72,000-kilogram (159,000 lb) Boeing 727 airplane 3.7 meters (12 ft) in 6.74 seconds.

The photograph above shows people who are combining forces to pull an airplane. Suppose you knew the mass of the plane and how hard the people were pulling. How much would the plane accelerate? The sample problem below shows how Newton's second law helps you calculate the acceleration.

Calculating Acceleration

Sample Problem

If a team pulls with a combined force of 9000 N on an airplane with a mass of 30,000 kg, what is the acceleration of the airplane?

What do you know? mass = 30,000 kg, force = 9000 N

What do you want to find out? acceleration

Rearrange the formula: $a = \dfrac{F}{m}$

Substitute into the formula: $a = \dfrac{9000 \text{ N}}{30,000 \text{ kg}}$

Calculate and simplify: $a = \dfrac{9000 \text{ N}}{30,000 \text{ kg}} = \dfrac{9000 \text{ kg} \cdot \text{m/s}^2}{30,000 \text{ kg}} = 0.3 \text{ m/s}^2$

Check that your units agree: Unit is m/s^2.
Unit for acceleration is m/s^2.
Units agree.

Answer: $a = 0.3 \text{ m/s}^2$

Practice the Math

1. Half the people on the team decide not to pull the airplane. The combined force of those left is 4500 N, while the airplane's mass is still 30,000 kg. What will be the acceleration?
2. A girl pulls a wheeled backpack with a force of 3 N. If the backpack has a mass of 6 kg, what is its acceleration?

Mass and Acceleration

Mass is also a variable in Newton's second law. If the same force acts on two objects, the object with less mass will have the greater acceleration. For instance, if you push a soccer ball and a bowling ball with equal force, the soccer ball will have a greater acceleration.

If objects lose mass, they can gain acceleration if the force remains the same. When a rocket is first launched, most of its mass is the fuel it carries. As the rocket burns fuel, it loses mass. As the mass continually decreases, the acceleration continually increases.

APPLY This NASA launch rocket accelerates with enough force to lift about 45 cars off the ground. As the rocket loses fuel, will it accelerate more or less? Why?

Calculating Mass

Sample Problem

A model rocket is accelerating at 2 m/s². The force on it is 1 N. What is the mass of the rocket?

What do you know? acceleration = 2 m/s², force = 1 N

What do you want to find out? mass

Rearrange the formula: $m = \dfrac{F}{a}$

Substitute into the formula: $m = \dfrac{1 \text{ N}}{2 \text{ m/s}^2}$

Calculate and simplify: $m = \dfrac{1 \text{ N}}{2 \text{ m/s}^2} = \dfrac{1 \text{ kg} \cdot \text{m/s}^2}{2 \text{ m/s}^2} = 0.5 \text{ kg}$

Check that your units agree: Unit is kg. Unit of mass is kg. Units agree.

Answer: m = 0.5 kg

Practice the Math

1. Another model rocket is accelerating at a rate of 3 m/s² with a force of 1 N. What is the mass of the rocket?
2. A boy pushes a shopping cart with a force of 10 N, and the cart accelerates 1 m/s². What is the mass of the cart?

Forces can change the direction of motion.

Usually, we think of a force as either speeding up or slowing down the motion of an object, but force can also make an object change direction. If an object changes direction, it is accelerating. Newton's second law says that if you apply a force to an object, the direction in which the object accelerates is the same as the direction of the force. You can change the direction of an object without changing its speed. For example, a good soccer player can control the motion of a soccer ball by applying a force that changes the ball's direction but not its speed.

CHECK YOUR READING How can an object accelerate when it does not change speed?

Chapter 2: Forces 53

INVESTIGATE Motion and Force

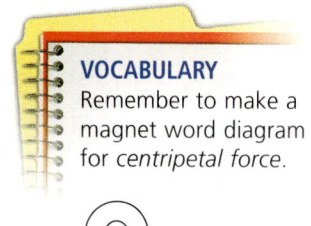

What affects circular motion?

PROCEDURE

1. Spread newspaper over your work surface. Place the paper plate down on the newspaper.

2. Practice rolling the marble around the edge of the plate until you can roll it around completely at least once.

3. Cut out a one-quarter slice of the paper plate. Put a dab of paint on the edge of the plate where the marble will leave it. Place the plate back down on the newspaper.

4. Hypothesize: How will the marble move once it rolls off the plate? Why?

5. Roll the marble all the way around the paper plate into the cut-away section and observe the resulting motion as shown by the trail of paint.

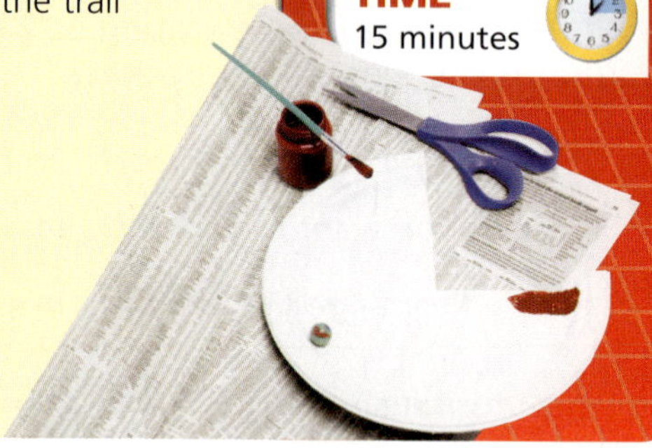

WHAT DO YOU THINK?
- Did your observations support your hypothesis?
- What forces affected the marble's motion after it left the plate?

CHALLENGE How will changing the speed at which you roll the marble change your results? Repeat the activity to test your prediction.

SKILL FOCUS
Hypothesizing

MATERIALS
- newspaper
- paper plate
- marble
- scissors
- poster paint
- paintbrush

TIME
15 minutes

VOCABULARY
Remember to make a magnet word diagram for *centripetal force*.

Centripetal Force

When you were younger, you may have experimented with using force to change motion. Perhaps you and a friend took turns swinging each other in a circle. If you remember this game, you may also remember that your arms got tired because they were constantly pulling your friend as your friend spun around. It took force to change the direction of your friend's motion. Without that force, your friend could not have kept moving in a circle.

Any force that keeps an object moving in a circle is known as a **centripetal force** (sehn-TRIHP-ih-tuhl). This force points toward the center of the circle. Without the centripetal force, the object would go flying off in a straight line. When you whirl a ball on a string, what keeps the ball moving in a circle? The force of the string turns the ball, changing the ball's direction of motion. When the string turns, so does the ball. As the string changes direction, the force from the string also changes direction. The force is always pointing along the string toward your hand, the center of the circle. The centripetal force on the whirling ball is the pull from the string. If you let go of the string, the ball would fly off in the direction it was headed when you let go.

CHECK YOUR READING How does centripetal force change the motion of an object?

54 Unit: Motion and Forces

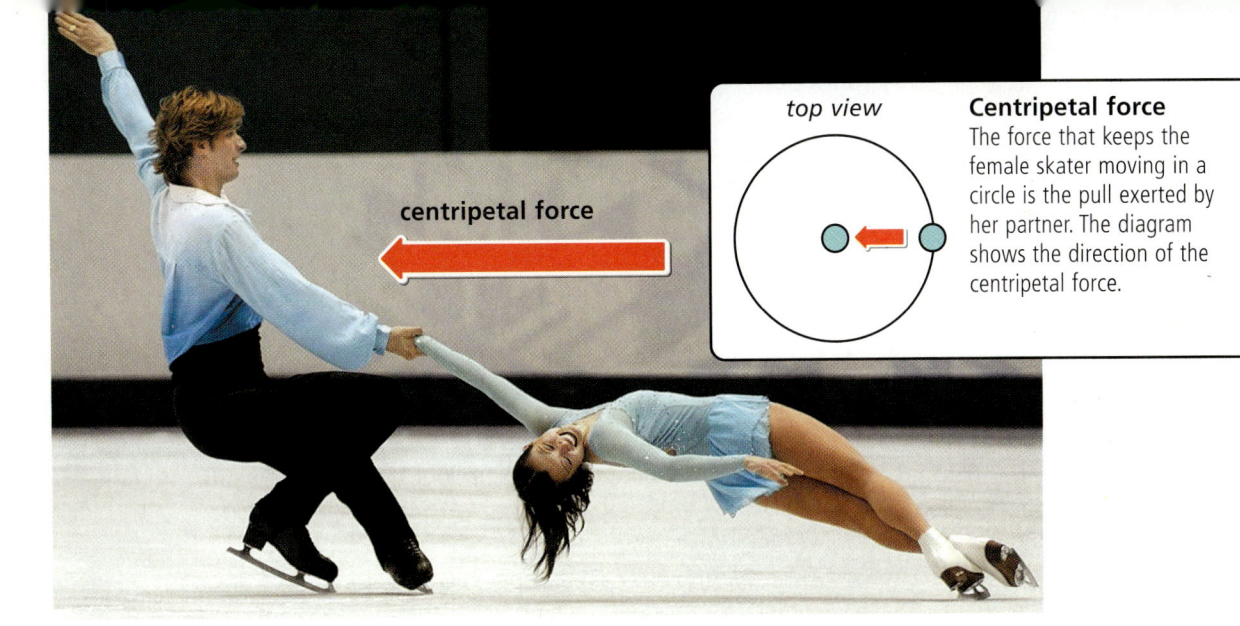

Centripetal force The force that keeps the female skater moving in a circle is the pull exerted by her partner. The diagram shows the direction of the centripetal force.

top view

centripetal force

Circular Motion and Newton's Second Law

Suppose the male skater shown above spins his partner faster. Her direction changes more quickly than before, so she accelerates more. To get more acceleration, he must apply more force. The same idea holds for a ball you whirl on a string. You have to pull harder on the string when you whirl the ball faster, because it takes more centripetal force to keep the ball moving at the greater speed.

You can apply the formula for Newton's second law even to an object moving in a circle. If you know the size of the centripetal force acting upon the object, you can find its acceleration. A greater acceleration requires a greater centripetal force. A more massive object requires a greater centripetal force to have the same circular speed as a less massive object. But no matter what the mass of an object is, if it moves in a circle, its force and acceleration are directed toward the center of the circle.

CHECK YOUR READING How does increasing the centripetal force on an object affect its acceleration?

2.2 Review

KEY CONCEPTS

1. If the force acting upon an object is increased, what happens to the object's acceleration?
2. How does the mass of an object affect its acceleration?
3. What force keeps an object moving in a circle? In what direction does this force act?

CRITICAL THINKING

4. **Infer** Use Newton's second law to determine how much force is being applied to an object that is traveling at a constant velocity.
5. **Calculate** What force is needed to accelerate an object 5 m/s² if the object has a mass of 10 kg?

CHALLENGE

6. **Synthesize** Carlos pushes a 3 kg box with a force of 9 N. The force of friction on the box is 3 N in the opposite direction. What is the acceleration of the box? **Hint:** Combine forces to find the net force.

Chapter 2: **Forces** 55

MATH in SCIENCE

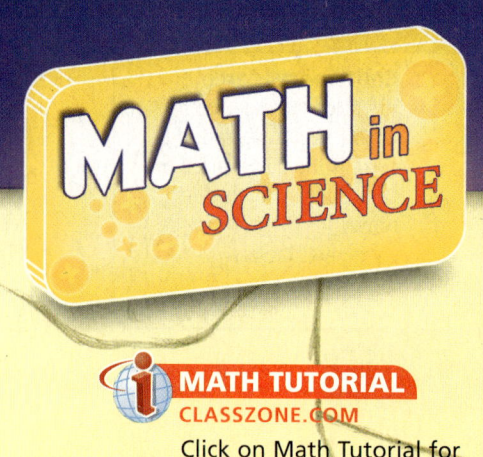

SKILL: USING SIGNIFICANT FIGURES

MATH TUTORIAL
CLASSZONE.COM
Click on Math Tutorial for more help with rounding decimals.

The AbioCor artificial heart, which has a mass of about 0.9 kg, is designed to fit entirely inside the human body.

Meaningful Numbers

A student doing a science report on artificial hearts reads that a certain artificial heart weighs about 2 pounds. The student then writes that the mass of the artificial heart is 0.907185 kilograms. Someone reading this report might think that the student knows the mass to a high precision, when actually he knows it only to one meaningful number.

When you make calculations, the number of digits to include in your answer depends in part on the number of meaningful digits, or significant figures, in the numbers you are working with.

Example

In an experiment to find acceleration, a scientist might record the following data.

Force = 3.1 N   mass = 1.450 kg

In this example, force is given to two significant figures, and mass is given to four significant figures.

(1) Use a calculator and the formula $a = F/m$ to find the acceleration. The display on the calculator shows

2.1379310345

(2) To determine how many of the digits in this answer are really meaningful, look at the measurement with the least number of significant figures. In this example, force is given to two significant figures. Therefore, the answer is meaningful only to two significant figures.

(3) Round the calculated number to two digits.

ANSWER acceleration = 2.1 m/s²

Answer the following questions.

For each pair of measurements, calculate the acceleration to the appropriate number of digits.

1. Force = 3.100 N   mass = 3.1 kg

2. Force = 2 N   mass = 4.2 kg

3. Force = 1.21 N   mass = 1.1000 kg

CHALLENGE Suppose a scientist measures a force of 3.25 N and a mass of 3.3 kg. She could round the force to two significant figures and then divide, or she could divide and then round the answer. Compare these two methods. Which method do you think is more accurate?

56 Unit: Motion and Forces

KEY CONCEPT
2.3 Forces act in pairs.

BEFORE, you learned
- A force is a push or a pull
- Increasing the force on an object increases the acceleration
- The acceleration of an object depends on its mass and the force applied to it

NOW, you will learn
- How Newton's third law relates action/reaction pairs of forces
- How Newton's laws work together

VOCABULARY

Newton's third law p. 57

THINK ABOUT

How do jellyfish move?

Jellyfish do not have much control over their movements. They drift with the current in the ocean. However, jellyfish do have some control over their up-and-down motion. By squeezing water out of its umbrella-like body, the jellyfish shown here applies a force in one direction to move in the opposite direction. If the water is forced downward, the jellyfish moves upward. How can a person or an object move in one direction by exerting a force in the opposite direction?

Newton's third law relates action and reaction forces.

COMBINATION NOTES
In your notebook, make an outline and draw a diagram about Newton's third law.

Newton made an important observation that explains the motion of the jellyfish. He noticed that forces always act in pairs. **Newton's third law** states that every time one object exerts a force on another object, the second object exerts a force that is equal in size and opposite in direction back on the first object. As the jellyfish contracts its body, it applies a downward force on the water. The water applies an equal force back on the jellyfish. It is this equal and opposite force on the jellyfish that pushes it up. This is similar to what happens when a blown-up balloon is released. The balloon pushes air out the end, and the air pushes back on the balloon and moves it forward.

CHECK YOUR READING What moves the jellyfish through the water?

Chapter 2: Forces 57

Action and Reaction Pairs

The force that is exerted on an object and the force that the object exerts back are known together as an action/reaction force pair. One force in the pair is called the action force, and the other is called the reaction force. For instance, if the jellyfish pushing on the water is the action force, the water pushing back on the jellyfish is the reaction force. Likewise, if the balloon pushing the air backward is the action force, the air pushing the balloon forward is the reaction force.

You can see many examples of action and reaction forces in the world around you. Here are three:

- You may have watched the liftoffs of the space shuttle on television. When the booster rockets carrying the space shuttle take off, their engines push fuel exhaust downward. The exhaust pushes back on the rockets, sending them upward.

- When you bang your toe into the leg of a table, the same amount of force that you exert on the table is exerted back on your toe.

- Action and reaction forces do not always result in motion. For example, if you press down on a table, the table resists the push with the same amount of force, even though nothing moves.

CHECK YOUR READING Identify the action/reaction forces in each example described above.

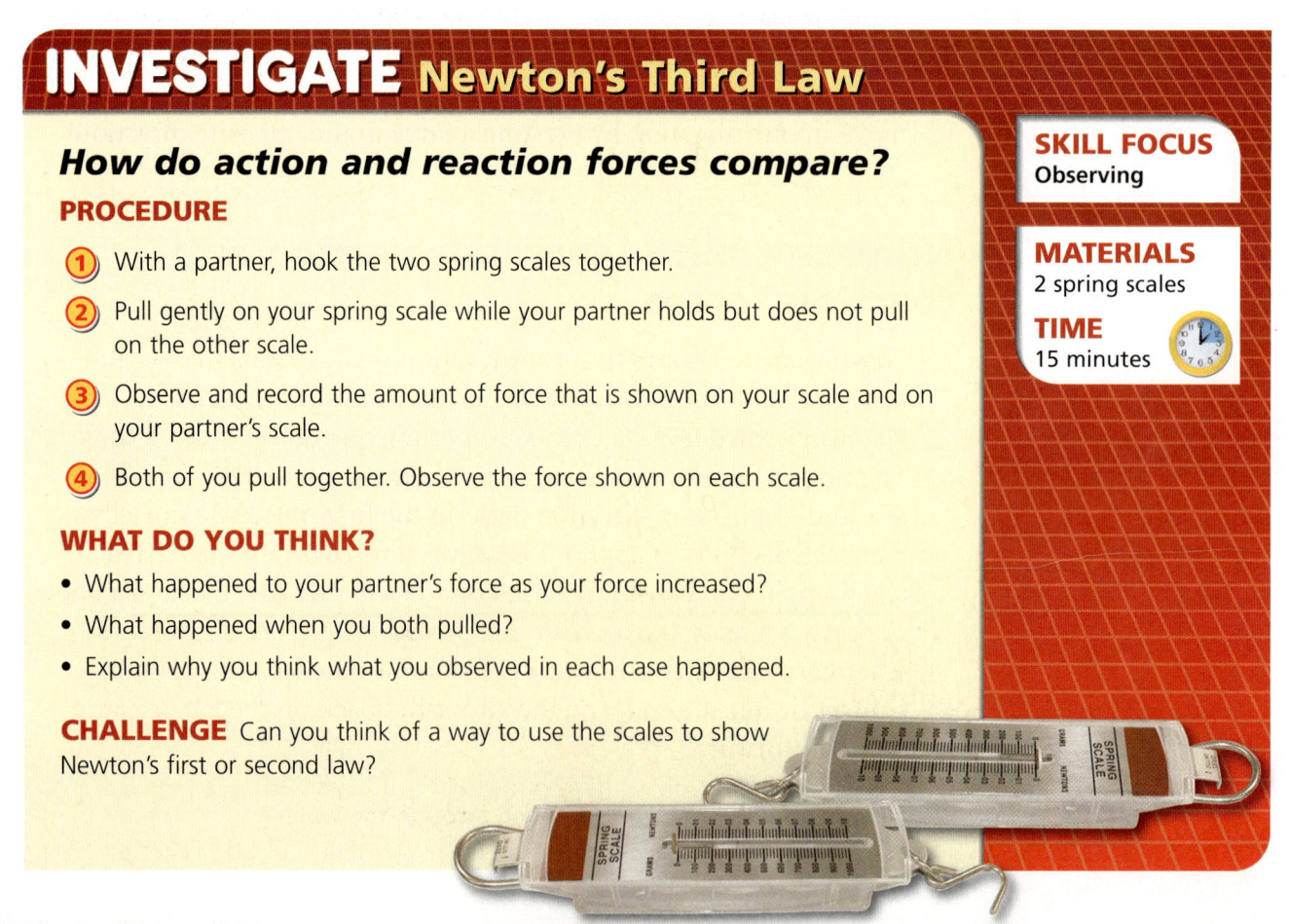

INVESTIGATE Newton's Third Law

How do action and reaction forces compare?

PROCEDURE

1. With a partner, hook the two spring scales together.
2. Pull gently on your spring scale while your partner holds but does not pull on the other scale.
3. Observe and record the amount of force that is shown on your scale and on your partner's scale.
4. Both of you pull together. Observe the force shown on each scale.

WHAT DO YOU THINK?
- What happened to your partner's force as your force increased?
- What happened when you both pulled?
- Explain why you think what you observed in each case happened.

CHALLENGE Can you think of a way to use the scales to show Newton's first or second law?

SKILL FOCUS
Observing

MATERIALS
2 spring scales

TIME
15 minutes

Action and Reaction Forces Versus Balanced Forces

Because action and reaction forces are equal and opposite, they may be confused with balanced forces. Keep in mind that balanced forces act on a single object, while action and reaction forces act on different objects.

Balanced Forces If you and a friend pull on opposite sides of a backpack with the same amount of force, the backpack doesn't move, because the forces acting on it are balanced. In this case, both forces are exerted on one object—the backpack.

Action and Reaction As you drag a heavy backpack across a floor, you can feel the backpack pulling on you with an equal amount of force. The action force and the reaction force are acting on two different things—one is acting on the backpack, and the other is acting on you.

The illustration below summarizes Newton's third law. The girl exerts an action force on the boy by pushing him. Even though the boy is not trying to push the girl, an equal and opposite reaction force acts upon the girl, causing her to move as well.

Newton's Third Law

When one object exerts a force on another object, the second object exerts an equal and opposite force on the first object.

1 One Skater Pushes

reaction force — action force

The action force from the girl sets the boy in motion.

2 Both Skaters Move

Even though the boy does not do anything, the reaction force from him sets the girl in motion as well.

READING VISUALS How does the direction of the force on the girl relate to her motion?

Newton's Three Laws of Motion

All three of Newton's laws work together to help describe how an object will move.

Newton's First Law

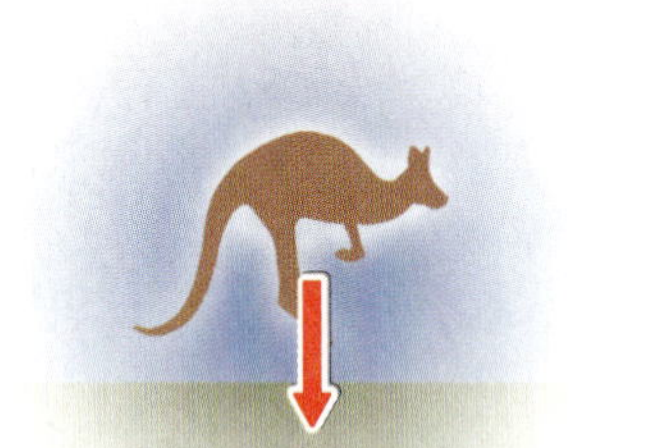

force of gravity

This kangaroo has jumped, setting itself in motion. If no other forces acted on it, the kangaroo would continue to move through the air with the same motion. Instead, the force of gravity will bring this kangaroo back to the ground.

Newton's Second Law

acceleration

The large kangaroo does not have as much acceleration as a less massive kangaroo would if it used the same force to jump. However, the more massive kangaroo can increase its acceleration by increasing the force of its jump.

Newton's Third Law

action force   reaction force

A kangaroo applies an action force on the ground with its powerful back legs. The reaction force from the ground can send the kangaroo as far as 8 meters (26 ft) through the air.

READING VISUALS What forces are involved in a kangaroo jump?

Common Name: Red kangaroo
Scientific Name: *Macropus rufus*
Home: Australia
Top Speed: 65 km/h (40 mi/h)
Maximum Leap: 8 m (26 ft)

AUSTRALIA

Newton's three laws describe and predict motion.

Newton's three laws can explain the motion of almost any object, including the motion of animals. The illustrations on page 60 show how all three of Newton's laws can be used to describe how kangaroos move. The three laws are not independent of one another; they are used together to explain the motion of objects.

You can use the laws of motion to explain how other animals move as well. For example, Newton's laws explain why a squid moves forward while squirting water out behind it. These laws also explain that a bird is exerting force when it speeds up to fly away or when it changes its direction in the air.

You can also use Newton's laws to make predictions about motion. If you know the force acting upon an object, then you can predict how that object's motion will change. For example, if you want to send a spacecraft to Mars, you must be able to predict exactly where Mars will be by the time the spacecraft reaches it. You must also be able to control the force on your spacecraft so that it will arrive at the right place at the right time.

Knowing how Newton's three laws work together can also help you win a canoe race. In order to start the canoe moving, you need to apply a force to overcome its inertia. Newton's second law might affect your choice of canoes, because a less massive canoe is easier to accelerate than a more massive one. You can also predict the best position for your paddle in the water. If you want to move straight ahead, you push backward on the paddle so that the canoe moves forward. Together, Newton's laws can help you explain and predict how the canoe, or any object, will move.

RESOURCE CENTER
CLASSZONE.COM
Find out more about Newton's laws of motion.

COMBINATION NOTES
Make an outline and draw a diagram showing how all three of Newton's laws apply to the motion of one object.

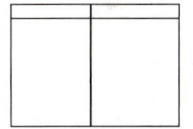

2.3 Review

KEY CONCEPTS

1. Identify the action/reaction force pair involved when you catch a ball.
2. Explain the difference between balanced forces and action/reaction forces.
3. How do Newton's laws of motion apply to the motion of an animal, such as a cat that is running?

CRITICAL THINKING

4. **Apply** A man pushes on a wall with a force of 50 N. What are the size and the direction of the force that the wall exerts on the man?
5. **Evaluate** Jim will not help push a heavy box. He says, "My force will produce an opposite force and cancel my effort." Evaluate Jim's statement.

CHALLENGE

6. **Calculate** Suppose you are holding a basketball while standing still on a skateboard. You and the skateboard have a mass of 50 kg. You throw the basketball with a force of 10 N. What is your acceleration before and after you throw the ball?

Chapter 2: Forces 61

CHAPTER INVESTIGATION

Newton's Laws of Motion

OVERVIEW AND PURPOSE As you know, rocket engineers consider Newton's laws when designing rockets and planning rocket flights. In this investigation you will use what you have learned about Newton's laws to
- build a straw rocket
- improve the rocket's performance by modifying one design element

▶ Problem
Write It Up

What aspects of a model rocket affect the distance it flies?

▶ Hypothesize
Write It Up

After step 8 in the procedure, write a hypothesis to explain what you predict will happen during the second set of trials. Your hypothesis should take the form of an "If . . . , then . . . , because . . ." statement.

▶ Procedure

1. Make a data table like the one shown on the sample notebook page.

2. Insert the straw with the smaller diameter into one of the bottles. Seal the mouth of the bottle tightly with modeling clay so that air can escape only through the straw. This is the rocket launcher.

3. Cut two thin strips of paper, one about 8 cm long and the other about 12 cm long. Connect the ends of the strips to make loops.

4. To create the rocket, place the straw with the larger diameter through the smaller loop and tape the loop to the straw at one end. Attach the other loop to the other end of the straw in the same way. Both loops should be attached to the same side of the straw to stabilize your rocket in flight.

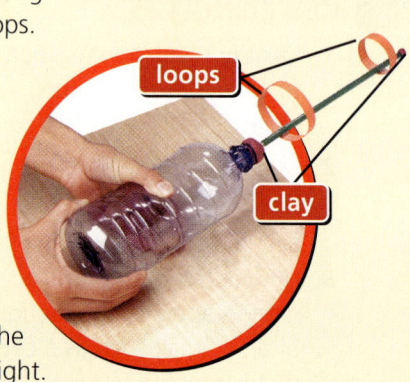

MATERIALS
- 2 straws with different diameters
- several plastic bottles, in different sizes
- modeling clay
- scissors
- construction paper
- meter stick
- tape

62 Unit: Motion and Forces

5. Use a small ball of modeling clay to seal the end of the straw near the smaller loop.

6. Slide the open end of the rocket over the straw on the launcher. Place the bottle on the edge of a table so that the rocket is pointing away from the table.

7. Test launch your rocket by holding the bottle with two hands and squeezing it quickly. Measure the distance the rocket lands from the edge of the table. Practice the launch several times. Remember to squeeze with equal force each time.

8. Launch the rocket four times. Keep the amount of force you use constant. Measure the distance the rocket travels each time, and record the results in your data table.

9. List all the variables that may affect the distance your rocket flies. Change the rocket or launcher to alter one variable. Launch the rocket and measure the distance it flies. Repeat three more times, and record the results in your data table.

Observe and Analyze

1. **RECORD OBSERVATIONS** Draw a diagram of both of your bottle rockets. Make sure your data table is complete.

2. **IDENTIFY VARIABLES** What variables did you identify, and what variable did you modify?

Conclude

1. **COMPARE** How did the flight distances of the original rocket compare with those of the modified rocket?

2. **ANALYZE** Compare your results with your hypothesis. Do the results support your hypothesis?

3. **IDENTIFY LIMITS** What possible limitations or errors did you experience or could you have experienced?

4. **APPLY** Use Newton's laws to explain why the rocket flies.

5. **APPLY** What other real-life example can you think of that demonstrates Newton's laws?

INVESTIGATE Further

CHALLENGE Why does the rocket have paper loops taped to it? Determine how the flight of the rocket is affected if one or both loops are completely removed. Hypothesize about the function of the paper loops and design an experiment to test your hypothesis.

Newton's Laws of Motion

Problem What aspects of a model rocket affect the distance it flies?

Hypothesize

Observe and Analyze

Table 1. Flight Distances of Original and Modified Rocket

Trial Number	Original Rocket Distance Rocket Flew (cm)	Modified Rocket Distance Rocket Flew (cm)
1		
2		
3		
4		

Conclude

KEY CONCEPT
2.4 Forces transfer momentum.

BEFORE, you learned
- A force is a push or a pull
- Newton's laws help to describe and predict motion

NOW, you will learn
- What momentum is
- How to calculate momentum
- How momentum is affected by collisions

VOCABULARY

momentum p. 64
collision p. 66
conservation of momentum p. 67

EXPLORE Collisions

What happens when objects collide?

PROCEDURE

1. Roll the two balls toward each other on a flat surface. Try to roll them at the same speed. Observe what happens. Experiment by changing the speeds of the two balls.

2. Leave one ball at rest, and roll the other ball so that it hits the first ball. Observe what happens. Then repeat the experiment with the balls switched.

MATERIALS
2 balls of different masses

WHAT DO YOU THINK?
- How did varying the speed of the balls affect the motion of the balls after the collision?
- What happened when one ball was at rest? Why did switching the two balls affect the outcome?

Objects in motion have momentum.

If you throw a tennis ball at a wall, it will bounce back toward you. What would happen if you could throw a wrecking ball at the wall at the same speed that you threw the tennis ball? The wall would most likely break apart. Why would a wrecking ball have a different effect on the wall than the tennis ball?

A moving object has a property that is called momentum. **Momentum** (moh-MEHN-tuhm) is a measure of mass in motion; the momentum of an object is the product of its mass and its velocity. At the same velocity, the wrecking ball has more momentum than the tennis ball because the wrecking ball has more mass. However, you could increase the momentum of the tennis ball by throwing it faster.

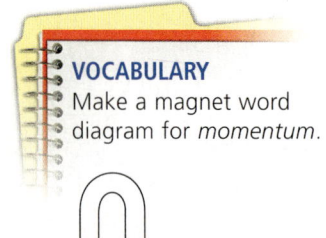

VOCABULARY
Make a magnet word diagram for *momentum*.

64 Unit: Motion and Forces

Momentum is similar to inertia. Like inertia, the momentum of an object depends on its mass. Unlike inertia, however, momentum takes into account how fast the object is moving. A wrecking ball that is moving very slowly, for example, has less momentum than a fast-moving wrecking ball. With less momentum, the slower-moving wrecking ball would not be able to do as much damage to the wall.

To calculate an object's momentum, you can use the following formula:

$$\text{momentum} = \text{mass} \cdot \text{velocity}$$
$$p = mv$$

In this formula, p stands for momentum, m for mass, and v for velocity. In standard units, the mass of an object is given in kilograms (kg), and velocity is given in meters per second (m/s). Therefore, the unit of momentum is the kilogram-meter per second (kg · m/s). Notice that the unit of momentum combines mass, length, and time.

Like force, velocity, and acceleration, momentum is a vector—it has both a size and a direction. The direction of an object's momentum is the same as the direction of its velocity. You can use speed instead of velocity in the formula as long as you do not need to know the direction of motion. As you will read later, it is important to know the direction of the momentum when you are working with more than one object.

CHECK YOUR READING How do an object's mass and velocity affect its momentum?

> **REMINDER**
> Inertia is the resistance of an object to changes in its motion.

> **RESOURCE CENTER**
> CLASSZONE.COM
> Explore momentum.

Calculating Momentum

Sample Problem

What is the momentum of a 1.5 kg ball moving at 2 m/s?

What do you know?   mass = 1.5 kg, velocity = 2 m/s

What do you want to find out?   momentum

Write the formula: $p = mv$

Substitute into the formula: p = 1.5 kg · 2 m/s

Calculate and simplify: p = 3 kg · m/s

Check that your units agree: Unit is kg · m/s.
   Unit of momentum is kg · m/s. Units agree.

Answer: p = 3 kg · m/s

Practice the Math

1. A 3 kg ball is moving with a velocity of 1 m/s. What is the ball's momentum?
2. What is the momentum of a 0.5 kg ball moving 0.5 m/s?

Chapter 2: **Forces** 65

INVESTIGATE Momentum

What happens when objects collide?
PROCEDURE

1. Set up two parallel rulers separated by one centimeter. Place a line of five marbles, each touching the next, in the groove between the rulers.

2. Roll a marble down the groove so that it collides with the line of marbles, and observe the results.

3. Repeat your experiment by rolling two and then three marbles at the line of marbles. Observe the results.

WHAT DO YOU THINK?
- What did you observe when you rolled the marbles?
- Why do you think the marbles moved the way they did?

CHALLENGE Use your answers to write a hypothesis explaining your observations. Design your own marble experiment to test this hypothesis. Do your results support your hypothesis?

SKILL FOCUS
Observing

MATERIALS
- 2 rulers
- 8 marbles

TIME
20 minutes

Momentum can be transferred from one object to another.

If you have ever ridden in a bumper car, you have experienced collisions. A **collision** is a situation in which two objects in close contact exchange energy and momentum. As another car bumps into the back of yours, the force pushes your car forward. Some of the momentum of the car behind you is transferred to your car. At the same time, the car behind you slows because of the reaction force from your car. You gain momentum from the collision, and the other car loses momentum. The action and reaction forces in collisions are one way in which objects transfer momentum.

If two objects involved in a collision have very different masses, the one with less mass has a greater change in velocity. For example, consider what happens if you roll a tennis ball and a bowling ball toward each other so that they collide. Not only will the speed of the tennis ball change, but the direction of its motion will change as it bounces back. The bowling ball, however, will simply slow down. Even though the forces acting on the two balls are the same, the tennis ball will be accelerated more during the collision because it has less mass.

CHECK YOUR READING How can a collision affect the momentum of an object?

Momentum is conserved.

During a collision between two objects, each object exerts a force on the other. The colliding objects make up a system—a collection of objects that affect one another. As the two objects collide, the velocity and the momentum of each object change. However, as no other forces are acting on the objects, the total momentum of both objects is unchanged by the collision. This is due to the conservation of momentum. The principle of **conservation of momentum** states that the total momentum of a system of objects does not change, as long as no outside forces are acting on that system.

READING TIP

A light blue-green arrow shows the momentum of an individual object.

A dark blue-green arrow shows the total momentum.

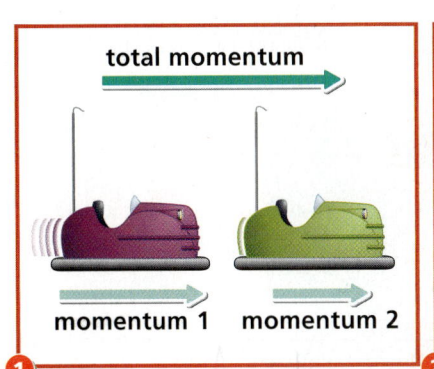

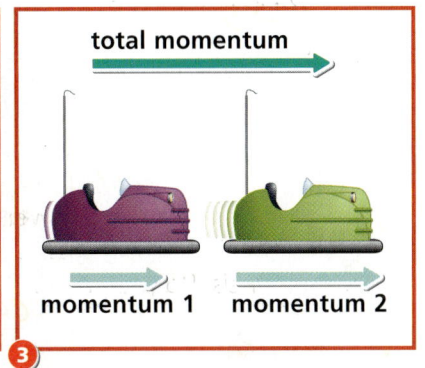

① Before the collision The momentum of the first car is greater than the momentum of the second car. Their combined momentum is the total momentum of the system.

② During the collision The forces on the two cars are equal and opposite, as described by Newton's third law. Momentum is transferred from one car to the other during the collision.

③ After the collision The momentum lost by one car was gained by the other car. The total momentum of the system remains the same as it was before the collision.

How much an object's momentum changes when a force is applied depends on the size of the force and how long that force is applied. Remember Newton's third law—during a collision, two objects are acted upon by equal and opposite forces for the same length of time. This means that the objects receive equal and opposite changes in momentum, and the total momentum does not change.

You can find the total momentum of a system of objects before a collision by combining the momenta of the objects. Because momentum is a vector, like force, the direction of motion is important. To find the total momentum of objects moving in the same direction, add the momenta of the objects. For two objects traveling in opposite directions, subtract one momentum from the other. Then use the principle of conservation of momentum and the formula for momentum to predict how the objects will move after they collide.

READING TIP

The plural of *momentum* is *momenta*.

CHECK YOUR READING What is meant by "conservation of momentum"? What questions do you have about the application of this principle?

Chapter 2: **Forces** 67

Two Types of Collisions

When bumper cars collide, they bounce off each other. Most of the force goes into changing the motion of the cars. The two bumper cars travel separately after the collision, just as they did before the collision. The combined momentum of both cars after the collision is the same as the combined momentum of both cars before the collision.

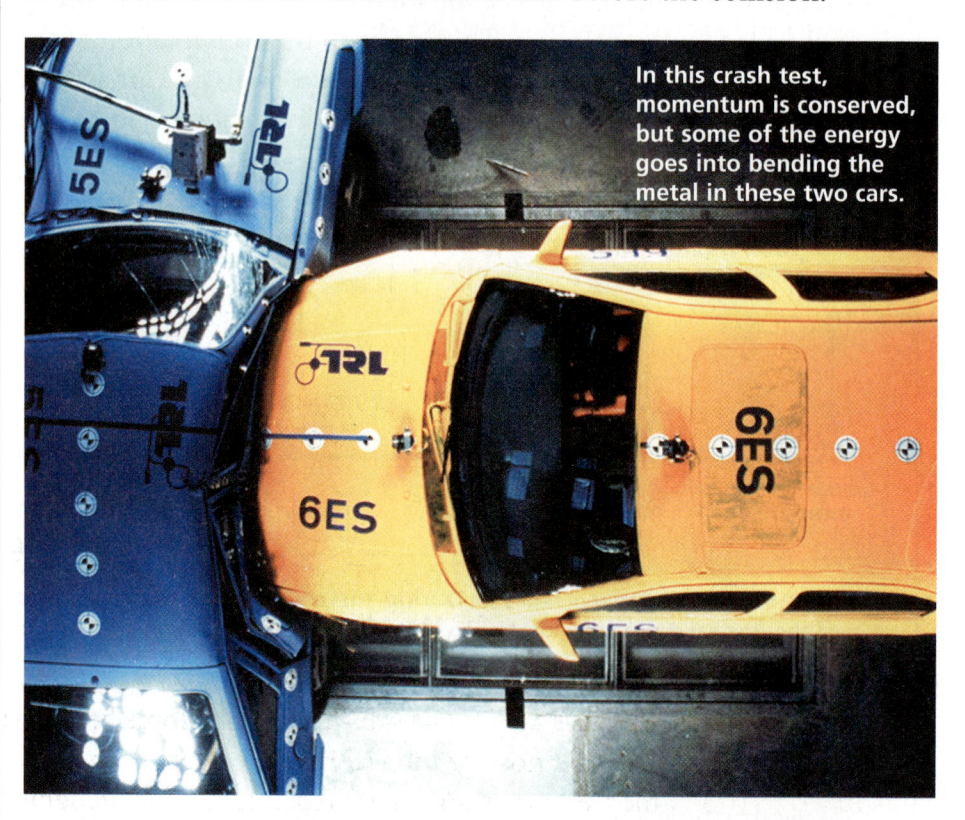

In this crash test, momentum is conserved, but some of the energy goes into bending the metal in these two cars.

When two cars collide during a crash test, momentum is also conserved during the collision. Unlike the bumper cars, however, which separate, the two cars shown in the photograph above stick and move together after the collision. Even in this case, the total momentum of both cars together is the same as the total momentum of both cars before the collision. Before the crash shown in the photograph, the yellow car had a certain momentum, and the blue car had no momentum. After the crash, the two cars move together with a combined momentum equal to the momentum the yellow car had before the collision.

CHECK YOUR READING Compare collisions in which objects separate with collisions in which objects stick together.

Momentum and Newton's Third Law

Collisions are not the only events in which momentum is conserved. In fact, momentum is conserved whenever the only forces acting on objects are action/reaction force pairs. Conservation of momentum is really just another way of looking at Newton's third law.

When a firefighter turns on a hose, water comes out of the nozzle in one direction, and the hose moves back in the opposite direction. You can explain why by using Newton's third law. The water is forced out of the hose. A reaction force pushes the hose backward. You can also use the principle of conservation of momentum to explain why the hose moves backward:

- Before the firefighter turns on the water, the hose and the water are not in motion, so the hose/water system has no momentum.
- Once the water is turned on, the water has momentum in the forward direction.
- For the total momentum of the hose and the water to stay the same, the hose must have an equal amount of momentum in the opposite direction. The hose moves backward.

If the hose and the water are not acted on by any other forces, momentum is conserved. Water is pushed forward, and the hose is pushed backward. However, the action and reaction force pair acting on the hose and the water are not usually the only forces acting on the hose/water system, as shown in the photograph above. There the firefighters are holding the hose steady.

The force the firefighters apply is called an outside force because it is not being applied by the hose or the water. When there is an outside force on a system, momentum is not conserved. Because the firefighters hold the hose, the hose does not move backward, even though the water has a forward momentum.

Firefighters must apply a force to the water hose to prevent it from flying backward when the water comes out.

CHECK YOUR READING Under what condition is momentum not conserved? What part of the paragraph above tells you?

2.4 Review

KEY CONCEPTS

1. How does increasing the speed of an object change its momentum?
2. A car and a truck are traveling at the same speed. Which has more momentum? Why?
3. Give two examples showing the conservation of momentum. Give one example where momentum is not conserved.

CRITICAL THINKING

4. **Predict** A performing dolphin speeds through the water and hits a rubber ball originally at rest. Describe what happens to the velocities of the dolphin and the ball.
5. **Calculate** A 50 kg person is running at 2 m/s. What is the person's momentum?

CHALLENGE

6. **Apply** A moving train car bumps into another train car with the same mass. After the collision, the two cars are coupled and move off together. How does the final speed of the two train cars compare with the initial speed of the moving train cars before the collision?

Chapter 2: Forces 69

Chapter Review

the BIG idea
Forces change the motion of objects in predictable ways.

CONTENT REVIEW
CLASSZONE.COM

KEY CONCEPTS SUMMARY

2.1 Forces change motion.

Newton's first law
Objects at rest remain at rest, and objects in motion remain in motion with the same velocity, unless acted upon by an unbalanced force.

unbalanced force → object at rest

object in motion ← unbalanced force

VOCABULARY
force p. 41
net force p. 43
Newton's first law p. 45
inertia p. 46

2.2 Force and mass determine acceleration.

Newton's second law
The acceleration of an object increases with increased force and decreases with increased mass, and is in the same direction as the force.

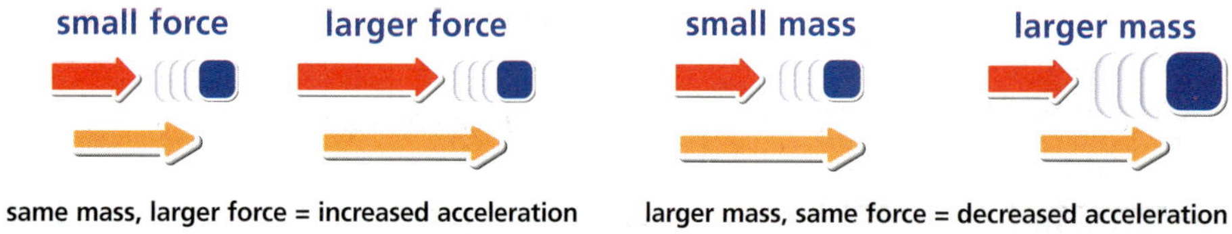

small force   larger force   small mass   larger mass

same mass, larger force = increased acceleration

larger mass, same force = decreased acceleration

VOCABULARY
Newton's second law p. 50
centripetal force p. 54

2.3 Forces act in pairs.

Newton's third law
When one object exerts a force on another object, the second object exerts an equal and opposite force on the first object.

reaction force   action force

VOCABULARY
Newton's third law p. 57

2.4 Forces transfer momentum.

- Momentum is a property of a moving object.
- Forces in collisions are equal and opposite.
- Momentum is conserved in collisions.

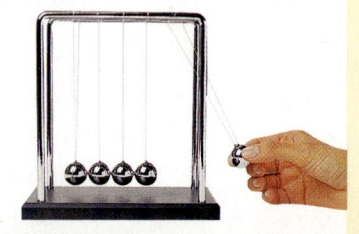

VOCABULARY
momentum p. 64
collision p. 66
conservation of momentum p. 67

C 70 Unit: Motion and Forces

Reviewing Vocabulary

Copy and complete the chart below. If the left column is blank, give the correct term. If the right column is blank, give an example from real life.

Term	Example from Real Life
1. acceleration	
2. centripetal force	
3.	The pull of a handle on a wagon
4. inertia	
5. mass	
6. net force	
7. Newton's first law	
8. Newton's second law	
9.	When you're walking, you push backward on the ground, and the ground pushes you forward with equal force.
10. momentum	

Reviewing Key Concepts

Multiple Choice *Choose the letter of the best answer.*

11. Newton's second law states that to increase acceleration, you
    a. increase force
    b. decrease force
    c. increase mass
    d. increase inertia

12. What units are used to measure force?
    a. kilograms
    b. meters
    c. newtons
    d. seconds

13. A wagon is pulled down a hill with a constant velocity. All the forces on the wagon are
    a. balanced
    b. unbalanced
    c. increasing
    d. decreasing

14. An action force and its reaction force are
    a. equal in size and direction
    b. equal in size and opposite in direction
    c. different in size but in the same direction
    d. different in size and in direction

15. John pulls a box with a force of 4 N, and Jason pulls the box from the opposite side with a force of 3 N. Ignore friction. Which of the following statements is true?
    a. The box moves toward John.
    b. The box moves toward Jason.
    c. The box does not move.
    d. There is not enough information to determine if the box moves.

16. A more massive marble collides with a less massive one that is not moving. The total momentum after the collision is equal to
    a. zero
    b. the original momentum of the more massive marble
    c. the original momentum of the less massive marble
    d. twice the original momentum of the more massive marble

Short Answer *Write a short answer to each question.*

17. List the following objects in order, from the object with the least inertia to the object with the most inertia: feather, large rock, pencil, book. Explain your reasoning.

18. During a race, you double your velocity. How does that change your momentum?

19. Explain how an object can have forces acting on it but not be accelerating.

20. A sea scallop moves by shooting jets of water out of its shell. Explain how this works.

Thinking Critically

Use the information in the photographs below to answer the next four questions.

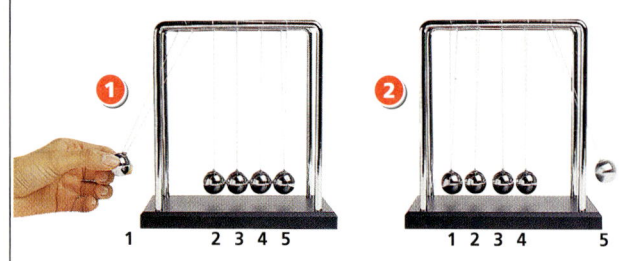

The photographs above show a toy called Newton's Cradle. In the first picture (1), ball 1 is lifted and is being held in place.

21. Are the forces on ball 1 balanced? How do you know?

22. Draw a diagram showing the forces acting on ball 2. Are these forces balanced?

In the second picture (2), ball 1 has been let go.

23. Ball 1 swung down, hit ball 2, and stopped. Use Newton's laws to explain why ball 1 stopped.

24. Use the principle of conservation of momentum to explain why ball 5 swung into the air.

Copy the chart below. Write what will happen to the object in each case.

Cause	Effect
25. Balanced forces act on an object.	
26. Unbalanced forces act on an object.	
27. No force acts on an object.	

28. **INFER** A baseball is three times more massive than a tennis ball. If the baseball and the tennis ball are accelerating equally, what can you determine about the net force on each?

Using Math Skills in Science

Complete the following calculations.

29. What force should Lori apply to a 5 kg box to give it an acceleration of 2 m/s^2?

30. If a 10 N force accelerates an object 5 m/s^2, how massive is the object?

31. Ravi applies a force of 5 N to a wagon with a mass of 10 kg. What is the wagon's acceleration?

32. Use the information in the photograph on the right to calculate the momentum of the shopping cart.

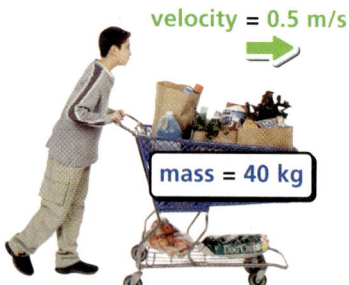

velocity = 0.5 m/s

mass = 40 kg

the BIG idea

33. **PREDICT** Look again at the tug of war pictured on pages 38–39. Describe what information you need to know to predict the outcome of the game. How would you use that information and Newton's laws to make your prediction?

34. **WRITE** Pick an activity you enjoy, such as running or riding a scooter, and describe how Newton's laws apply to that activity.

35. **SYNTHESIZE** Think of a question you have about Newton's laws that is still unanswered. What information do you need in order to answer the question? How might you find the information?

UNIT PROJECTS

If you need to do an experiment for your unit project, gather the materials. Be sure to allow enough time to observe results before the project is due.

Standardized Test Practice

Analyzing Data

To test Newton's second law, Jodie accelerates blocks of ice across a smooth, flat surface. The table shows her results. (For this experiment, you can ignore the effects of friction.)

Accelerating Blocks of Ice

Mass (kg)	1.0	1.5	2.0	2.5	3.0	3.5	4.0
Acceleration (m/s^2)	4.0	2.7	2.0	1.6	1.3	1.1	1.0

Study the data table and then answer the questions that follow.

1. The data show that as mass becomes greater, acceleration
   a. increases
   b. decreases
   c. stays the same
   d. cannot be predicted

2. From the data, you can tell that Jodie was applying a force of
   a. 1 N
   b. 2 N
   c. 3 N
   d. 4 N

3. If Jodie applied less force to the ice blocks, the accelerations would be
   a. greater
   b. less
   c. the same
   d. inconsistent

4. If Jodie applied a force of 6 N to the 2 kg block of ice, the acceleration would be
   a. 2 m/s^2
   b. 4 m/s^2
   c. 3 m/s^2
   d. 5 m/s^2

5. The average mass of the ice blocks she pushed was
   a. 1.5 kg
   b. 2.5 kg
   c. 3 kg
   d. 4 kg

6. If Jodie used a 3.25 kg block in her experiment, the force would accelerate the block somewhere between
   a. 1.0 and 1.1 m/s^2
   b. 1.1 and 1.3 m/s^2
   c. 1.3 and 1.6 m/s^2
   d. 1.6 and 2.0 m/s^2

Extended Response

Answer the two questions in detail. Include some of the terms shown in the word box. Underline each term you use in your answer.

Newton's second law	velocity
mass	inertia
gravity	balanced forces
centripetal force	unbalanced forces

7. Tracy ties a ball to a string and starts to swing the ball around her head. What forces are acting on the ball? What happens if the string breaks?

8. Luis is trying to pull a wagon loaded with rocks. What can he do to increase the wagon's acceleration?

CHAPTER 3

Gravity, Friction, and Pressure

the BIG idea

Newton's laws apply to all forces.

Key Concepts

SECTION 3.1
Gravity is a force exerted by masses.
Learn about gravity, weight, and orbits.

SECTION 3.2
Friction is a force that opposes motion.
Learn about friction and air resistance.

SECTION 3.3
Pressure depends on force and area.
Learn about pressure and how forces act on objects in fluids.

SECTION 3.4
Fluids can exert a force on objects.
Learn how fluids apply forces to objects and how forces are transmitted through fluids.

Internet Preview

CLASSZONE.COM

Chapter 3 online resources: Content Review, Simulation, two Visualizations, three Resource Centers, Math Tutorial, Test Practice

C 74 Unit: Motion and Forces

What forces are acting on this snowboarder? What forces are acting on the snow?

EXPLORE the BIG idea

Let It Slide
Make a ramp using a board and some books. Slide an object down the ramp. Change the surface of the ramp using various materials such as sandpaper.

Observe and Think What effects did different surfaces have on the motion of the object? What may have caused these effects?

Under Pressure
Take two never-opened plastic soft-drink bottles. Open and reseal one of them. Squeeze each bottle.

Observe and Think How did the fluid inside each bottle react to your force? What may have caused the difference in the way the bottles felt?

Internet Activity: Gravity
Go to **ClassZone.com** to explore gravity. Learn more about the force of gravity and its effect on you, objects on Earth, and orbits of planets and satellites. Explore how gravity determines weight, and find out how your weight would be different on other planets.

Observe and Think What would you weigh on Mars? What would you weigh on Neptune?

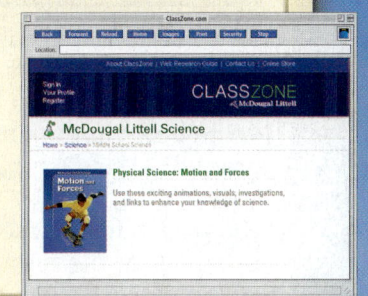

NSTA scilinks.org
SciLinks
Pressure Code: MDL006

Chapter 3: **Gravity, Friction, and Pressure** 75

CHAPTER 3
Getting Ready to Learn

CONCEPT REVIEW

- The motion of an object will not change unless acted upon by an unbalanced force.
- The acceleration of an object depends on force and mass.
- For every action force there is an equal and opposite reaction.

VOCABULARY REVIEW

force p. 41
Newton's first law p. 45
Newton's second law p. 50
Newton's third law p. 57
density See Glossary.

CONTENT REVIEW
CLASSZONE.COM
Review concepts and vocabulary.

TAKING NOTES

SUPPORTING MAIN IDEAS

Make a chart to show main ideas and the information that supports them. Copy the main ideas. Below each main idea, add supporting information, such as reasons, explanations, and examples.

VOCABULARY STRATEGY

Write each new vocabulary term in the center of a **four square** diagram. Write notes in the squares around each term. Include a definition, some characteristics, and some examples of the term. If possible, write some things that are not examples of the term.

See the Note-Taking Handbook on pages R45–R51.

SCIENCE NOTEBOOK

Force of gravity depends on mass and distance.
→ More mass = more gravitational force
→ More distance = less gravitational force

Definition	Characteristics
force of gravity acting on an object	• changes if gravity changes • measured in newtons

WEIGHT

Examples	Nonexamples
A 4 kg bowling ball weighs 39 N.	Mass in kg is not a weight.

76 Unit: Motion and Forces

3.1 KEY CONCEPT
Gravity is a force exerted by masses.

BEFORE, you learned
- Every action force has an equal and opposite reaction force
- Newton's laws are used to describe the motions of objects
- Mass is the amount of matter an object contains

NOW, you will learn
- How mass and distance affect gravity
- What keeps objects in orbit

VOCABULARY

gravity p. 77
weight p. 79
orbit p. 80

EXPLORE Downward Acceleration

How do the accelerations of two falling objects compare?

PROCEDURE

1. Make a prediction: Which ball will fall faster?
2. Drop both balls from the same height at the same time.
3. Observe the balls as they hit the ground.

MATERIALS
- golf ball
- Ping-Pong ball

WHAT DO YOU THINK?
- Were the results what you had expected?
- How did the times it took the two balls to hit the ground compare?

VOCABULARY
Create a four square diagram for *gravity* in your notebook.

Masses attract each other.

When you drop any object—such as a pen, a book, or a football—it falls to the ground. As the object falls, it moves faster and faster. The fact that the object accelerates means there must be a force acting on it. The downward pull on the object is due to gravity. **Gravity** is the force that objects exert on each other because of their masses. You are familiar with the force of gravity between Earth and objects on Earth.

Gravity is present not only between objects and Earth, however. Gravity is considered a universal force because it acts between any two masses anywhere in the universe. For example, there is a gravitational pull between the Sun and the Moon. Even small masses attract each other. The force of gravity between dust and gas particles in space helped form the solar system.

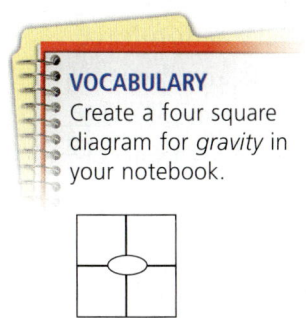

CHECK YOUR READING Why is gravity considered a universal force?

Chapter 3: Gravity, Friction, and Pressure 77

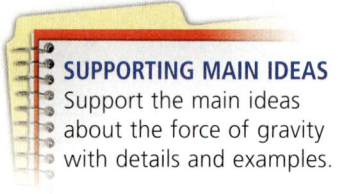

SUPPORTING MAIN IDEAS
Support the main ideas about the force of gravity with details and examples.

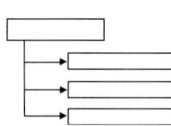

The Force of Gravity

If there is a force between all masses, why are you not pulled toward your desk by the desk's gravity when you walk away from it? Remember that the net force on you determines how your motion changes. The force of gravity between you and the desk is extremely small compared with other forces constantly acting on you, such as friction, the force from your muscles, Earth's gravity, and the gravitational pull from many other objects. The strength of the gravitational force between two objects depends on two factors, mass and distance.

The Mass of the Objects The more mass two objects have, the greater the force of gravity the masses exert on each other. If one of the masses is doubled, the force of gravity between the objects is doubled.

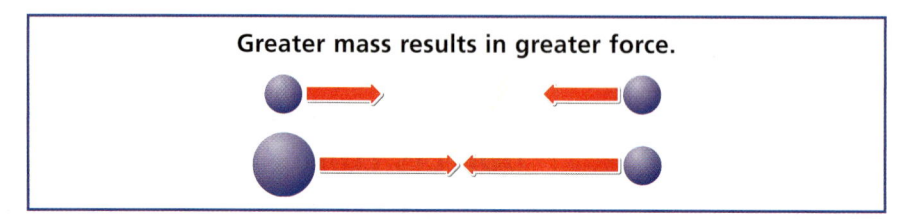

Greater mass results in greater force.

The Distance Between the Objects As distance between the objects increases, the force of gravity decreases. If the distance is doubled, the force of gravity is one-fourth as strong as before.

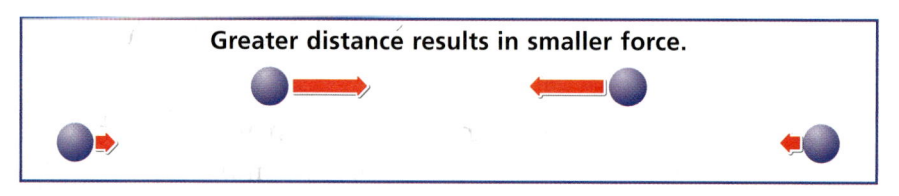

Greater distance results in smaller force.

CHECK YOUR READING How do mass and distance affect the force of gravity?

Gravity on Earth

The force of gravity acts on both masses equally, even though the effects on both masses may be very different. Earth's gravity exerts a downward pull on a dropped coin. Remember that every action force has an equal and opposite reaction force. The coin exerts an equal upward force on Earth. Because the coin has an extremely small mass compared with Earth, the coin can be easily accelerated. Earth's acceleration due to the force of the coin is far too small to notice because of Earth's large mass.

The acceleration due to Earth's gravity is called g and is equal to 9.8 m/s^2 at Earth's surface. You can calculate the force of gravity on an object using the object's mass and this acceleration. The formula that expresses Newton's second law is $F = ma$. If you use g as the acceleration, the formula for calculating the force due to gravity on a mass close to Earth's surface becomes $F = mg$.

78 Unit: Motion and Forces

Acceleration Due to Gravity

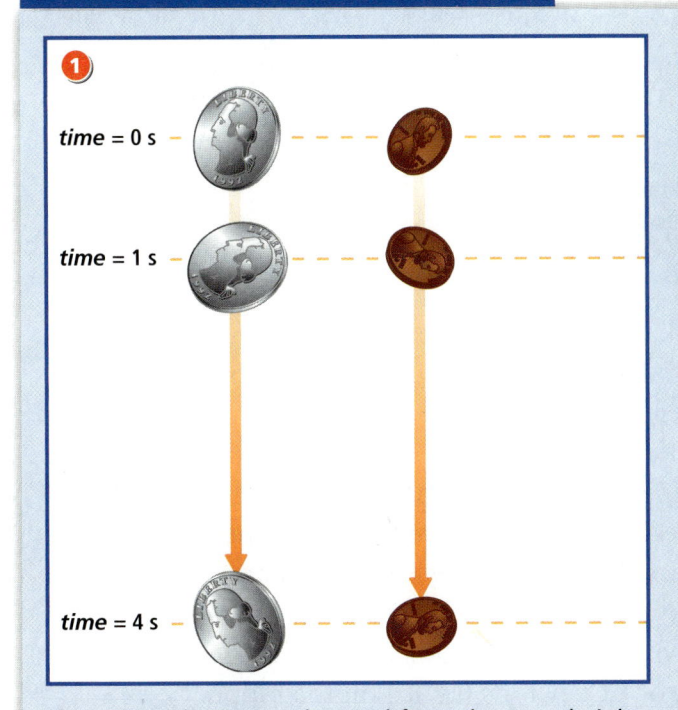

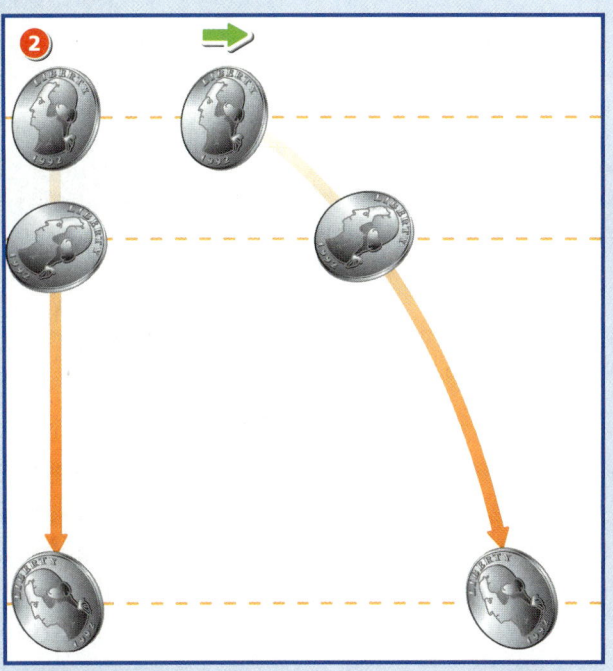

① time = 0 s
time = 1 s
time = 4 s

If any two objects are dropped from the same height in a vacuum, they fall at the same rate even if they have different masses.

②

If an object has a velocity in the horizontal direction when it falls, the horizontal velocity does not change its downward acceleration.

In a vacuum—that is, where there is no air—all falling objects have the same acceleration.

① The quarter falls at the same rate as the penny when they are dropped together. Because the quarter has more mass, gravity exerts more force on it. But greater mass also means more inertia, so the greater force does not produce a larger acceleration. Objects with different masses fall with the same acceleration.

② A coin that is dropped falls at the same rate as one that is thrown forward. Horizontal velocity does not affect acceleration due to gravity. Because gravity is directed downward, it changes only the downward velocity of the coin, not its forward velocity.

VISUALIZATION
CLASSZONE.COM
Explore how objects fall at the same rate in a vacuum.

CHECK YOUR READING Compare the times it takes two objects with different masses to fall from the same height.

Weight and Mass

While weight and mass are related, they are not the same properties. Mass is a measure of how much matter an object contains. **Weight** is the force of gravity on an object. Mass is a property that an object has no matter where it is located. Weight, on the other hand, depends on the force of gravity acting on that object.

Chapter 3: **Gravity, Friction, and Pressure** 79

On Earth
Mass = 50 kg
Weight = 490 N

On the Moon
Mass = 50 kg
Weight = 82 N

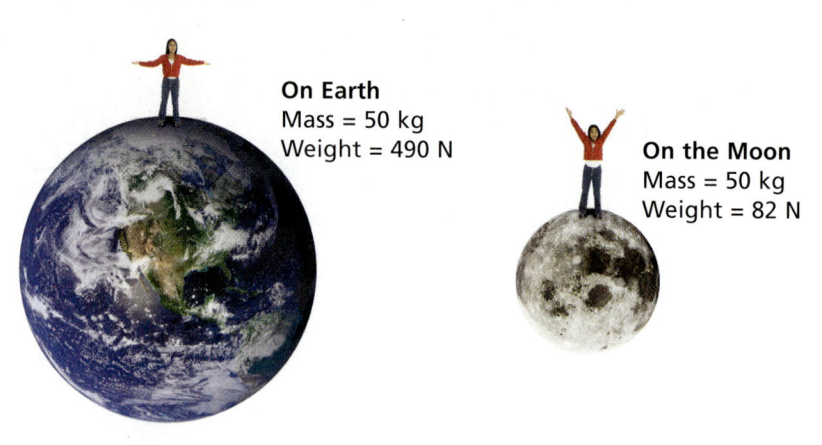

When you use a balance, you are measuring the mass of an object. A person with a mass of 50 kilograms will balance another mass of 50 kilograms whether she is on Earth or on the Moon. Traveling to the Moon would not change how much matter a person is made of. When you use a spring scale, such as a bathroom scale, to measure the weight of an object, however, you are measuring how hard gravity is pulling on an object. The Moon is less massive than Earth, and its gravitational pull is one-sixth that of Earth's. A spring scale would show that a person who has a weight of 490 newtons (110 lb) on Earth would have a weight of 82 newtons (18 lb) on the Moon.

Gravity keeps objects in orbit.

Sir Isaac Newton hypothesized that the force that pulls objects to the ground—gravity—also pulls the Moon in its orbit around Earth. An **orbit** is the elliptical path one body, such as the Moon, follows around another body, such as Earth, due to the influence of gravity. The centripetal force keeping one object in orbit around another object is due to the gravitational pull between the two objects. In the case of the Moon's orbit, the centripetal force is the gravitational pull between the Moon and Earth. Similarly, Earth is pulled around the Sun by the gravitational force between Earth and the Sun.

You can think of an object orbiting Earth as an object that is falling around Earth rather than falling to the ground. Consider what happens to the ball in the illustration on page 81. A dropped ball will fall about five meters during the first second it falls. Throwing the ball straight ahead will not change that falling time. What happens as you throw faster and faster?

Earth is curved. This fact is noticeable only over very long distances. For every 8000 meters you travel, Earth curves downward about 5 meters. If you could throw a ball at 8000 meters per second, it would fall to Earth in such a way that its path would curve the same amount that Earth curves. Since the ball would fall along the curve of Earth, the ball would never actually land on the ground. The ball would be in orbit.

> **READING TIP**
> An ellipse is shaped as shown below. A circle is a special type of ellipse.

80 Unit: Motion and Forces

Orbits

An object in orbit, like an object falling to the ground, is pulled toward Earth's center. If the object moves far enough forward as it falls, it orbits around Earth instead of hitting the ground.

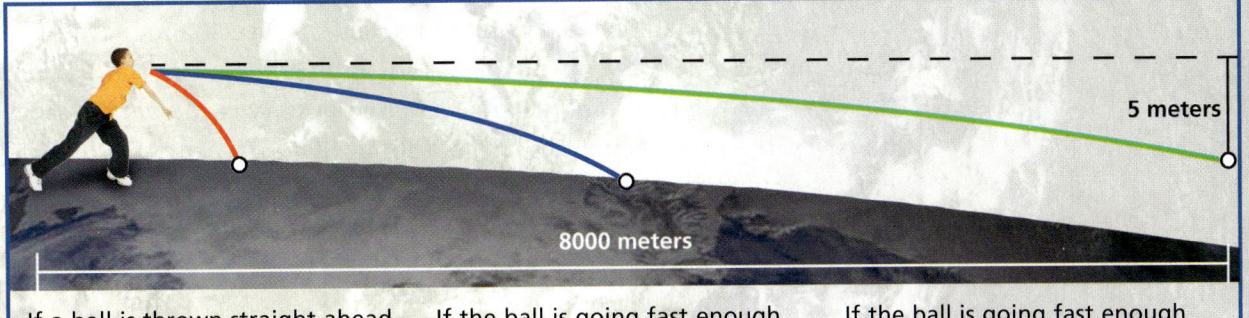

5 meters

8000 meters

If a ball is thrown straight ahead from a 5-meter height, it will drop 5 meters in the first second it falls. At low speeds, the ball will hit the ground after 1 second.

If the ball is going fast enough, the curvature of Earth becomes important. While the ball still drops 5 meters in the first second, it must fall farther than 5 meters to hit the ground.

If the ball is going fast enough to travel 8000 meters forward as it drops downward 5 meters, it follows the curvature of Earth. The ball will fall around Earth, not into it.

A ball thrown horizontally at 8000 m/s will not hit Earth during its fall. Gravity acts as a centripetal force, continually pulling the ball toward Earth's center. The ball circles Earth in an orbit.

Real-World Application
A satellite is launched upward until it is above Earth's atmosphere. The engine then gives the satellite a horizontal speed great enough to keep it in orbit.

➡ = force

➡ = velocity

READING VISUALS Compare the direction of the velocity with the direction of the force for an object in a circular orbit.

Chapter 3: **Gravity, Friction, and Pressure** 81

Spacecraft in Orbit

The minimum speed needed to send an object into orbit is approximately 8000 meters per second. At this speed, the path of a falling object matches the curve of Earth's surface. If you launch a spacecraft or a satellite at a slower speed, it will eventually fall to the ground.

A spacecraft launched at a greater speed can reach a higher orbit than one launched at a lower speed. The higher the orbit, the weaker the force from Earth's gravity. The force of gravity is still very strong, however. If a craft is in a low orbit—about 300 kilometers (190 mi)—Earth's gravitational pull is about 91 percent of what it is at Earth's surface. The extra distance makes a difference in the force of only about 9 percent.

If a spacecraft is launched with a speed of 11,000 meters per second or more, it is moving too fast to go into an orbit. Instead, the spacecraft will ultimately escape the pull of Earth's gravity altogether. The speed that a spacecraft needs to escape the gravitational pull of an object such as a planet or a star is called the escape velocity. A spacecraft that escapes Earth's gravity will go into orbit around the Sun unless it is also going fast enough to escape the Sun's gravity.

CHECK YOUR READING Did any facts in the text above surprise you? If so, which surprised you and why?

INVESTIGATE Gravity

How does gravity affect falling objects?

PROCEDURE

1. Carefully use the pencil to punch a hole that is the width of the pencil in the side of the cup, about one-third of the way up from the bottom.
2. Holding your finger over the hole, fill the cup three-fourths full of water.
3. Hold the cup above the dishpan. Predict what will happen if you remove your finger from the hole. Remove your finger and observe what happens.
4. With your finger over the hole, refill the cup to the same level as in step 2. Predict how the water will move if you hold the cup 50 cm above the dishpan and drop the cup and its contents straight down into the pan.
5. Drop the cup and observe what happens to the water while the cup is falling.

WHAT DO YOU THINK?
- What happened to the water in step 3? in step 5?
- How did gravity affect the water when you dropped the cup?

CHALLENGE Why did the water behave differently the second time?

SKILL FOCUS
Predicting

MATERIALS
- pencil
- paper cup
- water
- dishpan

TIME
15 minutes

82 Unit: Motion and Forces

People in Orbit

When an elevator you are riding in accelerates downward, you may feel lighter for a short time. If you were standing on a scale during the downward acceleration, the scale would show that you weighed less than usual. Your mass would not have changed, nor would the pull of gravity. What would cause the apparent weight loss?

When the elevator is still, the entire force of your weight presses against the scale. When the elevator accelerates downward, you are not pressing as hard on the scale, because the scale is also moving downward. Since the scale measures how hard you are pushing on it, you appear to weigh less. If you and the scale were in free fall—a fall due entirely to gravity—the scale would fall as fast as you did. You would not press against the scale at all, so you would appear to be weightless.

A spacecraft in orbit is in free fall. Gravity is acting on the astronauts and on the ship—without gravity, there could be no orbit. However, the ship and the astronauts are falling around Earth at the same rate. While astronauts are in orbit, their weight does not press against the floor of the spacecraft. The result is an environment, called a microgravity environment, in which objects behave as if there were no gravity. People and objects simply float as if they were weightless.

Astronaut Mae Jemison is shown here working in a microgravity environment.

CHECK YOUR READING Why do astronauts float when they are in orbit?

3.1 Review

KEY CONCEPTS

1. What effect would increasing the mass of two objects have on the gravitational attraction between them?
2. What effect would decreasing the distance between objects have on their gravitational attraction to each other?
3. How does gravity keep the Moon in orbit around Earth?

CRITICAL THINKING

4. **Compare** How does the size of the force exerted by Earth's gravity on a car compare with the size of the force the car exerts on Earth?
5. **Apply** What would be the effect on the mass and the weight of an object if the object were taken to a planet with twice the gravity of Earth?

CHALLENGE

6. **Synthesize** Precision measurements of the acceleration due to gravity show that the acceleration is slightly different in different locations on Earth. Explain why the force of gravity is not exactly the same everywhere on Earth's surface. **Hint:** Think about the details of Earth's surface.

Chapter 3: Gravity, Friction, and Pressure 83

EXTREME SCIENCE

GRAVITY IN THE EXTREME

Bending Light

You know that gravity can pull objects toward each other, but did you know that gravity can also affect light? Very extreme sources of gravity cause the normally straight path of a light beam to bend.

Going in Circles

Although Earth is massive, the effects of its gravity on light are not noticeable. However, scientists can model what a familiar scene might look like with an extreme source of gravity nearby. The image to the left shows how the light from the Seattle Space Needle could be bent almost into circles if an extremely small yet extremely massive object, such as a black hole, were in front of it.

Seeing Behind Galaxies

How do we know that gravity can bend light? Astronomers, who study space, have seen the phenomenon in action. If a very bright but distant object is behind a very massive one, such as a large galaxy, the mass of the galaxy bends the light coming from the distant object. This effect, called gravitational lensing, can produce multiple images of the bright object along a ring around the massive galaxy. Astronomers have observed gravitational lensing in their images.

Facts About Bending Light

- Gravitational lensing was predicted by Albert Einstein in the early 1900s, but the first example was not observed until 1979.
- The masses of distant galaxies can be found by observing their effect on light.

Seeing Quadruple
This gravitational lens is called the Einstein Cross. The four bright objects that ring the central galaxy are all images of the same very bright yet very distant object that is located 20 times farther away than the central galaxy.

EXPLORE

1. **INFER** Why are you unable to notice the gravitational bending of light by an object such as a large rock?
2. **CHALLENGE** Look at the photographs in the Resource Center. Find the multiple images of the distant objects and the more massive object bending the light from them.

RESOURCE CENTER CLASSZONE.COM Find out more information about gravitational lenses.

3.2 Friction is a force that opposes motion.

KEY CONCEPT

BEFORE, you learned
- Gravity is the attractive force masses exert on each other
- Gravity increases with greater mass and decreases with greater distance
- Gravity is the centripetal force keeping objects in orbit

NOW, you will learn
- How friction affects motion
- About factors that affect friction
- About air resistance

VOCABULARY

friction p. 85
fluid p. 88
air resistance p. 89

THINK ABOUT

What forces help you to walk?

As a person walks, she exerts a backward force on the ground. A reaction force moves her forward. But some surfaces are harder to walk on than others. Ice, for example, is harder to walk on than a dry surface because ice is slippery. How can different surfaces affect your ability to walk?

Friction occurs when surfaces slide against each other.

Have you ever pushed a heavy box across the floor? You probably noticed that it is easier to push the box over some surfaces than over others. You must apply a certain amount of force to the box to keep it moving. The force that acts against your pushing force is called friction. **Friction** is a force that resists the motion between two surfaces in contact.

When you try to slide two surfaces across each other, the force of friction resists the sliding motion. If there were no friction, the box would move as soon as you applied any force to it. Although friction can make some tasks more difficult, most activities, including walking, would be impossible without it. Friction between your feet and the ground is what provides the action and reaction forces that enable you to walk.

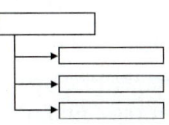

SUPPORTING MAIN IDEAS
Take notes about friction, including details and examples.

Chapter 3: Gravity, Friction, and Pressure 85

RESOURCE CENTER
CLASSZONE.COM
Learn more about friction, forces, and surfaces.

REMINDER
Remember that balanced forces on an object do not change the object's motion.

Forces and Surfaces

If you look down from a great height, such as from the window of an airplane, a flat field appears to be smooth. If you were to walk in the field, however, you would see that the ground has many bumps and holes. In the same way, a flat surface such as a piece of plastic may look and feel smooth. However, if you look at the plastic through a strong microscope, you see that it has tiny bumps and ridges. Friction depends on how these bumps and ridges on one surface interact with and stick to the bumps and ridges on other surfaces. There are several factors that determine the friction between two surfaces.

Types of Surfaces Friction between two surfaces depends on the materials that make up the surfaces. Different combinations of surfaces produce different frictional forces. A rubber hockey puck sliding across ice has a smaller frictional force on it than the same puck sliding across a wooden floor. The friction between rubber and ice is less than the friction between rubber and wood.

Motion of the Surfaces You need a larger force to start something moving than you do to keep something moving. If you have ever tried to push a heavy chair, you may have noticed that you had to push harder and harder until the chair suddenly accelerated forward.

As you apply a force to push a chair or any other object that is not moving, the frictional force keeping it from sliding increases so the forces stay balanced. However, the frictional force has a limit to how

Friction and Motion

Before Object Moves

applied force
friction

When an object is standing still, there is a maximum force needed to overcome friction and start it moving. Any force less than this will be exactly balanced by the force of friction, and the object will not move.

While Object Moves

acceleration
applied force
friction

Once the object is moving, the frictional force remains constant. This constant force is less than the maximum force needed to start the object moving.

Unit: Motion and Forces

large it can be. When your force is greater than this limit, the forces on the chair are no longer balanced, and the chair moves. The frictional force remains at a new lower level once the chair is moving.

Force Pressing the Surfaces Together The harder two surfaces are pushed together, the more difficult it is for the surfaces to slide over each other. When an object is placed on a surface, the weight of the object presses on that surface. The surface exerts an equal and opposite reaction force on the object. This reaction force is one of the factors that determines how much friction there is.

If you push a chair across the floor, there will be a certain amount of friction between the chair and the floor. Increasing the weight of the chair increases the force pushing the surfaces together. The force of friction between the chair and the floor is greater when a person is sitting in it than when the chair was empty.

Friction depends on the total force pressing the surfaces together, not on how much area this force acts over. Consider a rectangular cardboard box. It can rest with its smaller or larger side on the floor. The box will have the same force from friction regardless of which side sits on the floor. The larger side has more area in contact with the floor than the smaller side, but the weight of the box is more spread out on the larger side.

CHECK YOUR READING What factors influence frictional force? Give two examples.

Friction and Weight

Less Weight

The force of friction depends on the total force pushing the surfaces together. Here the weight of the chair is the force pressing the surfaces together.

More Weight

The weight of the chair increases when someone sits in it. The force of friction is now greater than when the chair was empty.

Chapter 3: **Gravity, Friction, and Pressure** 87

Friction produces sparks between a match head and a rough surface. The heat from friction eventually lights the match.

Friction and Heat

Friction between surfaces produces heat. You feel heat produced by friction when you rub your hands together. As you rub, friction causes the individual molecules on the surface of your hands to move faster. As the individual molecules in an object move faster, the temperature of the object increases. The increased speed of the molecules on the surface of your hands produces the warmth that you feel.

The heat produced by friction can be intense. The friction that results from striking a match against a rough surface produces enough heat to ignite the flammable substance on the head of the match. In some machines, such as a car engine, too much heat from friction can cause serious damage. Substances such as oil are often used to reduce friction between moving parts in machines. Without motor oil, a car's engine parts would overheat and stop working.

Motion through fluids produces friction.

As you have seen, two objects falling in a vacuum fall with the same acceleration. Objects falling through air, however, have different accelerations. This difference occurs because air is a fluid. A **fluid** is a substance that can flow easily. Gases and liquids are fluids.

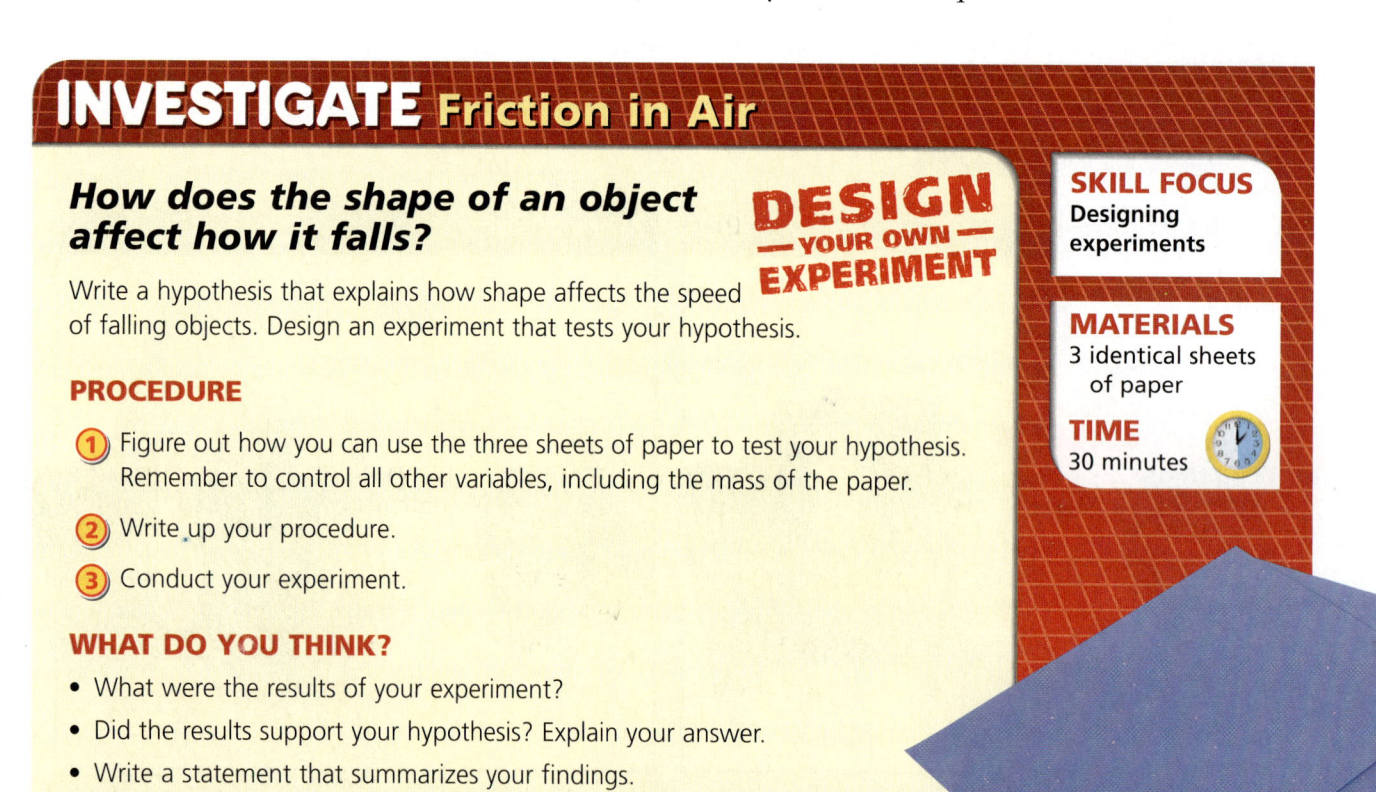

INVESTIGATE Friction in Air

How does the shape of an object affect how it falls?

DESIGN YOUR OWN EXPERIMENT

Write a hypothesis that explains how shape affects the speed of falling objects. Design an experiment that tests your hypothesis.

PROCEDURE

1. Figure out how you can use the three sheets of paper to test your hypothesis. Remember to control all other variables, including the mass of the paper.
2. Write up your procedure.
3. Conduct your experiment.

WHAT DO YOU THINK?

- What were the results of your experiment?
- Did the results support your hypothesis? Explain your answer.
- Write a statement that summarizes your findings.

CHALLENGE What other variable might affect falling time? How could you test it?

SKILL FOCUS
Designing experiments

MATERIALS
3 identical sheets of paper

TIME
30 minutes

Unit: Motion and Forces

When an object moves through a fluid, it pushes the molecules of the fluid out of the way. At the same time, the molecules of the fluid exert an equal and opposite force on the object that slows it down. This force resisting motion through a fluid is a type of friction that is often called drag. Friction in fluids depends on the shape of the moving object. Objects can be designed either to increase or reduce the friction caused by a fluid. Airplane designs, for example, improve as engineers find ways to reduce drag.

The friction due to air is often called **air resistance.** Air resistance differs from the friction between solid surfaces. Air resistance depends on surface area and the speed of an object in the following ways:

- An object with a larger surface area comes into contact with more molecules as it moves than an object with a smaller surface area. This increases the air resistance.
- The faster an object moves through air, the more molecules it comes into contact with in a given amount of time. As the speed of the object increases, air resistance increases.

When a skydiver jumps out of a plane, gravity causes the skydiver to accelerate toward the ground. As the skydiver falls, his body pushes against the air. The air pushes back—with the force of air resistance. As the skydiver's speed increases, his air resistance increases. Eventually, air resistance balances gravity, and the skydiver reaches terminal velocity, which is the final, maximum velocity of a falling object. When the skydiver opens his parachute, air resistance increases still further, and he reaches a new, slower terminal velocity that enables him to land safely.

When the force of air resistance equals the force from gravity, a skydiver falls at a constant speed.

CHECK YOUR READING How do speed and surface area affect air resistance?

3.2 Review

KEY CONCEPTS

1. How does friction affect forward motion? Give an example.
2. Describe two ways to change the frictional force between two solid surfaces.
3. How does air resistance affect the velocity of a falling object?

CRITICAL THINKING

4. **Infer** What two sources of friction do you have to overcome when you are walking?
5. **Synthesize** If you push a chair across the floor at a constant velocity, how does the force of friction compare with the force you exert? Explain.

CHALLENGE

6. **Synthesize** If you push a book against a wall hard enough, it will not slide down even though gravity is pulling it. Use what you know about friction and Newton's laws of motion to explain why the book does not fall.

Chapter 3: **Gravity, Friction, and Pressure** 89

MATH in SCIENCE

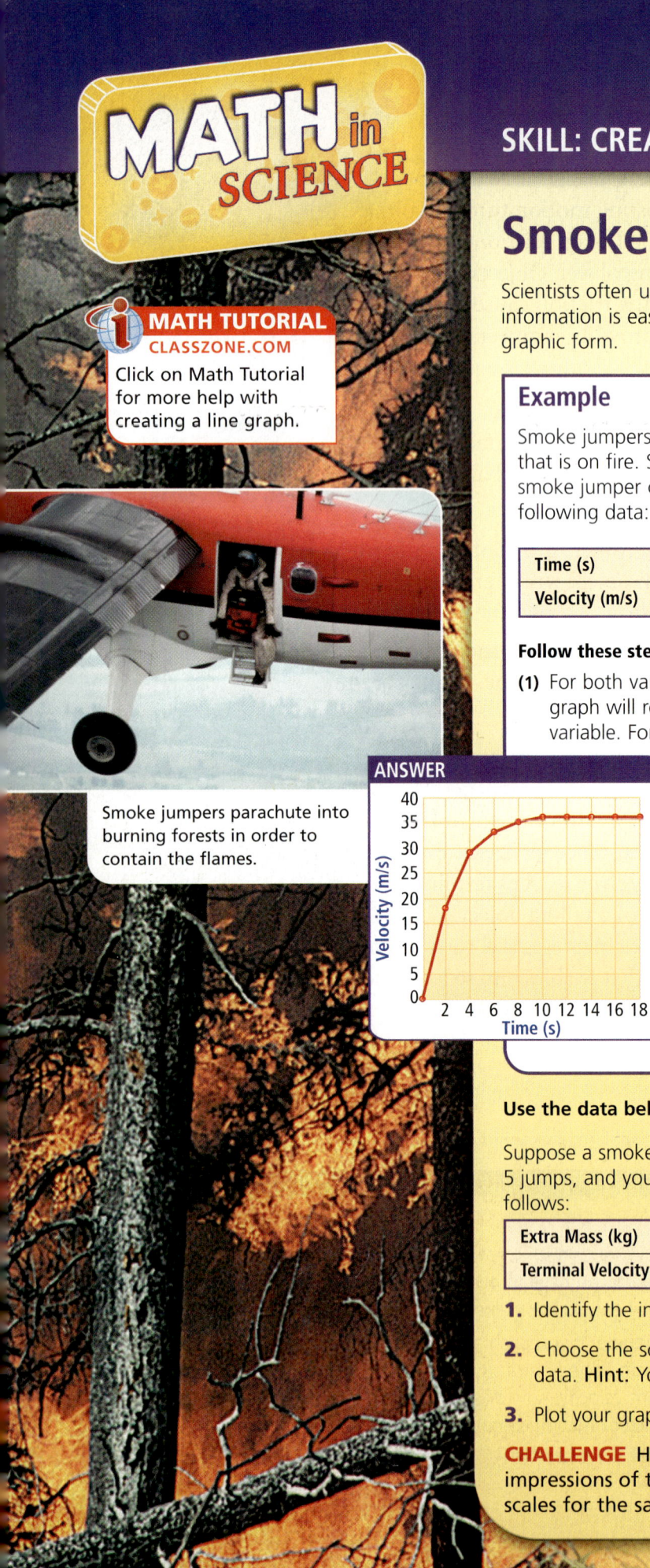

SKILL: CREATING A LINE GRAPH

Smoke Jumpers in Action

Scientists often use graphs as a way to present data. Sometimes information is easier to understand when it is presented in graphic form.

Example

Smoke jumpers are firefighters who parachute down into a forest that is on fire. Suppose you measured how the velocity of a smoke jumper changed as he was free-falling, and recorded the following data:

Time (s)	0	2	4	6	8	10	12	14	16	18
Velocity (m/s)	0	18	29	33	35	36	36	36	36	36

Follow these steps to make a line graph of the data in the table.

(1) For both variables, decide the scale that each box on your graph will represent and what range you will show for each variable. For the above time data you might choose a range of 0 to 18 s, with each interval representing 2 s. For velocity, a range of 0 to 40 m/s with intervals of 5 m/s each is reasonable.

(2) Determine the dependent and independent variables. In this example, the velocity depends on the falling time, so velocity is the dependent variable.

(3) Plot the independent variable along the horizontal axis, or *x*-axis. Plot the dependent variable along the vertical axis, or *y*-axis. Connect the points with a smooth line.

Use the data below to answer the following questions.

Suppose a smoke jumper varied the mass of his equipment over 5 jumps, and you measured his different terminal velocities as follows:

Extra Mass (kg)	0	5	10	15	20
Terminal Velocity (m/s)	36	37	38	39	40

1. Identify the independent and dependent variables.

2. Choose the scales and intervals you would use to graph the data. **Hint:** Your velocity range does not have to start at 0 m/s.

3. Plot your graph.

CHALLENGE How do different scales give different impressions of the data? Try comparing several different scales for the same data.

MATH TUTORIAL
CLASSZONE.COM
Click on Math Tutorial for more help with creating a line graph.

Smoke jumpers parachute into burning forests in order to contain the flames.

KEY CONCEPT
3.3 Pressure depends on force and area.

BEFORE, you learned
- Frictional forces oppose motion when surfaces resist sliding
- Frictional force depends on the surface types and the total force pushing them together
- Air resistance is a type of friction on objects moving through air

NOW, you will learn
- How pressure is determined
- How forces act on objects in fluids
- How pressure changes in fluids

VOCABULARY
pressure p. 91
pascal p. 92

EXPLORE Pressure

How does surface area affect pressure?

PROCEDURE

1. Place the pencil flat on the Styrofoam board. Balance the book on top of the pencil. After 5 seconds, remove the book and the pencil. Observe the Styrofoam.

2. Balance the book on top of the pencil in an upright position as shown. After 5 seconds, remove the book and the pencil. Observe the Styrofoam.

MATERIALS
- sharpened pencil
- Styrofoam board
- book

WHAT DO YOU THINK?
- How did the effect on the Styrofoam change from step 1 to step 2?
- What do you think accounts for any differences you noted?

VOCABULARY
Create a four square diagram for *pressure* in your notebook.

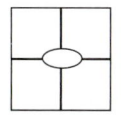

Pressure describes how a force is spread over an area.

Pressure is a measure of how much force is acting on a certain area. In other words, pressure describes how concentrated a force is. When a cat lies down on your lap, all the force of the cat's weight is spread out over a large area of your lap. If the cat stands up, however, all the force from the cat's weight is concentrated into its paws. The pressure the cat exerts on you increases when the cat stands up in your lap.

While the increased pressure may make you feel as if there is more force on you, the force is actually the same. The cat's weight is simply pressing on a smaller area. How you feel a force when it is pressing on you depends on both the force and the area over which it is applied.

Chapter 3: Gravity, Friction, and Pressure 91

One way to increase pressure is to increase force. If you press a wall with your finger, the harder you press, the more pressure you put on the wall. But you can also increase the pressure by decreasing the area. When you push a thumbtack into a wall, you apply a force to the thumbtack. The small area of the sharp point of the thumbtack produces a much larger pressure on the wall than the area of your finger does. The greater pressure from the thumbtack can pierce the wall, while the pressure from your finger alone cannot.

The following formula shows exactly how pressure depends on force and area:

$$\text{Pressure} = \frac{\text{Force}}{\text{Area}} \qquad P = \frac{F}{A}$$

In this formula, P is the pressure, F is the force in newtons, and A is the area over which the force is exerted, measured in square meters (m^2). The unit for pressure is the **pascal** (Pa). One pascal is the pressure exerted by one newton (1 N) of force on an area of one square meter (1 m^2). That is, one pascal is equivalent to one N/m^2.

Sometimes knowing pressure is more useful than knowing force. For example, many surfaces will break or crack if the pressure on them is too great. A person with snowshoes can walk on top of snow, while a person in hiking boots will sink into the snow.

READING TIP
Notice that when a unit, such as pascal or newton, is named for a person, the unit is not capitalized but its abbreviation is.

COMPARE How does the pressure from her snowshoes compare to the pressure from her boots?

Calculating Pressure

▶ **Sample Problem**

A winter hiker weighing 500 N is wearing snowshoes that cover an area of 0.2 m^2. What pressure does the hiker exert on the snow?

What do you know?   Area = 0.2 m^2, Force = 500 N

What do you want to find out?   Pressure

Write the formula: $P = \dfrac{F}{A}$

Substitute into the formula: $P = \dfrac{500 \text{ N}}{0.2 \text{ m}^2}$

Calculate and simplify: $P = 2500 \dfrac{N}{m^2} = 2500 \text{ N/m}^2$

Check that your units agree: Unit is N/m^2.
Unit of pressure is Pa, which is also N/m^2.
Units agree.

Answer: $P = 2500$ Pa

▶ **Practice the Math**

1. If a winter hiker weighing 500 N is wearing boots that have an area of 0.075 m^2, how much pressure is exerted on the snow?
2. A pressure of 2000 Pa is exerted on a surface with an area of 20 m^2. What is the total force exerted on the surface?

Pressure acts in all directions in fluids.

Fluids are made of loosely connected particles that are too small to see. These particles are in constant, rapid motion. The motion is random, which means particles are equally likely to move in any direction. Particles collide with—or crash into—one another and into the walls of a container holding the fluid. The particles also collide with any objects in the fluid.

As particles collide with an object in the fluid, they apply a constant force to the surfaces of the object. This force produces a pressure against the surfaces that the particles come in contact with. A fluid contains many particles, each moving in a different direction, and the force from each particle can be exerted in any direction. Therefore, the pressure exerted by the fluid acts on an object from all directions.

The diver in the picture below experiences a constant pressure from the particles—or molecules—in the water. Water molecules are constantly hitting her body from all directions. The collisions on all parts of her body produce a net force on the surface of her body.

SIMULATION
CLASSZONE.COM
Explore how a fluid produces pressure.

CHECK YOUR READING How does understanding particle motion help you understand fluid pressure?

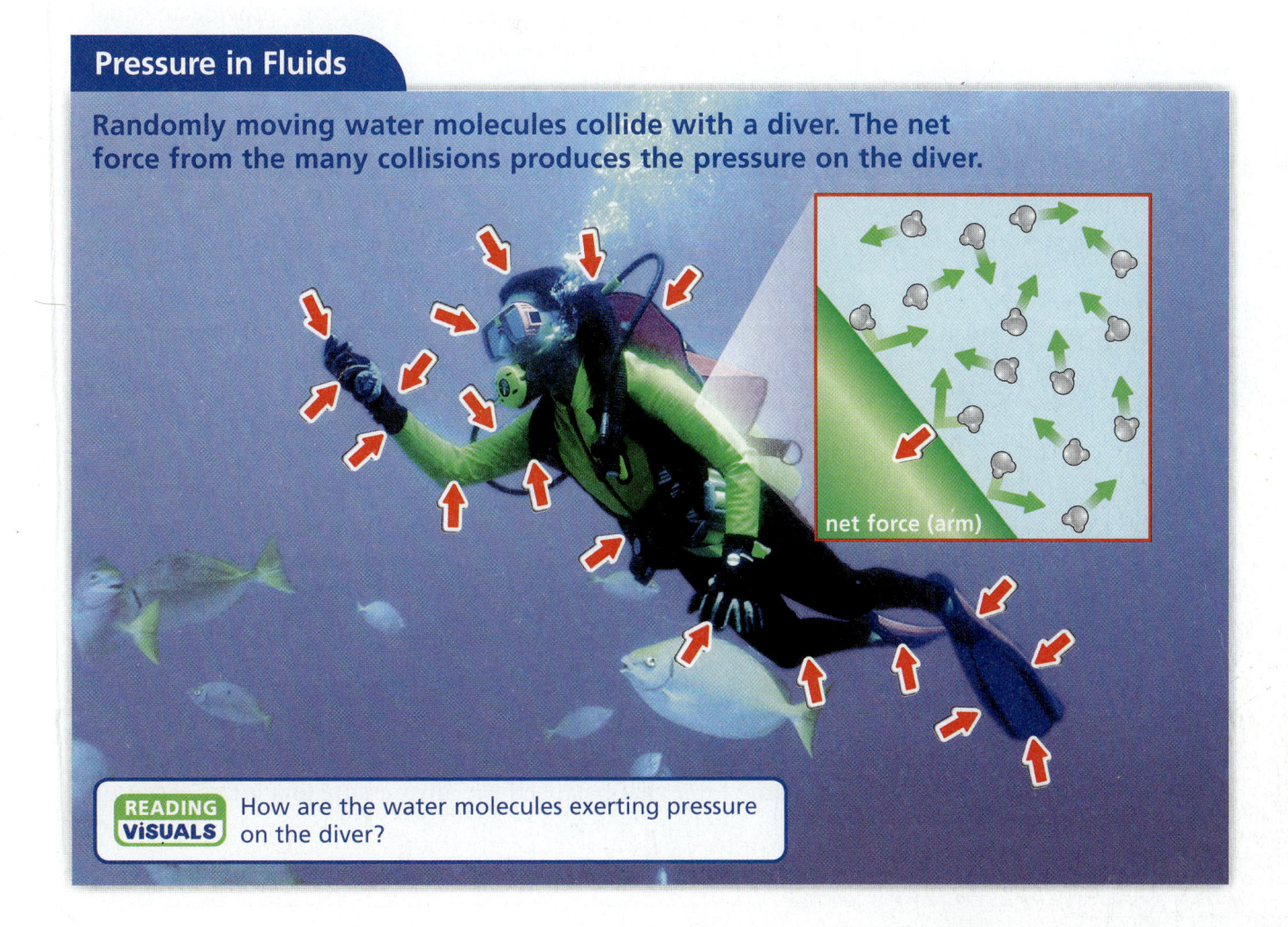

Pressure in Fluids

Randomly moving water molecules collide with a diver. The net force from the many collisions produces the pressure on the diver.

net force (arm)

READING VISUALS How are the water molecules exerting pressure on the diver?

Chapter 3: **Gravity, Friction, and Pressure** 93

Pressure in fluids depends on depth.

The pressure that a fluid exerts depends on the density and the depth of the fluid. Imagine that you have a tall cylinder sitting on the palm of your hand. As you fill the cylinder with water, the force of the water's weight exerts more and more pressure on your hand. The force of the water's weight increases as you put in more water.

Suppose you had two identical cylinders of water sitting on your hand. The cylinders would push with twice the weight of a single cylinder, but the force would be spread over twice the area. Therefore, the pressure would still be the same. The pressure does not depend on the total volume of the fluid, only on the depth and density.

Pressure in Air

Although you do not notice the weight of air, air exerts pressure on you at all times. At sea level, air exerts a pressure on you equal to about 100,000 pascals. This pressure is called atmospheric pressure and is referred to as one atmosphere. At this pressure, every square centimeter of your body experiences a force of ten newtons (2.2 lb). You do not notice it pushing your body inward, however, because the materials in your body provide an equal outward pressure that balances the air pressure.

Changing Elevation Air has weight. The more air there is above you, the greater the weight of that air. As you climb a mountain, the column of air above you is shorter and weighs less, so the pressure of air on you at higher elevations is less than one atmosphere.

Changing Density The air at the top of a column presses down on the air below it. The farther down the column, the more weight there is above to press downward. Air at lower elevations is more compressed, and therefore denser, than air at higher elevations.

Effects on Pressure Pressure is exerted by individual molecules colliding with an object. In denser air, there are more molecules—and therefore more collisions. An increase in the number of collisions results in an increase in the force, and therefore pressure, exerted by the air.

As you travel up a mountain, the air pressure on you decreases. For a short time, the pressure on the inside surface of your eardrum may continue to push out with the same force that balanced the air pressure at a lower elevation. The eardrum is pushed outward, and you may feel pain until your internal pressure adjusts to the new air pressure.

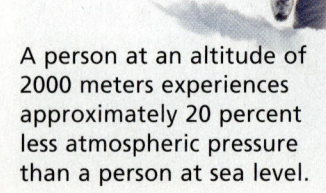

A person at an altitude of 2000 meters experiences approximately 20 percent less atmospheric pressure than a person at sea level.

Pressure in Water

Unlike air molecules, water molecules are already very close together. The density of water does not change very much with depth. However, the deeper you go underwater, the more water there is above you. The weight of that water above you produces the water pressure acting on your body. Just as air pressure increases at lower elevations, water pressure increases with greater water depth.

Water exerts more pressure on you than air does because water has a greater density than air. Therefore, the change in weight of the column of water above you as you dive is greater for each meter that you descend than it is in air. There is a greater difference in pressure if you dive ten meters farther down in the ocean than if you walked ten meters down a mountain. In fact, ten meters of water above you applies about as much pressure on you as the entire atmosphere does.

If you were to dive 1000 meters (3300 ft) below the surface of the ocean, the pressure would be nearly 100 times greater than pressure from the atmosphere. The force of this pressure would collapse your lungs unless you were protected by special deep-sea diving equipment. As scientists explore the ocean to greater depths, new underwater vehicles are designed that can withstand the increase in water pressure. Some whales, however, can dive to a depth of 1000 meters without being injured. As these whales dive to great depths, their lungs are almost completely collapsed by the pressure. However, the whales have adapted to the collapse—they store most of their oxygen intake in their muscles and blood instead of within their lungs.

A deep-diving whale at 1000 meters below the surface experiences about 34 times more pressure than a turtle diving to a depth of 20 meters (65 ft).

CHECK YOUR READING Why is water pressure greater than air pressure?

3.3 Review

KEY CONCEPTS

1. How is pressure related to force and surface area?
2. Describe the way in which a fluid exerts pressure on an object immersed in it.
3. How does changing elevation affect air pressure? How does changing depth affect water pressure?

CRITICAL THINKING

4. **Calculate** If a board with an area of 3 m² has a 12 N force exerted on it, what is the pressure on the board?
5. **Infer** What might cause a balloon blown up at a low altitude to burst if it is taken to a higher altitude?

CHALLENGE

6. **Synthesize** During cold winters, ice can form on small lakes and ponds. Many people enjoy skating on the ice. Occasionally, a person skates on thin ice and breaks through it. Why do rescue workers lie flat on the ice instead of walking upright when reaching out to help rescue a skater?

Chapter 3: **Gravity, Friction, and Pressure** 95

CHAPTER INVESTIGATION

Pressure in Fluids

OVERVIEW AND PURPOSE When you put your hand under a faucet, you experience water pressure. Underwater explorers also experience water pressure. In this investigation you will
- change the depth and volume of a column of water
- determine what factors affect pressure

▶ Problem

What factors affect water pressure?

▶ Hypothesize

Write two hypotheses to explain what you expect to happen to the water pressure as you change the depth and volume of the water column. Your hypotheses (one for depth, one for volume) should take the form of "If . . . , then . . . , because . . ." statements.

▶ Procedure

1. Create a data table like the one shown on the sample notebook page.

2. Using a nail, poke a hole in the side of each bottle 4 cm from the bottom of the bottle.

3. Set up the materials as shown on the left. Put a ruler in the small bottle so that the lower numbers are at the bottom.

4. Put your finger over the hole so no water will squirt out. Add or remove water (by lifting your finger off the hole) so that the water level is exactly at the 12 cm mark.

5. Release your finger from the hole, while your partner reads the exact mark where the water hits the meter stick. Cover the hole immediately after your partner reads the distance the water squirted. Record the distance on the line for this depth in your table.

MATERIALS
- nail
- 2 plastic bottles, small and large, with tops cut off
- ruler
- plastic container
- meter stick
- coffee can
- water

6. Add or remove water so that the water level is now exactly at the 11 cm mark. Repeat step 5.

7. Continue adding, removing, and squirting water at each whole centimeter mark until no more water squirts from the bottle.

8. Repeat steps 4–7 two more times for a total of three trials.

9. Repeat steps 4–8 using the large bottle.

Observe and Analyze

1. **RECORD OBSERVATIONS** Be sure that your data table is complete.

2. **GRAPH** Construct a graph showing distance versus depth. Draw two curves, one for the small bottle and one for the large bottle. Use different colors for the two curves.

3. **IDENTIFY VARIABLES AND CONSTANTS** List the variables and constants for the experiment using the small bottle and the experiment using the large bottle.

4. **ANALYZE** Is the depth greater when the bottle is more full or more empty? When did the water squirt farther, when the bottle was more full or more empty?

5. **ANALYZE** Did the water squirt farther when you used the small or the large bottle?

Conclude

1. **INTERPRET** Answer the question posed in the problem.

2. **ANALYZE** Examine your graph and compare your results with your hypotheses. Do your results support your hypotheses?

3. **INFER** How does depth affect pressure? How does volume affect pressure?

4. **IDENTIFY LIMITS** What possible limitations or errors did you experience or could you have experienced with this investigation?

5. **APPLY** Dams store water for irrigation, home use, and hydroelectric power. Explain why dams must be constructed so that they are much thicker at the bottom than at the top.

6. **APPLY** Have you ever dived to the bottom of a swimming pool to pick up a coin? Describe what you felt as you swam toward the bottom.

INVESTIGATE Further

CHALLENGE Repeat the investigation using a liquid with a density that is quite different from water. Measure the distance the liquid travels, and graph the new data in a different color. Is there a difference? Why do you think there is or is not a difference in pressure between liquids of different densities?

Pressure in Fluids

Problem What factors affect water pressure?

Hypothesize

Observe and Analyze

Table 1. Distance Water Squirted with Small Bottle

Depth of water small bottle (cm)	Trial 1	Trial 2	Trial 3	Average
12				
11				
10				

Table 2. Distance Water Squirted with Large Bottle

Depth of water large bottle (cm)	Trial 1	Trial 2	Trial 3	Average
12				
11				
10				

Conclude

Chapter 3: **Gravity, Friction, and Pressure**

KEY CONCEPT
3.4 Fluids can exert a force on objects.

BEFORE, you learned
- Pressure depends on force and area
- Pressure acts in all directions in fluids
- Density is mass divided by volume

NOW, you will learn
- How fluids apply forces to objects
- How the motion of a fluid affects the pressure it exerts
- How forces are transmitted through fluids

VOCABULARY
buoyant force p. 98
Bernoulli's principle p. 100
Pascal's principle p. 102

EXPLORE Forces in Liquid
How does water affect weight?

PROCEDURE

1. Tie a piece of string to the middle of the pencil. Tie 4 paper clips to each end of the pencil as shown.
2. Move the middle string along the pencil until the paper clips are balanced and the pencil hangs flat.
3. While keeping the pencil balanced, slowly lower the paper clips on one end of the pencil into the water. Observe what happens.

MATERIALS
- 3 pieces of string
- pencil
- 8 paper clips
- cup full of water

WHAT DO YOU THINK?
- How did the water affect the balance between the two sets of paper clips?
- Did the water exert a force on the paper clips? Explain.

Fluids can exert an upward force on objects.

If you drop an ice cube in air, it falls to the floor. If you drop the ice cube into water, it may sink a little at first, but the cube quickly rises upward until it floats. You know that gravity is pulling downward on the ice, even when it is in the water. If the ice cube is not sinking, there must be some force balancing gravity that is pushing upward on it.

The upward force on objects in a fluid is called **buoyant force**, or buoyancy. Buoyancy is why ice floats in water. Because of buoyant force, objects seem lighter in water. For example, it is easier to lift a heavy rock in water than on land because the buoyant force pushes upward on the rock, reducing the net force you need to lift it.

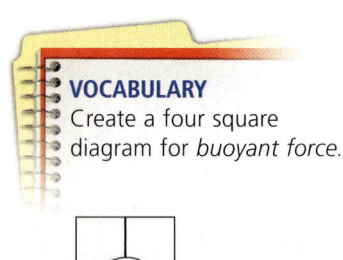

VOCABULARY
Create a four square diagram for *buoyant force*.

98 Unit: Motion and Forces

Buoyancy

The photograph on the right shows a balloon that has been pushed into a beaker of water. Remember that in a fluid, pressure increases with depth. This means that there is greater pressure acting on the bottom of the balloon than on the top of it. The pressure difference between the top and bottom of the balloon produces a net force that is pushing the balloon upward.

When you push a balloon underwater, the water level rises because the water and the balloon cannot be in the same place at the same time. The volume of the water has not changed, but some of the water has been displaced, or moved, by the balloon. The volume of the displaced water is equal to the volume of the balloon. The buoyant force on the balloon is equal to the weight of the displaced water. A deflated balloon would displace less water and would therefore have a smaller buoyant force on it.

CHECK YOUR READING Why does increasing the volume of an object increase the buoyant force on it when it is in a fluid?

Density and Buoyancy

Whether or not an object floats in a fluid depends on the densities of both the object and the fluid. Density is a measure of the amount of matter packed into a unit volume. The density of an object is equal to its mass divided by its volume, and is commonly measured in grams per cubic centimeter (g/cm^3).

If an object is less dense than the fluid it is in, the fluid the object displaces can weigh more than the object. A wooden ball that is pushed underwater, as in the beaker below and on the left, rises to the top and floats. An object rising in a liquid has a buoyant force acting upon it that is greater than its own weight. If an object is floating in a liquid, the buoyant force is balancing the weight.

READING TIP

Remember that both air and water are fluids, and water has a greater density than air. Therefore, water has a greater buoyant force.

If the object is more dense than the fluid it is in, the object weighs more than the fluid it displaces. A glass marble placed in the beaker on the far right sinks to the bottom because glass is denser than water. The weight of the water the marble displaces is less than the weight of the marble. A sinking object has a weight that is greater than the buoyant force on it.

Chapter 3: **Gravity, Friction, and Pressure** 99

The motion of a fluid affects its pressure.

The motion of a fluid affects the amount of pressure it exerts. A faster-moving fluid exerts less pressure as it flows over the surface of an object than a slower moving fluid. For example, wind blowing over a chimney top decreases the pressure at the top of the chimney. The faster air has less pressure than the slower-moving air in the fireplace. The increased pressure difference more effectively pulls the smoke from a fire out of the fireplace and up the chimney.

Bernoulli's Principle

Bernoulli's principle, named after Daniel Bernoulli (buhr-NOO-lee), a Swiss mathematician who lived in the 1700s, describes the effects of fluid motion on pressure. In general, **Bernoulli's principle** says that an increase in the speed of the motion of a fluid decreases the pressure within the fluid. The faster a fluid moves, the less pressure it exerts on surfaces or openings it flows over.

CHECK YOUR READING What is the relationship between the speed of a fluid and the pressure that the fluid exerts?

INVESTIGATE Bernoulli's Principle

How does the speed of air affect air pressure?

PROCEDURE

1. Use the pen to mark off intervals of 1 cm along the length of one of the straws.
2. Put a drop of food coloring in the cup of water and stir it. Place the marked straw into the cup and hold it upright so that the water level in the straw is at one of the marks. The straw should not touch the bottom of the cup.
3. Position the second straw as shown. Blow across the open end of the marked straw. Observe the level of the water in the marked straw as you blow.
4. Blow harder and then softer. Observe the water level as you change the speed of the air.

WHAT DO YOU THINK?
- What happened to the water in the straw as you blew?
- How did the speed of the air relate to the changes you observed?

CHALLENGE What results would you expect if you blew over the top of a tube with a closed bottom instead of the straw? Explain.

SKILL FOCUS
Observing

MATERIALS
- pen
- ruler
- two clear straws
- clear plastic cup filled with water
- food coloring

TIME
15 minutes

Applying Bernoulli's Principle

Bernoulli's principle has many applications. One important application is used in airplanes. Airplane wings can be shaped to take advantage of Bernoulli's principle. Certain wing shapes cause the air flowing over the top of the wing to move faster than the air flowing under the wing. Such a design improves the lifting force on a flying airplane.

Many racecars, however, have a device on the rear of the car that has the reverse effect. The device is designed like an upside-down airplane wing. This shape increases the pressure on the top of the car. The car is pressed downward on the road, which increases friction between the tires and the road. With more friction, the car is less likely to skid as it goes around curves at high speeds.

A prairie-dog colony also shows Bernoulli's principle in action. The mounds that prairie dogs build over some entrances to their burrows help to keep the burrows well-ventilated.

1. Air closer to the ground tends to move at slower speeds than air higher up. The air over an entrance at ground level generally moves slower than the air over an entrance in a raised mound.

2. The increased speed of the air over a raised mound entrance decreases the pressure over that opening.

3. The greater air pressure over a ground-level entrance produces an unbalanced force that pushes air through the tunnels and out the higher mound entrance.

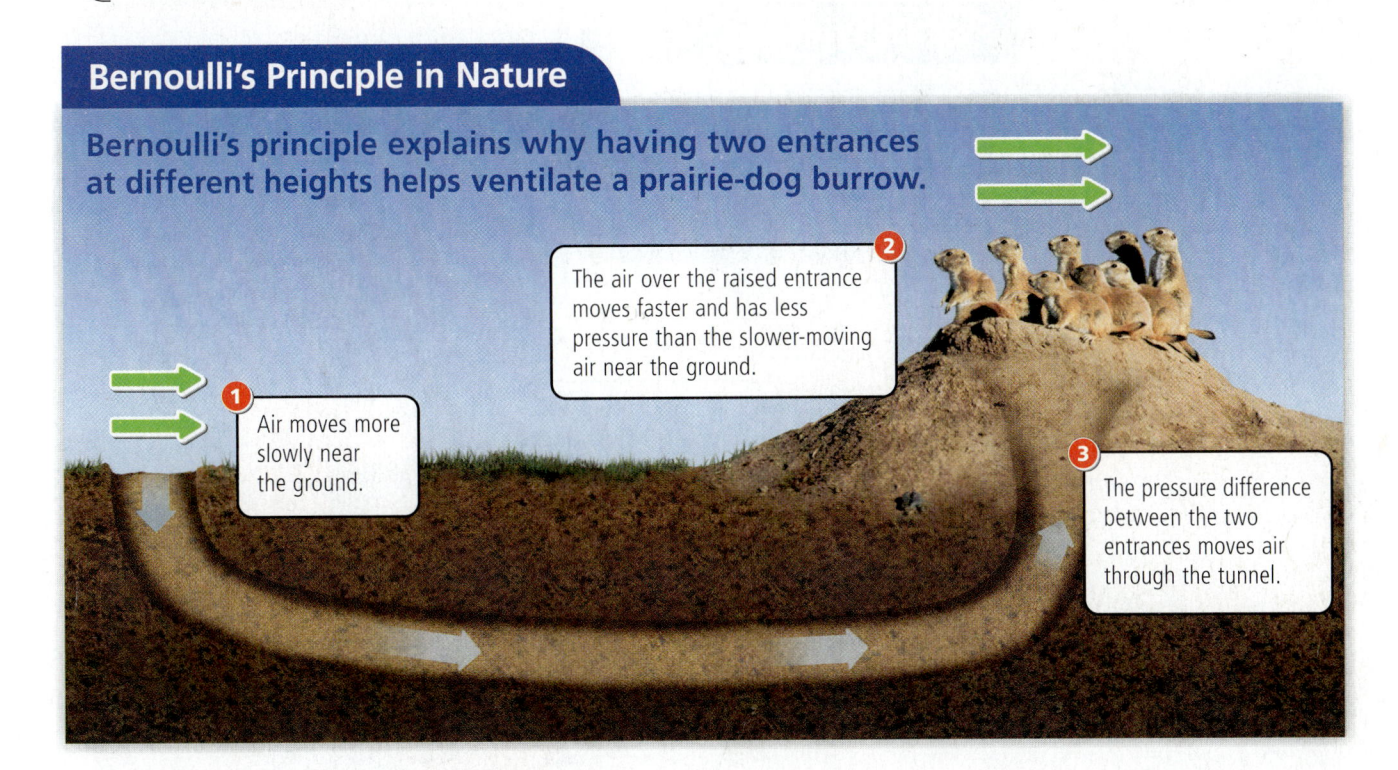

Bernoulli's Principle in Nature

Bernoulli's principle explains why having two entrances at different heights helps ventilate a prairie-dog burrow.

1. Air moves more slowly near the ground.

2. The air over the raised entrance moves faster and has less pressure than the slower-moving air near the ground.

3. The pressure difference between the two entrances moves air through the tunnel.

Chapter 3: **Gravity, Friction, and Pressure** 101

Forces can be transmitted through fluids.

Imagine you have a bottle full of water. You place the bottle cap on it, but you do not tighten the cap. You give the bottle a hard squeeze and the cap falls off. How was the force you put on the bottle transferred to the bottle cap?

Pascal's Principle

In the 1600s Blaise Pascal (pa-SKAL), a French scientist for whom the unit of measure called the pascal was named, experimented with fluids in containers. One of his key discoveries is called Pascal's principle. **Pascal's principle** states that when an outside pressure is applied at any point to a fluid in a container, that pressure is transmitted throughout the fluid with equal strength.

You can use Pascal's principle to transmit a force through a fluid. Some car jacks lift cars using Pascal's principle. These jacks contain liquids that transmit and increase the force that you apply.

① The part of the jack that moves down and pushes on the liquid is called a piston. As you push down on the piston, you increase the pressure on the liquid.

② The increase in pressure is equal to your applied force divided by the area of the downward-pushing piston. This increase in pressure is transmitted throughout the liquid.

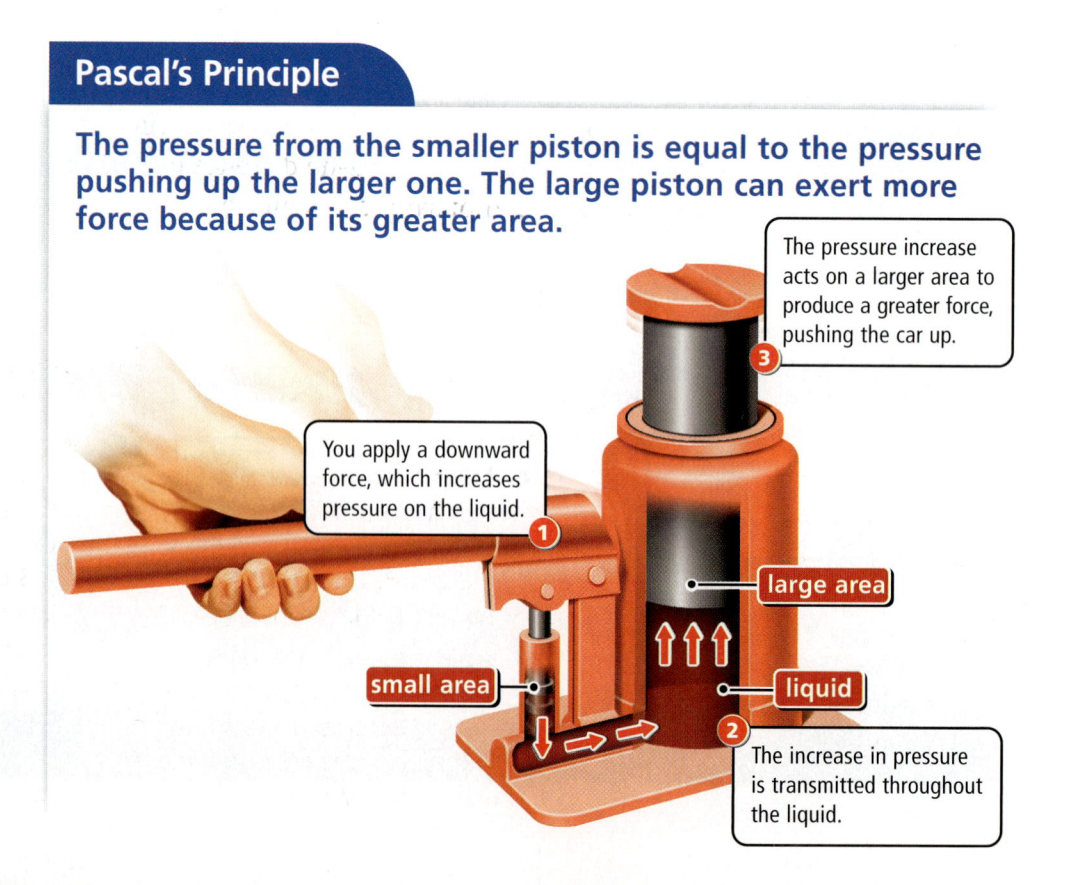

Pascal's Principle

The pressure from the smaller piston is equal to the pressure pushing up the larger one. The large piston can exert more force because of its greater area.

You apply a downward force, which increases pressure on the liquid. ①

② The increase in pressure is transmitted throughout the liquid.

③ The pressure increase acts on a larger area to produce a greater force, pushing the car up.

small area | liquid | large area

3) The increased pressure pushes upward on another piston, which raises the car. This piston has a large area compared with the first piston, so the upward force is greater than the downward force. A large enough area produces the force needed to lift a car. However, the larger piston does not move upward as far as the smaller one moved downward.

CHECK YOUR READING Describe how pressure is transmitted through a fluid.

Hydraulics

Machines that use liquids to transmit or increase a force are called hydraulic (hy-DRAW-lihk) machines. The advantage to using a liquid instead of a gas is that when you squeeze a liquid, its volume does not change much. The molecules in a liquid are so close together that it is hard to push the molecules any closer. Gas molecules, however, have a lot of space between them. If you apply pressure to a gas, you decrease its volume.

The hydraulic arm on the garbage truck lifts and empties trash cans.

Although hydraulic systems are used in large machines such as garbage trucks, research is being done on using hydraulics on a much smaller scale. Researchers are developing a storage chip similar to a computer chip that uses hydraulics rather than electronics. This chip uses pipes and pumps to move fluid into specific chambers on a rubber chip. Researchers hope that a hydraulic chip system will eventually allow scientists to use a single hand-held device to perform chemical experiments with over a thousand different liquids.

3.4 Review

KEY CONCEPTS

1. Why is there an upward force on objects in water?
2. How does changing the speed of a fluid affect its pressure?
3. If you push a cork into the neck of a bottle filled with air, what happens to the pressure inside the bottle?

CRITICAL THINKING

4. **Infer** Ebony is a dark wood that has a density of 1.2 g/cm^3. Water has a density of 1.0 g/cm^3. Will a block of ebony float in water? Explain.
5. **Analyze** When you use a spray bottle, you force air over a small tube inside the bottle. Explain why the liquid inside the bottle comes out.

CHALLENGE

6. **Synthesize** If you apply a force of 20 N downward on a car jack piston with an area of 2.5 cm^2, what force will be applied to the upward piston if it has an area of 400 cm^2? Hint: Remember that pressure equals force divided by area.

3 Chapter Review

the BIG idea
Newton's laws apply to all forces.

CONTENT REVIEW
CLASSZONE.COM

KEY CONCEPTS SUMMARY

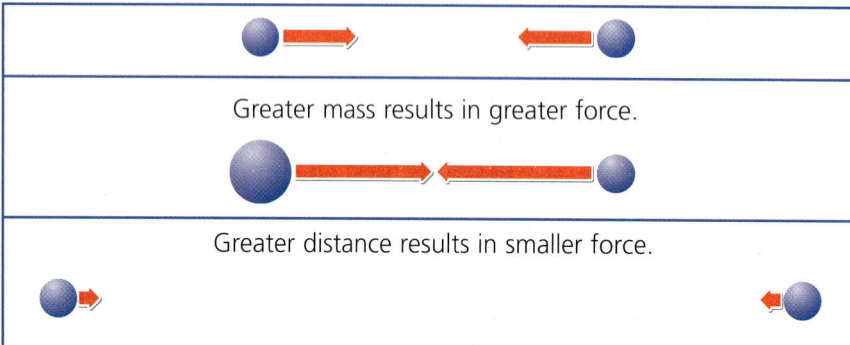

3.1 Gravity is a force exerted by masses.

Greater mass results in greater force.

Greater distance results in smaller force.

VOCABULARY
gravity p. 77
weight p. 79
orbit p. 80

3.2 Friction is a force that opposes motion.

Frictional force depends on—
- types of surfaces
- motion of surfaces
- force pressing surfaces together

Air resistance is a type of friction.

friction

VOCABULARY
friction p. 85
fluid p. 88
air resistance p. 89

3.3 Pressure depends on force and area.

$$\text{Pressure} = \frac{\text{Force}}{\text{Area}}$$

Pressure in a fluid acts in all directions.

VOCABULARY
pressure p. 91
pascal p. 92

3.4 Fluids can exert a force on objects.

- Buoyant force is equal to the weight of the displaced fluid.
- A faster-moving fluid produces less pressure than a slower-moving one.
- Pressure is transmitted through fluids.

VOCABULARY
buoyant force p. 98
Bernoulli's principle p. 100
Pascal's principle p. 102

104 Unit: Motion and Forces

Reviewing Vocabulary

Write a sentence describing the relationship between each pair of terms.

1. gravity, weight
2. gravity, orbit
3. pressure, pascal
4. fluid, friction
5. density, buoyant force
6. fluid, Bernoulli's principle

Reviewing Key Concepts

Multiple Choice *Choose the letter of the best answer.*

7. Which force keeps Venus in orbit around the Sun?
   a. gravity
   b. friction
   c. hydraulic
   d. buoyancy

8. You and a classmate are one meter apart. If you move farther away, how does the gravitational force between you and your classmate change?
   a. It increases.
   b. It decreases.
   c. It stays the same.
   d. It disappears.

9. You kick a ball on a level sidewalk. It rolls to a stop because
   a. there is no force on the ball
   b. gravity slows the ball down
   c. air pressure is pushing down on the ball
   d. friction slows the ball down

10. You push a chair at a constant velocity using a force of 5 N to overcome friction. You stop to rest, then push again. To start the chair moving again, you must use a force that is
    a. greater than 5 N
    b. equal to 5 N
    c. greater than 0 N but less than 5 N
    d. 0 N

11. How could you place an empty bottle on a table so that it produces the greatest amount of pressure on the table?

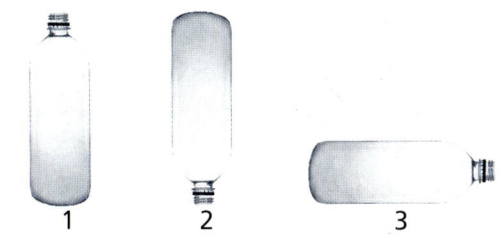

    a. position 1
    b. position 2
    c. position 3
    d. All positions produce the same pressure.

12. As you climb up a mountain, air pressure
    a. increases
    b. decreases
    c. stays the same
    d. changes unpredictably

13. If you squeeze a balloon in the middle, what happens to the air pressure inside the balloon?
    a. It increases only in the middle.
    b. It decreases only in the middle.
    c. It increases throughout.
    d. It decreases throughout.

Short Answer *Write a short answer to each question.*

14. How does the force of attraction between large masses compare with the force of attraction between small masses at the same distance?

15. Explain why a satellite in orbit around Earth does not crash into Earth.

16. You are pushing a dresser with drawers filled with clothing. What could you do to reduce the friction between the dresser and the floor?

17. Why is water pressure greater at a depth of 20 feet than it is at a depth of 10 feet?

18. If you blow over the top of a small strip of paper, the paper bends upward. Why?

Thinking Critically

19. **APPLY** Explain why an iron boat can float in water, while an iron cube cannot.

20. **COMPARE** How does the friction between solid surfaces compare with the friction between a moving object and a fluid?

21. **APPLY** Explain why a block of wood gets warm when it is rubbed with sandpaper.

22. **PREDICT** The Moon's orbit is gradually increasing. Each year the Moon is about 3.8 cm farther from Earth than the year before. How does this change affect the force of gravity between Earth and the Moon?

23. **APPLY** The Moon has one-sixth the gravity of Earth. Why would it be easier to launch spacecraft into orbit around the Moon than around Earth?

Use the photograph below to answer the next three questions.

24. **APPLY** A skydiver jumps out of a plane. After he reaches terminal velocity, he opens his parachute. Draw a sketch showing the forces of air resistance and gravity on the skydiver after the parachute opens. Use a longer arrow for a greater force.

25. **SYNTHESIZE** Air is a fluid, which produces a small buoyant force on the skydiver. How does this buoyant force change after he opens his parachute? Why?

26. **INFER** The Moon has no atmosphere. Would it be safe to skydive on the Moon? Why or why not?

27. **INFER** When oil and water are mixed together, the two substances separate and the oil floats to the top. How does the density of oil compare with the density of water?

28. **COMPARE** Three flasks are filled with colored water as shown below. How does the water pressure at the bottom of each flask compare with the water pressure at the bottom of the other two?

1   2   3

Using Math Skills in Science

Complete the following calculations.

29. How much force does a 10 kg marble exert on the ground?

30. A force of 50 N is applied on a piece of wood with an area of 0.5 m². What is the pressure on the wood?

the BIG idea

31. **ANALYZE** Look again at the picture on pages 74–75. What forces are acting on the snowboarder? on the snow? Use Newton's laws to explain how these forces enable the snowboarder to move down the hill.

32. **SYNTHESIZE** Choose two concepts discussed in this chapter, and describe how Newton's laws relate to those concepts.

UNIT PROJECTS

Check your schedule for your unit project. How are you doing? Be sure that you have placed data or notes from your research into your project folder.

Standardized Test Practice

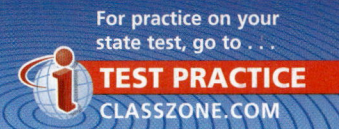

Interpreting Diagrams

Study the diagram and then answer the questions that follow.

Bernoulli's principle states that an increase in the speed of the motion of a fluid decreases the pressure exerted by the fluid. The diagram below relates the movement of a curve ball in baseball to this principle. The ball is shown from above.

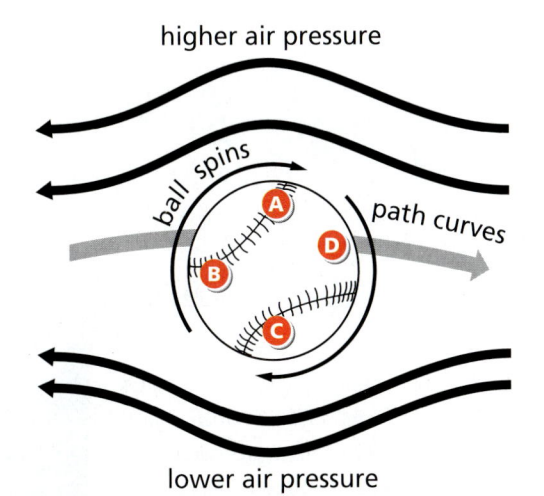

1. To which of these properties does Bernoulli's principle apply?
   a. air pressure
   b. temperature
   c. air resistance
   d. density

2. Where is the air moving fastest in the diagram?
   a. region A
   b. region B
   c. region C
   d. region D

3. Because the ball is spinning, the air on one side is moving faster than on the other side. This causes the ball to curve due to the
   a. air molecules moving slowly and evenly around the ball
   b. forward motion of the ball
   c. difference in air pressure on the ball
   d. changing air temperature around the ball

4. If the baseball were spinning as it moved forward underwater, instead of through the air, how would the pressure of the fluid act on the ball?
   a. The water pressure would be the same on all sides.
   b. The water pressure would vary as air pressure does.
   c. The water pressure would be greatest on the side where air pressure was least.
   d. The water pressure would prevent the ball from spinning.

Extended Response

Answer the two questions below in detail. Include some of the terms from the word box. Underline each term you use in your answer.

acceleration	air resistance	density
fluid	friction	gravity
mass	pressure	velocity

5. If a feather and a bowling ball are dropped from the same height, will they fall at the same rate? Explain.

6. A balloon filled with helium or hot air can float in the atmosphere. A balloon filled with air from your lungs falls to the ground when it is released. Why do these balloons behave differently?

TIMELINES in Science

UNDERSTANDING FORCES

In ancient times, people thought that an object would not move unless it was pushed. Scientists came up with ingenious ways to explain how objects like arrows stayed in motion. Over time, they came to understand that all motion could be described by three basic laws. Modern achievements such as suspension bridges and space exploration are possible because of the experiments with motion and forces performed by scientists and philosophers over hundreds of years.

This timeline shows just a few of the many steps on the path toward understanding forces. Notice how scientists used the observations and ideas of previous thinkers as a springboard for developing new theories. The boxes below the timeline show how technology has led to new insights and to applications of those ideas.

350 B.C.
Aristotle Discusses Motion

The Greek philosopher Aristotle states that the natural condition of an object is to be at rest. A force is necessary to keep the object in motion. The greater the force, the faster the object moves.

EVENTS

400 B.C.   350 B.C.   300 B.C.

APPLICATIONS AND TECHNOLOGY

TECHNOLOGY

Catapulting into History

As early as 400 B.C., armies were using objects in motion to do work. Catapults, or machines for hurling stones and spears, were used as military weapons. Five hundred years later, the Roman army used catapults mounted on wheels. In the Middle Ages, young trees were sometimes bent back, loaded with an object, and then released like a large slingshot. Today catapult technology is used to launch airplanes from aircraft carriers. A piston powered by steam propels the plane along the deck of the aircraft carrier until it reaches takeoff speed.

250 B.C.
Levers and Buoyancy Explained
The Greek inventor Archimedes uses a mathematical equation to explain how a small weight can balance a much larger weight near a lever's fulcrum. He also explains buoyancy, which provides a way of measuring volume.

A.D. 1121
Force Acting on Objects Described
Persian astronomer al-Khazini asserts that a force acts on all objects to pull them toward the center of Earth. This force varies, he says, depending on whether the object moves through air, water, or another medium. His careful notes and drawings illustrate these principles.

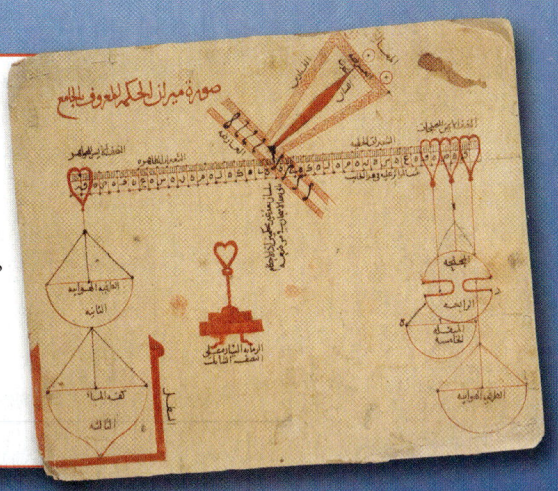

1150
Perpetual-Motion Machine Described
Indian mathematician and physicist Bhaskara describes a wheel that uses closed containers of liquid to turn forever without stopping. If it worked, his idea would promise an unending source of power that does not rely on an external source.

250 B.C.   A.D. 1100   1150   1200

APPLICATION
The First Steam-Powered Engine
In the first century A.D., Hero of Alexandria, a Greek inventor, created the first known steam engine, called the aeolipile. It was a hollow ball with two cylinders jutting out in opposite directions. The ball was suspended above a kettle that was filled with water and placed over a fire. As the water boiled, steam caused the ball to spin. The Greeks never used this device for work. In 1690, Sir Isaac Newton formulated the principle of the aeolipile in scientific terms in his third law of motion. A steam engine designed for work was built in 1698. The aeolipile is the earliest version of steam-powered pumps, steam locomotives, jet engines, and rockets.

Timelines in Science 109

1638
Objects Need No Force to Keep Moving
Italian astronomer Galileo Galilei says that an object's natural state is either in constant motion or at rest. Having observed the motion of objects on ramps, he concludes that an object in motion will slow down or speed up only if a force is exerted on it. He also claims that all objects dropped near the surface of Earth fall with the same acceleration due to the force of gravity.

1494
Perpetual-Motion Machine Impossible
Italian painter and engineer Leonardo da Vinci proves that it is impossible to build a perpetual-motion machine that works. He states that the force of friction keeps a wheel from turning forever without more force being applied.

1687
An Object's Motion Can Be Predicted
English scientist Sir Isaac Newton publishes his three laws of motion, which use Galileo's ideas as a foundation. He concludes that Earth exerts a gravitational force on objects on its surface and that Earth's gravity keeps the Moon in orbit.

1500　1550　1600　1650　1700　1750　1800

APPLICATION
A New and Improved Steam Engine
Scottish scientist James Watt designed steam engines that were much more efficient, and much smaller, than older models. About 500 of Watt's engines were in use by 1800. His pump engines drew water out of coal mines, and his rotating engines were used in factories and cotton mills. Watt's steam engines opened the way to the Industrial Revolution. They were used in major industries such as textile manufacturing, railroad transportation, and mining. Watt's steam technology also opened up new areas of research in heat, kinetic energy, and motion.

1919
Gravity Bends Light
A solar eclipse confirms German-American physicist Albert Einstein's modification of Newton's laws. Einstein's theory states that the path of a light beam will be affected by nearby massive objects. During the eclipse, the stars appear to shift slightly away from one another because their light has been bent by the Sun's gravity.

2001
Supercomputers Model Strong Force
Scientists have been using supercomputers to model the force that holds particles in the nucleus of an atom together. This force, called the strong force, cannot be measured directly in the same way that gravity and other forces can. Instead, computer models allow scientists to make predictions that are then compared with experimental results.

RESOURCE CENTER
CLASSZONE.COM
Get current research on force and motion.

1850 1900 1950 2000

TECHNOLOGY
Science Propels Exploration of Outer Space
An increased understanding of forces made space exploration possible. In 1926 American scientist Robert H. Goddard constructed and tested the first liquid-propelled rocket. A replica of Goddard's rocket can be seen at the National Air and Space Museum in Washington, D.C. In 1929 Goddard launched a rocket that carried the first scientific payload, a barometer and a camera.

Many later achievements—including the 1969 walk on the Moon—are a direct result of Goddard's trail-blazing space research.

INTO THE FUTURE
Since ancient times, scientists and philosophers have tried to explain how forces move objects. We now know that the laws of gravity and motion extend beyond Earth. Engineers have designed powerful spacecraft that can carry robots—and eventually people—to Mars and beyond. Rockets using new technology travel farther on less fuel than liquid-fueled rockets do.

Space travel and related research will continue to unravel the mysteries of forces in the universe. For example, recent observations of outer space provide evidence of an unidentified force causing the universe to expand rapidly. As people venture beyond Earth, we may learn new and unexpected things about the forces we have come to understand so far. The timeline shown here is just the beginning of our knowledge of forces.

ACTIVITIES
Reliving History
Bhaskara's design for a perpetual-motion machine involved a wheel with containers of mercury around the rim. As the wheel turned, the mercury would move in such a way that the wheel would always be heavier on one side—and stay in motion. Now we know that this theory goes against the laws of physics. Observe a wheel, a pendulum, or a swing. Think about why it cannot stay in motion forever.

Writing About Science
Suppose you won a trip to outer space. Write a letter accepting or refusing the prize. Give your reasons.

Timelines in Science 111 C

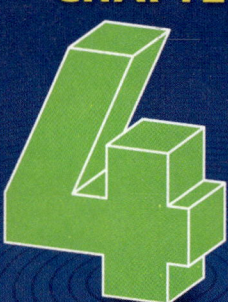

CHAPTER 4
Work and Energy

the BIG idea
Energy is transferred when a force moves an object.

Key Concepts

SECTION 4.1
Work is the use of force to move an object.
Learn about the relationship between force and work.

SECTION 4.2
Energy is transferred when work is done.
Learn how energy is related to work.

SECTION 4.3
Power is the rate at which work is done.
Learn to calculate power from work and energy.

Which takes more work, lifting a box or holding a box? Why?

Internet Preview
CLASSZONE.COM
Chapter 4 online resources: Content Review, Simulation, Visualization, two Resource Centers, Math Tutorial, Test Practice

112 Unit: Motion and Forces

EXPLORE the BIG idea

Bouncing Ball

Drop a large ball on a hard, flat floor. Let it bounce several times. Notice the height the ball reaches after each bounce.

Observe and Think
How did the height change? Why do you think this happens? Sketch the path of the ball through several bounces.

Power Climbing

Walk up a flight of stairs wearing a backpack. Run up the same flight of stairs wearing the backpack.

Observe and Think
Compare and contrast both trips up the stairs. Which one took greater effort? Did you apply the same force against gravity each time?

Internet Activity: Work

Go to **ClassZone.com** to simulate lifting weights of different masses. Determine how much work is done in lifting each weight by watching your progress on a work meter.

Observe and Think
Do you think more work will be done if the weights are lifted higher?

NSTA scilinks.org **SCLINKS**

Potential and Kinetic Energy **Code: MDL007**

Chapter 4: **Work and Energy** 113

CHAPTER 4
Getting Ready to Learn

CONCEPT REVIEW

- Forces change the motion of objects in predictable ways.
- Velocity is a measure of the speed and direction of an object.
- An unbalanced force produces acceleration.

VOCABULARY REVIEW

velocity p. 22
force p. 41

See Glossary for definitions.
energy, mass

CONTENT REVIEW
CLASSZONE.COM
Review concepts and vocabulary.

TAKING NOTES

MAIN IDEA WEB

Write each new blue heading in a box. Then write notes in boxes around it that give important terms and details about that blue heading.

CHOOSE YOUR OWN STRATEGY

Take notes about new vocabulary terms using one or more of the strategies from earlier chapters—**description wheel, magnet words,** or **four square.** Feel free to mix and match the strategies or use a different strategy.

See the Note-Taking Handbook on pages R45–R51.

SCIENCE NOTEBOOK

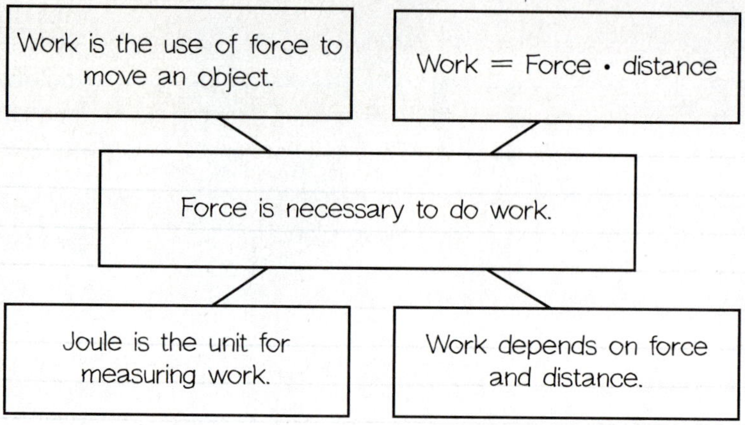

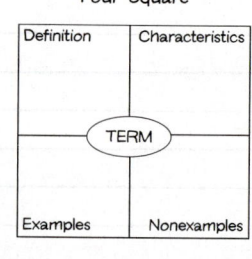

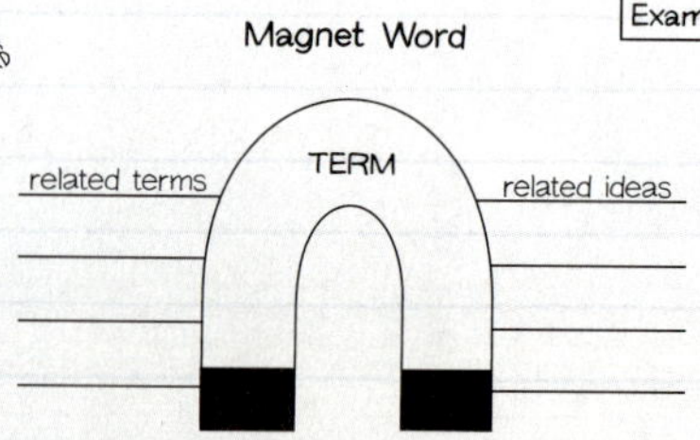

- Work is the use of force to move an object.
- Work = Force · distance
- Force is necessary to do work.
- Joule is the unit for measuring work.
- Work depends on force and distance.

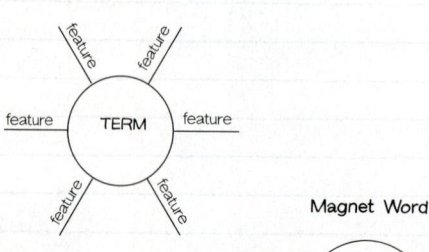

Description Wheel — feature / feature / feature / feature / feature / feature around TERM

Four Square — Definition | Characteristics / Examples | Nonexamples, with TERM in center

Magnet Word — related terms / TERM / related ideas

114 Unit: Motion and Forces

4.1
KEY CONCEPT
Work is the use of force to move an object.

BEFORE, you learned
- An unbalanced force produces acceleration
- Weight is measured in newtons

NOW, you will learn
- How force and work are related
- How moving objects do work

VOCABULARY

work p. 115
joule p. 117

EXPLORE Work
How do you work?

PROCEDURE

1. Lift a book from the floor to your desktop. Try to move the book at a constant speed.

2. Now lift the book again, but stop about halfway up and hold the book still for about 30 seconds. Then continue lifting the book to the desktop.

MATERIALS
book

WHAT DO YOU THINK?
- Do you think you did more work the first time you lifted the book or the second time you lifted the book?
- What do you think *work* means?

VOCABULARY
You might want to make a description wheel diagram in your notebook for *work*.

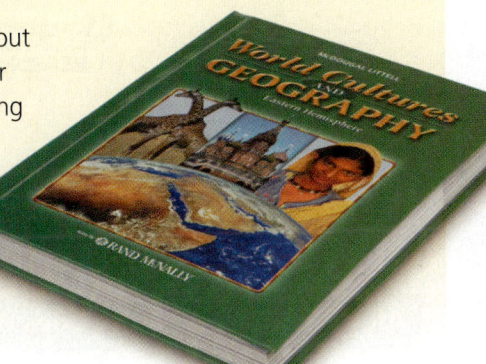

Force is necessary to do work.

What comes to mind when you think of work? Most people say they are working when they do anything that requires a physical or mental effort. But in physical science, **work** is the use of force to move an object some distance. In scientific terms, you do work only when you exert a force on an object and move it. According to this definition of work, reading this page is not doing work. Turning the page, however, would be work because you are lifting the page.

Solving a math problem in your head is not doing work. Writing the answer is work because you are moving the pencil across the paper. If you want to do work, you have to use force to move something.

CHECK YOUR READING How does the scientific definition of work differ from the familiar definition?

Chapter 4: **Work and Energy** 115

RESOURCE CENTER
CLASSZONE.COM

Learn more about work.

Force, Motion, and Work

Work is done only when an object that is being pushed or pulled actually moves. If you lift a book, you exert a force and do work. What if you simply hold the book out in front of you? No matter how tired your muscles may become from holding the book still, you are not doing work unless you move the book.

The work done by a force is related to the size of the force and the distance over which the force is applied. How much work does it take to push a grocery cart down an aisle? The answer depends on how hard you push the cart and the length of the aisle. If you use the same amount of force, you do more work pushing a cart down a long aisle than a short aisle.

Work is done only by the part of the applied force that acts in the same direction as the motion of an object. Suppose you need to pull a heavy suitcase on wheels. You pull the handle up at an angle as you pull the suitcase forward. Only the part of the force pulling the suitcase forward is doing work. The force with which you pull upward on the handle is not doing work because the suitcase is not moving upward—unless you are going uphill.

CHECK YOUR READING Give two examples of when you are applying a force but not doing work.

Work

Work is done by force that acts in the same direction as the motion of an object.

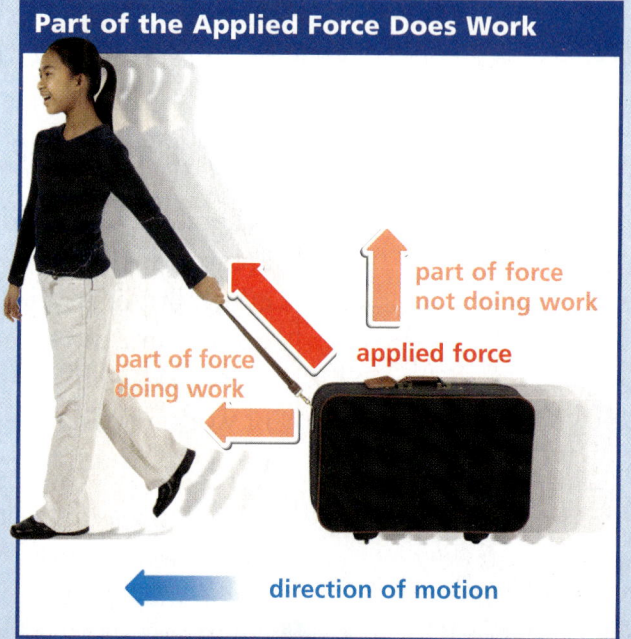

All of the Applied Force Does Work

applied force

direction of motion

Part of the Applied Force Does Work

part of force not doing work

applied force

part of force doing work

direction of motion

READING VISUALS How does changing the direction of the applied force change the amount of the force that is doing work?

116 Unit: Motion and Forces

Calculating Work

Work is a measure of how much force is applied over a certain distance. You can calculate the work a force does if you know the size of the force applied to an object and the distance over which the force acts. The distance involved is the distance the object moved in the direction of that force. The calculation for work is shown in the following formula:

$$\text{Work} = \text{Force} \cdot \text{distance}$$
$$W = Fd$$

You read in previous chapters that you can measure force in newtons. You also know that you can measure distance in meters. When you multiply a force in newtons times a distance in meters, the product is a measurement called the newton-meter (N·m), or the **joule** (jool).

The joule (J) is the standard unit used to measure work. One joule of work is done when a force of one newton moves an object one meter. To get an idea of how much a joule of work is, lift an apple (which weighs about one newton) from your foot to your waist (about one meter).

Use the formula for work to solve the problem below.

This man is doing work when he applies force to lift his body.

Calculating Work

▶ **Sample Problem**

How much work is done if a person lifts a barbell weighing 450 N to a height of 2 m?

What do you know?   force needed to lift = 450 N, distance = 2 m

What do you want to find out?   Work

Write the formula: $W = Fd$

Substitute into the formula: $W = 450 \text{ N} \cdot 2 \text{ m}$

Calculate and simplify: $W = 900 \text{ N·m}$

Check that your units agree: Unit is newton-meter (N·m).
Unit of work is joule, which is N·m.
Units agree.

Answer: $W = 900 \text{ J}$

▶ **Practice the Math**

1. If you push a cart with a force of 70 N for 2 m, how much work is done?
2. If you did 200 J of work pushing a box with a force of 40 N, how far did you push the box?

▼ **REMINDER**

You know that $W = Fd$. You can manipulate the formula to find force or distance.
$d = \dfrac{W}{F}$ and $F = \dfrac{W}{d}$

Chapter 4: **Work and Energy** 117

Objects that are moving can do work.

MAIN IDEA WEB
Remember to organize your notes in a web as you read.

You do work when you pick up your books, hit a baseball, swim a lap, or tap a keyboard. These examples show that you do work on objects, but objects can also do work.

For example, in a bowling alley, the bowling balls do work on the pins they hit. Outdoors, the moving air particles in a gust of wind do work that lifts a leaf off the ground. Moving water, such as the water in a river, also does work. If the windblown leaf lands in the water, it might be carried downstream by the current. As the leaf travels downstream, it might go over the edge of a waterfall. In that case, the gravitational force of Earth would pull the leaf and water down.

You can say that an object or person does work on an object, or that the force the object or person is exerting does work. For example, you could say that Earth (an object) does work on the falling water, or that gravity (a force) does work on the water.

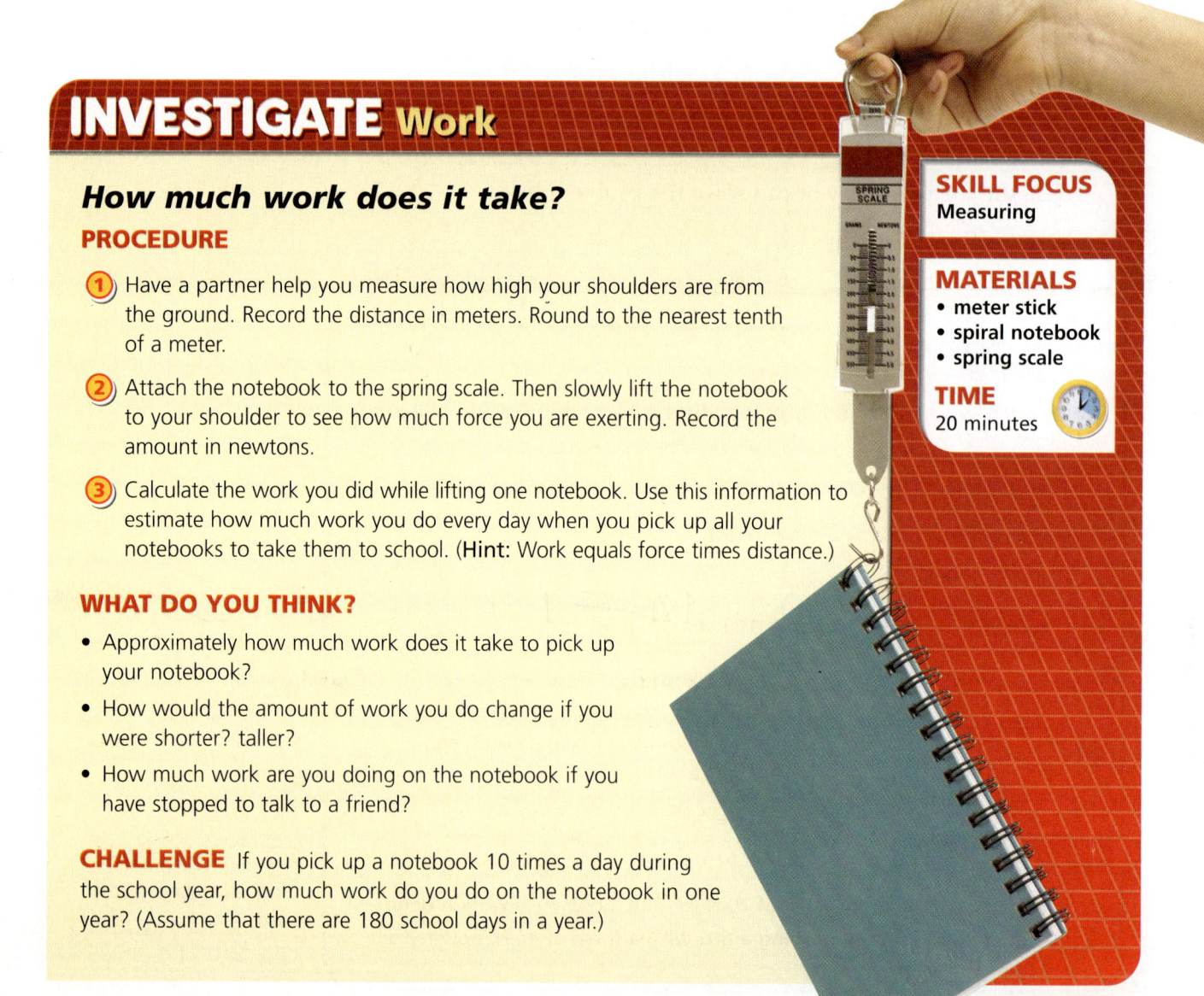

INVESTIGATE Work

How much work does it take?
PROCEDURE

1) Have a partner help you measure how high your shoulders are from the ground. Record the distance in meters. Round to the nearest tenth of a meter.

2) Attach the notebook to the spring scale. Then slowly lift the notebook to your shoulder to see how much force you are exerting. Record the amount in newtons.

3) Calculate the work you did while lifting one notebook. Use this information to estimate how much work you do every day when you pick up all your notebooks to take them to school. (**Hint:** Work equals force times distance.)

WHAT DO YOU THINK?
- Approximately how much work does it take to pick up your notebook?
- How would the amount of work you do change if you were shorter? taller?
- How much work are you doing on the notebook if you have stopped to talk to a friend?

CHALLENGE If you pick up a notebook 10 times a day during the school year, how much work do you do on the notebook in one year? (Assume that there are 180 school days in a year.)

SKILL FOCUS
Measuring

MATERIALS
- meter stick
- spiral notebook
- spring scale

TIME
20 minutes

118 Unit: Motion and Forces

APPLY How could you increase the work done by this water wheel?

Throughout history, people have taken advantage of the capability of objects in motion to do work. Many early cultures built machines such as water wheels to use the force exerted by falling water, and windmills to use the force exerted by moving air. In a water wheel like the one in the photograph, gravity does work on the water. As the water falls, it also can do work on any object that is put in its path. Falling water can turn a water wheel or the turbine of an electric generator.

The water wheel shown above uses the work done by water to turn gears that run a mill and grind grain. In the same way, windmills take advantage of the force of moving air particles. The wind causes the sails of a windmill to turn. The turning sails do work to run machinery or an irrigation system.

CHECK YOUR READING Describe how a water wheel does work.

4.1 Review

KEY CONCEPTS

1. If you push very hard on an object but it does not move, have you done work? Explain.
2. What two factors do you need to know to calculate how much work was done in any situation?
3. Was work done on a book that fell from a desk to the floor? If so, what force was involved?

CRITICAL THINKING

4. **Synthesize** Work is done on a ball when a soccer player kicks it. Is the player still doing work on the ball as it rolls across the ground? Explain.
5. **Calculate** Tina lifted a box 0.5 m. The box weighed 25 N. How much work did Tina do on the box?

CHALLENGE

6. **Analyze** Ben and Andy each pushed an empty grocery cart. Ben used twice the force, but they both did the same amount of work. Explain.

Chapter 4: **Work and Energy** 119

MATH in SCIENCE

SKILL: WORKING WITH AVERAGES

MATH TUTORIAL
CLASSZONE.COM
Click on Math Tutorial for more help with finding the mean.

Eliminating Extreme Values

A value that is far from most others in a set of data is called an outlier. Outliers make it difficult to find a value that might be considered average. Extremely high or extremely low values can throw off the mean. That is why the highest and lowest figures are ignored in some situations.

Example

The data set below shows the work an escalator does to move 8 people of different weights 5 meters. The work was calculated by multiplying the force needed to move each person by a distance of 5 meters.

| 4850 J | 1600 J | 3400 J | 2750 J |
| 2950 J | 1750 J | 3350 J | 3800 J |

The mean amount of work done is 3056 J.

(1) To calculate an adjusted mean, begin by identifying a high outlier in the data set.

High outlier: 4850

(2) Discard this value and find the new mean.

1600 J + 3400 J + 2750 J + 2950 J + 1750 J + 3350 J + 3800 J
= 19,600 J

Mean = $\frac{19,600 \text{ J}}{7}$ = 2800 J

ANSWER The mean amount of work done for this new data set is 2800 J.

Answer the following questions.

1. After ignoring the high outlier in the data set, does this new mean show a more typical level of work for the data set? Why or why not?

2. Do you think the lowest value in the data set is an outlier? Remove it and calculate the new average. How did this affect the results?

3. Suppose the heaviest person in the original data set were replaced by a person weighing the same as the lightest person. What would be the new mean for the data set?

CHALLENGE The median of a data set is the middle value when the values are written in numerical order. Find the median of the adjusted data set (without the high outlier). Compare it with the original and adjusted means. Why do you think it is closer to one than the other?

4.2 Energy is transferred when work is done.

KEY CONCEPT

BEFORE, you learned
- Work is the use of force to move an object
- Work can be calculated

NOW, you will learn
- How work and energy are related
- How to calculate mechanical, kinetic, and potential energy
- What the conservation of energy means

VOCABULARY

potential energy p. 122
kinetic energy p. 122
mechanical energy p. 125
conservation of energy p. 126

THINK ABOUT

How is energy transferred?

School carnivals sometimes include dunk tanks. The goal is to hit a target with a ball, causing a person sitting over a tank of water to fall into the water. You do work on the ball as you throw with your arm. If your aim is good, the ball does work on the target. How do you transfer your energy to the ball?

MAIN IDEA WEB
Remember to add boxes to your main idea web as you read.

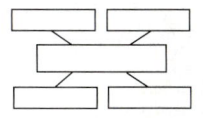

Work transfers energy.

When you change the position and speed of the ball in the carnival game, you transfer energy to the ball. Energy is the ability of a person or an object to do work or to cause a change. When you do work on an object, some of your energy is transferred to the object. You can think of work as the transfer of energy. In fact, both work and energy are measured in the same unit, the joule.

The man in the photograph above converts one form of energy into another form when he uses his muscles to toss the ball. You can think of the man and the ball as a system, or a group of objects that affect one another. Energy can be transferred from the man to the ball, but the total amount of energy in the system does not change.

CHECK YOUR READING How are work and energy related?

Chapter 4: Work and Energy 121

Work changes potential and kinetic energy.

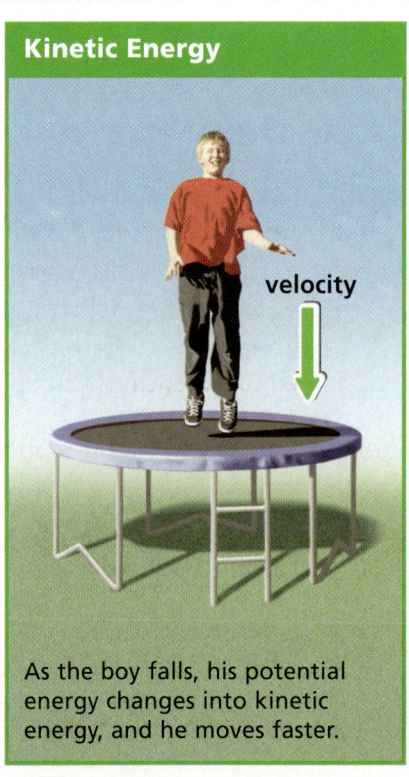

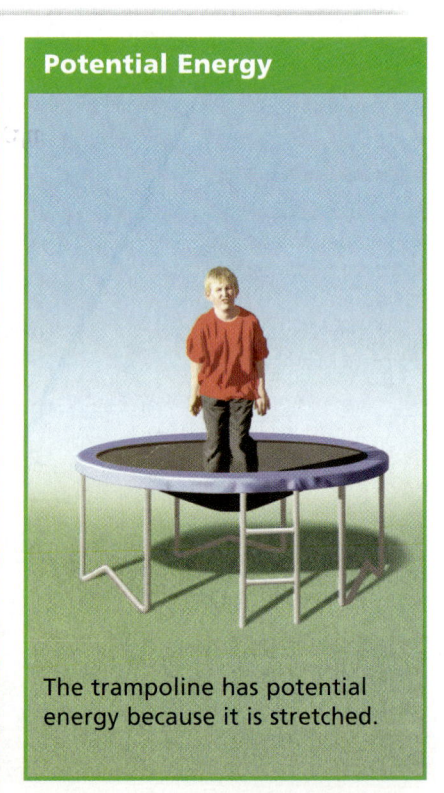

When you throw a ball, you transfer energy to it and it moves. By doing work on the ball, you can give it **kinetic energy** (kuh-NEHT-ihk), which is the energy of motion. Any moving object has some kinetic energy. The faster an object moves, the more kinetic energy it has.

When you do work to lift a ball from the ground, you give the ball a different type of energy, called potential energy. **Potential energy** is stored energy, or the energy an object has due to its position or its shape. The ball's position in your hand above the ground means that it has the potential to fall to the ground. The higher you lift the ball, the more work you do, and the more potential energy the ball has.

You can also give some objects potential energy by changing their shape. For example, if you are holding a spring, you can do work on the spring by squeezing it. After you do the work, the spring has potential energy because it is compressed. This type of potential energy is called elastic potential energy. Just as position gives the spring the potential to fall, compression gives the spring the potential to expand.

READING TIP
The word *potential* comes from the Latin word *potentia*, which means "power." The word *kinetic* comes from the Greek word *kinetos,* which means "moving."

Potential and Kinetic Energy

Potential Energy
The boy has potential energy based on his position because gravity will pull him back down.

Kinetic Energy
As the boy falls, his potential energy changes into kinetic energy, and he moves faster.

Potential Energy
The trampoline has potential energy because it is stretched.

Calculating Gravitational Potential Energy

Potential energy caused by gravity is called gravitational potential energy. Scientists must take gravitational potential energy into account when launching a spacecraft. Designers of roller coasters must make sure that roller-coaster cars have enough potential energy at the top of a hill to reach the top of the next hill. You can use the following formula to calculate the gravitational potential energy of an object:

Gravitational Potential Energy = mass · gravitational acceleration · height
$$GPE = mgh$$

Recall that g is the acceleration due to Earth's gravity. It is equal to 9.8 m/s^2 at Earth's surface.

The diver in the photograph below has given herself gravitational potential energy by climbing to the diving board. If you know her mass and the height of the board, you can calculate her potential energy.

Calculating Potential Energy

Sample Problem

What is the gravitational potential energy of a girl who has a mass of 40 kg and is standing on the edge of a diving board that is 5 m above the water?

What do you know?	mass = 40 kg, gravitational acceleration = 9.8 m/s^2, height = 5 m
What do you want to find out?	Gravitational Potential Energy
Write the formula:	$GPE = mgh$
Substitute into the formula:	GPE = 40 kg · 9.8 m/s^2 · 5 m
Calculate and simplify:	GPE = 1960 kg m^2/s^2
Check that your units agree:	kg m^2/s^2 = kg · m/s^2 · m = N·m = J
	Unit of energy is J. Units agree.
Answer:	GPE = 1960 J

> **REMINDER**
> A newton (N) is a kg · m/s^2, and a joule (J) is a N·m.

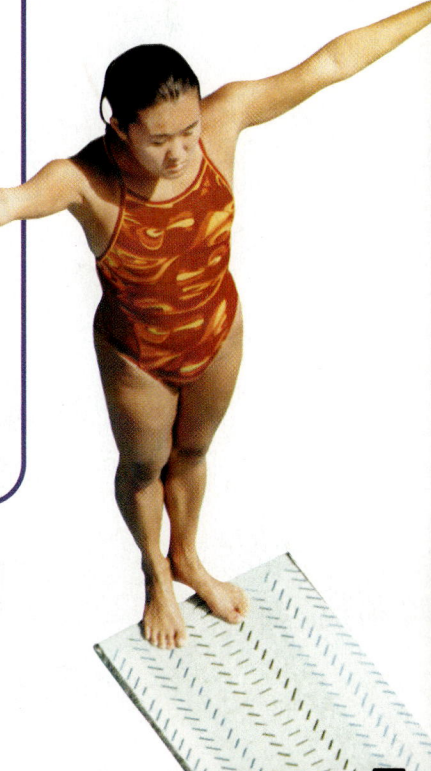

Practice the Math

1. An apple with a mass of 0.1 kg is attached to a branch of an apple tree 4 m from the ground. How much gravitational potential energy does the apple have?
2. If you lift a 2 kg box of toys to the top shelf of a closet, which is 3 m high, how much gravitational potential energy will the box of toys have?

The formula for gravitational potential energy is similar to the formula for work *(W = Fd)*. The formula for GPE also has a force *(mg)* multiplied by a distance *(h)*. To understand why *mg* is a force, remember two things: force equals mass times acceleration, and *g* is the acceleration due to Earth's gravity.

Chapter 4: **Work and Energy** 123

Calculating Kinetic Energy

The girl on the swing at left has kinetic energy. To find out how much kinetic energy she has at the bottom of the swing's arc, you must know her mass and her velocity. Kinetic energy can be calculated using the following formula:

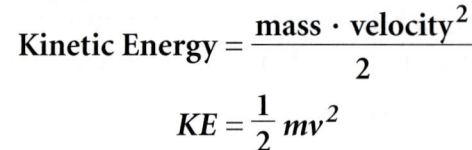

$$\text{Kinetic Energy} = \frac{\text{mass} \cdot \text{velocity}^2}{2}$$

$$KE = \frac{1}{2}mv^2$$

Notice that velocity is squared while mass is not. Increasing the velocity of an object has a greater effect on the object's kinetic energy than increasing the mass of the object. If you double the mass of an object, you double its kinetic energy. Because velocity is squared, if you double the object's velocity, its kinetic energy is four times greater.

Calculating Kinetic Energy

Sample Problem

What is the kinetic energy of a girl who has a mass of 40 kg and a velocity of 3 m/s?

What do you know? mass = 40 kg, velocity = 3 m/s

What do you want to find out? Kinetic Energy

Write the formula: $KE = \frac{1}{2}mv^2$

Substitute into the formula: $KE = \frac{1}{2} \cdot 40 \text{ kg} \cdot (3 \text{ m/s})^2$

Calculate and simplify: $KE = \frac{1}{2} \cdot 40 \text{ kg} \cdot \frac{9 \text{ m}^2}{\text{s}^2}$

$$= \frac{360 \text{ kg} \cdot \text{m}^2}{2 \text{ s}^2}$$

$$= 180 \text{ kg} \cdot \text{m}^2/\text{s}^2$$

Check that your units agree: $\frac{\text{kg} \cdot \text{m}^2}{\text{s}^2} = \frac{\text{kg} \cdot \text{m}}{\text{s}^2} \cdot \text{m} = \text{N} \cdot \text{m} = \text{J}$

Unit of energy is J. Units agree.

Answer: $KE = 180$ J

Practice the Math

1. A grasshopper with a mass of 0.002 kg jumps up at a speed of 15 m/s. What is the kinetic energy of the grasshopper?
2. A truck with a mass of 6000 kg is traveling north on a highway at a speed of 17 m/s. A car with a mass of 2000 kg is traveling south on the same highway at a speed of 30 m/s. Which vehicle has more kinetic energy?

Calculating Mechanical Energy

Mechanical energy is the energy possessed by an object due to its motion or position—in other words, it is the object's combined potential energy and kinetic energy. A thrown baseball has mechanical energy as a result of both its motion (kinetic energy) and its position above the ground (gravitational potential energy). Any object that has mechanical energy can do work on another object.

Once you calculate an object's kinetic and potential energy, you can add the two values together to find the object's mechanical energy.

Mechanical Energy = Potential Energy + Kinetic Energy

$$ME = PE + KE$$

For example, a skateboarder has a potential energy of 200 joules due to his position at the top of a hill and a kinetic energy of 100 joules due to his motion. His total mechanical energy is 300 joules.

VOCABULARY
Use a vocabulary strategy to help you remember *mechanical energy*.

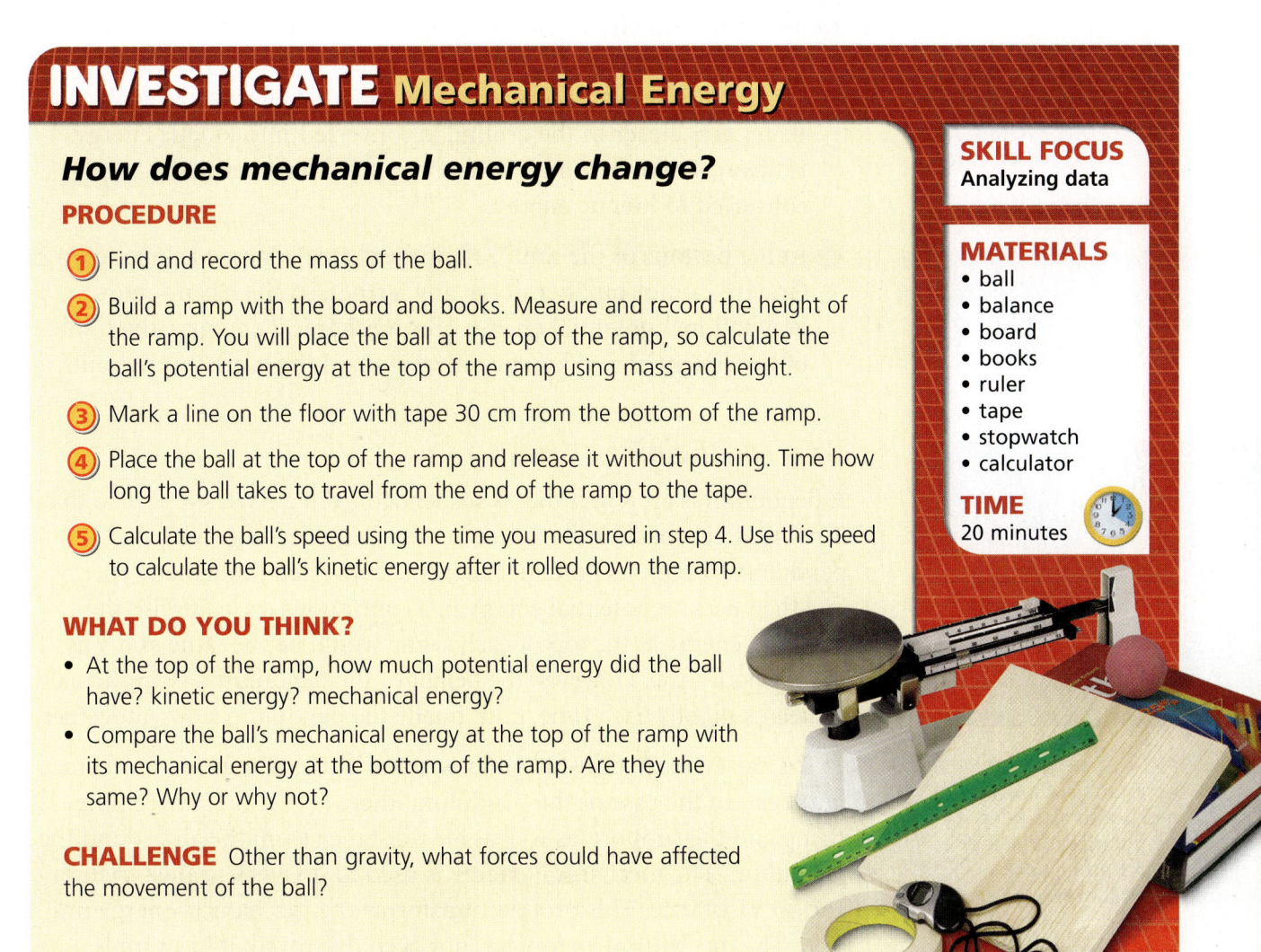

CHECK YOUR READING How is mechanical energy related to kinetic and potential energy?

INVESTIGATE Mechanical Energy

How does mechanical energy change?
PROCEDURE

1. Find and record the mass of the ball.
2. Build a ramp with the board and books. Measure and record the height of the ramp. You will place the ball at the top of the ramp, so calculate the ball's potential energy at the top of the ramp using mass and height.
3. Mark a line on the floor with tape 30 cm from the bottom of the ramp.
4. Place the ball at the top of the ramp and release it without pushing. Time how long the ball takes to travel from the end of the ramp to the tape.
5. Calculate the ball's speed using the time you measured in step 4. Use this speed to calculate the ball's kinetic energy after it rolled down the ramp.

WHAT DO YOU THINK?
- At the top of the ramp, how much potential energy did the ball have? kinetic energy? mechanical energy?
- Compare the ball's mechanical energy at the top of the ramp with its mechanical energy at the bottom of the ramp. Are they the same? Why or why not?

CHALLENGE Other than gravity, what forces could have affected the movement of the ball?

SKILL FOCUS
Analyzing data

MATERIALS
- ball
- balance
- board
- books
- ruler
- tape
- stopwatch
- calculator

TIME
20 minutes

Chapter 4: **Work and Energy** 125

VISUALIZATION
CLASSZONE.COM

Observe how potential and kinetic energy are transferred on an amusement park ride.

The total amount of energy is constant.

You know that energy is transferred when work is done. No matter how energy is transferred or transformed, all of the energy is still present somewhere in one form or another. This is known as the **law of conservation of energy.** As long as you account for all the different forms of energy involved in any process, you will find that the total amount of energy never changes.

Conserving Mechanical Energy

Look at the photograph of the in-line skater on page 127. As she rolls down the ramp, the amounts of kinetic energy and potential energy change. However, the total—or the mechanical energy—stays the same. In this example, energy lost to friction is ignored.

① At the top of the ramp, the skater has potential energy because gravity can pull her downward. She has no velocity; therefore, she has no kinetic energy.

② As the skater rolls down the ramp, her potential energy decreases because the elevation decreases. Her kinetic energy increases because her velocity increases. The potential energy lost as the skater gets closer to the ground is converted into kinetic energy. Halfway down the ramp, half of her potential energy has been converted to kinetic energy.

③ At the bottom of the ramp, all of the skater's energy is kinetic. Gravity cannot pull her down any farther, so she has no more gravitational potential energy. Her mechanical energy—the total of her potential and kinetic energy—stays the same throughout.

Losing Mechanical Energy

A pendulum is an object that is suspended from a fixed support so that it swings freely back and forth under the influence of gravity. As a pendulum swings, its potential energy is converted into kinetic energy and then back to potential energy in a continuous cycle. Ideally, the potential energy at the top of each swing would be the same as it was the previous time. However, the height of the pendulum's swing actually decreases slightly each time, until finally the pendulum stops altogether.

In most energy transformations, some of the energy is transformed into heat. In the case of the pendulum, there is friction between the string and the support, as well as air resistance from the air around the pendulum. The mechanical energy is used to do work against friction and air resistance. This process transforms the mechanical energy into heat. The mechanical energy has not been destroyed; it has simply changed form and been transferred from the pendulum.

APPLY Energy must occasionally be added to a pendulum to keep it swinging. What keeps a grandfather clock's pendulum swinging regularly?

Conserving Mechanical Energy

The potential energy and kinetic energy in a system or process may vary, but the total energy remains unchanged.

① Top of Ramp

At the top of the ramp, the skater's mechanical energy is equal to her potential energy because she has no velocity.

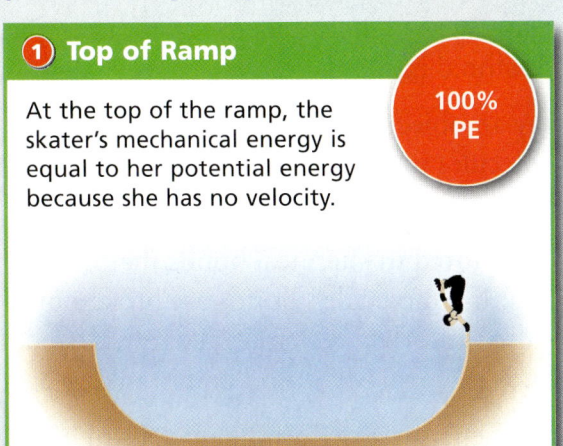

100% PE

② Halfway Down Ramp

As the skater goes down the ramp, she loses height but gains speed. The potential energy she loses is equal to the kinetic energy she gains.

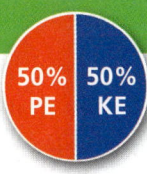

50% PE | 50% KE

③ Bottom of Ramp

As the skater speeds along the bottom of the ramp, all of the potential energy has changed to kinetic energy. Her mechanical energy remains unchanged.

100% KE

Fabiola da Silva is a professional in-line skater who was born in Brazil but now lives in California.

READING VISUALS How do the skater's kinetic and potential energy change as she skates up and down the ramp? (Assume she won't lose any energy to friction.)

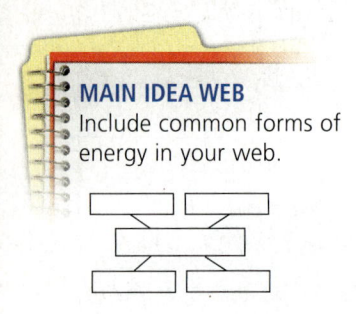

MAIN IDEA WEB Include common forms of energy in your web.

Forms of Energy

As you have seen, mechanical energy is a combination of kinetic energy and potential energy. Other common forms of energy are discussed below. Each of these forms of energy is also a combination of kinetic energy and potential energy. Chemical energy, for example, is potential energy when it is stored in bonds.

Thermal energy is the energy an object has due to the motion of its molecules. The faster the molecules in an object move, the more thermal energy the object has.

Chemical energy is the energy stored in chemical bonds that hold chemical compounds together. If a molecule's bonds are broken or rearranged, energy is released or absorbed. Chemical energy is used to light up fireworks displays. It is also stored in food and in matches.

Nuclear energy is the potential energy stored in the nucleus of an atom. In a nuclear reaction, a tiny portion of an atom's mass is turned into energy. The source of the Sun's energy is nuclear energy. Nuclear energy can be used to run power plants that provide electricity.

Electromagnetic energy is the energy associated with electrical and magnetic interactions. Energy that is transferred by electric charges or current is often called electrical energy. Another type of electromagnetic energy is radiant energy, the energy carried by light, infrared waves, and x-rays.

It is possible to transfer, or convert, one energy form into one or more other forms. For example, when you rub your hands together on a cold day, you convert mechanical energy to thermal energy. Your body converts chemical energy stored in food to thermal and mechanical energy (muscle movement).

4.2 Review

KEY CONCEPTS

1. Explain the relationship between work and energy.
2. How are potential energy and kinetic energy related to mechanical energy?
3. When one form of energy changes into one or more other forms of energy, what happens to the total amount of energy?

CRITICAL THINKING

4. **Infer** Debra used 250 J of energy to roll a bowling ball. When the ball arrived at the end of the lane, it had only 200 J of energy. What happened to the other 50 J?
5. **Calculate** A satellite falling to Earth has a kinetic energy of 182.2 billion J and a potential energy of 1.6 billion J. What is its mechanical energy?

CHALLENGE

6. **Apply** At what point in its motion is the kinetic energy of the end of a pendulum greatest? At what point is its potential energy greatest? When its kinetic energy is half its greatest value, how much potential energy did it gain?

128 Unit: Motion and Forces

Think SCIENCE

SKILL: ISOLATING VARIABLES

How Do They Do It?

Some women in Kenya and other African countries walk many miles every day carrying heavy loads on their heads without an increase in their heart rate. Most have done it since they were children. Scientists have studied African women to learn how they do this.

▸ Variables

In scientific research, variables must be chosen and tested. Variables are usually compared with a control group—that is, a group for whom all potential variables are held constant. Scientists first asked several Kenyan women to walk on a treadmill. The scientists measured the women's heart rate and how much oxygen they used while carrying different weights on their heads. They found that the women could carry as much as 20 percent of their own body weight without using extra oxygen or increasing their heart rate.

The same scientists asked subjects in a control group in the United States to walk on a treadmill. The people in this group wore helmets lined with different amounts of lead. Even the lightest load caused their heart rate and oxygen consumption to increase.

If you were studying the way these African women carry loads, what variables would you choose to isolate? What control group would you use? Here are some variables and controls to consider:

- carrying the load on the head compared with carrying it on the back
- weight of the load
- women compared with men
- African women compared with other women
- method of walking

▸ Isolate the Variables

On Your Own Design an experiment that could test one of the variables without interference from other variables. Can each variable be tested independently?

As a Group Discuss each variable and see if the group agrees that it can be tested independently. Can you eliminate any of the variables based on information on this page?

CHALLENGE How would you measure the amount of energy used for the variable you chose?

Women in many countries, like this woman from Abidjan, Ivory Coast, balance heavy loads as they walk.

Chapter 4: **Work and Energy** 129

4.3 Power is the rate at which work is done.

KEY CONCEPT

BEFORE, you learned
- Mechanical energy is a combination of kinetic energy and potential energy
- Mechanical energy can be calculated
- Work transfers energy

NOW, you will learn
- How power is related to work and time
- How power is related to energy and time
- About common uses of power

VOCABULARY

power p. 130
watt p. 131
horsepower p. 132

EXPLORE Power

How does time affect work?

PROCEDURE

1. Place the cups side by side. Put all of the marbles in one cup.
2. Place each marble, one by one, into the other cup. Time how long it takes to do this.
3. Set the timer for half that amount of time. Then repeat step 2 in that time.

WHAT DO YOU THINK?
- Did you do more work the first time or the second time? Why?
- What differences did you notice between the two tries?

MATERIALS
- 2 plastic cups
- 10 marbles
- stopwatch

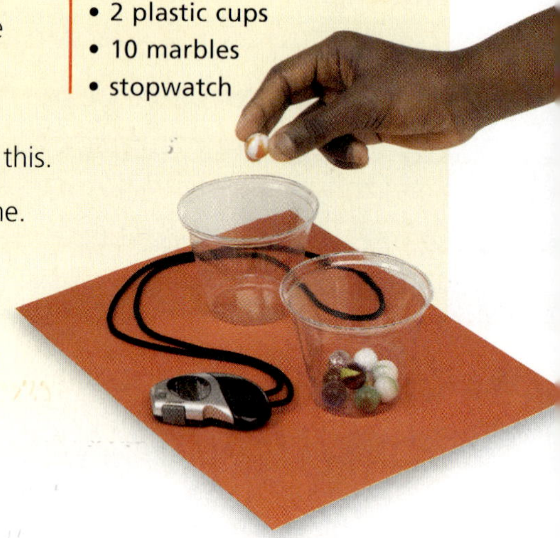

VOCABULARY
Use a vocabulary strategy to help you remember the meaning of *power*.

Power can be calculated from work and time.

If you lift a book one meter, you do the same amount of work whether you lift the book quickly or slowly. However, when you lift the book quickly, you increase your **power**—the rate at which you do work. A cook increases his power when he beats eggs rapidly instead of stirring them slowly. A runner increases her power when she breaks into a sprint to reach the finish line.

The word *power* has different common meanings. It is used to mean a source of energy, as in a power plant, or strength, as in a powerful engine. When you talk about a powerful swimmer, for example, you would probably say that the swimmer is very strong or very fast. If you use the scientific definition of power, you would instead say that a powerful swimmer is one who does the work of moving herself through the water in a short time.

Each of the swimmers shown in the photograph above is doing work—that is, she is using a certain force to move a certain distance. It takes time to cover that distance. The power a swimmer uses depends on the force, the distance, and the time it takes to cover that distance. The more force the swimmer uses, the more power she has. Also, the faster she goes, the more power she has because she is covering the same distance in a shorter time. Swimmers often increase their speed toward the end of a race, which increases their power, making it possible for them to reach the end of the pool in less time.

CHECK YOUR READING Summarize in your own words the difference between work and power.

Calculating Power from Work

You know that a given amount of work can be done by a slow-moving swimmer over a long period of time or by a fast-moving swimmer in a short time. Likewise, a given amount of work can be done by a low-powered motor over a long period of time or by a high-powered motor in a short time.

Because power is a measurement of how much work is done in a given time, power can be calculated based on work and time. To find power, divide the amount of work by the time it takes to do the work.

$$\text{Power} = \frac{\text{Work}}{\text{time}} \qquad P = \frac{W}{t}$$

Remember that work is measured in joules. Power is often measured in joules of work per second. The unit of measurement for power is the **watt** (W). One watt is equal to one joule of work done in one second. If an object does a large amount of work, its power is usually measured in units of 1000 watts, or kilowatts.

READING TIP

W (in italicized type) is the letter that represents the variable *Work*. W, not italicized, is the abbreviation for watt.

Chapter 4: **Work and Energy** 131

Resource Center
CLASSZONE.COM

Find out more about power.

Calculating Power from Work

▶ **Sample Problem**

An Antarctic explorer uses 6000 J of work to pull his sled for 60 s. What power does he need?

What do you know?   Work = 6000 J, time = 60 s

What do you want to find out?   Power

Write the formula: $P = \dfrac{W}{t}$

Substitute into the formula: $P = \dfrac{6000 \text{ J}}{60 \text{ s}}$

Calculate and simplify: $P = 100$ J/s $= 100$ W

Check that your units agree: $\dfrac{\text{J}}{\text{s}} = \text{W}$

Unit of power is W. Units agree.

Answer: $P = 100$ W

▶ **Practice the Math**

1. If a conveyor belt uses 10 J to move a piece of candy a distance of 3 m in 20 s, what is the conveyor belt's power?
2. An elevator uses a force of 1710 N to lift 3 people up 1 floor. Each floor is 4 m high. The elevator takes 8 s to lift the 3 people up 2 floors. What is the elevator's power?

Horsepower

James Watt, the Scottish engineer for whom the watt is named, improved the power of the steam engine in the mid-1700s. Watt also developed a unit of measurement for power called the horsepower. **Horsepower** is based on what it sounds like—the amount of work a horse can do in a minute. In Watt's time, people used horses to do many different types of work. For example, horses were used on farms to pull plows and wagons.

Watt wanted to explain to people how powerful his steam engine was compared with horses. After observing several horses doing work, Watt concluded that an average horse could move 150 pounds a distance of 220 feet in 1 minute. Watt called this amount of power 1 horsepower. A single horsepower is equal to 745 watts. Therefore, a horsepower is a much larger unit of measurement than a watt.

Today horsepower is used primarily in connection with engines and motors. For example, you may see a car advertised as having a 150-horsepower engine. The power of a motorboat, lawn mower, tractor, or motorcycle engine is also referred to as horsepower.

Both the horse and the tractor use power to pull objects around a farm.

132 Unit: Motion and Forces

INVESTIGATE Power

How much power do you have?
PROCEDURE

1. Measure a length of 5 meters on the floor. Mark the beginning and the end of the 5 meters with masking tape.
2. Attach the object to the spring scale with a piece of string. Slowly pull the object across the floor using a steady amount of force. Record the force and the time it takes you to pull the object.

WHAT DO YOU THINK?
- How much power did you use to pull the object 5 meters?
- How do you think you could increase the power you used? decrease the power?

CHALLENGE How quickly would you have to drag the object along the floor to produce 40 watts of power?

SKILL FOCUS
Measuring

MATERIALS
- meter stick
- masking tape
- 100 g object
- spring scale
- string
- stopwatch

TIME
15 minutes

Power can be calculated from energy and time.

Sometimes you may know that energy is being transferred, but you cannot directly measure the work done by the forces involved. For example, you know that a television uses power. But there is no way to measure all the work every part of the television does in terms of forces and distance. Because work measures the transfer of energy, you can also think of power as the amount of energy transferred over a period of time.

Calculating Power from Energy

When you turn on a television, it starts using energy. Each second the television is on, a certain amount of electrical energy is transferred from a local power plant to your television. If you measure how much energy your television uses during a given time period, you can find out how much power it needs by using the following formula:

$$\text{Power} = \frac{\text{Energy}}{\text{time}} \qquad P = \frac{E}{t}$$

This formula should look familiar to you because it is very similar to the formula used to calculate power from work.

Chapter 4: **Work and Energy** 133

The photograph shows Hong Kong, China, at night. Every second, the city uses more than 4 billion joules of electrical energy!

You can think about power as any kind of transfer of energy in a certain amount of time. It is useful to think of power in this way if you cannot directly figure out the work used to transfer the energy. Power calculated from transferred energy is also measured in joules per second, or watts.

You have probably heard the term *watt* used in connection with light bulbs. A 60-watt light bulb requires 60 joules of energy every second to shine at its rated brightness.

CHECK YOUR READING In what situations is it useful to think of power as the transfer of energy in a certain amount of time?

REMINDER

Remember that energy and work are both measured in joules.

Calculating Power from Energy

Sample Problem

A light bulb used 600 J of energy in 6 s. What is the power of the light bulb?

What do you know? Energy = 600 J, time = 6 s

What do you want to find out? Power

Write the formula: $P = \dfrac{E}{t}$

Substitute into the formula: $P = \dfrac{600 \text{ J}}{6 \text{ s}}$

Calculate and simplify: $P = 100$ J/s

Check that your units agree: Unit is J/s. Unit for power is W, which is also J/s. Units agree.

Answer: $P = 100$ W

Practice the Math

1. A laptop computer uses 100 J every 2 seconds. How much power is needed to run the computer?
2. The power needed to pump blood through your body is about 1.1 W. How much energy does your body use when pumping blood for 10 seconds?

Everyday Power

Many appliances in your home rely on electricity for energy. Each appliance requires a certain number of joules per second, the power it needs to run properly. An electric hair dryer uses energy. For example, a 600-watt hair dryer needs 600 joules per second. The wattage of the hair dryer indicates how much energy per second it needs to operate.

The dryer works by speeding up the evaporation of water on the surface of hair. It needs only two main parts to do this: a heating coil and a fan turned by a motor.

① When the hair dryer is plugged into an outlet and the switch is turned on, electrical energy moves electrons in the wires, creating a current.

② This current runs an electric motor that turns the fan blades. Air is drawn into the hair dryer through small holes in the casing. The turning fan blades push the air over the coil.

③ The current also makes the heating coil become hot.

④ The fan pushes heated air out of the dryer.

Most hair dryers have high and low settings. At the high power setting, the temperature is increased, more air is pushed through the dryer, and the dryer does its work faster. Some dryers have safety switches that shut off the motor when the temperature rises to a level that could burn your scalp. Insulation keeps the outside of the dryer from becoming hot to the touch.

Many other appliances, from air conditioners to washing machines to blenders, need electrical energy to do their work. Take a look around you at all the appliances that help you during a typical day.

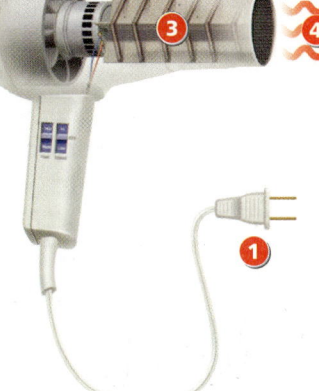

4.3 Review

KEY CONCEPTS

1. How is power related to work?
2. Name two units used for power, and give examples of when each unit might be used.
3. What do you need to know to calculate how much energy a light bulb uses?

CRITICAL THINKING

4. **Apply** Discuss different ways in which a swimmer can increase her power.
5. **Calculate** Which takes more power: using 15 N to lift a ball 2 m in 5 seconds or using 100 N to push a box 2 m in 1 minute?

CHALLENGE

6. **Analyze** A friend tells you that you can calculate power by using a different formula from the one given in this book. The formula your friend gives you is as follows:

    Power = force • speed

    Do you think this is a valid formula for power? Explain.

CHAPTER INVESTIGATION

Work and Power

OVERVIEW AND PURPOSE People in wheelchairs cannot use steps leading up to a building's entrance. Sometimes there is a machine that can lift a person and wheelchair straight up to the entrance level. At other times, there is a ramp leading to the entrance. Which method takes more power?

▶ Problem

How does a ramp affect the amount of energy, work, and power used to lift an object?

▶ Hypothesize

Write a hypothesis to explain how the potential energy, the amount of work done, and the power required to lift an object straight up compare with the same quantities when the object is moved up a ramp. Your hypothesis should take the form of an "If . . . , then . . . , because . . ." statement.

MATERIALS
- board
- chair
- meter stick
- string
- small wheeled object
- spring scale
- stopwatch

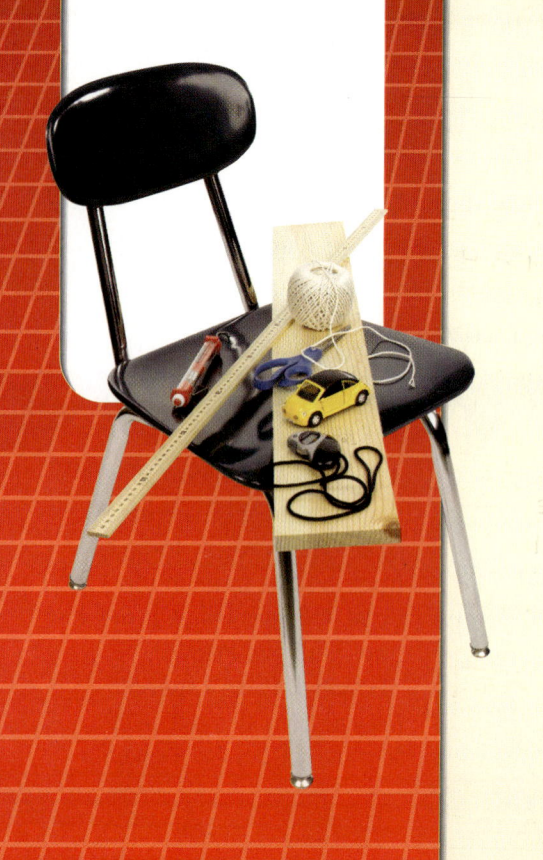

▶ Procedure

1. Make a data table like the one shown.

2. Lean the board up against the chair seat to create a ramp.

3. Measure and record the vertical distance from the floor to the top of the ramp. Also measure and record the length of the ramp.

4. Tie the string around the wheeled object. Make a loop so that you can hook the string onto the spring scale. Measure and record the weight of the object in newtons.

5. Lift the object straight up to the top of the ramp without using the ramp, as pictured.

136 Unit: Motion and Forces

6. On the spring scale, read and record the newtons of force needed to lift the object. Time how long it takes to lift the object from the floor to the top of the ramp. Conduct three trials and average your results. Record your measurements in the data table.

7. Drag the object from the bottom of the ramp to the top of the ramp with the spring scale, and record the newtons of force that were needed to move the object and the time it took. Conduct three trials and average your results.

Observe and Analyze *Write It Up*

1. **RECORD OBSERVATIONS** Draw the setup of the procedure. Be sure your data table is complete.

2. **IDENTIFY VARIABLES AND CONSTANTS** List the variables and constants in your notebook.

3. **CALCULATE**

   Potential Energy Convert centimeters to meters. Then calculate the gravitational potential energy (GPE) of the object at the top of the ramp. (Recall that weight equals mass times gravitational acceleration.)

   Gravitational Potential Energy = weight • height

   Work Calculate the work done, first when the object was lifted and then when it was pulled. Use the appropriate distance.

   Work = Force • distance

   Power Calculate the power involved in both situations.

   $$\text{Power} = \frac{\text{Work}}{\text{time}}$$

Conclude *Write It Up*

1. **COMPARE** How did the distance through which the object moved when it was pulled up the ramp differ from the distance when it was lifted straight up? How did the amount of force required differ in the two situations?

2. **COMPARE** How does your calculated value for potential energy compare with the values you obtained for work done?

3. **INTERPRET** Answer the question posed in the problem.

4. **ANALYZE** Compare your results with your hypothesis. Did your results support your hypothesis?

5. **IDENTIFY LIMITS** What possible limitations or sources of error could you have experienced?

6. **APPLY** A road going up a hill usually winds back and forth instead of heading straight to the top. How does this affect the work a car does to get to the top? How does it affect the power involved?

INVESTIGATE Further

CHALLENGE Design a way to use potential energy to move the car up the ramp. What materials can you use? Think about the materials in terms of potential energy—that is, how high they are from the ground or how stretched or compressed they are.

Work and Power

Problem How does the amount of energy, work, and power used to lift an object?

Hypothesize

Observe and Analyze

Measured length of ramp = _____ cm

Height object is being lifted = _____ cm

Measured weight of the object = _____ N

Table 1. Measurements for Lifting the Object with and Without the Ramp

	Trial No.	Force (N)	Time (s)
Straight up	1		
	2		
	3		
	Average		
Ramp	1		

Chapter 4: Work and Energy 137

Chapter Review

the BIG idea

Energy is transferred when a force moves an object.

CONTENT REVIEW
CLASSZONE.COM

KEY CONCEPTS SUMMARY

4.1 Work is the use of force to move an object.

Work is done by a force that acts in the same direction as the motion of an object.

Work = Force · distance

VOCABULARY
work p. 115
joule p. 117

4.2 Energy is transferred when work is done.

The amounts of potential energy and kinetic energy in a system or process may vary, but the total amount of energy remains unchanged.

$$GPE = mgh$$

$$KE = \frac{1}{2}mv^2$$

$$ME = PE + KE$$

VOCABULARY
potential energy p. 122
kinetic energy p. 122
mechanical energy p. 125
conservation of energy p. 126

4.3 Power is the rate at which work is done.

Power can be calculated from work and time.

$$Power = \frac{Work}{time}$$

Power can be calculated from energy and time.

$$Power = \frac{Energy}{time}$$

Power is measured in watts (W) and sometimes horsepower (hp).

VOCABULARY
power p. 130
watt p. 131
horsepower p. 132

138 Unit: Motion and Forces

Reviewing Vocabulary

Make a four square diagram for each of the terms listed below. Write the term in the center. Define it in one square. Write characteristics, examples, and formulas (if appropriate) in the other squares. A sample is shown below.

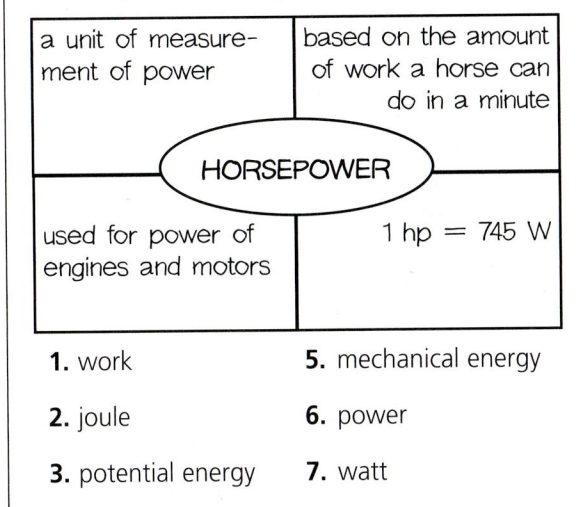

a unit of measurement of power	based on the amount of work a horse can do in a minute
HORSEPOWER	
used for power of engines and motors	1 hp = 745 W

1. work
2. joule
3. potential energy
4. kinetic energy
5. mechanical energy
6. power
7. watt

Reviewing Key Concepts

Multiple Choice *Choose the letter of the best answer.*

8. Work can be calculated from
   a. force and speed
   b. force and distance
   c. energy and time
   d. energy and distance

9. If you balance a book on your head, you are not doing work on the book because
   a. doing work requires moving an object
   b. you are not applying any force to the book
   c. the book is doing work on you
   d. the book has potential energy

10. Energy that an object has because of its position or shape is called
    a. potential energy   c. thermal energy
    b. kinetic energy   d. chemical energy

11. Suppose you are pushing a child on a swing. During what space of time are you doing work on the swing?
    a. while you hold it back before letting go
    b. while your hands are in contact with the swing and pushing forward
    c. after you let go of the swing and it continues to move forward
    d. all the time the swing is in motion

12. A falling ball has a potential energy of 5 J and a kinetic energy of 10 J. What is the ball's mechanical energy?
    a. 5 J   c. 15 J
    b. 10 J   d. 50 J

13. The unit that measures one joule of work done in one second is called a
    a. meter   c. newton-meter
    b. watt   d. newton

14. By increasing the speed at which you do work, you increase your
    a. force   c. energy
    b. work   d. power

15. A ball kicked into the air will have the greatest gravitational potential energy
    a. as it is being kicked
    b. as it starts rising
    c. at its highest point
    d. as it hits the ground

Short Answer *Answer each of the following questions in a sentence or two.*

16. How can you tell if a force you exert is doing work?

17. How does a water wheel do work?

18. State the law of conservation of energy. How does it affect the total amount of energy in any process?

19. Explain why a swing will not stay in motion forever after you have given it a push. What happens to its mechanical energy?

20. What are two ways to calculate power?

21. Why did James Watt invent a unit of measurement based on the work of horses?

Thinking Critically

22. SYNTHESIZE A weightlifter holds a barbell above his head. How do the barbell's potential energy, kinetic energy, and mechanical energy change as it is lifted and then lowered to the ground?

23. SYNTHESIZE What happens when you wind up a toy car and release it? Describe the events in terms of energy.

Use the photograph below to answer the next three questions.

24. APPLY When the boy first pushes on the chair, the chair does not move due to friction. Is the boy doing work? Why or why not?

25. ANALYZE For the first two seconds, the boy pushes the chair slowly at a steady speed. After that, he pushes the chair at a faster speed. How does his power change if he is using the same force at both speeds? How does his work change?

26. SYNTHESIZE As the boy pushes the chair, he does work. However, when he stops pushing, the chair stops moving and does not have any additional kinetic or potential energy. What happened to the energy he transferred by doing work on the chair?

27. APPLY A bouncing ball has mechanical energy. Each bounce, however, reaches a lower height than the last. Describe what happens to the mechanical, potential, and kinetic energy of the ball as it bounces several times.

28. CONNECT When you do work, you transfer energy. Where does the energy you transfer come from?

Using Math Skills in Science

Complete the following calculations.

29. Use the information in the photograph below to calculate the work the person does in lifting the box.

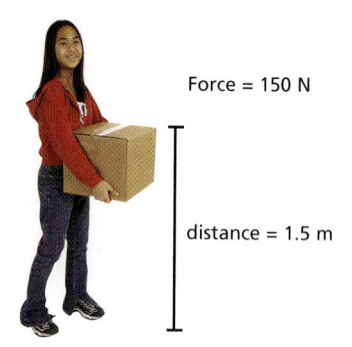

Force = 150 N
distance = 1.5 m

30. If you did 225 J of work to pull a wagon with a force of 25 N, how far did you pull it?

31. A kite with a mass of 0.05 kg is caught on the roof of a house. The house is 10 m high. What is the kite's gravitational potential energy? (Recall that $g = 9.8$ m/s^2.)

32. A baseball with a mass of 0.15 kg leaves a pitcher's hand traveling 40 m/s toward the batter. What is the baseball's kinetic energy?

33. Suppose it takes 150 J of force to push a cart 10 m in 60 s. Calculate the power.

34. If an electric hair dryer uses 1200 W, how much energy does it need to run for 2 s?

the BIG idea

35. SYNTHESIZE Look back at the photograph of the person lifting a box on pages 112–113. Describe the picture in terms of work, potential energy, kinetic energy, and power.

36. WRITE Think of an activity that involves work. Write a paragraph explaining how the work is transferring energy and where the transferred energy goes.

UNIT PROJECTS

If you need to create graphs or other visuals for your project, be sure you have grid paper, poster board, markers, or other supplies.

Standardized Test Practice

For practice on your state test, go to...
TEST PRACTICE
CLASSZONE.COM

Understanding Experiments

Read the following description of an experiment. Then answer the questions that follow.

James Prescott Joule is well known for a paddle-wheel experiment he conducted in the mid-1800s. He placed a paddle wheel in a bucket of water. Then he set up two weights on either side of the bucket. As the weights fell, they turned the paddle wheel. Joule recorded the temperature of the water before and after the paddle wheel began turning. He found that the water temperature increased as the paddle wheel turned.

Based on this experiment, Joule concluded that the falling weights released mechanical energy, which was converted into heat by the turning wheel. He was convinced that whenever mechanical force is exerted, heat is produced.

1. Which principle did Joule demonstrate with this experiment?
   a. When energy is converted from one form to another, some energy is lost.
   b. The amount of momentum in a system does not change as long as there are no outside forces acting on the system.
   c. One form of energy can be converted into another form of energy.
   d. When one object exerts a force on another object, the second object exerts an equal and opposite force on the first object.

2. Which form of energy was released by the weights in Joule's experiment?
   a. electrical
   b. mechanical
   c. nuclear
   d. heat

3. Which form of energy was produced in the water?
   a. chemical
   b. electrical
   c. nuclear
   d. heat

4. Based on Joule's finding that movement causes temperature changes in water, which of the following would be a logical prediction?
   a. Water held in a container should increase in temperature.
   b. Water at the base of a waterfall should be warmer than water at the top.
   c. Water with strong waves should be colder than calm water.
   d. Water should increase in temperature with depth.

Extended Response

Answer the two questions below in detail. Include some of the terms from the word box. Underline each term you use in your answer.

| potential energy | conservation of energy | force |
| kinetic energy | power | work |

5. A sledder has the greatest potential energy at the top of a hill. She has the least amount of potential energy at the bottom of a hill. She has the greatest kinetic energy when she moves the fastest. Where on the hill does the sledder move the fastest? State the relationship between kinetic energy and potential energy in this situation.

6. Andre and Jon are moving boxes of books from the floor to a shelf in the school library. Each box weighs 15 lb. Andre lifts 5 boxes in one minute. Jon lifts 5 boxes in 30 seconds. Which person does more work? Which person applies more force? Which person has the greater power? Explain your answers.

Chapter 4: **Work and Energy** 141

CHAPTER 5
Machines

the BIG idea

Machines help people do work by changing the force applied to an object.

Key Concepts

SECTION 5.1
Machines help people do work.
Learn about machines and how they are used to do work.

SECTION 5.2
Six simple machines have many uses.
Learn about levers and inclined planes and the other simple machines that are related to them.

SECTION 5.3
Modern technology uses compound machines.
Learn how scientists are using nanotechnology and robots to create new ways for machines to do work.

Internet Preview

CLASSZONE.COM
Chapter 5 online resources: Content Review, Simulation, four Resource Centers, Math Tutorial, Test Practice

Balls move through this sculpture. What do you think keeps the balls in motion?

EXPLORE the BIG idea

Changing Direction

Observe how a window blind works. Notice how you use a downward force to pull the blind up. Look around you for other examples.

Observe and Think Why does changing the direction of a force make work easier?

Shut the Door!

Find a door that swings freely on its hinges. Stand on the side where you can push the door to close it. Open the door. Push the door closed several times, placing your hand closer to or farther from the hinge each time.

Observe and Think Which hand placement made it easiest to shut the door? Why do you think that is so?

Internet Activity: Machines

Go to **ClassZone.com** to learn more about the simple machines in everyday objects. Select an item and think about how it moves and does its job. Then test your knowledge of simple machines.

Observe and Think What other objects contain simple machines?

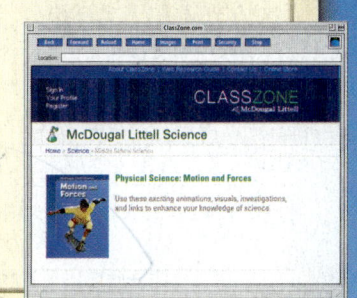

NSTA scilinks.org
SCLINKS

Simple Machines Code: MDL008

Chapter 5: **Machines** 143

CHAPTER 5
Getting Ready to Learn

CONCEPT REVIEW

- Work is done when a force moves an object over a distance.
- Energy can be converted from one form to another.
- Energy is transferred when work is done.

VOCABULARY REVIEW

work p. 115
mechanical energy p. 125
power p. 130

See Glossary for definitions.
energy, technology

CONTENT REVIEW
CLASSZONE.COM
Review concepts and vocabulary.

TAKING NOTES

CHOOSE YOUR OWN STRATEGY

Take notes using one or more of the strategies from earlier chapters—**outline, combination notes, supporting main ideas,** and **main idea web.** Feel free to mix and match the strategies, or use an entirely different note-taking strategy.

VOCABULARY STRATEGY

Draw a **word triangle** diagram for each new vocabulary term. On the bottom line, write and define the term. Above that, write a sentence that uses the term correctly. At the top, draw a small picture to show what the term looks like.

See the Note-Taking Handbook on pages R45–R51.

SCIENCE NOTEBOOK

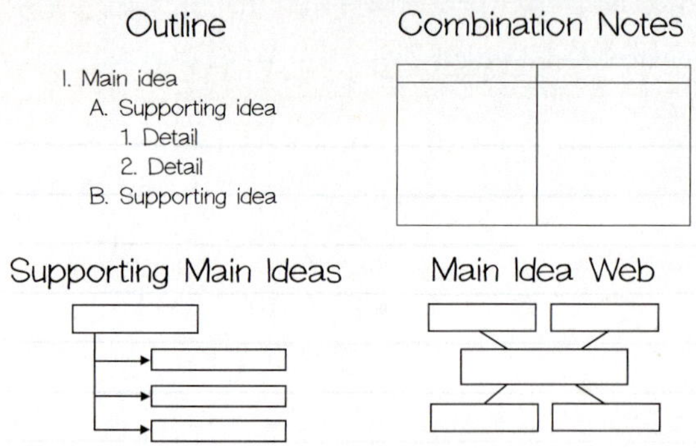

Outline
I. Main idea
  A. Supporting idea
    1. Detail
    2. Detail
  B. Supporting idea

Combination Notes

Supporting Main Ideas

Main Idea Web

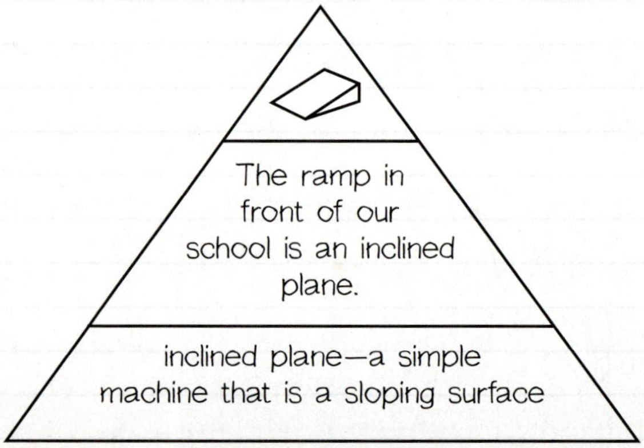

The ramp in front of our school is an inclined plane.

inclined plane—a simple machine that is a sloping surface

Unit: Motion and Forces

KEY CONCEPT

5.1 Machines help people do work.

◀ **BEFORE, you learned**
- Work is done when a force is exerted over a distance
- Some work can be converted to heat or sound energy

▶ **NOW, you will learn**
- How machines help you do work
- How to calculate a machine's efficiency

VOCABULARY

machine p. 145
mechanical advantage p. 147
efficiency p. 150

EXPLORE Machines

How do machines help you work?

PROCEDURE

1. Look at one of the machines closely. Carefully operate the machine and notice how each part moves.

2. Sketch a diagram of the machine. Try to show all of the working parts. Add arrows and labels to show the direction of motion for each part.

MATERIALS
various small machines

WHAT DO YOU THINK?
- What is the function of the machine?
- How many moving parts does it have?
- How do the parts work together?
- How does this machine make work easier?

Machines change the way force is applied.

For thousands of years, humans have been improving their lives with technology. Technology is the use of knowledge to create products or tools that make life easier. The simplest machine is an example of technology.

A **machine** is any device that helps people do work. A machine does not decrease the amount of work that is done. Instead, a machine changes the way in which work is done. Recall that work is the use of force to move an object. If, for example, you have to lift a heavy box, you can use a ramp to make the work easier. Moving the box up a ramp—which is a machine—helps you do the work by reducing the force you need to lift the box.

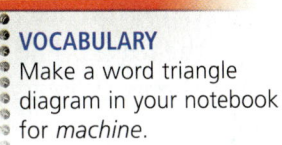

VOCABULARY
Make a word triangle diagram in your notebook for *machine*.

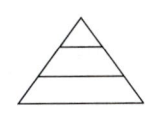

Chapter 5: **Machines** 145

If machines do not reduce the amount of work required, how do they help people do work? Machines make work easier by changing

- the size of the force needed to do the work and the distance over which the force is applied
- the direction in which the force is exerted

Machines can be powered by different types of energy. Electronic machines, such as computers, use electrical energy. Mechanical machines, such as a rake, use mechanical energy. Often this mechanical energy is supplied by the person who is using the machine.

Changing Size and Distance

Some machines help you do work by changing the size of the force needed. Have you ever tried to open a door by turning the doorknob's shaft instead of the handle? This is not easy to do. It takes less force to turn the handle of the doorknob than it does to turn the shaft. Turning the handle makes opening the door easier, even though you must turn it through a greater distance.

A rake is a machine that changes a large force over a short distance to a smaller force over a larger distance.

If a machine—such as a doorknob attached to a shaft—allows you to exert less force, you must apply that force over a greater distance. The total amount of work remains the same whether it is done with a machine or not. You can think of this in terms of the formula for calculating work—work is force times distance. Because a machine does not decrease the amount of work to be done, less force must mean greater distance.

A doorknob allows you to apply a smaller force over a greater distance. Some machines allow you to apply a greater input force over a shorter distance. Look at the boy using a rake, which is a machine. The boy moves his hands a short distance to move the end of the rake a large distance, allowing him to rake up more leaves.

Input force is the force exerted on a machine. Output force is the force that a machine exerts on an object. The boy in the photograph is exerting an input force on the rake. As a result, the rake exerts an output force on the leaves. The work the boy puts into the rake is the same as the work he gets out of the rake. However, the force he applies is greater than the force the rake can apply to the leaves. The output force is less than the input force, but it acts over a longer distance.

CHECK YOUR READING How can a rake help you do work? Use the word *force* in your answer.

Changing Direction

Machines also can help you work by changing the direction of a force. Think of raising a flag on a flagpole. You pull down on the rope, and the flag moves up. The rope system is a machine that changes the direction in which you exert your force. The rope system does not change the size of the force, however. The force pulling the flag upward is equal to your downward pull.

A shovel is a machine that can help you dig a hole. Once you have the shovel in the ground, you push down on the handle to lift the dirt up. You can use some of the weight of your body as part of your input force. That would not be possible if you were lifting the dirt by using only your hands. A shovel also changes the size of the force you apply, so you need less force to lift the dirt.

Mechanical Advantage of a Machine

When machines help you work, there is an advantage—or benefit—to using them. The number of times a machine multiplies the input force is called the machine's **mechanical advantage** (MA). To find a machine's mechanical advantage, divide the output force by the input force.

$$\text{Mechanical Advantage} = \frac{\text{Output Force}}{\text{Input Force}}$$

For machines that allow you to apply less force over a greater distance—such as a doorknob—the output force is greater than the input force. Therefore, the mechanical advantage of this type of machine is greater than 1. For example, if the input force is 10 newtons and the output force is 40 newtons, the mechanical advantage is 40 N divided by 10 N, or 4.

For machines that allow you to apply greater force over a shorter distance—such as a rake—the output force is less than the input force. In this case, the mechanical advantage is less than 1. If the input force is 10 newtons and the output force is 5 newtons, the mechanical advantage is 0.5. However, such a machine allows you to move an object a greater distance.

Sometimes changing the direction of the force is more useful than decreasing the force or the distance. For machines that change only the direction of a force—such as the rope system on a flagpole—the input force and output force are the same. Therefore, the mechanical advantage of the machine is 1.

APPLY How does the rope system help the man raise the flag?

NOTE-TAKING STRATEGY
Remember to organize your notes in a chart or web as you read.

Work transfers energy.

Machines transfer energy to objects on which they do work. Every time you open a door, the doorknob is transferring mechanical energy to the shaft. A machine that lifts an object gives it potential energy. A machine that causes an object to start moving, such as a baseball bat hitting a ball, gives the object kinetic energy.

Energy

When you lift an object, you transfer energy to it in the form of gravitational potential energy—that is, potential energy caused by gravity. The higher you lift an object, the more work you must do and the more energy you give to the object. This is also true if a machine lifts an object. The gravitational potential energy of an object depends on its height above Earth's surface, and it equals the work required to lift the object to that height.

Recall that gravitational potential energy is the product of an object's mass, gravitational acceleration, and height $(GPE = mgh)$. In the diagram on page 149, the climber wants to reach the top of the hill. The higher she climbs, the greater her potential energy. This energy comes from the work the climber does. The potential energy she gains equals the amount of work she does.

Work

As you have seen, when you use a machine to do work, there is always an exchange, or tradeoff, between the force you use to do the work and the distance over which you apply that force. You apply less force over a longer distance or greater force over a shorter distance.

To reach the top of the hill, the climber must do work. Because she needs to increase her potential energy by a certain amount, she must do the same amount of work to reach the top of the hill whether she climbs a steep slope or a gentle slope.

The sloping surface of the hill acts like a ramp, which is a simple machine called an inclined plane. You know that machines make work easier by changing the size or direction of a force. How does this machine make the climber's work easier?

As the climber goes up the hill, she is doing work against gravity.

❶ One side of the hill is a very steep slope—almost straight up. If the climber takes the steep slope, she climbs a shorter distance, but she must use more force.

❷ Another side of the hill is a long, gentle slope. Here the climber travels a greater distance but uses much less effort.

148 Unit: Motion and Forces

If the climber uses the steep slope, she must lift almost her entire weight. The inclined plane allows her to exert her input force over a longer distance; therefore, she can use just enough force to overcome the net force pulling her down the inclined plane. This force is less than her weight. In many cases, it is easier for people to use less force over a longer distance than it is for them to use more force over a shorter distance.

Energy and Work

To reach the top of the hill, the climber must do at least as much work as the amount of potential energy she needs to gain.

① The Short Route

By climbing straight up the steep slope, the climber covers a shorter distance but must apply more force against gravity.

② The Long Route

By climbing the gentle slope, the climber covers more distance but uses less force. The work does not decrease even though the force does.

READING VISUALS What combination of forces makes it more difficult to climb a steep slope? How might climbers try to overcome this problem?

Chapter 5: **Machines** 149

VOCABULARY
Write your own definition of *efficiency* in a word triangle.

Output work is always less than input work.

The work you do on a machine is called the input work, and the work the machine does in turn is called the output work. A machine's **efficiency** is the ratio of its output work to the input work. An ideal machine would be 100 percent efficient. All of the input work would be converted to output work. Actual machines lose some input work to friction.

You can calculate the efficiency of a machine by dividing the machine's output work by its input work and multiplying that number by 100.

$$\text{Efficiency (\%)} = \frac{\text{Output work}}{\text{Input work}} \cdot 100$$

Recall that work is measured in joules. Suppose you do 600 J of work in using a rope system to lift a box. The work done on the box is 540 J. You would calculate the efficiency of the rope system as follows:

$$\text{Efficiency} = \frac{540 \text{ J}}{600 \text{ J}} \cdot 100 = 90\%$$

CHECK YOUR READING What is a machine's efficiency? How does it affect the amount of work a machine can do?

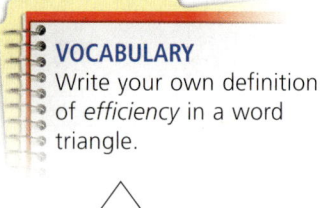

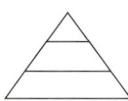

APPLY The mail carrier is riding a motorized human transport machine. Suppose the machine has an efficiency of 70 percent. How much work is lost in overcoming friction on the sidewalk and in the motor?

Efficiency
The work you put into a machine will always be greater than the work done by the machine. Some input work is always lost in overcoming friction.

Efficiency and Energy

You know that work transfers energy and that machines make work easier. The more mechanical energy is lost in the transfer to other forms of energy, the less efficient the machine. Machines lose some energy in the form of heat due to friction. The more moving parts a machine has, the more energy it loses to friction because the parts rub together. Machines can lose energy to other processes as well.

For example, a car engine has an efficiency of only about 25 percent. It loses much of the energy supplied by its fuel to heat from combustion. By comparison, a typical electric motor has more than an 80 percent efficiency. That means the motor converts more than 80 percent of the input energy into mechanical energy, or motion.

Many appliances come with energy guides that can help a buyer compare the energy efficiency of different models. A washing machine with the highest energy rating may not always save the most energy, however, because users may have to run those machines more often.

INVESTIGATE Efficiency

What is the efficiency of a ramp?

PROCEDURE

1. Build a ramp as shown. Measure the vertical height of the ramp and the length of the ramp in centimeters. Convert these distances to meters and record.

2. Attach the block to the spring scale and measure the force in newtons needed to lift the block straight up. Record this force as the output force. Multiply the output force by the height of the ramp in meters to get the output work. Record the output work.

3. Use the spring scale to pull the block up the ramp with a constant force. Record the force measured on the spring scale as the input force. Multiply the input force by the length of the ramp in meters to get the input work. Record the input work.

4. Use the input work and output work from steps 2 and 3 to calculate the efficiency of the ramp. Record your results.

WHAT DO YOU THINK?
- How did your input work compare with your output work?
- What could you do to increase the efficiency of the ramp?

CHALLENGE Would adding sandpaper on the surface of the ramp increase or decrease the efficiency of the ramp? Why? Test your hypothesis.

SKILL FOCUS
Analyzing data

MATERIALS
- board
- books
- meter stick
- wooden block with eye hook
- spring scale
for Challenge:
- sandpaper

TIME
20 minutes

Chapter 5: **Machines** 151

Proper maintenance can help keep a bicycle running as efficiently as possible.

Increasing Efficiency

Because all machines lose input work to friction, one way to improve the efficiency of a machine is by reducing friction. Oil is used to reduce friction between the moving parts of car engines. The use of oil makes engines more efficient.

Another machine that loses input work is a bicycle. Bicycles lose energy to friction and to air resistance. Friction losses result from the meeting of the gears, from the action of the chain on the sprocket, and from the tires changing shape against the pavement. A bicycle with poorly greased parts or other signs of poor maintenance requires more force to move. For a mountain bike that has had little maintenance, as much as 15 percent of the total work may be lost to friction. A well-maintained Olympic track bike, on the other hand, might lose only 0.5 percent.

CHECK YOUR READING What is a common way to increase a machine's efficiency?

5.1 Review

KEY CONCEPTS

1. In what ways can a machine change a force?
2. How is a machine's efficiency calculated?
3. Why is a machine's actual output work always less than its input work?

CRITICAL THINKING

4. **Apply** How would the input force needed to push a wheelchair up a ramp change if you increased the height of the ramp but not its length?
5. **Compare** What is the difference between mechanical advantage and efficiency?

CHALLENGE

6. **Apply** Draw and label a diagram to show how to pull down on a rope to raise a load of construction materials.

152 Unit: Motion and Forces

MATH in SCIENCE

SKILL: CHANGING RATIOS TO PERCENTS

MATH TUTORIAL
CLASSZONE.COM
Click on Math Tutorial for more help with percents and fractions.

How Efficient Are Machines?

A hammer is used to pound in nails. It can also be used to pry nails out of wood. When used to pry nails, a hammer is a machine called a lever. Like all machines, the hammer is not 100 percent efficient.

Efficiency is the amount of work a machine does divided by the amount of work that is done on the machine. To calculate efficiency, you must first find the ratio of the machine's output work to the input work done on the machine. A ratio is the comparison of two numbers by means of division. You convert the ratio to a decimal by dividing. Then convert the decimal to a percent.

Example

A person is doing 1000 joules of work on a hammer to pry up a nail. The hammer does 925 joules of work on the nail to pull it out of the wood.

(1) Find the ratio of output work to input work.

$$\frac{\text{Output work}}{\text{Input work}} = \frac{925 \text{ J}}{1000 \text{ J}} = 0.925$$

(2) To convert the decimal to a percent, multiply 0.925 by 100 and add a percent sign.

$$0.925 \cdot 100 = 92.5\%$$

ANSWER The efficiency of the hammer is 92.5 percent. This means that the hammer loses 7.5 percent of the input work to friction and other products.

No machine, no matter how large or small, is 100 percent efficient. Some of the input energy is lost to sound, heat, or other products.

Answer the following questions.

1. A construction worker does 1000 J of work in pulling down on a rope to lift a weight tied to the other end. If the output work of the rope system is 550 J, what is the ratio of output work to input work? What is the efficiency of the rope system?

2. If a machine takes in 20,000 J and puts out 5000 J, what is its efficiency?

3. You do 6000 J of work to pull a sled up a ramp. After you reach the top, you discover that the sled had 3600 J of work done on it. What is the efficiency of the ramp?

CHALLENGE If you put 7000 J of work into a machine with an efficiency of 50 percent, how much work will you get out?

Chapter 5: **Machines** 153

5.2 Six simple machines have many uses.

KEY CONCEPT

BEFORE, you learned
- Machines help you work by changing the size or direction of a force
- The number of times a machine multiplies the input force is the machine's mechanical advantage

NOW, you will learn
- How six simple machines change the size or direction of a force
- How to calculate mechanical advantage

VOCABULARY
simple machine p. 154
lever p. 155
fulcrum p. 155
wheel and axle p. 156
pulley p. 156
inclined plane p. 158
wedge p. 158
screw p. 159

EXPLORE Changing Forces

How can you change a force?

PROCEDURE
1. Lay one pencil on a flat surface. Place the other pencil on top of the first pencil and perpendicular to it, as shown. Place the book on one end of the top pencil.
2. Push down on the free end of the top pencil to raise the book.
3. Change the position of the bottom pencil so that it is closer to the book and repeat step 2. Then move the bottom pencil closer to the end of the pencil you are pushing on and repeat step 2.

MATERIALS
- 2 pencils
- small book

WHAT DO YOU THINK?
- How did changing the position of the bottom pencil affect how much force you needed to lift the book?
- At which position is it easiest to lift the book? most difficult?

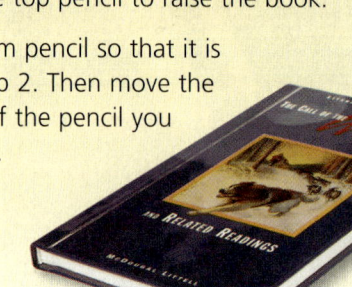

NOTE-TAKING STRATEGY
As you read, remember to take notes about the main ideas and supporting details.

There are six simple machines.

You have read about how a ramp and a shovel can help you do work. A ramp is a type of inclined plane, and a shovel is a type of lever. An inclined plane and a lever are both simple machines. **Simple machines** are the six machines on which all other mechanical machines are based. In addition to the inclined plane and the lever, simple machines include the wheel and axle, pulley, wedge, and screw. As you will see, the wheel and axle and pulley are related to the lever, and the wedge and screw are related to the inclined plane. You will read about each of the six simple machines in detail in this section.

154 Unit: Motion and Forces

Lever

A **lever** is a solid bar that rotates, or turns, around a fixed point. The bar can be straight or curved. The fixed point is called the **fulcrum.** A lever can multiply the input force. It can also change the direction of the input force. If you apply a force downward on one end of a lever, the other end can lift a load.

The way in which a lever changes an input force depends on the positions of the fulcrum, the input force, and the output force in relation to one another. Levers with different arrangements have different uses. Sometimes a greater output force is needed, such as when you want to pry up a bottle cap. At other times you use a greater input force on one end to get a higher speed at the other end, such as when you swing a baseball bat. The three different arrangements, sometimes called the three classes of levers, are shown in the diagram below.

CHECK YOUR READING What two parts are needed to make a lever?

Levers

Levers can be classified according to where the fulcrum is.

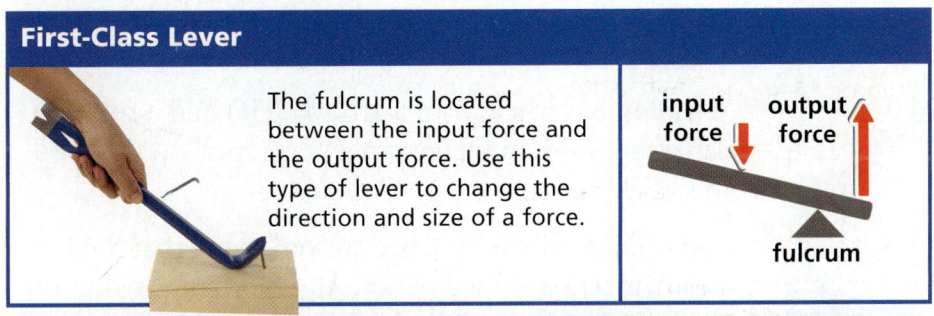

READING TIP
The lengths of the arrows in the diagram represent the size of the force.

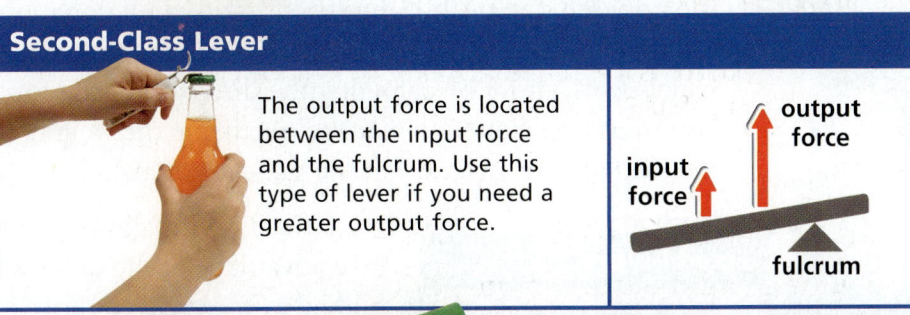

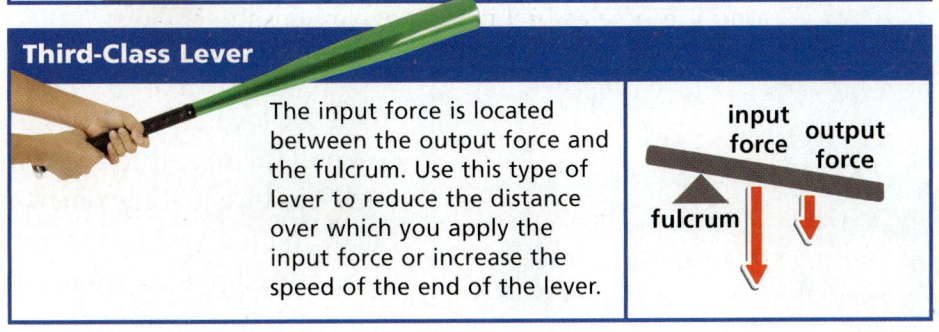

First-Class Lever

The fulcrum is located between the input force and the output force. Use this type of lever to change the direction and size of a force.

Second-Class Lever

The output force is located between the input force and the fulcrum. Use this type of lever if you need a greater output force.

Third-Class Lever

The input force is located between the output force and the fulcrum. Use this type of lever to reduce the distance over which you apply the input force or increase the speed of the end of the lever.

Chapter 5: **Machines** 155

Wheel and Axle

Wheel and Axle

A **wheel and axle** is a simple machine made of a wheel attached to a shaft, or axle. The wheels of most means of transportation—such as a bicycle and a car—are attached to an axle. The wheel and axle act like a rotating collection of levers. The axle at the wheel's center is like a fulcrum. Other examples of wheels and axles are screwdrivers, steering wheels, doorknobs, and electric fans.

Depending on your purpose for using a wheel and axle, you might apply a force to turn the wheel or the axle. If you turn the wheel, your input force is transferred to the axle. Because the axle is smaller than the wheel, the output force acts over a shorter distance than the input force. A driver applies less force to a steering wheel to get a greater turning force from the axle, or steering column. This makes it easier to steer the car.

If, instead, you turn the axle, your force is transferred to the wheel. Because the wheel is larger than the axle, the force acts over a longer distance. A car also contains this use of a wheel and axle. The engine turns the drive axles, which turn the wheels.

CHECK YOUR READING Compare the results of putting force on the axle with putting force on the wheel.

Pulley

A **pulley** is a wheel with a grooved rim and a rope or cable that rides in the groove. As you pull on the rope, the wheel turns.

A pulley that is attached to something that holds it steady is called a fixed pulley. An object attached to the rope on one side of the wheel rises as you pull down on the rope on the other side of the wheel. The fixed pulley makes work easier by changing the direction of the force. You must apply enough force to overcome the weight of the load and any friction in the pulley system.

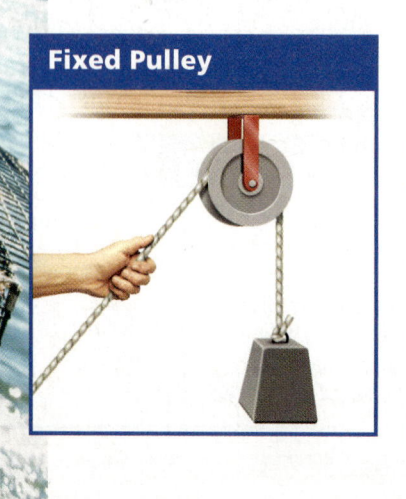

Fixed Pulley

A fixed pulley allows you to take advantage of the downward pull of your weight to move a load upward. It does not, however, reduce the force you need to lift the load. Also, the distance you pull the rope through is the same distance that the object is lifted. To lift a load two meters using a fixed pulley, you must pull down two meters of rope.

In a movable pulley setup, one end of the rope is fixed, but the wheel can move. The load is attached to the wheel. The person pulling the rope provides the output force that lifts the load. A single movable pulley does not change the direction of the force. Instead, it multiplies the force. Because the load is supported by two sections of rope, you need only half the force you would use with a fixed pulley to lift it. However, you must pull the rope through twice the distance.

CHECK YOUR READING How does a single fixed pulley differ from a single movable pulley?

Movable Pulley

A combination of fixed and movable pulleys is a pulley system called a block and tackle. A block and tackle is used to haul and lift very heavy objects. By combining fixed and movable pulleys, you can use more rope sections to support the weight of an object. This reduces the force you need to lift the object. The mechanical advantage of a single pulley can never be greater than 2. If engineers need a pulley system with a mechanical advantage greater than 2, they often use a block-and-tackle system.

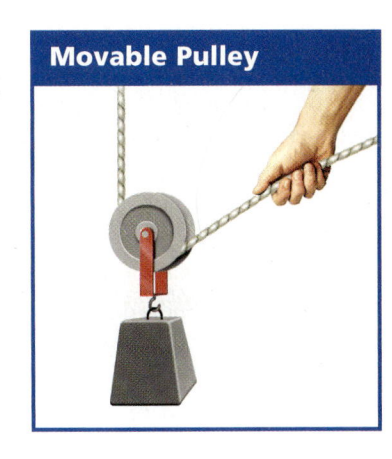

INVESTIGATE Pulleys

What is the mechanical advantage of a pulley system?

PROCEDURE

1. Hang the mass on the spring scale to find its weight in newtons. Record this weight as your output force.

2. Tie the top of one pulley to the ring stand.

3. Attach the mass to the second pulley.

4. Attach one end of the second pulley's rope to the bottom of the first pulley. Then thread the free end of the rope through the second pulley. Loop the rope up and over the first pulley, as shown.

5. Attach the spring scale to the free end of the rope. Pull down to lift the mass. Record the force you used as your input force. Calculate the mechanical advantage of this pulley system.
   Hint: The mechanical advantage can be calculated by dividing the output force by the input force.

WHAT DO YOU THINK?
- How did your input force compare with your output force?
- What caused the results you observed?

CHALLENGE Explain what the mechanical advantage would be for a pulley system that includes another movable pulley.

SKILL FOCUS
Inferring

MATERIALS
- 100 g mass
- spring scale
- 2 pulleys with rope
- ring stand

TIME
20 minutes

Chapter 5: **Machines** 157

Inclined Plane

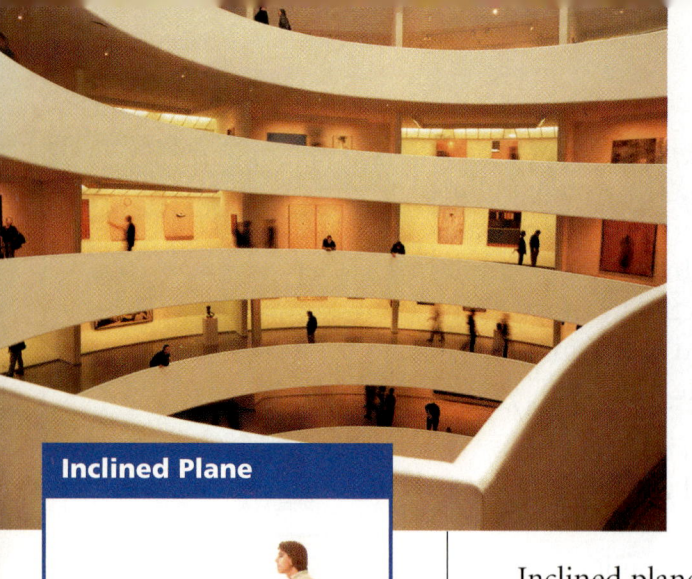

Inclined Plane

Recall that it is difficult to lift a heavy object straight up because you must apply a force great enough to overcome the downward pull of the force of gravity. For this reason people often use ramps. A ramp is an **inclined plane,** a simple machine that is a sloping surface. The photograph at the left shows the interior of the Guggenheim Museum in New York City. The levels of the art museum are actually one continuous inclined plane.

Inclined planes make the work of raising an object easier because they support part of the weight of the object while it is being moved from one level to another. The surface of an inclined plane applies a reaction force on the object resting on it. This extra force on the object helps to act against gravity. If you are pushing an object up a ramp, you have to push with only enough force to overcome the smaller net force that pulls the object down parallel to the incline.

The less steep an inclined plane is, the less force you need to push or pull an object on the plane. This is because a less steep plane supports more of an object's weight than a steeper plane. However, the less steep an inclined plane is, the farther you must go to reach a certain height. While you use less force, you must apply that force over a greater distance.

Wedge

CHECK YOUR READING How do inclined planes help people do work? Your answer should mention force.

Wedge

A **wedge** is a simple machine that has a thick end and a thin end. Wedges are used to cut, split, or pierce objects—or to hold objects together. A wedge is a type of inclined plane, but inclined planes are stationary, while wedges often move to do work.

Some wedges are single, movable inclined planes, such as a doorstop, a chisel, or an ice scraper. Another kind of wedge is made of two back-to-back inclined planes. Examples include the blade of an axe or a knife. In the photograph at the left, a sculptor is using a chisel to shape stone. The sculptor applies an input force on the chisel by tapping its thicker end with a mallet. That force pushes the thinner end of the chisel into the stone. As a result, the sides of the thinner end exert an output force that separates the stone.

The angle of the cutting edge determines how easily a wedge can cut through an object. Thin wedges have small angles and need less input force to cut than do thick wedges with large angles. That is why a sharp knife blade cuts more easily than a dull one.

You also can think of a wedge that cuts objects in terms of how it changes the pressure on a surface. The thin edges of a wedge provide a smaller surface area for the input force to act on. This greater pressure makes it easier to break through the surface of an object. A sharp knife can cut through an apple skin, and a sharp chisel can apply enough pressure to chip stone.

A doorstop is a wedge that is used to hold objects together. To do its job, a doorstop is pressed tip-first under a door. As the doorstop is moved into position, it lifts the door slightly and applies a force to the bottom of the door. In return, the door applies pressure to the doorstop and causes the doorstop to press against the floor with enough force to keep the doorstop—and the door—from moving.

Screw

A **screw** is an inclined plane wrapped around a cylinder or cone to form a spiral. A screw is a simple machine that can be used to raise and lower weights as well as to fasten objects. Examples of screws include drills, jar lids, screw clamps, and nuts and bolts. The spiraling inclined plane that sticks out from the body of the screw forms the threads of the screw.

In the photograph at right, a person is using a screwdriver, which is a wheel and axle, to drive a screw into a piece of wood. Each turn of the screwdriver pushes the screw farther into the wood. As the screw is turned, the threads act like wedges, exerting an output force on the wood. If the threads are very close together, the force must be applied over a greater distance—that is, the screw must be turned many times—but less force is needed.

The advantage of using a screw instead of a nail to hold things together is the large amount of friction that keeps the screw from turning and becoming loose. Think of pulling a nail out of a piece of wood compared with pulling a screw from the same piece of wood. The nail can be pulled straight out. The screw must be turned through a greater distance to remove it from the wood.

Notice that the interior of the Guggenheim Museum shown on page 158 is not only an inclined plane. It is also an example of a screw. The inclined plane is wrapped around the museum's atrium, which is an open area in the center.

Screw

CHECK YOUR READING Explain how a screw moves deeper into the wood as it is turned.

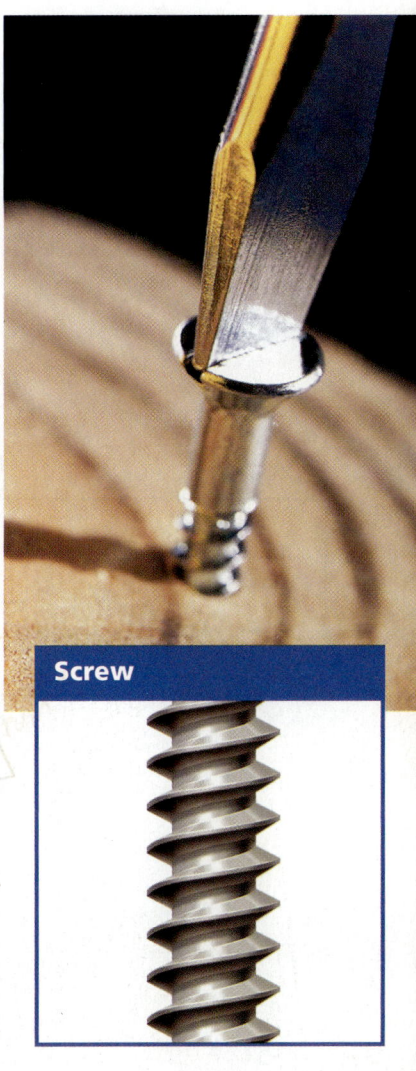

Chapter 5: **Machines** 159

The mechanical advantage of a machine can be calculated.

Recall that the number of times a machine multiplies the input force is the machine's mechanical advantage. You can calculate a machine's mechanical advantage using this formula:

$$\text{Mechanical Advantage} = \frac{\text{Output Force}}{\text{Input Force}}$$

$$MA = \frac{F_{out}}{F_{in}}$$

This formula works for all machines, regardless of whether they are simple machines or more complicated machines.

If a machine decreases the force you use to do work, the distance over which you have to apply that force increases. It is possible to use this idea to calculate the mechanical advantage of a simple machine without knowing what the input and output forces are. To make this calculation, however, you must assume that your machine is not losing any work to friction. In other words, you must assume that your machine is 100 percent efficient. The mechanical advantage that you calculate when making this assumption is called the ideal mechanical advantage.

Inclined Plane You can calculate the ideal mechanical advantage of an inclined plane by dividing its length by its height.

$$\text{Ideal Mechanical Advantage} = \frac{\text{length of incline}}{\text{height of incline}}$$

$$IMA = \frac{l}{h}$$

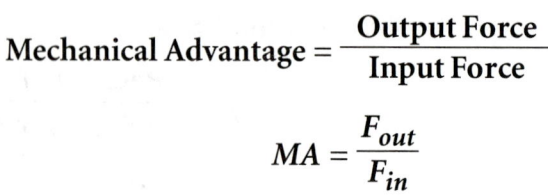

READING TIP

Scientists often consider the way in which an object will behave under ideal conditions, such as when there is no friction.

160 Unit: Motion and Forces

Be sure to use the length of the incline in your calculation, as shown in the diagram, and not the length of the base. If the mover in the photograph on page 160 increased the length of the ramp, he would increase the ramp's mechanical advantage. However, he would also increase the distance over which he had to carry the box.

Wheel and Axle To calculate the ideal mechanical advantage of a wheel and axle, use the following formula:

$$\text{Ideal Mechanical Advantage} = \frac{\text{Radius of input}}{\text{Radius of output}}$$

$$IMA = \frac{R_{in}}{R_{out}}$$

The Ferris wheel below is a giant wheel and axle. A motor applies an input force to the Ferris wheel's axle, which turns the wheel. In this example, the input force is applied to the axle, so the radius of the axle is the input radius in the formula above. The output force is applied by the wheel, so the radius of the wheel is the output radius.

For a Ferris wheel, the input force is greater than the output force. The axle turns through a shorter distance than the wheel does. The ideal mechanical advantage of this type of wheel and axle is less than 1.

Sometimes, as with a steering wheel, the input force is applied to turn the wheel instead of the axle. Then the input radius is the wheel's radius, and the output radius is the axle's radius. In this case, the input force on the wheel is less than the output force applied by the axle. The ideal mechanical advantage of this type of wheel and axle is greater than 1.

SIMULATION
CLASSZONE.COM

Explore the mechanical advantage of an inclined plane.

REMINDER
The radius is the distance from the center of the wheel or axle to any point on its circumference.

Chapter 5: **Machines** 161

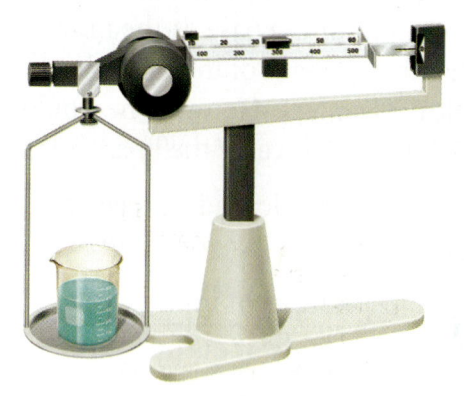

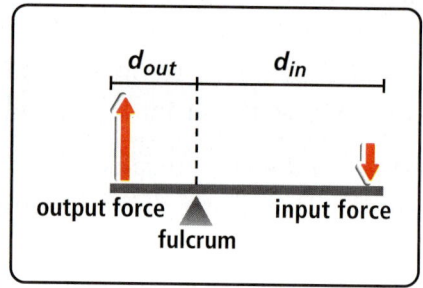

Lever The beam balance above is a lever. The beam is the solid bar that turns on a fixed point, or fulcrum. The fulcrum is the beam's balance point. When you slide the weight across the beam, you are changing the distance between the input force and the fulcrum. The mechanical advantage depends on the distances of the input force and output force from the fulcrum. The output force is applied to balance the beaker.

To calculate the ideal mechanical advantage of a lever, use the following formula:

$$\text{Ideal Mechanical Advantage} = \frac{\text{distance from input force to fulcrum}}{\text{distance from output force to fulcrum}}$$

$$IMA = \frac{d_{in}}{d_{out}}$$

This formula applies to all three arrangements of levers. If the distance from the input force to the fulcrum is greater than the distance from the output force to the fulcrum, the ideal mechanical advantage is greater than 1. The beam balance is an example of this type of lever.

5.2 Review

KEY CONCEPTS

1. Name the six simple machines and give an example of each.
2. Explain how a screw changes the size of the force needed to push it into wood.
3. To calculate mechanical advantage, what two things do you need to know?

CRITICAL THINKING

4. **Synthesize** How is a pulley similar to a wheel and axle?
5. **Calculate** What is the ideal mechanical advantage of a wheel with a diameter of 30 cm fixed to an axle with a diameter of 4 cm if the axle is turned?

CHALLENGE

6. **Infer** How can you increase a wedge's mechanical advantage? Draw a diagram to show your idea.

CONNECTING SCIENCES

PHYSICAL SCIENCE AND LIFE SCIENCE

A Running Machine

Marlon Shirley, who lives in Colorado, lost his lower left leg due to an accident at the age of five. He is a champion sprinter who achieved his running records while using a prosthesis (prahs-THEE-sihs), or a device used to replace a body part. Like his right leg, his prosthetic leg is a combination of simple machines that convert the energy from muscles in his body to move him forward. The mechanical system is designed to match the forces of his right leg.

Legs as Levers

Compare Marlon Shirley's artificial leg with his right leg. Both legs have long rods—one made of bone and the other of metal—that provide a strong frame. These rods act as levers. At the knee and ankle, movable joints act as fulcrums for these levers to transfer energy between the runner's body and the ground.

How Does It Work?

1. As the foot—real or artificial—strikes the ground, the leg stops moving forward and downward and absorbs the energy of the change in motion. The joints in the ankle and knee act as fulcrums as the levers transfer the energy to the muscle in the upper leg. This muscle acts like a spring to store the energy.

2. When the runner begins the next step, the energy is transferred back into the leg from the upper leg muscle. The levers in the leg convert the energy into forward motion of the runner's body.

The people who design prosthetic legs study the natural motion of a runner to learn exactly how energy is distributed and converted to motion so that they can build an artificial leg that works well with the real leg.

Other parts of the human body can act like simple machines. For example, teeth work like wedges.

EXPLORE

1. **VISUALIZE** Run across a room, paying close attention to the position of one of your ankles and knees as you move. Determine where the input force, output force, and fulcrum are in the lever formed by your lower leg.

2. **CHALLENGE** Use the library or the Internet to learn more about mechanical legs used in building robots that walk. How do the leg motions of these robots resemble your walking motions? How are they different?

RESOURCE CENTER
CLASSZONE.COM
Find out more about artificial limbs.

Chapter 5: **Machines** 163

KEY CONCEPT

5.3 Modern technology uses compound machines.

BEFORE, you learned
- Simple machines change the size or direction of a force
- All machines have an ideal and an actual mechanical advantage

NOW, you will learn
- How simple machines can be combined
- How scientists have developed extremely small machines
- How robots are used

VOCABULARY

compound machine p. 164
nanotechnology p. 167
robot p. 169

THINK ABOUT

How does a tow truck do work?

When a car is wrecked or disabled, the owner might call a towing service. The service sends a tow truck to take the car to be repaired. Tow trucks usually are equipped with a mechanism for freeing stuck vehicles and towing, or pulling, them. Look at the tow truck in the photograph at the right. What simple machines do you recognize?

VOCABULARY
Remember to write a definition for *compound machine* in a word triangle.

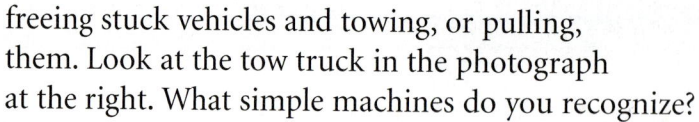

Compound machines are combinations of simple machines.

Like the tow truck pictured above, many of the more complex devices that you see or use every day are combinations of simple machines. For example, a pair of scissors is a combination of two levers. The cutting edges of those levers are wedges. A fishing rod is a lever with the fishing line wound around a wheel and axle, the reel. A machine that is made of two or more simple machines is called a **compound machine.**

In a very complex compound machine, such as a car, the simple machines may not be obvious at first. However, if you look carefully at a compound machine, you should be able to identify forms of levers, pulleys, and wheels and axles.

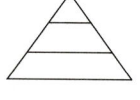

CHECK YOUR READING How are simple machines related to compound machines?

The gears in the photograph and diagram are spur gears, the most common type of gear.

Gears

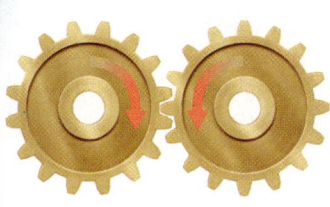

Gears

Gears are based on the wheel and axle. Gears have teeth on the edge of the wheel that allow one gear to turn another. A set of gears forms a compound machine in which one wheel and axle is linked to another.

Two linked gears that are the same size and have the same number of teeth will turn at the same speed. They will move in opposite directions. In order to make them move in the same direction, a third gear must be added between them. The gear that turns another gear applies the input force; the gear that is turned exerts the output force. A difference in speed between two gears—caused by a difference in size and the distance each turns through—produces a change in force.

CHECK YOUR READING How do gears form a compound machine?

Mechanical Advantage of Compound Machines

The mechanical advantage of any compound machine is equal to the product of the mechanical advantages of all the simple machines that make up the compound machine. For example, the ideal mechanical advantage of a pair of scissors would be the product of the ideal mechanical advantages of its two levers and two wedges.

The mechanical advantage of a pair of gears with different diameters can be found by counting the teeth on the gears. The mechanical advantage is the ratio of the number of teeth on the output gear to the number of teeth on the input gear. If there are more than two gears, count only the number of teeth on the first and last gears in the system. This ratio is the mechanical advantage of the whole gear system.

Compound machines typically must overcome more friction than simple machines because they tend to have many moving parts. Scissors, for example, have a lower efficiency than one lever because there is friction at the point where the two levers are connected. There is also friction between the blades of the scissors as they close.

Chapter 5: **Machines** 165

APPLY What simple machines do you see in this Jaws of Life cutting tool?

Modern technology creates new uses for machines.

Sophisticated modern machinery is often based on or contains simple machines. Consider Jaws of Life tools, which are used to help rescue people who have been in accidents. These cutters, spreaders, and rams are powered by hydraulics, the use of fluids to transmit force. When every second counts, these powerful machines can be used to pry open metal vehicles or collapsed concrete structures quickly and safely. The cutters are a compound machine made up of two levers—much like a pair of scissors. Their edges are wedges.

Contrast this equipment with a drill-like machine so small that it can be pushed easily through human arteries. Physicians attach the tiny drill to a thin, flexible rod and push the rod through a patient's artery to an area that is blocked. The tip rotates at extremely high speeds to break down the blockage. The tiny drill is a type of wheel and axle.

Microtechnology and Nanotechnology

Manufacturers make machines of all sizes by shaping and arranging pieces of metal, plastic, and other materials. Scientists have used technology to create very small machines through miniaturization—the making of smaller and smaller, or miniature, parts. Micromachines are too small to be seen by the naked eye but are visible under a microscope. There is a limit, however, to how far micromachines can be shrunk.

To develop even tinier machines, scientists needed a new approach. Scientists have used processes within the human body as their model. For example, inside the body a protein molecule carries materials back and forth within a cell on regular paths that are similar to little train tracks. The natural machines in the human body inspired scientists to develop machines that could be 1000 times smaller than the diameter of a human hair.

READING TIP

Micro-means "one-millionth." For example, a microsecond is one-millionth of a second. *Nano*-means "one-billionth." A nanosecond is one-billionth of a second.

These extremely tiny machines are products of **nanotechnology,** the science and technology of building electronic circuits and devices from single atoms and molecules. Scientists say that they create these machines, called nanomachines, from the bottom up. Instead of shaping already formed material—such as metal and plastic—they guide individual atoms of material to arrange themselves into the shapes needed for the machine parts.

Tools enable scientists to see and manipulate single molecules and atoms. The scanning tunneling microscope can create pictures of individual atoms. To manipulate atoms, special tools are needed to guide them into place. Moving and shaping such small units presents problems, however. Atoms tend to attach themselves to other atoms, and the tools themselves are also made of atoms. Thus it is difficult to pick up an atom and place it in another position using a tool because the atom might attach itself to the tool.

RESOURCE CENTER
CLASSZONE.COM
Learn more about nanomachines.

CHECK YOUR READING Compare the way in which nanomachines are constructed with the way in which larger machines are built.

Nanomachines are still mostly in the experimental stage. Scientists have many plans for nanotechnology, including protecting computers from hackers and performing operations inside the body. For example, a nanomachine could be injected into a person's bloodstream, where it could patrol and search out infections before they become serious problems. When the machine had completed its work, it could switch itself off and be passed out of the body. Similar nanomachines could carry anti-cancer drugs to specific cells in the body.

Nanotechnology could also be used to develop materials that repel water and dirt and make cleaning jobs easy. Nanoscale biosensors could be used to detect harmful substances in the environment. Another possible use for nanotechnology is in military uniforms that can change color— the perfect camouflage.

In the future, nanotechnology may change the way almost everything is designed and constructed. As with any new technology, it will be important to weigh both the potential risks and benefits.

This microgear mechanism could be used in a micromachine that includes microscopic sensors and tiny robots.

Chapter 5: **Machines** 167

A Robot at Work

Scientists are using a robot to unlock the secrets of the Great Pyramid in Egypt.

EGYPT

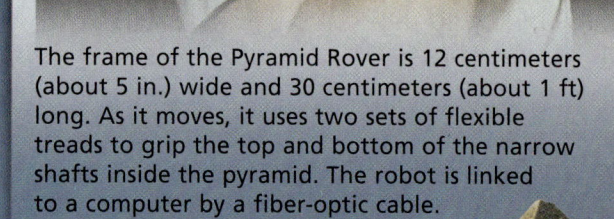

The frame of the Pyramid Rover is 12 centimeters (about 5 in.) wide and 30 centimeters (about 1 ft) long. As it moves, it uses two sets of flexible treads to grip the top and bottom of the narrow shafts inside the pyramid. The robot is linked to a computer by a fiber-optic cable.

second door
miniature camera
Pyramid Rover body
first door
computer

shaft explored by Pyramid Rover
Queen's Chamber
entrance

READING VISUALS What simple machines do you think might be part of the Pyramid Rover?

168 Unit: Motion and Forces

Robots

Humans have always taken risks to do jobs in places that are dangerous or difficult to get to. More and more often, robots can be used to do these jobs. A **robot** is a machine that works automatically or by remote control. When many people hear the word *robot,* they think of a machine that looks or moves like a person. However, most robots do not resemble humans at all. That is because they are built to do things humans cannot do or to go places where it is difficult for humans to go.

The Pyramid Rover, shown on page 168, is an example of a robot developed to go where people cannot. After a camera revealed a door at the end of an eight-inch-square shaft inside the Great Pyramid, the Pyramid Rover was sent through the shaft to explore the area. While researchers remained in the Queen's Chamber in the center of the pyramid, the robot climbed the shaft until it came to a door. Using ultrasound equipment mounted on the robot, researchers determined that the door was three inches thick. The robot drilled a hole in the door for a tiny camera and a light to pass through. The camera then revealed another sealed door!

Many companies use robots to manufacture goods quickly and efficiently. Robots are widely used for jobs such as welding, painting, and assembling products. Robots do some repetitive work better than humans, because robots do not get tired or bored. Also, they do the task in exactly the same way each time. Robots are very important to the automobile and computer industries.

RESOURCE CENTER
CLASSZONE.COM
Find out more about the Pyramid Rover and other robots.

CHECK YOUR READING How are robots better than humans at some jobs?

5.3 Review

KEY CONCEPTS

1. How do you estimate the mechanical advantage of a compound machine?
2. What are some uses of nanotechnology? Can you think of other possible uses for nanomachines?
3. What are three types of jobs that robots can do?

CRITICAL THINKING

4. **Synthesize** What factors might limit how large or how small a machine can be?
5. **Infer** How do you think the size of a gear compared with other gears in the same system affects the speed of its rotation?

CHALLENGE

6. **Apply** Robots might be put to use replacing humans in firefighting and other dangerous jobs. Describe a job that is dangerous. Tell what a robot must be able to do and what dangers it must be able to withstand to accomplish the required tasks.

CHAPTER INVESTIGATION

Design a Machine

DESIGN — YOUR OWN —

OVERVIEW AND PURPOSE
Although simple machines were developed thousands of years ago, they are still used today for a variety of purposes. Tasks such as cutting food with a knife, using a screwdriver to tighten a screw, and raising a flag on a flagpole all require simple machines. Activities such as riding a bicycle and raising a drawbridge make use of compound machines. In this investigation you will use what you have learned about simple and compound machines to
- choose a machine to design
- build your machine, test it, and calculate its mechanical advantage and efficiency

MATERIALS
- 500 g object
- 100 g object
- meter stick
- spring scale
- pulleys with rope
- board
- stick or pole

Procedure

1. Make a data table like the one shown on page 171.

2. From among the three choices listed below, choose which problem you are going to solve.

Carnival Game You work for a company that builds carnival games. Your supervisor has asked you to build a game in which a simple machine moves a 500-gram object from the bottom of the game 1 meter up to the top. This simple machine can be powered only by the person operating the game.

Video Game Contest The marketing department of a video game company is holding a contest. Candidates are asked to submit a working model of a compound machine that will move a 500-gram object a distance of 1 meter. The winning design will be used in a new video game the company hopes to sell. This compound machine must include at least 2 simple machines.

Construction Company You work for a construction company. Your boss has asked you to design a machine for lifting. Your first step is to build a scale model. The model must be a compound machine with a mechanical advantage of 5 that can move a 500-gram object a distance of 1 meter. You also can use a 100-gram object in your design.

170 Unit: Motion and Forces

3 Brainstorm design ideas on paper. Think of different types of machines you might want to build. Choose one machine to build.

4 Build your machine. Use your machine to perform the task of moving a 500-gram object a distance of 1 meter.

If you chose the third problem, test your compound machine to determine if it has a mechanical advantage of 5. If not, modify your machine and retest it.

5 Record all measurements in your data table.

Observe and Analyze *Write It Up*

1. **RECORD OBSERVATIONS** Make a sketch of your machine.

2. **CALCULATE** Use your data to calculate the mechanical advantage and efficiency of your machine. Use the formulas below.

$$\text{Mechanical Advantage} = \frac{\text{Output Force}}{\text{Input Force}}$$

$$\text{Efficiency (\%)} = \frac{\text{Output work}}{\text{Input work}} \cdot 100$$

3. **ANALYZE**

   Carnival Game Add arrows to the drawing of your machine to show the forces involved and the direction of those forces. If your goal was to move the ball from the top of the game to the bottom at a constant speed, how would your machine and diagram have to be changed?

   Video Game Contest Does your machine change the size of the force, the direction of the force, or both? If you used a pulley system (two or more pulleys working together), describe the advantages of using such a system.

   Construction Company Determine whether force or distance is changed by each simple machine in your compound machine. In what ways might you improve your machine to increase its efficiency?

Conclude *Write It Up*

1. **INFER** How might changing the arrangement of the parts in your machine affect the machine's mechanical advantage?

2. **IDENTIFY LIMITS** What was the hardest part about designing and constructing your machine?

3. **APPLY** If you needed to lift a large rock from a hole at a construction site, which type of simple machine would you use and why? Which type of compound machine would be useful?

INVESTIGATE Further

CHALLENGE If you made a simple machine, how would you combine it with another simple machine to increase its mechanical advantage?

If you made a compound machine, redesign it to increase its efficiency or mechanical advantage. What made the difference and why?

Draw a plan for the new machine. Circle the parts that were changed. If you have time, build your new machine.

Design a Machine

Observe and Analyze

Table 1. Machine Data

Output force	Input force	Mechanical Advantage
Output work	Input work	Efficiency

Sketch

Chapter 5: **Machines** 171

Chapter Review

the BIG idea

Machines help people do work by changing the force applied to an object.

CONTENT REVIEW
CLASSZONE.COM

KEY CONCEPTS SUMMARY

5.1 Machines help people do work.

When you use a machine to do work, there is always an exchange, or tradeoff, between the force you use and the distance over which you apply that force. You can use less force over a greater distance or a greater force over a shorter distance to do the same amount of work.

VOCABULARY
machine p. 145
mechanical advantage p. 147
efficiency p. 150

5.2 Six simple machines have many uses.

Simple machines change the size and/or direction of a force.

changes direction   changes size   changes both

input force
output force
fulcrum

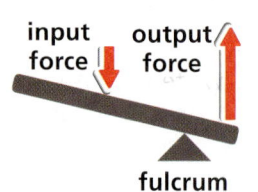

VOCABULARY
simple machine p. 154
lever p. 155
fulcrum p. 155
wheel and axle p. 156
pulley p. 156
inclined plane p. 158
wedge p. 158
screw p. 159

5.3 Modern technology uses compound machines.

- Compound machines are combinations of simple machines.

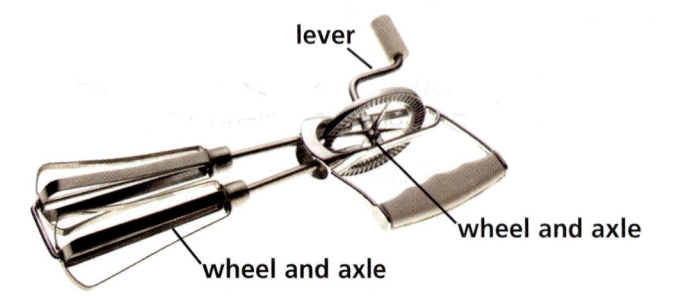

lever
wheel and axle
wheel and axle

- Modern technology creates new uses for machines.
  —Microtechnology and nanotechnology
  —Robots

VOCABULARY
compound machine p. 164
nanotechnology p. 167
robot p. 169

172 Unit: Motion and Forces

Reviewing Vocabulary

Write the name of the simple machine shown in each illustration. Give an example from real life for each one.

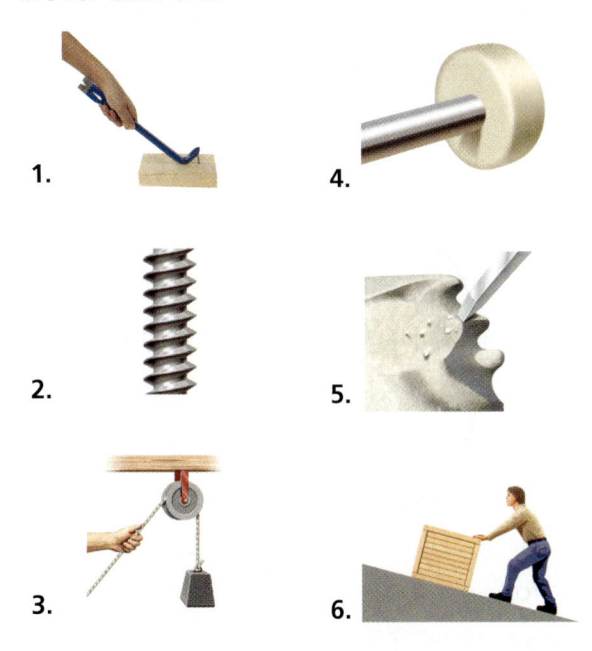

1.
2.
3.
4.
5.
6.

Copy the chart below, and write the definition for each term in your own words. Use the meaning of the term's root to help you.

Term	Root Meaning	Definition
7. machine	having power	
8. nanotechnology	one-billionth	
9. simple machine	basic	
10. efficiency	to accomplish	
11. compound machine	put together	
12. robot	work	
13. fulcrum	to support	

Reviewing Key Concepts

Multiple Choice *Choose the letter of the best answer.*

14. Machines help you work by
    a. decreasing the amount of work that must be done
    b. changing the size and/or direction of a force
    c. decreasing friction
    d. conserving energy

15. To calculate mechanical advantage, you need to know
    a. time and energy
    b. input force and output force
    c. distance and work
    d. size and direction of a force

16. A machine in which the input force is equal to the output force has a mechanical advantage of
    a. 0   c. 1
    b. between 0 and 1   d. more than 1

17. You can increase a machine's efficiency by
    a. increasing force   c. increasing distance
    b. reducing work   d. reducing friction

18. Levers turn around a
    a. fixed point called a fulcrum
    b. solid bar that rotates
    c. wheel attached to an axle
    d. sloping surface called an inclined plane

19. When you bite into an apple, your teeth act as what kind of simple machine?
    a. lever   c. wedge
    b. pulley   d. screw

Short Answer *Answer each of the following questions in a sentence or two.*

20. Describe the simple machines that make up scissors.

21. How do you calculate the mechanical advantage of a compound machine?

22. How did scientists use processes inside the human body as a model for making nanomachines?

Chapter 5: **Machines** 173

Thinking Critically

23. SYNTHESIZE How is a screw related to an inclined plane?

24. INFER Which simple machine would you use to raise a very heavy load to the top of a building? Why?

25. APPLY If you reached the top of a hill by using a path that wound around the hill, would you do more work than someone who climbed a shorter path? Why or why not? Who would use more force?

26. APPLY You are using a board to pry a large rock out of the ground when the board suddenly breaks apart in the middle. You pick up half of the board and use it to continue prying up the rock. The fulcrum stays in the same position. How has the mechanical advantage of the board changed? How does it change your work?

27. SYNTHESIZE What is the difference between a single fixed pulley and a single movable pulley? Draw a diagram to illustrate the difference.

Use the information in the diagram below to answer the next three questions.

4 m
1.5 m

28. SYNTHESIZE What is the mechanical advantage of the ramp? By how many times does the ramp multiply the man's input force?

29. SYNTHESIZE If the ramp's length were longer, what effect would this have on its mechanical advantage? Would this require the man to exert more or less input force?

30. INFER If the ramp's length stayed the same but the height was raised, how would this change the input force required?

Using Math Skills in Science

Complete the following calculations.

31. You swing a hockey stick with a force of 10 N. The stick applies 5 N of force on the puck. What is the mechanical advantage of the hockey stick?

32. Your input work on a manual lawn mower is 125,000 J. The output work is 90,000 J. What is the efficiency of the lawn mower?

33. If a car engine has a 20 percent efficiency, what percentage of the input work is lost?

34. A steering wheel has a radius of 21 cm. The steering column on which it turns has a radius of 3 cm. What is the mechanical advantage of this wheel and axle?

35. Two gears with the same diameter form a gear system. Each gear has 24 teeth. What is the mechanical advantage of this gear system?

the BIG idea

36. DRAW CONCLUSIONS Look back at the photograph on pages 142–143. Name the simple machines you see in the photograph. How do you think they work together to move balls through the sculpture? How has your understanding changed as to the way in which machines help people work?

37. SYNTHESIZE Think of a compound machine you have used recently. Explain which simple machines it includes and how they helped you do work.

38. PREDICT How do you think nanotechnology will be useful in the future? Give several examples.

UNIT PROJECTS

Evaluate all of the data, results, and information from your project folder. Prepare to present your project to the class. Be ready to answer questions posed by your classmates about your results.

174 Unit: Motion and Forces

Standardized Test Practice

For practice on your state test, go to...
TEST PRACTICE
CLASSZONE.COM

Analyzing Graphics

The Archimedean screw is a mechanical device first used more than 2000 years ago. It consists of a screw inside a cylinder. One end of the device is placed in water. As the screw is turned with a handle, its threads carry water upward. The Archimedean screw is still used in some parts of the world to pump water for irrigating fields. It can also be used to move grain in mills.

Study the illustration of an Archimedean screw. Then answer the questions that follow.

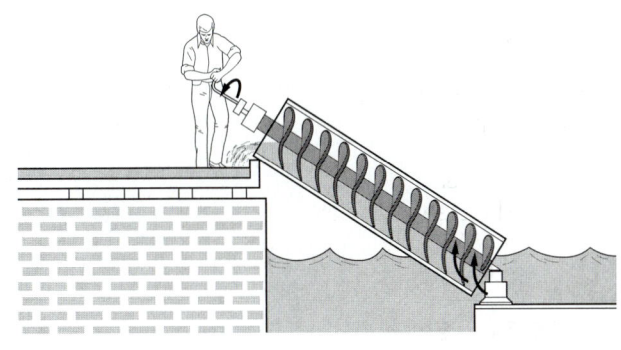

1. Which type of simple machine moves water in the cylinder?
   a. block and tackle
   b. pulley
   c. screw
   d. wedge

2. Which type of simple machine is the handle?
   a. wheel and axle
   b. inclined plane
   c. pulley
   d. wedge

3. What is the energy source for the Archimedean screw?
   a. the water pressure inside the screw
   b. the person who is turning the handle
   c. falling water that is turning the screw
   d. electrical energy

4. How is the Archimedean screw helping the person in the illustration do work?
   a. by decreasing the input force needed to lift the water
   b. by decreasing the work needed to lift the water
   c. by decreasing the distance over which the input force is applied
   d. by keeping the water from overflowing its banks

5. If the threads on the Archimedean screw are closer together, the input force must be applied over a greater distance. This means that the person using it must turn the handle
   a. with more force
   b. fewer times but faster
   c. in the opposite direction
   d. more times with less effort

Extended Response

Answer the two questions below in detail.

6. A playground seesaw is an example of a lever. The fulcrum is located at the center of the board. People seated at either end take turns applying the force needed to move the other person. If one person weighs more than the other, how can they operate the seesaw? Consider several possibilities in your answer.

7. Picture two gears of different sizes turning together. Suppose you can apply a force to turn the larger gear or the smaller gear, and it will turn the other. Discuss what difference it would make whether you turned the larger or smaller gear. Describe the input work you would do on the gear you are turning and the output work that gear would do on the other gear.

Chapter 5: **Machines** 175 **C**

UNIT D

Waves, Sound, and Light

transfer of energy

EM wave

MECHANICAL WAVE

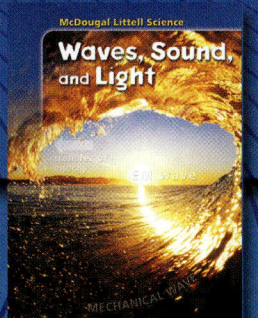

Waves, Sound, and Light
Contents Overview

Unit Features
FRONTIERS IN SCIENCE Sound Medicine — 2
TIMELINES IN SCIENCE The Story of Light — 106

1 Waves — 6
the BIG idea
Waves transfer energy and interact in predictable ways.

2 Sound — 34
the BIG idea
Sound waves transfer energy through vibrations.

3 Electromagnetic Waves — 70
the BIG idea
Electromagnetic waves transfer energy through radiation.

4 Light and Optics — 110
the BIG idea
Optical tools depend on the wave behavior of light.

FRONTIERS in Science

SOUND Medicine

How will sound waves be used in the future of medicine?

SCIENTIFIC AMERICAN FRONTIERS

View the video segment "Each Sound Is a Present" to learn how advances in medicine are restoring people's hearing.

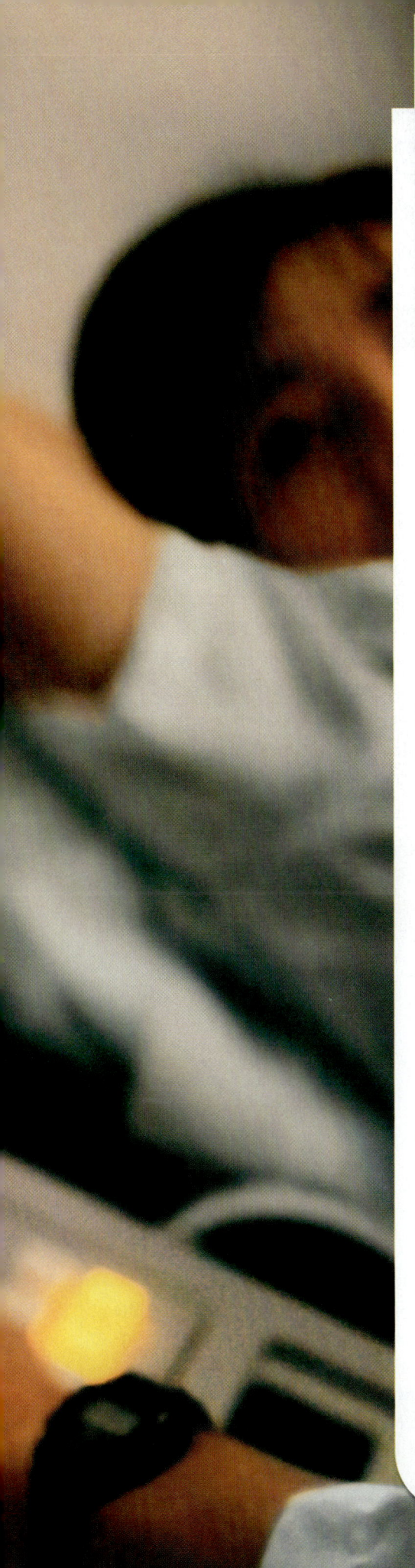

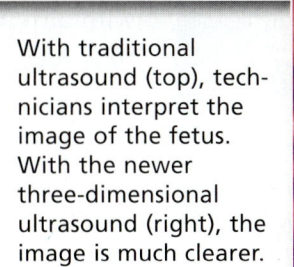

With traditional ultrasound (top), technicians interpret the image of the fetus. With the newer three-dimensional ultrasound (right), the image is much clearer.

Seeing Inside the Body

Have you ever wondered what the inside of your body looks like? Doctors have tried for many years to find ways of seeing what goes on inside a person's body that makes that person sick. Around 100 years ago, scientists found that a kind of wave called x-rays could be used to make images of the bones inside a person. This common method of seeing inside a body, is used mainly to show bones and teeth. However, repeated exposure to x-rays can be damaging to body cells. In the 1960s doctors started using a different kind of wave called ultrasound to make images of the organs inside the body.

Waves are now used in many medical applications. For example, cochlear implants use radio waves to help people hear. Ultrasound now has many new medical applications, from breaking up kidney stones to monitoring the flow of blood in the body.

Sound and Ultrasound

Sound is a type of wave, a vibration in the air. Humans can hear a wide range of different sounds, from very low pitches to very high. Sounds that are higher in pitch than humans can hear are referred to as ultrasound. They are no different from sounds we can hear, except they vibrate much faster than human ears can detect. Many animals can detect ultrasound; for example, dog whistles are in the ultrasound range.

Frontiers in Science 3 D

Imagining and Echolocation

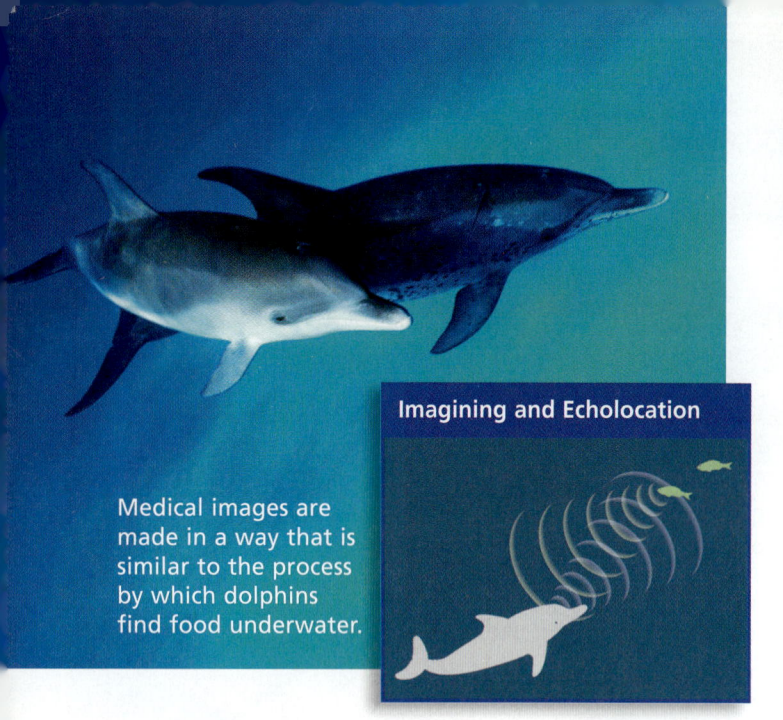

Medical images are made in a way that is similar to the process by which dolphins find food underwater.

The technology of ultrasound in medicine is based upon a process similar to that used by bats and dolphins to find food, a process called echolocation. The animal emits an ultrasound click or chirp and then listens for an echo. The echo indicates that an object has reflected the sound back to the animal. Over time, these animals have evolved the ability to judge the distance of the object by noting the time required for the sound to travel to the object and return. Echolocation enables bats to capture flying insects at night and dolphins to catch fish in the ocean depths, where light doesn't penetrate.

Similarly, in ultrasound imaging, a machine sends a beam of ultrasound into a person's body and detects any echoes. The waves reflect whenever they strike a boundary between two objects with different densities. A computer measures the time required for the wave to travel to the boundary and reflect back; this information is used to determine the location and shape of the organ. The computer can then generate a live image of the organ inside the body.

Ultrasound imaging has been used most often to monitor the development of a fetus inside its mother and to observe the valves of the heart. Blood flow can be color coded with faster flow in one color and slower flow in another color. The colors make it easier to see the location of blockages affecting the rate of flow in the blood vessels. This helps doctors detect blockages and diagnose heart problems.

SCIENTIFIC AMERICAN FRONTIERS

View the "Each Sound Is a Present" segment of your *Scientific American Frontiers* video to learn how a cochlear implant restores hearing to a young girl.

IN THIS SCENE FROM THE VIDEO
A young girl's cochlear implant is turned on for the first time.

HEARING IS A GIFT A recent development in technology is about to give seven-year-old Kelley Flynn something she has always wanted —better hearing. Kelley has been almost completely deaf since she was two years old, and now she is losing the little hearing she does have. The development is a device called a cochlear implant. Cochlear implants work inside the ear, stimulating the brain when a sound is detected.

Normally, sound travels as vibrations from the outer ear, through the middle ear to the inner ear, where thousands of tiny cells—called hair cells— register the quality of the sound and send a signal to the brain. In a cochlear implant, tiny electrical sensors, or electrodes, mimic the hair cells by registering the sound and sending a signal to the brain. The signals get to the electrodes through a system including a computer, microphone, and radio transmitter and receiver. Using this system, people with little or no hearing are able to sense sounds.

D 4 Unit: Waves, Sound, and Light

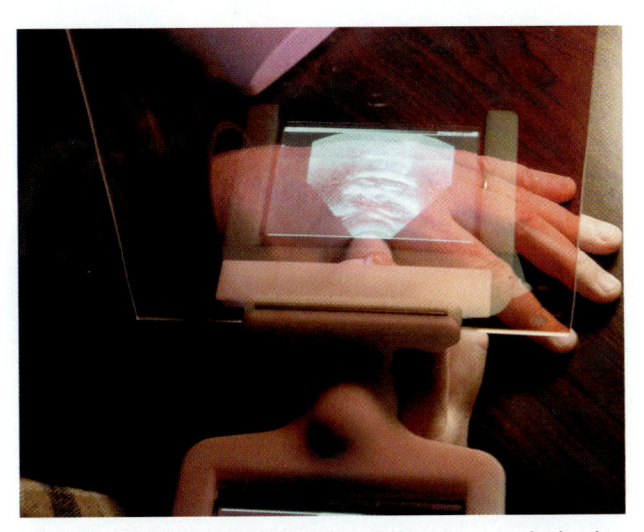

Recent advances in ultrasound technology include the development of portable devices that display images of the body, such as this hand-held device.

Advances in Ultrasound

Waves, including ultrasound, transfer energy. Physical therapists often use this fact when applying ultrasound to sore joints, heating the muscles and ligaments so they can move more freely. If the ultrasound waves are given stronger intensity and sharper focus, they can transfer enough energy to break up kidney stones in the body. The use of focused sound waves is now being tested for its ability to treat other problems, such as foot injuries.

Other recent advances in medical ultrasound include the development of devices that produce clearer images and use equipment that is smaller in size. In the late 1990's portable ultrasound devices were developed that allow the technology to be brought to the patient.

UNANSWERED Questions

As scientists learn more about the use of sound and other types of waves, new questions will arise.

- Will new methods of imaging the body change the way diseases are diagnosed?
- How closely do sounds heard using a cochlear implant resemble sounds heard by the ear?

UNIT PROJECTS

As you study this unit, work alone or with a group on one of these projects.

Magazine Article

Write a magazine article about the medical uses of ultrasound.

- Collect information about medical ultrasound and take notes about applications that interest you.
- If possible, conduct an interview with a medical practitioner who uses ultrasound.
- Read over all your notes and decide what information to include in your article.

Make a Music Video

Make a music video for a song of your choice, and explain how the video uses sound waves and light waves.

- Plan the sound portion of the video, including how the music will be played and amplified.
- For the lighting, use colored cellophane or gels to mix different colors of light. Explain your choices.
- Rehearse the video. Record the video and present it to the class.

Design a Demonstration

Design a hands-on demonstration of echolocation.

- Research the use of echolocation by animals.
- Design a demonstration of echolocation using a tennis ball and an obstacle.
- Present your demonstration to the class.

CAREER CENTER
CLASSZONE.COM

Learn more about careers in audiology.

CHAPTER 1: Waves

the BIG idea

Waves transfer energy and interact in predictable ways.

Key Concepts

SECTION 1.1 Waves transfer energy.
Learn about forces and energy in wave motion.

SECTION 1.2 Waves have measurable properties.
Learn how the amplitude, wavelength, and frequency of a wave are measured.

SECTION 1.3 Waves behave in predictable ways.
Learn about reflection, refraction, diffraction, and interference.

Internet Preview

CLASSZONE.COM

Chapter 1 online resources: Content Review, Simulation, Visualization, two Resource Centers, Math Tutorial, Test Practice

What is moving these surfers?

EXPLORE the BIG idea

How Can Energy Be Passed Along?

Stand several videos up in a line. Knock over the first video, and notice the motion of the other videos.

Observe and Think Write down your observations. How far did each video move? What traveled from the beginning to the end of the line? Where did the energy to move the last video come from?

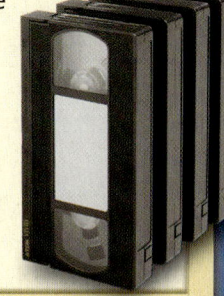

How Can You Change a Wave?

Fill a large bowl half-full of water. Dip a pencil into the water and pull it out quickly. Observe the wave that forms. Now try tapping the bowl with the eraser end of your pencil. What will happen if you use more energy to make the waves? Less energy?

Observe and Think What happened to the size of the waves? The speed? Why do you think that is so?

Internet Activity: Waves

Go to **ClassZone.com** to simulate the effect that different degrees of force have on a wave.

Observe and Think What do you think would happen to the wave if you increased the number of times the flapper moved? What other ways could you affect the wave in the pool?

NSTA scilinks.org **SCLINKS**
Seismic Waves Code: MDL027

Chapter 1: **Waves** 7 D

CHAPTER 1

Getting Ready to Learn

CONCEPT REVIEW

- Forces change the motion of objects in predictable ways.
- Energy can be transferred from one place to another.

VOCABULARY REVIEW

See Glossary for definitions.

force
kinetic energy
potential energy

CONTENT REVIEW
CLASSZONE.COM
Review concepts and vocabulary.

TAKING NOTES

COMBINATION NOTES

To take notes about a new concept, write an explanation of the concept in a table. Then make a sketch of the concept and label it so you can study it later.

VOCABULARY STRATEGY

Write each new vocabulary term in the center of a **four square** diagram. Write notes in the squares around each term. Include a definition, some characteristics, and some examples of the term. If possible, write some things that are not examples of the term.

See the Note-Taking Handbook on pages R45–R51.

SCIENCE NOTEBOOK

Concept	Explanation	Sketch
Forces and waves	Forces move a medium up and down or back and forth. A wave moves forward.	direction of force / direction of wave

Definition	Characteristics
A disturbance that transfers energy from one place to another	Matter moves in place. Energy travels entire distance.

WAVE

Examples	Nonexamples
Water wave	Ball rolling
Sound wave	Water rushing downstream

Unit: Waves, Sound, and Light

KEY CONCEPT
Waves transfer energy.

1.1

◁ BEFORE, you learned
- Forces can change an object's motion
- Energy can be kinetic or potential

▷ NOW, you will learn
- How forces cause waves
- How waves transfer energy
- How waves are classified

VOCABULARY
wave p. 9
medium p. 11
mechanical wave p. 11
transverse wave p. 13
longitudinal wave p. 14

EXPLORE Waves
How will the rope move?

PROCEDURE

1. Tie a ribbon in the middle of a rope. Then tie one end of the rope to a chair.
2. Holding the loose end of the rope in your hand, stand far enough away from the chair that the rope is fairly straight.
3. Flick the rope by moving your hand up and down quickly. Observe what happens.

MATERIALS
- ribbon
- rope
- chair

WHAT DO YOU THINK?
- How did the rope move? How did the ribbon move?
- What do you think starts a wave, and what keeps it going?

A wave is a disturbance.

You experience the effects of waves every day. Every sound you hear depends on sound waves. Every sight you see depends on light waves. A tiny wave can travel across the water in a glass, and a huge wave can travel across the ocean. Sound waves, light waves, and water waves seem very different from one another. So what, exactly, is a wave?

A **wave** is a disturbance that transfers energy from one place to another. Waves can transfer energy over distance without moving matter the entire distance. For example, an ocean wave can travel many kilometers without the water itself moving many kilometers. The water moves up and down—a motion known as a disturbance. It is the disturbance that travels in a wave, transferring energy.

READING TIP
To *disturb* means to agitate or unsettle.

CHECK YOUR READING How does an ocean wave transfer energy across the ocean?

Chapter 1: **Waves** 9 **D**

Forces and Waves

You know that a force is required to change the motion of an object. Forces can also start a disturbance, sending a wave through a material. The following examples describe how forces cause waves.

READING TIP
As you read each example, think of how it is similar to and different from the other examples.

Example 1 Rope Wave Think of a rope that is tied to a doorknob. You apply one force to the rope by flicking it upward and an opposite force when you snap it back down. This sends a wave through the rope. Both forces—the one that moves the rope up and the one that moves the rope down—are required to start a wave.

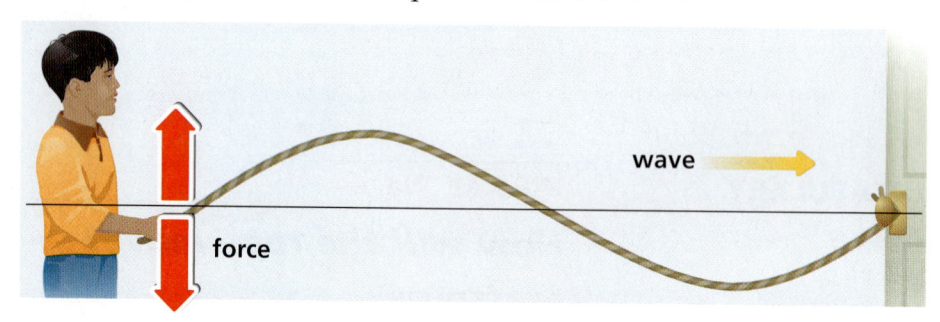

Example 2 Water Wave Forces are also required to start a wave in water. Think of a calm pool of water. What happens if you apply a force to the water by dipping your finger into it? The water rushes back after you remove your finger. The force of your finger and the force of the water rushing back send waves across the pool.

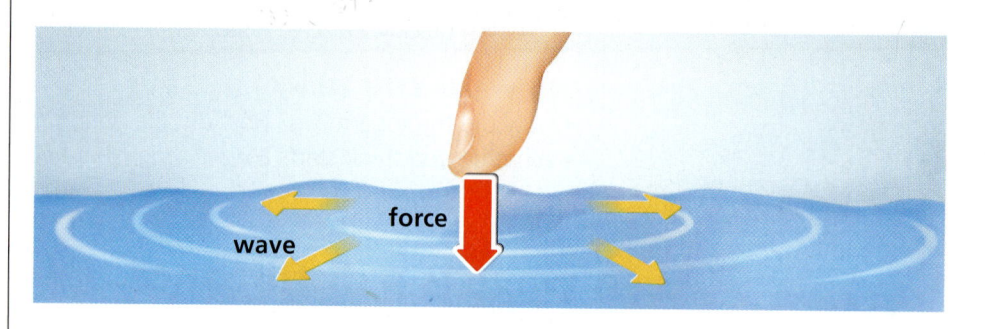

Example 3 Earthquake Wave An earthquake is a sudden release of energy that has built up in rock as a result of the surrounding rock pushing and pulling on it. When these two forces cause the rock to suddenly break away and move, the energy is transferred as a wave through the ground.

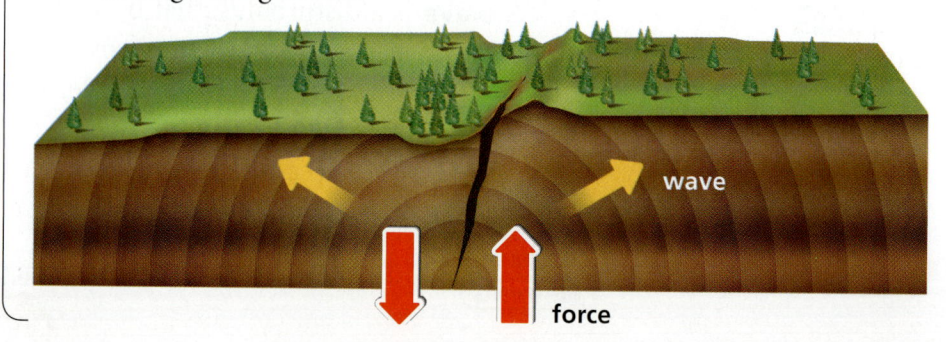

10 Unit: Waves, Sound, and Light

Materials and Waves

A rope tied to a doorknob, water, and the ground all have something in common. They are all materials through which waves move. A **medium** is any substance that a wave moves through. Water is the medium for an ocean wave; the ground is the medium for an earthquake wave; the rope is the medium for the rope wave. In the next chapter, you will learn that sound waves can move through many mediums, including air.

Waves that transfer energy through matter are known as **mechanical waves.** All of the waves you have read about so far, even sound waves, are mechanical waves. Water, the ground, a rope, and the air are all made up of matter. Later, you will learn about waves that can transfer energy through empty space. Light is an example of a wave that transfers energy through empty space.

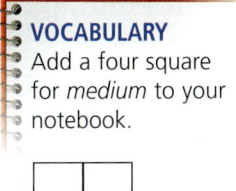

VOCABULARY
Add a four square for *medium* to your notebook.

CHECK YOUR READING How are all mechanical waves similar?

Energy and Waves

The waves caused by an earthquake are good examples of energy transfer. The disturbed ground shakes from side to side and up and down as the waves move through it. Such waves can travel kilometers away from their source. The ground does not travel kilometers away from where it began; it is the energy that travels in a wave. In the case of an earthquake, it is kinetic energy, or the energy of motion, that is transferred.

This photograph was taken after a 1995 earthquake in Japan. A seismic wave transferred enough energy through the ground to bend the railroad tracks, leaving them in the shape of a wave.

A Wave Model

When these fans do "the wave" in a stadium, they are modeling the way a disturbance travels through a medium.

Each person only moves up and down.

The wave can move all the way around the stadium.

READING VISUALS In which direction do people move when doing the stadium wave? In which direction does the wave move?

Look at the illustration of people modeling a wave in a stadium. In this model, the crowd of people represents a wave medium. The people moving up and down represent the disturbance. The transfer of the disturbance around the stadium represents a wave. Each person only moves up and down, while the disturbance can move all the way around the stadium.

Ocean waves are another good example of energy transfer. Ocean waves travel to the shore, one after another. Instead of piling up all the ocean water on the shore, however, the waves transfer energy. A big ocean wave transfers enough kinetic energy to knock someone down.

CHECK YOUR READING How does the stadium wave differ from a real ocean wave?

Waves can be classified by how they move.

As you have seen, one way to classify waves is according to the medium through which they travel. Another way to classify waves is by how they move. You have read that some waves transfer an up-and-down or a side-to-side motion. Other waves transfer a forward-and-backward motion.

Transverse Waves

Think again about snapping the rope with your hand. The action of your hand causes a vertical, or up-and-down, disturbance in the rope. However, the wave it sets off is horizontal, or forward. This type of wave is known as a transverse wave. In a **transverse wave,** the direction in which the wave travels is perpendicular, or at right angles, to the direction of the disturbance. *Transverse* means "across" or "crosswise." The wave itself moves crosswise as compared with the vertical motion of the medium.

READING TiP
Perpendicular means at a 90° angle.

Transverse Wave

direction of disturbance   direction of wave

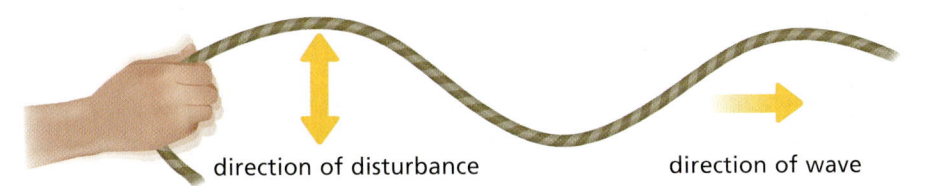

Water waves are also transverse. The up-and-down motion of the water is the disturbance. The wave travels in a direction that is perpendicular to the direction of the disturbance. The medium is the water, and energy is transferred outward in all directions from the source.

CHECK YOUR READING What is a transverse wave? Find two examples in the paragraphs above.

INVESTIGATE Wave Types

How do waves compare?

SKILL FOCUS
Comparing

PROCEDURE

1. Place the spring toy on the floor on its side. Stretch out the spring. To start a disturbance in the spring, take one end and move it from side to side. Observe the movement in the spring. Remember that a transverse wave travels at right angles to the disturbance.

2. Put the spring toy on the floor in the same position as before. Think about how you could make a different kind of disturbance to produce a different kind of wave. (**Hint:** Suppose you push the spring in the direction of the wave you expect to make.) Observe the movement in the spring.

MATERIALS
spring toy

TIME
10 minutes

WHAT DO YOU THINK?
- Compare the waves you made. How are they alike? How are they different?
- What kind of wave did you produce by moving the spring from side to side?

CHALLENGE Can you think of a third way to make a wave travel through a spring?

Chapter 1: **Waves** 13 **D**

Longitudinal Waves

READING TIP
The word *long* can help you remember longitudinal waves. The disturbance moves along the length of the spring.

Another type of wave is a longitudinal wave. In a **longitudinal wave** (LAHN-jih-TOOD-n-uhl), the wave travels in the same direction as the disturbance. A longitudinal wave can be started in a spring by moving it forward and backward. The coils of the spring move forward and bunch up and then move backward and spread out. This forward and backward motion is the disturbance. Longitudinal waves are sometimes called compressional waves because the bunched-up area is known as a compression. How is a longitudinal wave similar to a transverse wave? How is it different?

Longitudinal Wave

direction of disturbance

Time 1

compression

Time 2

direction of wave

Time 3

RESOURCE CENTER
CLASSZONE.COM
Learn more about waves.

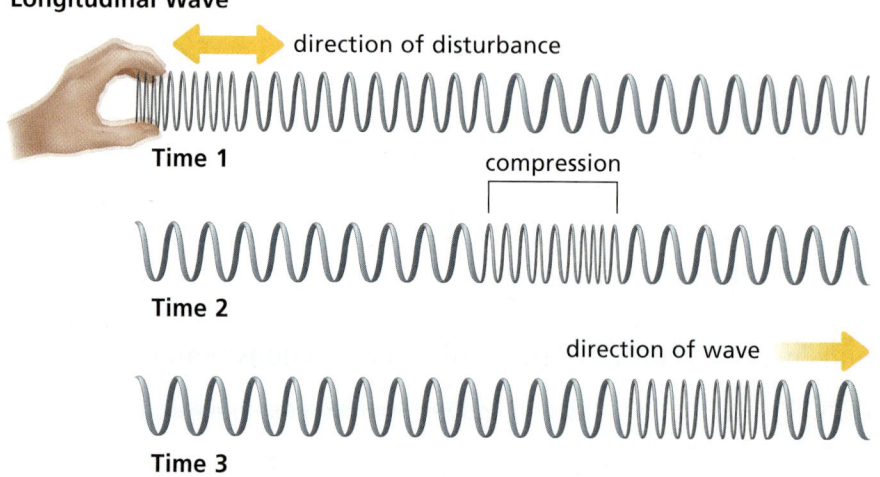

Sound waves are examples of longitudinal waves. Imagine a bell ringing. The clapper inside the bell strikes the side and makes it vibrate, or move back and forth rapidly. The vibrating bell pushes and pulls on nearby air molecules, causing them to move forward and backward. These air molecules, in turn, set more air molecules into motion. A sound wave pushes forward. In sound waves, the vibrations of the air molecules are in the same direction as the movement of the wave.

1.1 Review

KEY CONCEPTS

1. Describe how forces start waves.
2. Explain how a wave can travel through a medium and yet the medium stays in place. Use the term *energy* in your answer.
3. Describe two ways in which waves travel, and give an example of each.

CRITICAL THINKING

4. **Analyze** Does water moving through a hose qualify as a wave? Explain why or why not.
5. **Classify** Suppose you drop a cookie crumb in your milk. At once, you see ripples spreading across the surface of the milk. What type of waves are these? What is the disturbance?

CHALLENGE

6. **Predict** Suppose you had a rope long enough to extend several blocks down the street. If you were to start a wave in the rope, do you think it would continue all the way to the other end of the street? Explain why or why not.

D 14 Unit: Waves, Sound, and Light

MATH in SCIENCE

SKILL: MEAN, MEDIAN, AND MODE

MATH TUTORIAL
CLASSZONE.COM

Click on Math Tutorial for more help with finding the mean, median, and mode.

Wave Heights

Tracking stations throughout the world's oceans measure and record the height of water waves that pass beneath them. The data recorded by the stations can be summarized as average wave heights over one hour or one day.

How would you summarize the typical wave heights over one week? There are a few different ways in which data can be summarized. Three common ways are finding the mean, median, and mode.

Example

Wave height data for one week are shown below.

| 1.2 m | 1.5 m | 1.4 m | 1.7 m | 2.0 m | 1.4 m | 1.3 m |

(1) Mean To find the mean of the data, divide the sum of the values by the number of values.

$$\text{Mean} = \frac{1.2 + 1.5 + 1.4 + 1.7 + 2.0 + 1.4 + 1.3}{7} = 1.5 \text{ m}$$

ANSWER The mean wave height is 1.5 m.

(2) Median To find the median of the data, write the values in order from least to greatest. The value in the middle is the median.

1.2 m   1.3 m   1.4 m   (1.4 m)   1.5 m   1.7 m   2.0 m

ANSWER The median wave height is 1.4 m.

(3) Mode The mode is the number that occurs most often.

ANSWER The mode for the data is also 1.4 m.

Use the data to answer the following questions.

The data below show wave heights taken from a station off the coast of Florida over two weeks.

| Wk 1 | 1.2 m | 1.1 m | 1.1 m | 1.5 m | 4.7 m | 1.2 m | 1.1 m |
| Wk 2 | 0.7 m | 0.8 m | 0.9 m | 0.8 m | 1.0 m | 1.1 m | 0.8 m |

1. Find the mean, median, and mode of the data for Week 1.

2. Find the mean, median, and mode of the data for Week 2.

CHALLENGE A storm carrying strong winds caused high waves on the fifth day of the data shown above for Week 1. Which of the following was most affected by the high value—the mean, median, or mode?

Before going out on the water, boaters can check reports on wave conditions in their area.

Chapter 1: **Waves** 15 D

1.2 Waves have measurable properties.

BEFORE, you learned
- Forces cause waves
- Waves transfer energy
- Waves can be transverse or longitudinal

NOW, you will learn
- How amplitude, wavelength, and frequency are measured
- How to find a wave's speed

VOCABULARY

crest p. 17
trough p. 17
amplitude p. 17
wavelength p. 17
frequency p. 17

THINK ABOUT

How can a wave be measured?

This enormous wave moves the water high above sea level as it comes crashing through. How could you find out how high a water wave actually goes? How could you find out how fast it is traveling? In what other ways do you think a wave can be measured? Read on to find out.

COMBINATION NOTES
Use combination notes in your notebook to describe how waves can be measured.

Waves have amplitude, wavelength, and frequency.

The tallest ocean wave ever recorded was measured from the deck of a ship during a storm. An officer on the ship saw a wave reach a height that was level with a point high on the ship, more than 30 meters (100 ft)! Height is a property of all waves—from ripples in a glass of water to gigantic waves at surfing beaches—and it can be measured.

The speed of a water wave is another property that can be measured—by finding the time it takes for one wave peak to travel a set distance. Other properties of a wave that can be measured include the time between waves and the length of a single wave. Scientists use the terms *amplitude*, *wavelength*, and *frequency* to refer to some commonly measured properties of waves.

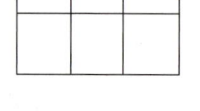

CHECK YOUR READING What are three properties of a wave that can be measured?

16 Unit: Waves, Sound, and Light

Measuring Wave Properties

A **crest** is the highest point, or peak, of a wave. A **trough** is the lowest point, or valley, of a wave. Suppose you are riding on a boat in rough water. When the boat points upward and rises, it is climbing to the crest of a wave. When it points downward and sinks, the boat is falling to the trough of the wave.

① **Amplitude** for a transverse wave is the distance between a line through the middle of a wave and a crest or trough. In an ocean wave, amplitude measures how far the wave rises above, or dips below, its original position, or rest position.

Amplitude is an important measurement, because it indicates how much energy a wave is carrying. The bigger the amplitude, the more energy the wave has. Find amplitude on the diagram below.

② The distance from one wave crest to the very next crest is called the **wavelength.** Wavelength can also be measured from trough to trough. Find wavelength on the diagram below.

③ The number of waves passing a fixed point in a certain amount of time is called the **frequency.** The word *frequent* means "often," so frequency measures how often a wave occurs. Frequency is often measured by counting the number of crests or troughs that pass by a given point in one second. Find frequency on the diagram below.

VOCABULARY
Remember to add a four square to your notebook for each new term on this page.

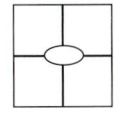

CHECK YOUR READING How is amplitude related to energy?

Wave Properties

Distance above or below rest position

water level at rest

② **Wavelength** is the distance from one crest or trough to the next.

crest

① **Amplitude** is the distance a medium moves above or below its position at rest.

trough

fixed point

③ **Frequency** is the number of waves passing a fixed point in a certain amount of time.

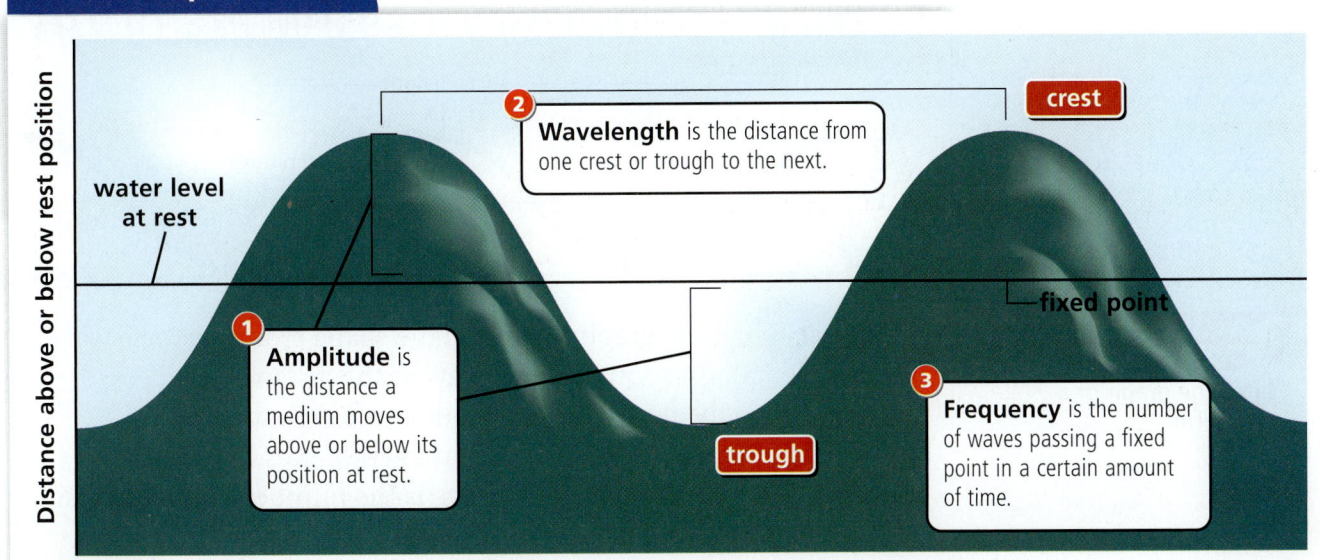

READING VISUALS How many wavelengths are shown in this diagram? How do you know?

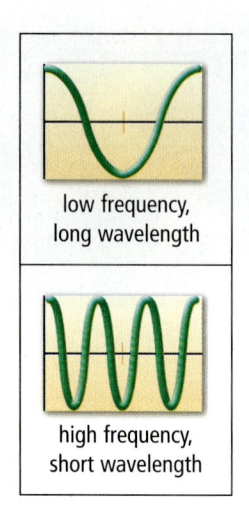

low frequency, long wavelength

high frequency, short wavelength

How Frequency and Wavelength Are Related

The frequency and wavelength of a wave are related. When frequency increases more wave crests pass a fixed point each second. That means the wavelength shortens. So, as frequency increases, wavelength decreases. The opposite is also true—as frequency decreases, wavelength increases.

Suppose you are making waves in a rope. If you make one wave crest every second, the frequency is one wave per second (1/s). Now suppose you want to increase the frequency to more than one wave per second. You flick the rope up and down faster. The wave crests are now closer together. In other words, their wavelengths have decreased.

REMINDER
Frequency is the number of waves that pass a given point in a certain amount of time.

Graphing Wave Properties

The graph of a transverse wave looks much like a wave itself. The illustration on page 19 shows the graph of an ocean wave. The measurements for the graph come from a float, or buoy (BOO-ee), that keeps track of how high or low the water goes. The graph shows the position of the buoy at three different points in time. These points are numbered. Since the graph shows what happens over time, you can see the frequency of the waves.

Unlike transverse waves, longitudinal waves look different from their graphs. The graph of a longitudinal wave in a spring is drawn below. The coils of the spring get closer and then farther apart as the wave moves through them.

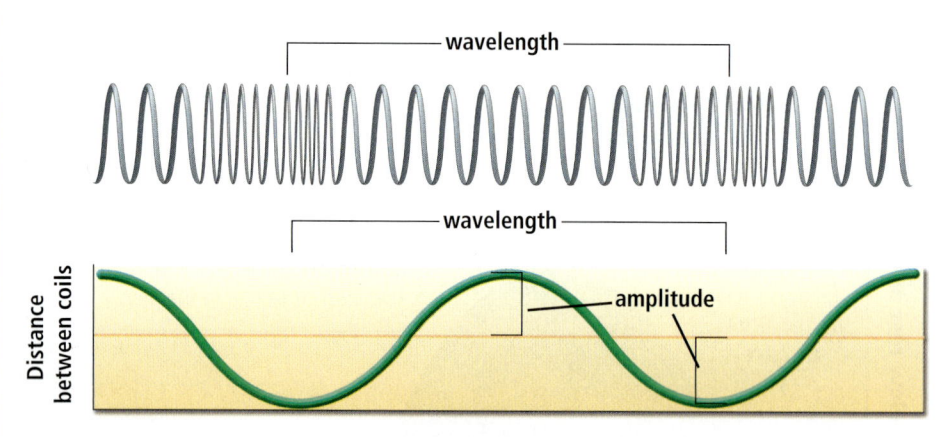

VISUALIZATION
CLASSZONE.COM
Watch the graph of a wave form.

The shape of the graph resembles the shape of a transverse wave. The wavelength on a longitudinal wave is the distance from one compression to the next. The amplitude of a longitudinal wave measures how compressed the medium gets. Just as in a transverse wave, frequency in a longitudinal wave is the number of waves passing a fixed point in a certain amount of time.

CHECK YOUR READING How are longitudinal waves measured?

D 18 Unit: Waves, Sound, and Light

Graphing a Wave

The graph of a transverse wave looks like a wave itself. The graph shows what happens over time.

The buoy moves up and down as the waves pass.

1 **Time: 0 s** The buoy is below the rest position.

2 **Time: 1 s** The buoy is equal with the rest position.

3 **Time: 2 s** The buoy is above the rest position.

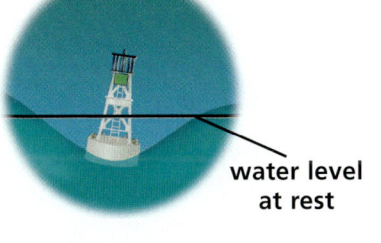

water level at rest

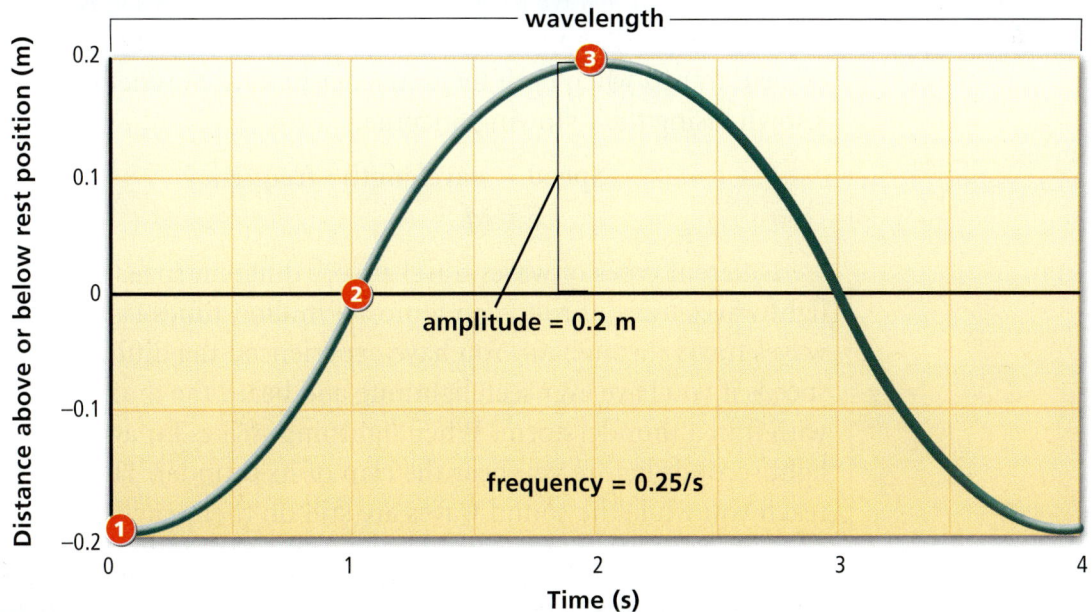

wavelength

amplitude = 0.2 m

frequency = 0.25/s

Distance above or below rest position (m)

Time (s)

READING VISUALS How many seconds does it take for one wave to pass? How much of the wave passes in one second?

Chapter 1: **Waves** 19

INVESTIGATE Frequency

How can you change frequency?

PROCEDURE

1. Tie 3 washers to a string. Tape the string to the side of your desk so that it can swing freely. The swinging washers can model wave action.
2. Pull the washers slightly to the side and let go. Find the frequency by counting the number of complete swings that occur in 1 minute.
3. Make a table in your notebook to record both the length of the string and the frequency.
4. Shorten the string by moving and retaping it. Repeat for 5 different lengths. Keep the distance you pull the washers the same each time.

WHAT DO YOU THINK?
- How did changing the length of the string affect the frequency?
- How does this model represent a wave? How does it differ from a wave?

CHALLENGE How could you vary the amplitude of this model? Predict how changing the amplitude would affect the frequency.

SKILL FOCUS
Collecting data

MATERIALS
- 3 metal washers
- piece of string
- tape
- stopwatch
- meter stick

TIME
30 minutes

Wave speed can be measured.

In addition to amplitude, wavelength, and frequency, a wave's speed can be measured. One way to find the speed of a wave is to time how long it takes for a wave to get from one point to another. Another way to find the speed of a wave is to calculate it. The speed of any wave can be determined when both the frequency and the wavelength are known, using the following formula:

$$\text{Speed} = \text{wavelength} \cdot \text{frequency}$$
$$S = \lambda f$$

> **REMINDER**
> The symbol λ represents wavelength.

Different types of waves travel at very different speeds. For example, light waves travel through air almost a million times faster than sound waves travel through air. You have experienced the difference in wave speeds if you have ever seen lightning and heard the thunder that comes with it in a thunderstorm. When lightning strikes far away, you see the light seconds before you hear the clap of its thunder. The light waves reach you while the sound waves are still on their way.

How fast do you think water waves can travel? Water waves travel at different speeds. You can calculate the speed using wavelength and frequency.

Suppose you wish to calculate the speed of an ocean wave with a wavelength of 16 meters and a frequency of 0.31 wave per second. When working through the problem in the example below, it is helpful to think of the frequency as

$$f = 0.31 \text{ (wave)/s}$$

even though the units for frequency are just 1/second. You can think of wavelengths as "meters per wave," or

$$\lambda = 16 \text{ m/(wave)}$$

RESOURCE CENTER
CLASSZONE.COM
Find out more about wave speed.

Calculating Wave Speed

▶ **Sample Problem**

An ocean wave has a wavelength of 16 meters and a frequency of 0.31 wave per second. What is the speed of the wave?

What do you know? wavelength = 16 m, frequency = 0.31 $\frac{\text{(wave)}}{\text{s}}$

What do you want to find out? Speed

Write the formula: $S = \lambda f$

Substitute into the formula: $S = 16 \frac{m}{\text{(wave)}} \cdot 0.31 \frac{\text{(wave)}}{s}$

Calculate and simplify: $16 \frac{m}{\cancel{\text{(wave)}}} \cdot 0.31 \frac{\cancel{\text{(wave)}}}{s} = 5 \frac{m}{s}$

Check that your units agree: Unit is m/s. Unit for speed is m/s. Units agree.

Answer: $S = 5$ m/s

▶ **Practice the Math**

1. In a stormy sea, 2 waves pass a fixed point every second, and the waves are 10 m apart. What is the speed of the waves?
2. In a ripple tank, the wavelength is 0.1 cm, and 10 waves occur each second. What is the speed of the waves (in cm/s)?

1.2 Review

KEY CONCEPTS

1. Make a simple diagram of a wave, labeling amplitude, frequency, and wavelength. For frequency, you will need to indicate a span of time, such as one second.
2. What two measurements of a wave do you need to calculate its speed?

CRITICAL THINKING

3. **Observe** Suppose you are watching water waves pass under the end of a pier. How can you figure out their frequency?
4. **Calculate** A wave has a speed of 3 m/s and a frequency of 6 (waves)/s. What is its wavelength?

CHALLENGE

5. **Apply** Imagine you are on a boat in the middle of the sea. You are in charge of recording the properties of passing ocean waves into the ship's logbook. What types of information could you record? How would this information be useful? Explain your answer.

CHAPTER INVESTIGATION

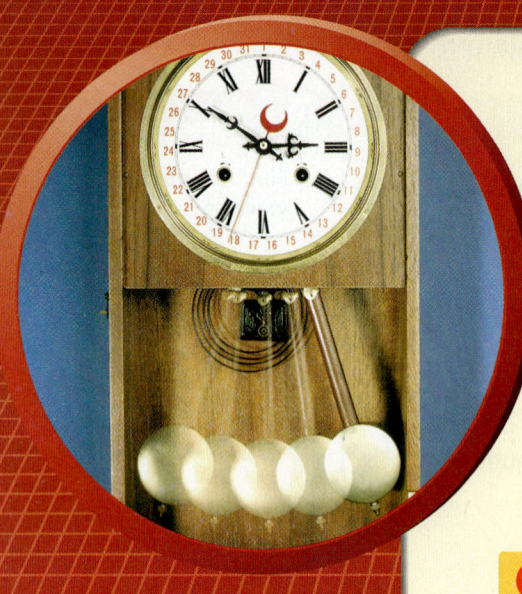

Wavelength

OVERVIEW AND PURPOSE The pendulum on a grandfather clock keeps time as it swings back and forth at a steady rate. The swings of a pendulum can be recorded as a wave with measurable properties. How do the properties of the pendulum affect the properties of the waves it produces? In this investigation you will use your understanding of wave properties to
- construct a pendulum and measure the waves it produces, and
- determine how the length of the pendulum affects the wavelength of the waves.

MATERIALS
- 1/2 sheet white paper
- tape
- scissors
- string
- meter stick
- fine sand
- graduated cylinder
- 2 sheets colored construction paper

▶ Problem

How does changing the length of a pendulum affect the wavelength?

▶ Hypothesize

Write a hypothesis in "If . . . , then . . . , because . . ." form to answer the problem question.

▶ Procedure

1. Make a data table like the one shown on the sample notebook page.

2. Make a cone with the half-sheet of paper by rolling it and taping it as shown. The hole in the bottom of the cone should be no larger than a pea.

3. Cut a hole in each side of the cone and tie the ends of the string to the cone to make a pendulum.

4. Hold the string on the pendulum so that the distance from your fingers holding the string to the bottom of the cone is 20 cm.

5. Cover the bottom of the cone with your fingertip. While you hold the cone, have your partner pour about 40 mL of sand into the cone.

D 22 Unit: Waves, Sound, and Light

6. Hold the pendulum about 5 cm above the construction paper as shown. Pull the pendulum from the bottom to one side of the construction paper. Be careful not to move the pendulum at the top, or to pull the pendulum over the edge of the paper.

7. Let the pendulum go while your partner gently pulls the paper forward so that the sand makes waves on the paper. Be sure to pull the paper at a steady rate. Let the remaining sand pile up on the end of the paper.

8. Measure the wavelength from crest to crest or trough to trough. Record the wavelength in your table.

9. Run two more trials, repeating steps 5–8. Be sure to pull the paper at the same speed for each trial. Calculate the average wavelength over all three trials, and record it in your table.

10. Repeat steps 4–8, changing the length of the pendulum to 30 cm and then to 40 cm.

Observe and Analyze

1. **RECORD OBSERVATIONS** Draw the setup of your procedure. Be sure your data table is complete.

2. **IDENTIFY VARIABLES AND CONSTANTS** Identify the variables and constants that affected the wave produced by the moving pendulum. List them in your notebook.

3. **ANALYZE** What patterns can you find in your data? For example, do the numbers increase or decrease as you read down each column?

Conclude

1. **INFER** Answer your problem question.

2. **INTERPRET** Compare your results with your hypothesis. Do your data support your hypothesis?

3. **IDENTIFY LIMITS** What possible limitations or sources of error could have affected your results?

4. **APPLY** Suppose you were examining the tracing made by a seismograph, a machine that records an earthquake wave. What would happen if you increased the speed at which the paper ran through the machine? What do you think the amplitude of the tracing represents?

INVESTIGATE Further

CHALLENGE Revise your experiment to change one variable other than the length of the pendulum. Run a new trial, changing the variable you choose but keeping everything else constant. How did changing the variable affect the wave produced?

Wavelength

Problem How does changing the length of a pendulum affect the wavelength?

Hypothesize

Observe and Analyze

Table 1. Wavelengths Produced by Pendulums

Pendulum Length (cm)	Trial 1	Trial 2	Trial 3	Average Wavelength (cm)
20				
30				
40				

Conclude

Chapter 1: **Waves** 23

KEY CONCEPT
1.3 Waves behave in predictable ways.

BEFORE, you learned
- Waves transfer energy
- Amplitude, wavelength, and frequency can be measured

NOW, you will learn
- How waves change as they encounter a barrier
- What happens when waves enter a new medium
- How waves interact with other waves

VOCABULARY

reflection p. 25
refraction p. 25
diffraction p. 26
interference p. 27

EXPLORE Reflection

How do ripples reflect?

PROCEDURE

1. Put a few drops of food coloring into the pan of water.
2. Dip the pencil in the water at one end of the pan to make ripples in the water.
3. Observe the ripples as they reflect off the side of the pan. Draw a sketch of the waves reflecting.

MATERIALS
- wide pan, half full of water
- food coloring
- pencil

WHAT DO YOU THINK?
- What happens when the waves reach the side of the pan?
- Why do you think the waves behave as they do?

COMBINATION NOTES
Use combination notes in your notebook to describe how waves interact with materials.

Waves interact with materials.

You have read that mechanical waves travel through a medium like air, water, or the ground. In this section, you will read how the motion of waves changes when they encounter a new medium. For instance, when an ocean wave rolls into a ship or a sound wave strikes a solid wall, the wave encounters a new medium.

When waves interact with materials in these ways, they behave predictably. All waves, from water waves to sound waves and even light waves, show the behaviors that you will learn about next. Scientists call these behaviors reflection, refraction, and diffraction.

CHECK YOUR READING What behaviors do all waves have in common?

24 Unit: Waves, Sound, and Light

Reflection

What happens to water waves at the end of a swimming pool? The waves cannot travel through the wall of the pool. Instead, the waves bounce off the pool wall. The bouncing back of a wave after it strikes a barrier is called **reflection.**

Remember what you have learned about forces. A water wave, like all waves, transfers energy. When the water wave meets the wall of the pool, it pushes against the wall. The wall applies an equal and opposite force on the water, sending the wave back in another direction. In the illustration on the right, you can see water waves reflecting off a barrier.

Sound and light waves reflect too. Sound waves reflecting off the walls of a canyon produce an echo. Light waves reflecting off smooth metal behind glass let you see an image of yourself in the mirror. The light waves bounce off the metal just as the water waves bounce off the pool wall. You will learn more about how sound and light waves reflect in the next chapters.

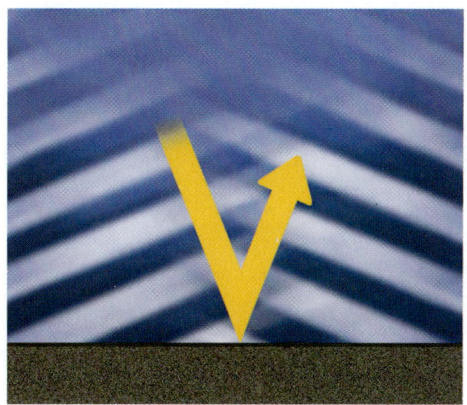

Reflection Water waves move in predictable ways. Here waves are shown from above as they reflect off a barrier.

CHECK YOUR READING How would you define *reflection* in your own words?

Refraction

Sometimes, a wave does not bounce back when it encounters a new medium. Instead, the wave continues moving forward. When a wave enters a new medium at an angle, it bends, or refracts. **Refraction** is the bending of a wave as it enters a new medium at an angle other than 90 degrees. Refraction occurs because waves travel at different speeds in different mediums. Because the wave enters the new medium at an angle, one side of the wave enters the new medium before the rest of the wave. When one side of a wave speeds up or slows down before the other side, it causes the wave to bend.

You have probably noticed the refraction of light waves in water. Objects half-in and half-out of water look broken or split. Look at the photograph of the straw in the glass. What your eyes suggest—that the straw is split—is not real, is it? You are seeing the refraction of light waves caused by the change of medium from air to water. You will learn more about the refraction of light waves in Chapter 4.

Refraction Light waves refract as they pass from air to water, making this straw look split.

Chapter 1: **Waves** 25

Diffraction

You have seen how waves reflect off a barrier. For example, water waves bounce off the side of a pool. But what if the side of the pool had an opening in it? Sometimes, waves interact with a partial barrier, such as a wall with an opening. As the waves pass through the opening, they spread out, or diffract. **Diffraction** is the spreading out of waves through an opening or around the edge of an obstacle. Diffraction occurs with all types of waves.

Diffraction through an opening

Look at the photograph on the right. It shows water waves diffracting as they pass through a small gap in a barrier. In the real world, ocean waves diffract through openings in cliffs or rock formations.

Similarly, sound waves diffract as they pass through an open doorway. Turn on a TV or stereo, and walk into another room. Listen to the sound with the door closed and then open. Then try moving around the room. You can hear the sound wherever you stand because the waves spread out, or diffract, through the doorway and reflect from the walls.

INVESTIGATE Diffraction

How can you make a wave diffract?

SKILL FOCUS
Predicting

PROCEDURE

1. Put a few drops of food coloring into the container of water.
2. Experiment with quick motions of the ruler to set off waves in the container.
3. Place the block on its side in the center of the container. Set the bag of sand on the block to hold it down. Predict how the waves will interact with the barrier you have added.
4. Make another set of waves, and observe how they interact with the barrier.

MATERIALS
- wide pan of water
- food coloring
- ruler
- wooden block
- bag of sand

TIME
20 minutes

WHAT DO YOU THINK?
- How did you make the waves diffract?
- How did your observations compare with your prediction?

CHALLENGE How could you change the experiment to make the effect of the diffraction more obvious?

D 26 Unit: Waves, Sound, and Light

Diffraction also occurs as waves pass the edge of an obstacle. The photograph at the right shows water waves diffracting as they pass an obstacle. Ocean waves also diffract in this way as they pass large rocks in the water.

Light waves diffract around the edge of an obstacle too. The edges of a shadow appear fuzzy because of diffraction. The light waves spread out, or diffract, around the object that is making the shadow.

Diffraction around an obstacle

CHECK YOUR READING Describe what happens when waves diffract.

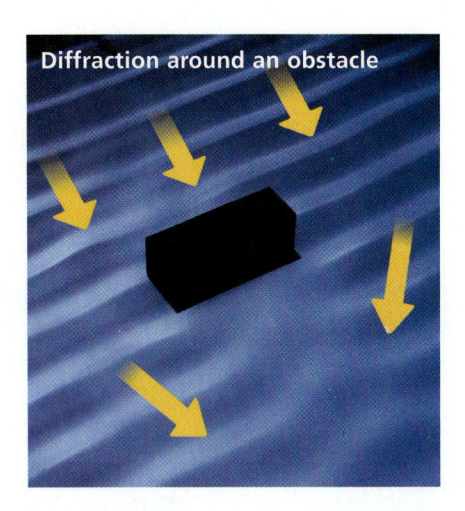

Waves interact with other waves.

Just as waves sometimes interact with new mediums, they can also interact with other waves. Two waves can add energy to or take away energy from each other in the place where they meet. **Interference** is the meeting and combining of waves.

Waves Adding Together

Suppose two identical waves coming from opposite directions come together at one point. The waves' crests and troughs are aligned briefly, which means they join up exactly. When the two waves merge into a temporary, larger wave, their amplitudes are added together. When the waves separate again, they have their original amplitudes and continue in their original directions.

The adding of two waves is called constructive interference. It builds up, or constructs, a larger wave out of two smaller ones. Look at the diagram at the right to see what happens in constructive interference.

Because the waves in the example joined together perfectly, the amplitude of the new wave equals the combined amplitudes of the 2 original waves. For example, if the crest of a water wave with an amplitude of 1 meter (3.3 ft) met up with the crest of another wave with an amplitude of 1 meter (3.3 ft), there would be a 2 meter (6.6 ft) crest in the spot where they met.

Constructive Interference

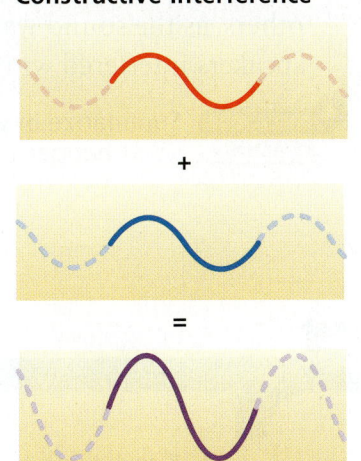

When two wave crests with amplitudes of 1 m each combine, a wave with an amplitude of 2 m is formed.

Chapter 1: **Waves** 27 **D**

Waves Canceling Each Other Out

Imagine again that two very similar waves come together. This time, however, the crest of one wave joins briefly with the trough of the other. The energy of one wave is subtracted from the energy of the other. The new wave is therefore smaller than the original wave. This process is called destructive interference. Look at the diagram below to see what happens in destructive interference.

For example, if a 2-meter (6.6 ft) crest met up with a 1-meter (3.3 ft) trough, there would be a temporary crest of only 1 meter (3.3 ft) where they met. If the amplitudes of the two original waves are identical, the two waves can cancel each other out completely!

When identical waves meet, they are usually not aligned. Instead, the crests meet up with crests in some places and troughs in others. As a result, the waves add in some places and subtract in others. The photograph on the left shows a pattern resulting from waves both adding and subtracting on the surface of a pond. Have you ever listened to music on stereo speakers that were placed at a distance from each other? The music may have sounded loud in some places and soft in others, as the sound waves from the two speakers interfered with each other.

Wave interference produces this pattern on a pond as two sets of waves interact.

Destructive Interference

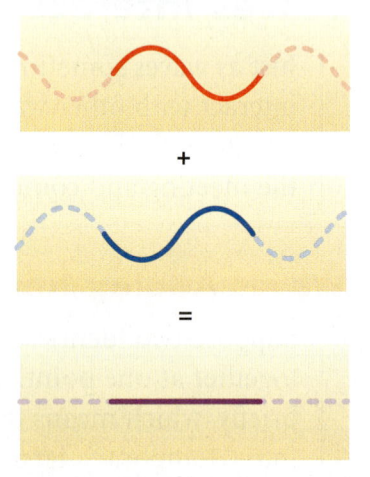

When a 1 m wave crest meets a 1 m wave trough, the amplitudes cancel each other out. A wave with an amplitude of 0 m is formed where they meet.

CHECK YOUR READING Summarize in your own words what happens during interference.

1.3 Review

KEY CONCEPTS
1. Explain what happens when waves encounter a medium that they cannot travel through.
2. Describe a situation in which waves would diffract.
3. Describe two ways that waves are affected by interference.

CRITICAL THINKING
4. **Synthesize** Explain how reflection and diffraction can happen at the same time in a wave.
5. **Compare** How is interference similar to net force? How do you think the two concepts might be related? **Hint:** Think about how forces are involved in wave motion.

CHALLENGE
6. **Predict** Imagine that you make gelatin in a long, shallow pan. Then you scoop the gelatin out of one end of the pan and add icy cold water to the exact same depth as the gelatin. Now suppose you set off waves at the water end. What do you think will happen when the waves meet the gelatin?

CONNECTING SCIENCES

PHYSICAL SCIENCE AND EARTH SCIENCE

Tsunamis!

Tsunamis (tsu-NAH-mees) are among the most powerful waves on Earth. They can travel fast enough to cross the Pacific Ocean in less than a day! When they reach shore, these powerful waves strike with enough force to destroy whole communities.

What Causes Tsunamis?

Tsunamis are caused by an undersea volcanic eruption, an earthquake, or even a landslide. This deep-sea event sends out a series of waves. Surprisingly, if you were out at sea, you would not even notice these powerful waves. The reason has to do with the physics of waves—their velocity, wavelength, and amplitude.

A tsunami generated by a powerful earthquake struck Japan in 1983. The photograph above shows a scene before the tsunami struck. What changes do you see in the picture below showing the scene after the tsunami struck?

Diagram of a Wave

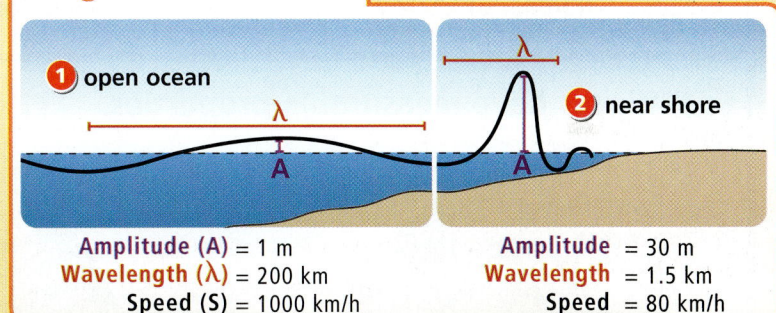

① open ocean
Amplitude (A) = 1 m
Wavelength (λ) = 200 km
Speed (S) = 1000 km/h

② near shore
Amplitude = 30 m
Wavelength = 1.5 km
Speed = 80 km/h

The Changing Wave

① On the open ocean, the waves of a tsunami are barely visible. The amplitude of the waves is less than a few meters, but the energy of the waves extends to the sea floor. The tsunami's wavelength is extremely long—up to 200 kilometers (120 mi). These long, low waves can travel as fast as a jet—almost 1000 kilometers per hour (600 mi/h).

② Near shore, the waves slow down as they approach shallow water. As their velocity drops, their wavelengths get shorter, but their amplitude gets bigger. All the energy that was spread out over a long wave in deep water is now compressed into a huge wave that can reach a height of more than 30 meters (100 ft).

Individual tsunami waves may arrive more than an hour apart. Many people have lost their lives returning home between waves, making the fatal mistake of thinking the danger was over.

EXPLORE

1. **VISUALIZE** Look at ② on the diagram. How tall is 30 meters (100 ft)? Find a 100-foot building or structure near you to visualize the shore height of a tsunami.

2. **CHALLENGE** Use library or Internet resources to prepare a chart on the causes and effects of a major tsunami event.

Chapter 1: Waves

Chapter Review

the BIG idea

Waves transfer energy and interact in predictable ways.

CONTENT REVIEW
CLASSZONE.COM

KEY CONCEPTS SUMMARY

1.1 Waves transfer energy.

Transverse Wave
direction of disturbance
direction of wave
transfer of energy

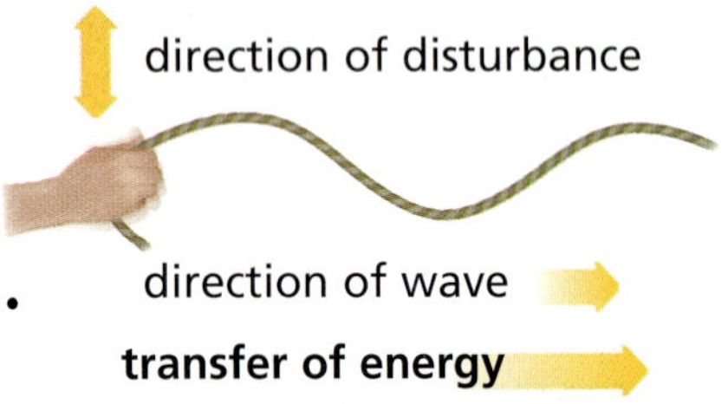

Longitudinal Wave
direction of disturbance
direction of wave
transfer of energy

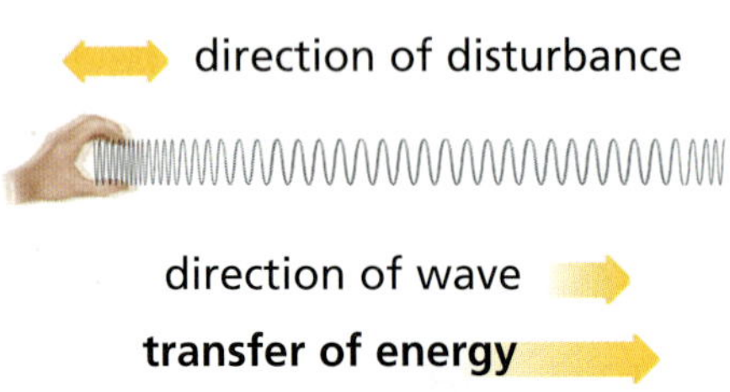

VOCABULARY
wave p. 9
medium p. 11
mechanical wave p. 11
transverse wave p. 13
longitudinal wave p. 14

1.2 Waves have measurable properties.

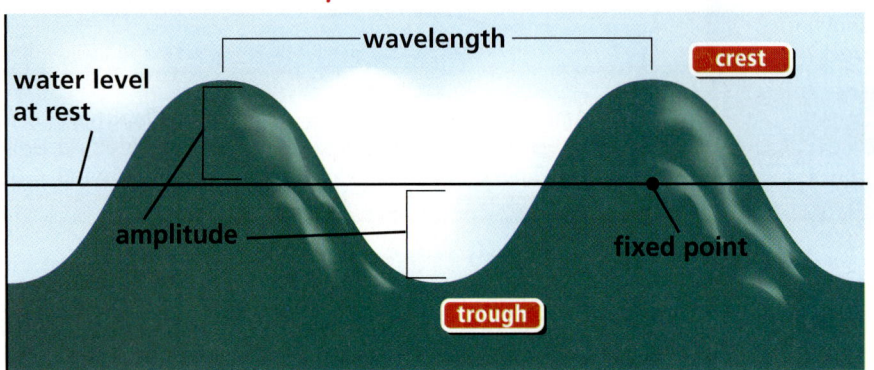

wavelength
crest
water level at rest
amplitude
fixed point
trough

Frequency is the number of waves passing a fixed point in a certain amount of time.

VOCABULARY
crest p. 17
trough p. 17
amplitude p. 17
wavelength p. 17
frequency p. 17

1.3 Waves behave in predictable ways.

Reflection   Refraction    Diffraction

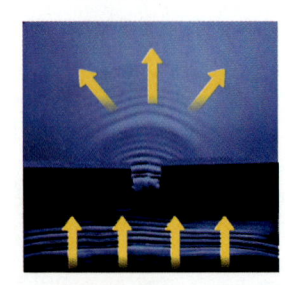

VOCABULARY
reflection p. 25
refraction p. 25
diffraction p. 26
interference p. 27

D 30 Unit: Waves, Sound, and Light

Reviewing Vocabulary

Draw a word triangle for each of the terms below. On the bottom row, write the term and your own definition of it. Above that, write a sentence in which you use the term correctly. At the top, draw a small picture to show what the term looks like. A sample is completed for you.

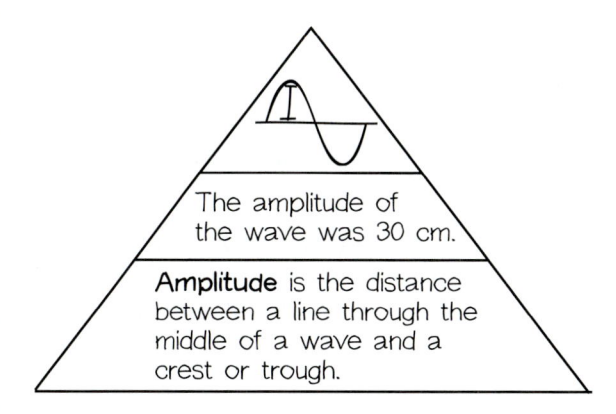

> The amplitude of the wave was 30 cm.
>
> **Amplitude** is the distance between a line through the middle of a wave and a crest or trough.

1. transverse wave
2. diffraction
3. frequency
4. medium
5. crest
6. interference
7. reflection
8. trough
9. refraction
10. wavelength

Reviewing Key Concepts

Multiple Choice *Choose the letter of the best answer.*

11. The direction in which a transverse wave travels is
    a. the same direction as the disturbance
    b. toward the disturbance
    c. from the disturbance downward
    d. at right angles to the disturbance

12. An example of a longitudinal wave is a
    a. water wave
    b. stadium wave
    c. sound wave
    d. rope wave

13. Which statement best defines a wave medium?
    a. the material through which a wave travels
    b. a point halfway between the crest and trough of a wave
    c. the distance from one wave crest to the next
    d. the speed at which waves travel in water

14. As you increase the amplitude of a wave, you also increase the
    a. frequency   c. speed
    b. wavelength   d. energy

15. To identify the amplitude in a longitudinal wave, you would measure areas of
    a. reflection   c. crests
    b. compression   d. refraction

16. Which statement describes the relationship between frequency and wavelength?
    a. When frequency increases, wavelength increases.
    b. When frequency increases, wavelength decreases.
    c. When frequency increases, wavelength remains constant.
    d. When frequency increases, wavelength varies unpredictably.

17. For wave refraction to take place, a wave must
    a. increase in velocity
    b. enter a new medium
    c. increase in frequency
    d. merge with another wave

18. Which setup in a wave tank would best enable you to demonstrate diffraction?
    a. water only
    b. water and sand
    c. water and food coloring
    d. water and a barrier with a small gap

19. Two waves come together and interact to form a new, smaller wave. This process is called
    a. destructive interference
    b. constructive interference
    c. reflective interference
    d. positive interference

Chapter 1: **Waves** 31

Thinking Critically

Use the diagram below to answer the next two questions.

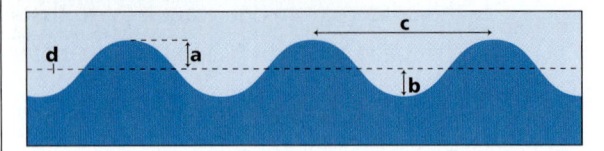

20. What two letters in the diagram measure the same thing? What do they both measure?

21. In the diagram above, what does the letter c measure?

Use the diagram below to answer the next three questions. The diagram shows waves passing a fixed point.

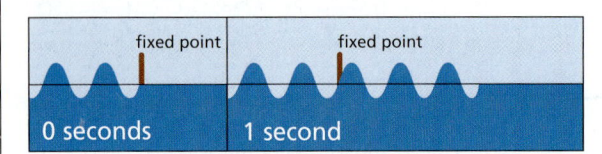

22. At 0 seconds, no waves have passed. How many waves have passed after 1 second?

23. What is being measured in the diagram?

24. How would you write the measurement taken in the diagram?

25. **EVALUATE** Do you think the following is an accurate definition of medium? Explain your answer.

    A **medium** is any solid through which waves travel.

26. **APPLY** Picture a pendulum. The pendulum is swinging back and forth at a steady rate. How could you make it swing higher? How is swinging a pendulum like making a wave?

27. **PREDICT** What might happen to an ocean wave that encounters a gap or hole in a cliff along the shore?

28. **EVALUATE** Do you think *interference* is an appropriate name for the types of wave interaction you read about in Section 1.3? Explain your answer.

Using Math in Science

29. At what speed is the wave below traveling if it has a frequency of 2/s?

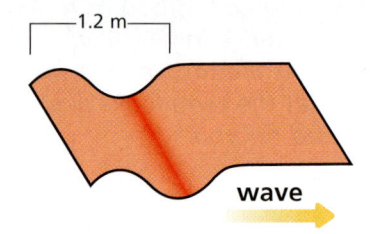

30. An ocean wave has a wavelength of 9 m and a frequency of 0.42/s. What is the wave's speed?

31. Suppose a sound wave has a frequency of 10,000/s. The wave's speed is 340 m/s. Calculate the wavelength of this sound wave.

32. A water wave is traveling at a speed of 2.5 m/s. The wave has a wavelength of 4 m. Calculate the frequency of this water wave.

the BIG idea

33. **INTERPRET** Look back at the photograph at the start of the chapter on pages 6–7. How does this photograph illustrate a transfer of energy?

34. **SYNTHESIZE** Describe three situations in which you can predict the behavior of waves.

35. **SUMMARIZE** Write a paragraph summarizing this chapter. Use the big idea from page 6 as the topic sentence. Then write an example from each of the key concepts listed under the big idea.

UNIT PROJECTS

If you are doing a unit project, make a folder for your project. Include in your folder a list of the resources you will need, the date on which the project is due, and a schedule to track your progress. Begin gathering data.

Standardized Test Practice

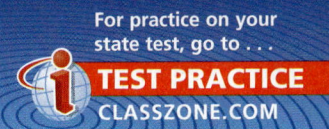

For practice on your state test, go to . . .
TEST PRACTICE
CLASSZONE.COM

Interpreting Diagrams

Study the illustration below and then answer the questions.

The illustration below shows a wave channel, a way of making and studying water waves. The motor moves the rod, which moves the paddle back and forth. The movement of the paddle makes waves, which move down the length of the channel. The material behind the paddle absorbs the waves generated in that direction.

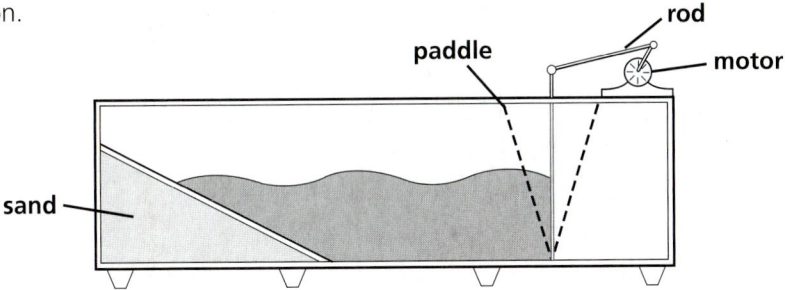

1. An experimenter can adjust the position of the rod on the arm of the motor. Placing it closer to the motor makes shallower waves. Placing it farther from the motor makes deeper waves. What property of waves does this affect?
   a. amplitude
   b. direction
   c. frequency
   d. wavelength

2. By changing motor speeds, an experimenter can make the paddle move faster or slower. What property of waves does this affect?
   a. amplitude
   b. direction
   c. trough depth
   d. wavelength

3. Sand is piled up in the channel at the end of the tank opposite the motor. When waves pass over this sand, their wavelengths shorten. Assuming that the speed of the waves stays the same, their frequency
   a. stays the same
   b. increases
   c. decreases
   d. cannot be predicted

4. Suppose there was no sand at the end of the tank opposite the paddle. In that case, the waves would hit the glass wall. What would they do then?
   a. stop
   b. reflect
   c. refract
   d. diffract

Extended Response

Answer the two questions below in detail.

5. Suppose temperatures in one 10-day period were as follows: 94°, 96°, 95°, 97°, 95°, 98°, 99°, 97°, 99°, and 98°. Make a simple line graph of the data. In what ways is the series of temperatures similar to a wave, and in what ways does it differ?

6. Lydia and Bill each drop a ball of the same size into the same tank of water but at two different spots. Both balls produce waves that spread across the surface of the water. As the two sets of waves cross each other, the water forms high crests in some places. What can you say about both waves? Explain your answer.

Chapter 1: **Waves** 33 **D**

CHAPTER 2 Sound

the BIG idea

Sound waves transfer energy through vibrations.

Key Concepts

**SECTION 2.1
Sound is a wave.**
Learn how sound waves are produced and detected.

**SECTION 2.2
Frequency determines pitch.**
Learn about the relationship between the frequency of a sound wave and its pitch.

**SECTION 2.3
Intensity determines loudness.**
Learn how the energy of a sound wave relates to its loudness.

**SECTION 2.4
Sound has many uses.**
Learn how sound waves are used to detect objects and to make music.

Internet Preview

CLASSZONE.COM

Chapter 2 online resources: Content Review, two Visualizations, three Resource Centers, Math Tutorial, Test Practice

How is this guitar player producing sound?

EXPLORE the BIG idea

What Gives a Sound Its Qualities?

Tap your finger lightly on a table. Then tap it hard. Try scratching the table with your finger. Now, place your head on the table so that your ear is flat against its surface. Tap the table again.

Observe and Think
How did the sounds differ each time? What did you feel?

How Does Size Affect Sound?

Hang three large nails of different sizes from the edge of a table so that they are not touching. Tap each nail with a metal spoon to make it vibrate. Listen to the sounds that are made by tapping each nail.

Observe and Think Which nail produced the highest sound? the lowest? How does the size of a vibrating object affect its sound?

Internet Activity: Sound

Go to **ClassZone.com** to discover how particles move as sound waves move through the air.

Observe and Think
How are the sound waves in the animation similar to the waves you have already learned about?

NSTA scilinks.org
SciLINKS
What Is Sound? Code: MDL028

Chapter 2: Sound 35 D

CHAPTER 2
Getting Ready to Learn

CONCEPT REVIEW

- A wave is a disturbance that transfers energy from one place to another.
- Mechanical waves are waves that travel through matter.

VOCABULARY REVIEW

medium p. 11
longitudinal wave p. 14
amplitude p. 17
wavelength p. 17
frequency p. 17

CONTENT REVIEW
CLASSZONE.COM
Review concepts and vocabulary.

TAKING NOTES

OUTLINE

As you read, copy the headings on your paper in the form of an outline. Then add notes in your own words that summarize what you have read.

VOCABULARY STRATEGY

Place each vocabulary term at the center of a **description wheel** diagram. Write some words on the spokes describing it.

See the Note-Taking Handbook on pages R45–R51.

SCIENCE NOTEBOOK

I. Sound is a type of mechanical wave.
   A. How sound waves are produced
      1.
      2.
      3.
   B. How sound waves are detected
      1.
      2.
      3.

Description wheel for VIBRATION:
- rapid back-and-forth motion
- can produce a sound
- can make with vocal cords
- usually too small to see

2.1 KEY CONCEPT
Sound is a wave.

BEFORE, you learned
- Waves transfer energy
- Waves have wavelength, amplitude, and frequency

NOW, you will learn
- How sound waves are produced and detected
- How sound waves transfer energy
- What affects the speed of sound waves

VOCABULARY
sound p. 37
vibration p. 37
vacuum p. 41

EXPLORE Sound
What is sound?

PROCEDURE

1. Tie the middle of the string to the spoon handle.
2. Wrap the string ends around your left and right index fingers. Put the tips of these fingers gently in your ears and hold them there.
3. Stand over your desk so that the spoon dangles without touching your body or the desk. Then move a little to make the spoon tap the desk lightly. Listen to the sound.

MATERIALS
- piece of string
- large metal spoon

WHAT DO YOU THINK?
- What did you hear when the spoon tapped the desk?
- How did sound travel from the spoon to your ears?

OUTLINE
Start an outline for this heading. Remember to leave room for details.

I. Main idea
  A. Supporting idea
    1. Detail
    2. Detail
  B. Supporting idea

Sound is a type of mechanical wave.

In the last chapter, you read that a mechanical wave travels through a material medium. Such mediums include air, water, and solid materials. Sound is an example of a mechanical wave. **Sound** is a wave that is produced by a vibrating object and travels through matter.

The disturbances that travel in a sound wave are vibrations. A **vibration** is a rapid, back-and-forth motion. Because the medium vibrates back and forth in the same direction as the wave travels, sound is a longitudinal wave. Like all mechanical waves, sound waves transfer energy through a medium.

CHECK YOUR READING What do sound waves have in common with other mechanical waves? Your answer should include the word *energy*.

Chapter 2: Sound 37 D

How Sound Waves Are Produced

READING TIP
When you see the word *push* or *pull,* think of force.

The disturbances in a sound wave are vibrations that are usually too small to see. Vibrations are also required to start sound waves. A vibrating object pushes and pulls on the medium around it and sends out waves in all directions.

You have a sound-making instrument within your own body. It is the set of vocal cords within the voice box, or larynx, in your throat. Put several of your fingers against the front of your throat. Now hum. Do you feel the vibrations of your vocal cords?

Your vocal cords relax when you breathe to allow air to pass in and out of your windpipe. Your vocal cords tense up and draw close together when you are about to speak or sing. The illustration below shows how sound waves are produced by the human vocal cords.

① Your muscles push air up from your lungs and through the narrow opening between the vocal cords.

② The force of the air causes the vocal cords to vibrate.

③ The vibrating vocal cords produce sound waves.

CHECK YOUR READING How do human vocal cords produce sound waves?

How Vocal Cords Produce Sound

Sound waves are produced by vibrations.

enlargement of vocal cords

① Air is pushed up from the lungs.

② The **vocal cords** vibrate in the larynx.

③ Sound waves are produced.

READING VISUALS What starts the vibrations in the vocal cords?

D 38 Unit: Waves, Sound, and Light

How Sound Waves Are Detected

The shape of a human ear helps it collect sound waves. Picture a satellite dish. It collects radio waves from satellites. Your ear works in much the same way. Actually, what we typically call the ear is only the outer section of the ear. The illustration below shows the main parts of the human ear.

❶ Your outer ear collects sound waves and reflects them into a tiny tube called the ear canal. At the end of the ear canal is a thin, skin-like membrane stretched tightly over the opening, called the eardrum. When sound waves strike the eardrum, they make it vibrate.

❷ The middle ear contains three tiny, connected bones called the hammer, anvil, and stirrup. These bones carry vibrations from the eardrum to the inner ear.

❸ One of the main parts of the inner ear, the cochlea (KAWK-lee-uh), contains about 30,000 hair cells. Each of these cells has tiny hairs on its surface. The hairs bend as a result of the vibrations. This movement triggers changes that cause the cell to send electrical signals along nerves to your brain. Only when your brain receives and processes these signals do you actually hear a sound.

READING TIP
As you read each numbered description here, match it to the number on the illustration below.

How the Ear Detects Sound

Sound waves are detected in the human ear, beginning with vibrations of the eardrum.

- The vibrations travel through the **hammer, anvil,** and **stirrup** to the inner ear.
- Cells in the **cochlea** detect the vibrations and send a message to the brain.
- Sound waves cause the **eardrum** to vibrate.

outer ear | middle ear | inner ear

Enlargement of hairs on a single cell in the cochlea (magnified 2185x)

READING VISUALS How do vibrations get from the eardrum to the cochlea?

Chapter 2: **Sound** 39

Sound waves vibrate particles.

You can see the motion of waves in water. You can even ride them with a surfboard. But you cannot see air. How, then, can you picture sound waves moving through air? Sound waves transfer the motion of particles too small to see from one place to another.

For example, think about a drum that has been struck. What happens between the time the drum is struck and the sound is heard?

- The drum skin vibrates rapidly. It pushes out and then in, over and over again. Of course, this happens very, very fast. The vibrating drum skin pushes against nearby particles in the air. The particles in the air become bunched together, or compressed.
- When the drum skin pushes the opposite way, a space opens up between the drum's surface and the particles. The particles rush back in to fill the space.
- The back-and-forth movement, or vibration, of the particles is the disturbance that travels to the listener. Both the bunched up areas, or compressions, and the spaces between the compressions are parts of the wave.

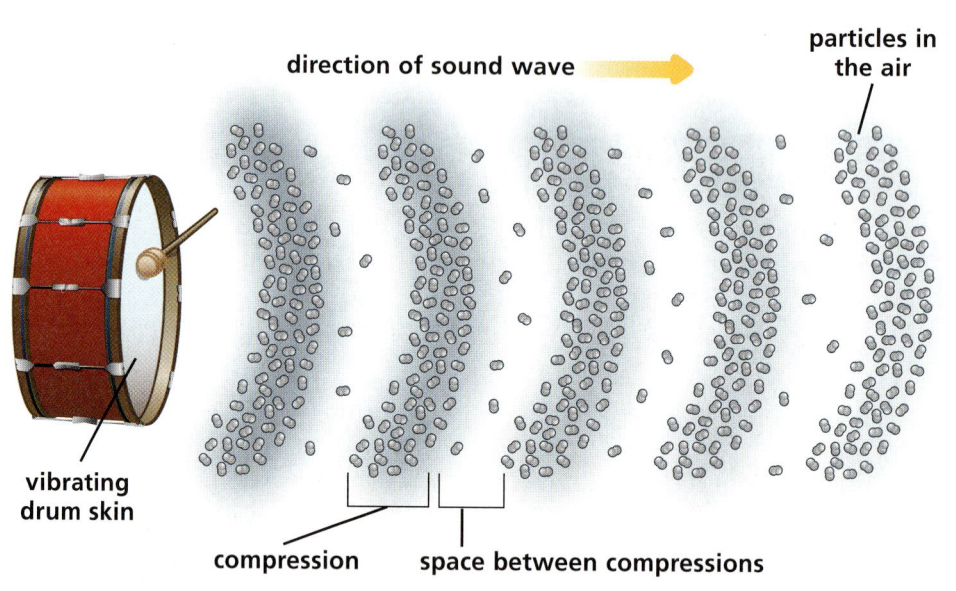

direction of sound wave

particles in the air

vibrating drum skin

compression   space between compressions

Notice that the waves consist of repeating patterns of compressions and spaces between the compressions. The compressions are areas of high air pressure. The spaces between the compressions are areas of low air pressure. The high- and low-pressure air pushes and pulls on the surrounding air, which then pushes and pulls on the air around that. Soon a sound wave has traveled through the air and has transferred kinetic energy from one place to another.

> **REMINDER**
> Kinetic energy is the energy of motion.

> **CHECK YOUR READING**
> Summarize in your own words how sound travels through air.

In the middle 1600s, scientists began to do experiments to learn more about air. They used pumps to force the air out of enclosed spaces to produce a vacuum. A **vacuum** is empty space. It has no particles—or very, very few of them. Robert Boyle, a British scientist, designed an experiment to find out if sound moves through a vacuum.

Boyle put a ticking clock in a sealed jar. He pumped some air out of the jar and still heard the clock ticking. Then he pumped more air out. The ticking grew quieter. Finally, when Boyle had pumped out almost all the air, he could hear no ticking at all. Boyle's experiment demonstrated that sound does not travel through a vacuum.

The photograph at the right shows equipment that is set up to perform an experiment similar to Boyle's. A bell is placed in a sealed jar and powered through the electrical connections at the top. The sound of the loudly ringing bell becomes quieter as air is pumped out through the vacuum plate.

Sound is a mechanical wave. It can move only through a medium that is made up of matter. Sound waves can travel through air, solid materials, and liquids, such as water, because all of these mediums are made up of particles. Sound waves cannot travel through a vacuum.

Sound Experiment
- connections
- sealed jar
- bell
- vacuum plate

INFER As air is pumped out of the jar, the sound of the bell becomes quieter. Why do you think the bell is suspended?

CHECK YOUR READING How did Boyle's experiment show that sound cannot travel through a vacuum?

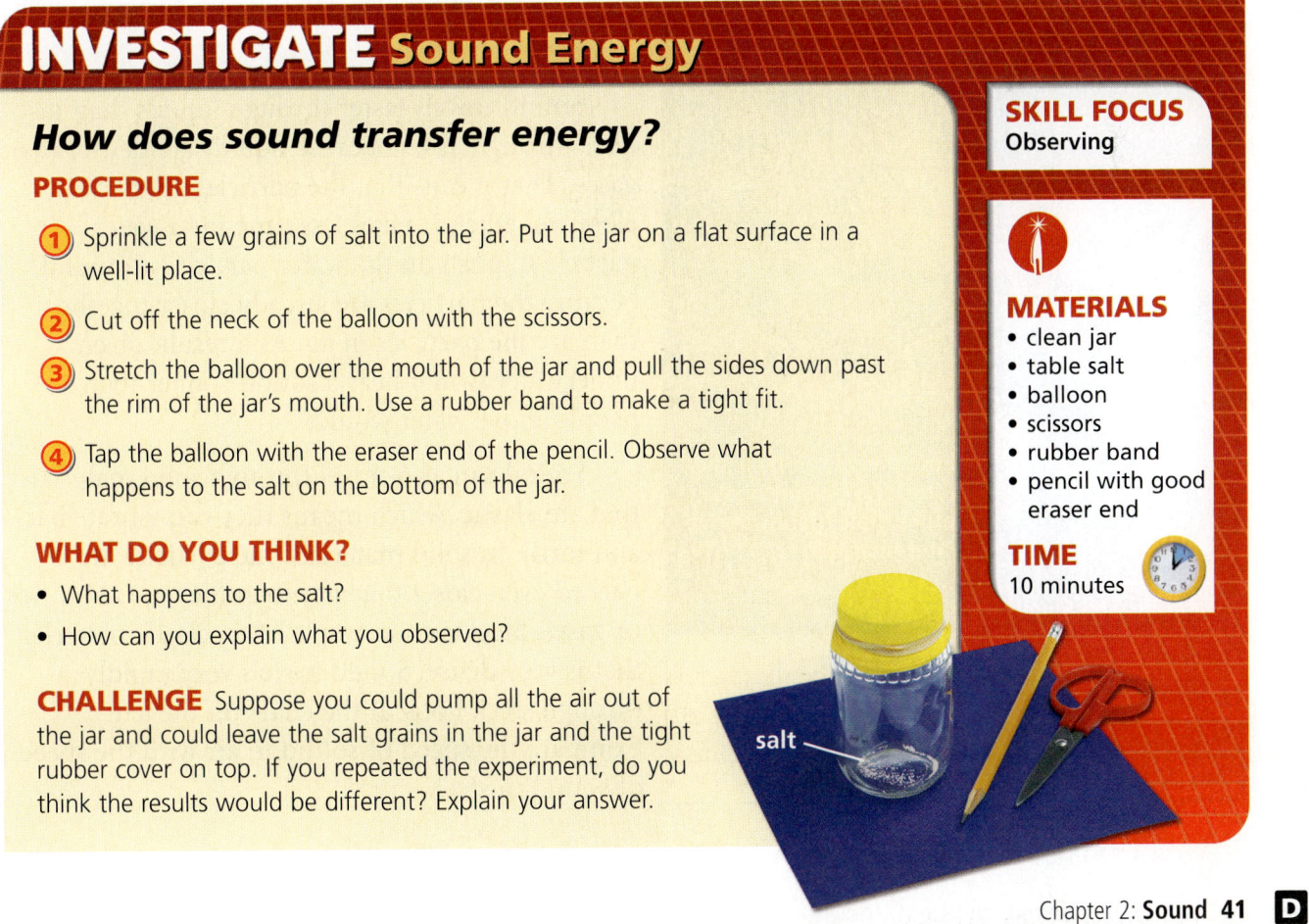

INVESTIGATE Sound Energy

How does sound transfer energy?

PROCEDURE

1. Sprinkle a few grains of salt into the jar. Put the jar on a flat surface in a well-lit place.
2. Cut off the neck of the balloon with the scissors.
3. Stretch the balloon over the mouth of the jar and pull the sides down past the rim of the jar's mouth. Use a rubber band to make a tight fit.
4. Tap the balloon with the eraser end of the pencil. Observe what happens to the salt on the bottom of the jar.

WHAT DO YOU THINK?
- What happens to the salt?
- How can you explain what you observed?

CHALLENGE Suppose you could pump all the air out of the jar and could leave the salt grains in the jar and the tight rubber cover on top. If you repeated the experiment, do you think the results would be different? Explain your answer.

SKILL FOCUS
Observing

MATERIALS
- clean jar
- table salt
- balloon
- scissors
- rubber band
- pencil with good eraser end

TIME
10 minutes

Chapter 2: Sound 41

The speed of sound depends on its medium.

Suppose you are in the baseball stands during an exciting game. A pitch flies from the mound toward home plate, and you see the batter draw back, swing, and hit the ball high. A split second later you hear the crack of the bat meeting the ball. You notice that the sound of the hit comes later than the sight. Just how fast does sound travel?

Sound travels more slowly than light, and it does not always travel at the same speed. Two main factors affect the speed of sound: the material that makes up the medium—such as air or water—and the temperature. If we know the medium and the temperature, however, we can predict the speed of sound.

CHECK YOUR READING Which two factors affect the speed of sound?

The Effect of the Material

You have probably heard sounds in more than one medium. Think about the medium in which you most often hear sound—air. You listen to a radio or a compact disk player. You hear the siren of a fire truck. These sound waves travel through air, a mixture of gases.

Now think about going swimming. You dip below the water's surface briefly. Someone jumps into the water nearby and splashes water against the pool wall. You hear strange underwater sounds. These sound waves travel through water, a liquid.

Sound travels faster through liquids than it does through gases because liquids are denser than gases. That means that the particles are packed closer together. It takes less time for a water particle to push on the water particles around it because the particles are already closer together than are the particles in air. As a result, divers underwater would hear a sound sooner than people above water would.

Sound can also travel through solid materials that are elastic, which means they can vibrate back and forth. In solid materials, the particles are packed even closer together than they are in liquids or gases. Steel is an example of an elastic material that is very dense. Sound travels very rapidly through steel. Look at the chart on the left. Compare the speed of sound in air with the speed of sound in steel.

These divers can hear the motor of a distant boat before their friends above water hear it.

Materials and Sound Speeds

Medium	State	Speed of Sound
Air (20°C)	Gas	344 m/s (769 mi/h)
Water (20°C)	Liquid	1,400 m/s (3,130 mi/h)
Steel (20°C)	Solid	5,000 m/s (11,200 mi/h)

The Effect of Temperature

Sound also travels faster through a medium at higher temperatures than at lower ones. Consider the medium of air, a mixture of gases. Gas particles are not held tightly together as are particles in solids. Instead, the gas particles bounce all around. The higher the temperature, the more the gas particles wiggle and bounce. It takes less time for particles that are already moving quickly to push against the particles around them than it takes particles that are moving slowly. Sound, therefore, travels faster in hot air than in cold air.

Look at the picture of the snowboarders. The sound waves they make by yelling will travel more slowly through air than similar sounds made on a hot day. If you could bear to stand in air at a temperature of 100°C (212°F—the boiling point of water) and listen to the same person yelling, you might notice that the sound of the person's voice reaches you faster.

The chart on the right shows the speed of sound in air at two different temperatures. Compare the speed of sound at the temperature at which water freezes with the speed of sound at the temperature at which water boils. Sound travels about 17 percent faster in air at 100°C than in air at 0°C.

These snowboarders' shouts reach their friends more slowly in this cold air than they would in hot air.

Temperature and Sound Speeds

Medium	Temperature	Speed of Sound
Air	0°C (32°F)	331 m/s (741 mi/h)
Air	100°C (212°F)	386 m/s (864 mi/h)

CHECK YOUR READING What is the difference between the speed of sound in air at 0°C and at 100°C?

2.1 Review

KEY CONCEPTS

1. Describe how sound waves are produced.
2. Describe how particles move as energy is transferred through a sound wave.
3. Explain how temperature affects the speed of sound.

CRITICAL THINKING

4. **Predict** Would the sound from a distant train travel faster through air or through steel train tracks? Explain.
5. **Evaluate** Suppose an audience watching a science fiction movie hears a loud roar as a spaceship explodes in outer space. Why is this scene unrealistic?

CHALLENGE

6. **Evaluate** A famous riddle asks this question: If a tree falls in the forest and there is no one there to hear it, is there any sound? What do you think? Give reasons for your answer.

Chapter 2: Sound 43

Extreme Science

SURPASSING THE SPEED OF SOUND

RESOURCE CENTER
CLASSZONE.COM
Find out more about supersonic aircraft.

Sonic Booms

Airplanes traveling faster than the speed of sound can produce an incredibly loud sound called a sonic boom. The sonic boom from a low-flying airplane can rattle and even break windows!

How It Works

Breaking the Barrier

The sound waves produced by this airplane begin to pile up and produce a pressure barrier.

This airplane has broken through the pressure barrier and has produced a loud boom.

This photograph may actually show the wake of a sonic boom. It was taken on a very humid day, and water vapor may have condensed in the low-pressure part of the sound wave.

When an airplane reaches extremely high speeds, it actually catches up to its own sound waves. The waves start to pile up and form a high-pressure area in front of the plane. If the airplane has enough acceleration, it breaks through the barrier, making a sonic boom. The airplane gets ahead of both the pressure barrier and the sound waves and is said to be traveling at supersonic speeds—speeds faster than the speed of sound.

Boom and It's Gone

If an airplane that produces a boom is flying very high, it may be out of sight by the time the sonic boom reaches a hearer on the ground. To make a sonic boom, a plane must be traveling faster than about 1240 kilometers per hour (769 mi/h)! The sound does not last very long—about one-tenth of a second for a small fighter plane to one-half second for a supersonic passenger plane.

Boom Notes

- The pilot of an airplane cannot hear the sonic boom because the sound waves are behind the plane.
- Lightning heats particles in the air so rapidly that they move faster than the speed of sound and cause a shock wave, which is what makes the boom of thunder. If a lightning strike is very close, you will hear a sharp crack.
- Large meteors enter the atmosphere fast enough to make a sonic boom.

EXPLORE

1. **PREDICT** Specially designed cars have traveled faster than the speed of sound. Would you expect them to produce a sonic boom?
2. **CHALLENGE** The space shuttles produce sonic booms when they are taking off and landing, but not while they are orbiting Earth, even though they are moving much faster than 1240 km/h. Can you explain why?

Unit: Waves, Sound, and Light

KEY CONCEPT
2.2 Frequency determines pitch.

◀ **BEFORE, you learned**
- Sound waves are produced by vibrations
- Frequency measures the number of waves passing a fixed point per second

▶ **NOW, you will learn**
- How the frequency of a wave affects the way it sounds
- How sound quality differs from pitch
- How the Doppler effect works

VOCABULARY

pitch p. 45
hertz p. 46
ultrasound p. 46
resonance p. 48
Doppler effect p. 50

EXPLORE Pitch

Why does the sound change?

PROCEDURE

① Hold the ruler flat on the edge of a desk so that it sticks out about 25 centimeters beyond the edge.

② With your free hand, push the tip of the ruler down and then let it go. As the ruler vibrates, slide it back onto the desk. Listen to the sounds the ruler makes.

MATERIALS
ruler

WHAT DO YOU THINK?
- What happened to the sound as you slid the ruler back onto the desk?
- Describe the motion of the ruler.

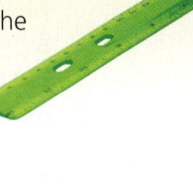

Pitch depends on the frequency of a sound wave.

VOCABULARY
Remember to add a description wheel in your notebook for each new term.

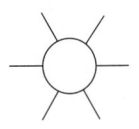

When you listen to music, you hear both high and low sounds. The characteristic of highness or lowness of a sound is called **pitch**. The frequency of a sound wave determines the pitch of the sound you hear. Remember that frequency is the number of waves passing a fixed point in a given period of time. A high-frequency wave with short wavelengths, such as that produced by a tiny flute, makes a high-pitched sound. A low-frequency wave with long wavelengths, such as the one produced by the deep croak of a tuba, makes a low-pitched sound. An object vibrating very fast produces a high-pitched sound, while an object vibrating slower produces a lower-pitched sound.

CHECK YOUR READING How is frequency related to pitch?

Chapter 2: **Sound** 45 **D**

High and Low Frequencies

Frequency is a measure of how often a wave passes a fixed point. One complete wave can also be called a cycle. The unit for measuring frequency, and also pitch, is the hertz. A **hertz** (Hz) is one complete wave, or cycle, per second. For example, a wave with a frequency of 20 hertz has 20 cycles per second. In a wave with a frequency of 100 hertz, 100 waves pass a given point every second. The diagram below shows how frequency and pitch are related.

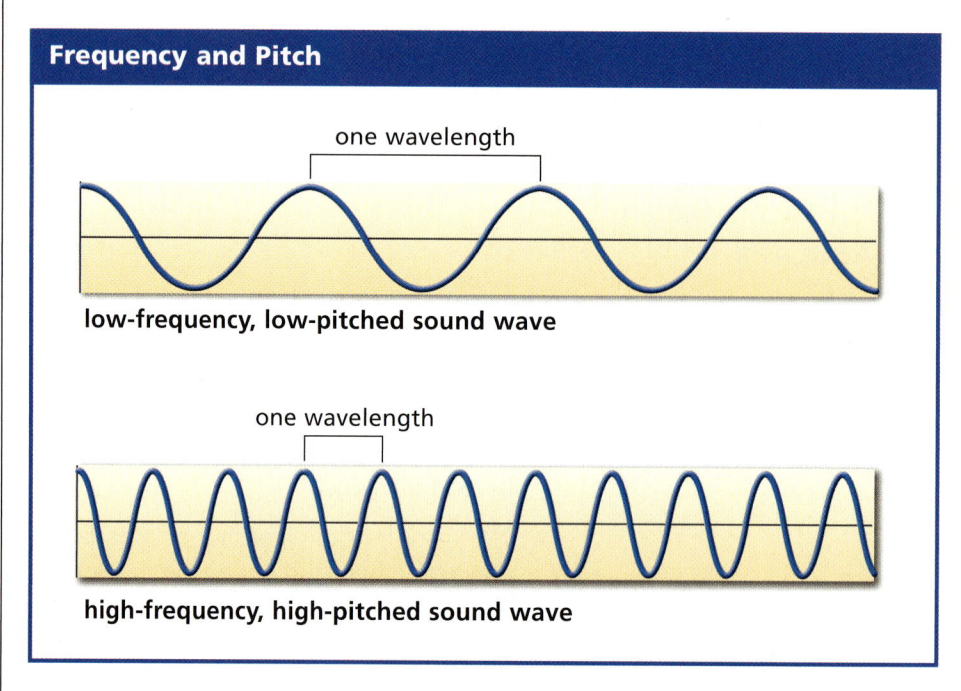

Frequency and Pitch

one wavelength

low-frequency, low-pitched sound wave

one wavelength

high-frequency, high-pitched sound wave

Human ears can hear a wide range of pitches. Most people with good hearing can hear sounds in the range of 20 hertz to 20,000 hertz. The note of middle C on a piano, for example, has a frequency of 262 hertz.

Sound waves with wavelengths below 20 hertz are called infrasound. People cannot hear sounds in this range. Infrasound waves have a very long wavelength and can travel great distances without losing much energy. Elephants may use infrasound to communicate over long distances. Some of the waves that elephants use travel through the ground instead of the air, and they may be detected by another elephant up to 32 kilometers (about 20 miles) away.

The highest frequency that humans can hear is 20,000 hertz. Sound waves in the range above 20,000 hertz are called **ultrasound.** Though people cannot hear ultrasound, it is very useful. Later in this chapter, you will learn about some of the uses of ultrasound. Many animals can hear sound waves in the ultrasound range. The chart on page 47 shows the hearing ranges of some animals.

> **READING TIP**
> The prefix *infra* means "below," and the prefix *ultra* means "beyond."

CHECK YOUR READING What is the range of frequencies that humans can hear?

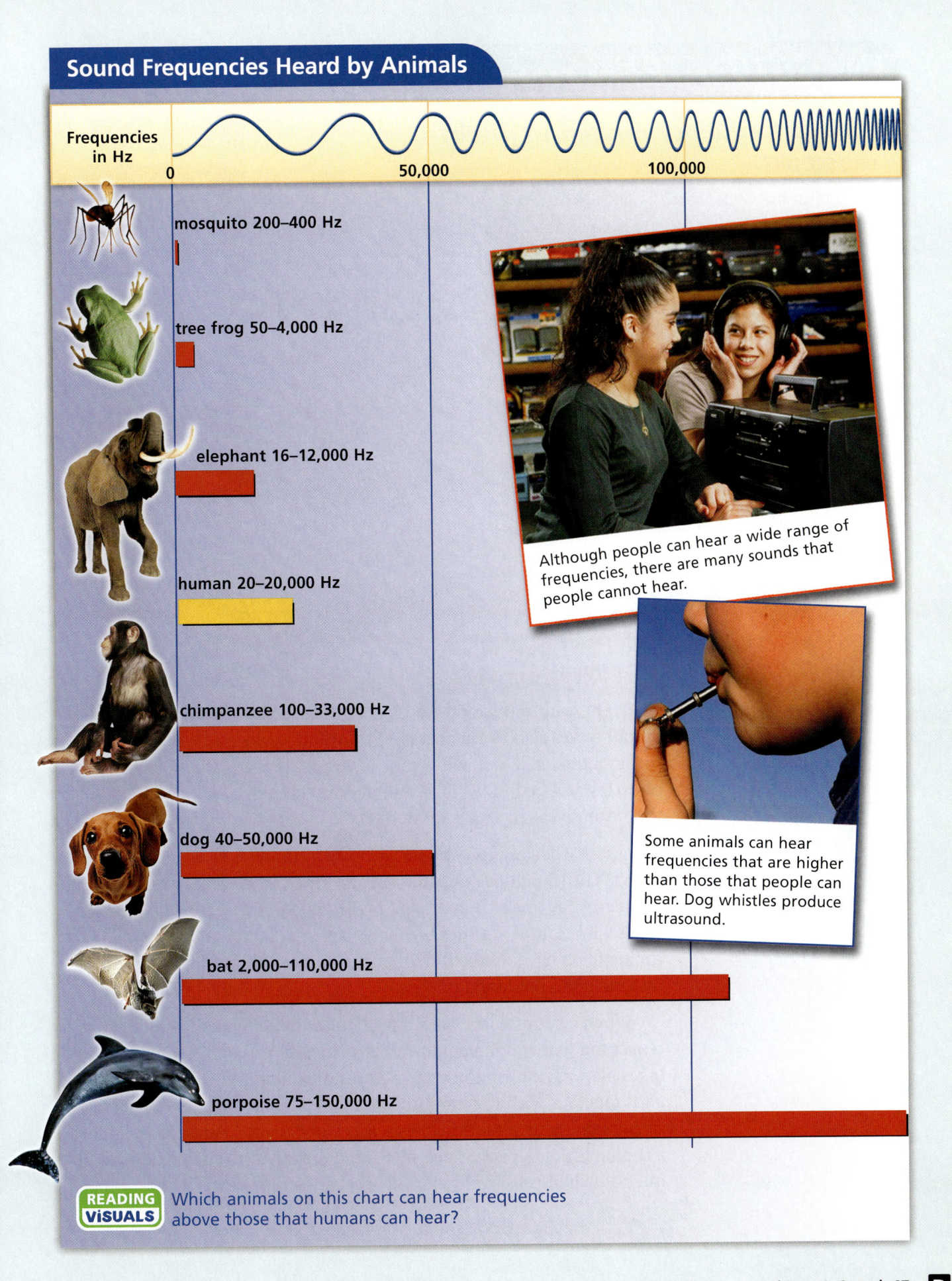

Sound Frequencies Heard by Animals

Frequencies in Hz: 0 — 50,000 — 100,000

- mosquito 200–400 Hz
- tree frog 50–4,000 Hz
- elephant 16–12,000 Hz
- human 20–20,000 Hz
- chimpanzee 100–33,000 Hz
- dog 40–50,000 Hz
- bat 2,000–110,000 Hz
- porpoise 75–150,000 Hz

Although people can hear a wide range of frequencies, there are many sounds that people cannot hear.

Some animals can hear frequencies that are higher than those that people can hear. Dog whistles produce ultrasound.

READING VISUALS Which animals on this chart can hear frequencies above those that humans can hear?

Chapter 2: **Sound** 47 **D**

INVESTIGATE Sound Frequency

How is frequency related to pitch?

PROCEDURE

1. Stretch the rubber bands around the open box.
2. Pull one of the rubber bands tightly across the open part of the box so that it vibrates with a higher frequency than the looser rubber band. Tape the rubber band in place.
3. Pluck each rubber band and listen to the sound it makes.

WHAT DO YOU THINK?
- Which rubber band produces a sound wave with a higher pitch?
- How is frequency related to pitch?

CHALLENGE Suppose you are tuning a guitar and want to make one of the strings sound higher in pitch. Do you tighten or loosen the string? Explain your answer.

SKILL FOCUS
Inferring

MATERIALS
- 2 rubber bands of different sizes
- small open box
- tape

TIME
20 minutes

Natural Frequencies

You have read that sound waves are produced by vibrating objects. Sound waves also cause particles in the air to vibrate as they travel through the air. These vibrations have a frequency, or a number of cycles per second. All objects have a frequency at which they vibrate called a natural frequency.

You may have seen a piano tuner tap a tuning fork against another object. The tuner does this to make the fork vibrate at its natural frequency. He or she then listens to the pitch produced by the tuning fork's vibrations and tunes the piano string to match it. Different tuning forks have different frequencies and can be used to tune instruments to different pitches.

When a sound wave with a particular frequency encounters an object that has the same natural frequency, constructive interference takes place. The amplitude of the sound from the vibrating object adds together with the amplitude of the initial sound wave. The strengthening of a sound wave in this way is called **resonance.** When a tuning fork is struck, a nearby tuning fork with the same natural frequency will also begin to vibrate because of resonance.

CHECK YOUR READING How is natural frequency related to resonance?

Sound Quality

Have you ever noticed that two singers can sing exactly the same note, or pitch, and yet sound very different? The singers produce sound waves with their vocal cords. They stretch their vocal cords in just the right way to produce sound waves with a certain frequency. That frequency produces the pitch that the note of music calls for. Why, then, don't the singers sound exactly the same?

Each musical instrument and each human voice has its own particular sound, which is sometimes called the sound quality. Another word for sound quality is timbre (TAM-buhr). Timbre can be explained by the fact that most sounds are not single waves but are actually combinations of waves. The pitch that you hear is called the fundamental tone. Other, higher-frequency pitches are called overtones. The combination of pitches is the main factor affecting the quality of a sound.

Another factor in sound quality is the way in which a sound starts and stops. Think about a musician who is crashing cymbals. The cymbals' sound blasts out suddenly. A sound produced by the human voice, on the other hand, starts much more gently.

CHECK YOUR READING What are two factors that affect sound quality? Which sentences above tell you?

The illustration below shows oscilloscope (uh-SIHL-uh-SKOHP) screens. An oscilloscope is a scientific instrument that tracks an electrical signal. The energy of a sound wave is converted into a signal and displayed on an oscilloscope screen. The screens below show sound wave diagrams made by musicians playing a piano and a clarinet. Both of these musical instruments are producing the same note, or pitch. Notice that the diagrams look slightly different from each other. Each has a different combination of overtones, producing a unique sound quality.

Both oscilloscope images at left show diagrams of sound waves of the same pitch produced on two different instruments. The waves, however, have different sound qualities.

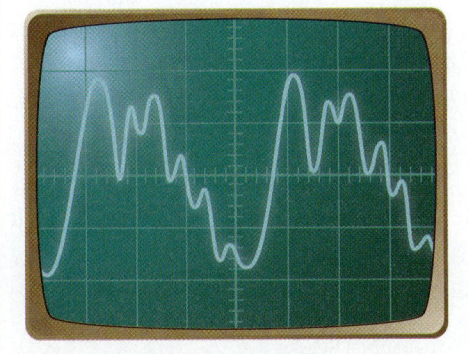

piano

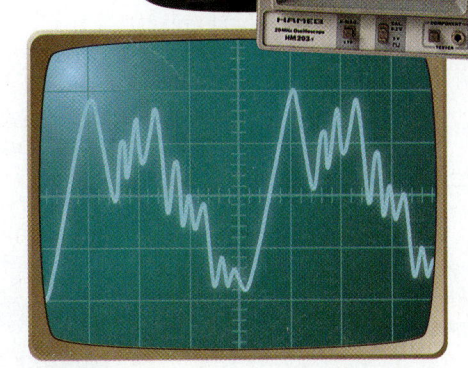

clarinet

Chapter 2: **Sound** 49

The motion of the source of a sound affects its pitch.

Sometimes in traffic, a screeching siren announces that an ambulance must pass through traffic. Drivers slow down and pull over to the side, leaving room for the ambulance to speed by. Suppose you are a passenger in one of these cars. What do you hear?

When the ambulance whizzes past you, the pitch suddenly seems to drop. The siren on the ambulance blasts the same pitches again and again. What has made the difference in what you hear is the rapid motion of the vehicle toward you and then away from you. The motion of the source of a sound affects its pitch.

DESCRIPTION WHEEL
Make a description wheel in your notebook for the Doppler effect.

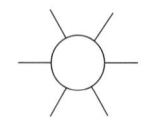

The Doppler Effect

In the 1800s an Austrian scientist named Christian Doppler hypothesized about sound waves. He published a scientific paper about his work. In it, he described how pitch changes when a sound source moves rapidly toward and then away from a listener. Doppler described the scientific principle we notice when a siren speeds by. The **Doppler effect** is the change in perceived pitch that occurs when the source or the receiver of a sound is moving.

Before long, a Dutch scientist learned of Doppler's work. In 1845 he staged an experiment to test the hypothesis that Doppler described. In the experiment, a group of trumpet players were put on a train car. Other musicians were seated beside the railroad track. Those musicians had perfect pitch—that is, the ability to identify a pitch just by listening to it. The train passed by the musicians while the trumpeters on the train played their instruments. The musicians recorded the pitches they heard from one moment to the next. At the end of the demonstration, the musicians reported that they had heard the pitch of the trumpets fall as the train passed. Their experiment showed that the Doppler effect exists.

CHECK YOUR READING How does the motion of a sound's source affect its pitch?

To listeners outside a train, the sound made by the train seems higher in pitch while it approaches them than while it speeds away.

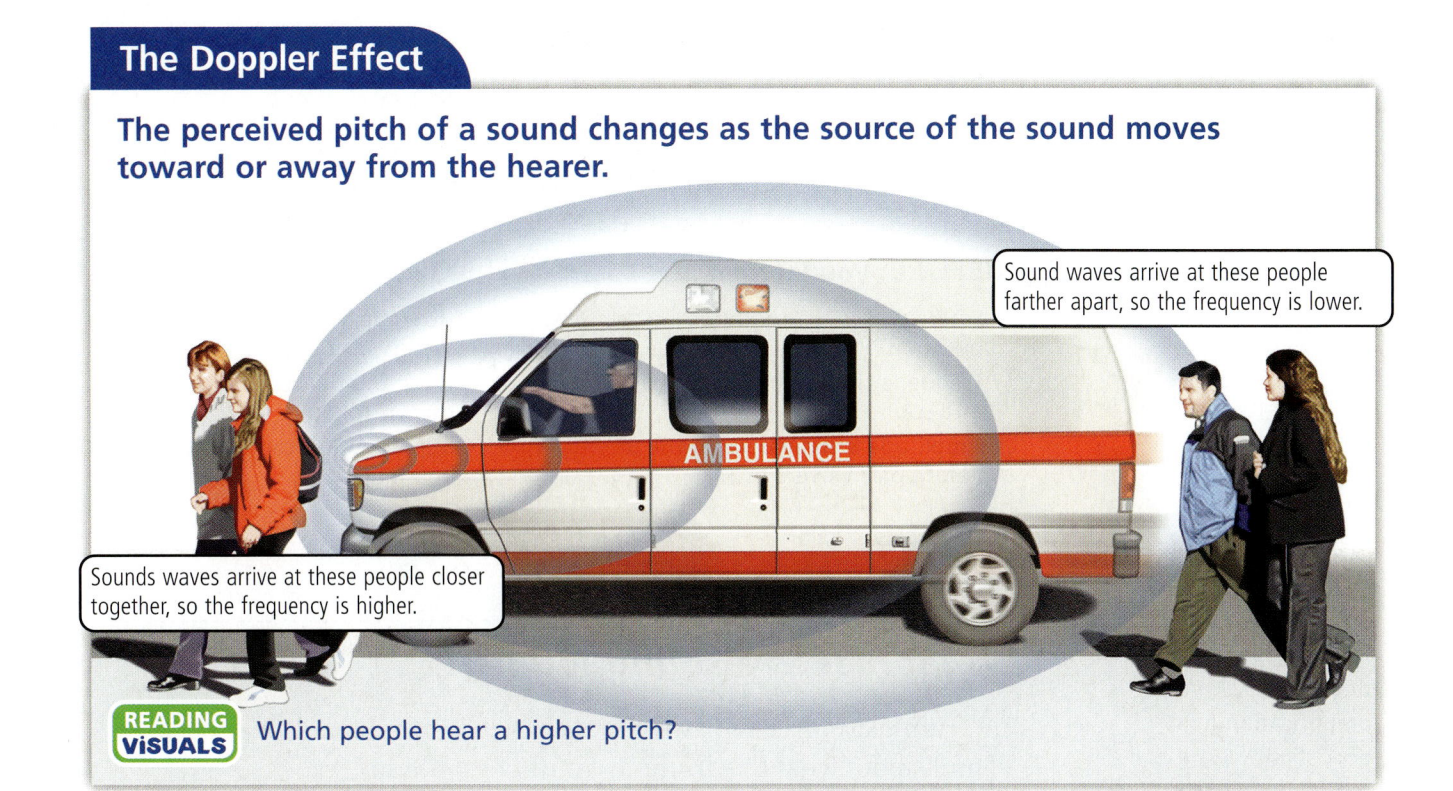

The Doppler Effect

The perceived pitch of a sound changes as the source of the sound moves toward or away from the hearer.

Sound waves arrive at these people farther apart, so the frequency is lower.

Sounds waves arrive at these people closer together, so the frequency is higher.

READING VISUALS Which people hear a higher pitch?

Frequency and Pitch

Again imagine sitting in a car as an ambulance approaches. The siren on the ambulance continually sends out sound waves. As the ambulance pulls closer to you, it catches up with the sound waves it is sending out. As a result, the sound waves that reach your ears are spaced closer together. The frequency, and therefore the pitch, is higher when it reaches you. As the ambulance continues, it gets farther and farther away from you, while the sound waves still move toward you. Now the waves arrive farther and farther apart. As the frequency decreases, you hear a lower pitch.

VISUALIZATION CLASSZONE.COM
Explore the Doppler effect.

2.2 Review

KEY CONCEPTS

1. Describe what is different about the sound waves produced by a low note and a high note on a musical instrument.
2. Explain why two people singing the same pitch do not sound exactly the same.
3. How does perceived pitch change as a sound source passes a listener?

CRITICAL THINKING

4. **Apply** How could you produce vibrations in a tuning fork without touching it? Explain your answer.
5. **Predict** Suppose you could view the waves produced by a high-pitched and a low-pitched voice. Which wave would display the greater number of compressions in 1 s? Why?

CHALLENGE

6. **Infer** Offer a possible explanation for why no one noticed the Doppler effect before the 1800s.

Chapter 2: **Sound** 51 **D**

2.3 Intensity determines loudness.

KEY CONCEPT

BEFORE, you learned
- Sound waves are produced by vibrations
- Frequency determines the pitch of a sound
- Amplitude is a measure of the height of a wave crest

NOW, you will learn
- How the intensity of a wave affects its loudness
- How sound intensity can be controlled
- How loudness can affect hearing

VOCABULARY

intensity p. 52
decibel p. 52
amplification p. 55
acoustics p. 55

THINK ABOUT

What makes a sound louder?

A drum player has to play softly at some times and loudly at others. Think about what the drummer must do to produce each type of sound. If you could watch the drummer in the photograph in action, what would you see? How would the drummer change the way he moves the drumsticks to make a loud, crashing sound? What might he do to make a very soft sound?

Intensity depends on the amplitude of a sound wave.

OUTLINE
Make an outline for this heading. Remember to include main ideas and details.

I. Main idea
   A. Supporting idea
      1. Detail
      2. Detail
   B. Supporting idea

Earlier you read that all waves carry energy. The more energy a sound wave carries, the more intense it is and the louder it will sound to listeners. The **intensity** of a sound is the amount of energy its sound wave has. A unit called the **decibel** (dB) is used to measure sound intensity. The faint rustling of tree leaves on a quiet summer day can hardly be heard. Some of the softest sounds measure less than 10 decibels. On the other hand, the noise from a jet taking off or the volume of a TV set turned all the way up can hurt your ears. Very loud sounds measure more than 100 decibels. Remember that amplitude is related to wave energy. The greater the amplitude, the more intensity a sound wave has and the louder the sound will be.

CHECK YOUR READING How is energy related to loudness?

D 52 Unit: Waves, Sound, and Light

INVESTIGATE Loudness

How is amplitude related to loudness?

PROCEDURE

1. Cut a notch in the middle of both ends of the cardboard. Stretch the rubber band around the cardboard so that it fits into the notches as shown.
2. Mark lines on the cardboard at one and four centimeters away from the rubber band.
3. Slide the pencils under the rubber band at each end.
4. Pull the rubber band to the one-centimeter line and let it go so that it vibrates with a low amplitude. Notice the sound it makes. Pull the rubber band to the four-centimeter line and let it go again. This time the amplitude is higher. Notice the sound it makes this time.

WHAT DO YOU THINK?

- How did the loudness of the sounds compare?
- How is amplitude related to loudness?

CHALLENGE Using what you learned from experimenting with the rubber band, explain why swinging a drumstick harder on a drum would make a louder sound than swinging a drumstick lightly.

SKILL FOCUS
Observing

MATERIALS
- piece of cardboard
- scissors
- large rubber band
- 2 pencils
- ruler

TIME
15 minutes

The drummer varies the loudness of a sound by varying the energy with which he hits the drum. Loudness is also affected by the distance between the source and the listener.

Have you ever wondered why sound gradually dies out over distance? Think about someone walking away from you with a radio. When the radio is close, the radio seems loud. As the person walks away, the sound grows fainter and fainter. Sound waves travel in all directions from their source. As the waves travel farther from the radio, their energy is spread out over a greater area. This means that their intensity is decreased. The sound waves with lower intensities are heard as quieter sounds.

Other forces can take energy away from sound waves, too. Forces can act within the medium of a sound wave to decrease the intensity of the waves. This effect on sound is probably a good thing. Imagine what the world would be like if every sound wave continued forever!

Approximate Sound Intensities

dB	Examples
10	leaves rustling
20	light rainfall
30	whisper
50	conversation
60	dog barking
70	traffic
90	lawn mower
100	motorcycle
120	amplified music
140	firecrackers
150	airplane taking off

20 dB light rainfall

150 dB airplane taking off nearby

90 dB lawn mower

60 dB dog barking

10 dB leaves rustling in gentle breeze

READING VISUALS What is the source of the most intense sound in this picture? the least intense?

The intensity of sound can be controlled.

REMINDER
Remember, amplitude is related to wave energy.

Over time and distance, a sound wave gets weaker and weaker until the sound becomes undetectable. The pitch, however, does not typically change as the sound grows weaker. In other words, even as the amplitude decreases, the frequency stays the same.

Sometimes it is desirable to change sound intensity without changing the pitch and quality of a sound. We can do this by adding energy to or taking energy away from a sound wave. As you have already seen, intensity is the amount of energy in a sound wave. Changing the intensity of a sound wave changes its amplitude.

Sound intensity can be controlled in many ways. Mufflers on cars and trucks reduce engine noise. Have you ever heard a car with a broken muffler? You were probably surprised at how loud it was. Burning fuel in an engine produces hot gases that expand and make a very loud noise. A muffler is designed to absorb some of the energy of the sound waves and so decrease their amplitude. As a result, the intensity of the sound you hear is much lower than it would be without the muffler.

CHECK YOUR READING How could you change the intensity of a sound without changing the pitch?

D 54 Unit: Waves, Sound, and Light

Amplification

In addition to being reduced, as they are in a muffler, sound waves can be amplified. The word *amplify* may remind you of *amplitude*, the measure of the height of a wave's crest. These words are related. To amplify something means to make it bigger. **Amplification** is the increasing of the strength of an electrical signal. It is often used to increase the intensity of a sound wave.

When you listen to a stereo, you experience the effects of amplification. Sound input to the stereo is in the form of weak electrical signals from a microphone. Transistors in an electronic circuit amplify the signals. The electrical signals are converted into vibrations in a coil in your stereo's speaker. The coil is attached to a cone, which also vibrates and sends out sound waves. You can control the intensity of the sound waves by adjusting your stereo's volume.

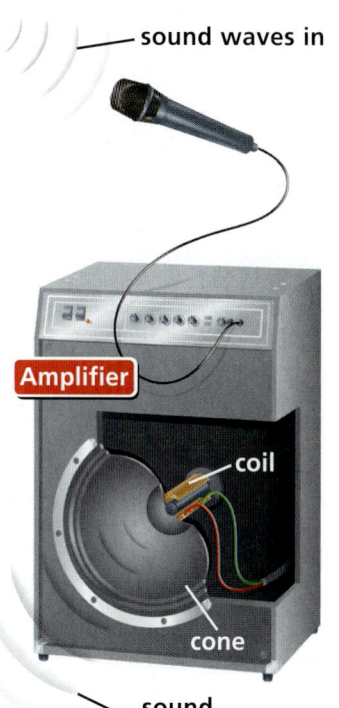

Acoustics

The scientific study of sound is called **acoustics** (uh-KOO-stihks). Acoustics involves both how sound is produced and how it is received and heard by humans and animals.

Acoustics also refers to the way sound waves behave inside a space. Experts called acoustical engineers help design buildings to reduce unwanted echoes. An echo is simply a reflected sound wave. To control sound intensity, engineers design walls and ceilings with acoustical tiles. The shapes and surfaces of acoustical tiles are designed to absorb or redirect some of the energy of sound waves.

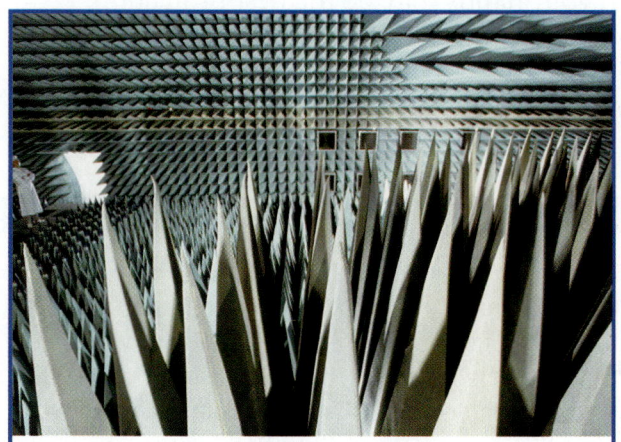

The pointed tiles in this sound-testing room are designed to absorb sound waves and prevent any echoes.

The shapes and surfaces in this concert hall direct sound waves to the audience.

READING VISUALS **COMPARE AND CONTRAST** Imagine sound waves reflecting off the surfaces in the two photographs above. How do the reflections differ?

Chapter 2: Sound 55

Intense sound can damage hearing.

When a train screeches to a stop in a subway station, the sound of the squealing brakes echoes off the tunnel walls. Without thinking about it, you cover your ears with your hands. This response helps protect your ears from possible damage.

In the first section of this chapter, you read about the main parts of the human ear. The part of the inner ear called the cochlea is lined with special cells called hair cells. As you have seen, these cells are necessary for hearing.

The hair cells are extremely sensitive. This sensitivity makes hearing possible, but it also makes the cells easy to damage. Continual exposure to sounds of 90 dB or louder can damage or destroy the cells. This is one reason why being exposed to very loud noises, especially for more than a short time, is harmful to hearing.

healthy hair cells

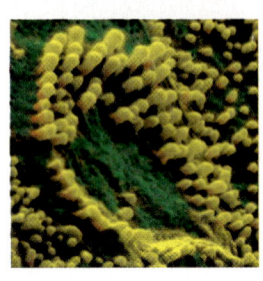

damaged hair cells

CHECK YOUR READING How do high-intensity sounds damage hearing?

Using earplugs can prevent damage from too much exposure to high-intensity sounds such as amplified music. The intensity at a rock concert is between 85 and 120 dB. Ear protection can also protect the hearing of employees in factories and other noisy work sites. In the United States, there are laws that require employers to reduce sounds at work sites to below 90 dB or to provide workers with ear protection.

RESOURCE CENTER CLASSZONE.COM
Find out more about sound and protecting your hearing.

Even a brief, one-time exposure to an extremely loud noise can destroy hair cells. Noises above 130 dB are especially dangerous. Noises above 140 dB are even painful. It is best to avoid such noises altogether. If you find yourself exposed suddenly to such a noise, covering your ears with your hands may be the best protection.

2.3 Review

KEY CONCEPTS

1. Explain how the terms *intensity, decibel,* and *amplitude* are related.
2. Describe one way in which sound intensity can be controlled.
3. How do loud sounds cause damage to hearing?

CRITICAL THINKING

4. **Synthesize** A wind chime produces both soft and loud sounds. If you could see the waves, how would they differ?
5. **Design an Experiment** How could you demonstrate that sound dies away over distance? Suppose you could use three volunteers, a radio, and a tape recorder.

CHALLENGE

6. **Apply** Which of these acoustical designs would be best for a concert hall? Why?
   a. bare room with hard walls, floor, and ceiling
   b. room padded with sound-absorbing materials such as acoustical tile
   c. room with some hard surfaces and some sound padding

MATH in SCIENCE

SKILL: INTERPRETING GRAPHS

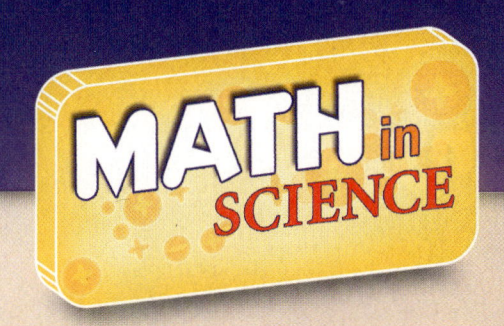

MATH TUTORIAL
CLASSZONE.COM

Click on Math Tutorial for more help with interpreting line graphs.

Measuring Hearing Loss

An audiogram is a graph that can be used to determine if a patient has hearing loss. The vertical axis shows the lowest intensity, in decibels, that the patient can hear for each frequency tested. Notice that intensity is numbered from top to bottom on an audiogram.

To determine the lowest intensity heard at a given frequency, find the frequency on the horizontal axis. Follow the line straight up until you see the data points, shown as ✶ for the right ear and ● for the left ear. Look to the left to find the intensity. For example, the lowest intensity heard in both ears at 250 Hz is 10 dB.

Audiogram for Patient A

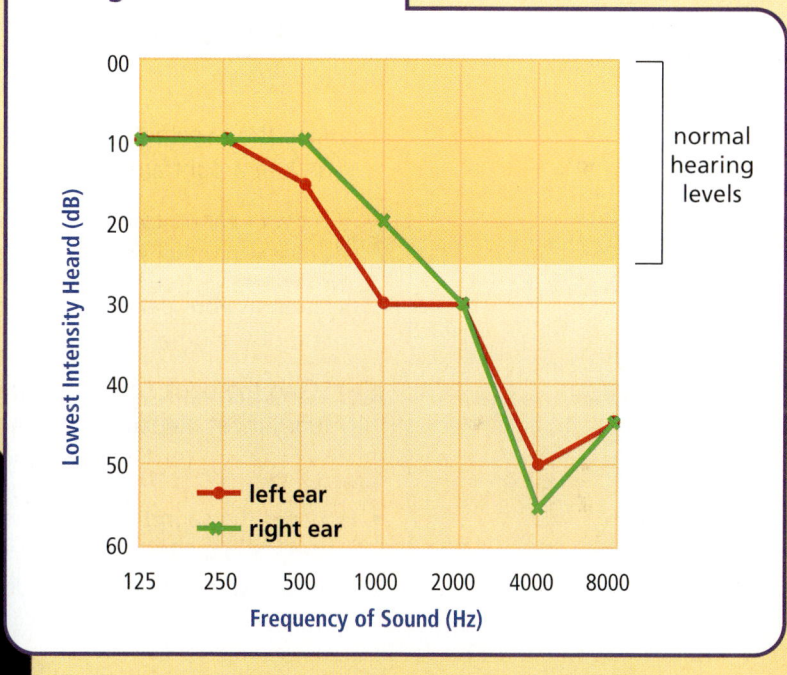

[Graph: Lowest Intensity Heard (dB) vs Frequency of Sound (Hz); normal hearing levels shaded; left ear and right ear plotted]

Use the graph to answer the following questions.

1. What is the lowest intensity heard in the patient's left ear at 1000 Hz? the right ear at the same frequency?

2. At which frequencies are the data points for both ears within normal hearing levels?

3. Data points outside the normal hearing levels indicate hearing loss. At which frequencies are the data points for both ears outside the normal levels?

CHALLENGE A dip in the graph at 3000 to 4000 Hz is a sign that the hearing loss was caused by exposure to loud noises. The patient is referred to a specialist for further testing. Should Patient A get further testing? Why or why not?

This air traffic ground controller wears ear protection to prevent hearing loss.

KEY CONCEPT
2.4 Sound has many uses.

◀ **BEFORE, you learned**
- Sound waves are produced by vibrations
- Sound waves have amplitude, frequency, and wavelength

▶ **NOW, you will learn**
- How ultrasound is used
- How musical instruments work
- How sound can be recorded and reproduced

VOCABULARY

echolocation p. 59
sonar p. 59

EXPLORE Echoes

How can you use sound to detect an object?

PROCEDURE

1. Tape the two cardboard tubes onto your desk at a right angle as shown.
2. Put your ear up to the end of one of the tubes. Cover your other ear with your hand.
3. Listen as your partner whispers into the outside end of the other tube.
4. Stand the book upright where the tubes meet. Repeat steps 2 and 3.

MATERIALS
- 2 cardboard tubes
- tape
- book

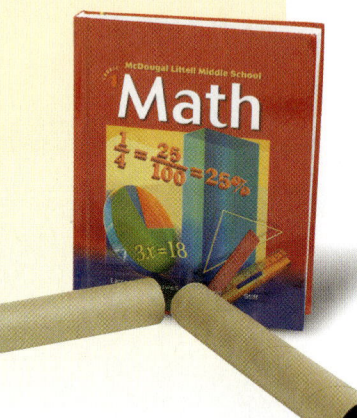

WHAT DO YOU THINK?
- How did the sound change when you added the book?
- How can an echo be used to detect an object?

Ultrasound waves are used to detect objects.

A ringing telephone, a honking horn, and the sound of a friend's voice are all reminders of how important sound is. But sound has uses that go beyond communication. For example, some animals and people use reflected ultrasound waves to detect objects. Some animals, such as bats, use the echoes of ultrasound waves to find food. People use ultrasound echoes to detect objects underwater or even to produce images of the inside of the body.

CHECK YOUR READING Other than communication, what are three uses of sound?

Echolocation

Sending out ultrasound waves and interpreting the returning sound echoes is called **echolocation** (*echo + location*). Bats flying at night find their meals of flying insects by using echolocation. They send out as many as 200 ultrasound squeaks per second. By receiving the returning echoes, they can tell where prey is and how it is moving. They can also veer away from walls, trees, and other big objects.

VOCABULARY
Make description wheels for the terms *echolocation* and *sonar* to help you remember them later.

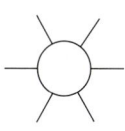

sound waves emitted by bat

sound waves reflected off prey

A number of animals that live in water use echolocation, too. Dolphins, toothed whales, and porpoises produce ultrasound squeaks or clicks. They listen to the returning echo patterns to find fish and other food in the water.

Sonar

People use the principles of echolocation to locate objects underwater. During World War I (1914–1918), scientists developed instruments that used sound waves to locate enemy submarines. Instruments that use echolocation to locate objects are known as **sonar.** Sonar stands for "sound navigation and ranging." The sonar machines could detect sounds coming from submarine propellers. Sonar devices could also send out ultrasound waves and then use the echoes to locate underwater objects. The information from the echoes could then be used to form an image on a screen.

Later, people found many other uses for sonar. Fishing boats use sonar to find schools of fish. Oceanographers—scientists who study the ocean—use it to map the sea floor. People have even used sonar to find ancient sunken ships in deep water.

This woman is using sonar to monitor for submarines.

Sonar is used to locate sunken ships. The image of the sunken ship above was produced on the basis of information from sonar.

Medical Uses of Ultrasound

Ultrasound has many uses in medicine. Because ultrasound waves are not heard by humans, ultrasound can be used at very high intensities. For example, high-intensity vibrations from ultrasound waves are used to safely break up kidney stones in patients. The energy transferred by ultrasound waves is also used to clean medical equipment.

One of the most important medical uses of ultrasound is the ultrasound scanner. This device relies on the same scientific principle as sonar. It sends sound waves into a human body and then records the waves that are reflected from inside the body. Information from these echoes forms a picture on a screen. The ultrasound scanner is used to examine internal organs such as the heart, pancreas, bladder, ovaries, and brain. Doppler ultrasound is a technology that can detect the movement of fluids through the body and is used to examine blood flow.

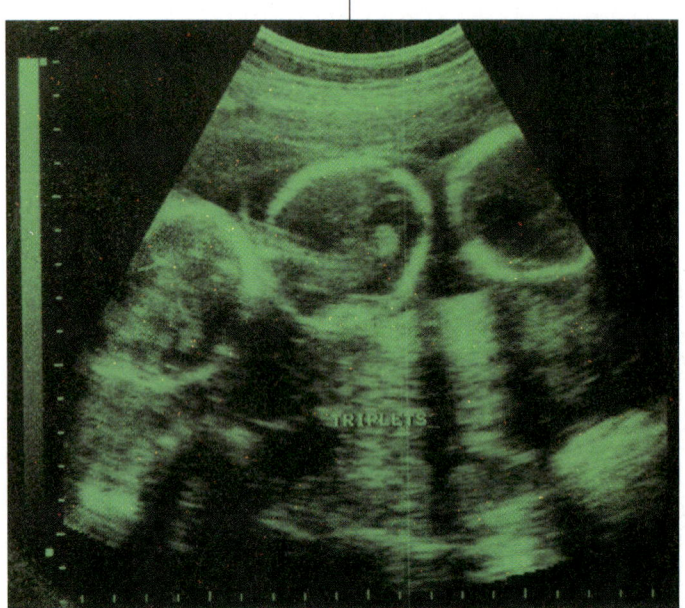

The image of these triplets was produced by reflected ultrasound waves.

CHECK YOUR READING How is an ultrasound scanner similar to sonar?

One of the most well-known uses of ultrasound is to check on the health of a fetus during pregnancy. Problems that are discovered may possibly be treated early. The scan can also reveal the age and gender of the fetus and let the expecting parents know if they will be having twins or triplets. Ultrasound is safer than other imaging methods, such as the x-ray, which might harm the development of the fetus.

Sound waves can produce music.

Why are some sounds considered noise and other sounds considered music? Music is sound with clear pitches or rhythms. Noise is random sound; that means it has no intended pattern.

Musical instruments produce pitches and rhythms when made to vibrate at their natural frequencies. Some musical instruments have parts that vibrate at different frequencies to make different pitches. All of the pitches, together with the resonance of the instrument itself, produce its characteristic sound. The three main types of musical instruments are stringed, wind, and percussion. Some describe electronic instruments as a fourth type of musical instrument. Look at the illustration on the next page to learn more about how each type of musical instrument works.

RESOURCE CENTER
CLASSZONE.COM
Explore musical instruments from around the world.

How Musical Instruments Work

The way a musical instrument vibrates when it is played determines the sound it produces.

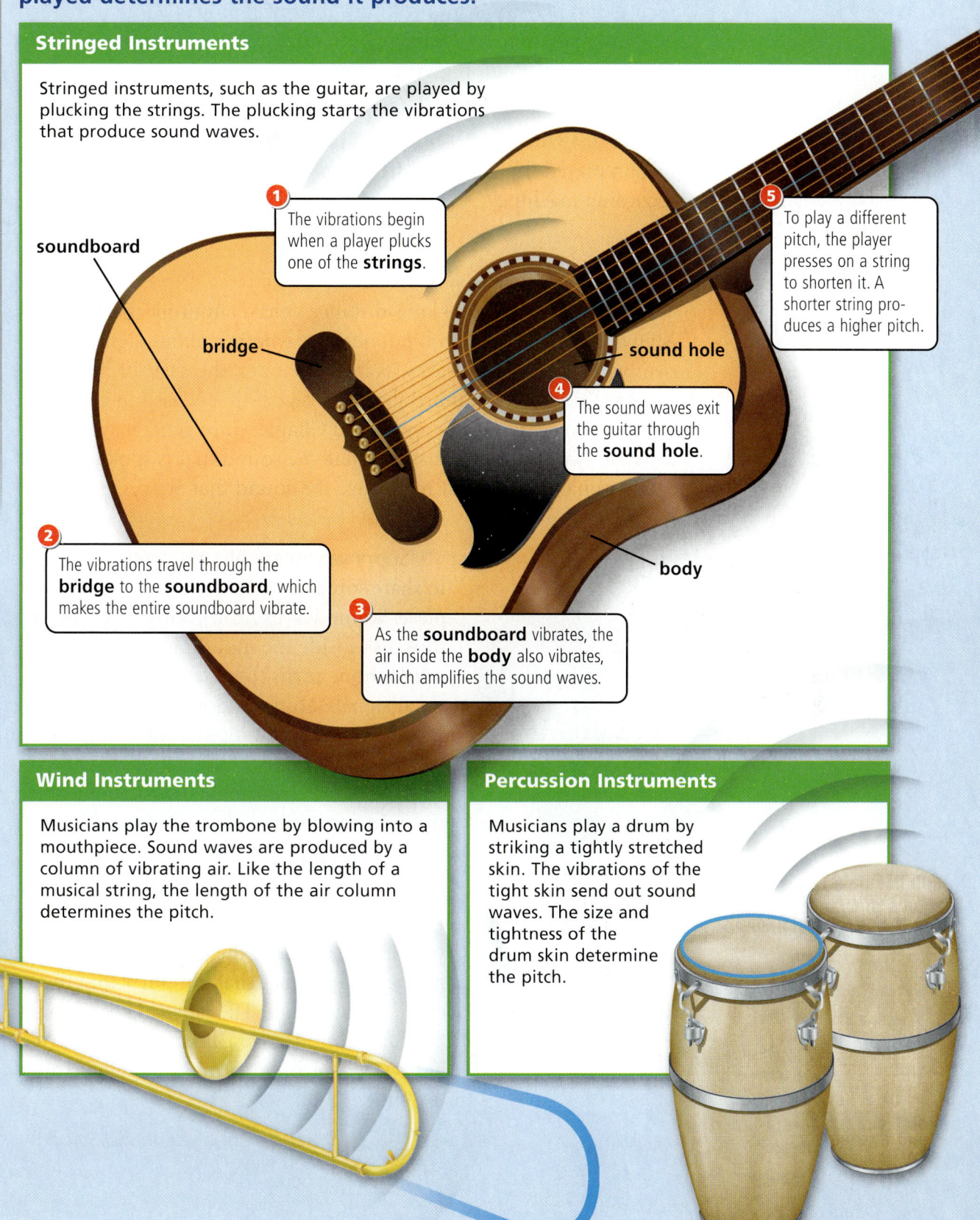

Stringed Instruments

Stringed instruments, such as the guitar, are played by plucking the strings. The plucking starts the vibrations that produce sound waves.

soundboard

bridge

sound hole

body

1 The vibrations begin when a player plucks one of the **strings**.

2 The vibrations travel through the **bridge** to the **soundboard**, which makes the entire soundboard vibrate.

3 As the **soundboard** vibrates, the air inside the **body** also vibrates, which amplifies the sound waves.

4 The sound waves exit the guitar through the **sound hole**.

5 To play a different pitch, the player presses on a string to shorten it. A shorter string produces a higher pitch.

Wind Instruments

Musicians play the trombone by blowing into a mouthpiece. Sound waves are produced by a column of vibrating air. Like the length of a musical string, the length of the air column determines the pitch.

Percussion Instruments

Musicians play a drum by striking a tightly stretched skin. The vibrations of the tight skin send out sound waves. The size and tightness of the drum skin determine the pitch.

Chapter 2: **Sound** 61

Sound can be recorded and reproduced.

For most of human history, people had no way to send their voices farther than they could shout. Nor could people before the 1800s record and play back sound. The voices of famous people were lost when they died. Imagine having a tape or a compact disk recording of George Washington giving a speech!

Then in the late 1800s, two inventions changed the world of sound. In 1876, the telephone was invented. And in 1877, Thomas Edison played the first recorded sound on a phonograph, or sound-recording machine.

READING TIP
The prefix *phono* means "sound," and the suffix *graph* means "writing."

The Telephone

The telephone has made long-distance voice communication possible. Many people today use cell phones. But whether phone signals travel over wires or by microwaves, as in cell phones, the basic principles are similar. You will learn more about the signal that is used in cell phones when you read about microwaves in Chapter 3. In general, a telephone must do two things. It must translate the sound that is spoken into it into a signal, and it must reproduce the sound that arrives as a signal from somewhere else.

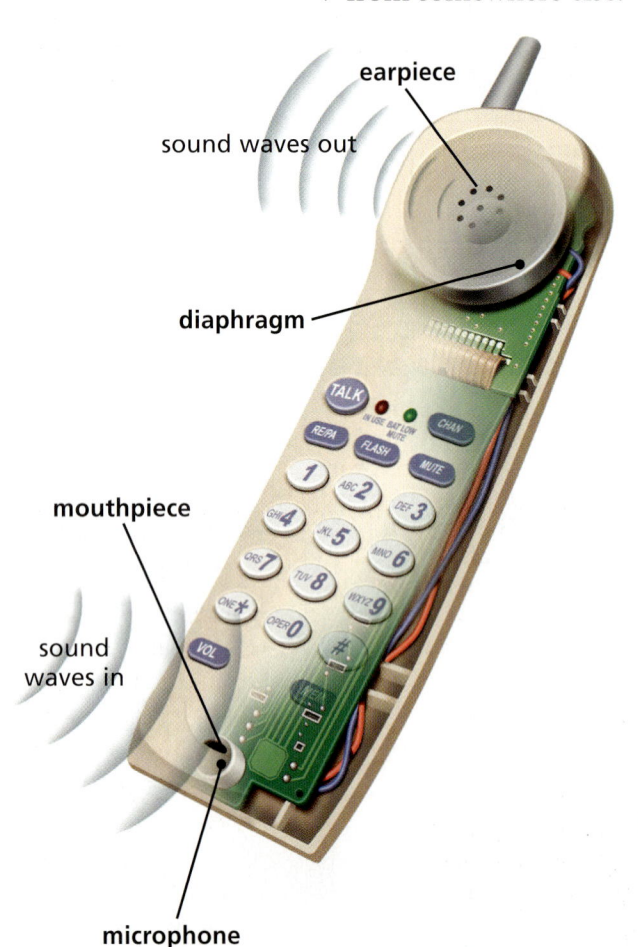

Suppose you are phoning your best friend to share some news. You speak into the mouthpiece. Sound waves from your voice cause a thin disk inside the mouthpiece to vibrate. A microphone turns these vibrations into electrical signals. Your handset sends these signals over wire to a switching station. Computers in the switching station connect phone callers and keep them connected until they finish their conversation.

Your friend receives the news by listening to the earpiece on his handset. There the process is more or less reversed. The electrical signals that arrive in the earpiece are turned into vibrations that shake another thin disk called a diaphragm. The vibrating diaphragm produces sound waves. The sound your friend hears is a copy of your voice, though it sounds like the real you.

CHECK YOUR READING What part of a telephone detects sound waves?

Recorded Sound

Sound occurs in real time, which means it is here for a moment and then gone. That is why Thomas Edison's invention of the phonograph—a way to preserve sound—was so important.

Edison's phonograph had a needle connected to a diaphragm that could pick up sound waves. The vibrations transferred by the sound waves were sent to a needle that cut into a piece of foil. The sound waves were translated into bumps along the grooves cut into the foil. These grooves contained all the information that was needed to reproduce the sound waves. Look at the image on top at the right to view an enlargement of record grooves. To play back the sound, Edison used another needle to track along the grooves etched in the foil. Later, phonographs were developed that changed sound waves into electrical signals that could be amplified.

Most people today listen to music on audio tapes or CDs. Tape consists of thin strips of plastic coated with a material that can be magnetized. Sounds that have been turned into electrical signals are stored on the tape as magnetic information. A CD is a hard plastic disc that has millions of microscopic pits arranged in a spiral. The bottom photograph at the right shows an enlargement of pits on the surface of a CD. These pits contain the information that a CD player can change into electrical signals, which are then turned into sound waves.

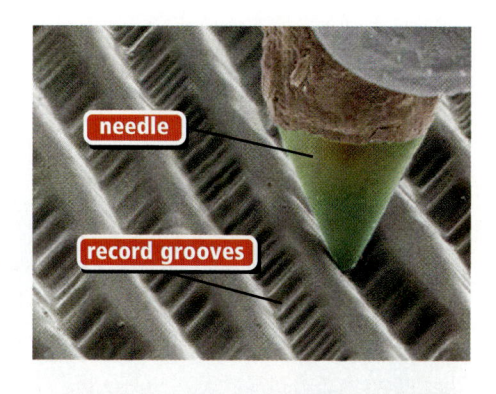

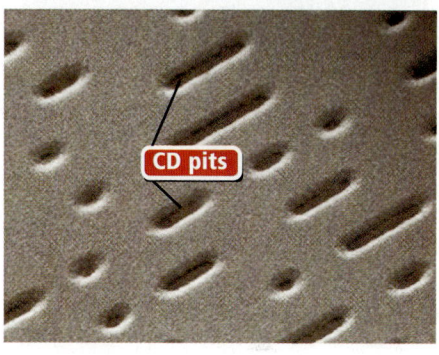

The images above were taken by a scanning electron micrograph (SEM). Both the record grooves (top) and CD pits (bottom) store all of the information needed to reproduce sound.

CHECK YOUR READING Describe three devices on which sound is recorded.

2.4 Review

KEY CONCEPTS

1. Describe one medical use of ultrasound.
2. How are vibrations produced by each of the three main types of musical instruments?
3. How does a telephone record and reproduce sound?

CRITICAL THINKING

4. **Model** Draw a simple diagram to show how telephone communication works. Begin your diagram with the mouthpiece and end with the earpiece.
5. **Classify** The pitch of a musical instrument is changed by shortening the length of a vibrating column of air. What type of instrument is it?

CHALLENGE

6. **Synthesize** How is the earpiece of a telephone similar to the amplifier you read about in Section 3? Look again at the diagram of the amplifier on page 55 to help you find similarities.

Chapter 2: Sound 63 D

CHAPTER INVESTIGATION

Build a Stringed Instrument

OVERVIEW AND PURPOSE

People make music by plucking strings, blowing through tubes, and striking things. Part of each musical instrument vibrates to produce sounds that form the building blocks of music. In this lab, you will use what you have learned about sound to

- make a simple stringed instrument and see how the vibrating string produces sounds and
- change the design so that your stringed instrument produces more than one pitch.

DESIGN YOUR OWN

MATERIALS
- book
- 3–5 rubber bands
- 2 pencils
- ruler
- shoebox
- scissors

▶ Problem   *Write It Up*

How does the length of a string affect the pitch of the sound it produces when plucked?

▶ Hypothesize   *Write It Up*

Write a hypothesis to explain how changing the length of the string affects the pitch of sound that is produced. Your hypothesis should take the form of an "If . . . , then . . . , because . . ." statement. Complete steps 1–3 before writing your hypothesis.

▶ Procedure

1. Make a data table like the one shown. Try out the following idea for a simple stringed instrument. Stretch a rubber band around a textbook. Put two pencils under the rubber band to serve as bridges.

2. Put the bridges far apart at either end of the book. Find the string length by measuring the distance between the two bridges. Record this measurement in your **Science Notebook.** Pluck the rubber band to make it vibrate. Watch it vibrate and listen to the sound it makes.

3. Move the bridges closer together. What effect does this have on the length of the string? Measure and record the new length. How does this affect the tone that is produced? Record your observations.

64 Unit: Waves, Sound, and Light

4. Make a musical instrument based on the principles you just identified. Begin by stretching rubber bands of the same weight or thickness over the box.

5. If necessary, reinforce the box with an extra layer of cardboard or braces so that it can withstand the tension of the rubber bands without collapsing.

6. Place pencils under the rubber bands at each end of the box. Arrange one pencil at an angle so that each string is a different length. Record the length of each string and your observations of the sounds produced. Experiment with the placement of the bridges.

7. You might also try putting one bridge at the center of the box and plucking on either side of it. How does this affect the range of pitches your instrument produces?

8. Experiment with the working model to see how you can vary the sounds. Try this variation: cut a hole in the center of the box lid. Put the lid back on the box. Replace the rubber bands and bridges. How does the hole change the sound quality?

Observe and Analyze

1. **RECORD OBSERVATIONS** Draw a picture of your completed instrument design. Be sure your data table is complete.

2. **ANALYZE** Explain what effect moving the bridges farther apart or closer together has on the vibrating string.

3. **SYNTHESIZE** Using what you have learned from this chapter, write a paragraph that explains how your instrument works. Be sure to describe how sound waves of different frequencies and different intensities can be produced on your instrument.

Conclude

1. **INTERPRET** Answer the question posed in the problem.

2. **ANALYZE** Compare your results with your hypothesis. Did your results support your hypothesis?

3. **EVALUATE** Describe any difficulties with or limitations of the materials that you encountered as you made your instrument.

4. **APPLY** Based on your experiences, how would you explain the difference between music and noise?

INVESTIGATE Further

CHALLENGE Stringed instruments vary the pitch of musical sounds in several other ways. In addition to the length of the string, pitch depends on the tension, weight, and thickness of the string. Design an experiment to test one of these variables. How does it alter the range of sounds produced by your stringed instrument?

Build a Stringed Instrument

Problem How does the length of a string affect the pitch of the sound it produces when plucked?

Hypothesize

Observe and Analyze

Simple instrument: initial string length _____
Simple instrument: new string length _____

Table 1. Stringed Instrument Sound Observations

Stringed Instrument Designs	Length of Strings (cm)	Observations About Pitch and Sound Quality
Bridges at each end		
Bridge in middle		
After adding sound hole		

Conclude

2 Chapter Review

the BIG idea
Sound waves transfer energy through vibrations.

CONTENT REVIEW
CLASSZONE.COM

KEY CONCEPTS SUMMARY

2.1 Sound is a wave.

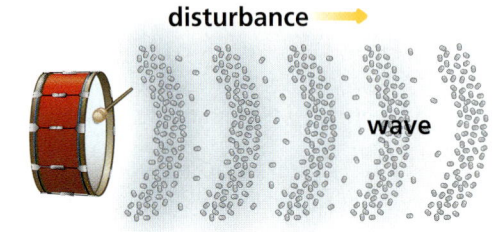

Sound is a longitudinal wave that travels through a material medium, such as air.

VOCABULARY
sound p. 37
vibration p. 37
vacuum p. 41

2.2 Frequency determines pitch.

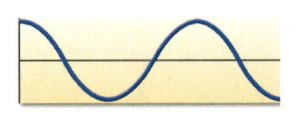

A sound wave with a lower frequency and longer wavelength is perceived to have a lower pitch.

A sound wave with a higher frequency and shorter wavelength is perceived to have a higher pitch.

VOCABULARY
pitch p. 45
hertz p. 46
ultrasound p. 46
resonance p. 48
Doppler effect p. 50

2.3 Intensity determines loudness.

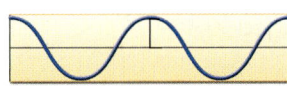

A sound wave with a lower amplitude and energy is perceived as a softer sound.

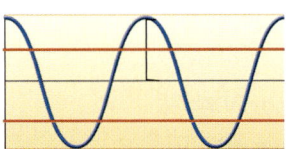

A sound wave with a higher amplitude and energy is perceived as a louder sound.

VOCABULARY
intensity p. 52
decibel p. 52
amplification p. 55
acoustics p. 55

2.4 Sound has many uses.

Human uses of sound:
sonar
ultrasound
music
telephone
recording

Bats use sound to locate objects.

VOCABULARY
echolocation p. 59
sonar p. 59

Reviewing Vocabulary

Copy and complete the chart below by using vocabulary terms from this chapter.

Property of Wave	Unit of Measurement	Characteristic of Sound
Frequency	1.	2.
3.	4.	loudness

Make a frame for each of the vocabulary words listed below. Write the word in the center. Decide what information to frame it with. Use definitions, examples, descriptions, parts, or pictures. An example is shown.

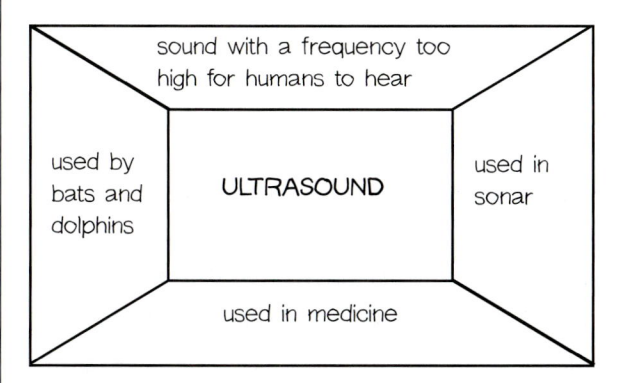

```
        sound with a frequency too
        high for humans to hear
used by                          used in
bats and    ULTRASOUND           sonar
dolphins
           used in medicine
```

5. resonance
6. Doppler effect
7. amplification
8. acoustics
9. echolocation
10. sonar

Reviewing Key Concepts

Multiple Choice *Choose the letter of the best answer.*

11. Sound is a mechanical wave, so it always
    a. travels through a vacuum
    b. has the same amplitude
    c. is made by a machine
    d. travels through matter

12. Which unit is a measure of sound frequency?
    a. hertz
    b. decibel
    c. amp
    d. meter

13. In which of the following materials would sound waves move fastest?
    a. water
    b. cool air
    c. hot air
    d. steel

14. Which of the following effects is caused by amplification?
    a. wavelength increases
    b. amplitude increases
    c. frequency decreases
    d. decibel measure decreases

15. The frequency of a sound wave determines its
    a. pitch
    b. loudness
    c. amplitude
    d. intensity

16. As sound waves travel away from their source, their
    a. intensity increases
    b. energy increases
    c. intensity decreases
    d. frequency decreases

17. A telephone mouthpiece changes sound waves into
    a. electric signals
    b. vibrations
    c. CD pits
    d. grooves on a cylinder

Short Answer *Look at the diagrams of waves below. For the next two items, choose the wave diagram that best fits the description, and explain your choice.*

a.   b.   c.

18. the sound of a basketball coach blowing a whistle during practice

19. the sound of a cow mooing in a pasture

Chapter 2: **Sound** 67

Thinking Critically

Look at the photograph of an instrument above. Write a short answer to the next two questions.

20. **HYPOTHESIZE** How might sound waves be produced using the instrument in the photograph?

21. **APPLY** How might a person playing the instrument in the photograph vary the intensity?

22. **COMMUNICATE** Two people are singing at the same pitch, yet they sound different. Explain why.

23. **SEQUENCE** Copy the following sequence chart on your paper. Write the events in the correct sequence on the chart.

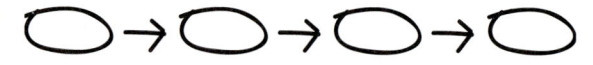

○ → ○ → ○ → ○

Events
 a. Sound waves race out from the wind chime.
 b. Forces in air gradually weaken the chime sound.
 c. A breeze makes a wind chime vibrate.
 d. A person nearby hears the wind chime.

24. **COMPARE AND CONTRAST** Write a description of the similarities and differences between each of the following pairs of terms: frequency—amplitude; intensity—amplitude; pitch—quality; fundamental tone—overtones.

Using Math in Science

Read the line graph below showing freeway noise levels at a toll collector's booth. Use the data in the graph to answer the next four questions.

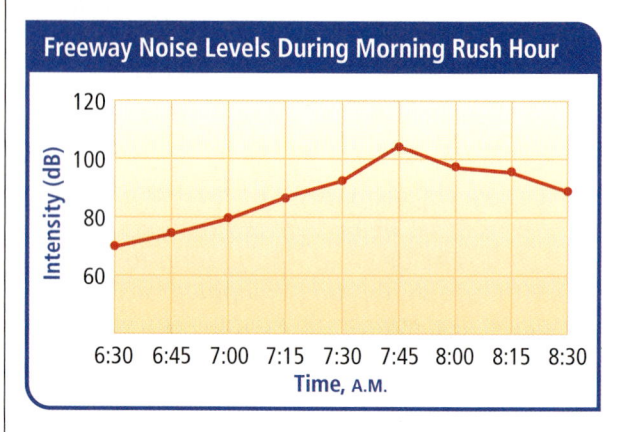

Freeway Noise Levels During Morning Rush Hour

25. Which is the noisiest quarter-hour?

26. Estimate the loudest level of sound that the toll collector is exposed to.

27. If ear protection should be worn for a sound level above 90 dB, should the toll collector wear hearing protection? If so, during which times?

28. Describe how you could turn the line graph into a bar graph. Would the bar graph be as informative? Explain your answer.

the BIG idea

29. **ANALYZE** Look back at the picture at the start of the chapter on pages 34–35. How are sound waves being produced?

30. **SUMMARIZE** Write a paragraph summarizing this chapter. Use the Big Idea on page 34 as your topic sentence. Write examples of each key concept listed on page 34.

UNIT PROJECTS

Check your schedule for your unit project. How are you doing? Be sure that you've placed data or notes from your research in your project folder.

Standardized Test Practice

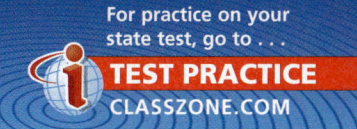

For practice on your state test, go to...
TEST PRACTICE
CLASSZONE.COM

Analyzing Experiments

Read the following description of the way scientists study animals' hearing. Then answer the questions below.

Scientists test the hearing ranges of a human by making a sound and asking the person to say whether it was heard. This cannot be done with animals. Scientists use different methods to find animals' hearing ranges. In some experiments, they train animals—by rewarding them with food or water—to make specific behaviors when they hear a sound. Another method is to study an animal's nervous system for electrical reactions to sounds.

Researchers have found that dogs and cats can hear a wide range of sounds. Both dogs and cats can hear much higher frequencies than humans can. Lizards and frogs can only hear sounds in a much narrower range than humans can. Elephants can hear a wider range than lizards and frogs but not as wide a range as dogs and cats. Elephants can hear the lowest frequency sounds of all these animals.

1. What type of behavior would be best for scientists to train animals to make as a signal that they hear a sound?
   a. a typical motion that the animal makes frequently
   b. a motion that is difficult for the animal to make
   c. a motion the animal makes rarely but does make naturally
   d. a complicated motion of several steps

2. According to the passage, which animals can hear sounds with the highest frequencies?
   a. cats
   b. elephants
   c. frogs
   d. lizards

3. The high-pitched sounds of car brakes are sometimes more bothersome to pet dogs than they are to their owners. Based on the experimental findings, what is the best explanation for that observation?
   a. The dogs hear high-intensity sounds that their owners cannot hear.
   b. The dogs hear low-intensity sounds that their owners cannot hear.
   c. The dogs hear low-frequency sounds that their owners cannot hear.
   d. The dogs hear high-frequency sounds that their owners cannot hear.

4. Which animal hears sounds with the longest wavelengths?
   a. cat
   b. dog
   c. elephant
   d. frog

Extended Response

Answer the two questions below in detail. Include some of the terms from the word box in your answer. Underline each term you use in your answer.

| amplitude | distance | Doppler effect |
| frequency | pitch | wavelength |

5. Suppose you are riding in a car down the street and pass a building where a fire alarm is sounding. Will the sound you hear change as you move up to, alongside, and past the building? Why or why not?

6. Marvin had six glass bottles that held different amounts of water. He blew air into each bottle, producing a sound. How would the sounds produced by each of the six bottles compare to the others? Why?

Chapter 2: **Sound** 69 D

CHAPTER 3
Electromagnetic Waves

the BIG idea

Electromagnetic waves transfer energy through radiation.

How does this phone stay connected?

Key Concepts

SECTION 3.1 Electromagnetic waves have unique traits.
Learn how electromagnetic waves differ from mechanical waves.

SECTION 3.2 Electromagnetic waves have many uses.
Learn about the behaviors and uses of different types of electromagnetic waves.

SECTION 3.3 The Sun is the source of most visible light.
Learn about the natural and artificial production of light.

SECTION 3.4 Light waves interact with materials.
Learn how light waves behave in a material medium.

Internet Preview

CLASSZONE.COM

Chapter 3 online resources: Content Review, Simulation, Visualization, two Resource Centers, Math Tutorial, Test Practice.

EXPLORE the BIG idea

What Melts the Ice Cubes?

Put an ice cube in each of two sandwich bags, and place the bags in sunlight. Cover one with a sheet of white paper, and cover the other with a sheet of black paper. Lift the sheets of paper every five minutes and observe the cubes. Continue until they are melted.

Observe and Think
What did you notice about the way the ice cubes melted? How can you explain what you observed?

What Is White Light Made Of?

Use the shiny side of a compact disk (CD) to reflect light from the Sun onto a sheet of white paper. If bright sunlight is not available, use a flashlight. Try holding the CD at different angles and at different distances from the paper.

Observe and Think
What did you see on the paper? Where do you think that what you observed came from?

Internet Activity: Electromagnetic Waves

Go to **ClassZone.com** to explore images of the Sun based on different wavelengths.

Observe and Think
Why can we see only some of the waves coming from the Sun?

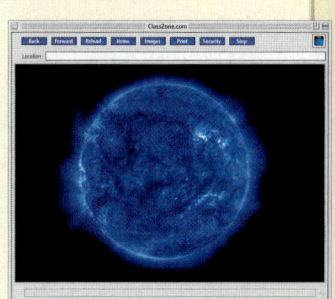

NSTA scilinks.org
SCLINKS
Light and Color Code: MDL029

Chapter 3: Electromagnetic Waves 71 D

CHAPTER 3
Getting Ready to Learn

CONCEPT REVIEW

- A wave is a disturbance that transfers energy.
- Mechanical waves have a medium.
- Waves can be measured.
- Waves react to a change in medium.

VOCABULARY REVIEW

mechanical wave p. 11
wavelength p. 17
frequency p. 17
reflection p. 25
field *See Glossary.*

CONTENT REVIEW
CLASSZONE.COM
Review concepts and vocabulary.

TAKING NOTES

SUPPORTING MAIN IDEAS

Make a chart to show main ideas and the information that supports them. Copy each blue heading. Below each heading, add supporting information, such as reasons, explanations, and examples.

VOCABULARY STRATEGY

Write each new vocabulary term in the center of a **frame game** diagram. Decide what information to frame it with. Use examples, descriptions, parts, sentences that use the term in context, or pictures. You can change the frame to fit each term.

See the Note-Taking Handbook on pages R45–R51.

SCIENCE NOTEBOOK

MAIN IDEA
Electromagnetic waves have unique properties.

→ EM waves are disturbances in a field rather than in a medium.

→ EM waves can travel through a vacuum.

→ EM waves travel at the speed of light.

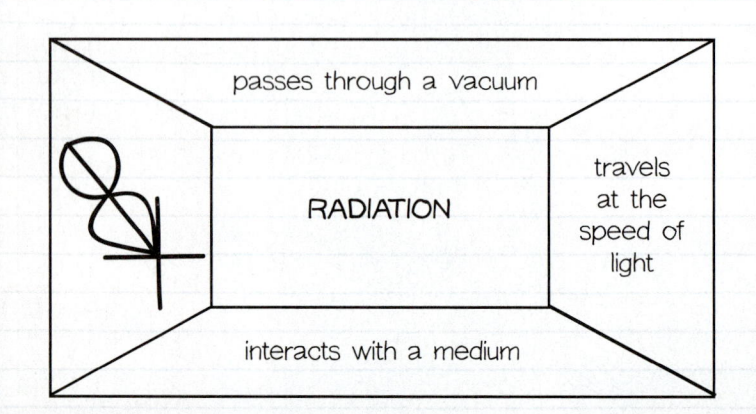

---

passes through a vacuum

RADIATION

travels at the speed of light

interacts with a medium

KEY CONCEPT
3.1 Electromagnetic waves have unique traits.

BEFORE, you learned
- Waves transfer energy
- Mechanical waves need a medium to travel

NOW, you will learn
- How electromagnetic waves differ from mechanical waves
- Where electromagnetic waves come from
- How electromagnetic waves transfer energy

VOCABULARY
electromagnetic wave p. 73
radiation p. 75

EXPLORE Electromagnetic Waves

How does the signal from a remote control travel?

PROCEDURE

1. Turn the TV on and off using the remote control.
2. Work with a partner to try to turn on the TV by aiming the remote control at the mirror.

MATERIALS
- TV with remote control unit
- mirror with stand

WHAT DO YOU THINK?
How did you have to position the remote control and the mirror in order to operate the TV? Why do you think this worked?

An electromagnetic wave is a disturbance in a field.

Did you know that you are surrounded by thousands of waves at this very moment? Waves fill every cubic centimeter of the space around you. They collide with or pass through your body all the time.

Most of these waves are invisible, but you can perceive many of them. Light is made up of these waves, and heat can result from them. Whenever you use your eyes to see, or feel the warmth of the Sun on your skin, you are detecting their presence. These waves also allow radios, TVs, and cell phones to send or receive information over long distances. These waves have the properties shared by all waves, yet they are different from mechanical waves in important ways. This second type of wave is called an electromagnetic wave. An **electromagnetic wave** (ih-LEHK-troh-mag-NEHT-ihk) is a disturbance that transfers energy through a field. Electromagnetic waves are also called EM (EE-EHM) waves.

VOCABULARY
Create a frame game diagram for the term *electromagnetic wave*.

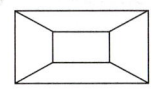

Chapter 3: **Electromagnetic Waves** 73 D

A field is an area around an object where the object can apply a force—a push or a pull—to another object without touching it. You have seen force applied through a field if you have ever seen a magnet holding a card on the door of a refrigerator. The magnet exerts a pull on the door, even though it does not touch the door. The magnet exerts a force through the magnetic field that surrounds the magnet. When a disturbance occurs in an electric or magnetic field rather than in a medium, the wave that results is an electromagnetic wave.

VISUALIZATION
CLASSZONE.COM
Learn more about the nature of EM waves.

How EM Waves Form

EM waves occur when electrically charged atomic particles move. Charged particles exert an electric force on each other, so they have electric fields. A moving charged particle creates a magnetic force, so a moving charge also has a magnetic field around it.

When electrically charged particles move quickly, they can start a disturbance of electric and magnetic fields. The fields vibrate at right angles to each other, as shown in the diagram above. The EM wave travels in the form of these vibrating fields. As you read in Chapter 1, waves have the properties of wavelength and frequency. In an EM wave, both the electric and the magnetic fields have these properties.

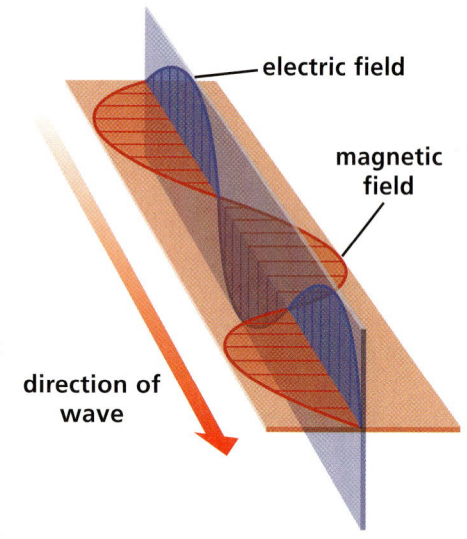

CHECK YOUR READING What are the two types of fields that make up an EM wave?

Sources of EM Waves

Many of the EM waves present in Earth's environment come from the Sun. The Sun's high temperature allows it to give off countless EM waves. Other stars give off as many EM waves as the Sun, but because these bodies are so far away, fewer of their EM waves reach Earth. In addition to the Sun, technology is a source of EM waves that humans use for a wide variety of purposes.

EM waves from the Sun provide most of the energy for the environment on Earth. Some of the energy goes into Earth's surface, which then gives off EM waves of different wavelengths.

CHECK YOUR READING What are two sources of EM waves on Earth?

Electromagnetic waves can travel in a vacuum.

Energy that moves in the form of EM waves is called **radiation** (RAY-dee-AY-shuhn). Radiation is different from the transfer of energy through a medium by a mechanical wave. A mechanical wave must vibrate the medium as it moves, and this uses some of the wave's energy. Eventually, every mechanical wave will give up all of its energy to the medium and disappear. An EM wave can travel without a material medium—that is, in a vacuum or space empty of matter—and does not lose energy as it moves. In theory, an EM wave can travel forever.

READING TIP

EM waves are also called rays. The words *radiation* and *radiate* come from the Latin word *radius*, which means "ray" or "spoke of a wheel."

How EM Waves Travel in a Vacuum

Because they do not need a medium, EM waves can pass through outer space, which is a near vacuum. Also, because they do not give up energy in traveling, EM waves can cross the great distances that separate stars and galaxies. For example, rays from the Sun travel about 150 million kilometers (93 million mi) to reach Earth. Rays from the most distant galaxies travel for billions of years before reaching Earth.

Usually, EM waves spread outward in all directions from the source of the disturbance. The waves then travel until something interferes with them. The farther the waves move from their source, the more they spread out. As they spread out, there are fewer waves in a given area and less energy is transferred. Only a very small part of the energy radiated from the Sun is transferred to Earth. But that energy is still a great amount—enough to sustain life on the planet.

The Speed of EM Waves in a Vacuum

In a vacuum, EM waves travel at a constant speed, and they travel very fast—about 300,000 kilometers (186,000 mi) per second. In 1 second, an EM wave can travel a distance greater than 7 times the distance around Earth. Even at this speed, rays from the Sun take about 8 minutes to reach Earth. This constant speed is called the speed of light. The vast distances of space are often measured in units of time traveled at this speed. For example, the Sun is about 8 light-minutes away from Earth. The galaxy shown in the photograph is 60 million light-years from Earth.

The light and other EM waves from this galaxy took approximately 60 million years to reach Earth.

CHECK YOUR READING How are EM waves used to measure distances in space?

Chapter 3: Electromagnetic Waves 75 D

MATH in SCIENCE

SKILL: USING EXPONENTS

MATH TUTORIAL
CLASSZONE.COM

Click on Math Tutorial for more help with positive and negative exponents.

EM Frequencies

The Chandra X-Ray Observatory in the photograph is a space telescope that detects high-frequency EM waves called x-rays. A wave's frequency is the number of peaks that pass a given point in 1 second. EM frequencies usually run from about 100 Hz to about 1 trillion trillion Hz. If written in standard form (using zeros), 1 trillion trillion would look like this:

1,000,000,000,000,000,000,000,000

Because this number is hard to read, it would be helpful to write it more simply. Using exponents, 1 trillion trillion can be written as **10^{24}**.

Exponents can also be used to simplify very small numbers. For example, the wavelength of a wave with a frequency of 10^{24} Hz is about one ten-thousandth of one trillionth of a meter. That number can be written in standard form as **0.000,000,000,000,000,1 m**. Using exponents, the number can be written more simply as **10^{-16} m**.

Examples

Large Numbers

To write a multiple of 10 in exponent form, just count the zeros. Then, use the total as the exponent.

(1) 10,000 has 4 zeros.

(2) 4 is the exponent.

ANSWER 10^4 is the way to write 10,000 using exponents.

Decimals

To convert a decimal into exponent form, count the number of places to the right of the decimal point. Then, use the total with a negative sign as the exponent.

(1) 0.000,001 has 6 places to the right of the decimal point.

(2) Add a negative sign to make the exponent −6.

ANSWER 10^{-6} is the way to write 0.000,001 using exponents.

Answer the following questions.

Write each number using an exponent.
1. 10,000,000
2. 0.000,01
3. 100,000
4. 0.0001
5. 10,000,000,000
6. 0.000,000,001

Write the number in standard form.
7. 10^8
8. 10^{-8}
9. 10^{11}
10. 10^{-12}
11. 10^{17}
12. 10^{-15}

CHALLENGE Using exponents, multiply 10^2 by 10^3. Explain how you got your result.

The top photograph shows a visible-light image of the Crab Nebula. The bottom photograph shows the same nebula as it appears at higher x-ray frequencies.

D 78 Unit: Waves, Sound, and Light

KEY CONCEPT
3.2 Electromagnetic waves have many uses.

BEFORE, you learned
- EM waves transfer energy through fields
- EM waves have measurable properties
- EM waves interact with matter

NOW, you will learn
- How EM waves differ from one another
- How different types of EM waves are used

VOCABULARY
electromagnetic spectrum p. 80
radio waves p. 82
microwaves p. 83
visible light p. 84
infrared light p. 84
ultraviolet light p. 85
x-rays p. 86
gamma rays p. 86

EXPLORE Radio Waves
How can you make radio waves?

PROCEDURE

1. Tape one end of one length of wire to one end of the battery. Tape one end of the second wire to the other end of the battery.
2. Wrap the loose end of one of the wires tightly around the handle of the fork.
3. Turn on the radio to the AM band and move the selector past all stations until you reach static.
4. Hold the fork close to the radio. Gently pull the free end of wire across the fork's prongs.

WHAT DO YOU THINK?
- What happens when you stroke the prongs with the wire?
- How does changing the position of the dial affect the results?

MATERIALS
- two 25 cm lengths of copper wire
- C or D battery
- electrical tape
- metal fork
- portable radio

EM waves have different frequencies.

It might seem hard to believe that the same form of energy browns your toast, brings you broadcast television, and makes the page you are now reading visible. Yet EM waves make each of these events possible. The various types of EM waves differ from each other in their wavelengths and frequencies.

The frequency of an EM wave also determines its characteristics and uses. Higher-frequency EM waves, with more electromagnetic vibrations per second, have more energy. Lower-frequency EM waves, with longer wavelengths, have less energy.

REMINDER
Remember that frequency is the number of waves that pass a given point per second. The shorter the wavelength, the higher the frequency.

Chapter 3: **Electromagnetic Waves** 79 D

RESOURCE CENTER
CLASSZONE.COM

Learn more about the electromagnetic spectrum.

The Electromagnetic Spectrum

The range of all EM frequencies is known as the **electromagnetic spectrum** (SPEHK-truhm), or EM spectrum. The spectrum can be represented by a diagram like the one below. On the left are the waves with the longest wavelengths and the lowest frequencies and energies. Toward the right, the wavelengths become shorter, and the frequencies and energies become higher. The diagram also shows different parts of the spectrum: radio waves, microwaves, infrared light, visible light, ultraviolet light, x-rays, and gamma rays.

The EM spectrum is a smooth, gradual progression from the lowest frequencies to the highest. Divisions between the different parts of the spectrum are useful, but not exact. As you can see from the diagram below, some of the sections overlap.

The Electromagnetic Spectrum

Frequency in Hertz (1 hertz = 1 wavelength/second)

10^4 10^5 10^6 10^7 10^8 10^9 10^{10} 10^{11} 10^{12} 10^{13}

Radio Waves

Microwaves

Infrared Light

This woman is speaking on the radio. **Radio waves** are used for radio and television broadcasts. They are also used for cordless phones, garage door openers, alarm systems, and baby monitors.

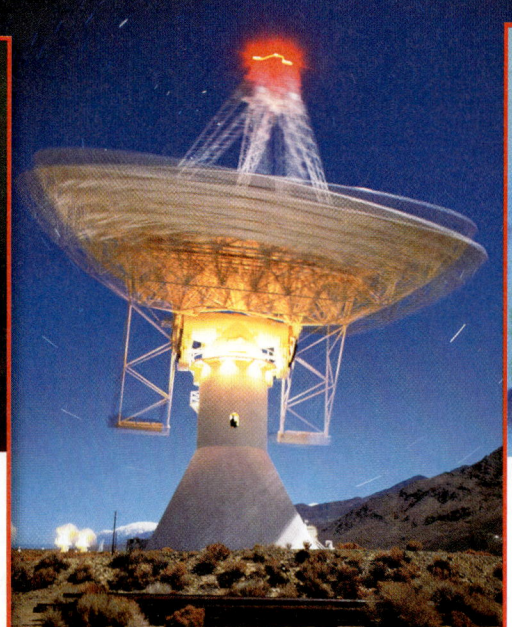

Not all astronomy involves visible light. Telescopes like the one above pick up **microwaves** from space. Microwaves are also used for radar, cell phones, ovens, and satellite communications.

The amount of **infrared light** an object gives off depends on its temperature. Above, different colors indicate different amounts of infrared light.

D   80   Unit: Waves, Sound, and Light

Measuring EM Waves

Because all EM waves move at the same speed in a vacuum, the frequency of an EM wave can be determined from its wavelength. EM wavelengths run from about 30 kilometers for the lowest-frequency radio waves to trillionths of a centimeter for gamma rays. EM waves travel so quickly that even those with the largest wavelengths have very high frequencies. For example, a low-energy radio wave with a wavelength of 30 kilometers has a frequency of 10,000 cycles per second.

EM wave frequency is measured in hertz (Hz). One hertz equals one cycle per second. The frequency of the 30-kilometer radio wave mentioned above would be 10,000 Hz. Gamma ray frequencies reach trillions of trillions of hertz.

SUPPORTING MAIN IDEAS
Write details that support the main idea that EM waves form a spectrum based on frequency.

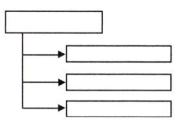

CHECK YOUR READING Why is wavelength all you need to know to calculate EM wave frequency in a vacuum?

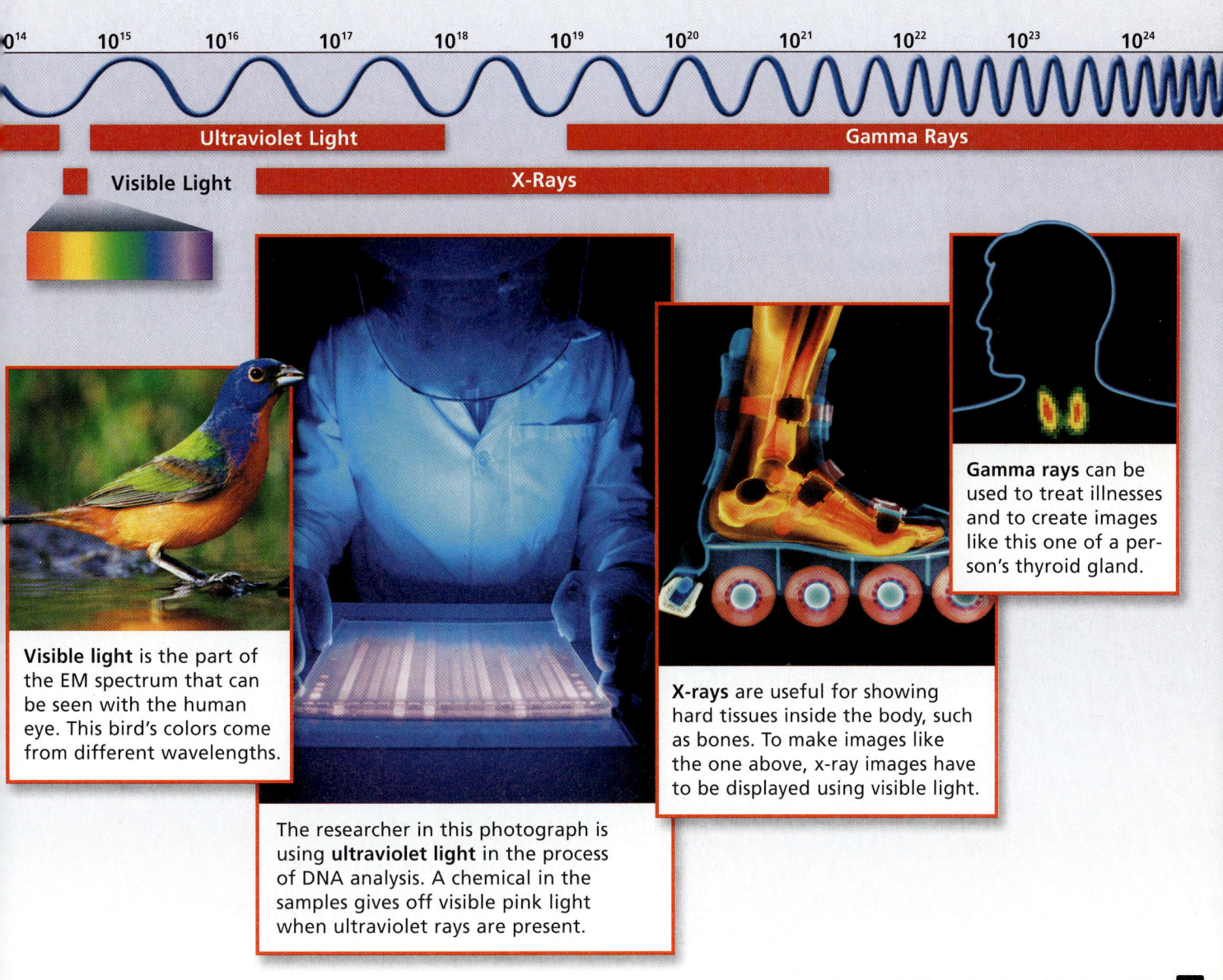

10^{14} 10^{15} 10^{16} 10^{17} 10^{18} 10^{19} 10^{20} 10^{21} 10^{22} 10^{23} 10^{24}

Ultraviolet Light

Gamma Rays

Visible Light

X-Rays

Visible light is the part of the EM spectrum that can be seen with the human eye. This bird's colors come from different wavelengths.

The researcher in this photograph is using **ultraviolet light** in the process of DNA analysis. A chemical in the samples gives off visible pink light when ultraviolet rays are present.

X-rays are useful for showing hard tissues inside the body, such as bones. To make images like the one above, x-ray images have to be displayed using visible light.

Gamma rays can be used to treat illnesses and to create images like this one of a person's thyroid gland.

Chapter 3: **Electromagnetic Waves** 81

Radio waves and microwaves have long wavelengths and low frequencies.

Radio waves are EM waves that have the longest wavelengths, the lowest frequencies, and the lowest energies. Radio waves travel easily through the atmosphere and many materials. People have developed numerous technologies to take advantage of the properties of radio waves.

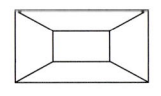

Radio Waves

Radio was the first technology to use EM waves for telecommunication, which is communication over long distances. A radio transmitter converts sound waves into radio waves and broadcasts them in different directions. Radio receivers in many locations pick up the radio waves and convert them back into sound waves.

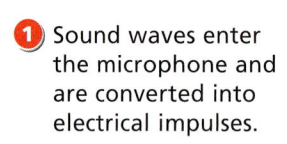

VOCABULARY
Make a frame game diagram for *radio waves* and the other types of EM waves.

1 Sound waves enter the microphone and are converted into electrical impulses.

2 The electrical impulses are converted into radio waves and broadcast by the transmitter.

3 The radio waves reach a radio receiver and are converted back into sound.

AM Signal

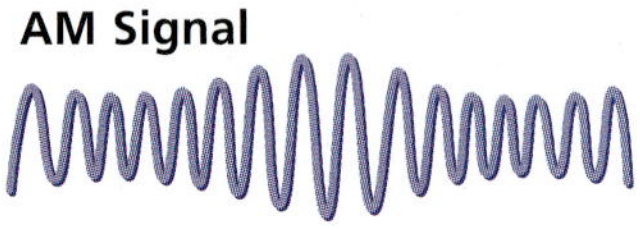

Information is encoded in the signal by varying the radio wave's amplitude.

FM Signal

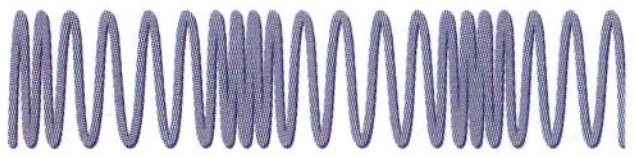

Information is encoded in the signal by varying the radio wave's frequency.

Different radio stations broadcast radio waves at different frequencies. To pick up a particular station, you have to tune your radio to the frequency for that station. The numbers you see on the radio—such as 670 or 99.5—are frequencies.

Simply transmitting EM waves at a certain frequency is not enough to send music, words, or other meaningful sounds. To do that, the radio transmitter must attach information about the sounds to the radio signal. The transmitter attaches the information by modulating—that is, changing—the waves slightly. Two common ways of modulating radio waves are varying the amplitude of the waves and varying the frequency of the waves. Amplitude modulation is used for AM radio, and frequency modulation is used for FM radio.

You might be surprised to learn that broadcast television also uses radio waves. The picture part of a TV signal is transmitted using an AM signal. The sound part is transmitted using an FM signal.

CHECK YOUR READING What two properties of EM waves are used to attach information to radio signals?

Microwaves

A type of EM waves called microwaves comes next on the EM spectrum. **Microwaves** are EM waves with shorter wavelengths, higher frequencies, and higher energy than other radio waves. Microwaves get their name from the fact that their wavelengths are generally shorter than those of radio waves. Two important technologies that use microwaves are radar and cell phones.

Radar The term *radar* stands for "radio detection and ranging." Radar came into wide use during World War II (1939–1945) as a way of detecting aircraft and ships from a distance and estimating their locations. Radar works by transmitting microwaves, receiving reflections of the waves from objects the waves strike, and converting these patterns into visual images on a screen. Today, radar technology is used to control air traffic at airports, analyze weather conditions, and measure the speed of a moving vehicle.

Radar led to the invention of the microwave oven. The discovery that microwaves could be used to cook food was made by accident when microwaves melted a candy bar inside a researcher's pocket.

Cell Phones A cell phone is actually a radio transmitter and receiver that uses microwaves. Cell phones depend on an overlapping network of cells, or areas of land several kilometers in diameter. Each cell has at its center a tower that sends and receives microwave signals. The tower connects cell phones inside the cell to each other or to the regular wire-based telephone system. These two connecting paths are shown below.

> **READING TiP**
> As you read about the different categories of EM waves, refer to the diagram on pages 80 and 81.

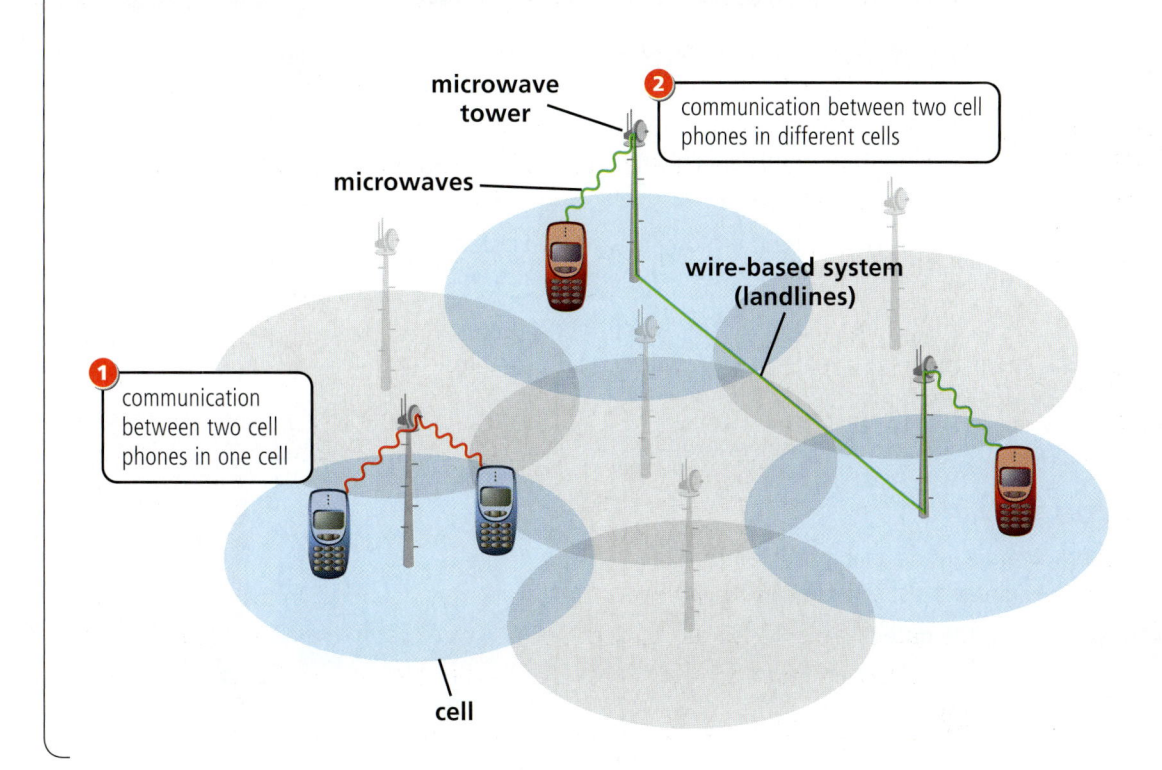

- microwave tower
- microwaves
- ② communication between two cell phones in different cells
- wire-based system (landlines)
- ① communication between two cell phones in one cell
- cell

Chapter 3: **Electromagnetic Waves** 83

Infrared, visible, and ultraviolet light have mid-range wavelengths and frequencies.

Visible light is the part of the EM spectrum that human eyes can see. It lies between 10^{14} Hz and 10^{15} Hz. We perceive the longest wavelengths of visible light as red and the shortest as violet. This narrow band is very small compared with the rest of the spectrum. In fact, visible light is only about 1/100,000 of the complete EM spectrum. The area below visible light and above microwaves is the infrared part of the EM spectrum. Above visible light is the ultraviolet part of the spectrum. You will read more about visible light in the next section.

READING TIP
Infrared means "below red." *Ultraviolet* means "beyond violet."

Infrared Light

The **infrared light** part of the spectrum consists of EM frequencies between microwaves and visible light. Infrared radiation is the type of EM wave most often associated with heat. Waves in this range are sometimes called heat rays. Although you cannot see infrared radiation, you can feel it as warmth coming from the Sun, a fire, or a radiator. Infrared lamps are used to provide warmth in bathrooms and to keep food warm after it is cooked. Infrared rays also help to cook food—for example, in a toaster or over charcoal.

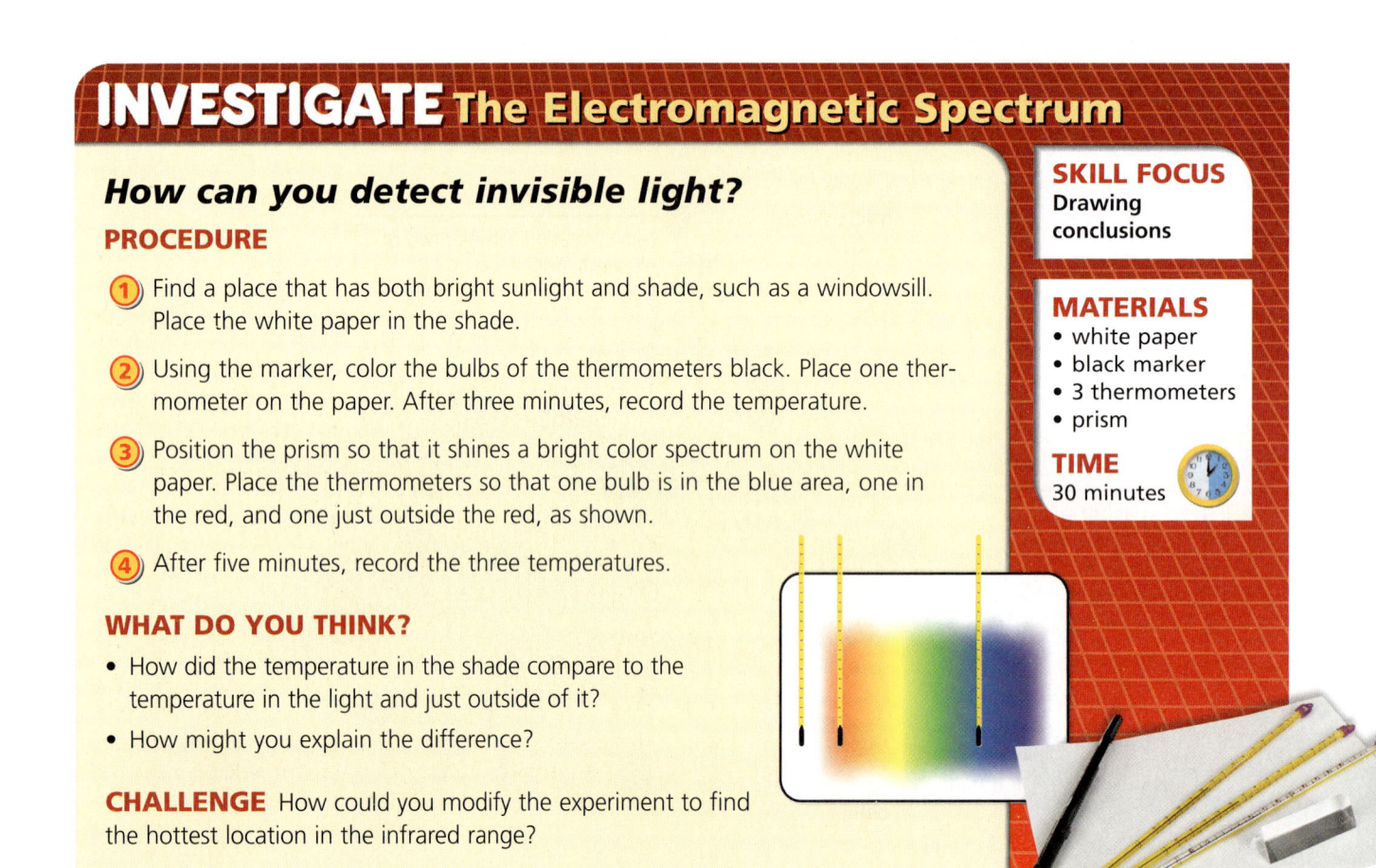

INVESTIGATE The Electromagnetic Spectrum

How can you detect invisible light?
PROCEDURE

1. Find a place that has both bright sunlight and shade, such as a windowsill. Place the white paper in the shade.
2. Using the marker, color the bulbs of the thermometers black. Place one thermometer on the paper. After three minutes, record the temperature.
3. Position the prism so that it shines a bright color spectrum on the white paper. Place the thermometers so that one bulb is in the blue area, one in the red, and one just outside the red, as shown.
4. After five minutes, record the three temperatures.

WHAT DO YOU THINK?
- How did the temperature in the shade compare to the temperature in the light and just outside of it?
- How might you explain the difference?

CHALLENGE How could you modify the experiment to find the hottest location in the infrared range?

SKILL FOCUS
Drawing conclusions

MATERIALS
- white paper
- black marker
- 3 thermometers
- prism

TIME
30 minutes

Some animals, such as pit viper snakes, can actually see infrared light. Normally, human beings cannot see infrared light. However, infrared scopes and cameras convert infrared radiation into visible wavelengths. They do this by representing different levels of infrared radiation with different colors of visible light. This technology can create useful images of objects based on the objects' temperatures.

CHECK YOUR READING How do human beings perceive infrared radiation?

In this infrared image, warmer areas appear red and orange, while cooler ones appear blue, green, and purple.

Ultraviolet Light

The **ultraviolet light** part of the EM spectrum consists of frequencies above those of visible light and partially below those of x-rays. Because ultraviolet (UV) light has higher frequencies than visible light, it also carries more energy. The waves in this range can damage your skin and eyes. Sunblock and UV-protection sunglasses are designed to filter out these frequencies.

Ultraviolet light has beneficial effects as well. Because it can damage cells, UV light can be used to sterilize medical instruments and food by killing harmful bacteria. In addition, UV light causes skin cells to produce vitamin D, which is essential to good health. Ultraviolet light can also be used to treat skin problems and other medical conditions.

Like infrared light, ultraviolet light is visible to some animals. Bees and other insects can see higher frequencies than people can. They see nectar guides—marks that show where nectar is located—that people cannot see with visible light. The photographs below show how one flower might look to a person and to a bee.

This photograph shows the flower as it appears in visible light.

This photograph shows the flower as it might appear to a bee in ultraviolet light. Bees are able to see nectar guides in the UV range.

Chapter 3: **Electromagnetic Waves** 85

X-rays and gamma rays have short wavelengths and high frequencies.

At the opposite end of the EM spectrum from radio waves are x-rays and gamma rays. Both have very high frequencies and energies. **X-rays** have frequencies from about 10^{16} Hz to 10^{21} Hz. **Gamma rays** have frequencies from about 10^{19} Hz to more than 10^{24} Hz. Like other EM waves, x-rays and gamma rays are produced by the Sun and by other stars. People have also developed technologies that use these EM frequencies.

X-rays allow us to see inside the body.

X-rays pass easily through the soft tissues of the body, but many are absorbed by denser matter such as bone. If photographic film is placed behind the body and x-rays are aimed at the film, only the x-rays that pass through the body will expose the film. This makes x-ray images useful for diagnosing bone fractures and finding dense tumors. But too much exposure to x-rays can damage tissue. Even in small doses, repeated exposure to x-rays can cause cancer over time. When you have your teeth x-rayed, you usually wear a vest made out of lead for protection. Lead blocks high-frequency radiation.

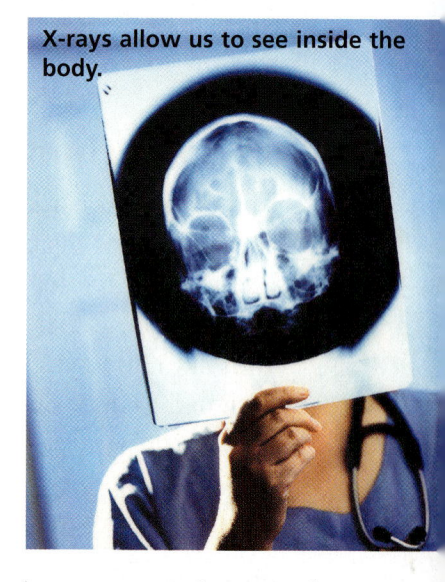

Gamma rays have the highest frequencies and energies of any EM waves. Gamma rays are produced by some radioactive substances as well as by the Sun and other stars. Gamma rays can penetrate the soft and the hard tissues of the body, killing normal cells and causing cancer cells to develop. If carefully controlled, this destructive power can be beneficial. Doctors can also use gamma rays to kill cancer cells and fight tumors.

3.2 Review

KEY CONCEPTS

1. What two properties of EM waves change from one end of the EM spectrum to the other?
2. Describe two uses for microwave radiation.
3. How are EM waves used in dentistry and medicine?

CRITICAL THINKING

4. **Infer** Why do you think remote controls for TVs, VCRs, and stereos use infrared light rather than ultraviolet light?
5. **Apply** For a camera to make images of where heat is escaping from a building in winter, what type of EM wave would it need to record?

CHALLENGE

6. **Synthesize** When a person in a car is talking on a cell phone, and the car moves from one cell to another, the conversation continues without interruption. How might this be possible?

Think SCIENCE

SKILL: DETERMINING RELEVANCE

Are Cell Phones Harmful?

In 1993, a man appearing on a popular television talk show claimed that cell phone radiation had caused his wife's brain cancer. Since that time, concerned scientists have conducted more than a dozen studies. None of them have shown clear evidence of a connection between cell phones and cancer. However, researchers have made a number of experimental observations.

▷ Experimental Observations

Here are some results from scientists' investigations.

1. Substances that cause cancer work by breaking chemical bonds in DNA.
2. Only EM radiation at ultraviolet frequencies and above can break chemical bonds.
3. Microwave radiation may make it easier for molecules called free radicals to damage DNA bonds.
4. Other factors such as psychological stress may cause breaks in DNA bonds.
5. Performing multiple tasks like driving and talking on the phone reduces the brain's ability to perform either task.
6. Exposing the brain to microwave radiation may slow reaction times.

▷ Hypotheses

Here are some hypotheses that could be used for further research.

A. Microwaves from cell phones can break DNA bonds.
B. Cell phones may contribute to cancer.
C. Holding and talking into a cell phone while driving increases a person's risk of having an accident.
D. Worrying about cell phones may be a health risk.

▷ Determining Relevance

On Your Own On a piece of paper, write down each hypothesis. Next to the hypothesis write each observation that you think is relevant. Include your reasons.

As a Group Discuss how each observation on your list is or is not relevant to a particular hypothesis.

CHALLENGE Based on the observations listed above, write a question that you think would be a good basis for a further experiment. Then explain how the answer to this question would be helpful.

Talking on a cell phone while driving may increase the risk of accidents.

Chapter 3: **Electromagnetic Waves** 87

KEY CONCEPT
3.3 The Sun is the source of most visible light.

BEFORE, you learned
- Visible light is part of the EM spectrum
- EM waves are produced both in nature and by technology

NOW, you will learn
- How visible light is produced by materials at high temperatures
- How some living organisms produce light
- How humans produce light artificially

VOCABULARY
incandescence p. 89
luminescence p. 89
bioluminescence p. 89
fluorescence p. 91

THINK ABOUT

Why is light important?

This railroad worm has eleven pairs of green lights on its sides and a red light on its head. The animal probably uses these lights for illumination and to frighten away predators. Almost every living organism, including humans, depends on visible light. Think of as many different ways as you can that plants, animals, and people use light. Then, think of all the sources of visible light that you know of, both natural and artificial. Why is light important to living organisms?

Light comes from the Sun and other natural sources.

RESOURCE CENTER
CLASSZONE.COM
Learn more about visible light.

It is hard to imagine life without light. Human beings depend on vision in countless ways, and they depend on light for vision. Light is the only form of EM radiation for which human bodies have specialized sensory organs. The human eye is extremely sensitive to light and color and the many kinds of information they convey.

Most animals depend on visible light to find food and to do other things necessary for their survival. Green plants need light to make their own food. Plants, in turn, supply food directly or indirectly for nearly all other living creatures. With very few exceptions, living creatures depend on light for their existence.

CHECK YOUR READING How is plants' use of light important to animals?

D 88 Unit: Waves, Sound, and Light

Most of the visible light waves in the environment come from the Sun. The Sun's high temperature produces light of every wavelength. The production of light by materials at high temperatures is called **incandescence** (IHN-kuhn-DEHS-uhns). When a material gets hot enough, it gives off light by glowing or by bursting into flames.

Other than the Sun, few natural sources of incandescent light strongly affect life on Earth. Most other stars give off as much light as the Sun, or even more, but little light from stars reaches Earth because they are so far away. Lightning produces bright, short-lived bursts of light. Fire, which can occur naturally, is a lower-level, longer-lasting source of visible light. The ability to make and use fire was one of the first light technologies, making it possible for human beings to see on a dark night or inside a cave.

CHECK YOUR READING   Why does little light reach Earth from stars other than the Sun?

Some living things produce visible light.

Many organisms produce their own visible light, which they use in a variety of ways. They produce this light through luminescence. **Luminescence** is the production of light without the high temperatures needed for incandescence. The production of light by living organisms is called **bioluminescence.** Bioluminescent organisms produce light from chemical reactions rather than from intense heat. Bioluminescence enables organisms to produce light inside their tissues without being harmed.

Bioluminescent organisms include insects, worms, fish, squid, jellyfish, bacteria, and fungi. Some of these creatures have light-producing organs that are highly complex. These organs might include light-producing cells but also reflectors, lenses, and even color filters.

The firefly, a type of beetle, uses bioluminescence to attract mates. A chemical reaction in its abdomen allows the firefly to glow at specific intervals. The pattern of glowing helps fireflies of the same species identify each other at night. Most often, the male flashes a signal while flying, and the female responds with a flash. After they have identified each other, the fireflies may continue to exchange flashes until the male has located the female.

VOCABULARY
Don't forget to make word frames for the terms *luminescence* and *bioluminescence.*

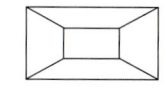

Chapter 3: **Electromagnetic Waves** 89

The process of bioluminescence is very efficient. Almost all of the energy released by the chemical reactions of bioluminescence is converted into light. Very little heat is produced. Researchers in lighting technology wanted for years to imitate this efficiency, and that became possible with the development of light-emitting diodes (LEDs). LEDs produce little heat, converting almost all of the incoming electrical energy into light.

CHECK YOUR READING How is bioluminescence different from incandescence?

A female firefly responds to a male's signal.

Human technologies produce visible light.

Human beings invented the first artificial lighting when they learned to make and control fire. For most of human history, people have made light with devices that use fire in some form, such as oil lamps, candles, and natural gas lamps. After the discovery of electricity, people began to make light through a means other than fire. However, the technique of using a very hot material as a light source stayed the same until the invention of fluorescent lighting. In recent years, "cool" lighting has become much more common.

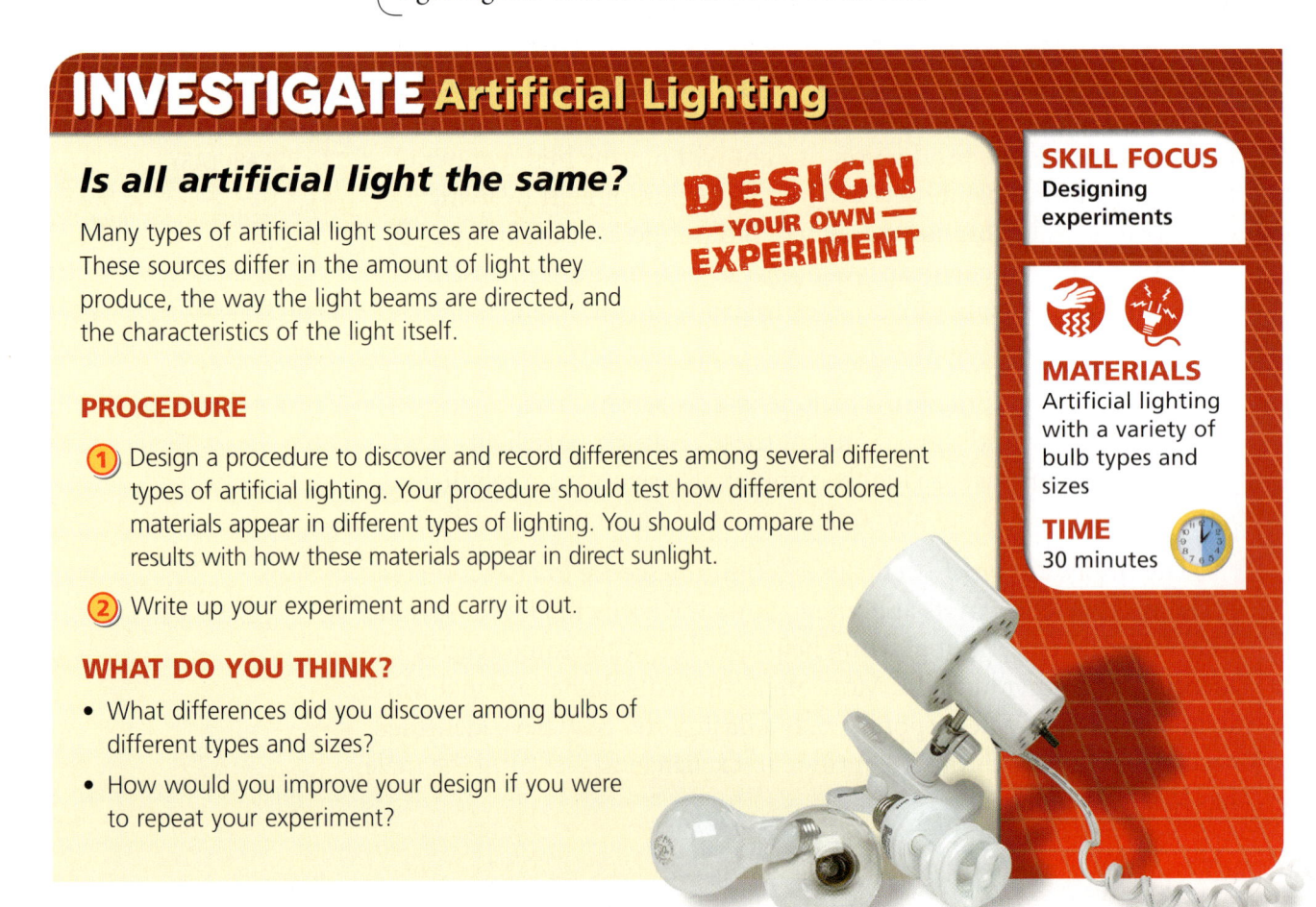

INVESTIGATE Artificial Lighting

Is all artificial light the same?
Many types of artificial light sources are available. These sources differ in the amount of light they produce, the way the light beams are directed, and the characteristics of the light itself.

DESIGN YOUR OWN EXPERIMENT

PROCEDURE

1. Design a procedure to discover and record differences among several different types of artificial lighting. Your procedure should test how different colored materials appear in different types of lighting. You should compare the results with how these materials appear in direct sunlight.
2. Write up your experiment and carry it out.

WHAT DO YOU THINK?
- What differences did you discover among bulbs of different types and sizes?
- How would you improve your design if you were to repeat your experiment?

SKILL FOCUS
Designing experiments

MATERIALS
Artificial lighting with a variety of bulb types and sizes

TIME
30 minutes

Unit: Waves, Sound, and Light

Incandescent and Fluorescent Lighting

The development of the electric light bulb in the late 1800s made light available at a touch. An ordinary light bulb is a sealed glass tube with a thin tungsten wire running through it. This wire is called a filament. When electrical current passes through the filament, the tungsten gets hotter and begins to glow. Because these light bulbs use high temperatures to produce light, they are called incandescent bulbs.

Tungsten can become very hot—about 3500 degrees Celsius (6300°F)—without melting. At such high temperatures, tungsten gives off a bright light. However, the tungsten filament also produces much infrared radiation. In fact, the filament produces more infrared light than visible light. As a result, incandescent bulbs waste a lot of energy that ends up as heat. At such high temperatures, tungsten also slowly evaporates and collects on the inside of the bulb. Eventually, the filament weakens and breaks, and the bulb burns out.

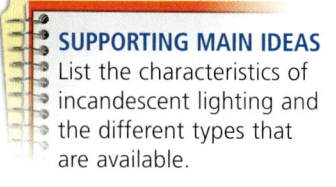

SUPPORTING MAIN IDEAS
List the characteristics of incandescent lighting and the different types that are available.

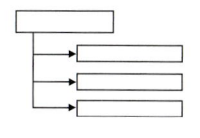

CHECK YOUR READING What causes ordinary light bulbs to burn out?

Since the 1980s, halogen (HAL-uh-juhn) bulbs have come into wide use. Halogen bulbs have several advantages over ordinary incandescent bulbs. They contain a gas from the halogen group. This gas combines with evaporating tungsten atoms and deposits the tungsten back onto the filament. As a result, the filament lasts longer. The filament can also be raised to a higher temperature without damage, so it produces more light. Halogen bulbs, which are made of quartz, resist heat better than glass.

Incandescent Light Bulb
- tungsten filament 
- glass bulb

Halogen Light Bulb
- tungsten filament
- halogen gas mixture
- quartz bulb

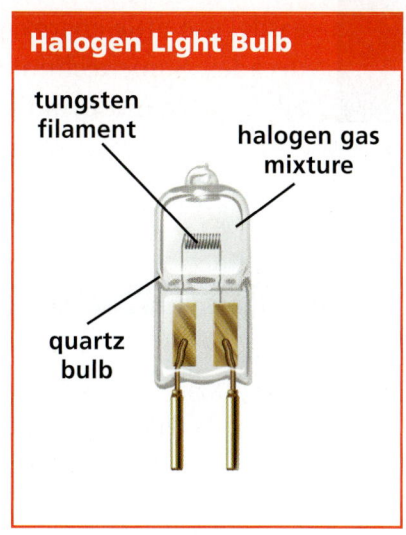

Fluorescent Light Bulb
- mercury vapor and other gases
- phosphor coating
- electric current
- electrode

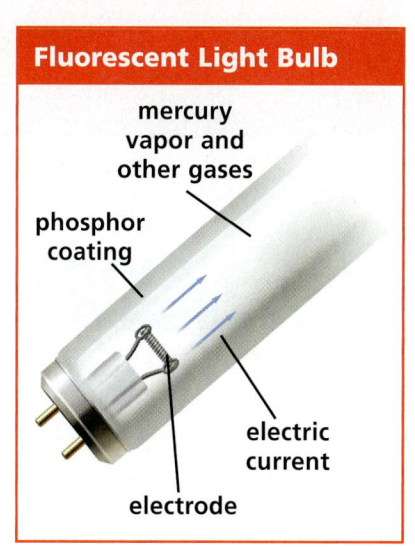

Many electric lights in use today are fluorescent. **Fluorescence** (flu-REHS-uhns) occurs when a material absorbs EM radiation of one wavelength and gives off EM radiation of another. Fluorescent bulbs are filled with a mixture of mercury vapor and other gases that give off ultraviolet light when an electric current passes through them.

Chapter 3: **Electromagnetic Waves** 91

The insides of the bulbs are coated with a powder called phosphor that fluoresces. Phosphor absorbs ultraviolet light and gives off visible light. Because fluorescent lighting is cool and does not waste much energy as heat, it is more efficient and more economical than incandescent lighting.

CHECK YOUR READING Why are fluorescent lights more efficient than incandescent lights?

Other Types of Artificial Lighting

Like fluorescent lights, many other artificial light sources use a gas in place of a filament. For example, neon lights use gas-filled tubes to produce light. However, instead of ultraviolet light, the gas gives off visible light directly. The colors of neon lights come from the particular mixtures of gases and filters used. Vapor lights, which are commonly used for street lights, work in a similar way. In a vapor light, a material such as sodium is heated until it becomes a gas, or vapor. The vapor responds to an electric current by glowing brightly.

One of fastest-growing types of artificial lighting is the light emitting diode, or LED. LEDs do not involve bulbs, filaments, or gases. Instead, they produce light electronically. A diode is a type of semiconductor—a device that regulates electric current. An LED is a semiconductor that converts electric energy directly into visible light.

LEDs have many advantages over traditional forms of lighting. They produce a very bright light, do not break easily, use little energy, produce little heat, and can last for decades. Some technologists believe that LEDs will eventually replace most traditional forms of artificial lighting.

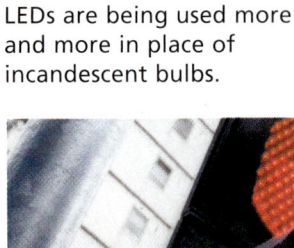

LEDs are being used more and more in place of incandescent bulbs.

3.3 Review

KEY CONCEPTS
1. Describe natural, nonliving sources of incandescent light.
2. What advantages does bioluminescence have over incandescence as a way for living organisms to produce light?
3. What are some advantages and disadvantages of artificial incandescent lighting?

CRITICAL THINKING
4. **Classify** Make a chart summarizing the different types of artificial lighting discussed in this section.
5. **Infer** Why do you think moonlight does not warm you, even though the Moon reflects light from the hot Sun?

CHALLENGE
6. **Compare and Contrast** What does LED lighting have in common with bioluminescence? How are the two different?

92 Unit: Waves, Sound, and Light

KEY CONCEPT
3.4 Light waves interact with materials.

◀ **BEFORE, you learned**
- Mechanical waves respond to a change in medium
- Visible light is made up of EM waves
- EM waves interact with a new medium in the same ways that mechanical waves do

▶ **NOW, you will learn**
- How the wave behavior of light affects what we see
- How light waves interact with materials
- Why objects have color
- How different colors are produced

VOCABULARY

transmission p. 93
absorption p. 93
scattering p. 95
polarization p. 96
prism p. 97
primary colors p. 98
primary pigments p. 99

EXPLORE Light and Matter

How can a change in medium affect light?

PROCEDURE

1. Fill the container with water.
2. Add 10 mL (2 tsp) of milk to the water. Put on the lid, and gently shake the container until the milk and water are mixed.
3. In a dark room, shine the light at one side of the container from about 5 cm (2 in.) away. Observe what happens to the beam of light.

MATERIALS
- clear plastic container with lid
- water
- measuring spoons
- milk
- flashlight

WHAT DO YOU THINK?
- What happened to the beam of light from the flashlight?
- Why did the light behave in this way?

Light can be reflected, transmitted, or absorbed.

You have read that EM waves can interact with a material medium in the same ways that mechanical waves do. Three forms of interaction play an especially important role in how people see light. One form is reflection. Most things are visible because they reflect light. The two other forms of interaction are transmission and absorption.

Transmission (trans-MIHSH-uhn) is the passage of an EM wave through a medium. If the light reflected from objects did not pass through the air, windows, or most of the eye, we could not see the objects. **Absorption** (uhb-SAWRP-shun) is the disappearance of an EM wave into the medium. Absorption affects how things look, because it limits the light available to be reflected or transmitted.

VOCABULARY
Don't forget to make word frames for *transmission* and *absorption*.

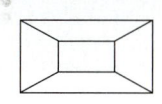

Chapter 3: **Electromagnetic Waves** 93 **D**

How Materials Transmit Light

Materials can be classified according to the amount and type of light they transmit.

① Transparent (trans-PAIR-uhnt) materials allow most of the light that strikes them to pass through. It is possible to see objects through a transparent material. Air, water, and clear glass are transparent. Transparent materials are used for items such as windows, light bulbs, thermometers, sandwich bags, and clock faces.

② Translucent (trans-LOO-suhnt) materials transmit some light, but they also cause it to spread out in all directions. You can see light through translucent materials, but you cannot see objects clearly through them. Some examples are lampshades, frosted light bulbs, frosted windows, sheer fabrics, and notepaper.

③ Opaque (oh-PAYK) materials do not allow any light to pass through them, because they reflect light, absorb light, or both. Heavy fabrics, construction paper, and ceramic mugs are opaque. Shiny materials may be opaque mainly because they reflect light. Other materials, such as wood and rock, are opaque mainly because they absorb light.

CHECK YOUR READING What is the difference between translucent and opaque materials?

This stained-glass window contains transparent, translucent, and opaque materials.

94 Unit: Waves, Sound, and Light

A light filter is a material that is transparent to some kinds of light and opaque to others. For example, clear red glass transmits red light but absorbs other wavelengths. Examples of light filters are the colored covers on taillights and traffic lights, infrared lamp bulbs, and UV-protected sunglasses. Filters that transmit only certain colors are called color filters.

Scattering

Sometimes fine particles in a material interact with light passing through the material to cause scattering. **Scattering** is the spreading out of light rays in all directions, because particles reflect and absorb the light. Fog or dust in the air, mud in water, and scratches or smudges on glass can all cause scattering. Scattering creates glare and makes it hard to see through even a transparent material. Making the light brighter causes more scattering, as you might have noticed if you have ever tried to use a flashlight to see through fog.

Fine particles, such as those in fog, scatter light and reduce visibility.

Scattering is what makes the sky blue. During the middle of the day, when the Sun is high in the sky, molecules in Earth's atmosphere scatter the blue part of visible light more than they scatter the other wavelengths. This process makes the sky light and blue. It is too bright to see the faint stars beyond Earth's atmosphere. At dawn and dusk, light from the Sun must travel farther through the atmosphere before it reaches your eyes. By the time you see it, the greens and blues are scattered away and the light appears reddish. At night, because there is so little sunlight, the sky is dark and you can see the stars.

SUPPORTING MAIN IDEAS
Be sure to add to your chart the different ways light interacts with materials.

CHECK YOUR READING How does scattering make the sky blue?

Chapter 3: **Electromagnetic Waves** 95

Polarization

Polarizing filters reduce glare and make it easier to see objects. **Polarization** (POH-luhr-ih-ZAY-shuhn) is a quality of light in which all of its waves vibrate in the same direction. Remember that EM waves are made of electric and magnetic fields vibrating at right angles to each other. Polarization describes the electric fields of a light wave. When all of the electric fields of a group of light waves vibrate in the same direction, the light is polarized.

Light can be polarized by a particular type of light filter called a polarizing filter. A polarizing filter acts on a light wave's electric field like the bars of a cage. The filter allows through only waves whose electric fields vibrate in one particular direction. Light that passes through the filter is polarized. In the illustration below, these waves are shown in darker yellow.

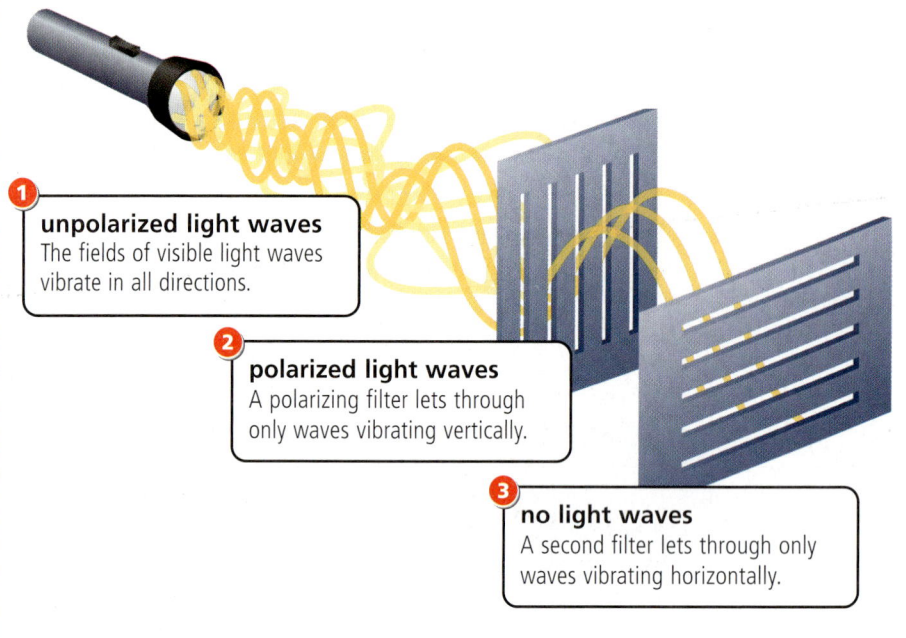

Light reflecting off the surface of this pond causes glare.

A polarizing filter reduces glare, making it possible to see objects under the water.

1 unpolarized light waves
The fields of visible light waves vibrate in all directions.

2 polarized light waves
A polarizing filter lets through only waves vibrating vertically.

3 no light waves
A second filter lets through only waves vibrating horizontally.

What do you think happens when polarized light passes into a second polarizing filter? If the direction of the second filter is the same as the first, then all of the light will pass through the second filter. The light will still be polarized. If the second filter is at a right angle to the first, as in the illustration above, then no light at all will pass through the second filter.

Wavelengths determine color.

The section of the EM spectrum called visible light is made up of many different wavelengths. When all of these wavelengths are present together, as in light from the Sun or a light bulb, the light appears white.

96 Unit: Waves, Sound, and Light

Seen individually, different wavelengths appear as different colors of light. This fact can be demonstrated by using a prism. A **prism** is a tool that uses refraction to spread out the different wavelengths that make up white light. The prism bends some of the wavelengths more than others. The lightwaves, bent at slightly different angles, form a color spectrum. The color spectrum could be divided into countless individual wavelengths, each with its own color. However, the color spectrum is usually divided into seven named color bands. In order of decreasing wavelength, the bands are red, orange, yellow, green, blue, indigo, and violet. You see a color spectrum whenever you see a rainbow.

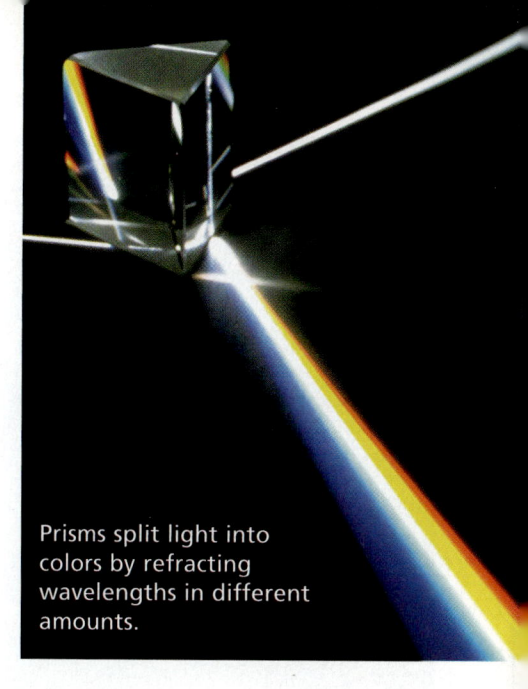

Prisms split light into colors by refracting wavelengths in different amounts.

Color Reflection and Absorption

The color of an object or material is determined by the wavelengths it absorbs and those it reflects. An object has the color of the wavelengths it reflects. A material that reflects all wavelengths of visible light appears white. A material that absorbs all wavelengths of visible light appears black. A green lime absorbs most wavelengths but reflects green, so the lime looks green, as shown below.

SUPPORTING MAIN IDEAS
Describe the roles of reflection and absorption in color.

① In this simplified diagram, light of all colors strikes the lime.

② The lime absorbs all wavelengths except green.

③ The lime reflects mostly green, so it appears green.

The color that an object appears to the eye depends on another factor besides the wavelengths the object absorbs and reflects. An object can reflect only wavelengths that are in the light that shines on it. In white light, a white object reflects all the wavelengths of visible light and appears white. If you shine only red light on a white piece of paper, however, the paper will appear red, not white, because only red light is available to be reflected.

In summary, two factors determine the color of an object: first, the wavelengths that the object itself reflects or absorbs, and second, the wavelengths present in the light that shines on the object.

CHECK YOUR READING What color band or bands does a red apple absorb? a white flower?

Chapter 3: **Electromagnetic Waves** 97 **D**

Primary Colors of Light

The human eye can detect only three color bands: red, green, and blue. Your brain perceives these three colors and various mixtures of them as all the colors. These three colors of light, which can be mixed to produce all possible colors, are called **primary colors.** When all three colors are mixed together equally, they appear white, or colorless. Whenever colored light is added to a mixture, specific wavelengths are added. Mixing colors by adding wavelengths is called additive color mixing.

An example of the practical use of primary colors is a color television or computer monitor. The screen is divided into thousands of tiny bundles of red, green, and blue dots, or pixels. A television broadcast or DVD sends signals that tell the monitor which pixels to light up and when to do so. By causing only some pixels to give off light, the monitor can mix the three colors to create an amazing variety of colorful images.

Primary colors of light combine to make the secondary colors yellow, cyan (light blue), and magenta (dark pink).

CHECK YOUR READING What does an equal mix of all three primary colors produce?

INVESTIGATE Mixing Colors

What is black ink made of?

PROCEDURE

1. Trim each of the filter papers to a disk about 10 cm (4 in.) in diameter. Make two parallel cuts about 1 cm (.5 in.) apart and 5 cm (2 in.) long from the edge of each disk toward the center. Fold the paper to make a flap at a right angle.

2. Use a different marker to make a dark spot in the middle of the flap on each disk.

3. Fill each of the cups with water. Set one of the disks on top of each cup so that the water covers the end of the flap but does not reach the ink spot.

4. After 15 minutes, examine each of the flaps.

WHAT DO YOU THINK?

- What did you observe about the effects of water on the ink spots?
- How do the three different samples compare?

CHALLENGE Write a hypothesis to explain what you observed about the colors in a black marker.

SKILL FOCUS
Observing

MATERIALS
- 3 coffee filters
- scissors
- 3 brands of black felt-tip marker
- 3 cups
- water

TIME
30 minutes

98 Unit: Waves, Sound, and Light

Primary Pigments

Remember that two factors affect an object's color. One is the wavelengths present in the light that shines on the object. The other is the wavelengths that the object's material reflects or absorbs. Materials can be mixed to produce colors just as light can. Materials that are used to produce colors are called pigments. The **primary pigments** are cyan, yellow, and magenta. You can mix primary pigments just as you can mix primary colors to produce all the colors.

The primary pigment colors are the same as the secondary colors of light. The secondary pigment colors are red, blue, and green—the same as the primary colors of light.

The effect of mixing pigments is different from the effect of mixing light. Remember that a colored material absorbs all wavelengths except those of the color it reflects. Yellow paint absorbs all wavelengths except yellow. Because pigments absorb wavelengths, whenever you mix pigments, you are subtracting wavelengths rather than adding them. Mixing colors by subtracting wavelengths is called subtractive color mixing. When all three primary pigments are mixed together in equal amounts, all wavelengths are subtracted. The result is black—the absence of reflected light.

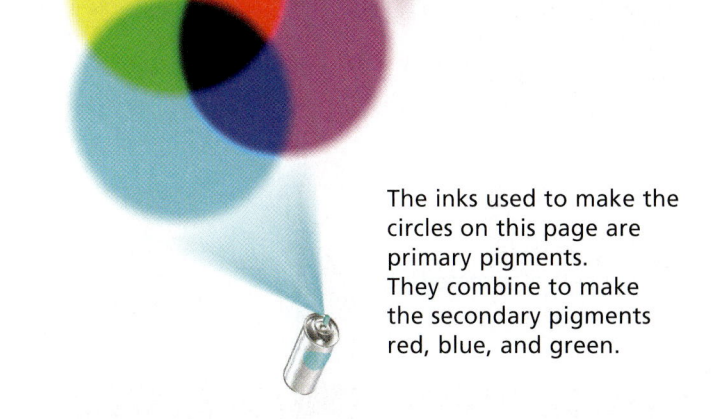

The inks used to make the circles on this page are primary pigments. They combine to make the secondary pigments red, blue, and green.

CHECK YOUR READING How is mixing pigments different from mixing light?

3.4 Review

KEY CONCEPTS

1. What are some ways in which materials affect how light is transmitted?
2. How does a polarizing filter reduce glare?
3. In order for an object to appear white, which wavelengths must the light contain and the object reflect?

CRITICAL THINKING

4. **Apply** Imagine that you are a firefighter searching a smoke-filled apartment. Would using a stronger light help you see better? Explain your answer.
5. **Predict** Higher-energy EM waves penetrate farthest into a dense medium. What colors are more likely to penetrate to the bottom of a lake?

CHALLENGE

6. **Synthesize** If you focus a red light, a green light, and a blue light on the same part of a black curtain, what color will the curtain appear to be? Why?

Chapter 3: **Electromagnetic Waves** 99 **D**

CHAPTER INVESTIGATION

Wavelength and Color

OVERVIEW AND PURPOSE Lighting directors use color filters to change the look of a scene. The color an object appears depends on both the wavelengths of light shining on it and the wavelengths of light it reflects. In this exercise, you will investigate the factors that affect these wavelengths and so affect the color of an object. You will
- make a light box
- study the effect of different colors of light on objects of different colors

MATERIALS
- 3 sheets of acetate (red, blue, and green)
- ruler
- scissors
- shoe box
- masking tape
- light source
- 4 solid-colored objects (white, black, red, and yellow)

Problem

How does the appearance of objects of different colors change in different colors of light?

Hypothesize

Read the procedure below and look at the sample notebook page. Predict what color each object will appear in each color of light. Give a reason for each prediction.

Procedure

1. Draw a data table like the one in the sample **Science Notebook.**

2. Make 3 color filters by cutting a 10 cm (4 in.) square from each color of acetate.

3. Make a 3 cm (1 in.) wide hole in the middle of the top of the box. This will be the viewing hole.

4. Make an 8 cm (3 in.) hole in one end of the box. This will be the light hole.

5. You will observe each of the four colored objects four times—with no filter and with the red, blue, and green filters. Use masking tape to position the filters in the light hole, as shown.

step 5

D 100 Unit: Waves, Sound, and Light

6. Place the light box on a flat surface near a strong white light source, such as sunlight or a bright lamp. Position the box with the uncovered light hole facing the light source. Place the white object inside the box, look through the eyehole, and observe the object's color. Record your observations.

7. Use the light box to test each of the combinations of object color and filter shown in the table on the sample notebook page. Record your results.

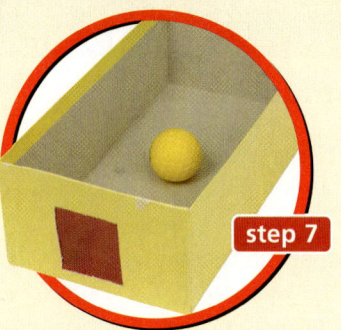

Observe and Analyze *Write It Up*

1. **RECORD OBSERVATIONS** Be sure your data table is complete.

2. **COMPARE** What color did the red object appear to be when viewed with a blue filter? a red filter?

Conclude *Write It Up*

1. **INTERPRET** Answer your problem question.

2. **ANALYZE** Compare your results to your predictions. How do the results support your hypothesis?

3. **IDENTIFY VARIABLES** What different variables affected the outcome of your experiment?

4. **INFER** Why do colors of objects appear to change in different types of light?

5. **IDENTIFY LIMITS** What possible limitations or sources of error could have affected your results?

6. **APPLY** If you were going to perform on a stage that was illuminated using several different color filters, what color clothing should you wear in order to look as bright and colorful as possible?

INVESTIGATE Further

CHALLENGE Perform this experiment using different kinds of artificial light. Try it with a low-wattage incandescent bulb, a high-wattage incandescent bulb, a fluorescent bulb, or a full-spectrum bulb. How do different kinds of artificial light affect the colors that objects appear to be?

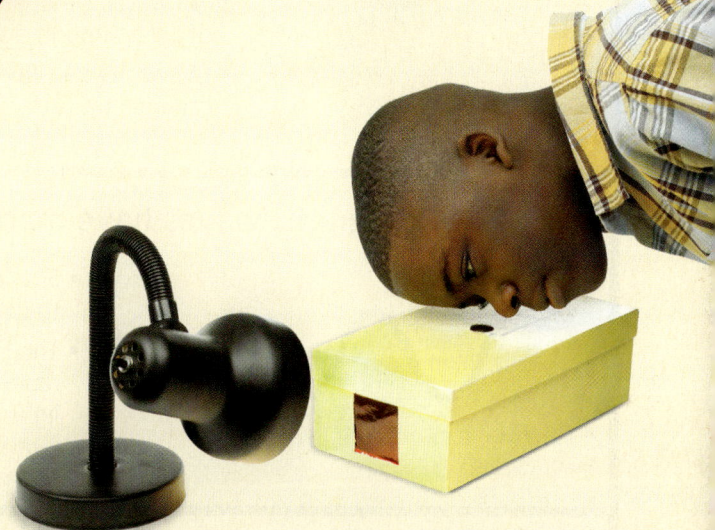

Wavelength and Color

Problem
How does the appearance of objects of different colors change in different colors of light?

Hypothesize

Observe and Analyze
Table 1. Predicted and Observed Colors of Objects with Different Colored Filters

Predicted	no filter	red filter	blue filter	green filter
white object				
black object				
red object				
yellow object				
Observed	no filter	red filter	blue filter	green filter
white object				

Chapter 3: **Electromagnetic Waves** 101

3 Chapter Review

the BIG idea
Electromagnetic waves transfer energy through radiation.

CONTENT REVIEW
CLASSZONE.COM

KEY CONCEPTS SUMMARY

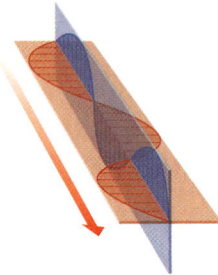

3.1 Electromagnetic waves have unique traits.

- Electromagnetic (EM) waves are made of vibrating electric and magnetic fields.
- EM waves travel at the speed of light through a vacuum.
- EM waves transfer energy and can interact with matter.

VOCABULARY
electromagnetic wave p. 73
radiation p. 75

3.2 Electromagnetic waves have many uses.

- EM waves are grouped by frequency on the EM spectrum.
- The EM spectrum is divided into radio waves, microwaves, infrared light, visible light, ultraviolet light, x-rays, and gamma rays.

VOCABULARY
EM spectrum p. 80
radio waves p. 82
microwaves p. 83
visible light p. 84
infrared light p. 84
ultraviolet light p. 85
x-rays p. 86
gamma rays p. 86

3.3 The Sun is the source of most visible light.

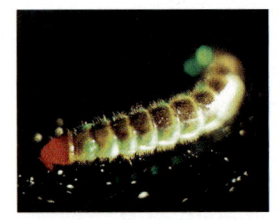

- Most visible light in the environment comes from the Sun.
- Many living organisms produce visible light for their own use.
- Humans produce visible light artificially.

VOCABULARY
incandescence p. 89
luminescence p. 89
bioluminescence p. 89
fluorescence p. 91

3.4 Light waves interact with materials.

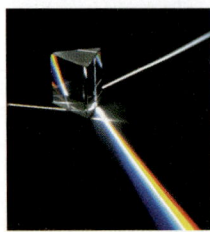

- Reflection, transmission, and absorption affect what light we see.
- Light can be scattered and polarized.
- Visible light is made up of many wavelengths.
- The primary colors are red, blue, and green.
- The primary pigments are yellow, cyan, and magenta.

VOCABULARY
transmission p. 93
absorption p. 93
scattering p. 95
polarization p. 96
prism p. 97
primary colors p. 98
primary pigments p. 99

D 102 Unit: Waves, Sound, and Light

Reviewing Vocabulary

Make a four-square diagram for each of the listed terms. Write the term in the center. Define the term in one square. Write characteristics, examples, and nonexamples in other squares. A sample is shown below.

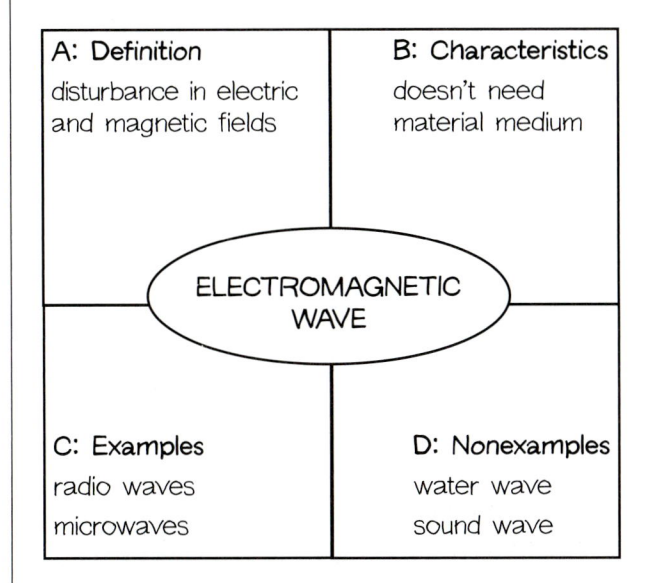

A: Definition	B: Characteristics
disturbance in electric and magnetic fields	doesn't need material medium

ELECTROMAGNETIC WAVE

C: Examples	D: Nonexamples
radio waves microwaves	water wave sound wave

1. gamma rays
2. infrared light
3. transmission
4. absorption
5. pigment
6. radiation
7. bioluminescence
8. EM spectrum
9. incandescence
10. polarization

Reviewing Key Concepts

Multiple Choice *Choose the letter of the best answer.*

11. An electromagnetic wave is a disturbance that transfers energy through a field. In this sense, a disturbance is the same as a
    a. confusion
    b. magnification
    c. vibration
    d. conflict

12. Unlike mechanical waves, EM waves can travel through
    a. a vacuum
    b. water
    c. the ground
    d. air

13. A light year is a measure of
    a. time
    b. distance
    c. speed
    d. wavelength

14. The Sun and a light bulb both produce light through
    a. bioluminescence
    b. incandescence
    c. luminescence
    d. polarization

15. Which of the following types of light bulb converts ultraviolet waves into visible light waves?
    a. incandescent
    b. fluorescent
    c. halogen
    d. tungsten

16. An object seen through translucent material appears less clear than one seen through transparent material because the translucent material
    a. transmits none of the light coming from the object
    b. reflects all the light coming from the object
    c. transmits all the light coming from the object
    d. diffuses some light coming from the object

17. An object appears red because it
    a. reflects light waves of all colors
    b. reflects light waves of red
    c. absorbs light waves of red
    d. transmits light waves of all colors

18. Primary colors of light can combine to make
    a. black light
    b. white light
    c. primary pigments
    d. ultraviolet light

Short Answer *Write a short answer to each question.*

19. What vibrates in an EM wave?

20. How can EM waves be used to measure distance?

21. Describe how microwaves are used in communications.

22. What two properties of an EM wave change as you move from one part of the EM spectrum to another?

23. How does visible light differ from other EM waves? How is it similar?

24. Explain briefly how an incandescent light bulb works.

Chapter 3: **Electromagnetic Waves** 103

Thinking Critically

The diagram below shows how far different wavelengths of visible light penetrate into ocean water. Use information from this diagram to answer the next three questions.

25. OBSERVE An EM wave can interact with a material in different ways. Which type of interaction keeps some light waves from reaching the ocean floor?

26. PREDICT How would violet light behave in the same water? Think of where violet is on the color spectrum.

27. SYNTHESIZE How is the apparent color of objects near the ocean floor affected by the interactions shown in the diagram?

28. ANALYZE Under what circumstances can an EM wave begin to convert some of its electromagnetic energy into other forms of energy?

29. ANALYZE What two things must be true about the light source and the material of an object for you to see an object as red?

30. PREDICT If you shine a blue light on a white object, what color will the object appear to be? What color light would you need to add to make the white object appear white?

31. APPLY Why might incandescent lighting become less common in the future? Explain your reasoning.

32. IDENTIFY CAUSE AND EFFECT Liquid crystal displays like the ones used in some calculators work by polarizing light. Describe how two polarizing filters could cause the numbers on the display panel to appear black.

33. COMPARE AND CONTRAST In what way would a sieve be a good model for a polarizing light filter? In what ways would it not be?

34. CONTRAST In what ways is a fluorescent bulb more efficient than incandescent and halogen bulbs?

35. PREDICT What color will a white object appear to be if you look at it through a blue filter?

the BIG idea

36. ANALYZE Return to the question on page 70. Answer the question again, using what you have learned in the chapter.

37. SUMMARIZE Write a summary of this chapter. Use the Big Idea statement from page 70 as the title for your summary. Use the Key Concepts listed on page 70 as the topic sentences for each paragraph. Provide an example for each key concept.

38. ANALYZE Describe all of the EM wave behaviors and interactions that occur when a radiator warms a kitten.

UNIT PROJECTS

Check your schedule for your unit project. How are you doing? Be sure that you've placed data or notes from your research in your project folder.

Standardized Test Practice

Interpreting Diagrams

The diagram below shows part of the electromagnetic (EM) spectrum. The lower band shows frequency in hertz. The upper band shows part of the spectrum used by different technologies.

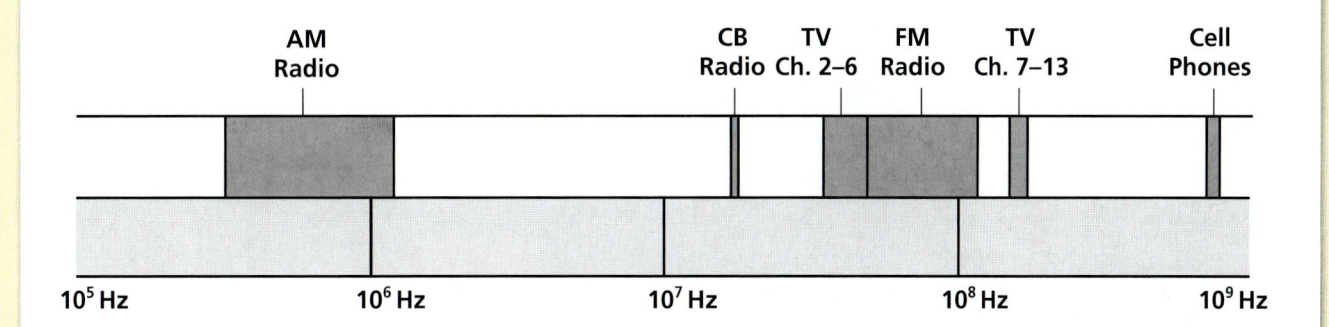

| AM Radio | | CB Radio | TV Ch. 2–6 | FM Radio | TV Ch. 7–13 | Cell Phones |

10^5 Hz 10^6 Hz 10^7 Hz 10^8 Hz 10^9 Hz

Use the diagram to answer the following questions.

1. Which of the technologies listed below uses the highest frequencies?
   a. AM radio
   b. CB radio
   c. FM radio
   d. TV channels 2–6

2. If you were receiving a signal at a frequency of nearly 10^9 Hz, what would you be using?
   a. a CB radio
   b. an AM radio
   c. an FM radio
   d. a cell phone

3. A television station broadcasts its video signal at 10^6 Hz and its audio signal at 10^8 Hz. To receive the broadcasts, your television would need to use the technologies of
   a. both AM and FM radio
   b. both CB and AM radio
   c. both CB and FM radio
   d. both CB radio and cell phone transmissions

4. Signals with similar frequencies sometimes interfere with each other. For this reason, you might expect interference in which of the following?
   a. lower television channels from cell phones
   b. upper television channels from FM radio
   c. lower television channels from FM radio
   d. upper television channels from cell phones

Extended Response

Answer the two questions below in detail. Include some of the terms from the word box. Underline each term you use in your answer.

| frequency | energy | interaction |
| field | medium | vacuum |

5. What are the similarities and differences between mechanical waves and electromagnetic waves?

6. What are some advantages and disadvantages of different types of artificial lighting?

Chapter 3: Electromagnetic Waves 105

TIMELINES in Science

THE STORY OF LIGHT

Light has fascinated people since ancient times. The earliest ideas about light were closely associated with beliefs and observations about vision. Over the centuries, philosophers and scientists developed an increasingly better understanding of light as a physical reality that obeyed the laws of physics.

With increased understanding of the nature and behavior of light has come the ability to use light as a tool. Many applications of light technology have led to improvements in human visual abilities. People can now make images of a wide range of objects that were invisible to earlier generations. The study of light has also led to technologies that do not involve sight at all.

This timeline shows just a few of the many steps on the road to understanding light. The boxes below the timeline show how these discoveries have been applied and developed into new technologies.

400 B.C.
Light Travels in a Straight Line
Observing the behavior of shadows, Chinese philosopher Mo-Ti finds that light travels in a straight line. His discovery helps explain why light passing through a small opening forms an upside-down image.

300 B.C.
Reflection Obeys Law
Greek mathematician Euclid discovers that light striking mirrors obeys the law of reflection. The angle at which light reflects off a mirror is equal to the angle at which it strikes the mirror.

EVENTS

450 B.C.   425 B.C.   400 B.C.   375 B.C.   350 B.C.   325 B.C.   300 B.C.

APPLICATIONS AND TECHNOLOGY

APPLICATION

Camera Obscura

The principle described by Mo-Ti in 400 B.C. led to the development of the camera obscura. When light from an object shines through a small hole into a dark room, an image of the object appears on the far wall. The darkened room is called, in Latin, *camera obscura*. Because light travels in a straight line, the highest points on the object appear at the lowest points on the image; thus, the image appears upside down. Room-sized versions of the camera obscura like the one shown here were a popular attraction in the late 1800s.

A.D. 1000
Eyes Do Not Shoot Rays
Egyptian mathematician and astronomer Ali Alhazen publishes his *Book of Optics*. A diagram of the eye, from this book, is shown below. Alhazen proves that light travels from objects to the eyes, not the other way around. The previously accepted theory, put forth by Greek philosopher Plato centuries ago, claimed that light travels from the eyes to objects.

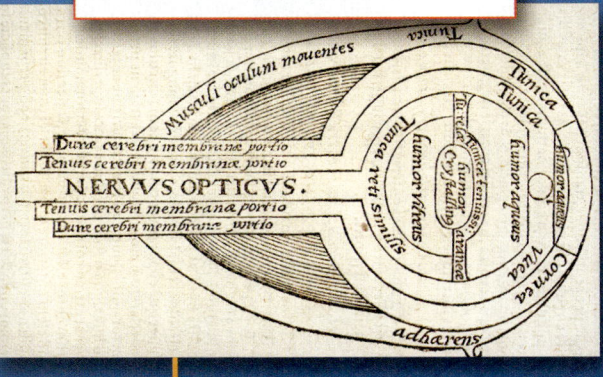

1666
White Light Is Made of Colors
British scientist Isaac Newton makes a remarkable discovery. After studying the effects of a prism on white light, Newton realizes that white light is actually made up of different colors. This contradicts the long-held belief that white light is pure light, and that colored light gets its color from the impurities of different materials.

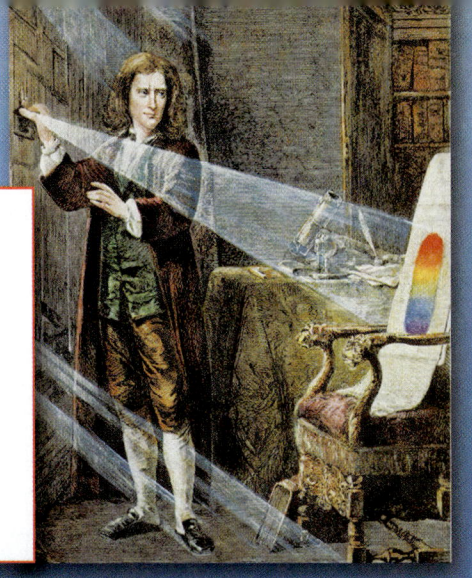

1676
Light Speeds Into Distance
Looking through a telescope, Danish astronomer Olaus Roemer observes one of Jupiter's moons "setting" earlier and earlier as Earth approaches the planet—and later and later as Earth moves farther away. Roemer infers that distance affects the time it takes light to travel from Jupiter to Earth. He estimates the speed of light as 230,000 kilometers per second.

TECHNOLOGY
Reflecting Telescopes
Early astronomers such as Galileo used refracting telescopes. These telescopes, which used a lens to gather light, were difficult to focus because of the uneven refraction of different wavelengths. Isaac Newton built the first reflecting telescope, which overcame this difficulty by using a mirror to gather light and focus an image. All major astronomical telescopes, including the Hubble Space Telescope, now use mirrors.

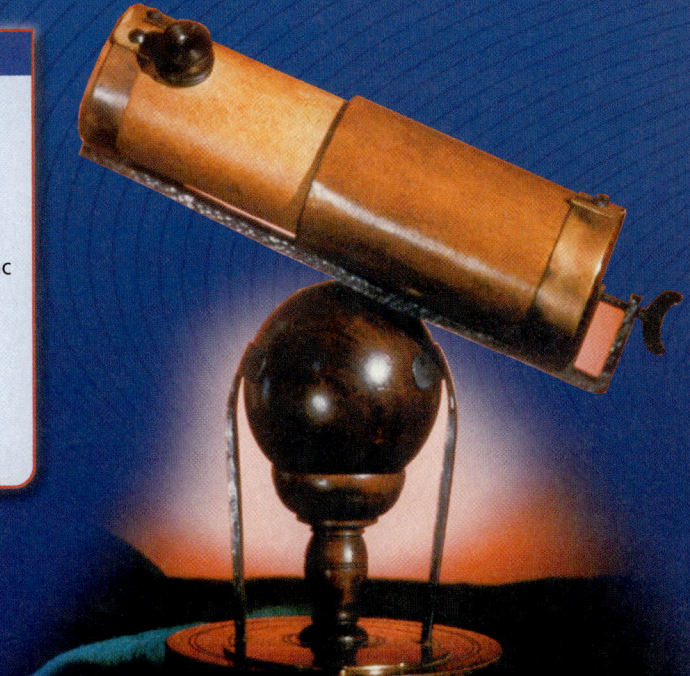

Timelines in Science 107 D

1821
Light Waves Move Like Ripples in a Pond
French physicist Augustin-Jean Fresnel confirms the theory that light waves are transverse waves. Like water waves, light waves vibrate at right angles to the direction of their travel. This theory helps to explain many observed behaviors of light, including diffraction fringes like those surrounding this mountain climber.

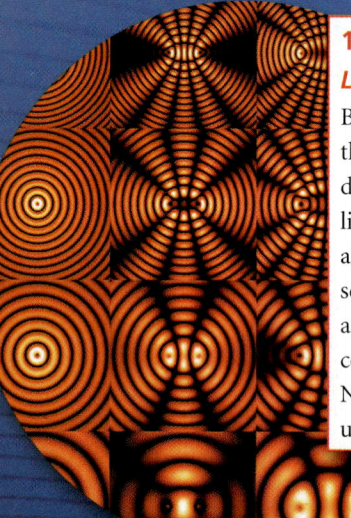

1801
Light Makes Waves
British scientist Thomas Young finds that beams of light can interact to produce an interference pattern. He aims light through two slits and observes alternating light and dark bands on a screen. Young concludes that light acts as if it were made up of waves, which contradicts the theory put forth by Newton and others that light is made up of particles.

1887
No Medium Needed
U.S. scientists Albert Michelson and Edward Morley disprove the theory that light, like other waves, must have a medium. The men devise an experiment to detect the effect of ether—material that light supposedly uses to move through space—on a light beam. The experiment shows that no ether exists and therefore that light waves need no medium.

1750   1775   1800   1825   1850   1875   1900

APPLICATION
Holograms
Holograms are used today to create images for art, communications, and research. A hologram is an interference pattern created by a collision between the two halves of a split laser beam. One half shines on film, and the other half shines on the object. The object reflects this second beam onto the film, where it creates an interference pattern with the first beam. This interference pattern captures a three-dimensional image of the object, as in this hologram of a shark.

TECHNOLOGY
Gravitational Lenses
As part of his theory of relativity, Albert Einstein predicted that light would bend in a gravitational field. His theory was confirmed in 1919. During a solar eclipse, scientists witnessed the bending of light from more distant stars as that light passed near the Sun. Astronomers take advantage of this effect to get a better look at objects deep in space. Sometimes light from a distant object passes through a closer object's gravitational field on its way to Earth. By analyzing images of the object, scientists can learn more about it.

1960
Light Beams Line Up
U.S. inventor Theodore Harold Maiman builds a working laser by stimulating emission of light in a cylinder of ruby crystal. Laser light waves all have the same wavelength, and their peaks occur together.

2001
Light Is Completely Stopped
After slowing light to the speed of a bicycle, Danish physicist Lene Vestergaard Hau brings it to a complete halt in a supercold medium. Controlling the speed of light could revolutionize computers, communications, and other electronic technology.

RESOURCE CENTER
CLASSZONE.COM
Learn more about current research involving light.

1925   1950   1975   2000

APPLICATION

Lasers in Eye Surgery
For centuries, people have used corrective lenses to help their eyes focus images more clearly. Today, with the help of lasers, doctors can correct the eye itself. Using an ultraviolet laser, doctors remove microscopic amounts of a patient's cornea to change the way it refracts light. As a result, the eye focuses images exactly on the retina. For many nearsighted people, the surgery results in 20/20 vision or better.

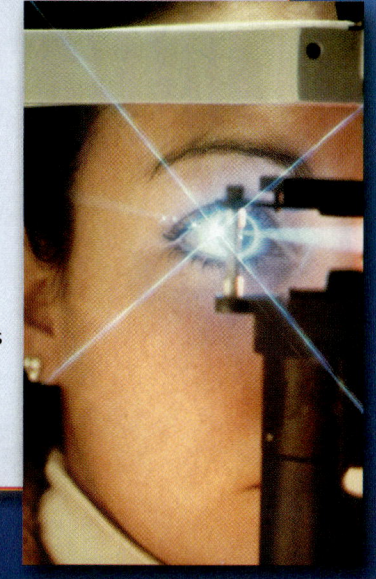

INTO THE FUTURE

Much of our current knowledge in science, from the workings of our bodies to the universe as a whole, is founded upon experiments that used light. Evidence from new light applications will continue to shape our knowledge. In the future, the nature of light, itself, may again come into question as new experiments are performed.

As new light microscopes are developed, scientists will gain more detailed information about how systems within our bodies work, such as how our brain cells interact with each other to perform a complex task. With powerful telescopes, scientists will gain a better understanding of the universe at its beginnings and how galaxies are formed.

Finally, as we continue to study the behavior of light, we may continue to modify its very definition. Sometimes considered a stream of particles, and other times considered waves, light is now understood to have qualities of both particles and waves.

ACTIVITIES

Make a Camera Obscura
Take a small box and paint the interior black. On one side, make a pinhole. On a side next to that one, make a hole about 5 cm in diameter.

On a bright, sunny day, hold the box so that sunlight enters the box through the pinhole. Fit your eye snugly against the larger hole and look inside.

Writing About Science
Lasers are currently used in entertainment, medicine, communication, supermarkets, and so on. Write a prediction about a specific use of lasers in the future. You might describe a new invention.

Timelines in Science 109 D

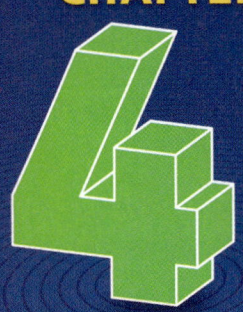

CHAPTER 4
Light and Optics

the BIG idea

Optical tools depend on the wave behavior of light.

How can this device help a person to see better?

Key Concepts

SECTION 4.1
Mirrors form images by reflecting light.
Learn how mirrors use reflection to create images.

SECTION 4.2
Lenses form images by refracting light.
Learn how lenses use refraction to create images.

SECTION 4.3
The eye is a natural optical tool.
Learn about how eyes work as optical tools.

SECTION 4.4
Optical technology makes use of light waves.
Learn about complex optical tools.

Internet Preview

CLASSZONE.COM

Chapter 4 online resources: Content Review, Simulation, Visualization, three Resource Centers, Math Tutorial, Test Practice.

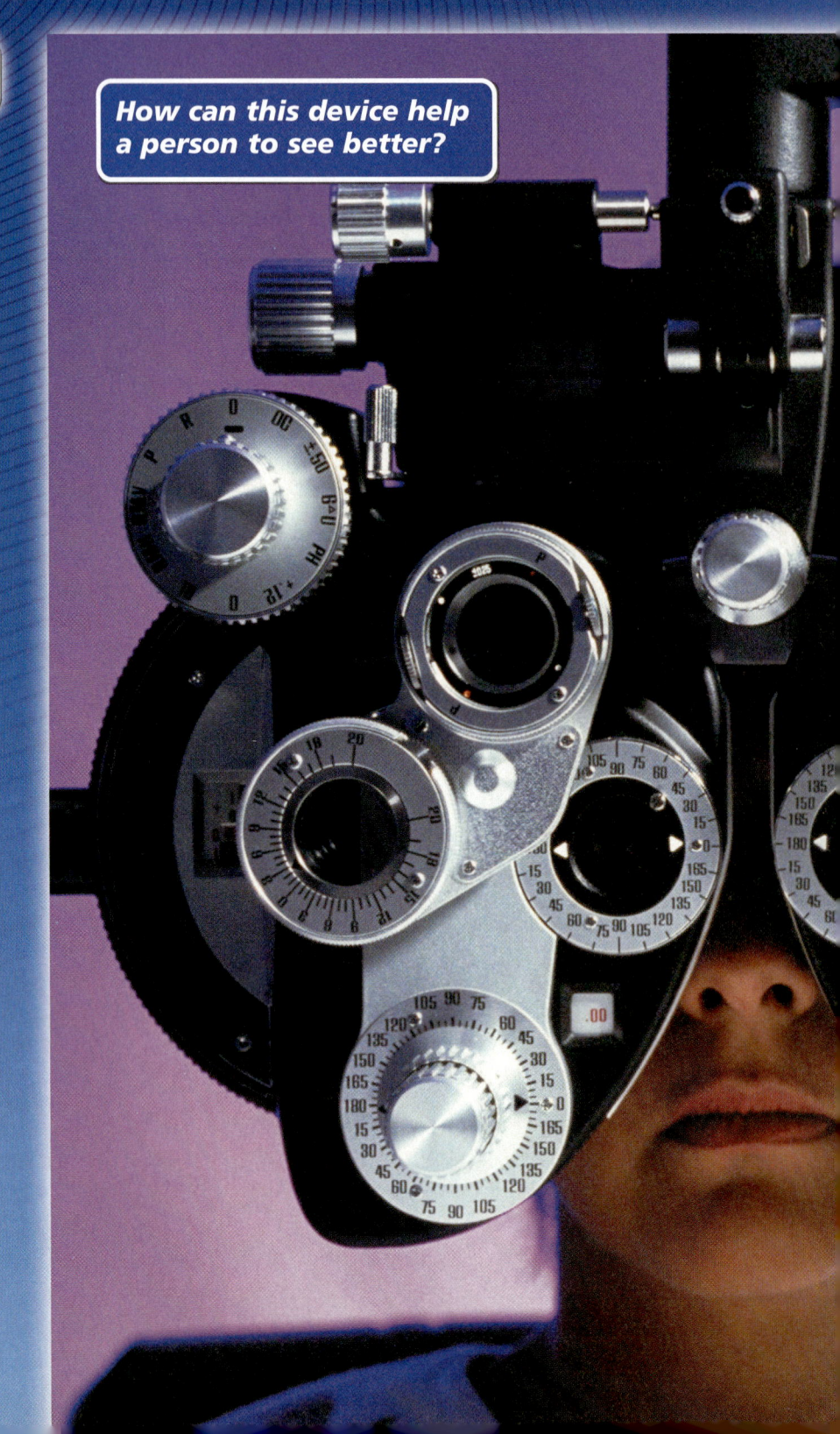

D 110 Unit: Waves, Sound, and Light

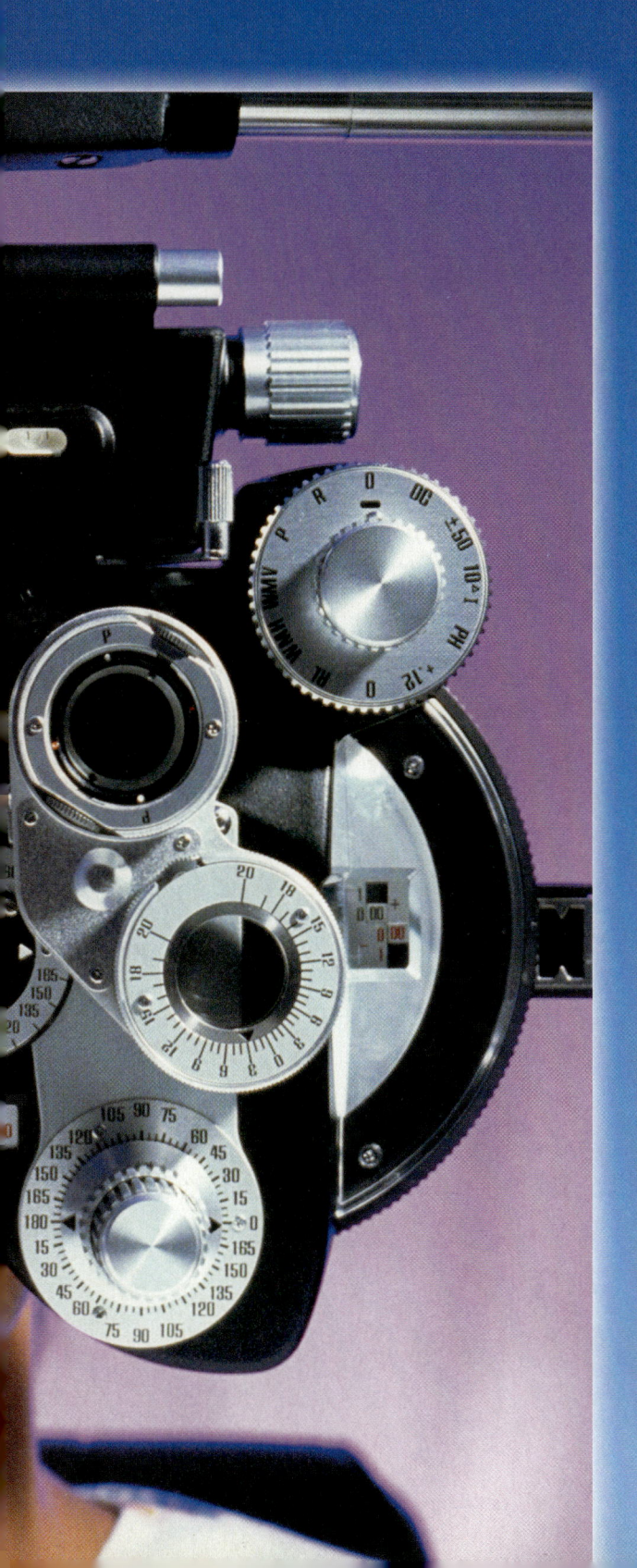

EXPLORE the BIG idea

How Does a Spoon Reflect Your Face?

Look at the reflection of your face in the bowl of a shiny metal spoon. How does your face look? Is it different from what you would expect? Now turn the spoon over and look at your face in the round side. How does your face look this time?

Observe and Think Why do the two sides of the spoon affect the appearance of your face in these ways?

Why Do Things Look Different Through Water?

Fill a clear, round jar with straight, smooth sides with water. Look through the jar at different objects in the room. Experiment with different distances between the objects and the jar and between yourself and the jar.

Observe and Think How does the jar change the way things look? What do you think causes these changes?

Internet Activity: Optics

Go to **ClassZone.com** to learn more about optics.

Observe and Think How does research in optics benefit other areas of scientific investigation?

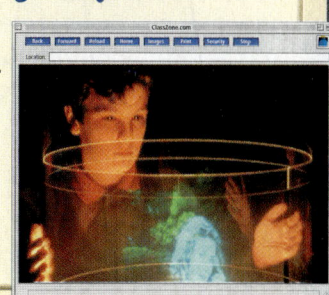

NSTA scilinks.org SCLINKS

Lenses Code: MDL030

Chapter 4: **Light and Optics** 111

CHAPTER 4
Getting Ready to Learn

CONCEPT REVIEW

- Light tends to travel in a straight line.
- The speed of light is affected by a material medium.
- Reflection and refraction are two ways light interacts with materials.

VOCABULARY REVIEW

reflection p. 25
refraction p. 25
visible light p. 84

CONTENT REVIEW
CLASSZONE.COM
Review concepts and vocabulary.

TAKING NOTES

COMBINATION NOTES

To take notes about a new concept, first make an informal outline of the information. Then make a sketch of the concept and label it so you can study it later.

CHOOSE YOUR OWN STRATEGY

Take notes about new vocabulary terms, using one or more of the strategies from earlier chapters—**four square**, **description wheel**, or **frame game**. Feel free to mix and match the strategies, or to use an entirely different vocabulary strategy.

See the Note-Taking Handbook on pages R45–R51.

SCIENCE NOTEBOOK

NOTES
The angle of incidence (x) equals the angle of reflection (y).

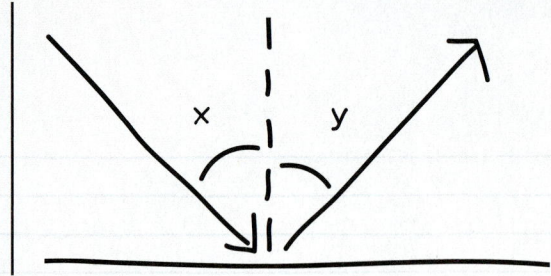

FOUR SQUARE
Definition	Characteristics
TERM	
Examples	Nonexamples

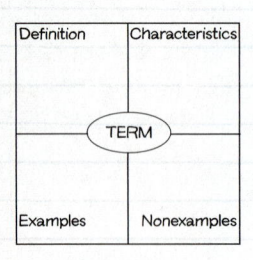

DESCRIPTION WHEEL
feature / feature / feature / feature / feature — TERM

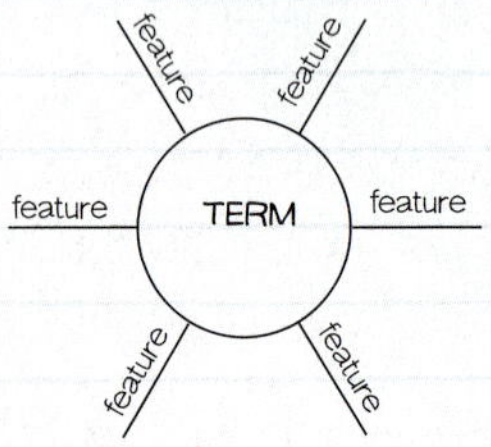

FRAME GAME
example / sketch / TERM / sentence / description

112 Unit: Waves, Sound, and Light

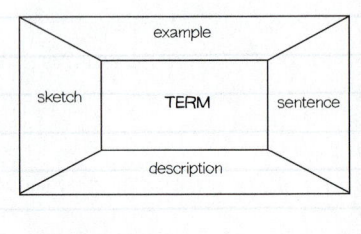

KEY CONCEPT
4.1 Mirrors form images by reflecting light.

BEFORE, you learned
- EM waves interact with materials
- Light can be reflected

NOW, you will learn
- About the science of optics
- How light is reflected
- How mirrors form images

VOCABULARY
optics p. 113
law of reflection p. 114
regular reflection p. 114
diffuse reflection p. 114
image p. 115
convex p. 116
concave p. 116
focal point p. 117

EXPLORE Reflection

How does surface affect reflection?

PROCEDURE

1. Tear off a square sheet of aluminum foil. Look at your reflection in the shiny side of the foil.
2. Turn the foil over and look at your reflection in the dull side.
3. Crumple up the piece of foil, then smooth it out again, shiny side up. Again, look at your reflection in the foil.

MATERIALS
aluminum foil

WHAT DO YOU THINK?
- How did the three reflections differ from one another?
- What might explain these differences?

COMBINATION NOTES
Don't forget to include sketches of important concepts in your notebook.

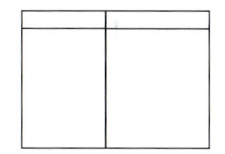

Optics is the science of light and vision.

Optics (AHP-tihks) is the study of visible light and the ways in which visible light interacts with the eye to produce vision. Optics is also the application of knowledge about visible light to develop tools—such as eyeglasses, mirrors, magnifying lenses, cameras, and lasers—that extend vision or that use light in other ways.

Mirrors, lenses, and other optical inventions are called optical tools. By combining optical tools, inventors have developed powerful instruments to extend human vision. For example, the microscope uses a combination of mirrors and lenses to make very small structures visible. Telescopes combine optical tools to extend vision far into space. As you will see, some of the latest optical technology—lasers—use visible light in ways that do not involve human vision at all.

Chapter 4: Light and Optics 113 **D**

Mirrors use regular reflection.

You have read that when light waves strike an object, they either pass through it or they bounce off its surface. Objects are made visible by light waves, or rays, bouncing off their surfaces. In section 3 you will see how the light waves create images inside the human eye.

Light rays bounce off objects in a very predictable way. For example, look at the diagram on the left below. Light rays from a flashlight strike a mirror at an angle of 60° as measured from the normal, an imaginary line perpendicular to the surface of the mirror. This angle is called the angle of incidence. The angle at which the rays reflect off the mirror, called the angle of reflection, is also 60° as measured from the normal. The example illustrates the **law of reflection,** which states that the angle of reflection equals the angle of incidence. As you can see in the second diagram, holding the flashlight at a different angle changes both the angle of incidence and the angle of reflection. However, the two angles remain equal.

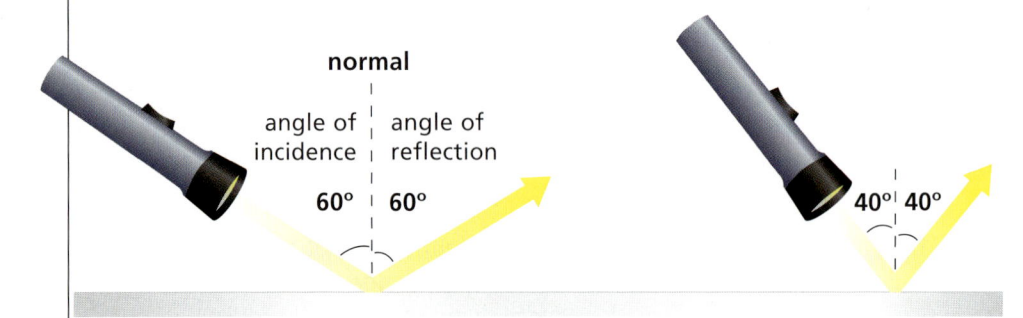

The angle of reflection equals the angle of incidence.

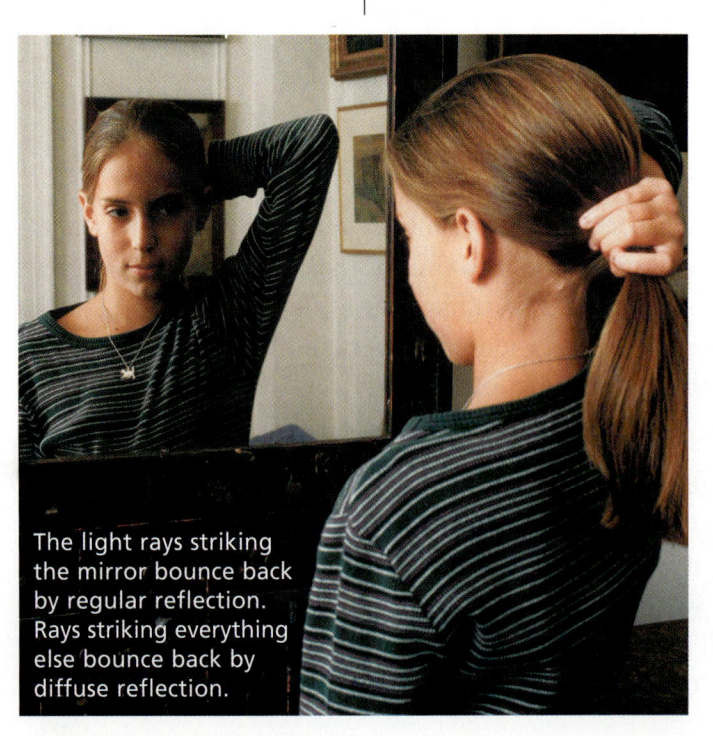

The light rays striking the mirror bounce back by regular reflection. Rays striking everything else bounce back by diffuse reflection.

If the surface of an object is very smooth, like a mirror, light rays that come from the same direction will bounce off in the same new direction. The reflection of parallel light rays all in the same direction is called **regular reflection.**

If the surface is not very smooth—even if it feels smooth to the touch, like a piece of paper—light rays striking it from the same direction bounce off in many new directions. Each light ray follows the law of reflection, but rays coming from the same direction bounce off different bumps and hollows of the irregular surface. The reflection of parallel light rays in many different directions is called **diffuse reflection.**

INVESTIGATE The Law of Reflection

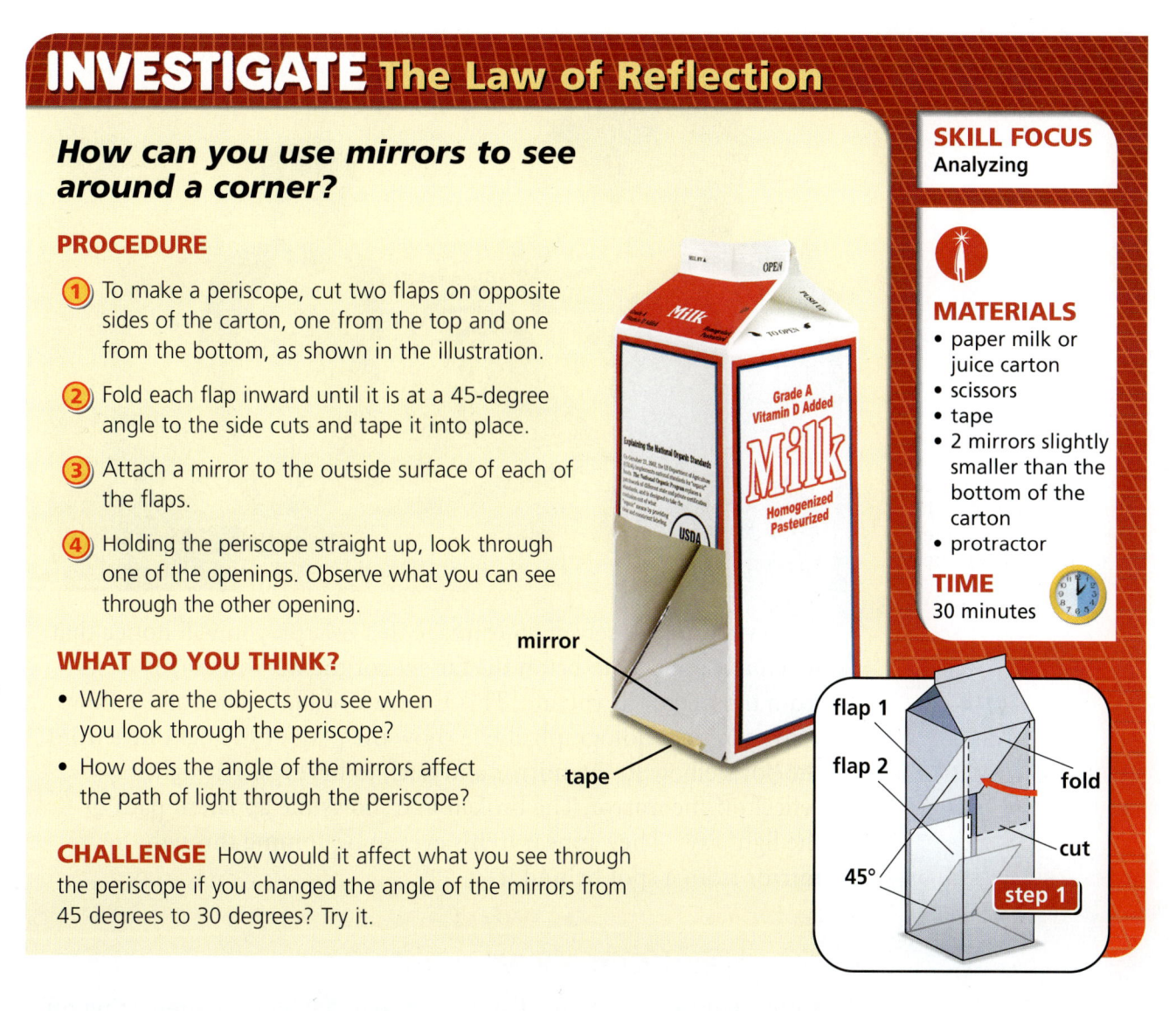

How can you use mirrors to see around a corner?

PROCEDURE

1. To make a periscope, cut two flaps on opposite sides of the carton, one from the top and one from the bottom, as shown in the illustration.

2. Fold each flap inward until it is at a 45-degree angle to the side cuts and tape it into place.

3. Attach a mirror to the outside surface of each of the flaps.

4. Holding the periscope straight up, look through one of the openings. Observe what you can see through the other opening.

WHAT DO YOU THINK?
- Where are the objects you see when you look through the periscope?
- How does the angle of the mirrors affect the path of light through the periscope?

CHALLENGE How would it affect what you see through the periscope if you changed the angle of the mirrors from 45 degrees to 30 degrees? Try it.

SKILL FOCUS
Analyzing

MATERIALS
- paper milk or juice carton
- scissors
- tape
- 2 mirrors slightly smaller than the bottom of the carton
- protractor

TIME
30 minutes

Shape determines how mirrors form images.

When you look in a mirror, you see an image of yourself. An **image** is a picture of an object formed by waves of light. The image of yourself is formed by light waves reflecting off you, onto the mirror, and back toward your eyes. Mirrors of different shapes can produce images that are distorted in certain ways.

VISUALIZATION
CLASSZONE.COM
See reflection in action.

Flat Mirrors

Your image in a flat mirror looks exactly like you. It appears to be the same size as you, and it's wearing the same clothes. However, if you raise your right hand, the image of yourself in the mirror will appear to raise its left hand. That is because you see the image as a person standing facing you. In fact, your right hand is reflected on the right side of the image, and your left on the left side.

CHECK YOUR READING If you wink your left eye while looking in the mirror, which eye in the image of you will wink?

Chapter 4: **Light and Optics** 115

The solid line shows the actual path of light. The broken line shows where the light appears to be coming from.

If you look closely at your image in a mirror, you will notice that it actually appears to be on the far side of the mirror, exactly as far from the mirror as you are. This is a trick of light. The solid yellow arrows in the photograph above show the path of the light rays from the boy's elbow to the mirror and back to his eyes. The light rays reflect off the mirror. The broken line shows the apparent path of the light rays. They appear to his eyes to be coming through the mirror from a spot behind it.

Concave and Convex Mirrors

VOCABULARY
Try making sketches to help you remember the new terms on this page.

Unlike light rays hitting a flat mirror, parallel light rays reflecting off a curved mirror do not move in the same direction. A **convex** mirror is curved outward, like the bottom of a spoon. In a convex mirror, parallel light rays move away from each other, as you can see in the diagram below on the left. A **concave** mirror is curved inward toward the center, like the inside of a spoon. Parallel light rays reflecting off a concave mirror move toward each other, as shown on the right.

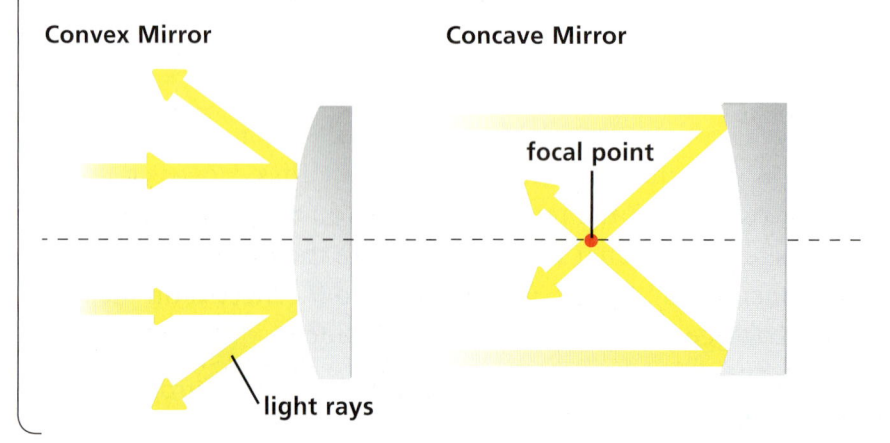

Convex Mirror

Concave Mirror

focal point

light rays

116 Unit: Waves, Sound, and Light

The rays striking a concave mirror cross and then move apart again. The point at which the rays meet is called the **focal point** of the mirror. The distance between the mirror and its focal point depends on the shape of the curve.

The images formed in these mirrors depend on the curve of the mirror's surface and the distance of the object from the mirror. Your image in a curved mirror may appear larger or smaller than you are, and it may even be upside down.

Convex Mirror

Your image in a convex mirror appears smaller than you.

Concave Mirror, Far Away

If you are standing far away, your image in a concave mirror appears upside down and smaller than you.

Concave Mirror, Up Close

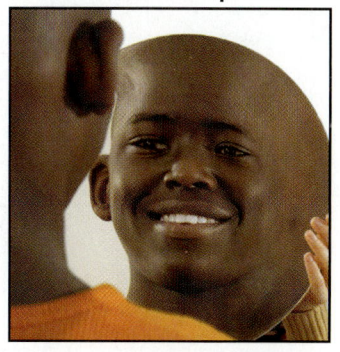

If you are standing inside the focal point, your image in a concave mirror appears right-side up and larger.

All rays parallel to a line through the center of the mirror are reflected off the mirror and pass through the mirror's focal point. Rays from the top of the object are reflected downward and those from the bottom are reflected upward.

CHECK YOUR READING How does your distance from the mirror affect the way your image appears in a concave mirror?

4.1 Review

KEY CONCEPTS

1. Explain the term *optics* in your own words.
2. How is diffuse reflection similar to regular reflection? How is it different?
3. Describe the path that light rays take when they form an image of your smile when you look into a flat mirror.

CRITICAL THINKING

4. **Infer** Imagine seeing your reflection in a polished table top. The image is blurry and hard to recognize. What can you tell about the surface of the table from your observations?
5. **Analyze** Why do images formed by concave mirrors sometimes appear upside down?

CHALLENGE

6. **Synthesize** Draw the letter *R* below as it would appear if you held the book up to (a) a flat mirror and (b) a convex mirror.

R

Chapter 4: **Light and Optics** 117

MATH in SCIENCE

SKILL: MEASURING ANGLES

Send Help!

Survival kits often contain a small mirror that can be used to signal for help. If you were lost in the desert and saw a search plane overhead, you could use the mirror to reflect sunlight toward the plane and catch the pilot's attention. To aim your signal, you would use the law of reflection. The angle at which a ray of light bounces off a mirror—the angle of reflection—is always equal to the angle at which the ray strikes the mirror—the angle of incidence.

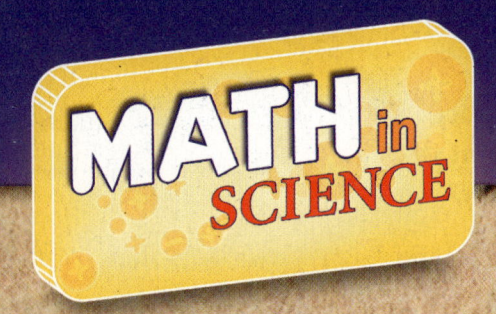

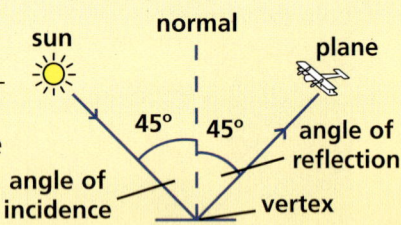

MATH TUTORIAL
CLASSZONE.COM

Click on Math Tutorial for more help with measuring angles.

Example

Measure the angle of incidence using a protractor as follows:

(1) Place the center mark of the protractor over the vertex of the angle formed by the incident ray and the normal.

(2) Place the left 0° mark of the protractor on the incident ray.

(3) Read the number where the normal crosses the scale (35°).

(4) The angle of incidence is 35°.

ANSWER Therefore, the angle of reflection will be 35°.

Copy each of the following angles of incidence, extend its sides, and use a protractor to measure it.

1.   2.   3.   4.

CHALLENGE Copy the drawing below. Use a protractor to find the angle of reflection necessary to signal the plane from point A.

• A

A mirror can be used to signal for help.

D 118 Unit: Waves, Sound, and Light

KEY CONCEPT
4.2 Lenses form images by refracting light.

◁ BEFORE, you learned
- Waves can refract when they move from one medium to another
- Refraction changes the direction of a wave

▷ NOW, you will learn
- How a material medium can refract light
- How lenses control refraction
- How lenses produce images

VOCABULARY
lens p. 121
focal length p. 123

EXPLORE Refraction

How does material bend light?

PROCEDURE

1. Place the pencil in the cup, as shown in the photograph. Look at the cup from the side so that you see part of the pencil through the cup.

2. Fill the cup one-third full with water and repeat your observations.

3. Gently add oil until the cup is two-thirds full. After the oil settles into a separate layer, observe.

MATERIALS
- clear plastic cup
- pencil
- water
- mineral oil

WHAT DO YOU THINK?
- How did the appearance of the pencil change when you added the water? the oil?
- What might explain these changes?

A medium can refract light.

When sunlight strikes a window, some of the light rays reflect off the surface of the glass. Other rays continue through the glass, but their direction is slightly changed. This slight change in direction is called refraction. Refraction occurs when a wave strikes a new medium—such as the window—at an angle other than 90° and keeps going forward in a slightly different direction.

Refraction occurs because one side of the wave reaches the new medium slightly before the other side does. That side changes speed, while the other continues at its previous speed, causing the wave to turn.

CHECK YOUR READING How does the motion of a light wave change when it refracts?

Chapter 4: **Light and Optics** 119 **D**

COMBINATION NOTES
Sketch the ways light is refracted when it moves into a denser medium and into a thinner medium.

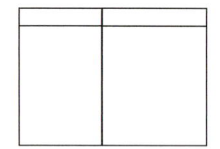

READING TIP
A dense medium has more mass in a given volume than a thin medium.

Refraction of Light

Recall that waves travel at different speeds in different mediums. The direction in which a light wave turns depends on whether the new medium slows the wave down or allows it to travel faster. Like reflection, refraction is described in terms of an imaginary line—called the normal—that is perpendicular to the new surface. If the medium slows the wave, the wave will turn toward the normal. If the new medium lets the wave speed up, the wave will turn away from the normal. The wave in the diagram below turns toward the normal as it slows down in the new medium.

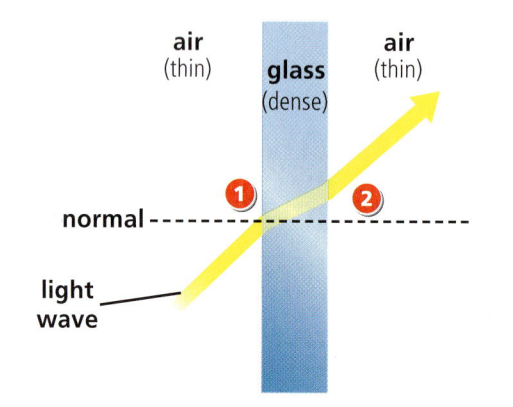

① Waves moving at an angle into a denser medium turn toward the normal.

② Waves moving at an angle into a thinner medium turn away from the normal.

Light from the Sun travels toward Earth through the near vacuum of outer space. Sunlight refracts when it reaches the new medium of Earth's upper atmosphere. Earth's upper atmosphere is relatively thin and refracts light only slightly. Denser materials, such as water and glass, refract light more.

By measuring the speed of light in different materials and comparing this speed to the speed of light in a vacuum, scientists have been able to determine exactly how different materials refract light. This knowledge has led to the ability to predict and control refraction, which is the basis of much optical technology.

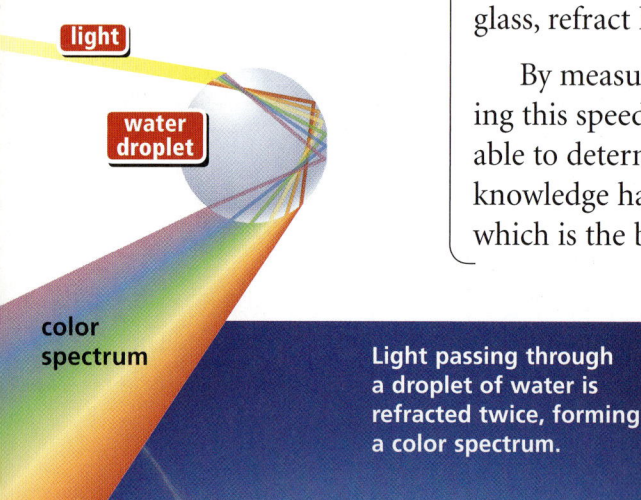

Light passing through a droplet of water is refracted twice, forming a color spectrum.

Refraction and Rainbows

You've seen rainbows in the sky after a rainstorm or hovering in the spray of a sprinkler. Rainbows are caused by refraction and reflection of light through spherical water drops, which act as prisms. Just as a prism separates the colors of white light, producing the color spectrum, each water drop separates the wavelengths of sunlight to produce a spectrum. Only one color reaches your eye from each drop. Red appears at the top of a rainbow because it is coming from higher drops, while violet comes from lower drops.

Shape determines how lenses form images.

When you look at yourself in a flat mirror, you see your image clearly, without distortions. Similarly, when you look through a plain glass window, you can see what is on the other side clearly. Just as curved mirrors distort images, certain transparent mediums called lenses alter what you see through them. A **lens** is a clear optical tool that refracts light. Different lenses refract light in different ways and form images useful for a variety of purposes.

READING TIP
Distort means to change the shape of something by twisting or moving the parts around.

Convex and Concave Lenses

Like mirrors, lenses can be convex or concave. A convex lens is curved outward; a concave lens is curved inward. A lens typically has two sides that are curved, as shown in the illustration below.

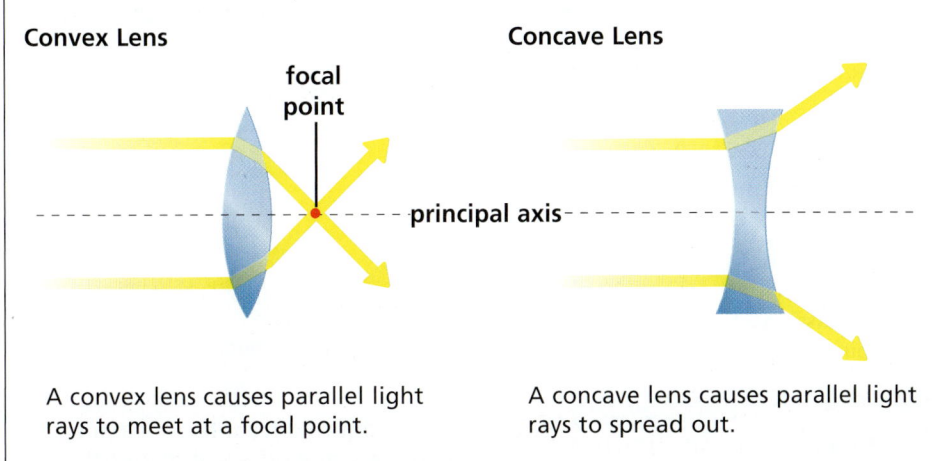

Convex Lens

focal point

principal axis

A convex lens causes parallel light rays to meet at a focal point.

Concave Lens

A concave lens causes parallel light rays to spread out.

Convex Parallel light rays passing through a convex lens are refracted inward. They meet at a focal point on the other side of the lens. The rays are actually refracted twice—once upon entering the lens and once upon leaving it. This is because both times they are entering a new medium at an angle other than 90 degrees. Rays closest to the edges of the lens are refracted most. Rays passing through the center of the lens—along the principal axis, which connects the centers of the two curved surfaces—are not refracted at all. They pass through to the same focal point as all rays parallel to them.

REMINDER
The focal point is the point at which parallel light rays meet after being reflected or refracted.

Concave Parallel light rays that pass through a concave lens are refracted outward. As with a convex lens, the rays are refracted twice. Rays closest to the edges of the lens are refracted most; rays at the very center of the lens pass straight through without being deflected. Because they are refracted away from each other, parallel light rays passing through a concave lens do not meet.

CHECK YOUR READING Compare what happens to parallel light rays striking a concave mirror with those striking a concave lens.

Chapter 4: **Light and Optics** 121

How a Convex Lens Forms an Image

A convex lens forms an image by refracting light rays. Light rays reflected from an object are refracted when they enter the lens and again when they leave the lens. They meet to form the image.

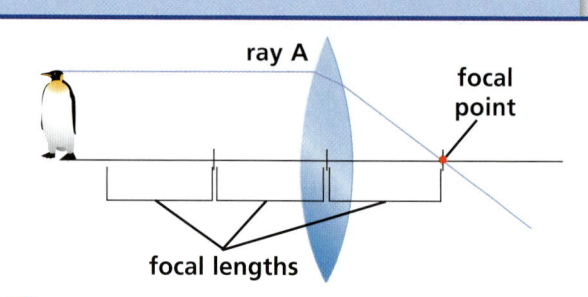

1 Light rays reflect off the penguin in all directions, and many enter the lens. Here a single ray (A) from the top of the penguin enters the lens and is refracted downward.

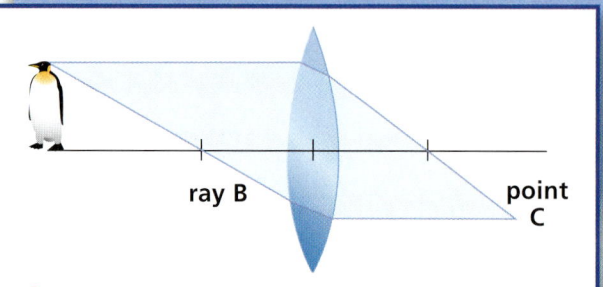

2 Another light ray (B) from the top of the penguin passes through the lens at the bottom and meets the first ray at point C. All of the rays from the top of the penguin passing through the lens meet at this point.

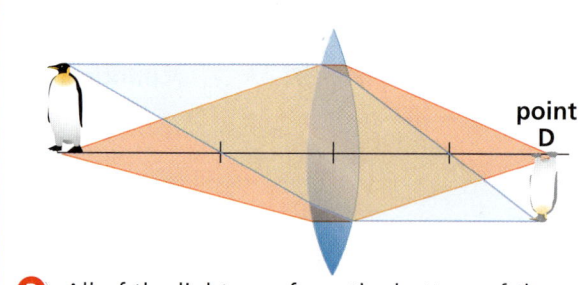

3 All of the light rays from the bottom of the penguin meet at a different point (D). Light rays from all parts of the penguin meet at corresponding points on the image.

READING VISUALS Where do light rays reflected from the middle of the penguin meet?

Images Formed by Lenses

When light rays from an object pass through a lens, an image of the object is formed. The type of image depends on the lens and, for convex lenses, on the distance between the lens and the object.

Notice the distance between the penguin and the lens in the illustration on page 122. The distance is measured in terms of a **focal length,** which is the distance from the center of the lens to the lens's focal point. The penguin is more than two focal lengths from the camera lens, which means the image formed is upside down and smaller.

If the penguin were between one and two focal lengths away from a convex lens, the image formed would be upside down and larger. Overhead projectors form this type of image, which is then turned right side up by a mirror and projected onto a screen for viewing.

Finally, if an object is less than one focal length from a convex lens, it will appear right side up and larger. In order to enlarge an object so that you can see details, you hold a magnifying lens close to the object. In the photograph, you see a face enlarged by a magnifying lens. The boy's face is less than one focal length from the lens.

If you look at an object through a concave lens, you'll see an image of the object that is right side up and smaller than the object normally appears. In the case of concave lenses, the distance between the object and the lens does not make a difference in the type of image that is formed. In the next section you'll see how the characteristics of the images formed by different lenses play a role in complex optical tools.

SIMULATION
CLASSZONE.COM
Work with convex and concave lenses to form images.

CHECK YOUR READING When will an image formed by a convex lens be upside down?

4.2 Review

KEY CONCEPTS

1. What quality of a material affects how much it refracts light?
2. How does the curve in a lens cause it to refract light differently from a flat piece of glass?
3. How does a camera lens form an image?

CRITICAL THINKING

4. **Infer** You look through a lens and see an image of a building upside down. What type of lens are you looking through?
5. **Make a Model** Draw the path of a light ray moving at an angle from air into water. Write a caption to explain the process.

CHALLENGE

6. Study the diagram on the opposite page. Describe the light rays that would pass through the labeled focal point. Where are they coming from, and how are they related to each other?

Chapter 4: Light and Optics 123

CHAPTER INVESTIGATION

Looking at Lenses

OVERVIEW AND PURPOSE Optical tools such as microscopes, telescopes, and eyeglasses use lenses to create images of objects. In this lab, you will use what you have learned about light and lenses to
- experiment with a convex lens to focus images of objects
- determine what makes it possible to focus images of objects.

▶ Procedure

PART A

1. Make a data table like the one shown on the sample notebook page.

2. Draw a stick figure on one index card. Assemble the cards, clay, and lens as shown in the photograph.

3. Position the convex lens so that you can see an enlarged, right-side up image of the stick figure. Measure the distances between the lens and the card, and between the lens and your eye. Record the distances in your data table.

4. Position the lens so that you can see an enlarged, upside down image of the stick figure. Measure the distances between the lens and the object, and between the lens and your eye. Record the distances in your data table.

5. Position the lens so that you can see a reduced, upside down image of the stick figure. Measure the distances between the lens and the object, and between the lens and your eye. Record the distances in your data table.

MATERIALS
- index cards
- marker
- modeling clay
- convex lens
- books
- meter stick
- flashlight
- masking tape
- white poster board

D 124 Unit: Waves, Sound, and Light

PART B

6. Put an arrow made of tape on the lens of the flashlight as shown.

7. Assemble poster board and clay to make a screen. Arrange the flashlight, lens, and screen as shown below right.

8. Shine the beam from the flashlight through the lens to form an enlarged, upside down image on the screen. Measure the distances between the lens and the flashlight and between the lens and the screen.

9. Position the light and screen to produce a reduced, upside down image. Measure the distances between the lens and the flashlight and between the lens and the screen.

10. Position the light and screen to produce an enlarged right-side up image.

Observe and Analyze *Write It Up*

1. **RECORD OBSERVATIONS** Draw pictures of each setup in steps 3–9 to show what happened. Be sure your data table is complete.

2. **ANALYZE** What was the distance from the lens to the object in step 3? Answer this question for each of the other steps. How do the distances compare?

3. **ANALYZE** What happened when you tried to form the three types of images on the screen? How can you explain these results?

Conclude *Write It Up*

1. **ANALYZE** What conclusions can you draw about the relationship between the distances you measured and the type of image that was produced?

2. **IDENTIFY LIMITS** Describe possible sources of error in your procedure or any places where errors might have occurred.

3. **APPLY** What kind of lenses are magnifying glasses? When a magnifying glass produces a sharp clear image, where is the object located in relation to the lens?

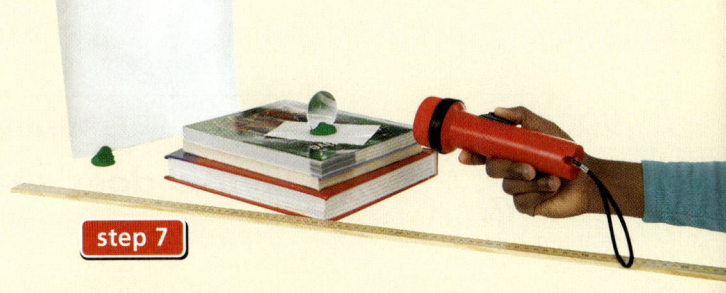

INVESTIGATE Further

CHALLENGE If you were to repeat steps 8 and 9 with a concave lens, you would not be able to focus an image on the screen. Why not?

Looking at Lenses
Observe and Analyze
Table 1. Distances from Lens

Image	Object	Eye
Object enlarged and right-side up		
Object enlarged and upside down		
Object reduced and upside down		

	Flashlight	Screen
Object enlarged and right-side up		
Object enlarged and upside down		
Object reduced and upside down		

Conclude

Chapter 4: **Light and Optics** 125

KEY CONCEPT
4.3 The eye is a natural optical tool.

BEFORE, you learned
- Mirrors and lenses focus light to form images
- Mirrors and lenses can alter images in useful ways

NOW, you will learn
- How the eye depends on natural lenses
- How artificial lenses can be used to correct vision problems

VOCABULARY

cornea p. 127
pupil p. 127
retina p. 127

EXPLORE Focusing Vision

How does the eye focus an image?

PROCEDURE

1. Position yourself so you can see an object about 6 meters (20 feet) away.
2. Close one eye, hold up your index finger, and bring it as close to your open eye as you can while keeping the finger clearly in focus.
3. Keeping your finger in place, look just to the side at the more distant object and focus your eye on it.
4. Without looking away from the more distant object, observe your finger.

WHAT DO YOU THINK?
- How does the nearby object look when you are focusing on something distant?
- What might be happening in your eye to cause this change in the nearby object?

The eye gathers and focuses light.

The eyes of human beings and many other animals are natural optical tools that process visible light. Eyes transmit light, refract light, and respond to different wavelengths of light. Eyes contain natural lenses that focus images of objects. Eyes convert the energy of light waves into signals that can be sent to the brain. The brain interprets these signals as shape, brightness, and color. Altogether, these processes make vision possible.

In this section, you will learn how the eye works. You will also learn how artificial lenses can be used to improve vision.

How Light Travels Through the Human Eye

1 Light enters the eye through the **cornea** (KAWR-nee-uh), a transparent membrane that covers the eye. The cornea acts as a convex lens and does most of the refracting in the eye.

2 The light then continues through the **pupil,** a circular opening that controls how much light enters the eye. The pupil is surrounded by the iris, which opens and closes to change the size of the pupil.

3 Next the light passes through the part of the eye called the lens. The lens is convex on both sides. It refracts light to make fine adjustments for near and far objects. Unlike the cornea, the lens is attached to tiny muscles that contract and relax to control the amount of refraction that occurs and to move the focal point.

4 The light passes through the clear center of the eye and strikes the **retina** (REHT-uhn-uh). The retina contains specialized cells that respond to light. Some of these cells send signals through the optic nerve to the brain. The brain interprets these signals as images.

READING TIP
The word *lens* can refer both to an artificial optical tool and to a specific part of the eye.

How the Human Eye Forms an Image

The cornea and lens together focus a reduced, inverted image on the retina.

1. Light from an object is refracted by the **cornea.**
2. The light passes through the iris and the **pupil.**
3. The **lens** refracts the light more.
4. An image is focused on the **retina.**

iris

optic nerve

READING VISUALS What part of the illustration explains why the image is focused upside down? Explain your answer.

Chapter 4: **Light and Optics** 127

How the Eye Forms Images

COMBINATION NOTES
Make a chart showing how light interacts with different parts of the eye.

For you to see an object clearly, your eye must focus an image of the object on your retina. The light reflected from each particular spot on the object must converge on a matching point on your retina. Many such points make up an image of an entire object. Because the light rays pass through the lens's focal point, the image is upside down. The brain interprets this upside down image as an object that is right-side up.

For a complete image to be formed in the eye and communicated to the brain, more than the lens and the cornea are needed. The retina also plays an important role. The retina contains specialized cells that detect brightness and color and other qualities of light.

Rod Cells Rod cells distinguish between white and black and shades of gray. Rods respond to faint light, so they help with night vision.

Cone Cells Cone cells respond to different wavelengths of light, so they detect color. There are three types of cones, one for each of the colors red, blue, and green. Cones respond to other colors with combinations of these three, as the screen of a color monitor does. The brain interprets these combinations as the entire color spectrum.

CHECK YOUR READING Which type of cell in the retina detects color?

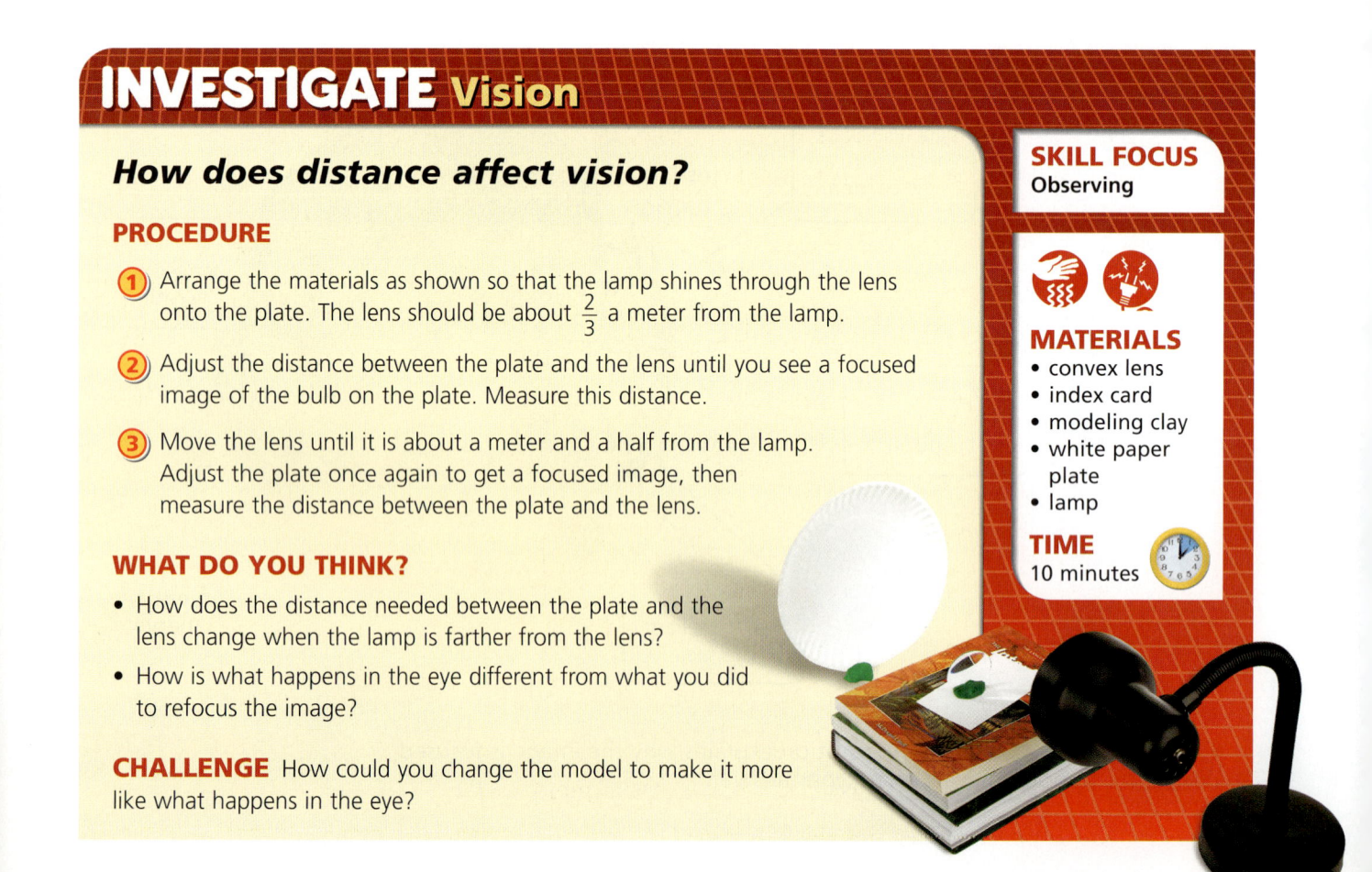

INVESTIGATE Vision

How does distance affect vision?

PROCEDURE

1. Arrange the materials as shown so that the lamp shines through the lens onto the plate. The lens should be about $\frac{2}{3}$ a meter from the lamp.

2. Adjust the distance between the plate and the lens until you see a focused image of the bulb on the plate. Measure this distance.

3. Move the lens until it is about a meter and a half from the lamp. Adjust the plate once again to get a focused image, then measure the distance between the plate and the lens.

WHAT DO YOU THINK?
- How does the distance needed between the plate and the lens change when the lamp is farther from the lens?
- How is what happens in the eye different from what you did to refocus the image?

CHALLENGE How could you change the model to make it more like what happens in the eye?

SKILL FOCUS
Observing

MATERIALS
- convex lens
- index card
- modeling clay
- white paper plate
- lamp

TIME
10 minutes

D 128 Unit: Waves, Sound, and Light

Corrective lenses can improve vision.

What happens when the image formed by the lens of the eye does not fall exactly on the retina? The result is that the image appears blurry. This can occur either because of the shape of the eye or because of how the lens works. Artificial lenses can be used to correct this problem.

Corrective Lenses

A person who is nearsighted cannot see objects clearly unless they are near. Nearsightedness occurs when the lens of the eye focuses the image in front of the retina. The farther away the object is, the farther in front of the retina the image forms. This problem can be corrected with glasses made with concave lenses. The concave lenses spread out the rays of light before they enter the eye. The point at which the rays meet then falls on the retina.

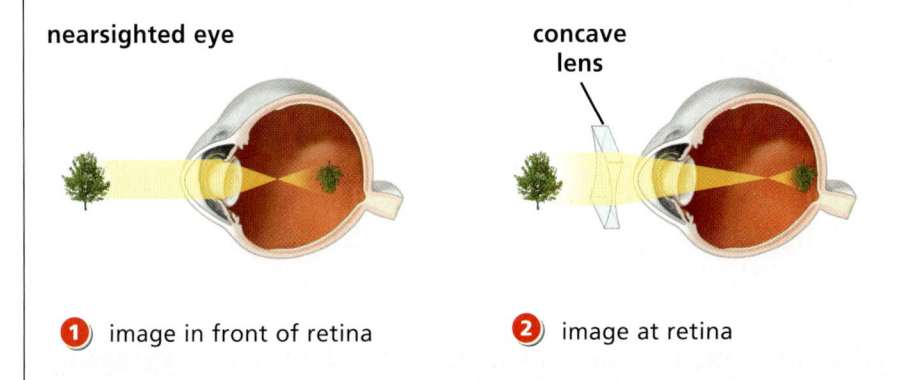

nearsighted eye

concave lens

① image in front of retina

② image at retina

Objects are clearer to a farsighted person when the objects are farther away. Farsightedness occurs when the lens of the eye focuses an object's image behind the retina. This condition can result from aging, which may make the lens less flexible. The closer the object is, the farther behind the retina the image forms. Farsightedness can be corrected with glasses made from convex lenses. The convex lenses bend the light rays inward before they enter the eye. The point at which the rays meet then falls on the retina.

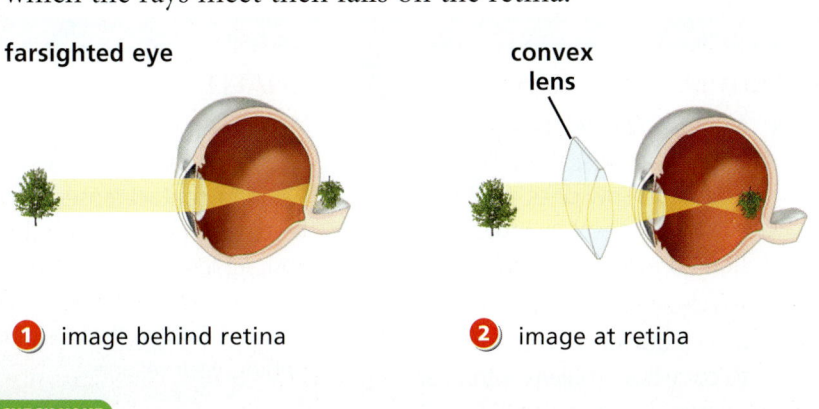

READING TiP

Nearsighted people can see objects near to them best. *Farsighted* people can see objects better when the objects are farther away.

farsighted eye

convex lens

① image behind retina

② image at retina

CHECK YOUR READING What kind of lens is used for correcting nearsightedness?

Surgery and Contact Lenses

Wearing glasses is an effective way to correct vision. It is also possible to change the shape of the cornea to make the eye refract properly. The cornea is responsible for two-thirds of the refraction that takes place inside the eye. As you know, the eye's lens changes shape to focus an image, but the shape of the cornea does not ordinarily change.

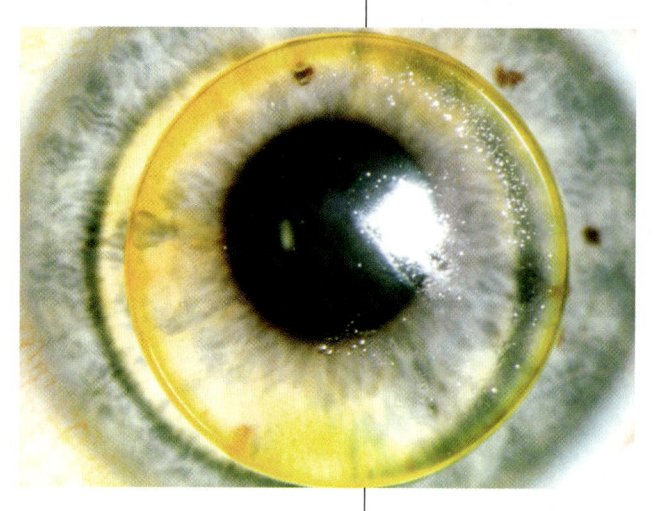

However, using advanced surgical technology, doctors can change the shape of the cornea. By doing this, they change the way light rays focus in the eye so that the image lines up with the retina. To correct for nearsightedness, surgeons remove tissue from the center of the cornea. This flattens the cornea and makes it less convex so that it will refract less. To correct for farsightedness, surgeons remove tissue from around the edges of the cornea. This increases the cornea's curvature to make it refract more. Surgery changes the shape of the cornea permanently and can eliminate the need for eyeglasses.

Contact lenses also correct vision by changing the way the cornea refracts light. Contact lenses are corrective lenses that fit directly onto the cornea. The lenses actually float on a thin layer of tears. The moisture, the contact lens, and the cornea all function together. The lens of the eye then focuses the light further. Because the change is temporary, contacts, like eyeglasses, can be adapted to new changes in the eye.

Contact lenses fit directly onto the cornea, changing the way light is refracted as it enters a person's eye.

CHECK YOUR READING What are two ways of changing the way the cornea refracts light to correct vision?

4.3 Review

KEY CONCEPTS

1. Where are images focused in an eye with perfect vision?
2. What causes people with nearsightedness to see blurry images of objects at a distance?
3. What kind of lens is used for correcting farsightedness? Why?

CRITICAL THINKING

4. **Make a Model** Draw a diagram to answer the following question: How does a convex lens affect the way a nearsighted eye focuses an image?
5. **Analyze** What distance would an eye doctor need to measure to correct a problem with nearsightedness or farsightedness?

CHALLENGE

6. **Apply** A person alternates between wearing glasses and wearing contact lenses to correct farsightedness. Are the contact lenses more or less convex than the lenses of the glasses? Explain the reasoning behind your response.

D 130 Unit: Waves, Sound, and Light

KEY CONCEPT

4.4 Optical technology makes use of light waves.

◀ BEFORE, you learned

- Mirrors are optical tools that use reflection
- Lenses are optical tools that use refraction
- The eye is a natural optical tool
- Lenses can correct vision

▶ NOW, you will learn

- How mirrors and lenses can be combined to make complex optical tools
- How optical tools are used to extend natural vision
- How laser light is made and used in optical technology

VOCABULARY

laser p. 135
fiber optics p. 137

EXPLORE Combining Lenses

How can lenses be combined?

PROCEDURE

1) Assemble the lenses, clay, and index cards as shown in the photograph.

2) Line the lenses up so that you have a straight line of sight through them.

3) Experiment with different distances between
   - the lenses
   - the far lens and an object
   - the near lens and your eye
   Find an arrangement that allows you to see a clear image of an object through both lenses.

MATERIALS
- 2 convex lenses
- modeling clay
- 2 index cards

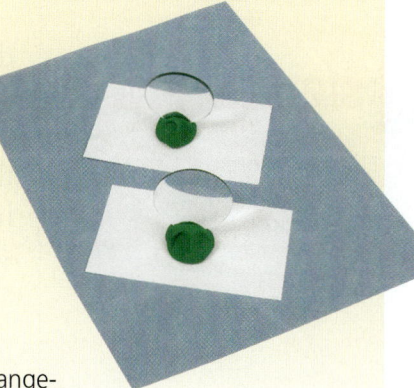

WHAT DO YOU THINK?
- What kind of image could you see? What arrangement or arrangements work best to produce an image?
- How do you think the lenses are working together to focus the image?

Mirrors and lenses can be combined to make more powerful optical tools.

COMBINATION NOTES
As you read this section, make a list of optical tools. Add sketches to help you remember important concepts.

If you know about submarines, then you know how much they depend on their periscopes to see above the water. Periscopes are made by combining mirrors. Lenses can also be combined. In the eye, for example, the cornea and the eye's lens work together to focus an image. Mirrors and lenses can be combined with each other, as they are in an overhead projector. Many of the most powerful and complex optical tools are based on different combinations of mirrors and lenses.

Chapter 4: **Light and Optics** 131 **D**

Microscopes

Microscopes are used to see objects that are too small to see well with the naked eye. An ordinary microscope works by combining convex lenses. The lens closer to the object is called the objective. The object is between one and two focal lengths from this lens, so the lens focuses an enlarged image of the object inside the microscope.

The other microscope lens—the one you look through—is called the eyepiece. You use this lens to look at the image formed by the objective. Like a magnifying glass, the eyepiece lens forms an enlarged image of the first image.

Very small objects do not reflect much light. Most microscopes use a lamp or a mirror to shine more light on the object.

CHECK YOUR READING Which types of images do the lenses in a microscope form?

Telescopes

Telescopes are used to see objects that are too far away to see well with the naked eye. One type of telescope, called a refracting telescope, is made by combining lenses. Another type of telescope, called a reflecting telescope, is made by combining lenses and mirrors.

Refracting telescopes combine convex lenses, just as microscopes do. However, the objects are far away from the objective lens instead of near to it. The object is more than two focal lengths from the objective lens, so the lens focuses a reduced image of the object inside the telescope. The eyepiece of a telescope then forms an enlarged image of the first image, just as a microscope does. This second image enlarges the object.

Reflecting telescopes work in the same way that refracting telescopes do. However, there is no objective lens where light enters the telescope. Instead, a concave mirror at the opposite end focuses an image of the object. A small flat mirror redirects the image to the side of the telescope. With this arrangement, the eyepiece does not interfere with light on its way to the concave mirror. The eyepiece then forms an enlarged image of the first image.

Both refracting and reflecting telescopes must adjust for the small amount of light received from distant objects. The amount of light gathered can be increased by increasing the diameter of the objective lens or mirror. Large mirrors are easier and less expensive to make than large lenses. So reflecting telescopes can produce brighter images more cheaply than refracting telescopes.

CHECK YOUR READING How is a reflecting telescope different from a refracting telescope?

RESOURCE CENTER
CLASSZONE.COM
Find out more about microscopes and telescopes.

D 132 Unit: Waves, Sound, and Light

Microscopes and Telescopes

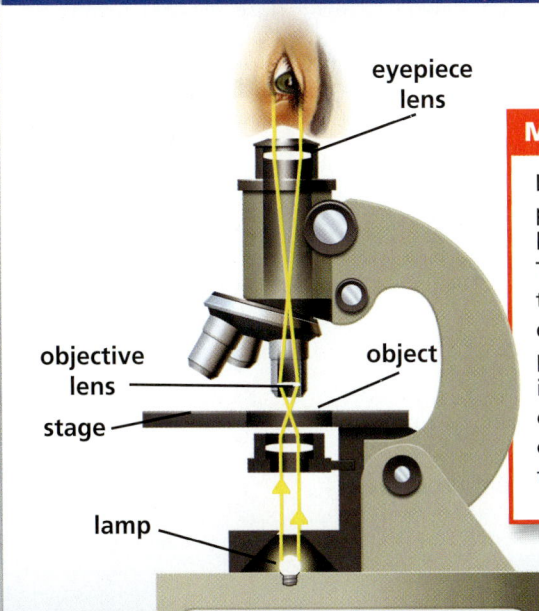

Microscope

Light from an object passes through a convex lens called an objective. The objective lens focuses the light to form an enlarged image. The eyepiece lens enlarges the image even more. The one-celled algae at right, called diatoms, appear 400 times their normal size.

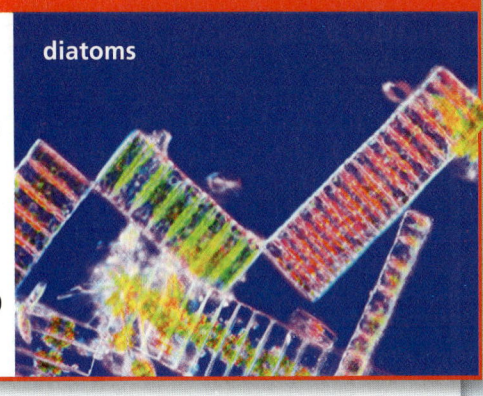

eyepiece lens, objective lens, stage, object, lamp

diatoms

Refracting Telescope

The objective lens gathers and focuses light from a distant object to form an image of the object. The eyepiece enlarges the image. The telescope image of the Moon at left shows fine details of the lunar surface.

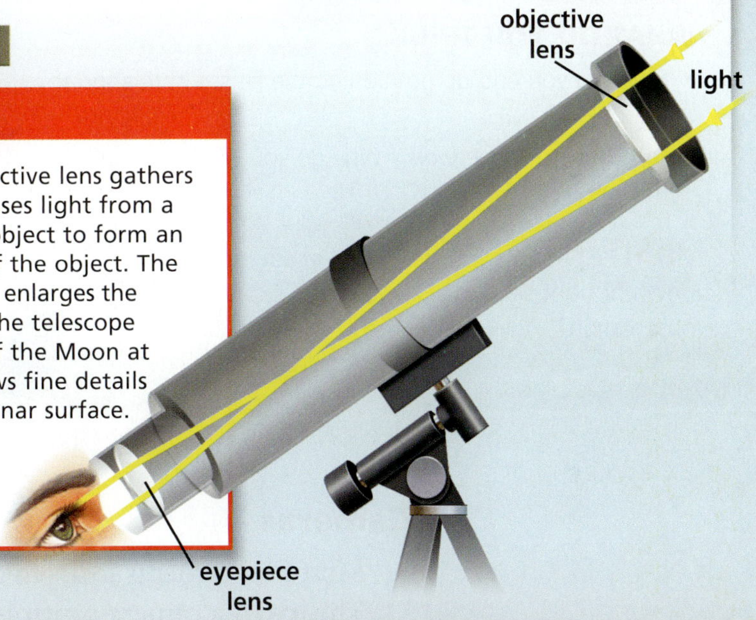

surface of the Moon

objective lens, light, eyepiece lens

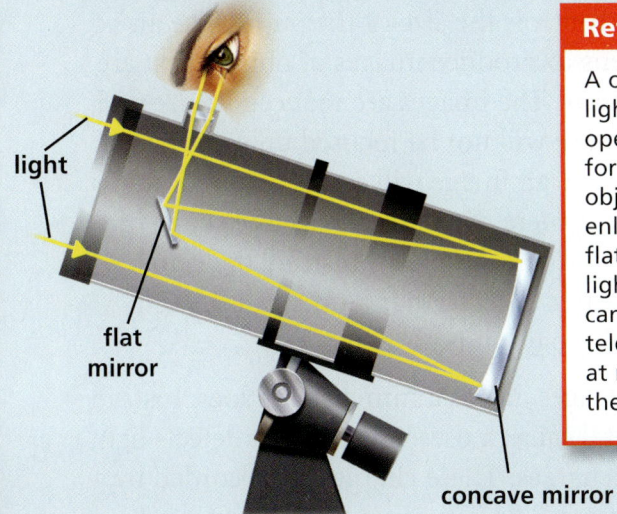

Reflecting Telescope

A concave mirror gathers light through a wide opening and focuses it to form an image of the object. The eyepiece lens enlarges the image. The flat mirror redirects the light so that the eyepiece can be out of the way. The telescope image of Saturn at right shows details of the planet's rings.

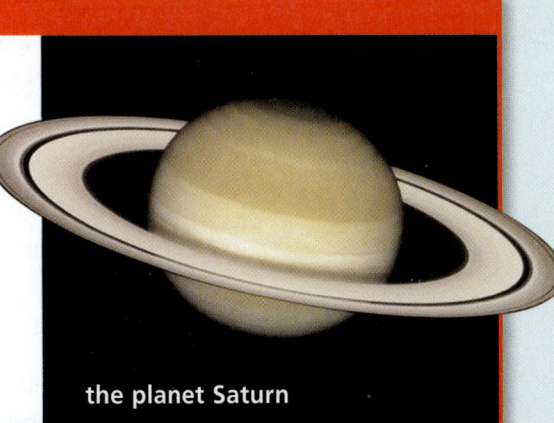

light, flat mirror, concave mirror

the planet Saturn

READING VISUALS Which type of telescope is similar in construction to a microscope?

Chapter 4: **Light and Optics** 133

INVESTIGATE Optical Tools

How can you make a simple telescope?

Use what you have learned about how a telescope works to build one. Figure out how far apart the two lenses need to be and use that information to construct a working model.

DESIGN YOUR OWN

SKILL FOCUS
Making models

MATERIALS
- 2 convex lenses
- 2 cardboard tubes
- duct tape

TIME
30 minutes

PROCEDURE

1. Decide how the lenses should be positioned in relation to an object you select to view.
2. Adjust the lenses until you get a clear image.
3. Use the other materials to fix the lenses into place and to make it possible to adjust the distance between them.

WHAT DO YOU THINK?

- How did you end up positioning the lenses in relation to the object?
- Did your telescope work? Why do you think you got this result?

CHALLENGE Is your telescope image upside down or right-side up? How can you explain this observation?

Cameras

Most film cameras focus images in the same way that the eye does. The iris of a camera controls the size of the aperture, an opening for light, just as the iris of an eye controls the size of the pupil. Like an eye, a camera uses a convex lens to produce images of objects that are more than two focal lengths away. The images are reduced in size and upside down. In the eye, an image will not be focused unless it falls exactly on the retina. In a camera, an image will not be focused unless it falls exactly on the film. The camera does not change the shape of its lens as the eye does to change the focal point. Instead, the camera allows you to move the lens nearer to or farther away from the film until the object you want to photograph is in focus.

A digital camera focuses images just as a film camera does. Instead of using film, though, the digital camera uses a sensor that detects light and converts it into electrical charges. These charges are recorded by a small computer inside the camera. The computer can then reconstruct the image immediately on the camera's display screen.

READING TIP
The term *digital* is often used to describe technology involving computers. Computers process information digitally, that is, using numbers.

D 134 Unit: Waves, Sound, and Light

How Cameras Work

A camera focuses an image in the same way as an eye.

film camera

light
lens
iris
aperture
film

READING VISUALS What part of a camera corresponds to the pupil of an eye?

Eye and Camera

lens
image
pupil
retina

film
iris
lens
aperture
image

Digital Camera

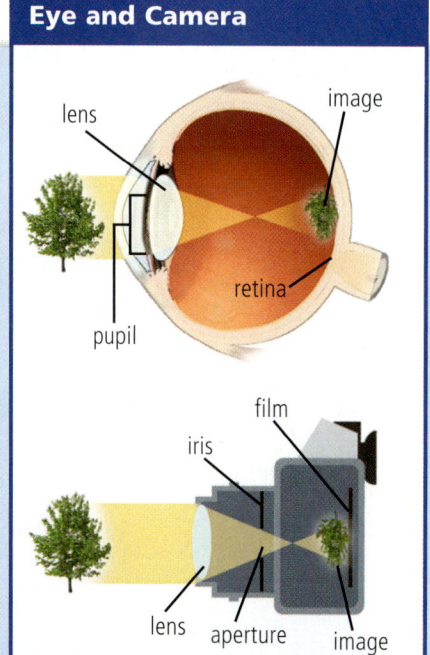

A **digital camera** records images digitally, that is, using a computer.

Lasers use light in new ways.

A **laser** (LAY-zuhr) is a device that produces an intense, concentrated beam of light that is brighter than sunlight. The word *laser* means "light amplification by stimulated emission of radiation." Laser light has many uses. It carries a lot of energy and can be controlled precisely.

Ordinary visible light is made up of many different wavelengths. Even colored light usually contains many different wavelengths. But a laser beam is made up of light waves with a single wavelength and a pure color. In addition, the waves are in phase, which means the peaks are lined up so they match exactly.

REMINDER
The peak of a wave is where it has the greatest energy.

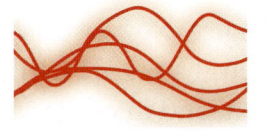

Visible light waves of different wavelengths

Light waves of a single wavelength

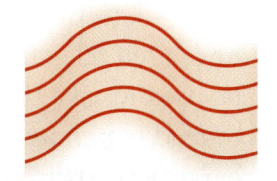

Single wavelength waves in phase

Chapter 4: **Light and Optics** 135

Light waves in a laser beam are highly concentrated and exactly parallel. Ordinary light spreads out, growing more faint as it gets farther from its source. Laser light spreads out very little. After traveling 1 kilometer (0.6 mi), a laser beam may have a diameter of only one meter.

Making Laser Light

A laser is made in a special tube called an optical cavity. A material that is known to give off a certain wavelength of light, such as a ruby crystal, is placed inside the tube. Next, an energy source, such as a bright flash of light, stimulates the material, causing it to emit, or give off, light waves. Both ends of the crystal are mirrored so that they reflect light back and forth between them. One end is mirrored more than the other. As the light waves pass through the crystal, they cause the material to give off more light waves—all perfectly parallel, all with the same wavelength, and all with their crests and troughs lined up. Eventually the beam becomes concentrated and strong enough to penetrate the less-mirrored end of the crystal. What comes out of the end is a laser beam.

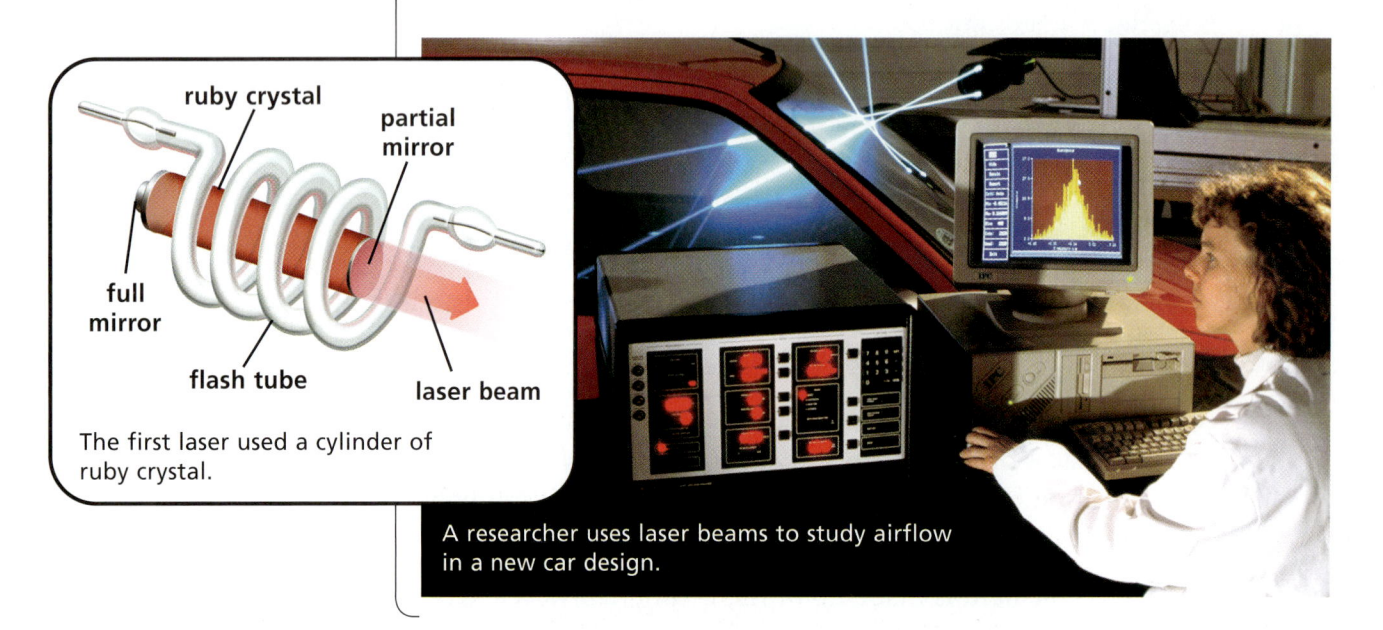

**RESOURCE CENTER
CLASSZONE.COM**
Learn more about lasers.

The first laser used a cylinder of ruby crystal.

A researcher uses laser beams to study airflow in a new car design.

Visual Uses of Lasers

Lasers are used today in an amazing variety of ways. One of these ways is to create devices that do the kind of work the human eye does—detecting and interpreting light waves. For example, surveyors once used telescopes to measure distances and angles. Now lasers can be used to take these measurements more precisely. Lasers are used to read bar codes, to scan images and pages of text, and to create holograms—three-dimensional images that appear to hover in the air. Holograms, which are hard to reproduce, are sometimes used in important documents so that the documents cannot be duplicated.

D 136 Unit: Waves, Sound, and Light

Fiber Optics

Some laser applications use visible light in ways that have nothing to do with vision. One of the fastest growing technologies is fiber optics. **Fiber optics** is technology based on the use of laser light to send signals through transparent wires called optical fibers. Fiber optics makes use of a light behavior called total internal reflection. Total internal reflection occurs when all of the light inside a medium reflects off the inner surface of the medium.

When light strikes the inner surface of a transparent medium, it may pass through the surface or it may be reflected back into the medium. Which one occurs depends on the angle at which the light hits the surface. For example, if you look through the sides of an aquarium, you can see what is behind it. But if you look at the surface of the water from below, it will act like a mirror, reflecting the inside of the aquarium.

Laser light is very efficient at total internal reflection. It can travel long distances inside clear fibers of glass or other materials. Light always travels in a straight line; however, by reflecting off the sides of the fibers, laser light inside fibers can go around corners and even completely reverse direction.

CHECK YOUR READING What is total internal reflection? What questions do you have about this light behavior?

optical fibers

Fiber optics is important in communications, because it can be used to transmit information very efficiently. Optical fibers can carry more signals than a corresponding amount of electrical cable. Optical cables can be used in place of electrical wires for telephone lines, cable television, and broadband Internet connections.

Fiber optics also has visual uses. For example, fiber optics is used in medicine to look inside the body. Using optical cable, doctors can examine organs and diagnose illnesses without surgery or x-rays. Optical fibers can also deliver laser light to specific points inside the body to help surgeons with delicate surgery.

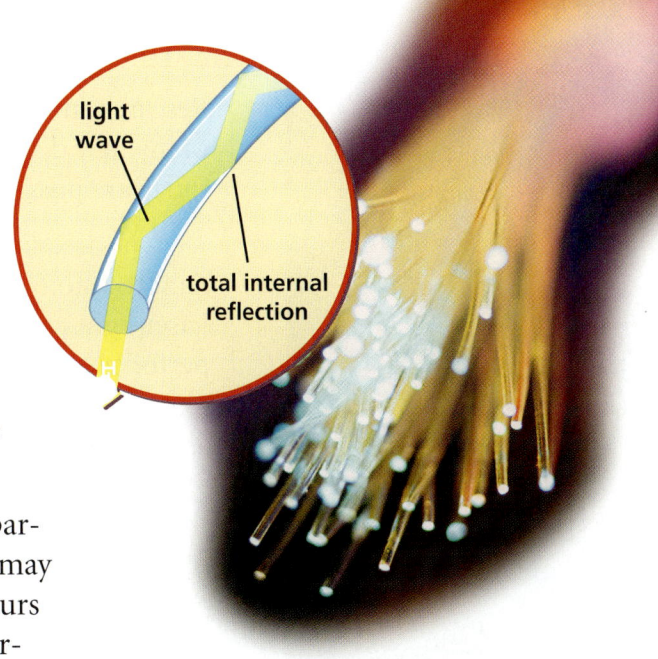

This surgeon uses fiber optics to see inside a patient's body.

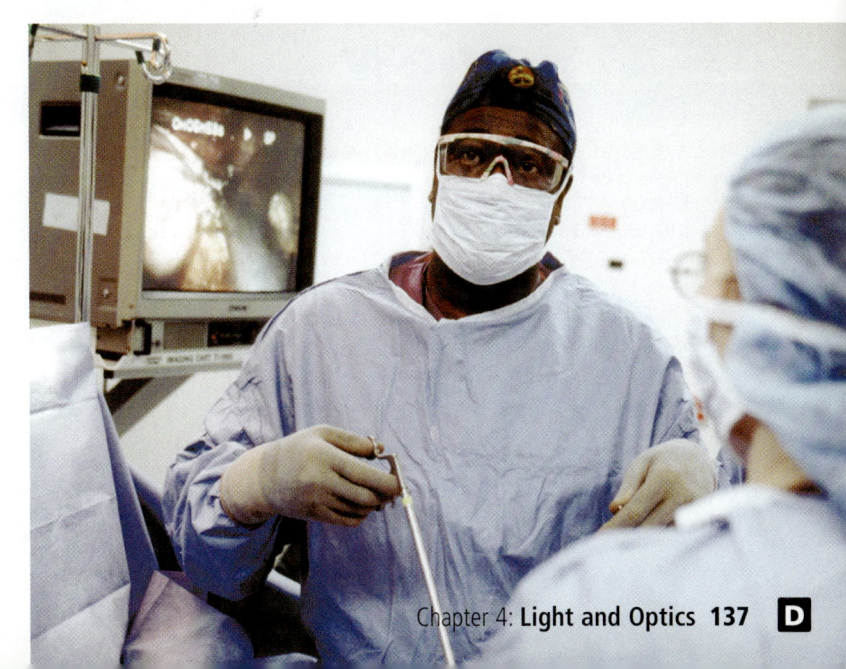

Chapter 4: **Light and Optics** 137

Future Uses of Lasers

Research involving new uses of lasers continues at an amazing pace. Many new discoveries and developments in science and technology today are possible only because of lasers.

One area of research in which lasers have made a big impact is nanotechnology—the development of super-tiny machines and tools. Laser light can be controlled very precisely, so scientists can use it to perform extremely fine operations. For example, lasers could be used to cut out parts to make molecule-size motors. Lasers can also be used as "optical tweezers" to handle extremely small objects such as molecules. Scientists are even beginning to use lasers to change the shape of molecules. They do this by varying the laser's wavelength.

Future applications of lasers are also sure to involve new ways of transferring energy. Remember that a wave is a disturbance that transfers energy. Laser light is made up of EM waves. EM waves can move energy over great distances without losing any of it. When EM waves encounter a material medium, their energy can then be converted into other forms and put to use.

One possible future use of lasers is to supply energy to spacecraft. Scientists imagine a day when orbiting space stations will make rockets unnecessary. A cable between the ground and the station will make it possible for a "space elevator" to escape Earth's gravity by climbing up the cable. The elevator will be powered by an Earth-based laser. A device on board the elevator will convert the laser's energy into electrical power.

In this artist's illustration, a space elevator of the future draws power from a laser beam to climb to an orbiting space station.

4.4 Review

KEY CONCEPTS

1. How do refracting and reflecting telescopes use convex lenses and mirrors?
2. What is different about the way a camera focuses images from the way an eye focuses images?
3. How is laser light different from ordinary light?

CRITICAL THINKING

4. **Predict** What would happen to laser light if it passed through a prism?
5. **Analyze** What are two ways reflection is involved in fiber optics?

CHALLENGE

6. **Apply** How could the speed of light and a laser beam be used to measure the distance between two satellites?

SCIENCE on the JOB

PHOTOGRAPHER

Optics in Photography

Photographers use the science of optics to help them make the best photographs possible. For example, a portrait photographer chooses the right equipment and lighting to make each person look his or her best. A photographer needs to understand how light reflects, refracts, and diffuses to achieve just the right effect.

Using Reflection

A gold-colored reflector reflects only gold-colored wavelengths of light onto the subject. Photographers use these to fill in shadows and add warmth.

without gold reflector

with gold reflector

Using Diffusion

When light is directed toward a curved reflective surface, the light scatters in many directions. This diffused light produces a softer appearance than direct light.

direct light

diffused light

Using Refraction

Lenses refract light in different ways. A long lens makes the subject appear closer. A wide-angle lens includes more space around the subject.

long lens

wide-angle lens

EXPLORE

1. **COMPARE** Find photos of people and compare them to the photos above. Which would have been improved by the use of a gold reflector? a long lens? diffused light?

2. **CHALLENGE** Using a disposable camera and a desk lamp, experiment with photography yourself. Try using a piece of paper as a reflector and observe its effects on the photograph. What happens if you use more than one reflector? What happens if you use a different color of paper?

Chapter 4 Review

the BIG idea
Optical tools depend on the wave behavior of light.

CONTENT REVIEW
CLASSZONE.COM

KEY CONCEPTS SUMMARY

4.1 Mirrors form images by reflecting light.

- Light rays obey the law of reflection.
- Mirrors work by regular reflection.
- Curved mirrors can form images that are distorted in useful ways.

VOCABULARY
optics p. 113
law of reflection p. 114
regular reflection p. 114
diffuse reflection p. 114
image p. 115
convex p. 116
concave p. 116
focal point p. 117

4.2 Lenses form images by refracting light.

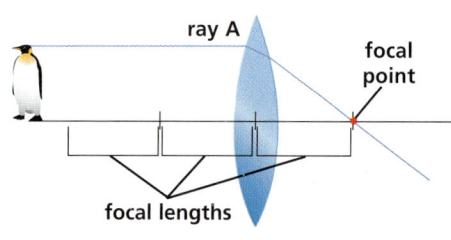

- Lenses have curved surfaces that refract parallel light waves in different amounts.
- Convex lenses bend light inward toward a focal point.
- Concave lenses spread light out.
- Lenses form a variety of useful images.

VOCABULARY
lens p. 121
focal length p. 123

4.3 The eye is a natural optical tool.

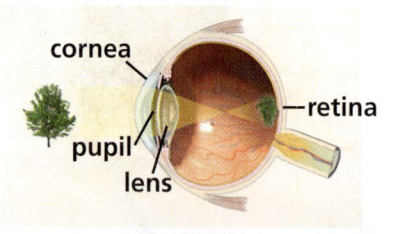

- The eyes of humans and many animals use lenses to focus images on the retina.
- The retina detects images and sends information about them to the brain.

VOCABULARY
cornea p. 127
pupil p. 127
retina p. 127

4.4 Optical technology makes use of light waves.

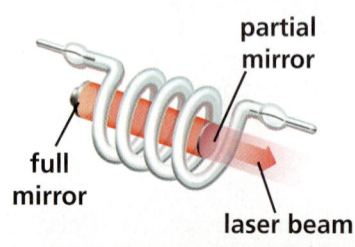

- Many optical tools are made by combining mirrors and lenses.
- Examples of optical tools include telescopes, microscopes, cameras, and lasers.
- Lasers have a wide variety of uses.

VOCABULARY
laser p. 135
fiber optics p. 137

D 140 Unit: Waves, Sound, and Light

Reviewing Vocabulary

For each item below, fill in the blank. If the right column is blank, give a brief description or definition. If the left column is blank, give the correct term.

Term	Description
1.	shape like the inside of a bowl
2. convex	
3.	science of light, vision, and related technology
4.	picture of object formed by light rays
5. focal point	
6.	controls the amount of light entering the eye
7.	distance between mirror or lens and place where light rays meet
8. fiber optics	
9. law of reflection	
10.	concentrated, parallel light waves of a single wavelength

Reviewing Key Concepts

Multiple Choice *Choose the letter of the best answer.*

11. What shape is a mirror that reflects parallel light rays toward a focal point?
    a. convex
    b. flat
    c. concave
    d. regular

12. According to the law of reflection, a light ray striking a mirror
    a. continues moving through the mirror in the same direction
    b. moves into the mirror at a slightly different angle
    c. bounces off the mirror toward the direction it came from
    d. bounces off the mirror at the same angle it hits

13. Reflecting telescopes focus images using
    a. several mirrors
    b. several lenses
    c. both mirrors and lenses
    d. either a mirror or a lens, but not both

14. Ordinary light differs from laser light in that ordinary light waves
    a. all have the same wavelength
    b. tend to spread out
    c. stay parallel to one another
    d. all have their peaks lined up

15. Nearsighted vision is corrected when lenses
    a. reflect light away from the eye
    b. allow light rays to focus on the retina
    c. allow light to focus slightly past the retina
    d. help light rays reflect regularly

16. Lasers do work similar to that of human vision when they are used to
    a. perform surgery
    b. send phone signals over optical cable
    c. scan bar codes at the grocery store
    d. change the shape of molecules

Short Answer *Write a short answer to each question.*

17. Name one optical tool, describe how it works, and explain some of its uses.

18. How are the images that are produced by a convex mirror different from those produced by a concave mirror?

19. Describe what typically happens to a ray of light from the time it enters the eye until it strikes the retina.

20. How do lenses correct nearsightedness and farsightedness?

21. What does a refracting telescope have in common with a simple microscope?

22. Describe two ways the distance of an object from a lens can affect the appearance of the object's image.

Chapter 4: **Light and Optics** 141

Thinking Critically

INTERPRET *In the four diagrams below, light rays are shown interacting with a material medium. For the next four questions, choose the letter of the diagram that answers the question.*

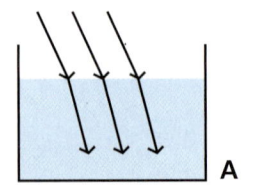

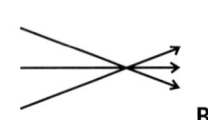

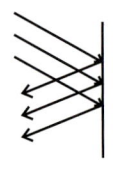

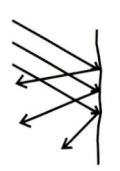

A

B

C

D

23. Which diagram shows regular reflection?

24. Which diagram shows diffuse reflection?

25. Which diagram shows refraction?

26. Which diagram shows light rays converging at a focal point?

COMPARE AND CONTRAST *Copy the chart below. For each pair of terms, write down one way they are alike (compare) and one way they are different (contrast).*

Terms	Compare	Contrast
27. flat mirror, curved mirror		
28. convex lens, concave lens		
29. focal point, focal length		
30. nearsighted, farsighted		
31. simple microscope, refracting telescope		
32. regular reflection, total internal reflection		

33. **INFER** What is the approximate focal length of the eye's lens? How do you know?

34. **ANALYZE** Why is laser light used in fiber optics?

35. **APPLY** In order to increase the magnification of a magnifying glass, would you need to make the convex surfaces of the lens more or less curved?

36. **APPLY** Describe a possible use for laser light not mentioned in the chapter. What characteristics of laser light does this application make use of?

the BIG idea

37. **SYNTHESIZE** Using what you have learned in this chapter, describe two possible uses of an optical tool like the one shown on pages 110–111. Explain what wave behaviors of light would be involved in these uses. Then explain how these uses could benefit the person in the photo.

38. **APPLY** Make a sketch of an optical tool that would use three mirrors to make a beam of light return to its source. Your sketch should include:
    - the path of light waves through the tool
    - labels indicating the names of parts and how they affect the light
    - several sentences describing one possible use of the tool

UNIT PROJECTS

Evaluate all the data, results, and information from your project folder. Prepare to present your project.

142 Unit: Waves, Sound, and Light

Standardized Test Practice

For practice on your state test, go to...
TEST PRACTICE
CLASSZONE.COM

Interpreting Diagrams

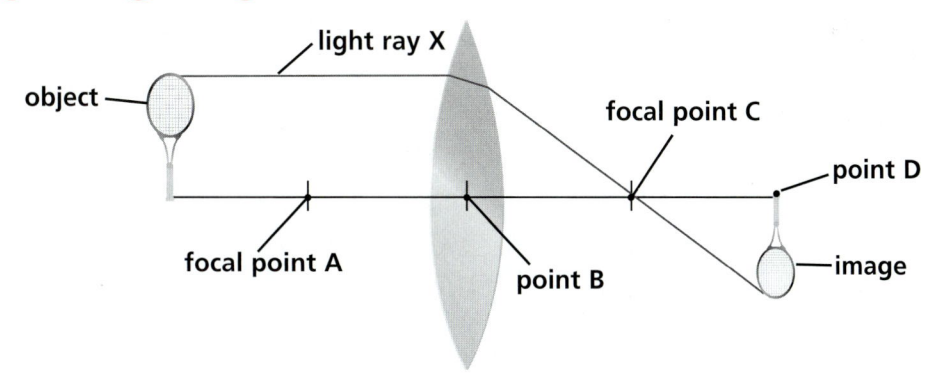

Study the diagram above and then answer the questions that follow.

1. What kind of lens is shown in the diagram?
   a. concave
   b. convex
   c. flat
   d. prism

2. What happens to parallel light rays passing through this type of lens?
   a. They become polarized.
   b. They form a rainbow.
   c. They bend inward.
   d. They bend outward.

3. All light rays parallel to light ray X will pass through what point?
   a. point A
   b. point B
   c. point C
   d. point D

4. How far is the object in the diagram from the lens?
   a. less than one focal length
   b. one focal length
   c. about two focal lengths
   d. more than three focal lengths

5. Where would you position a screen in order to see the image in focus on the screen?
   a. at point A
   b. at point B
   c. at point C
   d. at point D

Extended Response

Answer the two questions below in detail. Include some of the terms from the word box. Underline each term you use in your answer.

concave	focal point	real image
convex	refraction	virtual image
flat mirror	reflection	magnifying glass

6. What kind of mirror would you use to see what is happening over a broad area? Why?

7. Choose one of the following optical tools and explain how it uses mirrors and/or lenses to form an image: camera, telescope, periscope, microscope.

Chapter 4: **Light and Optics** 143

UNIT E

Electricity and Magnetism

magnet

ATTRACT

magnetic field

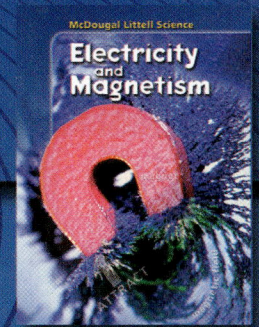

Electricity and Magnetism
Contents Overview

Unit Features
FRONTIERS IN SCIENCE Electronics in Music   2
TIMELINES IN SCIENCE The Story of Electronics   72

1 Electricity   6
the BIG idea
Moving electric charges transfer energy.

2 Circuits and Electronics   40
the BIG idea
Circuits control the flow of electric charge.

3 Magnetism   76
the BIG idea
Current can produce magnetism, and magnetism can produce current.

FRONTIERS in Science

Electronics in *Music*

How are electronics changing the way we make and listen to music?

SCIENTIFIC AMERICAN FRONTIERS

View the video segment "Toy Symphony" to learn about some creative new ways in which music and electronics can be combined.

The quality of amplified sound waves can be controlled using electronics. Controls on this soundboard are adjusted in preparation for an outdoor concert.

Catching a Sound Wave

Everyone knows that music and electronics go together. If you want to hear music, you turn on a radio or TV, choose a CD or DVD to play, or listen to a computer file downloaded in MP3. All of these formats use electronics to record, play, and amplify music. Some of the most recent developments in music also use electronics to produce the music in the first place. For example, the orchestral music playing in the background of the last blockbuster movie you saw may not have been played by an orchestra at all. It may have been produced electronically on a computer.

Music consists of sound, and sound is a wave. Inside your TV or stereo equipment, electronic circuits represent sound waves as analog signals or digital signals. In analog recordings a peak in the original sound wave corresponds to a peak in the current. Radio and TV broadcasts are usually analog signals. The sound wave is converted to electromagnetic waves sent out through the air. Your radio or TV set receives these waves and converts them back to a sound wave.

In digital sound recordings the system samples the incoming sound wave at frequent intervals of time, such as 44,100 times per second. The system measures the height of each wave and assigns it a number. The numbers form a digital signal. This information can then be stored and transmitted. The playback electronics, such as CD players and DVD players, convert the signal back to a sound wave for you to hear.

Digital Devices

In a compact disc (CD), the numbers representing the sound wave are coded into a series of microscopic pits in a long spiral track burned into the plastic of the CD. A laser beam scans the track and reads the pits, converting the data back into numbers. This information is then converted into sound waves by an electronic circuit in the CD player. CDs can store up to 74 minutes of music because the pits are only a few millionths of a meter in size. Digital videodiscs (DVDs) often have several layers, each with a separate data track, and use even smaller tracks and pits than CDs use. As a result, a DVD can store seven times as much information as a CD.

The amount of computer space needed to represent a song in normal digital format is too large to store very many songs on a single device. However, the development of a compression program called MP3 decreases the size of a typical song to one-tenth its original size. This enables you to buy and download a song from the Internet in minutes instead of hours and store files on your computer or MP3 player without taking up too much space.

MP3 players store digital files that are compressed in size.

Making Music

These advances in recording and playing music enables you to listen to music, whatever your taste in music happens to be. Electronic technology also allows you to change the music or even generate your own music, as shown in the video. Recording engineers used to work with large electronic consoles with hundreds of switches in order to blend different singers and background demonstrated by concert violinist Joshua Bell. As Joshua plays the violin, a computer registers the movements of the bow and produces new and different sounds from the movements. Other musical electronic devices in the lab are designed to allow someone with little or no experience with an instrument to play and compose music.

With Beatbugs—small interactive devices—kids can play music and collaborate with others. They can also compose and edit their own music. Using new computer software, a ten-year-old boy was able to compose an entire symphony played by the German Symphony Orchestra.

SCIENTIFIC AMERICAN FRONTIERS

View the "Toy Symphony" segment of your *Scientific American Frontiers* video to learn how electronic devices allow people to interact with music in new ways.

IN THIS SCENE FROM THE VIDEO Kids play with Beatbugs at MIT's Media Lab.

PLAYING WITH SOUNDS At the Massachusetts Institute of Technology (MIT) Media Lab, Tod Machover and his colleagues have invented several new musical instruments that are based on electronics. One such invention is the hyperviolin,

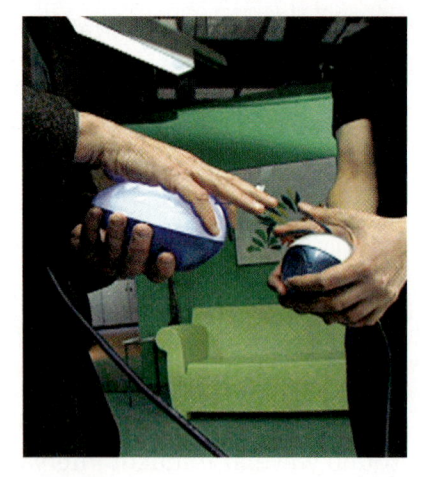

4 Unit: Electricity and Magnetism

Home recording studios are possible because of new electronic technology.

instruments or to add special effects such as echoes or distortion. Now this can all be done on a laptop computer, using the Musical Instrument Digital Interface (MIDI).

MIDI technology is an advancement in digital technology. Whereas CD, DVD, and MP3 files represent the sound waves themselves, MIDI files represent the instructions for another device—such as an electronic instrument—to play the music. With MIDI, you can connect an electronic keyboard directly to a computer and compose and edit your own music, layer in the sounds of different instruments, and dub in special effects. Once you understand how to use electronics to produce the sound waves you want, you can become your own favorite band.

UNANSWERED Questions

Every year, scientists develop new technologies affecting the way we produce and listen to music. As advances in music technology are made, new question arise.

- Are there electronic sounds that no one has heard before?
- How will the development of music technology affect who is producing music?
- What type of devices will people be using to listen to music in 50 years?

UNIT PROJECTS

As you study this unit, work alone or with a group on one of these projects.

Multimedia Presentation

Put together an informative presentation that explains how electric guitars work.

- Gather information about electric guitars. Learn how they use both electricity and magnetism.
- Give a presentation that uses mixed media, such as a computer slide show, model, poster, or tape recording.

Build a Radio

Build a working radio from simple materials.

- Using books or the Internet, find instructions for building a simple crystal radio.
- Collect the materials and assemble the radio. Modify the design of the radio to improve it.
- Demonstrate the radio to the class and explain how it works.

Design an Invention

Design an electronic invention.

- Select a purpose for your invention, such as a toy, a fan, or a burglar alarm. Write a paragraph that explains the purpose of your invention.
- Draw a sketch of your design and modify it if necessary.
- Make a pamphlet to advertise your invention. If possible, build the invention and include photographs of it in the pamphlet.

CAREER CENTER
CLASSZONE.COM

Learn more about careers in music and computer science.

CHAPTER 1
Electricity

the BIG idea

Moving electric charges transfer energy.

Key Concepts

SECTION 1.1
Materials can become electrically charged.
Learn how the movement of electrons builds static charges and how static charges are used in technology.

SECTION 1.2
Charges can move from one place to another.
Learn what factors control the movement of charges.

SECTION 1.3
Electric current is a flow of charge.
Learn how electric current is measured and how it can be produced.

Internet Preview

CLASSZONE.COM
Chapter 1 online resources: Content Review, two Simulations, two Resource Centers, Math Tutorial, Test Practice.

What keeps this dragon glowing brightly?

EXPLORE the BIG idea

How Do the Pieces of Tape Interact?

Cut three strips of tape. Press two onto your shirt. Peel them off and hold them close to each other, without touching. Observe. Hold one of them close to the third strip. Observe.

Observe and Think
How did the strips of tape behave in each case? Can you think of an explanation?

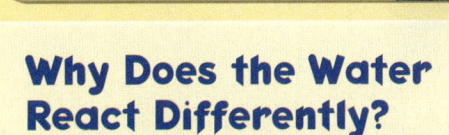

Why Does the Water React Differently?

Open a faucet just enough to let flow a thin stream of water. Run a comb through your hair a few times, and then hold it near the stream of water. Observe the behavior of the water. Touch the comb to the stream of water briefly and then hold it near the stream again.

Observe and Think How did the interaction of the comb and the stream change after you touched the comb to the water?

Internet Activity: Static Electricity

Go to **ClassZone.com** to learn more about materials and static electricity.

Observe and Think What role does the type of material play in static electricity?

NSTA scilinks.org
SCLINKS

Electricity Code: MDL065

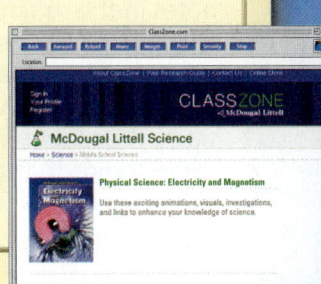

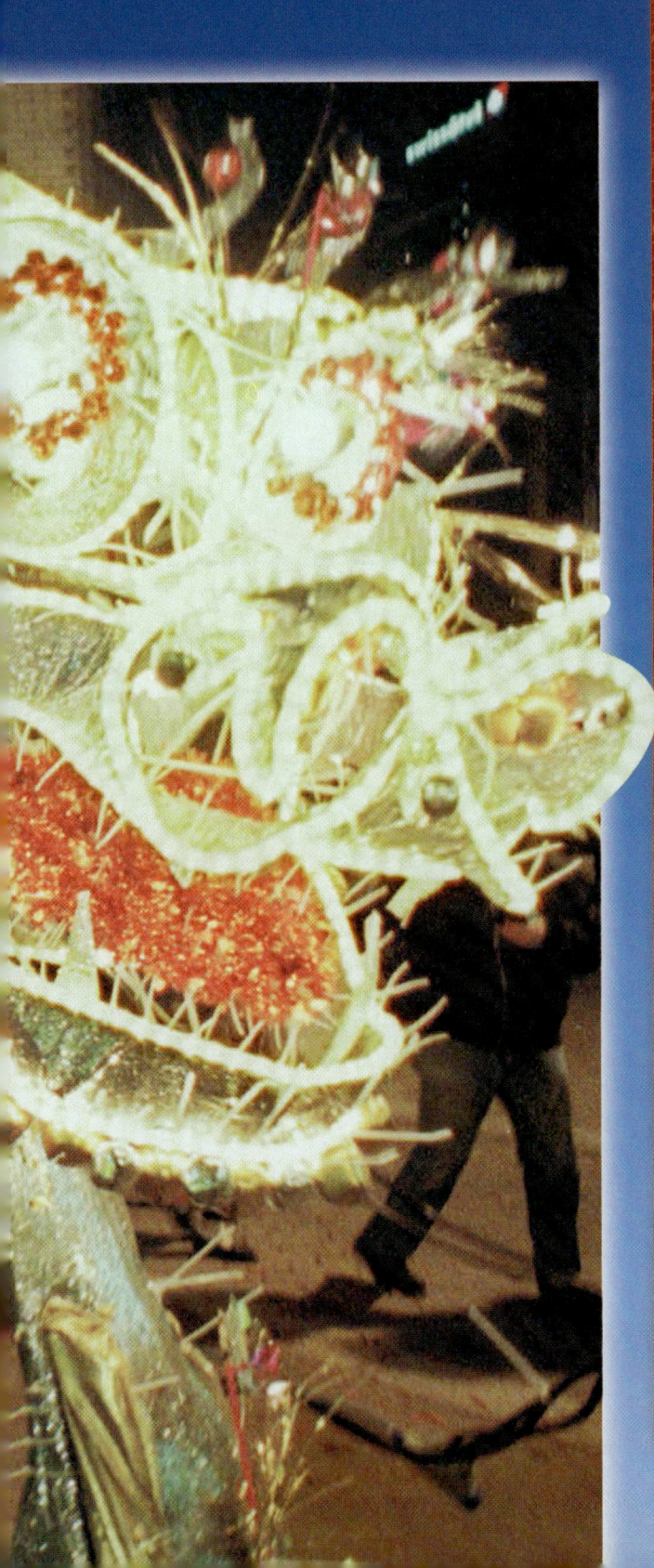

Chapter 1: **Electricity** 7

CHAPTER 1
Getting Ready to Learn

◁ CONCEPT REVIEW

- Matter is made of particles too small to see.
- Energy and matter can move from one place to another.
- Electromagnetic energy is one form of energy.

◁ VOCABULARY REVIEW

See Glossary for definitions.

atom
electron
joule
proton

CONTENT REVIEW
CLASSZONE.COM
Review concepts and vocabulary.

▷ TAKING NOTES

COMBINATION NOTES

To take notes about a new concept, first make an informal outline of the information. Then make a sketch of the concept and label it so you can study it later.

VOCABULARY STRATEGY

Write each new vocabulary term in the center of a **four square** diagram. Write notes in the squares around each term. Include a definition, some characteristics, and some examples of the term. If possible, write some things that are not examples of the term.

See the Note-Taking Handbook on pages R45–R51.

SCIENCE NOTEBOOK

NOTES
How static charges are built
- Contact
- Induction
- Charge polarization

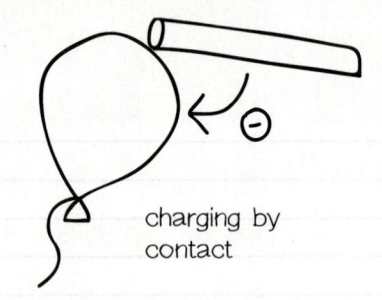

charging by contact

Definition	Characteristics
imbalance of charge in material	results from movement of electrons; affected by type of material
Examples	Nonexample
clinging laundry, doorknob shock, lightning	electricity from an electrical outlet

(STATIC CHARGE)

E 8 Unit: Electricity and Magnetism

KEY CONCEPT

1.1 Materials can become electrically charged.

BEFORE, you learned
- Atoms are made up of particles called protons, neutrons, and electrons
- Protons and electrons are electrically charged

NOW, you will learn
- How charged particles behave
- How electric charges build up in materials
- How static electricity is used in technology

VOCABULARY
electric charge p. 10
electric field p. 10
static charge p. 11
induction p. 13

EXPLORE Static Electricity

How can materials interact electrically?

PROCEDURE

1. Hold the newspaper strips firmly together at one end and let the free ends hang down. Observe the strips.

2. Put the plastic bag over your other hand, like a mitten. Slide the plastic down the entire length of the strips and then let go. Repeat several times.

3. Notice how the strips of paper are hanging. Describe what you observe.

MATERIALS
- 2 strips of newspaper
- plastic bag

WHAT DO YOU THINK?
- How did the strips behave before step 2? How did they behave after step 2?
- How might you explain your observations?

COMBINATION NOTES
As you read this section, write down important ideas about electric charge and static charges. Make sketches to help you remember these concepts.

Electric charge is a property of matter.

You are already familiar with electricity, static electricity, and magnetism. You know electricity as the source of power for many appliances, including lights, tools, and computers. Static electricity is what makes clothes stick together when they come out of a dryer and gives you a shock when you touch a metal doorknob on a dry, winter day. Magnetism can hold an invitation or report card on the door of your refrigerator.

You may not know, however, that electricity, static electricity, and magnetism are all related. All three are the result of a single property of matter—electric charge.

Chapter 1: Electricity 9 **E**

VOCABULARY
Make a four square diagram for the term *electric charge* and the other vocabulary terms in this section.

The smallest unit of a material that still has the characteristics of that material is an atom or a molecule. A molecule is two or more atoms bonded together. Most of an atom's mass is concentrated in the nucleus at the center of the atom. The nucleus contains particles called protons and neutrons. Much smaller particles called electrons move at high speeds outside the nucleus.

Protons and electrons have electric charges. **Electric charge** is a property that allows an object to exert an electric force on another object without touching it. Recall that a force is a push or a pull. The space around a particle through which an electric charge can exert this force is called an **electric field.** The strength of the field is greater near the particle and weaker farther away.

All protons have a positive charge (+), and all electrons have a negative charge (−). Normally, an atom has an equal number of protons and electrons, so their charges balance each other, and the overall charge on the atom is neutral.

Particles with the same type of charge—positive or negative—are said to have like charges, and particles with different charges have unlike charges. Particles with like charges repel each other, that is, they push each other away. Particles with unlike charges attract each other, or pull on each other.

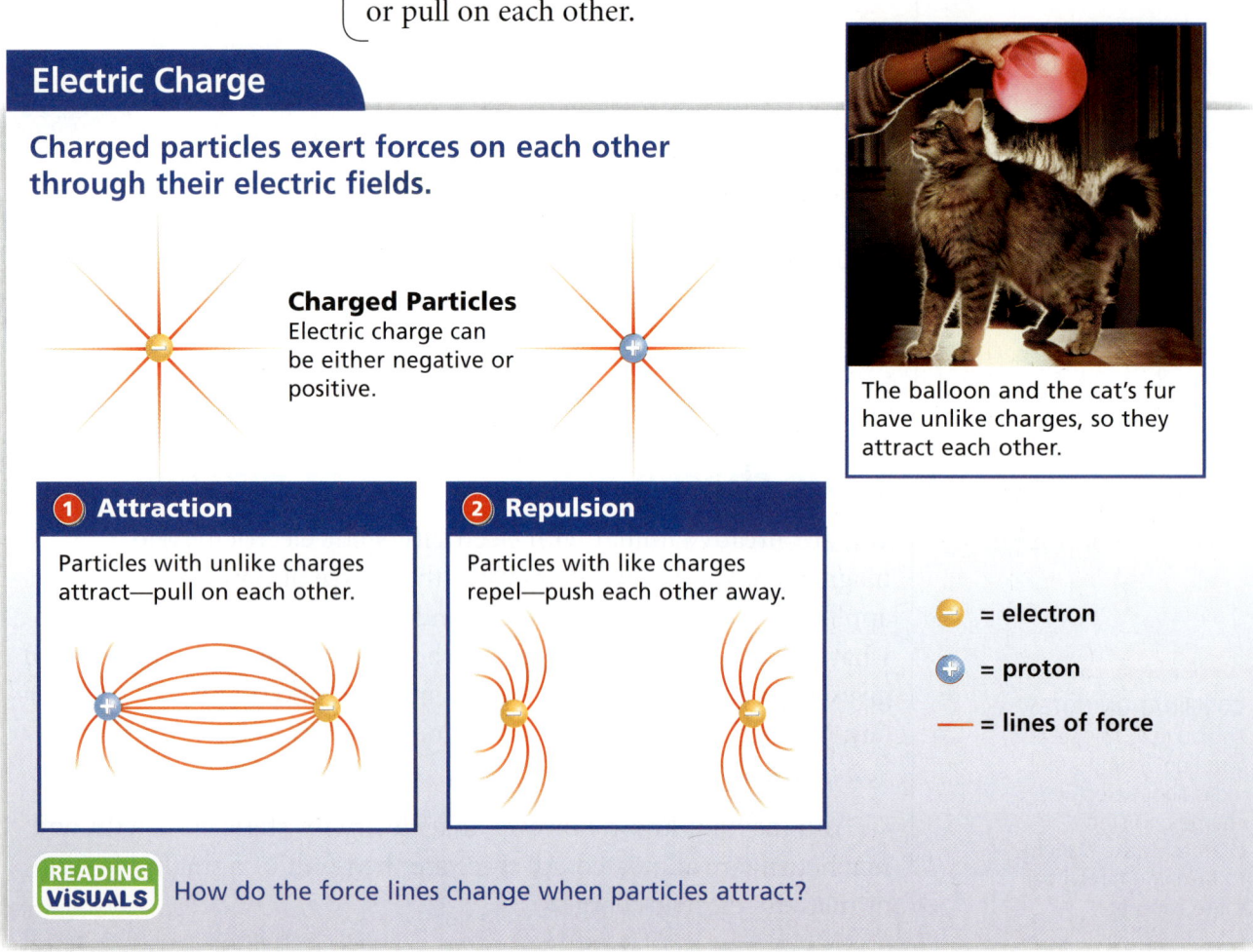

Electric Charge

Charged particles exert forces on each other through their electric fields.

Charged Particles
Electric charge can be either negative or positive.

The balloon and the cat's fur have unlike charges, so they attract each other.

① Attraction
Particles with unlike charges attract—pull on each other.

② Repulsion
Particles with like charges repel—push each other away.

⊖ = electron
⊕ = proton
— = lines of force

READING VISUALS How do the force lines change when particles attract?

10 Unit: Electricity and Magnetism

Static charges are caused by the movement of electrons.

You have read that protons and electrons have electric charges. Objects and materials can also have charges. A **static charge** is a buildup of electric charge in an object caused by the presence of many particles with the same charge. Ordinarily, the atoms that make up a material have a balance of protons and electrons. A material develops a static charge—or becomes charged—when it contains more of one type of charged particle than another.

If there are more protons than electrons in a material, the material has a positive charge. If there are more electrons than protons in a material, it has a negative charge. The amount of the charge depends on how many more electrons or protons there are. The total number of unbalanced positive or negative charges in an object is the net charge of the object. Net charge is measured in coulombs (KOO-LAHMZ). One coulomb is equivalent to more than 10^{19} electrons or protons.

Electrons can move easily from one atom to another. Protons cannot. For this reason, charges in materials usually result from the movement of electrons. The movement of electrons through a material is called conduction. If electrons move from one atom to another, the atom they move to develops a negative charge. The atom they move away from develops a positive charge. Atoms with either a positive or a negative charge are called ions.

A static charge can build up in an uncharged material when it touches or comes near a charged material. Static charges also build up when some types of uncharged materials come into contact with each other.

> **READING TiP**
> The word *static* comes from the Greek word *statos*, which means "standing."

> **REMINDER**
> 10^{19} is the same as 1 followed by 19 zeros.

Charging by Contact

When two uncharged objects made of certain materials—such as rubber and glass—touch each other, electrons move from one material to the other. This process is called charging by contact. It can be demonstrated by a balloon and a glass rod, as shown below.

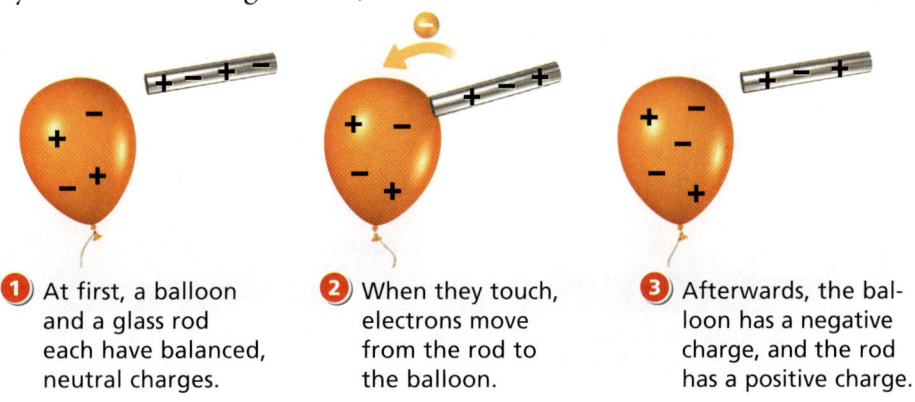

① At first, a balloon and a glass rod each have balanced, neutral charges.

② When they touch, electrons move from the rod to the balloon.

③ Afterwards, the balloon has a negative charge, and the rod has a positive charge.

Chapter 1: **Electricity** 11 **E**

metal globe

connection to globe

conveyor belt

source of electrons

As the sphere takes on a negative charge, electrons spread out over this student's skin and hair. Because her hairs all have the same charge, they repel one another.

A Van de Graaff generator is a device that builds up a strong static charge through contact. This device is shown at left. At the bottom of the device, a rubber conveyer belt rubs against a metal brush and picks up electrons. At the top, the belt rubs against metal connected to the sphere, transferring electrons to the sphere. As more and more electrons accumulate on the sphere, the sphere takes on a strong negative charge. In the photograph, the student touches the sphere as it is being charged. Some of the electrons spread across her arm to her head. The strands of her hair, which then all have a negative charge, repel one another.

CHECK YOUR READING How can a Van de Graaff generator make a person's hair stand on end?

How Materials Affect Static Charging

Charging by contact occurs when one material's electrons are attracted to another material more than they are attracted to their own. Scientists have determined from experience which materials are likely to give up or to accept electrons. For example, glass gives up electrons to wool. Wool accepts electrons from glass, but gives up electrons to rubber. The list at left indicates how some materials interact. Each material tends to give up electrons to anything below it on the list and to accept electrons from anything above it. The farther away two materials are from each other on the list, the stronger the interaction.

When you walk across a carpet, your body can become either positively or negatively charged. The type of charge depends on what materials the carpet and your shoes are made of. If you walk in shoes with rubber soles across a wool carpet, you will probably become negatively charged, because wool gives up electrons to rubber. But if you walk in wool slippers across a rubber mat, you will probably become positively charged.

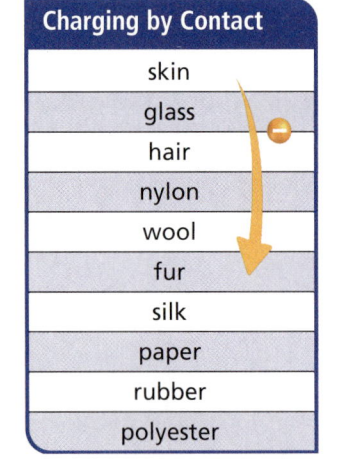

Charging by Contact
skin
glass
hair
nylon
wool
fur
silk
paper
rubber
polyester

Materials higher on the list tend to give up electrons to materials lower on the list.

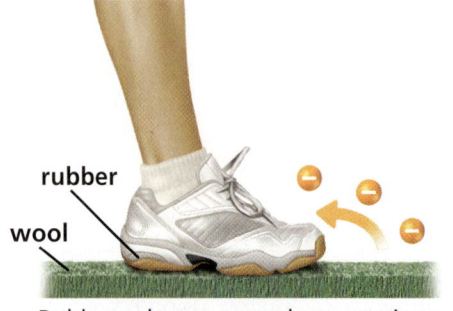

rubber
wool
Rubber soles on a wool carpet give a person a negative charge.

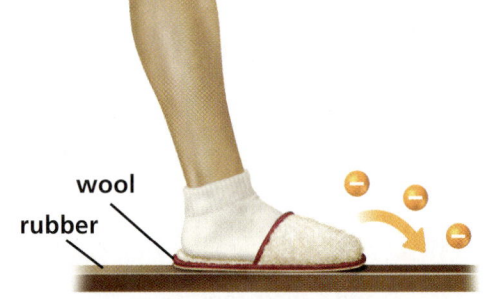

wool
rubber
Wool slippers on a rubber mat give a person a positive charge.

E 12 Unit: Electricity and Magnetism

Charging by Induction

Charging can occur even when materials are not touching if one of the materials already has a charge. Remember that charged particles push and pull each other through their electric fields without touching. The pushing and pulling can cause a charge to build in another material. The first charge is said to induce the second charge. The buildup of a charge without direct contact is called **induction.**

READING TIP

Induce and *induction* both contain the Latin root *ducere,* which means "to lead."

Induction can produce a temporary static charge. Consider what happens when a glass rod with a negative charge is brought near a balloon, as shown below. The unbalanced electrons in the rod repel the electrons in the material of the balloon. Many electrons move to the side of the balloon that is farthest away from the rod. The side of the balloon that has more electrons becomes negatively charged. The side of the balloon with fewer electrons becomes positively charged. When the rod moves away, the electrons spread out evenly once again.

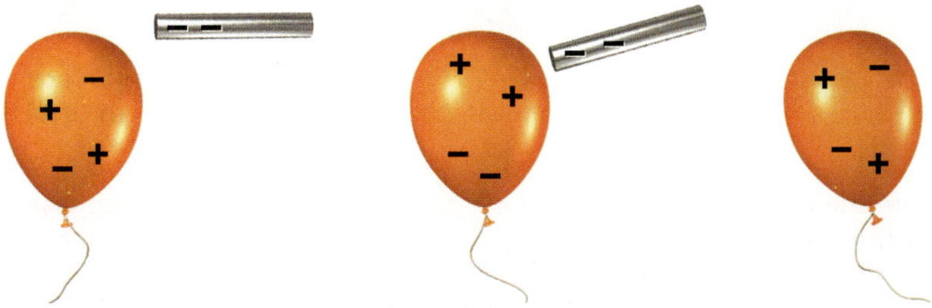

① At first, the rod has a negative charge and the balloon has a balanced charge.

② When the rod comes close to the balloon, electrons in the balloon move away from the rod.

③ When the rod moves away, electrons in the balloon spread out evenly as before.

If the electrons cannot return to their original distribution, however, induction can leave an object with a stable static charge. For example, if a negatively charged rod approaches two balloons that are touching each other, electrons will move to the balloon farther from the rod. If the balloons are then separated, preventing the electrons from moving again, the balloon with more electrons will have a negative charge and the one with fewer electrons will have a positive charge. When the rod is taken away, the balloons keep their new charges.

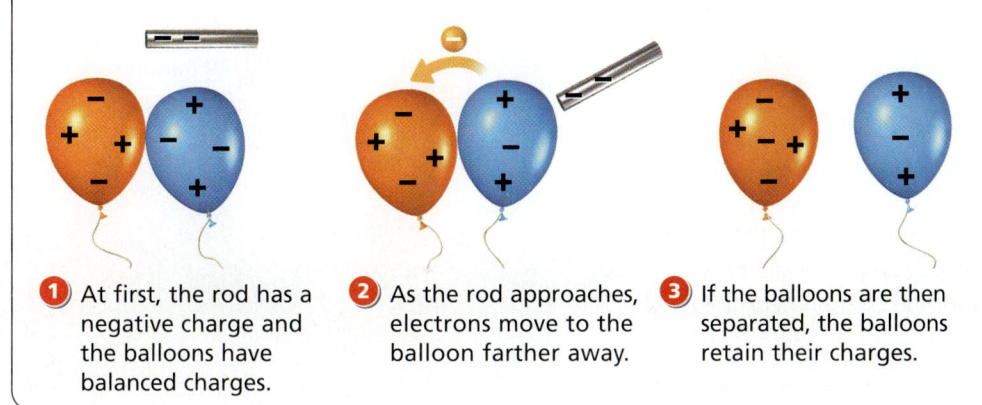

① At first, the rod has a negative charge and the balloons have balanced charges.

② As the rod approaches, electrons move to the balloon farther away.

③ If the balloons are then separated, the balloons retain their charges.

Chapter 1: **Electricity** 13 **E**

Charge Polarization

Induction can build a charge by changing the position of electrons, even when electrons do not move between atoms. Have you ever charged a balloon by rubbing it on your head, and then stuck the balloon to a wall? When you bring the balloon close to the wall, the balloon's negative charge pushes against the electrons in the wall. If the electrons cannot easily move away from their atoms, the negative charges within the atoms may shift to the side away from the balloon. When this happens, the atoms are said to be polarized. The surface of the wall becomes positively charged, and the negatively charged balloon sticks to it.

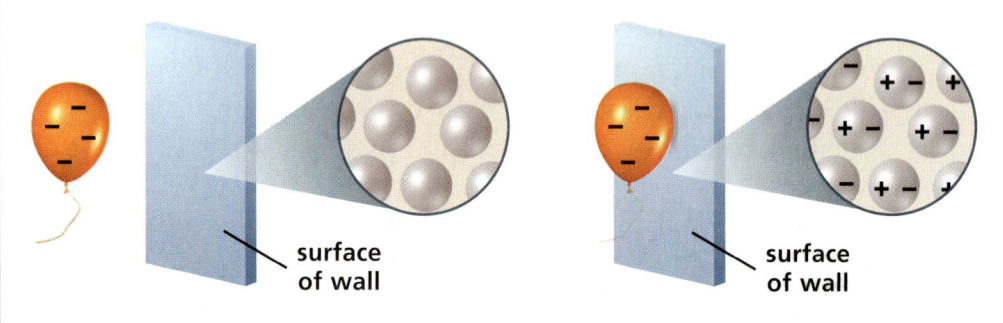

① Before the charged balloon comes near the wall, the atoms in the surface of the wall are not polarized.

② As the balloon nears the wall, atoms in the surface of the wall become polarized and attract the balloon.

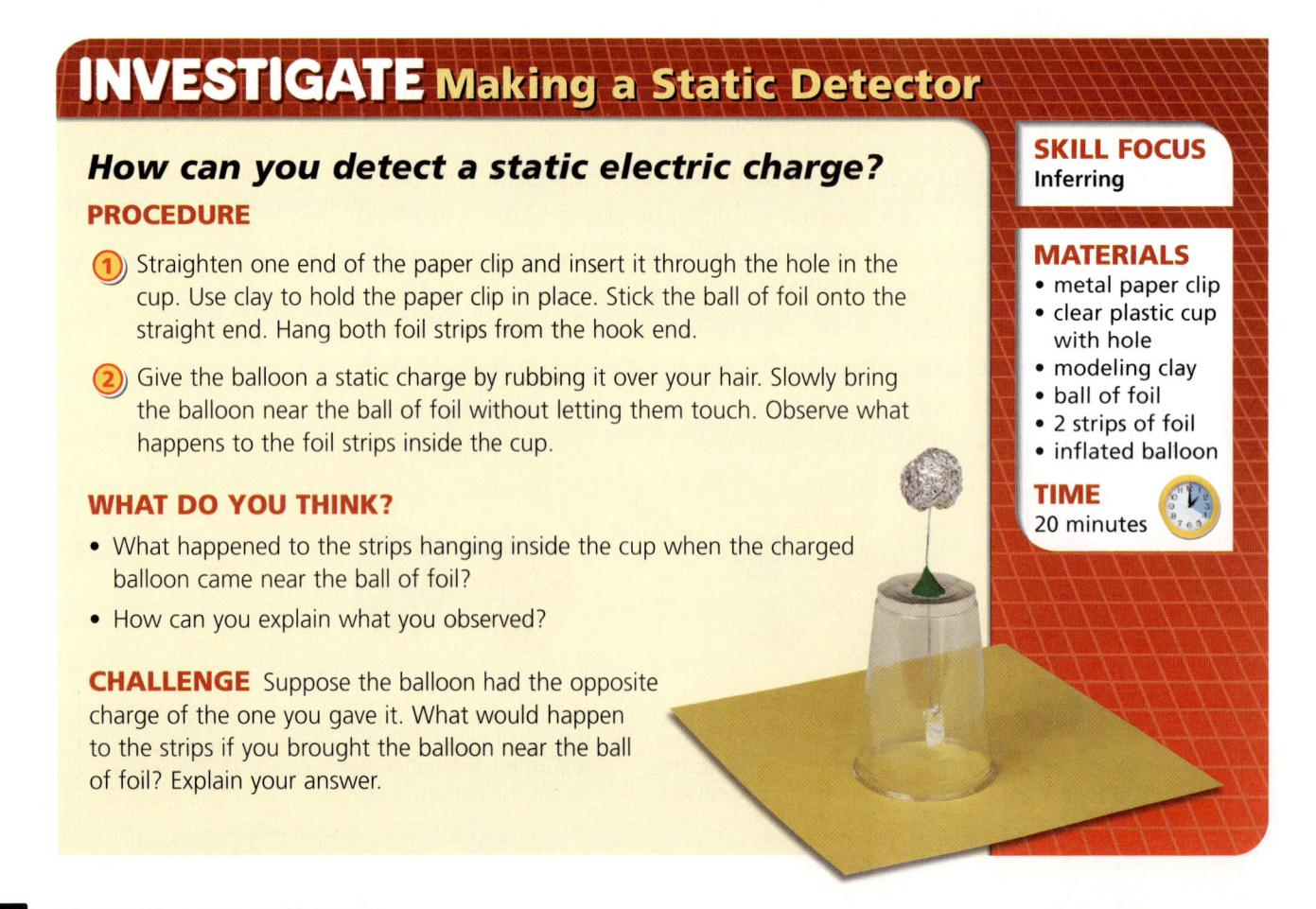

INVESTIGATE Making a Static Detector

How can you detect a static electric charge?

PROCEDURE

① Straighten one end of the paper clip and insert it through the hole in the cup. Use clay to hold the paper clip in place. Stick the ball of foil onto the straight end. Hang both foil strips from the hook end.

② Give the balloon a static charge by rubbing it over your hair. Slowly bring the balloon near the ball of foil without letting them touch. Observe what happens to the foil strips inside the cup.

WHAT DO YOU THINK?
- What happened to the strips hanging inside the cup when the charged balloon came near the ball of foil?
- How can you explain what you observed?

CHALLENGE Suppose the balloon had the opposite charge of the one you gave it. What would happen to the strips if you brought the balloon near the ball of foil? Explain your answer.

SKILL FOCUS
Inferring

MATERIALS
- metal paper clip
- clear plastic cup with hole
- modeling clay
- ball of foil
- 2 strips of foil
- inflated balloon

TIME
20 minutes

14 Unit: Electricity and Magnetism

Technology uses static electricity.

Static charges can be useful in technology. An example is the photocopy machine. Photocopiers run on electricity that comes to them through wires from the power plant. But static charges play an important role in how they work.

How a Photocopier Works

A photocopier uses static charges to make copies.

Input An original document goes into the copier. A bright light shines on the page.

Inside the Copier The letters or images are transferred from the original to the copy, as shown in the box at right.

Output Heat fixes the toner to the paper, creating a permanent copy of the original.

Labels: mirror, original, toner cartridge, lamp, drum 1, drum 2, heating element, paper

Inside the Copier

1 A mirror reflects light from white areas of the original onto drum 1, which is positively charged. These lighted areas of the drum become negatively charged.

2 Negatively charged toner (powdered ink) is attracted to the positive areas of drum 1 in the pattern of the original.

3 Drum 1 rolls against a fresh, positively charged piece of paper on drum 2. The toner on drum 1 sticks to the paper.

READING VISUALS Why does the copy have the same pattern of light and dark areas as the original?

Chapter 1: **Electricity** 15

Static electricity is also used in making cars. When new cars are painted, the paint is given an electric charge and then sprayed onto the car in a fine mist. The tiny droplets of paint stick to the car more firmly than they would without the charge. This process results in a coat of paint that is very even and smooth.

Another example of the use of static electricity in technology is a device called an electrostatic air filter. This device cleans air inside buildings with the help of static charges. The filter gives a static charge to pollen, dust, germs, and other particles in the air. Then an oppositely charged plate inside the filter attracts these particles, pulling them out of the air. Larger versions of electrostatic filters are used to remove pollutants from industrial smokestacks.

CHECK YOUR READING How can static charges help clean air?

1.1 Review

KEY CONCEPTS
1. How do a positive and a negative particle interact?
2. Describe how the movement of electrons between two objects with balanced charges could cause the buildup of electric charge in both objects.
3. Describe one technological use of static electricity.

CRITICAL THINKING
4. **Infer** A sock and a shirt from the dryer stick together. What does this tell you about the charges on the sock and shirt?
5. **Analyze** You walk over a rug and get a shock from a doorknob. What do the materials of the rug and the shoes have to do with the type of charge your body had?

CHALLENGE
6. **Apply** Assume you start with a negatively charged rod and two balloons. Describe a series of steps you could take to create a positively charged balloon, pick up negatively charged powder with the balloon, and drop the powder from the balloon.

CONNECTING SCIENCES

PHYSICAL SCIENCE AND LIFE SCIENCE

Electric Eels

An electric eel is a slow-moving fish with no teeth and poor eyesight. It lives in the murky waters of muddy rivers in South America. Instead of the senses that most animals use—vision, hearing, smell, and touch—an electric eel uses electricity to find its next meal. Since the fish that it eats often can swim much faster than the eel, it also uses electricity to catch its prey.

Electric Sense

An electric eel actually has three pairs of electric organs in its body. Two of them build electric charge for stunning prey and for self-defense. The third electric organ builds a smaller charge that helps in finding prey. The charge produces an electric field around the eel. Special sense organs on its body detect small changes in the electric field caused by nearby fish and other animals.

Shocking Organs

The electric eel builds an electric charge with a series of thousands of cells called electrocytes. Every cell in the series has a positive end and a negative end. Each electrocyte builds only a small charge. However, when all of the cells combine their charge, they can produce about five times as much electricity as a standard electrical outlet in a house. The charge is strong enough to paralyze or kill a human. Typically, though, the charge is used to stun or kill small fish, which the eel then swallows whole. Electric charge can also be used to scare away predators.

EXPLORE

1. **INFER** Electric eels live for 10 to 20 years, developing a stronger shock as they grow older. What could account for this increase in electric charge?
2. **CHALLENGE** Sharks and other animals use electricity also. Use the library or Internet to find out how.

An electric eel (Electrophorus electricus) can deliver a jolt five times as powerful as an electrical outlet.

Chapter 1: **Electricity** 17 **E**

KEY CONCEPT
1.2 Charges can move from one place to another.

BEFORE, you learned
- Static charges are built up by the separation of electrons from protons
- Materials affect how static charges are built up
- Energy is the ability to cause change

NOW, you will learn
- How charges move
- How charges store energy
- How differences in materials affect the movement of charges

VOCABULARY
electric potential p. 19
volt p. 19
conductor p. 22
insulator p. 22
resistance p. 23
ohm p. 23
grounding p. 25

EXPLORE Static Discharge
How can you observe electrical energy?

PROCEDURE
1. Rub the balloon against the wool cloth several times to give the balloon a static charge.
2. Slowly bring the balloon toward the middle part of the fluorescent bulb until a spark jumps between them.

MATERIALS
- inflated balloon
- wool cloth
- fluorescent light bulb

WHAT DO YOU THINK?
- What happened in the fluorescent bulb when the spark jumped?
- How might you explain this observation?

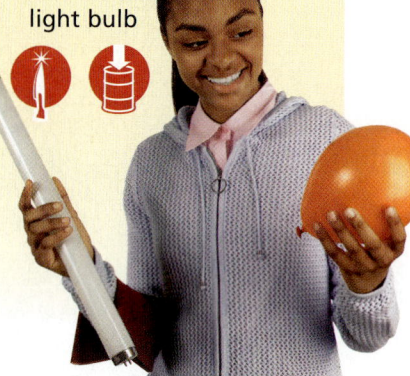

Static charges have potential energy.

You have read how a static charge is built up in an object such as a balloon. Once it is built up, the charge can stay where it is indefinitely. However, the charge can also move to a new location. The movement of a static charge out of an object is known as static discharge. When a charge moves, it transfers energy that can be used to do work.

What causes a charge to move is the same thing that builds up a charge in the first place—that is, the force of attraction or repulsion between charged particles. For example, suppose an object with a negative charge touches an object with a positive charge. The attraction of the unbalanced electrons in the first object to the unbalanced protons in the second object can cause the electrons to move to the second object.

> **REMINDER**
> Energy can be either kinetic (energy of motion) or potential (stored energy). Energy is measured in joules.

CHECK YOUR READING What can cause a charge to move?

18 Unit: Electricity and Magnetism

Electric Potential Energy

Potential energy is stored energy an object may have because of its position. Water in a tower has gravitational potential energy because it is high above the ground. The kinetic energy—energy of motion—used to lift the water to the top of the tower is stored as potential energy. If you open a pipe below the tower, the water moves downward and its potential energy is converted back into kinetic energy.

Similarly, electric potential energy is the energy a charged particle has due to its position in an electric field. Because like charges repel, for example, it takes energy to push a charged particle closer to another particle with a like charge. That energy is stored as the electric potential energy of the first particle. When the particle is free to move again, it quickly moves away, and its electric potential energy is converted back into kinetic energy.

When water moves downward out of a tower and some of its potential energy is converted into kinetic energy, its potential energy decreases. Similarly, when a charged particle moves away from a particle with a like charge, its electric potential energy decreases. The water and the particle both move from a state of higher potential energy to one of lower potential energy.

Like water in a tower, a static charge has potential energy. Just as gravity moves water down the supply pipe attached under the tank, the electric potential energy of a charge moves the charge along an electrical pathway.

Electric Potential

To push a charged particle closer to another particle with the same charge takes a certain amount of energy. To push two particles into the same position near that particle takes twice as much energy, and the two particles together have twice as much electric potential energy as the single particle. Although the amount of potential energy is higher, the amount of energy per unit charge at that position stays the same. **Electric potential** is the amount of electric potential energy per unit charge at a certain position in an electric field.

Electric potential is measured in units called volts, and voltage is another term for electric potential. A potential of one **volt** is equal to one joule of energy per coulomb of charge.

Just as water will not flow between two towers of the same height, a charge will not move between two positions with the same electric potential. For a charge to move, there must be a difference in potential between the two positions.

Charge Movement

When water moves from a higher to a lower position, some of its potential energy is used to move it. Along the way, some of its potential energy can be used to do other work, such as turning a water wheel. Similarly, when a charge moves, some of its electric potential energy is used in moving the charge and some of it can be used to do other work. For example, moving an electric charge through a material can cause the material to heat up, as in a burner on an electric stove.

You can see how a moving charge transfers energy when you get a shock from static electricity. As you walk across a rug, a charge builds up on your body. Once the charge is built up, it cannot move until you come in contact with something else. When you reach out to touch a doorknob, the charge has a path to follow. The electric potential energy of the charge moves the charge from you to the doorknob.

Why do you get a shock? Recall that the force of attraction or repulsion between charged particles is stronger when they are close together. As your hand gets closer to the doorknob, the electric potential of the static charge increases. At a certain point, the difference in electric potential between you and the doorknob is great enough to move the charge through the air to the doorknob. As the charge moves, some of its potential energy is changed into the heat, light, and sound of a spark.

CHECK YOUR READING What two factors determine whether a static charge will move?

Lightning

RESOURCE CENTER
CLASSZONE.COM
Find out more about lightning and lightning safety.

The shock you get from a doorknob is a small-scale version of lightning. Lightning is a high-energy static discharge. This static electricity is caused by storm clouds. Lightning comes from the electric potential of millions of volts, which releases large amounts of energy in the form of light, heat, and sound. As you read about how lightning forms, follow the steps in the illustration on page 21.

① **Charge Separation** Particles of moisture inside a cloud collide with the air and with each other, causing the particles to become electrically charged. Wind and gravity separate charges, carrying the heavier, negatively charged particles to the bottom of the cloud and the lighter, positively charged particles to the top of the cloud.

② **Charge Buildup** Through induction, the negatively charged particles at the bottom of the cloud repel electrons in the ground, causing the surface of the ground to build up a positive charge.

③ **Static Discharge** When the electric potential, or voltage, created by the difference in charges is large enough, the negative charge moves from the cloud to the ground. The energy released by the discharge produces the flash of lightning and the sound of thunder.

How Lightning Forms

Lightning is a type of static discharge. Storm clouds may develop very large charges, each with an electric potential of millions of volts.

1 Charge Separation

Collisions between particles in storm clouds separate charges. Negatively charged particles collect at the bottom of the cloud.

2 Charge Buildup

The negatively charged bottom part of the cloud induces a positive charge in the surface of the ground.

3 Static Discharge

The charge jumps through the air to the ground. Energy released by the discharge causes thunder and lightning.

READING VISUALS How is lightning like the shock you can get from a doorknob? How is it different?

COMBINATION NOTES
Make notes on the different ways materials can affect charge movement. Use sketches to help explain the concepts.

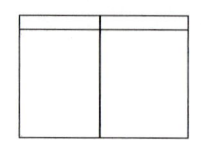

Materials affect charge movement.

After you walk across a carpet, a charge on your skin has no place to go until you touch or come very close to something. That is because an electric charge cannot move easily through air. However, a charge can move easily through the metal of a doorknob.

Conductors and Insulators

A material that allows an electric charge to pass through it easily is called a **conductor**. Metals such as iron, steel, copper, and aluminum are good conductors. Most wire used to carry a charge is made of copper, which conducts very well.

A material that does not easily allow a charge to pass through it is called an **insulator**. Plastic and rubber are good insulators. Many types of electric wire are covered with plastic, which insulates well. The plastic allows a charge to be conducted from one end of the wire to the other, but not through the sides of the wire. Insulators are also important in electrical safety, because they keep charges away from the body.

CHECK YOUR READING What is the difference between a conductor and an insulator?

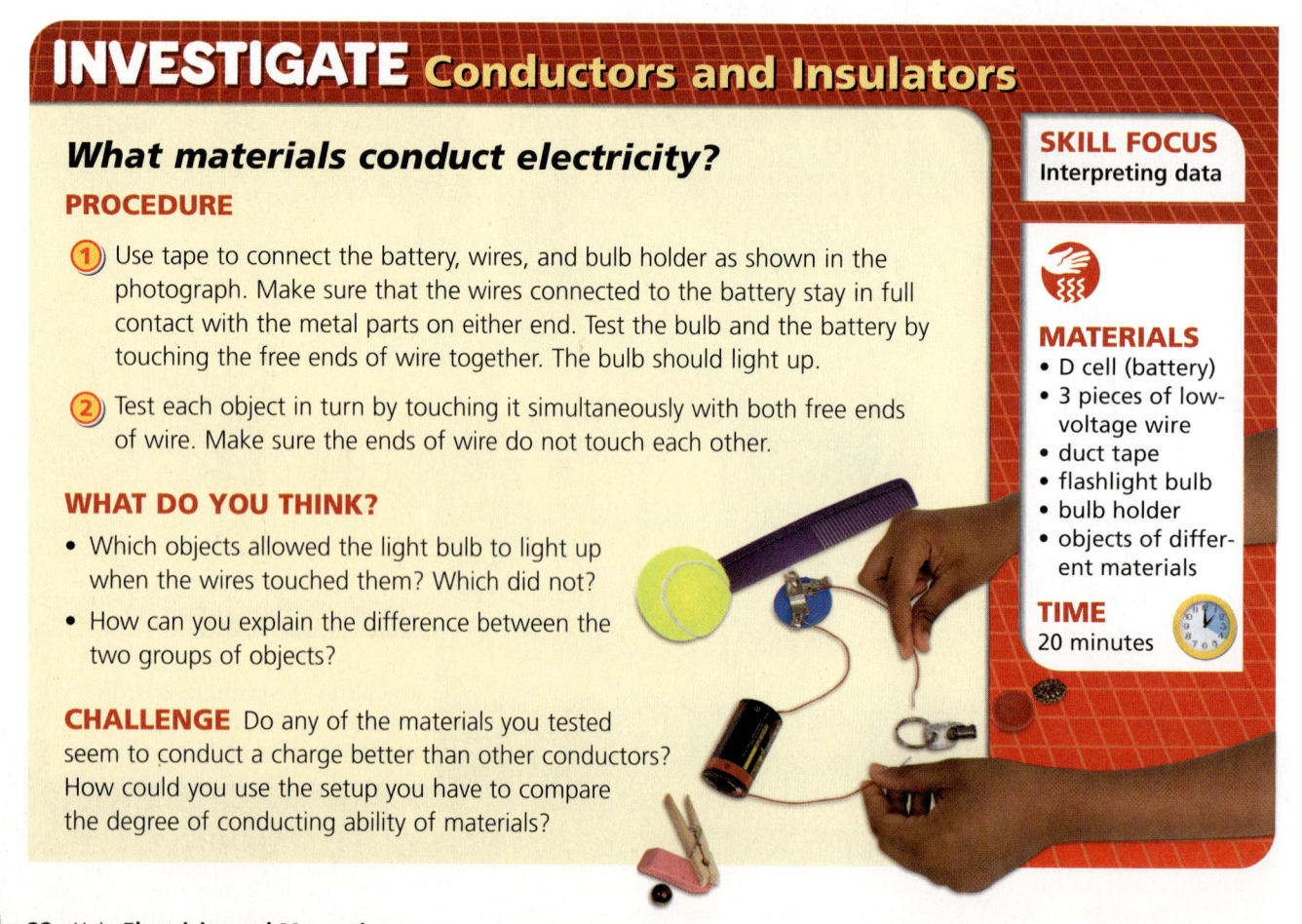

INVESTIGATE Conductors and Insulators

What materials conduct electricity?
PROCEDURE

1. Use tape to connect the battery, wires, and bulb holder as shown in the photograph. Make sure that the wires connected to the battery stay in full contact with the metal parts on either end. Test the bulb and the battery by touching the free ends of wire together. The bulb should light up.

2. Test each object in turn by touching it simultaneously with both free ends of wire. Make sure the ends of wire do not touch each other.

WHAT DO YOU THINK?
- Which objects allowed the light bulb to light up when the wires touched them? Which did not?
- How can you explain the difference between the two groups of objects?

CHALLENGE Do any of the materials you tested seem to conduct a charge better than other conductors? How could you use the setup you have to compare the degree of conducting ability of materials?

SKILL FOCUS
Interpreting data

MATERIALS
- D cell (battery)
- 3 pieces of low-voltage wire
- duct tape
- flashlight bulb
- bulb holder
- objects of different materials

TIME
20 minutes

Electrons can move freely in a material with low resistance, such as the copper wire in these power lines. Electrons cannot move freely in a material with high resistance, such as the ceramic insulator this worker is putting in place or his safety gloves.

Resistance

Think about the difference between walking through air and walking through waist-deep water. The water resists your movement more than the air, so you have to work harder to walk. If you walked waist-deep in mud, you would have to work even harder.

Materials resist the movement of a charge in different amounts. Electrical **resistance** is the property of a material that determines how easily a charge can move through it. Electrical resistance is measured in units called **ohms.** The symbol for ohms is the Greek letter *omega* (Ω).

Most materials have some resistance. A good conductor such as copper, though, has low resistance. A good insulator, such as plastic or wood, has high resistance.

Like a thick drink in a straw, an electric charge moves more easily through a short, wide pathway than a long, narrow one.

Resistance depends on the amount and shape of the material as well as on the type of material itself. A wire that is thin has more resistance than a wire that is thick. Think of how you have to work harder to drink through a narrow straw than a wide one. A wire that is long has more resistance than a wire that is short. Again, think of how much harder it is to drink through a long straw than a short one.

CHECK YOUR READING What three factors affect how much resistance an object has?

Chapter 1: **Electricity** 23 **E**

By taking advantage of resistance, we can use an electric charge to do work. When a moving charge overcomes resistance, some of the charge's electrical energy changes into other forms of energy, such as light and heat. For example, the filament of a light bulb is often made of tungsten, a material with high resistance. When electricity moves through the tungsten, the filament gives off light, which is useful. However, the bulb also gives off heat. Because light bulbs are not usually used to produce heat, we think of the heat they produce as wasted energy.

A three-way light bulb has two filaments, each with a different level of resistance. The one with higher resistance produces brighter light. Both together give the brightest setting.

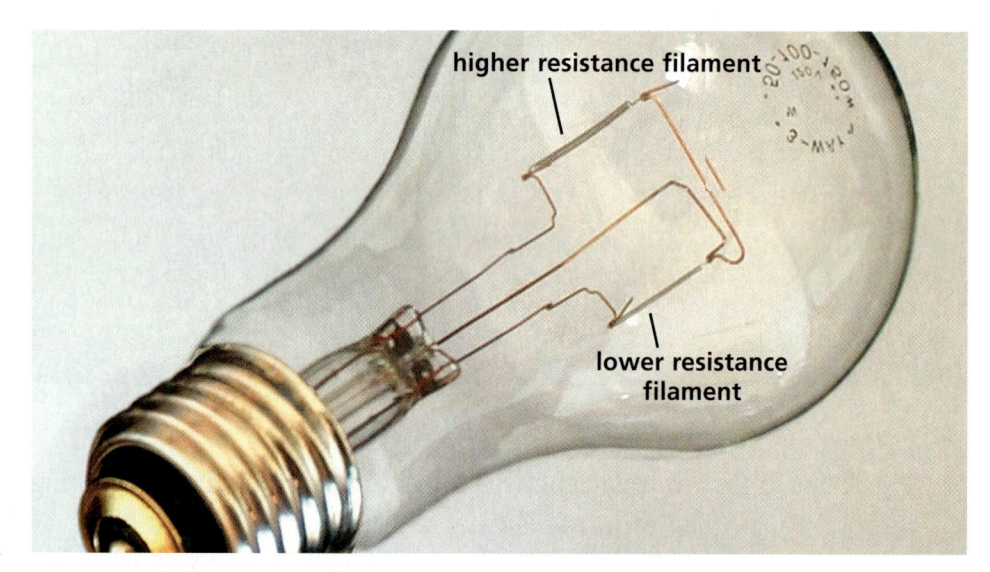

higher resistance filament

lower resistance filament

A material with low resistance is one that a charge can flow through with little loss of energy. Materials move electricity more efficiently when they have low resistances. Such materials waste less energy, so more is available to do work at the other end. That is why copper is used for electrical wiring. Even copper has some resistance, however, and using it wastes some energy.

Superconductors

Scientists have known for many years that some materials have practically no resistance at extremely low temperatures. Such materials are called superconductors, because they conduct even better than good conductors like copper. Superconductors have many uses. They can be used in power lines to increase efficiency and conserve energy, and in high-speed trains to reduce friction. Engineers are also testing superconducting materials for use in computers and other electronic devices. Superconductors would make computers work faster and might also be used to make better motors and generators.

Because superconductors must be kept extremely cold, they have not always been practical. Scientists are solving this problem by developing superconductors that will work at higher temperatures.

CHECK YOUR READING How much resistance does a superconducting material have?

Grounding

If a charge can pass through two different materials, it will pass through the one with the lower resistance. This is the principle behind an important electrical safety procedure—grounding. **Grounding** means providing a harmless, low-resistance path—a ground—for electricity to follow. In many cases, this path actually leads into the ground, that is, into the Earth.

Grounding is used to protect buildings from damage by lightning. Most buildings have some type of lightning rod, which is made from a material that is a good conductor. The rod is placed high up, so that it is closer to the lightning charge. The rod is connected to a conductor cable, and the cable is attached to a copper pole, which is driven into the ground.

Because of the rod's low resistance, lightning will strike the rod before it will strike the roof, where it might have caused a fire. Lightning hits the rod and passes harmlessly through the cable into the ground.

Grounding provides a path for electric current to travel into the ground, which can absorb the charge and make it harmless. The charge soon spreads out so that its voltage in any particular spot is low.

CHECK YOUR READING What is a ground cable?

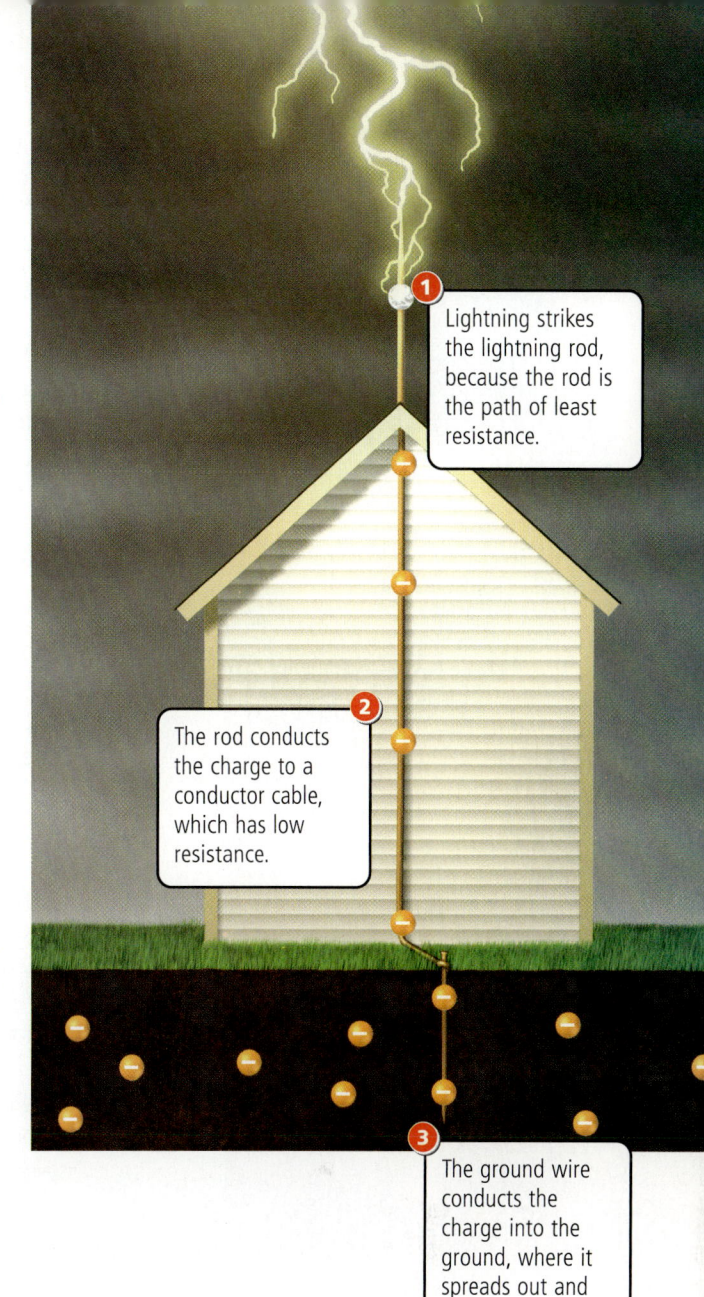

1. Lightning strikes the lightning rod, because the rod is the path of least resistance.
2. The rod conducts the charge to a conductor cable, which has low resistance.
3. The ground wire conducts the charge into the ground, where it spreads out and becomes harmless.

1.2 Review

KEY CONCEPTS

1. Explain what happens when you get a static electric shock as you touch a doorknob.
2. What is electric potential?
3. What three factors affect how much electrical resistance an object has?
4. How can a lightning rod protect a building from fire?

CRITICAL THINKING

5. **Infer** Object A has a positive charge. After Object A touches Object B, A still has a positive charge and the same amount of charge. What can you infer about the charge of B?
6. **Analyze** Why do lightning rods work better if they are placed high up, closer to the lightning charge?

CHALLENGE

7. **Apply** Could the same material be used as both a conductor and an insulator? Explain your answer.

Chapter 1: **Electricity** 25

CHAPTER INVESTIGATION

Lightning

OVERVIEW AND PURPOSE Lightning is a form of static discharge. During storms, electric charges build up within clouds. Lightning occurs when these charges move. In this experiment, you will
- model the buildup of charges that can occur during a storm
- model a lightning strike
- use a ground to control the path of discharge

Procedure

1. Draw a data table like the one on the sample notebook page.

2. Firmly press a lump of clay onto the inside bottom of one aluminum pan (A) to make a handle. Press another lump onto the underside of the other pan (B) as shown.

3. Place the foam plate upside down on a flat surface. Without touching the plate with your bare skin, rub the bottom of the plate vigorously with the wool cloth for 1–2 minutes.

4. Pick up aluminum pan A by the handle and hold it about 5 cm above the foam plate. Drop the pan so that it rests centered on top of the foam plate as shown. Be careful not to touch the pan or the plate.

5. Make the room as dark as possible. Slowly lower aluminum pan B over the rim of the first pan until they touch. Describe what occurs and where, in your notebook.

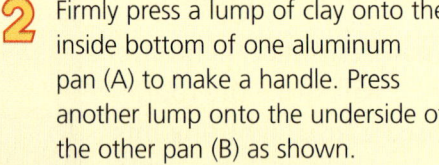

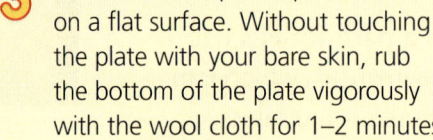

MATERIALS
- modeling clay
- 2 aluminum pie pans
- foam plate
- wool cloth
- paper clip

6. Repeat steps 3–5 two more times, recording your observations in your notebook.

7. Open the paper clip partway, as shown. Repeat steps 3–4. Then, instead of using the second aluminum pan, slowly bring the pointed end of the paper clip toward the rim of the first pan until they touch. Record your observations.

8. Repeat step 7 two more times, touching the paper clip to the aluminum pan in different places.

Observe and Analyze *Write It Up*

1. **RECORD OBSERVATIONS** Be sure your data table is complete. Draw pictures to show how the procedure varied between steps 5–6 and steps 7–8.

2. **ANALYZE** What did you observe in step 5 when the two aluminum pans touched? What do you think caused this to occur?

3. **COMPARE** How were your observations when you touched the aluminum pan with the paper clip different from those you made when you touched it with the other pan? How can you explain the difference?

Conclude *Write It Up*

1. **ANALYZE** Use the observations recorded in your data table to answer the following question: When you used the paper clip, why were you able to control the point at which the static discharge occurred?

2. **INFER** What charges did the foam plate and aluminum pan have before you began the experiment? after you dropped the pan on the plate? after you touched the pan with the paper clip?

3. **IDENTIFY VARIABLES** What variables and controls affected the outcome of your experiment?

4. **IDENTIFY LIMITS** What limitations or sources of error could have affected your results?

5. **APPLY** In your experiment, what corresponds to storm clouds and lightning? How did the paper clip work like a lightning rod?

INVESTIGATE Further

CHALLENGE Where did the charge go when you touched the pie pan with the paper clip? Write a hypothesis to explain what happens in this situation and design an experiment to test your hypothesis.

Lightning
Observe and Analyze
Table 1. Observations of Static Discharge

Trial	Observations
With second aluminum pan	
1	
2	
3	
With paper clip	
4	
5	
6	

Conclude

Chapter 1: **Electricity** 27

1.3 Electric current is a flow of charge.

KEY CONCEPT

BEFORE, you learned
- Charges move from higher to lower potential
- Materials can act as conductors or insulators
- Materials have different levels of resistance

NOW, you will learn
- About electric current
- How current is related to voltage and resistance
- About different types of electric power cells

VOCABULARY
electric current p. 28
ampere p. 29
Ohm's law p. 29
electric cell p. 31

EXPLORE Current

How does resistance affect the flow of charge?

PROCEDURE

1. Tape the pencil lead flat on the posterboard.
2. Connect the wires, cell, bulb, and bulb holder as shown in the photograph.
3. Hold the wire ends against the pencil lead about a centimeter apart from each other. Observe the bulb.
4. Keeping the wire ends in contact with the lead, slowly move them apart. As you move the wire ends apart, observe the bulb.

MATERIALS
- pencil lead
- posterboard
- electrical tape
- 3 lengths of wire
- D cell battery
- flashlight bulb
- bulb holder

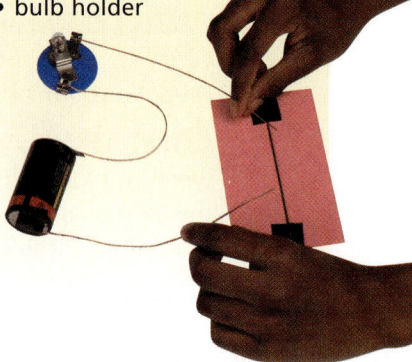

WHAT DO YOU THINK?
- What happened to the bulb as you moved the wire ends apart?
- How might you explain your observation?

Electric charge can flow continuously.

Static charges cannot make your television play. For that you need a different type of electricity. You have learned that a static charge contains a specific, limited amount of charge. You have also learned that a static charge can move and always moves from higher to lower potential. However, suppose that, instead of one charge, an electrical pathway received a continuous supply of charge and the difference in potential between the two ends of the pathway stayed the same. Then, you would have a continuous flow of charge. Another name for a flow of charge is **electric current.** Electric current is the form of electricity used to supply energy in homes, schools, and other buildings.

VOCABULARY
Don't forget to make a four square diagram for the term *electric current*.

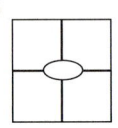

Current, Voltage, and Resistance

Electric current obeys the same rules as moving static charges. Charge can flow only if it has a path to follow, that is, a material to conduct it. Also, charge can flow only from a point of higher potential to one of lower potential. However, one concept that does not apply to a moving static charge applies to current. Charge that flows steadily has a certain rate of flow. This rate can be measured. The standard unit of measure for current is the **ampere,** or amp. An amp is the amount of charge that flows past a given point per unit of time. One amp equals one coulomb per second. The number of amps—or amperage—of a flowing charge is determined by both voltage and resistance.

Electric current, or amperage, can be compared to the flow of water through a pipe. Electric potential, or voltage, is like pressure pushing the water through the pipe. Resistance, or ohms, is like the diameter of the pipe, which controls how much water can flow through. Water pressure and pipe size together determine the rate of water flow. Similarly, voltage and resistance together determine the rate of flow of electric charge.

COMBINATION NOTES
In your notes, try making a sketch to help you remember how current, voltage, and resistance differ.

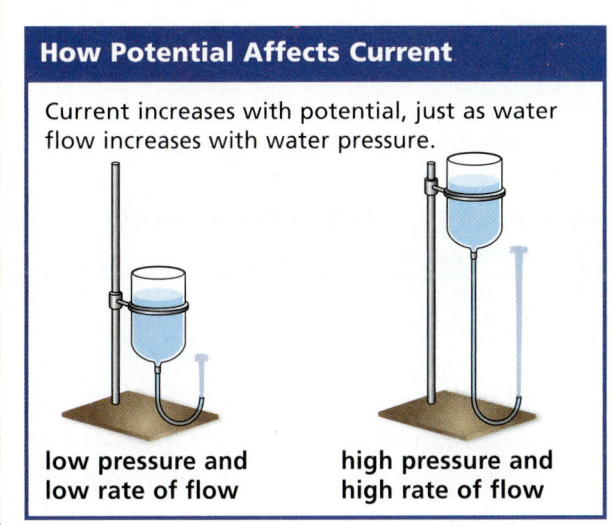

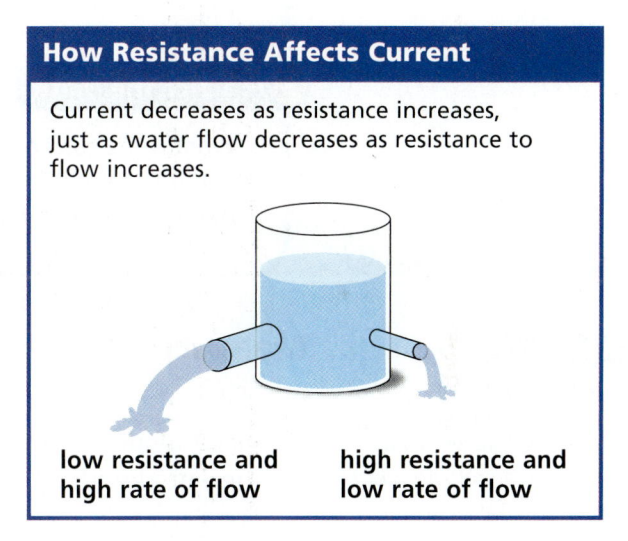

How Potential Affects Current
Current increases with potential, just as water flow increases with water pressure.

low pressure and low rate of flow

high pressure and high rate of flow

How Resistance Affects Current
Current decreases as resistance increases, just as water flow decreases as resistance to flow increases.

low resistance and high rate of flow

high resistance and low rate of flow

Ohm's Law

You now have three important measurements for the study of electricity: volts, ohms, and amps. The scientist for whom the ohm is named discovered a mathematical relationship among these three measurements. The relationship, called **Ohm's law,** is expressed in the formula below.

$$\text{Current} = \frac{\text{Voltage}}{\text{Resistance}} \quad I = \frac{V}{R}$$

I is current measured in amps (A), *V* is voltage measured in volts (V), and *R* is resistance measured in ohms (Ω).

SIMULATION CLASSZONE.COM
See Ohm's law in action.

CHECK YOUR READING What two values do you need to know to calculate the amperage of electric current?

Chapter 1: **Electricity** 29 **E**

You have read that current is affected by both voltage and resistance. Using Ohm's law, you can calculate exactly how much it is affected and determine the exact amount of current in amps. Use the formula for current to solve the sample problem below.

Calculating Current

Sample Problem

What is the current in an electrical pathway with an electric potential of 120 volts and a resistance of 60 ohms?

What do you know? voltage = 120 V, resistance = 60 Ω

What do you want to find out? current

Write the formula: $I = \dfrac{V}{R}$

Substitute into the formula: $I = \dfrac{120 \text{ V}}{60 \text{ Ω}}$

Calculate and simplify: $I = 2$ A

Check that your units agree: Unit is amps. Unit of current is amps. Units agree.

Answer: 2 A

Practice the Math

1. What is the current in an electrical pathway in which the voltage is 220 V and the resistance is 55 Ω?
2. An electrical pathway has a voltage of 12 volts and a resistance of 24 ohms. What is the current?

Measuring Electricity

READING TIP

The terms *voltmeter*, *ohmmeter*, *ammeter*, and *multimeter* are all made by adding a prefix to the word *meter*.

Volts, ohms, and amps can all be measured using specific electrical instruments. Volts can be measured with a voltmeter. Ohms can be measured with an ohmmeter. Amps can be measured with an ammeter. These three instruments are often combined in a single electrical instrument called a multimeter.

To use a multimeter, set the dial on the type of unit you wish to measure. For example, the multimeter in the photograph is being used to test the voltage of a 9-volt battery. The dial is set on volts in the 0–20 range. The meter shows that the battery's charge has an electric potential of more than 9 volts, which means that the battery is good. A dead battery would have a lower voltage.

CHECK YOUR READING   What does an ohmmeter measure?

INVESTIGATE Electric Cells

How can you produce electric current?

PROCEDURE

1. Insert the paper clip and the penny into the lemon, as shown in the photograph. The penny and paper clip should go about 3 cm into the lemon. They should be close, but not touching.

2. On the multimeter, go to the DC volts (V⎓) section of the dial and select the 0–2000 millivolt range (2000 m).

3. Touch one of the leads of the multimeter to the paper clip. Touch the other lead to the penny. Observe what is shown on the display of the multimeter.

WHAT DO YOU THINK?
- What did you observe on the display of the multimeter?
- How can you explain the reading on the multimeter?

CHALLENGE Repeat this experiment using different combinations of fruits or vegetables and metal objects. Which combinations work best?

SKILL FOCUS
Inferring

MATERIALS
- paper clip
- penny
- large lemon
- multimeter

For Challenge
- additional fruits or vegetables
- metal objects

TIME
20 minutes

Electric cells supply electric current.

Electric current can be used in many ways. Two basic types of device have been developed for producing current. One type produces electric current using magnets. You will learn more about this technology in Chapter 3. The other type is the **electric cell,** which produces electric current using the chemical or physical properties of different materials.

Electrochemical Cells

An electrochemical cell is an electric cell that produces current by means of chemical reactions. As you can see in the diagram, an electrochemical cell contains two strips made of different materials. The strips are called electrodes. The electrodes are suspended in a third material called the electrolyte, which interacts chemically with the electrodes to separate charges and produce a flow of electrons from the negative terminal to the positive terminal.

Batteries are made using electrochemical cells. Technically, a battery is two or more cells connected to each other. However, single cells, such as C cells and D cells, are often referred to as batteries.

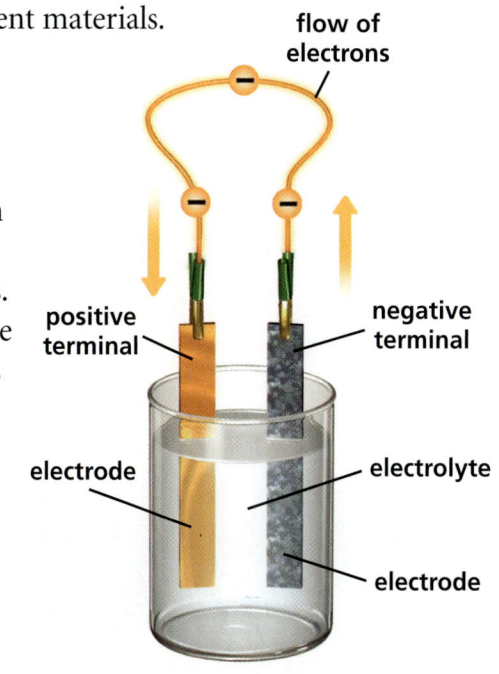

Chapter 1: **Electricity** 31 **E**

Resource Center
CLASSZONE.COM

Learn more about electrochemical cells.

Primary Cells The electrochemical cell shown on page 31 is called a wet cell, because the electrolyte is a liquid. Most household batteries in use today have a solid paste electrolyte and so are called dry cells. Both wet cells and dry cells are primary cells. Primary cells produce electric current through chemical reactions that continue until one or more of the chemicals is used up.

The primary cell on page 33 is a typical zinc-carbon dry cell. It has a negative electrode made of zinc. The zinc electrode is made in the shape of a can and has a terminal—in this case, a wide disk of exposed metal—on the bottom of the cell. The positive electrode consists of a carbon rod and particles of carbon and manganese dioxide. The particles are suspended in an electrolyte paste. The positive electrode has a terminal—a smaller disk of exposed metal—at the top of the rod. A paper separator prevents the two electrodes from coming into contact inside the cell.

When the two terminals of the cell are connected—for example, when you turn on a flashlight—a chemical reaction between the zinc and the electrolyte produces electrons and positive zinc ions. The electrons flow through the wires connecting the cell to the flashlight bulb, causing the bulb to light up. The electrons then travel through the carbon rod and combine with the manganese dioxide. When the zinc and manganese dioxide stop reacting, the cell dies.

CHECK YOUR READING Why are most household batteries called dry cells?

Storage Cells Some batteries produce current through chemical reactions that can be reversed inside the battery. These batteries are called storage cells, secondary cells, or rechargeable batteries. A car battery like the lead-acid battery shown on page 33 is rechargeable. The battery has a negative electrode of lead and a positive electrode of lead peroxide. As the battery produces current, both electrodes change chemically into lead sulfate, and the electrolyte changes into water.

When storage cells are producing current, they are said to be discharging. Whenever a car engine is started, the battery discharges to operate the ignition motor. A car's battery can also be used when the car is not running to operate the lights or other appliances. If the battery is used too long in discharge mode, it will run down completely.

While a car is running, however, the battery is continually being charged. A device called an alternator, which is run by the car's engine, produces current. When electrons flow into the battery in the reverse direction from discharging, the chemical reactions that produce current are reversed. The ability of the battery to produce current is renewed.

CHECK YOUR READING What kind of battery can be charged by reversing chemical reactions?

Unit: Electricity and Magnetism

Batteries

Both primary cells and storage cells produce electricity through chemical reactions.

Flashlights use **primary cells.**

Car batteries and cell phones use **storage cells.**

Primary Cell

Primary cells produce electric current through chemical reactions. The reactions continue until the chemicals are used up.

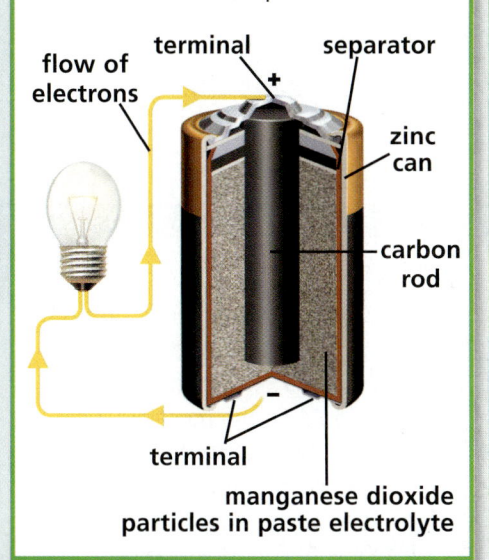

flow of electrons
terminal
separator
zinc can
carbon rod
terminal
manganese dioxide particles in paste electrolyte

Storage Cell

① Discharging Storage cells produce current through chemical reactions that can be reversed in the battery.

starter motor
flow of electrons
alternator
lead sulfate
mostly water

② Charging Sending current through the battery in the opposite direction reverses the chemical reactions.

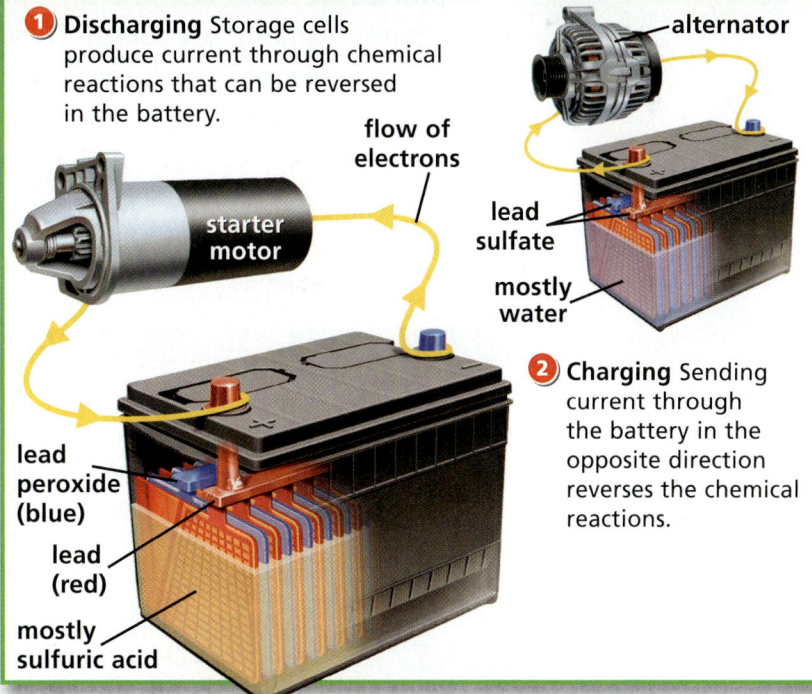

lead peroxide (blue)
lead (red)
mostly sulfuric acid

READING VISUALS In which direction do electrons flow when a storage cell is being charged?

Chapter 1: **Electricity** 33 **E**

READING TIP

The word *solar* comes from the Latin word *sol*, which means the Sun.

Solar Cells

Some materials, such as silicon, can absorb energy from the Sun or other sources of light and then give off electrons, producing electric current. Electric cells made from such materials are called solar cells.

Solar cells are often used to make streetlights come on automatically at night. Current from the cell operates a switch that keeps the lights turned off. When it gets dark, the current stops, the switch closes, and the streetlights come on.

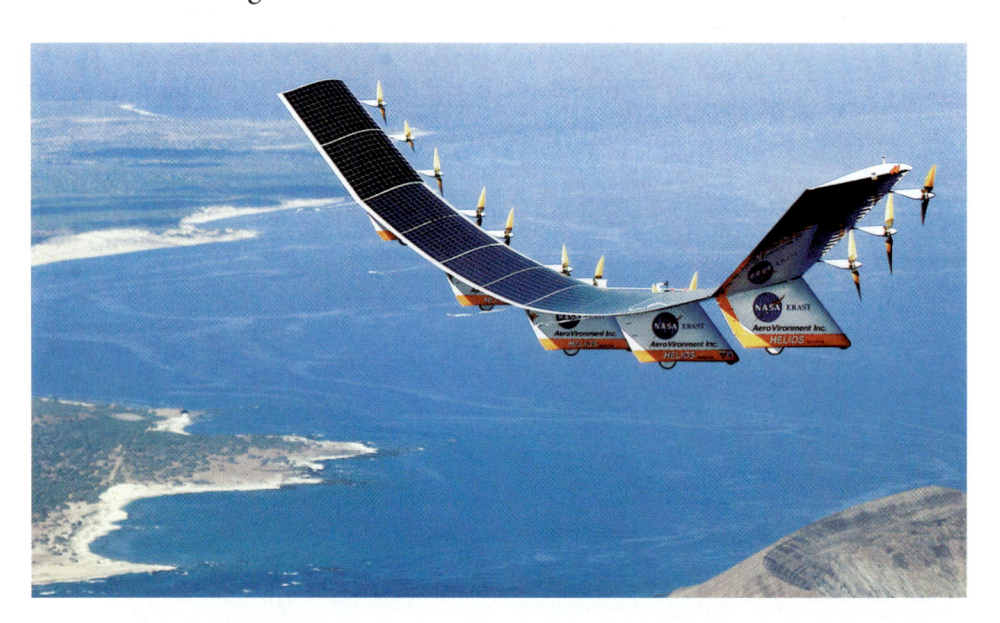

This NASA research aircraft is powered only by the solar cells on its upper surface.

Many houses and other buildings now get at least some of their power from solar cells. Sunlight provides an unlimited source of free, environmentally safe energy. However, it is not always easy or cheap to use that energy. It must be collected and stored because solar cells do not work at night or when sunlight is blocked by clouds or buildings.

CHECK YOUR READING Where do solar cells get their energy?

1.3 Review

KEY CONCEPTS

1. How is electric current different from a static charge that moves?
2. How can Ohm's law be used to calculate the electrical resistance of a piece of wire?
3. How do rechargeable batteries work differently from nonrechargeable ones?

CRITICAL THINKING

4. **Infer** Electrical outlets in a house maintain a steady voltage, even when the amount of resistance on them changes. How is this possible?
5. **Analyze** Why don't solar cells eventually run down as electrochemical cells do?

CHALLENGE

6. **Apply** Several kinds of electric cells are discussed in this section. Which do you think would be the most practical source of electrical energy on a long trek through the desert? Explain your reasoning.

34 Unit: Electricity and Magnetism

MATH in SCIENCE

SKILL: USING VARIABLES

MATH TUTORIAL
CLASSZONE.COM
Click on Math Tutorial for more help with equations.

Which Formula Is Best?

A rock band needs an amplifier, and an amplifier needs a volume control. A volume control works by controlling the amount of resistance in an electrical pathway. When resistance goes down, the current—and the volume—go up. Ohm's law expresses the relationship among voltage (V), resistance (R), and amperage (I). If you know the values of two variables, you can use Ohm's law to find the third. The law can be written in three ways, depending on which variable you wish to find.

$$I = \frac{V}{R} \qquad R = \frac{V}{I} \qquad V = IR$$

A simple way to remember these three versions of the formula is to use the pyramid diagram below. Cover up the variable you are looking for. The visible part of the diagram will give you the correct formula to use.

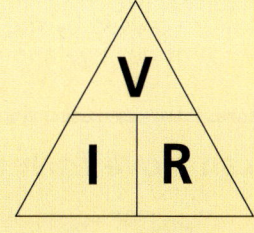

Example

What is the voltage of a battery that produces a current of 1 amp through a wire with a resistance of 9 ohms?

(1) You want to find voltage, so cover up the V in the pyramid diagram. To find V, the correct formula to use is $V = IR$.

(2) Insert the known values into the formula. $V = 1 \text{ A} \cdot 9 \ \Omega$

(3) Solve the equation to find the missing variable. $1 \cdot 9 = 9$

ANSWER 9 volts

Answer the following questions.

1. What is the voltage of a battery that sends 3 amps of current through a wire with a resistance of 4 ohms?

2. What is the resistance of a wire in which the current is 2 amps if the battery producing the current has a voltage of 220 volts?

3. What is the amperage of a current at 120 volts through a wire with a resistance of 5 ohms?

CHALLENGE Dimmer switches also work by varying resistance. A club owner likes the way the lights look at 1/3 normal current. The normal current is 15 amps. The voltage is constant at 110 V. How much resistance will he need?

A volume control works by changing the amount of resistance to the flow of current.

Chapter 1: Electricity 35

Chapter Review

the BIG idea
Moving electric charges transfer energy.

CONTENT REVIEW
CLASSZONE.COM

KEY CONCEPTS SUMMARY

1.1 Materials can become electrically charged.

Electric charge is a property of matter.

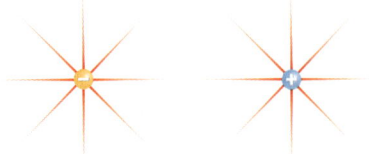

Electrons have a negative charge.   Protons have a positive charge.   Unlike charges attract.   Like charges repel.

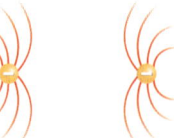

Static charges are caused by the movement of electrons, resulting in an imbalance of positive and negative charges.

VOCABULARY
electric charge p. 10
electric field p. 10
static charge p. 11
induction p. 13

1.2 Charges can move from one place to another.

Charge movement is affected by
- electric potential, measured in volts
- resistance, measured in ohms

A conductor has low resistance.
An insulator has high resistance.
A ground is the path of least resistance.

VOCABULARY
electric potential p. 19
volt p. 19
conductor p. 22
insulator p. 22
resistance p. 23
ohm p. 23
grounding p. 25

1.3 Electric current is a flow of charge.

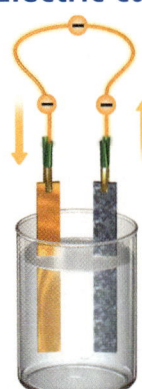

Electric current is measured in amperes, or amps.
Ohm's law states that current equals voltage divided by resistance.
Electrochemical cells produce electric current through chemical reactions.

VOCABULARY
electric current p. 28
ampere p. 29
Ohm's law p. 29
electric cell p. 31

Reviewing Vocabulary

Copy the chart below, and write each term's definition. Use the meanings of the underlined roots to help you.

Word	Root	Definition
EXAMPLE current	to run	continuous flow of charge
1. static charge	standing	
2. induction	into + to lead	
3. electric cell	chamber	
4. conductor	with + to lead	
5. insulator	island	
6. resistance	to stop	
7. electric potential	power	
8. grounding	surface of Earth	

Write a vocabulary term to match each clue.

9. In honor of scientist Alessandro Volta (1745–1827)

10. In honor of the scientist who discovered the relationship among voltage, resistance, and current

11. The amount of charge that flows past a given point in a unit of time.

Reviewing Key Concepts

Multiple Choice *Choose the letter of the best answer.*

12. An electric charge is a
    a. kind of liquid
    b. reversible chemical reaction
    c. type of matter
    d. force acting at a distance

13. A static charge is different from electric current in that a static charge
    a. never moves
    b. can either move or not move
    c. moves only when resistance is low enough
    d. moves only when voltage is high enough

14. Charging by induction means charging
    a. with battery power
    b. by direct contact
    c. at a distance
    d. using solar power

15. Electric potential describes
    a. the electric potential energy per unit charge
    b. the electric kinetic energy per unit charge
    c. whether an electric charge is positive or negative
    d. how an electric charge is affected by gravity

16. A superconductor is a material that, when very cold, has no
    a. amperage
    b. resistance
    c. electric charge
    d. electric potential

17. Ohm's law says that when resistance goes up, current
    a. increases
    b. decreases
    c. stays the same
    d. matches voltage

18. Electrochemical cells include
    a. all materials that build up a charge
    b. primary cells and storage cells
    c. batteries and solar cells
    d. storage cells and lightning rods

Short Answer *Write a short answer to each question.*

19. What determines whether a charge you get when walking across a rug is positive or negative?

20. What is the difference between resistance and insulation?

21. What is one disadvantage of solar cells?

Thinking Critically

Use the diagram of an electrochemical cell below to answer the next three questions.

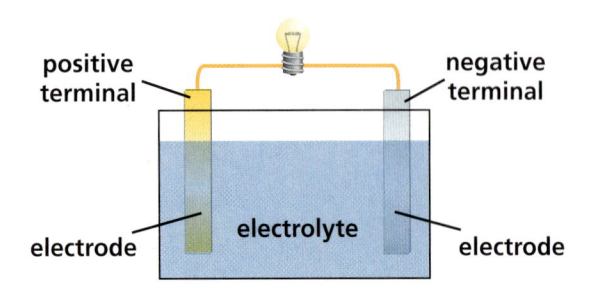

22. ANALYZE In which direction do electrons flow between the two terminals?

23. PREDICT What changes will occur in the cell as it discharges?

24. ANALYZE What determines whether the cell is rechargeable or not?

Use the graph below to answer the next three questions.

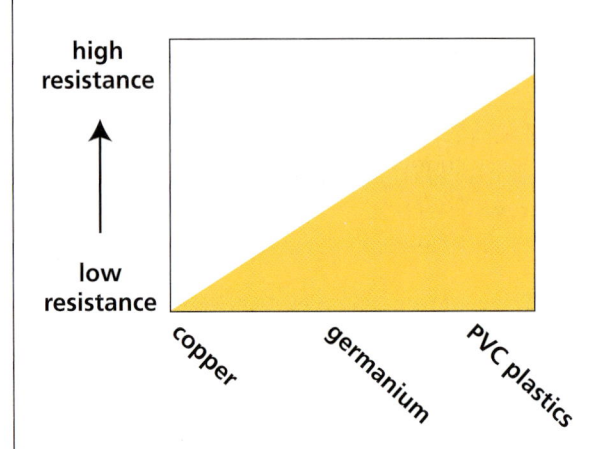

25. INFER Which material could you probably use as an insulator?

26. INFER Which material could be used in a lightning rod?

27. APPLY Materials that conduct electrons under some—but not all—conditions are known as semiconductors. Which material is probably a semiconductor?

Using Math in Science

Use the formula for Ohm's law to answer the next four questions.

$$I = \frac{V}{R}$$

28. An electrical pathway has a voltage of 240 volts and a current of 10 amperes. What is the resistance?

29. A 240-volt air conditioner has a resistance of 8 ohms. What is the current?

30. An electrical pathway has a current of 1.2 amperes and resistance of 40 ohms. What is the voltage?

31. An electrical pathway has a voltage of 400 volts and resistance of 2000 ohms. What is the current?

the BIG idea

32. INFER Look back at the photograph on pages 6 and 7. Based on what you have learned in this chapter, describe what you think is happening to keep the dragon lit.

33. COMPARE AND CONTRAST Draw two simple diagrams to compare and contrast static charges and electric current. Add labels and captions to make your comparison clear. Then write a paragraph summarizing the comparison.

UNIT PROJECTS

If you are doing a unit project, make a folder for your project. Include in your folder a list of the resources you will need, the date on which the project is due, and a schedule to keep track of your progress. Begin gathering data.

Standardized Test Practice

Interpreting Diagrams

Use the illustration below to answer the following questions. Assume that the balloons start off with no net charge.

1. What will happen if a negatively charged rod is brought near one of the balloons without touching it?
   a. The balloons will move toward each other.
   b. The balloons will move away from each other.
   c. Electrons on the balloons will move toward the rod.
   d. Electrons on the balloons will move away from the rod.

2. What will happen if a positively charged rod is brought near one of the balloons without touching it?
   a. The balloons will move toward each other.
   b. The balloons will move away from each other.
   c. Electrons on the balloons will move toward the rod.
   d. Electrons on the balloons will move away from the rod.

3. In the previous question, the effect of the rod on the balloons is an example of
   a. charging by contact
   b. charge polarization
   c. induction
   d. conduction

4. What will happen if a negatively charged rod is brought near one of the balloons and the balloons are then separated?
   a. The balloon farthest from the rod will become positively charged.
   b. The balloon farthest from the rod will become negatively charged.
   c. Both balloons will become positively charged.
   d. Both balloons will have no net charge.

5. If you rub one balloon in your hair to charge it and then move it close to the other balloon, the balloons will
   a. not move
   b. move away from each other
   c. move toward the ground
   d. move toward each other

6. What will happen if a negatively charged rod is brought near one of the balloons, then taken away, and the balloons are then separated?
   a. The balloon farthest from the rod will become positively charged.
   b. The balloon farthest from the rod will become negatively charged.
   c. Both balloons will become positively charged.
   d. Both balloons will have no net charge.

Extended Response

Answer the two questions below in detail. Include some of the terms from the word box. Underline each term that you use in your answers.

| charge separation | recharging | resistance |
| source of current | static charge | induce |

7. Describe the events leading up to and including a bolt of lightning striking Earth from a storm cloud.

8. Explain the advantages and disadvantages of storage cells over other types of electric cells.

CHAPTER 2
Circuits and Electronics

the BIG idea
Circuits control the flow of electric charge.

Key Concepts

SECTION 2.1
Charge needs a continuous path to flow.
Learn how circuits are used to control the flow of charge.

SECTION 2.2
Circuits make electric current useful.
Learn about series circuits and parallel circuits.

SECTION 2.3
Electronic technology is based on circuits.
Learn about computers and other electronic devices.

How can circuits control the flow of charge?

Internet Preview
CLASSZONE.COM
Chapter 2 online resources: Content Review, Simulation, Visualization, two Resource Centers, Math Tutorial, Test Practice

EXPLORE the BIG idea

Will the Flashlight Still Work?

Experiment with a flashlight to find out if it will work in any of the following arrangements: with one of the batteries facing the wrong way, with a piece of paper between the batteries, or with one battery removed. In each case, switch on the flashlight and observe.

Observe and Think When did the flashlight work? Why do you think it worked or did not work in each case?

What's Inside a Calculator?

Use a small screwdriver to open a simple calculator. Look at the circuit board inside.

Observe and Think How do you think the metal lines relate to the buttons on the front of the calculator? to the display? What is the source of electrical energy? How is it connected to the rest of the circuit?

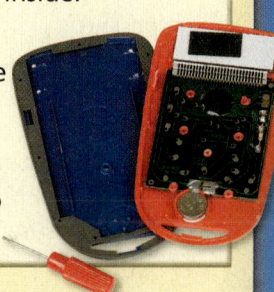

Internet Activity: Circuits

Go to **ClassZone.com** to build a virtual circuit. See if you can complete the circuit and light the bulb.

Observe and Think What parts are necessary to light the bulb? What happened when you opened the switch? closed the switch?

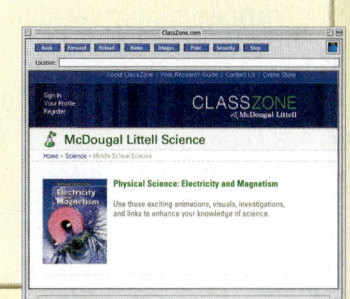

NSTA scilinks.org SciLINKS
Electronic Circuits Code: MDL066

Chapter 2: **Circuits and Electronics** 41

CHAPTER 2
Getting Ready to Learn

CONCEPT REVIEW

- Energy can change from one form to another.
- Energy can move from one place to another.
- Current is the flow of charge through a conductor.

VOCABULARY REVIEW

electric current p. 28
electric potential p. 18
conductor p. 22
resistance p. 23
ampere p. 29

CONTENT REVIEW
CLASSZONE.COM
Review concepts and vocabulary.

TAKING NOTES

OUTLINE

As you read, copy the headings on your paper in the form of an outline. Then add notes in your own words that summarize what you read.

VOCABULARY STRATEGY

Write each new vocabulary term in the center of a **frame game** diagram. Decide what information to frame it with. Use examples, descriptions, parts, sentences that use the term in context, or pictures. You can change the frame to fit each term.

See the Note-Taking Handbook on pages R45–R51.

SCIENCE NOTEBOOK

I. ELECTRIC CHARGE FLOWS IN A LOOP.
   A. THE PARTS OF A CIRCUIT
      1. voltage source
      2. connection
      3. electrical device
      4. switch

	Electrical device	
Part of a circuit	**RESISTOR**	Light bulb is an example
	Slows the flow of charge	

E 42 Unit: Electricity and Magnetism

KEY CONCEPT
2.1 Charge needs a continuous path to flow.

BEFORE, you learned
- Current is the flow of charge
- Voltage is a measure of electric potential
- Materials affect the movement of charge

NOW, you will learn
- About the parts of a circuit
- How a circuit functions
- How safety devices stop current

VOCABULARY
circuit p. 43
resistor p. 44
short circuit p. 46

EXPLORE Circuits

How can you light the bulb?

PROCEDURE

1. Tape one end of a strip of foil to the negative terminal, or the flat end, of the battery. Tape the other end of the foil to the tip at the base of the light bulb, as shown.

2. Tape the second strip of foil to the positive terminal, or the raised end, of the battery.

3. Find a way to make the bulb light.

WHAT DO YOU THINK?
- How did you make the bulb light?
- Can you find other arrangements that make the bulb light?

MATERIALS
- 2 strips of aluminum foil
- electrical tape
- D cell (battery)
- light bulb

VOCABULARY
Use a frame game diagram to record the term *circuit* in your notebook.

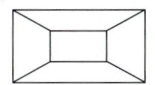

Electric charge flows in a loop.

In the last chapter, you read that current is electric charge that flows from one place to another. Charge does not flow continuously through a material unless the material forms a closed path, or loop. A **circuit** is a closed path through which a continuous charge can flow. The path is provided by a low-resistance material, or conductor, usually wire. Circuits are designed to do specific jobs, such as light a bulb.

Circuits can be found all around you and serve many different purposes. In this chapter, you will read about simple circuits, such as the ones in flashlights, and more complex circuits, such as the ones that run toys, cameras, computers, and more.

CHECK YOUR READING How are circuits related to current?

Chapter 2: Circuits and Electronics 43 **E**

The Parts of a Circuit

The illustration below shows a simple circuit. Circuits typically contain the following parts. Some circuits contain many of each part.

> **REMINDER**
> Remember, a battery consists of two or more cells.

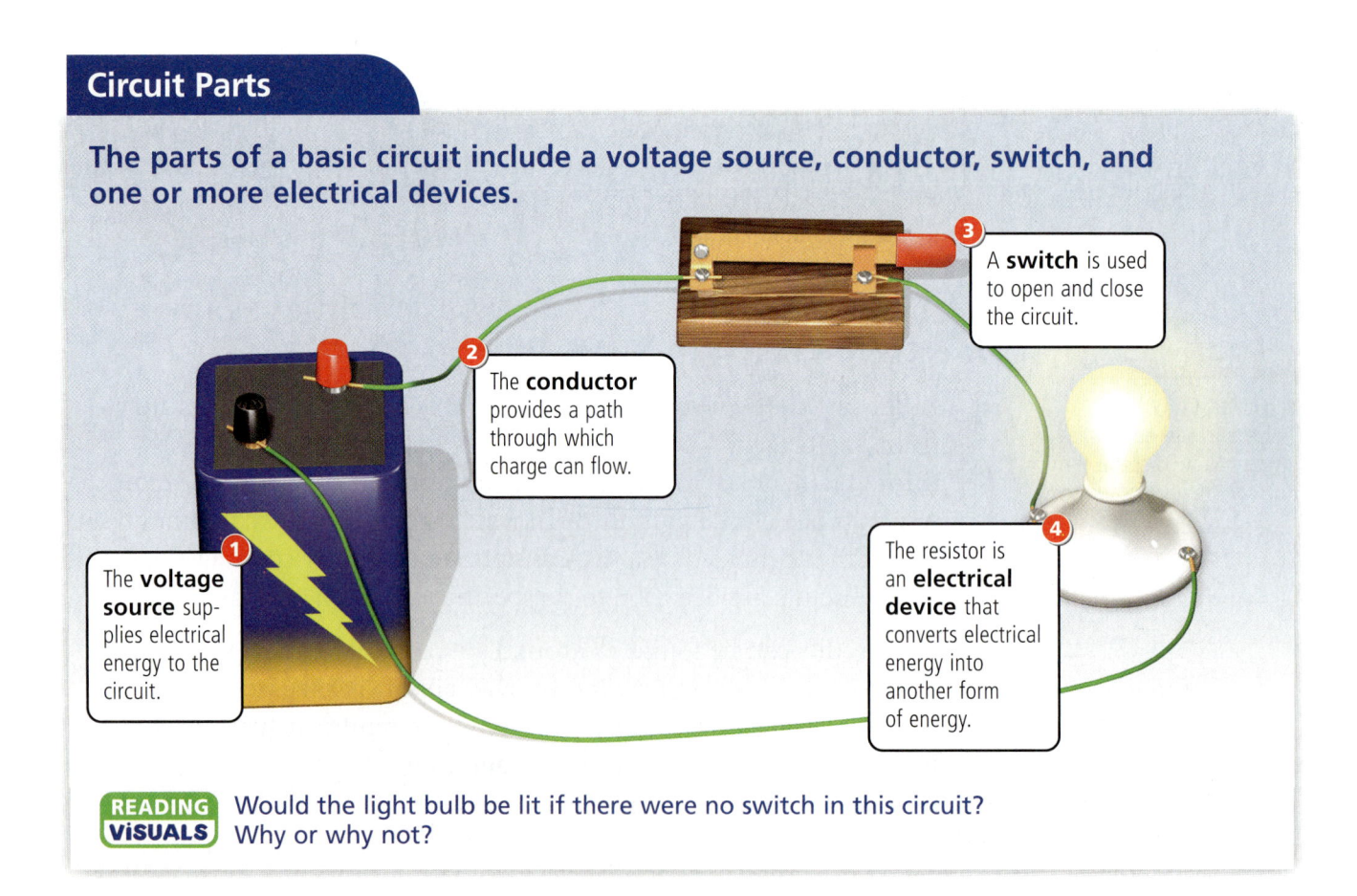

❶ Voltage Source The voltage source in a circuit provides the electric potential for charge to flow through the circuit. Batteries are often the voltage sources in a circuit. A power plant may also be a voltage source. When you plug an appliance into an outlet, a circuit is formed that goes all the way to a power plant and back.

❷ Conductor A circuit must be a closed path in order for charge to flow. That means that there must be a conductor, such as wire, that forms a connection from the voltage source to the electrical device and back.

❸ Switch A switch is a part of a circuit designed to break the closed path of charge. When a switch is open, it produces a gap in the circuit so that the charge cannot flow.

❹ Electrical Device An electrical device is any part of the circuit that changes electrical energy into another form of energy. A **resistor** is an electrical device that slows the flow of charge in a circuit. When the charge is slowed, some energy is converted to light or heat. A light bulb is an example of a resistor.

Circuit Parts

The parts of a basic circuit include a voltage source, conductor, switch, and one or more electrical devices.

❶ The **voltage source** supplies electrical energy to the circuit.

❷ The **conductor** provides a path through which charge can flow.

❸ A **switch** is used to open and close the circuit.

❹ The resistor is an **electrical device** that converts electrical energy into another form of energy.

READING VISUALS Would the light bulb be lit if there were no switch in this circuit? Why or why not?

44 Unit: Electricity and Magnetism

Open and Closed Circuits

Current in a circuit is similar to water running through a hose. The flow of charge differs from the flow of water in an important way, however. The water does not require a closed path to flow. If you cut the hose, the water continues to flow. If you cut a wire, the charge stops flowing.

Batteries have connections at both ends so that charge can follow a closed path to and from the battery. The cords that you see on appliances might look like single cords but actually contain at least two wires. The wires connect the device to a power plant and back to make a closed path.

Switches work by opening and closing the circuit. A switch that is on closes the circuit and allows charge to flow through the electrical devices. A switch that is off opens the circuit and stops the current.

REMINDER
Current requires a closed loop.

CHECK YOUR READING How are switches used to control the flow of charge through a circuit?

Standard symbols are used to represent the parts of a circuit. Some common symbols are shown in the circuit diagrams below. The diagrams represent the circuit shown on page 44 with the switch in both open and closed positions. Electricians and architects use diagrams such as these to plan the wiring of a building.

Circuit Diagrams

Symbols are used to represent the parts of a circuit. The circuit diagrams below show the circuit from page 44 in both an open and closed position.

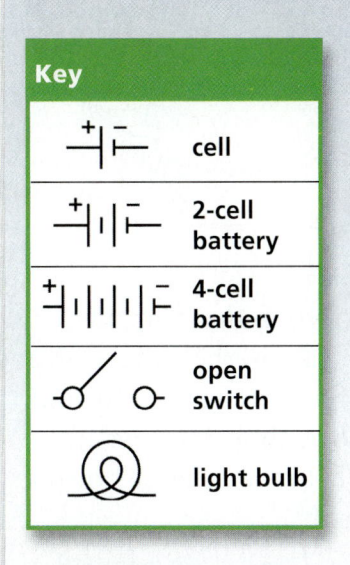

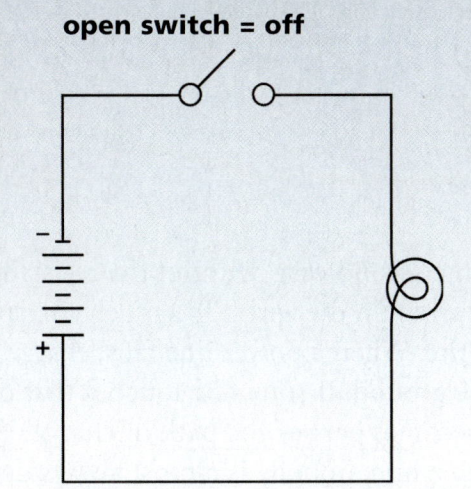

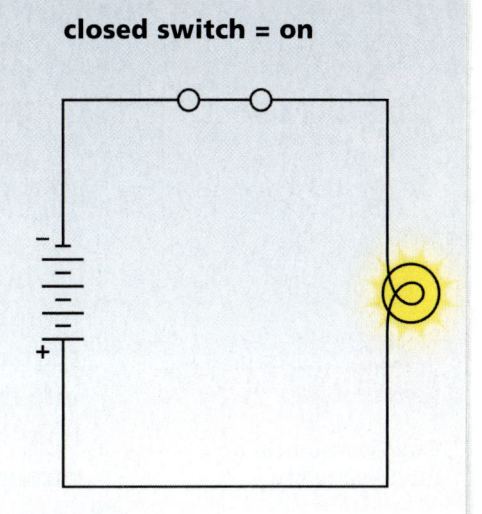

Key
- cell
- 2-cell battery
- 4-cell battery
- open switch
- light bulb

open switch = off

closed switch = on

READING VISUALS Would charge flow through the circuit diagrammed on the left? Why or why not?

Chapter 2: **Circuits and Electronics** 45 **E**

OUTLINE
Add this heading to your outline, along with supporting ideas.

I. Main idea
   A. Supporting idea
      1. Detail
      2. Detail
   B. Supporting idea

Current follows the path of least resistance.

Since current can follow only a closed path, why are damaged cords so dangerous? And why are people warned to stay away from fallen power lines? Although current follows a closed path, the path does not have to be made of wire. A person can become a part of the circuit, too. Charge flowing through a person is dangerous and sometimes deadly.

Current follows the path of least resistance. Materials with low resistance, such as certain metals, are good conductors. Charge will flow through a copper wire but not the plastic coating that covers it because copper is a good conductor and plastic is not. Water is also a good conductor when mixed with salt from a person's skin. That is why it is dangerous to use electrical devices near water.

Short Circuits

A **short circuit** is an unintended path connecting one part of a circuit with another. The current in a short circuit follows a closed path, but the path is not the one it was intended to follow. The illustration below shows a functioning circuit and a short circuit.

❶ **Functioning Circuit** The charge flows through one wire, through the light bulb, and then back through the second wire to the outlet.

❷ **Short Circuit** The cord has been damaged and the two wires inside have formed a connection. Now the path of least resistance is through one wire and back through the second wire.

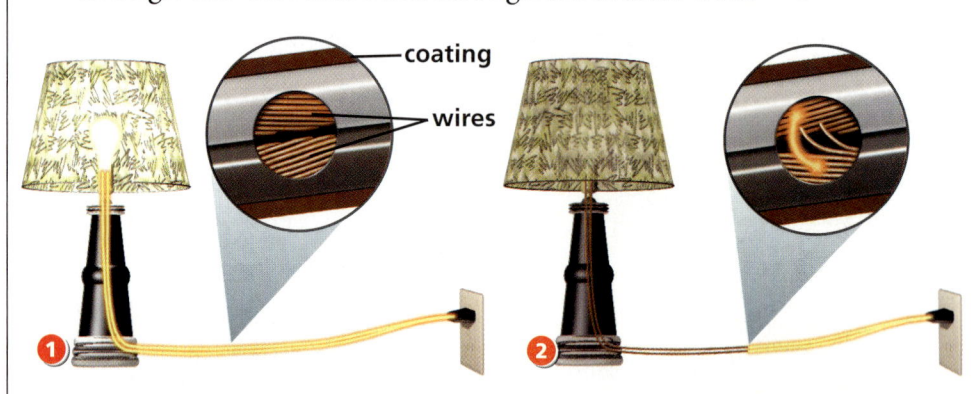

RESOURCE CENTER
CLASSZONE.COM

Explore resources on electrical safety.

In the second case, without the resistance from the lamp, there is more current in the wires. Too much current can overheat the wires and start a fire. When a power line falls, charge flows along the wire and into the ground. If someone touches that power line, the person's body becomes part of the path of charge. That much charge flowing through a human body is almost always deadly.

CHECK YOUR READING Why are short circuits dangerous?

E 46 Unit: Electricity and Magnetism

Grounding a Circuit

Recall that when lightning strikes a lightning rod, charge flows into the ground through a highly conductive metal rod rather than through a person or a building. In other words, the current follows the path of least resistance. The third prong on some electrical plugs performs a similar function. A circuit that connects stray current safely to the ground is known as a grounded circuit. Because the third prong grounds the circuit, it is sometimes called the ground.

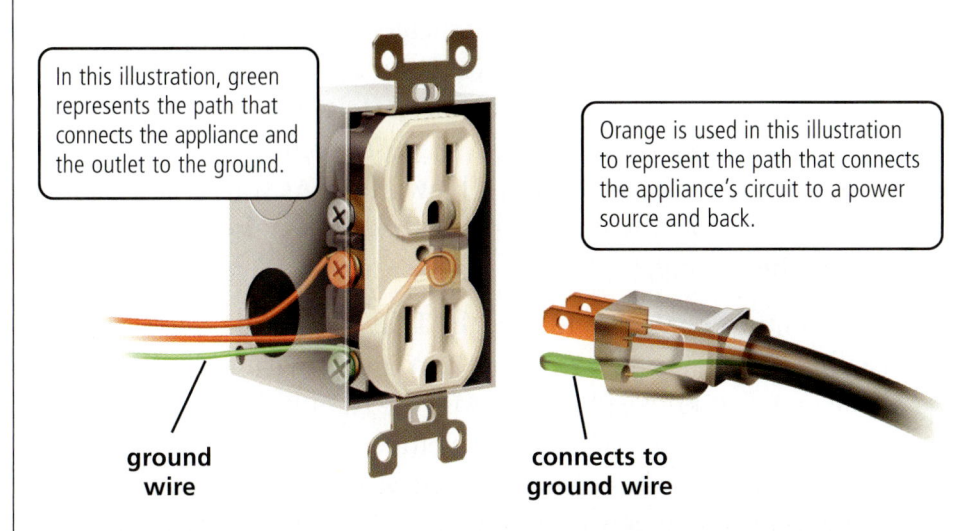

In this illustration, green represents the path that connects the appliance and the outlet to the ground.

Orange is used in this illustration to represent the path that connects the appliance's circuit to a power source and back.

ground wire

connects to ground wire

Normally, charge flows through one prong, along a wire to an appliance, then back along a second wire to the second prong. If there is a short circuit, the charge might flow dangerously to the outside of the shell of the appliance. If there is a ground wire, the current will flow along the third wire and safely into the ground, along either a buried rod or a cold water pipe.

CHECK YOUR READING What is the purpose of a ground wire?

Safety devices control current.

Suppose your living room wiring consists of a circuit that supplies current to a television and several lights. One hot evening, you turn on an air conditioner in the living room window. The wires that supply current to the room are suddenly carrying more current than before. The lights in the room become dim. Too much current in a circuit is dangerous. How do you know if there is too much current in a wire?

Fortunately, people have been using electric current for over a hundred years. An understanding of how charge flows has led to the development of safety devices. These safety devices are built into circuits to prevent dangerous situations from occurring.

⚠ SAFETY TIPS

- Never go near a fallen power line.
- Never touch an electrical appliance when you are in the shower or bathtub.
- Always dry your hands thoroughly before using an electrical appliance.
- Never use an electrical cord that is damaged in any way.
- Never bend or cut a ground prong in order to make a grounded plug fit into an ungrounded outlet.

Chapter 2: **Circuits and Electronics** 47

How Fuses Work

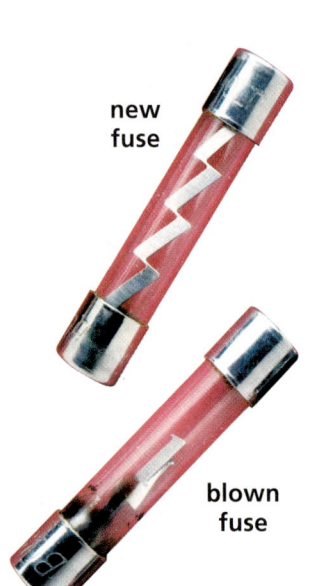

If you turn on an air conditioner in a room full of other electrical appliances that are already on, the circuit could overheat. But if the circuit contains a fuse, the fuse will automatically shut off the current. A fuse is a safety device that opens a circuit when there is too much current in it. Fuses are typically found in older homes and buildings. They are also found in cars and electrical appliances like air conditioners.

A fuse consists of a thin strip of metal that is inserted into the circuit. The charge in the closed circuit flows through the fuse. If too much charge flows through the fuse, the metal strip melts. When the strip has melted and the circuit is open, the fuse is blown. The photographs on the left show a new fuse and a blown fuse. As you can see, charge cannot flow across the melted strip. It has broken the circuit and stopped the current.

How much current is too much? That varies. The electrician who installs a circuit knows how much current the wiring can handle. He or she uses that knowledge to choose the right kind of fuse. Fuses are measured in amperes, or amps. Remember that amperage is a measure of current. If a fuse has blown, it must be replaced with a fuse of the same amperage. But a fuse should be replaced only after the problem that caused it to blow has been fixed.

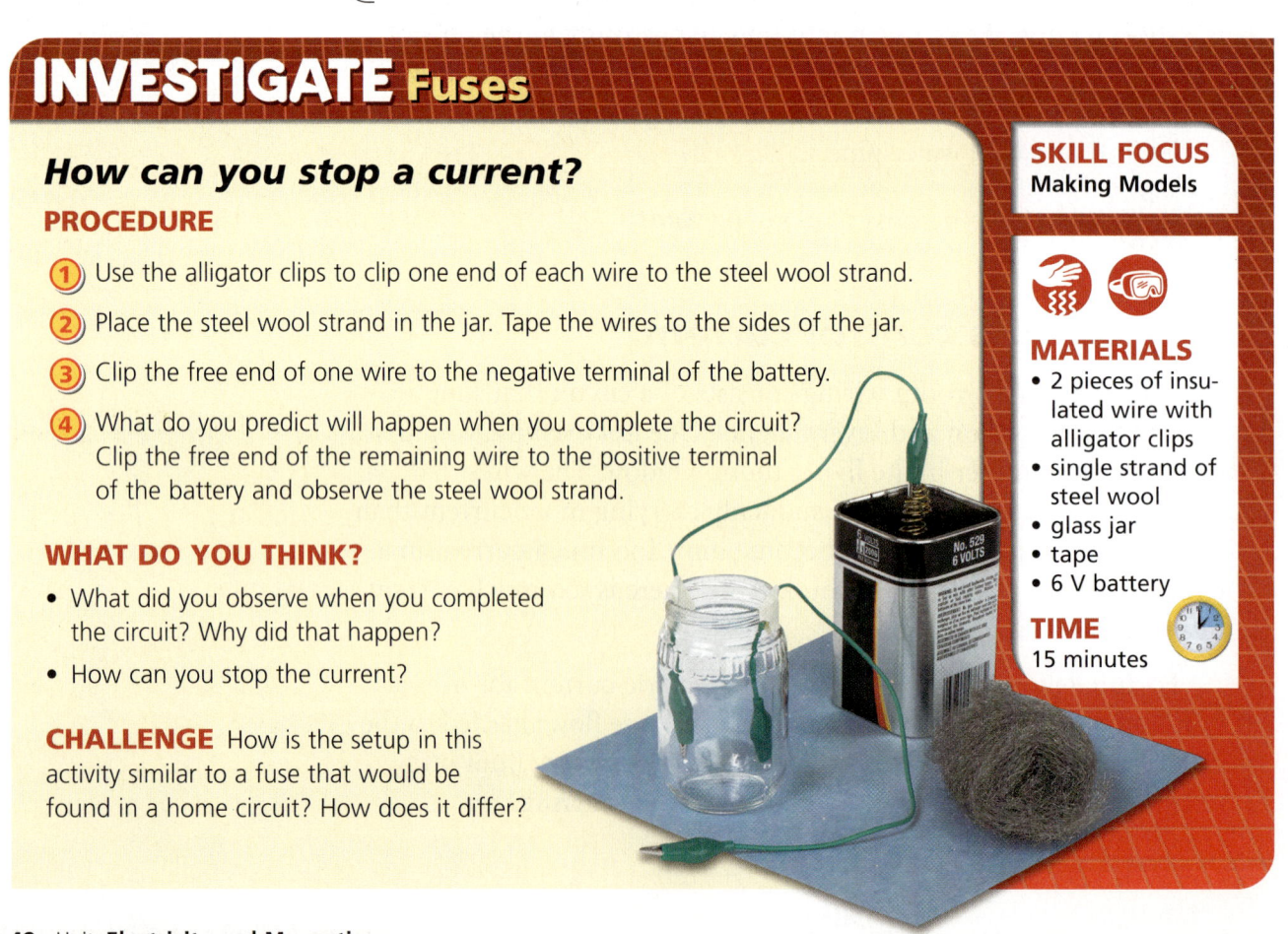

new fuse

blown fuse

INVESTIGATE Fuses

How can you stop a current?
PROCEDURE

1. Use the alligator clips to clip one end of each wire to the steel wool strand.
2. Place the steel wool strand in the jar. Tape the wires to the sides of the jar.
3. Clip the free end of one wire to the negative terminal of the battery.
4. What do you predict will happen when you complete the circuit? Clip the free end of the remaining wire to the positive terminal of the battery and observe the steel wool strand.

WHAT DO YOU THINK?
- What did you observe when you completed the circuit? Why did that happen?
- How can you stop the current?

CHALLENGE How is the setup in this activity similar to a fuse that would be found in a home circuit? How does it differ?

SKILL FOCUS
Making Models

MATERIALS
- 2 pieces of insulated wire with alligator clips
- single strand of steel wool
- glass jar
- tape
- 6 V battery

TIME
15 minutes

Other Safety Devices

Most modern homes do not use fuses. Instead, they use safety devices called circuit breakers. Circuit breakers, unlike fuses, do not have to be replaced every time they open the circuit. Like fuses, circuit breakers automatically open the circuit when too much charge flows through it. If the circuit becomes overloaded or there is a short circuit, the wire and the breaker grow hot. That makes a piece of metal inside the breaker expand. As it expands, it presses against a switch. The switch is then flipped to the off position and the current is stopped. Once the problem is solved, power can be restored manually by simply flipping the switch back. The illustration on the right shows a circuit breaker.

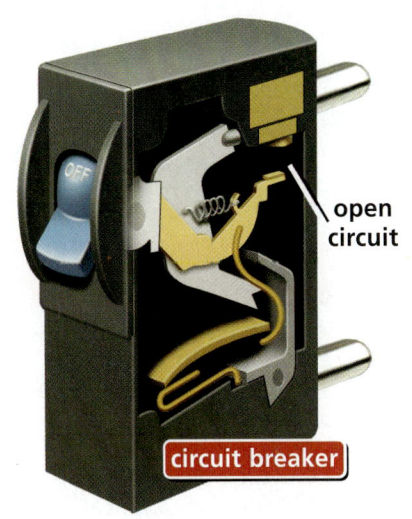

CHECK YOUR READING How are circuit breakers similar to fuses?

The photograph at the bottom right shows another safety device—a ground-fault circuit interrupter (GFCI) outlet. Sometimes a little current leaks out of an outlet or an appliance. Often it is so small you do not notice it. But if you happen to have wet hands, touching even a small current can be very dangerous.

GFCI outlets are required in places where exposure to water is common, such as in kitchens and bathrooms. A tiny circuit inside the GFCI outlet monitors the current going out and coming in. If some of the current starts to flow through an unintended path, there will be less current coming in to the GFCI. If that happens, a circuit breaker inside the GFCI outlet opens the circuit and stops the current. To close the circuit again, you push "Reset."

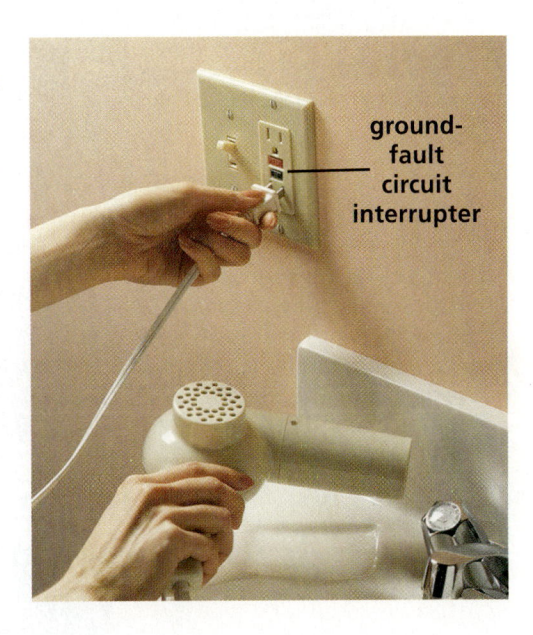

2.1 Review

KEY CONCEPTS

1. Describe three parts of a circuit and explain what each part does.
2. Explain the function of a ground wire.
3. What do fuses and circuit breakers have in common?

CRITICAL THINKING

4. **Apply** Suppose you have built a circuit for a class project. You are using a flat piece of wood for its base. How could you make a switch out of a paperclip and two nails?
5. **Communicate** Draw a diagram of a short circuit. Use the symbols for the parts of a circuit.

CHALLENGE

6. **Evaluate** A fuse in a home has blown and the owner wants to replace it with a fuse that can carry more current. Why might the owner's decision lead to a dangerous situation?

Chapter 2: **Circuits and Electronics** 49

SCIENCE on the JOB

ELECTRICIAN

The Science of Electrical Work

Electricians are the professionals who know how to control and modify electrical installations safely. They are the people who install the wiring and fixtures that deliver current to the appliances in your home. They also inspect equipment and wiring to locate and correct problems. High-voltage current can cause injuries, or even death, if not handled correctly. The electrician uses science to build and repair electrical systems safely.

Choosing the Wire

Different types and thicknesses of wire have different amounts of resistance and can carry different amounts of current without overheating. The electrician knows which type of wire is suitable for each application.

Installing Safety Devices

Circuit breakers shut off a circuit when the wires carry too much current. This safety device protects the wires from overheating. The electrician chooses circuit breakers with the appropriate amperage for each circuit.

Using Circuit Diagrams

Circuit diagrams are used to map all of the circuits in a project. The electrician determines how many electrical devices each one will contain and knows how much energy those devices will use.

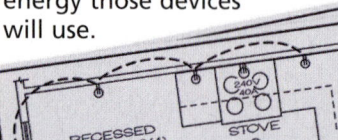

EXPLORE

1. **INFER** Look around the room you're in for electrical outlets. Why do you think each one is located where it is? Do you think they all connect appliances to the same circuit? Explain how this is possible.

2. **CHALLENGE** Suppose you are planning the wiring for the lighting in a room. Draw a diagram of the room's layout and indicate where the wires, lighting fixtures, and switches will be located.

KEY CONCEPT
2.2 Circuits make electric current useful.

BEFORE, you learned
- Charge flows in a closed circuit
- Circuits have a voltage source, conductor, and one or more electrical devices
- Current follows the path of least resistance

NOW, you will learn
- How circuits are designed for specific purposes
- How a series circuit differs from a parallel circuit
- How electrical appliances use circuits

VOCABULARY
series circuit p. 52
parallel circuit p. 53

THINK ABOUT
How does it work?

You know what a telephone does. But did you ever stop to think about how the circuits and other electrical parts inside of it work together to make it happen?

This photo shows an old telephone that has been taken apart to reveal its circuits. As you can see, there are a lot of different parts. Each one has a function. Pick two or three of the parts. What do you think each part does? How do you think it works? How might it relate to the other parts inside the telephone?

OUTLINE
Remember to include this heading in your outline.

I. Main idea
   A. Supporting idea
      1. Detail
      2. Detail
   B. Supporting idea

Circuits are constructed for specific purposes.

How many things around you right now use electric current? Current is used to transfer energy to so many things because it is easy to store, distribute, and turn off and on. Each device that uses current is a part of at least one circuit—the circuit that supplies its voltage.

Most electrical appliances have many circuits inside of them that are designed to carry out specific functions. Those circuits may be designed to light bulbs, move motor parts, or calculate. Each of those circuits may have thousands—or even millions—of parts. The functions that a circuit can perform depend on how those parts are set up within the circuit.

CHECK YOUR READING Why is the design of a circuit important?

Chapter 2: Circuits and Electronics 51 **E**

Circuits can have multiple paths.

Even a simple circuit can contain several parts. When you flip the light switch in your classroom, how many different lights go on? If you count each light bulb or each fluorescent tube, there might be as many as ten or twelve light bulbs. There is more than one way those light bulbs could be connected in one circuit. Next, you will read about two simple ways that circuits can be constructed.

Series Circuits

READING TIP
The word *series* means a number of things arranged one after another.

A **series circuit** is a circuit in which current follows a single path. That means that all of the parts in a series circuit are part of the same path. The photograph and diagram below show a series circuit. The charge coming from the D cell flows first through one light bulb, and then through the next one.

Series Circuit

Each device in a series circuit is wired on a single path.

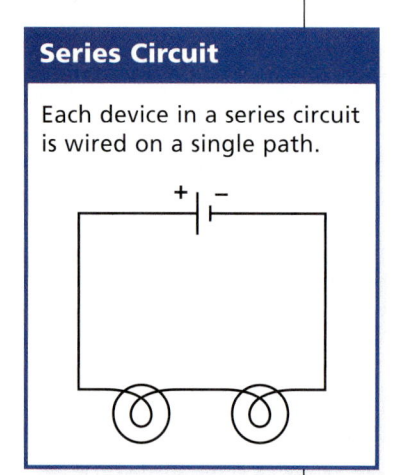

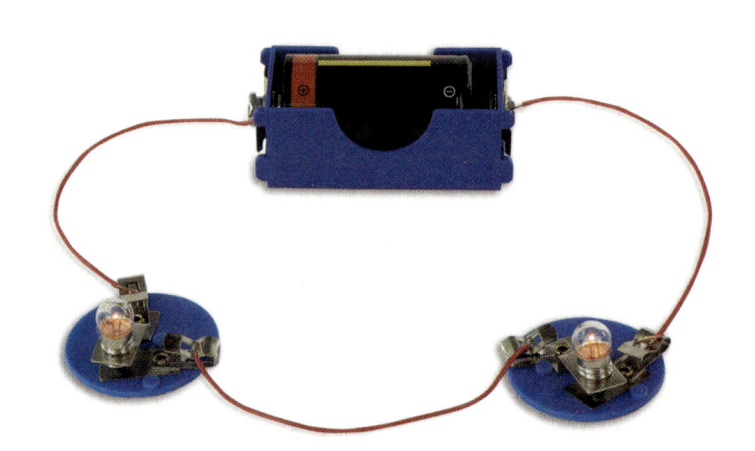

A series circuit uses a minimal amount of wire. However, a disadvantage of a series circuit is that all of the elements must be in working order for the circuit to function. If one of the light bulbs burns out, the circuit will be broken and the other bulb will be dark, too. Series circuits have another disadvantage. Light bulbs and other resistors convert some energy into heat and light. The more light bulbs that are added to a series circuit, the less current there is available, and the dimmer all of the bulbs become.

CHECK YOUR READING Give two disadvantages of a series circuit.

If voltage sources are arranged in series, the voltages will add together. Sometimes batteries are arranged in series to add voltage to a circuit. For example, the circuits in flashlights are usually series circuits. The charge flows through one battery, through the next, through the bulb, and back to the first battery. The flashlight is brighter than it would be if its circuit contained only a single battery.

52 Unit: Electricity and Magnetism

Parallel Circuits

A **parallel circuit** is a circuit in which current follows more than one path. Each path is called a branch. The current divides among all possible branches, so that the voltage is the same across each branch. The photograph and diagram below show a simple parallel circuit.

Parallel Circuit

Each device in a parallel circuit has its own connection to the voltage source.

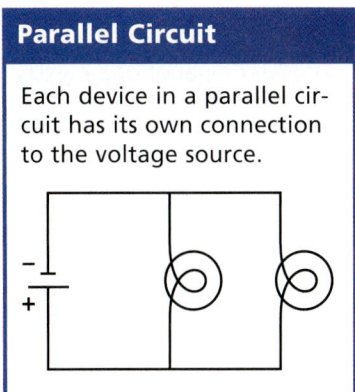

Parallel circuits require more wire than do series circuits. On the other hand, there is more than one path on which the charge may flow. If one bulb burns out, the other bulb will continue to glow. As you add more and more light bulbs to a series circuit, each bulb in the circuit grows dimmer and dimmer. Because each bulb you add in a parallel circuit has its own branch to the power source, the bulbs burn at their brightest.

A flashlight contains batteries wired in a series circuit. Batteries can be wired in parallel, too. If the two positive terminals are connected to each other and the two negative terminals are connected to each other, charge will flow from both batteries. Adding batteries in parallel will not increase the voltage supplied to the circuit, but the batteries will last longer.

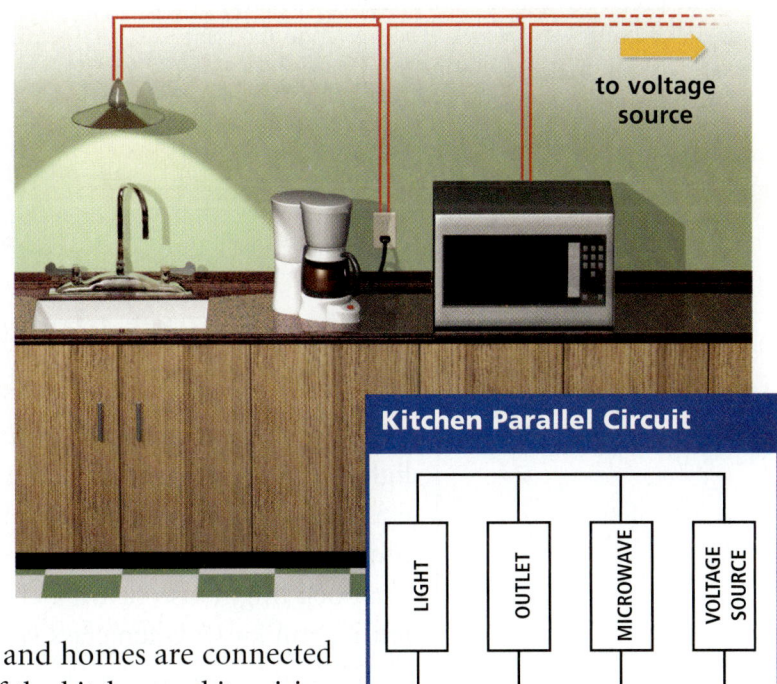

to voltage source

Kitchen Parallel Circuit

The circuits in most businesses and homes are connected in parallel. Look at the illustration of the kitchen and its wiring. This is a parallel circuit, so even if one electrical device is switched off, the others can still be used. The circuits within many electrical devices are combinations of series circuits and parallel circuits. For example, a parallel circuit may have branches that contain several elements arranged in series.

CHECK YOUR READING Why are the circuits in buildings and homes arranged in parallel?

Chapter 2: **Circuits and Electronics** 53

INVESTIGATE Circuits

How can you produce brighter light?
PROCEDURE

1. Clip one end of a wire to the light bulb and the other end to the negative terminal of one battery to form a connection.

2. Use another wire to connect the positive terminal of the battery with the negative terminal of a second battery, as shown in the photograph.

3. Use a third wire to connect the positive terminal of the second battery to the light bulb. Observe the light bulb.

4. Remove the wires. Find a way to reconnect the wires to produce the other type of circuit.

WHAT DO YOU THINK?
- Which circuit produced brighter light? What type of circuit was it?
- Why did the light bulb glow brighter in that circuit?

CHALLENGE Suppose you wanted to construct a new circuit consisting of four light bulbs and only one battery. How would you arrange the light bulbs so that they glow at their brightest? Your answer should be in the form of either a diagram or a sketch of the circuit.

SKILL FOCUS
Inferring

MATERIALS
- 4 insulated wires with alligator clips
- small light bulb in a holder
- 2 batteries in holders

TIME
15 minutes

Circuits convert electrical energy into other forms of energy.

We use electrical energy to do many things besides lighting a string of light bulbs. For example, a circuit in a space heater converts electrical energy into heat. A circuit in a fan converts electrical energy into motion. A circuit in a bell converts electrical energy into sound. That bell might also be on a circuit that makes it ring at certain times, letting you know when class is over.

Branches, switches, and other elements in circuits allow for such control of current that our calculators and computers can use circuits to calculate and process information for us. All of these things are possible because voltage is electric potential that can be converted into energy in a circuit.

CHECK YOUR READING Name three types of energy that electrical energy can be converted into.

A toaster is an example of an electrical appliance containing a circuit that converts energy from one form to another. In a toaster, electrical energy is converted into heat. Voltage is supplied to the toaster by plugging it into a wall outlet, which completes the circuit from a power plant. The outlet is wired in parallel with other outlets, so the appliance will always be connected to the same amount of voltage.

① When you push the handle down, a piece of metal connects to contact points on a circuit board that act as a switch and run current through the circuit.

② Charge flows through a resistor in the circuit called a heating element. The heating element is made up of a type of wire that has a very high resistance. As charge flows through the heating element, electrical energy is converted into heat.

③ The holder in the toaster is loaded onto a timed spring. After a certain amount of time passes, the spring is released, the toast pops up, and the circuit is opened. The toaster shuts off automatically, and your toast is done.

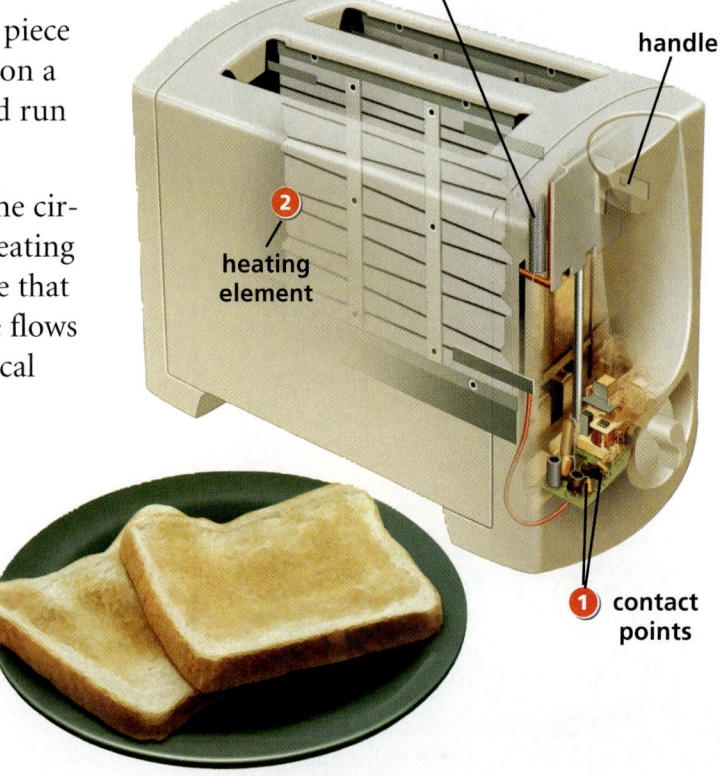

CHECK YOUR READING Summarize the way a circuit in a toaster works. (Remember that a summary includes only the most important information.)

2.2 Review

KEY CONCEPTS

1. **Explain** how a circuit can perform a specific function.
2. How are series circuits and parallel circuits similar? How do they differ?
3. Describe three electrical appliances that use circuits to convert electrical energy into other forms of energy.

CRITICAL THINKING

4. **Analyze** Why are the batteries of flashlights often arranged in series and not in parallel?
5. **Infer** You walk past a string of small lights around a window frame. Only two of the bulbs are burned out. What can you tell about the string of lights?

CHALLENGE

6. **Apply** Explain how the circuit in a space heater converts electrical energy into heat. Draw a diagram of the circuit, using the standard symbols for circuit diagrams.

Chapter 2: **Circuits and Electronics** 55

MATH in SCIENCE

SKILL: SOLVING PERCENT PROBLEMS

MATH TUTORIAL
CLASSZONE.COM
Click on Math Tutorial for more help with percents and proportions.

Voltage Drop

A voltage drop occurs when current passes through a wire or an electrical device. The higher the resistance of a wire, the greater the voltage drop. Too much voltage drop can cause the device to overheat.

The National Electric Code—a document of guidelines for electricians—states that the voltage drop across a wire should be no more than 5 percent of the voltage from the voltage source. To find 5 percent of a number, you can set up the calculation as a proportion.

Example

The lighting in a hotel includes many fixtures that will be arranged on long wires. The electrician needs to know the maximum voltage drop allowed in order to choose the proper wire. The circuit will use a voltage source of 120 V. What is 5% of 120?

(1) Write the problem as a proportion.

$$\frac{\text{voltage drop}}{\text{voltage}} = \frac{\text{percent}}{100}$$

(2) Substitute.

$$\frac{\text{voltage drop}}{120} = \frac{5}{100}$$

(3) Calculate and simplify.

$$\frac{\text{voltage drop}}{120} \cdot 120 = \frac{5}{100} \cdot 120$$

$$\text{voltage drop} = 6$$

ANSWER The maximum voltage drop in the wire is 6 V.

Use the proportion to answer the following questions.

1. If the voltage source is increased to 277 V, what is the maximum voltage drop in the wire?

2. To be on the safe side, the electrician decided to find a wire with a voltage drop that is 3 percent of the voltage from the voltage source. What is the voltage drop in the wire?

CHALLENGE A student wants to hang a string of lights outside and connect it to an extension cord. The voltage drop across the extension cord is 3.1 V. The outlet supplies 240 V. Does the voltage drop in the extension cord meet the code guidelines?

The many lights in this spectacular display in Kobe, Japan, produce a large voltage drop. The appropriate type of wire must be used to supply its current.

KEY CONCEPT
2.3 Electronic technology is based on circuits.

BEFORE, you learned
- Charge flows in a closed loop
- Circuits are designed for specific purposes
- Electrical appliances use circuits

NOW, you will learn
- How information can be coded
- How computer circuits use digital information
- How computers work

VOCABULARY

electronic p. 57
binary code p. 58
digital p. 58
analog p. 60
computer p. 61

EXPLORE Codes

How can information be coded?

PROCEDURE

1) Write the numbers 1 to 26 in your notebook. Below each number, write a letter of the alphabet. This will serve as your key.

2) On a separate piece of paper, write the name of the street you live on using numbers instead of words. For each letter of the word, use the number that is directly above it on your key.

3) Exchange messages with a partner and use your key to decode your partner's information.

MATERIALS
- notebook
- small piece of paper

WHAT DO YOU THINK?
- How can information be coded?
- Under what types of circumstances would information need to be coded?

Electronics use coded information.

A code is a system of symbols used to send a message. Language is a code, for example. The symbols used in written language are lines and shapes. The words on this page represent meanings coded into the form of letters. As you read, your brain decodes the lines and shapes that make up each word, and you understand the message that is encoded.

An **electronic** device is a device that uses electric current to represent coded information. In electronics, the signals are variations in the current. Examples of electronic devices include computers, calculators, CD players, game systems, and more.

RESOURCE CENTER
CLASSZONE.COM
Find out more about electronics.

CHECK YOUR READING Describe the signals used in electronic devices.

Chapter 2: Circuits and Electronics 57

Binary Code

The English alphabet contains only 26 letters, yet there is no limit to the number of messages that can be expressed with it. That is because the message is conveyed not only by the letters that are chosen but also by the order in which they are placed.

Many electronic devices use a coding system with only two choices, as compared with the 26 in the alphabet. A coding system consisting of two choices is a **binary code.** As with a language, complex messages can be sent using binary code. In electronics, the two choices are whether an electric current is on or off. Switches in electronic circuits turn the current on and off. The result is a message represented in pulses of current.

It may be hard to imagine how something as complex as a computer game can be expressed with pulses of current. But it is a matter of breaking down information into smaller and smaller steps. You may have played the game 20 questions. In that game, you receive a message by asking someone only yes-or-no questions. The player answering the questions conveys the message only in *yes*'s and *no*'s, a binary code.

The diagram on the left shows how a decision-making process can be written in simple steps. The diagram is similar to a computer program, which tells a computer what to do. Each step of the process has been broken down into a binary question. If you determine exactly what you mean by *cold* and *hot,* then anyone using this program—or even a computer—would arrive at the same conclusion for a given set of conditions.

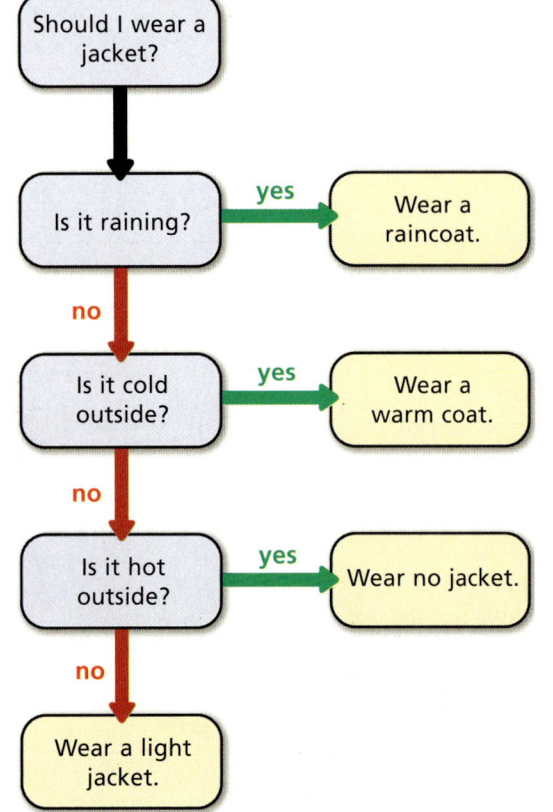

CHECK YOUR READING How can a process be broken down into simple steps?

Digital Information

You can think of the yes-or-no choices in a binary system as being represented by the numbers 0 and 1. Information that is represented as numbers, or digits, is called **digital** information. In electronics, a circuit that is off is represented by 0, and a circuit that is on is represented by 1.

Digital information is represented in long streams of digits. Each 0 or 1 is also known as a bit, which is short for *bi*nary dig*it*. A group of 8 bits is known as a byte. You might have heard the term *gigabyte* in reference to the amount of information that can be stored on a computer. One gigabyte is equal to about 1 billion bytes. That's 8 billion 0s and 1s!

Computers, digital cameras, CD players, DVD players, and other devices use digital information. Digital information is used in electronic devices more and more. There are at least two reasons for this:

- Digital information can be copied many times without losing its quality. The 1s are always copied as 1s, and the 0s are always copied as 0s.
- Digital information can be processed, or worked with, on computers.

For example, a photograph taken on a digital camera can be input to a computer in the form of digital information. Once the photograph is on a computer, the user can modify it, copy it, store it, and send it.

Many portable devices such as game systems and MP3 players can also be used with computers. Because computers and the devices use the same type of information, computers can be used to add games, music, and other programs to the devices. The photograph at right of a watch shows an example of a portable device that uses digital information.

This watch also functions as an MP3 player—it can store songs as digital files.

CHECK YOUR READING Why is digital information often used in electronic devices?

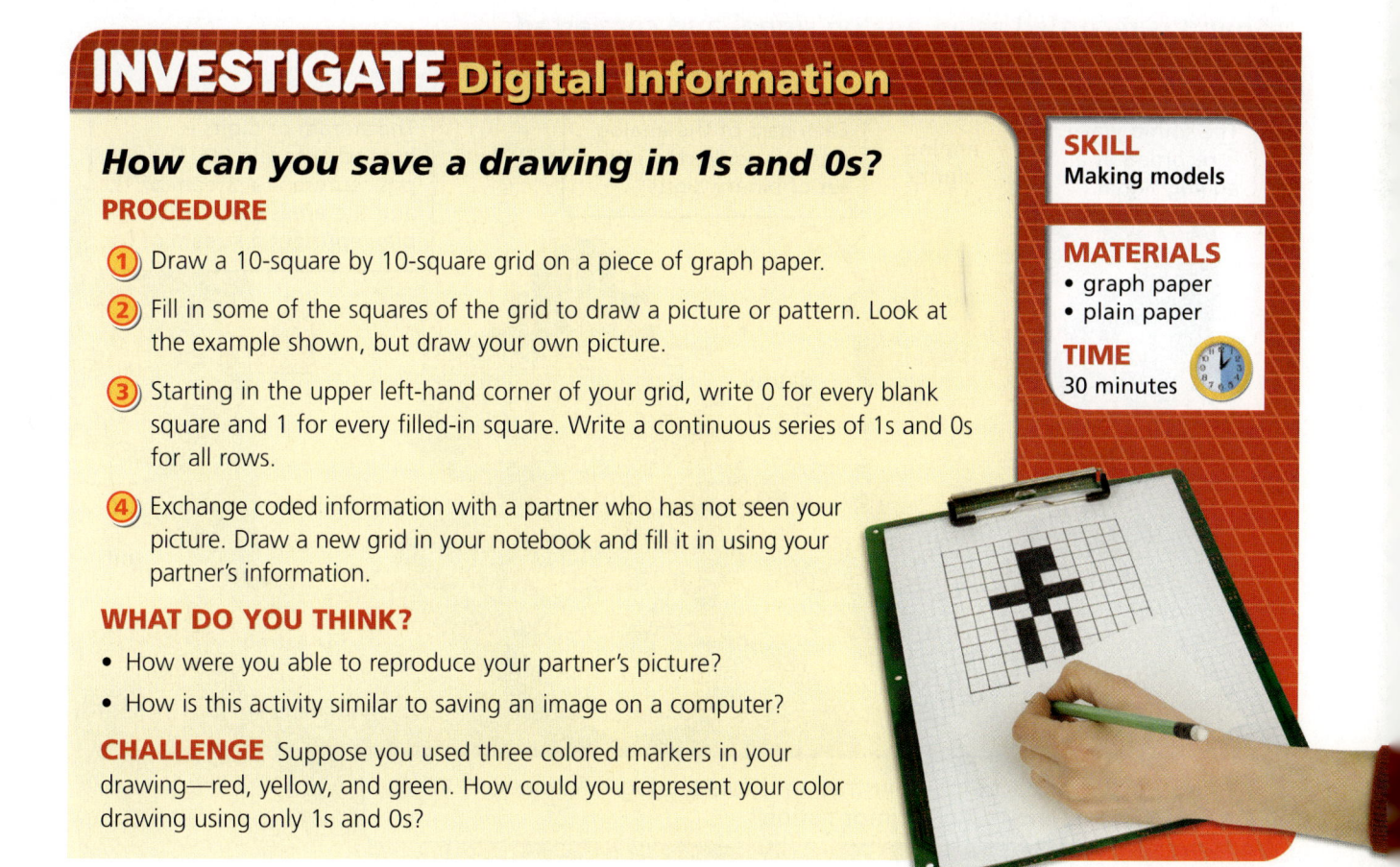

INVESTIGATE Digital Information

How can you save a drawing in 1s and 0s?

PROCEDURE

1. Draw a 10-square by 10-square grid on a piece of graph paper.
2. Fill in some of the squares of the grid to draw a picture or pattern. Look at the example shown, but draw your own picture.
3. Starting in the upper left-hand corner of your grid, write 0 for every blank square and 1 for every filled-in square. Write a continuous series of 1s and 0s for all rows.
4. Exchange coded information with a partner who has not seen your picture. Draw a new grid in your notebook and fill it in using your partner's information.

WHAT DO YOU THINK?

- How were you able to reproduce your partner's picture?
- How is this activity similar to saving an image on a computer?

CHALLENGE Suppose you used three colored markers in your drawing—red, yellow, and green. How could you represent your color drawing using only 1s and 0s?

SKILL Making models

MATERIALS
- graph paper
- plain paper

TIME 30 minutes

Chapter 2: **Circuits and Electronics** 59

Analog to Digital

Some electronic devices use a system of coding electric current that differs from the digital code. Those electronics use analog information. **Analog** information is information that is represented in a continuous but varying form.

For example, a microphone records sound waves as analog information. The analog signal that is produced varies in strength as the sound wave varies in strength, as shown below. In order for the signal to be burned onto a CD, it is converted into digital information.

① The sound waves are recorded in the microphone as an analog electrical signal.

② The signal is sent through a computer circuit that measures, or samples, each part of the wave. The signal is sampled many thousands of times every second.

③ Each measurement of the wave is converted into a stream of digits. Microscopic pits representing the stream of digits are burned onto the CD. A stereo converts the signal from digital back to analog form, making it possible for people to hear what was recorded.

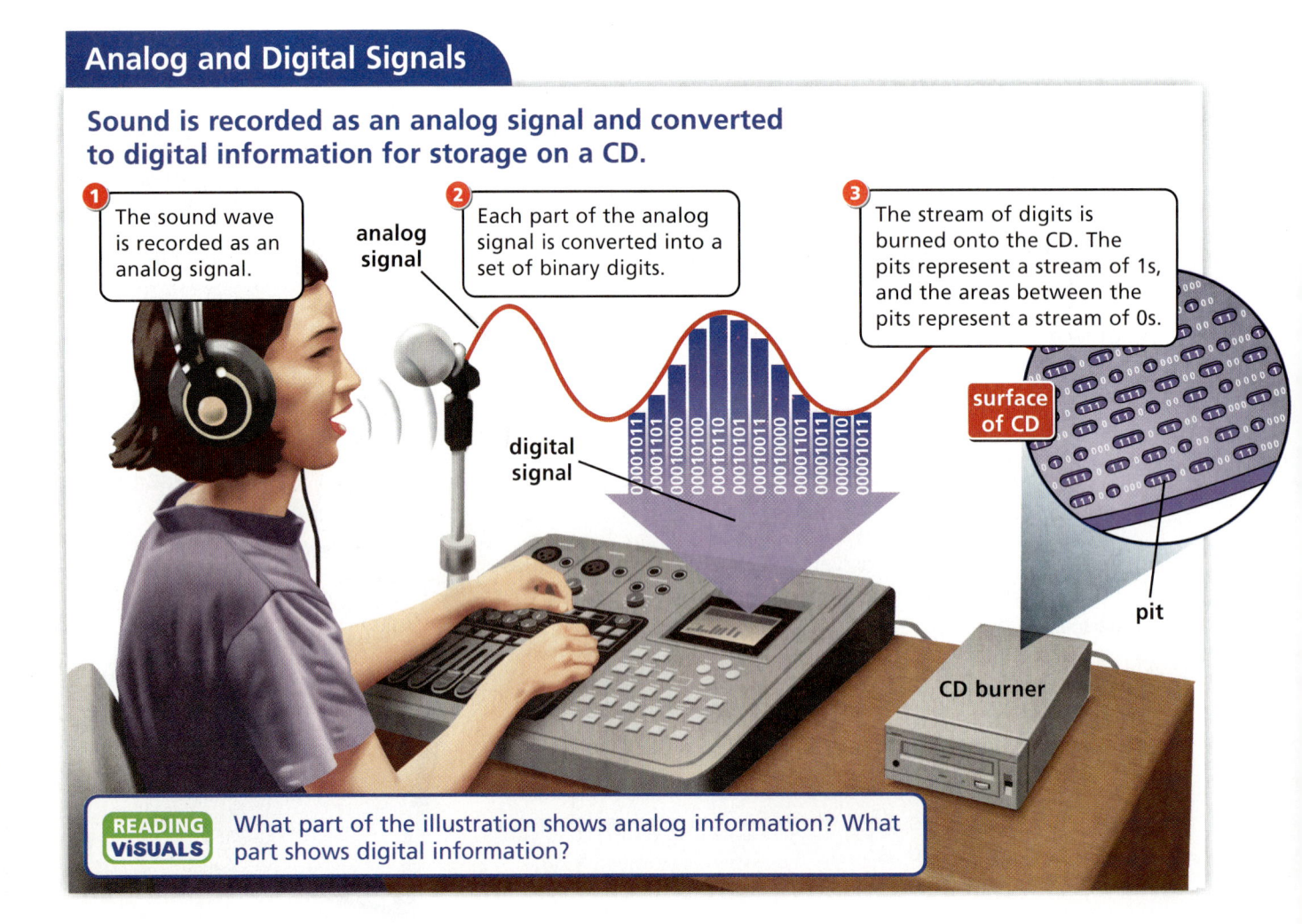

Analog and Digital Signals

Sound is recorded as an analog signal and converted to digital information for storage on a CD.

① The sound wave is recorded as an analog signal.

② Each part of the analog signal is converted into a set of binary digits.

③ The stream of digits is burned onto the CD. The pits represent a stream of 1s, and the areas between the pits represent a stream of 0s.

analog signal

digital signal

surface of CD

pit

CD burner

READING VISUALS What part of the illustration shows analog information? What part shows digital information?

60 Unit: Electricity and Magnetism

Computer circuits process digital information.

A **computer** is an electronic device that processes digital information. Computers have been important in science and industry for a long time. Scientists use computers to gather, store, process, and share scientific data. As computers continue to get faster, smaller, and less expensive, they are turning up in many places.

Suppose you get a ride to the store. If the car you're riding in is a newer car, it probably has a computer inside it. At the store, you buy a battery, and the clerk records the sale on a register that is connected to a computer. You put the battery in your camera and take a picture, and the camera has a computer inside it.

VOCABULARY
Remember to make a frame game diagram for *computer*.

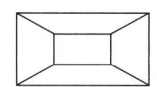

Integrated Circuits

The first digital computer weighed 30 tons and took up a whole room. After 60 years of development, computers the size of a postage stamp are able to complete the same tasks in less time. New technology in computer circuits has led to very small and powerful computers.

Computers process information on circuits that contain many switches, branches, and other elements that allow for a very fine control of current. An integrated circuit is a miniature electronic circuit. Tiny switches, called transistors, in these circuits turn off and on rapidly, signaling the stream of digits that represent information. Over a million of these switches may be on one small integrated circuit!

CHECK YOUR READING How do integrated circuits signal digital information?

Most integrated circuits are made from silicon, an element that is very abundant in Earth's crust. When silicon is treated with certain chemicals, it becomes a good semiconductor. A semiconductor is a material that is more conductive than an insulator but less conductive than a conductor. Silicon is a useful material in computers because the flow of current in it can be finely controlled.

Microscopic circuits are etched onto treated silicon with chemicals or lasers. Transistors and other circuit parts are constructed layer by layer on the silicon. A small, complex circuit on a single piece of silicon is known as a silicon chip, or microchip.

This integrated circuit is smaller than the common ant, *Camponotus pennsylvanicus,* which ranges in length from 6 to 17 mm.

OUTLINE
Use an outline to take notes about personal computers.

I. Main idea
   A. Supporting idea
      1. Detail
      2. Detail
   B. Supporting idea

Personal Computers

When you think of a computer, you probably think of a monitor, mouse, and keyboard—a personal computer (PC). All of the physical parts of a computer and its accessories are together known as hardware. Software refers to the instructions, or programs, and languages that control the hardware. The hardware, software, and user of a computer all work together to complete tasks.

CHECK YOUR READING What is the difference between hardware and software?

Computers have two kinds of memory. As the user is working, information is saved on the computer's random-access memory, or RAM. RAM is a computer's short-term memory. Most computers have enough RAM to store billions of bits. Another type of memory is called read-only memory, or ROM. ROM is a computer's long-term memory, containing the programs to start and run the computer. ROM can save information even after a computer is turned off.

The illustration below shows how a photograph is scanned, modified, and printed using a personal computer. The steps fall into four main functions—input, storage, processing, and output.

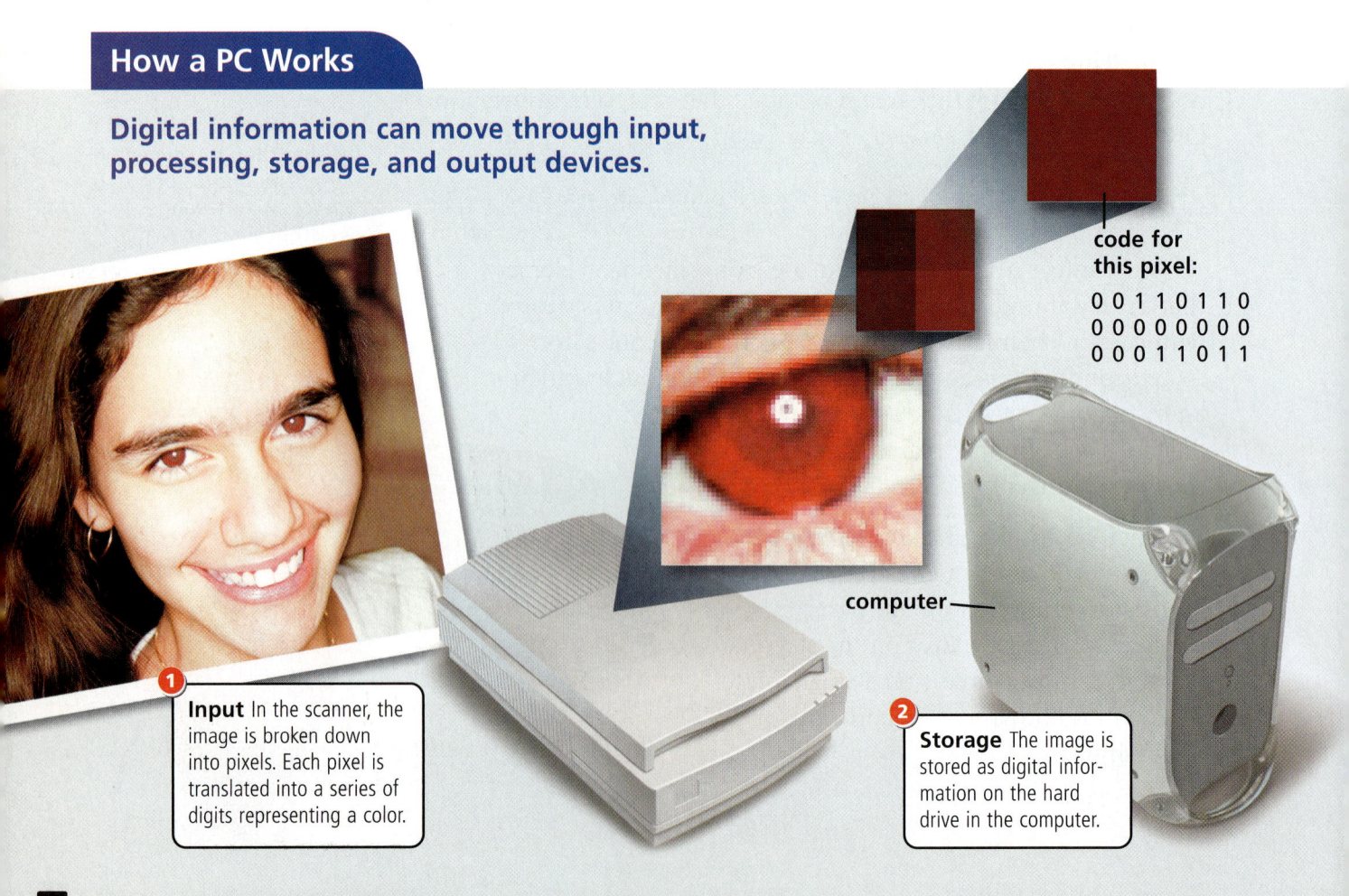

How a PC Works

Digital information can move through input, processing, storage, and output devices.

code for this pixel:
0 0 1 1 0 1 1 0
0 0 0 0 0 0 0 0
0 0 0 1 1 0 1 1

computer

1 Input In the scanner, the image is broken down into pixels. Each pixel is translated into a series of digits representing a color.

2 Storage The image is stored as digital information on the hard drive in the computer.

E 62 Unit: Electricity and Magnetism

① Input The user scans the photograph on a scanner. Each small area, or pixel, of the photograph is converted into a stream of digits. The digital information representing the photograph is sent to the main computer circuit, which is called the central processing unit, or CPU.

② Storage The user saves the photograph on a magnetic storage device called the hard drive. Small areas of the hard drive are magnetized in one of two directions. The magnetized areas oriented in one direction represent 1s, and the areas oriented in the opposite direction represent 0s, as a way to store the digital information.

③ Processing The photograph is converted back into pixels on the monitor, or screen, for the user to see. The computer below has a software program installed for altering photographs. The user adds more input to the computer with the mouse and the keyboard to improve the photograph.

④ Output The user sends the improved photograph to a printer. The printer converts the digital information back to pixels, and the photograph is printed.

VISUALIZATION
CLASSZONE.COM
See how hard drives store information.

CHECK YOUR READING During which one of the four main computer functions is information converted into digital information?

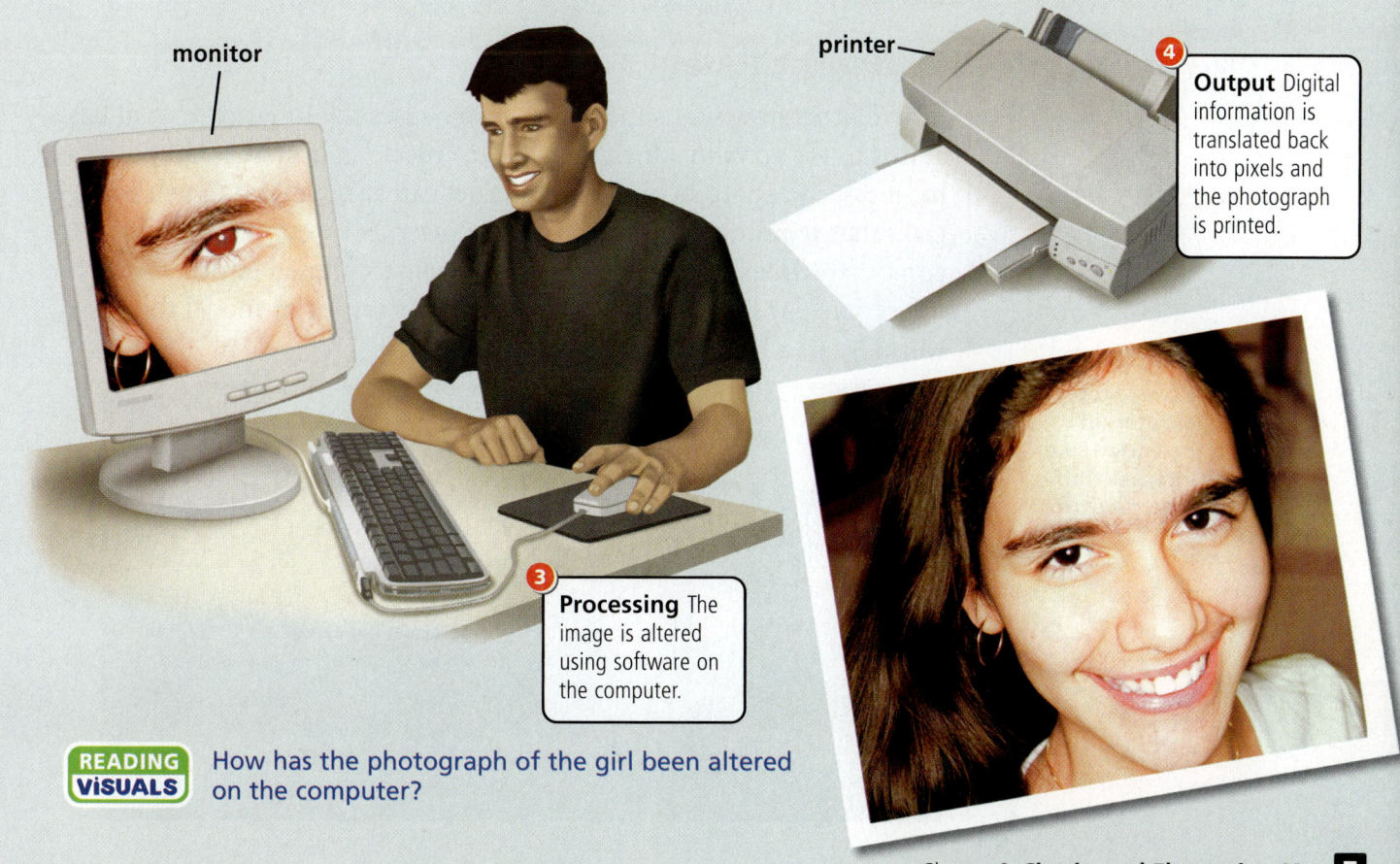

monitor

printer

④ Output Digital information is translated back into pixels and the photograph is printed.

③ Processing The image is altered using software on the computer.

READING VISUALS How has the photograph of the girl been altered on the computer?

Chapter 2: **Circuits and Electronics** 63 **E**

Computers can be linked with other computers.

You may have been at a computer lab or a library and had to wait for a printer to print something for you. Offices, libraries, and schools often have several computers that are all connected to the same printer. A group of computers that are linked together is known as a network. Computers can also be linked with other computers to share information. The largest network of computers is the Internet.

The Origin of the Internet

People have been using computer networks to share information on university campuses and military bases for decades. The computers within those networks were connected over telephone systems from one location to another. But those networks behaved like a series circuit. If the link to one computer was broken, the whole network of links went down.

The network that we now call the Internet is different. The United States Department of Defense formed the Internet by linking computers on college campuses across the country. Many extra links were formed, producing a huge web of connected computers. That way, if some links are broken, others still work.

CHECK YOUR READING How does the Internet differ from earlier networks?

The Internet Today

The Internet now spans the world. E-mail uses the Internet. E-mail has added to the ways in which people can "meet," communicate, conduct business, and share stories. The Internet can also be used to work on tasks that require massive computing power. For example, millions of computers linked together, along with their combined information, might one day be used to develop a cure for cancer or model the workings of a human mind.

This map shows a representation of Internet traffic in the early 1990s. A map of Internet traffic now would be even more full of lines.

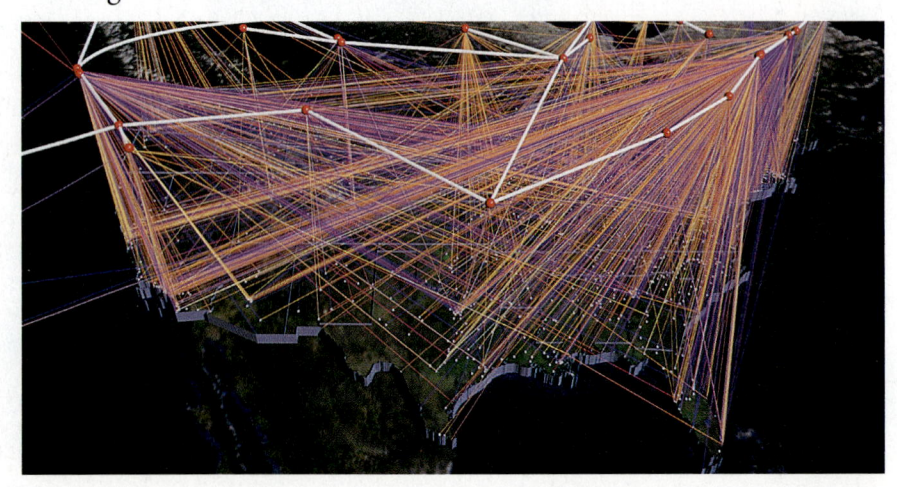

When you think of the Internet, you might think of the World Wide Web, or the Web. The Web consists of all of the information that can be accessed on the Internet. This information is stored on millions of host computers all over the world. The files that you locate are called Web pages. Each Web page has an address that begins with *www*, which stands for World Wide Web. The system allows you to search or surf through all of the information that is available on it. You might use the Web to research a project. Millions of people use the Web every day to find information, to shop, or for entertainment.

You may have heard of the Bronze Age or the Iron Age in your history class. Digital information and the Internet have had such a strong impact on the way we do things that some people refer to the era we live in as the Information Age.

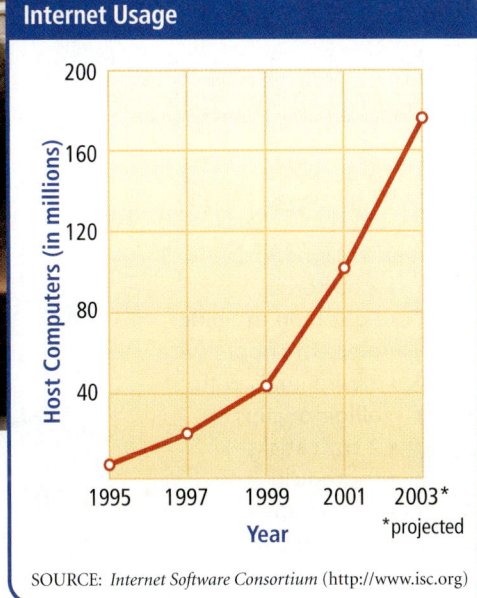

Internet Usage

SOURCE: *Internet Software Consortium* (http://www.isc.org)

2.3 Review

KEY CONCEPTS

1. Describe an example of coded information.
2. What is digital information? Give three examples of devices that use digital information.
3. Give an example of each of the following in terms of computers: input, storage, processing, and output.

CRITICAL THINKING

4. **Compare** Morse code uses a signal of dots and dashes to convey messages. How is Morse code similar to digital code?
5. **Infer** The word *integrated* means "brought together to form a whole." How does that definition apply to an integrated circuit?

CHALLENGE

6. **Predict** Computers as we know them did not exist 50 years ago, and now they are used for many purposes. How do you think people will use computers 50 years from now? Write a paragraph describing what you think the computers of the future will be like and how they will be used.

Chapter 2: **Circuits and Electronics** 65

CHAPTER INVESTIGATION

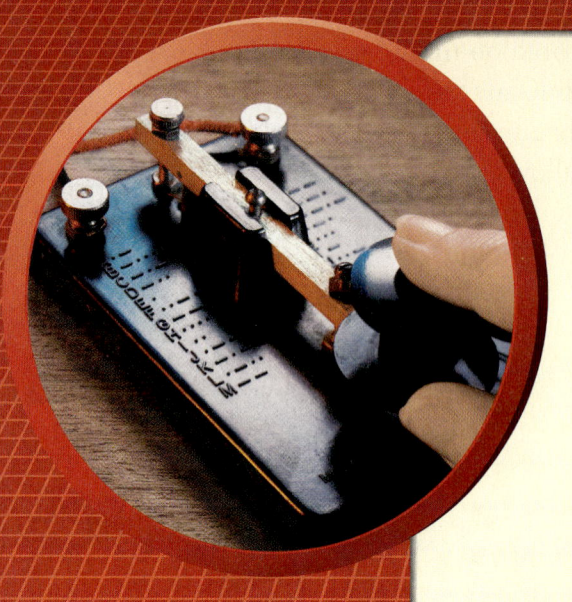

Design an Electronic Communication Device

OVERVIEW AND PURPOSE
The telegraph was one of the first inventions to demonstrate that machines could be used to communicate over long distances. In a telegraph, messages are sent as electrical signals along a wire from a sending device to a receiver.

Like modern computers, the telegraph uses a binary code. The code is called Morse code—a combination of short and long signals—to stand for letters and symbols. In this lab, you will use what you have learned about circuits to
- design a battery-powered device that uses Morse code
- build and test your design

DESIGN YOUR OWN

MATERIALS
- 2 batteries
- light bulb in holder
- piece of copper wire
- 2 wire leads with alligator clips
- 2 craft sticks
- toothpick
- paper clip
- piece of cardboard
- clothespin
- aluminum foil
- rubber band
- scissors
- tape
- wire cutters
- Morse Code Chart

Problem

A toy company has contracted you to design and build a new product for kids. They want a communication device that is similar to a telegraph. Kids will use the device to communicate with each other in Morse code. The company's market research has shown that parents do not like noisy toys, so the company wants a device that uses light rather than sound as a signal.

Procedure

1. Brainstorm ideas for a communication device that can use Morse code. Look at the available materials and think how you could make a circuit that contains a light bulb and a switch.

2. Describe your proposed design and/or draw a sketch of it in your **Science Notebook.** Include a list of the materials that you would need to build it.

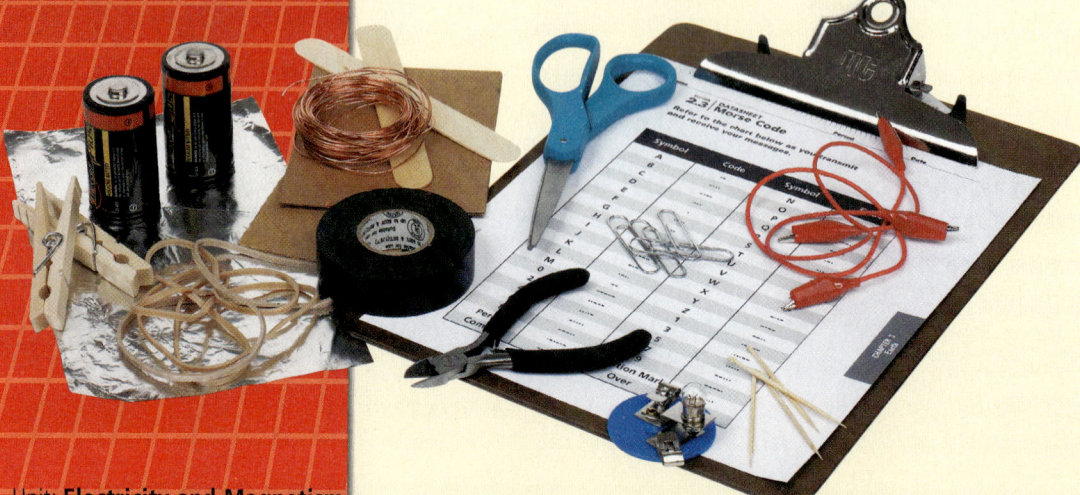

Unit: Electricity and Magnetism

3. Show your design to a team member. Consider the constraints of each of your designs, such as what materials are available, the complexity of the design, and the time available.

4. Choose one idea or combine two ideas into a final design to test with your group. Build a sample version of your device, called a prototype.

5. Test your device by writing a short question. Translate the question into Morse code. Make long and short flashes of light on your device to send your message. Another person on your team should write down the message received in Morse code, translate the message, and send an answer.

6. Complete at least two trials. Each time, record the question in English, the question in code, the answer in code, and the answer in English.

7. Write a brief evaluation of how well the signal worked. Use the following criteria for your evaluation for each trial.
   - What errors, if any, occurred while you were sending the signal?
   - What errors, if any, occurred while you were receiving the signal?
   - Did the translated answer make sense? Why or why not?

Observe and Analyze

1. **MODEL** Draw a sketch of your final design. Label the parts. Next to your sketch, draw a circuit diagram of your device.

2. **INFER** How do the parts of your circuit allow you to control the flow of current?

3. **COMPARE** How is the signal that is used in your system similar to the digital information used by computers to process information? How does the signal differ?

4. **APPLY** A small sheet of instructions will be packaged with the device. Write a paragraph for the user that explains how to use it. Keep in mind that the user will probably be a child.

Conclude

1. **EVALUATE** What problems, if any, did you encounter when testing your device? How might you improve upon the design?

2. **IDENTIFY LIMITS** What are the limitations of your design? You might consider its estimated costs, where and how kids will be able to use it, and the chances of the device breaking.

3. **APPLY** How might you modify your design so that it could be used by someone with limited vision?

4. **SYNTHESIZE** Write down the steps that you have used to develop this new product. Your first step was to brainstorm an idea.

INVESTIGATE Further

CHALLENGE Design another system of communication that uses your own code. The signal should be in the form of flags. Make a table that lists what the signals mean and write instructions that explain how to use the system to communicate.

Design an Electronic Communication Device
Observe and Analyze
Table 1. Prototype Testing

	Trial 1	Trial 2
Question (English)		
Question (code)		
Answer (code)		
Answer (English)		
Evaluation		

Conclude

Chapter 2: **Circuits and Electronics** 67

2 Chapter Review

the BIG idea
Circuits control the flow of electric charge.

CONTENT REVIEW
CLASSZONE.COM

KEY CONCEPTS SUMMARY

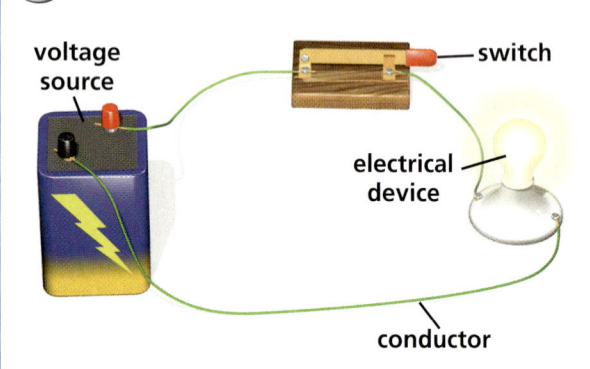

2.1 Charge needs a continuous path to flow.

Charge flows in a closed path. Circuits provide a closed path for current. Circuit parts include voltage sources, switches, conductors, and electrical devices such as resistors.

VOCABULARY
circuit p. 43
resistor p. 44
short circuit p. 46

2.2 Circuits make electric current useful.

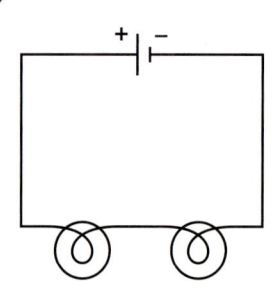

Each device in a **series circuit** is wired on a single path.

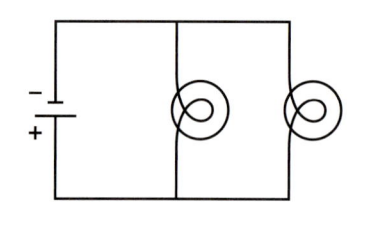

Each device in a **parallel circuit** has its own connection to the voltage source.

VOCABULARY
series circuit p. 52
parallel circuit p. 53

2.3 Electronic technology is based on circuits.

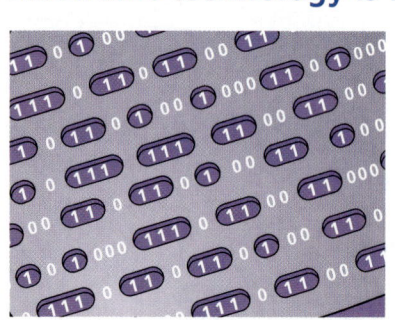

Electronic devices use electrical signals to represent coded information. Computers process information in digital code which uses 1s and 0s to represent the information.

VOCABULARY
electronic p. 57
binary code p. 58
digital p. 58
analog p. 60
computer p. 61

E 68 Unit: Electricity and Magnetism

Reviewing Vocabulary

Draw a Venn diagram for each of the term pairs below. Write the terms above the circles. In the center, write characteristics that the terms have in common. In the outer circles write the ways in which they differ. A sample diagram has been completed for you.

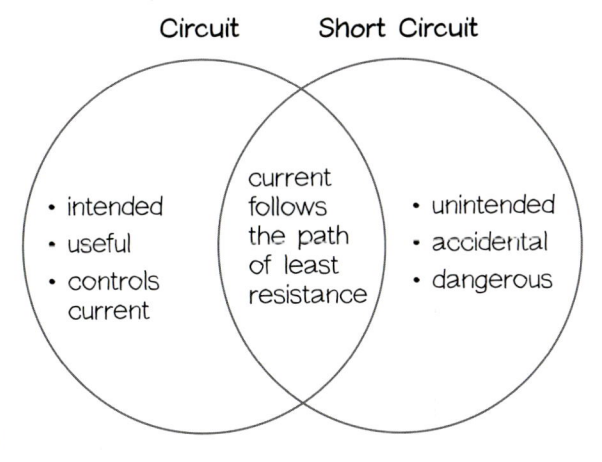

Circuit — Short Circuit
- intended
- useful
- controls current

current follows the path of least resistance

- unintended
- accidental
- dangerous

1. resistor; switch
2. series circuit; parallel circuit
3. digital; analog
4. digital; binary code
5. electronic; computer

Reviewing Key Concepts

Multiple Choice *Choose the letter of the best answer.*

6. Current always follows
   a. a path made of wire
   b. a path containing an electrical device
   c. a closed path
   d. an open circuit

7. When you open a switch in a circuit, you
   a. form a closed path for current
   b. reverse the current
   c. turn off its electrical devices
   d. turn on its electrical devices

8. Which one of the following parts of a circuit changes electrical energy into another form of energy?
   a. resistor
   b. conductor
   c. base
   d. voltage source

9. A circuit breaker is a safety device that
   a. must be replaced after each use
   b. has a wire that melts
   c. supplies voltage to a circuit
   d. stops the current

10. What happens when more than one voltage source is added to a circuit in series?
    a. The voltages are added together.
    b. The voltages cancel each other out.
    c. The voltages are multiplied together.
    d. The voltage of each source decreases.

11. Which of the following is an electronic device?
    a. flashlight
    b. calculator
    c. lamp
    d. electric fan

12. Which word describes the code used in digital technology?
    a. binary
    b. analog
    c. alphabetical
    d. Morse

13. Computers process information that has been
    a. broken down into simple steps
    b. converted into heat
    c. represented as a wave
    d. coded as an analog signal

Short Answer *Write a short answer to each question.*

14. How can hardware, software, and the user of a computer work together to complete a task?

15. Describe three parts of a personal computer and explain the main function of each.

Chapter 2: **Circuits and Electronics** 69

Thinking Critically

Use the illustrations below to answer the next two questions.

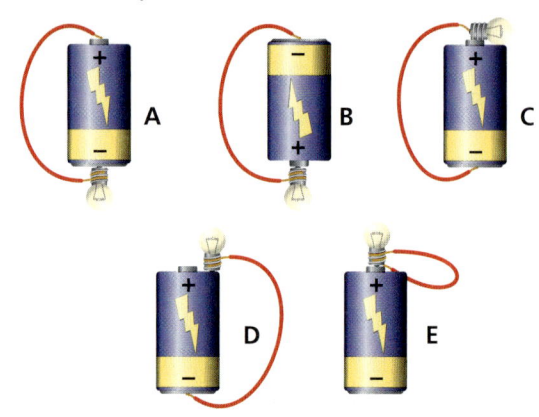

A B C

D E

16. PREDICT In which arrangement(s) above will the light bulb glow? For each arrangement in which you think the bulb will not glow, explain your reasoning.

17. APPLY Which arrangement could be used as a battery tester? List the materials that you would use to make a battery tester.

Use the diagram below to answer the next five questions.

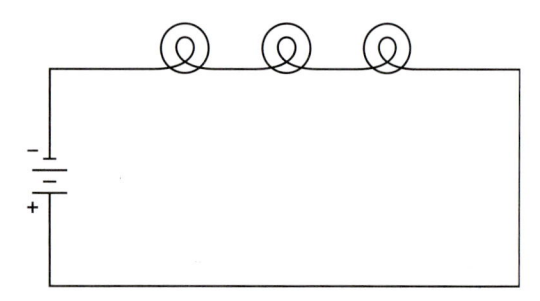

18. Is this a series circuit or a parallel circuit?

19. Explain what would happen if you unscrewed one of the bulbs in the circuit.

20. Explain what would happen if you wired three more bulbs into the circuit.

21. Draw and label a diagram of the same elements wired in the other type of circuit. Does your sketch involve more or fewer pieces of wire? How many?

22. Imagine you want to install a switch into your circuit. Where would you add the switch? Explain your answer.

23. ANALYZE Look for a pattern in the digital codes below, representing the numbers 1–10. What is the code for the number 11? How do you know?

0001; 0010; 0011; 0100; 0101; 0110; 0111; 1000; 1001; 1010

24. APPLY A computer circuit contains millions of switches that use temperature-dependent materials to operate lights, sounds, and a fan. How many different types of energy is current converted to in the computer circuit? Explain.

25. ANALYZE A music recording studio makes a copy of a CD that is itself a copy of another CD. Explain why the quality of the copied CDs is the same as the original CD.

26. INFER A new watch can be programmed to perform specific tasks. Describe what type of circuit the watch might contain.

27. SYNTHESIZE Explain how the Internet is like a worldwide parallel circuit.

the BIG idea

28. ANALYZE Look back at the photograph on pages 40–41. Think about the answer you gave to the question. How has your understanding of circuits changed?

29. SYNTHESIZE Explain how the following statement relates to electric circuits: "Energy can change from one form to another and can move from one place to another."

30. SUMMARIZE Write a paragraph summarizing how circuits control current. Using the heading at the top of page 43 as your topic sentence. Then give an example from each red and blue heading on pages 43–45.

UNIT PROJECTS

If you need to do an experiment for your unit project, gather the materials. Be sure to allow enough time to observe results before the project is due.

Standardized Test Practice

For practice on your state test, go to...
TEST PRACTICE
CLASSZONE.COM

Interpreting Diagrams

The four circuit diagrams below use the standard symbols for the parts of a circuit.

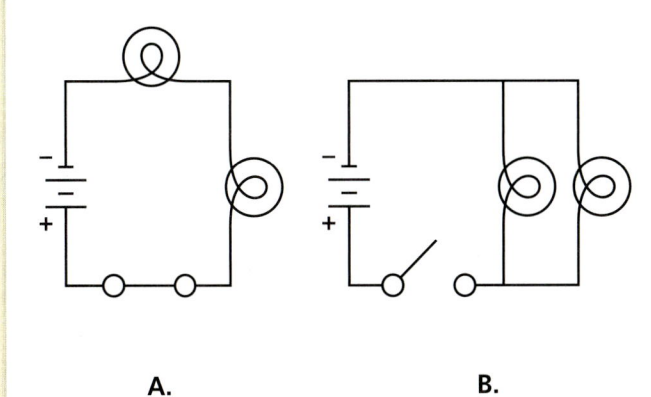

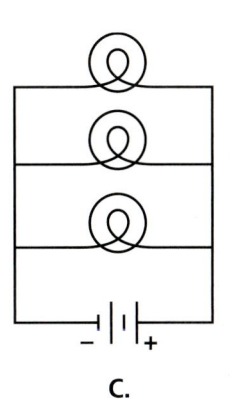

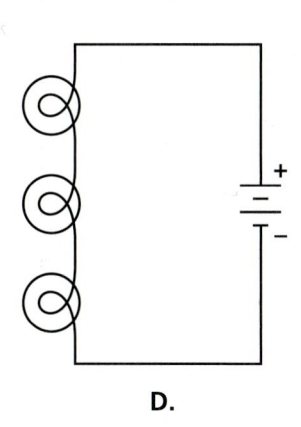

A.   B.   C.   D.

Study the diagrams and answer the questions that follow.

1. Which diagram shows a series circuit, with one voltage source and two light bulbs?
  a. A **c.** C
  b. B **d.** D

2. Which diagram shows a parallel circuit powered by a battery, with three light bulbs?
  a. A **c.** C
  b. B **d.** D

3. The light bulbs in these diagrams limit the flow of charge and give off heat and light. Under which category of circuit parts do light bulbs belong?
  a. switches **c.** resistors
  b. conductors **d.** voltage sources

4. In which diagram would the light bulbs be dark?
  a. A **c.** C
  b. B **d.** D

5. If all light bulbs and voltage sources were equal, how would the light from each of the bulbs in diagram C compare to the light from each of the bulbs in diagram A?
  a. The bulbs in diagram C would give less light than the bulbs in diagram A.
  b. The bulbs in diagram C would give more light than the bulbs in diagram A.
  c. The bulbs in diagram C would give the same amount of light as the bulbs in diagram A.
  d. It cannot be determined which bulbs would give more light.

Extended Response

Answer the two questions below in detail. Include some of the terms from the word box. Underline each term you use in your answer.

| flow of charge | electric current | binary code |
| open circuit | digital | signal |

6. What are two types of safety devices designed to control electric current and prevent dangerous accidents? How does each work?

7. Explain how an electronic circuit differs from an electric circuit. What role do electronic circuits play in computer operations?

Chapter 2: **Circuits and Electronics** 71   **E**

TIMELINES in Science

THE STORY OF ELECTRONICS

Inventions such as the battery, the dynamo, and the motor created a revolution in the production and use of electrical energy. Think of how many tools and appliances that people depend on every day run on electric current. Try to imagine not using electricity in any form for an entire day.

The use of electricity as an energy source only begins the story of how electricity has changed our lives. Parts of the story are shown on this timeline. Research in electronics has given us not only electrical versions of machines that already existed but also entirely new technologies.

These technologies include computers. Electricity is used as a signal inside computers to code and transmit information. Electricity can even mimic some of the processes of logical reasoning and decision making, giving computers the power to solve problems.

600 B.C.
Thales Studies Static Electricity
Greek philosopher-scientist Thales of Miletus discovers that when he rubs amber with wool or fur, the amber attracts feathers and straw. The Greek word for amber, *elektron*, is the origin of the word *electricity*.

EVENTS

640 B.C. 620 B.C. 600 B.C. A.D. 1740

APPLICATIONS AND TECHNOLOGY

APPLICATION
Leyden Jar
In 1745 German inventor Ewald Georg von Kleist invented a device that would store a static charge. The device, called a Leyden jar, was a glass container filled with water. A wire ran from the outside of the jar through the cork into the water. The Leyden jar was the first capacitor, an electronic component that stores and releases charges. Capacitors have been key to the development of computers.

72 Unit: Electricity and Magnetism

1752
Franklin Invents Lightning Rod

To test his hypothesis that lightning is caused by static electric charges, U.S. inventor Ben Franklin flies a kite during a thunderstorm. A metal key hangs from the kite strings. Sparks jump from the key to Franklin's knuckle, showing that the key has a static charge. On the basis of this experiment, Franklin invents the lightning rod.

1776
Bassi Gives Physics a Boost

Italian scholar Laura Bassi, one of the first women to hold a chair at a major European university, is named professor of experimental physics. Bassi uses her position to establish one of the world's first electrical laboratories.

1800
Volta Invents Battery

Italian scientist Alessandro Volta creates the first battery by stacking round plates of metal separated by disks soaked in salt water. Volta's discovery refutes the competing belief that electricity must be created by living beings.

1760   1780   1800   1820   1840

TECHNOLOGY
The Difference Engine

Around 1822 British mathematician Charles Babbage developed the first prototype of a machine that could perform calculations mechanically. Babbage's "difference engine" used disks connected to rods with hand cranks to calculate mathematical tables. Babbage's invention came more than 100 years before the modern computer.

Timelines in Science 73 E

1879
Edison Improves Dynamo

To help bring electric lights to the streets of New York City, U.S. inventor Thomas Edison develops an improved dynamo, or generator. Edison's dynamo, known as a long-legged Mary Ann, operates at about twice the efficiency of previous models.

1904
Vacuum Tube Makes Debut

British inventor Ambrose Fleming modifies a light bulb to create an electronic vacuum tube. Fleming's tube, which he calls a valve, allows current to flow in one direction but not the other and can be used to detect weak radio signals.

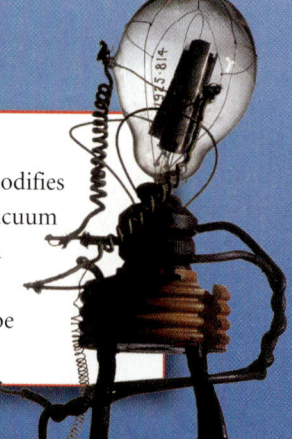

1947
Transistor Invented

A transistor—a tiny electronic switch made out of a solid material called a semiconductor—is introduced to regulate the flow of electricity. Transistors, which do not produce excess heat and never burn out, can replace the vacuum tube in electronic circuitry and can be used to make smaller, cheaper, and more powerful computers.

1860   1880   1900   1920   1940

APPLICATION

First Electronic Digital Computer

Electronic Numerical Integrator and Computer (ENIAC) was the first digital computer. It was completed and installed in 1944 at the Moore School of Electrical Engineering at the University of Pennsylvania. Weighing more than 30 tons, ENIAC contained 19,000 vacuum tubes, 70,000 resistors, and 6000 switches, and it used almost 200 kilowatts of electric power. ENIAC could perform 5000 additions per second.

1958
Chip Inventors Think Small
Jack Kilby, a U.S. electrical engineer, conceives the idea of making an entire circuit out of a single piece of germanium. The integrated circuit, or "computer chip," is born. This invention enables computers and other electronic devices to be made much smaller than before.

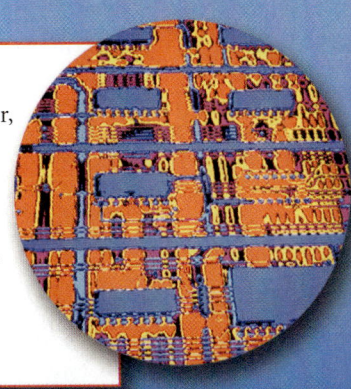

2001
Scientists Shrink Circuits to Atomic Level
Researchers succeed in building a logic circuit, a kind of transistor the size of a single molecule. The molecule, a tube of carbon atoms called a carbon nanotube, can be as small as 10 atoms across—500 times smaller than previous transistors. Computer chips, which currently contain over 40 million transistors, could hold hundreds of millions or even billions of nanotube transistors.

RESOURCE CENTER
CLASSZONE.COM
Explore current research in electronics and computers.

1960   1980   2000

TECHNOLOGY
Miniaturization
Miniaturization has led to an explosion of computer technology. As circuits have shrunk, allowing more components in less space, computers have become smaller and more powerful. They have also become easier to integrate with other technologies, such as telecommunications. When not being used for a phone call, this cell phone can be used to connect to the Internet, to access e-mail, and even to play computer games.

INTO THE FUTURE
Electronic computer components have become steadily smaller and more efficient over the years. However, the basic mechanism of a computer—a switch that can be either on or off depending on whether an electric charge is present—has remained the same. These switches represent the 1s and 0s, or the "bits," of binary code.

Quantum computing is based on an entirely new way of representing information. In quantum physics, individual subatomic particles can be described in terms of three states rather than just two. Quantum bits, or "qubits," can carry much more information than the binary bits of ordinary computers. Using qubits, quantum computers could be both smaller and faster than binary computers and perform operations not possible with current technology.

Quantum computing is possible in theory, but the development of hardware that can process qubits is just beginning. Scientists are currently looking for ways to put the theory into practice and to build computers that will make current models look as bulky and as slow as ENIAC.

ACTIVITIES

Reliving History
Make a Leyden jar capacitor. Line the inside of a jar with aluminum foil. Stop the jar with clay. Insert a copper wire through the plug so that one end touches the foil and the other sticks out of the jar about 2 centimeters.

To test for a voltage difference between the wire and the glass, touch one end of a multimeter to the exposed wire and the other end to the glass. Run a comb through your hair several times and touch it to the wire. Test the voltage difference again.

Writing About Science
Learn more about the current state of electronic circuit miniaturization. Write up the results of your research in the form of a magazine article.

CHAPTER 3 Magnetism

the BIG idea

Current can produce magnetism, and magnetism can produce current.

Key Concepts

SECTION 3.1 Magnetism is a force that acts at a distance.
Learn how magnets exert forces.

SECTION 3.2 Current can produce magnetism.
Learn about electromagnets and their uses.

SECTION 3.3 Magnetism can produce current.
Learn how magnetism can produce an electric current.

SECTION 3.4 Generators supply electrical energy.
Learn how generators are used in the production of electrical energy.

Internet Preview

CLASSZONE.COM

Chapter 3 online resources: Content Review, Simulation, Visualization, three Resource Centers, Math Tutorial, Test Practice

What force is acting on this compass needle?

EXPLORE the BIG idea

Is It Magnetic?
Experiment with a magnet and several objects made of different materials.

Observe and Think Which objects are attracted to the magnet? Why do you think the magnet attracts some objects and not others?

How Can You Make a Chain?
Hang a paper clip on the end of a magnet. Then hang a second paper clip by touching it to the end of the first paper clip. Add more paper clips to make a chain.

Observe and Think How many paper clips did you add? What held the chain together?

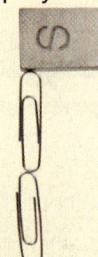

Internet Activity: Electromagnets
Go to **ClassZone.com** to work with a virtual electromagnet. Explore how current and magnetism are related.

Observe and Think What happens when you increase the voltage?

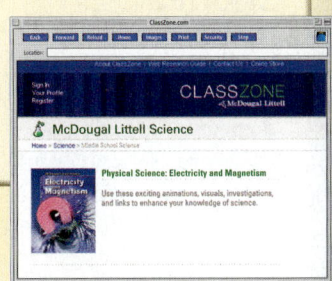

NSTA SciLINKS
scilinks.org
Electromagnetism Code: MDL067

Chapter 3: **Magnetism** 77 **E**

CHAPTER 3
Getting Ready to Learn

CONCEPT REVIEW

- Energy can change from one form to another.
- A force is a push or a pull.
- Power is the rate of energy transfer.

VOCABULARY REVIEW

electric current p. 28
circuit p. 43
kinetic energy See Glossary.

CONTENT REVIEW
CLASSZONE.COM
Review concepts and vocabulary.

TAKING NOTES

MAIN IDEA WEB

Write each new blue heading in a box. Then write notes in boxes around the center box that give important terms and details about that blue heading.

VOCABULARY STRATEGY

Place each vocabulary term at the center of a **description wheel** diagram. As you read about the term, write some words describing it on the spokes.

See the Note-Taking Handbook on pages R45–R51.

SCIENCE NOTEBOOK

- Magnetism is the force exerted by magnets.
- All magnets have two poles.
- Magnets attract and repel other magnets.
- Opposite poles attract, and like poles repel.
- Magnets have magnetic fields of force around them.

MAGNETIC DOMAINS
- Magnetic fields of atoms point in the same direction.
- In magnets, they line up.
- Magnetic materials have them.
- Nonmagnetic materials don't have them.

78 Unit: Electricity and Magnetism

KEY CONCEPT

3.1 Magnetism is a force that acts at a distance.

◀ BEFORE, you learned
- A force is a push or pull
- Some forces act at a distance
- Atoms contain charged particles

▶ NOW, you will learn
- How magnets attract and repel other magnets
- What makes some materials magnetic
- Why a magnetic field surrounds Earth

VOCABULARY
magnet p. 79
magnetism p. 80
magnetic pole p. 80
magnetic field p. 81
magnetic domain p. 82

EXPLORE Magnetism

How do magnets behave?

PROCEDURE

1. Clamp the clothespin on the dowel so that it makes a stand for the magnets, as shown.

2. Place the three magnets on the dowel. If there is a space between pairs of magnets, measure and record the distance between them.

3. Remove the top magnet, turn it over, and replace it on the dowel. Record your observations. Experiment with different arrangements of the magnets and record your observations.

MATERIALS
- clothespin
- wooden dowel
- 3 disk magnets
- ruler

WHAT DO YOU THINK?
- How did the arrangement of the magnets affect their behavior?
- What evidence indicates that magnets exert a force?

VOCABULARY
Make a description wheel for the term *magnet*.

Magnets attract and repel other magnets.

Suppose you get home from school and open the refrigerator to get some milk. As you close the door, it swings freely until it suddenly seems to close by itself. There is a magnet inside the refrigerator door that pulls it shut. A **magnet** is an object that attracts certain other materials, particularly iron and steel.

There may be quite a few magnets in your kitchen. Some are obvious, like the seal of the refrigerator and the magnets that hold notes to its door. Other magnets run the motor in a blender, provide energy in a microwave oven, operate the speakers in a radio on the counter, and make a doorbell ring.

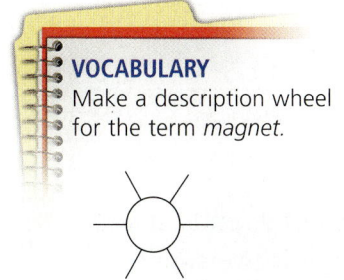

Chapter 3: Magnetism 79 **E**

Magnetism

The force exerted by a magnet is called **magnetism.** The push or pull of magnetism can act at a distance, which means that the magnet does not have to touch an object to exert a force on it. When you close the refrigerator, you feel the pull before the magnet actually touches the metal frame. There are other forces that act at a distance, including gravity and static electricity. Later you will read how the force of magnetism is related to electricity. In fact, magnetism is the result of a moving electric charge.

You may be familiar with magnets attracting, or pulling, metal objects toward them. Magnets can also repel, or push away, objects. The train in the photograph at the left is called a maglev train. The word *maglev* is short for *mag*netic *lev*itation, or lifting up. As you can see in the diagram, the train does not touch the track. Magnetism pushes the entire train up and pulls it forward. Maglev trains can move as fast as 480 kilometers per hour (300 mi/h).

The train is pushed up by magnets beneath it and pulled forward by magnets ahead of it.

CHECK YOUR READING How can a train operate without touching the track?

Magnetic Poles

RESOURCE CENTER
CLASSZONE.COM
Find out more about magnetism.

The force of magnetism is not evenly distributed throughout a magnet. **Magnetic poles** are the parts of a magnet where the magnetism is the strongest. Every magnet has two magnetic poles. If a bar magnet is suspended so that it can swing freely, one pole of the magnet always points toward the north. That end of the magnet is known as the north-seeking pole, or north pole. The other end of the magnet is called the south pole. Many magnets are marked with an *N* and an *S* to indicate the poles.

As with electric charges, opposite poles of a magnet attract and like poles—or poles that are the same—repel, or push each other away. Every magnet has both a north pole and a south pole. A horseshoe magnet is like a bar magnet that has been bent into the shape of a *U*. It has a pole at each of its ends. If you break a bar magnet between the two poles, the result is two smaller magnets, each of which has a north pole and a south pole. No matter how many times you break a magnet, the result is smaller magnets.

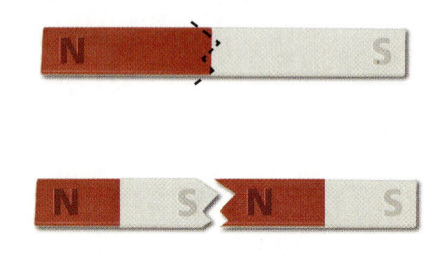

E 80 Unit: Electricity and Magnetism

Magnetic Fields

You have read that magnetism is a force that can act at a distance. However magnets cannot exert a force on an object that is too far away. A **magnetic field** is the region around a magnet in which the magnet exerts force. If a piece of iron is within the magnetic field of a magnet, it will be pulled toward the magnet. Many small pieces of iron, called iron filings, are used to show the magnetic field around a magnet. The iron filings form a pattern of lines called magnetic field lines.

READING TIP

Thin red lines in the illustrations below indicate the magnetic field.

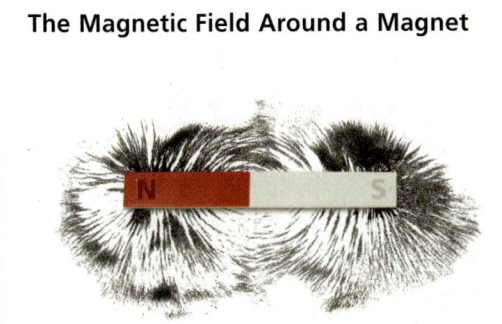

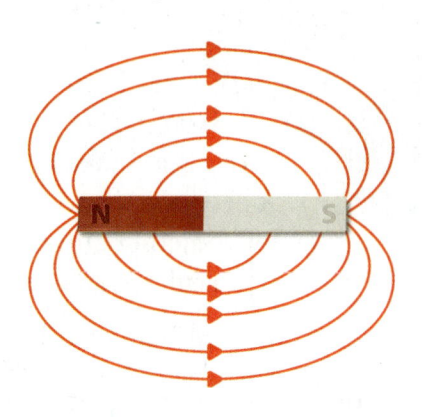

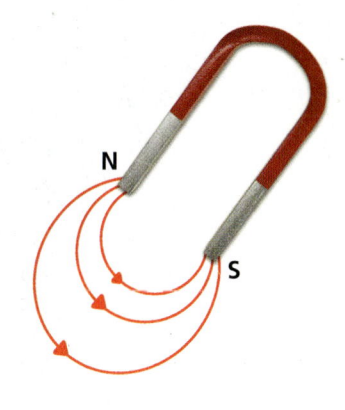

The Magnetic Field Around a Magnet

The arrangement of the magnetic field lines depends on the shape of the magnet, but the lines always extend from one pole to the other pole. The magnetic field lines are always shown as starting from the north pole and ending at the south pole. In the illustrations above, you can see that the lines are closest together near the magnets' poles. That is where the force is strongest. The force is weaker farther away from the magnet.

CHECK YOUR READING Where is the magnetic field of a magnet the strongest?

What happens to the magnetic fields of two magnets when the magnets are brought together? As you can see below, each magnet has an effect on the field of the other magnet. If the magnets are held so that the north pole of one magnet is close to the south pole of the other, the magnetic field lines extend from one magnet to the other. The magnets pull together. On the other hand, if both north poles or both south poles of two magnets are brought near one another, the magnets repel. It is very difficult to push like poles of strong magnets together because magnetic repulsion pushes them apart.

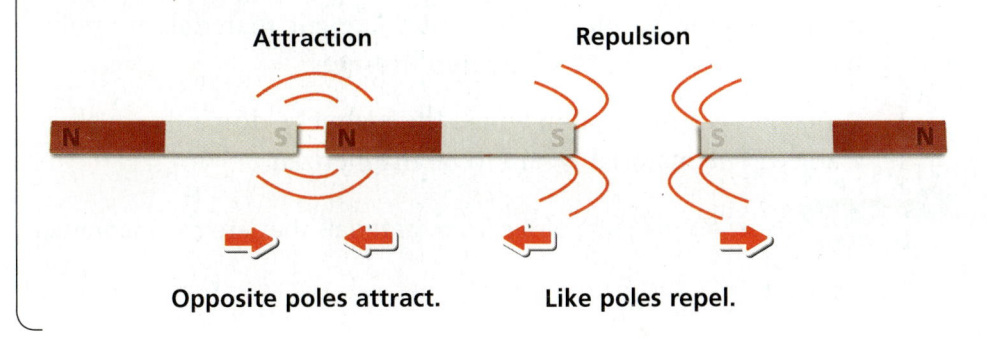

Attraction — Opposite poles attract.

Repulsion — Like poles repel.

Chapter 3: **Magnetism** 81

Some materials are magnetic.

Some magnets occur naturally. Lodestone is a type of mineral that is a natural magnet and formed the earliest magnets that people used. The term *magnet* comes from the name *Magnesia,* a region of Greece where lodestone was discovered. Magnets can also be made from materials that contain certain metallic elements, such as iron.

If you have ever tried picking up different types of objects with a magnet, you have seen that some materials are affected by the magnet and other materials are not. Iron, nickel, cobalt, and a few other metals have properties that make them magnetic. Other materials, such as wood, cannot be made into magnets and are not affected by magnets. Whether a material is magnetic or not depends on its atoms—the particles that make up all matter.

You read in Chapter 1 that the protons and electrons of an atom have electric fields. Every atom also has a weak magnetic field, produced by the electron's motion around a nucleus. In addition, each electron spins around its axis, an imaginary line through its center. The spinning motion of the electrons in magnetic materials increases the strength of the magnetic field around each atom. The magnetic effect of one electron is usually cancelled by another electron that spins in the opposite direction.

Inside Magnetic Materials

READING TIP
The red arrows in the illustration on page 83 are tiny magnetic fields.

The illustration on page 83 shows how magnets and the materials they affect differ from other materials.

① In a material that is not magnetic, such as wood, the magnetic fields of the atoms are weak and point in different directions. The magnetic fields cancel each other out. As a result, the overall material is not magnetic and could not be made into a magnet.

② In a material that is magnetic, such as iron, the magnetic fields of a group of atoms align, or point in the same direction. A **magnetic domain** is a group of atoms whose magnetic fields are aligned. The domains of a magnetic material are not themselves aligned, so their fields cancel one another out. Magnetic materials are pulled by magnets and can be made into magnets.

③ A magnet is a material in which the magnetic domains are all aligned. The material is said to be magnetized.

CHECK YOUR READING How do magnets differ from materials that are not magnetic?

How Magnets Differ from Other Materials

Magnets, and the materials they attract, contain small regions called magnetic domains. In a magnet, the domains are aligned.

Nonmagnetic Materials

Magnet

Magnetic Materials

① Nonmagnetic Materials

Some materials, like wood, are not magnetic. The tiny magnetic fields of their spinning electrons point in different directions and cancel each other out.

② Magnetic Materials

magnetic domain

Other materials, like iron, are magnetic. Magnetic materials have magnetic domains, but the fields of the domains point in different directions.

③ Magnets

When a material is magnetized, the magnetic fields of all the domains point in the same direction.

READING VISUALS Do the paper clips in this photograph contain magnetic domains? Why or why not?

Chapter 3: **Magnetism** 83 **E**

Temporary and Permanent Magnets

If you bring a magnet near a paper clip that contains iron, the paper clip is pulled toward the magnet. As the magnet nears the paper clip, the domains within the paper clip are attracted to the magnet's nearest pole. As a result, the domains within the paper clip become aligned. The paper clip develops its own magnetic field.

You can make a chain of paper clips that connect to one another through these magnetic fields. However, if you remove the magnet, the chain falls apart. The paper clips are temporary magnets, and their domains return to a random arrangement when the stronger magnetic field is removed.

Placing magnetic materials in very strong magnetic fields makes permanent magnets, such as the ones you use in the experiments in this chapter. You can make a permanent magnet by repeatedly stroking a piece of magnetic material in the same direction with a strong magnet. This action aligns the domains. However, if you drop a permanent magnet, or expose it to high temperatures, some of the domains can be shaken out of alignment, weakening its magnetism.

CHECK YOUR READING How can you make a permanent magnet?

Earth is a magnet.

People discovered long ago that when a piece of lodestone was allowed to turn freely, one end always pointed toward the north. Hundreds of years ago, sailors used lodestone in the first compasses for navigation. A compass works because Earth itself is a large magnet. A compass is simply a magnet that is suspended so that it can turn freely. The magnetic field of the compass needle aligns itself with the much larger magnetic field of Earth.

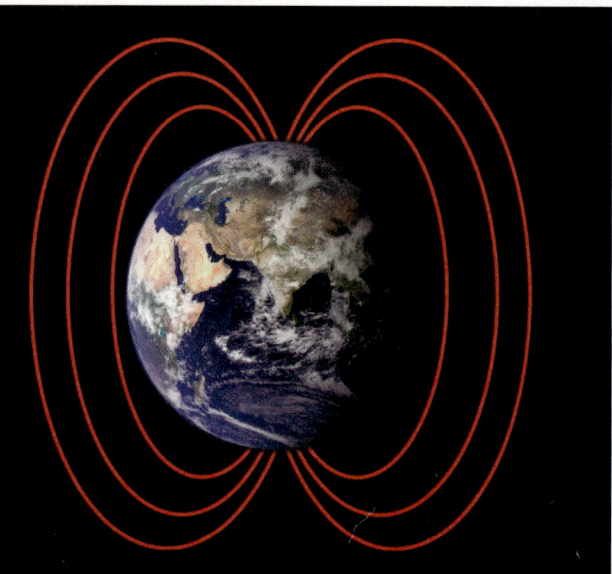

Earth's Magnetic Field

The magnetic field around Earth acts as if there were a large bar magnet that runs through Earth's axis. Earth's axis is the imaginary line through the center of Earth around which it rotates. The source of the magnetic field that surrounds Earth is the motion of its core, which is composed mostly of iron and nickel. Charged particles flow within the core. Scientists have proposed several explanations of how that motion produces the magnetic field, but the process is not yet completely understood.

CHECK YOUR READING What is the source of Earth's magnetic field?

INVESTIGATE Earth's Magnetic Field

What moves a compass needle?

PROCEDURE

1. Gently place the aluminum foil on the water so that it floats.
2. Rub one pole of the magnet along the needle, from one end of the needle to the other. Lift up the magnet and repeat. Do this about 25 times, rubbing in the same direction each time. Place the magnet far away from your set-up.
3. Gently place the needle on the floating foil to act as a compass.
4. Turn the foil so that the needle points in a different direction. Observe what happens when you release the foil.

WHAT DO YOU THINK?

- What direction did the needle move when you placed it in the bowl?
- What moved the compass's needle?

CHALLENGE How could you use your compass to answer a question of your own about magnetism?

SKILL FOCUS
Inferring

MATERIALS
- small square of aluminum foil
- bowl of water
- strong magnet
- sewing needle

TIME
15 minutes

Earth's magnetic field affects all the magnetic materials around you. Even the cans of food in your cupboard are slightly magnetized by this field. Hold a compass close to the bottom of a can and observe what happens. The magnetic domains in the metal can have aligned and produced a weak magnetic field. If you twist the can and check it again several days later, you can observe the effect of the domains changing their alignment.

Sailors learned many centuries ago that the compass does not point exactly toward the North Pole of Earth's axis. Rather, the compass magnet is currently attracted to an area 966 kilometers (600 mi) from the end of the axis of rotation. This area is known as the magnetic north pole. Interestingly, the magnetic poles of Earth can reverse, so that the magnetic north pole becomes the magnetic south pole. This has happened at least 400 times over the last 330 million years. The most recent reversal was about 780,000 years ago.

The evidence that the magnetic north and south poles reverse is found in rocks in which the minerals contain iron. The iron in the minerals lines up with Earth's magnetic field as the rock forms. Once the rock is formed, the domains remain in place. The evidence for the reversing magnetic field is shown in layers of rocks on the ocean floor, where the domains are arranged in opposite directions.

Magnetism and the Atmosphere

A constant stream of charged particles is released by reactions inside the Sun. These particles could be damaging to living cells if they reached the surface of Earth. One important effect of Earth's magnetic field is that it turns aside, or deflects, the flow of the charged particles.

Observers view a beautiful display of Northern Lights in Alaska.

Many of the particles are deflected toward the magnetic poles, where Earth's magnetic field lines are closest together. As the particles approach Earth, they react with oxygen and nitrogen in Earth's atmosphere. These interactions can be seen at night as vast, moving sheets of color—red, blue, green or violet—that can fill the whole sky. These displays are known as the Northern Lights or the Southern Lights.

CHECK YOUR READING Why do the Northern Lights and the Southern Lights occur near Earth's magnetic poles?

3.1 Review

KEY CONCEPTS

1. What force causes magnets to attract or repel one another?
2. Why are some materials magnetic and not others?
3. Describe three similarities between Earth and a bar magnet.

CRITICAL THINKING

4. **Apply** A needle is picked up by a magnet. What can you say about the needle's atoms?
5. **Infer** The Northern Lights can form into lines in the sky. What do you think causes this effect?

CHALLENGE

6. **Infer** Hundreds of years ago sailors observed that as they traveled farther north, their compass needle tended to point toward the ground as well as toward the north. What can you conclude about the magnet inside Earth from this observation?

Think SCIENCE

SKILL: EVALUATING CONCLUSIONS

Can Magnets Heal People?

Many people believe that a magnetic field can relieve pain and cure injuries or illnesses. They point out that human blood cells contain iron and that magnets attract iron.

⊙ Claims

Here are some claims from advertisements and published scientific experiments.

> a. In an advertisement, a person reported back pain that went away overnight when a magnetic pad was taped to his back.
>
> b. In an advertisement, a person used magnets to treat a painful bruise. The pain reportedly stopped soon after the magnet was applied.
>
> c. In a research project, people who had recovered from polio, but still had severe pain, rated the amount of pain they experienced. People who used magnets reported slightly more pain relief than those who used fake magnets that looked like the real magnets.
>
> d. A research project studied people with severe muscle pain. Patients who slept on magnetic pads for six months reported slightly less pain than those who slept on nonmagnetic pads or no pads.
>
> e. A research project studied people with pain in their heels, placing magnets in their shoes. About sixty percent of people with real magnets reported improvements. About sixty percent of people with fake magnets also reported improvements.

⊙ Controls

Scientists use control groups to determine whether a change was a result of the experimental variable or some other cause. A control group is the same as an experimental group in every way except for the variable that is tested. For each of the above cases, was a control used? If not, can you think of some other explanation for the result?

⊙ Evaluating Conclusions

On Your Own Evaluate each claim or report separately. Based on all the evidence, can you conclude that magnets are useful for relieving pain? What further evidence would help you decide?

As a Group Find advertisements for companies that sell magnets for medical use. Do they provide information about how their tests were conducted and how you can contact the doctors or scientists involved?

CHALLENGE Design an experiment, with controls, that would show whether or not magnets are useful for relieving pain.

Some people believe that pads containing magnets, such as these, can relieve pain.

KEY CONCEPT
3.2 Current can produce magnetism.

BEFORE, you learned
- Electric current is the flow of charge
- Magnetism is a force exerted by magnets
- Magnets attract or repel other magnets

NOW, you will learn
- How an electric current can produce a magnetic field
- How electromagnets are used
- How motors use electromagnets

VOCABULARY

electromagnetism p. 89
electromagnet p. 90

EXPLORE Magnetism from Electric Current

What is the source of magnetism?

PROCEDURE

1. Tape one end of the wire to the battery.
2. Place the compass on the table. Place the wire so that it is lying beside the compass, parallel to the needle of the compass. Record your observations.
3. Briefly touch the free end of the wire to the other end of the battery. Record your observations.
4. Turn the battery around and tape the other end to the wire. Repeat steps 2 and 3.

MATERIALS
- electrical tape
- copper wire
- AA cell (battery)
- compass

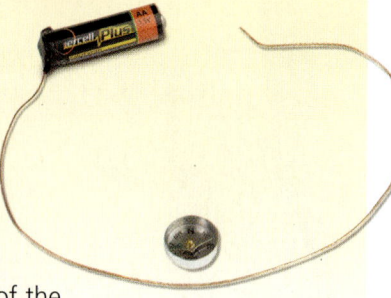

WHAT DO YOU THINK?
- What did you observe?
- What is the relationship between the direction of the battery and the direction of the compass needle?

An electric current produces a magnetic field.

> **REMINDER**
> Current is the flow of electrons through a conductor.

Like many discoveries, the discovery that electric current is related to magnetism was unexpected. In the 1800s, a Danish physicist named Hans Christian Oersted (UR-stehd) was teaching a physics class. Oersted used a battery and wire to demonstrate some properties of electricity. He noticed that as an electric charge passed through the wire, the needle of a nearby compass moved.

When he turned the current off, the needle returned to its original direction. After more experiments, Oersted confirmed that there is a relationship between magnetism and electricity. He discovered that an electric current produces a magnetic field.

E 88 Unit: Electricity and Magnetism

Electromagnetism

The relationship between electric current and magnetism plays an important role in many modern technologies. **Electromagnetism** is magnetism that results from an electric current. When a charged particle such as an electron moves, it produces a magnetic field. Because an electric current generally consists of moving electrons, a current in a wire produces a magnetic field. In fact, the wire acts as a magnet. Increasing the amount of current in the wire increases the strength of the magnetic field.

VOCABULARY
Remember to record *electromagnetism* in your notebook.

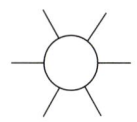

You have seen how magnetic field lines can be drawn around a magnet. The magnetic field lines around a wire are usually illustrated as a series of circles. The magnetic field of a wire actually forms the shape of a tube around the wire. The direction of the current determines the direction of the magnetic field. If the direction of the electric current is reversed, the magnetic field still exists in circles around the wire, but is reversed.

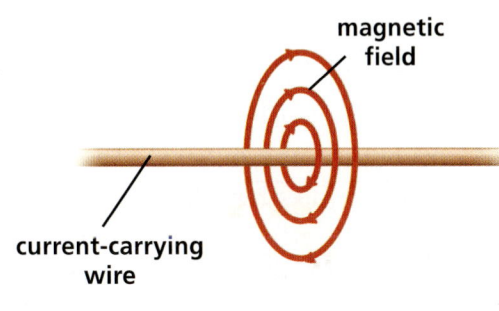

If the wire is shaped into a loop, the magnetism becomes concentrated inside the loop. The field is much stronger in the middle of the loop than it is around a straight wire. If you wind the wire into a coil, the magnetic force becomes stronger with each additional turn of wire as the magnetic field becomes more concentrated.

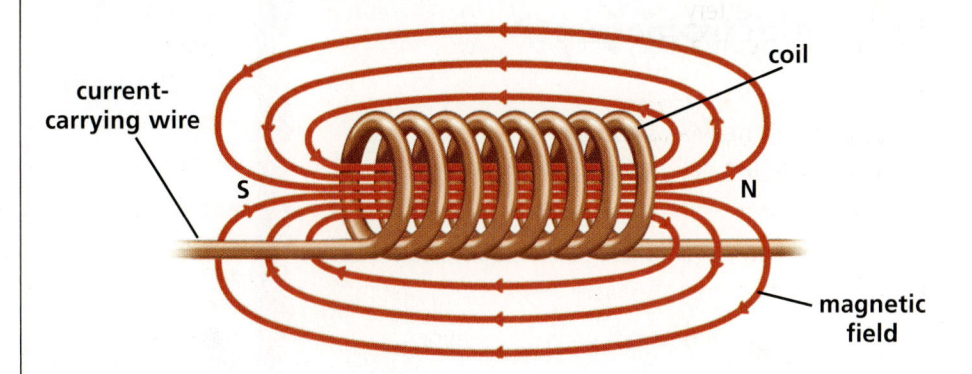

A coil of wire with charge flowing through it has a magnetic field that is similar to the magnetic field of a bar magnet. Inside the coil, the field flows in one direction, forming a north pole at one end. The flow outside the coil returns to the south pole. The direction of the electric current in the wire determines which end of the coil becomes the north pole.

CHECK YOUR READING — How is a coil of wire that carries a current similar to a bar magnet?

Chapter 3: **Magnetism** 89

Making an Electromagnet

Recall that a piece of iron in a strong magnetic field becomes a magnet itself. An **electromagnet** is a magnet made by placing a piece of iron or steel inside a coil of wire. As long as the coil carries a current, the metal acts as a magnet and increases the magnetic field of the coil. But when the current is turned off, the magnetic domains in the metal become random again and the magnetic field disappears.

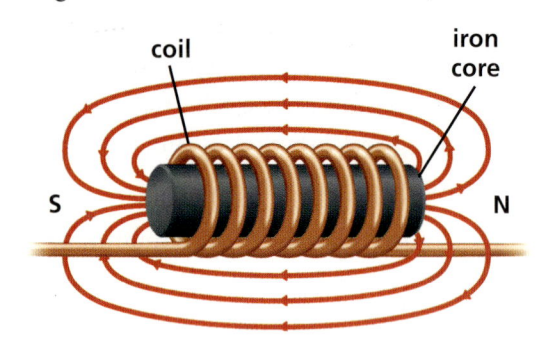

By increasing the number of loops in the coil, you can increase the strength of the electromagnet. Electromagnets exert a much more powerful magnetic field than a coil of wire without a metal core. They can also be much stronger than the strongest permanent magnets made of metal alone. You can increase the field strength of an electromagnet by adding more coils or a stronger current. Some of the most powerful magnets in the world are huge electromagnets that are used in scientific instruments.

CHECK YOUR READING How can you increase the strength of an electromagnet?

INVESTIGATE Electromagnets

How can you make an electromagnet?
PROCEDURE

1. Starting about 25 cm from one end of the wire, wrap the wire in tight coils around the nail. The coils should cover the nail from the head almost to the point.

2. Tape the two batteries together as shown. Tape one end of the wire to a free battery terminal.

3. Touch the point of the nail to a paper clip and record your observations.

4. Connect the other end of the wire to the other battery terminal. Again touch the point of the nail to a paper clip. Disconnect the wire from the battery. Record your observations.

WHAT DO YOU THINK?
- What did you observe?
- Did you make an electromagnet? How do you know?

CHALLENGE Do you think the result would be different if you used an aluminum nail instead of an iron nail? Why?

SKILL FOCUS
Observing

MATERIALS
- insulated wire
- large iron nail
- 2 D cells
- electrical tape
- paper clip

TIME
20 minutes

Uses of Electromagnets

Because electromagnets can be turned on and off, they have more uses than permanent magnets. The photograph below shows a powerful electromagnet on a crane. While the electric charge flows through the coils of the magnet, it lifts hundreds of cans at a recycling plant. When the crane operator turns off the current, the magnetic field disappears and the cans drop from the crane.

A permanent magnet would not be nearly as useful for this purpose. Although you could use a large permanent magnet to lift the cans, it would be hard to remove them from the magnet.

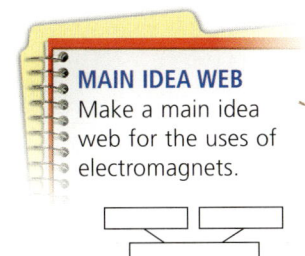

MAIN IDEA WEB
Make a main idea web for the uses of electromagnets.

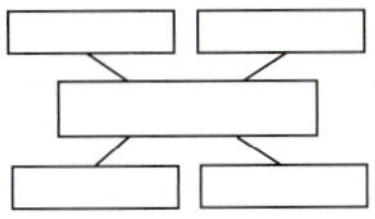

This powerful electromagnet can be turned on and off to collect and move cans at a recycling plant.

wire supplying electric current

electromagnet

You use an electromagnet every time you store information on a computer. The computer hard drive contains disks that have billions of tiny magnetic domains in them. When you save a file, a tiny electromagnet in the computer is activated. The magnetic field of the electromagnet changes the orientation of the small magnetic domains. The small magnets store your file in a form that can be read later by the computer. A similar system is used to store information on magnetic tape of an audiocassette or videocassette. Sound and pictures are stored on the tape by the arrangement of magnets embedded in the plastic film.

Magnetic information is often stored on credit cards and cash cards. A black strip on the back of the card contains information about the account number and passwords. The cards can be damaged if they are frequently exposed to magnetic fields. For example, cards should not be stored with their strips facing each other, or near a magnetic clasp on a purse or wallet. These magnetic fields can change the arrangement of the tiny magnetic domains on the card and erase the stored information.

Chapter 3: Magnetism 91 **E**

Motors use electromagnets.

Because magnetism is a force, magnets can be used to move things. Electric motors convert the energy of an electric current into motion by taking advantage of the interaction between current and magnetism.

There are hundreds of devices that contain electric motors. Examples include power tools, electrical kitchen appliances, and the small fans in a computer. Almost anything with moving parts that uses current has an electric motor.

Motors

Page 93 shows how a simple motor works. The photograph at the top of the page shows a motor that turns the blades of a fan. The illustration in the middle of the page shows the main parts of a simple motor. Although they may look different from each other, all motors have similar parts and work in a similar way. The main parts of an electrical motor include a voltage source, a shaft, an electromagnet, and at least one additional magnet. The shaft of the motor turns other parts of the device.

Recall that an electromagnet consists of a coil of wire with current flowing through it. Find the electromagnet in the illustration on page 93. The electromagnet is placed between the poles of another magnet.

When current from the voltage source flows through the coil, a magnetic field is produced around the electromagnet. The poles of the magnet interact with the poles of the electromagnet, causing the motor to turn.

① The poles of the magnet push on the like poles of the electromagnet, causing the electromagnet to turn.

② As the motor turns, the opposite poles pull on each other.

③ When the poles of the electromagnet line up with the opposite poles of the magnet, a part of the motor called the commutator reverses the polarity of the electromagnet. Now, the poles push on each other again and the motor continues to turn.

The illustration of the motor on page 93 is simplified so that you can see all of the parts. If you saw the inside of an actual motor, it might look like the illustration on the left. Notice that the wire is coiled many times. The electromagnet in a strong motor may coil hundreds of times. The more coils, the stronger the motor.

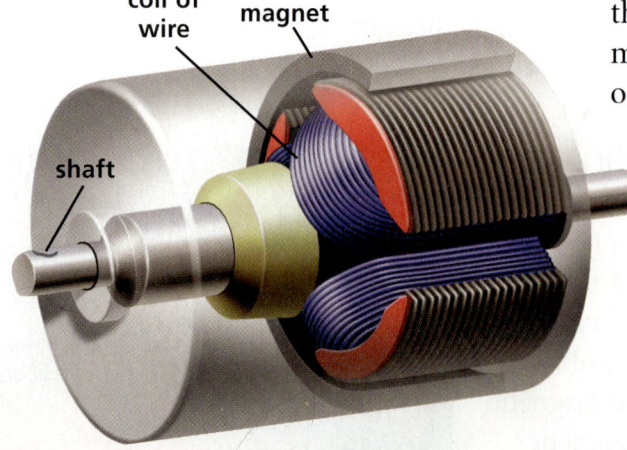

VISUALIZATION CLASSZONE.COM
See a motor in motion.

CHECK YOUR READING What causes the electromagnet in a motor to turn?

How a Motor Works

Although motors may look different from each other, they all have similar parts and work in a similar way.

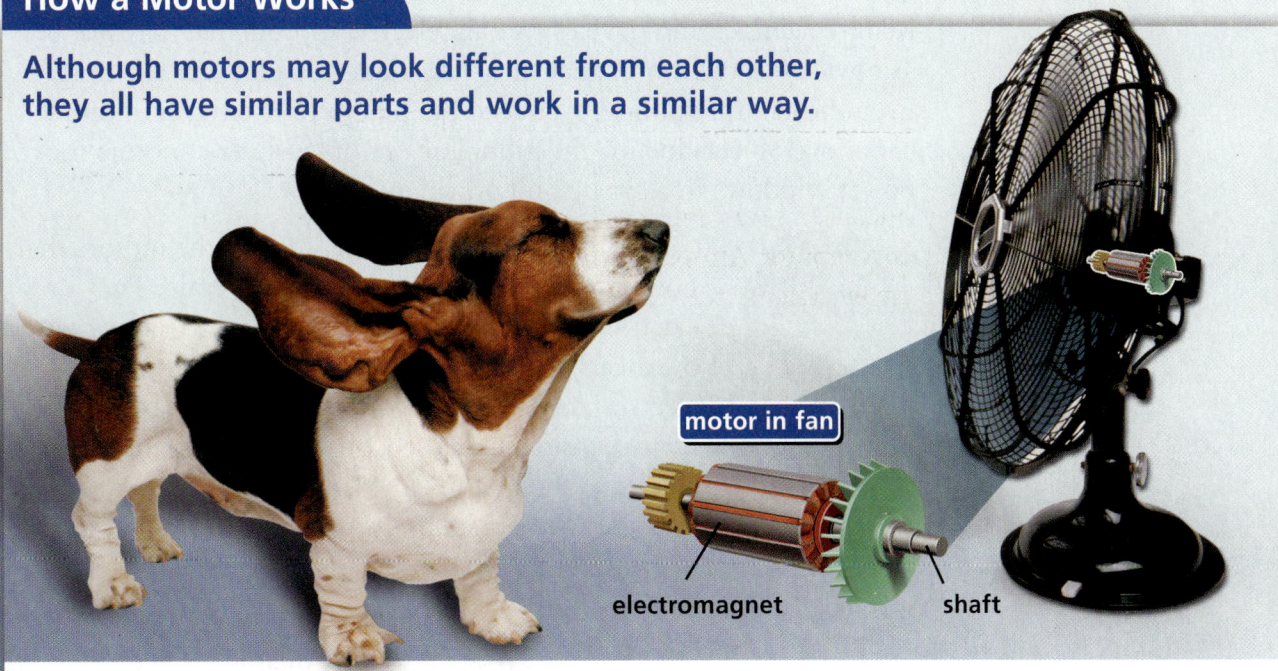

motor in fan

electromagnet   shaft

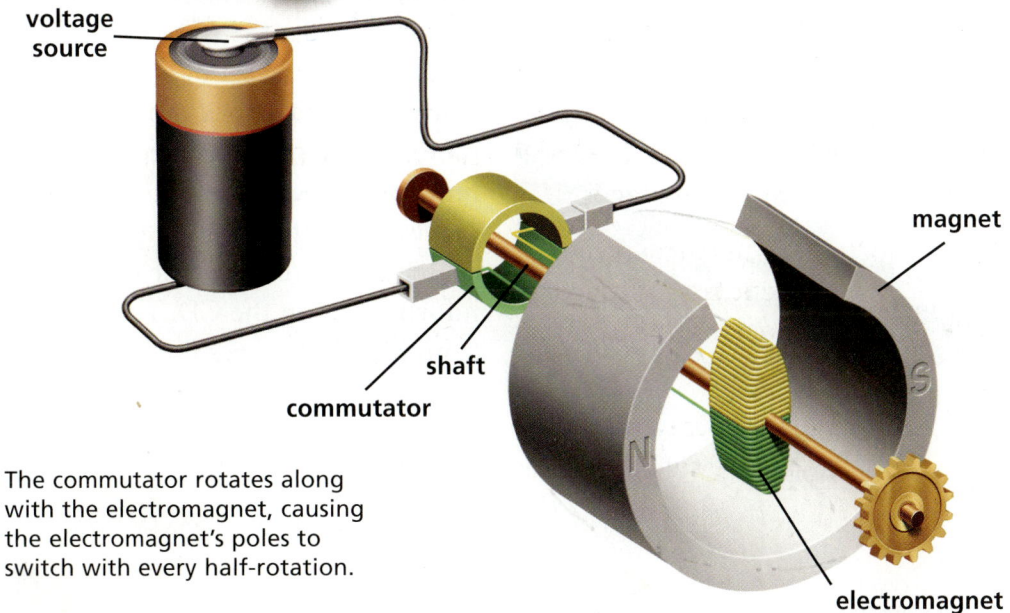

voltage source

shaft
commutator
magnet
electromagnet

The commutator rotates along with the electromagnet, causing the electromagnet's poles to switch with every half-rotation.

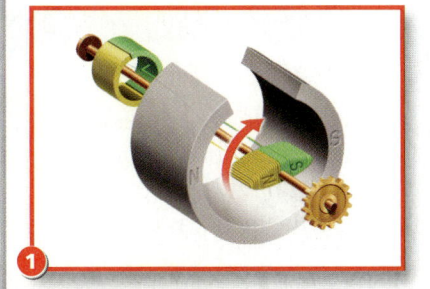

1 Like poles of the magnets push on each other.

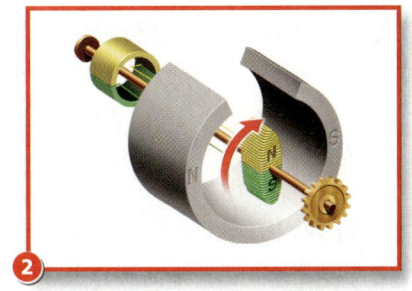

2 As the motor turns, opposite poles attract.

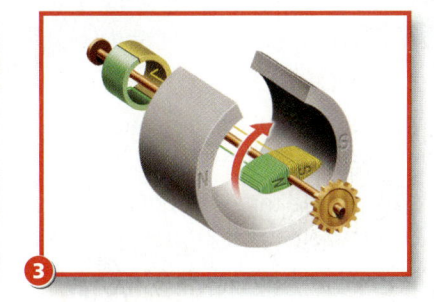

3 The electromagnet's poles are switched, and like poles again repel.

READING VISUALS Would a motor work without an electromagnet? Why or why not?

Chapter 3: **Magnetism** 93

Uses of Motors

Many machines and devices contain electric motors that may not be as obvious as the motor that turns the blades of a fan, for example. Even though the motion produced by the motor is circular, motors can move objects in any direction. For example, electric motors move power windows in a car up and down.

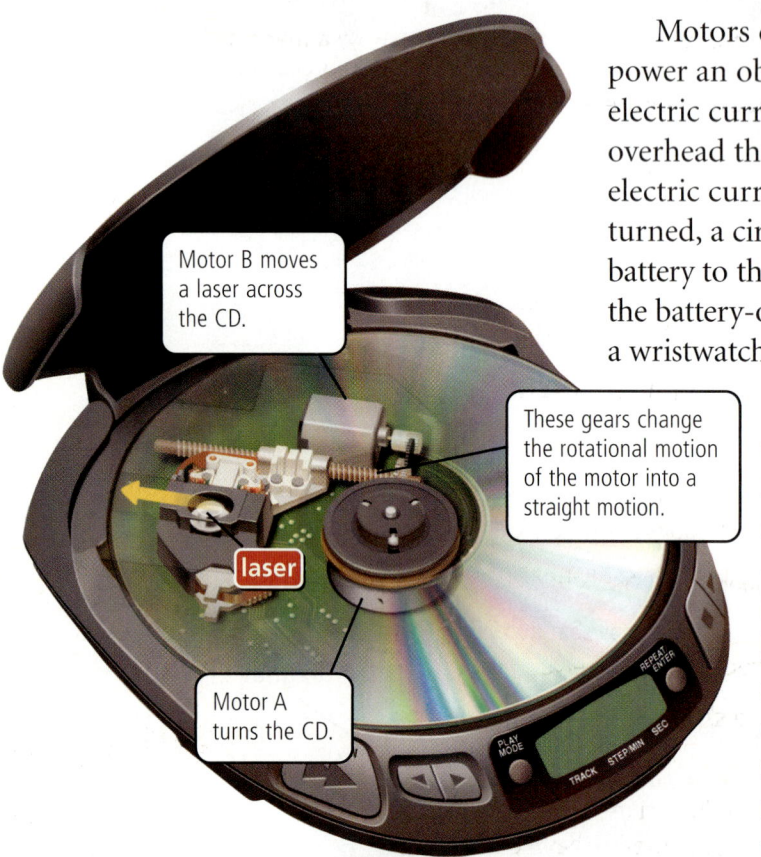

Motors can be very large, such as the motors that power an object as large as a subway train. They draw electric current from a third rail on the track or wires overhead that carry electric current. A car uses an electric current to start the engine. When the key is turned, a circuit is closed, producing a current from the battery to the motor. Other motors are very small, like the battery-operated motors that move the hands of a wristwatch.

The illustration on the left shows the two small motors in a portable CD player. Motor A causes the CD to spin. Motor B is connected to a set of gears. The gears convert the rotational motion of the motor into a straight-line motion, or linear motion. As the CD spins, a laser moves straight across the CD from the center outward. The laser reads the information on the CD. The motion from Motor B moves the laser across the CD.

Motor B moves a laser across the CD.

These gears change the rotational motion of the motor into a straight motion.

Motor A turns the CD.

CHECK YOUR READING Explain the function served by each motor in a CD player.

3.2 Review

KEY CONCEPTS
1. Explain how electric current and magnetism are related.
2. Describe three uses of electromagnets.
3. Explain how electrical energy is converted to motion in a motor.

CRITICAL THINKING
4. **Contrast** How does an electromagnet differ from a permanent magnet?
5. **Apply** Provide examples of two things in your home that use electric motors, and explain why they are easier to use because of the motors.

CHALLENGE
6. **Infer** Why is it necessary to change the direction of the current in the coil of an electric motor as it turns?

KEY CONCEPT
3.3 Magnetism can produce current.

BEFORE, you learned
- Magnetism is a force exerted by magnets
- Electric current can produce a magnetic field
- Electromagnets can make objects move

NOW, you will learn
- How a magnetic field can produce an electric current
- How a generator converts energy
- How direct current and alternating current differ

VOCABULARY
generator p. 96
direct current p. 97
alternating current p. 97
transformer p. 99

EXPLORE Energy Conversion

How can a motor produce current?

PROCEDURE

1. Touch the wires on the motor to the battery terminals to see how the motor operates.
2. Connect the wires to the light bulb.
3. Roll the shaft, or the movable part of the motor, between your fingers. Observe the light bulb.
4. Now spin the shaft rapidly. Record your observations.

MATERIALS
- small motor
- AA cell (battery)
- light bulb in holder

WHAT DO YOU THINK?
- How did you produce current?
- What effect did your motion have on the amount of light produced?

MAIN IDEA WEB
Make a main idea web in your notebook for this heading.

Magnets are used to generate an electric current.

In the 1830s, about ten years after Oersted discovered that an electric current produces magnetism, physicists observed the reverse effect—a moving magnetic field induces an electric current. When a magnet moves inside a coiled wire that is in a circuit, an electric current is generated in the wire.

It is often easier to generate an electric current by moving a wire inside a magnetic field. Whether it is the magnet or the wire that moves, the effect is the same. Current is generated as long as the wire crosses the magnetic field lines.

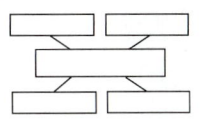

CHECK YOUR READING What must happen for a magnetic field to produce an electric current?

Chapter 3: **Magnetism** 95 **E**

Generating an Electric Current

A **generator** is a device that converts the energy of motion, or kinetic energy, into electrical energy. A generator is similar to a motor in reverse. If you manually turn the shaft of a motor that contains a magnet, you can produce electric current.

The illustration below shows a portable generator that provides electrical energy to charge a cell phone in an emergency. The generator produces current as you turn the handle. Because it does not need to be plugged in, the generator can be used wherever and whenever it is needed to recharge a phone. The energy is supplied by the person turning the handle.

❶ As the handle is turned, it rotates a series of gears. The gears turn the shaft of the generator.

❷ The rotation of the shaft causes coils of wire to rotate within a magnetic field.

❸ As the coils of the wire cross the magnetic field line, electric current is generated. The current recharges the battery of the cell phone.

CHECK YOUR READING What is the source of energy for a cell phone generator?

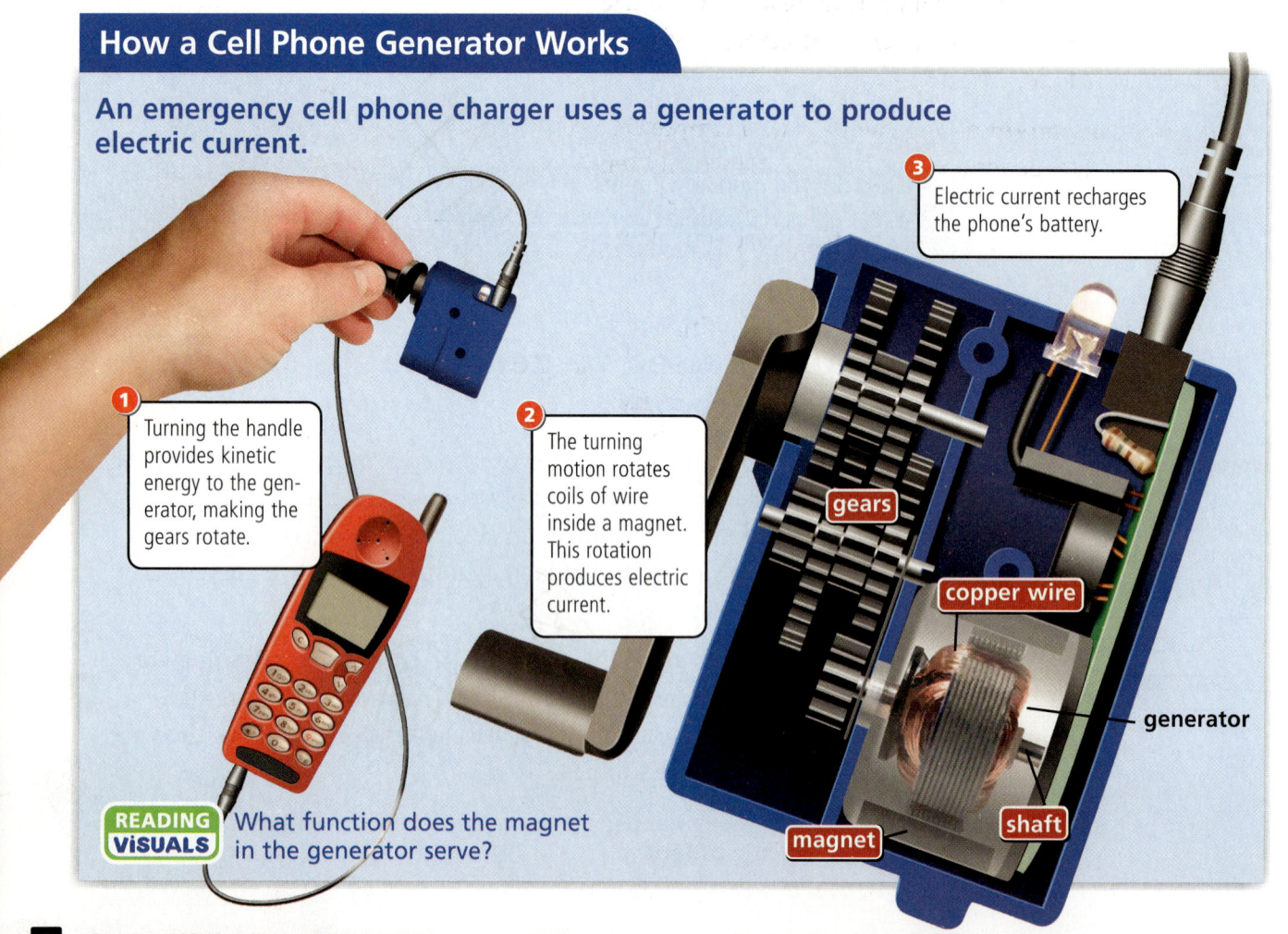

How a Cell Phone Generator Works

An emergency cell phone charger uses a generator to produce electric current.

❶ Turning the handle provides kinetic energy to the generator, making the gears rotate.

❷ The turning motion rotates coils of wire inside a magnet. This rotation produces electric current.

❸ Electric current recharges the phone's battery.

gears

copper wire

generator

magnet

shaft

READING VISUALS What function does the magnet in the generator serve?

96 Unit: Electricity and Magnetism

Direct and Alternating Currents

Think about how current flows in all of the circuits that you have studied so far. Electrons flow from one end of a battery or generator, through the circuit, and eventually back to the battery or generator. Electrons that flow in one direction produce one of two types of current.

- A **direct current** (DC) is electric charge that flows in one direction only. Direct current is produced by batteries and by DC generators such as the cell phone generator.
- An **alternating current** (AC) is a flow of electric charge that reverses direction at regular intervals. The current that enters your home and school is an alternating current.

CHECK YOUR READING What is the difference between direct current and alternating current?

Direct currents and alternating currents are produced by different generators. In an AC generator, the direction in which charge flows depends upon the direction in which the magnet moves in relation to the coil. Because generators use a rotating electromagnet, the poles of the electromagnet alternate between moving toward and moving away from the magnet. The result is a current that reverses with each half-rotation of the coil.

The illustration on the right shows a simple DC generator. DC generators are very similar to AC generators. The main difference is that DC generators have a commutator that causes the current to flow in only one direction.

Many things in your home can work with either direct or alternating currents. In light bulbs, for instance, the resistance to motion of the electrons in the filament makes the filament glow. It doesn't matter in which direction the current is moving.

Some appliances can use only direct current. The black box that is on the plug of some devices is an AC–DC converter. AC–DC converters change the alternating current to direct current. For example, laptop computers use converters like the one shown in the photograph on the right. In a desktop computer, the converter is part of the power supply unit.

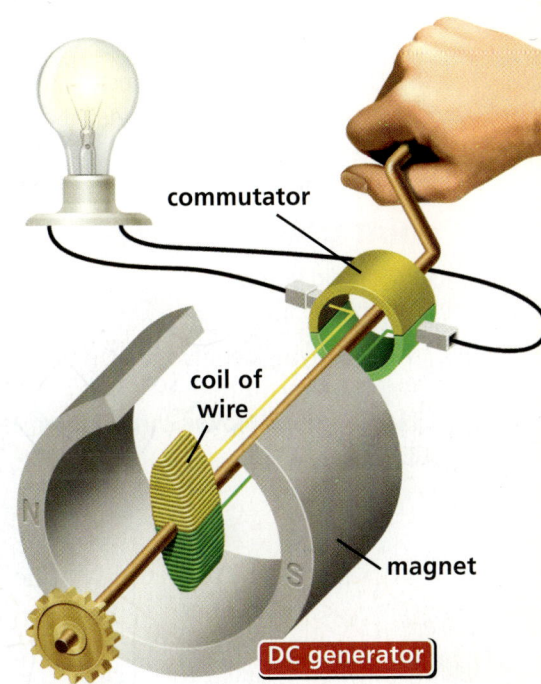

Chapter 3: **Magnetism** 97

INVESTIGATE Electric Current

How can you identify the current?
PROCEDURE

1. Wrap the wire tightly around the middle of the compass 10–15 times. Leave about 30 cm of wire free at each end. Tape the wire to the back of the compass to keep it in place.

2. Sand the ends of the wire with sandpaper to expose about 2 cm of copper on each end. Arrange the compass on your desk so that the needle is parallel to, or lined up with, the coil. This will serve as your current detector.

3. Tape one end of the wire to one terminal of the battery. Touch the other end of the wire to the other battery terminal. Record your observations.

4. Observe the current detector as you tap the end of the wire to the battery terminal at a steady pace. Speed up or slow down your tapping until the needle of the compass alternates back and forth. Record your observations.

WHAT DO YOU THINK?
- What did you observe?
- What type of current did you detect in step 3? in step 4? How did you identify the type of current?

CHALLENGE How is this setup similar to an AC generator?

SKILL FOCUS
Inferring

MATERIALS
- piece of wire
- compass
- ruler
- tape
- sandpaper
- D cell (battery)

TIME
15 minutes

The energy that powers a car comes from burning gasoline, but the car also contains many devices that use electrical energy. Some of them are familiar—the headlights, turn signals, radio, power windows, and door locks. Others may be less familiar, such as the spark plugs that ignite the gasoline, the fuel and oil pumps that move fluids in the engine, and the air conditioner.

A car's engine includes a generator to provide current to its electrical devices. As the engine runs, it converts gasoline to kinetic energy. Some of that energy is transferred to the generator by a belt attached to its shaft. Inside the generator, a complex coil of copper wires turns in a magnetic field, generating a current that operates the electrical devices of the car.

The generator also recharges the battery, so that power is available when the engine is not running. Because the generator in most cars supplies alternating current, a car generator is usually called an alternator.

CHECK YOUR READING What function does a generator in a car serve?

Magnets are used to control voltage.

A **transformer** is a device that increases or decreases voltage. Transformers use magnetism to control the amount of voltage. A transformer consists of two coils of wire that are wrapped around an iron ring.

An alternating current from the voltage source in the first coil produces a magnetic field. The iron ring becomes an electromagnet. Because the current alternates, the magnetic field is constantly changing. The second coil is therefore within a changing magnetic field. Current is generated in the second coil. If the two coils have the same number of loops, the voltage in the second coil will be the same as the voltage in the first coil.

A change in the voltage is caused when the two coils have different numbers of loops. If the second coil has fewer loops than the first, as in the illustration, the voltage is decreased. This is called a step-down transformer. On the other hand, if the second coil has more loops than the first, the voltage in the second circuit will be higher than the original voltage. This transformer is called a step-up transformer.

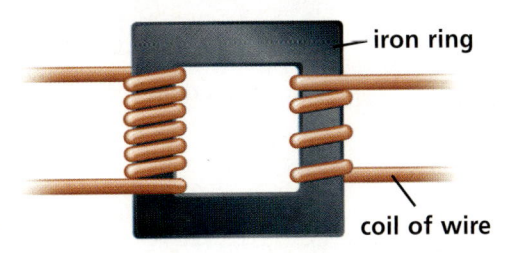

Step-Down Transformer
— iron ring
— coil of wire

Transformers are used in the distribution of current. Current is sent over power lines from power plants at a very high voltage. Step-down transformers on utility poles, such as the one pictured on the right, reduce the voltage available for use in homes. Sending current at high voltages minimizes the amount of energy lost to resistance along the way.

3.3 Review

KEY CONCEPTS

1. What is necessary for a magnetic field to produce an electric current?
2. Explain how electric generators convert kinetic energy into electrical energy.
3. Compare and contrast the ways in which direct current and alternating current are generated.

CRITICAL THINKING

4. **Apply** Many radios can be operated either by plugging them into the wall or by using batteries. How can a radio use either source of current?
5. **Draw Conclusions** Suppose that all of the electrical devices in a car stop working. Explain what the problem might be.

CHALLENGE

6. **Apply** European power companies deliver current at 220 V. Draw the design for a step-down transformer that would let you operate a CD player made to work at 110 V in France.

Chapter 3: **Magnetism** 99

CHAPTER INVESTIGATION

Build a Speaker

OVERVIEW AND PURPOSE Speakers are found on TVs, computers, telephones, stereos, amplifiers, and other devices. Inside a speaker, magnetism and electric current interact to produce sound. The current produces a magnetic field that acts on another magnet and causes vibrations. The vibrations produce sound waves. In this lab, you will
- construct a speaker
- determine how the strength of the magnet affects the speaker's volume

▶ Problem

How does the strength of the magnet used to make a speaker affect the loudness of sound produced by the speaker?

▶ Hypothesize

Write a hypothesis that explains how you expect the strength of a magnet to affect the loudness of sound produced by the speaker, and why. Your hypothesis should be in the form of an "if . . . , then . . . , because . . ." statement.

▶ Procedure

1. Make a data table similar to the one shown on the sample notebook page.

2. Test the strength of each magnet by measuring the distance at which a paper clip will move to the magnet, as shown. Record the measurements in your **Science Notebook.**

3. Starting about 6 cm from the end of the wire, wrap the wire around the marker 50 times to make a coil.

MATERIALS
- 3 magnets of different strengths
- paper clip
- ruler
- piece of wire
- marker
- cup
- masking tape
- 2 wire leads with alligator clips
- stereo system

4. Carefully slide the coil off the marker. Wrap the ends of the wire around the coil to keep it in the shape of a circle, as shown.

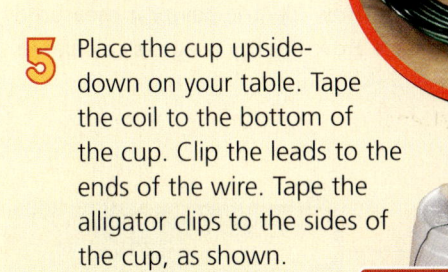

step 4

5. Place the cup upside-down on your table. Tape the coil to the bottom of the cup. Clip the leads to the ends of the wire. Tape the alligator clips to the sides of the cup, as shown.

coil
step 5

6. Take turns attaching the alligator clips to the stereo as instructed by your teacher. Place each magnet on the table near the stereo. Test the speaker by holding the cup directly over each magnet and listening. Record your observations.

Observe and Analyze
Write It Up

1. **RECORD OBSERVATIONS** Be sure to record your observations in the data table.
2. **INFER** Why is the coil of wire held near the magnet?
3. **APPLY** The diaphragm on a speaker vibrates to produce sound. What part of your stereo is the diaphragm?
4. **IDENTIFY** What was the independent variable in this experiment? What was the dependent variable?

Conclude
Write It Up

1. **INTERPRET** Which magnet produced the loudest noise when used with your speaker? Answer the question posed in the problem.
2. **ANALYZE** Compare your results with your hypothesis. Did your results support your hypothesis?
3. **IDENTIFY LIMITS** Describe possible limitations or sources of error in the procedure or any places where errors might have occurred.
4. **APPLY** You have built a simple version of a real speaker. Apply what you have learned in this lab to explain how a real speaker might work.

INVESTIGATE Further

CHALLENGE In what ways might you vary the design of the speaker to improve its functioning? Review the procedure to identify variables that might be changed to improve the speaker. Choose one variable and design an experiment to test that variable.

Build a Speaker

Problem How does the strength of the magnet used to make a speaker affect the loudness of sound produced by the speaker?

Hypothesize

Observe and Analyze

Table 1. Strength of Magnet and Loudness of Sound

Magnet	Strength (paper clip distance)	Observations
1		
2		
3		

Conclude

Chapter 3: **Magnetism** 101

KEY CONCEPT
3.4 Generators supply electrical energy.

◄ **BEFORE, you learned**
- Magnetism is a force exerted by magnets
- A moving magnetic field can generate an electric current in a conductor
- Generators use magnetism to produce current

► **NOW, you will learn**
- How power plants generate electrical energy
- How electric power is measured
- How energy usage is calculated

VOCABULARY

electric power p. 102
watt p. 104
kilowatt p. 104
kilowatt-hour p. 105

THINK ABOUT

How can falling water generate electrical energy?

This photograph shows the Hoover Dam on the Nevada/Arizona border, which holds back a large lake, almost 600 feet deep, on the Colorado River. It took thousands of workers nearly five years to build the dam, and it cost millions of dollars. One of the main purposes of the Hoover Dam is the generation of current. Think about what you have read about generators. How could the energy of falling water be used to generate current?

VOCABULARY
Use a description wheel to take notes about *electrical power*.

Generators provide most of the world's electrical energy.

The tremendous energy produced by falling water provides the turning motion for large generators at a power plant. The power plant at the Hoover Dam supplies energy to more than a million people.

Other sources of energy at power plants include steam from burning fossil fuels, nuclear reactions, wind, solar heating, and ocean tides. Each source provides the energy of motion to the generators, producing electrical energy. **Electric power** is the rate at which electrical energy is generated from another source of energy.

CHECK YOUR READING What do power plants that use water, steam, and wind all have in common?

How does the power plant convert the energy of motion into electrical energy? Very large generators in the plant hold powerful electromagnets surrounded by massive coils of copper wire. The illustration below shows how the energy from water falling from the reservoir to the river far below a dam is converted to electrical energy.

RESOURCE CENTER
CLASSZONE.COM
Find out more about dams that generate current.

❶ As the water falls from the reservoir, its kinetic energy increases and it flows very fast. The falling stream of water turns a fan-like device, called a turbine, which is connected to the generator's shaft.

❷ The rotation of the shaft turns powerful electromagnets that are surrounded by the coil of copper wires. The coil is connected to a step-up transformer that sends high-voltage current to power lines.

❸ Far from the plant, step-down transformers reduce the voltage so that current can be sent through smaller lines to neighborhoods. Another transformer reduces the voltage to the level needed to operate lights and appliances.

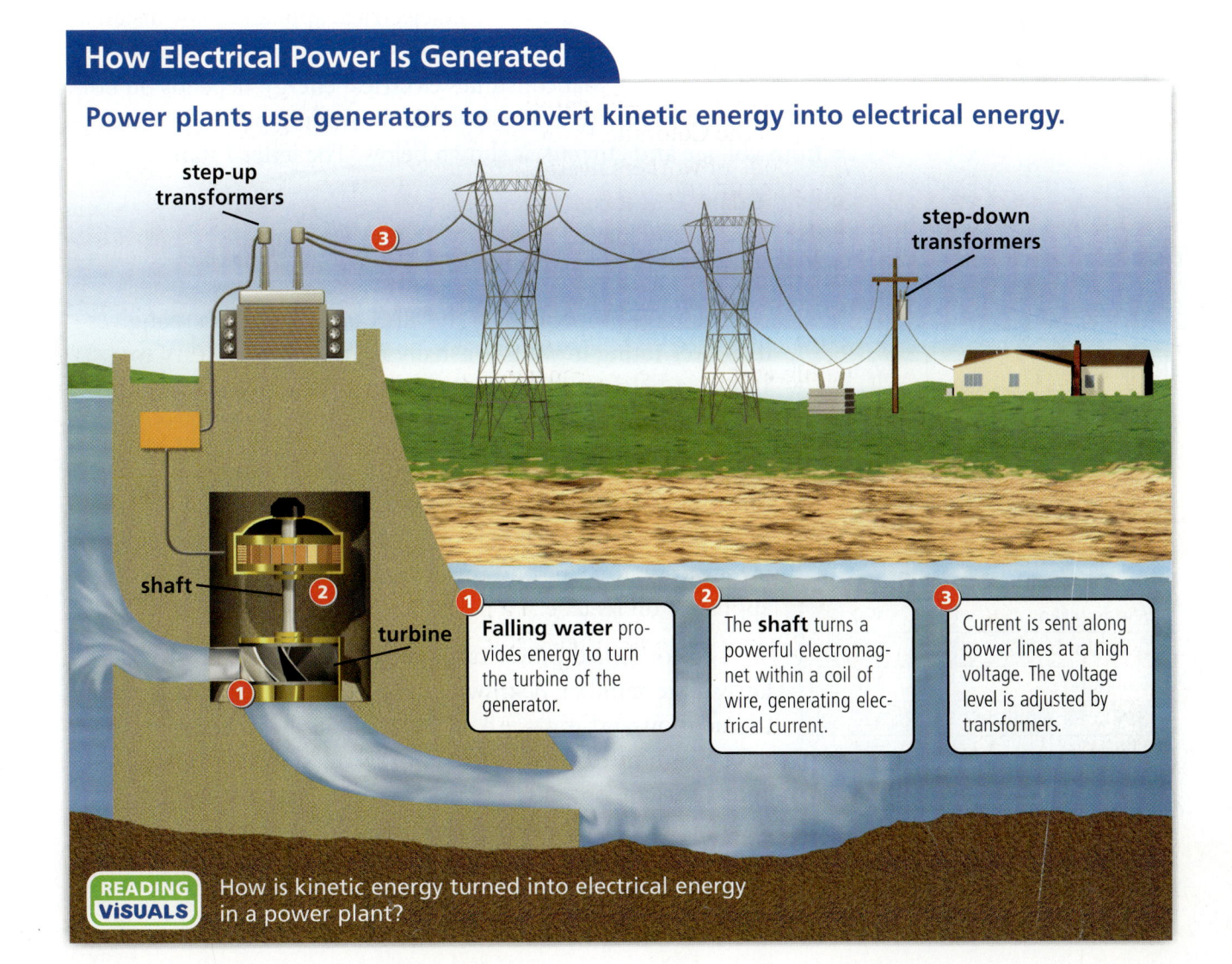

How Electrical Power Is Generated

Power plants use generators to convert kinetic energy into electrical energy.

step-up transformers

step-down transformers

shaft

turbine

❶ **Falling water** provides energy to turn the turbine of the generator.

❷ The **shaft** turns a powerful electromagnet within a coil of wire, generating electrical current.

❸ Current is sent along power lines at a high voltage. The voltage level is adjusted by transformers.

READING VISUALS How is kinetic energy turned into electrical energy in a power plant?

Chapter 3: **Magnetism** 103

Electric power can be measured.

You have read that electric power is the rate at which electrical energy is generated from another source of energy. Power also refers to the rate at which an appliance converts electrical energy back into another form of energy, such as light, heat, or sound.

In order to provide electrical energy to homes and factories, power companies need to know the rate at which energy is needed. Power can be measured so that companies can determine how much energy is used and where it is used. This information is used to figure out how much to charge customers, and it is used to determine whether more electrical energy needs to be generated. To provide energy to an average home, a power plant needs to burn about four tons of coal each year.

> RESOURCE CENTER
> CLASSZONE.COM
> Learn more about energy use and conservation.

Watts and Kilowatts

The unit of measurement for power is the **watt** (W). Watts measure the rate at which energy is used by an electrical appliance. For instance, a light bulb converts energy to light and heat. The power rating of the bulb, or of any device that consumes electrical energy, depends on both the voltage and the current. The formula for finding power, in watts, from voltage and current, is shown below. The letter I stands for current.

$$\text{Electric Power} = \text{Voltage} \cdot \text{Current}$$
$$P = VI$$

You have probably seen the label on a light bulb that gives its power rating in watts—usually in the range of 40 W to 100 W. A brighter bulb converts energy at a higher rate than one with a lower power rating.

The chart at the left shows typical power ratings, in watts, for some appliances that you might have in your home. The exact power rating depends on how each brand of appliance uses energy. You can find the actual power rating for an appliance on its label.

The combined power rating in a building is likely to be a fairly large number. A **kilowatt** (kW) is a unit of power equal to one thousand watts. All of the appliances in a room may have a combined power rating of several kilowatts, but all appliances are not in use all of the time. That is why energy is usually calculated based on how long the appliances are in use.

Typical Power Ratings	
Appliance	**Watts**
DVD player	20
Radio	20
Video game system	25
Electric blanket	60
Light bulb	75
Stereo system	100
Window fan	100
Television	110
Computer	120
Computer monitor	150
Refrigerator	700
Air conditioner	1000
Microwave oven	1000
Hair dryer	1200
Clothes dryer	3000

CHECK YOUR READING Explain what kilowatts are used to measure.

INVESTIGATE Power

How would you use your electrical energy?

PROCEDURE

1. On a sheet of graph paper, outline a box that is 10 squares long by 18 squares wide. The box represents a room that is wired to power a total of 1800 W. Each square represents 10 W of power.

2. From the chart on page 104, choose appliances that you want in your room. Using colored pencils, fill in the appropriate number of boxes for each appliance.

3. All of the items that you choose must fit within the total power available, represented by the 180 squares.

WHAT DO YOU THINK?

- How did you decide to use your electrical energy?
- Could you provide enough energy to operate everything you wanted at one time?

CHALLENGE During the summer, power companies sometimes cannot produce enough energy for the demand. Why do you think that happens?

SKILL FOCUS
Making models

MATERIALS
- graph paper
- colored pencils

TIME
30 minutes

Calculating Energy Use

The electric bill for your energy usage is calculated based on the rate at which energy is used, or the power, and the amount of time it is used at that rate. Total energy used by an appliance is determined by multiplying its power consumption by the amount of time that it is used.

Energy used = Power • time

$$E = Pt$$

The kilowatt-hour is the unit of measurement for energy usage. A **kilowatt-hour** (kWh) is equal to one kilowatt of power for a one-hour period. Buildings usually have meters that measure how many kilowatt-hours of energy have been used. The meters display four or five small dials in a row, as shown in the photograph on the right. Each dial represents a different place value—ones, tens, hundreds, or thousands. For example, the meter in the photograph shows that the customer has used close to 9000 kWh of energy—8933 kWh, to be exact. To find how much energy was used in one month, the last month's reading is subtracted from this total.

Chapter 3: **Magnetism** 105

To determine the number of kilowatt-hours of energy used by an appliance, find its wattage on the chart on page 104 or from the label. Then, substitute it into the formula along with the number of hours it was in use. Solve the sample problems below.

Finding Energy Used

Sample Problem

How much energy is used to dry clothes in a 3 kW dryer for 30 minutes?

What do you know?	Power = 3.0 kW, time = 0.5 hr
What do you want to find out?	Energy used
Write the formula:	$E = Pt$
Substitute into the formula:	$E = 3.0 \text{ kW} \cdot 0.5 \text{ hr}$
Calculate and simplify:	$E = 1.5$ kWh
Check that your units agree:	Unit is kWh. Unit for energy used is kWh. Units agree.
Answer:	1.5 kWh

Practice the Math

1. All of the appliances in a computer lab are in use for 6 hours every day and together use 3.3 kW. How much energy has been used in 1 day?
2. How much energy is used when a 1.2 kW hair dyer is in use for 0.2 hr?

Energy prices vary, but you can estimate the cost of using an electrical appliance by using a value of about 8 cents/kWh. You can calculate how much energy you can save by turning off the lights or television when you are not using them. Although the number may seem small, try multiplying your savings over the course of a month or year.

3.4 Review

KEY CONCEPTS

1. How do power plants generate electrical energy from kinetic energy?
2. Explain what watts measure.
3. How is energy use determined?

CRITICAL THINKING

4. **Apply** Think about reducing energy usage in your home. What changes would make the largest difference in the amount of energy used?
5. **Calculate** How much energy is used if a 3000 W clothes dryer is used for 4 hours?

CHALLENGE

6. **Calculate** An electric bill for an apartment shows 396 kWh of energy used over one month. The appliances in the apartment have a total power rating of 2.2 kW. How many hours were the appliances in use?

MATH in SCIENCE

SKILL: USING SIGNIFICANT FIGURES

MATH TUTORIAL
CLASSZONE.COM
Click on Math Tutorial for more help with rounding decimals.

Energy Calculations

Significant figures are meaningful digits in a number. Calculations can sometimes produce answers with more significant figures than are accurately known. Scientists use rules to determine how to round their answers. The rule for writing an answer to a multiplication problem is shown below.

Rule: Your answer may show only as many significant figures as the number in the problem with the fewest significant figures.

Generally, a significant figure is any digit shown except for a zero, unless the zero is contained between two nonzero digits or between a nonzero digit and a decimal point. For example, the number 40.3 has three significant figures, but the number 5.90 has only two significant figures. The number 0.034 has three significant figures, and the number 0.8 has only one significant figure.

Example

A computer uses 6.5 kWh of energy per day. If the computer is left on all the time, how much energy does it use in a year?

(1) Solve the problem.

$$E = 6.5 \frac{\text{kWh}}{\text{day}} \cdot 365 \frac{\text{days}}{\text{year}} = 2372.5 \frac{\text{kWh}}{\text{year}}$$

(2) Look at the number with the fewest significant figures. The number 6.5 has two significant figures, and the number 365 has three significant figures. Therefore, the answer is only meaningful to two significant figures.

(3) Round the answer to two significant figures.

ANSWER $E = 2400 \frac{\text{kWh}}{\text{year}}$

Answer the following questions. Write your answers using the significant figure rule for multiplication.

1. How much energy is used in a year by a computer that uses 1.7 kWh/day?

2. An energy-efficient computer uses 0.72 kWh/day. How much energy does it use in a week?

3. How much energy is used in one year if a 0.27 kW computer is on for 3 hours/day? (**Hint:** Use the formula $E = Pt$.)

CHALLENGE The energy usage of a computer is measured to be 0.058030 kWh. How many significant figures does this measurement have?

Chapter 3: **Magnetism** 107

Chapter Review

the BIG idea

Current can produce magnetism, and magnetism can produce current.

CONTENT REVIEW
CLASSZONE.COM

KEY CONCEPTS SUMMARY

3.1 Magnetism is a force that acts at a distance.

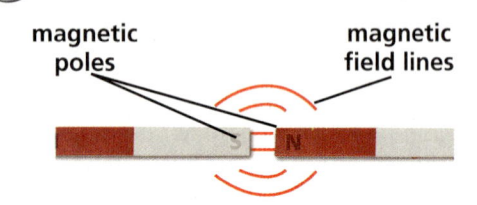

All magnets have a north and south pole. The like poles of two magnets repel each other and the opposite poles attract.

Opposite poles attract.

VOCABULARY
magnet p. 79
magnetism p. 80
magnetic pole p. 80
magnetic field p. 81
magnetic domain p. 82

3.2 Current can produce magnetism.

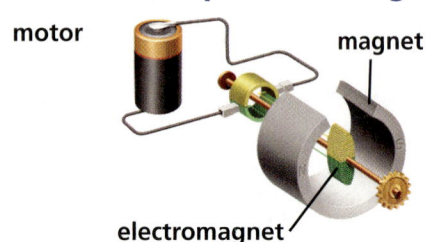

A magnet that is produced by electric current is called an electromagnet. Motors use electromagnets to convert electrical energy into the energy of motion.

VOCABULARY
electromagnetism p. 89
electromagnet p. 90

3.3 Magnetism can produce current.

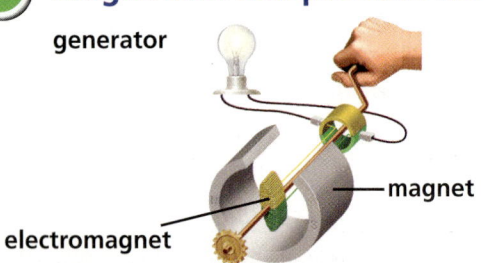

Magnetism can be used to produce electric current. In a generator the energy of motion is converted into electrical energy.

VOCABULARY
generator p. 96
direct current p. 97
alternating current p. 97
transformer p. 99

3.4 Generators supply electrical energy.

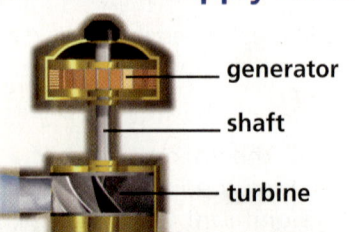

Generators at power plants use large magnets to produce electric current, supplying electrical energy to homes and businesses.

VOCABULARY
electric power p. 102
watt p. 104
kilowatt p. 104
kilowatt-hour p. 105

E 108 Unit: Electricity and Magnetism

Reviewing Vocabulary

Draw a cluster diagram for each of the terms below. Write the vocabulary term in the center circle. In another circle, write the definition of the term in your own words. Add other circles that give examples or characteristics of the term. A sample diagram is completed for you.

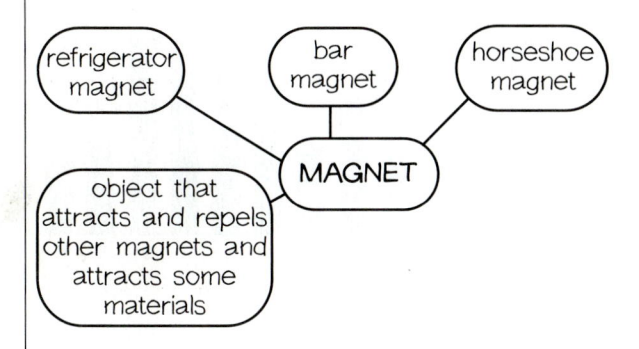

- refrigerator magnet
- bar magnet
- horseshoe magnet
- MAGNET
- object that attracts and repels other magnets and attracts some materials

1. magnetism
2. magnetic pole
3. magnetic field
4. magnetic domain
5. electromagnet
6. generator
7. direct current
8. alternating current
9. transformer
10. electric power
11. watt
12. kilowatt-hour

Reviewing Key Concepts

Multiple Choice *Choose the letter of the best answer.*

13. Magnetic field lines flow from a magnet's
    a. north pole to south pole
    b. south pole to north pole
    c. center to the outside
    d. outside to the center

14. Which of the following is characteristic of magnetic materials?
    a. Their atoms are all aligned.
    b. Their atoms are arranged in magnetic domains.
    c. They are all nonmetals.
    d. They are all made of lodestone.

15. The Earth's magnetic field helps to protect living things from
    a. ultraviolet light
    b. meteors
    c. the Northern Lights
    d. charged particles

16. To produce a magnetic field around a copper wire, you have to
    a. place it in Earth's magnetic field
    b. run a current through it
    c. supply kinetic energy to it
    d. place it near a strong magnet

17. An electric current is produced when a wire is
    a. stationary in a magnetic field
    b. moving in a magnetic field
    c. placed between the poles of a magnet
    d. coiled around a magnet

18. In a generator, kinetic energy is converted into
    a. light energy
    b. chemical energy
    c. electrical energy
    d. nuclear energy

19. In an AC circuit, the current moves
    a. back and forth
    b. from one end of a generator to the other
    c. from one end of a battery to the other
    d. in one direction

20. What is the function of the turbine in a power plant?
    a. to increase the voltage
    b. to convert DC to AC
    c. to cool the steam
    d. to turn the coil or magnet

21. The two factors needed to measure usage of electrical energy in a building are
    a. power and time
    b. power and voltage
    c. voltage and time
    d. current and voltage

Thinking Critically

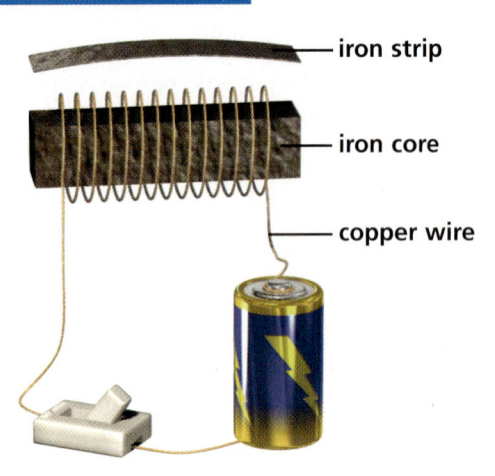

- iron strip
- iron core
- copper wire

Refer to the device in the illustration above to answer the next three questions.

22. APPLY What will happen when the switch is closed?

23. PREDICT What effect will switching the direction of the current have on the operation of the device?

24. CONTRAST If the iron strip is replaced with a thin magnet, how would that affect the answers to the previous two questions?

25. APPLY Coal is burned at a power plant to produce steam. The rising steam turns a turbine. Describe how the motion of the turbine produces current at the plant.

26. CONNECT List three things that you use in your everyday life that would not exist without the discovery of electromagnetism.

27. APPLY A radio for use during power outages works when you crank a handle. How is the radio powered? How can it keep operating even after you stop turning the crank?

28. HYPOTHESIZE Use your understanding of magnetic materials and the source of Earth's magnetic field to form a hypothesis about the difference between Earth and the Moon that accounts for the fact that the Moon does not have a magnetic field.

Using Math in Science

Some electric bills include a bar graph of energy usage similar to the one shown below. Use the information provided in the graph to answer the next four questions.

12-Month Usage (kWh)

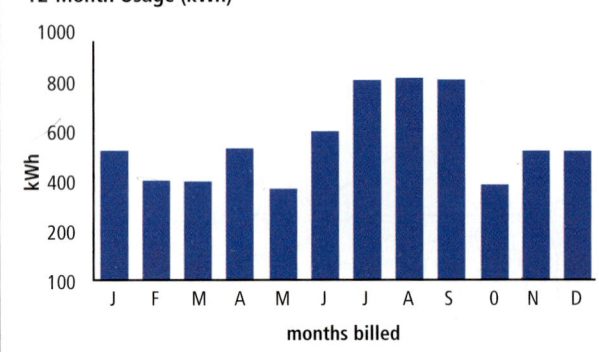

(bar graph showing kWh by month J F M A M J J A S O N D, months billed)

29. The first bar in the graph shows energy usage for the month of January. About how much energy, in kWh, was used in January?

30. If the appliances in the building have a combined power rating of 2 kW, how many hours were they in use during the month of March? (**Hint:** Use the formula $E = Pt$.)

31. The cost of energy was 8 cents per kWh. How much was charged for energy usage in May?

32. The most energy is used when the air conditioner is on. During which three months was the air conditioner on?

the BIG idea

33. ANALYZE Look back at pages 76–77. Think about the answer you gave to the question about the large photograph. How has your understanding of magnetism changed? Give examples.

34. SUMMARIZE Write a paragraph summarizing the first three pages of this chapter. Use the heading at the top of page 79 as your topic sentence. Explain each red and blue heading.

UNIT PROJECTS

Evaluate all the data, results, and information from your project folder. Prepare to present your project.

Standardized Test Practice

For practice on your state test, go to...
TEST PRACTICE
CLASSZONE.COM

Analyzing Tables

The table below lists some major advances in the understanding of electromagnetism.

Scientist	Year	Advance
William Gilbert	1600	proposes distinction between magnetism and static electricity
Pieter van Musschenbroek	1745	develops Leyden jar, which stores electric charge
Benjamin Franklin	1752	shows that lightning is a form of electricity
Charles Augustin de Coulomb	1785	proves mathematically that, for electricity and magnetism, force changes with distance
Alessandro Volta	1800	invents battery, first device to generate a continuous current
Hans Christian Oersted	1820	announces he had used electric current to produce magnetic effects
André Marie Ampère	1820	shows that wires carrying current attract and repel each other, just like magnets
Georg Simon Ohm	1827	studies how well different wires conduct electric current
Michael Faraday	1831	produces electricity with a magnet; invents first electric generator

Use the table above to answer the next four questions.

1. Which scientist first produced a device that allowed experimenters to hold an electric charge for later use?
 a. Coulomb
 b. Franklin
 c. Ohm
 d. van Musschenbroek

2. Which scientist developed the first device that could be used to provide a steady source of current to other devices?
 a. Ampère
 b. Faraday
 c. Volta
 d. Gilbert

3. Which scientist had the first experimental evidence that current could produce magnetism?
 a. Gilbert
 b. Faraday
 c. van Musschenbroek
 d. Oersted

4. Why was Coulomb's work important?
 a. He showed that electricity and magnetism could be stored.
 b. He showed that electricity and magnetism behave similarly.
 c. He proved that electricity and magnetism were different.
 d. He proved that electricity and magnetism were the same.

Extended Response

Answer the two questions below in detail. Include some of the terms from the word box. Underline each term you use in your answer.

| appliance | current | generator |
| motor | coil | kilowatt-hour |

5. How are electromagnets produced? How can the strength of these devices be increased? How can electromagnets be used in ways that permanent magnets cannot?

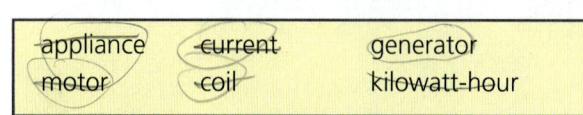

6. Alix chats online for an average of about an hour a day 6 days a week. Her computer has a power rating of 270 watts. She has a hair dryer with a power rating of 1200 watts. She uses it twice a week for about 15 minutes at a time. Which device is likely to use more power over the course of a year? Why?

Chapter 3: **Magnetism** 111

Student Resource Handbooks

Scientific Thinking Handbook — R2

- Making Observations — R2
- Predicting and Hypothesizing — R3
- Inferring — R4
- Identifying Cause and Effect — R5
- Recognizing Bias — R6
- Identifying Faulty Reasoning — R7
- Analyzing Statements — R8

Lab Handbook — R10

- Safety Rules — R10
- Using Lab Equipment — R12
- The Metric System and SI Units — R20
- Precision and Accuracy — R22
- Making Data Tables and Graphs — R23
- Designing an Experiment — R28

Math Handbook — R36

- Describing a Set of Data — R36
- Using Ratios, Rates, and Proportions — R38
- Using Decimals, Fractions, and Percents — R39
- Using Formulas — R42
- Finding Areas — R43
- Finding Volumes — R43
- Using Significant Figures — R44
- Using Scientific Notation — R44

Note-Taking Handbook — R45

- Note-Taking Strategies — R45
- Vocabulary Strategies — R50

Student Resources R1

Scientific Thinking Handbook

Making Observations

An **observation** is an act of noting and recording an event, characteristic, behavior, or anything else detected with an instrument or with the senses.

Observations allow you to make informed hypotheses and to gather data for experiments. Careful observations often lead to ideas for new experiments. There are two categories of observations:

- **Quantitative observations** can be expressed in numbers and include records of time, temperature, mass, distance, and volume.
- **Qualitative observations** include descriptions of sights, sounds, smells, and textures.

EXAMPLE

A student dissolved 30 grams of Epsom salts in water, poured the solution into a dish, and let the dish sit out uncovered overnight. The next day, she made the following observations of the Epsom salt crystals that grew in the dish.

Table 1. Observations of Epsom Salt Crystals

Quantitative Observations	Qualitative Observations
• mass = 30 g • mean crystal length = 0.5 cm • longest crystal length = 2 cm	• Crystals are clear. • Crystals are long, thin, and rectangular. • White crust has formed around edge of dish.

To determine the mass, the student found the mass of the dish before and after growing the crystals and then used subtraction to find the difference.

The student measured several crystals and calculated the mean length. (To learn how to calculate the mean of a data set, see page R36.)

Photographs or sketches are useful for recording qualitative observations.

Epsom salt crystals

MORE ABOUT OBSERVING

- Make quantitative observations whenever possible. That way, others will know exactly what you observed and be able to compare their results with yours.
- It is always a good idea to make qualitative observations too. You never know when you might observe something unexpected.

Predicting and Hypothesizing

A **prediction** is an expectation of what will be observed or what will happen. A **hypothesis** is a tentative explanation for an observation or scientific problem that can be tested by further investigation.

EXAMPLE

Suppose you have made two paper airplanes and you wonder why one of them tends to glide farther than the other one.

1. Start by asking a question.
2. Make an educated guess. After examination, you notice that the wings of the airplane that flies farther are slightly larger than the wings of the other airplane.
3. Write a prediction based upon your educated guess, in the form of an "If . . . , then . . ." statement. Write the independent variable after the word *if*, and the dependent variable after the word *then*.
4. To make a hypothesis, explain why you think what you predicted will occur. Write the explanation after the word *because*.

---

1. Why does one of the paper airplanes glide farther than the other?

2. The size of an airplane's wings may affect how far the airplane will glide.

3. Prediction: If I make a paper airplane with larger wings, then the airplane will glide farther.

   To read about independent and dependent variables, see page R30.

4. Hypothesis: If I make a paper airplane with larger wings, then the airplane will glide farther, because the additional surface area of the wing will produce more lift.

   Notice that the part of the hypothesis after because adds an explanation of why the airplane will glide farther.

MORE ABOUT HYPOTHESES

- The results of an experiment cannot prove that a hypothesis is correct. Rather, the results either support or do not support the hypothesis.
- Valuable information is gained even when your hypothesis is not supported by your results. For example, it would be an important discovery to find that wing size is not related to how far an airplane glides.
- In science, a hypothesis is supported only after many scientists have conducted many experiments and produced consistent results.

Scientific Thinking Handbook **R3**

Inferring

An **inference** is a logical conclusion drawn from the available evidence and prior knowledge. Inferences are often made from observations.

EXAMPLE

A student observing a set of acorns noticed something unexpected about one of them. He noticed a white, soft-bodied insect eating its way out of the acorn.

The student recorded these observations.

Observations
- There is a hole in the acorn, about 0.5 cm in diameter, where the insect crawled out.
- There is a second hole, which is about the size of a pinhole, on the other side of the acorn.
- The inside of the acorn is hollow.

Here are some inferences that can be made on the basis of the observations.

Inferences
- The insect formed from the material inside the acorn, grew to its present size, and ate its way out of the acorn.
- The insect crawled through the smaller hole, ate the inside of the acorn, grew to its present size, and ate its way out of the acorn.
- An egg was laid in the acorn through the smaller hole. The egg hatched into a larva that ate the inside of the acorn, grew to its present size, and ate its way out of the acorn.

When you make inferences, be sure to look at all of the evidence available and combine it with what you already know.

MORE ABOUT INFERENCES

Inferences depend both on observations and on the knowledge of the people making the inferences. Ancient people who did not know that organisms are produced only by similar organisms might have made an inference like the first one. A student today might look at the same observations and make the second inference. A third student might have knowledge about this particular insect and know that it is never small enough to fit through the smaller hole, leading her to the third inference.

Identifying Cause and Effect

In a **cause-and-effect relationship,** one event or characteristic is the result of another. Usually an effect follows its cause in time.

There are many examples of cause-and-effect relationships in everyday life.

Cause	Effect
Turn off a light.	Room gets dark.
Drop a glass.	Glass breaks.
Blow a whistle.	Sound is heard.

Scientists must be careful not to infer a cause-and-effect relationship just because one event happens after another event. When one event occurs after another, you cannot infer a cause-and-effect relationship on the basis of that information alone. You also cannot conclude that one event caused another if there are alternative ways to explain the second event. A scientist must demonstrate through experimentation or continued observation that an event was truly caused by another event.

EXAMPLE

Make an Observation

Suppose you have a few plants growing outside. When the weather starts getting colder, you bring one of the plants indoors. You notice that the plant you brought indoors is growing faster than the others are growing. You cannot conclude from your observation that the change in temperature was the cause of the increased plant growth, because there are alternative explanations for the observation. Some possible explanations are given below.

- The humidity indoors caused the plant to grow faster.
- The level of sunlight indoors caused the plant to grow faster.
- The indoor plant's being noticed more often and watered more often than the outdoor plants caused it to grow faster.
- The plant that was brought indoors was healthier than the other plants to begin with.

To determine which of these factors, if any, caused the indoor plant to grow faster than the outdoor plants, you would need to design and conduct an experiment.

See pages R28–R35 for information about designing experiments.

Scientific Thinking Handbook **R5**

Recognizing Bias

Television, newspapers, and the Internet are full of experts claiming to have scientific evidence to back up their claims. How do you know whether the claims are really backed up by good science?

Bias is a slanted point of view, or personal prejudice. The goal of scientists is to be as objective as possible and to base their findings on facts instead of opinions. However, bias often affects the conclusions of researchers, and it is important to learn to recognize bias.

When scientific results are reported, you should consider the source of the information as well as the information itself. It is important to critically analyze the information that you see and read.

SOURCES OF BIAS

There are several ways in which a report of scientific information may be biased. Here are some questions that you can ask yourself:

1. **Who is sponsoring the research?**

   Sometimes, the results of an investigation are biased because an organization paying for the research is looking for a specific answer. This type of bias can affect how data are gathered and interpreted.

2. **Is the research sample large enough?**

   Sometimes research does not include enough data. The larger the sample size, the more likely that the results are accurate, assuming a truly random sample.

3. **In a survey, who is answering the questions?**

   The results of a survey or poll can be biased. The people taking part in the survey may have been specifically chosen because of how they would answer. They may have the same ideas or lifestyles. A survey or poll should make use of a random sample of people.

4. **Are the people who take part in a survey biased?**

   People who take part in surveys sometimes try to answer the questions the way they think the researcher wants them to answer. Also, in surveys or polls that ask for personal information, people may be unwilling to answer questions truthfully.

SCIENTIFIC BIAS

It is also important to realize that scientists have their own biases because of the types of research they do and because of their scientific viewpoints. Two scientists may look at the same set of data and come to completely different conclusions because of these biases. However, such disagreements are not necessarily bad. In fact, a critical analysis of disagreements is often responsible for moving science forward.

Identifying Faulty Reasoning

Faulty reasoning is wrong or incorrect thinking. It leads to mistakes and to wrong conclusions. Scientists are careful not to draw unreasonable conclusions from experimental data. Without such caution, the results of scientific investigations may be misleading.

EXAMPLE

Scientists try to make generalizations based on their data to explain as much about nature as possible. If only a small sample of data is looked at, however, a conclusion may be faulty. Suppose a scientist has studied the effects of the El Niño and La Niña weather patterns on flood damage in California from 1989 to 1995. The scientist organized the data in the bar graph below.

The scientist drew the following conclusions:

1. The La Niña weather pattern has no effect on flooding in California.
2. When neither weather pattern occurs, there is almost no flood damage.
3. A weak or moderate El Niño produces a small or moderate amount of flooding.
4. A strong El Niño produces a lot of flooding.

Flood and Storm Damage in California

SOURCE: *Governor's Office of Emergency Services, California*

For the six-year period of the scientist's investigation, these conclusions may seem to be reasonable. However, a six-year study of weather patterns may be too small of a sample for the conclusions to be supported. Consider the following graph, which shows information that was gathered from 1949 to 1997.

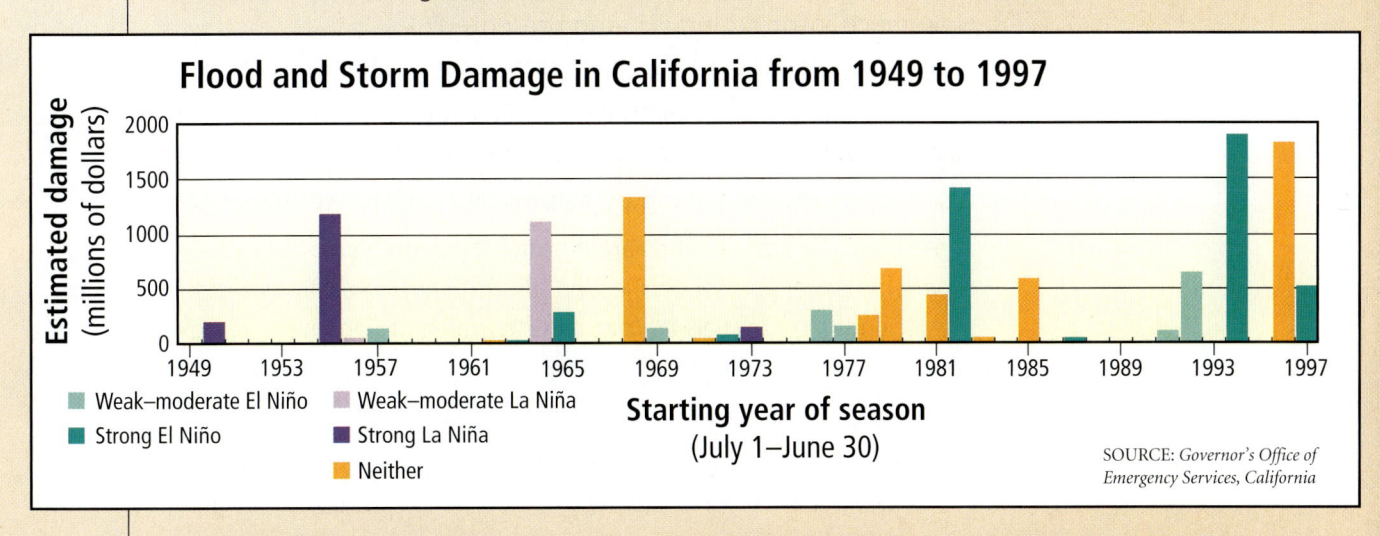

Flood and Storm Damage in California from 1949 to 1997

SOURCE: *Governor's Office of Emergency Services, California*

The only one of the conclusions that all of this information supports is number 3: a weak or moderate El Niño produces a small or moderate amount of flooding. By collecting more data, scientists can be more certain of their conclusions and can avoid faulty reasoning.

Scientific Thinking Handbook R7

Analyzing Statements

To **analyze** a statement is to examine its parts carefully. Scientific findings are often reported through media such as television or the Internet. A report that is made public often focuses on only a small part of research. As a result, it is important to question the sources of information.

Evaluate Media Claims

To **evaluate** a statement is to judge it on the basis of criteria you've established. Sometimes evaluating means deciding whether a statement is true.

Reports of scientific research and findings in the media may be misleading or incomplete. When you are exposed to this information, you should ask yourself some questions so that you can make informed judgments about the information.

1. **Does the information come from a credible source?**

   Suppose you learn about a new product and it is stated that scientific evidence proves that the product works. A report from a respected news source may be more believable than an advertisement paid for by the product's manufacturer.

2. **How much evidence supports the claim?**

   Often, it may seem that there is new evidence every day of something in the world that either causes or cures an illness. However, information that is the result of several years of work by several different scientists is more credible than an advertisement that does not even cite the subjects of the experiment.

3. **How much information is being presented?**

   Science cannot solve all questions, and scientific experiments often have flaws. A report that discusses problems in a scientific study may be more believable than a report that addresses only positive experimental findings.

4. **Is scientific evidence being presented by a specific source?**

   Sometimes scientific findings are reported by people who are called experts or leaders in a scientific field. But if their names are not given or their scientific credentials are not reported, their statements may be less credible than those of recognized experts.

Differentiate Between Fact and Opinion

Sometimes information is presented as a fact when it may be an opinion. When scientific conclusions are reported, it is important to recognize whether they are based on solid evidence. Again, you may find it helpful to ask yourself some questions.

1. **What is the difference between a fact and an opinion?**

    A **fact** is a piece of information that can be strictly defined and proved true. An **opinion** is a statement that expresses a belief, value, or feeling. An opinion cannot be proved true or false. For example, a person's age is a fact, but if someone is asked how old they feel, it is impossible to prove the person's answer to be true or false.

2. **Can opinions be measured?**

    Yes, opinions can be measured. In fact, surveys often ask for people's opinions on a topic. But there is no way to know whether or not an opinion is the truth.

HOW TO DIFFERENTIATE FACT FROM OPINION

Human Activities and the Environment

Unfortunately, human use of fossil fuels is one of the most significant developments of the past few centuries. Humans rely on fossil fuels, a nonrenewable energy resource, for more than 90 percent of their energy needs.

This careless misuse of our planet's resources has resulted in pollution, global warming, and the destruction of fragile ecosystems. For example, oil pipelines carry more than one million barrels of oil each day across tundra regions. Transporting oil across such areas can only result in oil spills that poison the land for decades.

Opinions
Notice words or phrases that express beliefs or feelings. The words *unfortunately* and *careless* show that opinions are being expressed.

Opinion
Look for statements that speculate about events. These statements are opinions, because they cannot be proved.

Facts
Statements that contain statistics tend to be facts. Writers often use facts to support their opinions.

Scientific Thinking Handbook R9

Lab Handbook

Safety Rules

Before you work in the laboratory, read these safety rules twice. Ask your teacher to explain any rules that you do not completely understand. Refer to these rules later on if you have questions about safety in the science classroom.

Directions

- Read all directions and make sure that you understand them before starting an investigation or lab activity. If you do not understand how to do a procedure or how to use a piece of equipment, ask your teacher.
- Do not begin any investigation or touch any equipment until your teacher has told you to start.
- Never experiment on your own. If you want to try a procedure that the directions do not call for, ask your teacher for permission first.
- If you are hurt or injured in any way, tell your teacher immediately.

Dress Code

goggles
apron
gloves

- Wear goggles when
  — using glassware, sharp objects, or chemicals
  — heating an object
  — working with anything that can easily fly up into the air and hurt someone's eye
- Tie back long hair or hair that hangs in front of your eyes.
- Remove any article of clothing—such as a loose sweater or a scarf—that hangs down and may touch a flame, chemical, or piece of equipment.
- Observe all safety icons calling for the wearing of eye protection, gloves, and aprons.

Heating and Fire Safety

fire safety
heating safety

- Keep your work area neat, clean, and free of extra materials.
- Never reach over a flame or heat source.
- Point objects being heated away from you and others.
- Never heat a substance or an object in a closed container.
- Never touch an object that has been heated. If you are unsure whether something is hot, treat it as though it is. Use oven mitts, clamps, tongs, or a test-tube holder.
- Know where the fire extinguisher and fire blanket are kept in your classroom.
- Do not throw hot substances into the trash. Wait for them to cool or use the container your teacher puts out for disposal.

Electrical Safety

electrical safety

- Never use lamps or other electrical equipment with frayed cords.
- Make sure no cord is lying on the floor where someone can trip over it.
- Do not let a cord hang over the side of a counter or table so that the equipment can easily be pulled or knocked to the floor.
- Never let cords hang into sinks or other places where water can be found.
- Never try to fix electrical problems. Inform your teacher of any problems immediately.
- Unplug an electrical cord by pulling on the plug, not the cord.

Chemical Safety

chemical safety

poison

fumes

- If you spill a chemical or get one on your skin or in your eyes, tell your teacher right away.
- Never touch, taste, or sniff any chemicals in the lab. If you need to determine odor, waft. Wafting consists of holding the chemical in its container 15 centimeters (6 in.) away from your nose, and using your fingers to bring fumes from the container to your nose.
- Keep lids on all chemicals you are not using.
- Never put unused chemicals back into the original containers. Throw away extra chemicals where your teacher tells you to.
- Pour chemicals over a sink or your work area, not over the floor.
- If you get a chemical in your eye, use the eyewash right away.
- Always wash your hands after handling chemicals, plants, or soil.

Wafting

Glassware and Sharp-Object Safety

sharp objects

- If you break glassware, tell your teacher right away.
- Do not use broken or chipped glassware. Give these to your teacher.
- Use knives and other cutting instruments carefully. Always wear eye protection and cut away from you.

Animal Safety

- Never hurt an animal.
- Touch animals only when necessary. Follow your teacher's instructions for handling animals.
- Always wash your hands after working with animals.

Cleanup

disposal

- Follow your teacher's instructions for throwing away or putting away supplies.
- Clean your work area and pick up anything that has dropped to the floor.
- Wash your hands.

Lab Handbook R11

Using Lab Equipment

Different experiments require different types of equipment. But even though experiments differ, the ways in which the equipment is used are the same.

Beakers

- Use beakers for holding and pouring liquids.
- Do not use a beaker to measure the volume of a liquid. Use a graduated cylinder instead. (See page R16.)
- Use a beaker that holds about twice as much liquid as you need. For example, if you need 100 milliliters of water, you should use a 200- or 250-milliliter beaker.

Test Tubes

- Use test tubes to hold small amounts of substances.
- Do not use a test tube to measure the volume of a liquid.
- Use a test tube when heating a substance over a flame. Aim the mouth of the tube away from yourself and other people.
- Liquids easily spill or splash from test tubes, so it is important to use only small amounts of liquids.

Test-Tube Holder

- Use a test-tube holder when heating a substance in a test tube.
- Use a test-tube holder if the substance in a test tube is dangerous to touch.
- Make sure the test-tube holder tightly grips the test tube so that the test tube will not slide out of the holder.
- Make sure that the test-tube holder is above the surface of the substance in the test tube so that you can observe the substance.

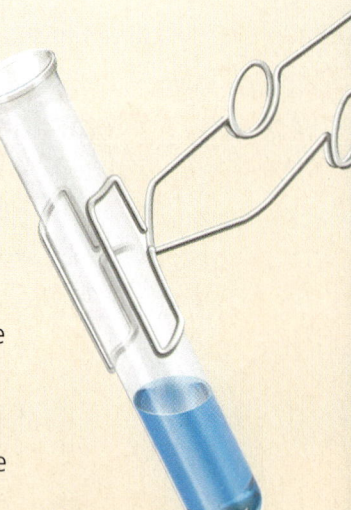

Test-Tube Rack

- Use a test-tube rack to organize test tubes before, during, and after an experiment.
- Use a test-tube rack to keep test tubes upright so that they do not fall over and spill their contents.
- Use a test-tube rack that is the correct size for the test tubes that you are using. If the rack is too small, a test tube may become stuck. If the rack is too large, a test tube may lean over, and some of its contents may spill or splash.

Forceps

- Use forceps when you need to pick up or hold a very small object that should not be touched with your hands.
- Do not use forceps to hold anything over a flame, because forceps are not long enough to keep your hand safely away from the flame. Plastic forceps will melt, and metal forceps will conduct heat and burn your hand.

Hot Plate

- Use a hot plate when a substance needs to be kept warmer than room temperature for a long period of time.
- Use a hot plate instead of a Bunsen burner or a candle when you need to carefully control temperature.
- Do not use a hot plate when a substance needs to be burned in an experiment.
- Always use "hot hands" safety mitts or oven mitts when handling anything that has been heated on a hot plate.

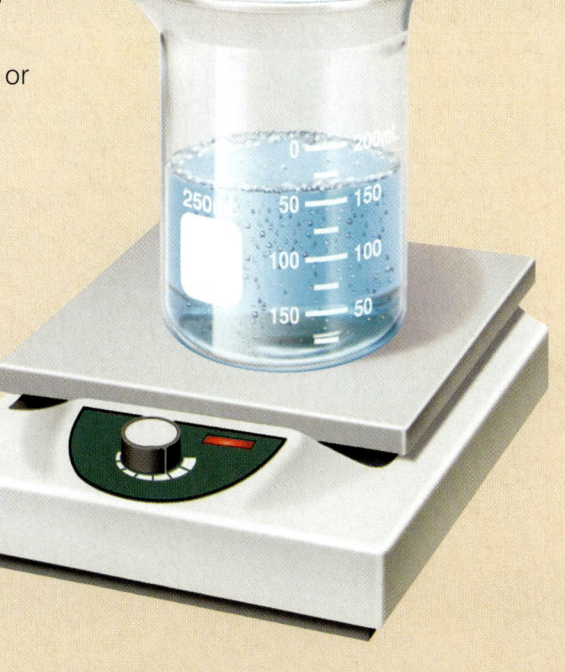

Lab Handbook **R13**

Microscope

Scientists use microscopes to see very small objects that cannot easily be seen with the eye alone. A microscope magnifies the image of an object so that small details may be observed. A microscope that you may use can magnify an object 400 times—the object will appear 400 times larger than its actual size.

Eyepiece Objects are viewed through the eyepiece. The eyepiece contains a lens that commonly magnifies an image 10 times.

Coarse Adjustment This knob is used to focus the image of an object when it is viewed through the low-power lens.

Fine Adjustment This knob is used to focus the image of an object when it is viewed through the high-power lens.

Low-Power Objective Lens This is the smallest lens on the nosepiece. It magnifies an image approximately 10 times.

Arm The arm supports the body above the stage. Always carry a microscope by the arm and base.

Stage Clip The stage clip holds a slide in place on the stage.

Base The base supports the microscope.

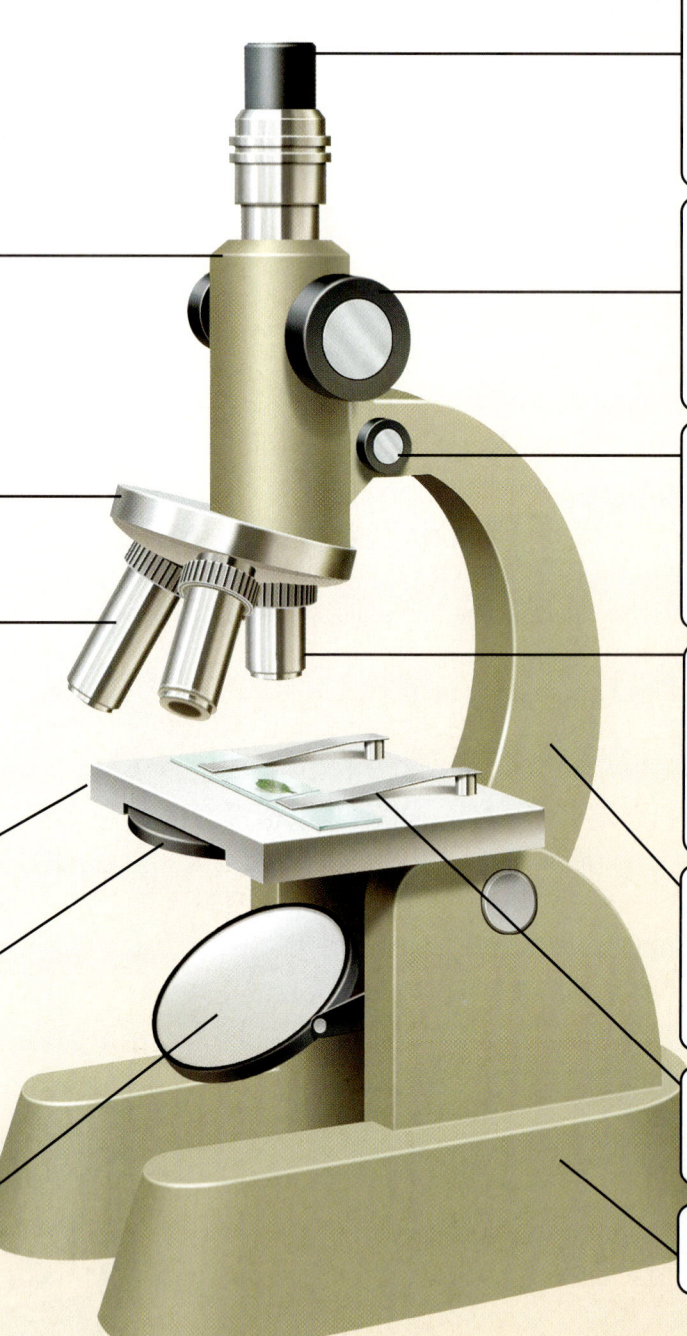

Body The body separates the lens in the eyepiece from the objective lenses below.

Nosepiece The nosepiece holds the objective lenses above the stage and rotates so that all lenses may be used.

High-Power Objective Lens This is the largest lens on the nosepiece. It magnifies an image approximately 40 times.

Stage The stage supports the object being viewed.

Diaphragm The diaphragm is used to adjust the amount of light passing through the slide and into an objective lens.

Mirror or Light Source Some microscopes use light that is reflected through the stage by a mirror. Other microscopes have their own light sources.

LAB HANDBOOK

R14   Student Resources

VIEWING AN OBJECT

1. Use the coarse adjustment knob to raise the body tube.
2. Adjust the diaphragm so that you can see a bright circle of light through the eyepiece.
3. Place the object or slide on the stage. Be sure that it is centered over the hole in the stage.
4. Turn the nosepiece to click the low-power lens into place.
5. Using the coarse adjustment knob, slowly lower the lens and focus on the specimen being viewed. Be sure not to touch the slide or object with the lens.
6. When switching from the low-power lens to the high-power lens, first raise the body tube with the coarse adjustment knob so that the high-power lens will not hit the slide.
7. Turn the nosepiece to click the high-power lens into place.
8. Use the fine adjustment knob to focus on the specimen being viewed. Again, be sure not to touch the slide or object with the lens.

MAKING A SLIDE, OR WET MOUNT

1 Place the specimen in the center of a clean slide.

2 Place a drop of water on the specimen.

3 Place a cover slip on the slide. Put one edge of the cover slip into the drop of water and slowly lower it over the specimen.

4 Remove any air bubbles from under the cover slip by gently tapping the cover slip.

5 Dry any excess water before placing the slide on the microscope stage for viewing.

Lab Handbook **R15**

Spring Scale (Force Meter)

- Use a spring scale to measure a force pulling on the scale.
- Use a spring scale to measure the force of gravity exerted on an object by Earth.
- To measure a force accurately, a spring scale must be zeroed before it is used. The scale is zeroed when no weight is attached and the indicator is positioned at zero.
- Do not attach a weight that is either too heavy or too light to a spring scale. A weight that is too heavy could break the scale or exert too great a force for the scale to measure. A weight that is too light may not exert enough force to be measured accurately.

Graduated Cylinder

- Use a graduated cylinder to measure the volume of a liquid.
- Be sure that the graduated cylinder is on a flat surface so that your measurement will be accurate.
- When reading the scale on a graduated cylinder, be sure to have your eyes at the level of the surface of the liquid.
- The surface of the liquid will be curved in the graduated cylinder. Read the volume of the liquid at the bottom of the curve, or meniscus (muh-NIHS-kuhs).
- You can use a graduated cylinder to find the volume of a solid object by measuring the increase in a liquid's level after you add the object to the cylinder.

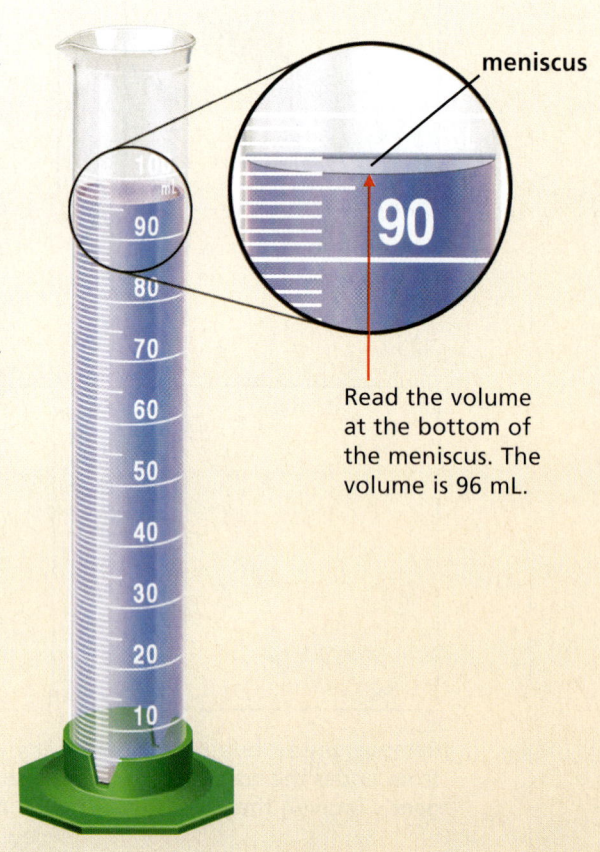

Read the volume at the bottom of the meniscus. The volume is 96 mL.

R16 Student Resources

Metric Rulers

- Use metric rulers or meter sticks to measure objects' lengths.
- Do not measure an object from the end of a metric ruler or meter stick, because the end is often imperfect. Instead, measure from the 1-centimeter mark, but remember to subtract a centimeter from the apparent measurement.
- Estimate any lengths that extend between marked units. For example, if a meter stick shows centimeters but not millimeters, you can estimate the length that an object extends between centimeter marks to measure it to the nearest millimeter.
- **Controlling Variables** If you are taking repeated measurements, always measure from the same point each time. For example, if you're measuring how high two different balls bounce when dropped from the same height, measure both bounces at the same point on the balls—either the top or the bottom. Do not measure at the top of one ball and the bottom of the other.

EXAMPLE

How to Measure a Leaf

1. Lay a ruler flat on top of the leaf so that the 1-centimeter mark lines up with one end. Make sure the ruler and the leaf do not move between the time you line them up and the time you take the measurement.

2. Look straight down on the ruler so that you can see exactly how the marks line up with the other end of the leaf.

3. Estimate the length by which the leaf extends beyond a marking. For example, the leaf below extends about halfway between the 4.2-centimeter and 4.3-centimeter marks, so the apparent measurement is about 4.25 centimeters.

4. Remember to subtract 1 centimeter from your apparent measurement, since you started at the 1-centimeter mark on the ruler and not at the end. The leaf is about 3.25 centimeters long (4.25 cm – 1 cm = 3.25 cm).

Lab Handbook **R17**

Triple-Beam Balance

This balance has a pan and three beams with sliding masses, called riders. At one end of the beams is a pointer that indicates whether the mass on the pan is equal to the masses shown on the beams.

1. Make sure the balance is zeroed before measuring the mass of an object. The balance is zeroed if the pointer is at zero when nothing is on the pan and the riders are at their zero points. Use the adjustment knob at the base of the balance to zero it.

2. Place the object to be measured on the pan.

3. Move the riders one notch at a time away from the pan. Begin with the largest rider. If moving the largest rider one notch brings the pointer below zero, begin measuring the mass of the object with the next smaller rider.

4. Change the positions of the riders until they balance the mass on the pan and the pointer is at zero. Then add the readings from the three beams to determine the mass of the object.

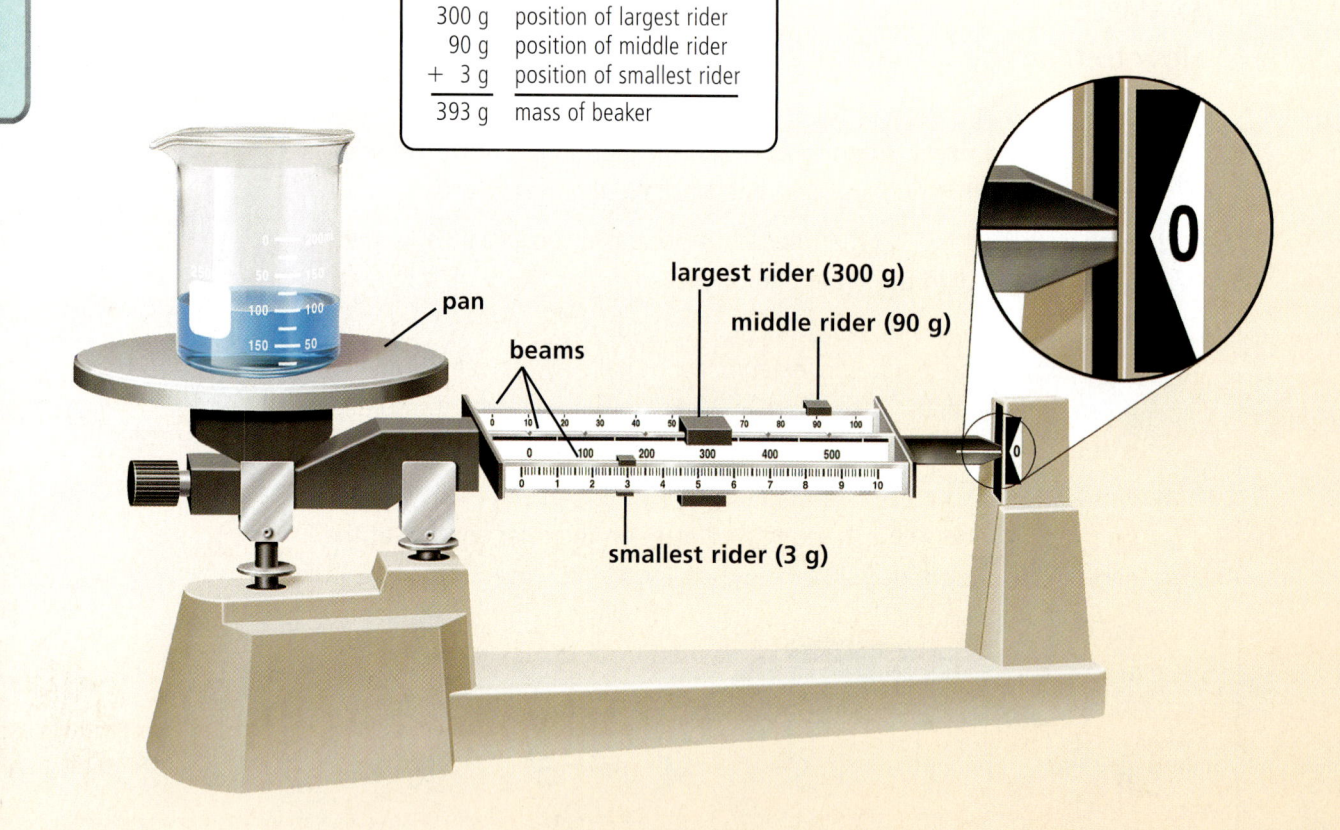

300 g	position of largest rider
90 g	position of middle rider
+ 3 g	position of smallest rider
393 g	mass of beaker

R18 Student Resources

Double-Pan Balance

This type of balance has two pans. Between the pans is a pointer that indicates whether the masses on the pans are equal.

1. Make sure the balance is zeroed before measuring the mass of an object. The balance is zeroed if the pointer is at zero when there is nothing on either of the pans. Many double-pan balances have sliding knobs that can be used to zero them.

2. Place the object to be measured on one of the pans.

3. Begin adding standard masses to the other pan. Begin with the largest standard mass. If this adds too much mass to the balance, begin measuring the mass of the object with the next smaller standard mass.

4. Add standard masses until the masses on both pans are balanced and the pointer is at zero. Then add the standard masses together to determine the mass of the object being measured.

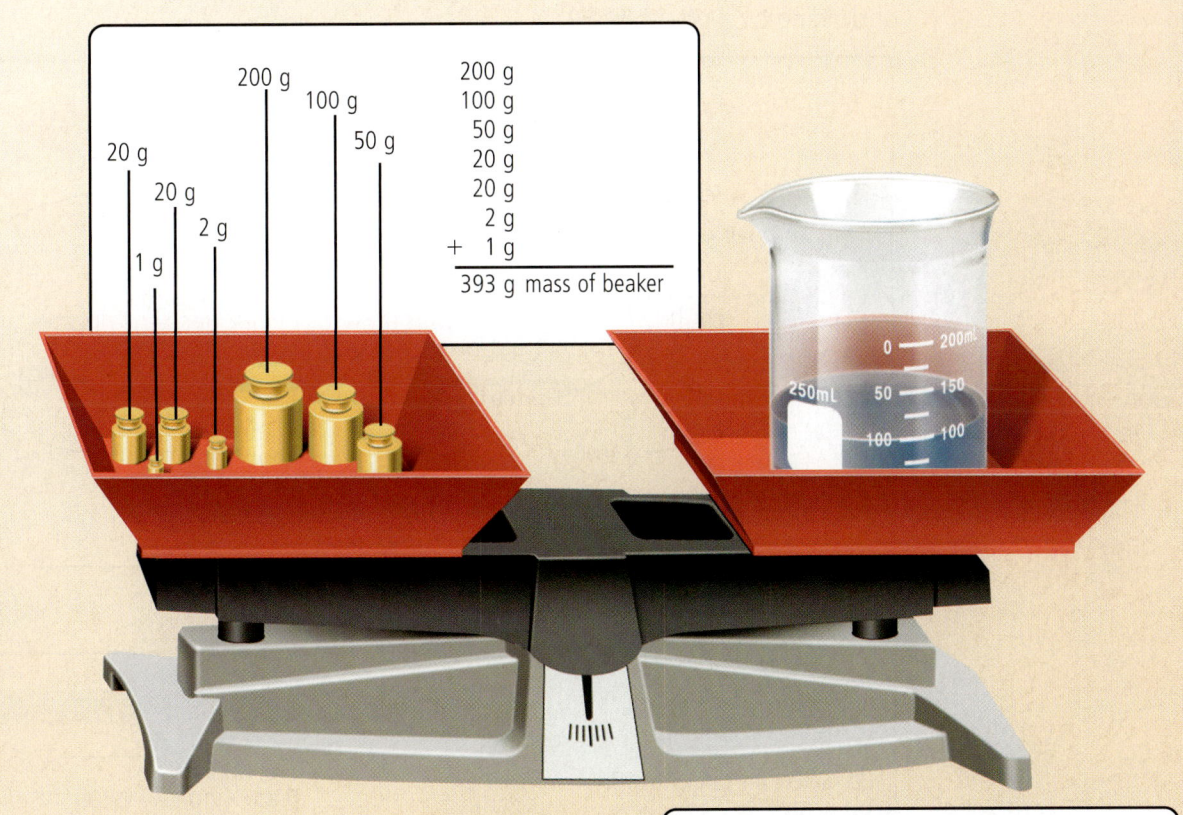

```
      200 g
         100 g         200 g
                         100 g
              50 g       50 g
  20 g                   20 g
      20 g               20 g
                          2 g
        2 g            + 1 g
    1 g              ─────────
                      393 g mass of beaker
```

Never place chemicals or liquids directly on a pan. Instead, use the following procedure:

❶ Determine the mass of an empty container, such as a beaker.

❷ Pour the substance into the container, and measure the total mass of the substance and the container.

❸ Subtract the mass of the empty container from the total mass to find the mass of the substance.

Lab Handbook R19

The Metric System and SI Units

Scientists use International System (SI) units for measurements of distance, volume, mass, and temperature. The International System is based on multiples of ten and the metric system of measurement.

Basic SI Units		
Property	Name	Symbol
length	meter	m
volume	liter	L
mass	kilogram	kg
temperature	kelvin	K

SI Prefixes		
Prefix	Symbol	Multiple of 10
kilo-	k	1000
hecto-	h	100
deca-	da	10
deci-	d	0.1 ($\frac{1}{10}$)
centi-	c	0.01 ($\frac{1}{100}$)
milli-	m	0.001 ($\frac{1}{1000}$)

Changing Metric Units

You can change from one unit to another in the metric system by multiplying or dividing by a power of 10.

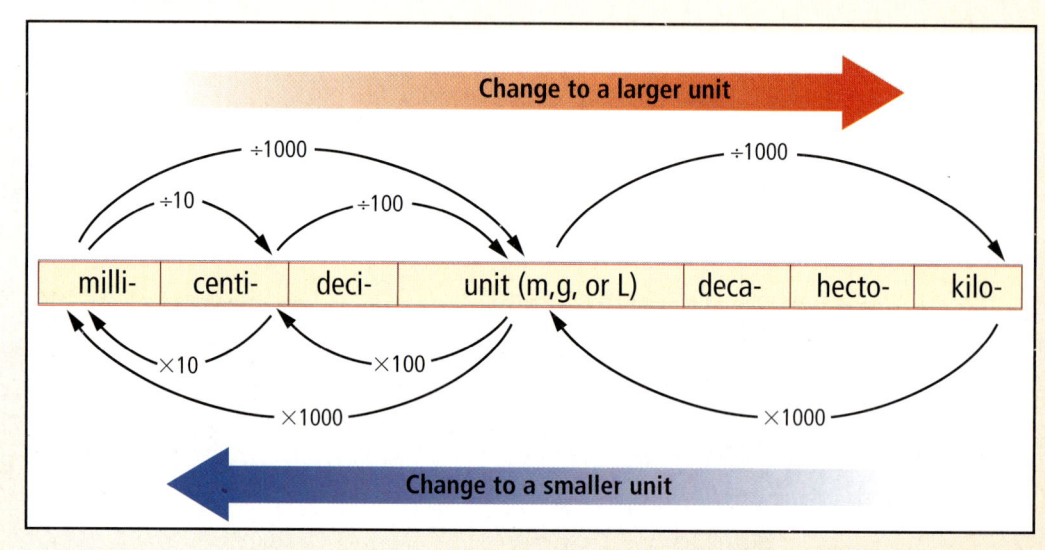

Change to a larger unit →

milli- | centi- | deci- | unit (m, g, or L) | deca- | hecto- | kilo-

← **Change to a smaller unit**

Example

Change 0.64 liters to milliliters.
(1) Decide whether to multiply or divide.
(2) Select the power of 10.
ANSWER 0.64 L = 640 mL

Change to a smaller unit by multiplying.
mL ← × 1000 ← L
0.64 × 1000 = 640.

Example

Change 23.6 grams to kilograms.
(1) Decide whether to multiply or divide.
(2) Select the power of 10.
ANSWER 23.6 g = 0.0236 kg

Change to a larger unit by dividing.
g → ÷ 1000 → kg
23.6 ÷ 1000 = 0.0236

Temperature Conversions

Even though the kelvin is the SI base unit of temperature, the degree Celsius will be the unit you use most often in your science studies. The formulas below show the relationships between temperatures in degrees Fahrenheit (°F), degrees Celsius (°C), and kelvins (K).

$$°C = \frac{5}{9}(°F - 32)$$

$$°F = \frac{9}{5}°C + 32$$

$$K = °C + 273$$

See page R42 for help with using formulas.

Examples of Temperature Conversions

Condition	Degrees Celsius	Degrees Fahrenheit
Freezing point of water	0	32
Cool day	10	50
Mild day	20	68
Warm day	30	86
Normal body temperature	37	98.6
Very hot day	40	104
Boiling point of water	100	212

Converting Between SI and U.S. Customary Units

Use the chart below when you need to convert between SI units and U.S. customary units.

SI Unit	From SI to U.S. Customary			From U.S. Customary to SI		
Length	When you know	multiply by	to find	When you know	multiply by	to find
kilometer (km) = 1000 m	kilometers	0.62	miles	miles	1.61	kilometers
meter (m) = 100 cm	meters	3.28	feet	feet	0.3048	meters
centimeter (cm) = 10 mm	centimeters	0.39	inches	inches	2.54	centimeters
millimeter (mm) = 0.1 cm	millimeters	0.04	inches	inches	25.4	millimeters
Area	When you know	multiply by	to find	When you know	multiply by	to find
square kilometer (km^2)	square kilometers	0.39	square miles	square miles	2.59	square kilometers
square meter (m^2)	square meters	1.2	square yards	square yards	0.84	square meters
square centimeter (cm^2)	square centimeters	0.155	square inches	square inches	6.45	square centimeters
Volume	When you know	multiply by	to find	When you know	multiply by	to find
liter (L) = 1000 mL	liters	1.06	quarts	quarts	0.95	liters
	liters	0.26	gallons	gallons	3.79	liters
	liters	4.23	cups	cups	0.24	liters
	liters	2.12	pints	pints	0.47	liters
milliliter (mL) = 0.001 L	milliliters	0.20	teaspoons	teaspoons	4.93	milliliters
	milliliters	0.07	tablespoons	tablespoons	14.79	milliliters
	milliliters	0.03	fluid ounces	fluid ounces	29.57	milliliters
Mass	When you know	multiply by	to find	When you know	multiply by	to find
kilogram (kg) = 1000 g	kilograms	2.2	pounds	pounds	0.45	kilograms
gram (g) = 1000 mg	grams	0.035	ounces	ounces	28.35	grams

Precision and Accuracy

When you do an experiment, it is important that your methods, observations, and data be both precise and accurate.

low precision

precision, but not accuracy

precision and accuracy

Precision

In science, **precision** is the exactness and consistency of measurements. For example, measurements made with a ruler that has both centimeter and millimeter markings would be more precise than measurements made with a ruler that has only centimeter markings. Another indicator of precision is the care taken to make sure that methods and observations are as exact and consistent as possible. Every time a particular experiment is done, the same procedure should be used. Precision is necessary because experiments are repeated several times and if the procedure changes, the results will change.

EXAMPLE

Suppose you are measuring temperatures over a two-week period. Your precision will be greater if you measure each temperature at the same place, at the same time of day, and with the same thermometer than if you change any of these factors from one day to the next.

Accuracy

In science, it is possible to be precise but not accurate. **Accuracy** depends on the difference between a measurement and an actual value. The smaller the difference, the more accurate the measurement.

EXAMPLE

Suppose you look at a stream and estimate that it is about 1 meter wide at a particular place. You decide to check your estimate by measuring the stream with a meter stick, and you determine that the stream is 1.32 meters wide. However, because it is hard to measure the width of a stream with a meter stick, it turns out that you didn't do a very good job. The stream is actually 1.14 meters wide. Therefore, even though your estimate was less precise than your measurement, your estimate was actually more accurate.

Making Data Tables and Graphs

Data tables and graphs are useful tools for both recording and communicating scientific data.

Making Data Tables

You can use a **data table** to organize and record the measurements that you make. Some examples of information that might be recorded in data tables are frequencies, times, and amounts.

EXAMPLE

Suppose you are investigating photosynthesis in two elodea plants. One sits in direct sunlight, and the other sits in a dimly lit room. You measure the rate of photosynthesis by counting the number of bubbles in the jar every ten minutes.

1. Title and number your data table.
2. Decide how you will organize the table into columns and rows.
3. Any units, such as seconds or degrees, should be included in column headings, not in the individual cells.

Table 1. Number of Bubbles from Elodea

Time (min)	Sunlight	Dim Light
0	0	0
10	15	5
20	25	8
30	32	7
40	41	10
50	47	9
60	42	9

Always number and title data tables.

The data in the table above could also be organized in a different way.

Table 1. Number of Bubbles from Elodea

Light Condition	Time (min)						
	0	10	20	30	40	50	60
Sunlight	0	15	25	32	41	47	42
Dim light	0	5	8	7	10	9	9

Put units in column heading.

Lab Handbook R23

Making Line Graphs

You can use a **line graph** to show a relationship between variables. Line graphs are particularly useful for showing changes in variables over time.

EXAMPLE

Suppose you are interested in graphing temperature data that you collected over the course of a day.

Table 1. Outside Temperature During the Day on March 7

	\multicolumn{7}{c}{Time of Day}
	7:00 A.M.	9:00 A.M.	11:00 A.M.	1:00 P.M.	3:00 P.M.	5:00 P.M.	7:00 P.M.
Temp (°C)	8	9	11	14	12	10	6

1. Use the vertical axis of your line graph for the variable that you are measuring—temperature.
2. Choose scales for both the horizontal axis and the vertical axis of the graph. You should have two points more than you need on the vertical axis, and the horizontal axis should be long enough for all of the data points to fit.
3. Draw and label each axis.
4. Graph each value. First find the appropriate point on the scale of the horizontal axis. Imagine a line that rises vertically from that place on the scale. Then find the corresponding value on the vertical axis, and imagine a line that moves horizontally from that value. The point where these two imaginary lines intersect is where the value should be plotted.
5. Connect the points with straight lines.

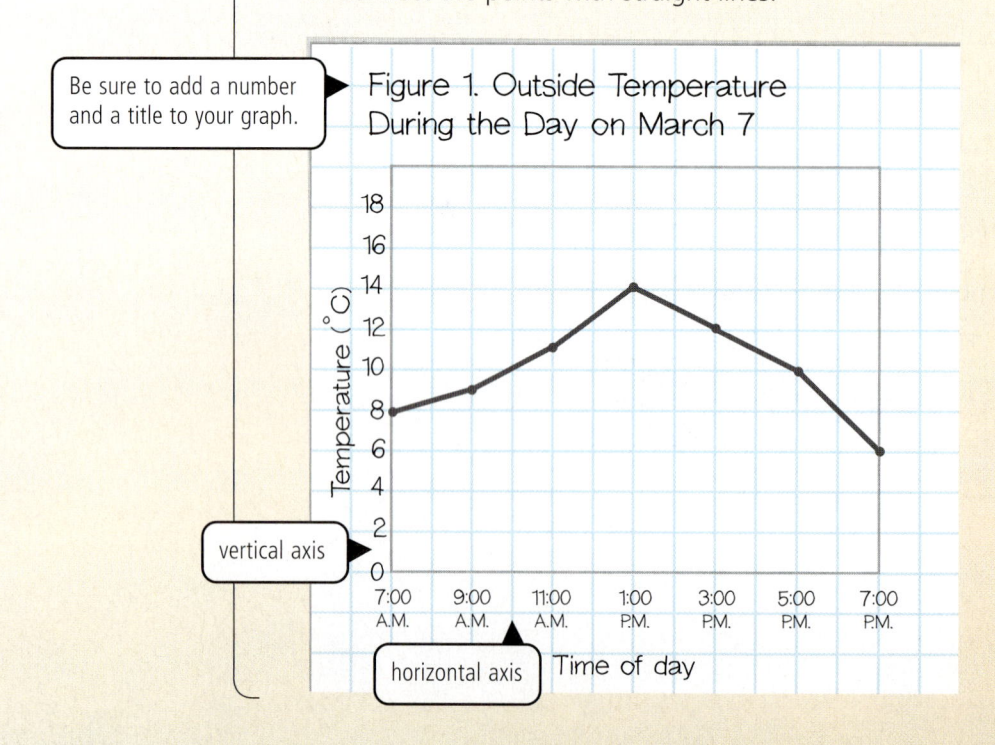

Be sure to add a number and a title to your graph.

Figure 1. Outside Temperature During the Day on March 7

vertical axis

horizontal axis — Time of day

R24 Student Resources

Making Circle Graphs

You can use a **circle graph,** sometimes called a pie chart, to represent data as parts of a circle. Circle graphs are used only when the data can be expressed as percentages of a whole. The entire circle shown in a circle graph is equal to 100 percent of the data.

EXAMPLE

Suppose you identified the species of each mature tree growing in a small wooded area. You organized your data in a table, but you also want to show the data in a circle graph.

1. To begin, find the total number of mature trees.

    56 + 34 + 22 + 10 + 28 = 150

2. To find the degree measure for each sector of the circle, write a fraction comparing the number of each tree species with the total number of trees. Then multiply the fraction by 360°.

    Oak: $\frac{56}{150} \times 360° = 134.4°$

3. Draw a circle. Use a protractor to draw the angle for each sector of the graph.
4. Color and label each sector of the graph.
5. Give the graph a number and title.

Table 1. Tree Species in Wooded Area

Species	Number of Specimens
Oak	56
Maple	34
Birch	22
Willow	10
Pine	28

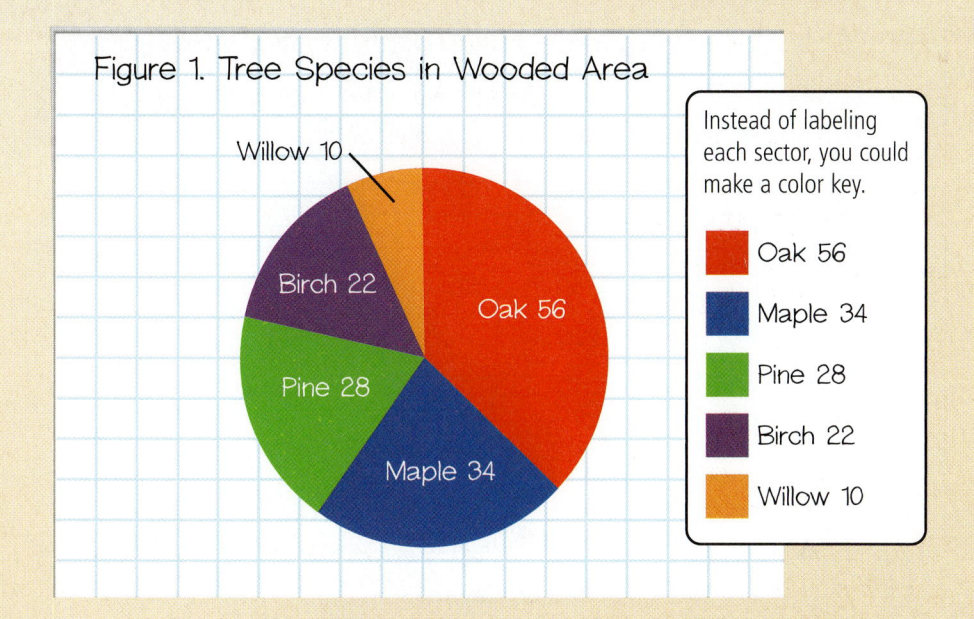

Figure 1. Tree Species in Wooded Area

Instead of labeling each sector, you could make a color key.

- Oak 56
- Maple 34
- Pine 28
- Birch 22
- Willow 10

Lab Handbook R25

Bar Graph

A **bar graph** is a type of graph in which the lengths of the bars are used to represent and compare data. A numerical scale is used to determine the lengths of the bars.

EXAMPLE

To determine the effect of water on seed sprouting, three cups were filled with sand, and ten seeds were planted in each. Different amounts of water were added to each cup over a three-day period.

Table 1. Effect of Water on Seed Sprouting

Daily Amount of Water (mL)	Number of Seeds That Sprouted After 3 Days in Sand
0	1
10	4
20	8

1. Choose a numerical scale. The greatest value is 8, so the end of the scale should have a value greater than 8, such as 10. Use equal increments along the scale, such as increments of 2.

2. Draw and label the axes. Mark intervals on the vertical axis according to the scale you chose.

3. Draw a bar for each data value. Use the scale to decide how long to make each bar.

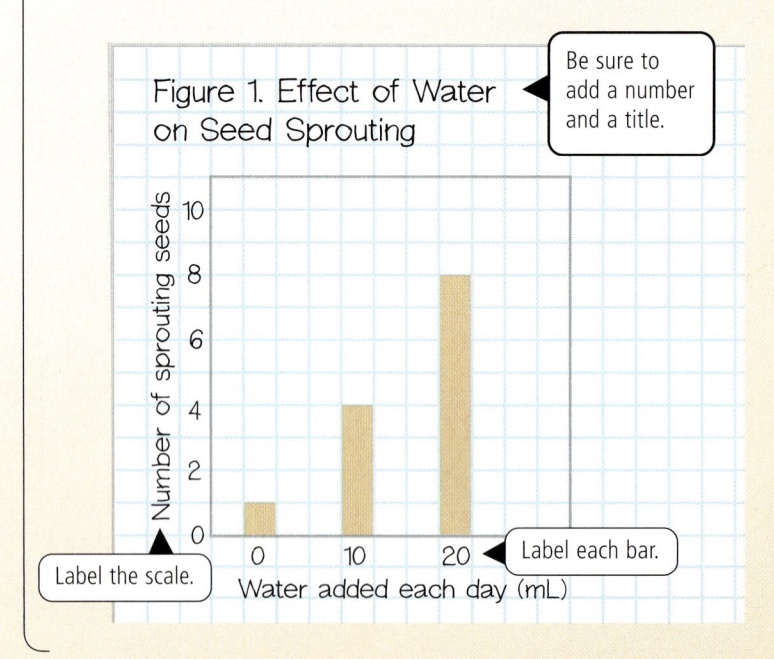

Figure 1. Effect of Water on Seed Sprouting

Double Bar Graph

A **double bar graph** is a bar graph that shows two sets of data. The two bars for each measurement are drawn next to each other.

EXAMPLE

The seed-sprouting experiment was done using both sand and potting soil. The data for sand and potting soil can be plotted on one graph.

1. Draw one set of bars, using the data for sand, as shown below.
2. Draw bars for the potting-soil data next to the bars for the sand data. Shade them a different color. Add a key.

Table 2. Effect of Water and Soil on Seed Sprouting

Daily Amount of Water (mL)	Number of Seeds That Sprouted After 3 Days in Sand	Number of Seeds That Sprouted After 3 Days in Potting Soil
0	1	2
10	4	5
20	8	9

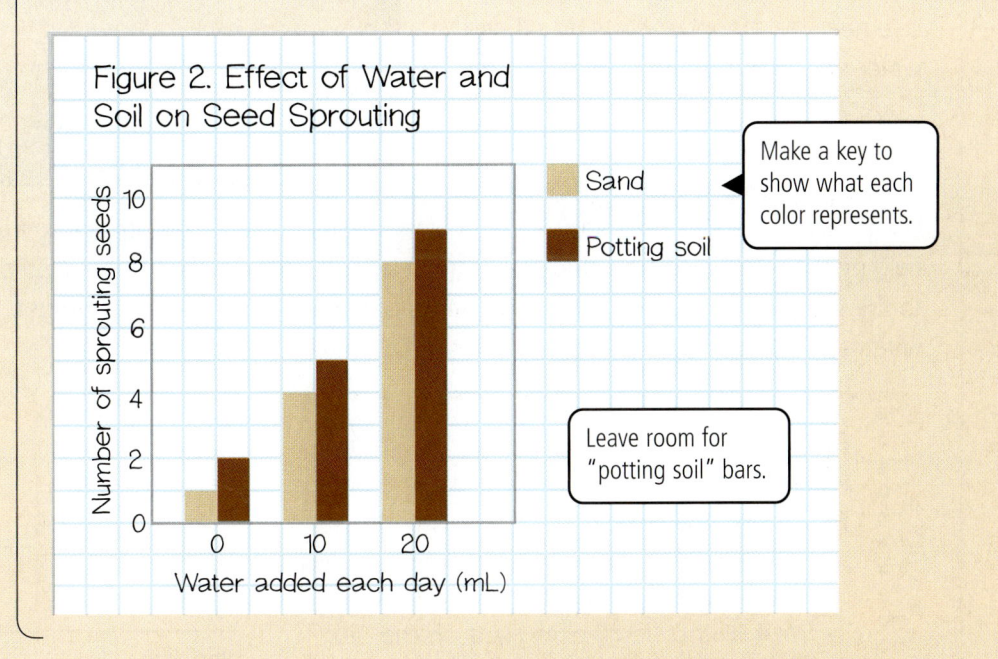

Figure 2. Effect of Water and Soil on Seed Sprouting

Make a key to show what each color represents.

Leave room for "potting soil" bars.

Lab Handbook **R27**

Designing an Experiment

Use this section when designing or conducting an experiment.

Determining a Purpose

You can find a purpose for an experiment by doing research, by examining the results of a previous experiment, or by observing the world around you. An **experiment** is an organized procedure to study something under controlled conditions.

1. Write the purpose of your experiment as a question or problem that you want to investigate.
2. Write down research questions and begin searching for information that will help you design an experiment. Consult the library, the Internet, and other people as you conduct your research.

> Don't forget to learn as much as possible about your topic before you begin.

EXAMPLE

Middle school students observed an odor near the lake by their school. They also noticed that the water on the side of the lake near the school was greener than the water on the other side of the lake. The students did some research to learn more about their observations. They discovered that the odor and green color in the lake came from algae. They also discovered that a new fertilizer was being used on a field nearby. The students inferred that the use of the fertilizer might be related to the presence of the algae and designed a controlled experiment to find out whether they were right.

Problem
How does fertilizer affect the presence of algae in a lake?

Research Questions
- Have other experiments been done on this problem? If so, what did those experiments show?
- What kind of fertilizer is used on the field? How much?
- How do algae grow?
- How do people measure algae?
- Can fertilizer and algae be used safely in a lab? How?

> **Research**
> As you research, you may find a topic that is more interesting to you than your original topic, or learn that a procedure you wanted to use is not practical or safe. It is OK to change your purpose as you research.

Writing a Hypothesis

A **hypothesis** is a tentative explanation for an observation or scientific problem that can be tested by further investigation. You can write your hypothesis in the form of an "If . . . , then . . . , because . . ." statement.

> **Hypothesis**
> If the amount of fertilizer in lake water is increased, then the amount of algae will also increase, because fertilizers provide nutrients that algae need to grow.

Hypotheses
For help with hypotheses, refer to page R3.

Determining Materials

Make a list of all the materials you will need to do your experiment. Be specific, especially if someone else is helping you obtain the materials. Try to think of everything you will need.

> **Materials**
> - 1 large jar or container
> - 4 identical smaller containers
> - rubber gloves that also cover the arms
> - sample of fertilizer-and-water solution
> - eyedropper
> - clear plastic wrap
> - scissors
> - masking tape
> - marker
> - ruler

Lab Handbook **R29**

Determining Variables and Constants

EXPERIMENTAL GROUP AND CONTROL GROUP

An experiment to determine how two factors are related always has two groups—a control group and an experimental group.

1. Design an experimental group. Include as many trials as possible in the experimental group in order to obtain reliable results.

2. Design a control group that is the same as the experimental group in every way possible, except for the factor you wish to test.

> **Experimental Group:** two containers of lake water with one drop of fertilizer solution added to each
>
> **Control Group:** two containers of lake water with no fertilizer solution added

Go back to your materials list and make sure you have enough items listed to cover both your experimental group and your control group.

VARIABLES AND CONSTANTS

Identify the variables and constants in your experiment. In a controlled experiment, a **variable** is any factor that can change. **Constants** are all of the factors that are the same in both the experimental group and the control group.

Hypothesis
If the amount of fertilizer in lake water is increased, then the amount of algae will also increase, because fertilizers provide nutrients that algae need to grow.

1. Read your hypothesis. The **independent variable** is the factor that you wish to test and that is manipulated or changed so that it can be tested. The independent variable is expressed in your hypothesis after the word *if*. Identify the independent variable in your laboratory report.

2. The **dependent variable** is the factor that you measure to gather results. It is expressed in your hypothesis after the word *then*. Identify the dependent variable in your laboratory report.

Table 1. Variables and Constants in Algae Experiment

Independent Variable	Dependent Variable	Constants
Amount of fertilizer in lake water	Amount of algae that grow	• Where the lake water is obtained • Type of container used • Light and temperature conditions where water will be stored

Set up your experiment so that you will test only one variable.

R30 Student Resources

MEASURING THE DEPENDENT VARIABLE

Before starting your experiment, you need to define how you will measure the dependent variable. An **operational definition** is a description of the one particular way in which you will measure the dependent variable.

Your operational definition is important for several reasons. First, in any experiment there are several ways in which a dependent variable can be measured. Second, the procedure of the experiment depends on how you decide to measure the dependent variable. Third, your operational definition makes it possible for other people to evaluate and build on your experiment.

EXAMPLE 1

An operational definition of a dependent variable can be qualitative. That is, your measurement of the dependent variable can simply be an observation of whether a change occurs as a result of a change in the independent variable. This type of operational definition can be thought of as a "yes or no" measurement.

Table 2. Qualitative Operational Definition of Algae Growth

Independent Variable	Dependent Variable	Operational Definition
Amount of fertilizer in lake water	Amount of algae that grow	Algae grow in lake water

A qualitative measurement of a dependent variable is often easy to make and record. However, this type of information does not provide a great deal of detail in your experimental results.

EXAMPLE 2

An operational definition of a dependent variable can be quantitative. That is, your measurement of the dependent variable can be a number that shows how much change occurs as a result of a change in the independent variable.

Table 3. Quantitative Operational Definition of Algae Growth

Independent Variable	Dependent Variable	Operational Definition
Amount of fertilizer in lake water	Amount of algae that grow	Diameter of largest algal growth (in mm)

A quantitative measurement of a dependent variable can be more difficult to make and analyze than a qualitative measurement. However, this type of data provides much more information about your experiment and is often more useful.

Writing a Procedure

Write each step of your procedure. Start each step with a verb, or action word, and keep the steps short. Your procedure should be clear enough for someone else to use as instructions for repeating your experiment.

> If necessary, go back to your materials list and add any materials that you left out.

Procedure

1. Put on your gloves. Use the large container to obtain a sample of lake water.

2. Divide the sample of lake water equally among the four smaller containers.

3. Use the eyedropper to add one drop of fertilizer solution to two of the containers.

> **Controlling Variables**
> The same amount of fertilizer solution must be added to two of the four containers.

4. Use the masking tape and the marker to label the containers with your initials, the date, and the identifiers "Jar 1 with Fertilizer," "Jar 2 with Fertilizer," "Jar 1 without Fertilizer," and "Jar 2 without Fertilizer."

5. Cover the containers with clear plastic wrap. Use the scissors to punch ten holes in each of the covers.

> **Controlling Variables**
> All four containers must receive the same amount of light.

6. Place all four containers on a window ledge. Make sure that they all receive the same amount of light.

7. Observe the containers every day for one week.

8. Use the ruler to measure the diameter of the largest clump of algae in each container, and record your measurements daily.

Recording Observations

Once you have obtained all of your materials and your procedure has been approved, you can begin making experimental observations. Gather both quantitative and qualitative data. If something goes wrong during your procedure, make sure you record that too.

Observations
For help with making qualitative and quantitative observations, refer to page R2.

For more examples of data tables, see page R23.

Table 4. Fertilizer and Algae Growth

	Experimental Group		Control Group		
Date and Time	Jar 1 with Fertilizer (diameter of algae in mm)	Jar 2 with Fertilizer (diameter of algae in mm)	Jar 1 without Fertilizer (diameter of algae in mm)	Jar 2 without Fertilizer (diameter of algae in mm)	Observations
5/3 4:00 P.M.	0	0	0	0	condensation in all containers
5/4 4:00 P.M.	0	3	0	0	tiny green blobs in jar 2 with fertilizer
5/5 4:15 P.M.	4	5	0	3	green blobs in jars 1 and 2 with fertilizer and jar 2 without fertilizer
5/6 4:00 P.M.	5	6	0	4	water light green in jar 2 with fertilizer
5/7 4:00 P.M.	8	10	0	6	water light green in jars 1 and 2 with fertilizer and in jar 2 without fertilizer
5/8 3:30 P.M.	10	18	0	6	cover off jar 2 with fertilizer
5/9 3:30 P.M.	14	23	0	8	drew sketches of each container

Notice that on the sixth day, the observer found that the cover was off one of the containers. It is important to record observations of unintended factors because they might affect the results of the experiment.

Use technology, such as a microscope, to help you make observations when possible.

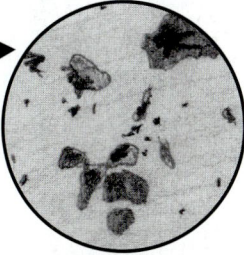

Drawings of Samples Viewed Under Microscope on 5/9 at 100x

Jar 1 with Fertilizer 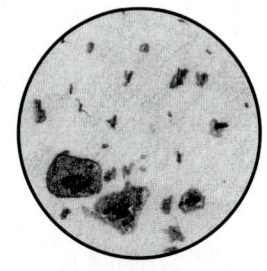 | Jar 2 with Fertilizer | Jar 1 without Fertilizer 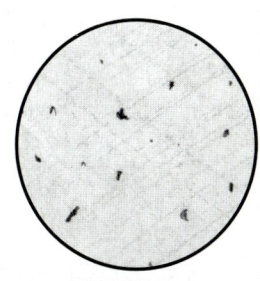 | Jar 2 without Fertilizer

Lab Handbook **R33**

Summarizing Results

To summarize your data, look at all of your observations together. Look for meaningful ways to present your observations. For example, you might average your data or make a graph to look for patterns. When possible, use spreadsheet software to help you analyze and present your data. The two graphs below show the same data.

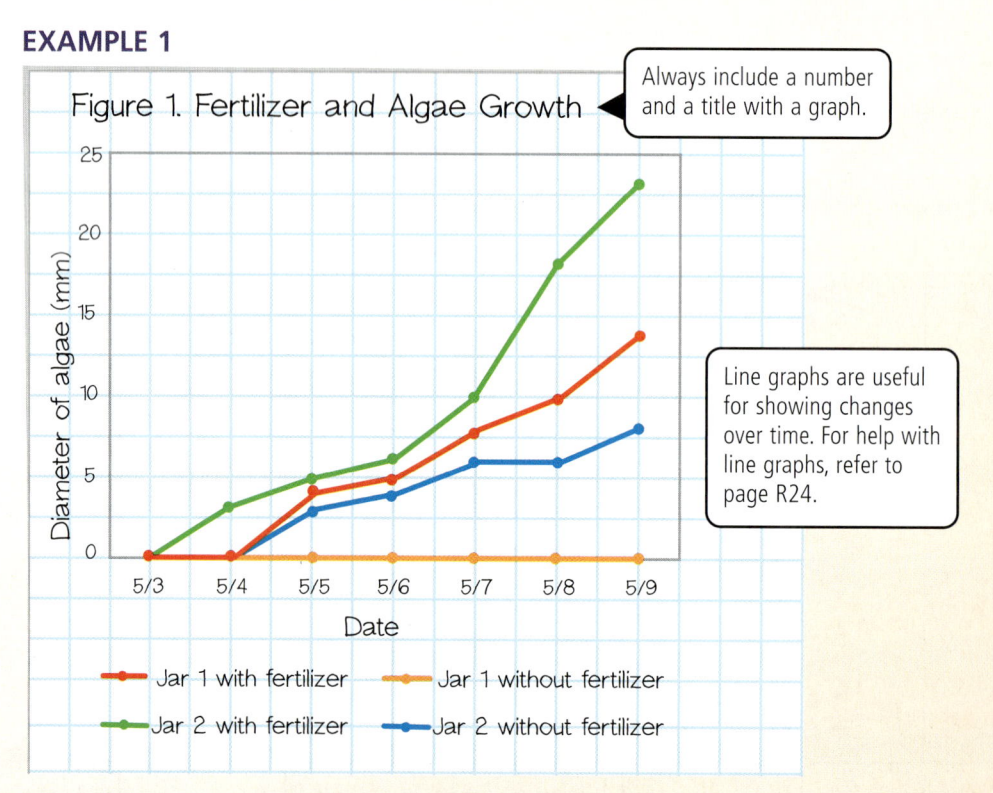

EXAMPLE 1

Figure 1. Fertilizer and Algae Growth

Always include a number and a title with a graph.

Line graphs are useful for showing changes over time. For help with line graphs, refer to page R24.

EXAMPLE 2

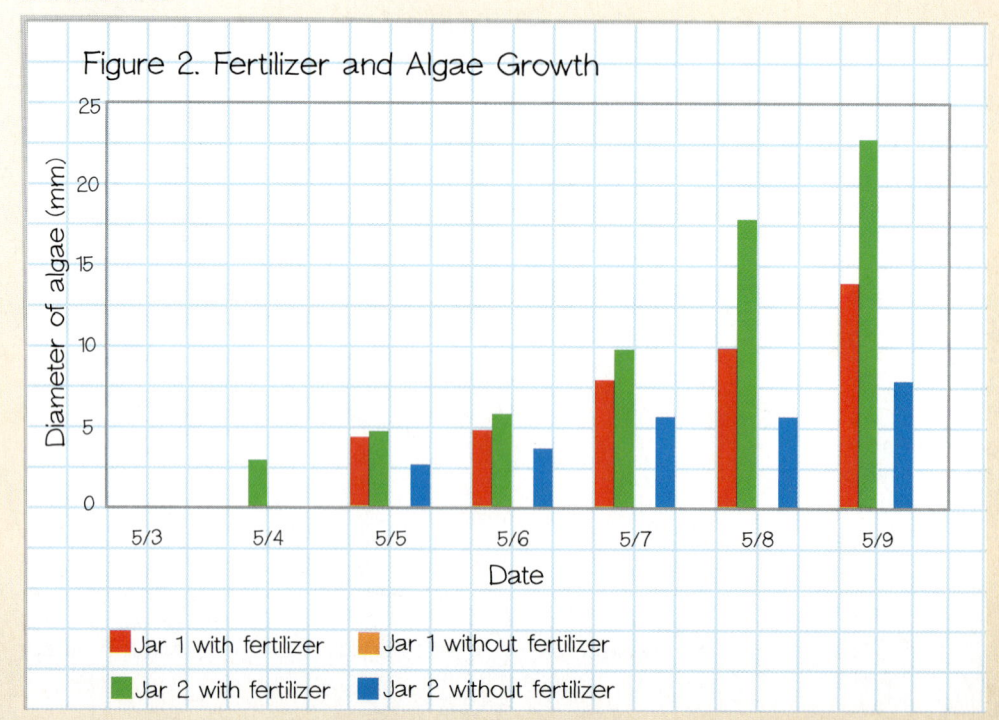

Figure 2. Fertilizer and Algae Growth

Bar graphs are useful for comparing different data sets. This bar graph has four bars for each day. Another way to present the data would be to calculate averages for the tests and the controls, and to show one test bar and one control bar for each day.

R34 Student Resources

Drawing Conclusions

RESULTS AND INFERENCES

To draw conclusions from your experiment, first write your results. Then compare your results with your hypothesis. Do your results support your hypothesis? Be careful not to make inferences about factors that you did not test.

For help with making inferences, see page R4.

Results and Inferences

The results of my experiment show that more algae grew in lake water to which fertilizer had been added than in lake water to which no fertilizer had been added. My hypothesis was supported. I infer that it is possible that the growth of algae in the lake was caused by the fertilizer used on the field.

Notice that you cannot conclude from this experiment that the presence of algae in the lake was due only to the fertilizer.

QUESTIONS FOR FURTHER RESEARCH

Write a list of questions for further research and investigation. Your ideas may lead you to new experiments and discoveries.

Questions for Further Research

- What is the connection between the amount of fertilizer and algae growth?
- How do different brands of fertilizer affect algae growth?
- How would algae growth in the lake be affected if no fertilizer were used on the field?
- How do algae affect the lake and the other life in and around it?
- How does fertilizer affect the lake and the life in and around it?
- If fertilizer is getting into the lake, how is it getting there?

Lab Handbook R35

Math Handbook

Describing a Set of Data

Means, medians, modes, and ranges are important math tools for describing data sets such as the following widths of fossilized clamshells.

13 mm   25 mm   14 mm   21 mm   16 mm   23 mm   14 mm

Mean

The **mean** of a data set is the sum of the values divided by the number of values.

Example

To find the mean of the clamshell data, add the values and then divide the sum by the number of values.

$$\frac{13 \text{ mm} + 25 \text{ mm} + 14 \text{ mm} + 21 \text{ mm} + 16 \text{ mm} + 23 \text{ mm} + 14 \text{ mm}}{7} = \frac{126 \text{ mm}}{7} = 18 \text{ mm}$$

ANSWER The mean is 18 mm.

Median

The **median** of a data set is the middle value when the values are written in numerical order. If a data set has an even number of values, the median is the mean of the two middle values.

Example

To find the median of the clamshell data, arrange the values in order from least to greatest. The median is the middle value.

13 mm   14 mm   14 mm   16 mm   21 mm   23 mm   25 mm

ANSWER The median is 16 mm.

Mode

The **mode** of a data set is the value that occurs most often.

> **Example**
>
> To find the mode of the clamshell data, arrange the values in order from least to greatest and determine the value that occurs most often.
>
> 13 mm   14 mm   14 mm   16 mm   21 mm   23 mm   25 mm
>
> **ANSWER** The mode is 14 mm.

A data set can have more than one mode or no mode. For example, the following data set has modes of 2 mm and 4 mm:

2 mm   2 mm   3 mm   4 mm   4 mm

The data set below has no mode, because no value occurs more often than any other.

2 mm   3 mm   4 mm   5 mm

Range

The **range** of a data set is the difference between the greatest value and the least value.

> **Example**
>
> To find the range of the clamshell data, arrange the values in order from least to greatest.
>
> 13 mm   14 mm   14 mm   16 mm   21 mm   23 mm   25 mm
>
> Subtract the least value from the greatest value.
>
> 13 mm is the least value.
> 25 mm is the greatest value.
>
> 25 mm − 13 mm = 12 mm
>
> **ANSWER** The range is 12 mm.

Using Ratios, Rates, and Proportions

You can use ratios and rates to compare values in data sets. You can use proportions to find unknown values.

Ratios

A **ratio** uses division to compare two values. The ratio of a value a to a nonzero value b can be written as $\frac{a}{b}$.

> **Example**
>
> The height of one plant is 8 centimeters. The height of another plant is 6 centimeters. To find the ratio of the height of the first plant to the height of the second plant, write a fraction and simplify it.
>
> $$\frac{8 \text{ cm}}{6 \text{ cm}} = \frac{4 \times \cancel{2}}{3 \times \cancel{2}} = \frac{4}{3}$$
>
> **ANSWER** The ratio of the plant heights is $\frac{4}{3}$.

You can also write the ratio $\frac{a}{b}$ as "a to b" or as $a:b$. For example, you can write the ratio of the plant heights as "4 to 3" or as 4:3.

Rates

A **rate** is a ratio of two values expressed in different units. A unit rate is a rate with a denominator of 1 unit.

> **Example**
>
> A plant grew 6 centimeters in 2 days. The plant's rate of growth was $\frac{6 \text{ cm}}{2 \text{ days}}$. To describe the plant's growth in centimeters per day, write a unit rate.
>
> *Divide numerator and denominator by 2:* $\quad \frac{6 \text{ cm}}{2 \text{ days}} = \frac{6 \text{ cm} \div 2}{2 \text{ days} \div 2}$
>
> *Simplify:* $\quad = \frac{3 \text{ cm}}{1 \text{ day}}$
>
> You divide 2 days by 2 to get 1 day, so divide 6 cm by 2 also.
>
> **ANSWER** The plant's rate of growth is 3 centimeters per day.

Proportions

A **proportion** is an equation stating that two ratios are equivalent. To solve for an unknown value in a proportion, you can use cross products.

Example

If a plant grew 6 centimeters in 2 days, how many centimeters would it grow in 3 days (if its rate of growth is constant)?

Write a proportion: $\dfrac{6 \text{ cm}}{2 \text{ days}} = \dfrac{x}{3 \text{ days}}$

Set cross products: $6 \text{ cm} \cdot 3 = 2x$

Multiply 6 and 3: $18 \text{ cm} = 2x$

Divide each side by 2: $\dfrac{18 \text{ cm}}{2} = \dfrac{2x}{2}$

Simplify: $9 \text{ cm} = x$

ANSWER The plant would grow 9 centimeters in 3 days.

Using Decimals, Fractions, and Percents

Decimals, fractions, and percentages are all ways of recording and representing data.

Decimals

A **decimal** is a number that is written in the base-ten place value system, in which a decimal point separates the ones and tenths digits. The values of each place is ten times that of the place to its right.

Example

A caterpillar traveled from point A to point C along the path shown.

A —— 36.9 cm —— B —— 52.4 cm —— C

ADDING DECIMALS To find the total distance traveled by the caterpillar, add the distance from A to B and the distance from B to C. Begin by lining up the decimal points. Then add the figures as you would whole numbers and bring down the decimal point.

```
  36.9 cm
+ 52.4 cm
---------
  89.3 cm
```

ANSWER The caterpillar traveled a total distance of 89.3 centimeters.

Example continued

SUBTRACTING DECIMALS To find how much farther the caterpillar traveled on the second leg of the journey, subtract the distance from A to B from the distance from B to C.

$$\begin{array}{r} 52.4 \text{ cm} \\ -36.9 \text{ cm} \\ \hline 15.5 \text{ cm} \end{array}$$

ANSWER The caterpillar traveled 15.5 centimeters farther on the second leg of the journey.

Example

A caterpillar is traveling from point D to point F along the path shown. The caterpillar travels at a speed of 9.6 centimeters per minute.

D • —— E • —————— 33.6 cm —————— • F

MULTIPLYING DECIMALS You can multiply decimals as you would whole numbers. The number of decimal places in the product is equal to the sum of the number of decimal places in the factors.

For instance, suppose it takes the caterpillar 1.5 minutes to go from D to E. To find the distance from D to E, multiply the caterpillar's speed by the time it took.

$$\begin{array}{r} 9.6 \\ \times\, 1.5 \\ \hline 480 \\ 96 \\ \hline 14.40 \end{array} \quad \begin{array}{l} 1 \text{ decimal place} \\ +1 \text{ decimal place} \\ \\ \\ 2 \text{ decimal places} \end{array}$$

Align as shown.

ANSWER The distance from D to E is 14.4 centimeters.

DIVIDING DECIMALS When you divide by a decimal, move the decimal points the same number of places in the divisor and the dividend to make the divisor a whole number.

For instance, to find the time it will take the caterpillar to travel from E to F, divide the distance from E to F by the caterpillar's speed.

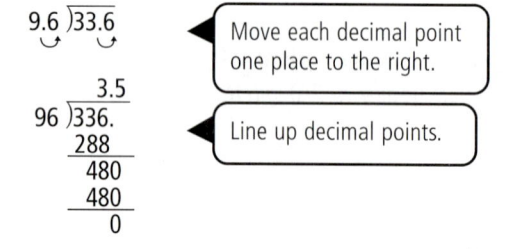

$$9.6\overline{)33.6}$$ ◀ Move each decimal point one place to the right.

$$\begin{array}{r} 3.5 \\ 96\overline{)336.} \\ \underline{288} \\ 480 \\ \underline{480} \\ 0 \end{array}$$ ◀ Line up decimal points.

ANSWER The caterpillar will travel from E to F in 3.5 minutes.

Fractions

A **fraction** is a number in the form $\frac{a}{b}$, where b is not equal to 0. A fraction is in **simplest form** if its numerator and denominator have a greatest common factor (GCF) of 1. To simplify a fraction, divide its numerator and denominator by their GCF.

> **Example**
>
> A caterpillar is 40 millimeters long. The head of the caterpillar is 6 millimeters long. To compare the length of the caterpillar's head with the caterpillar's total length, you can write and simplify a fraction that expresses the ratio of the two lengths.
>
> Write the ratio of the two lengths: $\frac{\text{Length of head}}{\text{Total length}} = \frac{6 \text{ mm}}{40 \text{ mm}}$
>
> Write numerator and denominator as products of numbers and the GCF: $= \frac{3 \times 2}{20 \times 2}$
>
> Divide numerator and denominator by the GCF: $= \frac{3 \times \cancel{2}^1}{20 \times \cancel{2}_1}$
>
> Simplify: $= \frac{3}{20}$
>
> **ANSWER** In simplest form, the ratio of the lengths is $\frac{3}{20}$.

Percents

A **percent** is a ratio that compares a number to 100. The word *percent* means "per hundred" or "out of 100." The symbol for *percent* is %.

For instance, suppose 43 out of 100 caterpillars are female. You can represent this ratio as a percent, a decimal, or a fraction.

Percent	Decimal	Fraction
43%	0.43	$\frac{43}{100}$

> **Example**
>
> In the preceding example, the ratio of the length of the caterpillar's head to the caterpillar's total length is $\frac{3}{20}$. To write this ratio as a percent, write an equivalent fraction that has a denominator of 100.
>
> Multiply numerator and denominator by 5: $\frac{3}{20} = \frac{3 \times 5}{20 \times 5}$
>
> $= \frac{15}{100}$
>
> Write as a percent: $= 15\%$
>
> **ANSWER** The caterpillar's head represents 15 percent of its total length.

Using Formulas

A **formula** is an equation that shows the general relationship between two or more quantities.

In science, a formula often has a word form and a symbolic form. The formula below expresses Ohm's law.

Word Form　　　　　　　**Symbolic Form**

Current = $\dfrac{\text{voltage}}{\text{resistance}}$　　　$I = \dfrac{V}{R}$

> The term *variable* is also used in science to refer to a factor that can change during an experiment.

In this formula, I, V, and R are variables. A mathematical **variable** is a symbol or letter that is used to represent one or more numbers.

Example

Suppose that you measure a voltage of 1.5 volts and a resistance of 15 ohms. You can use the formula for Ohm's law to find the current in amperes.

Write the formula for Ohm's law: $\quad I = \dfrac{V}{R}$

Substitute 1.5 volts for V and 15 ohms for R: $\quad I = \dfrac{1.5 \text{ volts}}{15 \text{ ohms}}$

Simplify: $\quad I = 0.1$ amp

ANSWER The current is 0.1 ampere.

If you know the values of all variables but one in a formula, you can solve for the value of the unknown variable. For instance, Ohm's law can be used to find a voltage if you know the current and the resistance.

Example

Suppose that you know that a current is 0.2 amperes and the resistance is 18 ohms. Use the formula for Ohm's law to find the voltage in volts.

Write the formula for Ohm's law: $\quad I = \dfrac{V}{R}$

Substitute 0.2 amp for I and 18 ohms for R: $\quad 0.2 \text{ amp} = \dfrac{V}{18 \text{ ohms}}$

Multiply both sides by 18 ohms: $\quad 0.2 \text{ amp} \cdot 18 \text{ ohms} = V$

Simplify: $\quad 3.6 \text{ volts} = V$

ANSWER The voltage is 3.6 volts.

Finding Areas

The area of a figure is the amount of surface the figure covers.

Area is measured in square units, such as square meters (m^2) or square centimeters (cm^2). Formulas for the areas of three common geometric figures are shown below.

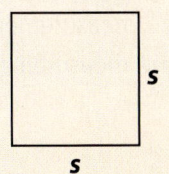

Area = (side length)^2
$A = s^2$

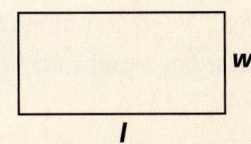

Area = length × width
$A = lw$

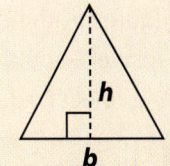

Area = $\frac{1}{2}$ × base × height
$A = \frac{1}{2} bh$

Example

Each face of a halite crystal is a square like the one shown. You can find the area of the square by using the steps below.

Write the formula for the area of a square: $A = s^2$

Substitute 3 mm for s: $= (3 \text{ mm})^2$

Simplify: $= 9 \text{ mm}^2$

ANSWER The area of the square is 9 square millimeters.

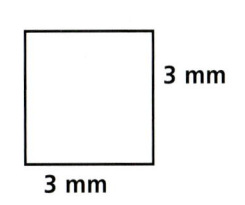

Finding Volumes

The volume of a solid is the amount of space contained by the solid.

Volume is measured in cubic units, such as cubic meters (m^3) or cubic centimeters (cm^3). The volume of a rectangular prism is given by the formula shown below.

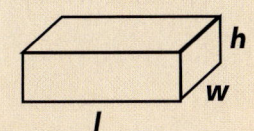

Volume = length × width × height
$V = lwh$

Example

A topaz crystal is a rectangular prism like the one shown. You can find the volume of the prism by using the steps below.

Write the formula for the volume of a rectangular prism: $V = lwh$

Substitute dimensions: $= 20 \text{ mm} \times 12 \text{ mm} \times 10 \text{ mm}$

Simplify: $= 2400 \text{ mm}^3$

ANSWER The volume of the rectangular prism is 2400 cubic millimeters.

Using Significant Figures

The **significant figures** in a decimal are the digits that are warranted by the accuracy of a measuring device.

When you perform a calculation with measurements, the number of significant figures to include in the result depends in part on the number of significant figures in the measurements. When you multiply or divide measurements, your answer should have only as many significant figures as the measurement with the fewest significant figures.

Example

Using a balance and a graduated cylinder filled with water, you determined that a marble has a mass of 8.0 grams and a volume of 3.5 cubic centimeters. To calculate the density of the marble, divide the mass by the volume.

Write the formula for density: $\text{Density} = \dfrac{\text{mass}}{\text{Volume}}$

Substitute measurements: $= \dfrac{8.0 \text{ g}}{3.5 \text{ cm}^3}$

Use a calculator to divide: $\approx 2.285714286 \text{ g/cm}^3$

ANSWER Because the mass and the volume have two significant figures each, give the density to two significant figures. The marble has a density of 2.3 grams per cubic centimeter.

Using Scientific Notation

Scientific notation is a shorthand way to write very large or very small numbers. For example, 73,500,000,000,000,000,000,000 kg is the mass of the Moon. In scientific notation, it is 7.35×10^{22} kg.

Example

You can convert from standard form to scientific notation.

Standard Form	Scientific Notation
720,000	7.2×10^5
5 decimal places left	Exponent is 5.
0.000291	2.91×10^{-4}
4 decimal places right	Exponent is −4.

You can convert from scientific notation to standard form.

Scientific Notation	Standard Form
4.63×10^7	46,300,000
Exponent is 7.	7 decimal places right
1.08×10^{-6}	0.00000108
Exponent is −6.	6 decimal places left

Note-Taking Handbook

Note-Taking Strategies

Taking notes as you read helps you understand the information. The notes you take can also be used as a study guide for later review. This handbook presents several ways to organize your notes.

Content Frame

1. Make a chart in which each column represents a category.
2. Give each column a heading.
3. Write details under the headings.

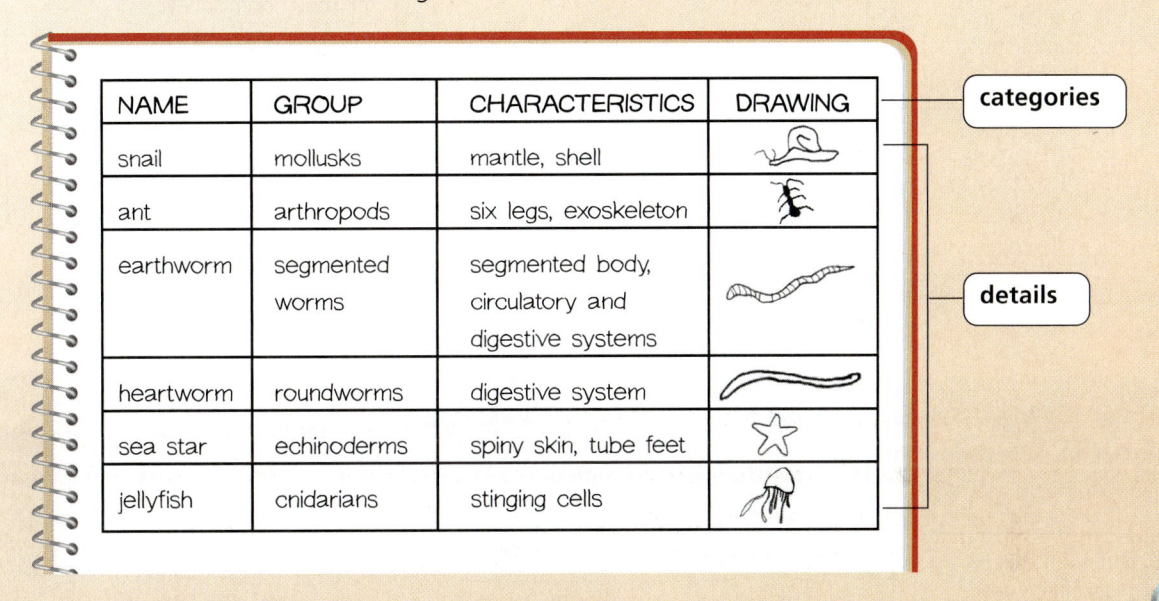

NAME	GROUP	CHARACTERISTICS	DRAWING
snail	mollusks	mantle, shell	
ant	arthropods	six legs, exoskeleton	
earthworm	segmented worms	segmented body, circulatory and digestive systems	
heartworm	roundworms	digestive system	
sea star	echinoderms	spiny skin, tube feet	
jellyfish	cnidarians	stinging cells	

- categories (top row)
- details (rows below)

Combination Notes

1. For each new idea or concept, write an informal outline of the information.
2. Make a sketch to illustrate the concept, and label it.

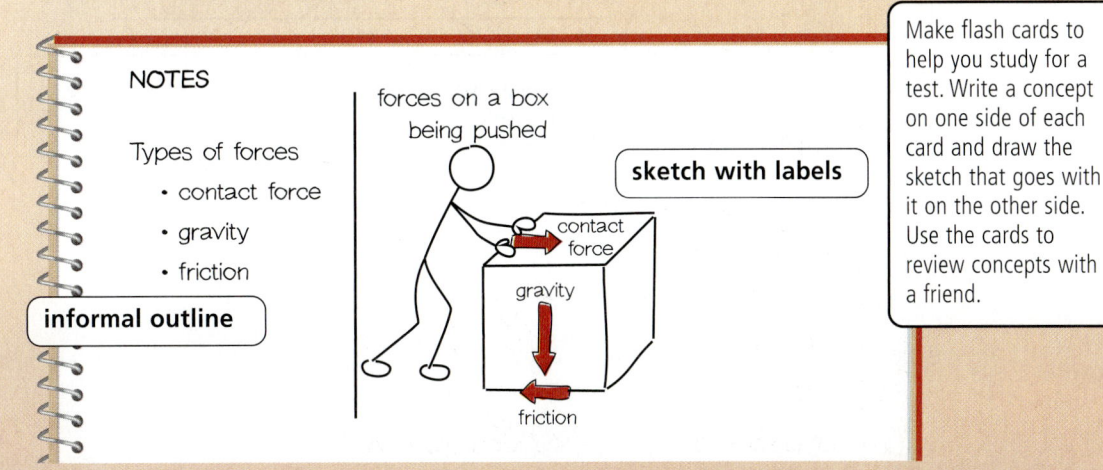

NOTES

Types of forces
- contact force
- gravity
- friction

informal outline

forces on a box being pushed

sketch with labels

- contact force
- gravity
- friction

Make flash cards to help you study for a test. Write a concept on one side of each card and draw the sketch that goes with it on the other side. Use the cards to review concepts with a friend.

Main Idea and Detail Notes

1. In the left-hand column of a two-column chart, list main ideas. The blue headings express main ideas throughout this textbook.
2. In the right-hand column, write details that expand on each main idea.

You can shorten the headings in your chart. Be sure to use the most important words.

> When studying for tests, cover up the detail notes column with a sheet of paper. Then use each main idea to form a question—such as "How does latitude affect climate?" Answer the question, and then uncover the detail notes column to check your answer.

MAIN IDEAS	DETAIL NOTES
1. Latitude affects climate. *(main idea 1)*	1. Places close to the equator are usually warmer than places close to the poles. 1. Latitude has the same effect in both hemispheres. *(details about main idea 1)*
2. Altitude affects climate. *(main idea 2)*	2. Temperature decreases with altitude. 2. Altitude can overcome the effect of latitude on temperature. *(details about main idea 2)*

Main Idea Web

1. Write a main idea in a box.
2. Add boxes around it with related vocabulary terms and important details.

> You can find definitions near highlighted terms.

- **definition of *work*:** Work is the use of force to move an object.
- **formula:** Work = force · distance
- **main idea:** Force is necessary to do work.
- **definition of *joule*:** The joule is the unit used to measure work.
- **important detail:** Work depends on the size of a force.

NOTE-TAKING HANDBOOK

Mind Map

1. Write a main idea in the center.
2. Add details that relate to one another and to the main idea.

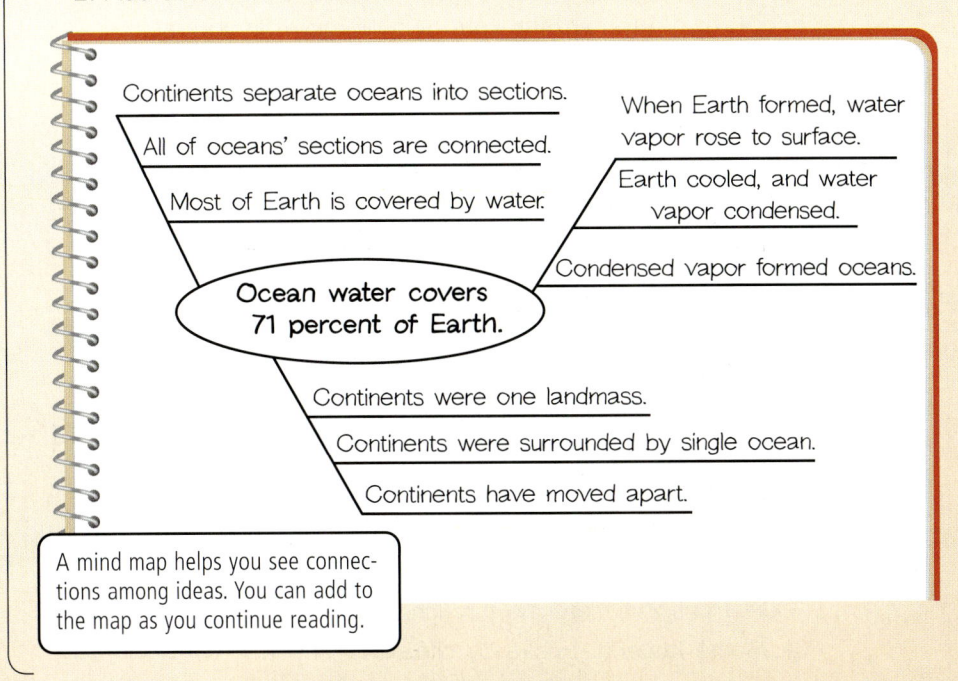

- Continents separate oceans into sections.
- All of oceans' sections are connected.
- Most of Earth is covered by water.
- When Earth formed, water vapor rose to surface.
- Earth cooled, and water vapor condensed.
- Condensed vapor formed oceans.

Ocean water covers 71 percent of Earth.

- Continents were one landmass.
- Continents were surrounded by single ocean.
- Continents have moved apart.

A mind map helps you see connections among ideas. You can add to the map as you continue reading.

Supporting Main Ideas

1. Write a main idea in a box.
2. Add boxes underneath with information—such as reasons, explanations, and examples—that supports the main idea.

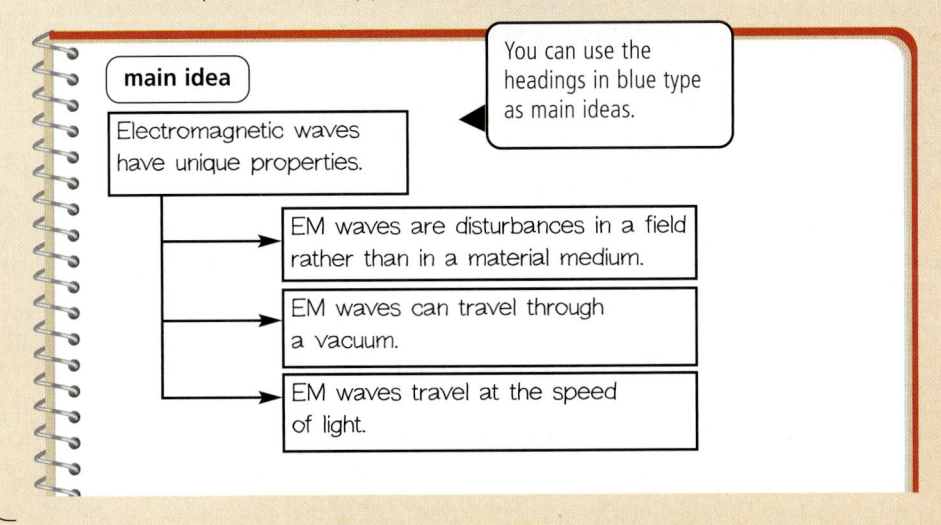

main idea

Electromagnetic waves have unique properties.

You can use the headings in blue type as main ideas.

- EM waves are disturbances in a field rather than in a material medium.
- EM waves can travel through a vacuum.
- EM waves travel at the speed of light.

Note-Taking Handbook R47

Outline

1. Copy the chapter title and headings from the book in the form of an outline.
2. Add notes that summarize in your own words what you read.

Cell Processes — **1st key idea**
I. Cells capture and release energy. — **1st subpoint of I**
   A. All cells need energy.
   B. Some cells capture light energy. — **2nd subpoint of I**
      1. Process of photosynthesis — **1st detail about B**
      2. Chloroplasts (site of photosynthesis) — **2nd detail about B**
      3. Carbon dioxide and water as raw materials
      4. Glucose and oxygen as products
   C. All cells release energy.
      1. Process of cellular respiration
      2. Fermentation of sugar to carbon dioxide
      3. Bacteria that carry out fermentation
II. Cells transport materials through membranes.
   A. Some materials move by diffusion.
      1. Particle movement from higher to lower concentrations
      2. Movement of water through membrane (osmosis)
   B. Some transport requires energy.
      1. Active transport
      2. Examples of active transport

Correct Outline Form
Include a title.

Arrange key ideas, subpoints, and details as shown.

Indent the divisions of the outline as shown.

Use the same grammatical form for items of the same rank. For example, if A is a sentence, B must also be a sentence.

You must have at least two main ideas or subpoints. That is, every A must be followed by a B, and every 1 must be followed by a 2.

Concept Map

1. Write an important concept in a large oval.
2. Add details related to the concept in smaller ovals.
3. Write linking words on arrows that connect the ovals.

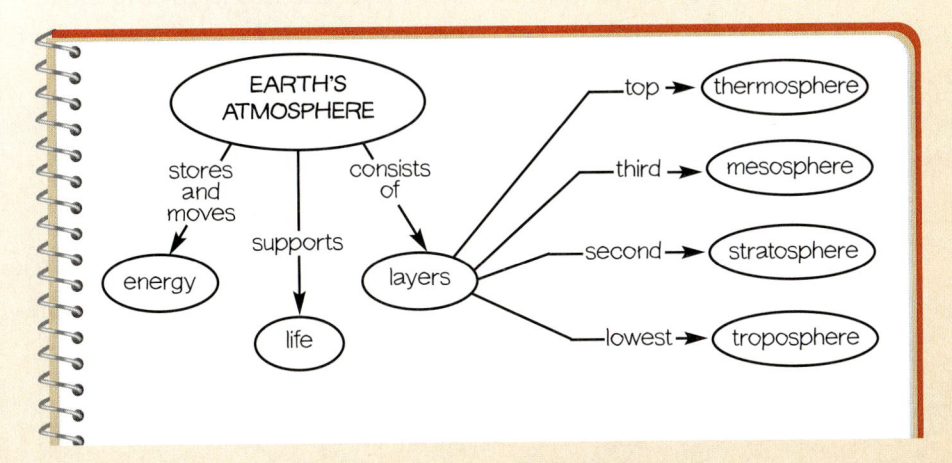

EARTH'S ATMOSPHERE
- stores and moves → energy
- supports → life
- consists of → layers
  - top → thermosphere
  - third → mesosphere
  - second → stratosphere
  - lowest → troposphere

The main ideas or concepts can often be found in the blue headings. An example is "The atmosphere stores and moves energy." Use nouns from these concepts in the ovals, and use the verb or verbs on the lines.

Venn Diagram

1. Draw two overlapping circles, one for each item that you are comparing.
2. In the overlapping section, list the characteristics that are shared by both items.
3. In the outer sections, list the characteristics that are peculiar to each item.
4. Write a summary that describes the information in the Venn diagram.

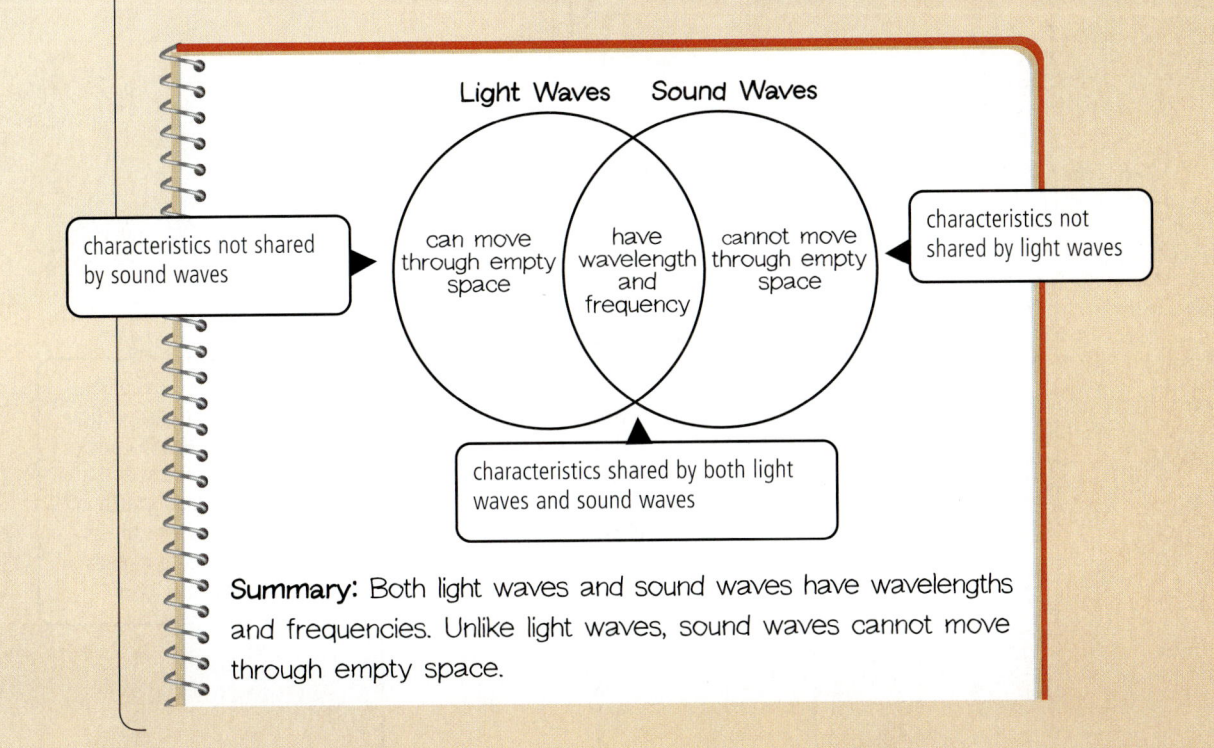

Light Waves | Sound Waves

- characteristics not shared by sound waves: can move through empty space
- characteristics shared by both light waves and sound waves: have wavelength and frequency
- characteristics not shared by light waves: cannot move through empty space

Summary: Both light waves and sound waves have wavelengths and frequencies. Unlike light waves, sound waves cannot move through empty space.

Vocabulary Strategies

Important terms are highlighted in this book. A definition of each term can be found in the sentence or paragraph where the term appears. You can also find definitions in the Glossary. Taking notes about vocabulary terms helps you understand and remember what you read.

Description Wheel

1. Write a term inside a circle.
2. Write words that describe the term on "spokes" attached to the circle.

When studying for a test with a friend, read the phrases on the spokes one at a time until your friend identifies the correct term.

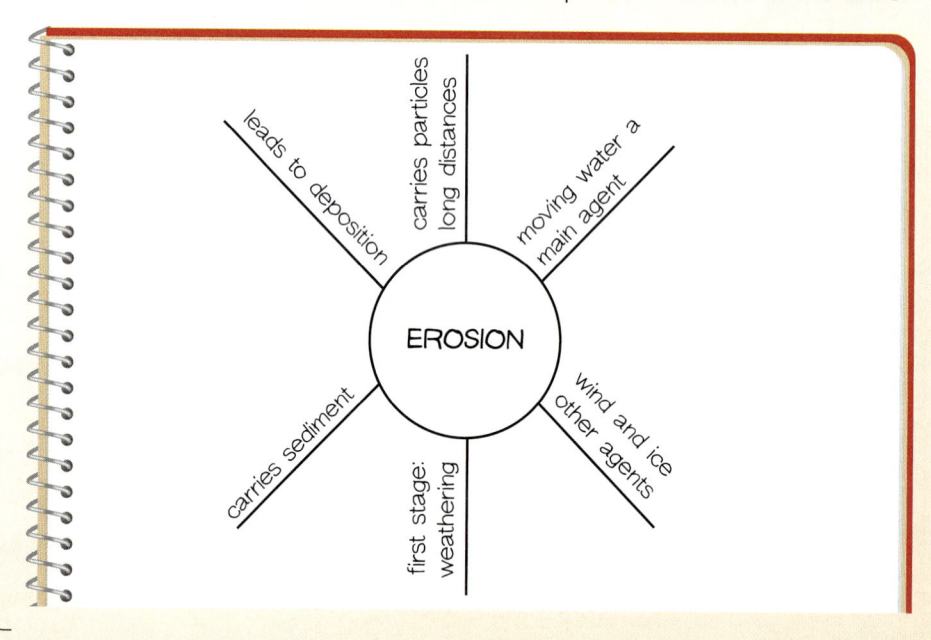

EROSION
- leads to deposition
- carries particles long distances
- moving water a main agent
- wind and ice other agents
- first stage: weathering
- carries sediment

Four Square

1. Write a term in the center.
2. Write details in the four areas around the term.

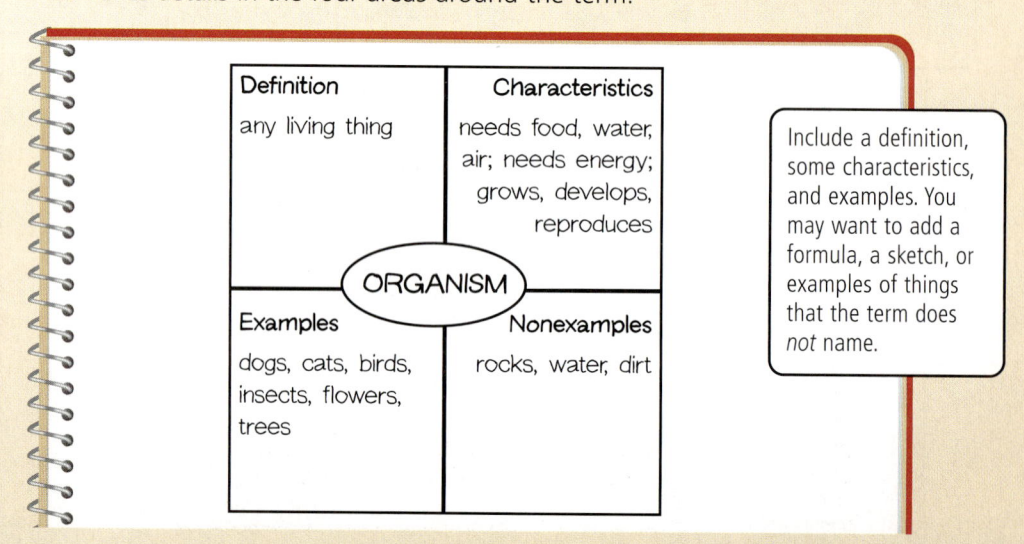

Definition	Characteristics
any living thing	needs food, water, air; needs energy; grows, develops, reproduces
Examples	Nonexamples
dogs, cats, birds, insects, flowers, trees	rocks, water, dirt

ORGANISM

Include a definition, some characteristics, and examples. You may want to add a formula, a sketch, or examples of things that the term does *not* name.

Frame Game

1. Write a term in the center.
2. Frame the term with details.

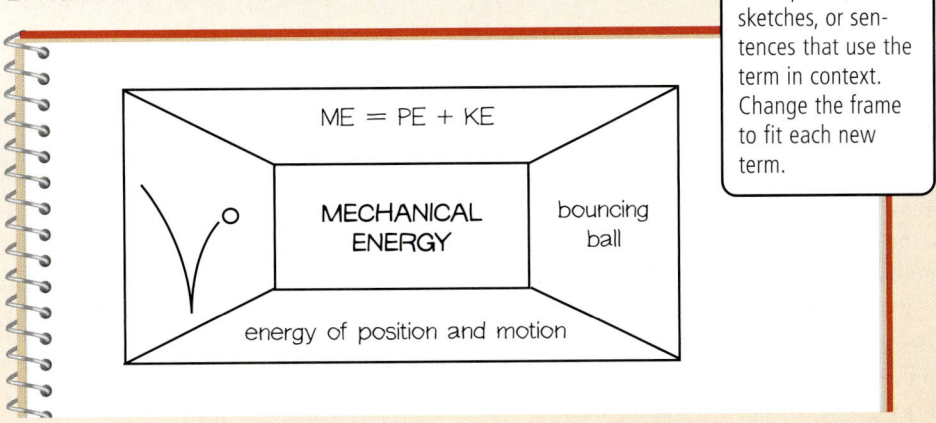

Include examples, descriptions, sketches, or sentences that use the term in context. Change the frame to fit each new term.

ME = PE + KE

MECHANICAL ENERGY

bouncing ball

energy of position and motion

Magnet Word

1. Write a term on the magnet.
2. On the lines, add details related to the term.

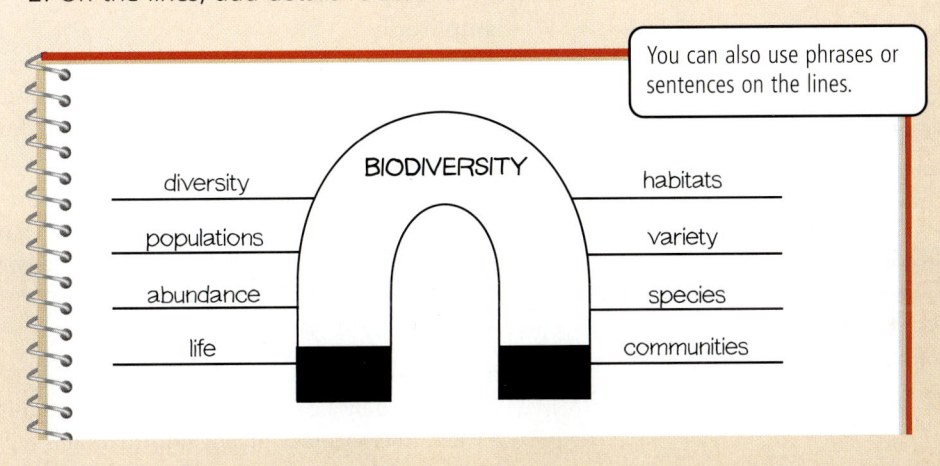

You can also use phrases or sentences on the lines.

BIODIVERSITY

diversity — habitats
populations — variety
abundance — species
life — communities

Word Triangle

1. Write a term and its definition in the bottom section.
2. In the middle section, write a sentence in which the term is used correctly.
3. In the top section, draw a small picture to illustrate the term.

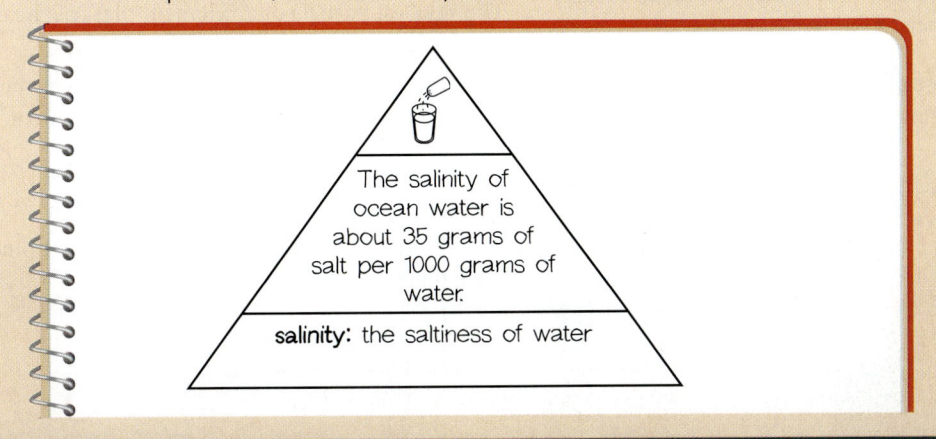

The salinity of ocean water is about 35 grams of salt per 1000 grams of water.

salinity: the saltiness of water

Note-Taking Handbook R51

Glossary

A

absorption (uhb-SAWRP-shuhn)
The disappearance of a wave into a medium. When a wave is absorbed, the energy transferred by the wave is converted into another form of energy, usually thermal energy. (p. D93)

absorción La desaparición de una onda dentro de un medio. Cuando se absorbe una onda, la energía transferida por la onda se convierte a otra forma de energía, normalmente a energía térmica.

acceleration
The rate at which velocity changes over time. (p. C25)

aceleración La razón a la cual la velocidad cambia con respecto al tiempo.

acid
A substance that can donate a proton to another substance and has a pH below 7. (p. B126)

ácido Una sustancia que puede donar un protón a otra sustancia y que tiene un pH menor a 7.

acoustics (uh-KOO-stihks)
The scientific study of sound; the behavior of sound waves inside a space. (p. D55)

acústica El estudio científico del sonido; el comportamiento de las ondas sonoras dentro de un espacio.

air resistance
The fluid friction due to air. (p. C89)

resistencia del aire La fricción fluida debida al aire.

alloy
A solid mixture composed of a metal and one or more other substances. (p. B134)

aleación Una mezcla sólida compuesta de un metal y una o más sustancias adicionales.

alternating current AC
Electric current that reverses direction at regular intervals. (p. E97)

corriente alterna Corriente eléctrica que invierte su dirección a intervalos regulares.

ampere amp
The unit of measurement of electric current, which is equal to one coulomb per second. The number of amps flowing through a circuit equals the circuit's amperage. (p. E29)

amperio La unidad de medición de la corriente eléctrica, la cual es igual a un culombio por segundo. El número de amperios fluyendo por un circuito es igual al amperaje del circuito.

amplification
The strengthening of an electrical signal, often used to increase the intensity of a sound wave. (p. D55)

amplificación El fortalecimiento de una señal eléctrica, a menudo se usa para aumentar la intensidad de una onda sonora.

amplitude
The maximum distance that a disturbance causes a medium to move from its rest position; the distance between a crest or trough of a wave and line through the center of a wave. (p. D17)

amplitud La distancia máxima que se mueve un medio desde su posición de reposo debido a una perturbación; la distancia entre una cresta o valle de una onda y una línea que pasa por el centro de la onda.

analog
Represented by a continuous but varying quantity, such as a wave. In electronics, analog information is represented by a continuous but varying electrical signal. (p. E60)

análogo Que es representado por una cantidad variante pero continua, como una onda. En la electrónica, la información análoga se representa mediante una señal eléctrica continua pero variante.

atom
The smallest particle of an element that has the chemical properties of that element. (p. A16)

átomo La partícula más pequeña de un elemento que tiene las propiedades químicas de ese elemento.

atomic mass
The average mass of the atoms of an element. (p. B17)

masa atómica La masa promedio de los átomos de un elemento.

R52 Physical Science

atomic mass number
The total number of protons and neutrons in an atom's nucleus.

número de masa atómica El número total de protones y neutrones que hay en el núcleo de un átomo.

atomic number
The number of protons in the nucleus of an atom. (p. B12)

número atómico El número de protones en el núcleo de un átomo.

B

base
A substance that can accept a proton from another substance and has a pH above 7. (p. B126)

base Una sustancia que puede aceptar un protón de otra sustancia y que tiene un pH superior a 7.

Bernoulli's principle
A statement that describes the effects of movement on fluid pressure. According to this principle, an increase in the speed of the motion of a fluid decreases the pressure within the fluid. (p. C100)

principio de Bernoulli Un enunciado que describe los efectos del movimiento sobre la presión de un líquido. De acuerdo a este principio, un aumento en la velocidad del movimiento de un fluido disminuye la presión dentro del líquido

binary code
A coding system in which information is represented by two figures, such as 1 and 0. (p. E58)

código binario Un sistema de codificación en el cual la información se representa con dos números, como el 1 y el 0.

bioluminescence
The production of light by living organisms. (p. D89)

bioluminiscencia La producción de luz por parte de organismos vivos.

boiling
A process by which a substance changes from its liquid state to its gas state. The liquid is heated to a specific temperature at which bubbles of vapor form within the liquid. (p. A54)

ebullición Un proceso mediante el cual una sustancia cambia de su estado líquido a su estado gaseoso se calienta el líquido a una determinada temperatura a la cual se forman burbujas de vapor dentro del líquido.

boiling point
The temperature at which a substance changes from its liquid state to its gas state through boiling. (p. A54)

punto de ebullición La temperatura a la cual una sustancia cambia de su estado líquido a su estado gaseoso mediante ebullición.

bond energy
The amount of energy in a chemical bond between atoms.

energía de enlace La cantidad de energía que hay en un enlace químico entre átomos.

buoyant force
The upward force on objects in a fluid; often called buoyancy. (p. C98)

fuerza flotante La fuerza hacia arriba que ejerce un fluido sobre un objeto inmerso en él, a menudo llamada flotación.

C

calorie
The amount of energy needed to increase the temperature of one gram of water by one degree Celsius. (p. A112)

caloría La cantidad de energía que se necesita para aumentar la temperatura de un gramo de agua un grado centígrado.

carbohydrate
A type of carbon-based molecule in living things. Carbohydrates include sugars and starches used for energy or as structural materials. Carbohydrate molecules contain carbon, hydrogen, and oxygen atoms.

carbohidrato Un tipo de molécula de los organismos vivos basada en el carbono. Los carbohidratos incluyen los azúcares y los almidones usados como fuente de energía o como materiales estructurales. Las moléculas de los carbohidrato contienen átomos de carbono, hidrógeno y oxígeno.

catalyst
A substance that increases the rate of a chemical reaction but is not consumed in the reaction. (p. B76)

catalizador Una sustancia que aumenta lel a ritmo velocidad de una reacción química pero que no es consumida en la reacción.

centripetal force (sehn-TRIHP-ih-tuhl)
Any force that keeps an object moving in a circle. (p. C54)

fuerza centrípeta Cualquier fuerza que mantiene a un objeto moviéndose en forma circular.

Glossary R53

chemical change
A change of one substance into another substance. (p. A46)

cambio químico La transformación de una sustancia a otra sustancia.

chemical formula
An expression that shows the number and types of atoms joined in a compound. (p. B43)

fórmula química Una expresión que muestra el número y los tipos de átomos unidos en un compuesto.

chemical property
A characteristic of a substance that describes how it can form a new substance. (p. A46)

propiedad química Una característica de una sustancia que describe como puede formar una nueva sustancia.

chemical reaction
The process by which chemical changes occur. In a chemical reaction, atoms are rearranged, and chemical bonds are broken and formed. (p. B69)

reacción química El proceso mediante el cual ocurren cambios químicos. En una reacción química, los átomos se reorganizan y los enlaces químicos se rompen y se vuelven a formar.

circuit
A closed path through which charge can flow. (p. E43)

circuito Una trayectoria cerrada por la cual puede fluir una carga.

coefficient
The number before a chemical formula that indicates how many molecules are involved in a chemical reaction.

coeficiente El número anterior a una fórmula química que indica cuántas moléculas están involucradas en una reaccíon química.

collision
A situation in which two objects in close contact exchange energy and momentum. (p. C66)

colisión Situación en la cual dos objetos en contacto cercano intercambian energía y momento.

compound
A substance made up of two or more different types of atoms bonded together. (p. A23)

compuesto Una sustancia formada por dos o más diferentes tipos de átomos enlazados.

compound machine
A machine that is made up of two or more simple machines. (p. C164)

máquina compuesta Una máquina que está hecha de dos o más máquinas simples.

computer
An electronic device that processes digital information. (p. E61)

computadora Un aparato electrónico que procesa información digital.

concave
Curved inward toward the center, like the inside of a spoon. (p. D116)

cóncavo Dicho de una superficie con curvatura hacia dentro, como la parte interna de una cuchara.

concentration
The amount of solute dissolved in a solvent at a given temperature.

concentración La cantidad de soluto disuelta en un solvente a una temperatura determinada.

condensation
The process by which a gas becomes a liquid. (p. A55)

condensación El proceso mediante el cual un gas se convierte en un líquido.

conduction
The process by which energy is transferred from a warmer object to a cooler object by means of physical contact. (p. A117)

conducción El proceso mediante el cual se transfiere energía de un objeto más caliente a un objeto más frío por medio de contacto físico.

conductor
1. A material that transfers energy easily. (p. A117)
2. A material that transfers electric charge easily. (p. E22)

conductor 1. Un material que transfiere energía fácilmente. 2. Un material que transfiere cargas eléctricas fácilmente.

convection
A process by which energy is transferred in gases and liquids, occurring when a warmer, less dense area of gas or liquid is pushed up by a cooler, more dense area of the gas or liquid. (p. A118)

convección Un proceso mediante el cual se transfiere energía en los gases y los líquidos; ocurre cuando un área más fría y más densa del gas o del líquido empuja hacia arriba un área más caliente y menos densa de gas o de líquido.

convex
Curved outward, like the underside of a spoon. (p. D116)

convexo Dicho de una superficie con curvatura hacia afuera, como la parte externa de una cuchara.

cornea (KAWR-nee-uh)
A transparent membrane that covers the eye. (p. D127)

córnea Una membrana transparente que cubre el ojo.

covalent bond
A pair of electrons shared by two atoms. (p. B50)

enlace covalente Un par de electrones compartidos por dos átomos.

crest
The highest point, or peak, of a wave. (p. D17)

cresta El punto más alto, o el pico, de una onda.

cycle
n. A series of events or actions that repeat themselves regularly; a physical and/or chemical process in which one material continually changes locations and/or forms. Examples include the water cycle, the carbon cycle, and the rock cycle.

v. To move through a repeating series of events or actions.

ciclo *s.* Una serie de eventos o acciones que se repiten regularmente; un proceso físico y/o químico en el cual un material cambia continuamente de lugar y/o forma. Ejemplos: el ciclo del agua, el ciclo del carbono y el ciclo de las rocas.

D

data
Information gathered by observation or experimentation that can be used in calculating or reasoning. *Data* is a plural word; the singular is *datum*.

datos Información reunida mediante observación o experimentación y que se puede usar para calcular o para razonar.

decibel dB
The unit used to measure the intensity of a sound wave. (p. D52)

decibel La unidad que se usa para medir la intensidad de una onda sonora.

degree
Evenly divided units of a temperature scale. (p. A106)

grado Unidades de una escala de temperatura distribuidas uniformemente.

density
A property of matter representing the mass per unit volume. (pp. A43, C99)

densidad Una propiedad de la materia que representa la masa por unidad de volumen.

diffraction
The spreading out of waves as they pass through an opening or around the edges of an obstacle. (p. D26)

difracción La dispersión de las ondas al pasar por una apertura o alrededor de los bordes de un obstáculo.

diffuse reflection
The reflection of parallel light rays in many different directions. (p. D114)

reflexión difusa La reflexión de rayos de luz paralelos en muchas direcciones diferentes.

digital
Represented by numbers. In electronics, digital information is represented by the numbers 1 and 0, signaled by a circuit that is either on or off. (p. E58)

digital Que es representado por números. En la electrónica, la información digital es representada por los números 1 y 0, señalados por un circuito que está encendido o apagado.

dilute
adj. Having a low concentration of solute. (p. B118)

v. To add solvent in order to decrease the concentration of a solution.

diluido *adj.* Que tiene una baja concentración de soluto.

diluir *v.* Agregar solvente para disminuir la concentración de una solución.

direct current DC
Electric current that flows in one direction only. (p. E97)

corriente directa Corriente eléctrica que fluye en una sola dirección.

Doppler effect
The change in perceived pitch that occurs when the source or the one who hears the sound is moving. (p. D50)

efecto Doppler El cambio en el tono percibido que ocurre cuando la fuente o el receptor de un sonido está en movimiento.

Glossary R55

E

echolocation
The sending out of high-pitched sound waves and the interpretation of the returning echoes. (p. D59)

ecolocación El envío de ondas sonoras de tono alto y la interpretación de los ecos que regresan.

efficiency
The percentage of the input work done on a machine that the machine can return in output work. A machine's output work divided by its input work and multiplied by 100. (p. C150)

eficiencia El porcentaje del trabajo de entrada suministrado a una máquina que la máquina puede devolver como trabajo de salida. El trabajo de salida de una máquina dividido por su trabajo de entrada y multiplicado por cien.

electric cell
A device that produces electric current using the chemical or physical properties of different materials. A battery consists of two or more cells linked together. (p. E31)

celda eléctrica Un aparato que produce corriente eléctrica usando las propiedades químicas o físicas de diferentes materiales. Una pila consiste de dos o más celdas conectadas.

electric charge
A property that allows one object to exert an electric force on another object without touching it. Electric charge can be positive or negative: positive charge is a property of the proton, while negative charge is a property of the electron. (p. E10)

carga eléctrica Una propiedad que permite a un objeto ejercer una fuerza eléctrica sobre otro objeto sin tocarlo. La carga eléctrica puede ser positiva o negativa: la carga positiva es una propiedad del protón mientras que la carga negativa es una propiedad del electrón.

electric current
A continuous flow of electric charge, which is measured in amperes. (p. E28)

corriente eléctrica Un flujo continuo de una carga eléctrica, el cual se mide en amperios.

electric field
An area surrounding a charged object, within which the object can exert an electric force on another object without touching it. (p. E10)

campo eléctrico Un área que rodea un objeto con carga, dentro del cual el objeto puede ejercer una fuerza eléctrica sobre otro objeto sin tocarlo.

electric potential
The amount of potential energy per unit charge that a static charge or electric current has. Electric potential is measured in volts and is often called voltage. (p. E19)

potencial eléctrico La cantidad de energía potencial por unidad de carga que tiene una carga estática o una corriente eléctrica. El potencial eléctrico se mide en voltios y a menudo se llama voltaje.

electric power
The rate at which electrical energy is generated from, or converted into, another source of energy, such as kinetic energy. (p. E102)

potencia eléctrica El ritmo al cual se genera energía eléctrica a partir de, o se convierte en, otra fuente de energía, como energía cinética.

electromagnet
A magnet that consists of a piece of iron or steel inside a coil of current-carrying wire. (p. E90)

electroimán Un imán que consiste de un pedazo de hierro o de acero dentro de una bobina de alambre por la cual fluye una corriente eléctrica.

electromagnetic spectrum   EM spectrum
The range of all electromagnetic frequencies, including the following types (from lowest to highest frequency): radio waves, microwaves, infrared light, visible light, ultraviolet light, x-rays, and gamma rays. (p. D80)

espectro electromagnético La escala de todas las frecuencias electromagnéticas, incluyendo los siguientes tipos (de la frecuencia más baja a la más alta): ondas de radio, microondas, luz infrarroja, luz visible, luz ultravioleta, rayos X y rayos gamma.

electromagnetic wave   EM wave
A type of wave, such as a light wave or radio wave, that does not require a medium to travel; a disturbance that transfers energy through a field. (p. D73)

onda electromagnética Un tipo de onda, como una onda luminosa o de radio, que no requiere un medio para propagarse; una perturbación que transfiere energía a través de un campo.

electromagnetism
Magnetism that results from the flow of electric charge. (p. E89)

electromagnetismo Magnetismo que resulta del flujo de una carga eléctrica.

electron
A negatively charged particle located outside an atom's nucleus. An electron is about 2000 times smaller than either a proton or neutron. (p. B11)

electrón Una partícula con carga negativa localizada fuera del núcleo de un átomo. Un electrón es como aproximadamente 2000 veces más pequeño que un protón o un neutrón.

electronic
adj. Operating by means of an electrical signal. An electronic device is a device that uses electric current to represent coded information. (p. E57)

n. An electronic device or system, such as a computer, calculator, CD player, or game system.

electrónico *adj.* Que opera por medio de una señal eléctrica. Un aparato electrónico es un aparato que usa corriente eléctrica para representar información codificada.

element
A substance that cannot be broken down into a simpler substance by ordinary chemical changes. An element consists of atoms of only one type. (p. A22)

elemento Una sustancia que no puede descomponerse en otra sustancia más simple por medio de cambios químicos normales. Un elemento consta de átomos de un solo tipo.

endothermic reaction
A chemical reaction that absorbs energy. (p. B87)

reacción endotérmica Una reacción química que absorbe energía.

energy
The ability to do work or to cause a change. For example, the energy of a moving bowling ball knocks over pins; energy from food allows animals to move and to grow; and energy from the Sun heats Earth's surface and atmosphere, which causes air to move. (p. A72)

energía La capacidad para trabajar o causar un cambio. Por ejemplo, la energía de una bola de boliche en movimiento tumba los pinos; la energía proveniente de su alimento permite a los animales moverse y crecer; la energía del Sol calienta la superficie y la atmósfera de la Tierra, lo que ocasiona que el aire se mueva.

energy efficiency
A measurement of usable energy after an energy conversion; the ratio of usable energy to the total energy after an energy conversion. (p. A83)

eficiencia energética Una medida de la energía utilizable después de una conversión energética; la razón entre la energía utilizable y el total de energía después de una conversión energética.

enzyme
A type of protein that is a catalyst for chemical reactions in living things. (p. B159)

enzima Un tipo de proteína que es un catalizador de reacciones químicas en organismos vivos.

evaporation
A process by which a substance changes from its liquid state to its gas state by random particle movement. Evaporation usually occurs at the surface of a liquid over a wide range of temperatures. (p. A53)

evaporación Un proceso mediante el cual una sustancia cambia de su estado líquido a su estado gaseoso por medio del movimiento aleatorio de las partículas. La evaporación normalmente ocurre en la superficie de un líquido en una amplia gama de temperaturas.

exothermic reaction
A chemical reaction that releases energy. (p. B87)

reacción exotérmica Una reacción química que libera energía.

experiment
An organized procedure to study something under controlled conditions. (p. xl)

experimento Un procedimiento organizado para estudiar algo bajo condiciones controladas.

F

fiber optics
Technology based on the use of laser light to send signals through transparent wires called optical fibers. This technology is often used in communications. (p. D137)

fibra óptica Tecnología basada en el uso de luz de láser para mandar señales por alambres transparentes llamados fibras ópticas. Esta tecnología se usa a menudo en comunicaciones.

field
An area around an object where the object can apply a force—such as gravitational force, magnetic force, or electrical force—on another object without touching it.

campo Un área alrededor de un objeto donde el objeto puede aplicar una fuerza, como fuerza gravitacional, fuerza magnética o fuerza eléctrica, sobre otro objeto sin tocarlo.

fluid
A substance that can flow easily, such as a gas or a liquid. (p. C88)

fluido Una sustancia que fluye fácilmente, como por ejemplo un gas o un líquido.

fluorescence (flu-REHS-uhns)
A phenomenon in which a material absorbs electromagnetic radiation of one wavelength and gives off electromagnetic radiation of a different wavelength. (p. D91)

fluorescencia Un fenómeno en el cual un material absorbe radiación electromagnética de una longitud de onda y emite radiación electromagnética de longitud de onda diferente.

focal length
The distance from the center of a convex lens to its focal point. (p. D123)

distancia focal La distancia del centro de un lente convexo a su punto focal.

focal point
The point at which parallel light rays reflected from a concave mirror come together; the point at which parallel light rays refracted by a convex lens come together. (p. D117)

punto focal El punto en el cual se unen los rayos paralelos de luz reflejados por un espejo cóncavo; el punto en el cual se unen los rayos paralelos de luz refractados por un lente convexo.

force
A push or a pull; something that changes the motion of an object. (p. C41)

fuerza Un empuje o un jalón; algo que cambia el movimiento de un objeto.

freezing
The process by which a substance changes from its liquid state into its solid state. (p. A52)

congelación El proceso mediante el cual una sustancia cambia de su estado líquido a su estado sólido.

freezing point
The temperature at which a substance changes from its liquid state to its solid state through freezing. (p. A52)

punto de congelación La temperatura a la cual una sustancia cambia de su estado líquido a su estado sólido mediante congelación.

frequency
The number of waves that pass a fixed point in a given amount of time, usually one second; the number of cycles per unit time. (p. D17)

frecuencia El número de ondas que pasan un punto fijo en un período de tiempo determinado, normalmente un segundo; el número de ciclos por unidad de tiempo.

friction
A force that resists the motion between two surfaces in contact. (p. C85)

fricción Una fuerza que resiste el movimiento entre dos superficies en contacto.

fulcrum
A fixed point around which a lever rotates. (p. C155)

fulcro Un punto fijo alrededor del cual gira una palanca.

G

gamma rays
Part of the electromagnetic spectrum that consists of waves with the highest frequencies; electromagnetic waves with frequencies ranging from more than 10^{19} hertz to more than 10^{24} hertz. (p. D86)

rayos gamma Parte del espectro electromagnético que consiste de ondas con las frecuencias más altas; las ondas electromagnéticas con frecuencias de más de 10^{19} hertzios hasta más de 10^{24} hertzios.

gas
Matter with no definite volume and no definite shape. The molecules in a gas are very far apart, and the amount of space between them can change easily. (p. A28)

gas Materia sin volumen definido ni forma definida. Las moléculas en un gas están muy separadas unas de otras, y la cantidad de espacio entre ellas puede cambiar fácilmente.

generator
A device that converts kinetic energy, or the energy of motion, into electrical energy. Generators produce electric current by rotating a magnet within a coil of wire or rotating a coil of wire within a magnetic field. (p. E96)

generador Un aparato que convierte energía cinética, o la energía del movimiento, a energía eléctrica. Los generadores producen corriente eléctrica al girar un imán dentro de una bobina de alambre o haciendo rotar una bobina de alambre dentro de un campo magnético.

gravity
The force that objects exert on each other because of their mass. (p. C77)

gravedad La fuerza que los objetos ejercen entre sí debido a su masa.

grounding
The creation of a harmless, low-resistance path—a ground—for electricity to follow. Grounding is an important electrical safety procedure. (p. E25)

conexión a tierra La creación de una trayectoria inofensiva, de baja resistencia—una tierra—para que la siga la electricidad. La conexión a tierra es un importante procedimiento de seguridad eléctrica.

group
A vertical column in the periodic table of the elements. Elements in a group have similar properties. (p. B22)

grupo Una columna vertical en la tabla periódica de los elementos. Los elementos en un grupo tienen propiedades similares.

H

half-life
The amount of time it takes for half of the nuclei of a radioactive isotope to decay into atoms of another element. (p. B32)

vida media La cantidad de tiempo que se necesita para que le toma a la mitad del núcleo de un isótopo radioactivo se en descomponganerse en átomos de otro elemento.

heat
1. The flow of energy from an object at a higher temperature to an object at a lower temperature. (p. A110) 2. Energy that is transferred from a warmer object to a cooler object.

calor 1. El flujo de energía de un objeto a mayor temperatura a un objeto a menor temperatura. 2. Energía que se transfiere de un objeto más caliente a un objeto más frío.

hertz Hz
The unit used to measure frequency. One hertz is equal to one complete cycle per second. (p. D46)

hercio La unidad usada para medir frecuencia. Un hercio es igual a un ciclo completo por segundo.

horizontal
Parallel to the horizon; level.

horizontal Paralelo al horizonte; nivelado.

horsepower hp
The unit of measurement of power for engines and motors. One horsepower equals 745 watts. (p. C132)

caballos de fuerza La unidad de medición de potencia para máquinas y motores. Un caballo de fuerza es igual a 745 vatios.

hydrocarbon
A compound that contains only carbon and hydrogen. (p. B163)

hidrocarburo Un compuesto que contiene solamente carbono e hidrógeno.

hypothesis
A tentative explanation for an observation or phenomenon. A hypothesis is used to make testable predictions. (p. xl)

hipótesi Una explicación provisional de una observación o de un fenómeno. Una hipótesis se usa para hacer predicciones que se pueden probar.

I

image
A picture of an object formed by rays of light. (p. D115)

imagen Reproducción de la figura de un objeto formada por rayos de luz.

incandescence (IHN-kuhn-DEHS-uhns)
1. The production of light by materials having high temperatures. (p. D89) 2. Light produced by an incandescent object.

incandescencia 1. La producción de luz por parte de materiales a altas temperaturas. 2. La luz producida por un objeto incandescente.

inclined plane
A simple machine that is a sloping surface, such as a ramp. (p. C158)

plano inclinado Una máquina simple que es una superficie en pendiente, como por ejemplo una rampa.

induction
The build-up of a static charge in an object when the object is close to, but not touching, a charged object. (p. E13)

inducción La acumulación de carga estática en un objeto cuando el objeto está cercano a, pero no en contacto con, un objeto con carga.

inertia (ih-NUR-shuh)
The resistance of an object to a change in the speed or the direction of its motion. (p. C46)

inercia La resistencia de un objeto al cambio de la velocidad o de la dirección de su movimiento.

infrared light
Part of the electromagnetic spectrum that consists of waves with frequencies between those of microwaves and visible light. (p. D84)

luz infrarroja Parte del espectro electromagnético que consiste de ondas con frecuencias entre las de las microondas y las de la luz visible.

Glossary **R59**

inorganic compound
A compound that is not considered organic. All compounds that do not contain carbon are inorganic, as are some types of carbon-containing compounds. (p. B148)

compuesto inorgánico Un compuesto que no se considera orgánico. Todos los compuestos que no contienen carbono son inorgánicos, al igual que algunos tipos de compuestos que contienen carbono.

insulator
1. A material that does not transfer energy easily. (p. A117) 2. A material that does not transfer electric charge easily. (p. E22)

aislante 1. Un material que no transfiere energía fácilmente. 2. Un material que no transfiere cargas eléctricas fácilmente.

intensity
The amount of energy of a wave, per wavelength. Intensity is associated with the amplitude of a sound wave and with the quality of loudness produced by the sound wave. (p. D52)

intensidad La cantidad de energía de una onda sonora, por longitud de onda. La intensidad está asociada con la amplitud de una onda sonora y con la calidad del volumen producido por la onda sonora.

interference
The meeting and combining of waves; the adding or subtracting of wave amplitudes that occurs as waves overlap. (p. D27)

interferencia El encuentro y la combinación de ondas; la suma o la resta de amplitudes de onda que ocurre cuando las ondas se traslapan.

ion
An atom or group of atoms that has a positive or negative electric charge. (p. B14)

ión Un átomo o un grupo de átomos que tiene una carga eléctrica positiva o negativa.

ionic bond
The electrical attraction between a negative ion and a positive ion. (p. B48)

enlace iónico La atracción eléctrica entre un ión negativo y un ión positivo.

isomer
Any of two or more compounds that contain the same atoms but that have different structures. (p. B152)

isómero Cualquiera de dos o más compuestos que contienen los mismos átomos pero que tienen estructuras diferentes.

isotope
An atom of one element that has a different number of neutrons than another atom of the same element. (p. B12)

isótopo Un átomo de un elemento que tiene un número diferente de neutrones que otro átomo del mismo elemento.

J

joule (jool) J
A unit used to measure energy and work. One calorie is equal to 4.18 joules of energy; one joule of work is done when a force of one newton moves an object one meter. (pp. A112, C117)

julio Una unidad que se usa para medir la energía y el trabajo. Una caloría es igual a 4.18 julios de energía; se hace un joule de trabajo cuando una fuerza de un newton mueve un objeto un metro.

K

kilowatt kW
A unit of measurement for power equal to 1000 watts. (p. E104)

kilovatio Una unidad de medición para la potencia equivalente a 1000 vatios.

kilowatt-hour kWh
The unit of measurement for electrical energy equal to one kilowatt of power over a one-hour period. (p. E105)

kilovatio-hora La unidad de medición de energía eléctrica igual a un kilovatio de potencia en un período de una hora.

kinetic energy (kuh-NEHT-ihk)
The energy of motion. A moving object has the most kinetic energy at the point where it moves the fastest. (pp. A74, C122)

energía cinética La energía de movimiento. Un objeto en movimiento tiene la mayor energía cinética en el punto en donde se mueve más rápidamente.

kinetic theory of matter (kuh-NEHT-ihk)
A theory stating that all matter is made of particles in motion. (p. A104)

teoría cinética de la materia Una teoría que establece que toda materia está compuesta de partículas en movimiento.

L

laser (LAY-zuhr)
A device that produces an intense, concentrated beam of light that can be brighter than sunlight. Lasers are often used in medicine and communications. (p. D135)

láser Un aparato que produce un intenso rayo de luz concentrado que es más brillante que la luz del Sol. Los láseres se usan a menudo en la medicina y las comunicaciones.

law
In science, a rule or principle describing a physical relationship that always works in the same way under the same conditions. The law of conservation of energy is an example.

ley En las ciencias, una regla o un principio que describe una relación física que siempre funciona de la misma manera bajo las mismas condiciones. La ley de la conservación de la energía es un ejemplo.

law of conservation of energy
A law stating that no matter how energy is transferred or transformed, it continues to exist in one form or another. (pp. A82, C126)

ley de la conservación de la energía Una ley que establece que no importa cómo se transfiere o transforma la energía, toda la energía sigue presente en alguna forma u otra.

law of conservation of mass
A law stating that atoms are not created or destroyed in a chemical reaction. (p. B79)

ley de la conservación de la masa Una ley que establece que los átomos ni se crean ni se destruyen en una reacción química.

law of conservation of momentum
A law stating that the amount of momentum a system of objects has does not change as long as there are no outside forces acting on that system. (p. C67)

ley de la conservación del momento Una ley que establece que la cantidad de momento que tiene un sistema de objetos no cambia mientras no haya fuerzas externas actuando sobre el sistema.

law of reflection
A law of physics stating that the angle at which light strikes a surface (the angle of incidence) equals the angle at which it reflects off the surface (the angle of reflection). (p. D114)

ley de la reflexión Una ley de la física que establece que el ángulo al cual la luz incide sobre una superficie (el ángulo de incidencia) es igual al ángulo al cual se refleja (ángulo de reflexión) de la superficie.

lens
A transparent optical tool that refracts light. (p. D121)

lente Una herramienta óptica transparente que refracta la luz.

lever
A solid bar that rotates, or turns, around a fixed point (fulcrum); one of the six simple machines. (p. C155)

palanca Una barra sólida que da vueltas o gira alrededor de un punto fijo (el fulcro); una de las seis máquinas simples.

lipid
A type of carbon-based molecule in living things. Lipids include fats and oils used for energy or as structural materials. (p. B156)

lípido Un tipo de molecula de los organismos vivos basada en el carbono. Los lípidos incluyen las grasas y los aceites usados como fuente de energía o como materiales estructurales.

liquid
Matter that has a definite volume but does not have a definite shape. The molecules in a liquid are close together but not bound to one another. (p. A28)

líquido Materia que tiene un volumen definido pero no tiene una forma definida. Las moléculas en un líquido están cerca unas de otras pero no están ligadas.

longitudinal wave (LAHN-jih-TOOD-uhn-uhl)
A type of wave in which the disturbance moves in the same direction that the wave travels. (p. D14)

onda longitudinal Un tipo de onda en la cual la perturbación se mueve en la misma dirección en la que viaja la onda.

luminescence
The production of light without the high temperatures needed for incandescence. (p. D89)

luminiscencia La producción de luz sin las altas temperaturas necesarias para la incandescencia.

M

machine
Any device that makes doing work easier. (p. C145)

máquina Cualquier aparato que facilita el trabajo.

magnet
An object that attracts certain other materials, particularly iron and steel. (p. E79)

imán Un objeto que atrae a ciertos otros materiales, especialmente al hierro y al acero.

GLOSSARY

Glossary R61

magnetic domain
A group of atoms whose magnetic fields align, or point in the same direction. Magnetic materials have magnetic domains, whereas nonmagnetic materials do not. (p. E83)

dominio magnético Un grupo de átomos cuyos campos magnéticos se alinean, o apuntan en la misma dirección. Los materiales magnéticos tienen dominios magnéticos mientras que los materiales no magnéticos no tienen.

magnetic field
An area surrounding a magnet within which the magnet can exert a force. Magnetic fields are concentrated into a pattern of lines that extend from the magnet's north pole to its south pole. (p. E81)

campo magnético Un área alrededor de un imán dentro del cual el imán puede ejercer una fuerza. Los campos magnéticos se concentran en un patrón de líneas que se extienden del polo norte del imán a su polo sur.

magnetic pole
One of two ends of a magnet where the magnetic force is the strongest. Every magnet has two poles.

polo magnético Uno de dos extremos de un imán donde la fuerza magnética es lo más fuerte. Todos los imanes tienen dos polos.

magnetism
The force exerted by a magnet. Opposite poles of two magnets attract, or pull together, whereas like poles of two magnets repel, or push apart. (p. E80)

magnetismo La fuerza que ejerce un imán. Los polos opuestos de dos imanes se atraen, o jalan hacia si, mientras que los polos iguales de dos imanes se repelen, o se empujan para alejarse uno del otro.

mass
A measure of how much matter an object is made of. (p. A10)

masa Una medida de la cantidad de materia de la que está compuesto un objeto.

matter
Anything that has mass and volume. Matter exists ordinarily as a solid, a liquid, or a gas. (p. A9)

materia Todo lo que tiene masa y volumen. Generalmente la materia existe como sólido, líquido o gas.

mechanical advantage
The number of times a machine multiplies the input force; output force divided by input force (p. C147)

ventaja mecánica El número de veces que una máquina multiplica la fuerza de entrada; la fuerza de salida dividida por la fuerza de entrada.

mechanical energy
A combination of the kinetic energy and potential energy an object has. (p. C125)

energía mecánica La combinación de la energía cinética y la energía potencial que tiene un objeto.

mechanical wave
A wave, such as a sound wave or a seismic wave, that transfers kinetic energy through matter. (p. D11)

onda mecánica Una onda, como una onda sonora o una onda sísmica, que transfiere energía cinética a través de la materia.

medium
A substance through which a wave moves. (p. D11)

medio Una sustancia a través de la cual se mueve una onda.

melting
The process by which a substance changes from its solid state to its liquid state. (p. A51)

fusión El proceso mediante el cual una sustancia cambia de su estado sólido a su estado líquido.

melting point
The temperature at which a substance changes from its solid state to its liquid state through melting. (p. A51)

punto de fusión La temperatura a la cual una sustancia cambia de su estado sólido a su estado líquido mediante fusión.

metal
An element that tends to be shiny, easily shaped, and a good conductor of electricity and heat. (p. B27)

metal Un elemento que tiende a ser brilloso, fácilmente deformable moldeado y buen conductor de electricidad y calor.

metallic bond
A certain type of bond in which nuclei float in a sea of electrons. (p. B56)

enlace metálico Cierto tipo de enlace en el cual los núcleos flotan en un mar de electrones.

metalloid
An element that has properties of both metals and nonmetals. (p. B30)

metaloide Un elemento que tiene propiedades de los metales así como de los no metales.

meter m
The international standard unit of length, about 39.37 inches.

metro La unidad estándar internacional de longitud, aproximadamente 39.37 pulgadas.

microwaves
Part of the electromagnetic spectrum that consists of waves with higher frequencies than radio waves, but lower frequencies than infrared waves. (p. D83)

microondas Parte del espectro electromagnético que consiste de ondas con frecuencias mayores a las ondas de radio, pero menores a las de las ondas infrarrojas.

mixture
A combination of two or more substances that do not combine chemically but remain the same individual substances. Mixtures can be separated by physical means. (p. A23)

mezcla Una combinación de dos o más sustancias que no se combinan químicamente sino que permanecen como sustancias individuales. Las mezclas se pueden separar por medios físicos.

molecule
A group of atoms that are held together by covalent bonds so that they move as a single unit. (pp. A18, B51)

molécula Un grupo de átomos que están unidos mediante enlaces covalentes de tal manera que se mueven como una sola unidad.

momentum (moh-MEHN-tuhm)
A measure of mass in motion. The momentum of an object is the product of its mass and velocity. (p. C64)

momento Una medida de la masa en movimiento. El momento de un objeto es el producto de su masa y su velocidad.

monomer
One of many small, repeating units linked together to form a polymer. (p. B166)

monómero Una de muchas unidades pequeñas que se repiten y están enlazadas unas con otras para formar un polímero.

motion
A change of position over time. (p. C11)

movimiento Un cambio de posición a través del tiempo.

N

nanotechnology
The science and technology of building electronic circuits and devices from single atoms and molecules. (p. C167)

nanotecnología La ciencia y tecnología de fabricar circuitos y aparatos electrónicos a partir de átomos y moléculas individuales.

net force
The overall force acting on an object when all of the forces acting on it are combined. (p. C43)

fuerza neta La fuerza resultante que actúa sobre un objeto cuando todas las fuerzas que actúan sobre él son combinadas.

neutral
Describing a solution that is neither an acid nor a base. A neutral solution has a pH of 7. (p. B129)

neutro Que describe una solución que no es un ácido ni una base. Una solución neutra tiene un pH de 7.

neutron
A particle that has no electric charge and is located in an atom's nucleus. (p. B11)

neutrón Una partícula que no tiene carga eléctrica y que se encuentra en el núcleo de un átomo.

Newton's first law
A scientific law stating that objects at rest remain at rest, and objects in motion remain in motion with the same velocity, unless acted on by an unbalanced force. (p. C45)

primera ley de Newton Una ley científica que establece que los objetos en reposo permanecen en reposo, y que los objetos en movimiento permanecen en movimiento con la misma velocidad, a menos que actúe sobre ellos una fuerza no balanceada.

Newton's second law
A scientific law stating that the acceleration of an object increases with increased force and decreases with increased mass. (p. C50)

segunda ley de Newton Una ley científica que establece que la aceleración de un objeto aumenta al incrementar la fuerza que actúa sobre él y disminuye al incrementar su masa.

Newton's third law
A scientific law stating that every time one object exerts a force on another object, the second object exerts a force that is equal in size and opposite in direction back on the first object. (p. C57)

tercera ley de Newton Una ley científica que establece que cada vez que un objeto ejerce una fuerza sobre otro objeto, el segundo objeto ejerce una fuerza de la misma magnitud y en dirección opuesta sobre el primer objeto.

nonmetal
An element that is not a metal and has properties generally opposite to those of a metal. (p. B29)

no metal Un elemento que no es un metal y que tiene propiedades generalmente opuestas a las de los metales.

nucleic acid
One of several carbon-based molecules that carry an organism's genetic code. One of the nucleic acids—DNA—contains the information needed to construct proteins. (p. B161)

ácido nucleico Una de varias moléculas basadas en el carbono que llevan el código genético de un organismo. Uno de los ácidos nucleicos, el ADN, contiene la información necesaria para construir proteínas.

nucleus
The central region of an atom where most of the atom's mass is found in protons and neutrons. (p. B11)

núcleo La región central de un átomo donde se encuentra la mayor parte de la masa del átomo en la forma de protones y neutrones.

O

ohm Ω
The unit of measurement for electrical resistance. (p. E23)

ohmio La unidad de medición para la resistencia eléctrica.

Ohm's law
The mathematical relationship among current, voltage, and resistance, expressed in the formula $I = V/R$ (current = voltage/resistance). (p. E29)

ley de Ohm La relación matemática entre la corriente, el voltaje y la resistencia, expresada en la fórmula $I = V/R$ (corriente = voltaje/resistencia).

optics (AHP-tihks)
The study of light, vision, and related technology. (p. D113)

óptica El estudio de la luz, la visión y la tecnología relacionada a ellas.

orbit
The elliptical path one celestial body follows around another celestial body. An object in orbit has a centripetal force acting on it that keeps the object moving in a circle or other ellipse. (p. C80)

órbita El camino elíptico que un cuerpo celeste sigue alrededor de otro cuerpo celeste. La fuerza centrípeta actúa sobre un objeto en órbita y lo mantiene en un movimiento circular o elíptico.

organic compound
A compound that is based on carbon. (p. B147)

compuesto orgánico Un compuesto basado en el carbono.

P, Q

parallel circuit
A circuit in which current follows more than one path. Each device that is wired in a parallel circuit has its own path to and from the voltage source. (p. E53)

circuito paralelo Un circuito en el cual la corriente sigue más de una trayectoria. Cada aparato que está conectado a un circuito paralelo tiene su propia trayectoria desde y hacia la fuente de voltaje.

particle
A very small piece of matter, such as an atom, molecule, or ion.

partícula Una cantidad muy pequeña de materia, como un átomo, una molécula o un ión.

pascal Pa
The unit used to measure pressure. One pascal is the pressure exerted by one newton of force on an area of one square meter, or one N/m^2. (p. C92)

pascal La unidad utilizada para medir presión. Un pascal es la presión ejercida por un newton de fuerza sobre un área de un metro cuadrado, o un N/m^2.

Pascal's principle
A statement that says when an outside pressure is applied at any point to a fluid in a container, that pressure is transmitted throughout the fluid with equal strength. (p. C102)

principio de Pascal Un enunciado que dice que cuando una presión externa es aplicada a cualquier punto de un líquido en un contenedor, esta presión es transmitida a través del fluido con igual fuerza.

period
A horizontal row in the periodic table of the elements. Elements in a period have varying properties. (p. B22)

período Un renglón horizontal en la tabla periódica de los elementos. Los elementos en un período tienen distintas propiedades.

periodic table
A table of the elements, arranged by atomic number, that shows the patterns in their properties. (p. B18)

tabla periódica Una tabla de los elementos, organizada en base a número atómico, que muestra los patrones en sus propiedades.

pH
The concentration of hydrogen ions in a solution; a measurement of acidity. (p. B129)

pH La concentración de iones de hidrógeno en una solución;, una medida de acidez.

photosynthesis
In green plants, the endothermic process in which light is absorbed and used to change carbon dioxide and water into glucose and oxygen. (p. B90)

fotosíntesis En plantas verdes, el proceso endotérmico en el cual se absorbe luz y se usa para cambiar dióxido de carbono y agua a glucosa y oxígeno.

physical change
A change in a substance that does not change the substance into a different one. (p. A44)

cambio físico Un cambio en una sustancia que no transforma la sustancia a otra sustancia.

physical property
A characteristic of a substance that can be observed without changing the identity of the substance. (p. A41)

propiedad física Una característica de una sustancia que se puede observar sin cambiar la identidad de la sustancia.

pitch
The quality of highness or lowness of a sound. Pitch is associated with the frequency of a sound wave—the higher the frequency, the higher the pitch. (p. D45)

tono La cualidad de un sonido de ser alto o bajo. El tono está asociado con la frecuencia de una onda sonora: entre más alta sea la frecuencia, más alto es el tono.

plastic
A polymer that can be molded or shaped. (p. B167)

plástico Un polímero que puede ser modelado o deformadomoldeado.

polar covalent bond
The unequal sharing of electrons between two atoms that gives rise to negative and positive regions of electric charge. (p. B51)

enlace polar covalente El compartir electrones desigualmente entre dos átomos y que lleva a la formación de regiones de carga eléctrica positiva y regiones de carga eléctrica negativa.

polarization (POH-luhr-ih-ZAY-shuhn)
A way of filtering light so that all of the waves vibrate in the same direction. (p. D96)

polarización Una manera de filtrar la luz para que todas las ondas vibren en la misma dirección.

polymer
A very large carbon-based molecule made of smaller, repeating units. (p. B166)

polímero Una molécula muy grande basada en el carbono compuesta de unidades más pequeñas que se repiten.

position
An object's location. (p. C9)

posición La ubicación de un objeto.

potential energy
Stored energy; the energy an object has due to its position, molecular arrangement, or chemical composition. (pp. A75, C122)

energía potencial Energía almacenada; o la energía que tiene un objeto debido a su posición, arreglo molecular o composición química.

power
The rate at which work is done. (p. C130)

potencia La razón a la cual se hace el trabajo.

precipitate
n. A solid substance that forms as a result of a reaction between chemicals in two liquids. (p. B72)

v. To come out of solution.

precipitado *s.* Una sustancia sólida que se forma como resultado de la reacción entre sustancias químicas en dos líquidos.

precipitar *v.* Salir de solución.

pressure
A measure of how much force is acting on a certain area; how concentrated a force is. Pressure is equal to the force divided by area. (p. C91)

presión Una medida de cuánta fuerza actúa sobre cierta área; el nivel de concentración de la fuerza. La presión es igual a la fuerza dividida entre el área.

primary colors
Three colors of light—red, green, and blue—that can be mixed to produce all possible colors. (p. D98)

colores primarios Tres colores de luz, rojo, verde y azul, que se pueden mezclar para producir todos los colores posibles.

primary pigments
Three colors of substances—cyan, yellow, and magenta—that can be mixed to produce all possible colors. (p. D99)

pigmentos primarios Tres colores de sustancias, cian, amarillo y magenta, que se pueden mezclar para producir todos los colores posibles.

prism
An optical tool that uses refraction to separate the different wavelengths that make up white light. (p. D97)

prisma Una herramienta óptica que usa la refracción para separar las diferentes longitudes de onda que componen la luz blanca.

product
A substance formed by a chemical reaction. A product is made by the rearrangement of atoms and bonds in reactants. (p. B71)

producto Una sustancia formada por una reacción química. Un producto se hace mediante la reorganización de los átomos y los enlaces en los reactivos.

protein
A macromolecule in living things that is made of smaller molecules called amino acids. (p. B158)

proteína Una macromolécula en organismos vivos compuesta de moléculas más pequeñas llamadas aminoácidos.

proton
A positively charged particle located in an atom's nucleus. (p. B11)

protón Una partícula con cargada positivamente localizada en el núcleo de un átomo.

pulley
A wheel with a grooved rim that turns on an axle; one of the six simple machines. (p. C156)

polea Una rueda con un canto acanalado que gira sobre un eje; una de las seis máquinas simples.

pupil
The circular opening in the iris of the eye that controls how much light enters the eye. (p. D127)

pupila La apertura circular en el iris del ojo que controla cuánta luz entra al ojo.

R

radiation (RAY-dee-AY-shuhn)
Energy that travels across distances in the form of electromagnetic waves. (pp. A119, D75)

radiación Energía que viaja a través de la distancia en forma de ondas electromagnéticas.

radioactivity
The process by which the nucleus of an atom of an element releases energy and particles. (p. B30)

radioactividad El proceso mediante el cual el núcleo de un átomo de un elemento libera energía y partículas.

radio waves
The part of the electromagnetic spectrum that consists of waves with the lowest frequencies. (p. D82)

ondas de radio La parte del espectro electromagnético que consiste de las ondas con las frecuencias más bajas.

reactant
A substance that is present at the beginning of a chemical reaction and is changed into a new substance. (p. B71)

reactivo Una sustancia que está presente en el comienzo de una reacción química y que se convierte en una nueva sustancia.

reactive
Likely to undergo a chemical change. (p. B26)

reactivo Que es probable que sufra un cambio químico.

reference point
A location to which another location is compared. (p. C10)

punto de referencia Una ubicación con la cual se compara otra ubicación.

reflection
The bouncing back of a wave after it strikes a barrier. (p. D25)

reflexión El rebote de una onda después de que incide sobre una barrera.

refraction
The bending of a wave as it crosses the boundary between two mediums at an angle other than 90 degrees. (p. D25)

refracción El doblamiento de una onda a medida que cruza el límite entre dos medios a un ángulo distinto a 90 grados.

regular reflection
The reflection of parallel light rays in the same direction. (p. D114)

reflexión especular La reflexión de rayos de luz paralelos en la misma dirección.

resistance
The property of a material that determines how easily a charge can move through it. Resistance is measured in ohms. (p. E29)

resistencia La propiedad de un material que determina qué tan fácilmente puede moverse una carga a través de él. La resistencia se mide en ohmios.

resistor
An electrical device that slows the flow of charge in a circuit. (p. E44)

resistencia Un aparato eléctrico que hace más lento el flujo de carga en un circuito.

resonance
The strengthening of a sound wave when it combines with an object's natural vibration. (p. D48)

resonancia El fortalecimiento de una onda sonora cuando se combina con la vibración natural de un objeto.

respiration
The exothermic process by which living things release energy from glucose and oxygen and produce carbon dioxide and water. (p. B94)

respiración El proceso exotérmico mediante el cual los organismos vivos liberan energía de la glucosa y del oxígeno y producen dióxido de carbono y agua.

retina (REHT-uhn-uh)
A light-sensitive membrane at the back of the inside of the eye. (p. D127)

retina Una membrana sensible a la luz en la parte trasera del interior del ojo.

robot
A machine that works automatically or by remote control. (p. C169)

robot Una máquina que funciona automáticamente o por control remoto.

S

saturated
Containing the maximum amount of a solute that can be dissolved in a particular solvent at a given temperature and pressure. (p. B118)

saturado Que contiene la máxima cantidad de soluto que se puede disolver en un solvente en particular a determinada temperatura y presión.

scattering
The spreading out of light rays in all directions as particles reflect and absorb the light. (p. D95)

dispersión La disipación de los rayos de luz en todas las direcciones a medida que las partículas reflejan y absorben la luz.

screw
A simple machine that is an inclined plane wrapped around a cylinder. A screw can be used to raise and lower weights as well as to fasten objects. (p. C159)

tornillo Una máquina simple que es un plano inclinado enrollado alrededor de un cilindro. Un tornillo se puede usar para levantar o bajar pesos y también para sujetar objetos.

second s
A unit of time equal to one-sixtieth of a minute.

segundo Una unidad de tiempo igual a una sesentava parte de un minuto.

series circuit
A circuit in which current follows a single path. Each device that is wired in a series circuit shares a path to and from the voltage source. (p. E52)

circuito en serie Un circuito en el cual la corriente sigue una sola trayectoria. Cada aparato conectado a un circuito en serie comparte una trayectoria desde y hacia la fuente de voltaje.

short circuit
An unintended and undesired path connecting one part of a circuit with another. (p. E46)

corto circuito Una trayectoria no intencionada y no deseada que conecta una parte de un circuito con otra.

simple machine
One of the basic machines on which all other mechanical machines are based. The six simple machines are the lever, inclined plane, wheel and axle, pulley, wedge, and screw. (p. C154)

máquina simple Una de las máquinas básicas sobre las cuales están basadas todas las demás máquinas mecánicas. Las seis máquinas simples son la palanca, el plano inclinado, la rueda y eje, la polea, la cuña y el tornillo.

solar cell
A type of technology in which light-sensitive materials convert sunlight into electrical energy. (p. A88)

celda solar Un tipo de tecnología en el cual materiales sensibles a la luz convierten luz solar a energía eléctrica.

solid
Matter that has a definite shape and a definite volume. The molecules in a solid are in fixed positions and are close together. (p. A28)

sólido La materia que tiene una forma definida y un volumen definido. Las moléculas en un sólido están en posiciones fijas y cercanas unas a otras.

solubility
The amount of solute that dissolves in a certain amount of a solvent at a given temperature and pressure to produce a saturated solution. (p. B119)

solubilidad La cantidad de soluto que se disuelve en cierta cantidad de solvente a determinada temperatura y presión para producir una solución saturada.

solute
In a solution, a substance that is dissolved in a solvent. (p. B112)

soluto En una solución, una sustancia que se disuelve en un solvente.

solution
A mixture of two or more substances that is identical throughout; a homogeneous mixture. (p. B111)

solución Una mezcla de dos o más sustancias que es idéntica en su totalidad;, una mezcla homogénea.

solvent
In a solution, the substance that dissolves a solute and makes up the largest percentage of a solution. (p. B112)

solvente En una solución, la sustancia que disuelve un soluto y que compone el porcentaje mayor de la una solución.

sonar
Instruments that use echolocation to locate objects underwater; acronym for "sound navigation and ranging." (p. D59)

sonar Instrumentos que usan la ecolocación para localizar objetos bajo agua; acrónimo en inglés para "navegación y determinación de distancias por sonido".

sound
A type of wave that is produced by a vibrating object and that travels through matter. (p. D37)

sonido Un tipo de onda que es producida por un objeto que vibra y que viaja a través de la materia.

specific heat
The amount of energy required to raise the temperature of one gram of a substance by one degree Celsius. (p. A113)

calor específico La cantidad de energía que se necesita para aumentar la temperatura de un gramo de una sustancia un grado centígrado.

speed
A measure of how fast something moves through a particular distance over a definite time period. Speed is distance divided by time. (p. C16)

rapidez Una medida del desplazamiento de un objeto a lo largo de una distancia específica en un período de tiempo definido. La rapidez es la distancia dividida entre el tiempo.

states of matter
The different forms in which matter can exist. Three familiar states are solid, liquid, and gas. (p. A27)

estados de la materia Las diferentes formas en las cuales puede existir la materia. Los tres estados conocidos son sólido, líquido y gas.

static charge
The buildup of electric charge in an object caused by the uneven distribution of charged particles. (p. E11)

carga estática La acumulación de carga eléctrica en un objeto ocasionada por la desigual distribución de partículas con carga.

sublimation
The process by which a substance changes directly from its solid state to its gas state without becoming a liquid first. (p. A53)

sublimación El proceso mediante el cual una sustancia cambia directamente de su estado sólido a su estado gaseoso sin convertirse primero en líquido.

subscript
A number written slightly below and to the right of a chemical symbol that shows how many atoms of an element are in a compound. (p. B43)

subíndice Un número que se escribe en la parte inferior a la derecha de un símbolo químico y que muestra cuantos átomos de un elemento están en un compuesto.

substance
Matter of a particular type. Elements, compounds, and mixtures are all substances.

sustancia La materia de cierto tipo. Los elementos, los compuestos y las mezclas son sustancias.

suspension
A mixture in which the different parts are identifiable as separate substances; a heterogeneous mixture. (p. B113)

suspensión Una mezcla en la cual las diferentes partes son identificables como sustancias distintas; una mezcla heterogénea.

system
A group of objects or phenomena that interact. A system can be as simple as a rope, a pulley, and a mass. It also can be as complex as the interaction of energy and matter in the four parts of the Earth system.

sistema Un grupo de objetos o fenómenos que interactúan. Un sistema puede ser algo tan sencillo como una cuerda, una polea y una masa. También puede ser algo tan complejo como la interacción de la energía y la materia en las cuatro partes del sistema de la Tierra.

T

technology
The use of scientific knowledge to solve problems or engineer new products, tools, or processes.
   tecnología El uso de conocimientos científicos para resolver problemas o para diseñar nuevos productos, herramientas o procesos.

temperature
A measure of the average amount of kinetic energy of the particles in an object. (p. A105)
   temperatura Una medida de la cantidad promedio de energía cinética de las partículas en un objeto.

terminal velocity
The final, maximum velocity of a falling object. (p. C89)
   velocidad terminal La velocidad máxima final de un objeto en caída libre.

theory
In science, a set of widely accepted explanations of observations and phenomena. A theory is a well-tested explanation that is consistent with all available evidence.
   teoría En las ciencias, un conjunto de explicaciones de observaciones y fenómenos que es ampliamente aceptado. Una teoría es una explicación bien probada que es consecuente con la evidencia disponible.

thermal energy
The energy an object has due to the motion of its particles; the total amount of kinetic energy of particles in an object. (p. A111)
   energía térmica La energía que tiene un objeto debido al movimiento de sus partículas; la cantidad total de energía cinética de las partículas en un objeto.

thermometer
A device for measuring temperature. (p. A107)
   termómetro Un aparato para medir la temperatura.

transformer
A device that uses electromagnetism to increase or decrease voltage. A transformer is often used in the distribution of current from power plants. (p. E99)
   transformador Un aparato que usa electromagnetismo para aumentar o disminuir el voltaje. A menudo se usa un transformador en la distribución de corriente desde las centrales eléctricas.

transmission (trans-MIHSH-uhn)
The passage of a wave through a medium. (p. D93)
   transmisión El paso de una onda a través de un medio.

transverse wave
A type of wave in which the disturbance moves at right angles, or perpendicular, to the direction in which the wave travels. (p. D13)
   onda transversal Un tipo de onda en el cual la perturbación se mueve en ángulo recto, o perpendicularmente, a la dirección en la cual viaja la onda.

trough (trawf)
The lowest point, or valley, of a wave (p. D17)
   valle El punto más bajo de una onda.

U

ultrasound
Sound waves with frequencies above 20,000 hertz, the upper limit of typical hearing levels in humans, used for medical purposes, among other things. (p. D46)
   ultrasonido Ondas sonoras con frecuencias superiores a 20,000 hertzios, el límite superior de los niveles auditivos típicos de los humanos. Estas ondas tienen usos médicos, entre otros.

ultraviolet light
The part of the electromagnetic spectrum that consists of waves with frequencies higher than those of visible light and lower than those of x-rays. (p. D85)
   luz ultravioleta La parte del espectro electromagnético que consiste de ondas con frecuencias superiores a las de luz visible y menores a las de los rayos X.

V

vacuum
A space containing few or no particles of matter. (p. D41)
   vacío Un espacio que no contiene partículas de materia o bien contiene muy pocas.

variable
Any factor that can change in a controlled experiment, observation, or model. (p. R30)
   variable Cualquier factor que puede cambiar en un experimento controlado, en una observación o en un modelo.

vector
A quantity that has both size and direction. (p. C22)
   vector Una cantidad que tiene magnitud y dirección.

velocity
A speed in a specific direction. (p. C22)
   velocidad Una rapidez en una dirección específica.

vertical
Going straight up or down from a level surface.

vertical Que está dispuesto hacia arriba o hacia abajo de una superficie nivelada.

vibration
A rapid, back-and-forth motion. (p. D37)

vibración Un movimiento rápido hacia delante y hacia atrás.

visible light
The part of the electromagnetic spectrum that consists of waves detectable by the human eye. (p. D84)

luz visible La parte del espectro electromagnético que consiste de ondas detectables por el ojo humano.

volt V
The unit of measurement for electric potential, which is equal to one joule per coulomb. The number of volts of an electric charge equals the charge's voltage. (p. E19)

voltio La unidad de medición para el potencial eléctrico, el cual es igual a un julio por segundo por culombio. El número de voltios de una carga eléctrica es igual al voltaje de la carga.

volume
An amount of three-dimensional space, often used to describe the space that an object takes up. (p. A11)

volumen Una cantidad de espacio tridimensional; a menudo se usa este término para describir el espacio que ocupa un objeto.

W

watt W
The unit of measurement for power, which is equal to one joule of work done or energy transferred in one second. For example, a 75 W light bulb converts electrical energy into heat and light at a rate of 75 joules per second. (pp. C131, E104)

vatio La unidad de medición de la potencia, el cual es igual a un julio de trabajo realizado o energía transferida en un segundo. Por ejemplo, una bombilla de 75 W convierte energía eléctrica a calor y luz a un ritmo de 75 julios por segundo.

wave
A disturbance that transfers energy from one place to another without requiring matter to move the entire distance. (p. D9)

onda Una perturbación que transfiere energía de un lugar a otro sin que sea necesario que la materia se mueva toda la distancia.

wavelength
The distance from one wave crest to the next crest; the distance from any part of one wave to the identical part of the next wave. (p. D17)

longitud de onda La distancia de una cresta de onda a la siguiente cresta; la distancia de cualquier parte de una onda a la parte idéntica de la siguiente onda.

wedge
A simple machine that has a thick end and a thin end. A wedge is used to cut, split, or pierce objects, or to hold objects together. (p. C158)

cuña Una máquina simple que tiene un extremo grueso y otro extremo delgado. Una cuña se usa para cortar, partir o penetrar objetos, o para mantener objetos juntos.

weight
The force of gravity on an object. (pp. A11, C79)

peso La fuerza de la gravedad sobre un objeto.

wheel and axle
A simple machine that is a wheel attached to a shaft, or axle. (p. C156)

rueda y eje Una máquina simple que es una rueda unida a una flecha, o a un eje.

work
The use of force to move an object over a distance. (p. C115)

trabajo El uso de fuerza para mover un objeto una distancia.

X, Y, Z

x-rays
The part of the electromagnetic spectrum that consists of waves with high frequencies and high energies; electromagnetic waves with frequencies ranging from more than 10^{16} hertz to more than 10^{21} hertz. (p. D86)

rayos X La parte del espectro electromagnético que consiste de las ondas con altas frecuencias y altas energías; las ondas electromagnéticas con frecuencias de más de 10^{16} hertzios hasta más de 10^{21} hertzios.

Index

Page numbers for definitions are printed in **boldface** type.
Page numbers for illustrations, maps, and charts are printed in *italics*.

A

absolute zero, A98
absorption, D**93**, D97
acceleration, C**25**, C25–31, C*26*, C*34*, C49–55, C*53*, C*60*
   average, C28
   force, mass, and, C50–53, C*50*, C*51*, C*52*, C*53*, C56, C*56*, C*67*, C*70*, C*86*
   gravitational, C78–79, C*79*, C*80*, C*81*, C123, C148, C*149*
   negative, C*26*, C*29*, C*30*, C31
   velocity, time, and, C25, C*26*, C27–31, C*28*, C*30*, C*34*
accuracy, **R22**
AC-DC converter, E97, E*97*
acetic acid, B128, B*128*, B129
acidity, measuring, B129
acid rain, B124, B131
acids, B124, B125–131, B**126**, B140
   acetic, B128, B*128*, B129
   acid-base neutralization, B124, B131
   Chapter Investigation, B132–33
   properties, B125, B127
   strength, B128–29
   testing for, B127
acoustics, D*55*, D**55**
actinides, B21
action and reaction, C57–60, C*59*, C*60*, C66, C*70*, C85, C158
aeolipile, C109, C*109*, C111
aerogel, A*59*
air, B52, B*52*
   density of, C94
   weight of, C*94*
air bags, B84, B*84*, C47
air conditioners, A91
air filter, E16
air pressure, C94, C100–101
air resistance, C**89**, C*89*, C152
alchemy, A97, A99
alkali metals, B27
alkaline earth metals, B27
alloys, B28, B**134**, B134–38, B140
   aluminum, B136, B138
   cobalt, B137
   gold, B134
   Internet activity, B109
   iron, B135–38
   liquid, B138

   in medicine, B137, B*137*
   memory, B135, B137
   in space flight, B138, B*138*
   titanium, B137, B*137*, B138
   in transportation, B136
   uses, B*135*, B136–38
alternating current (AC), E**97**
alternator, E98
altitude, air pressure and, C94
aluminum, B27, B*27*
amino acids, B158–59
   DNA and, B160–61
ammeter, E30
ammonia, B43, B*44*, B119, B128, B*129*
   molecular structure, B54, B*54*, B*129*
ampere (amp), E**29**, E36
amplification, D*55*, D**55**
amplitude, D16, D*17*, D**17**, D*18*, D*19*, D29, D55
AM waves, D82, D*82*
analog (information), E**60**
   conversion to digital, E60, E*60*
analysis, critical, R8
angle of incidence, D114, D*114*, D118
angle of reflection, D114, D*114*, D118
angles, measuring, D118
antacids, B125, B131
antifreeze, B116
anvil (ear), D39, D*39*
aperture, D134, D*135*
Archimedes, C109, C*109*
area, **R43**
   force, pressure, and, C91–95, C*92*, C*93*, C104
Aristotle, A96, C108, C*108*
aromatic compounds, B150
artificial lenses, D129–130
artificial light, D90–92
astatine, B22
astronomy, C84
atmosphere (unit of pressure), C94
atomic mass, B**17**, B24–25
atomic mass number, B**12**
atomic model, B*11*
atomic number, B**12**
atomic particles, B*11*, B11–12
atomic size, B23, B*23*
atomic theory of matter, A16

atoms, xxxi, **xxxi**, xxxiii, A**16**, A16–17, A34, B9–15, B34, B*34*, B104–07
  atomic number, B**12**
  carbon, B147, B152, B157
  change in identity, B30, B32
  in chemical reactions, B69, B71, B73, B79–81, B83
  compounds and, B41–42, B44, B*44*, B62
  electrons, B**11**, B*11*, B11–12, B106
  images of, A20, A*20*
  ion formation, B14–15, B48, B57
  mass, A17, B**17**, B24–25
  mass number, B12
  model, B*11*
  motion of, A19
  nanotechnology and, C167
  neutral, B12
  neutrons, B*11*, B**11**, B12–13, B*13*, B30, B34, B*34*
  nucleus, B*11*, B**11**, B34, B*34*, B106
  particles, B*11*, B11–12
  polarized, E14, E*14*
  protons, B**11**, B*11*, B34, B*34*, B126
  radioactive, B30–32
  ratios of, in compounds, B42, B44, B*44*
  size, B12, B23, B*23*
  structure, B11–12
  types, in Earth's crust, B10, B*10*
  types, in humans, B10, B*10*
audion, B106
audio tape, D63
automobile. *See* car.
averages, calculating, C120, **R36**
axle. *See* wheel and axle.

B

Babbage, Charles, E73
Bacon, Francis, A97
Bakelite, B167
balanced forces, C**43**, C43–47, C**45**, C59, C**86**
bases, B125–31, B**126**, B140
  acid-base neutralization, B131
  Chapter Investigation, B132–33
  properties, B125, B127
  strength, B128–29
  testing for, B127
Bassi, Laura, E73
batteries, B105, E31, E73
  car, E32, E*33*
  in parallel circuits, E53
  rechargeable, E32, E*33*
  in series circuits, E52
beetle, bombardier, B89, B*89*
benzene, B150
Bernoulli, Daniel, C100
Bernoulli's principle, C**100**, C100–101, C104
  in nature, C*101*

Bessemer process, B136
bias, **R6**
  scientific, R6
  sources of, R6
bicycles
  efficiency of, C*152*
  forces acting on, C44
binary code, E58
bioluminescence, D*88*, D**89**, D89–90
bit, E58
Black, Joseph, A97
block-and-tackle system. *See* pulley.
Bohr, Niels, B106
boiling, A*54*, A**54**, A64
boiling point, A**54**, B116
  of compounds, B57–58
  of hydrocarbons, B164
bond energy, B86–88
  in endothermic reactions, B87, B89, B*89*, B100
  in exothermic reactions, B87, B*88*, B100
bonds. *See* chemical bonds.
Boyle, Robert, B104
brass, B*135*
British thermal units (BTUs), A91
bromine, B22
bronze, B134–35, B*135*
buoyancy, C**98**, C98–99, C104, C109
  density and, C*99*
butane, B152
byte, E58

C

calcium, B16, B27, B42, B*42*
calcium chloride, B42, B*42*, B62
calorie, A**112**, A113
Calorie (food), A112
calorimeter, A112
calorimetry, A97
cameras, D134, D*135*, D139
  digital, D134, D*135*
car
  battery, E32, E*33*
  catalytic converter, B96, B*97*
  design of, xlii–xliii
  efficient, A87, A*87*
  fuel-cell powered, xliii, *xliii*
  gas consumption, xliii
  gasoline vs. electric, A77
  generator, E98
  hybrid, A87, A*87*
  hydrogen powered, A99
  pollution and, xliii, B96, B97
  solar-cell powered, A4, A5, A88, A*88*
  static electricity and, E16, E*16*
carbohydrates, B**155**, B155–56, B172

carbon, B16, B144–72
    atomic model, *xli*
    bonding, B148–49
    carbohydrates, B**155**, B155–56, B172
    chains, B150, B*151*, B152, B156, B164
    cycle, B164, B*164*
    forms of, B58–59, B*59*
    hydrocarbon, B96, B*97*, B**163**, B163–64, B*165*
    lipids, B**156**, B*156*, B56–57, B172
    in living things, B10, B16, B154–161, B164
    in materials, B163–69
    monomers, B**166**, B166–69, B172
    nanotubes, B153, B*153*
    nucleic acids, B**161**, B*160*, B172
    polymers, B**166**, B166–69, B172
    products, B*165*
    proteins, B**158**, B158–59, B*159*, B172
    rings, B150, B*151*
    structures, B147–52
carbon chains, B150, B*151*, B156, B164
    branched, B150, B152, B*152*
    straight, B150, B152, B*152*
carbon cycle, B164, B*164*
carbon dioxide, A*22*, A*48*, A53, B43, B51, B*51*, B90, B94–97, B*97*, B119, B122, B*148*
    formation, B80
carbon monoxide molecule, A18
carbon rings, B150, B*151*, B*155*, B*156*, B*160*, B169
carbon steel, B*135*
Carnot, Nicolas Sadi, A98
catalyst, B*76*, B**76**, B96
catalytic converter, B96, B*97*
catapult, C108, C*108*
cause-and-effect relationship, **R5**
CD (compact disc), D63, D*63*
CD (compact disc) player, E4, E94, E*94*
cell phone, D83, D*83*, D87
    generator, E4, E94, E*94*
cells
    cone, D**128**
    hair (ear), D39, D*39*, D56, D*56*
    rod, D**128**
celluloid, B167
cellulose, B156, B*156*, B167
Celsius, Anders, A97
Celsius scale, A97, A106, A*106*
    converting to Fahrenheit, A109
Chapter Investigations
    acids and bases, B132–33
    atomic masses, B24–25
    build a speaker, E100–101
    chemical bonds, B60–61
    chemical reactions, B92–93
    electronic devices, E66–67
    energy conversions, A84–85
    freezing point, A56–57
    insulators, A122–123

lenses, D124–125
lightning, E26–27
mass and volume, A14–15
polymers, B170–71
stringed instrument, D64–65
wavelength, D22–23
wavelength and color, D100–101
charge buildup, E11–13, E18
    in lightning, E20, E*21*
charge polarization, E14, E*14*
charging by contact, E*11*, E11–12
chemical bonds, B41, B47–62
    of carbon atoms, B148–51
    Chapter Investigation, B60–61
    in chemical reactions, B86–89, B*88*, B*89*
    comparison of, B52, B*52*
    covalent, B50, B*50*, B50–52, B*51*, B*52*, B58–59, B62
    double, B148–49, B*148*, B*149*, B*167*, B*172*
    electrons and, B47–48, B62, B148
    Internet activity, B39
    ionic, B*48*, B48–49, B*52*, B57–58, B62
    metallic, B**56**, B56–57, B*57*, B62, B148
    models, B*50*
    polar covalent, B**50**, B*51*, B*52*, B122–23, B*123*
    properties of substances and, B56–59
    single, B*148*, B148–49, B*149*, B*167*, B172
    structure of materials and, B53–54
    triple, B*148*, B148–49, B*149*, B*172*
chemical change, A**46**, A46–48, A64
    Internet activity, A39
    signs of, A47, A48
chemical compounds, B38–62
    aromatic, B150
    atoms and, B41–42, B44, B*44*, B62
    covalent, B54, B*54*, B58, B114, B*114*
    formulas, B43–44, B*44*
    inorganic, B*148*, B**148**
    ionic, B49, B*52*, B53, B57–58, B114, B*114*
    isomers, B**152**, B*152*, B169
    names of ionic compounds, B49
    new, B73
    organic, B**147**, B147–48, B*148*
    properties, B41–42, B56–59, B62
    with same elements, B44–45, B*45*
    structure, B53–54, B*54*
    substances and, B41
    synthesis, B73
chemical energy, xxxiv, A**73**, A76, C128
    of fossil fuels, A80
chemical equations, B80–84
    balancing, B81–84
    coefficients, B82–83
    conservation of mass, B80, B81, B84, B100
chemical formulas, B**43**, B43–44, B*44*
    how to write, B43
chemical properties, A**46**, A64.

chemical reactions, B66–100, B**69**, B100.
    See also chemical change.
  atoms and, B69, B71, B73, B79–81, B83
  catalyst in, B*76*, B**76**, B96
  in catalytic converters, B96, B*97*
  Chapter Investigation, B92–93
  chemical changes, B71, B*71*
  classification of, B73
  conservation of mass, B78–79, B*79*, B80, B81, B84, B100
  electronics and, B98–99, B*99*
  endothermic, B**87**, B*89*, B89–90, B100
  energy changes in, B86–91, B100
  equations of, B80–84
  evidence of, B72, B*72*, B100
  exothermic, B*87*, B**87**, B87–89, B*88*, B100
  in firefighting, B85
  in industry, B96–99, B100
  Internet activity, B67
  iodine clock, B77
  in living things, B88–89, B90, B91, B94–95, B100
  neutralization, B131
  photosynthesis, B**90**, B90–91, B94, B95
  products, B**71**
  rates and factors, B74–76, B*75*, B77
  reactants, B**71**
  respiration, B**94**, B94–95
  thermite reaction, B87, B*87*
chips, B98–99, B*99*
chloride ion, B15, B*15*, B*48*, B114, B126, B*126*, B128, B*128*
chlorine, B16, B22, B42, B*42*
  atom, B12, B13, B*13*, B15, B*15*
cholesterol, B157
circle graphs, A26
circuit diagram, E45, E*45*, E50
  of parallel circuit, E*53*
  of series circuit, E*52*
circuits, E**43**, E43–49
  in appliances, E54–55
  closed, E45, E*45*
  diagrams of, E45, E50, E52, E53
  electronic technology and, E57–65
  energy conversion, E54–55
  functioning, E46, E*46*
  fuses, E48, E*48*
  grounding, E47, E*47*
  integrated, E61, E*61*
  Internet activity, E41
  open, E45, E*45*
  parallel, E**53**, E*53*
  parts of, E44, E*44*
  paths of, E52–53
  safety devices and, E47–49, E50
  series, E**52**, E*52*
  short, E46, E*46*
  uses for, E51–55

closed circuit, E45, E*45*
cobalt alloys, B137
cochlea, D39, D*39*
code, E57
  binary, E58
coefficients, B82–83
collisions, C**66**, C*67*, C*68*, C*70*. See also momentum.
  of molecules and pressure, C93
colors, D96–99
  mixing, D98, D99, D*99*
  primary, D*98*, D**98**
  reflection and absorption, D97, D*97*
  wavelength and, D96–99, D100–101
color spectrum, D97
combustion, B*73*, B**73**
  gasoline, B96
  methane, B81, B*81*, B82, B*82*, B88, B*88*
  respiration, B**94**, B94–95
combustion reaction, B73
commutator, E*93*, E**97**, E*97*
compact disc (CD), D63, D*63*
compass, E84, E85
compounds, A**23**, A24, A34. See also chemical compounds.
  comparing mixtures with, A24
compressional waves, D14
compressions, D40, D*40*
computer chips, E75
computers, E**61**, E61–65, E68
  electromagnets and, E91
  first, E74
  functions of, E*62*, E63
  Internet and, E64–65
  miniaturization in, E75
  modeling forces, C111
  network, E64
  personal, E*62*, E62–63
  scientific use of, xli
concave lens, D*121*, D**121**
  images formed by, D123
  nearsightedness and, D129, D*129*
concave mirror, D*116*, D**116**, D*117*
  in telescopes, D132, D*133*
concentration, B74, B*75*, B**117**, B117–18
condensation, A*55*, A**55**, A64
conduction, A*117*, A**117**, A124, E11
conductors, A**117**, E**22**, E36, E44, E*44*, E68
cone cells, D**128**
conservation of energy, xxxv, A**82**, A92, C**126**, C*127*, C128, C*128*
conservation of mass, B78–79, B**79**, B100
conservation of matter, xxxiii
constants, **R30**
constructive interference, D27, D*27*
contact force, xxxvii, **xxxvii**, C*42*
contact lens, D130, D*130*
control group, C129, R30

R74 Physical Science

convection, A*118*, A**118**, A124
convex lens, D*121*, D**121**, D*122*, D*123*, D124–125
    in cameras, D134, D*135*
    farsightedness and, D129, D*129*
    images formed by, D123, D*123*
    in microscopes (objective lens), D132, D*133*
    in telescopes (objective lens), D132, D*133*
convex mirror, D*116*, D**116**, D*117*
cooking, with heat, A115
copper, B27, B*27*, B*62*
    properties of bonds in, B57, B*57*
cornea, D*127*, D**127**, D128, D130
    surgery on, D130
coulombs, E11, E19
covalent bond, B**50**, B*50*, B50–52, B*51*, B*52*, B58–59, B62
covalent compounds
    properties of, B58
    in solutions, B114, B*114*
    structure of, B54, B*54*
crest, D**17**, D30
critical analysis, R8
    of statements, R8–9
crystals, B53
    of ionic compounds, B49, B*49*
Curie, Marie, B30, B106
Curie, Pierre, B106
current (electrical), C135
    alternating, E97
    direct, E97
cycle, D46

D

Dalton, John, B11
dams, A80, A*80*
data,
    analyzing, xxxvi
    describing, R36–37
data tables, making, R23
da Vinci, Leonardo, C110
Davy, Humphrey, B105
decibel, D**52**, D54, D*54*
decimals, R**39**, R40
    adding, R39
    dividing, R40
    multiplying, R40
    in scientific notation, B33
    subtracting, R40
decomposition, B*73*, B**73**
    of sodium azide, B84
    of water, B71, B*71*, B89, B*89*
Deep Space 1 (spacecraft), C29
DeForest, Lee, B106
degrees, A**106**

density, A**43**, C**99**
    of air, C*94*
    buoyancy and, C99
    calculating, A43, A49
    identifying substances using, A59, A64
    mass, volume, and, C99
    of minerals, A63
    of water, C*95*
design, technological, xlii–xliii
destructive interference, D28, D*28*
dew, A*50*
Dewar, James, A98
diamond, B58, B*59*, B*62*
diesel fuel, B*151*, B*165*
diffraction, D**26**, D*26*, D26–27, D*27*, D30
diffuse reflection, D**114**
diffusion, D139, D*139*
digital cameras, D134, D*135*
digital (information), E**58**, E58–59
digital sound, E3–4
dilute, B*118*, B**118**, B140
direct current (DC), E**97**
direction of force, C42, C43, C147, C*149*. See also vectors.
discharge. See static discharge.
displacement, A13, A*13*, C99, C104
distance
    distance-time graph, C20, C*21*, C*30*, C31, C*34*
    force, work, and, C115–119
    gravity and, C78, C104
    measuring, C11, C24
    speed and, C16–19, C23, C24, C34
DNA, B*160*, B161
Doppler effect, D**50**, D*51*
Doppler ultrasound, D60
drag, C89. See also air resistance.
dry ice, A*22*, A53
DVDs, E4
dynamo, E74

E

ear, D39, D*39*
ear canal, D39
eardrum, D39, D*39*
Earth
    curvature of, C80, C*81*
    gravity of, C78, C79
    magnetic field of, E*84*, E84–85
    mass and weight on, C*80*
    orbit around Sun, C80
earthquakes, D10, D*10*, D11, D*11*
echolocation, D*59*, D59
Edison, Thomas, D62, D63, E74

Index **R75**

efficiency, A**83**, A86, A87, A91, A92, C**150**, C*150*, C150–152, C*153*
  calculating, C150, C*153*
  friction and, C*150*, C151, C156
  ideal mechanical advantage and, C160
Einstein, Albert, B10, C84, C111
einsteinium, B10
electrical devices, E44, E*44*
electrical energy, xxxiv, C128, C135, C146, C151, E108
  in cars, A87
  conversion of, A*81*
  conversion through circuits, E54–55
  generating through a power plant, E103, E*103*
  from solar cells, A88–89
electric car, A77
electric cell, E31. See also electrochemical cells.
electric charge, E9–10, E**10**, E*10*, E36
electric current, B105, E**28**, E28–34
  calculating, E29–30
  comparison of static charge and, E29
  distribution of, E99
  generating, E96
  paths of, E43–49
  production of, by magnetism, E95, E108
  production of magnetism, E88
electric eels, E17, E*17*
electric fan, A83, A*83*
electric field, D73–74, D*74*, E10, E*10*
electrician, E50
electricity, C128, C135, C146, C151, E6–36. See also electric charge; electric current; static charge.
  electric eel, E17
  electrician, E50
  electromagnetism, E*89*, E**89**. See also electromagnetic (EM) waves.
  induction, E*13*, E**13**, E13–14
  lightning, E20, E*21*, E26–27
  magnetism and, E88, E95
  measuring, E30
  movement of, E18–25, E36
  polarization, E14, E*14*
  safety devices, E47–49, E50
  safety tips, E47
  technology and, E15–16
electric potential, E**19**. See also voltage.
  effect on current, E29, E*29*
electric power, E**102**
  generating, E103, E*103*
  measuring, E104
  ratings of appliances, E104, E*104*
electric properties, A60, A64
electrochemical cells, E*31*, E36
  primary cells, E32, E*33*
  solar cells, E34, E*34*
  storage cells, E32, E*33*
electrolysis, B71, B*71*

electromagnetic energy, A*73*, A**73**, C128
  of Sun, A80, A119
electromagnetic (EM) waves, D70–101, D**73**. See also laser; light.
  artificial light, D90–92
  as a disturbance, D73–74
  formation of, D74, D*74*
  frequencies, D78, D79, D81
  gamma rays, D81, D*81*, D**86**
  infrared light, D80, D*80*, D**84**, D84–85, D*85*
  Internet activity, D71
  laser light and, D138
  light waves and materials, D93–99, D102
  measuring, D81
  microwaves, D77, D*77*, D80, D*80*, D**83**, D*83*
  radio waves, D79, D80, D*80*, D*82*, D**82**
  sources of, D74
  spectrum, D80–81
  sunlight, D88–89, D102
  traits, D73–77, D102
  travel of, D75
  ultraviolet light, D81, D*81*, D**85**, D*85*
  uses of, D79–86, D102
  visible light, D81, D*81*, D**84**
  x-rays, D81, D*81*, D**86**, D*86*
electromagnetic spectrum, D*80–81*, D**80–81**
electromagnetism, E89
electromagnets, E*90*, E**90**, E*93*, E108
  making an, E90
  in a power plant, E103
  Internet activity, E77
  uses of, E91–94
electron cloud, B*11*, B12, B34, B*34*
electronic devices, E**57**, E68, E72–75
  analog information and, E60
  Chapter Investigation, E66–67
  coded information and, E57–59
  computer. See computers.
  digital information and, E58–59
  music and, E2–5
Electronic Numerical Integrator and Computer (ENIAC), E74
electrons, B**11**, B*11*, B11–12, B106
  chemical bonds and, B47–48, B62
  discovery of, B105
  ion formation and, B*14*, B14–15, B*15*
  static charge and, E11, E*11*, E36
elements, xxxi, A**22**, B9–13
  atoms and, B11
  carbon. See carbon.
  compounds and, B41–45, B62
  density, trends of, B23
  in Earth's crust, B10, B*10*
  half-lives, B32, B*32*
  halogens, B22, B*22*, B29, B*29*
  in human body, B10, B*10*, B16
  ion formation and periodic table, B48

R76 Physical Science

metalloids, B30, B*30*, B34
metals, B**27**, B27–28
names and symbols, B10
noble gases, B29, B*29*
nonmetals, B**29**, B*29*, B34
organization of, B17, B34, B*34*
periodic table of, B17–23, B**18**, B*20–21*, B26–32
properties of, and compound properties, B41–42
rare earth (lanthanides), B21, B28, B*28*
reactive, B**26**, B27, B*27*
ellipse, C80
Empedocles, A96
endothermic reaction, B**87**, B*89*, B89–90, B100
   Chapter Investigation, B92–93
   photosynthesis, B**90**, B90–91, B94, B95
energy, xxxiv, **xxxv**, A68–92, A**72**, C121–128, C138. *See also* heat.
   bond energy, B87, B*88*, B*89*, B100
   changes in form. *See* energy conversion.
   chemical, xxxiv, A**73**, A76, A80, C128
   and chemical reactions, B86–91
   conservation of, xxxv, **xxxv**, A**82**, A92, C**126**, C*126*, C*127*, C128, C*138*
   efficiency, A**83**, A86, A87, A91, A92, C151, C152
   elastic potential, C122
   electrical, xxxiv, A*81*, A87, A88–89, C128, C135, C146, C151, E108
   electromagnetic, A**73**, A*73*, A80, A119, C128
   in endothermic reactions, B*89*, B89–90, B90–91, B100
   in exothermic reactions, B87–88, B*88*, B90–91, B100
   forms of, xxxiv, A71–76, A*81*, A92, C128
   Internet activity, A69
   kinetic, A74, A**74**, C**122**, C*122*, C**124**, C125–128, C*127*, C*138*, D11, E103, E*103*
   law of conservation of, **xxxv**, A**82**, A92
   mechanical, A**73**, A*81*, C**125**, C125–128, C*127*, C146, C151
   nuclear, A**73**, A*73*, C128
   potential, A74, A**75**, A*75*, A75–76, A*76*, A92, C**122**, C*122*, C*123*, C125–128, C*127*, C*138*, C148, C*149*, E19
   power, time, and, C133–136
   radiant, C128
   radiation, A*119*, A**119**, A124, D**75**
   solar, A4, A88–89, E34, E*34*
   sound, A**73**
   sources of, xxxv, A80, A*81*, A88–90
   storage and release, B90–91
   thermal, A**73**, A*73*, A98, A99, A*111*, A**111**, A114, A124, C128, C151
   transfer of, A111, A112, A116–121, A124, C121–128, C*122*, C133–135, C*134*, C*135*, C*149*, D9–12
   transformation of, C121, C122, C125–128, C*127*
   wasted, A83, A*83*, A86
   wind, A88, A90
energy conversion, A78–83, A*79*, A*81*, A92
   Chapter Investigation, A84–85
   between kinetic and potential energy, A79, A*79*–80, A81
   technology and, A86–91, A92
   uses for, A80, A*81*
   wasted energy and, A83, A*83*, A86
energy efficiency, A**83**, A87, A91, A92, C151, C152
energy transfer, A111, A112, A116–121, A124, C121–128, C*122*, C133–135, C*134*, C*135*, C*149*, D9–12
   EM waves, D76, D77
   laser, D138
   sound, D37, D41
energy usage
   appliances, E104, E*104*
   calculating, E105–106, E107
engine. *See also* motor.
   efficiency of car, C151, C152
   power of different types, C132
   steam, C109–110, C*109*, C*110*, C132
enzymes, B76, B*76*, B**159**
equations, chemical, B80–84
equator, C10
Europium, B28
evaluating, **R8**
   media claims, R8
evaporation, A*53*, A**53**, A64
evidence, collection of, xl
exothermic reaction, B*87*, B**87**, B87–89, B*88*, B100
   Chapter Investigation, B92–93
   in living things, B88–89, B*89*, B95
expansion joints, A108
experiment, **xl**. *See also* lab.
   conclusions, drawing, R35
   constants, determining, R30
   controlled, **R28**, R30
   designing, R28–35
   hypothesis, writing, R29
   materials, determining, R29
   observations, recording, R33
   procedure, writing, R32
   purpose, determining, R28
   results, summarizing, R34
   variables, R30–31, R32
experimental group, R30
exponents, B33, D78, **R44**
eye, D126–128, D*127*, D140
   compared with camera, D134, D*135*
   formation of image, D*127*, D128
eyepiece lens, D132, D*133*
eyesight. *See* vision.

F

fact, **R9**
　different from opinion, R9
Fahrenheit, Gabriel, A97
Fahrenheit scale, A97, A106, A*106*
　converting to Celsius, A109
farsightedness, D129, D*129*, D130
fatty acids, B127, B*156*, B156–57
faulty reasoning, **R7**
Fermi, Enrico, B10
fermium, B10
fiber optics, D**137**, D*137*
field, D73–74
filament, D91, D*91*
fires and chemical reactions, B85
first law of motion. *See* Newton's laws of motion.
Fleming, Ambrose, E74
floating. *See* buoyancy.
fluids, C**88**, C88–89, C*93*, C93–95, C98–103. *See also* liquid; hydraulics; water.
　friction in, C88–89, C*89*
　pressure in, C*93*, C93–95
　transmission of force through, C102–103, C104
fluorescence, D**91**
fluorescent light bulbs, D*91*, D91–92
fluorine, B22
FM waves, D82, D*82*
focal length, D*122*, D**123**
focal point, D*116*, D**117**, D*121*, D*122*
force, xxxvii, **xxxvii**, C38–70, C*41*, C*42*
　acceleration, mass, and, C*50*, C*51*, C*52*, C*53*, C*56*, C*67*, C*70*, C*86*
　action and reaction, C57–60, C*59*, C*60*, C66, C*70*, C*85*, C158
　applied, C*116*
　area and, C91–95, C104
　balanced, C*43*, C43–47, C*45*, C*59*, C*86*
　buoyancy, C**98**
　centripetal, C**54**, C*55*, C80, C*81*
　changing direction of, C42, C*43*, C147, C*149*
　contact, xxxvii, **xxxvii**, C*42*
　direction of motion changed by, C53–55
　distance, work, and, C115–119, C*116*, C*118*, C138
　electrical, xxxvii
　friction, xxxvii, **xxxvii**, C**85**, C*85*–89
　gravitational, **xxxvii**, xl, A11, A75, C42, C*42*, C77–84
　input, C146–147, C*146*, C149–153, C*155*, C160–162
　Internet activity, C39
　machines, work, and, C145–152, C*146*, C*147*, C155–162, C*155*, C*172*
　magnetic, xxxvii. *See also* magnetism.
　mass, distance, and, C77–85, C*78*, C104
　multiplication of, C146, C147
　needed to overcome friction, C*86*, C*87*, C*104*
　net, C**43**, C44, C*93*, C98, C*99*, C*149*
　output, C146–147, C*146*, C150–153, C*155*, C160–162
　physical, xxxvi–xxxvii
　strong, C111
　transmission through fluids, C102–103
　types of, C42
　unbalanced, C*43*, C43–47, C*45*, C*47*, C*70*
　waves and, D10
formulas, A91, **R42**. *See also* chemical formulas.
　density, A43, A49
　electrical power, E104
　energy use, E105–106
　Ohm's law, E**29**, E29–30, E35
　volume, A12
　wave speed, D20–21
fossil fuels
　vs. alternative energy sources, A4–5, A88
　energy of, A80
fractions, **R41**
frame of reference, C*13*. *See also* motion, observing.
Franklin, Benjamin, E73
free fall, C83, C90
freezing, A*52*, A**52**, A64
freezing point, A**52**, B115
　Chapter Investigation, A56–57
frequency, D16, D**17**, D*17*, D18, D30, D66
　Doppler effect and, D51
　electromagnetic, D78, D79
　natural, D48
　of sound waves, D45–51, D*46*
　wavelength and, D18, D*18*, D46
　fundamental tone, D49
friction, xxxvii, **xxxvii**, A98, C*42*, C44, C**85**, C85–89, C*86*, C*87*, C110.
　air resistance, C**89**, C*89*, C152
　compound machines and, C165
　efficiency and, C*150*, C151, C152, C156
　fluids and, C88–89, C*89*
　force needed to overcome, C*86*, C*87*, C*104*
　heat and, C*87*
　reducing, C152
　surfaces and, C86–88
　weight and, C*87*
fuel, future sources, A2–5
fuel cell, hydrogen, xliii, *xliii*
fuel injectors, A87
fulcrum, C109, C**155**, C*155*, C*162*, C163, C*172*
fullerene, B59, B*59*
fuses, E48, E*48*

G

Galilei, Galileo, C44, C110
   theory of motion, C44–45
gallium, B19
gamma rays, D80, D*81*, D**86**
gas, A**28**, A*29*, A32–33
   behavior of, A33, A*33*
   boiling, A*54*, A**54**, A64
   condensation, A*55*, A**55**, A64
   convection cycle, A118, A124
   evaporation, A*53*, A**53**, A64
   inert, B29, B*29*
   kinetic theory and, A104, A*104*
   studying, B104
   sublimation, A**53**
   volume and, A32, A*32*
gasoline, car consumption of, xliii
Gateway Arch (St. Louis), A108
gears, C*165*
   mechanical advantage of, C165
   used in nanotechnology, C*167*
Geiger counter, B30
generator, E**96**, E97–98, E102–103, E108
   car, E98
   cell phone, E96, E*96*
   DC, E97, E*97*
   Van de Graaff, E12, E*12*
germanium, E75
gigabyte, E58
glow sticks, B88, B94
glucose, B155–56. See also sugar.
   formula, B46
   model, B*155*
   in respiration, B94–95
glue, B55
Goddard, Robert H., C111
gold, A22, A*22*, B10, B12, B*12*, B134
graduated cylinder, A13, R16, R*16*
graphite, B59, B*59*, B*62*
graphs,
   bar, B162, R26, R31
   circle, A26, R25
   distance-time, C20, C*21*, C*30*, C31, C*34*
   double bar, R27
   line, B77, C*90*, R24, R34
   using, D57
   velocity-time, C*30*, C31, C*90*
   wave properties, D18, D*19*
gravity, xxxvii, xl, A11, A75, C42, C*42*, C60, C**77**, C77–84, C*78*, C*79*, C*104*
   acceleration, mass, and, C78–79, C*79*, C148, C*149*
   distance, mass, and, C77–85, C*78*, C*104*
   Earth's, C78–81, C*80*, C*81*, C123
   effect on light, C*84*, C111
   energy and, C123, C126, C*127*
   internet activity, C75
   orbit and, C80–83, C*81*
   weight and, C79–80, C*80*
   work and, C118–119, C*119*, C*158*
Greek philosophy, theory of motion in, C44, C108
ground-fault circuit interrupter (GFCI), E49, E*49*
grounding, E**25**, E*25*, E36
group, in periodic table, B*20*, B**22**, B*22*, B26–30, B34, B*34*

H

hair, B159, B*159*
hair cells, ear, D39, D*39*, D56, D*56*
hair dryer, energy use of, C*135*
Hales, Stephen, B104
half-life, B**32**
halogen light bulbs, D91, D*91*
halogens, B**22**, B*22*, B**29**, B*29*
hammer, D39, D*39*
hardware, E62
hearing loss, D56, D57
heat, A96–99, A**110**. See also temperature; energy.
   conduction, A*117*, A**117**
   convection, A*118*, A**118**
   cooking with, A115
   friction and, A98, C*87*, C151
   measuring, A112
   as motion, A97
   radiation, A*119*, A**119**
   vs. temperature, A110
   thermal energy and, A111, A*111*
   transfer of energy, A98, A111, A112, A116–121, A124
heating properties, A60, A*60*, A64
heat pack, chemical, B119
heat rays (infrared light), D**84**, D84–85, D*85*
hemoglobin, B16, B159, B*159*
hertz, D**46**, D47, D81
hexane, B172
holograms, D136
hormones, B157
horsepower, C132. See also power; Watt.
human body, elements in, B10, B*10*, B16
hybrid car, A87, A*87*
hydraulics, C*103*, C*166*
hydrocarbon, B96, B*97*, B**163**, B163–64, B*165*
hydrochloric acid, B44, B126, B128, B*128*, B129
   pH of, B129, B*130*
hydrogen, B10, B16
   compounds of, B44–45
   fuel cells and, xliii
   ions, B126, B128–31, B*128*
hypothesis, **xl**, xli, R3, **R3**, R29

Index R79

I

ice, xxxiii, A28, A30, A*30*
ice cream, B115
ideal mechanical advantage, C160–162
image, D**115**, D115–116, D*116*, D116–117, D*117*, D123, D133
incandescence, D**89**, D90–92
incandescent light bulb, D91, D*91*
incidence, angle of, D114, D*114*, D118
inclined plane, C*147*, C148, C*149*, C154, C**158**, C*158*, C159, C160. *See also* wedge.
    ideal mechanical advantage of, C*160*, C160–161
induction, E**13**, E*13*, E13–14
    in lightning, E20, E*21*
inert gases, B29, B*29*
inertia, C**46**, C*47*. *See also* momentum.
inference, **R4**, R35
infrared light, D**80**, D*80*, D**84**, D84–85, D*85*
infrared spectroscopy B4
infrared waves, C128
infrasound, D46
inner ear, D*39*
inorganic compounds, B**148**, B*148*
input, E*62*, E63
insulators, A**117**, A*120*, A120–121, E**22**, E36
    Chapter Investigation, A122–123
integrated circuits, E**61**, E*61*
intensity, sound, D**52**, D52–56, D*54*, D66
interference, D**27**, D*27*, D27–28, D*28*
International Space Station, B138, B*138*
International System of Units, R20–21
Internet, E64–65
    usage, E*65*
Internet activity
    alloys, B109
    chemical bonding, B39
    chemical reactions, B67
    energy, A69
    kinetic theory, A101
    periodic table, B7
    physical and chemical changes, A39
    polymers, B145
    scale, A7
Investigations. *See* Chapter Investigations.
iodine, B22, B50, B*50*
    molecular structure, B54, B*54*
iodine clock reaction, B77
ion engines, A3
ionic bond, B**48**, B*48*, B48–49, B*52*, B62
ionic compounds
    names of, B49
    properties of, B57–58
    in solutions, B114, B*114*, B123, B*123*
    structures of, B53

ions, B**14**
    acids and bases, B126, B128–31, B*128*, B*129*
    formation, B**14**, B14–15, B*15*, B48
    negative, B15, B*15*, B*48*, B48–49
    periodic table and, B22–23, B48, B*48*
    positive, B14, B*14*, B*48*, B48–49
iris, D127, D*127*
    camera, D134, D*135*
isobutane, B152
isomers, B**152**, B*152*, B169
isotopes, B**12**, B12–13, B*13*
    atomic mass number and, B17
    half-life, B32, B*32*
    radioactive, B30, B31–32

J

jellyfish, movement of, C*57*, C58
joule, A**112**, C**117**, C*123*, C*124*, C131
Joule, James, A98

K

kangaroos, movement of, C*60*
Kelvin, Lord, A98
keratin, B159, B*159*
Kevlar, B169, B*169*
Kilby, Jack, E75
kilowatt, C131, E**104**
kilowatt-hour, E**105**
kinetic energy, A**74**, A*74*, C**122**, C*122*, C*124*, C125–128, C*127*, C*138*, D11, E**103**, E*103*
    in cars, A87
    conversion to electrical energy, E103, E*103*
    conversion to potential energy, A*79*, A79–80, A*81*, A92
    mass and speed, A105
    of objects, A103
    of sound waves, D40
    temperature and, A105, A*105*, A124
    in wind, A90
kinetic theory of matter, A**104**, A*104*, A124
    Internet activity, A101
Kleist, Ewald Georg von, E72

L

lab, R10–35. *See also* experiment.
    equipment, R12–19
    safety, R10–11
laboratory equipment
    beaker, R12, *R12*
    beam balance, A10, A*14*
    double-pan balance, A10, A*10*, R19, *R19*
    force meter, R16, *R16*
    forceps, R13, *R13*

graduated cylinder, A*13*, A*14–15*, R16, *R16*
hot plate, R13, *R13*
meniscus, A15, R16, **R16**, *R16*
microscope, *xl*, A20, A*20*, D132, D*133*, R14, R14–15
ruler, metric, R17, *R17*
spring scale, A11, A*11*, R16, *R16*
test-tube holder, R12, *R12*
test-tube rack, R13, *R13*
test tube, R12, *R12*
triple-beam balance, A*14*, R18, *R18*
Langmuir, Irving, B106
lanthanides (rare earth elements), B21, B28, B*28*
laser, D*135*, D**135**, D135–138, D*136*
 chemical reaction and, *xl*
 fiber optics, D*137*, D**137**
 future uses, D138, D*138*
 making, D136
 visual uses, D136, D137
laser beams, D136, D*136*
latitude, C10, C*10*
Lavoisier, Antoine, B78–79, B*79*
law of conservation of energy, xxxv, A**82**, A92
law of conservation of mass, B78–79, B*79*, B100
 in chemical equations, B80, B81, B84
law of reflection, D**114**, D115, D116, D118
laws of motion. *See* Newton's laws of motion.
LEDs (light emitting diodes), D92, D*92*
lemon, pH, B*130*
lenses, D*121*, D**121**, D121–25, D140
 camera, D134, D*135*, D139, D*139*
 concave, D*121*, D**121**, D123, D129, D*129*
 contact, D130, D*130*
 convex, D*121*, D**121**, D*122*, D123, D124–125
 corrective, D129–130
 eyepiece, D132, D*133*
 gravitational, C*84*
 human eye, D127, D*127*
 long, D139, D*139*
 microscope, D132, D*133*
 mirrors and, D131
 objective, D132, D*133*
 telescope, D132, D*133*
 wide-angle, D139, D*139*
Leonardo da Vinci, C110
lever, C109, C*146*, C153, C154, C**155**, C*162*, C*172*
 compound machines using, C164, C165, C*166*, C*172*
 first-class, C*155*
 force and, C*155*
 ideal mechanical advantage of, C*162*
 in human body, C163
 real-world examples, C*163*, C164
 second-class, C*155*
 third-class, C*155*
Lewis, G.N., B106
Leyden jar, E72
lift, C101

light. *See also* optics.
 artificial, D90–92
 bending by gravity, C*84*, C111
 color, D96–101
 diffused, D139, D*139*
 infrared, D**84**, D84–85, D*85*
 materials and, D93–99, D102
 neon, D92
 refraction and, D*25*, D**25**, D30, D119–120, D*120*, D*122*
 speed of, D75
 sunlight, D88–89, D102
 ultraviolet, D**85**, D*85*
 visible, C128, D81, D*81*, D**84**, D*135*
 white, D96
light bulb, A86, D91, D*91*, E24, E*24*
light-emitting diode (LED), A87, A*87*, D92, D*92*
light filters, D95, D96
lightning, D20, D44, E20, E*21*
 Chapter Investigation, E26–27
lightning rod, E3
lights, efficient, A87
lipids, B**156**, B*156*, B156–57, B172
liquid, A28, A29, A32–33, A51–55. *See also* fluids; hydraulics; water.
 boiling, A*54*, A**54**, A64
 condensation, A*55*, A**55**, A64
 convection, A118, A124
 evaporation, A*53*, A**53**, A64
 freezing, A*52*, A**52**, A64
 kinetic energy and, A105, A*105*, A124
 kinetic theory and, A104, A*104*
lithium, B10
litmus paper, B127, B129
location, ways of describing, C9, C*10*
lodestone, E82, E84
logic circuit, E75
longitude, C10, C*10*
longitudinal waves, D**14**, D18, D*18*, D30
long lens, D139, D*139*
loudness, D52–56, D*54*, D66
luminescence, D**89**

M

machines, C108–110, C**145**, C145–169, C*146*, C*172*
 compound, C**164**, C164–169, C*172*
 efficiency of, C**150**, C*150*, C150–152, C**153**
 electronic, C146
 force, work, and, C145–152, C*146*, C147, C155–162, C*155*, C*172*
 Internet activity, C143
 mechanical advantage of, C**147**, C160–162
 perpetual motion, C109, C110
 robotic, C2–5, C*2*, C*4*, C168, C**169**
 simple, C146, C**154**, C154–162, C163, C*172*. *See also* inclined plane; lever; pulley; screw; wedge;

Index R81

wheel and axle.
maglev train, E80, E*80*
magnesium, B10, B27
magnetic domain, E**82**, E83
magnetic field, D74, D*74*, E**81**, E*81*, E89, E*89*, E108
    of Earth, E*84*, E84–85
magnetic force, xxxvii. *See also* magnetism.
magnetic poles, E**80**, E*80*, E85, E108
magnetic properties, A60, A*60*, A64
    used in separating minerals, A63
magnetism, xxxvii, E**80**, E108
    atmosphere and, E86
    control of voltage, E99
    electricity and, E88
    electromagnetism, E*89*, E**89**
    magnetic materials, E82, E*82*, E83
    production of electric current, E95, E108
magnets, *xxxix*, E**79**, E82, E108
    Earth, E*84*, E84–85
    healing properties of, E87
    permanent, E84
    temporary, E84
    vs. other materials, E*83*
manufacturing
    methods, C167
    robots used in, C169
Mars, exploration of, C2–5
Mars Exploration Rover (robot), C3–5, C*3*
mass, xxxi, **xxxi**, A**10**, A34, A41, C46, C49–53
    acceleration, gravitation, and, C78–79, C*79*, C148, C149
    Chapter Investigation, A14–15
    force, acceleration, and, C50, C51, C52, C53, C56, C67, C70, C86
    gravitation, distance, and, C77–85, C*78*, C*104*
    inertia and, C46
    measuring, A10
    momentum, velocity, and, C64–65, C*65*, C70
    as physical property, A41, A42
    specific heat and, A114
    thermal energy and, A114
    volume, density, and, C99
    weight and, compared, A11, C79–80, C*80*
math skills. *See also* units of measurement.
    angles, measuring, D118
    area, **R43**
    averages, C120, **R36**, **R37**
    bar graphs, B162
    circle graphs, A26, R25
    decimal, **R39**, R40
    describing a set of data, R36–37
    eliminating outlying values, C120
    examples, E35, E56, E107
    exponents, D78, **R44**
    formulas, A91, C18, C23, C51, C52, C53, C65, C92, C117, C123, C124, C125, C131, C133, E29, E104, E105, E107, **R42**
    fractions, **R41**
    graphs, using, D57
    line graphs, B77, C90
    mean, C120, D15, **R36**
    median, D15, **R36**
    metric conversions, A109
    mode, D15, **R37**
    percents, B139, C153, E56, **R41**
    proportions, **R39**
    range, **R37**
    rates, **R38**
    ratios, B46, C153, **R38**
    scientific notation, B33, D78, **R44**
    significant figures, C56, E107, **R44**
    units, C24
    variables, E35
    volume, **R43**
matter, xxx–xxxiii, **xxxi**, A**9**
    Aristotle's theory of, A96
    atoms and, A16–19, A34
    chemical properties and changes, A46–48, A64
    combinations of, A21–25, A34
    compound, A**23**, A24, A34
    conservation of, xvii
    density, A**43**, A49, A59, A63, A64
    electrical charge property, E9, E36
    element, A**22**
    forms of, xxx–xxxi
    gas, A**28**, A*29*, A32–33, A34, A104, A*104*, B29, B104
    kinetic theory and, A104, A*104*, A124
    liquid, A**28**, A*29*, A31, A34, A51–55, A104, A*104*
    mass and volume, A9–13, A34
    mixture, A**23**, A23–25, A34, A61–63, A64
    movement of, xxxiii
    particles and, xxx–xxxi, A27–28, A103
    physical change, A**44**, A*45*, A50–55, A64
    physical forces and, xxxvi
    physical properties, A**41**, A41–43, A*42*, A59–60, A64
    pure, A21–22, A**22**, A34
    solid, A**28**, A*29*, A30, A34, A48, A51, A51–52, A53, A64, A104, A*104*
    states of, A**27**, A27–33, A*29*, A34, A50–55, A104, A*104*, A124
mean, C120, D15, **R36**
measurement
    acceleration, C28, C51
    amplitude, D**17**
    area, C92, R43, **R43**
    density, C99
    distance, C11, C24
    Earth's gravity, C78
    energy, C121
    force, C51, C80
    frequency, D**17**, D30
    International System of Units (SI), R20–21
    mass, **xxxi**, xxxi, A**10**, A17, C51
    power, C131, C132

pressure, C92, C94
speed, C18
temperature, R21
volume, **xxxi**, A12–13, A14–15, **R43**
wavelength, D*17*, D30
weight, A**11**, C80
work, C117
mechanical advantage, C**147**, C157, C160. *See also* efficiency; machines.
calculating, C147
compound machines, C165
ideal, C160–162
mechanical energy, A73, C**125**, C125–128, C*127*, C*138*
conversion of, A*81*
mechanical waves, D**11**, D37, D41
median, D15, **R36**
medicine
alloys and, B137, B*137*
from nature, B2–5
radioactivity in, B31
medium, D**11**, D12, D41, D42–43, D75, D76, D119, D120, D*120*
EM waves, D75, D76
light, D93–99, D102
refraction in, D119, D120, D*120*
sound, D41, D42–43
total internal reflection and, D137, D*137*
melting, A**51**, A64
melting point, A**51**, A51–52
used in separating minerals, A63
Mendeleev, Dmitri, B18, B*18*, B19
mercury, B27
metallic bond, B**56**, B56–57, B*57*, B62
metalloids, B**30**, B*30*, B34
metals, B22, B**27**, B27–28
alkali, B27
alkaline earth, B27
alloys, B28, B109, B**134**, B134–38, B140
properties and bonds, B56–57
reactive, B27, B*27*
transition, B*27*, B27–28
methane, B*44*
bonding of, B*50*, B50–51
combustion, B81, B*81*, B82, B*82*, B88, B*88*
molecular structure, B54, B*54*
metric system, R20–21
changing metric units, R20, *R20*
converting between U.S. customary units, R21, *R21*
temperature conversion, A109, R21, *R21*
microchips, B98–99, B*99*, E61
microgears, C*167*
microgravity, C*83*
microscope, D132, D*133*, R14, R14–15. *See also* laboratory equipment.
making a slide or wet mount, R15, *R15*
scanning tunneling (STM), xl, A20, A*20*
viewing an object, R15

microtechnology, C166–167
microwave oven, D77, D*77*
microwaves, A73, D77, D*77*, D80, D*80*, D83, D*83*
middle ear, D39, D*39*
MIDI, E5
milk, pH, B*130*
minerals, separating, A63
mirrors, D113–117, D140
concave, D*116*, D**116**, D*117*
convex, D*116*, D**116**, D*117*
flat, D115–116, D*116*
lenses and, D131
mixtures, A**23**, A23–25, A34, B111. *See also* solutions.
comparing compounds with, A24
heterogeneous, A25
homogeneous, A25
separating, A61–63, A64
mode, D15, **R37**
molecular structure, B54, B*54*
studying, B4
molecule, xxxi, **xxxi**, A**18**, A34, B**51**
air, C94
collision of, C93–95
fluid, C*93*, C93–95
motion of, A19, A*19*
nanotechnology and, C166–167
water, C*93*, C94, C*95*
momentum, C**64**, C64–69, C*65*, C*67*, C*70*. *See also* inertia.
conservation of, C**67**, C*68*, C*69*
transfer of, C66, C*67*
velocity, mass, and, C64–65, C*65*, C*70*
monomers, B**166**, B172
Moon
exploration of, C111, C*111*
mass and weight on, C80
orbit around Earth, C80
mosaic, xl
motion, C6–34, C**11**, C*34*. *See also* inertia; Newton's laws of motion.
Aristotle and, C108
Bhaskara and, C109
circular, C54, C*55*
direction of, force, and, C53–55, C*55*, C*116*
direction of, work, and, C*116*
fluids, and, C88–89, C*89*, C100–101, C104
force, work, and, C115–119, C*116*, C*118*, C*138*, C148–149, C*149*
friction and, C42, C*42*, C44, C85, C86–87, C*86*, C*87*
Galileo and, C110
Internet activity, C7
Leonardo da Vinci and, C110
observing, C13–14, C*34*
perpetual, C109, C110, C126
relative, C13–14, C*14*, C34
motors, C151, E*92*, E92–94, E*93*, E108. *See also* engine.
electromagnets and, E92

Index **R83**

how they work, E92, E*93*
uses of, E94
multimeter, E30, E*30*
music, D60–61
electronics and, E2–5
musical instruments, D61, D*61*, D64

N

nanotechnology, C166–167, **C167**, C*167*, D138
nanotubes, carbon, B153, B*153*
natural frequencies, D48
natural medicines, B2–5
nearsightedness, D129, D*129*, D130
negative ions, B15, B*15*, B*48*, B48–49
neon lights, D92
Neptune, xl
Neptunium, B10
Nernst, Walther, A98
net charge, E11
network, computer, E64
neutral, B**129**, B*130*, B131, B140
neutral atoms, B12
neutralization reaction, B131
neutron, B**11**, B*11*, B34, B*34*
    number of, B12–13, B*13*
newton, A11
Newton, Sir Isaac, C44, C45, C80, C109, C110
Newton's laws of motion, C44, C45, C60, C61, C70, C109, C110, C111
    first, C44–47, **C45**, C*45*, C60
    second, C49–55, **C50**, C*50*, C55, C60, C78
    third, **C57**, C57–59, C*59*, C60, C67, C68–69
newton (unit of force), C51, C*92*, C*117*, C*123*
Nitinol, B135
nitrogen, B16, B51, B*51*
    compounds, B44
noble gases, B29, B*29*
Nomex, B169, B*169*
nonmetals, B29, B*29*, B34
nonpolar substances, B122–23, B*123*
normal line, D120, D*120*
Northern Lights, E86, E*86*
north pole, E81, E85
note-taking strategies, **R45–49**
    choose your own strategy, A102, A*102*
    combination notes, B68, B*68*, C40, C144, D8, D*8*, D112, D*112*, E8, E*8*, R45, R*45*
    concept map, R49, R*49*
    content frame, R45, R*45*
    main idea and detail notes, A8, A*8*, A102, A*102*, B40, B*40*, R46, R*46*
    main idea web, A40, A*40*, A102, A*102*, B8, B*8*, C114, C144, E78, E*78*, R46, R*46*
    mind map, A70, A*70*, A102, A*102*, B110, B*110*, R47, R*47*

outline, C8, C144, D36, D*36*, E42, E*42*, R48, R*48*
supporting main ideas, B146, B*146*, C76, C144, D72, D*72*, R47, R*47*
Venn diagram, R49, R*49*
nuclear energy, A73, A*73*, C128
nuclear magnetic resonance spectoscopy, B4
nucleic acids, B**161**, B*160*, B172
nucleus, B**11**, B*11*, B34, B*34*, B106
numbers. See also math skills.
    meaningful, C56
    outlying, C120

O

objective lens, D132, D*133*
observations, xl, **R2**, R5, R33
    qualitative, R2
    quantitative, R2
ocean waves. See waves, ocean.
ohmmeter, E30
ohms, E**23**, E29
Ohm's law, E**29**, E29–30, E35, E36
oil, A24
opaque materials, D94, D*94*
open circuit, E45, E*45*
operational definition, **R31**
opinion, **R9**
    different from fact, R9
optical fibers, D137, D*137*
optical tools, D131–139
optic nerve, D127, D*127*
optics, D110–139, D*113*. See also eye, visible light.
    fiber, D*137*, D**137**
    Internet activity, D111
    lenses and refraction, D119–125
    mirrors and reflection, D113–118
    photography, D139
    technology, D131–138, D140
orbit, C**80**, C80–83, C*81*. See also force, centripetal.
    humans in, C83
    velocity needed to achieve, C82
organic compounds, B**147**, B147–48, B*148*
oscilloscope, D49, D*49*
osmium, B23
outer ear, D39, D*39*
outliers, C120
output, E63, E*63*
overtone, D49
oxygen
    in combustion, B73, B*73*, B81, B*81*
    compounds, B44–45
    fuel cells and, xliii
    molecule, A18, A*18*
    in photosynthesis, B90, B45
    in respiration, B94–95
ozone molecule, A18, A*18*

P

pan balance, A10, A*10*, R19, R*19*
parallel circuit, E*53*, E**53**, E68
particle accelerators, B107
particles, xxx–xxxi
   atomic, B*11*, B11–12
   electric charge and, E10, E*10*
   kinetic theory, A*104*, A**104**, A124
   moving, A103
   speed of, A104, A105
   thermal expansion and, A108
Pascal, Blaise, C102
Pascal's principle, C102, C102–103, C*102*, C104
pascal (unit of pressure), C**92**, C94
pendulum, C*126*
percents, B139, C153, E56, **R41**
period, B*20*, B*22*, B**22**, B34, B*34*
periodic table, B17–30, B**18**, B*20–21*, B34, B*34*
   atomic size and, B23, B*23*
   density of elements and, B23
   group, B*20*, B*22*, B**22**, B34, B*34*
   halogens, B22, B*22*, B29, B*29*
   how to read, B19, B*19*
   Internet activity, B7
   Mendeleev's, B18, B*18*
   metalloids, B30, B*30*, B34
   metals, B27–28
   modern table, B19, B*20–21*
   noble gases, B29, B*29*
   nonmetals, B*29*, B**29**, B34
   organization of, B19, B22–23
   period, B*20*, B*22*, B**22**, B34, B*34*
   regions, B26, B*26*
   trends and patterns, B22–23
petroleum, B164, B*164*
pewter, B*135*
pH, B**129**, B*130*, B140
phonograph, D63
phospholipids, B157, B*157*
phosphorus, B16
photocopier, E15, E*15*
photography, D139
photoresist, B98–99
photosynthesis, B**90**, B90–91, B94
   equation, B95
physical change, A**44**, A*45*, A64
   Internet activity, A39
   states of matter and, A50–55
physical properties, A**41**, A41–43, A*42*, A64. See also mass; volume.
   color, A41, A*42*, A48
   density, A43, A**43**, A49, A59, A63, A64
   electric, A60, A64
   heating, A60, A*60*, A64
   magnetic, A60, A*60*, A63, A64
   shape, A41, A*42*
   size, A41
   solubility, A60, A64
   texture, A41, A*42*
   used to identify substances, A59–60, A64
   used to separate mixtures, A61–63, A64
physical science, xxix. See also science.
   unifying principles of, xxx–xxxvii
pitch, D**45**, D*46*, D47, D49, D*49*
   Doppler effect and, D50–51
plane, inclined, C*147*, C148, C*149*, C154, C**158**, C*158*, C159, C*160*
plastic, B**167**, B167–68
   recycling, B168, B*168*
pneumatic trough, B104
point of view. See frame of reference.
polar bears, A*120*, A121
polar covalent bond, B*51*, B**51**, B*52*
polarization, D*96*, D**96**
poles, magnetic, E**80**, E*80*, E81, E85, E108
pollution, xliii, C167
polymers, B**166**, B172
   Chapter Investigation, B170–71
   formation, B166–67, B*167*
   Internet activity, B145
   monomers and, B**166**, B167–69, B*167*, B*168*, B172
   new materials, B168–69
   plastics, B167–68
polypropylene, B166, B*167*
polystyrene, B*151*
positive ions, B14, B*14*, B48, B48–49
position, C**9**, C9–14, C*34*. See also reference point; motion.
   energy transfer, speed, and, C121
   potential energy and, C122
   ways of describing, C*10*
potassium, B16, B27
potential energy, A74, A*75*, A**75**, A75–76, A*76*, A92, C**122**, C*122*, C*123*, C125–128, C*127*, C*138*, C148, C*149*, E19
   chemical, xxxiv, A73, A76, A80
   conversion between kinetic energy and, A*79*, A79–80, A*81*, A92
pound, A11
power, C**130**, C130–135, C*132*, C138
   energy, time, and, C133–135, C*134*, C*135*, C138
   everyday usage, C*135*
   work, time, and, C130–132, C*132*, C138
power plants, E102, E*103*
praseodymium, B28
precipitate, A48, B*72*, B**72**, B118–19, B*119*
precision, **R22**
prediction, xl, **xl**, R3, **R3**
pressure, C**91**, C91–96
   air, C*94*
   area, force, and, C91–95, C*92*, C*93*, C104
   atmospheric, C*94*

Index R85

in fluids, C93, C93–95, C100–103, C101, C102, C104
solubility and, B122, B122
water, C93, C95
primary cells, E32, E33
primary colors, D98, D98, D102
primary pigments, D99, D99, D102
prime meridian, C10
principal axis, D121, D121
prism, D97, D97, D120, D120
processing, E63, E63
products, B71
propane, B44
properties. See physical properties; chemical properties.
proportions, A49, R39
propylene, B166, B167
proteins, B158, B158–59, B159, B172
DNA and, B160, B161
enzymes, B76, B76, B159
structural, B159, B159
transport, B159, B159
protons, B11, B11, B34, B34
in acids and bases, B126
relation to element, and, B12
static charge and, E11, E36
pulley, C147, C154, C156, C156, C157, C172
block-and-tackle system, using, C157
fixed, C156, C157
mechanical advantage of, C157
movable, C157
pupil, D127, D127
pure matter, A21–22, A22, A34

Q

quarks, B107
quartz, B98, B98

R

radar, D83
radiation, A119, A119, A124, D75
radioactivity, B30, B106
detection, B30
medical uses, B31, B31
radio waves, D79, D80, D82, D82
radius, C161
rainbows, D120, D120
ramp. See inclined plane.
random-access memory (RAM), E62
range, R37
rare earth elements (lanthanides), B21, B28, B28
rates, C17, R38
ratios, B46, C153, R38
reactants, B71
changes in, B74–75, B75

reaction, C57–60, C59, C60, C66, C77, C85, C158. See also chemical reactions; endothermic reaction; exothermic reaction.
combustion, B73
reactive, B26
reactive metals, B27, B27
read-only memory (ROM), E62
reasoning, faulty, R7
reference point, C10, C10, C34
reflecting telescope, D132, D133
reflection, D25, D25, D30, D97, D113, D114, D139
angle of, D114, D114, D118
diffuse, D114
law of, D114, D115, D116, D118
in photography, D139, D139
regular, D114, D114
total internal, D137, D137
refracting telescope, D132, D133
refraction, D25, D25, D30, D139
of light, D119–120, D120, D122
in photography, D139, D139
rainbows and, D120, D120
regular reflection, D114, D114
repulsion, E10, E81, E81
resistance, E23, E23, E23–24, E24, E29, E29, E36
effects on current, E29, E29
resistor, E44, E44
resonance, D48
respiration, B94, B94–95
equation, B95
retina, D127, D127, D128, D129–130
retinal, B152
RNA, B161
robots, C2–5, C2, C4, C168, C169, C169
Mars exploration and, C2–5
rocket, C111
rod cells, D128
rounding numbers, C56
ruby crystal, D136, D136
rust, A46

S

safety, R10–11
animal, R11
chemical, R11
clean up, R11
directions, R10
dress code, R10
electrical, R11
fire, R10
glassware, R11
heating, R10
icons, R10–11
lab, R10–11
sharp object, R11

salt, B131. *See also* sodium chloride.
    table, A23, A30
saturated, B**118**, B118–19
saturated fat, B157
scale (size), Internet activity, A7
scanning tunneling microscope, *xl*, A20, A*20*, B107
scattering, D*95*, D**95**
science, nature of, xxxviii–xli
Scientific American Frontiers, C2, C4
scientific notation, B33, D78, **R44**
scientific process, xxxix–xli
    asking questions, xxxix
    determining what is known, xxxix
    interpreting results, xli
    investigating, xl
    sharing results, xli
screw, C154, C*158*, C**159**, C*159*
seat belts, C*47*
secondary cells. *See* storage cells.
second law of motion. *See* Newton's laws of motion.
semiconductors, B30, B33, B*33*, B98, E61
separation
    of minerals, A63
    of mixtures, A61–62, A64
series circuits, E*52*, E**52**
short circuits, E*46*, E**46**
SI units. *See* International System of Units.
significant figures, C56, E107, **R44**
silicon, B98–99, B*99*, E61
    atoms of in Earth's crust, B10
sinking. *See* buoyancy.
SI units. *See* International System of Units.
skydiving, C89
slides, making, R15, R*15*
slope (steepness), C148, C*149*, C*160*
snowflakes, A30, A*30*
soap, B127, B*127*
    pH, B*130*
sodium, B16, B27, B*27*
    ion, B14, B*14*
sodium azide, B84
sodium chloride, B49, B*49*, B*52*, B140
    freezing point and, B115
    in solution, B114, B123, B*123*
sodium hydroxide, B126, B128, B*129*
    pH, B*130*
software, E62
soil, A25, A*25*
solar cells, A*88*, A**88**, A88–89, A92, E34, E*34*
solar energy, A4, A5, A88–89, A99
solid, A**28**, A*29*, A30, A34
    formation of, A48
    kinetic theory and, A104, A*104*
    melting of, A*51*, A51–52, A64
    sublimation, A**53**
solubility, A60, A64, B**119**, B119–23, B140
    changes in, B120–23

molecular structure and, B122–23, B*123*
pressure and, B122, B*122*
temperature and, B120–21, B*121*
solute, B**112**. *See also* solutions.
    change in solubility, B120–23
    concentration and, B117–18, B*118*, B140
    how they dissolve, B114, B*114*
solutions, B108–40, B**111**, B*113*, B140.
    See also solute; solvent.
    acidity, B129, B*130*
    acids, B125–31, B**126**, B140
    alloys, B**134**, B134–38, B140
    bases, B125–31, B**126**, B140
    concentrated, B118, B*118*, B140
    concentration, B**117**, B117–18
    dilute, B*118*, B**118**, B140
    gases, B112
    liquids, B112
    neutral, B**129**, B140
    saturated, B118
    solid, B112, B134–38
    solubility, B**119**, B119–23
    solvent-solute interactions, B114, B*114*
    supersaturated, B118–19, B*119*, B121
    types, B112
solvent, B**112**. *See also* solutions.
    boiling point, B116
    changing properties, B115–16
    freezing point, B115
    interaction with solutes, B114, B*114*
sonar, D*59*, D**59**
sonic booms, D44, D*44*
sound, D14, D34–65, D**37**, D66
    acoustics, D*55*, D**55**
    in air, D40, D*40*, D41, D42–43
    amplification, D*55*, D**55**
    changes in, D45
    Doppler effect, D**50**, D51
    different materials and, D42
    frequency and pitch, D45–51, D*46*, D66
    intensity, D**52**, D52–56, D*54*, D66
    Internet activity, D35
    loudness, D52–56, D*54*, D66
    mediums, D41, D42–43
    music, D60–61
    pitch, D**45**, D*46*, D47, D49, D*49*, D50–51, D66
    quality, D49
    recorded, D62, D63, D*63*
    sonic booms, D44, D*44*
    speed of, D42–44
    temperature and, D43
    ultrasound, D2–5, D**46**, D47, D58–60
    uses of, D2–5, D58–63, D66
    vibration, D**37**, D38, D40
    as a wave, D37–44, D*40*, D66
sound energy, A73

sound frequencies, D45–51, D*46*
   heard by animals, D47
   high and low, D46
   natural, D48
   sound quality, D49
sound waves, D14, D38, E3
   detection of, D39, D*39*
   mechanical wave, D37
   production of, D38, D*38*
   vibration of particles, D*40*, D40–41
Southern Lights, E86
south pole, E81, E85
spacecraft, C29, C*53*, C81–83, C*83*, C*169*
   fuel for, A2–4
   velocity needed to achieve orbit, C82
space elevator, D138, D*138*
Space Station, International, B138, B*138*
speakers, Chapter Investigation, E100–101
specific heat, A**113**
   in cooking, A115
   mass and, A114
spectroscopy, B4
speed, C12, C**16**, C16–23, C*17*, C*18*, C*23*, C*34*. See also velocity.
   average, C19, C23
   instantaneous, C19
   of light, D42, D75
   relation to velocity, C22–23
   time, distance, and, C16–23, C*17*, C*18*, C*20*, C*21*, C*24*, C*34*
   using distance-time graph to show, C20, C*21*
stainless steel, B*135*, B136, B137
Standardized Test Practice
   analyzing data, C73
   analyzing descriptions, B103
   analyzing experiments, A67, D69
   analyzing graphics, C175
   analyzing tables, E111
   interpreting diagrams, A127, C107, D33, D105, D143, E39, E71
   interpreting graphs, A37, A95, B143, C37
   interpreting tables, B37, B65, B175
   understanding experiments, C141
starch, B155, B*155*, B156
states of matter, A**27**, A27–33, A*29*, A34
   changes of, A50–55
   kinetic theory and, A104, A*104*, A124
static charge, E**11**, E11–12, E*12*, E36
   comparison of electric current and, E29
   materials affecting, E12, E*12*
   movement of, E18–25, E36
   potential energy and, E18–19
   technology and, E15–16
static discharge, E18
   lightning, E20, E*21*, E26–27
static electricity. See also static charge
   Internet activity, E7

steam engine, C109–110, C*109*, C*110*, C132
steel, B136
   carbon, B*135*
   stainless, B*135*, B136, B137
steering wheel, example of wheel and axle, C156
step-down transformer, E99, E*99*, E103, E*103*
step-up transformer, E99, E103, E*103*
stirrup, D39, D*39*
storage, E*62*, E63
storage cells, E32, E*33*
Styrofoam, A117
sublimation, A**53**
subscripts, B**43**
   in chemical equations, B83
   in chemical formulas, B43–44
substances
   identifying, A59–60, A64
   Greek classification of, A96
   properties used to identify, A58
   specific heat of, A113
sugar, B147, B*148*. See also glucose.
   solubility of, B*121*
   in solution, B114
Sun
   electromagnetic energy, A80
   radiation, A119, A*119*
   solar energy, A4, A5, A88–89, A92, A99
sunlight, D88–89, D102
superconductors, E24
supersonic speed, D44
surface area. See also pressure.
   air resistance and, C*89*
   in chemical reactions, B74–75, B75
suspension, B*113*, B**113**
switches, E44, E*44*, E45, E*45*, E68
   transistors, E61, E74
synthetic compounds, B4–5
synthesis reaction, B*73*, B**73**
systems. See energy, conservation of; momentum, conservation of.

T

tables, R23
taking notes. See note-taking strategies.
tarnish, A46, A*46*
technology
   acoustical engineering, D55, D*55*
   alloys, B28, B**134**, B134–139, B*135*
   alternative energy, A4–5, A88–90, A*88*, A99
   applications of Bernoulli's Principle, C101
   audiogram, D57, D*57*
   cameras and photography, D134, D*135*, D139
   carbon nanotubes, B153, B*153*
   cars, electric and hybrid, A77, A7, A*87*
   catalytic converter, B96, B*97*
   catapult, C108

cell phone, D83, D87
cells, electric and electrochemical, B105, **E31**, *E31*
cells, primary and storage, E32, *E33*
cells, solar, A4, **A88**, A88–89, E34, *E34*
chemical technology, B96
circuit, **E43**, E43–49, E51–55
cochlear implants, D4–5
compound machines, **C164**, C164–166, *C166*
computer modeling, C111
computer, *xli*, E59, **E61**, E61–65, *E62–63*, E74–75
corrective lenses, D129–130
digital devices, E3–4, E59–60, E94, *E94*
electric energy, A80, A83, *A83*, A88–89
electrical energy and appliances, xxxv, C135, *C135*
electrician, E50
electrolysis, B71, *B71*
electromagnets, **E90**, E90–93, *E93*
electronic products, B98–99, *B99*
electronics, **E57**, E57–60
electrostatic air filter, E16
elements in industry, B27–30
energy conversions, A80, *A81*, A86–87
energy efficiency, **A83**, A91
engineering and thermal expansion, A108
fiber optics, **D137**
gamma rays, *D81*, **D86**
generator, **E96**, *E96–97*, E96–98, E102–103
holograms, D108
hydraulics, C103
hydrogen fuel cells, xliii
infrared light, *D80*, **D84**, D84–85
insulators, A117, *A120*, A121–123
Internet, E64–65
lasers, *xl*, D109, **D135**, D135–136, D138
light-emitting diode (LED), A87, *A87*
lighting, D90–92
machines, **C145**
maglev train, E80, *E80*
magnets for medical use, E87
microchips, B98–99, E61
microscopes, xl, *xl*, D132, *D133*
microwaves, *D80*, **D83**
miniaturization, C166
motor, E92–94, *E93*
multimeter, E30, *E30*
Musical Instrument Digital Interface (MIDI), E5
musical instruments, D60–61, *D61*
nanotechnology, **C167**
nature of, xlii–xliii
objects used to do work, C119, *C119*
oscilloscope, D49, *D49*
particle accelerator, B107, *B107*
particle detector, *xxxviii*
petroleum, B164, *B165*
photocopier, E15, *E15*
plastics, **B167**, B167–168, *B168*
polymers, **B166**, B166–169, *B167*

propulsion, ion and beamed energy, A3, *A3*, A4
radar, D83
radio waves, *D80*, **D82**
radioactivity in medicine, B31
recorded sound devices, D63
robot, C2–5, *C2*, *C4*, *C168*, **C169**
scanning electron micrograph, *D63*
scanning tunneling microscope, xl, *xl*, A20, *A20*, *B55*, B107
semiconductor, B30, B98
sonar, **D59**, *D59*
sonic boom, D44, *D44*
spacecraft, *A2*, A3–4, C29, *C81*, C82, C111
spectroscopy, B4
steam engine, C109–110
superconductor, E24
telephone, D62, *D62*
telescope, reflecting and refracting, D107, D132, *D133*
thermometer, A97, **A107**
transformer, **E99**, *E99*
transistor, E61, E74
ultrasound, *D3*, D3–5, **D46**, D58-60
ultraviolet light, *D81*, **D85**
water treatment, A62
x-rays, *D81*, **D86**
Teflon, B168
telephone, D62, D*62*, D83
telescope, D*80*, D132, D*133*
television, D80, D82
temperature, A48, A96–98, **A**105, B75, B*75*. *See also* heat.
  convection and, A118
  conversion, A109, R21, *R21*
  in cooking, A115
  vs. heat, A110
  kinetic energy and, A105, *A105*, A124
  of lakes, A114, A118
  measuring, A106–107, A124
  reaction rate and, B75, B*75*
  scales, A106, *A106*
  solubility and, B120–21, B*121*
  specific heat and, A113
  speed of sound and, D43
  vs. thermal energy, A111
  unit conversion, R21, *R21*
terminal velocity, C89, C90
Thales of Miletus, E72
thermal energy, A*73*, A*73*, A*111*, **A**111, C128
  heat and, A111, A124
  mass and, A114
  from ponds, A99
thermal expansion, A108
thermite reaction, B87, B*87*
thermometer, A97, **A**107
thermos, A98, A*120*, A121
third law of motion. *See* Newton's laws of motion.

Index **R89**

Thompson, Benjamin, A98
Thomson, Joseph John, B105
timbre, D49
time
    distance, speed, and, C16–23, C*17*, C*18*, C*20*, C*21*, C*24*, C34
    distance-time graph, C20, C*21*, C30, C31, C*34*
    energy, power, and, C133–135, C*134*, C*135*, C138
    velocity, acceleration, and, C25, C*26*, C27–31, C*28*, C*30*, C*34*
    velocity-time graph, C*30*, C31, C90
    work, power, and, C130–132, C*132*, C138
titanium alloy, B137, B*137*, B138
total internal reflection, D137, D*137*
transformer, E*99*, E**99**
    in a power plant, E103, E*103*
transistors, E61, E74
transition metals, B*27*, B27–28
translucent materials, D94, D*94*
transmission, D**93**, D94–95
transparent materials, D94, D*94*
transportation, alloys and, B136
transverse waves, D**13**, D30
    graph of, D18, D*19*
trough, D**17**, D30
tsunamis, D29, D*29*
tungsten, D91, D*91*

U

ultrasound, D2–5, D**46**, D47, D58–60
ultrasound scanner, D2–5, D60, D*60*
ultraviolet light, D81, D*81*, D85, D**85**
units of measurement, C24. *See also* metric system.
    ampere (amp), E29
    British thermal unit (BTU), A91
    calorie, A**112**
    centimeter, A12
    coulomb, E11, E19
    decibel, D**52**
    degree, A**106**
    gram, A10
    hertz, D**46**, D47, D81
    horsepower, C132
    joule, A**112**, C117
    kilogram, A10, C51
    kilogram-meter per second (kg·m/s), C65
    kilometers per hour (km/h), C23
    kilowatt, E**104**
    kilowatt-hour, E**105**
    meter, A12
    meters per second (m/s), C18, C24
    meters per second squared (m/s^2), C28, C51
    newton, A11, C51–53
    ohm, E**23**
    pascal, C92
    pound, A11
    volt, E**19**, E29
    watt, C131, E**104**
    wavelength, D**17**, D30
unsaturated fat, B157

V

vacuum, D**41**, D75
    acceleration in, C79
    EM waves and, D75
vacuum flask, A98, A*120*, A121
vacuum tubes, E74
Van de Graaff generator, E12, E*12*
vanillin, B150, B*151*, B172
variables, E35, **R30**, R31, R32
    controlling, R17
    dependent, **R30**, R31
    independent, R30
    isolating, C129
vector, C**22**, C22
    acceleration, C26
    of force, C42
    momentum, C65
    velocity, C22
velocity, C**22**, C*22*, C25–31, C*26*, C*34*. *See also* speed.
    acceleration, time, and, C25, C*26*, C27–31, C*28*, C*30*, C*34*
    average, C23
    escape, C82
    kinetic energy, mass, and, C124, C126
    momentum, mass, and, C64–65, C65, C*70*
    needed to achieve orbit, C82
    relation to speed, C22–23
    terminal, C*89*, C90
    velocity-time graph, C*30*, C31, C89, C*90*
vibration, D**37**, D38–39, D40
visible light, C128, D81, D*81*, D**84**, D*135*. *See also* optics.
vision, D126–130
    correction of, D129–130
    farsightedness, D129, D*129*, D130
    formation of images, D*127*, D128
    nearsightedness, D129, D*129*, D130
vitamin E molecule, A18
vocabulary strategies, R50–51
    choose your own strategy, B110, B*110*
    description wheel, A102, A*102*, B40, B*40*, C8, C114, D36, D*36*, D112, D*112*, E78, E*78*, R50, *R50*
    four square, A8, A*8*, B68, B*68*, C76, C114, D8, D*8*, D112, D*112*, E8, E*8*, R50, *R50*
    frame game, A70, A*70*, B8, B*8*, D72, D*72*, D112, D*112*, E42, E*42*, R51, *R51*
    magnet word, A40, A*40*, B146, B*146*, C40, C114, R51, *R51*
    word triangle, C144, R51, *R51*
vocal cords, D38, D*38*
volt, E**19**, E29
Volta, Alessandro, B105, E73

voltage
    drop, E56
    magnetic control of, E99
    source, E44, E*44*, E52, E68
voltmeter, E30
volume, xxxi, **xxxi**, A**11**, A34, A41, R43, **R43**
    buoyancy, C109
    calculating, A12–13
    Chapter Investigation, A14–15
    displacement, A13, A*13*, C99, C104
    of liquid, A13
    mass, density and, C99
    as physical property, A41, A42

W

water, **xxxiii**, A28, B44, B45, B45, B51, B51, B52, C93, C94, C95. *See also* ice; buoyancy; hydraulics.
    electrolysis, B71, B*71*, B89, B*89*
    heat and temperature and, A110
    molecule, A18, A*18*, A19, A30, A*30*
    molecular structure, B54, B*54*
    oil and, A24, B122–23, B*123*
    pH, B*130*
    physical changes of, A44, A50
    physical states, B70, B*70*
    pressure in, C*93*, C*95*
    as solution, B124
    as solvent, B122–23, B*123*, B126
    specific heat of, A113
    used to power machines, C*119*
    vapor, xxxiii
water-treatment plants, A62
water wheels, C*119*
Watt, James, C110, C132
watt (unit of power), C**131**, E**104**
wavelength, D16, D*17*, D**17**, D30
    color and, D96–99, D100–101
    frequency and, D18, D*18*, D46
waves, D6–29, D**9**. *See also* light; medium; sound; sound waves.
    AM (amplitude modulation), D82, D*82*
    amplitude, D16, D*17*, D**17**
    behavior, D24–28
    classification, D12–14
    compressional, D14
    diffraction, D**26**, D*26*, D26–27, D*27*, D30
    electromagnetic, D70–101. *See also* electromagnetic waves.
    energy and, D9–14
    FM (frequency modulation), D82, D*82*
    frequency, D16, D*17*, D**17**, D18, D30, D45–66
    height, D15, D16
    Internet activity, D7
    longitudinal, D**14**, D18, D*18*, D30
    mechanical, D**11**, D37, D41
    model, D*12*
    ocean, D10, D12, D13, D15, D20–21
    properties, D16–21
    reflection, D*25*, D**25**, D30, D114–117, D*114*, D*116*, D*117*
    refraction, D*25*, D**25**, D30, D120, D*120*, D122
    rope, D9, D10, D*10*, D13, D*13*
    sound, D14, D34–65
    speed of, D16, D20–21, D44
    transverse, D**13**, D18, D*19*, D30
    wavelength, D16, D*17*, D**17**, D18, D30, D46, D96–101
wedge, C154, C**158**, C*158*, C159
    compound machines using, C165, C*172*
    real-world examples, C*158*, C159
    used to hold objects together, C159
    used to separate objects, C159
weight, A**11**, C**79**
    difference between mass and, A11
    friction and, C87
    gravitation and, C79–80, C*80*
    mass and, compared, C79–80, C*80*
    measuring, A11
weightlessness, C*83*
wet cell. *See* electrochemical cell.
wet mount, making a, R15, R*15*
whales, C95
wheel and axle, C154, C**156**, C*156*, C161, C*172*
    compound machines using, C164–165, C*165*, C166, C*172*
    mechanical advantage of, C*161*, C165
    real-world examples, C156, C*159*, C*161*
white light, D96
wide-angle lens, D139, D*139*
wind
    convection cycle, A118, A*118*
    energy, A88, A90
    used to power machines, C119
windmills, A90, A*90*, C119
wings, C101
wool, physical changes in, A44, A45, A*45*
work, C**115**, C115–135, C*118*, C*138*
    distance, force, and, C115–119, C*116*, C*118*, C138, C148–149, C*149*
    energy transfer and, C121, C126, C*127*
    gravitation and, C118–119, C*119*
    input, C150–152, C*150*, C153
    Internet activity, C113
    machines, force, and, C145–152, C*146*, C*147*, C155–162, C*155*, C172
    output, C150–152, C*150*, C153
    time, power, and, C130–132, C*132*, C138
World Wide Web, E65

X, Y, Z

x-rays, A73, B4, D81, D*81*, D86, D**86**
zero, absolute, A98

Index **R91**

Acknowledgments

Photography
Cover © Scott T. Smith/Corbis; **i** © Scott T. Smith/Corbis; **iii** *left (top to bottom)* Photograph of James Trefil by Evan Cantwell; Photograph of Rita Ann Calvo by Joseph Calvo; Photograph of Linda Carnine by Amilcar Cifuentes; Photograph of Sam Miller by Samuel Miller; *right (top to bottom)* Photograph of Kenneth Cutler by Kenneth A. Cutler; Photograph of Donald Steely by Marni Stamm; Photograph of Vicky Vachon by Redfern Photographics; **vi** © David Leahy/Getty Images; **vii** AP/Wide World Photos; **viii** © Digital Vision/PictureQuest; **x** © Arthur Tilley/Getty Images; **xi** © Mike Chew/Corbis; **xii** © Chip Simons/Getty Images; **xiii** © Alan Kearney/Getty Images; **xiv** © 2003 Barbara Ries; **xv** © Philip & Karen Smith/age fotostock america, inc.; **xx–xxi** Photographs by Sharon Hoogstraten; **xxx–xxxi** © Larry Hamill/age fotostock america, inc.; **xxxii–xxxiii** © Fritz Poelking/age fotostock america, inc.; **xxxiv–xxxv** © Galen Rowell/Corbis; **xxxvi–xxxvii** © Jack Affleck/SuperStock; **xxxviii** AP/Wide World Photos; **xxxix** © David Parker/IMI/University of Birmingham High, TC Consortium/Photo Researchers; **xl** *left* AP/Wide World Photos; *right* Washington University Record; **xli** *top* © Kim Steele/Getty Images; *bottom* Reprinted with permission from S. Zhou et al., SCIENCE 291:1944–47. © 2001 AAAS; **xlii–xliii** © Mike Fiala/Getty Images; **xliii** *left* © Derek Trask/Corbis; *right* AP/Wide World Photos; **xlviii** © The Chedd-Angier Production Company.

Matter and Energy
Divider © Scott T. Smith/Corbis; **A2–A3, A3** Courtesy of NASA/JPL/Caltech; **A4** *top* © Babakin Space Center, The Planetary Society; *bottom* © The Chedd-Angier Production Company; **A6–A7** © Steve Allen/Brand X Pictures; **A7, A9** Photographs by Sharon Hoogstraten; **A10** *left* © Antonio Mo/Getty Images; *right* © ImageState/Alamy; **A11** © Tom Stewart/Corbis; **A12, A13** Photographs by Sharon Hoogstraten; **A14** *top* © Stewart Cohen/Getty Images; *bottom* Photograph by Sharon Hoogstraten; **A14–A15, A15** Photographs by Sharon Hoogstraten; **A16** © Royalty-Free/Corbis; **A17** Photograph by Sharon Hoogstraten; **A18** © NatPhotos/Tony Sweet/Digital Vision; **A19** © Jake Rajs/Getty Images; **A20** Courtesy IBM Archives; **A21** Photograph by Sharon Hoogstraten; **A22** *left* © James L. Amos/Corbis; *right* © Omni Photo Communications, Inc./Index Stock; **A23** © Richard Laird/Getty Images; **A24** Photograph by Sharon Hoogstraten; **A25** © Royalty-Free/Corbis; **A26** © Nik Wheeler/Corbis; **A27** Photograph by Sharon Hoogstraten; **A30** © Robert F. Sisson/Getty Images; **A31** Photograph by Sharon Hoogstraten; **A34** *top* Photograph by Sharon Hoogstraten; *bottom left* © James L. Amos/Corbis; *bottom right* © Royalty-Free/Corbis; **A36** Photographs by Sharon Hoogstraten; **A38–A39** © David Leahy/Getty Images; **A39, A41** Photographs by Sharon Hoogstraten; **A42** *left* Photograph by Sharon Hoogstraten; *right* © Dan Lim/Masterfile; **A45** *top left* © Maryellen McGrath/Bruce Coleman Inc.; *top center* © Jean-Bernard Vernier/Corbis Sygma; *top right* © Angelo Cavalli/Getty Images; *bottom* © Garry Black/Masterfile; *inset* Photograph by Sharon Hoogstraten; **A46** © Mark C. Burnett/Stock, Boston Inc./PictureQuest; **A47** Photograph by Sharon Hoogstraten; **A48** © J. Westrich/Masterfile; **A49** *left* © Owen Franken/Corbis; *right* © Erich Lessing/Art Resource, New York; **A50** © ImageState/Alamy; **A51** *left* © Brand X Pictures; *right* © Peter Bowater/Alamy; **A52** © Royalty-Free/Corbis; **A53** © Winifred Wisniewski/Frank Lane Picture Agency/Corbis; **A54** © A. Pasieka/Photo Researchers; **A55** © Sean Ellis/Getty Images; **A56** *top* © Royalty-Free/Corbis; *bottom* Photograph by Sharon Hoogstraten; **A57, A58** Photographs by Sharon Hoogstraten; **A59** © Lawrence Livermore National Laboratory/Photo Researchers; **A60** *top left* © SPL/Photo Researchers; *top right* © Felix St. Clair Renard/Getty Images; *bottom* © David Young-Wolff/PhotoEdit; **A61** Photograph by Sharon Hoogstraten; **A62** © Alan Towse/Ecoscene/Corbis; **A63** © Robert Essel NYC/Corbis; *inset* © The Cover Story/Corbis; **A64** *top left* © Dan Lim/Masterfile; *top right* © Mark C. Burnett/Stock, Boston Inc./PictureQuest; *bottom* © David Young-Wolff/PhotoEdit; **A66** © Winifred Wisniewski/Frank Lane Picture Agency/Corbis; **A68–A69** AP/Wide World Photos; **A69, A71** Photographs by Sharon Hoogstraten; **A72** © Alan Schein Photography/Corbis; **A73** *top* © Patrick Ward/Corbis; *bottom* © NASA/Photo Researchers; **A74** AP/Wide World Photos; **A75** *top* © George H. H. Huey/Corbis; *bottom* Photograph by Sharon Hoogstraten; **A76** *top* © Vladimir Pcholkin/Getty Images; *bottom* © Thomas Beach; **A77** © Adam Gault/Digital Vision; **A78** © Bill Aron/PhotoEdit; **A79** © TempSport/Corbis; **A80** © Robert Cameron/Getty Images; **A81** *left* © Gunter Marx Photography/Corbis; *right* © Lester Lefkowitz/Corbis; **A82** © Left Lane Productions/Corbis; **A83** © Dorling Kindersley; **A84** *top* © Grant Klotz/Alaska Stock Images/PictureQuest; *bottom* Photograph by Sharon Hoogstraten; **A85, A86** Photographs by Sharon Hoogstraten; **A87** *top left* © Royalty-Free/Corbis; *top right* Thinkstock, LLC; *bottom* AP/Wide World Photos; **A88** © AFP/Corbis; *inset* © John Farmar; Cordaiy Photo Library Ltd./Corbis; **A89** *top* © Sally A. Morgan; Ecoscene/Corbis; *bottom* Photograph by Sharon Hoogstraten; **A90** © Joe Sohm/Visions of America, LLC/PictureQuest; **A91** © Michael S. Lewis/Corbis; **A92** *top* © Vladimir Pcholkin/Getty Images; *bottom* © AFP/Corbis; **A96** © Don Farrall/Getty Images; **A97** *top left* © Sheila Terry/Photo Researchers; *top center, top right* © Dorling Kindersley; *bottom* © SEF/Art Resource, New York; **A98** *top left* Mary Evans Picture Library; *top right, bottom* © Dorling Kindersley; **A99** © Mark Wiens/Masterfile; **A100–A101** © Steve Bloom/stevebloom.com; **A101, A103** Photographs by Sharon Hoogstraten; **A104** © Tracy Frankel/Getty Images; **A105** Photographs by Sharon Hoogstraten; **A106** © Daryl Benson/Masterfile

inset © Spencer Grant/PhotoEdit; **A107** Photograph by Sharon Hoogstraten; **A108** *top* © Steve Vidler/SuperStock; *bottom* © Chase Jarvis/Getty Images; **A109** © FogStock/Alamy; *inset* © Gordon Wiltsie/Getty Images; **A110** © David Bishop/Getty Images; **A111** Thinkstock, LLC; **A112** Photograph by Sharon Hoogstraten; **A113** © Richard Bickel/Corbis; **A115** *top left* © Jeremy Samuelson/FoodPix; *bottom left* © William Reavell-StockFood Munich/StockFood; *right* © Martin Jacobs/FoodPix; **A116** Photograph by Sharon Hoogstraten; **A117** © Brand X Pictures/Alamy; **A119** © ImageState Royalty Free/Alamy; **A120** *top left* E.C. Humphrey; *top right* Creatas®; *bottom* © Uwe Walz Gdt/age fotostock america, inc.; **A122** *top* © Nancy Ney/Corbis; *bottom* Photograph by Sharon Hoogstraten; **A123** Photograph by Sharon Hoogstraten; **A124** *top* Photographs by Sharon Hoogstraten; *bottom* Thinkstock, LLC.

Chemical Interactions
Divider © Photodisc/Getty Images; **B2–B3** © David Cavagnaro/Peter Arnold, Inc.; **B3** Joel Sartore/National Geographic Image Collection; **B4** © The Chedd-Angier Production Company; **B5** © Colin Cuthbert/Photo Researchers; **B6–B7** IBM Research, Almaden Research Center; **B7, B9** Photographs by Sharon Hoogstraten; **B10** NASA; **B12** © Pascal Goetgheluck/Photo Researchers; **B13** Photograph by Sharon Hoogstraten; **B16** © Cnri/Photo Researchers; **B17** Photograph by Sharon Hoogstraten; **B18** *left, right* The Granger Collection, New York; **B24** *top* © A. Hart-Davis/Photo Researchers; *bottom* Photograph by Sharon Hoogstraten; **B26** Photograph by Sharon Hoogstraten; **B27** *left* © Charles D. Winters/Photo Researchers; *center* © Rich Treptow/Visuals Unlimited; *right* © Corbis Images/PictureQuest; **B28** © Peter Christopher/Masterfile; **B29** © M. Gibbon/Robertstock.com; **30** © Superstock; **B31** *top* © Simon Fraser/Photo Researchers; *bottom* Photograph by Sharon Hoogstraten; **B33** © Alfred Pasieka/Photo Researchers; *inset* © John Walsh/Photo Researchers; **B38–B39** © Digital Vision/PictureQuest; **B39, B41** Photographs by Sharon Hoogstraten; **B42** *left* © Rich Treptow/Visuals Unlimited; *center, right* © E. R. Degginger/Color-Pic, Inc.; **B43, B45** Photograph by Sharon Hoogstraten; **B46** © Lawrence M. Sawyer/Photodisc/PictureQuest; **B47** © IFA/eStock Photography (PQ price control)/PictureQuest; **B49** © Runk and Schoenberger/Grant Heilman Photography, Inc.; **B52** © The Image Bank/Getty Images; **B53** Photograph by Sharon Hoogstraten; **B55** © Astrid & Hanns-Frieder Michler/Photo Researchers; *inset* © Volker Steger/Photo Researchers; **B56** Photograph by Sharon Hoogstraten; **B57** © David Wrobel/Visuals Unlimited; **B58** © Rob Blakers/photolibrary/PictureQuest; **B59** *left* © E. R. Degginger/Robertstock.com; *right* © C. Swartzell/Visuals Unlimited; **B60** *top* © David Young-Wolff/Getty Images; *bottom* Photograph by Sharon Hoogstraten; **B61** Photograph by Sharon Hoogstraten; **B62** *left* © Rich Treptow/Visuals Unlimited; *center, right* © E. R. Degginger/Color-Pic, Inc.; **B66–B67** From *General Chemistry* by P. W. Atkins, © 1989 by Peter Atkins. Used with permission of W.H. Freeman and Company; **B67, B69** Photographs by Sharon Hoogstraten; **B70** © Daryl Benson/Masterfile; **B72** *top left* © Science VU/Visuals Unlimited; *top right* © 1992 Richard Megna/Fundamental Photographs, NYC; *bottom left* © E. R. Degginger/Color-Pic, Inc.; *bottom right* © Larry Stepanowicz/Visuals Unlimited; **B74** Photograph by Sharon Hoogstraten; **B77** © Corbis Images/PictureQuest; *inset* © Andrew Lambert Photography/Photo Researchers; **B78** © Wally Eberhart/Visuals Unlimited; **B79** *top* The Granger Collection, New York; *bottom* Photograph by Sharon Hoogstraten; **B80** © William Ervin/Photo Researchers; **B82** © Maximilian Stock Ltd./Photo Researchers; **B84** © Index Stock; **B85** *left, inset* Courtesy of Chicago Fire Department; *center* Uline; *bottom right* Photograph by Sharon Hoogstraten; **B86** Photograph by Sharon Hoogstraten; **B87** *top* NASA; *bottom* © 1992 Richard Megna/Fundamental Photographs, NYC; **B88** © Jeffrey L. Rotman/Corbis; **B89** Thomas Eisner and Daniel Aneshansley, Cornell University; **B91** © Harald Sund/Brand X Pictures/PictureQuest; **B92** *top* AP/Wide World Photos; *bottom* Photographs by Sharon Hoogstraten; **B93** Photograph by Sharon Hoogstraten; **B94** © Runk and Schoenberger/Grant Heilman Photography, Inc.; **B95** Photograph by Sharon Hoogstraten; **B96** © Tom Yhlman/Visuals Unlimited; **B97** *background* © Conor Caffrey/Photo Researchers; **B98** © Arnold Fisher/Photo Researchers; **B99** *left to right* © Bruce Forster/Getty Images; © Colin Cuthbert/Photo Researchers; © Fontarnau-Gutiérrez/age fotostock america, inc.; © D. Roberts/Photo Researchers; **B100** © 1992 Richard Megna/ Fundamental Photographs, NYC; **B104** From Hales, *Vegetable Statiks* [1727]; **B105** *top* The Granger Collection, New York; *bottom* Mary Evans Picture Library; **B106** *top* AP/Wide World Photos; *bottom* © Dorling Kindersley; **B107** *top, bottom* © David Parker/Photo Researchers; **B108–B109** © Stephen Frink/Index Stock; **B109, B111** Photographs by Sharon Hoogstraten; **B112** © Richard Cummins/Corbis; **B113, B115** Photographs by Sharon Hoogstraten; **B116** © Peter & Georgina Bowater/Stock Connection/PictureQuest; *inset* © 2001 Kim Fennema/Visuals Unlimited; **B117, B118** Photographs by Sharon Hoogstraten; **B119** *left, right* © 1990 Richard Megna/Fundamental Photographs, NYC; **B120, B121** Photographs by Sharon Hoogstraten; **B122** © Stephen Frink/StephenFrink.com; **B123** Photograph by Sharon Hoogstraten; **B124** © Thom Lang/Corbis; **B125, B127, B129** Photographs by Sharon Hoogstraten; **B130** *top left* © Martyn F. Chillmaid/Photo Researchers; *top right* © Chuck Swartzell/Visuals Unlimited; *center left* © E. R. Degginger/Color-Pic, Inc.; *center right* © Phil Degginger/Color-Pic, Inc.; *bottom left* © Stockbyte; *bottom right* © E. R. Degginger/Color-Pic, Inc.; **B132** © Runk and Schoenberger/Grant Heilman Photography, Inc.; **B132–B133, B133, B134** Photographs by Sharon Hoogstraten; **B135** *top to bottom* © Photodisc/Getty Images; © Greg Pease/Stock Connection/PictureQuest; © Stockbyte; © S. Feld/Robertstock.com; Jellinek & Sampson, London/Bridgeman Art Library; **B136** © Joachim Messerschmidt/Bruce Coleman, Inc.; **B137** *top* © Princess Margaret Rose Hospital/Photo Researchers; *inset* © Klaus Rose/Okapia/Photo Researchers; *bottom* Photograph by Sharon Hoogstraten; **B138** NASA; **B139** © IFA/eStock Photography (PQ price control)/PictureQuest; **B140** © Joachim Messerschmidt/Bruce Coleman, Inc.; **B144–B145** © Jeff Greenberg/Index Stock/PictureQuest; **B145, B147** Photographs by Sharon Hoogstraten; **B148** *left* © E. R. Degginger/ Color-Pic, Inc.; *right* © Charles D.

Acknowlegments R93

Winters/Photo Researchers; **B149** Photograph by Sharon Hoogstraten; **B151** *top* © Claver Carroll/ age fotostock america, inc.; *bottom left* © Fabio Cardoso/age fotostock america, inc.; *bottom right* Photograph by Sharon Hoogstraten; **B153** *left* © S. J. Tans et al., Delft University of Technology/Photo Researchers; *right* Georgia Institute of Technology; **B154** Photograph by Sharon Hoogstraten; **B155** © Marcialis/StockFood; **B156** © John Durham/Photo Researchers; **B157** *top* © Meyer/ StockFood; *bottom* © SPL/Photo Researchers; **B158** Photograph by Sharon Hoogstraten; **B159** *left* © Andrew Syred/Photo Researchers; *right* © SCIMAT 2000/Photo Researchers; **B162** © Eising/StockFood; **B163** Photograph by Sharon Hoogstraten; **B165** *top* © Thomas Kitchin/Tom Stack & Associates; *center* © Superstock; *bottom left* © Bob Krist/Corbis; *bottom center* © Omni Photo Communications/ Index Stock; *bottom right* © Gary Rhijnsburger/Masterfile; **B167** *top Image* Club Graphics; *bottom* © 1994 CMCD, Inc.; **B168** *bottom left* © J. Blank/Robertstock.com; **B169** *left* © SuperStock; *right* © Cheryl A. Ertelt/Visuals Unlimited; **B170** *top* © E. R. Degginger/ Color-Pic, Inc.; *bottom* Photograph by Sharon Hoogstraten; **B171** Photograph by Sharon Hoogstraten; **B172** © SuperStock.

Motion and Forces
Divider © Brett Froomer/Getty Images, **C2–C3** Courtesy of NASA/JPL/Caltech; **C3** © Stocktrek/Corbis; **C4** *top* Courtesy of NASA/JPL/Caltech; *bottom* © The Chedd-Angier Production Company; **C6–C7** © Lester Lefkowitz/Corbis; **C7** Photographs by Sharon Hoogstraten; **C9** © Royalty-Free/Corbis; **C11** © Globus, Holway & Lobel/Corbis; **C12** *top* Photograph by Sharon Hoogstraten; *bottom* © The Image Group/Getty Images; **C14** *top* © Georgina Bowater/Corbis; *bottom* © SuperStock; **C15** © Graham Wheatley/ The Military Picture Library/Corbis; **C16, C17** Photographs by Sharon Hoogstraten; **C18** © Gunter Marx Photography/Corbis; **C19** Photograph by Sharon Hoogstraten; **C21** © Tom Brakefield/Corbis; **C22** © David M. Dennis/Animals Animals; **C23** © Kelly-Mooney Photography/Corbis; **C24** © Gallo Images/Corbis; **C25** © 1986 Richard Megna/Fundamental Photographs, NYC; **C27** Photograph by Sharon Hoogstraten; **C28** © Royalty-Free/Corbis; **C29** Courtesy of NASA/JPL/Caltech; **C30** © Robert Essel NYC/Corbis; **C32** *top* © Mark Jenkinson/Corbis; *bottom* Photographs by Sharon Hoogstraten; **C34** *top* © Globus, Holway & Lobel/Corbis; *center* Photograph by Sharon Hoogstraten; **C36** © David M. Dennis/Animals Animals; **C38–C39** © Arthur Tilley/Getty Images; **C39, C41** Photographs by Sharon Hoogstraten; **C42** © John Kelly/Getty Images; **C43** *left* © AFP/Corbis; *right* © Reuters NewMedia Inc./Corbis; **C44** © Michael Kevin Daly/Corbis; **C45** *left* © Jim Cummins/Getty Images; *right* © Piecework Productions/Getty Images; **C46** Photograph by Sharon Hoogstraten; **C47** © Jeffrey Lynch/Mendola Ltd.; **C48** *left, inset* © Bill Ross/Corbis; *right* Dr. Paula Messina, San Jose State University; **C49, C50** Photographs by Sharon Hoogstraten; **C52** AP/Wide World Photos; **C53** NASA; **C54** Photograph by Sharon Hoogstraten; **C55** AP/Wide World Photos; **C56** *top* Clare Hirn, Jewish Hospital, University of Louisville and ABIOMED; *bottom* John Lair, Jewish Hospital, University of Louisville and ABIOMED; **C57** © Danny Lehman/Corbis; **C58, C59** Photographs by Sharon Hoogstraten; **C60** © Photodisc/Getty Images; *background* © David C. Fritts/Animals Animals; **C62** *top* Digital image © 1996 Corbis/Original image courtesy of NASA/Corbis; *bottom* Photographs by Sharon Hoogstraten; **C64, C66** Photographs by Sharon Hoogstraten; **C68** © TRL Ltd./Photo Researchers; **C69** © Charles O'Rear/Corbis; **C70** *top* © Photodisc/Getty Images; *bottom* Photographs by Sharon Hoogstraten; **C71** © Siede Preis/ Getty Images; **C72** Photographs by Sharon Hoogstraten; **C74–C75** © Mike Chew/Corbis; **C75, C77** Photographs by Sharon Hoogstraten; **C80, C81** Photographs of models by Sharon Hoogstraten; **C80** *left* NASA; *right* © Photodisc/Getty Images; **C81** *top, bottom, background* NASA; **C82** Photograph by Sharon Hoogstraten; **C83** NASA; **C84** *left* © Royalty-Free/Corbis; *right* NASA/ESA; **C85** © John Beatty/Getty Images; **C86, C87** Photographs by Sharon Hoogstraten; **C88** *top* © Al Francekevich/Corbis; *bottom* Photograph by Sharon Hoogstraten; **C89** © Joe McBride/Getty Images; **C90** © NatPhotos/Tony Sweet/Digital Vision; *inset* © Michael S. Yamashita/Corbis; **C91** Photograph by Sharon Hoogstraten; **C92** © Wilson Goodrich/Index Stock; **C93** © Royalty-Free/Corbis; **C94** © Philip & Karen Smith/Getty Images; **C95** © Ralph A. Clevenger/Corbis; **C96** *top* © Stephen Frink/Corbis; *bottom* Photographs by Sharon Hoogstraten; **C98, C99, C100** Photographs by Sharon Hoogstraten; **C101** Photograph of prairie dogs © W. Perry Conway/Corbis; **C103** © Omni Photo Communications Inc./Index Stock; **C104** *top, bottom* Photographs by Sharon Hoogstraten; *center* © Royalty-Free/Corbis; **C105** Photograph by Sharon Hoogstraten; **C106** *left* © Joe McBride/Getty Images; *right* Photograph by Sharon Hoogstraten; **C108** *top* © Erich Lessing/Art Resource, New York; *bottom* © Dagli Orti/The Art Archive; **C109** *top left* © SPL/Photo Researchers; *top right* Sam Fogg Rare Books & Manuscripts; *bottom* © Dorling Kindersley; **C110** *left* © Victoria & Albert Museum, London/Art Resource, New York; *top right* Photo Franca Principe, Institute and Museum of the History of Science; *center right* © Scala/Art Resource, New York; *bottom right* © Dorling Kindersley; **C111** *top* © Gerald L. Schad/Photo Researchers; *bottom* NASA; **C112–C113** © Digital Vision; **C113** *top Image* Club Graphics; *center* Photograph by Sharon Hoogstraten; **C115, C116** Photographs by Sharon Hoogstraten; **C117** © Rob Lewine/Corbis; **C118** Photograph by Sharon Hoogstraten; **C119** © Reinhard Eisele/Corbis; **C120** © Roger Allyn Lee/ SuperStock; **C121** Chris Wipperman/KCPDSA; **C123** © Patrik Giardino/Corbis; **C124** © Tony Anderson/Getty Images; **C125** Photograph by Sharon Hoogstraten; **C126** © 1988 Paul Silverman/Fundamental Photographs, NYC; **C127** © Tony Donaldson/Icon Sports Media; **C129** © AFP/Corbis; **C130** Photograph by Sharon Hoogstraten; **C131** © Pete Saloutos/Corbis; **C132** © Digital Vision; **C133** Photograph by Sharon Hoogstraten; **C134** © Walter Hodges/Corbis; **C135** © Grantpix/Index Stock; **C136** *top* © David Young-Wolff/PhotoEdit; *bottom* Photographs by Sharon Hoogstraten; **C138** © Pete Saloutos/Corbis; **C140** Photographs by Sharon Hoogstraten; **C142–C143** © Balthazar Korab; **C145** Photograph by Sharon Hoogstraten; **C146** © David Young-Wolff/PhotoEdit; **C147** © Joseph Sohm/

ChromoSohm Inc./Corbis; **C149** © Brad Wrobleski/Masterfile; **C150** © Michael Macor/San Francisco Chronicle/Corbis SABA; **C151** Photograph by Sharon Hoogstraten; **C152** © Jean-Yves Ruszniewski/Corbis; **C153** © Royalty-Free/Corbis; *inset* © Felicia Martinez/ PhotoEdit; **C154, C155** Photographs by Sharon Hoogstraten; **C156** © Tom Stewart/Corbis; **C157** Photograph by Sharon Hoogstraten; **C158** *top* © David Butow/Corbis SABA; *bottom* © Peter Beck/Corbis; **C159** © Henryk T. Kaiser/Index Stock; **C160** © Tony Freeman/ PhotoEdit; **C161** © Todd A. Gipstein/Corbis; **C163** AP/Wide World Photos; **C164** © Tony Freeman/PhotoEdit; **C165** © Lester Lefkowitz/ Corbis; **C166** Hurst Jaws of Life; **C167** © David Parker/Photo Researchers; **C168** *top* AP/Wide World Photos; *bottom* © Robert Caputo/Stock Boston; *background* © Royalty-Free/Corbis; **C170** *top* © Photodisc/Getty Images; *bottom* Photograph by Sharon Hoogstraten; **C172** © ThinkStock/SuperStock; **C173** *top left* Photograph by Sharon Hoogstraten; **C174** © Tony Freeman/ PhotoEdit.

Waves, Sound, and Light
Divider © David Pu'u/Corbis; **D2–D3** © Paul Kuroda/SuperStock; **D3** *left* © B. Benoit/Photo Researchers; *right* © Powerstock/SuperStock; **D4** *top* © Stephen Frink/Corbis; *bottom* © The Chedd-Angier Production Company; **D5** © George Stetten, M.D., Ph.D; **D6–D7** © Peter Sterling/Getty Images; **D7, D9** Photographs by Sharon Hoogstraten; **D11** Photograph courtesy of Earthquake Engineering Research Institute Reconnaissance Team; **D12** © Michael Krasowitz/Getty Images; **D13** Photograph by Sharon Hoogstraten; **D15** © John Lund/Getty Images; **D16** © Greg Huglin/Superstock; **D17** © Arnulf Husmo/Getty Images; **D19** Richard Olsenius/National Geographic Image Collection; **D20** Photograph by Sharon Hoogstraten; **D22** *top* © 1990 Robert Mathena/ Fundamental Photographs, NYC; *bottom* Photographs by Sharon Hoogstraten; **D23, D24** Photographs by Sharon Hoogstraten; **D25** © 2001 Richard Megna/Fundamental Photographs, NYC; **D26** *top* © 1972 FP/Fundamental Photographs, NYC; *bottom* Photograph by Sharon Hoogstraten; **D27** © 1998 Richard Megna/Fundamental Photographs, NYC; **D28** © Hiroshi Hara/Photonica; **D29** Takaaki Uda, Public Works Research Institute, Japan/NOAA; **D30** *bottom center* © 2001 Richard Megna/Fundamental Photographs, NYC; *bottom right* © 1972 FP/Fundamental Photographs, NYC; **D34–D35** © Chip Simons/Getty Images; **D35, D37** Photographs by Sharon Hoogstraten; **D39** © Susumu Nishinaga/Photo Researchers; **D41** Photographs by Sharon Hoogstraten; **D42** © Jeff Rotman/Getty Images; **D43** © John Terence Turner/Getty Images; **D44** *left* © Reuters NewMedia Inc./Corbis; *background* © Jason Hindley/Getty Images; **D45** Photograph by Sharon Hoogstraten; **D47** *left (top to bottom)* © Will Crocker/Getty Images; © Dorling Kindersley; © Photodisc/Getty Images; © Dorling Kindersley; © Photodisc/Getty Images; © Stephen Dalton/Animals Animals; © Steve Bloom/Getty Images; *top right* © Don Smetzer/Getty Images; *bottom right* Brian Gordon Green/National Geographic Image Collection; **D48** Photograph by Sharon Hoogstraten; **D49** © Dorling Kindersley; **D50** © Michael Melford/Getty Images; **D52** © Tom Main/Getty Images; **D53** Photograph by Sharon Hoogstraten; **D55** *left* © Roger Ressmeyer/Corbis; *right* Symphony Center, Home of the Chicago Symphony Orchestra; **D56** © Yehoash Raphael, Kresge Hearing Research Institute, The University of Michigan; **D57** © Chris Shinn/Getty Images; **D58** Photograph by Sharon Hoogstraten; **D59** *top left* © Stephen Dalton/OSF/Animals Animals; *top right* © Paulo de Oliveira/Getty Images; *bottom left* © AFP/Corbis; *bottom right* U.S. Navy photo by Photographer's Mate 3rd Class Lawrence Braxton/Department of Defense; **D60** © Fetal Fotos; **D63** © Andrew Syred/Photo Researchers; **D64** *top left* © Reuters NewMedia Inc./Corbis; *bottom* Photographs by Sharon Hoogstraten; **D65** Photograph by Sharon Hoogstraten; **D66** *bottom left* © Stephen Dalton/OSF/Animals Animals; *bottom right* © Paulo de Oliveira/Getty Images; **D68** © Photodisc/Getty Images; **D70–D71** © Alan Kearney/Getty Images; **D71** *top, center* Photographs by Sharon Hoogstraten; *bottom* The EIT Consortium/NASA; **D73** Photograph by Sharon Hoogstraten; **D75** NASA, The Hubble Heritage Team, STScI, AURA; **D76** Photograph by Sharon Hoogstraten; **D78** *top* Palomar Observatory/Caltech; *center* NASA/MSFC/SAO; *bottom* NASA/CXC/ASU/J. Hester et al; *background* NASA/JHU/AUI/R. Giacconi et al.; **D79** Photograph by Sharon Hoogstraten; **D80** *left* © China Tourism Press/Getty Images; *center* © David Nunuk/Photo Researchers; *right* © Dr. Arthur Tucker/Photo Researchers; **D81** *left to right* © Jeremy Woodhouse/Getty Images; © Sinclair Stammers/Photo Researchers; © Hugh Turvey/Photo Researchers; © Alfred Pasieka/Photo Researchers; **D84** Photograph by Sharon Hoogstraten; **D85** *top* © Dr. Arthur Tucker/Photo Researchers; *bottom* © Thomas Eisner, Cornell University; **D86** © Martin Spinks; **D87** © Photodisc/Getty Images; *inset* © David Young-Wolff/Getty Images; **D88** Robert F. Sisson/National Geographic Image Collection; **D89** © George D. Lepp/Corbis; **D90** *top* © Raymond Blythe/OSF/Animals Animals; *bottom* Photograph by Sharon Hoogstraten; **D92** © Traffic Technologies; **D93** Photograph by Sharon Hoogstraten; **D94** © Jeff Greenberg/Visuals Unlimited; **D95** © Raymond Gehman/Corbis; **D96** © Charles Swedlund; **D97** *top* © Ace Photo Agency/Phototake; *bottom* © Dorling Kindersley; **D98** Photograph by Sharon Hoogstraten; **D100** *top* © Michael Newman/PhotoEdit; *bottom* Photographs by Sharon Hoogstraten; **D101** Photographs by Sharon Hoogstraten; **D102** *center right* Robert F. Sisson/National Geographic Image Collection; *bottom* © Ace Photo Agency/Phototake; **D106** *top* The Granger Collection, New York; *bottom* © Jack and Beverly Wilgus; **D107** *top* The Granger Collection, New York; *center left* Diagram of the eye from the *Opticae thesaurus. Alhazeni Arabis libri septem, nunc primum editi* by Ibn al-Haytham (Alhazen). Edited by Federico Risnero (Basleae, 1572), p. 6. Private collection, London; *center right* Courtesy of NASA/JPL/Caltech; *bottom* © Royal Greenwich Observatory/Photo Researchers; **D108** *top* © Stock Connection/Alamy; *center* © Florian Marquardt; *bottom* © Museum of Holography, Chicago; **D109** *top* © Bettmann/Corbis; *bottom* © Bob Masini/Phototake; **D110–D111** © Tom Raymond/Getty Images; **D111** *top, center* Photographs by Sharon Hoogstraten; *bottom* © Philippe Plaily/Photo Researchers; **D112**

Photograph by Sharon Hoogstraten; **D114** © Laura Dwight/Corbis; **D115** Photograph by Sharon Hoogstraten; **D116** © Michael Newman/PhotoEdit; **D117** Photographs by Sharon Hoogstraten; **D118** Peter McBride/Aurora; **D119** Photograph by Sharon Hoogstraten; **D120** © Richard H. Johnston/Getty Images; **D122** © Kim Heacox/Getty Images; *background* © Photodisc/Getty Images; **D123** © T. R. Tharp/Corbis; **D124** *top* © Ruddy Gold/age photostock america, inc.; *bottom* Photograph by Sharon Hoogstraten; **D125** Photographs by Sharon Hoogstraten; **D126** © CMCD, 1994; **D128** Photograph by Sharon Hoogstraten; **D130** © Argentum/Photo Researchers; **D131** Photograph by Sharon Hoogstraten; **D133** *top* © Andrew Syred/Photo Researchers; *center* Lunar and Planetary Institute, CIRS/Library; *bottom* NASA; **D134** Photograph by Sharon Hoogstraten; **D135** Use of Canon Powershot S45 courtesy of Canon USA; **D136** © Philippe Psaila/Photo Researchers; **D137** *top* © Photodisc/Getty Images; *bottom* © Tom Stewart/corbisstockmarket.com; **D138** Bradley C. Edwards, Ph.D.; **D139** *top* © Photodisc/Getty Images; *center* © PhotoFlex.com; *bottom* © Michael Goldman/Photis/PictureQuest; **D140** © Michael Newman/PhotoEdit.

Electricity and Magnetism
Divider © Nick Koudis/Getty Images; **E2–E3** © PHISH 2003; **3** © Jacques M. Chenet/Corbis; **E4** *top* © John Foxx/ImageState; *bottom* © The Chedd-Angier Production Company; **E5** © Stuart Hughes/Corbis; **E6–E7** AP/Wide World Photos; **E7, E9** Photographs by Sharon Hoogstraten; **E10** © Roger Ressmeyer/Corbis; **E12** © Charles D. Winters/Photo Researchers; **E14** Photograph by Sharon Hoogstraten; **E16** © Maximilian Stock Ltd./Photo Researchers; **E17** *left* © Ann and Rob Simpson; *right* © Patrice Ceisel/Visuals Unlimited; **E18** Photograph by Sharon Hoogstraten; **E19** © Steve Crise/Corbis; **E21** © A & J Verkaik/Corbis; **E22** Photograph by Sharon Hoogstraten; **E23** *top* © Tim Wright/Corbis; *bottom* © Leland Bobb/Corbis; **E24** © James D. Hooker/*Lighting Equipment News (UK)*; **E26** *top left* © Scott T. Smith; All other photographs by Sharon Hoogstraten; **E27, E28, E30, E31** Photographs by Sharon Hoogstraten; **E33** © Chip Simons 2003; **E34** Photo Courtesy of NASA/Getty Images; **E35** © Julian Hirshowitz/Corbis; **E36** © James D. Hooker/*Lighting Equipment News (UK)*; **E40–E41** © 2003 Barbara Ries; **E41, E43** Photographs by Sharon Hoogstraten; **E48** *left* © 1989 Paul Silverman/Fundamental Photographs, NYC; *right* Photograph by Sharon Hoogstraten; **E49** © Creative Publishing International, Inc.; **E50** *top left* © Gary Rhijnsburger/Masterfile; *center left* © Creative Publishing International, Inc.; **E51, E52, E53, E54** Photographs by Sharon Hoogstraten; **E56** © Robert Essel NYC/Corbis; **E57** Photograph by Sharon Hoogstraten; **E59** *top* AP/Wide World Photos; *bottom* Photograph by Sharon Hoogstraten; **E61** © Kurt Stier/Corbis; **E62, E63** © Gen Nishino/Getty Images; **E64** © Donna Cox and Robert Patterson/ National Center for Supercomputing Applications, University of Illinois, Urbana; **E65** AP/Wide World Photos; **E66** *top* © Sheila Terry/Photo Researchers; *bottom* Photograph by Sharon Hoogstraten; **E72** *top* © SPL/Photo Researchers; *bottom* The Granger Collection, New York; **E73** *top left* © Philadelphia Museum of Art/Corbis; *top right* © Archivo Iconografico, S.A./Corbis; *bottom* © Adam Hart-Davis/ Photo Researchers; **E74** *top* Science Museum/Science & Society Picture Library; *center left* © Bettmann/ Corbis; *center right* © Tony Craddock/Photo Researchers; *bottom* © Bettmann/Corbis; **E75** *top* © Alfred Pasieka/Photo Researchers; *bottom* AP/Wide World Photos; **E76–E77** © Philip & Karen Smith/age fotostock america, inc.; **E77, E79** Photographs by Sharon Hoogstraten; **E80** *top* © Michael S. Yamashita/ Corbis; *bottom* Photograph by Sharon Hoogstraten; **E81** Photographs by Sharon Hoogstraten; **E82** © The Natural History Museum, London; **E83** Photograph by Sharon Hoogstraten; **E84** NASA; **E85** Photograph by Sharon Hoogstraten; **E86** © Chris Madeley/Photo Researchers; **E87** © Brian Bahr/Getty Images; *inset* Courtesy of Discover Magnetics; **E88, E90** Photographs by Sharon Hoogstraten; **E91** *top* © George Haling/Photo Researchers; *bottom* © Dick Luria/Photo Researchers; **E93** © G. K. & Vikki Hart/Getty Images; **E95** Photograph by Sharon Hoogstraten; **E97** © Ondrea Barbe/ Corbis; **E98** Photograph by Sharon Hoogstraten; **E99** © Randy M. Ury/Corbis; **E100** *top* © Christopher Gould/Getty Images; *bottom* Photographs by Sharon Hoogstraten; **E101** Photographs by Sharon Hoogstraten; **E102** Bureau of Reclamation; **E104** Courtesy of General Electric; **E105** *top* Photograph by Sharon Hoogstraten; *bottom* © Maya Barnes/The Image Works; **E107** © Mark Richards/PhotoEdit; **E108** *top* Photograph by Sharon Hoogstraten.

Backmatter
R28 © Photodisc/Getty Images.

Illustrations and Maps
Accurate Art, Inc. **A127, C107, C175, D33**; Ampersand Design Group **A29, A115, B85, B97, C15, D139, E50**; Argosy **D10, D13, D14, D18, D19, D25, D30, D55, D61**; Eric Chadwick **D98, D99**; Steve Cowden **C122, D12, D51, D54, D82, E60, E62–E63, E68**; Stephen Durke **A10, A11, A18, A20, A22, A30, A32, A33, A34, A81, B11, B12, B13, B14, B15, B34, B48, B49, B50, B51, B52, B54, B59, B62, B64, B70, B71, B73, B88, B89, B97, B102, B114, B142, B148, B158, B159, B160, B172, B174, E11, E12, E13, E21, E25, E31, E36, E39, E44, E46, E53, E68, E103, E108, E110**; Patrick Gnan **B160**; Gary Hincks **B124**; KO Studios **B160**; Debbie Maizels **B160**; MapQuest.com, Inc. **A114, C10, C60, C129, C168**; Precision Graphics **B165**; Tony Randazzo/American Artists Rep. Inc. **C13**; Dan Stuckenschneider **C102, C135, C156, C157, C158, C159, C161, C162, C165, C172, C173, D62, D77, D91, D102, D133, D135, D136, D140, E15, E33, E47, E49, E55, E92, E93, E94, E96, E97, E108, R11–R19, R22, R32**; Dan Stukenschneider based on an illustration by Matt Cioffi **C168**; Bart Vallecoccia **D38, D39, D126, D127, D129, D135, D140**.

Formulas

Word Form	Symbolic Form	Purpose
Volume = length • width • height	$V = lwh$	to calculate the volume of a rectangular object
Density = $\frac{\text{mass}}{\text{Volume}}$	$D = \frac{m}{V}$	to calculate the density of an object
Speed = $\frac{\text{distance}}{\text{time}}$	$S = \frac{d}{t}$	to calculate the speed of an object
acceleration = $\frac{\text{final velocity} - \text{initial velocity}}{\text{time}}$	$a = \frac{v_{final} - v_{initial}}{t}$	to calculate the acceleration of an object
Force = mass • acceleration	$F = ma$	to calculate the force, mass, or acceleration of an object; called Newton's second law
momentum = mass • velocity	$p = mv$	to calculate the momentum of an object
Pressure = $\frac{\text{Force}}{\text{Area}}$	$P = \frac{F}{A}$	to calculate the pressure on an object
Work = Force • distance	$W = Fd$	to calculate work
Gravitational Potential Energy = mass • gravitational acceleration • height	$GPE = mgh$	to calculate the gravitational potential energy of an object
Kinetic Energy = $\frac{\text{mass} \cdot \text{velocity}^2}{2}$	$KE = \frac{1}{2}mv^2$	to calculate the kinetic energy of an object
Mechanical Energy = Potential Energy + Kinetic Energy	$ME = PE + KE$	to calculate the mechanical energy of an object
Power = $\frac{\text{Work}}{\text{time}}$	$P = \frac{W}{t}$	to calculate power based on work
Power = $\frac{\text{Energy}}{\text{time}}$	$P = \frac{E}{t}$	to calculate power based on energy
Efficiency (%) = $\frac{\text{Output work}}{\text{Input work}} \cdot 100$	$E(\%) = \frac{W_{out}}{W_{in}} \cdot 100$	to calculate the efficiency of a machine
Mechanical Advantage = $\frac{\text{Output work}}{\text{Input work}}$	$MA = \frac{F_{out}}{F_{in}}$	to calculate a machine's mechanical advantage
Speed = wavelength • frequency	$S = \lambda f$	to calculate the speed of a wave
Current = $\frac{\text{Voltage}}{\text{Resistance}}$	$I = \frac{V}{R}$	to calculate the relationships among current, voltage, and resistance; called Ohm's law
Electrical Power = Voltage • Current	$P = VI$	to calculate power
Energy used = Power • time	$E = Pt$	to calculate the total energy used

The Periodic Table of the Elements

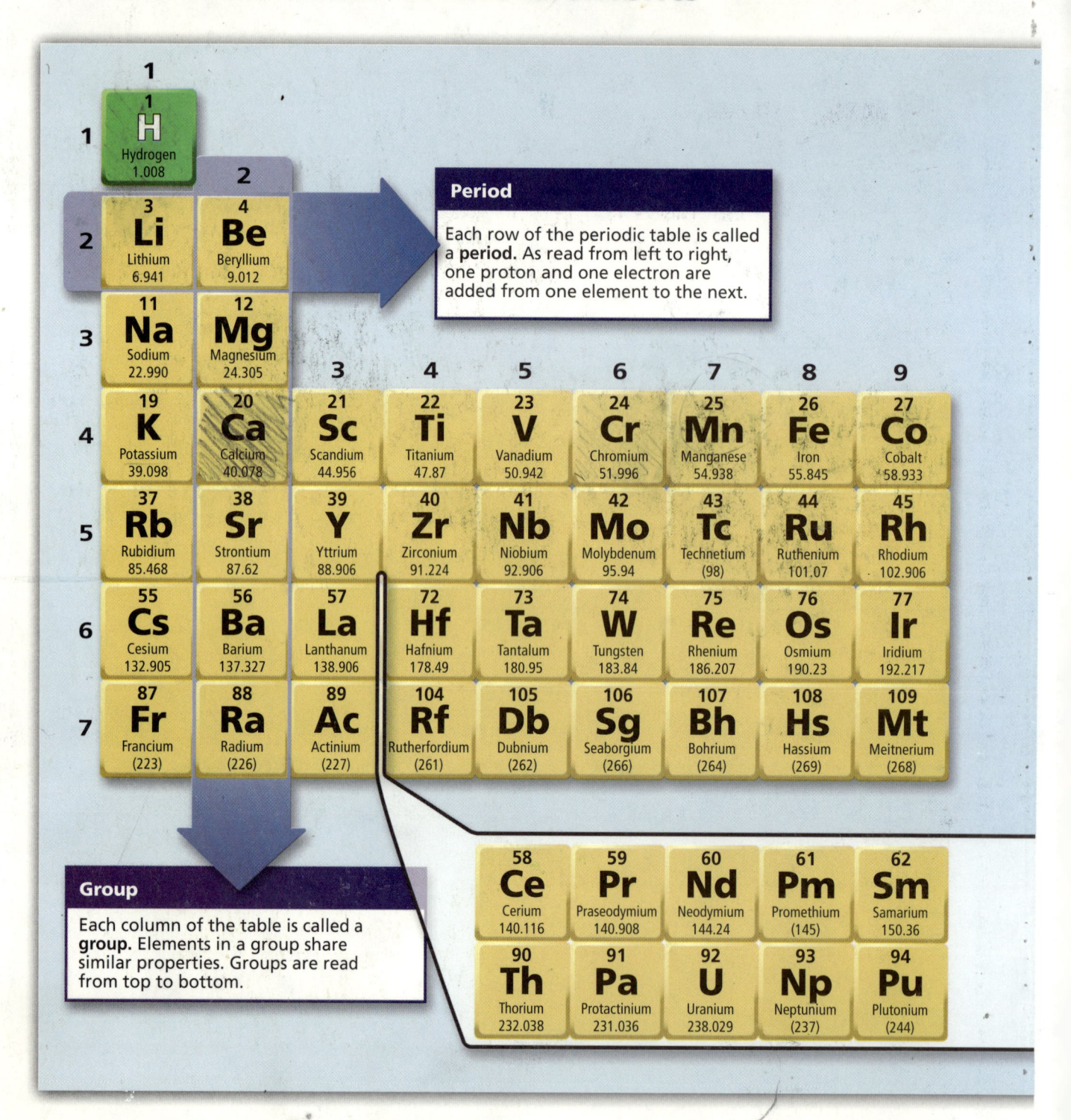

Group	1	2	3	4	5	6	7	8	9
1	1 **H** Hydrogen 1.008								
2	3 **Li** Lithium 6.941	4 **Be** Beryllium 9.012							
3	11 **Na** Sodium 22.990	12 **Mg** Magnesium 24.305							
4	19 **K** Potassium 39.098	20 **Ca** Calcium 40.078	21 **Sc** Scandium 44.956	22 **Ti** Titanium 47.87	23 **V** Vanadium 50.942	24 **Cr** Chromium 51.996	25 **Mn** Manganese 54.938	26 **Fe** Iron 55.845	27 **Co** Cobalt 58.933
5	37 **Rb** Rubidium 85.468	38 **Sr** Strontium 87.62	39 **Y** Yttrium 88.906	40 **Zr** Zirconium 91.224	41 **Nb** Niobium 92.906	42 **Mo** Molybdenum 95.94	43 **Tc** Technetium (98)	44 **Ru** Ruthenium 101.07	45 **Rh** Rhodium 102.906
6	55 **Cs** Cesium 132.905	56 **Ba** Barium 137.327	57 **La** Lanthanum 138.906	72 **Hf** Hafnium 178.49	73 **Ta** Tantalum 180.95	74 **W** Tungsten 183.84	75 **Re** Rhenium 186.207	76 **Os** Osmium 190.23	77 **Ir** Iridium 192.217
7	87 **Fr** Francium (223)	88 **Ra** Radium (226)	89 **Ac** Actinium (227)	104 **Rf** Rutherfordium (261)	105 **Db** Dubnium (262)	106 **Sg** Seaborgium (266)	107 **Bh** Bohrium (264)	108 **Hs** Hassium (269)	109 **Mt** Meitnerium (268)

Period
Each row of the periodic table is called a **period**. As read from left to right, one proton and one electron are added from one element to the next.

Group
Each column of the table is called a **group**. Elements in a group share similar properties. Groups are read from top to bottom.

58 **Ce** Cerium 140.116	59 **Pr** Praseodymium 140.908	60 **Nd** Neodymium 144.24	61 **Pm** Promethium (145)	62 **Sm** Samarium 150.36
90 **Th** Thorium 232.038	91 **Pa** Protactinium 231.036	92 **U** Uranium 238.029	93 **Np** Neptunium (237)	94 **Pu** Plutonium (244)

■ Metal   ■ Metalloid   ■ Nonmetal   **Fe** Solid   **Hg** Liquid   O Gas